See the Difference with Learning[...]

LearningCurve
macmillan learning

learningcurveworks.com

LearningCurve is a winning solution for everyone: students come to class better prepared and instructors have more flexibility to go beyond the basic facts and concepts in class. LearningCurve's game-like quizzes are book-specific and link back to the textbook in LaunchPad so that students can brush up on the reading when they get stumped by a question. The reporting features help instructors track overall class trends and spot topics that are giving students trouble so that they can adjust lectures and class activities.

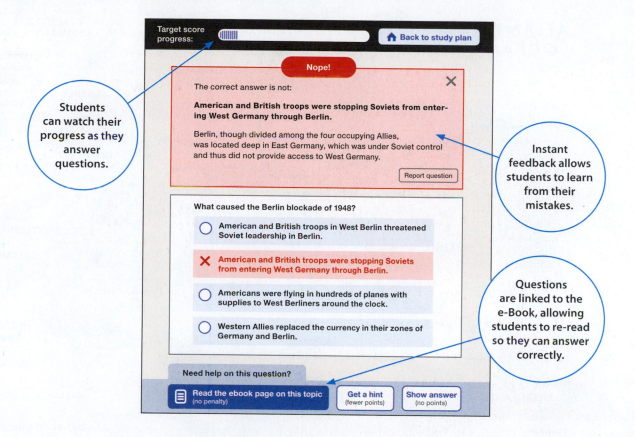

Students can watch their progress as they answer questions.

Target score progress:

Back to study plan

Nope!

The correct answer is not:

American and British troops were stopping Soviets from entering West Germany through Berlin.

Berlin, though divided among the four occupying Allies, was located deep in East Germany, which was under Soviet control and thus did not provide access to West Germany.

Report question

Instant feedback allows students to learn from their mistakes.

What caused the Berlin blockade of 1948?

○ American and British troops in West Berlin threatened Soviet leadership in Berlin.

✗ American and British troops were stopping Soviets from entering West Germany through Berlin.

○ Americans were flying in hundreds of planes with supplies to West Berliners around the clock.

○ Western Allies replaced the currency in their zones of Germany and Berlin.

Need help on this question?

Read the ebook page on this topic (no penalty)

Get a hint (fewer points)

Show answer (no points)

Questions are linked to the e-Book, allowing students to re-read so they can answer correctly.

LearningCurve is easy to assign, easy to customize, and easy to complete. See the difference LearningCurve makes in teaching and learning history.

CONCISE EDITION

A History of Western Society

TWELFTH EDITION

John P. McKay
University of Illinois at Urbana-Champaign

Bennett D. Hill
Late of *Georgetown University*

John Buckler
Late of *University of Illinois at Urbana-Champaign*

Clare Haru Crowston
University of Illinois at Urbana-Champaign

Merry E. Wiesner-Hanks
University of Wisconsin–Milwaukee

Joe Perry
Georgia State University

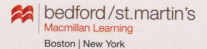
bedford/st.martin's
Macmillan Learning
Boston | New York

FOR BEDFORD/ST. MARTIN'S

Vice President, Editorial, Macmillan Learning Humanities: Edwin Hill
Publisher for History: Michael Rosenberg
Acquiring Editor for History: Laura Arcari
Director of Development for History: Jane Knetzger
Senior Developmental Editor: Leah R. Strauss
Senior Production Editor: Christina M. Horn
Senior Media Producer: Michelle Camisa
Senior Production Supervisor: Jennifer Wetzel
History Marketing Manager: Melissa Famiglietti
Media Editor: Jennifer Jovin
Associate Editor: Tess Fletcher
Editorial Assistant: Melanie McFadyen
Copy Editor: Jennifer Brett Greenstein

Indexer: Leoni Z. McVey
Cartography: Mapping Specialists, Ltd.
Photo Editor: Robin Fadool
Photo Researcher: Bruce Carson
Permissions Editor: Eve Lehmann
Senior Art Director: Anna Palchik
Text Design: Boynton Hue Studio
Cover Design: William Boardman
Cover Art: Peasant Girl, 1720 (oil on canvas)/Private Collection/Mondadori Portfolio/Electa/Ugo Allegri/ Bridgeman Images
Composition: Jouve
Printing and Binding: LSC Communications

Manufactured in the United States of America.

1 0 9 8 7 6
f e d c b a

For information, write: Bedford/St. Martin's, 75 Arlington Street, Boston, MA 02116   (617-399-4000)

ISBN 978-1-319-07358-9 (Combined Edition)
ISBN 978-1-319-07388-6 (Volume 1)
ISBN 978-1-319-07389-3 (Volume 2)

ACKNOWLEDGMENTS

Preface

We are pleased to publish the Concise Edition of *A History of Western Society*, Twelfth Edition. The Concise Edition provides our signature approach to history in a smaller, more affordable trim size. Featuring the full narrative of the parent text and select features, images, maps, and pedagogical tools, the Concise Edition continues to incorporate the latest and best scholarship in the field in an accessible, student-friendly manner. *A History of Western Society* grew out of the initial three authors' desire to infuse new life into the study of Western Civilization. The three current authors, Clare Haru Crowston, Merry E. Wiesner-Hanks, and Joe Perry, who first used the book as students or teachers and took over full responsibilities with the eleventh edition, continue to incorporate the latest and best scholarship in the field. All three of us regularly teach introductory history courses and thus bring insights into the text from the classroom, as well as from new secondary works and our own research in archives and libraries. In this new twelfth edition we aim to enhance the distinctive attention to daily life that sparks students' interest while also providing a number of innovative tools—both print and digital—designed to help students think historically and master the material.

Helping Instructors Teach with Digital Resources

We know that many students today are on a budget and that instructors want greater flexibility and more digital options in their choice of course materials. Accordingly, *A History of Western Society* is offered in Macmillan's premier learning platform, **LaunchPad**, an intuitive, interactive e-Book and course space. Free when packaged with the print text or available at a low price when used as stand-alone, LaunchPad grants students and teachers access to a wealth of online tools and resources built specifically for our text to enhance reading comprehension and promote in-depth study. Developed with extensive feedback from history instructors and students, **LaunchPad for *A History of***

Western Society includes the complete narrative of the print book; the companion reader, *Sources for Western Society*; and **LearningCurve**, an adaptive learning tool that is designed to get students to read before they come to class. With **new source-based questions in the test bank and in the LearningCurve**, instructors now have more ways to test students on their understanding of sources and narrative in the book.

This edition also includes **Guided Reading Exercises** that prompt students to be active readers of the chapter narrative and autograded **primary source quizzes** to test comprehension of written and visual sources. These features, plus **additional primary source documents, video tools for making video assignments, map activities, flashcards, and customizable test banks**, make LaunchPad a great asset for any instructor who wants to enliven the history of Western Civilization for students.

These new digital directions have not changed the central mission of the book, which is to introduce students to the broad sweep of Western Civilization in a fresh yet balanced manner. Every edition has incorporated new research to keep the book up-to-date and respond to the changing needs of readers and instructors, and we have continued to do this in the twelfth edition. As we have made these changes, large and small, we have sought to give students and teachers an integrated perspective so that they can pursue—on their own or in the classroom—the historical questions that they find particularly exciting and significant. To learn more about the benefits of LearningCurve and LaunchPad, see the "Versions and Supplements" section on page xiii.

The Story of *A History of Western Society*: Bringing the Past to Life for Students

At the point when *A History of Western Society* was first conceptualized, social history was dramatically changing the ways we understood the past, and the original authors decided to create a book that would re-create the lives of ordinary people in appealing human terms, while also giving major economic, political, cultural, and intellectual developments the attention they unquestionably deserve. The current authors remain committed to advancing this vision for today's classroom, with a broader definition of social history that brings the original idea into the twenty-first century.

History as a discipline never stands still, and over the last several decades cultural history has joined social history as a source of dynamism. Because of its emphasis on the ways people made sense of their lives, *A History of Western Society* has always included a large amount of cultural history, ranging from foundational works of philosophy and literature to popular songs and stories. This focus on cultural history has been enhanced in recent editions in a way that highlights the interplay between men's and women's lived experiences and the ways men and women reflect on these experiences to create meaning. The joint social and cultural perspective requires—fortunately, in our opinion—the inclusion of objects as well as texts as important sources for studying history, which has allowed us to incorporate the growing emphasis on material culture in the work of many historians. We know that engaging students' interest in the past is often a challenge, but we also know that the text's hallmark approach—the emphasis on daily life and individual experience in its social and cultural dimensions—connects with students and makes the past vivid and accessible.

"Life" Chapters Connect the Past to the Present

Although social and cultural history can be found in every chapter, they are particularly emphasized in the acclaimed "Life" chapters that spark student interest by making the past palpable and approachable in human terms. The five chapters are Chapter 4: Life in the Hellenistic World, 336–30 B.C.E.; Chapter 10: Life in Villages and Cities of the High Middle Ages, 1000–1300; Chapter 18: Life in the Era of Expansion, 1650–1800; Chapter 22: Life in the Emerging Urban Society, 1840–1914; and Chapter 30: Life in an Age of Globalization, 1990 to the Present. Because we

know that a key challenge of teaching history—and Western Civilization in particular—is encouraging students to appreciate the relevance of the past to our lives today.

Primary Sources and Historical Thinking

In response to the growing emphasis on historical thinking skills in the teaching of history at all levels, as well as to requests from our colleagues and current adopters, we have significantly expanded the book's primary source program to offer a wide variety of sources, both written and visual, presented in several ways. Available in print and in LaunchPad, **"Evaluating the Evidence"** (three in each chapter) features an individual source, with headnotes and questions that help students understand the source and connect it to the information in the rest of the chapter. Selected for their interest and carefully integrated into their historical context, these sources provide students with firsthand encounters with people of the past along with the means and tools for building historical skills, including chronological reasoning, explaining causation, evaluating context, and assessing perspective. The suggestions for essays based on the primary sources encourage students to further expand their skills as they use their knowledge to develop historical arguments and write historical analyses.

Those using LaunchPad will have access to an additional distinctive primary sources feature. **"Thinking Like a Historian"** (one in each chapter) groups at least five sources around a central question, with additional questions to guide students' analysis of the evidence and suggestions for essays that will allow them to put these sources together with what they have learned in class. Topics include "Land Ownership and Social Conflict in the Late Republic" (Chapter 5); "The Rights of Which Men?" (Chapter 19); and "The Conservative Reaction to Immigration and Islamist Terrorism" (Chapter 30).

In addition, in the print book we have quoted extensively from a wide range of primary sources in the narrative, demonstrating that such quotations are the "stuff" of history. We believe that our extensive use of **primary source extracts** as an integral part of the narrative as well as in extended form in the primary source boxes in LaunchPad will give students ample practice in thinking critically and historically.

Finally, **the companion reader, *Sources for Western Society*, Third Edition**, continues to provide a rich selection of documents to complement each chapter of the text. It is **FREE** when packaged with the textbook and is also available in LaunchPad.

Distinctive Essay Features Punctuate Larger Developments

In addition to the expanded primary source program, we are pleased to offer two unique boxed essay features in each chapter — **"Individuals in Society"** and, in LaunchPad, **"Living in the Past"** — that personalize larger developments and make them tangible.

To give students a chance to see the past through ordinary people's lives, each chapter in print and LaunchPad includes one of the popular **"Individuals in Society" biographical essays**, which offer brief studies of individuals or groups, informing students about the societies in which they lived. We have found that readers empathize with these human beings as they themselves seek to define their own identities. The spotlighting of individuals, both famous and obscure, perpetuates the book's continued attention to cultural and intellectual developments, highlights human agency, and reflects changing interests within the historical profession as well as the development of "microhistory." Features include essays on Aristophanes, the ancient Athenian playwright who mercilessly satirized the demagogues and thinkers of his day; Anna Jansz of Rotterdam, an Anabaptist martyr; Hürrem, a concubine who became a powerful figure in the Ottoman Empire during the sixteenth century; Rebecca Protten, a former slave and leader in the Moravian missionary movement; Samuel Crompton, the inventor of the spinning mule during the Industrial Revolution who struggled to control and profit from his invention; and Edward Snowden, a former CIA operative who leaked classified documents about American surveillance programs to the world press and was considered by some a hero and by others a traitor.

To introduce students to the study of material culture, **"Living in the Past"** essays in LaunchPad use social and cultural history to show how life in the past was both similar to and different from our lives today. These features are richly illustrated with images and artifacts and include a short essay and questions for analysis. We use these essays to explore the deeper ramifications of aspects of their own lives that students might otherwise take for granted, such as consumer goods, factories, and even currency. Students connect to the people of the past through a diverse range of topics such as "Farming in the Hellenistic World," "Roman Table Manners," "Child's Play," "Coffeehouse Culture," "The Immigrant Experience," "Nineteenth-Century Women's Fashion," and "The Supermarket Revolution."

Because we know that a key challenge of teaching history — and Western Civilization in particular — is encouraging students to appreciate the relevance of the past to our lives today, the five "Life" chapters each include in LaunchPad a feature called **"The Past Living Now"** that examines an aspect of life today with origins in the period covered in that chapter. Featuring engaging topics such as the development of the modern university (Chapter 10) and the dawn of commercialized sports (Chapter 18), these essays were conceived with student interest in mind.

New Coverage and Updates to the Narrative

This edition is enhanced by the incorporation of a wealth of new scholarship and subject areas that immerse students in the dynamic and ongoing work of history. Chapters 1–6 incorporate the exciting cross-disciplinary scholarship that has emerged over the last several decades on the Paleolithic and Neolithic eras, river valley civilizations, and the ancient Mediterranean. For example, archaeologists working at Göbekli Tepe in present-day Turkey have unearthed rings of massive, multi-ton, elaborately carved limestone pillars built around 9000 B.C.E. by groups of foragers, which has led to a rethinking of the links among culture, religion, and the initial development of agriculture. Similarly, new research on the peoples of Mesopotamia, based on cuneiform writing along with other sources, has led scholars to revise the view that Mesopotamians were fatalistic and to emphasize instead that they generally anticipated being well treated by the gods if they behaved morally.

Throughout these chapters, material on cross-cultural connections, the impact of technologies, and changing social relationships has been added. In Chapter 14, we have updated and expanded the coverage of the conquest of the Aztec and Inca Empires and the impact of the conquest on indigenous peoples, including new material on the economic exploitation of indigenous people, religious conversion, and European debates about indigenous people.

In Chapter 16, there are several significant revisions. First, there is more coverage of global/colonial issues and of the interaction between intellectual ideas and social change. Second, with regard to the Scientific Revolution, there is a new section called "Why Europe?" that asks why the Scientific Revolution happened in Europe, as well as an expanded discussion of the relationship between religion and science. Third, a new section called "The Social Life of the Enlightenment" draws attention to recent scholarship linking the ideas of the Enlightenment to the social changes of the eighteenth century; this section includes coverage of the impact of contact with non-Europeans, debates on race, and women's role in the Enlightenment. Chapter 20 pays increased attention to the global context of industrialization, including two new sections: "Why Britain?" explains why the Industrial Revolution originated in Britain and not elsewhere in the world, such as China or India; and "The Global Picture" discusses the global spread of industrialization. A new section on living standards for the working class addresses the impact of industrialization on working people.

Other additions include a streamlined discussion of the role of women in classical Athens (Chapter 3); updated coverage of medicine in the Hellenistic period (Chapter 4); new material on the Vikings of western Europe (Chapter 8); expanded treatment of the growth of Russia's land empire to complement attention to western European acquisition of overseas empires and new material on Peter the Great's campaigns against the Ottomans (Chapter 15); increased coverage of communities and identities of the Atlantic world with material on the way colonial contacts help create national European identities as well as "African" and "Indian" identities (Chapter 17); updated coverage of the history of the family, popular culture, and medicine, including material on the use of colonial plants as

medicines (Chapter 18); new material on the Congress of Vienna (Chapter 21) and expanded coverage of political ideologies of liberalism, republicanism, and nationalism (Chapters 21 and 23); new material on women's roles in the European colonies and on women and imperialism (Chapter 24); expanded coverage of the First World War in the Middle East, the collapse of the Ottoman Empire, and the postwar mandate system (Chapter 25); new discussion of Jewish resistance to the Holocaust and extended coverage of anti-Semitism and eugenics in Nazi Germany (Chapter 27); new material on violence and decolonization in the Algerian War of Independence (Chapter 28); and up-to-date coverage of contemporary events in the final chapter, including the refugee crisis, the euro crisis and Greek debt relief, Russian expansionism, issues surrounding terrorism and anti-Muslim sentiment in Europe, and the potential fragmentation of the European Union (Chapter 30).

Helping Students Understand the Narrative

We know firsthand and take seriously the challenges students face in understanding, retaining, and mastering so much material that is often unfamiliar. With the goal of making this the most student-centered edition yet, we continued to enhance the book's pedagogy on many fronts. To focus students' reading, each chapter opens with a **chapter preview with focus questions** keyed to the main chapter headings. These questions are repeated within the chapter and again in the **"Review & Explore" section** at the end of each chapter that provides helpful guidance for reviewing key topics.

To help students understand the bigger picture and prepare for exams, each chapter includes **"Looking Back, Looking Ahead" conclusions** that provide an insightful synthesis of the chapter's main developments, while connecting to events that students will encounter in the chapters to come. In this way students are introduced to history as an ongoing process of interrelated events. These conclusions are followed by **"Make Connections" questions** that prompt students to assess larger developments across chapters, thus allowing them to develop skills in evaluating change and continuity, making comparisons, and analyzing context and causation. To promote clarity and comprehension, boldface key terms in the text are defined in the margins and listed in the chapter review. **Phonetic spellings** are located directly after terms that readers are likely to find hard to pronounce. The **chapter chronologies**, which review major developments discussed in each chapter, mirror the key events of the chapter.

The high-quality art and map program has been thoroughly revised and features more than two hundred **contemporaneous illustrations**. As in earlier editions, all illustrations have been carefully selected to complement the text, and all include captions that inform students while encouraging them to read the text more deeply. High-quality **full-size maps** illustrate major developments in the narrative, and helpful **spot maps** are embedded in the narrative to locate areas under discussion. Finally, all of the full-color images and maps included in the parent text appear in LaunchPad.

In addition, whenever an instructor assigns the **LaunchPad e-Book** (which is free when bundled with the print book), students get full access to **LearningCurve**, an online adaptive learning tool that promotes mastery of the book's content and diagnoses students' trouble spots. With this adaptive quizzing, students accumulate points toward a target score as they go, giving the interaction a game-like feel. Feedback for incorrect responses explains why the answer is incorrect and directs students back to the text to review before they attempt to answer the question again. The end result is a better understanding of the key elements of the text. Instructors who actively assign LearningCurve report their students come to class prepared for discussion and their students enjoy using it. In addition, LearningCurve's reporting feature allows instructors to quickly diagnose which concepts students in their classes are struggling with so they can adjust lectures and activities accordingly. The LaunchPad e-Book with LearningCurve is thus an invaluable asset for instructors who need to support students in all settings, from traditional lectures to hybrid, online, and newer "flipped" classrooms. To learn more about the benefits of LearningCurve and LaunchPad, see the "Versions and Supplements" section on page xiii.

Acknowledgments

It is a pleasure to thank the instructors who reviewed the eleventh edition in preparation for the twelfth edition:

Robert Blackey, California State University, San Bernardino
Kevin Caldwell, Blue Ridge Community College
Amy Colon, SUNY Sullivan
Maia Conrad, Thomas Nelson Community College
Scott Gavorsky, Great Basin College
George Kaloudis, Rivier College
Roy Koepp, University of Nebraska at Kearney
Jesse Lynch, Shasta College
Michael McKeown, Daytona State College
Jennifer Morris, Mount St. Joseph University
Stephen Santelli, Northern Virginia Community College
Calvin Tesler, Lehigh University
Doris Tishkoff, Quinnipiac University

It is also a pleasure to thank the many editors who have assisted us over the years, first at Houghton Mifflin and now at Bedford/St. Martin's. At Bedford/St. Martin's, these include senior development editor Leah Strauss, senior production editor Christina Horn, associate editor Tess Fletcher and editorial assistant Melanie McFadyen, director of development Jane Knetzger, acquiring editor for history Laura Arcari, and publisher for history Michael Rosenberg. Other key contributors were photo researcher Bruce Carson, text permissions editor Eve Lehmann, text designer Cia Boynton, copy editor Jennifer Brett Greenstein, proofreaders Angela Morrison and Susan Zorn, indexer Leoni McVey, and cover designer Billy Boardman.

Many of our colleagues at the University of Illinois, the University of Wisconsin–Milwaukee, and Georgia State University continue to provide information and stimulation, often without even knowing it. We thank them for it. We also thank the many students over the years with whom we have used earlier editions of this book. Their reactions and opinions helped shape the revisions to this edition, and we hope it remains worthy of the ultimate praise that they bestowed on it: that it's "not boring like most textbooks." Merry

Wiesner-Hanks would, as always, also like to thank her husband, Neil, without whom work on this project would not be possible. Clare Haru Crowston thanks her husband, Ali, and her children, Lili, Reza, and Kian, who are a joyous reminder of the vitality of life that we try to showcase in this book. Joe Perry thanks his colleagues and students at Georgia State for their intellectual stimulation and is grateful to Joyce de Vries for her unstinting support and encouragement.

Each of us has benefited from the criticism of our coauthors, although each of us assumes responsibility for what he or she has written. Merry Wiesner-Hanks intensively reworked John Buckler's Chapters 1–6

and revised Chapters 7–13; Clare Crowston wrote and revised Chapters 14–19 and took responsibility for John McKay's Chapter 20; and Joe Perry took responsibility for John McKay's Chapters 21–24 and wrote and revised Chapters 25–30.

We'd especially like to thank the founding authors, John P. McKay, Bennett D. Hill, and John Buckler, for their enduring contributions and for their faith in each of us to carry on their legacy.

CLARE HARU CROWSTON
MERRY E. WIESNER-HANKS
JOE PERRY

Versions and Supplements

Adopters of *A History of Western Society* and their students have access to abundant print and digital resources and tools, including documents, assessment and presentation materials, the acclaimed Bedford Series in History and Culture volumes, and much more. The LaunchPad course space provides access to the narrative with all assignment and assessment opportunities at the ready. See below for more information, visit **macmillanlearning.com**, or contact your local Bedford/St. Martin's sales representative.

Get the Right Version for Your Class

To accommodate different course lengths and course budgets, *A History of Western Society* is available in several different formats, including a Concise Edition (narrative with select features, maps, and images), a Value Edition (narrative only in two colors with select maps and images), loose-leaf versions, and low-priced PDF e-Books. And for the best value of all, package a new print book with LaunchPad at no additional charge to get the best each format offers—a print version for easy portability and reading with a LaunchPad interactive e-Book and course space with LearningCurve and loads of additional assignment and assessment options.

- **Combined Edition** (Chapters 1–30): available in paperback, Concise Edition, Value Edition, loose-leaf, e-Book formats, and in LaunchPad

- **Volume 1, From Antiquity to the Enlightenment** (Chapters 1–16): available in paperback, Concise Edition, Value Edition, loose-leaf, e-Book formats, and in LaunchPad

- **Volume 2, From the Age of Exploration to the Present** (Chapters 14–30): available in paperback, Concise Edition, Value Edition, loose-leaf, e-Book formats, and in LaunchPad

- **Volume A, From Antiquity to 1500** (Chapters 1–12): available in paperback, e-Book formats, and in LaunchPad

- **Volume B, From the Later Middle Ages to 1815** (Chapters 11–19): available in paperback, e-Book formats, and in LaunchPad

- **Volume C, From the Revolutionary Era to the Present** (Chapters 19–30): available in paperback, e-Book formats, and in LaunchPad

- **Since 1300** (Chapters 11–30): available in paperback, e-Book formats, and in LaunchPad

As noted below, any of these volumes can be packaged with additional titles for a discount. To get ISBNs for discount packages, visit **macmillanlearning.com** or contact your Bedford/St. Martin's representative.

Assign LaunchPad— an Assessment-Ready Interactive e-Book and Course Space

Available for discount purchase on its own or for packaging with new books at no additional charge, LaunchPad is a breakthrough solution for today's courses. Intuitive and easy to use for students and instructors alike, LaunchPad is ready to use as is and can be edited, customized with your own material, and assigned quickly. LaunchPad for *A History of Western Society* provides Bedford/St. Martin's high-quality content all in one place, including the full interactive e-Book and companion reader, *Sources for Western Society*, plus LearningCurve formative quizzing; guided reading activities designed to help students read actively for key concepts; autograded quizzes for primary sources; and chapter summative quizzes. Through a wealth of formative and summative assessment, including the adaptive learning program of LearningCurve (see the full description ahead), students gain confidence and get into their reading before class. These features, plus additional primary source documents, video tools for making video assignments, map activities, flashcards, and customizable test banks, make LaunchPad an invaluable asset for any instructor.

LaunchPad easily integrates with course management systems, and with fast ways to build assignments, rearrange chapters, and add new pages, sections, or links, it lets teachers build the courses they want to teach and hold students accountable. For more information, visit **launchpadworks.com**, or to arrange a demo, contact us at **history@macmillan.com**.

Assign LearningCurve So Your Students Come to Class Prepared

Students using LaunchPad receive access to LearningCurve for *A History of Western Society*. Assigning LearningCurve in place of reading quizzes is easy for instructors, and the reporting features help instructors track overall class trends and spot topics that are giving students trouble so they can adjust their lectures and class activities. This online learning tool is popular with students because it was designed to help them rehearse content at their own pace in a nonthreatening, game-like environment. The feedback for wrong answers provides instructional coaching and sends students back to the book for review. Students answer as many questions as necessary to reach a target score, with repeated chances to revisit material they haven't mastered. When LearningCurve is assigned, students come to class better prepared.

Take Advantage of Instructor Resources

Bedford/St. Martin's has developed a rich array of teaching resources for this book and for this course. They range from lecture and presentation materials and assessment tools to course management options. Most can be found in LaunchPad or can be downloaded or ordered at **macmillanlearning.com**.

Bedford Coursepack for Blackboard, Canvas, Brightspace by D2L, or Moodle. We can help you integrate our rich content into your course management system. Registered instructors can download coursepacks that include our popular free resources and book-specific content for *A History of Western Society*.

Instructor's Manual. The *Instructor's Manual* offers both experienced and first-time instructors tools for presenting textbook material in engaging ways. It includes content learning objectives, annotated chapter outlines, and strategies for teaching with the textbook, plus suggestions on how to get the most out of LearningCurve and a survival guide for first-time teaching assistants.

Guide to Changing Editions. Designed to facilitate an instructor's transition from the previous edition of *A History of Western Society* to this new edition, this guide presents an overview of major changes as well as of changes in each chapter.

Online Test Bank. The test bank includes a mix of fresh, carefully crafted multiple-choice, matching, short-answer, and essay questions for each chapter. Many of the multiple-choice questions feature a map, an image, or a primary source excerpt as the prompt. All questions appear in easy-to-use test bank software that allows instructors to add, edit, re-sequence, and print questions and answers. Instructors can also export questions into a variety of course management systems.

The Bedford Lecture Kit: **Lecture Outlines, Maps, and Images.** Look good and save time with *The Bedford Lecture Kit.* These presentation materials include fully customizable multimedia presentations built around chapter outlines that are embedded with maps, figures, and images from the textbook and are supplemented by more detailed instructor notes on key points and concepts.

Print, Digital, and Custom Options for More Choice and Value

For information on free packages and discounts up to 50%, visit **macmillanlearning.com** or contact your local Bedford/St. Martin's sales representative.

***Sources for Western Society*,** **Third Edition.** This primary source collection — available in Volume 1, Volume 2, and Since 1300 versions — provides a revised and expanded selection of sources to accompany *A History of Western Society*, Twelfth Edition. Each chapter features five or six written and visual sources by well-known figures and ordinary individuals alike. With over fifty new selections — including a dozen new visual sources — and enhanced pedagogy throughout, this book gives students the tools to engage critically with canonical and lesser-known sources and prominent and ordinary voices. Each chapter includes a "Sources in Conversation" feature that presents differing views on key topics. This companion reader is an exceptional value for students and offers plenty of assignment options for instructors. Available free when packaged with the print text and included in the LaunchPad e-Book. Also available on its own as a downloadable PDF e-Book.

NEW *Bedford Custom Tutorials for History.* Designed to customize textbooks with resources relevant to individual courses, this collection of brief units, each sixteen pages long and loaded with examples, guides students through basic skills such as using historical evidence effectively, working with primary sources, taking effective notes, avoiding plagiarism and citing sources, and more. Up to two tutorials can be added to a Bedford/St. Martin's history survey title at no additional charge, freeing you to spend your class time focusing on content and interpretation. For more information, visit **macmillanlearning.com /historytutorials**.

The Bedford Series in History and Culture. More than one hundred titles in this highly praised series combine first-rate scholarship, historical narrative, and important primary documents for undergraduate courses. Each book is brief, inexpensive, and focused on a specific topic or period. Revisions of several bestselling titles, such as *The Prince by Niccolò Machiavelli with Related Documents*, edited by William J. Connell; *The Enlightenment: A Brief History with Documents*, by Margaret C. Jacob; *Candide by Voltaire with Related Documents*, edited by Daniel Gordon; and *The French Revolution and Human Rights: A Brief History with Documents*, by Lynn Hunt, are now available. For a complete list of titles, visit **macmillanlearning.com**. Package discounts are available.

Rand McNally Atlas of Western Civilization. This collection of over fifty full-color maps highlights social, political, and cross-cultural change and interaction from classical Greece and Rome to the postindustrial Western world. Each map is thoroughly indexed for fast reference. Free when packaged.

Trade Books. Titles published by sister companies Hill and Wang; Farrar, Straus and Giroux; Henry Holt and Company; St. Martin's Press; Picador; and Palgrave Macmillan are available at a 50% discount when packaged with Bedford/St. Martin's textbooks. For more information, visit **macmillanlearning.com /tradeup**.

A Pocket Guide to Writing in History. This portable and affordable reference tool by Mary Lynn Rampolla provides reading, writing, and research advice useful to students in all history courses. Concise yet comprehensive advice on approaching typical history assignments, developing critical reading skills, writing effective history papers, conducting research, using and documenting sources, and avoiding plagiarism — enhanced with practical tips and examples throughout — has made this slim reference a bestseller. Package discounts are available.

A Student's Guide to History. This complete guide to success in any history course provides the practical help students need to be successful. In addition to introducing students to the nature of the discipline, author Jules Benjamin teaches a wide range of skills from preparing for exams to approaching common writing assignments, and explains the research and documentation process with plentiful examples. Package discounts are available.

The Social Dimension of Western Civilization. Combining current scholarship with classic pieces, this reader's forty-eight secondary sources, compiled by Richard M. Golden, hook students with the fascinating and often surprising details of how everyday Western people worked, ate, played, celebrated, worshiped, married, procreated, fought, persecuted, and died. Package discounts are available.

The West in the Wider World: Sources and Perspectives. Edited by Richard Lim and David Kammerling Smith, the first college reader to focus on the central historical question "How did the West become the West?" offers a wealth of written and visual source materials that reveal the influence of non-European regions on the origins and development of Western Civilization. Package discounts are available.

Brief Contents

1 Origins, to 1200 B.C.E. 2

2 Small Kingdoms and Mighty Empires in the Near East, 1200–510 B.C.E. 34

3 The Development of Greek Society and Culture, ca. 3000–338 B.C.E. 60

4 *Life* in the Hellenistic World, 336–30 B.C.E. 92

5 The Rise of Rome, ca. 1000–27 B.C.E. 120

6 The Roman Empire, 27 B.C.E.–284 C.E. 152

7 Late Antiquity, 250–600 184

8 Europe in the Early Middle Ages, 600–1000 218

9 State and Church in the High Middle Ages, 1000–1300 250

10 *Life* in Villages and Cities of the High Middle Ages, 1000–1300 284

11 The Later Middle Ages, 1300–1450 322

12 European Society in the Age of the Renaissance, 1350–1550 356

13 Reformations and Religious Wars, 1500–1600 390

14 European Exploration and Conquest, 1450–1650 426

15 Absolutism and Constitutionalism, ca. 1589–1725 464

16 Toward a New Worldview, 1540–1789 504

17 The Expansion of Europe, 1650–1800 542

18 *Life* in the Era of Expansion, 1650–1800 574

19 Revolutions in Politics, 1775–1815 608

20 The Revolution in Energy and Industry, ca. 1780–1850 646

21 Ideologies and Upheavals, 1815–1850 680

22   *Life* in the Emerging Urban Society, 1840–1914   716

23   The Age of Nationalism, 1850–1914   752

24   The West and the World, 1815–1914   790

25   War and Revolution, 1914–1919   826

26   The Age of Anxiety, 1880–1940   866

27   Dictatorships and the Second World War, 1919–1945   902

28   Cold War Conflict and Consensus, 1945–1965   942

29   Challenging the Postwar Order, 1960–1991   982

30   *Life* in an Age of Globalization, 1990 to the Present   1020

Glossary   G-1

Index   I-1

About the Authors   I-66

Contents

Preface   vii

Versions and Supplements   xiii

Maps, Figures, and Tables   xxxv

Special Features   xxxviii

1 Origins

to 1200 B.C.E.   2

Understanding Western History   4
Describing the West • What Is Civilization?

The Earliest Human Societies   6
From the First Hominids to the Paleolithic Era • Planting
Crops • Implications of Agriculture • Trade and
Cross-Cultural Connections
Evaluating the Evidence 1.1 Paleolithic Venus
Figures   8

Civilization in Mesopotamia   12
Environment and Mesopotamian Development • The
Invention of Writing and the First Schools • Religion in
Mesopotamia • Sumerian Politics and Society
Evaluating the Evidence 1.2 Gilgamesh's Quest for
Immortality   18

Empires in Mesopotamia   19
The Akkadians and the Babylonians • Life Under
Hammurabi • Cultural Exchange in the Fertile Crescent

The Egyptians   23
The Nile and the God-King • Egyptian Religion •
Egyptian Society and Work • Egyptian Family Life • The
Hyksos and New Kingdom Revival • Conflict and
Cooperation with the Hittites
Evaluating the Evidence 1.3 Egyptian Home Life   27
Individuals in Society Hatshepsut and Nefertiti   31

LOOKING BACK / LOOKING AHEAD   32
REVIEW & EXPLORE   33

photo: Deir el-Medina, Thebes, Egypt/Bridgeman Images

2 Small Kingdoms and Mighty Empires in the Near East

1200–510 B.C.E.   34

Iron and the Emergence of New States   36
Iron Technology • The Decline of Egypt and the Emergence of Kush • The Rise of Phoenicia
Evaluating the Evidence 2.1 The Report of Wenamun   39

The Hebrews   40
The Hebrew State • The Jewish Religion • Hebrew Family and Society
Evaluating the Evidence 2.2 A Jewish Family Contract   45

Assyria, the Military Monarchy   46
Assyria's Long Road to Power • Assyrian Rule and Culture • The Neo-Babylonian Empire
Evaluating the Evidence 2.3 Assyrians Besiege a City   51

The Empire of the Persian Kings   52
Consolidation of the Persian Empire • Persian Religion • Persian Art and Culture
Individuals in Society Cyrus the Great   53

LOOKING BACK / LOOKING AHEAD   58

REVIEW & EXPLORE   59

3 The Development of Greek Society and Culture

ca. 3000–338 B.C.E.   60

Greece in the Bronze Age   62
Geography and Settlement • The Minoans • The Mycenaeans • Homer, Hesiod, and the Epic

The Development of the Polis in the Archaic Age   67
Organization of the Polis • Governing Structures • Overseas Expansion • The Growth of Sparta • The Evolution of Athens
Evaluating the Evidence 3.1 Hesiod, *Works and Days*   68

War and Turmoil in the Classical Period   75
The Persian Wars • Growth of the Athenian Empire • The Peloponnesian War • The Struggle for Dominance • Philip II and Macedonian Supremacy

Classical Greek Life and Culture   79
Athenian Arts in the Age of Pericles • Households and Work • Gender and Sexuality • Public and Personal Religion • The Flowering of Philosophy
Evaluating the Evidence 3.2 The Acropolis of Athens   80
Evaluating the Evidence 3.3 Sophocles, *Antigone*   82
Individuals in Society Aristophanes   84

LOOKING BACK / LOOKING AHEAD   90

REVIEW & EXPLORE   91

photo: British Museum, London, UK/De Agostini Picture Library/Bridgeman Images

photo: National Archaeological Museum, Athens, Greece/De Agostini Picture Library/G. Dagli Orti/Bridgeman Images

4 *Life* in the Hellenistic World
336–30 B.C.E.   92

Alexander's Conquests and Their Political Legacy   94
Military Campaigns • The Political Legacy
Evaluating the Evidence 4.1 Arrian on Alexander the Great   97

Building a Hellenized Society   99
Urban Life • Greeks in Hellenistic Cities • Greeks and Non-Greeks

The Economy of the Hellenistic World   104
Agriculture and Industry • Commerce

Religion and Philosophy in the Hellenistic World   107
Religion and Magic • Hellenism and the Jews • Philosophy and the People
Evaluating the Evidence 4.2 A Hellenistic Spell of Attraction   109

Hellenistic Science and Medicine   113
Science • Medicine
Individuals in Society Archimedes, Scientist and Inventor   114
Evaluating the Evidence 4.3 The Periplus of the Erythraean Sea   116

LOOKING BACK / LOOKING AHEAD   118

REVIEW & EXPLORE   119

5 The Rise of Rome
ca. 1000–27 B.C.E.   120

Rome's Rise to Power   122
The Geography of Italy • The Etruscans • The Founding of Rome • The Roman Conquest of Italy
Evaluating the Evidence 5.1 The Temple of Hercules Victor   128

The Roman Republic   129
The Roman State • Social Conflict in Rome

Roman Expansion   132
The Punic Wars • Rome Turns East

Roman Society   135
Roman Families • Greek Influence on Roman Culture • Opposing Views: Cato the Elder and Scipio Aemilianus
Evaluating the Evidence 5.2 A Woman's Actions in the Turia Inscription   137

The Late Republic   141
Reforms for Poor and Landless Citizens • Political Violence • Civil War
Individuals in Society Queen Cleopatra   146
Evaluating the Evidence 5.3 Cicero and the Plot to Kill Caesar   148

LOOKING BACK / LOOKING AHEAD   150

REVIEW & EXPLORE   151

6 The Roman Empire
27 B.C.E.–284 C.E.   152

Augustus's Reign   154
The Principate • Roman Expansion • The Flowering of
Latin Literature • Marriage and Morality
Evaluating the Evidence 6.1 Augustus, *Res
Gestae*   158
Evaluating the Evidence 6.2 Ovid, *The Art of
Love*   162
Evaluating the Evidence 6.3 Ara Pacis   163

Augustus's Successors   164
The Julio-Claudians and the Flavians • The Age of the
"Five Good Emperors"
Individuals in Society Pliny the Elder   166

Rome and the Provinces   168
Life in Imperial Rome • Approaches to Urban
Problems • Popular Entertainment • Prosperity in the
Roman Provinces • Trade and Commerce

The Coming of Christianity   175
Factors Behind the Rise of Christianity • The Life and
Teachings of Jesus • The Spread of Christianity • The
Growing Acceptance and Evolution of Christianity

The Empire in Disarray   180
Civil Wars and Military Commanders • Turmoil in
Economic Life

LOOKING BACK / LOOKING AHEAD   182

REVIEW & EXPLORE   183

7 Late Antiquity
250–600   184

**Reconstruction Under Diocletian
and Constantine**   186
Political Measures • Economic Issues • The Acceptance
of Christianity

The Growth of the Christian Church   190
The Church and Its Leaders • The Development of
Christian Monasticism • Monastery Life • Christianity
and Classical Culture • Christian Notions of Gender and
Sexuality • Saint Augustine on Human Nature, Will, and
Sin

Barbarian Society   196
Village and Family Life • Tribes and Hierarchies •
Customary and Written Law • Celtic and Germanic Religion
Evaluating the Evidence 7.1 Tacitus on Germanic
Society   198

Migration, Assimilation, and Conflict   200
Celtic and Germanic People in Gaul and Britain •
Visigoths and Huns • Germanic Kingdoms and
the End of the Roman Empire
Evaluating the Evidence 7.2 Battle Between Romans
and Goths   204

Christian Missionaries and Conversion   206
Missionaries' Actions • The Process of Conversion
Evaluating the Evidence 7.3 Gregory of Tours on the
Veneration of Relics   208

The Byzantine Empire   210
Sources of Byzantine Strength • The Law Code of
Justinian • Byzantine Intellectual Life • The Orthodox
Church
Individuals in Society Theodora of
Constantinople   214

LOOKING BACK / LOOKING AHEAD   216

REVIEW & EXPLORE   217

8 Europe in the Early Middle Ages

600–1000   218

The Spread of Islam   220

The Arabs • The Prophet Muhammad • The Teachings and Expansion of Islam • Sunni and Shi'a Divisions • Life in Muslim Spain • Muslim-Christian Relations • Cross-Cultural Influences in Science and Medicine

Evaluating the Evidence 8.1   The Muslim Conquest of Spain   225

Frankish Rulers and Their Territories   228

The Merovingians • The Rise of the Carolingians • The Warrior-Ruler Charlemagne • Carolingian Government and Society • The Imperial Coronation of Charlemagne

Evaluating the Evidence 8.2   The Capitulary de Villis   233

Early Medieval Culture   235

The Carolingian Renaissance • Northumbrian Learning and Writing

Individuals in Society   The Venerable Bede   238

Evaluating the Evidence 8.3   The Death of Beowulf   239

Invasions and Migrations   240

Vikings in Western Europe • Slavs and Vikings in Eastern Europe • Magyars and Muslims

Political and Economic Decentralization   245

Decentralization and the Origins of "Feudalism" • Manorialism, Serfdom, and the Slave Trade

LOOKING BACK / LOOKING AHEAD   248

REVIEW & EXPLORE   249

9 State and Church in the High Middle Ages

1000–1300   250

Political Revival and the Origins of the Modern State   252

England • France • Central Europe • Italy • The Iberian Peninsula

Evaluating the Evidence 9.1   Marriage and Wardship in the Norman Exchequer   254

Law and Justice   259

Local Laws and Royal Courts • The Magna Carta • Law in Everyday Life

Nobles   262

Origins and Status of the Nobility • Training, Marriage, and Inheritance • Power and Responsibility

The Papacy   265

The Gregorian Reforms • Emperor Versus Pope • Criticism and Heresy • The Popes and Church Law

Evaluating the Evidence 9.2   Pope Boniface VIII, *Unam Sanctam*   269

Monks, Nuns, and Friars   270

Monastic Revival • Life in Convents and Monasteries • The Friars

Individuals in Society   Hildegard of Bingen   272

Evaluating the Evidence 9.3   Brother Henry as Composer and Singer   275

The Crusades and the Expansion of Christianity   276

Background and Motives of the Crusades • The Course of the Crusades • Consequences of the Crusades • The Expansion of Christianity • Christendom

LOOKING BACK / LOOKING AHEAD   282

REVIEW & EXPLORE   283

10 *Life* in Villages and Cities of the High Middle Ages

1000–1300   284

Village Life   286
Slavery, Serfdom, and Upward Mobility • The
Manor • Work • Home Life • Childbirth and Child
Abandonment

Popular Religion   292
Christian Life in Medieval Villages • Saints and
Sacraments • Muslims and Jews • Rituals of Marriage
and Birth • Death and the Afterlife
Evaluating the Evidence 10.1   The Pilgrim's Guide to
Santiago de Compostela   297

Towns and Economic Revival   298
The Rise of Towns • Merchant and Craft Guilds • The
Revival of Long-Distance Trade • Business Procedures •
The Commercial Revolution
Individuals in Society   Francesco Datini   305

Urban Life   306
City Life • Servants and the Poor • Popular
Entertainment

Medieval Universities   309
Origins • Legal and Medical Training • Theology and
Philosophy • University Students
Evaluating the Evidence 10.2   Healthy Living   312

Literature and Architecture   315
Vernacular Literature and Drama • Churches and
Cathedrals
Evaluating the Evidence 10.3   Courtly Love
Poetry   316

LOOKING BACK / LOOKING AHEAD   320

REVIEW & EXPLORE   321

11 The Later Middle Ages

1300–1450   322

Prelude to Disaster   324
Climate Change and Famine • Social Consequences

The Black Death   326
Pathology • Spread of the Disease • Care of the
Sick • Economic, Religious, and Cultural Effects
Evaluating the Evidence 11.1   Dance of Death   331

The Hundred Years' War   332
Causes • English Successes • Joan of Arc and France's
Victory • Aftermath
Evaluating the Evidence 11.2   The Trial of Joan of
Arc   337

Challenges to the Church   339
The Babylonian Captivity and Great Schism • Critiques,
Divisions, and Councils • Lay Piety and Mysticism
Individuals in Society   Meister Eckhart   343

Social Unrest in a Changing Society   344
Peasant Revolts • Urban Conflicts • Sex in the
City • Fur-Collar Crime • Ethnic Tensions and
Restrictions • Literacy and Vernacular Literature
Evaluating the Evidence 11.3   Christine de Pizan, Advice
to the Wives of Artisans   348

LOOKING BACK / LOOKING AHEAD   354

REVIEW & EXPLORE   355

photo: Detail from the mosaic *The Triumph of the Cross*, Basilica of St. Clement,
Rome, Italy/De Agostini Picture Library/Gianni Dagli Orti/Bridgeman Images

photo: From *Cas de Nobles Hommes et Femmes*, 1465/Musée Condé, Chantilly,
France/Bridgeman Images

12 European Society in the Age of the Renaissance
1350–1550   356

Wealth and Power in Renaissance Italy   358
Trade and Prosperity • Communes and Republics of Northern Italy • City-States and the Balance of Power
Evaluating the Evidence 12.1 A Sermon of Savonarola   363

Intellectual Change   363
Humanism • Education • Political Thought • Christian Humanism • The Printed Word
Evaluating the Evidence 12.2 Thomas More, *Utopia*   369

Art and the Artist   373
Patronage and Power • Changing Artistic Styles • The Renaissance Artist
Individuals in Society Leonardo da Vinci   376

Social Hierarchies   379
Race and Slavery • Wealth and the Nobility • Gender Roles

Politics and the State in Western Europe   382
France • England • Spain
Evaluating the Evidence 12.3 A Gold Coin of Ferdinand and Isabella   386

LOOKING BACK / LOOKING AHEAD   388

REVIEW & EXPLORE   389

13 Reformations and Religious Wars
1500–1600   390

The Early Reformation   392
The Christian Church in the Early Sixteenth Century • Martin Luther • Protestant Thought • The Appeal of Protestant Ideas • The Radical Reformation and the German Peasants' War • Marriage, Sexuality, and the Role of Women
Evaluating the Evidence 13.1 Martin Luther, *On Christian Liberty*   396
Individuals in Society Anna Jansz of Rotterdam   400
Evaluating the Evidence 13.2 Domestic Scene   402

The Reformation and German Politics   404
The Rise of the Habsburg Dynasty • Religious Wars in Switzerland and Germany

The Spread of Protestant Ideas   407
Scandinavia • Henry VIII and the Reformation in England • Upholding Protestantism in England • Calvinism • The Reformation in Eastern Europe
Evaluating the Evidence 13.3 Elizabethan Injunctions About Religion   410

The Catholic Reformation   414
Papal Reform and the Council of Trent • New and Reformed Religious Orders

Religious Violence   418
French Religious Wars • The Netherlands Under Charles V • The Great European Witch-Hunt

LOOKING BACK / LOOKING AHEAD   424

REVIEW & EXPLORE   425

14 European Exploration and Conquest
1450–1650   426

World Contacts Before Columbus   428
The Trade World of the Indian Ocean • The Trading States of Africa • The Ottoman and Persian Empires • Genoese and Venetian Middlemen

The European Voyages of Discovery   432
Causes of European Expansion • Technology and the Rise of Exploration • The Portuguese Overseas Empire • Spain's Voyages to the Americas • Spain "Discovers" the Pacific • Early Exploration by Northern European Powers
Evaluating the Evidence 14.1 Columbus Describes His First Voyage   440

Conquest and Settlement   442
Spanish Conquest of the Aztec and Inca Empires • Portuguese Brazil • Colonial Empires of England and France • Colonial Administration

The Era of Global Contact   447
Indigenous Population Loss and Economic Exploitation • Life in the Colonies • The Columbian Exchange • Sugar and Slavery • Spanish Silver and Its Economic Effects • The Birth of the Global Economy
Evaluating the Evidence 14.2 Interpreting the Spread of Disease Among Natives   449
Individuals in Society Juan de Pareja   452

Changing Attitudes and Beliefs   457
Religious Conversion • European Debates About Indigenous Peoples • New Ideas About Race • Michel de Montaigne and Cultural Curiosity • William Shakespeare and His Influence
Evaluating the Evidence 14.3 Tenochtitlan Leaders Respond to Spanish Missionaries   458

LOOKING BACK / LOOKING AHEAD   462

REVIEW & EXPLORE   463

photo: Detail from a Namban Byobu Japanese painted screen/Museu Nacional de Soares dos Reis, Porto, Portugal/Bridgeman Images

15 Absolutism and Constitutionalism
ca. 1589–1725   464

Seventeenth-Century Crisis and Rebuilding   466
The Social Order and Peasant Life • Famine and Economic Crisis • The Thirty Years' War • Achievements in State-Building • Warfare and the Growth of Army Size • Popular Political Action

Absolutism in France and Spain   472
The Foundations of French Absolutism • Louis XIV and Absolutism • Life at Versailles • The French Economic Policy of Mercantilism • Louis XIV's Wars • The Decline of Absolutist Spain in the Seventeenth Century
Evaluating the Evidence 15.1 Letter from Versailles   475

Absolutism in Austria and Prussia   480
The Return of Serfdom in the East • The Austrian Habsburgs • Prussia in the Seventeenth Century • The Consolidation of Prussian Absolutism

The Development of Russia and the Ottoman Empire   484
Mongol Rule in Russia and the Rise of Moscow • Building the Russian Empire • The Reforms of Peter the Great • The Ottoman Empire
Evaluating the Evidence 15.2 Peter the Great and Foreign Experts   488
Individuals in Society Hürrem   492

Constitutional Rule in England and the Dutch Republic   492
Religious Divides and Civil War • The Puritan Protectorate • The Restoration of the English Monarchy • Constitutional Monarchy • The Dutch Republic in the Seventeenth Century • Baroque Art and Music
Evaluating the Evidence 15.3 John Locke, *Two Treatises of Government*   498

LOOKING BACK / LOOKING AHEAD   502

REVIEW & EXPLORE   503

photo: By Charles Le Brun (1619–1690), 1678/Museum of Fine Arts, Budapest, Hungary/Erich Lessing/Art Resource, NY

16 Toward a New Worldview
1540–1789   504

The Scientific Revolution   506
Why Europe? • Scientific Thought to 1500 • The Copernican Hypothesis • Brahe, Kepler, and Galileo: Proving Copernicus Right • Newton's Synthesis • Natural History and Empire • Magic and Alchemy
Evaluating the Evidence 16.1 Galileo Galilei, *The Sidereal Messenger*   512
Evaluating the Evidence 16.2 "An Account of a Particular Species of Cocoon"   514

Important Changes in Scientific Thinking and Practice   516
The Methods of Science: Bacon and Descartes • Medicine, the Body, and Chemistry • Science and Religion • Science and Society

The Rise and Spread of Enlightenment Thought   520
The Early Enlightenment • The Influence of the Philosophes • Enlightenment Movements Across Europe

The Social Life of the Enlightenment   526
Global Contacts • Enlightenment Debates About Race • Women and the Enlightenment • Urban Culture and Life in the Public Sphere
Evaluating the Evidence 16.3 Denis Diderot, "Supplement to Bougainville's Voyage"   528

Enlightened Absolutism   532
Frederick the Great of Prussia • Catherine the Great of Russia • The Austrian Habsburgs • Jewish Life and the Limits of Enlightened Absolutism
Individuals in Society Moses Mendelssohn and the Jewish Enlightenment   538

LOOKING BACK / LOOKING AHEAD   540

REVIEW & EXPLORE   541

17 The Expansion of Europe
1650–1800   542

Working the Land   544
The Legacy of the Open-Field System • New Methods of Agriculture • The Leadership of the Low Countries and England
Evaluating the Evidence 17.1 Arthur Young on the Benefits of Enclosure   548

The Beginning of the Population Explosion   549
Long-Standing Obstacles to Population Growth • The New Pattern of the Eighteenth Century

The Growth of Rural Industry   552
The Putting-Out System • The Lives of Rural Textile Workers • The Industrious Revolution

The Debate over Urban Guilds   556
Urban Guilds • Adam Smith and Economic Liberalism
Evaluating the Evidence 17.2 Adam Smith on the Division of Labor   558

The Atlantic World and Global Trade   559
Mercantilism and Colonial Competition • The Atlantic Economy • The Atlantic Slave Trade • Identities and Communities of the Atlantic World • The Atlantic Enlightenment • Trade and Empire in Asia and the Pacific
Evaluating the Evidence 17.3 Olaudah Equiano's Economic Arguments for Ending Slavery   566
Individuals in Society Rebecca Protten   568

LOOKING BACK / LOOKING AHEAD   572

REVIEW & EXPLORE   573

18 *Life* in the Era of Expansion
1650–1800   574

Marriage and the Family   576
Late Marriage and Nuclear Families • Work Away from Home • Premarital Sex and Community Controls • New Patterns of Marriage and Illegitimacy • Sex on the Margins of Society

Children and Education   581
Child Care and Nursing • Foundlings and Infanticide • Attitudes Toward Children • The Spread of Elementary Schools
Evaluating the Evidence 18.1   Parisian Boyhood   586

Popular Culture and Consumerism   587
Popular Literature • Leisure and Recreation • New Foods and Appetites • Toward a Consumer Society
Evaluating the Evidence 18.2   A Day in the Life of Paris   592
Individuals in Society   Rose Bertin, "Minister of Fashion"   595

Religious Authority and Beliefs   596
Church Hierarchy • Protestant Revival • Catholic Piety • Marginal Beliefs and Practices
Evaluating the Evidence 18.3   Advice to Methodists   599

Medical Practice   602
Faith Healing and General Practice • Improvements in Surgery • Midwifery • The Conquest of Smallpox

LOOKING BACK / LOOKING AHEAD   605

REVIEW & EXPLORE   606

19 Revolutions in Politics
1775–1815   608

Background to Revolution   610
Social Change • Growing Demands for Liberty and Equality • The Seven Years' War

The American Revolutionary Era, 1775–1789   613
The Origins of the Revolution • Independence from Britain • Framing the Constitution • Limitations of Liberty and Equality
Evaluating the Evidence 19.1   Abigail Adams, "Remember the Ladies"   619

Revolution in France, 1789–1791   620
Breakdown of the Old Order • The Formation of the National Assembly • Popular Uprising and the Rights of Man • A Constitutional Monarchy and Its Challenges
Evaluating the Evidence 19.2   Abbé Sieyès, *What Is the Third Estate?*   622

World War and Republican France, 1791–1799   627
The International Response • The Second Revolution and the New Republic • Total War and the Terror • The Thermidorian Reaction and the Directory
Evaluating the Evidence 19.3   Contrasting Visions of the Sans-Culottes   630

The Napoleonic Era, 1799–1815   633
Napoleon's Rule of France • Napoleon's Expansion in Europe • The Grand Empire and Its End

The Haitian Revolution, 1791–1804   638
Revolutionary Aspirations in Saint-Domingue • The Outbreak of Revolt • The War of Haitian Independence
Individuals in Society   Toussaint L'Ouverture   642

LOOKING BACK / LOOKING AHEAD   644

REVIEW & EXPLORE   645

photo: *A Market Day*, 1765, Central European School (oil on canvas)/© Sotheby's/akg-images

photo: *The Taking of the Bastille, 14 July 1789*/French School/Château de Versailles, France/Bridgeman Images

20 The Revolution in Energy and Industry
ca. 1780–1850   646

The Industrial Revolution in Britain   648
Why Britain? • Technological Innovations and Early Factories • The Steam Engine Breakthrough • Steam-Powered Transportation • Industry and Population
Individuals in Society Samuel Crompton   652

Industrialization in Europe and the World   658
National and International Variations • Industrialization in Continental Europe • Agents of Industrialization • The Global Picture

New Patterns of Working and Living   664
Work in Early Factories • Working Families and Children • The New Sexual Division of Labor • Living Standards for the Working Class
Evaluating the Evidence 20.1 Debate over Child Labor Laws   667
Evaluating the Evidence 20.2 The Testimony of Young Mine Workers   670

Relations Between Capital and Labor   672
The New Class of Factory Owners • Responses to Industrialization • The Early British Labor Movement • The Impact of Slavery
Evaluating the Evidence 20.3 Advice for Middle-Class Women   675

LOOKING BACK / LOOKING AHEAD   678

REVIEW & EXPLORE   679

21 Ideologies and Upheavals
1815–1850   680

The Aftermath of the Napoleonic Wars   682
The European Balance of Power • Metternich and Conservatism • Repressing the Revolutionary Spirit • Limits to Conservative Power and Revolution in South America
Evaluating the Evidence 21.1 The Karlsbad Decrees: Conservative Reaction in the German Confederation   689

The Spread of Radical Ideas   690
Liberalism and the Middle Class • The Growing Appeal of Nationalism • The Foundations of Modern Socialism • The Birth of Marxist Socialism

The Romantic Movement   695
The Tenets of Romanticism • Romantic Literature • Romanticism in Art and Music
Evaluating the Evidence 21.2 English Romantic Poets   697
Individuals in Society Germaine de Staël   699
Evaluating the Evidence 21.3 Jacob and Wilhelm Grimm, *Children's Stories and Household Tales*   700

Reforms and Revolutions Before 1848   702
National Liberation in Greece • Liberal Reform in Great Britain • Ireland and the Great Famine • The Revolution of 1830 in France

The Revolutions of 1848   708
A Democratic Republic in France • Revolution and Reaction in the Austrian Empire • Prussia, the German Confederation, and the Frankfurt National Parliament

LOOKING BACK / LOOKING AHEAD   714

REVIEW & EXPLORE   715

photo: *The Falcon Glassworks*, c. 1840, (oil on canvas)/© Museum of London/HIP/ The Image Works

photo: By Gustave Wappers (1803–1874), (oil on canvas)/Musée Royaux des Beaux-Arts de Belgique, Brussels, Belgium/© Leemage/Bridgeman Images

22 *Life* in the Emerging Urban Society

1840–1914 716

Taming the City 718
Industry and the Growth of Cities • The Advent of the Public Health Movement • The Bacterial Revolution • Improvements in Urban Planning • Public Transportation
Evaluating the Evidence 22.1 First Impressions of the World's Biggest City 720

Rich and Poor and Those in Between 725
The Distribution of Income • The People and Occupations of the Middle Classes • Middle-Class Culture and Values • The People and Occupations of the Working Classes • Working-Class Leisure and Religion

Changing Family Lifestyles 732
Middle-Class Marriage and Courtship Rituals • Middle- and Working-Class Sexuality • Prostitution • Separate Spheres and the Importance of Homemaking • Child Rearing • The Feminist Movement
Evaluating the Evidence 22.2 Stephan Zweig on Middle-Class Youth and Sexuality 734
Individuals in Society Franziska Tiburtius 742

Science and Thought 743
The Triumph of Science in Industry • Darwin and Natural Selection • The Modern University and the Social Sciences • Realism in Art and Literature
Evaluating the Evidence 22.3 Émile Zola and Realism in Literature 749

LOOKING BACK / LOOKING AHEAD 750

REVIEW & EXPLORE 751

photo: By Alexander Blaikley (1816–1903)/© Fine Art Photographic Library/Corbis

23 The Age of Nationalism

1850–1914 752

Napoleon III in France 754
France's Second Republic • Napoleon III's Second Empire

Nation Building in Italy, Germany, and the United States 757
Italy to 1850 • Cavour and Garibaldi in Italy • Growing Austro-Prussian Rivalry • Bismarck and the Austro-Prussian War • Taming the German Parliament • The Franco-Prussian War • Slavery and Nation Building in the United States
Evaluating the Evidence 23.1 The Struggle for the Italian Nation 759

The Modernization of Russia and the Ottoman Empire 766
The "Great Reforms" in Russia • The Russian Revolution of 1905 • Reform and Readjustment in the Ottoman Empire
Evaluating the Evidence 23.2 Eyewitness Accounts of Bloody Sunday 770

The Responsive National State, 1871–1914 772
The German Empire • Republican France • Great Britain and Ireland • The Austro-Hungarian Empire

The Nation and the People 778
Making National Citizens • Nationalism and Racism • Jewish Emancipation and Modern Anti-Semitism
Individuals in Society Theodor Herzl 782

Marxism and the Socialist Movement 783
The Socialist International • Labor Unions and Marxist Revisionism
Evaluating the Evidence 23.3 Adelheid Popp, the Making of a Socialist 784

LOOKING BACK / LOOKING AHEAD 788

REVIEW & EXPLORE 789

photo: By Gerolamo Induno (1825–1890), (oil on canvas)/Civico Museo del Risorgimento, Milano, Italy/De Agostini Picture Library/Alfredo Dagli Orti/Bridgeman Images

24 The West and the World
1815–1914   790

Industrialization and the World Economy   792
The Rise of Global Inequality • The World Market •
The Opening of China • Japan and the United States •
Western Penetration of Egypt

Global Migration Around 1900   799
The Pressure of Population • European Emigration •
Asian Emigration

Western Imperialism, 1880–1914   803
The European Presence in Africa Before 1880 • The
Scramble for Africa After 1880 • Imperialism in
Asia • Causes of the New Imperialism • A "Civilizing
Mission" • Orientalism • Critics of Imperialism
Evaluating the Evidence 24.1 Nativism in the United
States   804
Individuals in Society Cecil Rhodes   808
Evaluating the Evidence 24.2 The White Man's
Burden   814
Evaluating the Evidence 24.3 The Brown Man's
Burden   817

Responding to Western Imperialism   818
The Pattern of Response • Empire in India • The
Example of Japan • Toward Revolution in China

LOOKING BACK / LOOKING AHEAD   824

REVIEW & EXPLORE   825

25 War and Revolution
1914–1919   826

The Road to War   828
Growing International Conflict • The Mood of 1914 •
The Outbreak of War

Waging Total War   834
Stalemate and Slaughter on the Western Front • The
Widening War
Evaluating the Evidence 25.1 Poetry in the
Trenches   838

The Home Front   841
Mobilizing for Total War • The Social Impact •
Growing Political Tensions
Individuals in Society Vera Brittain   844
Evaluating the Evidence 25.2 Wartime Propaganda
Posters   845

The Russian Revolution   847
The Fall of Imperial Russia • The Provisional Government •
Lenin and the Bolshevik Revolution • Trotsky and the
Seizure of Power • Dictatorship and Civil War
Evaluating the Evidence 25.3 Peace, Land, and Bread for
the Russian People   851

The Peace Settlement   854
The End of the War • Revolution in Austria-Hungary
and Germany • The Treaty of Versailles • The Peace
Settlement in the Middle East • The Human Costs
of the War

LOOKING BACK / LOOKING AHEAD   864

REVIEW & EXPLORE   865

26 The Age of Anxiety
1880–1940   866

Uncertainty in Modern Thought   868
Modern Philosophy • The Revival of Christianity • The
New Physics • Freudian Psychology

Evaluating the Evidence 26.1 Friedrich Nietzsche
Pronounces the Death of God   870

**Modernism in Architecture, Art,
Literature, and Music**   875
Architecture and Design • New Artistic Movements •
Twentieth-Century Literature • Modern Music

Evaluating the Evidence 26.2 The Futurist
Manifesto   878

An Emerging Consumer Society   881
Mass Culture • The Appeal of Cinema • The Arrival of
Radio

The Search for Peace and Political Stability   885
Germany and the Western Powers • Hope in Foreign
Affairs • Hope in Democratic Government

Individuals in Society Gustav Stresemann   888

The Great Depression, 1929–1939   891
The Economic Crisis • Mass Unemployment • The New
Deal in the United States • The Scandinavian Response
to the Depression • Recovery and Reform in Britain and
France

Evaluating the Evidence 26.3 George Orwell on Life on
the Dole   896

LOOKING BACK / LOOKING AHEAD   900

REVIEW & EXPLORE   901

27 Dictatorships and the Second World War
1919–1945   902

Authoritarian States   904
Conservative Authoritarianism and Radical Totalitarian
Dictatorships • Communism and Fascism

Stalin's Soviet Union   907
From Lenin to Stalin • The Five-Year Plans • Life and
Culture in Soviet Society • Stalinist Terror and the Great
Purges

Evaluating the Evidence 27.1 Stalin Justifies the
Five-Year Plan   910

Evaluating the Evidence 27.2 Famine and Recovery on a
Soviet Collective Farm   913

Mussolini and Fascism in Italy   917
The Seizure of Power • The Regime in Action

Hitler and Nazism in Germany   919
The Roots of National Socialism • Hitler's Road to
Power • State and Society in Nazi Germany • Popular
Support for National Socialism • Aggression and
Appeasement

The Second World War   927
German Victories in Europe • Europe Under Nazi
Occupation • The Holocaust • Japanese Empire and the
War in the Pacific • The "Hinge of Fate" • Allied Victory

Evaluating the Evidence 27.3 Everyday Life in the
London Blitz   929

Individuals in Society Primo Levi   935

LOOKING BACK / LOOKING AHEAD   940

REVIEW & EXPLORE   941

28 Cold War Conflict and Consensus
1945–1965 942

Postwar Europe and the Origins of the Cold War 944
The Legacies of the Second World War • The Peace Settlement and Cold War Origins • West Versus East • Big Science in the Nuclear Age

The Western Renaissance/Recovery in Western Europe 954
The Search for Political and Social Consensus • Toward European Unity • The Consumer Revolution
Evaluating the Evidence 28.1 Western European Recovery and the Promise of Prosperity 956

Developments in the Soviet Union and the East Bloc 959
Postwar Life in the East Bloc • Reform and De-Stalinization • Foreign Policy and Domestic Rebellion • The Limits of Reform
Evaluating the Evidence 28.2 The Nixon-Khrushchev "Kitchen Debate" 962

The End of Empires 966
Decolonization and the Global Cold War • The Struggle for Power in Asia • Independence and Conflict in the Middle East • Decolonization in Africa
Evaluating the Evidence 28.3 Frantz Fanon on Violence, Decolonization, and Human Dignity 969

Postwar Social Transformations 975
Changing Class Structures • Patterns of Postwar Migration • New Roles for Women • Youth Culture and the Generation Gap
Individuals in Society Armando Rodrigues 977

LOOKING BACK / LOOKING AHEAD 980
REVIEW & EXPLORE 981

29 Challenging the Postwar Order
1960–1991 982

Reform and Protest in the 1960s 984
Cold War Tensions Thaw • The Affluent Society • The Counterculture Movement • The United States and Vietnam • Student Revolts and 1968 • The 1960s in the East Bloc
Evaluating the Evidence 29.1 Human Rights Under the Helsinki Accords 987

Crisis and Change in Western Europe 995
Economic Crisis and Hardship • The New Conservatism • Challenges and Victories for Women • The Rise of the Environmental Movement • Separatism and Right-Wing Extremism
Individuals in Society Margaret Thatcher 999
Evaluating the Evidence 29.2 Simone de Beauvoir's Feminist Critique of Marriage 1002

The Decline of "Developed Socialism" 1005
State and Society in the East Bloc • Dissent in Czechoslovakia and Poland • From Détente Back to Cold War • Gorbachev's Reforms in the Soviet Union
Evaluating the Evidence 29.3 Dissent in the Czechoslovak Socialist Republic 1008

The Revolutions of 1989 1012
The Collapse of Communism in the East Bloc • German Unification and the End of the Cold War • The Disintegration of the Soviet Union

LOOKING BACK / LOOKING AHEAD 1018
REVIEW & EXPLORE 1019

30 *Life* in an Age of Globalization

1990 TO THE PRESENT   1020

Reshaping the Soviet Union and the Former East Bloc   1022
Economic Shock Therapy in Russia • Russian Revival Under Vladimir Putin • Coping with Change in the Former East Bloc • Tragedy in Yugoslavia • Instability in the Former Soviet Republics
Evaluating the Evidence 30.1 President Putin on Global Security   1025

The New Global System   1033
The Global Economy • The New European Union • Supranational Organizations • The Human Side of Globalization • Life in the Digital Age
Individuals in Society Edward Snowden   1040

Ethnic Diversity in Contemporary Europe   1042
The Prospect of Population Decline • Changing Immigration Flows • Toward a Multicultural Continent • Europe and Its Muslim Population

Confronting Long-Term Challenges   1049
Growing Strains in U.S.-European Relations • Turmoil in the Muslim World • The Global Recession and the Viability of the Eurozone • Dependence on Fossil Fuels • Climate Change and Environmental Degradation • Promoting Human Rights
Evaluating the Evidence 30.2 William Pfaff, Will the French Riots Change Anything?   1050
Evaluating the Evidence 30.3 The Thessaloniki Programme   1058

LOOKING BACK / LOOKING AHEAD   1062

REVIEW & EXPLORE   1063

Glossary   G-1

Index   I-1

About the Authors   I-66

photo: *The Standing March* is the collaborative work by the French artist known as JR and the U.S. filmmaker Darren Aronofsky/photo: Eric Feferberg/AFP/Getty Images

Maps, Figures, and Tables

CHAPTER 1

Map 1.1 Spread of Cultures in the Ancient Near East, ca. 3000–1640 B.C.E.   13

Map 1.2 Empires and Migrations in the Eastern Mediterranean   29

Figure 1.1 Sumerian Writing   15

CHAPTER 2

Map 2.1 The Assyrian and Persian Empires, ca. 1000–500 B.C.E.   48

Spot Map The Kingdom of Kush, 1000 B.C.E.–300 C.E.   38

Spot Map Phoenician Settlements in the Mediterranean   40

Spot Map The Hebrew Exodus and State, ca. 1250–800 B.C.E.   42

CHAPTER 3

Map 3.1 Classical Greece, 500–338 B.C.E.   63

Map 3.2 Greek Colonization, ca. 750–550 B.C.E.   71

Map 3.3 The Peloponnesian War, 431–404 B.C.E.   77

Spot Map Spartan Expansion, ca. 750–500 B.C.E.   72

Spot Map The Persian Wars, 499–479 B.C.E.   75

Spot Map The Delian League, ca. 478–431 B.C.E.   76

CHAPTER 4

Map 4.1 Alexander's Conquests, 334–324 B.C.E.   95

Map 4.2 The Hellenistic World, ca. 263 B.C.E.   100

CHAPTER 5

Map 5.1 Roman Italy and the City of Rome, ca. 218 B.C.E.   123

Map 5.2 Roman Expansion During the Republic, ca. 282–44 B.C.E.   134

Spot Map The Etruscans, ca. 500 B.C.E.   124

CHAPTER 6

Map 6.1 Roman Expansion Under the Empire, 44 B.C.E.–180 C.E.   156

Map 6.2 Production and Trade in the Pax Romana, ca. 27 B.C.E.–180 C.E.   173

Spot Map Roman Britain, ca. 130 C.E.   167

CHAPTER 7

Map 7.1 The Division of the Roman World, 293   186

Map 7.2 The Spread of Christianity, to 600   189

Map 7.3 The Barbarian Migrations, ca. 340–500   201

Map 7.4 The Byzantine Empire, ca. 600   211

CHAPTER 8

Map 8.1 The Spread of Islam, 622–900   222

Map 8.2 Charlemagne's Conquests, ca. 768–814   232

Map 8.3 Invasions and Migrations of the Ninth and Tenth Centuries   241

Spot Map The Treaty of Verdun, 843   240

Spot Map Kievan Rus, ca. 1050   244

CHAPTER 9

Map 9.1 The Growth of the Kingdom of France, 1180–1314   255

Map 9.2 The Holy Roman Empire and the Kingdom of Sicily, ca. 1200   256

Map 9.3 The Reconquista, ca. 750–1492   259

Map 9.4 The Crusades   278

CHAPTER 10

Map 10.1 European Population Density, ca. 1300   300

Map 10.2 Trade and Manufacturing in Thirteenth-Century Europe   302

Map 10.3 Intellectual Centers of Medieval Europe   310

Spot Map The Hanseatic League, 1300–1400   303

CHAPTER 11

Map 11.1 The Course of the Black Death in Fourteenth-Century Europe   328

Map 11.2 The Hundred Years' War, 1337–1453   334

Map 11.3 Fourteenth-Century Revolts   345

Spot Map The Great Schism, 1378–1417   340

Spot Map The Hussite Revolution, 1415–1436   341

CHAPTER 12

Map 12.1 The Italian City-States, ca. 1494   361

Map 12.2 The Growth of Printing in Europe, 1448–1552   372

Map 12.3 The Unification of Spain and the Expulsion of the Jews, Fifteenth Century   385

Spot Map The Expansion of France, 1475–1500   383

CHAPTER 13

Map 13.1 The Global Empire of Charles V, ca. 1556   405

Map 13.2 Religious Divisions in Europe, ca. 1555   415

Spot Map The Route of the Spanish Armada, 1588   411

Spot Map The Netherlands, 1609   420

CHAPTER 14

Map 14.1 The Fifteenth-Century Afroeurasian Trading World   428

Map 14.2 Overseas Exploration and Conquest in the Fifteenth and Sixteenth Centuries   436

Map 14.3 Seaborne Trading Empires in the Sixteenth and Seventeenth Centuries   453

Spot Map Columbus's First Voyage to the New World, 1492–1493   438

Spot Map Invasion of Tenochtitlan, 1519–1521   442

CHAPTER 15

Map 15.1 Europe After the Thirty Years' War   470

Map 15.2 Europe After the Peace of Utrecht, 1715   479

Map 15.3 The Growth of Austria and Brandenburg-Prussia to 1748   483

Map 15.4 The Ottoman Empire at Its Height, 1566   490

Spot Map The Acquisitions of Louis XIV, 1668–1713   477

Spot Map The Expansion of Russia to 1725   486

Spot Map The English Civil War, 1642–1649   495

CHAPTER 16

Map 16.1 The Partition of Poland, 1772–1795   536

Spot Map The War of the Austrian Succession, 1740–1748   533

Spot Map The Pale of Settlement, 1791   539

CHAPTER 17

Map 17.1 Industry and Population in Eighteenth-Century Europe   554

Map 17.2 The Atlantic Economy in 1701   561

Spot Map Plantation Zones, ca. 1700   564

Spot Map India, 1805   571

Figure 17.1 The Growth of Population in England, 1550–1850   549

Figure 17.2 The Increase of Population in Europe, 1650–1850   551

Figure 17.3 Exports of English Manufactured Goods, 1700–1774   563

CHAPTER 18

Map 18.1 Literacy in France, ca. 1789   588

CHAPTER 19

Map 19.1 The Seven Years' War in Europe, North America, and India, 1755–1763   614

Map 19.2 Napoleonic Europe in 1812   636

Map 19.3 The War of Haitian Independence, 1791–1804   641

Spot Map The Great Fear, 1789   624

Spot Map Areas of Insurrection, 1793   629

Spot Map German Confederation of the Rhine, 1806   635

CHAPTER 20

Map 20.1 The Industrial Revolution in Great Britain, ca. 1850   656

Map 20.2 Continental Industrialization, ca. 1850   660

Spot Map Cottage Industry and Transportation in Eighteenth-Century Great Britain   648

Table 20.1 Per Capita Levels of Industrialization, 1750–1913   659

CHAPTER 21

Map 21.1 Europe in 1815   682

Map 21.2 Peoples of the Habsburg Monarchy, 1815   687

Map 21.3 The Revolutions of 1848   711

Spot Map Greek Independence, 1830   703

CHAPTER 22

Map 22.1 European Cities of 100,000 or More, 1800–1900   719

Map 22.2 The Modernization of Paris, ca. 1850–1870   723

Figure 22.1 The Decline of Death Rates in England and Wales, Germany, France, and Sweden, 1840–1913   722

Figure 22.2 The Decline of Birthrates in England and Wales, France, Germany, and Sweden, 1840–1913   740

CHAPTER 23

Map 23.1 The Unification of Italy, 1859–1870   758

Map 23.2 The Unification of Germany, 1864–1871   762

Map 23.3 Slavery in the United States, 1860   765

Map 23.4 Russian Expansion, 1856–1900   768

Spot Map U.S. Secession, 1860–1861   765

Spot Map The Crimean War, 1853–1856   766

CHAPTER 24

Map 24.1 European Investment to 1914   795

Map 24.2 The Partition of Africa   806

Map 24.3 Asia in 1914   810

Spot Map The Suez Canal, 1869   798

Spot Map The Great Rebellion, 1857–1858   819

Figure 24.1 The Growth of Average Income per Person in Industrialized Countries, Nonindustrialized Countries, and Great Britain, 1750–1970   792

Figure 24.2 Emigration from Europe by Decade, 1860–1940   800

Figure 24.3 Origins and Destinations of European Emigrants, 1851–1960   801

CHAPTER 25

Map 25.1 European Alliances at the Outbreak of World War I, 1914   829

Map 25.2 The Balkans, 1878–1914   833

Map 25.3 World War I in Europe and the Middle East, 1914–1918   836

Map 25.4 Territorial Changes After World War I   855

Spot Map The Schlieffen Plan   834

Spot Map The Battle of the Somme, 1916   837

Spot Map The Armenian Genocide, 1915–1918   839

Spot Map The Battle of Gallipoli   840

Figure 25.1 Casualties of World War I   862

CHAPTER 26

Map 26.1 The Great Depression in the United States and Europe, 1929–1939   892

Spot Map French Occupation of the Ruhr, 1923–1925   886

Spot Map British Unemployment, 1932   894

CHAPTER 27

Map 27.1 The Formation of the U.S.S.R.   909

Map 27.2 The Growth of Nazi Germany, 1933–1939   926

Map 27.3 World War II in Europe and Africa, 1939–1945   930

Map 27.4 The Holocaust, 1941–1945   933

Map 27.5 World War II in the Pacific   936

Spot Map Italy's Ethiopian Campaign, 1935–1936   919

Spot Map Vichy France, 1940   928

Spot Map Nazi Occupation of Poland and East-Central Europe, 1939–1942   931

CHAPTER 28

Map 28.1 The Aftermath of World War II in Europe, ca. 1945–1950   946

Map 28.2 Cold War Europe in the 1950s   950

Map 28.3 Decolonization in Africa and Asia, 1947 to the Present   967

Spot Map Israel, 1948   971

Spot Map The Suez Crisis, 1956   972

CHAPTER 29

Map 29.1 Pollution in Europe, ca. 1990   1004

Map 29.2 Democratic Movements in Eastern Europe, 1989   1013

Spot Map The Soviet War in Afghanistan, 1979–1989   1010

Spot Map The Reunification of Germany, 1990   1016

CHAPTER 30

Map 30.1 Russia and the Successor States, 1991–2015   1027

Map 30.2 The Breakup of Yugoslavia, 1991–2006   1030

Map 30.3 The European Union, 2016   1035

Map 30.4 Major Migration Routes into Contemporary Europe   1045

Spot Map Iraq, ca. 2010   1054

Spot Map Primary Oil and Gas Pipelines to Europe, ca. 2005   1059

Special Features

EVALUATING THE EVIDENCE

CHAPTER 1

1.1 Paleolithic Venus Figures   8

1.2 Gilgamesh's Quest for Immortality   18

1.3 Egyptian Home Life   27

CHAPTER 2

2.1 The Report of Wenamun   39

2.2 A Jewish Family Contract   45

2.3 Assyrians Besiege a City   51

CHAPTER 3

3.1 Hesiod, *Works and Days*   68

3.2 The Acropolis of Athens   80

3.3 Sophocles, *Antigone*   82

CHAPTER 4

4.1 Arrian on Alexander the Great   97

4.2 A Hellenistic Spell of Attraction   109

4.3 The Periplus of the Erythraean Sea   116

CHAPTER 5

5.1 The Temple of Hercules Victor   128

5.2 A Woman's Actions in the Turia Inscription   137

5.3 Cicero and the Plot to Kill Caesar   148

CHAPTER 6

6.1 Augustus, *Res Gestae*   158

6.2 Ovid, *The Art of Love*   162

6.3 Ara Pacis   163

CHAPTER 7

7.1 Tacitus on Germanic Society   198

7.2 Battle Between Romans and Goths   204

7.3 Gregory of Tours on the Veneration of Relics   208

CHAPTER 8

8.1 The Muslim Conquest of Spain   225

8.2 The Capitulary de Villis   233

8.3 The Death of Beowulf   239

CHAPTER 9

9.1 Marriage and Wardship in the Norman Exchequer   254

9.2 Pope Boniface VIII, *Unam Sanctam*   269

9.3 Brother Henry as Composer and Singer   275

CHAPTER 10

10.1 The Pilgrim's Guide to Santiago de Compostela   297

10.2 Healthy Living   312

10.3 Courtly Love Poetry   316

CHAPTER 11

11.1 Dance of Death   331

11.2 The Trial of Joan of Arc   337

11.3 Christine de Pizan, Advice to the Wives of Artisans   348

CHAPTER 12

12.1 A Sermon of Savonarola   363

12.2 Thomas More, *Utopia*   369

12.3 A Gold Coin of Ferdinand and Isabella   386

CHAPTER 13

13.1 Martin Luther, *On Christian Liberty*   396

13.2 Domestic Scene   402

13.3 Elizabethan Injunctions About Religion   410

CHAPTER 14

14.1 Columbus Describes His First Voyage   440

14.2 Interpreting the Spread of Disease Among Natives   449

14.3 Tenochtitlan Leaders Respond to Spanish Missionaries   458

CHAPTER 15

15.1 Letter from Versailles   475

15.2 Peter the Great and Foreign Experts   488

15.3 John Locke, *Two Treatises of Government*   498

CHAPTER 16

16.1   Galileo Galilei, *The Sidereal Messenger*   512

16.2   "An Account of a Particular Species of Cocoon"   514

16.3   Denis Diderot, "Supplement to Bougainville's Voyage"   528

CHAPTER 17

17.1   Arthur Young on the Benefits of Enclosure   548

17.2   Adam Smith on the Division of Labor   558

17.3   Olaudah Equiano's Economic Arguments for Ending Slavery   566

CHAPTER 18

18.1   Parisian Boyhood   586

18.2   A Day in the Life of Paris   592

18.3   Advice to Methodists   599

CHAPTER 19

19.1   Abigail Adams, "Remember the Ladies"   619

19.2   Abbé Sieyès, *What Is the Third Estate?*   622

19.3   Contrasting Visions of the Sans-Culottes   630

CHAPTER 20

20.1   Debate over Child Labor Laws   667

20.2   The Testimony of Young Mine Workers   670

20.3   Advice for Middle-Class Women   675

CHAPTER 21

21.1   The Karlsbad Decrees: Conservative Reaction in the German Confederation   689

21.2   English Romantic Poets   697

21.3   Jacob and Wilhelm Grimm, *Children's Stories and Household Tales*   700

CHAPTER 22

22.1   First Impressions of the World's Biggest City   720

22.2   Stephan Zweig on Middle-Class Youth and Sexuality   734

22.3   Émile Zola and Realism in Literature   749

CHAPTER 23

23.1   The Struggle for the Italian Nation   759

23.2   Eyewitness Accounts of Bloody Sunday   770

23.3   Adelheid Popp, the Making of a Socialist   784

CHAPTER 24

24.1   Nativism in the United States   804

24.2   The White Man's Burden   814

24.3   The Brown Man's Burden   817

CHAPTER 25

25.1   Poetry in the Trenches   838

25.2   Wartime Propaganda Posters   845

25.3   Peace, Land, and Bread for the Russian People   851

CHAPTER 26

26.1   Friedrich Nietzsche Pronounces the Death of God   870

26.2   The Futurist Manifesto   878

26.3   George Orwell on Life on the Dole   896

CHAPTER 27

27.1   Stalin Justifies the Five-Year Plan   910

27.2   Famine and Recovery on a Soviet Collective Farm   913

27.3   Everyday Life in the London Blitz   929

CHAPTER 28

28.1   Western European Recovery and the Promise of Prosperity   956

28.2   The Nixon-Khrushchev "Kitchen Debate"   962

28.3   Frantz Fanon on Violence, Decolonization, and Human Dignity   969

CHAPTER 29

29.1   Human Rights Under the Helsinki Accords   987

29.2   Simone de Beauvoir's Feminist Critique of Marriage   1002

29.3   Dissent in the Czechoslovak Socialist Republic   1008

CHAPTER 30

30.1   President Putin on Global Security   1025

30.2   William Pfaff, Will the French Riots Change Anything?   1050

30.3   The Thessaloniki Programme   1058

INDIVIDUALS IN SOCIETY

Hatshepsut and Nefertiti   31

Cyrus the Great   53

Aristophanes   84

Archimedes, Scientist and Inventor   114

Queen Cleopatra   146

Pliny the Elder   166

Theodora of Constantinople   214

The Venerable Bede   238

Hildegard of Bingen   272

Francesco Datini   305

Meister Eckhart   343

Leonardo da Vinci   376

Anna Jansz of Rotterdam   400

Juan de Pareja   452

Hürrem   492

Moses Mendelssohn and the Jewish
   Enlightenment   538

Rebecca Protten   568

Rose Bertin, "Minister of Fashion"   595

Toussaint L'Ouverture   642

Samuel Crompton   652

Germaine de Staël   699

Franziska Tiburtius   742

Theodor Herzl   782

Cecil Rhodes   808

Vera Brittain   844

Gustav Stresemann   888

Primo Levi   935

Armando Rodrigues   977

Margaret Thatcher   999

Edward Snowden   1040

A History of
Western Society

CONCISE EDITION

Understanding Western History
What do we mean by "the West" and "Western civilization"?

The Earliest Human Societies
How did early human societies develop and create new technologies and cultural forms?

Civilization in Mesopotamia
What kind of civilization did the Sumerians develop in Mesopotamia?

Empires in Mesopotamia
How did the Akkadian and Old Babylonian empires develop in Mesopotamia?

The Egyptians
How did the Egyptians create a prosperous and long-lasting society?

Life in New Kingdom Egypt, ca. 1500–1300 B.C.E. In this wall painting from the tomb of an official, a man guides a wooden ox-drawn plow through the soil, while the woman walking behind throws seed in the furrow. The painting was designed not to show real peasants working but to depict the servants who would spring to life to serve the deceased in the afterlife. Nevertheless, the gender division of labor and the plow itself are probably accurate. (Deir el-Medina, Thebes, Egypt/ Bridgeman Images)

1

Origins

TO 1200 B.C.E.

What is history? That seemingly simple question hides great complexities. If history is the story of humans, what does it mean to be human? As they have in the past, philosophers, religious leaders, politicians, physicians, and others wrestle with this question every day, as do scientists using technologies that were unavailable until very recently, such as DNA analysis and radiocarbon dating. Is all of the human past "history"? Previous generations of historians would generally have answered no, that history only began when writing began and everything before that was "prehistory." This leaves out most of the human story, however, and today historians no longer see writing as such a sharp dividing line. They explore all eras of the human past using many different types of sources, although they do still tend to pay more attention to written sources.

For most of their history, humans were foragers moving through the landscape, inventing ever more specialized tools. About 11,000 years ago, people in some places domesticated plants and animals, which many scholars describe as the most significant change in human history. They began to live in permanent villages, some of which grew into cities. They created structures of governance to control their more complex societies, along with military forces and taxation systems. Some invented writing to record taxes, inventories, and payments, and they later put writing to other uses, including the preservation of stories, traditions, and history. The first places where these new technologies and systems were introduced were the Tigris and Euphrates River Valleys of southwest Asia and the Nile Valley of northeast Africa, areas whose history became linked through trade connections, military conquests, and migrations. ■

Understanding Western History

Most human groups have left some record of themselves. Some left artifacts, others pictures or signs, and still others written documents. In many of these records, groups set up distinctions between themselves and others. Some of these distinctions are between small groups such as neighboring tribes, some between countries and civilizations, and some between vast parts of the world. Among the most enduring of the latter are the ideas of "the West" and "the East."

Describing the West

Ideas about the West and the distinction between West and East derived originally from the ancient Greeks. Greek civilization grew up in the shadow of earlier civilizations to the south and east of Greece, especially Egypt and Mesopotamia. Greeks defined themselves in relation to these more advanced cultures, which they saw as "Eastern." Greeks were also the first to use the word *Europe* for a geographic area, taking the word from the name of a minor goddess. They set Europe in opposition to "Asia" (also named for a minor goddess), by which they meant both what we now call western Asia and what we call Africa.

The Greeks passed this conceptualization on to the Romans, who saw themselves clearly as part of the West. For some Romans, Greece remained in the West, while other Romans came to view Greek traditions as vaguely "Eastern." To Romans, the East was more sophisticated and more advanced, but also decadent and somewhat immoral. Roman value judgments have continued to shape preconceptions, stereotypes, and views of differences between the West and the East—which in the past were also called the "Occident" and the "Orient"—to this day.

Greco-Roman ideas about the West were passed on to people who lived in western and northern Europe, who saw themselves as the inheritors of this classical tradition and thus as the West. When these Europeans established colonies outside of Europe beginning in the late fifteenth century, they regarded what they were doing as taking Western culture with them, even though many aspects of Western culture, such as Christianity, had actually originated in what Europeans by that point regarded as the East. With colonization, *Western* came to mean those cultures that included significant numbers of people of European ancestry, no matter where on the globe they were located.

In the early twentieth century educators and other leaders in the United States became worried that many people, especially young people, were becoming cut off from European intellectual and cultural traditions. They encouraged the establishment of college and university courses focusing on "Western civilization," the first of which was taught at Columbia University in 1919. In designing the course, the faculty included cultures that as far back as the ancient Greeks had been considered Eastern, such as Egypt and Mesopotamia. This conceptualization and the course spread to other colleges and universities, developing into what became known as the introductory Western civilization course, a staple of historical instruction for generations of college students.

After World War II divisions between the West and the East changed again. Now there was a new division between East and West within Europe, with *Western* coming to imply a capitalist economy and *Eastern* the Communist Eastern bloc. Thus, Japan was considered Western, and some Greek-speaking areas of Europe became Eastern. The collapse of communism in the Soviet Union and eastern Europe in the 1980s brought yet another refiguring, with much of eastern Europe joining the European Union, originally a Western organization.

At the beginning of the twenty-first century, *Western* still suggests a capitalist economy, but it also has certain cultural connotations, such as individualism and competition, which some see as negative and others as positive. Islamist radicals often describe their aims as an end to Western cultural, economic, and political influence, though Islam itself is generally described, along with Judaism and Christianity, as a Western monotheistic religion. Thus, throughout its long history, the meaning of "the West" has shifted, but in every era it has meant more than a geographical location.

What Is Civilization?

Just as the meaning of the word *Western* is shaped by culture, so is the meaning of the word *civilization*. In the ancient world, residents of cities generally viewed themselves as more advanced and sophisticated than rural folk—a judgment still made today. They saw themselves as more "civilized," a word that comes from the Latin adjective *civilis*, which refers to a citizen, either of a town or of a larger political unit such as an empire.

This depiction of people as either civilized or uncivilized was gradually extended to whole societies. Beginning in the eighteenth century, European scholars described any society in which political, economic, and social organizations operated on a large scale, not primarily through families and kin groups, as a **civilization**. Civilizations had cities; laws that governed human relationships; codes of manners and social conduct that regulated how people were to behave; and scientific, philosophical, and theological beliefs that explained the larger world. Civilizations also had some form of political organization, what political scientists call "the state," through which one group was able to coerce resources out of others to engage in group endeavors, such as building large structures or carrying out warfare. States established armies, bureaucracies, and taxation systems. Generally only societies that used writing were judged to be civilizations, because writing allowed more permanent expression of thoughts, ideas, and feelings. Human societies in which people were nomadic or lived in small villages without formal laws, and in which traditions were passed down orally, were not regarded as civilizations.

Until the middle of the twentieth century, historians often referred to the places where writing and cities developed as "cradles of civilization," proposing a model of

Chronology

ca. 250,000 B.C.E.	*Homo sapiens* evolve in Africa
250,000–9000 B.C.E.	Paleolithic era
9000 B.C.E.	Beginning of the Neolithic; crop raising; domestication of sheep and goats
ca. 7000 B.C.E.	Domestication of cattle; plow agriculture
ca. 5500 B.C.E.	Smelting of copper
ca. 3800 B.C.E.	Establishment of first Mesopotamian cities
ca. 3200 B.C.E.	Development of cuneiform and hieroglyphic writing
ca. 3100 B.C.E.	Unification of Upper and Lower Egypt
ca. 3000 B.C.E.	Development of wheeled transport; beginning of bronze technology
ca. 2500 B.C.E.	Bronze technology becomes common in many areas
ca. 2300 B.C.E.	Establishment of the Akkadian empire
ca. 1800 B.C.E.	Hyksos people begin to settle in the Nile Delta
1792–1750 B.C.E.	Hammurabi rules Babylon
1258 B.C.E.	Peace treaty between Egyptian pharaoh Ramesses II and Hittite king Hattusili III
ca. 1200 B.C.E.	"Bronze Age Collapse"; destruction and drought

A note on dates: This book generally uses the terms B.C.E. (Before the Common Era) and C.E. (Common Era) when giving dates, a system of chronology based on the Christian calendar and now used widely around the world.

civilization A large-scale system of human political, economic, and social organizations; civilizations have cities, laws, states, and often writing.

development for all humanity patterned on that of an individual life span. However, the idea that all human societies developed (or should develop) on a uniform process from a "cradle" to a "mature" civilization has now been largely discredited, and some historians choose not to use the term *civilization* at all because it could imply that some societies are superior to others.

Just as the notion of "civilization" has been questioned, so has the notion of "Western civilization." Ever since the idea of "Western civilization" was first developed, people have debated what its geographical extent and core values are. Are there certain beliefs, customs, concepts, and institutions that set Western civilization apart from other civilizations, and if so, when and how did these originate? How were these values and practices transmitted over space and time, and how did they change? No civilization stands alone, and each is influenced by its neighbors. Whatever Western civilization was—and is—it has been shaped by interactions with other societies, cultures, and civilizations, but the idea that there are basic distinctions between the West and the rest of the world in terms of cultural values has been very powerful for thousands of years, and it still shapes the way many people, including people in power, view the world.

The Earliest Human Societies

FOCUS QUESTION
How did early human societies develop and create new technologies and cultural forms?

Scientists who study the history of the earth use a variety of systems to classify and divide time. Geologists and paleontologists divide time into periods that last many millions of years, determined by the movements of continents and the evolution and extinction of plant and animal species. During the nineteenth century, archaeologists coined labels for eras of the human past according to the primary material out of which surviving tools had been made. Thus the earliest human era became the Stone Age, the next era the Bronze Age, and the next the Iron Age. They further divided the Stone Age into the **Paleolithic** (Old Stone) **era**, during which people used stone, bone, and other natural products to make tools and gained food largely by foraging—that is, by gathering plant products, trapping or catching small animals and birds, and hunting larger prey. This was followed by the **Neolithic** (New Stone) **era**, which saw the beginning of agricultural and animal domestication. People around the world adopted agriculture at various times, and some never did, but the transition between the Paleolithic and the Neolithic is usually set at about 9000 B.C.E., the point at which agriculture was first developed.

Paleolithic era The period of human history up to about 9000 B.C.E., when tools were made from stone and bone and people gained their food through foraging.

Neolithic era The period after 9000 B.C.E., when people developed agriculture, domesticated animals, and used tools made of stone and wood.

From the First Hominids to the Paleolithic Era

Using many different pieces of evidence from all over the world, archaeologists, paleontologists, and other scholars have developed a view of human evolution that has a widely shared basic outline, though there are disagreements about details. Sometime between 7 and 6 million years ago in southern and eastern Africa, groups of human ancestors (members of the biological "hominid" family) began to walk upright, which allowed them to carry things. About 3.4 million years ago some hominids began to use naturally occurring objects as tools, and around 2.5 million years ago one group in East Africa began to make simple tools, a feat that was accompanied by, and may have spurred, brain development. Groups migrated into much of Africa, and then into Asia and Europe; by about 600,000 years ago there were hominids throughout much of Afroeurasia.

About 200,000 years ago, again in East Africa, some of these early humans evolved into *Homo sapiens* ("thinking humans"), which had still larger and more complex brains that allowed for symbolic language and better social skills. *Homo sapiens* invented highly specialized tools made out of a variety of materials: barbed fishhooks and harpoons, snares and traps for catching small animals, bone needles for sewing clothing, awls for punching holes in leather, sharpened flint pieces bound to wooden or bone handles for hunting and cutting, and slings for carrying infants. They made regular use of fire for heat, light, and cooking, increasing the range of foods that were easily digestible. They also migrated, first across Africa, and by 70,000 years ago out of Africa into Eurasia. Eventually they traveled farther still, reaching Australia using rafts about 50,000 years ago and the Americas by about 15,000 years ago, or perhaps earlier. They moved into areas where other types of hominids lived, interacting with them and in some cases interbreeding with them. Gradually the other types of hominids became extinct, leaving *Homo sapiens* as the only survivors and the ancestors of all modern humans.

In the Paleolithic period humans throughout the world lived in ways that were similar to one another. Archaeological evidence and studies of modern foragers suggest that people generally lived in small groups of related individuals and moved throughout the landscape in search of food. In areas where food resources were especially rich, such as along seacoasts, they settled more permanently in one place, living in caves or building structures. They ate mostly plants, and much of the animal protein in their diet came from foods gathered or scavenged, such as insects and birds' eggs, rather than hunted directly. Paleolithic peoples did, however, hunt large game. Groups working together forced animals over cliffs, threw spears, and, beginning about 15,000 B.C.E., used bows to shoot projectiles so that they could stand farther away from their prey while hunting.

Paleolithic people were not differentiated by wealth, because in a foraging society it was not advantageous to accumulate material goods. Most foraging societies that exist today, or did so until recently, have some type of division of labor by sex, and also by age. Men are more often responsible for hunting, through which they gain prestige as well as meat, and women for gathering plant and animal products. This may or may not have been the case in the Paleolithic era, or there may have been a diversity of patterns.

Early human societies are often described in terms of their tools, but this misses a large part of the story. Beginning in the Paleolithic era, human beings have expressed themselves through what we would now term the arts or culture: painting and decorating walls and objects, making music, telling stories, dancing alone or in groups. Paleolithic evidence, particularly from after about 50,000 years ago, includes flutes, carvings, jewelry, and amazing paintings done on cave walls and rock outcroppings that depict animals, people, and symbols. Burials, paintings, and objects also suggest that people may have developed ideas about supernatural forces that controlled some aspects of the natural world and the humans in it, what we now term spirituality or religion. Spiritually adept men and women communicated with that unseen world, and objects such as carvings or masks were probably thought to have special healing or protective powers. (See "Evaluating the Evidence 1.1: Paleolithic Venus Figures," page 8.)

Paleolithic Venus Figures

Written sources provide evidence about the human past only after the development of writing, allowing us to read the words of people long dead. For most of human history, however, there were no written sources, so we "read" the past through objects. Interpreting written documents is difficult, and interpreting archaeological evidence is even more difficult and often contentious. For example, small stone statues of women with enlarged breasts and buttocks dating from the later Paleolithic period (roughly 33,000–9,000 B.C.E.) have been found in many parts of Europe. These were dubbed "Venus figures" by nineteenth-century archaeologists, who thought they represented Paleolithic standards of female beauty just as the goddess Venus represented classical standards. A reproduction of one of these statues, the six-inch-tall Venus of Lespugue made from a mammoth tusk about 25,000 years ago in southern France, is shown here.

EVALUATE THE EVIDENCE

1. As you look at this statue, does it seem to link more closely with fertility or with sexuality? How might your own situation as a twenty-first-century person shape your answer to this question?
2. Some scholars see Venus figures as evidence that Paleolithic society was egalitarian or female dominated, but others point out that images of female deities or holy figures are often found in religions that deny women official authority. Can you think of examples of the latter? Which point of view seems most persuasive to you?

(Museo Civico Palazzo Chiericati, Vicenza, Italy/De Agostini Picture Library/Alfredo Dagli Orti/Bridgeman Images)

Total human population grew very slowly during the Paleolithic. One estimate proposes that there were perhaps 500,000 humans in the world about 30,000 years ago. By about 10,000 years ago, this number had grown to 5 million—ten times as many people. This was a significant increase, but it took twenty thousand years. The low population density meant that human impact on the environment was relatively small, although still significant.

Planting Crops

Foraging remained the basic way of life for most of human history, and for groups living in extreme environments, such as tundras or deserts, it was the only possible way to survive. In a few especially fertile areas, however, the natural environment provided enough food that people could become more settled. About 15,000 years ago, the earth's climate entered a warming phase, and more parts of the world were able to support sedentary or semi-sedentary groups of foragers. In several of these places, foragers began planting seeds in the ground along with gathering wild grains, roots, and other foodstuffs. By observation, they learned the optimum times and places for planting. They removed unwanted plants through weeding and selected the seeds they planted in order to get crops that had favorable characteristics, such as larger edible parts. Through this human intervention, certain crops became domesticated, that is, modified by selective breeding so as to serve human needs.

Intentional crop planting first developed around 9000 B.C.E. in the area archaeologists call the **Fertile Crescent**, which runs from present-day Lebanon, Israel, and Jordan north to Turkey and then south and east to the Iran-Iraq border. In this area of mild climate, wild barley and wheat were abundant, along with fruit and nut trees, migrating ducks, and herds of gazelles and other animals. Over the next two millennia, intentional crop planting emerged for the most part independently in the Nile River Valley, western Africa, China, India, Papua New Guinea, Mesoamerica, and perhaps other places where the archaeological evidence has not survived.

Why, after living successfully as foragers for tens of thousands of years, did humans in so many parts of the world begin raising crops at about the same time? The answer to this question is not clear, but crop raising may have resulted from population pressures in those parts of the world where the warming climate provided more food through foraging. More food meant lower child mortality and longer life spans, which allowed populations to grow. People then had a choice: they could move to a new area — the solution that people had always relied on when faced with the problem of food scarcity — or they could develop ways to increase the food supply. They chose the latter and began to plant more intensively, beginning cycles of expanding population and intensification of land use that have continued to today.

A very recent archaeological find at Göbekli Tepe in present-day Turkey, at the northern edge of the Fertile Crescent, suggests that cultural factors may have played a role in the development of agriculture. Here, around 9000 B.C.E., hundreds of people came together to build rings of massive, multi-ton elaborately carved limestone pillars, and then covered them with dirt and built more. The people who created this site lived some distance away, where archaeological remains indicate that at the time they first carved the pillars, they ate wild game and plants, not crops. We can only speculate about why so many people expended the effort they did to carve these pillars and raise them into place, but the project may have unintentionally spurred the development of new methods of food production that would allow the many workers to be fed efficiently. Indeed, it is very near here that evidence of the world's oldest domesticated wheat has been discovered. Archaeologists speculate that, at least in this case, the symbolic, cultural, or perhaps religious importance of the structure can help explain why the people building it changed from foraging to agriculture.

Fertile Crescent An area of mild climate and abundant wild grain where agriculture first developed, in present-day Lebanon, Israel, Jordan, Turkey, and Iraq.

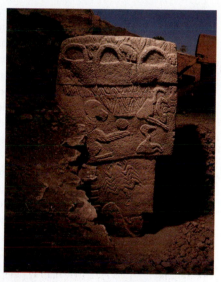

Pillar at Göbekli Tepe The huge limestone pillars arranged in rings at the Paleolithic site Göbekli Tepe are somewhat humanoid in shape, and the carvings are of dangerous animals, including lions, boars, foxes, snakes, vultures, and scorpions. The structure required enormous skill and effort of the people who built it, and clearly had great importance to them. (Vincent J. Musi/National Geographic Creative)

Implications of Agriculture

Whatever the reasons for the move from foraging to agriculture, within several centuries of initial crop planting, people in the Fertile Crescent, parts of China, and the Nile Valley were relying primarily on domesticated food products. They built permanent houses near one another in villages and planted fields around the villages. In addition, they invented storage containers for food, such as pottery made from fired clay and woven baskets.

A field of planted and weeded crops yields ten to one hundred times as much food — measured in calories — as the same area of naturally occurring plants. It also requires much more labor, however, which was provided both by the greater number of people in the community and by those people working longer hours. In contrast to the twenty hours a week foragers spent on obtaining food, farming peoples were often in the fields from dawn to dusk. Early farmers were also less healthy than foragers were; their narrower range of foodstuffs made them more susceptible to disease and nutritional deficiencies, such as anemia, and also made them shorter. Still, farmers came to outnumber foragers, and slowly larger and larger parts of Europe, China, South and Southeast Asia, and Africa became home to farming villages, a dramatic human alteration of the environment.

At roughly the same time that they domesticated certain plants, people also domesticated animals. The earliest animal to be domesticated was the dog, which separated genetically as a subspecies from wolves at least 15,000 years ago and perhaps much earlier. In about 9000 B.C.E., at the same time they began to raise crops, people in the Fertile Crescent domesticated wild goats and sheep, probably using them first for meat, and then for milk, skins, and eventually fleece. They began to breed the goats and sheep selectively for qualities that they wanted, including larger size, greater strength, better coats, increased milk production, and more even temperaments. Sheep and goats allow themselves to be herded, and people developed a new form of living, **pastoralism**, based on herding and raising livestock; sometimes people trained dogs to assist them. Eventually other grazing animals, including cattle, camels, horses, yak, and reindeer, also became the basis of pastoral economies in Central and West Asia, many parts of Africa, and far northern Europe.

> **pastoralism** An economic system based on herding flocks of goats, sheep, cattle, or other animals beneficial to humans.

Crop raising and pastoralism brought significant changes to human ways of life, but the domestication of certain large animals had an even bigger impact. Cattle and water buffalo were domesticated in some parts of Asia and North Africa, in which they occurred naturally, by at least 7000 B.C.E. Donkeys were domesticated by about 4000 B.C.E., and horses by about 2500 B.C.E. All these animals can be trained to carry people or burdens on their backs and pull against loads dragged behind them, two qualities that are rare among the world's animal species. The domestication of large animals dramatically increased the power available to humans to carry out their tasks, which had both an immediate effect in the societies in which this happened and a long-term effect when these societies later encountered other societies in which human labor remained the only source of power.

Sometime in the seventh millennium B.C.E., people attached wooden sticks to frames that animals dragged through the soil, thus breaking it up and allowing seeds to sprout more easily. These simple scratch plows, pulled by cattle and water buffalo, allowed Neolithic people to produce a significant amount of surplus food, which meant that some people in the community could spend their days performing other tasks, increasing the division of labor. Surplus food had to be stored, and some people began to specialize in making products for storage, such as pots, baskets, bags, bins, and other kinds of containers. Others specialized in making tools, houses, and other items needed in village life or for producing specific types of food. Families and households became increasingly interdependent, trading food for other commodities or services.

The division of labor allowed by plow agriculture contributed to the creation of social hierarchies, that is, the divisions between rich and poor, elites and common people, that have been a central feature of human society since the Neolithic era. Although no written records were produced during this era, archaeological evidence provides some clues about how the hierarchies might have developed. Villagers needed more complex rules about how food was to be distributed and how differ-ent types of work were to be valued than did foragers. Certain individuals must have begun to specialize in the determination and enforcement of these rules, and informal structures of power gradually became more formalized. Religious specialists probably developed more elaborate rituals to celebrate life passages and to appeal to the gods for help in times of difficulty, such as illness.

Individuals who were the heads of large families or kin groups had control over the labor of others, and this power became more significant when that labor brought material goods that could be stored. The ability to control the labor of others could also come from physical strength, a charismatic personality, or leadership talents, and such traits may also have led to greater wealth. Material goods—plows, sheep, cattle, sheds, pots, carts—gave one the ability to amass still more material goods, and the gap between those who had them and those who did not widened. Social hierarchies were reinforced over generations as children inherited goods and status from their parents. By the time writing was invented, social distinctions between elites—rulers, nobles, hereditary priests, and other privileged groups—and the rest of the popula-tion were already in existence.

Along with hierarchies based on wealth and power, the development of agricul-ture was intertwined with a hierarchy based on gender. In many places, plow agricul-ture came to be a male task, perhaps because of men's upper-body strength or because plow agriculture was difficult to combine with care for infants and small children. Men's responsibility for plowing and other agricultural tasks took them outside the household more often than women's duties did, enlarging their opportunities for leadership. This role may have led to their being favored as inheritors of family land and the right to farm communally held land, because when inheritance systems were established in later millennia, they often favored sons when handing down land. Accordingly, over generations, women's independent access to resources decreased.

The system in which men have more power and access to resources than women of the same social level, and in which some men are dominant over other men, is called **patriarchy** and is found in every society with written records, although the level of inequality varies. Men's control of property was rarely absolute, because the desire to keep wealth and property within a family or kin group often resulted in women's inheriting, owning, and in some cases managing significant amounts of wealth. Hierarchies of wealth and power thus intersected with hierarchies of gender in complex ways.

patriarchy A society in which most power is held by older adult men, especially those from the elite groups.

Trade and Cross-Cultural Connections

By 7000 B.C.E. or so, some agricultural villages in the Fertile Crescent may have had as many as ten thousand residents. One of the best known of these, Çatal Hüyük in what is now Turkey, shows evidence of trade as well as specialization of labor. Çatal Hüyük's residents lived in densely packed mud-brick houses with walls covered in white plaster that had been made with burned lime. The men and women of the town grew wheat, barley, peas, and almonds and raised sheep and perhaps cattle, though they also seem to have hunted. They made textiles, pots, figurines, baskets, carpets, copper and lead beads, and other goods, and decorated their houses with murals showing animal and human figures. They gathered, sharpened, and polished obsidian, a volcanic rock that could be used for knives, blades, and mirrors, and then traded it with neighboring towns, obtaining seashells and flint. From here the obsidian was exchanged still farther away, for Neolithic societies slowly developed local and then regional networks of exchange and communication.

Among the goods traded in some parts of the world was copper, which people hammered into shapes for jewelry and tools. Like most metals, in its natural state copper usually occurs mixed with other materials in a type of rock called ore, and by about 5500 B.C.E. people in the Balkans had learned that copper could be extracted from ore by heating it in a smelting process. Smelted copper was poured into molds and made into spear points, axes, chisels, beads, and other objects. Pure copper is soft, but through experimentation artisans learned that it would become harder if they mixed it with other metals such as zinc, tin, or arsenic during heating, creating an alloy called bronze.

Bronze Age The period in which the production and use of bronze implements became basic to society.

Because it was stronger than copper, bronze had a far wider range of uses, so much so that later historians decided that its adoption marked a new period in human history: the **Bronze Age**. Like all new technologies, bronze arrived at different times in different places, so the dates of the Bronze Age vary. It began about 3000 B.C.E. in some places, and by about 2500 B.C.E. bronze technology was having an impact in many parts of the world. The end of the Bronze Age came with the adoption of iron technology, which also varied from 1200 B.C.E. to 300 B.C.E. (see Chapter 2). All metals were expensive and hard to obtain, however, so stone, wood, and bone remained important materials for tools and weapons long into the Bronze Age.

Objects were not the only things traded over increasingly long distances during the Neolithic period, for people also carried ideas as they traveled on foot, boats, or camels, and in wagons or carts. Knowledge about the seasons and the weather was vitally important for those who depended on crop raising, and agricultural peoples in many parts of the world began to calculate recurring patterns in the world around them, slowly developing calendars. Scholars have demonstrated that people built circular structures of mounded earth or huge upright stones to help them predict the movements of the sun and stars, including Nabta Playa, erected about 4500 B.C.E. in the desert west of the Nile Valley in Egypt, and Stonehenge, erected about 2500 B.C.E. in southern England.

polytheism The worship of many gods and goddesses.

The rhythms of the agricultural cycle and patterns of exchange also shaped religious beliefs and practices. Among foragers, human fertility is a mixed blessing, as too many children can overtax food supplies, but among crop raisers and pastoralists, fertility—of the land, animals, and people—is essential. Thus in many places multiple gods came to be associated with patterns of birth, growth, death, and regeneration in a system known as **polytheism**. Like humans, the gods came to have a division of labor and a social hierarchy. There were rain-gods and sun-gods, sky-goddesses and moon-goddesses, gods that ensured the health of cattle or the growth of corn, goddesses of the hearth and home.

Civilization in Mesopotamia

FOCUS QUESTION

What kind of civilization did the Sumerians develop in Mesopotamia?

The origins of Western civilization are generally traced to an area that is today not seen as part of the West: Mesopotamia (mehs-oh-puh-TAY-mee-uh), the Greek name for the land between the Euphrates (yoo-FRAY-teez) and Tigris (TIGH-grihs) Rivers (Map 1.1). The earliest agricultural villages in Mesopotamia were in the northern, hilly parts of the river valleys, where there is abundant rainfall

MAP 1.1 Spread of Cultures in the Ancient Near East, ca. 3000–1640 B.C.E.   This map illustrates the spread of the Mesopotamian and Egyptian cultures through the semicircular stretch of land often called the Fertile Crescent. From this area, the knowledge and use of agriculture spread throughout western Asia, North Africa, and Europe.

for crops. Farmers had brought techniques of crop raising southward by about 5000 B.C.E., to the southern part of Mesopotamia, called Sumer. In this arid climate farmers developed irrigation on a large scale, which demanded organized group effort but allowed the population to grow. By about 3800 B.C.E., one of the agricultural villages, Uruk (OO-rook), had expanded significantly, becoming what many historians view as the world's first city, with a population that eventually numbered more than fifty thousand. People living in Uruk built large temples to honor their chief god and goddess, and also invented the world's first system of writing, through which they recorded information about their society. Over the next thousand years, other cities also grew in Sumer, trading with one another and adopting writing.

Environment and Mesopotamian Development

From the outset, geography had a profound effect on Mesopotamia, because here agriculture is possible only with irrigation. Consequently, the Sumerians and later civilizations built their cities along the Tigris and Euphrates Rivers and their branches. They used the rivers to carry agricultural and trade goods, and also to provide water for vast networks of irrigation channels.

The Tigris and Euphrates flow quickly at certain times of the year and carry silt down from the mountains and hills, causing floods. To prevent major floods, the Sumerians created massive hydraulic projects, including reservoirs, dams, and dikes as well as canals. In stories written later, they described their chief god, Enlil, as "the raging flood which has no rival," and believed that at one point there had been a massive flood, a tradition that also gave rise to the biblical story of Noah:

> A flood will sweep over the cult-centers;
> To destroy the seed of mankind . . .
> Is the decision, the word of the assembly of the gods.[1]

Judging by historical records, however, actual destructive floods were few.

In addition to water and transport, the rivers supplied fish, a major element of the Sumerian diet, and reeds, which were used for making baskets and writing implements. The rivers also provided clay, which was hardened to create bricks, the Sumerians' primary building material in a region with little stone. Clay was fired into pots, and inventive artisans developed the potter's wheel so that they could make pots that were stronger and more uniform than those made by earlier methods of coiling ropes of clay. The potter's wheel in turn appears to have led to the introduction of wheeled vehicles sometime in the fourth millennium B.C.E. Exactly where they were invented is hotly contested, but Sumer is one of the first locations in which they appeared. Wheeled vehicles, pulled by domesticated donkeys, led to road building, which facilitated settlement, trade, and conquest, although travel and transport by water remained far easier.

Cities and villages in Sumer and farther up the Tigris and Euphrates traded with one another, and even before the development of writing or kings, it appears that colonists sometimes set out from one city to travel hundreds of miles to the north or west to found a new city or to set up a community in an existing center. These colonies might well have provided the Sumerian cities with goods, such as timber and metal ores, that were not available locally. The cities of the Sumerian heartland continued to grow and to develop governments, and each one came to dominate the surrounding countryside, becoming city-states independent from one another, though not very far apart.

The city-states of Sumer continued to rely on irrigation systems that required cooperation and at least some level of social and political cohesion. The authority to run this system was, it seems, initially assumed by Sumerian priests. Encouraged and directed by their religious leaders, people built temples on tall platforms in the center of their cities. Temples grew into elaborate complexes of buildings with storage space for grain and other products and housing for animals. (Much later, by about 2100 B.C.E., some of the major temple complexes were embellished with a huge stepped pyramid, called a ziggurat, with a shrine on the top.) The Sumerians believed that humans had been created to serve the gods, who lived in the temples. The gods needed not only shelter but food, drink, and clothing. Surrounding the temple and other large buildings were the houses of ordinary citizens, each constructed around a central courtyard. To support the needs of the gods, including the temple constructions, and to support the religious leaders, temples owned large estates, including fields and orchards. Temple officials employed individuals to work the temple's land, paying the workers in rations of grain, oil, and wool.

By 2500 B.C.E. there were more than a dozen city-states in Sumer. Each city developed religious, political, and military institutions, and judging by the fact that people began to construct walls around the cities and other fortifications, warfare between cities was quite common. Presumably their battles were sometimes sparked by disputes over water, as irrigation in one area reduced or altered the flow of rivers in other areas.

The Invention of Writing and the First Schools

The origins of writing probably go back to the ninth millennium B.C.E., when Near Eastern peoples used clay tokens as counters for record keeping. By the fourth millennium, people had realized that impressing the tokens on clay, or drawing pictures of the tokens on clay, was simpler than making tokens. This breakthrough in turn suggested that more information could be conveyed by adding pictures of still other objects. The result was a complex system of pictographs in which each sign pictured an object, such as "star" (line A of Figure 1.1). These pictographs were the forerunners of the Sumerian form of writing known as **cuneiform** (kyou-NEE-uh-form), from the Latin term for "wedge shaped," used to describe the indentations made by a sharpened stylus in clay.

Scribes could combine pictographs to express meaning. For example, the sign for woman (line B) and the sign for mountain (line C) were combined, literally, into "mountain woman" (line D), which meant "slave woman" because the Sumerians regularly obtained their slave women from wars against enemies in the mountains. Pictographs were initially limited in that they could not represent abstract ideas, but the development of ideograms—signs that represented ideas—made writing more versatile. Thus the sign for star could also be used to indicate heaven, sky, or even god. The real breakthrough came when scribes started using signs to represent sounds. For instance, the symbol for "water" (two parallel wavy lines) could also be used to indicate "in," which sounded the same as the spoken word for "water" in Sumerian.

The development of the Sumerian system of writing was piecemeal, with scribes making changes and additions as they were needed. The system became so complicated that scribal schools were established, which by 2500 B.C.E. flourished throughout Sumer. Students at the schools were all male, and most came from families in the middle range of urban society. Each school had a master, teachers, and monitors. Discipline was strict, and students were caned for sloppy work and misbehavior. One graduate of a scribal school had few fond memories of the joy of learning:

cuneiform Sumerian form of writing; the term describes the wedge-shaped marks made by a stylus.

FIGURE 1.1 **Sumerian Writing**
(Source: S. N. Kramer, *The Sumerians: Their History, Culture and Character.* Copyright © 1963 by The University of Chicago Press. All rights reserved. Used by permission.)

> My headmaster read my tablet, said:
> "There is something missing," caned me.
> . . .
> The fellow in charge of silence said:
> "Why did you talk without permission," caned me.
> The fellow in charge of the assembly said:
> "Why did you stand at ease without permission," caned me.[2]

Scribal schools were primarily intended to produce individuals who could keep records of the property of temple officials, kings, and nobles. Thus writing first developed as a way to enhance the growing power of elites, not to record speech, although it later came to be used for that purpose, and the stories of gods, kings, and heroes were also written down. Hundreds of thousands of hardened clay tablets have survived from ancient Mesopotamia, and from them historians have learned about many aspects of life, including taxes and wages. Sumerians wrote numbers as well as words on clay tablets, and some surviving tablets show multiplication and division problems.

Mathematics was not just a theoretical matter to the people living in Mesopotamia, because the building of cities, palaces, temples, and canals demanded practical knowledge of geometry and trigonometry.

Religion in Mesopotamia

To Sumerians, and to later peoples in Mesopotamia as well, the world was controlled by gods and goddesses, who represented cosmic forces such as the sun, moon, water, and storms. Each city generally had a chief god or goddess, or sometimes several, with a large temple built in his or her honor. In Uruk, for example, one of the central temples was dedicated to the goddess Inanna, the goddess of love and sexuality, who was also associated with the planet Venus. In one widely told myth, Inanna descends to the underworld, setting off a long struggle among her worshippers to find a replacement. Another deity is found to take her place, but then Inanna returns, just as Venus sets and rises. The king of the gods was Enlil, who was believed to rule over the gods just as the king of a city-state ruled his population. Almost as powerful were the gods of the sun, of storms, and of freshwater.

The gods judged good and evil and would punish humans who lied or cheated. Gods themselves suffered for their actions, and sometimes for no reason at all, just as humans did. People believed that humans had been created to serve the gods and generally anticipated being well treated by the gods if they served them well. The best way to honor the gods was to make the temple as grand and impressive as possible, because the temple's size demonstrated the strength of the community and the power of its chief deity. Once it was built, the temple itself, along with the shrine on the top of the ziggurat, was often off-limits to ordinary people, who did not worship there as a spiritual community. Instead the temple was staffed by priests and priestesses who carried out rituals to honor the god or goddess. Kings and other political leaders might also visit the temple and carry out religious ceremonies from time to time, particularly when they thought the assistance of the gods was especially needed.

The peoples of Mesopotamia had many myths to account for the creation of the universe. According to one told by the Babylonians, in the beginning was the primeval sea, known as the goddess Tiamat, who gave birth to the gods. When Tiamat tried to destroy the gods, Marduk, the chief god of the Babylonians, proceeded to kill her and divide her body and thus created the sky and earth. These myths are the earliest known attempts to answer the question, how did it all begin?

Stories about the gods traveled with people when they moved up and down the rivers, so that gods often acquired new names and new characteristics over the centuries. Myths and stories about them were not written down until long after they had first been told, and often had many variations. Written texts were not an important part of Sumerian religious life, nor were they central to the religious practices of most of the other peoples in this region.

In addition to stories about gods, the Sumerians also told stories about heroes and kings, many of which were eventually reworked into the world's first epic poem, the

Epic of Gilgamesh (GIL-guh-mesh), which was later written down in Akkadian. An epic poem is a narration of the achievements, the labors, and sometimes the failures of heroes that embodies peoples' ideas about themselves. Historians can use epic poems to learn about various aspects of a society, and to that extent epics can be used as historical sources. The epic recounts the wanderings of Gilgamesh—the semihistorical king of Uruk—and his search for eternal life, and it grapples with enduring questions about life and death, friendship, humankind and deity, and immortality. (See "Evaluating the Evidence 1.2: Gilgamesh's Quest for Immortality," page 18.)

Sumerian Politics and Society

Exactly how kings emerged in Sumerian society is not clear. Scholars have suggested that during times of emergencies, a chief priest or perhaps a military leader assumed what was supposed to be temporary authority over a city. He established an army, trained it, and led it into battle. Temporary power gradually became permanent kingship, and sometime before 2450 B.C.E. kings in some Sumerian city-states began transferring their kingship to their sons, establishing patriarchal hereditary dynasties in which power was handed down through the male line. This is the point at which written records about kingship began to appear. The symbol of royal status was the palace, which came to rival the temple in grandeur.

Military leaders were sometimes able to conquer other cities, and in about 2350 B.C.E. Lugalzagesi, king of the city of Umma, conquered a number of other city-states and created a more unified state. Eventually he conquered Uruk as well, and declared in a long inscription that the god Enlil had given him a realm that extended from the Mediterranean to the Persian Gulf. Like many later rulers in all parts of the world, Lugalzagesi claimed territory far beyond what he actually held.

Kings made alliances with other powerful individuals, often through marriage. Royal family members were depended upon for many aspects of government. Kings worked closely with religious authorities and relied on ideas about the kings' connections with the gods, as well as the kings' military might, for their power. Royal children, both sons and daughters, were sometimes priests and priestesses in major temples. Acting together, priests, kings, and officials in Sumerian cities used force, persuasion, and taxation to maintain order, keep the irrigation systems working, and keep food and other goods flowing.

The king and his officials held extensive tracts of land, as did the temple; these lands were worked by the palace's or the temple's clients, free men and women who were dependent on the palace or the temple. They received crops and other goods in return for their labor. Although this arrangement assured the clients of a livelihood, the land they worked remained the possession of the palace or the temple. Some individuals and families owned land outright and paid their taxes in the form of agricultural products or items they made. At the bottom rung of society were slaves. Slavery predates written records, so like many other aspects of social hierarchies, we are not sure exactly how and when people first began to own other people. Like animals, slaves were a source

Mesopotamian Harpist   This small clay tablet, carved between 2000 B.C.E. and 1500 B.C.E., shows a seated woman playing a harp. Her fashionable dress and hat suggest that she is playing for wealthy people, perhaps at the royal court. Images of musicians are common in Mesopotamian art, indicating that music was important in Mesopotamian culture and social life. (Musée du Louvre, Paris/Erich Lessing/Art Resource, NY)

Gilgamesh's Quest for Immortality

The human desire to escape the grip of death appears in many cultures. The Epic of Gilgamesh *is perhaps the earliest recorded treatment of this topic. The oldest elements of the epic go back to stories told in the third millennium* B.C.E. *According to tradition, Gilgamesh was a king of the Sumerian city of Uruk. In the story, Gilgamesh is not fulfilling his duties as the king very well and sets out with his friend Enkidu to perform wondrous feats against fearsome agents of the gods. Together they kill several supernatural beings, and the gods decide that Enkidu must die. He foresees his own death in a dream.*

~

Listen again, my friend [Gilgamesh]! I had a dream in the
    night.
The sky called out, the earth replied,
I was standing in between them.
There was a young man, whose face was obscured.
His face was like that of an Anzu-bird.
He had the paws of a lion, he had the claws of an eagle.
He seized me by my locks, using great force against
    me. . . .
He seized me, drove me down to the dark house, dwelling
    of Erkalla's god [the underworld], . . .
On the road where travelling is one way only,
To the house where those who stay are deprived of light. . . .

Enkidu sickens and dies. Gilgamesh is distraught and determined to become immortal. He decides to journey to Ut-napishtim and his wife, the only humans who have eternal life. Everyone he meets along the way asks him about his appearance, and Gilgamesh always answers with the same words:

~

How could my cheeks not be wasted, nor my face dejected,
Nor my heart wretched, nor my appearance worn out,
Nor grief in my innermost being,
Nor my face like that of a long-distance traveller,
Nor my face weathered by wind and heat
Nor roaming open country clad only in a lionskin?
My friend was the hunted mule, wild ass of the mountain,
    leopard of open country,
Enkidu my friend was the hunted mule, wild ass of the
    mountain, leopard of open country.
We who met, and scaled the mountain,
Seized the Bull of Heaven [the sacred bull of the goddess
    Ishtar] and slew it,
Demolished Humbaba [the ogre who guards the forest of
    the gods] who dwelt in the Pine Forest,
Killed lions in the passes of the mountains,
My friend whom I love so much, who experienced every
    hardship with me,
Enkidu my friend whom I love so much, who experi-
    enced every hardship with me —
The fate of mortals conquered him!
For six days and seven nights I wept over him: I did not
    allow him to be buried
Until a worm fell out of his nose.
I was frightened and
I am afraid of Death, and so I roam open country.

---

of physical power for their owners, providing them an opportunity to amass more wealth and influence. Some Sumerian slaves were most likely prisoners of war and criminals who had lost their freedom as punishment for their crimes; others perhaps came into slavery to repay debts. Compared to many later societies, slaves were not widely used in Sumer, where most agricultural work was done by dependent clients. Slaves in Sumer also engaged in trade and made profits. They could borrow money, and many slaves were able to buy their freedom.

Each of the social categories included both men and women, but their experiences were not the same, for Sumerian society made distinctions based on gender. Most elite landowners were male, but women who held positions as priestesses or as queens ran their own estates, independently of their husbands and fathers. Some women owned businesses and took care of their own accounts. They could own property and distribute it to their offspring. Sons and daughters inherited from their parents, although a daughter received her inheritance in the form of a dowry, which technically remained hers but was managed by her husband or husband's family

The words of my friend weigh upon me. . . .
I roam open country on long journeys.
How, O how could I stay silent, how, O how could I keep
quiet?
My friend whom I love has turned to clay: Enkidu my
friend whom I love has turned to clay.
Am I not like him? Must I lie down too,
Never to rise, ever again?

*Gilgamesh finally reaches Ut-napishtim, to whom he tells his
story, and who says to him:*

Why do you prolong grief, Gilgamesh?
Since [the gods made you] from the flesh of gods and
mankind,
Since [the gods] made you like your father and mother
[Death is inevitable] . . . ,
Nobody sees the face of Death,
Nobody hears the voice of Death.
Savage Death just cuts mankind down.
Sometimes we build a house, sometimes we make a nest,
But then brothers divide it upon inheritance.
Sometimes there is hostility in [the land],
But then the river rises and brings flood-water. . . .
The Anunnaki, the great gods, assembled;
Mammitum [the great mother goddess] who creates fate
decreed destinies with them.
They appointed death and life.
They did not mark out days for death,
But they did so for life.

*Gilgamesh asks Ut-napishtim how he and his wife
can be immortal like the gods, if death is inevitable.*

*Ut-napishtim tells him the story of how they survived a flood
sent by the gods and the chief god Enlil blessed them with
eternal life. Gilgamesh wants this as well, but fails two
opportunities Ut-napishtim provides for him to achieve it. At
the end of the epic, he simply returns to Uruk with the boatman
Ur-shanabi, to whom he points out the glories of the city:*

Go up on to the wall of Uruk, Ur-shanabi, and walk
around,
Inspect the foundation platform and scrutinize the
brickwork! Testify that its bricks are baked bricks,
And that the Seven Counsellors must have laid its
foundations!
One square mile is city, one square mile is orchards, one
square mile is claypits, as well as the open ground of
Ishtar's temple.
Three square miles and the open ground comprise Uruk.

EVALUATE THE EVIDENCE

1. What does the *Epic of Gilgamesh* reveal about attitudes toward friendship in ancient Mesopotamia?
2. What does the epic tell us about views of the nature of human life? Where do human beings fit into the cosmic world?
3. Although at the end of his quest, Gilgamesh did not achieve personal immortality, how can his final words to Ur-shanabi be seen as a tribute to long-lasting human endeavors?

Source: *Myths from Mesopotamia: Creation, the Flood, Gilgamesh, and Others*, trans. Stephanie Dalley (Oxford: Oxford University Press, 1989), pp. 88–89, 103–104, 107, 108–109, 120. Used by permission of Oxford University Press.

after marriage. The Sumerians established the basic social, economic, and intellectual patterns of Mesopotamia, and they influenced their neighbors to the north and east.

Empires in Mesopotamia

The wealth of Sumerian cities also attracted non-Sumerian conquerors from the north, beginning with the Akkadians and then the Babylonians. Both of these peoples created large states in the valley of the Tigris and Euphrates. Hammurabi, one ruler of Babylon, proclaimed an extensive law code. Merchants traveled throughout the Fertile Crescent and beyond, carrying products and facilitating cultural exchange.

FOCUS QUESTION
How did the Akkadian and Old Babylonian empires develop in Mesopotamia?

The Akkadians and the Babylonians

In 2331 B.C.E. Sargon, the king of a city to the north of Sumer, conquered a number of Sumerian cities with what was probably the world's first permanent army

Victory Stele of Naram-Sin, King of Akkad   On this victory stele carved from sandstone about 2320 B.C.E., King Naram-Sin, Sargon's grandson, climbs a mountain above his soldiers and defeated enemies. Naram-Sin, under whose rule Akkad reached its largest size, is shown here as a god-king in a horned helmet, twice the size of the other men. (Musée du Louvre, Paris, France/De Agostini Picture Library/Gianni Dagli Orti/Bridgeman Images)

and created a large state. The symbol of his triumph was a new capital, the city of Akkad (AH-kahd). Sargon also expanded the Akkadian empire westward to North Syria, which became the breadbasket of the empire. He encouraged trading networks that brought in goods from as far away as the Indus River and what is now Turkey. Sargon spoke a different language than did the Sumerians, one of the many languages that scholars identify as belonging to the Semitic language family, which includes modern-day Hebrew and Arabic. However, Akkadians adapted cuneiform writing to their own language, and Akkadian became the diplomatic language used over a wide area.

Sargon tore down the defensive walls of Sumerian cities and appointed his own sons as their rulers to help him cement his power. He also appointed his daughter, Enheduana (2285–2250 B.C.E.), as high priestess in the city of Ur. Here she wrote a number of hymns, especially those in praise of the goddess Inanna, becoming the world's first author to put her name to a literary composition. For hundreds of years Enheduana's works were copied on clay tablets, which have been found in several cities in the area, indicating that people may have recited or read them.

Sargon's dynasty appears to have ruled Mesopotamia for about 150 years, during which time the Tigris and Euphrates Valleys attracted immigrants from many places. Then his empire collapsed, in part because of a period of extended drought, and the various city-states became independent again.

One significant city-state that arose in the wake of the Akkadian empire was settled by the Amorites (AM-uh-rites), who migrated in from the west, probably starting during the time of Sargon's empire. The Amorites were initially nomadic pastoralists, not agriculturalists, but they began to raise crops when they settled throughout Mesopotamia. One group of Amorites made their home in the city of Babylon along the middle Euphrates, where that river runs close to the Tigris. Positioned to dominate trade on both the Tigris and Euphrates Rivers, the city grew great because of its commercial importance and the sound leadership of a dynasty of Amorite rulers. Like other Amorite kingdoms of the time, Babylon was more than a city-state. It included smaller kingdoms whose rulers recognized the king of Babylon as their overlord.

Life Under Hammurabi

Hammurabi of Babylon (r. 1792–1750 B.C.E.) was initially a typical king of his era. As ruler of Babylon, he fought some of his neighbors, created treaties with others, taxed his people, expanded the city walls, and built temples. After he had ruled for thirty years, Babylon was attacked, and one of Hammurabi's allies did not provide the assistance he expected. Hammurabi defeated the attackers and also conquered his former ally and several other kingdoms, thus uniting most of Mesopotamia under his rule. The era from his reign to around 1595 B.C.E. is called the Old Babylonian period.

As had earlier rulers, Hammurabi linked his success with the will of the gods. He connected himself with the sun-god Shamash, the god of law and justice, and encouraged the spread of myths that explained how Marduk, the primary god of Babylon, had been elected king of the gods by the other deities in Mesopotamia. Marduk later became widely regarded as the chief god of Mesopotamia, absorbing the qualities and powers of other gods.

Hammurabi's most memorable accomplishment was the proclamation of an extensive law code, introduced about 1755 B.C.E. Hammurabi's was not the first law code in Mesopotamia; the earliest goes back to about 2100 B.C.E. Like the codes of the earlier lawgivers, **Hammurabi's law code** proclaimed that he issued his laws on divine authority "to establish law and justice in the language of the land, thereby promoting the welfare of the people." Hammurabi's code set a variety of punishments for breaking the law, including fines and physical punishment such as mutilation, whipping, and burning.

Hammurabi's code provides a wealth of information about daily life in Mesopotamia, although, like all law codes, it prescribes what the lawgivers hope will be the situation rather than providing a description of real life. We cannot know if its laws were enforced, but we can use it to see what was significant to people in Hammurabi's society. Because of farming's fundamental importance, the code dealt extensively with agriculture. Tenants faced severe penalties for neglecting the land or not working it at all. Since irrigation was essential to grow crops, tenants had to keep the canals and ditches in good repair. Anyone whose neglect of the canals resulted in damaged crops had to bear all the expense of the lost crops. Those tenants who could not pay the costs were forced into slavery.

Hammurabi gave careful attention to marriage and the family. As elsewhere in the Near East, marriage had aspects of a business agreement. The groom or his father offered the prospective bride's father a gift, and if this was acceptable, the bride's father provided his daughter with a dowry. As in Sumer, after marriage the dowry belonged to the woman (although the husband normally administered it) and was a means of protecting her rights and status. No marriage was considered legal without a contract, and although either party could break off the marriage, the cost was a stiff penalty. Fathers often contracted marriages while their children were still young, and once contracted, the children were considered to be wed even if they did not live together. Men were not allowed to take a second wife unless the first wife could not bear children or had a severe illness.

The penalty for adultery, defined as sex between a married woman and a man not her husband, was death. According to Hammurabi's code, "If the wife of a man has been caught while lying with another man, they shall bind them and throw them into the water."[3] A husband had the power to spare his wife by obtaining a pardon for her from the king. He could, however, accuse his wife of adultery even if he had not caught her in the act. In such a case she could try to clear herself, and if she was found innocent, she could take her dowry and leave her husband.

A father could not disinherit a son without just cause, and the code ordered the courts to forgive a son for his first offense. Men could adopt children into their families and include them in their wills, which artisans sometimes did to teach them the family trade, or wealthy landowners sometimes did to pass along land to able younger men, particularly if they had no children of their own.

The Code of Hammurabi demanded that the punishment fit the crime, calling for "an eye for an eye, and a tooth for a tooth," at least among equals. However, a higher-ranking man who physically hurt a commoner or slave, perhaps by breaking his arm or putting out his eye, could pay a fine to the victim instead of having his arm broken or losing his own eye. The fine for breaking an arm or otherwise hurting a commoner was huge—as much as five years' salary for a laborer—and commoners might have preferred to receive this rather than the less tangible recompense of seeing

Hammurabi's law code
A proclamation issued by Babylonian king Hammurabi to establish laws regulating many aspects of life.

Law Code of Hammurabi
Hammurabi ordered his code to be inscribed on stone pillars and set up in public throughout the Babylonian empire. At the top of the pillar, Hammurabi (left) is depicted receiving the rod and ring of authority from Shamash, the god of justice. (Musée du Louvre, Paris, France/De Agostini Picture Library/Gianni Dagli Orti/Bridgeman Images)

their assailant injured. As long as criminal and victim shared the same social status, however, the victim could demand exact vengeance.

Hammurabi's code began with legal procedure. There were no public prosecutors or district attorneys, so individuals brought their own complaints before the court. Each side had to produce witnesses to support its case. In cases of murder, the accuser had to prove the defendant guilty; any accuser who failed to do so was to be put to death. Another procedural regulation declared that once a judge had rendered a verdict, he could not change it. Anyone accused of witchcraft, even if the charges were not proved, underwent an ordeal by water. The defendant was thrown into the Euphrates, which was considered the instrument of the gods. A defendant who sank was guilty; a defendant who survived was innocent.

Consumer protection is not a modern idea; it goes back to Hammurabi's day. Merchants had to guarantee the quality of their goods and services. A boat builder who did sloppy work had to repair the boat at his own expense. House builders guaranteed their work with their lives. If inhabitants died when a house collapsed, the builder was put to death. A merchant who tried to increase the interest rate on a loan forfeited the entire amount. In these ways, Hammurabi's laws tried to ensure that consumers got what they paid for and paid a just price.

The practical impact of Hammurabi's code is much debated. There is disagreement about whether it recorded laws already established, promulgated new laws, recorded previous judicial decisions, or simply proclaimed what was just and proper. It is also unknown whether Hammurabi's proclamation was legally binding on the courts. Nevertheless, Hammurabi's code gives historians a valuable view into the lives of the Mesopotamians, and it influenced other law codes of the Near East, including those later written down in Hebrew Scripture.

Cultural Exchange in the Fertile Crescent

Law codes, preoccupied as they are with the problems of society, provide a bleak view of things, but other Mesopotamian documents give a happier glimpse of life. Countless wills and testaments show that husbands habitually left their estates to their wives, who in turn willed the property to their children. Financial documents prove that many women engaged in business without hindrance.

Mesopotamians found their lives lightened by holidays and religious festivals. Traveling merchants brought news from far away and swapped marvelous tales. The Mesopotamians enjoyed a vibrant and creative culture that left its mark on the entire Fertile Crescent. They made significant and sophisticated advances in mathematics using a numerical system based on units of sixty, ten, and six. They also developed the concept of place value—that the value of a number depends on where it stands in relation to other numbers.

Mesopotamian writing and merchandise, along with other aspects of the culture, spread far beyond the Tigris and Euphrates Valleys. Overland trade connected Sumer, Akkad, and Babylon with the eastern Mediterranean coast. Cities here were mercantile centers rich not only in manufactured goods but also in agricultural produce, textiles, and metals. The cities flourished under local rulers. People in Syria and elsewhere in the Middle East used Akkadian cuneiform to communicate in writing with their more distant neighbors. Cultural exchange remained a mixture of adoption and adaptation.

Southern and central Anatolia presented a similar picture of extensive contact between cultures. Major Anatolian cities with large local populations were also home to colonies of traders from Mesopotamia. Thousands of cuneiform tablets testify to centuries of commercial and cultural exchanges with Mesopotamia, and eventually with Egypt, which rose to power in the Nile Valley.

The Egyptians

At about the same time that Sumerian city-states expanded and fought with one another in the Tigris and Euphrates Valleys, a more cohesive state under a single ruler grew in the valley of the Nile River in North Africa. This was Egypt, which for long stretches of history was prosperous and secure behind desert areas on both sides of the Nile Valley. At various times groups migrated into Egypt seeking better lives or invaded and conquered Egypt. Often these newcomers adopted aspects of Egyptian religion, art, and politics, and the Egyptians also carried their traditions with them when they established an empire and engaged in trade.

FOCUS QUESTION
How did the Egyptians create a prosperous and long-lasting society?

The Nile and the God-King

The Greek historian and traveler Herodotus (heh-RAHD-uh-tuhs) in the fifth century B.C.E. called Egypt the "gift of the Nile." No other single geographical factor had such a fundamental and profound impact on the shaping of Egyptian life, society, and history as this river. The Nile flooded once a year for a period of several months, bringing fertile soil and moisture for farming, and agricultural villages developed along its banks by at least 6000 B.C.E. Although the Egyptians worried at times that these floods would be too high or too low, they also praised the Nile as a creative and comforting force:

Hail to thee, O Nile, that issues from the earth and comes to keep Egypt alive! . . .
He that waters the meadows which Re [Ra] created,
He that makes to drink the desert . . .
He who makes barley and brings emmer [wheat] into being . . .
He who brings grass into being for the cattle . . .
He who makes every beloved tree to grow . . .
O Nile, verdant art thou, who makest man and cattle to live.[4]

The Egyptians based their calendar on the Nile, dividing the year into three four-month periods: *akhet* (flooding), *peret* (growth), and *shemu* (harvest). Herodotus, accustomed to the rigors of Greek agriculture, was amazed by the ease with which the Egyptians seemed to raise crops. Egyptian texts, however, paint a different picture, recognizing the unrelenting work entailed in farming and the diseases from which people suffered. One of these was guinea worm disease, a parasitic illness caused by drinking contaminated water, evidence of which has also been found in Egyptian mummies. Treatment for guinea worm today is exactly the same as that recommended in ancient Egyptian medical texts: when the head of the worm emerges from the large blister it causes, wrap the worm around a stick and gradually pull it out.

Through the fertility of the Nile and their own hard work, Egyptians produced an annual agricultural surplus, which in turn sustained a growing and prosperous population. The Nile also unified Egypt. The river was the region's principal highway, promoting communication and trade throughout the valley.

Egypt was fortunate in that it was nearly self-sufficient—it had most of the materials required to address its basic needs. Besides having fertile soil, Egypt possessed enormous quantities of stone, which served as the raw material of architecture and sculpture, and abundant clay for pottery. The raw materials that Egypt lacked were close at hand. The Egyptians could obtain copper from Sinai (SIGH-nigh) and timber from Lebanon, and they traded with peoples farther away to obtain other materials that they needed.

The political power structures that developed in Egypt came to be linked with the Nile. Somehow the idea developed that a single individual, a king, was responsible for the rise and fall of the Nile. This belief came about before the development of writing in Egypt, so, as with the growth of priestly and royal power in Sumer, the precise details of its origins have been lost. The king came to be viewed as a descendant of the gods, and thus as a god himself.

Political unification most likely proceeded slowly, but stories told about early kings highlighted one who had united Upper Egypt—the upstream valley in the south—and Lower Egypt—the delta area of the Nile that empties into the Mediterranean Sea—into a single kingdom around 3100 B.C.E. In some sources he is called Narmer and in other sources Menes, but his fame as a unifier is the same, whatever his name, and he is generally depicted in carvings and paintings wearing the symbols of the two kingdoms. Historians later divided Egyptian history into dynasties, or families of kings. For modern historical purposes, however, it is more useful to divide Egyptian history into periods. The political unification of Egypt in the Archaic Period (3100–2660 B.C.E.) ushered in the period known as the Old Kingdom (2660–2180 B.C.E.), an era remarkable for prosperity and artistic flowering.

The focal point of religious and political life in the Old Kingdom was the king, who commanded wealth, resources, and people. The king's surroundings had to be worthy of a god, and only a magnificent palace was suitable for his home; in fact, the word **pharaoh**, which during the New Kingdom came to be used for the king, originally meant "great house." Just as the kings occupied a great house in life, so they reposed in great pyramids after death. Built during the Old Kingdom, these massive stone tombs contained all the things needed by the king in his afterlife. The pyramid also symbolized the king's power and his connection with the sun-god. After burial the entrance was blocked and concealed to ensure the king's undisturbed peace, although grave robbers later actually found the tombs fairly easy to plunder.

To ancient Egyptians, the king embodied the concept of **ma'at**, a cosmic harmony that embraced truth, justice, and moral integrity. Ma'at gave the king the right, authority, and duty to govern. To the people, the king personified justice and order—harmony among themselves, nature, and the divine.

Kings did not always live up to this ideal, of course. The two parts of Egypt were difficult to hold together, and several times in Egypt's long history there were periods of disunity, civil war, and chaos. During the First Intermediate Period (2180–2080 B.C.E.), rulers of various provinces asserted their independence from the king, and Upper and Lower Egypt were ruled by rival dynasties. There is evidence that the Nile's floods were unusually low during this period because of drought,

pharaoh The title given to the king of Egypt in the New Kingdom, from a word that meant "great house."

ma'at The Egyptian belief in a cosmic harmony that embraced truth, justice, and moral integrity; it gave the kings the right and duty to govern.

which contributed to instability just as it helped bring down the Akkadian empire. Warrior-kings reunited Egypt in the Middle Kingdom (2080–1640 B.C.E.) and expanded Egyptian power southward into Nubia.

Egyptian Religion

Like the Mesopotamians, the Egyptians were polytheistic, worshipping many gods of all types, some mightier than others. They developed complex ideas of their gods that reflected the world around them, and these views changed over the many centuries of Egyptian history as gods took on new attributes and often merged with one another. During the Old Kingdom, Egyptians considered the sun-god Ra the creator of life. He commanded the sky, earth, and under-world. This giver of life could also take it away without warn-ing. Ra was associated with the falcon-god Horus, the "lord of the sky," who served as the symbol of divine kingship.

Much later, during the New Kingdom (see page 28), the pharaohs of a new dynasty favored the worship of a different sun-god, Amon, whom they described as creating the entire cosmos by his thoughts. Amon brought life to the land and its people, they wrote, and he sustained both. Because he had helped them overthrow their enemies, Egyptians came to consider Amon the champion of fairness and justice, especially for the common people. Called the "vizier of the humble" and the "voice of the poor," Amon was also a magician and physician who cured ills, protected people from natural dangers, and watched over travelers. As his cult grew, Amon came to be identified with Ra, and eventually the Egyptians combined them into one sun-god, Amon-Ra.

The Egyptians likewise developed views of an afterlife that reflected the world around them and that changed over time. During the later part of the Old Kingdom, the walls of kings' tombs were carved with religious texts that provided spells that would bring the king back to life and help him ascend to Heaven, where he would join his divine father, Ra. Toward the end of the Old Kingdom, the tombs of powerful nobles also contained such inscriptions, an indication that more people expected to gain everlasting life, and a sign of the decentralization of power that would lead to the chaos of the First Intermediate Period. In the Middle Kingdom, new types of spells appeared on the coffins of even more people, a further expansion in admissions to the afterlife.

During the New Kingdom, a time when Egypt came into greater contact with the cultures of the Fertile Crescent, Egyptians developed more complex ideas about the afterlife, recording these in funerary manuscripts that have come to be known as the **Book of the Dead**, written to help guide the dead through the difficulties of the underworld. These texts explained that the soul left the body to become part of the divine after death and told of the god Osiris (oh-SIGH-ruhs), who died each year and was then brought back to life by his wife, Isis (IGH-suhs), when the Nile flooded. Osiris eventually became king of the dead, weighing dead humans' hearts to

Funeral Stele of a Wealthy Woman　This painted wooden stele shows Djed-amon-iu-ankh (right), a wealthy Egyptian woman who lived in the Third Intermediate Period, in a thin gown and with a cone of ointment on her head, and the sun-god Ra (left) in the form of Horus the falcon-god. Ra-Horus is holding a scepter in one hand and the ankh, the Egyptian symbol of life, in the other. Djed-amon-iu-ankh offers food and lotus flowers to the god, and the hieroglyphs above them describe the offering. Steles were erected in Egypt for funeral purposes and depicted the person memorialized in an attitude of reverence. (Egyptian National Museum, Cairo, Egypt/photo © Interfoto/Ancient Art & Architecture Collection, Ltd.)

Book of the Dead　Egyptian funerary manuscripts, written to help guide the dead through the difficulties they would encounter on the way to the afterlife.

determine whether they had lived justly enough to deserve everlasting life. Egyptians also believed that proper funeral rituals, in which the physical body was mummified, were essential for life after death, so Osiris was assisted by Anubis, the jackal-headed god of mummification.

New Kingdom pharaohs came to associate themselves with both Horus and Osiris, and they were regarded as avatars of Horus in life and Osiris in death. The pharaoh's wife was associated with Isis, for both the queen and the goddess were regarded as protectors.

Egyptian Society and Work

Egyptian society reflected the pyramids that it built. At the top stood the king, who relied on a sizable circle of nobles, officials, and priests to administer his kingdom. All of them were assisted by scribes, who used a writing system perhaps adapted from Mesopotamia and perhaps developed independently. Egyptian scribes actually created two writing systems: one called hieroglyphic for engraving important religious or political texts on stone or writing them on papyrus made from reeds growing in the Nile Delta, and a much simpler system called hieratic that allowed scribes to write more quickly. Hieratic writing was used for the documents of daily life, such as letters, contracts, and accounts, and also for medical and literary works. Students learned hieratic first, and only those from well-off families or whose families had high aspirations took the time to learn hieroglyphics. In addition to scribes, the cities of the Nile Valley were home to artisans of all types, along with merchants and other tradespeople. A large group of farmers made up the broad base of the social pyramid.

For Egyptians, the Nile formed an essential part of daily life. During the season of its flooding, from June to October, farmers worked on the pharaoh's building programs and other tasks away from their fields. When the water began to recede, they diverted some of it into ponds for future irrigation and began planting wheat and barley for bread and beer, using plows pulled by oxen or people to part the soft mud. From October to February farmers planted and tended crops, and then from February until the next flood they harvested them. Reapers with wooden sickles fixed with flint teeth cut the grain high, leaving long stubble. Women with baskets followed behind to gather the cuttings. Last came the gleaners—poor women, children, and old men who gathered anything left behind.

As in Mesopotamia, common people paid their obligations to their superiors in products and in labor, and many faced penalties if they did not meet their quota. One scribe described the scene at harvest time:

> And now the scribe lands on the river bank and is about to register the harvest-tax. The janitors carry staves and the Nubians rods of palm, and they say, Hand over the grain, though there is none. The farmer is beaten all over, he is bound and thrown into a well, soused and dipped head downwards. His wife has been bound in his presence and his children are in fetters.[5]

People's labor obligations in the Old Kingdom may have included forced work on the pyramids and canals, although recent research suggests that most people who built the pyramids were paid for their work. Some young men were drafted into the pharaoh's army, which served as both a fighting force and a labor corps.

Egyptian Home Life

This grave painting depicts an intimate moment in the life of an aristocratic family, with the father and mother in the center and their children around them. Often found in Egyptian tombs are statuettes of cats (see inset), which were both family pets and the symbol of the goddess Bastet.

EVALUATE THE EVIDENCE

1. What evidence do you find in the painting that Egyptian artists based the size of figures on people's status in the household?
2. Based on your reading, how might an image of a poor family differ from this depiction?

(family: From the Tomb of Ankerkhe, Workmen's Tombs, Deir el-Medina, Thebes, Egypt/ Bridgeman Images; cat: © The Trustees of the British Museum/Art Resource, NY)

Egyptian Family Life

The lives of all Egyptians centered around the family. Marriage was a business arrangement, just as in Mesopotamia, arranged by the couples' parents, and seems to have taken place at a young age. Once couples were married, having children, especially sons, was a high priority, as indicated by surviving charms to promote fertility and prayers for successful childbirth. Boys continued the family line, and only they could perform the proper burial rites for their father.

Wealthy Egyptians lived in spacious homes with attractive gardens and walls for privacy. (See "Evaluating the Evidence 1.3: Egyptian Home Life," above.) Such a house had an ample living room and a comfortable master bedroom with an attached bathroom. Smaller rooms served other purposes, including housing family members and servants, and providing space for cows, poultry, and storage. Poorer people lived in cramped quarters. Excavations at a city now called Tell el-Amarna show that residents' houses were about 16½ feet wide by 33 feet long. The family had narrow rooms for living, including two small rooms for sleeping and cooking. These small houses suggest that most Egyptians lived in small family groups, not as large extended families. The very poor lived in hovels with their animals.

Life in Egypt began at dawn with a bath and clean clothes. The Egyptians bathed several times a day because of the heat and used soda ash for soap. Rich and poor alike used perfumes as deodorants. Egyptians generally wore linen clothes, made from fibers of the flax plant, because there were few sheep in Egypt, and during this period they did not grow cotton. Because of the heat, men often wore only a kilt and women a sheath.

Marriage was apparently not celebrated by any ritual or religious act; it seems to have been purely a legal contract in which a woman brought one-third of her family's property to the marriage. The property continued to belong to her, though her husband managed it. She could obtain a divorce simply because she wanted it. If she did, she took her marriage portion with her and could also claim a share of the profits made during her marriage. Most Egyptian men had only one wife, but among the wealthy some had several wives or concubines. One wife, however, remained primary among the others. A husband could order his wife to her quarters and even beat her, but if a man treated his wife too violently, she could take him to court. If she won, her husband received one hundred lashes from a whip and surrendered his portion of their joint property to her. A man could dispense with his wife for any reason, just as she could leave him.

Ordinary women were expected to obey their fathers, husbands, and other men, but they possessed considerable economic and legal rights. They could own land in their own names and operate businesses. They could testify in court and bring legal action against men. Information from literature and art depicts a world in which ordinary husbands and wives enjoyed each other's company alone and together with family and friends. They held and attended parties together, and both participated in the festivities after dinner. Egyptian tomb monuments often show the couple happily standing together, arms around each other.

The Hyksos and New Kingdom Revival

While Egyptian civilization flourished in the Nile Valley, various groups migrated throughout the Fertile Crescent and then accommodated themselves to local cultures (Map 1.2). Some settled in the Nile Delta, including a group the Egyptians called Hyksos, which means "rulers of the uplands." Although they were later portrayed as a conquering horde, the Hyksos were actually migrants looking for good land, and their entry into the delta, which began around 1800 B.C.E., was probably gradual and generally peaceful.

The Hyksos brought with them the method of making bronze and casting it into tools and weapons that became standard in Egypt. They thereby brought Egypt fully into the Bronze Age culture of the Mediterranean world. Because bronze tools were sharper and more durable than the copper, stone, or bone tools they replaced, they made farming more efficient. The Hyksos also brought inventions that revolutionized Egyptian warfare, including bronze armor and weapons as well as horse-drawn chariots and the composite bow, made of laminated wood and horn, which was far more powerful than the simple wooden bow.

The migration of the Hyksos, combined with a series of famines and internal struggles for power, led Egypt to fragment politically in what later came to be known as the Second Intermediate Period (1640–1570 B.C.E.). During this time the Egyptians adopted bronze technology and new forms of weaponry from the Hyksos, while the newcomers began to worship Egyptian deities and modeled their political structure on that of the Egyptians.

In about 1570 B.C.E. a new dynasty of pharaohs arose, pushing the Hyksos out of the delta, subduing Nubia in the south, and conquering parts of Canaan in the northeast. In this way, these Egyptian warrior-pharaohs inaugurated what scholars refer to as the New Kingdom—a period in Egyptian history characterized by not only enormous wealth and conscious imperialism but also a greater sense of insecurity because of new contacts and military engagements. By expanding Egyptian power beyond the Nile Valley, the pharaohs created the first Egyptian empire, and they celebrated their triumphs with monuments on a scale unparalleled since the pyramids of the Old Kingdom. Even today the colossal granite statues of these pharaohs and the rich tomb objects testify to the might and splendor of the New Kingdom. They might also be testimony to an expansion of imported slave labor, although recently some scholars are rethinking the extent of slave labor in the New Kingdom.

MAP 1.2 Empires and Migrations in the Eastern Mediterranean　The rise and fall of empires in the eastern Mediterranean were shaped by internal developments, military conflicts, and the migration of peoples to new areas.

The New Kingdom pharaohs include a number of remarkable figures. Among these was Hatshepsut (r. ca. 1479–ca. 1458 B.C.E.), one of the few female pharaohs in Egypt's long history, who seized the throne for herself and used her reign to promote building and trade. Amenhotep III (r. ca. 1388–ca. 1350 B.C.E.) corresponded with other powerful kings in Babylonia and other kingdoms in the Fertile Crescent, sending envoys, exchanging gifts, and in some cases marrying their daughters. The kings promised friendship and active cooperation, referring to each other as "brothers," using this familial term to indicate their connection. They made alliances for offensive and defensive protection and swore to uphold one another's authority. Hence, the greatest powers of the period maintained peace, which facilitated the movement of gifts between kings and trade between ordinary people. Along with his chief royal wife, Tiye, who is known for her correspondence with foreign queens, Amenhotep is depicted on hundreds of statues, vases, amulets, and other objects, including two sixty-foot-tall statues that stood at the gate of his huge mortuary temple.

Amenhotep III was succeeded by his son, who took the name Akhenaton (ah-keh-NAH-tuhn) (r. 1351–1334 B.C.E.). He renamed himself as a mark of his changing religious ideas. Egyptians had long worshipped various sun-gods and aspects of the sun—Ra, Amon, Amon-Ra—but instead Akhenaton favored the worship of the god Aton (also spelled Aten), the visible disk of the sun. He was not a monotheist (someone who worships only one god), but he did order the erasure of the names of other sun-gods from the walls of buildings, the transfer of taxes from the traditional priesthood of Amon-Ra, and the building of huge new temples to Aton, especially at his new capital in the area now known as Amarna. In these temples Aton was to be worshipped in bright sunlight. Akhenaton also had artists portray him in more realistic ways than they had portrayed earlier pharaohs; he is depicted interacting with his children and especially with his wife Nefertiti (nehf-uhr-TEE-tee), who supported his new religious ideas. (See "Individuals in Society: Hatshepsut and Nefertiti," page 31.)

Akhenaton's new religion, imposed from above, failed to find a place among the people, however. After his death, traditional religious practices returned and the capital was moved back to Thebes. The priests of Amon-Ra led this restoration, but it was also supported by Akhenaton's son, who rejected the name he had been given that honored Aton and instead chose one that honored the traditional sun-god Amon. This son was Tutankhamon (r. 1333–1323 B.C.E.), whose short reign was not particularly noteworthy, and whose name would probably not be remembered except for the fact that his was the only tomb of an Egyptian king to be discovered nearly intact. The wealth of "King Tut's tomb," assembled for a boy-king who died unexpectedly at nineteen, can only suggest what must have originally been in the tomb of a truly powerful pharaoh.

The objects in the tomb have been studied intensively since it was first discovered in 1922 and have yielded much information about New Kingdom Egypt. In 2010 DNA analysis of Tutankhamon's mummy and other mummies from nearby tombs revealed, among other things, that he was the son of Akhenaton (there had been some doubt) and that his mother was probably one of Akhenaton's sisters. Brother-sister marriage was fairly common among Egyptian pharaohs, as it concentrated the family's power and connections with the gods. Marriage to close relatives can also cause genetic defects, however, and Tutankhamon seems to have suffered from several of these, including a malformed foot. Study of Tutankhamon's mummy also revealed that he suffered from malaria and had broken his leg shortly before he died. His high status did not make him immune to physical ailments.

Tutankhamon's short reign was also marked by international problems, including warfare on several of the borders of the Egyptian empire. His grandfather and father had engaged in extensive diplomatic relations with rulers of states dependent on Egypt and with other powerful kings, but Tutankhamon was less successful at these. He also died childless. His successors were court officials, and in 1298 B.C.E. one of them established a new dynasty whose members would reassert Egypt's imperial power and respond to new challenges.

Conflict and Cooperation with the Hittites

One of the key challenges facing the pharaohs after Tutankhamon was the expansion of the kingdom of the Hittites. At about the same time that the Sumerians were establishing city-states, speakers of Indo-European languages migrated into Anatolia. Indo-European is a large family of languages that includes English, most of the languages

INDIVIDUALS IN SOCIETY

Hatshepsut and Nefertiti

Egyptians understood the pharaoh to be an avatar of the god Horus, the source of law and morality, and the mediator between gods and humans. The pharaoh's connection with the divine stretched to members of his family, so that his siblings and children were also viewed as divine in some ways. Because of this, a pharaoh often took his sister or half-sister as one of his wives. This concentrated divine blood set the pharaonic family apart from other Egyptians (who did not generally marry close relatives) and allowed the pharaohs to imitate the gods, who in Egyptian mythology often married their siblings. A pharaoh chose one of his wives, often a relative, to be the "Great Royal Wife," or principal queen.

The familial connection with the divine allowed a handful of women to rule in their own right in Egypt's long history. We know the names of four female pharaohs, of whom the most famous was Hatshepsut (r. ca. 1479–ca. 1458 B.C.E.), the sister and wife of Thutmose II. After he died, she served as regent — adviser and co-ruler — for her young stepson Thutmose III. Hatshepsut sent trading expeditions and sponsored artists and architects, ushering in a period of artistic creativity and economic prosperity. She oversaw the construction of one of the world's great buildings, an elaborate terraced temple at Deir el-Bahri, which eventually served as her mortuary temple. Hatshepsut's status as a powerful female ruler was difficult for Egyptians to conceptualize, and she is often depicted in male dress or with a false beard, thus looking more like the male rulers who were the norm. After her death, Thutmose III tried to destroy all evidence that she had ever ruled, smashing statues and scratching her name off inscriptions, perhaps because of personal animosity and perhaps because he wanted to erase the fact that a woman had once been pharaoh. Only within recent decades have historians and archaeologists begun to (literally) piece together her story.

Though female pharaohs were very rare, many royal women had power through their position as "Great Royal Wives." The most famous was Nefertiti, the wife of Akhenaton. Her name means "the perfect (or beautiful) woman has come," and inscriptions also give her many other titles. Nefertiti used her position to spread the new religion of the sun-god Aton.

Together Nefertiti and Akhenaton built a new palace and capital city at Akhetaton, the present Amarna, away from the old centers of power. There they developed the cult of Aton to the exclusion of the traditional deities.

Painted limestone bust of Nefertiti. (Aegyptisches Museum, SMPK, Berlin, Germany/Bridgeman Images)

Granite head of Hatshepsut. (bpk, Berlin/Aegyptisches Museum, Staatliche Museen/Margarete Buesing/Art Resource, NY)

Nearly the only literary survival of their religious belief is the "Hymn to Aton," which declares Aton to be the only god. It describes Nefertiti as "the great royal consort whom he, Akhenaton, loves. The mistress of the Two Lands, Upper and Lower Egypt."

Nefertiti is often shown as being the same size as her husband, and in some inscriptions she is performing religious rituals that would normally have been carried out only by the pharaoh. The exact details of her power are hard to determine, however. An older theory held that her husband removed her from power, though there is also speculation that after his death she may have ruled secretly in her own right under a different name. Her tomb has long since disappeared. In the last decade individual archaeologists have claimed that several different mummies were Nefertiti, but most scholars dismiss these claims. Because her parentage is not known for certain, DNA testing such as that done on Tutankhamon's corpse would not reveal whether any specific mummy was Nefertiti.

QUESTIONS FOR ANALYSIS

1. Why might it have been difficult for Egyptians to accept a female ruler?
2. What opportunities do hereditary monarchies such as that of ancient Egypt provide for women? How does this fit with gender hierarchies in which men are understood as superior?

of modern Europe, Persian, and Sanskrit. It also includes Hittite, the language of a people who seem to have migrated into this area about 2300 B.C.E.

Information about the Hittites comes from archaeological sources, and also from written cuneiform tablets that provide details about politics and economic life. These records indicate that in the sixteenth century B.C.E. the Hittite king Hattusili I led his forces against neighboring kingdoms. Hattusili's grandson and successor, Mursili I, extended the Hittite conquests as far as Babylon. Upon his return home, the victorious Mursili was assassinated by members of his own family, which led to dynastic warfare. This pattern of expansion followed by internal conflict was repeated frequently, but when they were united behind a strong king, the Hittites were extremely powerful.

As the Hittites expanded southward, they came into conflict with the Egyptians, who were re-establishing their empire. The pharaoh Ramesses II engaged in numerous campaigns to retake Egyptian territory in Syria. He assembled a large well-equipped army with thousands of chariots and expected to defeat the Hittites easily, but was ambushed by them at the Battle of Kadesh in 1274 B.C.E. Returning to Egypt, Ramesses declared that he had won and had monuments carved commemorating his victory, including the giant temples at Abu Simbel in Nubia, which were also designed as a demonstration of Egypt's power over its southern neighbors. In reality, neither side gained much by the battle, though both sides seem to have recognized the impossibility of defeating the other.

In 1258 Ramesses II and the Hittite king Hattusili III concluded a peace treaty, which was recorded in both Egyptian hieroglyphics and Hittite cuneiform. Both of these have survived. Although peace treaties are known to have existed since the twenty-fourth century B.C.E., this is one of the best preserved. Returning to the language of cooperation established in earlier royal diplomacy, each side promised not to invade the other and to come to the other's aid if attacked. Each promised peace and brotherhood, and the treaty ended with a long oath to the gods, who would curse the one who broke the treaty and bless the one who kept it.

LOOKING BACK LOOKING AHEAD

The political and military story of waves of migrations, battles, and the rise and fall of empires can mask striking continuities across the Neolithic and Bronze Ages. The social patterns set in early agricultural societies — with most of the population farming the land, and a small number of elites who lived off their labor — lasted for millennia. Disrupted peoples and newcomers shared practical concepts of agriculture and metallurgy with one another, and wheeled vehicles allowed merchants to transact business over long distances. Merchants, migrants, and conquerors carried their gods and goddesses with them, and religious beliefs and practices blended and changed. Cuneiform tablets, wall inscriptions, and paintings testify to commercial exchanges and cultural accommodation, adoption, and adaptation.

The treaty of Ramesses II and Hattusili III brought peace between the Egyptians and the Hittites for a time, which was further enhanced by Ramesses II's marriage to a Hittite princess. This stability was not to last, however. Within several decades of the treaty, new peoples were moving into the eastern Mediterranean, disrupting trade and in some cases looting and destroying cities. There is evidence of drought, and some scholars have suggested a major volcanic explosion in Iceland cooled the climate for several years, leading to a series of poor harvests. Both the Egyptian and Hittite Empires shrank dramatically. All of these developments are part of a general "Bronze Age Collapse" that historians see as a major turning point.

Make Connections

Think about the larger developments and continuities within and across chapters.

1. What aspects of life in the Neolithic period continued with little change in the civilizations of Mesopotamia and Egypt? What were the most important differences?

2. Looking at your answers to question 1, do you think the distinction between "civilizations" and human cultures that were not "civilizations" discussed in the first part of this chapter is a valid one? Why or why not?

3. How were the societies that developed in Mesopotamia and Egypt similar to one another? Which of the characteristics you have identified as a similarity do you predict will also be found in later societies, and why?

1 REVIEW & EXPLORE

Review the Main Ideas

Answer the focus questions from each section of the chapter.

◆ What do we mean by "the West" and "Western civilization"? (p. 4)

◆ How did early human societies develop and create new technologies and cultural forms? (p. 6)

◆ What kind of civilization did the Sumerians develop in Mesopotamia? (p. 12)

◆ How did the Akkadian and Old Babylonian empires develop in Mesopotamia? (p. 19)

◆ How did the Egyptians create a prosperous and long-lasting society? (p. 23)

Identify Key Terms

Identify and explain the significance of each item below.

civilization (p. 5)
Paleolithic era (p. 6)
Neolithic era (p. 6)
Fertile Crescent (p. 9)
pastoralism (p. 10)
patriarchy (p. 11)
Bronze Age (p. 12)
polytheism (p. 12)
cuneiform (p. 15)
Hammurabi's law code (p. 21)
pharaoh (p. 24)
ma'at (p. 24)
Book of the Dead (p. 25)

NOTES

1. J. A. Black et al., *Electronic Text Corpus of Sumerian Literature* (http://etcsl.orinst.ox.ac.uk/), Oxford 1998–2006. Used by permission of Oxford University, ETCSL Project.

2. Quoted in S. N. Kramer, *The Sumerians: Their History, Culture, and Character*, p. 238. Copyright © 1963 by The University of Chicago. All rights reserved. Used by permission of the publisher.

3. James B. Pritchard, ed., *Ancient Near Eastern Texts Relating to the Old Testament—Third Edition with Supplement*, p. 171. © Reproduced with permission of PRINCETON UNIVERSITY PRESS, in the format Book via Copyright Clearance Center.

4. Ibid., p. 372.

5. Quoted in A. H. Gardiner, "Ramesside Texts Relating to the Taxation and Transport of Corn," *Journal of Egyptian Archaeology* 27 (1941): 19–20.

CHAPTER PREVIEW

Iron and the Emergence of New States
How did iron technology shape new states after 1200 B.C.E., including Kush and Phoenicia?

The Hebrews
How did the Hebrews create an enduring religious tradition?

Assyria, the Military Monarchy
What explains the rise and fall of the Assyrians?

The Empire of the Persian Kings
How did the Persians consolidate their power and control and influence the subjects of their extensive empire?

Life in the Persian Empire
Two men dressed in clothing of the Medes, one of the groups conquered by the Persians, drive a four-horse chariot in this small model made entirely of gold. In the nineteenth century a huge collection of silver and gold objects from the fifth and fourth centuries B.C.E. was found on the banks of the Oxus River in what is now Tajikistan. Most likely, the spot had been a ferry crossing and the objects had been buried long ago. (British Museum, London, UK/De Agostini Picture Library/Bridgeman Images)

2

Small Kingdoms and Mighty Empires in the Near East

1200–510 B.C.E.

The migrations, drought, and destruction of what scholars call the "Bronze Age Collapse" in the late thirteenth century B.C.E. ended the Hittite Empire and weakened the Egyptians. Much was lost, but the old cultures of the ancient Near East survived to nurture new societies. The technology for smelting iron, which developed in Anatolia as well as other places in the world, improved and spread, with iron weapons and tools becoming stronger and thus more important by about 1000 B.C.E. In the absence of powerful empires, the Phoenicians, Kushites, Hebrews, and many other peoples carved out small independent kingdoms until the Near East was a patchwork of them. The Hebrews created a new form of religious belief with a single god and wrote down their religious ideas and traditions in what later became the most significant written document from this period.

In the tenth century B.C.E. this jumble of small states gave way to an empire that for the first time embraced the entire Near East: the empire of the Assyrians. They assembled a huge army that used sophisticated military technology and brutal tactics, and they also developed effective administrative techniques and stunning artistic works. The Assyrian Empire lasted for about three hundred years and then broke apart with the rise of a new empire centered in Babylon. Beginning in 550 B.C.E. the Persians conquered the Medes—nomadic peoples who had settled in Iran—and then the Babylonians and Assyrians, creating the largest empire yet seen, stretching from Anatolia in the west to the Indus Valley in the east. The Persians established effective methods of governing their diverse subjects and built roads for conquest, trade, and communication. ■

Iron and the Emergence of New States

If the Bronze Age Collapse was a time of massive political and economic disruption, it was also a period of the spread of new technologies, especially iron. Even though empires shrank, many small kingdoms survived, each with cultures that combined elements shared across a wide area with local traditions. These states included several that developed on the borders of the shrinking Egyptian empire, including Kush and Phoenicia.

Iron Technology

Along with migration and drought, another significant development in the centuries around 1200 B.C.E. was the spread of iron tools and iron technology. Iron is the most common element in the earth, but most iron found on or near the earth's surface occurs in the form of ore, which must be smelted to extract the metal. This is also true of the copper and tin that are used to make bronze, but these can be smelted at much lower temperatures than iron. As artisans perfected bronze metalworking techniques, they also experimented with iron. They developed a long and difficult process for smelting iron, using charcoal and a bellows (which raised the temperature of the fire significantly) to extract the iron from the ore. This procedure was performed in an enclosed furnace, and the process was repeated a number of times as the ore was transformed into wrought iron, which could be hammered into shapes.

Exactly where and when the *first* smelted iron was produced is a matter of debate — many regions would like this honor — but it happened independently in several different places, including western Africa in what is now Nigeria, Anatolia (modern Turkey), and most likely India. In Anatolia, the earliest smelted weapon has been dated to about 2500 B.C.E., but there may have been some smelting earlier. Most of the iron produced was too brittle to be of much use until about 1100 B.C.E., however, when techniques improved and iron weapons gradually became stronger and cheaper than their bronze counterparts. Thus, in the schema of dividing history into periods according to the main material out of which tools are made (see Chapter 1), the **Iron Age** began in about 1100 B.C.E. Iron weapons became important items of trade around the Mediterranean and throughout the Tigris and Euphrates

Nubian Cylinder Sheath   This small silver sheath made about 520 B.C.E., perhaps for a dagger, depicts a winged goddess and the Egyptian god Amon-Ra (not shown in photograph). It and others like it were found in the tombs of Kushite kings and suggest ways that Egyptian artistic styles and religious ideas influenced cultures farther up the Nile. (Cylinder sheath of Amaninatake-lebte. Napatan Period, reign of King Amani-natake-lebte, 538–519 B.C. [gilded silver and colored paste]/Nubian/ Museum of Fine Arts, Boston, Massachusetts, USA/Harvard University–Boston Museum of Fine Arts Expedition/Bridgeman Images)

Valleys, and the technology for making them traveled as well. Iron appears to have been adopted more slowly in Egypt than in other parts of the Near East, so bronze remained important longer there. From Anatolia, iron objects were traded west into Greece and central Europe, and north into western Asia. By 500 B.C.E. knowledge of smelting had traveled these routes as well.

Ironworkers continued to experiment and improve their products. Somewhere in the Near East—again the exact location is disputed—ironworkers discovered that if the relatively brittle wrought iron objects were placed on a bed of burning charcoal and then cooled quickly, the outer layer would form into a layer of much harder material, steel. Goods made of cast or wrought iron were usually traded locally, but fine sword and knife blades of steel traveled long distances, and the knowledge of how to make them followed. Because it was fairly plentiful and relatively cheap when compared with bronze, iron has been called the "democratic metal." The transition from bronze to iron happened over many centuries, but iron (and even more so, steel) would be an important factor in history from this point on.

The Decline of Egypt and the Emergence of Kush

Although the treaty between the Egyptians and Hittites in 1258 B.C.E. seemed to indicate a future of peace and cooperation, this was not to be. Groups of seafaring peoples whom the Egyptians called "Sea Peoples" raided, migrated, and marauded in the eastern Mediterranean. Just who these people were and where they originated is much debated among scholars. They may have come from Greece, or islands in the Mediterranean such as Crete and Sardinia, or Anatolia (modern Turkey), or from all of these. Wherever they came from, their raids, combined with the expansion of the Assyrians (see page 46), led to the collapse of the Hittite Empire. The Hittite capital city of Hattusa was burned to the ground in 1180 B.C.E. by an army of many different peoples, and though small states re-emerged in Anatolia, these were very much under the influence of Assyria.

In Egypt, the pharaoh Ramesses III (r. 1186–1155 B.C.E.) defeated the Sea Peoples in both a land and sea battle, but these were costly, as were other military engagements. Ramesses appears to have also been the subject of an assassination plot, which he survived, but Egypt entered into a long period of political fragmentation and conquest by outsiders that scholars of Egypt refer to as the Third Intermediate Period (ca. 1070–712 B.C.E.). The long wars against invaders weakened and impoverished Egypt, causing political upheaval and economic decline. Scribes created somber

Chronology

ca. 1200 B.C.E.	"Bronze Age Collapse"; end of the Hittite Empire
ca. 1100 B.C.E.	Beginning of the Iron Age; Phoenicians begin to trade in the Mediterranean
ca. 1070–712 B.C.E.	Third Intermediate Period in Egypt
ca. 965–925 B.C.E.	Hebrew kingdom ruled by Solomon
911–609 B.C.E.	Neo-Assyrian Empire
727 B.C.E.	Kushite Dynasty established in Egypt
722 B.C.E.	Kingdom of Israel destroyed by the Assyrians
626–539 B.C.E.	Neo-Babylonian empire
ca. 600 B.C.E.	Ideas of Zoroaster gain prominence in Persia
587 B.C.E.	Kingdom of Judah destroyed by the Neo-Babylonians
587–538 B.C.E.	Babylonian Captivity of the Hebrews
550 B.C.E.	Cyrus the Great conquers the Medes and consolidates the Persian Empire
539 B.C.E.	Persians defeat the Neo-Babylonians
525 B.C.E.	Persians defeat the Egyptians and Nubians

Iron Age Period beginning about 1100 B.C.E., when iron became the most important material for tools and weapons.

portraits that no doubt exaggerated the negative, but were effective in capturing the mood:

> The land of Egypt was abandoned and every man was a law to himself. During many years there was no leader who could speak for others. Central government lapsed, small officials and headmen took over the whole land. Any man, great or small, might kill his neighbor. In the distress and vacuum that followed . . . men banded together to plunder one another. They treated the gods no better than men, and cut off the temple revenues.[1]

The decline of Egypt allowed new powers to emerge. South of Egypt was a region called Nubia, which as early as 2000 B.C.E. served as a conduit of trade through which ivory, gold, ebony, and other products flowed north from sub-Saharan Africa. Small kingdoms arose in this area, with large buildings and rich tombs. As Egypt expanded during the New Kingdom (see Chapter 1), it took over northern Nubia in what were sometimes brutal conquests, incorporating it into the growing Egyptian empire. The Nubians adopted many features of Egyptian culture, including Egyptian gods, the use of hieroglyphics, and the building of pyramids. Many Nubians became officials in the Egyptian bureaucracy and officers in the army, and there was significant intermarriage between the two groups.

With the contraction of the Egyptian empire in the Third Intermediate Period, an independent kingdom, **Kush**, rose in power in Nubia, with its capital at Napata in what is now Sudan. The Kushites conquered southern Egypt, and in 727 B.C.E. the Kushite king Piye (r. ca. 747–716 B.C.E.) swept through the Nile Valley to the delta in the north. United once again, Egypt enjoyed a brief period of peace during which the Egyptian culture continued to influence that of its conquerors. In the seventh century B.C.E. invading Assyrians pushed the Kushites out of Egypt, and the Kushite rulers moved their capital farther up the Nile to Meroë, where they built hundreds of pyramids. Meroë became a center for the production of iron, which was becoming the material of choice for weapons. Iron products from Meroë were the best in the world, smelted using wood from the vast forests in the area. They were traded to much of Africa and across the Red Sea and the Indian Ocean to India.

The Kingdom of Kush, 1000 B.C.E.–300 C.E.

Kush Kingdom in Nubia that adopted hieroglyphics and pyramids, and later conquered Egypt.

The Rise of Phoenicia

While Kush expanded in the southern Nile Valley, another group rose to prominence along the Mediterranean coast of modern Lebanon, the northern part of the area called Canaan in ancient sources. These Canaanites established the prosperous commercial centers of Tyre, Sidon, and Byblos, all cities still thriving today, and were master shipbuilders. With their stout ships, between about 1100 and 700 B.C.E. the residents of these cities became the seaborne merchants of the Mediterranean. (See "Evaluating the Evidence 2.1: The Report of Wenamun," at right.) Their most valued products were purple and blue textiles, from which originated their Greek name, **Phoenicians** (fih-NEE-shuhnz), meaning "Purple People."

Phoenicians Seafaring people from Canaan who traded and founded colonies throughout the Mediterranean and spread the phonetic alphabet.

The trading success of the Phoenicians brought them prosperity. In addition to textiles and purple dye, they began to manufacture goods for export, such as tools, weapons, and cookware. They worked bronze and iron, which they shipped processed or as ores, and made and traded glass products. Phoenician ships often

The Report of Wenamun

This account describes the trip of the Egyptian official Wenamun to purchase Lebanese wood to make a large ceremonial boat named Amon-user-he *for the god Amon-Ra. It is unknown whether this text describes a real mission, but the text reflects the political and economic situation in the decade from 1190 to 1180 B.C.E. Wenamun negotiated with the prince of Byblos, a Phoenician city-state in present-day Lebanon, for the timber, encountering great frustrations.*

When morning came, he [the prince of Byblos] sent and brought me up. . . . Then he spoke to me, saying: "On what business have you come?" I said to him: "I have come in quest of timber for the great noble bark of Amon-Ra, King of Gods. What your father did, what the father of your father did, you too will do it." So I said to him. He said to me: "True, they did it. If you pay me for doing it, I will do it. My relations carried out this business after Pharaoh had sent six ships laden with the goods of Egypt, and they had been unloaded into their storehouses. You, what have you brought for me? . . . What are these foolish travels they made you do?"

I said to him: "Wrong! These are not foolish travels that I am doing. There is no ship on the river that does not belong to [the god] Amon. His is the sea and his the Lebanon of which you say, 'It is mine.' It is a growing ground for [the ceremonial ship called] *Amon-user-he*, the lord of every ship. . . . You are prepared to haggle over the Lebanon with Amon, its lord? As to your saying, the former kings sent silver and gold: If they had owned life and health, they would not have sent these things. It was in place of life and health that they sent these things to your fathers! But Amon-Ra, King of Gods, he is the lord of life and health, and he was the lord of your fathers! They passed their lifetimes [making] offering to Amon. You too, you are the servant of Amon!" . . .

He placed my letter in the hand of his messenger; and he loaded the keel, the prow-piece, and the stern-piece, together with four other hewn logs, seven in all, and sent them to Egypt. His messenger who had gone to Egypt returned to me in Syria in the first month of winter, Smendes and Tentamun [the pharaoh and queen of the northern half of Egypt, Wenamun's employers] having sent: four jars and one *kakmen*-vessel of gold; five jars of silver; ten garments of royal linen; ten . . . garments of fine linen; five-hundred smooth linen mats; five-hundred ox-hides; five-hundred ropes; twenty sacks of lentils; and thirty baskets of fish. . . .

The prince rejoiced. He assigned three hundred men and three hundred oxen, and he set supervisors over them to have them fell the timbers. They were felled and they lay there during the winter. In the third month of summer they dragged them to the shore of the sea. The prince came out and stood by them, and he sent to me, saying: "Come!" . . . As I stood before him, he addressed me, saying: "Look, the business my fathers did in the past, I have done it, although you did not do for me what your fathers did for mine. Look, the last of your timber has arrived and is ready. Do as I wish, and come to load it."

EVALUATE THE EVIDENCE

1. How does Wenamun first attempt to get the prince of Byblos to give him the timber? What does the prince send in the first shipment? Why does he eventually provide more timber?
2. How does Wenamun's report reflect the decline of Egyptian power and wealth?

Source: Miriam Lichtheim, *Ancient Egyptian Literature: A Book of Readings*, vol. 2, *The New Kingdom* (Berkeley: University of California Press, 1976), pp. 226–228. © 2006 by the Regents of the University of California. Published by the University of California Press.

carried hundreds of jars of wine, and the Phoenicians introduced grape growing to new regions around the Mediterranean, dramatically increasing the wine available for consumption and trade. They imported rare goods and materials, including hunting dogs, gold, and ivory, from Persia in the east and their neighbors to the south. They also expanded their trade to Egypt, where they mingled with other local traders.

The variety and quality of the Phoenicians' trade goods generally made them welcome visitors. Moving beyond Egypt, they struck out along the coast of North Africa to establish new markets in places where they encountered little competition. In the ninth century B.C.E. they founded, in modern Tunisia, the city of

Phoenicia, ca. 750 B.C.E.
Area of Phoenician settlement
• Settlement
→ Phoenician trade route

Phoenician Settlements in the Mediterranean

Carthage (meaning "new city" in Phoenician), which prospered to become the leading city in the western Mediterranean, although it would one day struggle with Rome for domination of that region.

The Phoenicians planted trading posts and small farming communities along the coast, founding colonies in Spain and Sicily along with Carthage. Their trade routes eventually took them to the far western Mediterranean and beyond to the Atlantic coast of modern-day Portugal. The Phoenicians' voyages brought them into contact with the Greeks, to whom they introduced many aspects of the older and more urbanized cultures of Mesopotamia and Egypt.

The Phoenicians' overwhelming cultural achievement was the spread of a completely phonetic system of writing—that is, an alphabet. Writers of both cuneiform and hieroglyphics had developed signs that were used to represent sounds, but these were always used with a much larger number of ideograms. Sometime around 1800 B.C.E. workers in the Sinai Peninsula, which was under Egyptian control, began to write only with phonetic signs, with each sign designating one sound. This system vastly simplified writing and reading and spread among common people as a practical way to record things and communicate. Egyptian scribes and officials continued to use hieroglyphics, but the Phoenicians adopted the simpler system for their own language and spread it around the Mediterranean. The Greeks modified this alphabet and then used it to write their own language, and the Romans later based their alphabet—the script we use to write English today—on Greek. Alphabets based on the Phoenician alphabet were also created in the Persian Empire and formed the basis of Hebrew, Arabic, and various alphabets of South and Central Asia. The system invented by ordinary people and spread by Phoenician merchants is the origin of most of the world's phonetic alphabets today.

The Hebrews

FOCUS QUESTION
How did the Hebrews create an enduring religious tradition?

Yahweh The sole god in Hebrew monotheism; later anglicized as Jehovah.

The legacy of another people who took advantage of Egypt's collapse to found an independent state may have been even more far-reaching than that of the Phoenicians. For a period of several centuries, a people known as the Hebrews controlled first one and then two small states on the western end of the Fertile Crescent, Israel and Judah. Politically unimportant when compared with the Egyptians or Babylonians, the Hebrews created a new form of religious belief, a monotheism based on the worship of an all-powerful god they called **Yahweh** (YAH-way). Beginning in the late 600s B.C.E., they began to write down their religious ideas, traditions, laws, advice literature, prayers, hymns, history, and prophecies in a series of books. These were gathered together centuries later to form the Hebrew Bible, which Christians later adopted and termed the "Old Testament" to parallel specific Christian writings termed the "New Testament." These writings later became the core of the Hebrews' religion, Judaism, a word taken from the kingdom of Judah, the southern of the two Hebrew kingdoms and the one that was the primary force in developing religious traditions. (The word *Israelite*, often used as a synonym for *Hebrew*, refers to all people in this group, and not simply the residents of the northern kingdom of Israel.) Jews today revere these texts, as do many Christians, and Muslims respect them, all of which gives them particular importance.

The Hebrew State

Most of the information about the Hebrews comes from the Bible, which, like all ancient documents, must be used with care as a historical source. Archaeological evidence has supported many of its details, and because it records a living religious tradition, extensive textual and physical research into everything it records continues, with enormous controversies among scholars about how to interpret findings.

The Hebrews were nomadic pastoralists who may have migrated into the Nile Delta from the east, seeking good land for their herds of sheep and goats. According to the Hebrew Bible, they were enslaved by the Egyptians, but were led out of Egypt by a charismatic leader named Moses. The biblical account is very dramatic, and the events form a pivotal episode in the history of the Hebrews and the later religious practices of Judaism. Moses conveyed God's warning to the pharaoh that a series of plagues would strike Egypt, the last of which was the threat that all firstborn sons in Egypt would be killed. He instructed the Hebrews to prepare a hasty meal of a sacrificed lamb eaten with unleavened bread. The blood of the lamb was painted over the doors of Hebrew houses. At midnight Yahweh spread death over the land, but he passed over the Hebrew houses with the blood-painted doors. This event became known as the Passover, and later became a central religious holiday in Judaism. The next day a terrified pharaoh ordered the Hebrews out of Egypt. Moses then led them in search of what they understood to be the Promised Land, an event known as the Exodus, which was followed by forty years of wandering.

According to scripture, the Hebrews settled in the area between the Mediterranean and the Jordan River known as Canaan. They were organized into tribes, each tribe consisting of numerous families who thought of themselves as all related to one another and having a common ancestor. At first, good farmland, pastureland, and freshwater sources were held in common by each tribe. Common use of land was—and still is—characteristic of nomadic peoples. The Bible divides up the Hebrews at this point into twelve tribes, each named according to an ancestor.

In Canaan, the nomadic Hebrews encountered a variety of other peoples, whom they both learned from and fought. They slowly adopted agriculture, and not surprisingly, at times worshipped the agricultural gods of their neighbors, including Baal, an ancient fertility god represented as a golden calf. This was another example of the common historical pattern of newcomers adapting themselves to the culture of an older, well-established people.

The Bible reports that the greatest danger to the Hebrews came from a group known as the Philistines, who were most likely Greek-speaking people who had migrated to Canaan as

A Golden Calf   According to the Hebrew Bible, Moses descended from Mount Sinai, where he had received the Ten Commandments, to find the Hebrews worshipping a golden calf, which was against Yahweh's laws. In July 1990 an American archaeological team found this model of a gilded calf inside a pot. The figurine, which dates to about 1550 B.C.E., is strong evidence for the existence in Canaan of religious traditions that involved animals as divine symbols. (www.BibleLandPictures.com/Alamy Stock Photo)

Possible route of the Exodus, ca. 1250 B.C.E.

☐ Solomon's kingdom, ca. 950 B.C.E.

☐ Israel, ca. 800 B.C.E.

☐ Judah, ca. 800 B.C.E.

The Hebrew Exodus and State, ca. 1250–800 B.C.E.

part of the movement of the Sea Peoples and established a kingdom along the Mediterranean coast. The Philistines' superior technology and military organization at first made them invincible, but the Hebrews found a champion and a spirited leader in Saul. In the biblical account Saul and his men battled the Philistines for control of the land, often without success. In the meantime Saul established a monarchy over the twelve Hebrew tribes, becoming their king, an event conventionally dated to about 1025 B.C.E.

The Bible includes detailed discussion of the growth of the Hebrew kingdom. It relates that Saul's work was carried on by David of Bethlehem (r. ca. 1005–965 B.C.E.), who pushed back the Philistines and waged war against his other neighbors. To give his kingdom a capital, he captured the city of Jerusalem, which he enlarged, fortified, and made the religious and political center of his realm. David's military successes enlarged the kingdom and won the Hebrews unprecedented security, and his forty-year reign was a period of vitality and political consolidation.

David's son Solomon (r. ca. 965–925 B.C.E.) launched a building program that the biblical narrative describes as including cities, palaces, fortresses, and roads. The most symbolic of these projects was the Temple of Jerusalem, which became the home of the Ark of the Covenant, the chest that contained the holiest of Hebrew religious articles. The temple in Jerusalem was intended to be the religious heart of the kingdom, a symbol of Hebrew unity and Yahweh's approval of the kingdom built by Saul, David, and Solomon.

Evidence of this united kingdom may have come to light in August 1993 when an Israeli archaeologist found an inscribed stone slab that refers to a "king of Israel," and also to the "House of David." This discovery has been regarded by most scholars as the first mention of King David's dynasty outside of the Bible. The nature and extent of this kingdom continue to be disputed among archaeologists, who offer divergent datings and interpretations for the finds that are continuously brought to light.

Along with discussing expansion and success, the Bible also notes problems. Solomon's efforts were hampered by strife. The financial demands of his building program drained the resources of his people, and his use of forced labor for building projects further fanned popular resentment.

A united Hebrew kingdom did not last long. At Solomon's death his kingdom broke into political halves. The northern part became Israel, with its capital at Samaria, and the southern half became Judah, with Jerusalem remaining its center. War soon broke out between them, as recorded in the Bible, and the Assyrians wiped out the northern kingdom of Israel in 722 B.C.E. Judah survived numerous calamities until the Babylonians crushed it in 587 B.C.E. The survivors were forcibly relocated to Babylonia, a period commonly known as the Babylonian Captivity. In 539 B.C.E. the Persian king Cyrus the Great (see page 53) conquered the Babylonians and permitted some forty thousand exiles to return to Jerusalem. They rebuilt the temple, although politically the area was simply part of the Persian Empire.

The Jewish Religion

Torah The first five books of the Hebrew Bible, containing the most important legal and ethical Hebrew texts; later became part of the Christian Old Testament.

During and especially after the Babylonian Captivity, the most important legal and ethical Hebrew texts were edited and brought together in the **Torah**, the first five books of the Hebrew Bible. Here the exiles redefined their beliefs and practices, thereby establishing what they believed was the law of Yahweh. Fundamental to an understanding of the Jewish religion is the concept of the **Covenant**, an agreement that people believed to exist between themselves and Yahweh. According to the Bible, Yahweh appeared to the tribal leader Abraham, promising him that he would be blessed, as would his descendants, if they followed Yahweh. (Because Judaism, Christianity, and Islam all regard this event as foundational, they are referred to as the "Abrahamic religions.") Yahweh next appeared to Moses during the time he was leading the Hebrews out of Egypt, and Yahweh made a Covenant with the Hebrews: if they worshipped Yahweh as their only god, he would consider them his chosen people and protect them from their enemies. The Covenant was understood to be made with the whole people, not simply a king or an elite, and was renewed again several times in the accounts of the Hebrew people in the Bible. Individuals such as Abraham and Moses who acted as intermediaries between Yahweh and the Hebrew people were known as "prophets"; much of the Hebrew Bible consists of writings in their voices, understood as messages from Yahweh to which the Hebrews were to listen.

Worship was embodied in a series of rules of behavior that became known as the Ten Commandments, which Yahweh gave to Moses. These required certain kinds of religious observances and forbade the Hebrews to steal, kill, lie, or commit adultery, thus creating a system of ethical absolutes. From the Ten Commandments a complex system of rules of conduct was created and later written down as Hebrew law. The earliest part of this code, contained in the Torah, was most likely influenced by Hammurabi's code (see Chapter 1) and often called for harsh punishments. Later tradition, largely the work of the prophets who lived from the eighth to the fifth centuries B.C.E., put more emphasis on righteousness than on retribution.

Like the followers of other religions in the ancient Near East, Jews engaged in rituals through which they showed their devotion. They were also expected to please Yahweh by living up to high moral standards and by worshipping him above all other gods. The first of the Ten Commandments expresses this: "I am the Lord your God . . . you shall have no other gods besides me" (Exodus 20:2–3). Increasingly this was understood to be a commandment to worship Yahweh alone. The later prophets such as Isaiah created a system of ethical monotheism, in which goodness was understood to come from a single transcendent god, and in which religious obligations included fair and just behavior toward other people as well as rituals. They saw Yahweh as intervening directly in history and also working through individuals—both Hebrews and non-Hebrews—he had chosen to carry out his aims. (See "Individuals in Society: Cyrus the Great," page 53.) Judging by the many prophets (and a few prophetesses) in the Bible exhorting the Hebrews to listen to Yahweh, honor the Covenant, stop worshipping other gods, and behave properly, adherence to this system was a difficult challenge.

Like Mesopotamian deities, Yahweh punished people, but the Hebrews also believed he was a loving and forgiving god who would protect and reward all those who obeyed his commandments. A hymn recorded in the book of Psalms captures this idea:

> Blessed is every one who fears the Lord, who walks in his ways!
> You shall eat the fruit of the labor of your hands; you shall be happy, and it shall be well
>   with you.
> Your wife will be like a fruitful vine within your house;
> your children will be like olive shoots around your table.
> Lo, thus shall the man be blessed who fears the Lord. (Psalms 128:1–4)

Covenant An agreement that the Hebrews believed to exist between themselves and Yahweh, in which he would consider them his chosen people if they worshipped him as their only god.

The religion of the Hebrews was thus addressed to not only an elite but also the individual. Because kings or other political leaders were not essential to its practice, the rise or fall of a kingdom was not crucial to the religion's continued existence. Religious leaders were important in Judaism, but personally following the instructions of Yahweh was the central task for observant Jews in the ancient world.

Hebrew Family and Society

The Hebrews were originally nomadic, but they adopted settled agriculture in Canaan, and some lived in cities. The shift away from pastoralism affected more than just how people fed themselves. Communal use of land gave way to family or private ownership, and devotion to the traditions of Judaism came to replace tribal identity.

Family relationships reflected evolving circumstances. Marriage and the family were fundamentally important in Jewish life; celibacy was frowned upon, and almost all major Jewish thinkers and priests were married. Polygamy was allowed, but the typical marriage was probably monogamous. In the codes of conduct written down in the Hebrew Bible, sex between a married woman and a man not her husband was an "abomination," as were incest and sex between men. Men were free to have sexual relations with concubines, servants, and slaves, however.

As in Mesopotamia and Egypt, marriage was a family matter, too important to be left to the whims of young people. (See "Evaluating the Evidence 2.2: A Jewish Family Contract," page 45.) Although specific rituals may have been expected to ensure ritual purity in sexual relations, sex itself was viewed as part of Yahweh's creation and the bearing of children was seen in some ways as a religious function. Sons were especially desired because they maintained the family bloodline, while keeping ancestral property in the family. As in Mesopotamia, land was handed down within families, generally from father to son. A firstborn son became the head of the household at his father's death. Mothers oversaw the early education of the children, but as boys grew older, their fathers gave them more of their education. Both men and women were expected to know religious traditions so that they could teach their children and prepare for religious rituals and ceremonies. Women worked in the fields alongside their husbands in rural areas, and in shops in the cities. According to biblical codes, menstruation and childbirth made women ritually impure, but the implications of this in ancient times are contested by scholars.

Children, according to the book of Psalms, "are a heritage of the lord, and the fruit of the womb is his reward" (Psalms 128:3), and newly married couples were expected to begin a family at once. The desire for children to perpetuate the family was so strong that if a man died before he could sire a son, his brother was legally obliged to marry the widow. The son born of the brother was thereafter considered the offspring of the dead man. If the brother refused, the widow had her revenge by denouncing him to the elders and publicly spitting in his face.

The development of urban life among the Jews created new economic opportunities, especially in crafts and trades. People specialized in certain occupations, such as milling flour, baking bread, making pottery, weaving, and carpentry. As in most ancient societies, these crafts were family trades. Sons worked with their father, daughters with their mother. If the business prospered, the family might be assisted by a few paid workers or slaves. The practitioners of a craft usually lived in a

A Jewish Family Contract

During the time of Persian rule in Egypt, Jewish soldiers were stationed in Elephantine, a military post on the Nile. Historians have since recovered papyrus documents from that location, known as the Elephantine papyri, which provide information on all sorts of everyday social and economic matters, including marriage, divorce, property, slavery, and borrowing money. The text below is an agreement by a Jewish father regarding a house he had given to his daughter, probably as part of her dowry. It was written in Aramaic, the language of business in the Persian Empire.

On the 21st of Chisleu, that is the 1st of Mesore, year 6 of King Artaxerxes,* Mahseiah b. Yedoniah, a Jew of Elephantine, of the detachment of Haumadata, said to Jezaniah b. Uriah of the said detachment as follows: There is the site of 1 house belonging to me, west of the house belonging to you, which I have given to your wife, my daughter Mibtahiah, and in respect of which I have written her a deed. The measurements of the house in question are 8 cubits and a handbreadth by 11, *by the measuring-rod.*[†] Now do I, Mahseiah, say to you, Build and equip that site . . . and dwell thereon with your wife. But you may not sell that house or give it as a present to others; only your children by my daughter Mibtahiah shall have power over it after you

two. If tomorrow or some other day you build upon this land, and then my daughter divorces you and leaves you, she shall have no power to take it or give it to others; only your children by Mibtahiah shall have power over it, in return for the work which you shall have done. If, on the other hand, she recovers from you [in other words, if Jezaniah divorces *her*], she [may] take half the house, and [the] othe[r] half shall be at your disposal in return for the building which you will have done on that house. And again as to that half, your children by Mibtahiah shall have power over it after you. If tomorrow or another day I should institute suit or process against you and say I did not give you this land to build on and did not draw up this deed for you, I shall give you a sum of 10 *karshin* by royal weight, at the rate of 2 *R* to the ten, and no suit or process shall lie. This deed was written by ʿAtharshuri b. Nabuzeribni in the fortress of Syene at the dictation of Mahseiah.

Witnesses hereto (signatures)

EVALUATE THE EVIDENCE

1. How does Mahseiah seek to assist his daughter and his future grandchildren?
2. What does this contract reveal about the movement and mixtures of peoples in the Persian Empire, and about Persian methods of governing?

* This is the date of the document. Chisleu was a month in the Hebrew calendar, Mesore a seasonal period in the Egyptian calendar. Artaxerxes is most likely Artaxerxes I, king of Persia from 465 to 424 B.C.E., which means the year this agreement was drafted was 459 B.C.E.

† A cubit was the length of a forearm, roughly 20 inches; the house site was thus about 15 by 18 feet.

Source: James B. Pritchard, ed., *Ancient Near Eastern Texts Relating to the Old Testament — Third Edition with Supplement.* Reproduced with permission of PRINCETON UNIVERSITY PRESS, in the format Book via Copyright Clearance Center.

particular section of town, a custom still prevalent in the Near East today. Commerce and trade developed later than crafts. Trade with neighboring countries was handled by foreigners, usually Phoenicians. Jews dealt mainly in local trade, and in most instances craftsmen and farmers sold directly to their customers.

The Torah sets out rules about many aspects of life, including skin diseases, seminal emissions, childbirth, sexual actions, and animal sacrifices. Among these was the set of dietary laws known as *kashrut* (from which we derive the English word *kosher*, which means ritually pure and ready to be eaten), setting out what plants and animals Jews were forbidden to eat and how foods were to be prepared properly. Prohibited animals included pigs, rabbits, many birds, insects (except for locusts), and shellfish, as well as any animal not slaughtered in the proper way. Meat and dairy products were not to be eaten at the same meal or cooked in the same utensils. Later commentators

Hebrew Seal   This black stone seal dating from the seventh century B.C.E. depicts an archer shooting an arrow. The inscription beside him in ancient Hebrew letters means "for Hagab." Hagab was most likely the name of the official or army officer who would have used this seal on his letters and documents. Hagab chose to show himself dressed in Assyrian style, an indication of the Assyrian cultural influence that accompanied Assyrian military expansion. (Photo: Clara Amit. Courtesy, Israel Antiquities Authority)

sought to explain these laws as originating in concerns about health or hygiene, but the biblical text simply gives them as rules coming from Yahweh, sometimes expressed in terms of ritual purity or cleanliness. It is not clear how these rules were followed during the biblical period, because detailed interpretations were written down only much later, during the time of the Roman Empire, in the Talmud, a work that records civil and ceremonial law and Jewish traditions. Most scholars see the written laws as based on earlier oral traditions, but as with any law code, from Hammurabi's to contemporary ones, it is much easier to learn about what people were supposed to do according to the laws of the Torah than what they actually did.

Beliefs and practices that made Jews distinctive endured, but the Hebrew states did not. Small states like those of the Phoenicians and the Hebrews could exist only in the absence of a major power, and the beginning of the ninth century B.C.E. saw the rise of such a power: the Assyrians of northern Mesopotamia. They conquered the kingdom of Israel, the Phoenician cities, and eventually many other states as well.

Assyria, the Military Monarchy

FOCUS QUESTION
What explains the rise and fall of the Assyrians?

The Assyrian kingdom originated in northern Mesopotamia. The Assyrians built up the military and conquered many of their neighbors, including Babylonia, and took over much of Syria all the way to the Mediterranean. The Assyrians then moved into Anatolia, where the pressure they put on the Hittite Empire was one factor in its collapse. Assyria's success allowed it to become the leading power in the Near East, with an army that at times numbered many tens of thousands.

Assyria's Long Road to Power

The Assyrians had inhabited northern Mesopotamia since the third millennium B.C.E., forming a kingdom that grew and shrank in size and power over the centuries. They had long pursued commerce with the Babylonians in the south and the peoples of northern Syria and Anatolia in the north. During the time of Sargon of Akkad, they were part of the Akkadian empire, then independent, then part of the Babylonian empire under Hammurabi, then independent again (see Chapter 1). Warfare with the Babylonians and other Near Eastern states continued off and on, and in the thirteenth century B.C.E., under the leadership of a series of warrior-kings, the Assyrians slowly began to create a larger state.

The eleventh century B.C.E. — the time of the Bronze Age Collapse — was a period of instability and retrenchment in the Near East. The Assyrians did not engage in any new wars of conquest, but remained fairly secure within their borders. Under the leadership of King Adad-nirari II (r. 911–892 B.C.E.), Assyria began a campaign of expansion and domination, creating what scholars have termed the Neo-Assyrian Empire. Assyrian armies pushed in all directions, conquering, exacting tribute, and building new fortified towns, palaces, and temples. King Shalmaneser III (shal-muh-NEE-zuhr) (r. 858–823 B.C.E.) conquered all of Babylonia, Syria, Phoenicia, and much of the northern half of the Arabian peninsula. The next several turbulent centuries were marked by Assyrian military campaigns, constant efforts by smaller states to maintain or recover their independence, and eventual further Assyrian conquest.

Assyrian history is often told as a story of one powerful king after another, but among the successful Assyrian rulers there was one queen, Shammuramat, whose name in Greek became Semiramis. She ruled with her husband and then as regent for her young son in 810–806 B.C.E. Although not much can be known for certain about the historical Queen Semiramis, many legends grew up about her, which were told throughout the ancient Near East, and later by Greek and Roman authors. Some emphasized her wisdom, beauty, and patronage of the arts, while others portrayed her as a sex-crazed sorceress. These stories cannot be used as evidence for the lives of women in the Assyrian Empire, but like the stories of Queen Cleopatra of Egypt (see Chapter 5), they can be used as evidence for the continuing fascination with the few women who held political power in the ancient world.

Eighth-century kings continued the expansion of Assyria, which established its capital at Nineveh (NIHN-uh-vuh) on the Tigris River. The kingdom of Israel and many other states fell; others, like the kingdom of Judah, became subservient to the warriors from the Tigris. In 717 B.C.E. Sargon II (r. 721–705 B.C.E.) led his army in a sweeping attack along the coast of the eastern Mediterranean south of Phoenicia, where he defeated the armies of the Egyptian pharaoh. Sargon also lashed out at Assyria's traditional enemies to the north and then turned south against a renewed threat in Babylonia. By means of almost constant warfare, the Assyrians created an empire that stretched from east and north of the Tigris River to central Egypt (Map 2.1). Revolt against the Assyrians inevitably promised the rebels bloody battles and cruel sieges followed by surrender, accompanied by systematic torture and slaughter, or by deportations. Like many conquerors, the Assyrians recognized that relocated peoples were less likely to rebel because they were forced to create new lives for themselves far from their original homelands, and that simply relocating leaders might be enough to destroy opposition.

Assyrian methods were certainly harsh, but in practical terms Assyria's success was actually due primarily to the size of its army and the army's sophisticated and effective military organization. By Sargon's time, the Assyrians had invented the mightiest military machine the ancient Near East had ever seen, with perhaps seventy thousand men in the field in an era that typically saw armies of under ten thousand. The mainstay of the Assyrian army was the infantryman armed with an iron spear and sword and protected by helmet and armor. The Assyrian army also featured archers, some on foot, others on horseback, and still others in chariots — the latter ready to wield lances once they had expended their supply of arrows. Some infantry archers wore heavy armor.

MAP 2.1 The Assyrian and Persian Empires, ca. 1000–500 B.C.E.   The Assyrian Empire at its height around 650 B.C.E. included almost all of the old centers of power in the ancient Near East. By 513 B.C.E., however, the Persian Empire was far larger.

These soldiers served as a primitive field artillery whose job was to sweep the enemy's walls of defenders so that others could storm the defenses. Slingers (warriors who used slingshots) also served as artillery in pitched battles. For mobility on the battlefield, the Assyrians organized a corps of chariots.

Assyrian military genius was remarkable for the development of a wide variety of siege machinery and techniques, including excavation to undermine city walls and battering rams to knock down walls and gates. Never before in the Near East had anyone applied such technical knowledge to warfare. The Assyrians even invented the concept of a corps of engineers, who bridged rivers with pontoons or provided soldiers with inflatable skins for swimming. And the Assyrians knew how to coordinate their efforts, both in open battle and in siege warfare. Assyrian king Sennacherib's (r. 705–681 B.C.E.) account of his attacks on the kingdom of Judah, which was under the leadership of King Hezekiah (r. ca. 715–686 B.C.E.) in 701 B.C.E., provides a vivid portrait of the Assyrian war machine:

> As to Hezekiah, the Jew, he did not submit to my yoke, I laid siege to 46 of his strong cities, walled forts and to the countless small villages in their vicinity, and conquered them by means of well-stamped earth-ramps, and battering rams brought thus near to the walls combined with the attack by foot soldiers, using mines, breaches as well as sapper work. . . . Himself I made prisoner in Jerusalem, his royal residence, like a bird in a cage. I surrounded him with earthwork in order to molest those who were leaving his city's gate.[2]

Hezekiah's Tunnel When the Assyrians were attacking Jerusalem in the eighth century B.C.E., King Hezekiah ordered the building of a tunnel from the springs outside the city walls to bring freshwater into the city. It was constructed by teams operating from each end, guided by workers above listening for the ways their hammer blows sounded on the rock. The tunnel can still be walked through today, though at certain times of the year this means wading in water. (Photo © Zev Radovan/Bridgeman Images)

What Assyrian accounts do not mention is that the siege of Jerusalem was not successful. Although they had conquered many cities in Judah, the Assyrian armies gave up their attempts to conquer the entire kingdom and went home.

Sennacherib's campaign is also recorded several times in the Hebrew Bible, but there the point is very different. Instead of focusing on Assyrian might, the author stresses King Hezekiah's reliance on Yahweh. The biblical accounts attribute Judah's ability to withstand the Assyrian siege to an angel sent by Yahweh, but they also describe Hezekiah as taking practical measures to counter the Assyrian invasion. He "made weapons and shields in abundance," and also ordered the building of a tunnel that would divert water from the springs outside the walls of Jerusalem into the city, thus both limiting the water available for Assyrian troops and assuring the city of a steady supply:

> When Hezekiah saw that Sennacherib had come and intended to fight against Jerusalem, he planned with his officers and his mighty men to stop the water of the springs that were outside the city; and they helped him. A great many people were gathered, and they stopped all the springs and the brook that flowed through the land. (2 Chronicles 32:2–4)

The tunnel was completed and functioned, and is now a major tourist attraction. An inscription that was originally on the wall recording the way in which it was built has been dated to the eighth century B.C.E., and chemical analysis confirms this dating.

Assyrian Rule and Culture

Although the Assyrians gave up on conquering Judah, they won most of their battles, and they also knew how to use their victories to consolidate their power. The key to success in all empires is to get cooperation from some people in the regions you wish to dominate, and the Assyrians did this well. As early as the reign of Tiglath-pileser III, the Assyrian kings began to organize their conquered territories into an empire. The lands closest to Assyria became provinces governed by Assyrian officials. Kingdoms beyond the provinces were not annexed but became dependent states that followed Assyria's lead and also paid Assyria a hefty tribute. The Assyrian king chose these states' rulers either by regulating the succession of native kings or by supporting native kings who appealed to him. Against more distant states the Assyrian kings waged frequent war in order to conquer them outright or make the dependent states secure. (See "Evaluating the Evidence 2.3: Assyrians Besiege a City," at right.)

In the seventh century B.C.E. Assyrian power seemed firmly established. Yet the downfall of Assyria was swift and complete. Babylon finally won its independence from Assyria in 626 B.C.E. and joined forces with the Medes, an Indo-European-speaking people from Persia (modern Iran). Together the Babylonians and the Medes destroyed the Assyrian Empire in 612 B.C.E., paving the way for the rise of the Persians. The Hebrew prophet Nahum (NAY-uhm) spoke for many when he asked, "Nineveh is laid waste: who will bemoan her?" (Nahum 3:7). Their cities destroyed and their power shattered, the Assyrians disappeared from history, remembered only as a cruel people of the Old Testament who oppressed the Hebrews. Two hundred years later, when the Greek adventurer and historian Xenophon (ZEH-nuh-fuhn) passed by the ruins of Nineveh, he marveled at the extent of the former city but knew nothing of the Assyrians. The glory of their empire was forgotten.

Modern archaeology has brought the Assyrians out of obscurity. In 1839 the English archaeologist and traveler A. H. Layard began excavations at Nineveh. His findings electrified the world. Layard's workers unearthed masterpieces, including monumental sculpted figures—huge winged bulls, human-headed lions, and sphinxes—as well as brilliantly sculpted friezes. Among the most renowned of Layard's finds were the Assyrian palace reliefs, whose number has been increased by the discoveries of twentieth-century archaeologists. For the kings' palaces, Assyrian artists carved reliefs that showed scenes of war as a series of episodes that progressed from the time the army marched out until the enemy was conquered. In doing so, they created a visual narrative of events, a form still favored by comic-book artists and the authors of graphic novels.

Equally valuable were the numerous Assyrian cuneiform documents, which ranged from royal accounts of mighty military campaigns to simple letters by common people. The biggest find of these was the library of King Ashurbanipal (r. 668–627 B.C.E.), the last major Assyrian king, in the city of Nineveh. Like many Assyrian kings, Ashurbanipal was described as extremely cruel, but he was also well educated and deeply interested in literary and religious texts, especially those from what was already to him the ancient Mesopotamian past. Included in the tens of thousands of texts in his library were creation accounts from ancient Babylon (some most likely simply confiscated from the city of Babylon, which was part of the Assyrian Empire), the *Epic of Gilgamesh*, and many other mythological and religious texts, as well as word lists, chronicles, and royal documents. Some texts relate to medicine and astronomy, and others to foretelling the future or practicing magic. The clay tablets on which these were written are harder than normal, which many scholars think may have happened as a result of a fire that destroyed the city of Nineveh shortly after the end of Ashurbanipal's reign. Unfortunately, the English archaeologists who dug up his library in the nineteenth century did not follow the standards of excavation that later archaeologists would, and just shipped the tablets back to London all jumbled together without recording exactly where and how they had been found. Many broke and are still being pieced together more than a century after their discovery. Thus many questions that scholars have about the library are impossible to answer.

Assyrians Besiege a City

In this Assyrian carving made about 700 B.C.E., from the palace of King Sennacherib at Nineveh, troops attack the Jewish fortified town of Lachish using a variety of siege machinery. On the right, defending soldiers crowd a tower, while men and women carry sacks away from the city.

EVALUATE THE EVIDENCE

1. What means of attack do the Assyrians use against the besieged city? How does the artist convey the idea that Assyrian military might was overwhelming?
2. Based on what you have read in this chapter about King Sennacherib, why might he have chosen to have this particular scene portrayed in his palace?

(British Museum, London, UK/De Agostini Picture Library/G. Nimatallah/Bridgeman Images)

The Neo-Babylonian Empire

The decline of Assyria allowed another group of people, the Chaldeans, to create a new dynasty of kings and a somewhat smaller empire centered at Babylon. The Chaldeans were peoples that settled in southern Mesopotamia, where they established their rule, later extending it farther north. They grew strong enough to overthrow Assyrian rule in 626 B.C.E. with the help of another new people, the Medes, who had established themselves in modern western Iran (see page 52). The Neo- (or new) Babylonian empire they created was marked by an attempt at the restoration of past Babylonian greatness. Their most famous king, Nebuchadnezzar II (neh-buh-kuhd-NEH-zuhr) (r. 604–562 B.C.E.), thrust Babylonian power into Syria and Judah, destroying Jerusalem and forcibly deporting the residents to Babylonia.

The Chaldeans focused on solidifying their power and legitimizing their authority. Kings and priests consciously looked back to the great days of Hammurabi and other earlier kings. They instituted a religious revival that included restoring old temples and sanctuaries, as well as creating new ones in the same tradition. Part of their effort was commercial, as they sought to revive the economy in order to resurrect the image of Babylonian greatness. In their hands the city of Babylon grew and gained a reputation for magnificence and luxury. The city, it was said by later Greek and Roman writers, even housed hanging gardens, one of the "wonders of the ancient world." No contemporary written or archaeological sources confirm the existence of the hanging gardens, but they do confirm that Babylon was a bustling, thriving city.

The Neo-Babylonians preserved many basic aspects of older Babylonian law, literature, and government, yet they failed to bring peace and prosperity to Mesopotamia. Loss of important trade routes to the north and northeast reduced income, and additional misfortune came in the form of famine and plague. The Neo-Babylonian kingdom was weakened and ultimately conquered in 539 B.C.E. by its former allies the Medes, who had themselves found new allies, the Persians.

The Empire of the Persian Kings

FOCUS QUESTION
How did the Persians consolidate their power and control and influence the subjects of their extensive empire?

The Assyrians rose to power from a base in the Tigris and Euphrates River Valleys of Mesopotamia, which had seen many earlier empires. They were defeated by a coalition that included a Mesopotamian power—Babylon—but also a people with a base of power in a part of the world that had not been the site of earlier urbanized states: Persia (modern-day Iran), a stark land of towering mountains and flaming deserts, with a broad central plateau in the heart of the country (see Map 2.1). The Persians created an even larger empire than the Assyrians did, and one that stretched far to the east. Though as conquerors they willingly used force to accomplish their ends, they also used diplomacy to consolidate their power and generally allowed the peoples that they conquered to practice their existing customs and religions. Thus the Persian Empire was one of political unity and cultural diversity.

Consolidation of the Persian Empire

Iran's geographical position and topography explain its traditional role as the highway between western and eastern Asia. Nomadic peoples migrating south from the broad steppes of Russia and Central Asia have streamed into Iran throughout much of history. Confronting the uncrossable salt deserts, most have turned either westward or eastward, moving on until they reached the advanced and wealthy urban centers of Mesopotamia and India. Cities did emerge along these routes, however, and Iran became the area where nomads met urban dwellers.

Among the nomadic groups were Indo-European-speaking peoples who migrated into this area about 1000 B.C.E. with their flocks and herds. They were also horse breeders, and the horse gave them a decisive military advantage over those who already lived in the area. One of the Indo-European groups was the Medes, who settled in northern Iran with their capital at Ecbatana, the modern Hamadan. The Medes united under one king and joined the Babylonians in overthrowing the Assyrian Empire. With the rise of the Medes, the balance of power in western Asia shifted for the first time to the area east of Mesopotamia.

In 550 B.C.E. Cyrus the Great (r. 559–530 B.C.E.), king of the Persians and one of the most remarkable statesmen of antiquity, conquered the Medes. (See "Individuals in Society: Cyrus the Great," at right.) Cyrus's conquest of the Medes resulted not in slavery and slaughter but in the union of the two peoples. Having united Persia and Media, Cyrus set out to achieve two goals. First, he wanted to win control of the shore of the Mediterranean and thus of the terminal ports of the great trade routes that crossed Iran and Anatolia. Second, he strove to secure eastern Iran from the pressure of nomadic invaders.

INDIVIDUALS IN SOCIETY

Cyrus the Great

Cyrus (r. 559–530 B.C.E.), known to history as "the Great" and the founder of the Persian Empire, began life as a subject of the Medes, an Iranian people very closely related to the Persians. There are few surviving sources describing his early life, and even the date of his birth is uncertain. There are many legends, however, some originating in Persia and others in Greece, as many later Greek leaders and authors admired Cyrus. The Greek historian Herodotus records the legend that Cyrus was the grandson of Astyages, king of the Medes, who ordered him killed to eliminate him as a future threat. Cyrus, like the biblical Moses, escaped the plot and went on to rule both his own Persians and the Medes.

Another story recounted by Herodotus tells how Cyrus's playmates chose him king. He assigned them specific duties, and when one aristocratic boy refused to obey his orders, Cyrus had him "arrested." The boy's father later demanded that Cyrus explain his haughty behavior. Cyrus replied that the other boys had chosen him king, and he did his duty justly, as a king should. He told the man that if he had done anything wrong, he was there to take his punishment. The man and the other boys admired his calm sense of duty and responsibility. Through this anecdote, the historian projected Cyrus's intelligence and good qualities, revealed later in life, back into his boyhood.

Astyages eventually marched against the grown Cyrus and was defeated. Instead of enslaving the Medes, Cyrus incorporated them into the new kingdom of Persia, thus demonstrating his inclusive concept of rule. This relatively mild rule continued with his later conquests. He won the admiration of many Greeks, whom he allowed to continue their religious rituals and intellectual pursuits.

After conquering Babylonia, Cyrus allowed the Jews who had been in forced exile there to return to Jerusalem. Hebrew Scripture portrays Cyrus as divinely chosen, as evidenced by this biblical passage, probably written in the late sixth century B.C.E., shortly after the end of the Babylonian Captivity:

> Thus said the Lord to Cyrus, His anointed one —
> Whose right hand He has grasped,
> Treading down nations before him,
> Ungirding the loins of kings,
> Opening doors before him, and letting no gate stay shut:
> I will march before you, and level the hills that loom up;
> I will shatter doors of bronze
> And cut down iron bars.
> I will give you treasures concealed in the dark
> And secret hoards —
> So that you may know that it is I the Lord,
> The God of Israel, who call you by name. . . .
> It was I who roused him [Cyrus] for victory
> And who level all roads for him.
> He shall rebuild My city
> And let My exiled people go
> Without price and without payment
>   — said the LORD of hosts. (Isaiah 45:1–3, 13)

Cyrus died in 530 B.C.E. while campaigning in Central Asia. Though much of his life was spent at war, he knew how to govern conquered peoples effectively and acquired a reputation for benevolence and tolerance. Much about his life can never be known, but Cyrus appears to have been a practical man of sound judgment, keenly interested in foreign peoples and their ways of life.

Statue of Cyrus the Great at the Olympic Park in Sydney, Australia. A replica of a bas-relief in Cyrus's capital city of Pasargadae, this monument was erected in 1994 as a testament to the peaceful coexistence of many different peoples in the Persian Empire. (Visual Connection Archive)

QUESTIONS FOR ANALYSIS

1. How are the Greek stories, as told by Herodotus, and the biblical account similar in their portrayals of Cyrus? How are they different?
2. Herodotus, the Bible, and the inscription on the Cyrus cylinder discussed on page 54 have all been influential in establishing the largely positive historical view of Cyrus. What limitations might there be in using these as historical sources?

53

In a series of major campaigns, Cyrus achieved his goals. He conquered the various kingdoms of the Tigris and Euphrates Valleys, including Babylon in 539 B.C.E. A text written in cuneiform on a sixth-century-B.C.E. Babylonian clay cylinder presents Cyrus describing the way in which the main Babylonian god Marduk selected him to conquer Babylon and restore proper government and worship:

> I am Cyrus, king of the universe, the great king, the powerful king, king of Babylon, king of Sumer and Akkad, king of the four quarters of the world. . . . When I went as harbinger of peace i[nt]o Babylon I founded my sovereign residence within the palace amid celebration and rejoicing. Marduk, the great lord, bestowed on me as my destiny the great magnanimity of one who loves Babylon, and I every day sought him out in awe. My vast troops marched peaceably in Babylon, and the whole of [Sumer] and Akkad had nothing to fear. I sought the welfare of the city of Babylon and all its sanctuaries. As for the population of Babylon, . . . [w]ho as if without div[ine intention] had endured a yoke not decreed for them, I soothed their weariness, I freed them from their bonds. . . . Marduk, the great lord, rejoiced at [my good] deeds, and he pronounced a sweet blessing over me, Cyrus, the king who fears him, and over Cambyses, the son [my] issue, [and over] all my troops, that we might proceed further at his exalted command.[3]

We do not know who actually wrote this text, but whoever did made sure to portray Cyrus as someone who triumphed as the result of divine favor, not simply military conquest, and honored the gods of the regions he conquered.

Cyrus then swept into western Anatolia. Here his forces met those of the young kingdom of Lydia, a small state where gold may have first been minted into coins. Croesus (KREE-suhs), king of the Lydians, considered Cyrus an immediate threat and planned to attack his territory. Greek legends later related that Croesus consulted the oracle at Delphi, that is, the priestess of the temple to the god Apollo at Delphi, who was understood to convey the words of the god when she spoke. Speaking through the priestess, Apollo said of the invasion, "If you make war on the Persians, you will destroy a mighty empire" (Herodotus 1.53.3). Thinking that the oracle meant the Persian Empire, Croesus went ahead and was defeated; the oracle meant that he would destroy his own kingdom.

According to later Greek sources, Cyrus spared the life of Croesus, who then served him as an adviser. To the Greeks, Croesus became synonymous with enormous wealth, giving rise to the phrase "richer than Croesus." Recent scholarship has suggested that stories about Croesus's wealth were based primarily on the fact that Lydia was one of the earliest places where gold coins were minted. Historians studying Persian sources have also noted that the account of Croesus being spared and becoming an adviser to Cyrus might be an embellished story, yet another myth surrounding the kings of Lydia and Persia. The exact date and circumstances of Croesus's death have yet to be determined.

Whatever actually happened to Croesus, Cyrus's generals subdued the Greek cities along the coast of Anatolia, thus gaining him important ports on the Mediterranean. From Lydia, Cyrus marched to the far eastern corners of Iran and conquered the regions of Parthia and Bactria in Central Asia, though he ultimately died on the battlefield there.

After his victories, Cyrus made sure that the Persians were portrayed as liberators, and in some cases he was more benevolent than most conquerors were. According to his own account, he freed all the captive peoples who were living in forced exile in Babylonia. This included the Hebrews. He returned their sacred objects to them and allowed those who wanted to do so to return to Jerusalem, where he paid for the rebuilding of their temple.

Cyrus's successors continued Persian conquests, creating the largest empire the world had yet seen. In 525 B.C.E. Cyrus's son Cambyses (r. 530–522 B.C.E.) subdued the Egyptians and the Nubians. At Cambyses's death (the circumstances of which are disputed), Darius I (r. 521–486 B.C.E.) took over the throne and conquered Scythia in Central Asia, along with much of Thrace and Macedonia, areas north of the Aegean Sea. By 510 B.C.E. the Persians also ruled the western coast of Anatolia and many of the islands of the Aegean. Thus, within forty years, the Persians had transformed themselves from a subject people to the rulers of a vast empire that included all of the oldest kingdoms and peoples of the region, as well as many outlying areas (see Map 2.1). Unsurprisingly, Darius began to call himself "King of Kings." Invasions of Greece by Darius and his son Xerxes were unsuccessful, but the Persian Empire lasted another two hundred years, until it became part of the empire of Alexander the Great (see Chapter 4).

The Persians also knew how to preserve the empire they had won on the battle-field. Learning from the Assyrians, they created an efficient administrative system to govern the empire based in their newly built capital city of Persepolis near modern Shiraz, Iran. Under Darius, they divided the empire into districts and appointed either Persian or local nobles as administrators called **satraps** to head each one. The satrap controlled local government, collected taxes, heard legal cases, and maintained order. He was assisted by a council, and also by officials and army leaders sent from Persepolis who made sure that the satrap knew the will of the king and that the king knew what was going on in the provinces. This system lessened opposition to Persian rule by making local elites part of the system of government, although sometimes satraps used their authority to build up independent power.

Communication and trade were eased by a sophisticated system of roads linking the empire from the coast of Asia Minor to the valley of the Indus River. On the roads were way stations where royal messengers could get food and horses, a system that allowed messages to be communicated quickly, much like the famed pony express in the American West. These roads meant that the king was usually in close touch with officials and subjects. The roads also simplified the defense of the empire by making it easier to move Persian armies. In addition, the system allowed the easy flow of trade, which Persian rulers further encouraged by building canals, including one that linked the Red Sea and the Nile.

satraps Administrators in the Persian Empire who controlled local government, collected taxes, heard legal cases, and maintained order.

Persian Religion

Iranian religion was originally tied to nature. Ahuramazda (ah-HOOR-uh-MAZ-duh), the chief god, was the creator of all living creatures. Mithra, the sun-god whose cult would later spread throughout the Roman Empire, saw to justice and redemption. Fire was a particularly important god, and fire was often part of religious rituals. A priestly class, the Magi, developed among the Medes to officiate at sacrifices, chant prayers to the gods, and tend the sacred flame.

Around 600 B.C.E. the ideas of Zoroaster, a thinker and preacher whose dates are uncertain, began to gain prominence. Zoroaster is regarded as the author of key religious texts, later gathered together in a collection of sacred texts called the Avesta. He introduced new spiritual concepts to the Iranian people, stressing devotion to Ahuramazda alone and emphasizing the individual's responsibility to choose between the forces of creation, truth, and order and those of nothingness, chaos, falsehood, and disorder. Zoroaster taught that people possessed the free will to decide between these, and that they must rely on their own conscience to guide them through an active life in which they focused on "good thoughts, good words, and good deeds." Their decisions were crucial, he warned, for there would come a time of reckoning. At the end of time the forces of order would win, and the victorious Ahuramazda, like the Egyptian god Osiris (see Chapter 1), would preside over a last judgment to determine each person's eternal fate. Those who had lived according to good and truth would enter a divine kingdom. Liars and the wicked, denied this blessed immortality, would be condemned to eternal pain, darkness, and punishment. Thus Zoroaster preached a last judgment that led to a heaven or a hell.

Scholars—and contemporary Zoroastrians—debate whether Zoroaster saw the forces of disorder as a malevolent deity named Angra Mainyu who was co-eternal with and independent from Ahuramazda, or whether he was simply using this term to mean "evil thoughts" or "a destructive spirit." Later forms of **Zoroastrianism** followed each of these lines of understanding. Most Zoroastrians believed that the good Ahuramazda and the evil Angra Mainyu were locked together in a cosmic battle for the human race, a religious conceptualization that scholars call dualism, which was rejected in Judaism and Christianity. Some, however, had a more monotheistic interpretation and saw Ahuramazda as the only uncreated god.

Whenever he actually lived, Zoroaster's writings were spread by teachers, and King Darius began to use Zoroastrian language and images. Under the protection of the Persian kings, Zoroastrian ideas spread throughout Iran and the rest of the Persian Empire, and then beyond this into central China. It became the official religion of the later Persian Empire ruled by the Sassanid dynasty, and much later Zoroastrians migrated to western India, where they became known as Parsis and still live today. Zoroastrianism survived the fall of the Persian Empire to influence Christianity, Islam, and Buddhism, largely because of its belief in a just life on earth and a happy afterlife. Good behavior in the world, even though unrecognized at the time, would receive ample reward in the hereafter. Evil, no matter how powerful in life, would be punished after death. In some form or another, Zoroastrian concepts still pervade many modern religions, and Zoroastrianism still exists as a religion.

Persian Art and Culture

The Persians made significant contributions to art and culture. They produced amazing works in gold and silver, often with inlaid jewels and semiprecious stones such as deep blue lapis lazuli. They transformed the Assyrian tradition of realistic monumental sculpture from one that celebrated gory details of slaughter to one that showed both the Persians and their subjects as dignified. They noted and carved the physical features of their subjects, the way they wore their hair, their clothing, and their tools

Zoroastrianism Religion based on the ideas of Zoroaster that stressed devotion to the god Ahuramazda alone, and that emphasized the individual's responsibility to choose between good and evil.

King Darius Defeats His Enemies   King Darius of Persia proclaimed victory over his enemies with a written inscription and sculpture high on a cliff near Mount Behistun so all could see. He attributed his victory to Ahuramazda, the god of Zoroastrianism, whose symbol is carved above the chained prisoners. The proclamation itself was inscribed in three different cuneiform script languages, and it has been a vital tool for scholars as they have deciphered these ancient languages. (Photo © Zev Radovan/Bridgeman Images)

and weapons. Because they depicted both themselves and non-Persians realistically, Persian art serves as an excellent source for learning about the weapons, tools, clothing, and even hairstyles of many peoples of the area.

These carvings adorned temples and other large buildings in cities throughout the empire, and the Persians also built new cities from the ground up. The most spectacular of these was Persepolis, designed as a residence for the kings and an administrative and cultural center. The architecture of Persepolis combined elements found in many parts of the empire, including large, elegant columns topped by carvings of real and mythical animals. Underneath the city was a system of closed water pipes, drainage canals, and conduits that allowed water from nearby mountains to flow into the city without flooding it; provided water for households and plantings inside the city; and carried away sewage and waste from the city's many residents. The Persians thus further improved the technology for handling water that had been essential in this area since the time of the Sumerians.

The Persians allowed the peoples they conquered to maintain their own customs and beliefs, as long as they paid the proper amount of taxes and did not rebel. Their rule resulted in an empire that brought people together in a new political system, with a culture that blended older and newer religious traditions and ways of seeing the world. Even their opponents, including the Greeks who would stop their expansion and eventually conquer the Persian Empire, admired their art and institutions.

LOOKING BACK LOOKING AHEAD

During the centuries following the Bronze Age Collapse, natives and newcomers brought order to life across the ancient Near East. As Egypt fell, small kingdoms, including those of the Nubians, Phoenicians, and Hebrews, grew and prospered. Regular trade and communication continued, and new products and ideas were transported by sea and land. Beginning about 900 B.C.E. the Assyrians created a large state through military conquest that was often brutal, though they also developed effective structures of rule through which taxes flowed to their leaders. The Persians, an Iranian people whose center of power was east of Mesopotamia, then established an even larger empire, governing through local officials and building beautiful cities.

The lands on the northern shore of the Mediterranean were beyond the borders of the urbanized cultures and centralized empires of the ancient Near East, but maintained contact with them through trade and migration. As the Persian Empire continued to expand, it looked farther westward toward these lands, including Greece, as possible further conquests. Greek-speaking people living in Anatolia and traveling more widely throughout the area had also absorbed numerous aspects of Persian and other more urbanized cultures they had encountered. They learned of Near Eastern religions and myths, and of the sagas of heroic wars. They also acquired many of the advanced technologies developed by their eastern neighbors, including the use of bronze and later iron, the phonetic alphabet, wine growing, and shipbuilding. The Greeks combined these borrowings with their own traditions, ideas, and talents to create a distinct civilization, one that fundamentally shaped the subsequent development of Western society. Later empires, including the Romans, would adopt techniques of rule developed by the Persians, such as building roads and using local elites to serve as administrators.

Make Connections

Think about the larger developments and continuities within and across chapters.

1. How were the Assyrian and Persian Empires similar to the earlier empires of the Near East (Chapter 1) in terms of their technology and political structure? How were they different? What might explain the pattern of similarities and differences?

2. Most peoples in the ancient world gained influence over others and became significant in history through military conquest and the establishment of empires. By contrast, how did the Phoenicians and the Hebrews shape the development of Western civilization?

2 REVIEW & EXPLORE

Review the Main Ideas

Answer the focus questions from each section of the chapter.

◆ How did iron technology shape new states after 1200 B.C.E., including Kush and Phoenicia? (p. 36)

◆ How did the Hebrews create an enduring religious tradition? (p. 40)

◆ What explains the rise and fall of the Assyrians? (p. 46)

◆ How did the Persians consolidate their power and control and influence the subjects of their extensive empire? (p. 52)

Identify Key Terms

Identify and explain the significance of each item below.

Iron Age (p. 36)
Kush (p. 38)
Phoenicians (p. 38)
Yahweh (p. 40)
Torah (p. 42)
Covenant (p. 43)
satraps (p. 55)
Zoroastrianism (p. 56)

NOTES

1. James H. Breasted, *Ancient Records of Egypt*, vol. 4 (Chicago: University of Chicago Press, 1907), para. 398.

2. James B. Pritchard, ed., *Ancient Near Eastern Texts Relating to the Old Testament —Third Edition with Supplement,* p. 288. Reproduced with permission of PRINCETON UNIVERSITY PRESS, in the format Book via Copyright Clearance Center.

3. Cylinder inscription translation by Irving Finkel, curator of the Cuneiform Collection at the British Museum, www.britishmuseum .org. © The Trustees of the British Museum, 2016. Used by permission of the British Museum.

CHAPTER PREVIEW

Greece in the Bronze Age
How did the geography of Greece shape its earliest kingdoms, and what factors contributed to the decline of those kingdoms?

The Development of the Polis in the Archaic Age
What was the role of the polis in Greek society?

War and Turmoil in the Classical Period
What were the major wars of the classical period, and how did they shape Greek history?

Classical Greek Life and Culture
What were the lasting cultural and intellectual achievements of the classical period?

Religious Life in Hellenic Greece

This painted wooden slab from about 540 B.C.E., found in a cave near Corinth, shows adults and children about to sacrifice a sheep to the deities worshipped in this area. The participants are dressed in their finest clothes and crowned with garlands. Music adds to the festivities. Rituals such as this were a common part of religious life throughout Greece.

(National Archaeological Museum, Athens, Greece/De Agostini Picture Library/G. Dagli Orti/Bridgeman Images)

3

The Development of Greek Society and Culture

ca. 3000–338 B.C.E.

Humans came into Greece over many thousands of years, in waves of migrants whose place of origin and cultural characteristics have been the source of much scholarly debate. The first to arrive were hunter-gatherers, but techniques of agriculture and animal domestication had spread into Greece from Turkey by about 6500 B.C.E., after which small farming communities worked much of the land. Early settlers to Greece brought skills in making bronze weapons and tools, which became more common around 3000 B.C.E.

Although geographic conditions made farming difficult and limited the growth of early kingdoms, the people of ancient Greece built on the traditions and ideas of earlier societies to develop a culture that fundamentally shaped the intellectual and cultural traditions of Western civilization. They were the first to explore many of the questions about the world around them and the place of humans in it that continue to concern thinkers today. Drawing on their day-to-day experiences as well as logic and empirical observation, they developed ways of understanding and explaining the world around them, which grew into modern philosophy and science. They also created new political forms and new types of literature and art.

The history of the Greeks is divided into three broad periods: the Helladic period, which covered the Bronze Age, roughly 3000 B.C.E. to 1200 B.C.E.; the Hellenic period, from the Bronze Age Collapse to the death in 323 B.C.E. of Alexander the Great, the ruler of Macedonia, which by that point had conquered Greece; and the Hellenistic period, stretching from Alexander's death to the Roman conquest in 30 B.C.E. of the kingdom established in Egypt by Alexander's successors. This chapter focuses on the Greeks in the Bronze (Helladic) Age and most of the Hellenic period, which is further divided into the Dark Age, the Archaic age, and the classical period. Alexander's brief reign and the Hellenistic world are the subject of Chapter 4. ■

Greece in the Bronze Age

FOCUS QUESTION
How did the geography of Greece shape its earliest kingdoms, and what factors contributed to the decline of those kingdoms?

During the Bronze Age, which for Greek history is called the "Helladic period," early settlers in Greece began establishing small communities contoured by the mountains and small plains that shaped the land. These communities sometimes joined together to form kingdoms, most prominently the Minoan kingdom on the island of Crete and the Mycenaean kingdom on the mainland. The Minoan and Mycenaean societies flourished for centuries until the Bronze Age Collapse, when Greece entered a period of decline known as the Dark Age (ca. 1100–800 B.C.E.). Epic poems composed by Homer and Hesiod after the Dark Age provide the poets' versions of what life may have been like in these early Greek kingdoms.

Geography and Settlement

Hellas, as the Greeks still call their land, encompassed the Greek peninsula, the islands of the Aegean (ah-GEE-uhn) Sea, and the lands bordering the Aegean, an area known as the Aegean basin (Map 3.1). In ancient times this basin included the Greek settlements in Ionia, the western coast of the area known as Anatolia in modern western Turkey. Geography acts as an enormously divisive force in Greek life; mountains divide the land, and although there are good harbors on the sea, there are no navigable rivers. Much of the land is rocky and not very fertile, which meant that food availability was a constant concern.

The major regions of Greece were Thessaly and Macedonia in the north, and Boeotia (bee-OH-shuh) and the large island of Euboea (YOU-boh-ee-ah) in the center, lands marked by fertile plains that helped to sustain a strong population capable of serving as formidable cavalry and infantry. Immediately to the south of Boeotia was Attica, an area of thin soil in which olives and wine grapes flourished. Attica's harbors looked to the Aegean, which invited its inhabitants, the Athenians, to concentrate on maritime commerce. Still farther south, the Peloponnesus (peh-luh-puh-NEE-suhs), a large peninsula connected to the rest of mainland Greece by a very narrow isthmus at Corinth, was a patchwork of high mountains and small plains that divided the area into several regions. Beyond the coast, the islands of the Aegean served as stepping-stones to Anatolia.

The geographical fragmentation of Greece encouraged political fragmentation. Communications were poor, with rocky tracks far more common than roads. Early in Greek history several kingdoms did emerge, but the rugged terrain prohibited the growth of a great empire like those of Mesopotamia or Egypt. Instead tiny states became the most common form of government.

Chronology

3000 B.C.E.	Bronze tools and weapons become common in Greece	ca. 600–450 B.C.E.	Pre-Socratics develop ideas about the nature of the universe
ca. 1900 B.C.E.	Minoan culture begins to thrive on Crete	500–338 B.C.E.	Classical period; development of drama, philosophy, and major building projects in Athens
ca. 1650 B.C.E.	Mycenaean culture develops in Greece		
ca. 1300–1100 B.C.E.	"Bronze Age Collapse"; migration, destruction	499–479 B.C.E.	Persian wars
ca. 1100–800 B.C.E.	Dark Age; population declines; trade decreases; writing disappears	431–404 B.C.E.	Peloponnesian War
		427–347 B.C.E.	Life of Plato
ca. 800–500 B.C.E.	Archaic age; rise of the polis; Greek colonization of the Mediterranean; Homer and Hesiod compose epics and poetry	384–322 B.C.E.	Life of Aristotle
		371–362 B.C.E.	Thebes, with an alliance of city-states, rules Greece
ca. 750–500 B.C.E.	Sparta expands and develops a military state	338 B.C.E.	Philip II of Macedonia gains control of Greece
ca. 600–500 B.C.E.	Political reforms in Archaic Athens		

The Minoans

On the large island of Crete, Bronze Age farmers and fishermen began to trade their surpluses with their neighbors, and cities grew, housing artisans and merchants. Beginning about 2000 B.C.E. Cretans voyaged throughout the eastern Mediterranean and the Aegean, carrying the copper and tin needed for bronze and many other goods. Social hierarchies developed, and in many cities certain individuals came to

MAP 3.1 Classical Greece, 500–338 B.C.E.   In antiquity, the home of the Greeks included the islands of the Aegean and the western shore of Turkey as well as the Greek peninsula itself. Crete, the home of Minoan civilization, is the large island at the bottom of the map.

Minoan Bull-Leaping   A colorful fresco dating from around 1600 B.C.E. found at the palace of Knossos on Crete shows three people in a scene of bull-leaping. The outside figures are women, who are generally portrayed with light skin to represent women's association with the household, and the figure leaping over the bull is a man, whose reddish skin associates him with the outdoors. Bulls were venerated in Minoan culture, and this may be a scene of an actual ritual sport done at the palace, a spectacle celebrating human athletic prowess and mastery of nature. (National Archaeological Museum, Athens, Greece/Bridgeman Images)

Minoan   A wealthy and vibrant culture on Crete from around 1900 B.C.E. to 1450 B.C.E., ruled by a king with a large palace at Knossos.

hold power, although exactly how this happened is not clear. The Cretans began to use writing about 1900 B.C.E., in a form later scholars called Linear A. This has not been deciphered, but scholars know that the language of Crete was not related to Greek, so they do not consider the Cretans "Greek."

What we can know about the culture of Crete depends on archaeological and artistic evidence, and of this there is a great deal. At about the same time that writing began, rulers in several cities of Crete began to build large structures with hundreds of interconnected rooms. The largest of these, at Knossos (NOH-suhs), has over a thousand rooms along with pipes for bringing in drinking water and sewers to get rid of waste. The archaeologists who discovered these huge structures called them "palaces," and they named the flourishing and vibrant culture of this era **Minoan**, after a mythical king of Crete, Minos.

Few specifics are known about Minoan political life except that a king and a group of nobles stood at its head. Minoan life was long thought to have been relatively peaceful, but new excavations are revealing more and more walls around cities, which has called the peaceful nature of Minoan society into question, although there are no doubts that it was wealthy. In terms of their religious life, Minoans appear to have worshipped goddesses far more than gods. Whether this translated into more egalitarian gender roles for real people is unclear, but surviving Minoan art, including frescoes and figurines, shows women as well as men leading religious activities, watching entertainment, and engaging in athletic competitions, such as leaping over bulls.

Beginning about 1700 B.C.E. Minoan society was disrupted by a series of earthquakes and volcanic eruptions on nearby islands, some of which resulted in large tsunamis. The largest of these was a huge volcanic eruption that devastated the island of Thera to the north of Crete, burying the Minoan town there in lava and causing it to collapse into the sea. This eruption, one of the largest in recorded history, may have been the origin of the story of the mythical kingdom of Atlantis, a wealthy kingdom with beautiful buildings that had sunk under the ocean. The eruption on Thera was long seen as the most important cause of the collapse of Minoan civilization, but scholars using radiocarbon and other types of scientific dating have called this theory into question, as the eruption seems to have occurred somewhat earlier than 1600 B.C.E., and Minoan society did not collapse until more than two centuries later. In fact, new settlements and palaces were often built on Crete following the earthquakes and the eruption of Thera.

The Mycenaeans

As Minoan culture was flourishing on Crete, a different type of society developed on the mainland. This society was founded by groups who had migrated there during the period after 2000 B.C.E., and its members spoke an early form of Greek. By about 1650 B.C.E. one group of these immigrants had raised palaces and established cities at Thebes, Athens, Mycenae (migh-SEE-nee), and elsewhere. These palace-centers ruled by local kings formed a loose hegemony under the authority of the king of Mycenae, and the archaeologists who first discovered traces of this culture called it **Mycenaean** (migh-see-NEE-an).

As in Crete, the political unit in Mycenaean Greece was the kingdom, and the king and his warrior aristocracy stood at the top of society. The seat and symbol of the king's power was his palace, which was also the economic center of the kingdom. Within the palace's walls, royal artisans fashioned gold jewelry and rich ornaments, made and decorated fine pottery, forged weapons, prepared hides and wool for clothing, and manufactured the other goods needed by the king and his supporters. The Mycenaean economy was marked by an extensive division of labor, and at the bottom of the social scale were male and female slaves.

Palace scribes kept records with a script known as Linear B, which scholars realized was an early form of Greek and have learned to read. They thus consider the Mycenaeans the first truly "Greek" culture to emerge in this area. Information on Mycenaean culture comes through inscriptions and other forms of written records as well as buildings and other objects. All of these point to a society in which war was common. Mycenaean cities were all fortified by thick stone walls, and graves contain bronze spears, javelins, swords, helmets, and the first examples of metal armor known in the world. Mycenaean kingdoms appear to have fought regularly with one another.

Contacts between the Minoans and Mycenaeans were originally peaceful, and Minoan culture and trade goods flooded the Greek mainland. But most scholars think that around 1450 B.C.E., possibly in the wake of an earthquake that left Crete vulnerable, the Mycenaeans attacked Crete, destroying many towns and occupying Knossos. For about the next fifty years, the Mycenaeans ruled much of the island. The palaces at Knossos and other cities of the Aegean became grander as wealth gained through trade and tribute flowed into the treasuries of various Mycenaean kings. Linear B replaced Linear A as a writing system, a further sign of Mycenaean domination.

Prosperity, however, did not bring peace, and between 1300 and 1100 B.C.E. various kingdoms in and beyond Greece ravaged one another in a savage series of wars that destroyed both the Minoan and Mycenaean civilizations. Among these wars was perhaps one that later became known as the Trojan War, fought by Greeks in Ionia (see page 66).

The fall of the Minoans and Mycenaeans was part of what scholars see as a general collapse of Bronze Age civilizations in the eastern Mediterranean, including the end of the Egyptian New Kingdom and the fall of the Hittite Empire (see Chapters 1 and 2). This collapse appears to have had a number of causes: internal economic and social problems, including perhaps slave revolts; invasions and migrations by outsiders, who destroyed cities and disrupted trade and production; changes in warfare and weaponry, particularly the adoption of iron weapons, which made foot soldiers the most important factor in battles and reduced the power of kings and wealthy nobles fighting from chariots; and natural disasters such as volcanic

Mycenaean A Bronze Age culture that flourished in Greece from about 1650 B.C.E. to 1100 B.C.E., building fortified palaces and cities.

Mycenaean Dagger Blade   This scene in gold and silver on the blade of an iron dagger depicts hunters armed with spears and protected by shields defending themselves against charging lions. Judging by the number of hunting scenes in surviving Mycenaean art, the Mycenaeans seemed to enjoy the thrill and the danger of hunting. (National Archaeological Museum, Athens, Greece/Ancient Art & Architecture Collection, Ltd./Bridgeman Images)

eruptions, earthquakes, and droughts, which reduced the amount of food and contributed to famines. Mycenaean Greeks joined the migrating Sea Peoples and probably settled in Canaan; here they became the group known in the Bible as Philistines (see Chapter 2).

These factors worked together to usher in a period of poverty and disruption that historians of Greece have traditionally called the Dark Age (ca. 1100–800 B.C.E.). Cities were destroyed, population declined, villages were abandoned, and trade decreased. Migratory movements continued, including a group that later Greeks called the Dorians, who were originally thought to have been people speaking a language other than Greek invading from the north. Now the Dorians are generally regarded as Greek-speakers from the northern areas of the Greek mainland, and their movement is considered a combination of invasion and migration. Pottery became simpler, and jewelry and other grave goods became less ornate. Even writing, which had not been widespread previously, was a casualty of the chaos, and Linear A and B inscriptions were no longer produced.

The Bronze Age Collapse led to the widespread and prolonged movement of Greek peoples, both within Greece itself and beyond. They dispersed beyond mainland Greece farther south to the islands of the Aegean and in greater strength across the Aegean to the shores of Anatolia, arriving at a time when traditional states and empires had collapsed. By the conclusion of the Dark Age, the Greeks had spread their culture throughout the Aegean basin, and like many other cultures around the Mediterranean and the Near East, they had adopted iron.

Homer, Hesiod, and the Epic

Archaeological sources from the Dark Age are less rich than those from the periods that came after, and so they are often used in conjunction with literary sources written in later centuries to give us a more complete picture of the era. The Greeks, unlike the Hebrews, had no sacred book that chronicled their past. Instead they had epics, poetic tales of legendary heroes and of the times when people believed the gods still walked the earth. Of these, the *Iliad* and the *Odyssey* are the most important. Most scholars think they were composed in the eighth or seventh century B.C.E., with the *Iliad* appearing earlier than the *Odyssey*. By the fifth century B.C.E. they were attributed to a poet named Homer, though whether Homer was an actual historical individual is debated. Scholars also disagree about the ways in which the epics combine elements from the Bronze Age, the Dark Age, and the time in which they were written. What is not debated is their long-lasting impact, both on later Greek culture and on the Western world.

The *Iliad* recounts the tale of the Trojan War of the late Bronze Age. As Homer tells it, the Achaeans (uh-KEE-uhnz), the name he gives to the Mycenaeans, send an expedition to besiege the city of Troy to retrieve Helen, who was abducted by Paris, the Trojan king's son. The heart of the *Iliad*, however, concerns the quarrel between the Mycenaean king, Agamemnon, and the stormy hero of the poem, Achilles (uh-KIHL-eez), and how this brought suffering to the Achaeans. The first lines of the *Iliad* capture this well:

> Sing, O goddess, the anger of Achilles son of Peleus, that brought countless ills upon the Achaeans. Many a brave soul did it send hurrying down to Hades [underworld], and many a hero did it yield a prey to dogs and vultures.[1]

Ancient Greeks and Romans believed that the Trojan War was a real event embellished by poetic retelling, but by the modern era most people regarded it as a myth. Then in the late nineteenth century, the German businessman Heinrich Schliemann discovered and excavated the ruins of Troy. The city had actually been destroyed a number of times, including at least once in the late Mycenaean period, which provided evidence of the violence of this era, if not of the Trojan War itself. More recently, geologists studying the landscape features mentioned in the *Iliad* and historians examining written records from the Hittite and Egyptian Empires of the era have also confirmed the general picture portrayed in Homer's epic. Today most scholars think that the core of the story was a composite of many conflicts in Troy's past, although the characters are not historical.

Homer's *Odyssey* recounts the adventures of Odysseus (oh-DIH-see-uhs), a wise and fearless hero of the war at Troy, during his ten-year voyage home. He encounters many dangers, storms, and adventures, but he finally reaches his home and unites again with Penelope, the ideal wife, dedicated to her husband and family.

Both of Homer's epics portray engaging but flawed characters who are larger than life, yet human. The men and women at the center of the stories display the quality known as *arête* (ah-reh-TAY), that is, excellence and living up to one's fullest potential. Homer was also strikingly successful in depicting the great gods and goddesses, who generally sit on Mount Olympus in the north of Greece and watch the fighting at Troy like spectators at a baseball game, although they sometimes participate in the action.

Greeks also learned about the origin and descent of the gods and goddesses of their polytheistic system from another poet, Hesiod (HEH-see-uhd), who most scholars think lived sometime between 750 and 650 B.C.E. Hesiod made the gods the focus of his poem, the *Theogony*. By combining Mesopotamian myths, which the Hittites had adopted and spread to the Aegean, with a variety of Greek oral traditions, Hesiod forged a coherent story of the origin of the gods. At the beginning was "Chaos," the word Hesiod uses to describe the original dark emptiness. Then came several generations of deities, with the leader of each generation violently overthrowing his father to gain power. Despite this violence, Hesiod viewed the generation of gods who rule from Olympus as more just than those that came before. In another of Hesiod's poems, *Works and Days*, the gods watch over the earth, looking for justice and injustice, while leaving the great mass of men and women to live lives of hard work and endless toil. (See "Evaluating the Evidence 3.1: Hesiod, *Works and Days*," page 68.)

The Development of the Polis in the Archaic Age

Homer and Hesiod both lived in the era after the Dark Age, which later historians have termed the Archaic age (800–500 B.C.E.). The most important political change in this period was the development of the **polis** (PAH-luhs; plural *poleis*), a word generally translated as "city-state." With the polis, the Greeks established a new type of political structure. During the Archaic period, poleis established colonies throughout much of the Mediterranean, spreading Greek culture. Two particular poleis, each with a distinctive system of government, rose to prominence on the Greek mainland: Sparta and Athens.

FOCUS QUESTION

What was the role of the polis in Greek society?

polis Generally translated as "city-state," it was the basic political and institutional unit of Greece in the Hellenic period.

Hesiod, *Works and Days*

According to his description of himself in Works and Days *(ca. 700 B.C.E.), Hesiod was born in a small village he describes as "bad in winter, godawful in summer, nice never," with one brother, Perses, a lazy and irresponsible swindler who cheated him out of some of his inheritance but later came to him asking for money. Whether these details are true or not, they form the framework for his work, a speech full of advice addressed to his brother, but designed for a larger audience.*

And now I will tell a fable for princes who themselves understand. Thus said the hawk to the nightingale with speckled neck, while he carried her high up among the clouds, gripped fast in his talons, and she, pierced by his crooked talons, cried pitifully. To her he spoke disdainfully: "Miserable thing, why do you cry out? One far stronger than you now holds you fast, and you must go wherever I take you, songstress as you are. And if I please I will make my meal of you, or let you go. He is a fool who tries to withstand the stronger, for he does not get the mastery and suffers pain besides his shame." So said the swiftly flying hawk, the long-winged bird.

But you, Perses, listen to right and do not foster violence; for violence is bad for a poor man. Even the prosperous cannot easily bear its burden, but is weighed down under it when he has fallen into delusion. The better path is to go by on the other side towards Justice; for Justice beats Outrage when she comes at length to the end of the race. But only when he has suffered does the fool learn this. For Oath keeps pace with wrong judgements. There is a noise when Justice is being dragged in the way where those who devour bribes and give sentence with crooked judgements, take her. And she, wrapped in mist, follows to the city and haunts of the people, weeping, and bringing mischief to men, even to such as

have driven her forth in that they did not deal straightly with her. . . .

To you, foolish Perses, I will speak good sense. Badness can be got easily and in shoals: the road to her is smooth, and she lives very near us. But between us and Goodness the gods have placed the sweat of our brows: long and steep is the path that leads to her, and it is rough at the first; but when a man has reached the top, then is she easy to reach, though before that she was hard. . . .

Do not get base gain: base gain is as bad as ruin. Be friends with the friendly, and visit him who visits you. Give to one who gives, but do not give to one who does not give. A man gives to the free-handed, but no one gives to the close-fisted. Give is a good girl, but Take is bad and she brings death. For the man who gives willingly, even though he gives a great thing, rejoices in his gift and is glad in heart; but whoever gives way to shamelessness and takes something himself, even though it be a small thing, it freezes his heart. . . .

If your heart within you desires wealth, do these things and work with work upon work.

EVALUATE THE EVIDENCE

1. What does Hesiod's advice suggest about his notion of the role of humans in the world and their relationship with the gods?
2. Hesiod lived just after the period of the Greek Dark Age. How does *Works and Days* reflect the situation of his own society?

Source: Hugh G. Evelyn-White, *Works and Days* (Cambridge, Mass.: Harvard University Press; London: Heinemann Ltd, 1914).

Organization of the Polis

The Greek polis was not the first form of city-state to emerge. The earliest states in Sumer were also city-states, as were many of the small Mycenaean kingdoms. What differentiated the new Greek model from older city-states is the fact that the polis was more than a political institution; it was a community of citizens with their own customs and laws. With one exception, the poleis that emerged after 800 B.C.E. did not have kings but instead were self-governing. The physical, religious, and political forms of the polis varied from place to place, but everywhere the polis was relatively small, reflecting the fragmented geography of Greece. The very smallness of the polis enabled Greeks to see how they fit individually into the overall system—and how the individual parts made up the social whole. This notion of community was fundamental to the polis and was the very badge of Greekness.

Poleis developed from Dark Age towns, which were centers of administration, trade, and religion. When fully developed, each polis normally shared a surprisingly large number of features with other poleis. Physically a polis was a society of people who lived in a city (*asty*) and cultivated the surrounding countryside (*chora*). The countryside was essential to the economy of the polis and provided food to sustain the entire population. The city's water supply came from public fountains, springs, and cisterns. By the fifth century B.C.E. the city was generally surrounded by a wall. The city contained a point, usually elevated, called the acropolis, and a public square or marketplace called the agora (ah-guh-RAH). On the acropolis, which in the Dark Age was a place of refuge, people built temples, altars, public monuments, and various dedications to the gods of the polis. The agora was the political center of the polis. In the agora were shops, public buildings, and courts.

All poleis, with one exception, did not have standing armies. Instead they relied on their citizens for protection. Wealthy aristocrats often served as cavalry, which was never very important in military conflicts. The backbone of the army was the heavily armed infantry, or **hoplites**, ordinary citizens rather than members of the elite. Hoplites wore bronze helmets and leather and bronze body armor, which they purchased themselves. They carried heavy, round shields made of wood covered in bronze and armed themselves with iron-tipped spears and swords. They marched and fought in a close rectangular formation known as a phalanx, holding their shields together to form a solid wall, with the spears of the front row sticking out over the tops of the shields. As long as the phalanx stayed in formation, the hoplites presented an enemy with an impenetrable wall. This meant that commanders preferred to fight battles on open plains, where the hoplites could more easily maintain the phalanx, rather than in the narrow mountain passes that were common throughout much of Greece.

> **hoplites** Heavily armed citizens who served as infantrymen and fought to defend the polis.

Governing Structures

Each Greek polis had one of several different types of government. Monarchy, rule by a king, had been prevalent during the Mycenaean period, but afterward declined. The polis of Sparta (see page 71) had a system with two kings, but they were part of a more broadly based constitution. Sporadic periods of violent political and social upheaval often led to the seizure of power by one man, a type of government the Greeks called **tyranny**. Tyrants generally came to power by using their wealth or by negotiating to win a political following that toppled the existing legal government. In contrast to its contemporary meaning, however, tyranny in ancient Greece did not necessarily mean oppressive rule. Some tyrants used their power to benefit average citizens by helping to limit the power of the landowning aristocracy, which made them popular.

> **tyranny** Rule by one man who took over an existing government, generally by using his wealth to gain a political following.

Other types of government in the Archaic age were democracy and oligarchy. **Democracy** translates as "the power of the people" but was actually rule by citizens, not the people as a whole. Almost all Greek cities defined a citizen as an adult man with at least one or, at some times and places, two citizen parents. Thus citizens shared ancestry as well as a place of residence. Women were citizens for religious and reproductive purposes, but their citizenship did not give them the right to participate

> **democracy** A type of Greek government in which all citizens administered the workings of government.

in government. Free men who were not children of a citizen, resident foreigners (metics), and slaves were not citizens and had no political voice. Thus ancient Greek democracy did not reflect the modern concept that all people are created equal, but it did permit male citizens to share equally in determining the diplomatic and military policies of the polis, without respect to wealth. This comparatively broad basis of participation made Greek democracy an appealing model to some political thinkers across the ages, although others feared direct democracy and viewed it as "mob rule."

oligarchy A type of Greek government in which citizens who owned a certain amount of property ruled.

Oligarchy, which literally means "the rule of the few," was government by citizens who met a minimum property requirement. Many Greeks preferred oligarchy because it provided more political stability than democracy did. (Many of the Founding Fathers of the United States agreed, and they established a system in which the most important elections were indirect and only property owners had the right to vote.) Although oligarchy was the government of the prosperous, it left the door open to political and social advancement. If members of the polis obtained enough wealth to meet property or money qualifications, they could enter the governing circle.

Overseas Expansion

The development of the polis coincided with the growth of the Greek world in both wealth and numbers, bringing new problems. The increase in population created more demand for food than the land could supply. The resulting social and political tensions drove many people to seek new homes outside of Greece. In some cases the losers in a conflict within a polis were forced to leave. Other factors, largely intangible, played their part as well: the desire for a new start, a love of excitement and adventure, and curiosity about what lay beyond the horizon.

Greeks from the mainland and Ionia traveled throughout the Mediterranean, sailing in great numbers to Sicily and southern Italy, where there was ample space for expansion (Map 3.2). Here they established prosperous cities and often intermarried with local people. Some adventurous Greeks sailed farther west to Sardinia, France, Spain, and perhaps even the Canary Islands. In Sardinia they first established trading stations, and then permanent towns. From these new outposts Greek influence extended to southern France. The modern city of Marseilles, for example, began as a Greek colony and later sent settlers to southern Spain. In the far western Mediterranean the city of Carthage, established by the Phoenicians in the ninth century B.C.E., remained the dominant power. The Greeks traded with the Carthaginians but never conquered them.

Colonization changed the entire Greek world, both at home and abroad. In economic terms the expansion of the Greeks created a much larger market for agricultural and manufactured goods. From the east, especially from the northern coast of the Black Sea, came wheat. In return flowed Greek wine and olive oil, which could not be produced in the harsher climate of the north. Greek-manufactured goods, notably rich jewelry and fine pottery, circulated from southern Russia to Spain. During the same period the Greeks adopted the custom of minting coins from metal, first developed in the kingdom of Lydia in Anatolia. Coins provided many advantages over barter: they allowed merchants to set the value of goods in a determined system, they could be stored easily, and they allowed for more complex exchanges than did direct barter.

Colonization presented the polis with a huge challenge, for it required organization and planning on an unprecedented scale. The colonizing city, called the *metropolis*, or "mother city," first decided where to establish the colony, how to

MAP 3.2 Greek Colonization, ca. 750–550 B.C.E. The Greeks established colonies along the shores of the Mediterranean and the Black Sea, spreading Greek culture and creating a large trading network.

transport colonists to the site, and who would sail. Sometimes groups of people left willingly, and in other instances they left involuntarily after a civil war or other conflict. Then the metropolis collected and stored the supplies that the colonists would need both to feed themselves and to plant their first crop. All preparations ready, a leader, called an *oikist*, ordered the colonists to sail. Once the colonists landed, the oikist laid out the new polis, selected the sites of temples and public buildings, and established the government. Then he surrendered power to the new leaders. The colony was thereafter independent of the metropolis, a pattern that was quite different from most later systems of colonization. Colonization spread the polis and its values far beyond the shores of Greece.

The Growth of Sparta

Many different poleis developed during the Archaic period, but Sparta became the leading military power in Greece. To expand their polis, the Spartans did not establish colonies but set out in about 750 B.C.E. to conquer Messenia (muh-SEE-nee-uh), a rich, fertile region in the southwestern Peloponnesus. This conflict, called the First Messenian War by later Greek historians, lasted for twenty years and ended in a Spartan triumph. The Spartans appropriated Messenian land and turned the Messenians into **helots** (HEH-luhts), unfree residents forced to work state lands. Residents of coastal areas and the hills surrounding Messenia became a third group, known as *periokoi* (pehr-ee-OI-koi), who were free but had no political voice in the running of Sparta.

helots Unfree residents of Sparta forced to work state lands.

Spartan Expansion, ca. 750–500 B.C.E.

In about 650 B.C.E. Spartan exploitation and oppression of the Messenian helots, along with Sparta's defeat at the hands of a rival polis, led to a massive helot revolt that became known as the Second Messenian War. The Spartan poet Tyrtaeus, a contemporary of these events, vividly portrays the violence of the war:

> For it is a shameful thing indeed
> When with the foremost fighters
> An elder falling in front of the young men
> Lies outstretched,
> Having white hair and grey beard,
> Breathing forth his stout soul in the dust,
> Holding in his hands his genitals
> stained with blood.[2]

Finally, after some thirty years of fighting, the Spartans put down the revolt. Nevertheless, the political and social strain it caused led to a transformation of the Spartan polis. After the war, non-nobles who had shared in the fighting as hoplites appear to have demanded rights equal to those of the nobility and a voice in the government. (In more recent history, similar demands in the United States during the Vietnam War led to a lowering of the voting age to eighteen, to match the age at which soldiers were drafted.) Under intense pressure the aristocrats agreed to remodel the state into a new system.

The plan for the new system in Sparta was attributed to the lawgiver Lycurgus, who may or may not have been an actual person. According to later Greek sources, political distinctions among Spartan men were eliminated, and all citizens became legally equal. Governance of the polis was in the hands of two hereditary kings who were primarily military leaders. The kings were also part of the *Gerousia* (jeh-roo-SEE-ah), a council of men who had reached the age of sixty and thus retired from the Spartan army. The Gerousia deliberated on foreign and domestic matters and prepared legislation for the assembly, which consisted of all Spartan citizens. The real executive power of the polis was in the hands of five ephors (EH-fuhrs), or overseers, elected from and by all the citizens.

To provide for their economic needs, the Spartans divided the land of Messenia among all citizens. Helots worked the land, raised the crops, provided the Spartans with a certain percentage of their harvest, and occasionally served in the army. The Spartans kept the helots in line by means of systematic brutality and oppression.

In the system attributed to Lycurgus every citizen owed primary allegiance to Sparta. Suppression of the individual together with emphasis on military prowess led to a barracks state. Family life itself was sacrificed to the polis. Once Spartan boys reached the age of seven, they were enrolled in separate companies with other boys their age. They were required to live in the barracks and eat together in a common mess hall until age thirty. They slept outside on reed mats and underwent rugged physical and military training until they were ready to become frontline soldiers. For the rest of their lives, Spartan men kept themselves prepared for combat. Their military training never ceased, and the older men were expected to be models of endurance, frugality, and sturdiness. In battle Spartans were supposed to stand and die rather than retreat. Because men often did not see their wives or other women for long periods, not only in times of war but also in peace, their most meaningful relations were same-sex ones. The Spartan military leaders may have viewed such relationships as militarily advantageous because they believed that men would fight even more fiercely for lovers and comrades.

Spartans expected women in citizen families to be good wives and strict mothers of future soldiers. They were prohibited from wearing jewelry or ornate clothes. They, too, were supposed to exercise strenuously in the belief that hard physical training promoted the birth of healthy children. Xenophon (ca. 430–354 B.C.E.), a later Athenian admirer of the Spartans, commented:

> [Lycurgus had] insisted on the training of the body as incumbent no less on the female than the male; and in pursuit of the same idea instituted rival contests in running and feats of strength for women as for men. His belief was that where both parents were strong their progeny would be found to be more vigorous.[3]

An anecdote frequently repeated about one Spartan mother sums up Spartan military values. As her son was setting off to battle, the mother handed him his shield and advised him to come back either victorious, carrying the shield, or dead, being carried on it. Yet Spartan women were freer than many other Greek women. With men in military service much of their lives, women in citizen families owned land and ran the estates and were not physically restricted or secluded.

Along with the emphasis on military values for both sexes, the Spartan system served to instill in society the civic virtues of dedication to the state and a code of moral conduct. These aspects of Spartan society, along with Spartan military successes, were generally admired throughout the Greek world.

Spartan Hoplite   This bronze figurine portrays an armed foot soldier about to strike an enemy. His massive helmet with its full crest gives his head nearly complete protection, while a metal corselet covers his chest and back, and greaves (similar to today's shin guards) protect his lower legs. In his right hand he carries a thrusting spear (now broken off), and in his left a large, round shield. (bpk, Berlin/Antikensammlung, Staatliche Museen/Johannes Laurentius/Art Resource, NY)

The Evolution of Athens

Like Sparta, Athens faced pressing social, economic, and political problems during the Archaic period, but the Athenian response was far different from that of the Spartans. Instead of creating a state devoted to the military, the Athenians created a state that became a democracy.

For Athens the late seventh century B.C.E. was a time of turmoil, the causes of which are unclear. In 621 B.C.E. Draco (DRAY-koh), an Athenian aristocrat, under pressure from small landholders and with the consent of the nobles, published the first law code of the Athenian polis. His code was harsh—and for this reason his name is the origin of the word *draconian*—but it embodied the ideal that the law belonged to all citizens.

Yet the aristocracy still governed Athens oppressively, and the social and economic situation remained dire. Despite Draco's code, noble landholders continued to force small farmers and artisans into economic dependence. Many families were sold into slavery because of debt; others were exiled, and their land was mortgaged to the rich.

One person who recognized these problems clearly was Solon (SOH-luhn), an aristocrat and poet. Reciting his poems in the Athenian agora, where anyone could hear his call for justice and fairness, Solon condemned his fellow aristocrats for their greed and dishonesty. According to later sources, Solon's sincerity and good sense convinced other aristocrats that he was no crazed revolutionary. Moreover, he gained the trust of the common people, whose problems provoked them to demand access to political life, much as commoners in Sparta had. Around 594 B.C.E. the nobles elected Solon chief *archon* (AHR-kahn), or magistrate of the Athenian polis, with authority over legal, civic, and military issues.

Solon immediately freed all people enslaved for debt, recalled all exiles, canceled all debts on land, and made enslavement for debt illegal. Solon allowed non-nobles into the old aristocratic assembly, where they could take part in the election of magistrates, including the annual election of the city's nine archons.

Although Solon's reforms solved some immediate problems, they did not satisfy either the aristocrats or the common people completely, and they did not bring peace to Athens. During the sixth century B.C.E. the successful general Pisistratus (pigh-SIHS-trah-tuhs) declared himself tyrant, developing a base of followers from among the common people. He was exiled several times, but returned to power each time. Under his rule Athens prospered, and his building program began to transform the city into one of the splendors of Greece. He raised the civic consciousness and prestige of the polis by instituting new cultural festivals that brought people together. Although he had taken over control of the city by force, his reign as tyrant weakened the power of aristocratic families and aroused rudimentary feelings of equality in many Athenian men.

Athens became more democratic under the leadership of Cleisthenes (KLIGHS-thuh-neez), a wealthy and prominent aristocrat who had won the support of lower-status men and became the leader of Athens in 508 B.C.E. Cleisthenes created the *deme* (deem), a unit of land that kept the roll of citizens, or *demos*, within its jurisdiction. Men enrolled as citizens through their deme—much as we would register to vote in the voting district in which we live—instead of through their family group, which brought people of different families together and promoted community and democracy. The demes were grouped into ten tribes, which thus formed the link between the demes and the central government. Each tribe elected a military leader, or *strategos* (plural *strategoi*).

The democracy functioned on the idea that all full citizens were sovereign. In 487 B.C.E. the election of the city's nine archons was replaced by reappointment by lot, which meant that any citizen with a certain amount of property had a chance of becoming an archon. This system gave citizens prestige, although the power of the archons gradually dwindled as the strategoi became the real military leaders of the city. Legislation was in the hands of two bodies, the *boule* (boo-LAY), or council, composed of five hundred members, and the *ecclesia* (ek-lay-SEE-yah), the assembly of all citizens. By supervising the various committees of government and proposing bills to the ecclesia, the boule guided Athenian political life. It received foreign envoys and forwarded treaties to the ecclesia for ratification. It oversaw the granting of state contracts and was responsible for receiving many revenues. It held the democracy together. Nonetheless, the ecclesia had the final word. Open to all male citizens over eighteen years of age—about 10 percent of the population of the city—it met at a specific place to vote on matters presented to it.

War and Turmoil in the Classical Period

From the time of the Mycenaeans, violent conflict was common in Greek society, and this did not change in the fifth century B.C.E., the beginning of what scholars later called the classical period of Greek history, which they date from about 500 B.C.E. to the conquest of Greece by Philip of Macedon in 338 B.C.E. First, the Greeks beat back the armies of the Persian Empire. Then, turning their spears against one another, they destroyed their own political system in a century of warfare culminating in the Peloponnesian War. This war and its aftermath proved that the polis had reached the limits of its success as an effective political institution, with the attempts of various city-states to dominate the others leading only to incessant warfare. Many people went bankrupt, and the quality of life for most people changed for the worse. The Greeks' failure to unify against outsiders led to the rise of a dominant new power: the kingdom of Macedonia.

FOCUS QUESTION
What were the major wars of the classical period, and how did they shape Greek history?

The Persian Wars

In 499 B.C.E. the Greeks who lived in Ionia unsuccessfully rebelled against the Persian Empire, which had ruled the area for fifty years (see Chapter 2). The Athenians had provided halfhearted help to the Ionians in this failed rebellion, and in 490 B.C.E. the Persians retaliated against Athens, only to be surprisingly defeated by the Athenian hoplites at the Battle of Marathon. (According to legend, a Greek runner carried the victory message to Athens. When the modern Olympic games were founded in 1896, they included a long-distance running race between Marathon and Athens, a distance of about twenty-five miles, designed to honor the ancient Greeks. The marathon was set at its current distance of 26.2 miles for the London Olympics of 1908, so that the finish would be in front of the royal box in the stadium.)

In 480 B.C.E. the Persian king Xerxes I (r. 485–465 B.C.E.) personally led a massive invasion of Greece. Under the leadership of Sparta, many Greek poleis, though not all, joined together to fight the Persians. The first confrontations between the Persians and the Greeks occurred at the pass of Thermopylae (thuhr-MAWP-uh-lee), where an outnumbered Greek army, including three hundred top Spartan warriors, held off a much larger Persian force for several days. Before the fighting began, a report came in that when the Persian archers shot their bows the arrows darkened the sky. Herodotus (ca. 485–425 B.C.E.), a Greek historian born in the Persian-ruled city of Halicarnassus in Asia Minor, later wrote that one gruff Spartan, upon hearing this report, replied merely, "Fine, then we'll fight in the shade."[4] The Greeks at Thermopylae fought heroically, but the Persians won the battle after a local man showed them a hidden path over the mountains so that they could attack the Greeks from both sides. The victorious Persian army occupied and sacked Athens.

At the same time as the land battle of Thermopylae, Greeks and Persians fought one another in a naval battle at Artemisium off Boeotia. The Athenians, led by the general Themistocles, provided the heart of the naval forces with their fleet of triremes, oar-propelled warships. Storms wrecked many Persian ships, and neither side won a decisive victory. Only a month or so later, the Greek fleet met the Persian armada at Salamis, an island across from Athens. Though outnumbered, the Greek navy won an overwhelming victory by

The Persian Wars, 499–479 B.C.E.

outmaneuvering the Persians. The remnants of the Persian fleet retired, and in 479 B.C.E. the Greeks overwhelmed the Persian army at Plataea.

The wars provided a brief glimpse of what the Greeks could accomplish when they worked together. By defeating the Persians, the Greeks ensured that they would not be ruled by a foreign power. The decisive victories meant that Greek political forms and intellectual concepts would be handed down to later societies. Among the thoughtful Greeks who felt prompted to record and analyze these events was Herodotus, who traveled the Greek world to piece together the rise and fall of the Persian Empire. Like many other authors and thinkers, he was born elsewhere but moved to Athens and lived there for a time.

Growth of the Athenian Empire

The defeat of the Persians created a power vacuum in the Aegean, and the Athenians took advantage of the situation. Led by Themistocles, the Athenians and their allies formed the **Delian League**, a military alliance aimed at protecting the Aegean Islands, liberating Ionia from Persian rule, and keeping the Persians out of Greece. The league took its name from the small island of Delos, on which stood a religious center sacred to all parties. The Delian (DEE-lee-uhn) League was intended to be a free alliance under the leadership of Athens, but as the Athenians drove the Persians out of the Aegean, they also became increasingly imperialistic. Athens began reducing its allies to the status of subjects. Tribute was often collected by force, and the Athenians placed the economic resources of the Delian League under tighter and tighter control. Major allies revolted and were put down.

The aggressiveness of Athenian rule also alarmed Sparta and its allies. Relations between Athens and Sparta grew more hostile, particularly when Pericles (PEHR-uh-kleez) (ca. 494–429 B.C.E.), an aristocrat of solid intellectual ability, became the leading statesman in Athens. Pericles gained support among the ordinary citizens of Athens by introducing measures that broadened democracy, such as lowering the property requirement for the position of archon. Like the democracy he led, Pericles was aggressive and imperialistic. In 459 B.C.E. Sparta and Athens went to war over conflicts between Athens and some of Sparta's allies. The war ended in 445 B.C.E. with a treaty promising thirty years of peace, and no serious damage to either side. The treaty divided the Greek world between the two great powers, with each agreeing to respect the other and its allies.

Peace lasted thirteen years instead of thirty. Athens continued its severe policies toward its subject allies and came into conflict with Corinth, one of Sparta's leading supporters, over the island of Corcyra. In this climate of anger and escalation, Pericles decided to punish the city of Megara, which had switched allegiance from Sparta to Athens and then back again. In 432 B.C.E. Pericles persuaded the Athenians to pass a law that excluded the Megarians from trading with Athens and its empire, a restriction that would have meant economic disaster for the Megarians. In response the Spartans and their allies declared war.

The Peloponnesian War

At the outbreak of the war, which became known as the Peloponnesian (puh-luh-puh-NEE-zhuhn) War, the Spartan ambassador Melesippus warned the Athenians: "This day will be the beginning of great evil for the Greeks." Few men have ever

Delian League A military alliance led by Athens aimed at protecting the Aegean Islands, liberating Ionia from Persian rule, and keeping the Persians out of Greece.

- Delian League
- Allied with Delian League, 446 B.C.E.
- Athenian military settlement

Thasos

Corcyra

PERSIAN EMPIRE

BOEOTIA
Megara • • Athens
Corinth • Delos
• Sparta

The Delian League, ca. 478–431 B.C.E.

prophesied more accurately. The Peloponnesian War lasted a generation and brought in its wake disease, famine, civil wars, widespread destruction, and huge loss of life (Map 3.3). During the first Spartan invasion of Attica, which began in 431 B.C.E., many people sought refuge in Athens. Overcrowding and a lack of sanitation or clean water nurtured a dreadful plague that killed huge numbers, eventually claiming Pericles himself. The charismatic and eloquent Cleon became the leader of Athens and urged a more aggressive war strategy, doubling the tribute of Athens's allies to pay for it. Both Cleon and the leading Spartan general were killed in battle. Recognizing that ten years of war had resulted only in death, destruction, and stalemate, Sparta and Athens concluded the Peace of Nicias (NIH-shee-uhs) in 421 B.C.E.

The Peace of Nicias resulted in a cold war. But even cold war can bring horror and misery. Such was the case when in 416 B.C.E. the Athenians sent a fleet to the largely neutral island of Melos with an ultimatum: the Melians could surrender and pay tribute or perish. The Melians resisted. The Athenians conquered them, killed the men of military age, and sold the women and children into slavery.

The cold war grew hotter, thanks in part to the ambitions of Alcibiades (al-suh-BIGH-uh-dees) (ca. 450–404 B.C.E.), an aristocrat, a kinsman of Pericles, and a student of the philosopher Socrates (see page 89). An able but overconfident general, Alcibiades widened the war to further his own career and increase the power of Athens. He convinced the Athenians to attack Syracuse, the leading polis in Sicily, which would cut off the grain supply from Sicily to Sparta and its allies, allowing

MAP 3.3 The Peloponnesian War, 431–404 B.C.E. This map shows the alignment of states during the Peloponnesian War.

Athens to end the war and become the greatest power in Greece. The undertaking was vast, requiring an enormous fleet and thousands of sailors and soldiers, and ended in disaster. The Athenian historian Thucydides (thoo-SIHD-ih-dees) (ca. 460–ca. 399 B.C.E.), who saw action in the war himself and later tried to understand its causes, wrote the epitaph for the Athenians: "Infantry, fleet, and everything else were utterly destroyed, and out of many few returned home."[5]

The disaster in Sicily ushered in the final phase of the war, which was marked by three major developments: the renewal of war between Athens and Sparta, Persia's intervention in the war, and the revolt of many Athenian subjects. The year 413 B.C.E. saw Sparta's declaration of war against Athens and widespread revolt within the Athenian Empire, both supported by Alcibiades, who had defected to Sparta. The Persians threw their support behind the Spartans and built a fleet of ships for them; in exchange the Persians expected Ionia to be returned to them once the Spartans were successful. Now equipped with a fleet, the Spartans challenged the Athenians in the Aegean, and a long series of inconclusive naval battles followed.

The strain of war prompted the Athenians in 411 B.C.E. to recall Alcibiades from exile. He cheerfully double-crossed the Spartans and Persians, but even he could not restore Athenian fortunes. In 405 B.C.E. Spartan forces destroyed the last Athenian fleet at the Battle of Aegospotami, after which the Spartans blockaded Athens until it was starved into submission. In 404 B.C.E., after twenty-seven years of fighting, the Peloponnesian War was over, and the evils prophesied by the Spartan ambassador Melesippus in 431 B.C.E. had come true.

The Struggle for Dominance

The decades after the end of the Peloponnesian War were turbulent ones. The chief states—Sparta, Athens, and Thebes—each tried to create a political system in which it would dominate. When Athens surrendered to Sparta in 404 B.C.E., the Spartans used their victory to build an empire. Their decision brought them into conflict with Persia, which now demanded the return of Ionia to its control, as Sparta had promised earlier. From 400 to 386 B.C.E. the Spartans fought the Persians for Ionia, a conflict that eventually engulfed Greece itself. After years of stalemate the Spartans made peace with Persia and their own Greek enemies. The result was a treaty, the King's Peace of 386 B.C.E. in which the Greeks and Persians pledged themselves to live in harmony. This agreement cost Sparta its empire but not its position of dominance in Greece.

The Spartans were not long content with this situation, however, and decided to punish cities that had opposed Sparta during the war. They used naked force against old enemies even though they had formally agreed to peace. In 378 B.C.E. the Spartans launched an unprovoked attack on Athens. Together the Thebans and the Athenians created what was called the Second Athenian Confederacy, a federation of states to guarantee the terms of the peace treaty. The two fought Sparta until 371 B.C.E., when due to growing fear of Theban might, Athens made a separate peace with Sparta. Left alone, Thebes defended itself until later that year, when the brilliant Theban general Epaminondas (ih-pah-muh-NAHN-duhs) (ca. 418–362 B.C.E.) routed the Spartan army on the small plain of Leuctra and in a series of invasions eliminated Sparta as a major power.

The defeat of the once-invincible Spartans stunned the Greeks, who wondered how Thebes would use its victory. Epaminondas, also a gifted statesman, immediately grappled with the problem of how to translate military success into political reality. He concluded alliances with many Peloponnesian states but made no effort to dominate them, instead creating a federal league of cities in which people could marshal their resources, both human and material, to defend themselves from outside interference. Although he made Thebes the leader of this federation of cities, other city-states and leagues were bound to Thebes only by voluntary alliances. His premature death at the Battle of Mantinea in 362 B.C.E. put an end to his efforts, however.

Philip II and Macedonian Supremacy

While the Greek states exhausted themselves in endless conflicts, the new power of Macedonia arose in the north. The land, extensive and generally fertile, nurtured a large population. Whether the Macedonians should be considered Greeks is a controversial issue, among both scholars of the ancient world and Greeks and Macedonians living today. Macedonia had strong ties to the Greek poleis, but the government there developed as a kingdom, not a democracy or oligarchy.

The kings of Macedonia slowly built up their power over rival states, and in 359 B.C.E. the brilliant and cultured Philip II ascended to the throne. The young Philip had spent years in Thebes mastering diplomacy and warfare. With decades of effort he secured the borders of Macedonia against invaders from the north, and he then launched a series of military operations in the northwestern Aegean. By clever use of his wealth and superb army, he gained control of the area, and in 338 B.C.E. he won a decisive victory over Thebes and Athens that gave him command of Greece. Because the Greeks could not put aside their quarrels, they fell to an invader, and 338 B.C.E. is often seen as marking the end of the classical period.

After his victory, Philip led a combined army of soldiers from Macedonia and from many Greek states in an attempt to liberate the Ionian Greeks from Persian rule. Before he could launch this campaign, however, Philip fell to an assassin's dagger in 336 B.C.E. His young son Alexander vowed to carry on Philip's mission. He would succeed beyond all expectations.

Classical Greek Life and Culture

Despite the violence that dominated Greece for nearly two centuries beginning in 500 B.C.E., or to some degree because of it, playwrights and thinkers pondered the meaning of the universe and the role of humans in it, and artists and architects created new styles to celebrate Greek achievements. Thus, although warfare was one of the hallmarks of the classical period, intellectual and artistic accomplishments were as well.

FOCUS QUESTION
What were the lasting cultural and intellectual achievements of the classical period?

Athenian Arts in the Age of Pericles

In the midst of the warfare of the fifth century B.C.E., Pericles turned Athens into the showplace of Greece. He appropriated Delian League funds to pay for a huge building program to rebuild the city that had been destroyed during the Persian occupation in 480 B.C.E., and to display to all Greeks the glory of the Athenian polis. Workers erected temples and other buildings as patriotic memorials housing statues and carvings, often painted in bright colors, showing the gods in human form and

The Acropolis of Athens

(Lingbeek/Getty Images)

The natural rock formation of the Acropolis probably had a palace on top as early as the Mycenaean period, when the palace was also surrounded by a defensive wall. Temples were constructed beginning in the sixth century B.C.E., and after the Persian wars Pericles ordered the reconstruction and expansion of many of these, as well as the building of new and more magnificent temples and an extension of the defensive walls. The largest building is the Parthenon, a temple dedicated to the goddess Athena, which originally housed a forty-foot-tall statue of Athena made of ivory and gold sheets attached to a wooden frame. Much of the Parthenon was damaged when it was shelled during a war between Venice and the Ottoman Empire in the seventeenth century C.E., and air pollution continues to eat away at the marble.

EVALUATE THE EVIDENCE

1. Imagine yourself as an Athenian walking up the hill toward the Parthenon. What impression would the setting and the building itself convey?
2. What were the various functions of the Acropolis?

celebrating the Greek victory over the Persians. (The paint later washed away, leaving the generally white sculpture that we think of as "classical.") Many of the temples were built on the high, rocky Acropolis that stood in the center of the city, on top of the remains of temples that had been burned by the Persians, and sometimes incorporating these into their walls.

The Athenians normally hiked up the long approach to the Acropolis only for religious festivals, of which the most important and joyous was the Great Panathenaea, held every four years to honor the virgin goddess Athena and perhaps offer sacrifices to older deities as well. (See "Evaluating the Evidence 3.2: The Acropolis of Athens," above.) For this festival, Athenian citizens and legal noncitizen residents formed a huge procession to bring the statue of Athena in the Parthenon an exquisite robe, richly embroidered by the citizen women of Athens with mythological scenes. At the head of the procession walked an aristocratic young woman carrying an offering basket. She and other young unmarried women of the city had earlier left their toys and other marks of childhood in caves at the base of the Acropolis. Other richly dressed women followed her, most carrying gold and silver vessels containing wine and perfumes. Young men on horseback came next, followed by older men carrying staffs. Toward the rear came other young men carrying large pitchers of water and wine, or leading the bulls to the sacrifice. After the religious ceremonies, all the people joined in a feast.

Once the procession began, the marchers first saw the Propylaea, the ceremonial gateway whose columns appeared to uphold the sky. On the right was the small temple of Athena Nike, built to commemorate the victory over the Persians. The broad band of sculpture above its columns depicted the struggle between the Greeks and the Persians. To the left of the visitors stood the Erechtheum, a temple that housed several ancient shrines. On its southern side was the famous Portico of the Caryatids, a porch whose roof was supported by huge statues of young women. As visitors walked on, they obtained a full view of the Parthenon, the chief temple dedicated to Athena at the center of the Acropolis, with a huge painted ivory and gold statue of the goddess inside.

The development of drama was tied to the religious festivals of the city, especially those to the god of wine, Dionysus (see page 88). Drama was as rooted in the life of the polis as were the architecture and sculpture of the Acropolis. The polis sponsored the production of plays and required wealthy citizens to pay the expenses of their production. At the beginning of the year, dramatists submitted their plays to the chief archon of the polis. He chose those he considered best and assigned a theatrical troupe to each playwright. Many plays were highly controversial, containing overt political and social commentary, but the archons neither suppressed nor censored them.

Not surprisingly, given the incessant warfare, conflict was a constant element in Athenian drama, and playwrights used their art in attempts to portray, understand, and resolve life's basic conflicts. The Athenian dramatists examined questions about the relationship between humans and the gods, the demands of society on the individual, and the nature of good and evil. Aeschylus (EHS-kuh-lihs) (525–456 B.C.E.), the first of the great Athenian dramatists, was also the first to express the agony of the individual caught in conflict. In his trilogy of plays, *The Oresteia* (ohr-eh-STEE-uh), Aeschylus deals with the themes of betrayal, murder, and reconciliation, urging that reason and justice be applied to reconcile fundamental conflicts. The final play concludes with a prayer that civil dissension never be allowed to destroy the city and that the life of the city be one of harmony and grace.

Sophocles (SOFF-uh-klees) (496–406 B.C.E.) also dealt with matters personal and political. Perhaps his most famous plays are *Oedipus* (EHD-uh-puhs) *the King* and its sequel, *Oedipus at Colonus*. *Oedipus the King* is the tragic story of a man doomed by the gods to kill his father and marry his mother. Try as he might to avoid his fate, his every action brings him closer to its fulfillment. When at last he realizes that he has unwittingly carried out the decree of the gods, Oedipus blinds himself and flees into exile. In *Oedipus at Colonus*, Sophocles dramatizes the last days of the broken king, whose patient suffering and uncomplaining piety win him an exalted position. In the end the gods honor him for his virtue. The interpretation of these two plays has been hotly debated, but Sophocles seems to be saying that the gods only predict what is going to happen and do not determine it. It is up to the individual, not the gods, to decide whether things turn out tragically or not. (See "Evaluating the Evidence 3.3: Sophocles, *Antigone*," page 82.)

With Euripides (your-IHP-uh-dees) (ca. 480–406 B.C.E.) drama entered a new, and in many ways more personal, phase. To him the gods were far less important than human beings. The essence of Euripides's tragedy is the flawed character—men and women who bring disaster on themselves and their loved ones because their

The Discus Thrower This marble statue shows an athlete in mid-throw, capturing the tension in the muscles and tendons. The original was made about 450 B.C.E., perhaps by the sculptor Myron of Athens. As is true of so much Greek statuary, the original is lost, and this is a Roman copy. Athletes in Greece regularly competed nude, including in the Olympic games. (Victoria and Albert Museum, London, UK/Ancient Art and Architecture Collection Ltd./Bridgeman Images)

Sophocles, *Antigone*

The plays of Sophocles concern matters personal, political, and divine. In Antigone (an-TIH-guh-nee), produced in or before 441 B.C.E., Polyneices (pahl-eh-NIGH-sees) and Eteocles (eh-tee-OH-klees), the sons of King Oedipus of Thebes, have killed each other in a war over who would rule. Creon, the brother of Oedipus's wife, Jocasta (who is also Oedipus's mother, but that's the plot of another play; see page 81), is now king, and orders the body of Polyneices to be left to rot. Polyneices's sister (and Creon's niece) Antigone disobeys him, buries Polyneices, and carries out the proper funeral rituals. Creon condemns her to be walled up, so she hangs herself. Creon's son and Antigone's fiancé, Haemon, then kills himself, as does Creon's wife. The heart of the play is a series of confrontations between Creon and Antigone.

Creon *(to Antigone):*
You—tell me not at length but in a word.
You knew the order not to do this thing?

Antigone:
I knew, of course I knew. The word was plain.

Creon:
And still you dared to overstep these laws?

Antigone:
For me it was not Zeus who made that order.
Nor did that Justice who lives with the gods below
mark out such laws to hold among mankind.
Nor did I think your orders were so strong
that you, a mortal man, could over-run
the gods' unwritten and unfailing laws.
Not now, nor yesterday's, they always live,
and no one knows their origin in time
So not through fear of any man's proud spirit
would I be likely to neglect these laws,
draw on myself the gods' sure punishment.
I knew that I must die; how could I not?

even without your warning. If I die
before my time, I say it is a gain.
Who lives in sorrows many as are mine
how shall he not be glad to gain his death?
And so, for me to meet this fate, no grief.
But if I left that corpse, my mother's son,
dead and unburied I'd have cause to grieve
as now I grieve not.
And if you think my acts are foolishness
The foolishness may be in a fool's eye.

. . .

I go, without a friend, struck down by fate,
live to the hollow chambers of the dead.
What divine justice have I disobeyed?
Why, in my misery, look to the gods for help?
Can I call any of them my ally?
I stand convicted of impiety,
the evidence my pious duty done.
Should the gods think that this is righteousness,
in suffering I'll see my error clear.
But if it is the others who are wrong
I wish them no greater punishment than mine.

. . .

Look what I suffer, at whose command,
Because I respected the right.

EVALUATE THE EVIDENCE

1. How does Antigone justify what she has done? How does she describe the relationship between divine law and political law?
2. Given what was going on in Athens at the time that this play was performed, how can Antigone's words be seen as political commentary?

Source: *Sophocles I: Antigone*, trans. Elizabeth Wyckoff, in *The Complete Greek Tragedies* (Chicago: Phoenix Books, 1954), pp. 173–174, 190, 191. Copyright © 1954 by The University of Chicago. All rights reserved. Used by permission of the publisher.

passions overwhelm reason. Although Euripides's plays were less popular in his life-time than were those of Aeschylus and Sophocles, his work was to have a significant impact on Roman drama.

Writers of comedy treated the affairs of the polis and its politicians bawdily and often coarsely. Even so, their plays also were performed at religious festivals. Best known are the comedies of Aristophanes (eh-ruh-STAH-fuh-neez) (ca. 445–386 B.C.E.), a merciless critic of cranks and quacks. He commented snidely on Cleon, poked fun at Socrates (see page 89), and hooted at Euripides. (See "Individuals in

Society: Aristophanes," page 84.) Like Aeschylus, Sophocles, and Euripides, Aristophanes used his art to convey his ideas about human nature and the values of the polis.

Households and Work

In sharp contrast with the rich intellectual and cultural life of Periclean Athens stands the simplicity of its material life. The Athenians, like other Greeks, lived with comparatively few material possessions in houses that were rather simple. Well-to-do Athenians lived in houses consisting of a series of rooms opening onto a central courtyard, sometimes with bedrooms on an upper floor. Artisans often set aside a room to use as a shop or work area. Larger houses often had a dining room at the front where the men of the family ate and entertained guests at drinking parties called *symposia*, and a **gynaeceum** (also spelled *gynaikeion*), a room or section at the back where the women of the family and the female slaves worked, ate, and slept. Other rooms included the kitchen and bathroom. By modern standards there was not much furniture. In the men's dining room were couches, a sideboard, and small tables appropriate for social events. Cups and other pottery were often hung from pegs on the wall, as were hoplites' armor and, for aristocrats, the death masks of their relatives. In the courtyard were the well, a small altar, and a washbasin. If the family lived in the country, the stalls of the animals faced the courtyard. Country dwellers kept oxen for plowing, pigs for slaughtering, sheep for wool, goats for cheese, and mules and donkeys for transportation. Even in the city, chickens and perhaps a goat or two roamed the courtyard along with dogs and cats.

Cooking, done over a hearth in the house, provided welcome warmth in the winter. Baking and roasting were done in ovens. Meals consisted primarily of various grains, especially wheat and barley, as well as lentils, olives, figs, grapes, fish, and a little meat, foods that are now part of the highly touted "Mediterranean diet." The Greeks used olive oil for cooking, and also as an ointment and as lamp fuel.

The Greeks did not eat much meat. On special occasions, such as important religious festivals, the family ate the animal sacrificed to the god. The only Greeks who consistently ate meat were the Spartan warriors. They received a small portion of meat each day, together with the infamous Spartan black broth, a concoction of pork cooked in blood, vinegar, and salt. One Athenian, after tasting the broth, commented that he could easily understand why the Spartans were so willing to die.

In the city a man might support himself as a craftsman—a potter, bronze-smith, sailmaker, or tanner—or he could contract with the polis to work on public buildings. Certain crafts, including spinning and weaving, were generally done by women, who produced cloth for their own families and sold it. Men and women without skills worked as paid laborers but competed with slaves for work.

Slavery was commonplace in Greece, as it was throughout the ancient world. Slaves were usually foreigners and often "barbarians," people whose native language was not Greek. Most citizen households in Athens owned at least one slave. Slaves in Athens ranged widely in terms of their type of work and opportunities for escaping slavery. Some male slaves were skilled workers or well-educated teachers and tutors of writing, while others were unskilled laborers in the city, agricultural workers in the countryside, or laborers in mines, including the Athenian silver mines at Laurium. Female slaves worked in agriculture, or as domestic servants and nurses for children. Slaves received some protection under the law, and those who engaged in skilled labor for which they were paid could buy their freedom.

gynaeceum Women's quarters at the back of an Athenian house where the women of the family and the female slaves worked, ate, and slept.

I n 424 B.C.E., in the middle of the Peloponnesian War, citizens of Athens attending one of the city's regular dramatic festivals watched *The Knights*, in which two slaves complain about their fellow slave's power over their master Demos ("the people" in Greek) and everyone else around him. They run into a sausage seller and tell him that an oracle has predicted he will become more influential than their fellow slave and will eventually dominate the city, becoming what in ancient Greece was called a demagogue. He doesn't think this possible, as he is only a sausage seller, but the men tell him he is the perfect candidate: "Mix and knead together all the state business as you do for your sausages. To win the people, always cook them some savoury that pleases them. Besides, you possess all the attributes of a demagogue; a screeching, horrible voice, a perverse, crossgrained nature and the language of the market-place. In you all is united which is needful for governing." This leads to a series of shouted debates between the influential slave and the sausage maker, each one accusing the other of corruption and indecent behavior, and making ever more elaborate promises to the citizens of Athens. Ultimately the sausage seller wins, and the formerly domineering slave becomes a lowly sausage seller.

Although the forceful slave's name is never mentioned in the play, everyone knew he represented Cleon, at that point the leader of Athens, who had risen to power through populist speeches. The real Cleon may well have been among the thousands in the audience, as front-row seats at festivals were a reward he had just been given by the citizens of Athens for a military victory. Cleon had taken legal action against the playwright two years earlier for another play, accusing him of slandering the polis, but in this case he did nothing.

That playwright was Aristophanes, the only comic playwright in classical Athens from whom whole plays survive. Not much is known about Aristophanes's life, other than a few ambiguous clues in the plays. His first play, now lost, was produced in 427 B.C.E., and his last datable play, also now lost, in 386 B.C.E. (The dates of his life are inferred from these, as there is a comment in one play suggesting he was only eighteen when his first play

Roman copy of a Hellenistic bust depicting what Aristophanes might have looked like. (Musée du Louvre, Paris, France/De Agostini Picture Library/Bridgeman Images)

was produced.) He directed some of his own plays, won the theater competition several times, and had sons who were also comic playwrights. Even in his early plays, Aristophanes seems to have opposed anything that was new in Athens: new types of leaders (like Cleon), new styles in drama (Euripides was a standard target), new kinds of educators (such as the Sophists), new philosophy (especially that of Socrates). Everything and everyone was open to ridicule, and the more obscene the better: poets throw turds at each other, politicians collapse drunk and vomiting in the streets, military leaders walk around with huge erections when their wives refuse to have sex with them until they call off the war. Aristophanes combined kinds of comedy that today are often separated — political satire, complicated wordplay, celebrity slamming, cross-dressing, slapstick, dirty jokes, silly props, absurdity, audience taunting — and was a master at all of these.

QUESTIONS FOR ANALYSIS

1. How might political satires such as those of Aristophanes have both critiqued and reinforced civic values in classical Athens?
2. Can you think of more recent parallels to Aristophanes's political satires? What has been the response to these?

Gender and Sexuality

Citizenship was the basis of political power for men in ancient Athens and was inherited. After the middle of the fifth century B.C.E., people were considered citizens only if both parents were citizens, except for a few men given citizenship as a reward for service to the city. Adult male citizens were expected to take part in political decisions and be active in civic life, no matter what their occupation. They were also in charge of relations between the household and the wider community. Women in Athens and elsewhere in Greece, like those in Mesopotamia, brought dowries to their husbands upon marriage, which became the husband's to invest or use, though he was supposed to do this wisely.

Women did not play a public role in classical Athens, and we know the names of no female poets, artists, or philosophers. Women in wealthier citizen families probably spent most of their time at home in the gynaeceum, leaving the house only to attend some religious festivals, and perhaps occasionally plays. The main function of women from citizen families was to bear and raise children. Childbirth could be dangerous for both mother and infant, so pregnant women usually made sacrifices or visited temples to ask help from the gods. Women relied on their relatives, on friends, and on midwives to assist in the delivery.

In the gynaeceum women oversaw domestic slaves and hired labor, and together with servants and friends worked wool into cloth. Women personally cared for slaves who became ill and nursed them back to health, and cared for the family's material possessions as well. Women from noncitizen families lived freer lives than citizen women, although they worked harder and had fewer material comforts. They performed manual labor in the fields or sold goods or services in the agora, going about their affairs much as men did.

Among the services that some women and men sold was sex. Women who sold sexual services ranged from poor streetwalkers known as *pornai* to middle-status hired mistresses known as *palakai* to sophisticated courtesans known as *hetaerae,* who added intellectual accomplishments to physical beauty. Hetaerae accompanied men at dinner parties and in public settings where their wives would not have been welcome, serving men as social as well as sexual partners.

Same-sex relations were generally accepted in all of ancient Greece, not simply in Sparta. In classical Athens part of a male adolescent citizen's training might entail a hierarchical sexual and tutorial relationship with an adult man, who most likely was married and may have had female sexual partners as well. These relationships between young men and older men were often celebrated in literature and art, in part because Athenians regarded perfection as possible only in the male. Women were generally seen as inferior to men, dominated by their bodies rather than their minds. The perfect body was that of the young male, and perfect love was that between a young man and a slightly older man, not that between a man and a woman, who was marred by imperfection. The extent to which perfect love was sexual or spiritual was debated among the ancient Greeks. In one of his dialogues, the philosopher Plato (see page 89) argues that the best kind of love is one in which contemplation of the beloved leads to contemplation of the

Young Man and Hetaera In this scene painted on the inside of a drinking cup, a hetaera holds the head of a young man who has clearly had too much to drink. Sexual and comic scenes were common on Greek pottery, particularly on objects that would have been used at a private dinner party hosted by a citizen, known as a symposium. Wives did not attend symposia, but hetaerae and entertainers were often hired to perform for the male guests. (Painter: Makron, drinking cup [kylix], Greek, Late Archaic Period, about 490–480 B.C. Place of manufacture: Greece, Attica, Athens; ceramic, Red Figure; Height: 12.8 cm. [5 1/16 in.]; Diameter: 33.2 cm. [13 1/16 in.]/Museum of Fine Arts, Boston, Massachusetts, USA/Henry Lillie Pierce Fund, 01.8022/Photograph © 2015 Museum of Fine Arts, Boston. All Rights Reserved/ Bridgeman Images) divine, an intellectualized love that came to be known as "platonic." Plato was suspicious of the power of sexual passion because it distracted men from reason and the search for knowledge.

Along with praise of intellectualized love, Greek authors also celebrated physical sex and desire. The soldier-poet Archilochus (d. 652 B.C.E.) preferred "to light upon the flesh of a maid and ram belly to belly and thigh to thigh."[6] The lyric poet Sappho, who lived on the island of Lesbos in the northern Aegean Sea in the sixth century B.C.E., wrote often of powerful desire. One of her poems describes her reaction on seeing her beloved talking to someone else:

> He appears to me, that one, equal to the gods,
> the man who, facing you,
> is seated and, up close, that sweet voice of yours
> he listens to
>
> And how you laugh your charming laugh. Why it
> makes my heart flutter within my breast,
> because the moment I look at you, right then, for me,
> to make any sound at all won't work any more.
>
> My tongue has a breakdown and a delicate
> —all of a sudden—fire rushes under my skin.
> With my eyes I see not a thing, and there is a roar
> that my ears make.
> Sweat pours down me and a trembling
> seizes all of me; paler than grass
> am I, and a little short of death
> do I appear to me.[7]

Sappho's description of the physical reactions caused by love—and jealousy—reaches across the centuries. The Hellenic, and even more the Hellenistic, Greeks regarded her as a great lyric poet, although because some of her poetry is directed toward women, over the last century she has become better known for her sexuality than her writing. Today the English word *lesbian* is derived from Sappho's home island of Lesbos.

Same-sex relations did not mean that people did not marry, for Athenians saw the continuation of the family line as essential. Sappho, for example, appears to have been married and had a daughter. Sexual desire and procreation were both important aspects of life, but ancient Greeks did not necessarily link them.

Public and Personal Religion

Like most peoples of the ancient world, the Greeks were polytheists, worshipping a variety of gods and goddesses who were immortal but otherwise acted just like people. Migration, invasion, and colonization brought the Greeks into contact with other peoples and caused their religious beliefs to evolve. How much these contacts shaped Greek religion and other aspects of culture has been the subject of a fierce debate since the late 1980s, when in *Black Athena: The Afroasiatic Roots of Classical Civilization*, Martin Bernal proposed that the Greeks owed a great deal to the Egyptians and Phoenicians, and that scholars since the nineteenth century had purposely tried to cover this up to make the Greeks seem more European and less indebted to cultures in Africa and Asia.[8] Bernal's ideas are highly controversial, and most classicists do not accept his evidence, but they are part of a larger tendency among scholars in the last several decades— including those who vigorously oppose Bernal—to see the Greeks less in isolation from other groups and more in relation to the larger Mediterranean world.

Greek religion was primarily a matter of ritual, with rituals designed to appease the divinities believed to control the forces of the natural world. Processions, festivals, and sacrifices offered to the gods were frequently occasions for people to meet together socially, times of cheer or even drunken excess.

By the classical era the primary gods were understood to live metaphorically on Mount Olympus, the highest mountain in Greece. Zeus was the king of the gods and the most powerful of them, and he was married to Hera, who was also his sister (just as, in Egypt, Isis was Osiris's wife and sister; see Chapter 2). Zeus and Hera had several children, including Ares, the god of war. Zeus was also the father of the god Apollo, who represented the epitome of youth, beauty, and athletic skill, and who served as the patron god of music and poetry. Apollo's half sister Athena was a warrior-goddess who had been born from the head of Zeus.

The Greeks also honored certain heroes. A hero was born of a union of a god or goddess and a mortal and was considered an intermediate between the divine and the human. A hero displayed his divine origins by performing deeds beyond the ability of human beings. Herakles (or Hercules, as the Romans called him), the son of Zeus and the mortal woman Alcmene, was the most popular of the Greek heroes, defeating mythical opponents and carrying out impossible (or "Herculean") tasks. Devotees to Hercules believed that he, like other heroes, protected mortals from supernatural dangers and provided an ideal of vigorous masculinity.

The polis administered cults and festivals, and everyone was expected to participate in events similar to today's patriotic parades or ceremonies. Much religion was local and domestic, and individual families honored various deities privately in their homes. Many people also believed that magic rituals and spells were effective and sought the assistance of individuals reputed to have special knowledge or powers to cure disease, drive away ghosts, bring good weather, or influence the actions of others. Even highly educated Greeks sought the assistance of fortune-tellers and soothsayers, from the oracle at Delphi to local figures who examined the flights of birds or the entrails of recently slaughtered chickens for clues about what was going to happen in the future.

Along with public and family forms of honoring the gods, some Greeks also participated in what later historians have termed **mystery religions**, in which participants underwent an initiation ritual and gained secret knowledge that they were forbidden to reveal to the uninitiated. The Eleusinian mysteries, held at Eleusis in Attica, are one of the oldest of these. They centered on Demeter, the goddess of the harvest, whose lovely daughter Persephone (per-SEH-foh-nee), as the story goes, was taken by the god Hades to the underworld. In mourning, Demeter caused drought, and ultimately Zeus allowed Persephone to return to her, though she had to spend some months of the year in Hades. There is evidence of an agrarian ritual celebrating this mythological explanation for the cycle of the seasons as early as the Bronze Age, and in the sixth century B.C.E. the rulers of nearby Athens made the ritual open to all Greeks, women and slaves included. Many people flocked to the annual ceremonies and learned the mysteries, which by the fourth century B.C.E. appear to have promised life after death to those initiated into them.

mystery religions Belief systems that were characterized by secret doctrines, rituals of initiation, and sometimes the promise of rebirth or an afterlife.

Another somewhat secret religion was that of Dionysus (digh-uh-NIGH-suhs), the god of wine and powerful emotions. Dionysus appears to have been a god of non-Greek origin, though stories evolved to fit him into the Olympian system as a son of Zeus. He was killed and then reborn, which is why he, like Persephone, became the center of mystery religions offering rebirth. As the god of wine, he also represented freedom from the normal constraints of society, and his worshippers were reported to have danced ecstatically and even to have become a frenzied and uncontrolled mob. Whether or how often this actually happened is impossible to know, as contemporary Athenian writers who did not approve may have embellished their accounts of these wild rituals, and later scholars sometimes regarded them simply as fiction because chaotic orgies did not fit with their notions of the rational and orderly Greeks.

Greeks also shared some public Pan-Hellenic festivals, the chief of which were held at Olympia in honor of Zeus and at Delphi in honor of Apollo. The festivities at Olympia included athletic contests that have inspired the modern Olympic games. Held every four years, these games were for the glory of Zeus. They attracted visitors from all over the Greek world and lasted until the fourth century C.E., when they were banned by a Christian emperor because they were pagan. The Pythian (PIH-thee-uhn) games at Delphi were also held every four years and emphasized musical and literary contests as well as athletic prowess. Both the Olympic and the Pythian games were unifying factors in Greek life, bringing Greeks together culturally as well as religiously.

The Flowering of Philosophy

Just as the Greeks developed rituals to honor the gods, they spun myths and epics to explain the origin of the universe. Over time, however, as Greeks encountered other peoples with different beliefs, some of them began to question their old gods and myths, and they sought rational rather than supernatural explanations for natural phenomena. These Greek thinkers, based in Ionia, are called the Pre-Socratics because their rational efforts preceded those of the Athenians. They took individual facts and wove them into general theories that led them to conclude that, despite appearances, the universe is actually simple and subject to natural laws. Although they had little impact on the average Greek of their day, the Pre-Socratics began an intellectual revolution with their idea that nature was predictable, creating what we now call philosophy and science.

Drawing on their observations, the Pre-Socratics speculated about the basic building blocks of the universe. Thales (THAY-leez) (ca. 600 B.C.E.) thought the basic element of the universe was water, and Heraclitus (hehr-uh-KLIGH-tuhs) (ca. 500 B.C.E.) thought it was fire. Democritus (dih-MAW-kruh-tuhs) (ca. 460 B.C.E.) broke this down further and created the atomic theory, the idea that the universe is made up of invisible, indestructible particles. The culmination of Pre-Socratic thought was the theory that four simple substances make up the universe: fire, air, earth, and water.

The stream of thought started by the Pre-Socratics branched into several directions. Hippocrates (hih-PAW-kruh-teez) (ca. 470–400 B.C.E.), who lived on the island of Kos near present-day Turkey, became the most prominent physician and teacher of medicine of his time. He appears to have written several works, and his followers wrote many more. These medical writings became known as the "Hippocratic corpus," although it is impossible to say who actually wrote any specific work. Hippocrates sought natural explanations for diseases and seems to have advocated letting nature take its course and not intervening too much. Illness was caused not by evil spirits, he asserted, but by physical problems in the body, particularly by imbalances in what he saw as four basic bodily fluids: blood, phlegm, black bile, and yellow bile. In a healthy body these fluids, called humors, were in perfect balance, and the goal of medical treatment of the ill was to help the body bring them back into balance.

The **Sophists** (SOFF-ihsts), a group of thinkers in fifth-century-B.C.E. Athens, applied philosophical speculation to politics and language, questioning the beliefs and laws of the polis to understand their origin. They believed that excellence in both politics and language could be taught, and they provided lessons for the young men of Athens who wished to learn how to persuade others in the often-tumultuous Athenian democracy. Their later opponents criticized them for charging fees and also accused them of using rhetoric to deceive people instead of presenting the truth. (Today the word *sophist* is usually used in this sense, describing someone who deceives people with clever-sounding but false arguments.)

Socrates (SOK-ruh-teez) (ca. 469–399 B.C.E.), whose ideas are known only through the works of others, also applied philosophy to politics and to people. He seemed to many Athenians to be a Sophist because he also questioned Athenian traditions, although he never charged fees. His approach when exploring ethical issues and defining concepts was to start with a general topic or problem and to narrow the matter to its essentials. He did so by continuously questioning participants in a discussion or argument through which they developed critical thinking skills, a process known as the **Socratic method**. Because he posed questions rather than giving answers, it is difficult to say exactly what Socrates thought about many things, although he does seem to have felt that through knowledge people could approach the supreme good and thus find happiness. He clearly thought that Athenian leaders were motivated more by greed and opportunism than by a desire for justice in the war with Sparta, and he criticized Athenian democracy openly.

Socrates was viewed with suspicion by many because he challenged the traditional beliefs and values of Athens. The playwright Aristophanes satirized him and his followers in the riotously funny *The Clouds*, performed around 420 B.C.E. Twenty years later, after Athens's disastrous defeat at the hands of Sparta in the Peloponnesian War, Socrates came into serious conflict with the government. Charges were brought against him for corrupting the youth of the city, and for impiety, that is, for not believing in the gods honored in the city. Thus he was essentially charged with being unpatriotic because he criticized the traditions of the city and the decisions of government leaders. He was tried and imprisoned, and though he had several opportunities to escape, in 399 B.C.E. he drank the poison ordered as his method of execution and died.

Most of what we know about Socrates, including the details of his trial and death, comes from his student Plato (427–347 B.C.E.), who wrote dialogues in which Socrates asks questions and who also founded the Academy, a school dedicated to philosophy. Plato developed the theory that there are two worlds: the impermanent, changing world that we know through our senses, and the eternal, unchanging realm of "forms" that constitute the essence of true reality. According to Plato, true knowledge and the possibility of living a virtuous life come from contemplating ideal forms—what later came to be called **Platonic ideals**—not from observing the visible world. Thus if you want to understand justice, asserted Plato, you should think about what would make perfect justice, not study the imperfect examples of justice around you. Plato believed that the ideal polis could exist only when its citizens were well educated. From education came the possibility of determining all of the virtues of life and combining them into a system that would lead to an intelligent, moral, and ethical life.

Sophists A group of thinkers in fifth-century-B.C.E. Athens who applied philosophical speculation to politics and language and were accused of deceit.

Socratic method A method of inquiry used by Socrates based on asking questions, through which participants developed their critical thinking skills and explored ethical issues.

Platonic ideals In Plato's thought, the eternal unchanging ideal forms that are the essence of true reality.

Plato's student Aristotle (384–322 B.C.E.) also thought that true knowledge was possible, but he believed that such knowledge came from observation of the world, analysis of natural phenomena, and logical reasoning, not contemplation. Aristotle thought that everything had a purpose, so that to know something, one also had to know its function. Excellence—*arête* in Greek—meant performing one's function to the best of one's ability, whether one was a horse or a person. To the qualities of courage and strength that Homer had seen as essential to arête in people (see page 67), Aristotle added justice, generosity, temperance, and other moral virtues. The range of Aristotle's thought is staggering. His interests embraced logic, ethics, natural science, physics, politics, poetry, and art. He studied the heavens as well as the earth and judged the earth to be the center of the universe, with the stars and planets revolving around it.

Plato's idealism profoundly shaped Western philosophy, but Aristotle came to have an even wider influence; for many centuries in Europe, the authority of Aristotle's ideas was second only to the Bible's. His works—which are actually a combination of his lecture notes and those of his students, copied and recopied many times—were used as the ultimate proof that something was true, even if closer observation of the phenomenon indicated that it was not. Thus, ironically, Aristotle's authority was sometimes invoked in a way that contradicted his own ideas. Despite these limitations, the broader examination of the universe and the place of humans in it that Socrates, Plato, and Aristotle engaged in is widely regarded as Greece's most important intellectual legacy.

LOOKING BACK LOOKING AHEAD

The ancient Greeks built on the endeavors of earlier societies in the eastern Mediterranean, but they also added new elements, including drama, philosophy, science, and naturalistic art. They created governments that relied on the participation of citizens. These cultural and political achievements developed in a society that for many centuries was almost always at war, with the Persians and with each other. Those conflicts led many to wonder whether democracy was really a good form of government, and to speculate more widely about abstract ideals and the nature of the cosmos. The Greeks carried these ideas with them as they colonized much of the Mediterranean, in migrations that often resulted from the conflicts that were so common in Greece.

The classical Greeks had tremendous influence not only on the parts of the world in which they traveled or settled, but also on all of Western civilization from that point on. As you will see in Chapter 5, Roman art, religion, literature, and many other aspects of culture relied on Greek models. And as you will see in Chapter 12, European thinkers and writers made conscious attempts to return to classical ideals in art, literature, and philosophy during the Renaissance. In America political leaders from the Revolutionary era on decided that important government buildings should be modeled on the Parthenon or other temples, complete with marble statuary of their own heroes. In some ways, capitol buildings in the United States are perfect symbols of the legacy of Greece—gleaming ideals of harmony, freedom, democracy, and beauty that (as with all ideals) do not always correspond with realities.

Make Connections

Think about the larger developments and continuities within and across chapters.

1. What were the effects of the Bronze Age Collapse in Egypt, the Hittite Empire, Kush, Phoenicia, and Greece, and how did interactions among these societies change in this period of turmoil?

2. How were Greek understandings of the role of the gods in public and private life similar to those of the Egyptians and Sumerians? How were they different?

3. Looking at your own town or city, what evidence do you find of the cultural legacy of ancient Greece?

3 REVIEW & EXPLORE

Review the Main Ideas

Answer the focus questions from each section of the chapter.

◆ How did the geography of Greece shape its earliest kingdoms, and what factors contributed to the decline of those kingdoms? (p. 62)

◆ What was the role of the polis in Greek society? (p. 67)

◆ What were the major wars of the classical period, and how did they shape Greek history? (p. 75)

◆ What were the lasting cultural and intellectual achievements of the classical period? (p. 79)

Identify Key Terms

Identify and explain the significance of each item below.

Minoan (p. 64)
Mycenaean (p. 65)
polis (p. 67)
hoplites (p. 69)
tyranny (p. 69)
democracy (p. 69)
oligarchy (p. 70)
helots (p. 71)
Delian League (p. 76)
gynaeceum (p. 83)
mystery religions (p. 87)
Sophists (p. 89)
Socratic method (p. 89)
Platonic ideals (p. 89)

NOTES

1. Homer, *The Iliad*, trans. Samuel Butler (London: Longmans, Green, and Co., 1898), book 1, lines 1–5.
2. J. M. Edmonds, *Greek Elegy and Iambus* (Cambridge, Mass.: Harvard University Press, 1931), I.70, frag. 10.
3. *The Works of Xenophon*, trans. Henry G. Dakyns (London: Macmillan and Co., 1892), p. 296.
4. Herodotus, *Histories* 7.226.2. Works in Greek with no translator noted were translated by John Buckler.
5. Thucydides, *History of the Peloponnesian War* 7.87.6.
6. G. Tarditi, *Archilochus Fragmenta* (Rome: Edizioni dell'Ateno, 1968), frag. 112.
7. Gregory Nagy, *The Ancient Greek Hero in 24 Hours* (Cambridge, Mass.: Harvard University Press, 2013), p. 119. Used by permission of Gregory Nagy, Center for Hellenic Studies.
8. Martin Bernal, *Black Athena: The Afroasiatic Roots of Classical Civilization* (New Brunswick, N.J.: Rutgers University Press, 1991). Essays by classical scholars refuting Bernal can be found in Mary R. Lefkowitz and Guy Maclean Rogers, *Black Athena Revisited* (Durham: University of North Carolina Press, 1996).

CHAPTER PREVIEW

Alexander's Conquests and Their Political Legacy
How and why did Alexander the Great create an empire, and what was its political legacy?

Building a Hellenized Society
How did Greek ideas and traditions spread across the eastern Mediterranean and Near East?

The Economy of the Hellenistic World
What new economic connections were created in the Hellenistic period?

Religion and Philosophy in the Hellenistic World
How did religion and philosophy shape everyday life in the Hellenistic world?

Hellenistic Science and Medicine
How did science and medicine serve the needs of Hellenistic society?

Hellenistic Married Life
This small terra-cotta figurine from Myrina in what is now Turkey, made in the second century B.C.E., shows a newly married couple sitting on a bridal bed. The groom is drawing back the bride's veil, and she is exhibiting the modesty that was a desired quality in young women. Figurines representing every stage of life became popular in the Hellenistic period and were used for religious offerings in temples and sacred places. This one was found in a tomb.
(Musée du Louvre, Paris, France/Erich Lessing/Art Resource, NY)

4

Life in the Hellenistic World

336–30 B.C.E.

When his father was assassinated in 336 B.C.E., twenty-year-old Alexander inherited not only Philip's crown but also his determination to lead a united Greek force in fighting Persia. Alexander's invasion of the Persian Empire led to its downfall, but he died while planning his next campaign, only a little more than a decade after he had started. He left behind an empire that quickly broke into smaller kingdoms, but more important, his death ushered in an era, the Hellenistic, in which Greek culture, the Greek language, and Greek thought spread as far as India, blending with local traditions. The end of the Hellenistic period is generally set at 30 B.C.E., the year of the death of Cleopatra VII—a Greek ruler—and the Roman conquest of her kingdom of Egypt. The Romans had conquered much of what had been Alexander's empire long before this, but many aspects of Hellenistic culture continued to flourish under Roman governance, adapting to Roman ways of life. Thus rather than coming to an abrupt end in one specific year, the Hellenistic world gradually evolved into the Roman.

In many ways, life in the Hellenistic world was not much different from life in Hellenic Greece or from that in any other Iron Age agricultural society: most people continued to be farmers, raising crops and animals for their own needs and for paying rents and taxes to their superiors. Those who lived in cities, however, often ate foods and drank wine that came from far away, did business with people who were quite unlike them, and adopted religious practices and ways of thinking unknown to their parents. Hellenistic cities thus offer striking parallels to those of today. ■

Alexander's Conquests and Their Political Legacy

FOCUS QUESTION
How and why did Alexander the Great create an empire, and what was its political legacy?

Fully intending to carry out Philip's designs to lead the Greeks against the Persians, Alexander (r. 336–323 B.C.E.) proclaimed to the Greek world that the invasion of Persia was to be a mighty act of revenge for Xerxes's invasion of Greece in 480 B.C.E. (see Chapter 3) and more recent Persian interference in Greek affairs. Although he could not foresee this, Alexander's invasion ended up being much more. His campaign swept away the Persian Empire, which had ruled the area for over two hundred years. In its place Alexander established a Macedonian monarchy, and although his rule over these vast territories was never consolidated due to his premature death, he left behind a legacy of political and cultural influence, and a long period of war. Macedonian kings established dynasties, and Greek culture spread in this Hellenistic era.

Military Campaigns

Despite his youth, Alexander was well prepared to invade Persia. Philip had groomed his son to become king and had given him the best education possible, hiring the Athenian philosopher Aristotle to be his tutor. In 334 B.C.E. Alexander led an army of Macedonians and Greeks into Persian territory in Asia Minor. With him went a staff of philosophers to study the people of these lands, poets to write verses praising Alexander's exploits, scientists to map the area and study strange animals and plants, and a historian to write an account of the campaign. Alexander intended not only a military campaign but also an expedition of discovery.

In the next three years Alexander moved east into the Persian Empire, winning major battles at the Granicus River and Issus (Map 4.1). He moved into Syria and took most of the cities of Phoenicia and the eastern coast of the Mediterranean without a fight. His army successfully besieged the cities that did oppose him, including Tyre and Gaza, executing the men of military age afterwards and enslaving the women and children. He then turned south toward Egypt, which had earlier been conquered by the Persians. The Egyptians saw Alexander as a liberator, and he seized it without a battle. After honoring the priestly class, Alexander was proclaimed pharaoh, the legitimate ruler of the country. He founded a new capital, Alexandria, on the coast of the Mediterranean, which would later grow into an enormous city. He next marched to the oasis of Siwah, west of the Nile Valley, to consult the famous oracle of Zeus-Amon, a composite god who combined qualities of the Greek Zeus and the Egyptian Amon (see Chapter 1). No one will ever know what the priest told him, but henceforth Alexander called himself the son of Zeus.

Alexander left Egypt after less than a year and marched into Assyria, where at Gaugamela he defeated the Persian army. After this victory the principal Persian capital of Persepolis fell to him in a bitterly fought battle. There he performed a symbolic act of retribution by burning the royal buildings of King Xerxes, the invader of Greece during the Persian wars 150 years earlier. Alexander continued to pursue Darius, who appears to have been killed by Persian conspirators.

The Persian Empire had fallen and the war of revenge was over, but Alexander had no intention of stopping. Many of his troops had been supplied by Greek city-states that had allied with him; he released these troops from their obligations of military

Chronology

ca. 342–291 B.C.E.	Life of comedy writer Menander
340–270 B.C.E.	Life of Epicurus, on whose ideas Epicureanism was based
335–262 B.C.E.	Life of Zeno, on whose ideas Stoicism was based
334–324 B.C.E.	Alexander the Great's military campaigns
ca. 330–200 B.C.E.	Establishment of new Hellenistic cities
323 B.C.E.	Alexander dies at age thirty-two
323–ca. 300 B.C.E.	War of succession leads to the establishment of Antigonid, Ptolemaic, and Seleucid dynasties
ca. 287–212 B.C.E.	Life of Archimedes
ca. 280 B.C.E.	Founding of the library of Alexandria by the Ptolemies
168 B.C.E.	Roman overthrow of the Antigonid dynasty
166–164 B.C.E.	Revolt of the Maccabees in Judaea
30 B.C.E.	Roman conquest of Egypt; Ptolemaic dynasty ends

service, but then rehired them as mercenaries. Alexander then began his personal odyssey. With his Macedonian soldiers and Greek mercenaries, he set out to conquer more of Asia. He plunged deeper into the East, into lands completely unknown to the Greek world. It took his soldiers four additional years to conquer Bactria (in today's Afghanistan) and the easternmost parts of the now-defunct Persian Empire, but still Alexander was determined to continue his march.

MAP 4.1 Alexander's Conquests, 334–324 B.C.E. This map shows the course of Alexander's invasion of the Persian Empire. More important than the great success of his military campaigns were the founding of new cities and expansion of existing ones by Alexander and the Hellenistic rulers who followed him.

Amphora with Alexander and Darius at the Battle of Issus   Alexander, riding bareback, charges King Darius III, who is standing in a chariot. This detail from a jug was made within a decade after the battle, in a Greek colony in southern Italy, beyond the area of Alexander's conquests, a good indication of how quickly Alexander's fame spread. (Apulian amphora, ca. 330–320 B.C., by Darius Painter, from Ruvo in Magna Graecia, Italy/Museo Archeologico Nazionale, Naples, Italy/De Agostini Picture Library/ Alfredo Dagli Orti/Bridgeman Images)

In 326 B.C.E. Alexander crossed the Indus River and entered India (in the area that is now Pakistan). There, too, he saw hard fighting, and finally at the Hyphasis (HIH-fuh-sihs) River his troops refused to go farther. Alexander was enraged by the mutiny, for he believed he was near the end of the world. Nonetheless, the army stood firm, and Alexander relented. Still eager to explore the limits of the world, Alexander turned south to the Arabian Sea, and he waged a bloody and ruthless war against the people of the area. After reaching the Arabian Sea and turning west, he led his army through the grim Gedrosian Desert (now part of Pakistan and Iran). The army and those who supported the troops with supplies suffered fearfully, and many soldiers died along the way. Nonetheless, in 324 B.C.E. Alexander returned to Susa in the Greek-controlled region of Assyria, and in a mass wedding married the daughter of Darius as well as the daughter of a previous Persian king, a ceremony that symbolized both his conquest and his aim to unite Greek and Persian cultures. His mission was over, but Alexander never returned to his homeland of Macedonia. He died the next year in Babylon from fever, wounds, and excessive drinking. He was only thirty-two, but in just thirteen years he had created an empire that stretched from his homeland of Macedonia to India, gaining the title "the Great" along the way.

Alexander so quickly became a legend that he still seems superhuman. That alone makes a reasoned interpretation of his goals and character very difficult. His contemporaries from the Greek city-states thought he was a bloody-minded tyrant, but later Greek and Roman writers and political leaders admired him and even regarded him as a philosopher interested in the common good. That view influenced many later European and American historians, but this idealistic interpretation has generally been rejected after a more thorough analysis of the sources. The most common view today is that Alexander was a brilliant leader who sought personal glory through conquest and who tolerated no opposition. (See "Evaluating the Evidence 4.1: Arrian on Alexander the Great," at right.)

The Political Legacy

The main question at Alexander's death was whether his vast empire could be held together. Although he fathered a successor, the child was not yet born when Alexander died and was thus too young to assume the duties of kingship. (Later he and his mother, Roxana, were murdered by one of Alexander's generals, who viewed him as a threat.) This meant that Alexander's empire was a prize for the taking. Several of the chief Macedonian generals aspired to become sole ruler, which led to a civil war

Arrian on Alexander the Great

Arrian (ca. 86–160 C.E.) was a Greek military leader and historian who rose high in the ranks of the Roman army. He spent most of his career on the eastern border of the Roman Empire and thus lived in the heart of what had been Alexander's empire four hundred years earlier. He wrote a long history of Alexander's military campaigns based on accounts of Alexander's contemporaries, all of which are now lost, and modeled on the classical histories of war by Thucydides and Herodotus.

8. When [Alexander] arrived at Opis, he collected the Macedonians and announced that he intended to discharge from the army those who were useless for military service either from age or from being maimed in the limbs; and he said he would send them back to their own abodes. . . . [They were] offended by the speech which he delivered, thinking that now they were despised by him. . . . When Alexander heard this . . . , he ordered the most conspicuous of the men who had tried to stir up the multitude to sedition to be arrested. He himself pointed out with his hand to the shield-bearing guards those whom they were to arrest, to the number of thirteen; and he ordered these to be led away to execution. When the rest, stricken with terror, became silent, he mounted the platform again, and spoke as follows: . . .

10. ". . . Most of you have golden crowns, the eternal memorials of your valour and of the honour you receive from me. Whoever has been killed has met with a glorious end and has been honoured with a splendid burial. Brazen statues of most of the slain have been erected at home, and their parents are held in honour, being released from all public service and from taxation. But no one of you has ever been killed in flight under my leadership. And now I was intending to send back those of you who are unfit for service, objects of envy to those at home; but since you all wish to depart, depart all of you! Go back and report at home that your king Alexander, the conqueror of the Persians, Medes, Bactrians, and Sacians; . . . report that when you returned to Susa you deserted him and went away, handing him over to the protection of conquered foreigners. . . . Depart!"

11. Having thus spoken, he leaped down quickly from the platform, and entered the palace, where . . . on the third day he summoned the select Persians within, and among them he distributed the commands of the brigades. . . . But the Macedonians who heard the speech were thoroughly astonished. . . . [T]hey were no longer able to restrain themselves; but running in a body to the palace, they cast their weapons there in front of the gates as signs of supplication to the king. Standing in front of the gates, they shouted, beseeching to be allowed to enter, and saying that they were willing to surrender the men who had been the instigators of the disturbance. . . . When he [Alexander] was informed of this, he came out without delay. . . . After this Alexander offered sacrifice to the gods to whom it was his custom to sacrifice, and gave a public banquet, over which he himself presided, with the Macedonians sitting around him; and next to them the Persians; after whom came the men of the other nations, preferred in honour for their personal rank or for some meritorious action.

EVALUATE THE EVIDENCE

1. According to Arrian, how does Alexander react when his Macedonian troops disagree with his decision about sending some of them home? How do they then respond to his actions?
2. Arrian is generally favorable toward Alexander. In your opinion, does the incident related here show Alexander in a good light? Why might he have done what Arrian describes?

Source: From *The Greek Historians: The Complete and Unabridged Historical Works of Herodotus, Thucydides, Xenophon, Arrian* by Francis R. B. Godolphin, copyright 1942 & renewed 1970 by Random House. Used by permission of Random House, an imprint and division of Random House LLC. Any third party use of this material, outside of this publication, is prohibited. Interested parties must apply directly to Random House LLC for permission.

lasting for decades that tore Alexander's empire apart. By the end of this conflict, the most successful generals had carved out their own smaller monarchies, although these continued to be threatened by internal splits and external attacks.

Alexander's general Ptolemy (ca. 367–ca. 283 B.C.E.) was given authority over Egypt, and after fighting off rivals, established a kingdom and dynasty there, called the Ptolemaic (TAH-luh-MAY-ihk). In 304 B.C.E. he took the title of pharaoh, and

Royal Couple Cameo This Hellenistic cameo, designed to be worn as a necklace, probably portrays King Ptolemy II and his sister Arsinoe II, rulers of the Ptolemaic kingdom of Egypt. During the Hellenistic period portraits of queens became more common because of the increased importance of hereditary monarchies. (Kunthistorisches Museum, Vienna, Austria/ Erich Lessing/Art Resource, NY)

by the end of his long life he had a relatively stable realm to pass on to his son. For these successes he was later called Ptolemy Soter, "Ptolemy the Savior." The Ptolemaic dynasty would rule Egypt for nearly three hundred years, until the death of the last Ptolemaic ruler, Cleopatra VII, in 30 B.C.E. (see Chapter 5). Seleucus (ca. 358–281 B.C.E.), another of Alexander's officers, carved out a large kingdom, the Seleucid (SUH-loo-suhd), that stretched from the coast of Asia Minor to India, for which he was later called Seleucus Nicator, "Seleucus the Victor." He was assassinated in 281 B.C.E. on the order of the ruler of the Ptolemaic kingdom, but his son succeeded him, founding a dynasty that also lasted for centuries, although the kingdom itself shrank as independent states broke off in Pergamum, Bactria, Parthia, and elsewhere. Antigonus I (382–301 B.C.E.), a third general, became king of Macedonia and established the Antigonid (an-TIH-guh-nuhd) dynasty, which lasted until it was overthrown by the Romans in 168 B.C.E. Rome would go on to conquer the Seleucid and Ptolemaic kingdoms as well (see Chapters 5 and 6).

Hellenistic rulers amassed an enormous amount of wealth from their large kingdoms, and royal patronage provided money for the production of literary works and the research and development that allowed discoveries in science and engineering. To encourage obedience, Hellenistic kings often created ruler cults that linked the king's authority with that of the gods, or they adopted ruler cults that already existed, as Alexander did in Egypt. These deified kings were not considered gods as mighty as Zeus or Apollo, and the new ruler cults probably had little religious impact on the people being ruled. The kingdoms never won the deep emotional loyalty that Greeks had once felt for the polis, but the ruler cult was an easily understandable symbol of unity within the kingdom.

Hellenistic kingship was hereditary, which gave women who were members of royal families more power than any woman had in democracies such as Athens, where citizenship was limited to men. Wives and mothers of kings had influence over their husbands and sons, and a few women ruled in their own right when there was no male heir.

Greece itself changed politically during the Hellenistic period. To enhance their joint security, many poleis organized themselves into leagues of city-states, of which the two most extensive were the Aetolian (ee-TOH-lee-uhn) League in western and central Greece and the Achaean (uh-KEE-uhn) League in southern Greece. Until the arrival of the Romans in the eastern Mediterranean in the second century B.C.E. (see Chapter 5), the Hellenistic monarchies and Greek leagues of city-states waged frequent wars with one another that brought no lasting results. In terms of political stability and peace, these forms of government were no improvement on the Greek polis.

Hellenistic A term that literally means "like the Greek," used to describe the period after the death of Alexander the Great, when Greek culture spread.

Building a Hellenized Society

Alexander's most important legacy was clearly not political unity. Instead it was the spread of Greek ideas and traditions across a wide area, a process scholars later called **Hellenization**. To maintain contact with the Greek world as he moved farther eastward, he founded new cities and military colonies and expanded existing cities, settling Greek and Macedonian troops and veterans in them. Besides keeping the road back to Greece open, these settlements helped secure the countryside around them. This practice continued after his death, with more than 250 new cities founded in North Africa, West and Central Asia, and southeastern Europe. These cities and colonies became powerful instruments in the spread of Hellenism and in the blending of Greek and other cultures.

FOCUS QUESTION
How did Greek ideas and traditions spread across the eastern Mediterranean and Near East?

Hellenization The spread of Greek ideas, culture, and traditions to non-Greek groups across a wide area.

Urban Life

In many respects the Hellenistic city resembled a modern city. It was a cultural center with theaters, temples, and libraries. It was a seat of learning, a home of poets, writers, teachers, and artists. City dwellers could find amusement through plays, musical performances, animal fights, and gambling. The Hellenistic city was also an economic center that provided a ready market for grain and produce raised in the surrounding countryside. In short, the Hellenistic city offered cultural and economic opportunities for rich and poor alike.

To the Greeks, civilized life was unthinkable outside of a city, and Hellenistic kings often gave cities all the external trappings of a polis. Each had an assembly of citizens, a council to prepare legislation, and a board of magistrates to conduct political business. Yet, however similar to the Greek polis it appeared, such a city could not engage in diplomatic dealings, make treaties, pursue its own foreign policy, or wage its own wars. The city was required to follow royal orders, and the king often placed his own officials in it to see that his decrees were followed.

A Hellenistic city differed from a Greek polis in other ways as well. The Greek polis had one body of law and one set of customs. In the Hellenistic city Greeks represented an elite class. Natives and non-Greek foreigners who lived in Hellenistic cities usually possessed lesser rights than Greeks and often had their own laws. In some instances this disparity spurred natives to assimilate Greek culture in order to rise politically and socially.

The city of Pergamum in northwestern Anatolia is a good example of an older city that underwent changes in the Hellenistic period. Previously an important strategic site, Pergamum was transformed by its new Greek rulers into a magnificent city complete with all the typical buildings of the polis, including gymnasia, baths, and one of the finest libraries in the entire Hellenistic world. The new rulers erected temples to the traditional Greek deities, but they also built imposing temples to other gods. There was a Jewish population in the city, who may have established a synagogue. Especially in the agora, Greeks and indigenous people met to conduct business and exchange goods and ideas. Greeks felt as though they were at home, and the evolving culture mixed Greek and local elements.

The Bactrian city of Ay Khanoum on the Oxus River, on the border of modern Afghanistan, is a good example of a brand-new city where cultures met. Bactria and Parthia had been part of the Seleucid kingdom, but in the third century B.C.E. their

MAP 4.2 The Hellenistic World, ca. 263 B.C.E.   This map depicts the Hellenistic world after Alexander's death.

governors overthrew the Seleucids and established independent kingdoms in today's Afghanistan and Turkmenistan (Map 4.2). Bactria became an outpost of Hellenism, from which the rulers of China and India learned of sophisticated societies other than their own. It had Greek temples and administration buildings, and on a public square was a long inscription in Greek verse carved in stone, erected by a man who may have been a student of Aristotle and taken from a saying of the Oracle at Delphi:

> In childhood, learn good manners
> In youth, control your passions
> In middle age, practice justice
> In old age, be of good counsel
> In death, have no regrets.[1]

Along with this very public display of Greek ideals, the city also had temples to local deities and artwork that blended Greek and local styles (for an example, see the metal plate at right).

Greeks in Hellenistic Cities

The ruling dynasties of the Hellenistic world were Macedonian, and Macedonians and Greeks filled all the important political, military, and diplomatic positions. Besides building Greek cities, Hellenistic kings offered Greeks land and money as lures to further immigration.

Metal Plate from Ay Khanoum   This spectacular metal plate, made in the
Bactrian city of Ay Khanoum in the second century B.C.E., probably depicts
the goddess Cybele being pulled in a chariot by lions with the sun-god
above. Worship of Cybele, an earth-mother goddess, spread into
Greece from the east, and was then spread by her Greek followers as
they traveled and migrated. (National Museum of Afghanistan, Kabul/Pictures
from History/Bridgeman Images)

The Hellenistic monarchy, unlike the Greek polis,
did not depend solely on its citizens to fulfill its political needs, but instead relied on professionals. Talented
Greek men had the opportunity to rise quickly in the
government bureaucracy. Appointed by the king, these
administrators did not have to stand for election each
year, unlike many officials of Greek poleis. Since they held
their jobs year after year, they had ample time to create new
administrative techniques, and also time to develop ways to profit
personally from their positions.

Greeks also found ready employment in the armies and navies of the Hellenistic
monarchies. Alexander had proved the Greco-Macedonian style of warfare to be
far superior to that of other peoples, and Alexander's successors, themselves experienced officers, realized the importance of trained soldiers. Hellenistic kings were
reluctant to arm the local populations or to allow them to serve in the army, fearing
military rebellions among their conquered subjects. The result was the emergence of
professional armies and navies consisting primarily of Greeks, although drawn from
many areas of Greece and Macedonia, not simply from one polis. Unlike the citizen
hoplites of classical Greece, these men were full-time soldiers. Hellenistic kings paid
them well, often giving them land or leasing it to them as an incentive to remain
loyal.

Greeks were able to dominate other professions as well. Hellenistic kingdoms and
cities recruited Greek writers and artists to create Greek literature, art, and culture.
Greek architects, engineers, and skilled craftsmen found themselves in great demand
to produce the Greek-style buildings commissioned by the Hellenistic monarchs.
Architects and engineers would sometimes design and build whole cities, which they
laid out in checkerboard fashion and filled with typical Greek buildings. An enormous wave of construction took place during the Hellenistic period.

Increased physical and social mobility benefited some women as well as men.
More women learned to read than before, and they engaged in occupations in which
literacy was beneficial, including care of the sick. During the Hellenistic period
women continued to be required to have male guardians to buy, sell, or lease land;
to borrow money; and to represent them in other commercial transactions. (The
requirement of a male guardian was later codified in Roman law and largely maintained in Europe into the nineteenth century.) Yet often such a guardian was present
only to fulfill the letter of the law. The woman was the real agent and handled the
business being transacted.

Because of the opportunities the Hellenistic monarchies offered, many people
moved frequently. These were generally individual decisions, not part of organized

colonization efforts such as those that had been common in Archaic Greece (see Chapter 3). Once a Greek man had left home to take service with, for instance, the army or the bureaucracy of the Ptolemies, he had no incentive beyond his pay and the comforts of life in Egypt to keep him there. If the Seleucid king offered him more money or a promotion, he might well accept it and take his talents to Asia Minor. Thus professional Greek soldiers and administrators were very mobile and were apt to look to their own interests, not their kingdom's. Linguistic changes further facilitated the ease with which people moved. Instead of the different dialects spoken in Greece itself, a new Greek dialect called the *koine* (koy-NAY), which means "common," became the spoken language of traders, the royal court, the bureaucracy, and the army across the Hellenistic world.

As long as Greeks continued to migrate, the kingdoms remained stable and strong. In the process they drew an immense amount of talent from the Greek peninsula. However, the Hellenistic monarchies could not keep recruiting Greeks forever, in spite of their wealth and willingness to spend lavishly. In time the huge surge of immigration slowed greatly.

Greeks and Non-Greeks

Across the Hellenistic world the prevailing institutions and laws became Greek. Everyone, Greek or non-Greek, who wanted to find an official position or compete in business had to learn Greek. Those who did gained an avenue of social mobility, and as early as the third century B.C.E. local people in some Hellenistic cities began to rise in power and prominence. They adopted a Greek name and, if they were male, went to Greek educational institutions or sent their sons there. Hoping to impress the Greek elite, priests in Babylon and Alexandria composed histories of their areas in Greek. Once a man knew Greek, he could move more easily to another area for better opportunities, and perhaps even hide his non-Greek origins. He could also join a military unit and perhaps be deployed far from his place of origin. Thus learning Greek was an avenue of geographic mobility as well.

Cities granted citizenship to Hellenized local people and sometimes to Greek-speaking migrants, although there were fewer political benefits of citizenship than there had been in the classical period, because real power was held by monarchs, not citizens. Even a few women received honorary citizenship in Hellenistic cities because of aid they had provided in times of crisis. Being Greek became to some degree a matter of culture, not bloodlines.

Cultural influences in the other direction occurred less frequently, because they brought fewer advantages. Few Greeks learned a non-Greek language, unless they were required to because of their official position. Greeks did begin to worship local deities, but often these were somewhat Hellenized and their qualities blended with those of an existing Greek god or goddess. Greeks living in Egypt generally cremated their dead while Egyptians continued to mummify them, although by the first century B.C.E. Greeks and Romans sometimes mummified their dead as well, attaching realistic portraits painted on wooden panels to the mummies that have served as important sources about clothing and hairstyles.

Yet the spread of Greek culture was wider than it was deep. Hellenistic kingdoms were never entirely unified in language, customs, and thought. The principal reason for this phenomenon is that Greek culture generally did not extend far beyond the reaches of the cities. Many urban residents adopted the aspects of Hellenism that they found useful, but people in the countryside generally did not embrace it, nor were they encouraged to.

Ptolemaic Egypt provides an excellent example of this situation. The indigenous people were the foundation of the kingdom: they fed it by their labor in the fields and financed its operations with their taxes. Because of this, the Ptolemies tied local people to the land more tightly than they had been before, making it nearly impossible for them to leave their villages. The Ptolemies maintained separate legal systems for Greeks and Egyptians. The bureaucracy of the Ptolemies was relatively efficient, and the indigenous population was viciously and cruelly exploited. Even in times of hardship, the king's taxes came first, although payment might mean starvation. The people's desperation was summed up by one Egyptian, who scrawled the warning, "We are worn out; we will run away."[2] To many Egyptians, revolt or a life of banditry was preferable to working the land under the harsh Ptolemies.

The situation was somewhat different in the booming city of Alexandria, founded by Alexander to be a new seaport, where there had been a small village earlier. Within a century of its founding, it was probably the largest city in the world, with a population numbering in the hundreds of thousands. The ruling elite was primarily Greek, and the Ptolemies tried to keep the Greek and Egyptian populations apart, but this was not always possible. Although the Ptolemies encouraged immigration from Greece, the number of immigrants was relatively low, so intermarriage increased. And the Ptolemies themselves gave privileges to local priests, building temples and sponsoring rituals honoring the local gods. Priestly families became owners of large landed estates and engaged in other sorts of business as well, becoming loyal supporters of the Ptolemaic regime. Even the processions honoring local gods still celebrated Greekness, however, and sometimes became a flash point sparking protests by Egyptians.

In about 280 B.C.E. the Ptolemies founded a library in Alexandria that both glorified Greek culture and sponsored new scholarship. It came to contain hundreds of thousands of papyrus scrolls of Greek writings, including copies of such classic works as the poems of Homer, the histories of Herodotus and Thucydides, and the philosophical works of Plato and Aristotle, as well as newer accounts of scientific discoveries. The Ptolemies sent representatives to Greece to buy books, paid for copies made of any Greek books that were brought to Alexandria, and supported scholars who edited multiple versions of older books into a single authoritative version. The library became one of the foremost intellectual centers of the ancient world, pulling in Greek-speaking writers, scholars, scientists, and thinkers from far away and preserving Greek writings.

Greek culture spread more deeply in the Seleucid kingdom than in Egypt, although this was not because the Seleucids had an organized plan for Hellenizing the local population. The primary problem for the Seleucids was holding on to the territory they had inherited. To do this, they established cities and military colonies throughout the region to nurture a vigorous and large Greek-speaking population and to defend the kingdom from their Persian neighbors. Seleucid military colonies were generally founded near existing villages, thus exposing even rural residents to all aspects of Greek life. Many local people found Greek political and cultural forms attractive and imitated them. In Asia Minor and Syria, for instance, numerous villages and towns developed along Greek lines, and some of them grew into Hellenized cities.

Head of a Young Nubian
This bust, carved in black porphyry rock, was most likely made in Alexandria in the second or first century B.C.E. Hellenistic sculptors depicted the wide range of migrants to the city in stone, bronze, and marble. (From Alexandria, Egypt/Private Collection/ De Agostini Picture Library/Gianni Dagli Orti/Bridgeman Images)

The kings of Bactria and Parthia spread Greek culture even further. Some of these rulers converted to Buddhism, and the Buddhist ruler of the Mauryan Empire in northern India, Ashoka (ca. 269–233 B.C.E.), may have ordered translations of his laws into Greek for the Greek-speaking residents of Bactria and Parthia. In the second century B.C.E., after the collapse of the Mauryan Empire, Bactrian armies conquered part of northern India, establishing several small Indo-Greek states where the mixing of religious and artistic traditions was particularly pronounced.

The Economy of the Hellenistic World

FOCUS QUESTION
What new economic connections were created in the Hellenistic period?

Alexander's conquest of the Persian Empire not only changed the political face of the ancient world and led to a shared urban culture, but also brought the Near East and Egypt fully into the sphere of Greek economics. The Hellenistic period, however, did not see widespread improvements in the way people lived and worked. Cities flourished, but many people who lived in rural areas were actually worse off than they had been before, because of higher levels of rents and taxes. Alexander and his successors did link East and West in a broad commercial network, however. The spread of Greeks throughout the Near East and Egypt created new markets and stimulated trade.

Agriculture and Industry

Much of the revenue for the Hellenistic kingdoms was derived from agricultural products, rents paid by the tenants of royal land, and taxation of land. Trying to improve productivity, the rulers sponsored experiments on seed grain, selecting seeds that seemed the most hardy and productive. Egypt had a strong tradition of central authority dating back to the pharaohs, which the Ptolemies inherited and tightened. They had the power to mobilize local labor into the digging and maintenance of canals and ditches, and they even attempted to decree what crops Egyptian farmers would plant and what animals would be raised. Such centralized planning was difficult to enforce at the local level, however, especially because the officials appointed to do so switched positions frequently and concentrated most on extracting taxes. Thus, despite royal interest in agriculture and a more studied approach to it in the Hellenistic period, there is no evidence that agricultural productivity increased or that practices changed. Technology was applied to military needs, but not to those of food production.

Diodorus Siculus, a Greek historian who apparently visited Ptolemaic Egypt around 60 B.C.E., was surprised that Egyptians could feed all their children instead of resorting to the selective exposure of infants practiced in Greece. He decided that this was because of their less formal child-rearing habits:

> They feed their children in a sort of happy-go-lucky fashion that in its inexpensiveness quite surpasses belief; for they serve them with stews made of any stuff that is ready to hand and cheap, and give them such stalks as the byblos plant [the reeds from which papyrus is made] as can be roasted in the coals and the roots and the stems of marsh plants, either raw or boiled or baked. And since most of the children are reared without shoes or clothing because of the mildness of the climate of the country, the entire expense incurred by the parents of a child until it comes to maturity is not more than twenty drachmas. These are the leading reasons why Egypt has such an extraordinarily large population.[3]

Egyptian parents would probably have given other reasons, such as rents and taxes, for why their children had simple food and no shoes.

As with agriculture, although demand for goods increased during the Hellenistic period, no new techniques of production appear to have developed. Manual labor, not machinery, continued to turn out the raw materials and manufactured goods the Hellenistic world used.

Diodorus gives a picture of this hard labor, commenting about life in the gold mines owned by the kings:

> At the end of Egypt is a region bearing many mines and abundant gold, which is extracted with great pain and expense. . . . For kings of Egypt condemn to the mines criminals and prisoners of war, those who were falsely accused and those who were put into jail because of royal anger, not only them but sometimes also all of their relatives. Rounding them up, they assign them to the gold mines, taking revenge on those who were condemned and through their labors gaining huge revenues. The condemned—and they are very many—all of them are put in chains; and they work persistently and continually, both by day and throughout the night, getting no rest and carefully cut off from escape. For the guards, who are barbarian soldiers and who speak a different language, stand watch over them so that no man can either by conversation or friendly contact corrupt any of them.[4]

Apart from gold and silver, which were used primarily for coins and jewelry, bronze continued to be used for shields. Iron was utilized for weapons and tools.

Pottery remained an important commodity, and most of it was produced locally. The coarse pottery used in the kitchen for plates and cups changed little. Fancier pots and bowls, decorated with a shiny black glaze, came into use during the Hellenistic period. This ware originated in Athens, but potters in other places began to imitate its style, heavily cutting into the Athenian market. In the second century B.C.E. a red-glazed ware, often called Samian, burst on the market and soon dominated it. Pottery was often decorated with patterns and scenes from mythology, legend, and daily life. Potters often portrayed heroic episodes, such as battles from the *Iliad*, or gods, such as Dionysus at sea. Pots journeyed with Greek merchants, armies, and travelers, so these images spread knowledge of Greek religion and stories west as far as Portugal and east as far as Southeast Asia. Pottery thus served as a means of cultural exchange—of ideas as well as goods—among people scattered across huge portions of the globe.

Commerce

Alexander's conquest of the Persian Empire had immediate effects on trade. In the conquered Persian capitals Alexander had found vast sums of gold, silver, and other treasure. This wealth financed the creation of new cities, the building of roads, and the development of harbors. It also provided the thousands who participated in his expeditions with booty, with which they could purchase commodities. Whole new fields lay open to Greek merchants, who eagerly took advantage of the new opportunities. Commerce itself was a leading area where Greeks and non-Greeks met on grounds of common interest.

Trade was facilitated by the coining of money. Most of the great monarchies coined their money according to a uniform system, which meant that much of the money used in Hellenistic kingdoms had the same value. Traders were less in need of money changers than in the days when each major power coined money on a different standard.

Overland trade was conducted by caravan, and the backbone of this caravan trade was the camel — a shaggy, ill-tempered, but durable animal ideally suited to the harsh climate of the caravan routes. Luxury goods that were light, rare, and expensive traveled over the caravan routes to Alexandria or to the harbors of Phoenicia and Syria, from which they were shipped to Greece, Italy, and Spain. In time these luxury items became more commonplace, in part as the result of an increased volume of trade. Due to the prosperity of the period, more people could afford to buy gold, silver, ivory, precious stones, spices, and a host of other easily transportable goods. Perhaps the most prominent good in terms of volume was silk, and the trade in silk later gave the major east-west route its name: the Great Silk Road. In return the Greeks and Macedonians sent east manufactured goods, especially metal weapons, cloth, wine, and olive oil. Although these caravan routes can trace their origins to earlier times, they became far more prominent in the Hellenistic period. Business customs and languages of trade developed and became standardized, so that merchants from different nationalities could communicate in a way understandable to all of them.

The durability and economic importance of the caravan routes are amply demonstrated by the fact that the death of Alexander, the ensuing wars of his successors, and later regional conflicts had little effect on trade. Numerous mercantile cities grew up along these routes, and commercial contacts brought people from far-flung regions together, even if sometimes indirectly. The merchants and the caravan cities were links in a chain that reached from the Mediterranean Sea to India and beyond to China, along which ideas as well as goods were passed.

More economically important than the trade in luxury goods were commercial dealings in essential commodities like raw materials and grain and such industrial products as pottery. The Hellenistic monarchies usually raised enough grain for their own needs as well as a surplus for export. This trade in grain was essential for the cities of Greece and the Aegean, many of which could not grow enough. Fortunately for them, abundant wheat supplies were available nearby in Egypt and in the area north of the Black Sea (see Map 4.2).

Most trade in bulk commodities was seaborne, and the Hellenistic merchant ship was the workhorse of the day. The merchant ship had a broad beam and relied on sails for propulsion. It was far more seaworthy than the contemporary warship, the trireme (see Chapter 3), which was long, narrow, and built for speed. A small crew of experienced sailors could handle the merchant vessel easily. Maritime trade provided opportunities for workers in other industries and trades: sailors, shipbuilders, dockworkers, accountants, teamsters, and pirates. Piracy was always a factor in the Hellenistic world, so ships' crews had to be ready to defend their cargoes as well as transport them.

Cities in Greece often paid for their grain by exporting olive oil and wine. When agriculture and oil production developed in Syria, Greek products began to encounter competition from the Seleucid monarchy. Later in the Hellenistic period, Greek oil and wine, shipped in mass-produced pottery jugs called amphoras, found a lucrative market in Italy and throughout the Mediterranean.

Another significant commodity was fish, which for export was salted, pickled, or dried. This trade was especially important because fish provided poor people with protein, an essential element of their diet. Salt, too, was often imported, and there was a very small trade in salted meat, which was a luxury item. Far more important was the trade in honey, dried fruit, nuts, and vegetables. Of raw materials, wood was high in demand, but little trade occurred in manufactured goods.

Slaves were a staple of Hellenistic trade, traveling in all directions on both land and sea routes. A few lists of slaves owned by a single individual have survived, and these indicate that slaves in one area often came from far away, and from many different regions. Ancient authors cautioned against having too many slaves from one area together, as this might encourage them to revolt. War provided prisoners for the slave market; to a lesser extent, so did kidnapping and capture by pirates, although the origins of most slaves are unknown. Both old Greek states and new Hellenistic kingdoms were ready slave markets, and throughout the Mediterranean world slaves were almost always in demand. Slaves were to be found in the cities and temples of the Hellenistic world; in the shops, fields, armies, and mines; and in the homes of wealthier people. Their price varied depending on their age, sex, health, and skill level, and also—as with any commodity—on market conditions. Large-scale warfare increased the number of slaves available, so the price went down; during periods of relative peace, fewer people were enslaved through conquest, so the price went up.

Religion and Philosophy in the Hellenistic World

The mixing of peoples in the Hellenistic era influenced religion and philosophy. The Hellenistic kings built temples to the old Olympian gods and promoted rituals and ceremonies like those in earlier Greek cities, but new deities also gained prominence. More people turned to mystery religions, which blended Greek and non-Greek elements. Others turned to practical philosophies that provided advice on how to live a good life.

FOCUS QUESTION
How did religion and philosophy shape everyday life in the Hellenistic world?

Religion and Magic

When Hellenistic kings founded cities, they also built temples, staffed by priests and supported by taxes, for the Olympian gods of Greece. The transplanted religions, like those in Greece itself, sponsored literary, musical, and athletic contests, which were staged in beautiful surroundings among impressive new Greek-style buildings. These festivities offered bright and lively entertainment, both intellectual and physical. They fostered Greek culture and traditional sports and were attractive to socially aspiring individuals who adopted Greek culture.

Along with the traditional Olympian gods, Greeks and non-Greeks in the Hellenistic world also honored and worshipped deities that had not been important in the Hellenic period or that were a blend of imported Greek and indigenous gods and goddesses. Tyche (TIGH-kee), for example, was a new deity, the goddess and personification of luck, fate, chance, and fortune. Temples to her were built in major cities of the eastern Mediterranean, including Antioch and Alexandria, and her image was depicted on coins and bas-reliefs. Contemporaries commented that when no other cause could be found for an event, Tyche was responsible. Like the Olympians, she was unpredictable and sometimes malevolent.

Tyche could be blamed for bad things that happened, but Hellenistic people did not simply give in to fate. Instead they honored Tyche with public rituals and

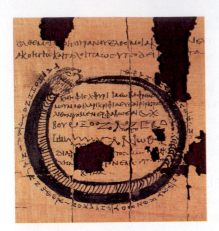

Hellenistic Magical Text   This text, written in Greek and Egyptian on papyrus, presents a magical incantation surrounded by a lion-headed snake. Both Hellenic and Hellenistic Greeks sought to know the future through various means of divination and to control the future through rituals and formulas that called on spirits and gods. (© British Library Board, PAP.121 fr 3)

more-private ceremonies, and they also turned to professionals who offered spells for various purposes. We generally make a distinction between religion and magic, but for Greeks there was not a clear line. Thus these people would write spells using both ordinary Greek words and special "magical" language known only to the gods, often instructing those who purchased them to carry out specific actions to accompany their words. Thousands of such spells survive, many of which are curse tables, intended to bring bad luck to a political, business, or athletic rival; or binding spells, meant to force a person to do something against his or her will. These binding spells included hundreds intended to make another person love the petitioner. They often invoke a large number of deities to assist the petitioner, reflecting the mixture of gods that was common in Hellenistic society. (See "Evaluating the Evidence 4.2: A Hellenistic Spell of Attraction," at right.)

Hellenistic kings generally did not suppress indigenous religious practices. Some kings limited the power of existing priesthoods, but they also subsidized them with public money. Priests continued to carry out the rituals that they always had, perhaps now adding the name "Zeus" to that of the local deity or composing their hymns in Greek.

Some Hellenistic kings intentionally sponsored new deities that mixed Egyptian and Greek elements. When Ptolemy I Soter established the Ptolemaic dynasty in Egypt, he thought that a new god was needed who would appeal to both Greeks and Egyptians. Working together, an Egyptian priest and a Greek priest combined elements of the Egyptian god Osiris (god of the afterlife) with aspects of the Greek gods Zeus, Hades (god of the underworld), and Asclepius (god of medicine) to create a new god, Serapis. Like Osiris, Serapis came to be regarded as the judge of souls, who rewarded virtuous and righteous people with eternal life. Like Asclepius, he was also a god of healing. Ptolemy I's successors made Serapis the protector and patron of Alexandria and built a huge temple in the god's honor in the city. His worship spread as intentional government policy, and he was eventually adopted by Romans as well, who blended him with their own chief god, Jupiter.

Increasingly, many people were attracted to mystery religions, so called because at the center of each was an inexplicable event that brought union with a god and was not to be divulged to anyone not initiated into them. Early mystery religions in the Hellenic period, such as those of Eleusis, were linked to specific gods in particular places, which meant that people who wished to become members had to travel (see Chapter 3). But new mystery religions, like Hellenistic culture in general, were not tied to a particular place; instead they were spread throughout the Hellenistic world. People did not have to undertake long and expensive pilgrimages just to become members. In that sense the mystery religions came to the people, for temples of the new deities sprang up wherever Greeks lived.

Mystery religions incorporated aspects of both Greek and non-Greek religions and claimed to save their adherents from the worst that fate could do. Most taught that by the rites of initiation, in which the secrets of the religion were shared, devotees became united with a deity who had also died and risen from the dead. The sacrifice of the god and his victory over death saved the devotee

A Hellenistic Spell of Attraction

Spells that have survived from the Hellenistic world include hundreds that are intended to make another person love the petitioner. Most of these are heterosexual, but a few involve men seeking men or women seeking women. This spell, inscribed on a lead tablet, is directed toward Anubis, the Egyptian dog-headed god of the underworld, and mentions a number of Egyptian and Greek deities associated with the underworld. Through this spell a woman named Sophia seeks to attract a woman named Gorgonia, although the spell itself is formulaic and was most likely written by a professional.

Fundament of the gloomy darkness, jagged-toothed dog, covered with coiling snakes, turning three heads, traveler in the recesses of the underworld, come, spirit-driver, with the Erinyes [or Furies, Greek goddesses of vengeance, often shown with snake hair and whips], savage with their stinging whips; holy serpents, maenads [frenzied female followers of Dionysus], frightful maidens, come to my wroth incantations. Before I persuade by force this one and you, render him immediately a fire-breathing daemon. Listen and do everything quickly, in no way opposing me in the performance of this action; for you are the governors of the earth. . . . By means of this corpse-daemon inflame the heart, the liver [which people also saw as a location of emotions], the spirit of Gorgonia, whom Nilogenia bore, with love and affection for Sophia, whom Isara bore. Constrain Gorgonia, whom Nilogenia bore, to cast herself

*Public baths were common in Hellenistic and Roman society as places where people went for recreation and relaxation as well as cleansing, much like today's spas. Here Sophia wants Gorgonia to meet her in a public bath, and Anubis wants to change himself into a female bath attendant so he can cast his spell on her more easily.

into the bath-house for the sake of Sophia, whom Isara bore; and you, become a bath-woman.* Burn, set on fire, inflame her soul, heart, liver, spirit with love for Sophia, whom Isara bore. Drive Gorgonia, whom Nilogenia bore, drive her, torment her body night and day, force her to rush forth from every place and every house, loving Sophia, whom Isara bore, she, surrendered like a slave, giving herself and all her possessions to her, because this is the will and command of the great god. . . . Blessed lord of the immortals, holding the scepters of Tartaros and of terrible, fearful Styx (?) and of life-robbing Lethe, the hair of Kerberos trembles in fear of you, you crack the loud whips of the Erinyes; the couch of Persephone delights you, when you go to the longed bed, whether you be the immortal Serapis, whom the universe fears, whether you be Osiris, star of the land of Egypt; your messenger is the all-wise boy; yours is Anubis, the pious herald of the dead. Come hither, fulfill my wishes, because I summon you by these secret symbols.

EVALUATE THE EVIDENCE

1. In the spell, what feelings does Sophia direct Anubis to create in Gorgonia, and what behavior is the expected result of these feelings?
2. What aspects of this spell appear distinctively Hellenistic? What aspects fit with modern understandings of sexual attraction?

from eternal death. Similarly, mystery religions demanded a period of preparation in which the converts strove to become pure and holy, that is, to live by the religion's precepts. Once aspirants had prepared themselves, they went through the initiation, usually a ritual of great emotional intensity symbolizing the entry into a new life.

Among the mystery religions the Egyptian cult of Isis spread widely. In Egyptian mythology Isis brought her husband Osiris back to life (see Chapter 1), and during the Hellenistic era this power came to be understood by her followers as extending to them as well. She promised to save any mortal who came to her, and her priests asserted that she had bestowed on humanity the gift of civilization and founded law and literature. Isis was understood to be a devoted mother as well as a devoted wife, and she became the goddess of marriage, conception, and childbirth. She became the most important goddess of the Hellenistic world, where Serapis was often regarded as her consort instead of Osiris. Devotion to Isis, and to many other mystery religions, later spread to the Romans as well as to the Greeks and non-Greeks who lived in Hellenistic cities.

Hellenism and the Jews

Jews in Hellenistic cities were generally treated the same as any other non-Greek group. At first they were seen as resident aliens. As they grew more numerous, they received permission to form a political corporation, a *politeuma* (pah-lih-TOO-mah), which gave them a great deal of autonomy. The Jewish politeuma, like the rest of the Hellenistic city, was expected to obey the king's commands, but there was virtually no royal interference with the Jewish religion. The Seleucid king Antiochus III (ca. 242–187 B.C.E.), for instance, recognized that most Jews were loyal subjects, and in his efforts to solidify his empire he endorsed their religious customs and ensured their autonomy.

Antiochus IV Epiphanes (r. 175–ca. 164 B.C.E.) broke with this pattern. He expanded the Seleucid kingdom and nearly conquered Egypt, but while he was there a revolt broke out in Judaea, led by Jews who opposed the Hellenized Jewish leader he had designated for them. Antiochus attacked Jerusalem, killing many, and restored his leader. According to Hebrew Scripture, he then banned Jewish practices and worship, ordered copies of the Torah burned, and set up altars to the Greek gods in Jewish temples. This sparked a widespread Jewish revolt that began in 166 B.C.E., called the Revolt of the Maccabees after the name of one of its leaders. Using guerrilla tactics, the Maccabees fought Syrian troops who were fighting under Seleucid commanders, retook Jerusalem, and set up a semi-independent state in 164 B.C.E. This state lasted for about a century, until it was conquered by the Romans. (The rededication of the temple in Jerusalem after the Maccabee victory is celebrated in the Jewish holiday of Hanukkah.)

Isis and Horus   In this small statue from Egypt, the goddess Isis is shown suckling her son Horus. Worship of Isis spread throughout the Hellenistic world; her followers believed that Isis offered them life after death, just as she had brought Horus's father, Osiris, back to life. (Musée du Louvre, Paris, France/Peter Willi/The Bridgeman Art Library)

Jews living in Hellenistic cities often embraced many aspects of Hellenism. The Revolt of the Maccabees is seen by some historians, in fact, as primarily a dispute between Hellenized Jews and those who wanted to retain traditional practices. So many Jews learned Greek, especially in Alexandria, that the Hebrew Bible was translated into Greek and services in the synagogue there came to be conducted in Greek. Jews often took Greek names, used Greek political forms, adopted Greek practice by forming their own trade associations, and put inscriptions on graves as the Greeks did. Some Jews were given the right to become full citizens of Hellenistic cities, although relatively few appear to have exercised that right. Citizenship would have allowed them to vote in the assembly and serve as magistrates, but it would also have obliged them to worship the gods of the city—a practice few Jews chose to follow.

Philosophy and the People

Philosophy during the Hellenic period was the exclusive province of the wealthy and educated, for only they had leisure enough to pursue philosophical studies (see Chapter 3). During the Hellenistic period, however, although philosophy was still directed toward the educated elite, it came to touch the lives of more men and women than ever before. There were several reasons for this development. First, much of Hellenistic life, especially in the new cities of the East, seemed unstable and without venerable traditions. Greeks were far more mobile than they had ever been before, but their very mobility left them feeling uprooted. Second, traditional religions had declined and there was a growing belief that one could do relatively little to change one's fate. One could honor Tyche, the goddess of fortune, through rituals in the hope that she would be kind, but to protect against the worst that Tyche could do, many Greeks also looked to philosophy. Philosophers themselves became much more numerous, and several new schools of philosophical thought caught the minds and hearts of many contemporary Greeks and some non-Greeks.

One of these was **Epicureanism** (eh-pih-kyou-REE-uh-nih-zuhm), a practical philosophy of serenity in an often-tumultuous world. Epicurus (eh-pih-KYOUR-uhs) (340–270 B.C.E.) was influenced by the atomic theory developed by the Pre-Socratic philosopher Democritus (see Chapter 3). Like Democritus, he thought that the world was made up of small pieces of matter that move in space, which determine the events of the world. Although he did not deny the existence of the gods, Epicurus taught that they had no effect on human life. Epicurus used observation and logic to study the world, and also to examine the human condition. He decided that the principal goods of human life were contentment and pleasure, which he defined as the absence of pain, fear, and suffering. By encouraging the pursuit of pleasure, he was not advocating drunken revels or sexual excess, which he thought caused pain, but moderation in food, clothing, and shelter.

> **Epicureanism** A system of philosophy based on the teachings of Epicurus, who viewed a life of contentment, free from fear and suffering, as the greatest good.

The writings of Epicurus survive only in fragments, but the third-century-C.E. biographer Diogenes Laertes quotes several of his letters. It is impossible to know if these are actual letters or not, but they express sentiments that fit with Epicurus's ideas, including these from a letter written at the end of his life, when he apparently suffered from kidney stones:

> I have written this letter to you on a happy day to me, which is also the last day of my life. For I have been attacked by a painful inability to urinate, and also dysentery, so violent that nothing can be added to the violence of my sufferings. But the cheerfulness of my mind, which comes from the recollection of all my philosophical contemplation, counterbalances all these afflictions. And I beg you to take care of the children of Metrodorus, in a manner worthy of the devotion shown by the young man to me, and to philosophy.[5]

Epicurus also taught that individuals could most easily attain peace and serenity by ignoring the outside world and looking into their personal feelings and reactions. This ideal was one to which anyone could aspire, no matter what their social standing. Epicurus is reported to have allowed slaves and even women to attend his school, a sharp contrast with the earlier philosopher Plato. Epicureanism taught its followers to ignore politics and issues, for politics led to tumult, which would disturb the soul. Although the Epicureans thought that the state originated through a social contract among individuals, they did not care about the political structure of the state. They were content to live under a democracy, oligarchy, monarchy, or any other form of government, and they never speculated about the ideal state.

Boy with a Goose   In the Hellenistic culture that developed across a huge area after Alexander the Great's conquests, wealthy urban residents wanted art that showed real people rather than gods. This statue of a little boy wrestling a goose, originally carved about 200 B.C.E., no doubt found an eager buyer. (Glyptothek, Staatliche Antikensammlung, Munich, Germany/photo © Vanni Archive/Art Resource, NY)

Zeno (335–262 B.C.E.), a philosopher from Cyprus, advanced a different concept of human beings and the universe. Zeno first came to Athens to form his own school, the Stoa, named after the covered walkways where he preferred to teach, and his philosophy, **Stoicism** (STOH-uh-sih-zuhm), in turn, came to be named for his school. Zeno and his followers considered nature an expression of divine will; in their view people could be happy only when living in accordance with nature. They stressed the unity of humans and the universe, stating that all people were obliged to help one another.

Unlike the Epicureans, the Stoics taught that people should participate in politics and worldly affairs. Yet this idea never led to the belief that individuals should try to change the order of things. The Stoics used the image of an actor in a play: the Stoic plays an assigned part but never tries to change the play. Like the Epicureans, they were indifferent to specific political forms. They believed that people should do their duty to the state in which they found themselves. To the Stoics, the important question was not whether they achieved anything, but whether they lived virtuous lives. The patient self-control and fortitude that the Stoics advocated made this a popular philosophy among the Romans later, and gave rise to the modern adjective *stoic* to convey these virtues.

The Stoics' most significant practical achievement was the creation of the concept of **natural law**. They concluded that because all people were kindred, partook of divine reason, and were in harmony with the universe, one law governed them all. This law was a part of the natural order of life, not something created by individual states or rulers. Thus natural law was an abstract matter of ethics, and applicable everywhere, not something that applied to everyday political or social life.

Individualistic and individualized themes emerge in Hellenistic art and literature as well as in philosophy. Sculptors looked to the works of the classical period such as the reliefs and statuary on the Athenian Acropolis for their models in terms of composition, but then created works that show powerful emotions and straining muscles. In contrast to the classical preference for the perfect human form, the artists and the people who bought their works wanted art that showed real people, including those suffering from trauma, disease, and the physical problems that came with aging. Hellenistic art was more naturalistic than Hellenic art—portraying the poor, old, and ugly as well as the young and beautiful.

As had Athens in the classical period, Hellenistic cities offered theater performances to their residents, paid for by the government. People tended to prefer revivals of the tragedies of Aeschylus, Sophocles, and Euripides (see Chapter 3) over newly written tragic works, but in comedy they wanted new material. This was provided by Menander (ca. 342–291 B.C.E.), whose more than one hundred comedies poked fun at current philosophies and social trends, including love, luck, money, and marriage.

Stoicism A philosophy, based on the ideas of Zeno, that people could be happy only when living in accordance with nature and accepting whatever happened.

natural law A Stoic concept that a single law that was part of the natural order of life governed all people.

Menander's comedies tended to be less political than those of Aristophanes, but they still commented on the ruler cults developed by Hellenistic kings, the dangers of the new professionalized mercenary armies to older values, and the conspicuous consumption of the newly rich.

Hellenistic Science and Medicine

In the scholarly realm, Hellenistic thinkers made advances in mathematics, astronomy, and mechanical design. Physicians used observation and dissection to better understand the way the human body works and to develop treatments for disease. Many of these developments occurred in Alexandria, where the Ptolemies did much to make the city an intellectual, cultural, and scientific center.

FOCUS QUESTION
How did science and medicine serve the needs of Hellenistic society?

Science

The main advances in Hellenistic science came in astronomy, geography, and mechanics. The most notable of the Hellenistic astronomers was Aristarchus (a-ruh-STAHR-kuhs) of Samos (ca. 310–230 B.C.E.). Aristarchus concluded that the sun is far larger than the earth and that the stars are enormously distant from the earth. He argued against the commonsense observation, which Aristotle had supported, that the earth was the center of the universe. Instead, Aristarchus developed the heliocentric theory—that the earth and planets revolve around the sun. His theory was discussed for several centuries, but was later forgotten when another astronomer working in Alexandria, Claudius Ptolemy (ca. 90–ca. 168 C.E.)—probably no relation to the ruling Ptolemies, as the name was a common one—returned to an earth-centered universe. Aristarchus's heliocentric theory was resurrected in the sixteenth century C.E. by the brilliant Polish astronomer Nicolaus Copernicus.

In geometry Hellenistic thinkers discovered little that was new, but Euclid (YOU-kluhd) (ca. 300 B.C.E.), a mathematician who lived in Alexandria, compiled a valuable textbook of existing knowledge. His *Elements of Geometry* rapidly became the standard introduction to geometry. Generations of students from the Hellenistic period to the twentieth century learned the essentials of geometry from it.

The greatest thinker of the Hellenistic period was Archimedes (ca. 287–212 B.C.E.), a native of Syracuse who was interested in nearly everything. (See "Individuals in Society: Archimedes, Scientist and Inventor," page 114.) A clever inventor, he devised new artillery for military purposes. In peacetime he perfected the water screw to draw water from a lower to a higher level. He also invented the compound pulley to lift heavy weights. His chief interest, however, lay in pure mathematics. He founded the science of hydrostatics (the study of fluids at rest) and discovered the principle that the volume of a solid floating in a liquid is equal to the volume of the liquid displaced by the solid.

Archimedes was willing to share his work with others, among them Eratosthenes (ehr-uh-TAHS-thuh-neez) (285–ca. 204 B.C.E.). Like Archimedes, he was a man of almost universal interests. From his native Cyrene in North Africa, Eratosthenes traveled to Athens, where he studied philosophy and mathematics. He refused to join any of the philosophical schools, for he was interested in too many things to follow any particular dogma. Around 245 B.C.E. King Ptolemy III invited Eratosthenes to

INDIVIDUALS IN SOCIETY
Archimedes, Scientist and Inventor

Archimedes (ca. 287–212 B.C.E.) was born in the Greek city of Syracuse in Sicily, an intellectual center where he pursued scientific interests. He was the most original thinker of his time and a practical inventor. In his book *On Plane Equilibriums* he dealt for the first time with the basic principles of mathematics, including the principle of the lever. He once said that if he were given a lever and a suitable place to stand, he could move the world. He also demonstrated how easily his compound pulley could move huge weights with little effort:

> A three-masted merchant ship of the royal fleet had been hauled on land by hard work and many hands. Archimedes put aboard her many men and the usual freight. He sat far away from her; and without haste, but gently working a compound pulley with his hand, he drew her towards him smoothly and without faltering, just as though she were running on the surface.*

He perfected what became known as the Archimedean screw, a pump to bring subterranean water up to irrigate fields, which he had observed in Egypt and which later came into wider use. He worked on issues involved with solid geometry, and in his treatise *On Floating Bodies* he founded the science of hydrostatics. He concluded that an object will float if it weighs less than the water it displaces, and that whenever a solid floats in a liquid, the volume of the solid equals the volume of the liquid displaced. The way he made his discovery has become famous:

> When he was devoting his attention to this problem, he happened to go to a public bath. When he climbed down into the bathtub there, he noticed that water in the tub equal to the bulk of his body flowed out. Thus, when he observed this method of solving the problem, he did not wait. Instead, moved with joy, he sprang out of the tub, and rushing home naked he

kept indicating in a loud voice that he had indeed discovered what he was seeking. For while running he was shouting repeatedly in Greek, "Eureka, eureka" ("I have found it, I have found it").†

War between Rome and Syracuse interrupted Archimedes's scientific life. In 213 B.C.E. during the Second Punic War, the Romans besieged the city. Hiero, its king and Archimedes's friend, asked the scientist for help in repulsing Roman attacks. Archimedes began to design and build remarkable devices that served as artillery. One weapon shot missiles to break up infantry attacks, and others threw huge masses of stones that fell on the enemy. For use against Roman warships, he is said to have designed a machine with beams from which large claws dropped onto the hulls of warships, hoisted them into the air, and dropped them back into the sea. Later Greek writers reported that he destroyed Roman ships with a series of polished mirrors that focused sunlight and caused the ships to catch fire. Modern experiments re-creating Archimedes's weapons have found that the claw might have been workable, but the mirrors probably were not, as they required a ship to remain stationary for the fire to ignite. It is not certain whether his war machines were actually effective, but later people recounted tales that the Romans became so fearful that whenever they saw a bit of rope or a stick of timber projecting over the wall, they shouted, "There it is — Archimedes is trying some engine on us," and fled. After many months the Roman siege was successful, however, and Archimedes was killed by a Roman soldier.

QUESTIONS FOR ANALYSIS

1. How did Archimedes combine theoretical mathematics and practical issues in his work?
2. What applications do you see in the world around you for the devices Archimedes improved or invented, such as the lever, the pulley, and artillery?

*Plutarch, *Life of Marcellus*. †Vitruvius, *On Architecture*, 9 Preface, 10.

Several of Archimedes's treatises were found on a palimpsest, a manuscript that had been scraped and washed so that another text could be written over it, thus reusing the expensive parchment. Reusing parchment was a common practice in the Middle Ages, but the original text can sometimes be reconstructed. Using digital processing with several types of light and X-rays to study this thirteenth-century-C.E. prayer book, scientists were slowly able to decipher the texts by Archimedes that were underneath, including one that had been completely lost. (Image by the Rochester Institute of Technology. Copyright resides with the owner of the Archimedes Palimpset)

Alexandria and made him the head of the library there. Eratosthenes continued his mathematical work and by letter struck up a friendship with Archimedes.

Eratosthenes used mathematics to further the geographical studies for which he is most famous. He concluded that the earth was a spherical globe and calculated the circumference of the earth geometrically, estimating it as about 24,675 miles. He was not wrong by much: the earth is actually 24,860 miles in circumference. He drew a map of the earth and discussed the shapes and sizes of land and ocean and the irregularities of the earth's surface. His idea that the earth was divided into large landmasses influenced other geographers and later shaped ordinary people's understanding of the world as well. Using geographical information gained by Alexander the Great's scientists, Eratosthenes declared that to get to India, a ship could sail around Africa or even sail directly westward, an idea that would not be tested until the end of the fifteenth century.

Other Greek geographers also turned their attention southward to Africa. During this period the people of the Mediterranean learned of the climate and customs of Ethiopia and gleaned some information about sub-Saharan Africa from Greek sailors and merchants who had traveled there. (See "Evaluating the Evidence 4.3: The Periplus of the Erythraean Sea," page 116.) Geographers incorporated these travelers' reports into their more theoretical works.

As the new artillery devised by Archimedes indicates, Hellenistic science was used for purposes of war as well as peace. Theories of mechanics were used to build machines that revolutionized warfare. Fully realizing the practical possibilities of the first effective artillery in Western history, Philip of Macedonia had introduced the machines to the broader world in the middle of the fourth century B.C.E. The catapult became the first and most widely used artillery piece, shooting ever-larger projectiles. Generals soon realized that they could also hurl burning bundles over the walls to start fires in the city. As the Assyrians had earlier, engineers built siege towers, large wooden structures that served as artillery platforms, and put them on wheels so that soldiers could roll them up to a town's walls. Once there, archers stationed on top of the siege towers swept the enemy's ramparts with arrows, while other soldiers manning catapults added missile fire. As soon as the walls were cleared, soldiers from the siege towers swept over the enemy's ramparts and into the city. To augment the siege towers, generals added battering rams that consisted of long, stout shafts housed in reinforced shells. Inside the shell the crew pushed the ram up to the wall and then heaved the shaft against the wall. Rams proved even more effective than catapults in bringing down large portions of walls.

Diodorus provided a description of these machines in his discussion of Philip's attack on the city of Perinthos in 340 B.C.E.:

> Philip launched a siege of Perinthos, advancing engines to the city and assaulting the walls in relays day after day. He built towers 120 feet tall that rose far above the towers of Perinthos. From their superior height he kept wearing down the besieged. He mined under the wall and also rocked it with battering-rams until he threw down a large section of it. The Perinthians fought stoutly and threw up a second wall. Philip rained down great destruction through his many and various arrow-shooting catapults. . . . Philip continually battered the walls with his rams and made breaches in them. With his arrow-firing catapults clearing the ramparts of defenders, he sent his soldiers in through the breaches in tight formation. He attacked with scaling-ladders the parts of the walls that had been cleared.[6]

The Periplus of the Erythraean Sea

A periplus was a manuscript that described a shoreline, along with ports and the distance between them; it was similar to the sailing logs used until the advent of modern navigation technology, or to the driving directions found through map Web sites today. The earliest peripli that survive (in later copies) date from the fifth century B.C.E. This particular periplus, written by a Greek-speaking merchant of Alexandria in the first century C.E., describes the coasts of the Red Sea, eastern Africa, and India, all of which the author appears to have visited personally.

1. Of the designated ports on the Erythraean Sea, and the market-towns around it, the first is the Egyptian port of Mussel Harbor. To those sailing down from that place, on the right hand, after eighteen hundred stadia [about two hundred miles], there is Berenice. The harbors of both are at the boundary of Egypt, and are bays opening from the Erythraean Sea.

2. On the right-hand coast next below Berenice is the country of the Berbers [or Barbaroi, that is, people who do not speak Greek]. . . . [A]nd behind them, further inland, in the country toward the west, there lies a city called Meroe. . . .

6. There are imported into these places, undressed cloth made in Egypt for the Berbers; robes from Arsinoe; cloaks of poor quality dyed in colors; double-fringed linen mantles; many articles of flint glass, and others of murrhine [a substance used to make glass], made in Diospolis; and brass, which is used for ornament and in cut pieces instead of coin; sheets of soft copper, used for cooking-utensils and cut up for bracelets and anklets for the women; iron, which is made into spears used against the elephants and other wild beasts, and in their wars. Besides these, small axes are imported, and adzes and swords; copper drinking-cups, round and large; a little coin for those coming to the market; wine of Laodicea [southern Turkey] and Italy, not much; olive oil, not much; for the king, gold and silver plate made after the fashion of the country, and for clothing, military cloaks, and thin coats of skin, of no great value. Likewise from the district of Ariaca [in India] across this sea, there are imported Indian iron, and steel, and Indian cotton cloth; the broad cloth called *monaché* and that called *sagmatogênê*, and girdles [wide belts], and coats of skin and mallow-colored cloth, and a few muslins, and colored lac [lacquer ware]. There are exported from these places ivory, and tortoise-shell and rhinoceros-horn. . . .

8. After Avalites there is another market-town, better than this, called Malao, distant a sail of about eight hundred stadia. The anchorage is an open roadstead, sheltered by a spit running out from the east. Here the natives are more peaceable. There are imported into this place the things already mentioned, and many tunics, cloaks from Arsinoe, dressed and dyed; drinking-cups, sheets of soft copper in small quantity, iron, and gold and silver coin, not much. There are exported from these places myrrh, a little frankincense (that known as far-side), the harder cinnamon, *duaca*, Indian copal and *macir*, which are imported into Arabia; and slaves, but rarely.

EVALUATE THE EVIDENCE

1. What types of merchandise are being traded along the east coast of Africa, and for what purposes?
2. What does this document suggest about consumers in the Hellenistic world, including those in Africa?

Source: Wilfred H. Schoff, trans., *The Periplus of the Erythraean Sea: Travel and Trade in the Indian Ocean by a Merchant of the First Century* (New York: Longmans, Green, and Co., 1912), pp. 22, 24–25.

For the Perinthians this grim story had a happy ending when their allies arrived to lift the siege, but many cities were successfully besieged and conquered with the new machines. Over time, Hellenistic generals built larger, more complex, and more effective machines. The earliest catapults could shoot only large arrows and small stones. By the time Alexander the Great besieged Tyre in 332 B.C.E., his catapults could throw stones big enough to knock down city walls.

If these new engines made waging war more efficient, they also added to the misery of the people, as war often directly involved the populations of cities. As it had in Periclean Athens (see Chapter 3), war often contributed to the spread of disease, and battlefields gave surgeons and physicians plenty of opportunities to test their ideas about how the human body would best heal.

Medicine

Doctors as well as scientists combined observation with theory during the Hellenistic period. They studied the writings attributed to Hippocrates (see Chapter 3) and generally accepted his theory of the four humors, but they also approached the study of medicine in a systematic, scientific fashion. The physician Herophilus (ca. 335–280 B.C.E.), for example, who lived in Alexandria, was the first to accurately describe the nervous system, and he differentiated between nerves and blood vessels and between motor and sensory nerves. Herophilus also closely studied the brain, which he considered the center of intelligence, and discerned the cerebrum and cerebellum. His younger contemporary Erasistratus (ca. 304–250 B.C.E.) also conducted research on the brain and nervous system and improved on Herophilus's work. To learn more about human anatomy, Herophilus and Erasistratus dissected human cadavers while their students watched. Human dissection was seen as unacceptable in most parts of the Hellenistic world, so they were probably the only scientists in antiquity to dissect human bodies, although animal dissection became very common in the Roman period. The story later spread that they had dissected living criminals, provided for them by the Ptolemaic kings of Egypt, but this may have just been a legend. They wrote works on various medical and anatomical topics, but only the titles and a few fragments quoted by later authors survive.

Because Herophilus and Erasistratus followed the teachings of Hippocrates, later writers on medicine labeled them "Dogmatists" or the "Dogmatic school," from the Greek word *dogma*, or philosophical idea. Along with their hands-on study of the human body, the Dogmatists also speculated about the nature of disease and argued that there were sometimes hidden causes for illness. Opposing them was an "Empiric school" begun by a student of Herophilus; these doctors held observation and experiment to be the only way to advance medical knowledge and viewed the search for hidden causes as useless. Later Greek and Roman physicians sometimes identified themselves with one or the other of these ways of thinking, but the labels were also sometimes simply used as insults to dismiss the ideas of a rival.

Whether undertaken by Dogmatists or Empiricists, medical study did not lead to effective cures for the infectious diseases that were the leading cause of death for most people, however, and people used a variety of ways to attempt to combat illness. Medicines prescribed by physicians or prepared at home often included natural products blended with materials understood to work magically. One treatment for fever, for example, was the liver of a cat killed when the moon was waning and preserved in salt. People also invoked Asclepius, the god of medicine, in healing rituals, or focused on other deities who were understood to have power over specific illnesses. They paid specialists to devise spells that would cure them or prevent them from becoming ill in the first place (see page 109). Women in childbirth gathered their female friends and relatives around them, and in larger cities could also hire experienced midwives who knew how to decrease pain and assist in the birthing process if something went wrong. People in the Hellenistic world may have thought that fate determined what would happen, but they also actively sought to make their lives longer and healthier.

LOOKING BACK LOOKING AHEAD

The conquests of Philip and Alexander broadened Greek and Macedonian horizons, but probably not in ways that they had intended. The empire that they created lasted only briefly, but the Hellenistic culture that developed afterwards took Greeks even beyond the borders of Alexander's huge empire as conquerors, merchants, artists, and sailors.

The Hellenistic world was largely conquered by the Romans, but in cultural terms the conquest was reversed: The Romans derived their alphabet from the Greek alphabet, though they changed the letters somewhat. Roman statuary was modeled on Greek and was often, in fact, made by Greek sculptors, who found ready customers among wealthy Romans. Furthermore, the major Roman gods and goddesses were largely the same as the Greek ones, though they had different names. Although the Romans did not seem to have been particularly interested in the speculative philosophy of Socrates and Plato, they were drawn to the more practical philosophies of the Epicureans and Stoics. And like the Hellenistic Greeks, many Romans turned from traditional religions to mystery religions that offered secret knowledge and promised eternal life. Among these was Christianity, a new religion that grew in the Roman Empire and whose most important early advocate was Paul of Tarsus, a well-educated Hellenized Jew who wrote in Greek. Significant aspects of Greek culture thus lasted long after the Hellenistic monarchies and even the Roman Empire were gone, shaping all subsequent societies in the Mediterranean and Near East.

Make Connections

Think about the larger developments and continuities within and across chapters.

1. How was Greek society in the Hellenistic era similar to that of the earlier Hellenic era examined in Chapter 3? How was it different? What would you judge to be more significant, the continuities or the changes?

2. Cities had existed in the Tigris and Euphrates Valleys and the Near East long before Alexander's conquests. What would residents of Sumer (Chapter 1), Babylon (Chapters 1 and 2), and Pergamum find unusual about one another's cities? What would seem familiar?

3. How would you compare religion in Egypt in the Old and New Kingdoms (Chapter 1) with religion in Hellenistic Egypt? What provides the best explanation for the differences you have identified?

4 REVIEW & EXPLORE

Review the Main Ideas

Answer the focus questions from each section of the chapter.

◆ How and why did Alexander the Great create an empire, and what was its political legacy? (p. 94)

◆ How did Greek ideas and traditions spread across the eastern Mediterranean and Near East? (p. 99)

◆ What new economic connections were created in the Hellenistic period? (p. 104)

◆ How did religion and philosophy shape everyday life in the Hellenistic world? (p. 107)

◆ How did science and medicine serve the needs of Hellenistic society? (p. 113)

Identify Key Terms

Identify and explain the significance of each item below.

Hellenistic (p. 98)
Hellenization (p. 99)
Epicureanism (p. 111)
Stoicism (p. 112)
natural law (p. 112)

NOTES

1. Ahmad Hasan Dani et al., *History of Civilizations of Central Asia* (Paris: UNESCO, 1992), p. 107.

2. Quoted in W. W. Tarn and G. T. Griffith, *Hellenistic Civilizations*, 3d ed. (Cleveland and New York: Meridian Books, 1961), p. 199.

3. All quotations from Diodorus are reprinted by permission of the publishers and the Trustees of the Loeb Classical Library from Diodorus of Sicily, *Biblioteca historica* 1.80–36, Loeb Classical Library Volume 279, with an English translation by C. H. Oldfather, pp. 275, 277.

Cambridge, Mass.: Harvard University Press. First published 1933. Loeb Classical Library® is a registered trademark of the President and Fellows of Harvard College.

4. Ibid., 3.12.1–3.

5. Diogenes Laertius, *Lives of Eminent Philosophers* 10.22, trans. C. D. Yonge, at Attalus (http://www.attalus.org/old/diogenes10a.html#22).

6. Diodorus 3.12.2–3.

Rome's Rise to Power
How did the Romans become the dominant power in Italy?

The Roman Republic
What were the key institutions of the Roman Republic?

Roman Expansion
How did the Romans take control of the Mediterranean world?

Roman Society
How did expansion affect Roman society and culture?

The Late Republic
What led to the fall of the Roman Republic?

Life in Etruscan Society

A fresco from an Etruscan tomb, painted about 470 B.C.E., shows dancers in an idyllic setting with olive trees, while other walls depict musicians and a banquet. The scenes are based on those on Greek pottery, evidence of the connections between the Etruscans and their Greek neighbors to the south. This tomb is one among many thousands in the Necropolis of Monterozzi in Tarquinia, just north of Rome, now a UNESCO World Heritage site.
(Wall painting from the Monterozzi Tomb, 6th–4th century B.C.E./Pictures from History/Bridgeman Images)

5

The Rise of Rome

ca. 1000–27 B.C.E.

The Hellenistic monarchies that arose after Alexander's conquests extended eastward and southward from Greece. The Greek colonies that had been established in southern Italy were not part of these monarchies, but culturally they became part of the Hellenistic world. To the north of the Greek city-states in the Italian peninsula, other people built their own societies. Among these were the people who later became the Romans, who settled on hills along the Tiber River in central Italy. Beginning in the sixth century B.C.E., the Romans gradually took over more and more territory in Italy through conquest and annexation. At about the same time, a group of aristocrats revolted against the kings ruling Rome and established a republican government in which the main institution of power was a political assembly, the Senate. Under the direction of the Senate, the Romans continued their political and military expansion, first to all of Italy, then throughout the western Mediterranean basin, and then to areas in the east that had been part of Alexander's empire. As they did, they learned about and incorporated Greek art, literature, philosophy, and religion, but the wars of conquest also led to serious problems that the Senate proved unable to handle.

Roman history is generally divided into three periods: the monarchical period, traditionally dated from 753 B.C.E. to 509 B.C.E., in which the city of Rome was ruled by kings; the republic, traditionally dated from 509 B.C.E. to 27 B.C.E., in which it was ruled by the Senate and expanded its power first to all of Italy and then beyond; and the empire, from 27 B.C.E. to 476 C.E., in which the vast Roman territories were ruled by an emperor. This chapter covers the first two of these periods. The Roman Empire will be discussed in Chapters 6 and 7. ■

Rome's Rise to Power

FOCUS QUESTION

How did the Romans become the dominant power in Italy?

The colonies established by Greek poleis (city-states) in the Hellenic era (see Chapter 3) included a number along the coast of southern Italy and Sicily, an area already populated by a variety of different groups that farmed, fished, and traded. So many Greek settlers came to this area and the Greek settlements there became so wealthy that it later became known as Magna Graecia—Greater Greece. Although Alexander the Great (see Chapter 4) created an empire that stretched from his homeland of Macedonia to India, his conquests did not reach as far as southern Italy and Sicily. Thus the Greek colonies there remained politically independent. They became part of the Hellenistic cultural world, however, and they transmitted much of that culture to people who lived farther north in the Italian peninsula. These included the Etruscans, who built the first cities north of Magna Graecia, and then the Romans, who eventually came to dominate the peninsula.

The Geography of Italy

The boot-shaped peninsula of Italy, with the island of Sicily at its toe, occupies the center of the Mediterranean basin (Map 5.1). To the south lies Africa; the distance between southwestern Sicily and the northern African coast is at one point only about a hundred miles. Italy and Sicily literally divide the Mediterranean into two basins and form the focal point between the two halves.

Like Greece and other Mediterranean lands, Italy enjoys a largely pleasant climate. The winters are rainy, but the summer months are dry. Because of the climate, the rivers of Italy usually carry little water during the summer, and some go entirely dry. Most of Italy's other rivers are unsuitable for regular large-scale shipping and never became major thoroughfares for commerce and communications. Yet the rivers nourished a bountiful agriculture that could produce enough crops for a growing population.

Geography encouraged Italy to look to the Mediterranean. In the north Italy is protected by the Alps, which form a natural barrier. The Alps retarded but did not prevent peoples from entering Italy by this route. From the north the Apennine Mountains run southward for the entire length of the Italian boot, cutting off access to the Adriatic Sea for those to their west. This barrier induced Italy to look west to Spain and Carthage rather than east to Greece, but it did not carve up the land in a way that would prevent the development of political unity.

In their southward course the Apennines leave two broad and fertile plains to their west: Latium and Campania. These plains attracted settlers and invaders from the time that peoples began to move into Italy. Among these peoples were those who would found Rome on the Tiber River in Latium.

This site enjoyed several advantages. The Tiber provided Rome with a constant source of water. Located at an easy crossing point on the Tiber, Rome thus stood astride the main avenue of communications between northern and southern Italy. Positioned amid seven hills, Rome was defensible and safe from the floods of the Tiber. It was also close to the sea through the port of Ostia. Thus Rome was in an excellent position to develop the resources of Latium and maintain contact with the rest of Italy.

Chronology

ca. 1000 B.C.E.	Earliest settlements in the area that became the city of Rome
753 B.C.E.	Traditional founding of the city of Rome
509 B.C.E.	Traditional date of establishment of the Roman Republic
451–449 B.C.E.	Laws of the Twelve Tables written and issued
387 B.C.E.	Gauls sack Rome
367 B.C.E.	Licinian-Sextian laws passed
ca. 265 B.C.E.	Romans control most of Italy
264–201; 149–146 B.C.E.	Punic Wars
133–121 B.C.E.	Reforms of the Gracchi
107–31 B.C.E.	Turmoil in the late republic
44 B.C.E.	Julius Caesar assassinated
31 B.C.E.	Octavian defeats Antony and Cleopatra at the Battle of Actium
27 B.C.E.	Senate issues decrees giving Octavian great power

MAP 5.1 Roman Italy and the City of Rome, ca. 218 B.C.E. As Rome expanded, it built roads linking major cities and offered various degrees of citizenship to the territories it conquered or with which it made alliances. The territories outlined in green that are separate from the Italian peninsula were added by 218 B.C.E., largely as a result of the Punic Wars.

123

The Etruscans, ca. 500 B.C.E.

Legend:
- Etruscan homeland
- Areas of expansion
- Etruscan city

ALPS · Corsica · Rome · Sardinia · Adriatic Sea · Tyrrhenian Sea · Sicily

The Etruscans

The culture that is now called Etruscan developed in north-central Italy about 800 B.C.E. Recent studies of DNA evidence have indicated that the Etruscans most likely originated in Turkey or elsewhere in the Near East, but migrated to Italy by at least 3000 B.C.E., and developed their culture there. The Etruscans spoke a language that was very different from Greek and Latin, although they adopted the Greek alphabet to write it. We know they wrote letters, records, and literary works, but once the Romans conquered them, knowledge of how to read and write Etruscan died out. Also, the writings themselves largely disappeared because many were written on linen books that did not survive; what remain are inscriptions on stone or engravings in metal. Modern scholars have learned to read Etruscan to some degree, but most of what we know about their civilization comes from archaeological evidence and from the writings of other peoples who lived around them at the same time.

The Etruscans established permanent settlements that evolved into cities resembling the Greek city-states, and they thereby built a rich cultural life, full of art and music, that became the foundation of civilization in much of Italy. The Etruscans spread their influence over the surrounding countryside, which they farmed and mined for its rich mineral resources. They traded natural products, especially iron, with their Greek neighbors to the south and with other peoples throughout the Mediterranean, including the Phoenicians, in exchange for a variety of goods.

Etruscan cities appear to have been organized in leagues, and beginning about 750 B.C.E. the Etruscans expanded southward into central Italy through military actions on land and sea and through the establishment of colony cities. Written records of battles all come from the side of the Etruscans' opponents, but objects found in graves indicate that military values were important in their society, as wealthy men were buried with bronze armor and shields and iron weapons. In the process of expansion they encountered a small collection of villages subsequently called Rome.

The Founding of Rome

Archaeological evidence indicates that the ancestors of the Romans began to settle on the hills east of the Tiber during the early Iron Age, around 1000 B.C.E. to 800 B.C.E. Archaeological sources provide the most important information about this earliest period of Roman history, but later Romans told a number of stories about the founding of Rome. These mix legend and history, but they illustrate the traditional ethics, morals, and ideals of Rome.

The Romans' foundation myths were told in a number of different versions. In the most common of these, Romulus and Remus founded the city of Rome, an event later Roman authors dated precisely to 753 B.C.E. These twin brothers were the sons of the war god Mars, and their mother, Rhea Silvia, was a descendant of Aeneas, a brave and pious Trojan who left Troy after it was destroyed by the Greeks in the Trojan War (see Chapter 3). The brothers, who were left to die by a jealous uncle, were raised

Etruscan Figure of a Mother and Son This bronze Etruscan sculpture from the sixth to fourth century B.C.E. shows a mother and child. The influence of Hellenistic Greek art is evident in the musculature of the little boy and the drape of the woman's clothing. The holders at the sides may have held candles. (Candelabra-shaped cymatium, bronze, 6th–4th century B.C.E./Museo Civico Archeologico, Bologna, Italy/ De Agostini Picture Library/akg-images)

by a female wolf. When they were grown, they decided to build a city in the hills that became part of Rome, but they quarreled over which hill should be the site of the city. Romulus chose one hill and started to build a wall around it, and Remus chose another. After Remus jumped mockingly over Romulus's wall, Romulus killed him and named the city after himself. He also established a council of advisers later called the Senate, which means "council of old men."

Romulus and his mostly male followers expanded their power over the neighboring Sabine peoples, in part by abducting and marrying their women. The Sabine women then arranged a peace by throwing themselves between their brothers and their husbands, convincing them that killing kin would make the men cursed. The Romans, favored by the gods, continued their rise to power. Despite its tales of murder and kidnapping, this founding myth ascribes positive traits to the Romans: they are descended from gods and heroes, can thrive in wild and tough settings, will defend their boundaries at all costs, and mix with other peoples rather than simply conquering them. Also, the story portrays women who were ancestors of Rome as virtuous and brave.

Later Roman historians continued the story by describing a series of kings after Romulus—the traditional number is seven—each elected by the Senate. According to tradition, the last three kings were Etruscan, and another tale about female virtue was told to explain why the Etruscan kings were overthrown. In this story, of which there are several versions, the son of King Tarquin, the Etruscan king who ruled Rome, raped Lucretia, a virtuous Roman wife, in her own home. As related by the historian Livy (59 B.C.E.–17 C.E.) in his massive history of the Roman Republic, Lucretia summoned her husband and father to the house, told them what had happened, and demanded they seek vengeance:

> One after another they tried to comfort her. They told her she was helpless, and therefore innocent; that he alone was guilty. It was the mind, they said, that sinned, not the body: without intention there could never be guilt. "What is due to him," Lucretia said, "is for you to decide. As for me I am innocent of fault, but I will take my punishment. Never shall Lucretia provide a precedent for unchaste women to escape what they deserve." With these words she drew a knife from under her robe, drove it into her heart, and fell forward, dead.[1]

Her father and husband and the other Roman nobles, continued Livy, swore on the bloody knife to avenge Lucretia's death by throwing out the Etruscan kings, and they did. Whether any of this story was true can never be known, but Romans generally accepted it as history, and dated the expulsion of the Etruscan kings to 509 B.C.E. They thus saw this year as marking the end of the monarchical period and the dawn of the republic, which had come about because of a wronged woman and her demands.

Most historians today view the idea that Etruscan kings ruled the city of Rome as legendary, but they stress the influence of the Etruscans on Rome. The Etruscans transformed Rome from a relatively large town to a real city with walls, temples, a drainage system, and other urban structures. The Romans adopted the Etruscan alphabet, which the Etruscans themselves had adopted from the Greeks. Romans adopted the use of a bundle of rods tied together with an ax emerging from the center, which symbolized the Etruscan kings' power. This ceremonial object was called the fasces (FAS-eez) and was carried first by Etruscan officials and then by Romans.

(In the twentieth century Mussolini would use the fasces as the symbol of his political party, the Fascists, and it is also used by many other governmental groups, including some in the United States.) Even the toga, the white woolen robe worn by citizens, came from the Etruscans, as did gladiatorial combat honoring the dead. In engineering and architecture the Romans adopted some design elements and the basic plan of their temples, along with paved roads, from the Etruscans.

In this early period the city of Rome does appear to have been ruled by kings, as were most territories in the ancient world. A hereditary aristocracy also developed—again, an almost universal phenomenon—which advised the kings and may have played a role in choosing them. And sometime in the sixth century B.C.E. a group of aristocrats revolted against these kings and established a government in which the main institution of power would be in the **Senate**, an assembly of aristocrats, rather than a single monarch. Executive power was in the hands of Senate leaders called **consuls**, but there were always two of them and they were elected for one-year terms only, not for life. Rome thereby became a republic, not a monarchy. Thus at the core of the myths was a bit of history.

Under kings and then the Senate, the villages along the Tiber gradually grew into a single city, whose residents enjoyed contacts with the larger Mediterranean world. Temples and public buildings began to grace Rome, and the Forum (see Map 5.1), a large plaza between two of Rome's hills, became a public meeting place similar to the Greek agora (see Chapter 3). The Capitoline Hill became the city's religious center when the temple of Jupiter Optimus Maximus (Jupiter the Best and Greatest) was built there. In addition, trade in metalwork became common, and wealthier Romans began to import fine Greek vases and other luxuries.

The Roman Conquest of Italy

In the years following the establishment of the republic, the Romans fought numerous wars with their neighbors on the Italian peninsula. The Roman army was made up primarily of citizens of Rome conscripted through an annual levy; any man aged sixteen to forty-six was eligible for the military draft and was then assigned to a legion for a particular campaign, with a maximum of six years. Those who could afford it bought their own weapons and armor. War also involved diplomacy, at which the Romans became masters. At an early date they learned the value of alliances, which became a distinguishing feature of Roman expansion in Italy. Alliances with the towns around them in Latium provided a large population that could be tapped for military needs; men from these towns were organized into troops called auxiliaries who fought with the legions.

These wars of the early republic later became the source of legends that continued to express Roman values. One of these involved the aristocrat Cincinnatus, who had been expelled from the Senate and forced to pay a huge fine because of the actions of his son. As the story goes, in 458 B.C.E. he was plowing the fields of his small farm when the Senate asked him to return and assume the office of dictator. This position, which had been created very early in the republic, was one in which one man would be given ultimate powers for six months in order to handle a serious crisis such as an invasion or rebellion. (Like the word *tyrant* in ancient Greece, *dictator* did not have its current negative meaning in the early Roman Republic.) At this point the armies of the Aequi, a neighboring group, had surrounded Roman forces commanded by both consuls, and Rome was in imminent danger of catastrophe. Cincinnatus, wiping his sweat, listened to the appeal of his countrymen and led the Roman infantry in victory over the Aequi. He then returned to his farm, becoming a legend among later Romans as a man of

Senate The assembly that was the main institution of power in the Roman Republic, originally composed only of aristocrats.

consuls Primary executives in the Roman Republic, elected for one-year terms, who commanded the army in battle, administered state business, and supervised financial affairs.

simplicity who put his civic duty to Rome before any consideration of personal interest or wealth, and who willingly gave up power for the greater good. The Roman Senate actually chose many more men as dictator in the centuries after Cincinnatus, and not until the first century B.C.E. would any try to abuse this position. No subsequent dictator achieved the legendary reputation of Cincinnatus, however. For George Washington and other leaders of the American War of Independence, he became the symbolic model of a leader who had performed selfless service but then stepped down from power. When in 1783 they decided to form a patriotic society, they named it after him: the Society of the Cincinnati (from which the Ohio city takes its name).

In 387 B.C.E. the Romans suffered a major setback when the Celts—or Gauls, as the Romans called them—invaded the Italian peninsula from the north, destroyed a Roman army, and sacked the city of Rome. (For more on the Gauls, see Chapter 7.) More intent on loot than on conquest, the Gauls agreed to abandon Rome in return for a thousand pounds of gold. As the story was later told, when the Gauls provided their own scale, the Romans howled in indignation. The Gallic chieftain Brennus then threw his sword on the scale, exclaiming "*Vae victis*" (woe to the conquered). These words, though legendary, were used by later Romans as an explanation for why they would not surrender, and the city of Rome was not sacked again until 410 C.E.

The Romans rebuilt their city and recouped their losses. They brought Latium and their Latin allies fully under their control and conquered Etruria (see Map 5.1). Starting in 343 B.C.E. they turned south and grappled with the Samnites in a series of bitter wars for the possession of Campania. The Samnites were a formidable enemy and inflicted serious losses on the Romans, and in response the Romans reorganized their army to create the mobile legion, a flexible unit of soldiers capable of fighting anywhere. The Romans won out in the end and continued their expansion southward.

In 280 B.C.E., alarmed by Roman expansion, the Greek city of Tarentum in southern Italy called for help from Pyrrhus (PIHR-uhs), king of Epirus in western Greece. A relative of Alexander the Great and an excellent general, Pyrrhus won two furious battles but suffered heavy casualties—thus the phrase "Pyrrhic victory" is still used today to describe a victory involving severe losses. According to the later historian Plutarch, Roman bravery and tenacity led Pyrrhus to comment: "If we win one more battle with the Romans, we'll be completely washed up."[2]

The Romans and the Carthaginians had made a series of treaties to help one another (see page 132), and the Carthaginians attacked Sicily, drawing the armies of Pyrrhus away from Italy for a while and relieving pressure on the Romans. The Romans threw new legions against Pyrrhus's army, which in the end left southern Italy. The Romans made formal alliances with many of the cities of Magna Graecia and then turned north again. Their superior military institutions, organization, and large supply of soldiers allowed them to conquer or take into their sphere of influence most of Italy by about 265 B.C.E.

As they expanded their territory, the Romans spread their religious traditions throughout Italy, blending them with local beliefs and practices. Religion for the Romans was largely a matter of honoring the state and the family. The main goal of religion was to secure the peace of the gods, what was termed *pax deorum*, and to harness divine power for public and private enterprises. Religious rituals were an important way of expressing common values, which for Romans meant those evident in their foundation myths: bravery, morality, seriousness, family, and home. The sacred fire at the shrine of the goddess Vesta in the city of Rome, for example, was

The Temple of Hercules Victor

This round temple, dating from the second century B.C.E., is the oldest surviving marble building in Rome and was imported from Greece. It once contained a statue of the mythical hero Hercules and was dedicated to him at this spot, where legend told he killed a monster who had stolen some cattle.

EVALUATE THE EVIDENCE

1. Looking at the picture of the temples on the Acropolis in Athens on page 80, what stylistic similarities do you see between those buildings and this temple?

2. How do those similarities, and the fact that this temple was dedicated to Hercules, provide evidence for Roman adoption of Greek religion and culture?

(© Justin Kase z12z/Alamy Stock Photo)

attended by the vestal virgins, young women chosen from aristocratic families. Vesta was the goddess of hearth and home, whose protection was regarded as essential to Roman well-being. The vestal virgins were important figures at major public rituals, though at several times of military loss and political crisis they were also charged with negligence of duty or unchastity, another link between female honor and the Roman state. Along with the great gods, the Romans believed in spirits who inhabited fields, forests, crossroads, and even the home itself. These were to be honored with rituals and gifts so that they would remain favorable instead of becoming hostile.

Victorious generals made sure to honor the gods of people they had conquered and by doing so transformed them into gods they could also call on for assistance in their future campaigns. Greek deities and mythical heroes were absorbed into the Roman pantheon. Their names were changed to Roman names, so that Zeus (the king of the gods), for example, became Jupiter, and Herakles (the semidivine hero) became Hercules, but their personal qualities and powers were largely the same. (See "Evaluating the Evidence 5.1: The Temple of Hercules Victor," above.)

Once they had conquered an area, the Romans built roads, many of which continued to be used for centuries and can still be seen today. These roads provided an easy route for communication between the capital and outlying areas, allowed for the quick movement of armies, and offered an efficient means of trade. They were the tangible sinews of unity, and many were marvels of engineering, as were the stone bridges the Romans built over Italy's many rivers.

In politics the Romans shared full Roman citizenship with many of their oldest allies, particularly the inhabitants of the cities of Latium. In other instances they granted citizenship without the franchise, that is, without the right to vote or hold Roman office. These allies were subject to Roman taxes and calls for military service, but ran their own local affairs. The extension of Roman citizenship strengthened the state and increased its population and wealth, although limitations on this extension would eventually become a source of conflict (see page 130).

The Roman Republic

Along with citizenship, the republican government was another important institution of Roman political life. Unlike the Greeks, the Romans rarely speculated on the ideal state or on political forms. Instead they created institutions, magistracies, and legal concepts to deal with practical problems and govern their ever-expanding state. These institutions were not static, but changed over time to allow a broader access to power and address new problems.

FOCUS QUESTION
What were the key institutions of the Roman Republic?

The Roman State

The Romans summed up their political existence in a single phrase: *senatus populusque Romanus*, "the Senate and the Roman people," which they abbreviated "SPQR." This sentiment reflects the republican ideal of shared government rather than power concentrated in a monarchy. It stands for the beliefs, customs, and laws of the republic—the unwritten constitution that evolved over two centuries to meet the demands of the governed. SPQR became a shorthand way of saying "Rome," just as U.S.A. says "the United States of America."

In the early republic social divisions determined the shape of politics. Political power was in the hands of a hereditary aristocracy—the **patricians**, whose privileged legal status was determined by their birth as members of certain families. Patrician men dominated the affairs of state, provided military leadership in time of war, and monopolized knowledge of law and legal procedure. The common people of Rome, the **plebeians** (plih-BEE-uhns), were free citizens with a voice in politics, but they had few of the patricians' political and social advantages. While some plebeian merchants increased their wealth in the course of Roman expansion and came to rival the patricians economically, most plebeians were poor artisans, small farmers, and landless urban dwellers.

patricians The Roman hereditary aristocracy, who held most of the political power in the republic.

plebeians The common people of Rome, who were free but had few of the patricians' advantages.

The Romans created several assemblies through which men elected high officials and passed legislation. The earliest was the Centuriate Assembly, in which citizens were organized into groups called centuries based loosely around their status in the military. Each citizen was assigned to a century depending on his status and amount of wealth, and the patricians possessed the majority of centuries. When an election was ordered, each century met separately and voted as a bloc, which meant that the patricians could easily outvote the plebeians. In 471 B.C.E. plebeian men won the right to meet in an assembly of their own, the *concilium plebis*, and to pass ordinances.

The highest officials of the republic were the two consuls, who were elected for one-year terms by the Centuriate Assembly. At a later time Romans believed that the consulship had initially been open only to patrician men, although surviving lists of consuls actually show that a few early consuls were plebeians. The consuls commanded the army in battle, administered state business, presided over the Senate and assemblies, and supervised financial affairs. In effect, they ran the state. The consuls appointed quaestors (KWEH-stuhrs) to assist them in their duties, and in 421 B.C.E. the quaestorship became an elective office open to plebeian men. The quaestors took charge of the public treasury and investigated crimes, reporting their findings to the consuls.

In 366 B.C.E. the Romans created a new office, that of praetor (PREE-tuhr). When the consuls were away from Rome, the praetors could act in their place; they could also command armies, be governors in the provinces, interpret law, and administer justice. Other officials included the powerful censors, who had many responsibilities, the most important being supervision of public morals, the power to determine who lawfully could hold public office and sit in the Senate, the registration of citizens, the taking of a census, and the leasing of public contracts.

The most important institution of the republic was the Senate, a political assembly that by tradition was established by Romulus and in reality most likely originated in the monarchical period as a council of the heads of powerful families who advised the king. By the time written records begin for Roman history, the Senate was already in existence. During the republic the Senate grew to several hundred members, all of whom had previously been elected to one of the high positions, which automatically conferred Senate membership. Because the Senate sat year after year with the same members, while high officials changed annually, it provided stability and continuity. It passed formal decrees that were technically "advice" to the magistrates, who were not bound to obey them but usually did. It directed the magistrates on the conduct of war and had the power over the expenditure of public money. In times of emergency it could name a dictator. Technically the Senate could not pass binding legislation during the republican period. Its decisions had to be put to the Centuriate Assembly for a vote before they could become law, but patricians dominated both groups and generally agreed on legislative matters.

Within the city of Rome itself the Senate's powers were limited by laws and traditions, but as Rome expanded, the Senate had greater authority in the outlying territories. The Romans divided the lands that they conquered into provinces, and the Senate named the governors for these, most of whom were former consuls or praetors. Another responsibility of the Senate was to handle relations between Rome and other powers.

A lasting achievement of the Romans was their development of law. Roman civil law, the *ius civile*, consisted of statutes, customs, and forms of procedure that regulated the lives of citizens. As the Romans came into more frequent contact with foreigners, the consuls and praetors applied a broader *ius gentium*, the "law of the peoples," to such matters as peace treaties, the treatment of prisoners of war, and the exchange of diplomats. In the ius gentium all sides were to be treated the same regardless of their nationality. By the late republic Roman jurists had widened this principle still further into the concept of *ius naturale*, "natural law," based in part on Stoic beliefs (see Chapter 4). Natural law, according to these thinkers, is made up of rules that govern human behavior that come from applying reason rather than customs or traditions, and so apply to all societies. In reality, Roman officials generally interpreted the law to the advantage of Rome, of course, at least to the extent that the strength of Roman armies allowed them to enforce it. But Roman law came to be seen as one of the most important contributions Rome made to the development of Western civilization.

Social Conflict in Rome

Struggle of the Orders
A conflict in which the plebeians sought political representation and safeguards against patrician domination.

Inequality between plebeians and patricians led to a conflict known as the **Struggle of the Orders**. In this conflict the plebeians sought to increase their power by taking advantage of the fact that Rome's survival depended on its army, which needed plebeians to fill the ranks of the infantry. According to tradition, in 494 B.C.E. the plebeians literally walked out of Rome and refused to serve in the army. Their general strike worked, and the patricians grudgingly made important concessions. They allowed the plebeians to elect their own officials, the **tribunes**, who presided over the concilium plebis, could bring plebeian grievances to the Senate for resolution, and could also veto the decisions of the consuls. Thus, as in Archaic age Greece (see Chapter 3), political rights were broadened because of military needs for foot soldiers.

The law itself was the plebeians' primary target. Only the patricians knew what the law was, and only they could argue cases in court. All too often they used the law for their own benefit. The plebeians wanted the law codified and published, but many patricians, including Cincinnatus and his son, vigorously opposed attempts by plebeians to gain legal rights. After much struggle, in 449 B.C.E. the patricians surrendered their legal monopoly and codified and published the Laws of the Twelve Tables, so called because they were inscribed on twelve bronze plaques. The Laws of the Twelve Tables covered many legal issues, including property ownership, guardianship, inheritance, procedure for trials, and punishments for various crimes. The penalty set for debt was strict:

> Unless they make a settlement [with their creditor], debtors shall be held in bonds for sixty days. During that time they shall be brought before the praetor's court in the meeting place on three successive market days, and the amount for which they are judged liable shall be announced; on the third market day they shall suffer capital punishment or be delivered for sale abroad, across the Tiber.[3]

Debtors no doubt made every effort to settle with their creditors. The patricians also made legal procedures public so that plebeians could argue cases in court. Later, in 445 B.C.E., the patricians passed a law, the *lex Canuleia*, that for the first time allowed patricians and plebeians to marry one another.

Licinius and Sextius were plebeian tribunes in the fourth century B.C.E. who mounted a sweeping assault on patrician privilege. Wealthy plebeians wanted the opportunity to provide political leadership for the state. After a ten-year battle the Licinian-Sextian laws passed in 367 B.C.E., giving wealthy plebeians access to all the offices of Rome, including the right to hold one of the two consulships. Once plebeians could hold the consulship, they could also sit in the Senate and advise on policy. They also gained such cosmetic privileges as wearing the purple-bordered toga, the symbol of aristocracy. Though decisive, this victory did not end the Struggle of the Orders. That happened only in 287 B.C.E. with the passage of the *lex Hortensia*, which gave the resolutions of the concilium plebis, the plebeian assembly, the force of law for patricians and plebeians alike.

The long Struggle of the Orders had resulted in an expansion of power to wealthy plebeians, but once certain plebeian families could hold the consulship and become members of the Senate, they became as guarded of their privileges and as uninterested in the problems of the average plebeian as the patricians had formerly been. Theoretically, all men could aspire to the highest political offices. In reality, political power had been expanded only slightly and still resided largely in a group of wealthy families, some of whom happened to be plebeian. Access to the highest political offices was still difficult for any plebeian, who often had to get the support of patrician families if he wanted a political career.

tribunes Plebeian-elected officials; tribunes brought plebeian grievances to the Senate for resolution and protected plebeians from the arbitrary conduct of patrician magistrates.

patron-client system An informal system of patronage in which free men promised their votes to a more powerful man in exchange for his help in legal or other matters.

Networks of support were actually important for all Romans involved in public life, not simply aspiring plebeians. Roman politics operated primarily through a **patron-client system** whereby free men promised their votes to a more powerful man in exchange for his help in legal or other matters. The more powerful patron looked after his clients, and his clients' support helped the patron advance his career.

Roman Expansion

FOCUS QUESTION
How did the Romans take control of the Mediterranean world?

As the republican government was developing, Roman territory continued to expand. Unlike Alexander the Great, the Romans did not map out grandiose strategies to conquer the world. Rather they responded to situations as they arose. This meant, however, that they sought to eliminate any state they saw as a military threat.

The Punic Wars

As they pushed southward, incorporating the southern Italian peninsula into their growing territory, the Romans confronted another great power in the western Mediterranean, the Carthaginians. The city of Carthage had been founded by Phoenicians as a trading colony in the eighth century B.C.E. (see Chapter 2). It commanded one of the best harbors on the northern African coast and was surrounded by fertile farmland. By the fourth century B.C.E. the Carthaginians began to expand their holdings, and they engaged in war with the Etruscans and with the Greek cities of southern Italy and Sicily. They had one of the largest navies in the Mediterranean and were wealthy enough to hire mercenaries to do much of their fighting. At the end of a long string of wars, the Carthaginians had created and defended a mercantile empire that stretched from western Sicily to the western end of the Mediterranean (see Map 5.1).

Punic Wars A series of three wars between Rome and Carthage in which Rome emerged the victor.

Beginning in the fifth century B.C.E. the Romans and the Carthaginians made a series of treaties with one another that defined their spheres of influence, and they worked together in the 270s B.C.E. to defeat Pyrrhus. But the Greek cities that became Roman allies in southern Italy and Sicily, including Syracuse, saw Carthage as a competitor in terms of trade. This competition led to the first of the three **Punic Wars** between Rome and Carthage. The First Punic War lasted for twenty-three years (264–241 B.C.E.). The Romans quickly learned that they could not hold Sicily unless they controlled the sea. Thus they hired Greeks from Syracuse to build and sail ships for them, engineering some of their vessels based on wrecked Carthaginian warships. The Romans adapted what they knew best, land warfare, to fighting at sea, rigging gangplanks to cross over to the Carthaginian ships and seize them. Of the seven major naval battles they fought with the Carthaginians, the Romans won six and finally wore their opponents down with superior resources and military might. In 241 B.C.E. the Romans took possession of Sicily, which became their first real province.

The peace treaty between Rome and Carthage brought no peace, as both powers had their sights set on dominating the western half of the Mediterranean. In 238 B.C.E. the Romans took advantage of Carthaginian weakness to seize Sardinia and Corsica. The Carthaginians responded by expanding their holdings in Spain, under the leadership of the commander Hamilcar Barca. With him he took his ten-year-old son, Hannibal, whom he had earlier led to an altar where he had made the boy swear to be an enemy to Rome forever. In the following years Hamilcar and his son-in-law Hasdrubal (HAHZ-droo-buhl) subjugated much of southern Spain and in the process rebuilt Carthaginian power. Rome first made a treaty with Hasdrubal setting the boundary between Carthaginian and Roman interests at the Ebro River, and then began to extend its own influence in Spain.

In 221 B.C.E. Hannibal became the Carthaginian commander in Spain and laid siege to Saguntum (suh-GUHN-tum), a Roman-allied city that lay within the sphere of Carthaginian interest and was making raids into Carthaginian territories. The Romans declared war, claiming that Carthage had attacked a friendly city. So began the Second Punic War, one of the most desperate wars ever fought by Rome. In 218 B.C.E. Hannibal marched an army of tens of thousands of troops—and, more famously, several dozen war elephants—from Spain across what is now France and over the Alps into Italy. Once there, he defeated one Roman army after another, and in 216 B.C.E. he won his greatest victory at the Battle of Cannae (KAH-nee). The exact number of Roman deaths is unknown, but ancient historians place it between fifty thousand and seventy thousand. Hannibal then spread devastation throughout the Italian peninsula, and a number of cities in central and southern Italy rebelled against Rome because it appeared to them that Hannibal would be victorious. Syracuse, Rome's ally during the First Punic War, also went over to the Carthaginians. Yet Hannibal was not able to win areas near Rome in central Italy, as Roman allies there, who had been extended citizenship rights, remained loyal. Hannibal's allies, who included Philip V, the Antigonid king of Macedonia (see Chapter 4), did not supply him with enough food and supplies to sustain his troops, and Rome fought back.

In 210 B.C.E. Rome found its answer to Hannibal in the young commander Scipio Africanus. Scipio copied Hannibal's methods of mobile warfare and guerrilla tactics and made more extensive use of cavalry than had earlier Roman commanders. In the following years Scipio operated in Spain, which in 207 B.C.E. he wrested from the Carthaginians. That same year the Romans sealed Hannibal's fate in Italy. At the Battle of Metaurus the Romans destroyed a major Carthaginian army coming to reinforce Hannibal. Scipio then struck directly at Carthage itself, prompting the Carthaginians to recall Hannibal from Italy to defend their homeland.

In 202 B.C.E., at the town of Zama near Carthage (Map 5.2), Scipio defeated Hannibal in a decisive battle. The Carthaginians sued for peace and the Roman Senate agreed, on terms that were very favorable to the Romans. Hannibal himself later served as a military adviser at the Seleucid court in its battle with Rome, and then as an adviser to one of the small kingdoms in Anatolia.

The Second Punic War contained the seeds of still other wars. Unabated fear of Carthage combined with the encouragement of Cato the Elder (see page 140) led to the Third Punic War, a needless, unjust, and savage conflict that ended in 146 B.C.E. when Scipio Aemilianus, the grandson by adoption of Scipio Africanus, destroyed the hated rival and burned Carthage to the ground. Scipio's friend Polybius, a Greek historian and military leader, later reported that as the Roman conqueror watched the city burn, he said, "I fear and foresee that

Triumphal Column of Gaius Duilius This is a replica of a monument celebrating Rome's first naval victory in the First Punic War in 260 B.C.E., a battle in which the admiral Gaius Duilius destroyed fifty Carthaginian ships. Models of the prows of the enemy ships are shown projecting from the column. The original was erected in the Roman Forum several centuries after the war to look back to earlier Roman glories, a common practice among Roman military and political leaders. (Museo della Civiltà Romana/© Vanni Archive/Art Resource, NY)

MAP 5.2 Roman Expansion During the Republic, ca. 282–44 B.C.E.   Rome expanded in all directions, first west and then east, eventually controlling every shore of the Mediterranean.

someday someone will give the same order about my fatherland."[4] It would, however, be centuries before an invader would stand before the gates of Rome.

During the war with Hannibal, the Romans had invaded the Iberian Peninsula, an area rich in material resources and the home of fierce warriors. They met with bloody and determined resistance. Not until 133 B.C.E., after years of brutal and ruthless warfare, did Scipio Aemilianus finally conquer Spain. Scipio's victory meant that Roman language, law, and culture, fertilized by Greek influences, would in time permeate this entire region, although it would be another century before the Iberian Peninsula was completely pacified.

Rome Turns East

During the Second Punic War, King Philip V of Macedonia made an alliance with Hannibal against Rome. The Romans, in turn, allied themselves with the Aetolian League of Greek city-states. The cities of the league bore the brunt of the fighting on the Greek peninsula until after the Romans had defeated Hannibal in 202 B.C.E. Then the Roman legions were deployed against Macedonian phalanxes, and the Macedonians were defeated in a series of wars. Roman armies also won significant victories against the forces of the Seleucid emperors, and that empire shrank. After the Battle of Pydna in 168 B.C.E., the Romans deported the important Macedonian leaders to Rome and reshaped the Macedonian kingdom to their liking. In 148 B.C.E. they made Macedonia into a Roman province. Another decisive victory came in 146 B.C.E., when the Romans attacked the city of Corinth, which was part of another league of Greek city-states, the Achaean League. Just as they had at Carthage earlier that year, the Romans destroyed the city, looting it for treasure. In 133 B.C.E. the king of Pergamum bequeathed his kingdom to the Romans. The Ptolemies of Egypt retained formal control of their kingdom, but they obeyed Roman wishes in terms of trade policy.

The Romans had used the discord and disunity of the Hellenistic world to divide and conquer it. Once they had done so, they faced the formidable challenge of governing it without further warfare, which they met by establishing the first Roman provinces in the East. Declaring the Mediterranean *mare nostrum*, "our sea," the Romans began to create political and administrative machinery to hold the Mediterranean together under a political system of provinces ruled by governors sent from Rome. Not all Romans were joyful over Rome's conquest of the Mediterranean world; some considered the victory a misfortune. The historian Sallust (86–34 B.C.E.), writing from hindsight, complained that the acquisition of an empire was the beginning of Rome's troubles:

> But when through labor and justice our Republic grew powerful, great kings defeated in war, fierce nations and mighty peoples subdued by force, when Carthage the rival of the Roman people was wiped out root and branch, all the seas and lands lay open, then fortune began to be harsh and to throw everything into confusion. The Romans had easily borne labor, danger, uncertainty, and hardship. To them leisure, riches—otherwise desirable—proved to be burdens and torments. So at first money, then desire for power grew great. These things were a sort of cause of all evils.[5]

Roman Society

Sallust was not alone in his feelings. By the second century B.C.E. the Romans ruled much of the Mediterranean world, and tremendous wealth poured into Rome. Roman institutions, social patterns, and ways of thinking changed to meet the new era. Some looked nostalgically back at what they fondly considered the good old days and idealized the traditional agrarian and family-centered way of life. Others embraced the new urban life and eagerly accepted Greek culture.

FOCUS QUESTION
How did expansion affect Roman society and culture?

Roman Families

The core of traditional Roman society was the family, although the word "family" (*familia*) in ancient Rome actually meant all those under the authority of a male head of household, including nonrelated slaves and servants. In poor families this group might be very small, but among the wealthy it could include hundreds of slaves and servants.

The male head of household was called the **paterfamilias**. Just as slave owners held power over their slaves, fathers held great power over their children, which technically lasted for their children's whole lives. Initially this seems to have included power over life and death, but by the second century B.C.E. that had been limited by

paterfamilias The oldest dominant male of the family, who held great power over the lives of family members.

law and custom. Fathers continued to have the power to decide how family resources should be spent, however, and sons did not inherit until after their fathers had died.

In the early republic, legal authority over a woman generally passed from her father to her husband on marriage, but the Laws of the Twelve Tables allowed it to remain with her father even after a marriage. That was advantageous to the father, and could also be to the woman, for her father might be willing to take her side in a dispute with her husband, and she could return to her birth family if there was quarreling or abuse. By the late republic more and more marriages were of this type, and during the time of the empire (27 b.c.e.–476 c.e.) almost all of them were.

In order to marry, both spouses had to be free Roman citizens. Most citizens did marry, with women of wealthy families marrying in their midteens and non-elite women in their late teens. Grooms were generally somewhat older than their brides. Marital agreements, especially among the well-to-do, were stipulated with contracts between the families involved. According to Roman law, marriage required a dowry, a payment of money, property, and/or goods that went from the bride's family to the groom. Roman law also prohibited marriages between slaves, between a slave and a free person, and initially between plebeians and patricians, although that changed in the fifth century b.c.e. (see page 131). If their owner allowed it, slaves could enter a marriage-like relationship called *contubernium*, which benefited their owner, as any children produced from it would be his. People who were not slaves or citizens certainly lived together in marriage-like relationships, but these had no standing before the law and their children could not legally inherit.

Weddings were central occasions in a family's life, with spouses chosen carefully by parents, other family members, or marriage brokers. Professional fortune-tellers were frequently consulted to determine whether a match was good or what day would be especially lucky or auspicious for a couple to marry. The ceremony typically began with the bride welcoming the groom and the wedding party to her home for a feast, and then later the whole group progressed with much noise to the groom's household. It would be very unlucky if the bride tripped while going into the house, so the groom often carried her across the doorstep. The bride's entrance into the groom's house marked the point at which the two were married. As elsewhere in the ancient world, no public officials or priests were involved.

Women could inherit and own property under Roman law, though they generally received a smaller portion of any family inheritance than their brothers did. A woman's inheritance usually came as her dowry on marriage. In the earliest Roman marriage laws, men could divorce their wives without any grounds while women could not divorce their husbands, but by the second century b.c.e. these laws had changed, and both men and women could initiate divorce. By then women had also gained greater control over their dowries and other family property, perhaps because Rome's military conquests meant that many husbands were away for long periods of time and women needed some say over family finances. (See "Evaluating the Evidence 5.2: A Woman's Actions in the Turia Inscription," at right.)

Although marriages were arranged by families primarily for the handing down of property to legitimate children, the Romans, somewhat contradictorily, viewed the model marriage as one in which husbands and wives were loyal to one another and shared interests and activities. The Romans praised women, like Lucretia of old, who were virtuous and loyal to their husbands and devoted to their children. Such praises

A Woman's Actions in the Turia Inscription

Because they were carved in stone, most funeral inscriptions from ancient Rome are very short. One of the few surviving long inscriptions about a woman is from a tombstone from the first century B.C.E. Neither she nor her husband — the speaker in the inscription — has been identified with certainty, though she is traditionally called "Turia," and he may have been a Roman official named Quintus Lucretius Vespillo. Both of them were caught up in the unrest of the civil wars of the late republic.

~

You became an orphan suddenly before the day of our wedding, when both your parents were murdered together in the solitude of the countryside. It was mainly due to your efforts that the death of your parents was not left unavenged. I had left for Macedonia, and your sister's husband Cluvius had gone to the Province of Africa.

So strenuously did you perform your filial duty by your persistent demands and your pursuit of justice that we could not have done more if we had been present. But these merits you have in common with that most virtuous lady your sister.

. . . Then pressure was brought to bear on you and your sister to accept the view that your father's will, by which you and I were heirs, had been invalidated by his having contracted a [fictitious purchase] with his wife. If that was the case, then you together with all your father's property would necessarily come under the guardianship of those who pursued the matter; your sister would be left without any share at all of that inheritance. . . .

You defended our common cause by asserting the truth, namely, that the will had not in fact been broken. . . .

They gave way before your firm resolution and did not pursue the matter any further. Thus you on your own brought to a successful conclusion the defence you took up of your duty to your father, your devotion to your sister, and your faithfulness towards me. . . .

You provided abundantly for my needs during my flight [into political exile] and gave me the means for a dignified manner of living, when you took all the gold and jewellery from your own body and sent it to me and over and over again enriched me in my absence with servants, money and provisions, showing great ingenuity in deceiving the guards posted by our adversaries.

You begged for my life when I was abroad — it was your courage that urged you to this step — and because of your entreaties I was shielded by the clemency of those against whom you marshalled your words. But whatever you said was always said with undaunted courage.

Meanwhile when a troop of men collected by Milo, whose house I had acquired by purchase when he was in exile, tried to profit by the opportunities provided by the civil war and break into our house to plunder, you beat them back successfully and were able to defend our home.

EVALUATE THE EVIDENCE

1. What actions does the Roman woman in this tombstone inscription take to defend and support her family and husband?
2. How did the military campaigns and civil wars of the Roman Republic affect women's lives, and how did they shape what were regarded as admirable qualities in Roman women?

Source: Mary R. Lefkowitz and Maureen B. Fant, eds., *Women's Life in Greece and Rome: A Source Book in Translation*, Second Edition, pp. 135–137. © 1982, 1992 M. B. Fant and M. R. Lefkowitz. Reprinted with permission of The Johns Hopkins University Press and Bloomsbury Publishing Plc.

emerge in literature, and also in epitaphs on tombstones, such as this one from around 130 B.C.E.:

> Stranger, my message is short. Stand by and read it through. Here is the unlovely tomb of a lovely woman. Her parents called her Claudia by name. She loved her husband with all her heart. She bore two sons; of these she leaves one on earth; under the earth she has placed the other. She was charming in converse, yet gentle in bearing. She kept house, she made wool. That's my last word. Go your way.[6]

Traditionally minded Romans thought that mothers should nurse their own children and personally see to their welfare. Non-elite Roman women did nurse their own children, although wealthy women increasingly employed slaves as wet nurses and to help them raise the children. Very young children were under their mother's care, and most children learned the skills they needed from their own parents. For children from wealthier urban families, opportunities for formal education increased in the late republic. Boys and girls might be educated in their homes by tutors, who were often Greek slaves, and boys also might go to a school, paid for by their parents.

Most people in the expanding Roman Republic lived in the countryside. Farmers used oxen and donkeys to plow their fields, collecting the dung of the animals for fertilizer. Besides spreading manure, some farmers fertilized their fields by planting lupines and beans and plowing them under when they began to pod. Forage crops for animals to eat included clover, vetch, and alfalfa. Along with crops raised for local consumption and to pay their rents and taxes, many farmers raised crops to be sold. These included wheat, flax for making linen cloth, olives, and wine grapes.

Most Romans worked long days, and an influx of slaves from Rome's wars and conquests provided additional labor for the fields, mines, and cities. To the Romans, slavery was a misfortune that befell some people, but it did not entail any racial theories. Slave boys and girls were occasionally formally apprenticed in trades such as leatherworking, weaving, or metalworking. Well-educated slaves served as tutors or accountants, ran schools, and designed and made artwork and buildings. For loyal slaves the Romans always held out the possibility of freedom, and **manumission**, the freeing of individual slaves by their masters, was fairly common, especially for household slaves. Nonetheless, slaves rebelled from time to time, sometimes in large-scale revolts put down by Roman armies (see page 145).

> **manumission** The freeing of individual slaves by their masters.

Membership in a family did not end with death, as the spirits of the family's ancestors were understood to remain with the family. They and other gods regarded as protectors of the household—collectively these were called the *lares* and *penates*—were represented by small statues that stood in a special cupboard or a niche in the wall. The statues were taken out at meals and given small bits of food, or food was thrown into the household's hearth for them. The lares and penates represented the gods at family celebrations such as weddings, and families took the statues with them when they moved. They were honored in special rituals and ceremonies, although the later Roman poet Ovid (43 B.C.E.–17 C.E.) commented that these did not have to be elaborate:

> The spirits of the dead ask for little.
> They are more grateful for piety than for an expensive gift—
> Not greedy are the gods who haunt the Styx [the river that bordered the underworld] below.
> A rooftile covered with a sacrificial crown,
> Scattered kernels, a few grains of salt,
> Bread dipped in wine, and loose violets—
> These are enough.[7]

Greek Influence on Roman Culture

Many aspects of life did not change greatly during the Roman expansion. Most people continued to marry and form families, and to live in the countryside with the rhythm of their days and years determined by the needs of their crops. But with the conquest of the Mediterranean world, Rome became a great city, and many other cities emerged as well. The spoils of war went to build theaters, stadiums, and other places of amusement. Romans and Italian townspeople began to spend more of their time in leisure pursuits.

This new urban culture reflected Hellenistic influences. Romans developed a liking for Greek literature, and it became common for an educated Roman to speak both Latin and Greek. The poet Horace (64–8 B.C.E.) summed it up well: "Captive Greece captured her rough conqueror and introduced the arts into rustic Latium."[8]

The new Hellenism profoundly stimulated the growth and development of Roman art and literature. The Roman conquest of the Hellenistic East resulted in wholesale confiscation of Greek paintings and sculpture to grace Roman temples, public buildings, and private homes. Roman artists copied many aspects of Greek art, but used art, especially portraiture, to communicate Roman values. Portrait busts in stone were a favored art form. Those who commissioned them wanted to be portrayed as individuals, but also as representing certain admirable qualities, such as wisdom or dignity.

In literature the Greek influence was also strong. Roman authors sometimes wrote histories and poetry in Greek, or translated Greek classics into Latin. The poet Ennius (EHN-ee-uhs) (239–169 B.C.E.), the father of Latin poetry, studied Greek philosophy, wrote comedies in Latin, and adapted many of Euripides's tragedies for the Roman stage. Plautus (ca. 254–184 B.C.E.) brought a bawdy humor to his reworkings of Greek plays. The Roman dramatist Terence (ca. 195–159 B.C.E.), a follower of Scipio, wrote comedies of refinement and grace that owed their essentials to Greek models. All early Roman literature was derived from that of the Greeks, but it flourished because it also spoke to Roman ways of thinking.

The conquest of the Mediterranean world and the wealth it brought gave the Romans leisure, and Hellenism influenced how they spent their free time. Many rich urban dwellers changed their eating habits by consuming elaborate meals of exotic dishes. During the second century B.C.E. the Greek custom of bathing also gained popularity in the Roman world. In the early republic Romans had bathed infrequently, especially in the winter. Increasingly Romans built large public buildings containing pools and exercise rooms, and by the period of the early empire baths had become an essential part of any Roman city. Architects built intricate systems of aqueducts to supply the bathing establishments with water. The baths contained hot-air rooms to induce a good sweat and pools of hot and cold water to finish the actual bathing.

Conservative Romans railed against this Greek custom, calling it a waste of time and

Roman Bath   This Roman bath in Bath, England (a city to which it gave its name), was built beginning in the first century C.E. around a natural hot spring. The Romans spread the custom of bathing, which they had adopted from the Greeks, to the outer reaches of their empire. In addition to hot water, bathers used oil for massage and metal scrapers (inset) to clean and exfoliate their skin. Many Roman artifacts have been unearthed at Bath, including a number of curse tablets, small tablets made of lead calling on the gods to harm someone, which were common in the Greco-Roman world. Not surprisingly, many of the curse tablets found at Bath relate to the theft of clothing while people were bathing. (bath: Photo © Neil Holmes/Bridgeman Images; artifact: © The Trustees of the British Museum/Art Resource, NY)

an encouragement to idleness and immorality. They were correct in that bathing establishments were more than just places to take a bath. They came to include gymnasia where men exercised and played ball, snack bars where people dined and chatted, and even libraries and lecture halls. Women also had opportunities to bathe, generally in separate facilities or at separate times.

The baths were socially important places where men and women went to see and be seen. Social climbers tried to talk to the right people and wangle invitations to dinner; politicians took advantage of the occasion to discuss the affairs of the day; marriages were negotiated by wealthy fathers. Baths were also places where people could buy sex, as the women and men who worked in bathhouses often made extra income through prostitution. Because of this, moralists portrayed them as dens of iniquity, but they were seen by most Romans as a normal part of urban life.

Opposing Views: Cato the Elder and Scipio Aemilianus

In addition to disagreeing over public baths, Romans differed greatly in their opinions about Hellenism and other new social customs. Two men, Marcus Cato (234–149 B.C.E.) and Scipio Aemilianus (185–129 B.C.E.), both of whom were military commanders and consuls, the highest office in the Roman Republic, can serve as representatives of these opposing views.

Marcus Cato, called Cato the Elder, was a plebeian and owned a small rural estate, but his talent caught the eye of high patrician officials and he became their client. He fought in the Second Punic War under Scipio Africanus and then returned to Rome, where he worked his way up through various offices. In 195 B.C.E. he was elected consul. A key issue facing Cato was the heated debate over the repeal of the Oppian Law, which had been passed twenty years earlier, right after Rome's disastrous loss to Carthage at the Battle of Cannae. Rome needed money to continue the war, and the law decreed that no woman was to own more than a small amount of gold, or wear clothing trimmed in purple, or drive a chariot in the city of Rome itself. These were all proclaimed to be luxuries that wasted money and undermined the war effort. The law was passed in part for financial reasons, but also had gendered social implications, as there was no corresponding law limiting men's conspicuous consumption. By 195 B.C.E. the war was over and this restriction on women's spending had lost its economic rationale. Roman women publicly protested against it, and Cato led the battle to prevent its repeal. He declared that women were like animals and would engage in an orgy of shopping if the law were lifted, and that Roman society would be destroyed by women's spending. The women's actions were more effective than Cato's speeches, however, and the law was lifted, although later in his political career Cato pushed for other laws forbidding women from wearing fancy clothing or owning property.

Women's spending was not the only problem destroying Roman society, according to Cato. Although he made certain his older son learned Greek as an essential tool in Roman society, he instructed the boy not to take Greek ideas too seriously and viewed the influx of Greek culture in general as dangerous. Cato set himself up as the defender of what he saw as traditional Roman values: discipline, order, morality, frugality, and an agrarian way of life. He even criticized his superior Scipio Africanus for being too lenient toward his troops and spending too much money. Cato proclaimed his views in speeches at the Senate, through his decisions when acting as a military commander, and also in his written works, which were all in Latin. His only work to survive in its entirety is a manual for running large agricultural estates written for the absentee landowners who were becoming more common. In this he advises the adoption of any measures that would increase efficiency and profitability, including selling off old or sickly slaves as soon as possible.

Cato held the office of censor, and he attempted to remove from the lists of possible officeholders anyone who did not live up to his standards. Late in life he was a diplomat to Carthage, and after seeing that the city had recovered economically from the war with Rome, he came home declaring, "Carthage must be destroyed." He repeated this often enough that shortly after his death the Romans decided to do just this in the Third Punic War.

Ironically, the mission to Carthage was led by Scipio Aemilianus, the grandson of Scipio Africanus and an avid devotee of Hellenism. Like his grandfather, Scipio believed that broader views had to replace the old Roman narrowness. Rome was no longer a small city on the Tiber; it was the capital of the world, and Romans had to adapt themselves to that fact. Scipio became an innovator in both politics and culture. He developed a more personal style of politics that looked unflinchingly at the broader problems that the success of Rome brought to its people. He embraced Hellenism wholeheartedly. Perhaps more than anyone else of his day, Scipio represented the new Roman—imperial, cultured, and independent.

In his education and interests, too, Scipio broke with the past. As a boy he had received the traditional Roman training, learning to read and write Latin and becoming acquainted with the law. He mastered the fundamentals of rhetoric and learned how to throw the javelin, fight in armor, and ride a horse. But as a young man he formed a lasting friendship with the historian Polybius, who after being brought to Rome as a war hostage was his tutor. Polybius actively encouraged him in his study of Greek and in his intellectual pursuits. In later life Scipio's love of Greek learning, rhetoric, and philosophy became legendary. Scipio also promoted the spread of Hellenism in Roman society, and his views became more widespread than those of Cato. In general, Rome absorbed and added what it found useful from Hellenism, just as earlier it had absorbed aspects of Etruscan culture.

The Late Republic

The wars of conquest created serious problems for the Romans. The republican constitution had suited the needs of a simple city-state but was inadequate to meet the requirements of Rome's new position in international affairs. New armies had to be provided for defense, and systems of administration and tax collection had to be created to support the republic. Moreover, the people of the Roman Republic came away from the war with differing needs and expectations. Roman generals, who had commanded huge numbers of troops for long periods of time, acquired great power and ambition and were becoming too mighty for the state to control. At the same time, non-Roman inhabitants of Italy who had fought in the wars of expansion began to agitate for full Roman citizenship, including the right to vote. Some individuals, including military contractors, profited greatly from the foreign wars, while average soldiers gained little.

These problems, complex and explosive, largely account for the turmoil of the late republic (133–27 B.C.E.). This era produced some of Rome's most famous figures: the Gracchi brothers, Marius, Sulla, Cicero, Crassus, Pompey, and Julius Caesar, among others.

FOCUS QUESTION
What led to the fall of the Roman Republic?

Reforms for Poor and Landless Citizens

Hannibal's operations and the warfare in Italy had left the countryside a shambles. The prolonged fighting had also drawn untold numbers of Roman and Italian men away from their farms for long periods. Conscripted legionaries were required to serve in their units until a military campaign was over, which might be many years. Women often ran the farms in their absence, but with so many men away fighting they did not have enough workers to keep the land under full cultivation. When the legionaries returned to their farms in Italy, they encountered an appalling situation. All too often their farms looked like those they had destroyed in their wars of conquest: land was untilled, buildings were falling down, and animals were wandering.

The wars of conquest had also made some men astoundingly rich, and the newly wealthy invested their money in land. Land won by conquest was generally declared public land, and although officially there was a limit on how much public land one individual could hold, this law was often ignored. Wealthy people rented public land—though rents were frequently not collected—and bought up small farms, often at very low prices, to create huge estates, which the Romans called **latifundia** (lah-tuh-FUHN-dee-uh). The owners of the latifundia occasionally hired free men as day laborers, but they preferred to use slaves, who could not strike or be drafted into the army. Using slave labor, and farming on a large scale, owners of latifundia could raise crops at a lower cost than could small farmers.

latifundia Huge agricultural estates owned by wealthy absentee landowners and worked by slaves.

Confronted by these conditions, veterans and their families took what they could get for their broken and bankrupt farms and tried their luck elsewhere. Sometimes large landowners simply appropriated public land and the small farms of former soldiers, and there was little that veterans could do about it. Gradually agriculture in Italy was transformed from subsistence farming to an important source of income for the Roman ruling class.

Most veterans migrated to the cities, especially to Rome. Although some found work, most did not. Industry and small manufacturing were generally in the hands of slaves, and even when work was available, slave labor kept the wages of free men low. Instead of a new start, veterans and their families encountered slum-like living conditions and continued dependency on others. If they were Roman citizens, they could vote in citizens' assemblies, however, and tended to back anyone who offered them better prospects.

Growing numbers of landless citizens held ominous consequences for the strength of Rome's armies. The Romans had always believed that only landowners should serve in the army, for only they had something to fight for. Landless men, even if they were Romans and lived in Rome, could not be conscripted into the army. These landless men may have been veterans of major battles and numerous campaigns, but once they lost their land, they became ineligible for further military service. The landless ex-legionaries wanted to be able to serve in the army again, and they were willing to support any leader who would allow them to.

One man who recognized the plight of Rome's veterans, peasant farmers, and urban poor was the aristocratic military leader Tiberius Gracchus (tigh-BEER-ee-uhs GRAK-uhs) (163–133 B.C.E.). After his election as tribune in 133 B.C.E., Tiberius proposed reforms that would help make land ownership more equitable. Although his reforms enjoyed the support of some distinguished and popular members of the Senate, they angered those who had usurped large tracts of public land for their own use, who bitterly resisted Tiberius's efforts. This was to be expected, yet he unquestionably made

Coin Showing a Voter   This coin from 63 B.C.E. shows a citizen wearing a toga dropping a voting tablet into a voting urn, the Roman equivalent of today's ballot box. The tablet has a *V* on it, meaning a yes vote, and the coin has an inscription giving the name of the moneyer, the official who controlled the production of coins and decided what would be shown on them. Here the moneyer, Lucius Cassius Longinus, depicted a vote held fifty years earlier regarding whether an ancestor of his should be named prosecutor in a trial charging three vestal virgins with unchastity. As was common among moneyers, Longinus chose this image as a means to advance his political career, in this case by suggesting his family's long history of public office. (Bibliothèque Nationale de France [BnF]/Snark/Art Resource, NY)

additional problems for himself by making decisions and taking actions in ways that, while within his rights as a tribune, were unprecedented.

Many powerful Romans became suspicious of Tiberius's growing influence with the people. Some considered him a tyrant, a concept that came from the Greeks for someone who gained power outside the normal structures and against the traditional ruling class. When he sought to be re-elected as tribune, riots erupted among his opponents and supporters, and a group of senators beat Tiberius to death in cold blood. Thus some of the very people who directed the affairs of state and administered the law had taken the law into their own hands. The death of Tiberius was the beginning of an era of political violence.

Although Tiberius was dead, his land bill was law. Furthermore, Tiberius's brother Gaius Gracchus (153–121 B.C.E.) took up the cause of reform. Gaius (GAY-uhs) was a veteran soldier with an enviable record, and when he became tribune he demanded even more extensive reform than had his brother. To help the urban poor, Gaius pushed legislation to provide them with cheap grain for bread. He defended his brother's land law and proposed that Rome send many of its poor and propertyless people out to form colonies, including one on the site where Carthage had once stood. The prospect of new homes, land, and a fresh start gave the urban poor new hope and made Gaius popular among them.

Like his brother Tiberius, Gaius aroused a great deal of personal and factional opposition. When Gaius failed in 121 B.C.E. to win the tribunate for the third time, he feared for his life. In desperation he armed his staunchest supporters, whereupon the Senate ordered the consul to restore order. Gaius was killed, and many of his supporters died in the turmoil.

Political Violence

The death of Gaius brought little peace, and trouble came from two sources: the outbreak of new wars in the Mediterranean basin and further political unrest in Rome. In 112 B.C.E. Rome declared war against the rebellious Jugurtha (joo-GUHR-thuh), king of Numidia in North Africa. Numidia had been one of Rome's client kingdoms, a kingdom still ruled by its own king but subject to Rome. Client kingdoms followed Rome's lead in foreign affairs but conducted their own internal business according to their own laws and customs. The benefits of these relationships were mutual, for the client kingdoms enjoyed the protection of Rome while defending Rome's borders, but they were not relationships between equals: Rome always remained the senior partner. In time many of these states became provinces of the Roman Empire (see Chapters 6 and 7).

The Roman legions made little headway against Jugurtha until 107 B.C.E., when Gaius Marius (MEHR-ee-uhs), a politician not from the traditional Roman aristocracy, became consul and led troops to Numidia. A man of fierce vigor and courage, Marius saw the army as the tool of his ambition. He took the unusual but not wholly unprecedented step of recruiting an army by permitting landless men to serve in the legions, thus tapping Rome's vast reservoir of poor citizens; the state provided them with weapons and armor and promised them pay. Marius was unable to defeat Jugurtha directly, but his assistant, Sulla, bribed Jugurtha's father-in-law to betray him, and Jugurtha was captured and later executed in Rome. Marius later claimed this as a victory.

Fighting was also going on at Rome's northern border, where two German peoples, the Cimbri and Teutones, were moving into Gaul and later into northern Italy. After the Germans had defeated Roman armies sent to repel them, the Senate sent Marius to lead the campaign against them. Before engaging the Germans, Marius encouraged enlistments by promising his volunteers land after the war. Poor and landless citizens flocked to him. Marius and his army conquered the Germans, but when Marius proposed a bill to grant land to his troops once they had retired from military service, the Senate refused to act, in effect turning its back on the soldiers of Rome. It was a disastrous mistake. Henceforth the legionaries expected their commanders—not the Senate or the state—to protect their interests, and the Roman army gradually changed from an army of citizen conscripts into an army of paid soldiers.

Rome was dividing into two political factions, both of whom wanted political power. The *populares* attempted to increase their power through the plebeian assembly and the power of the tribunes, while the *optimates* employed the traditional means of patron-client relationships and working primarily through the Senate. Both of these factions were represented in the Senate, and both had their favored general. Marius was the general backed by the populares, who from 104 B.C.E. to 100 B.C.E. elected him consul every year, although this was technically illegal and put unprecedented power into a Roman military commander's hands.

The favored general of the optimates was Sulla, who had earlier been Marius's assistant. In 90 B.C.E. many Roman allies in the Italian peninsula rose up against Rome because they were expected to pay taxes and serve in the army, but they had no voice in political decisions because they were not full citizens. This revolt became known as the Social War, so named from the Latin word *socius*, or "ally." Sulla's armies gained a number of victories over the Italian allies, and Sulla gained prestige through his success in fighting them. In the end, however, the Senate agreed to give many allies Roman citizenship in order to end the fighting.

Sulla's military victories led to his election as consul in 88 B.C.E., and he was given command of the Roman army in a campaign against Mithridates, the king of a state that had gained power and territory in what is now northern Turkey and was expanding into Greece. Before he could depart, however, the populares gained the upper hand in the assembly, revoked his consulship, and made Marius the commander of the troops against Mithridates. Riots broke out. Sulla fled the city and returned at the head of an army, an unprecedented move by a Roman general. He quelled the riots, put down his opponents, made some political changes that reduced the power of the assembly, and left again, this time to fight Mithridates.

Sulla's forces were relatively successful against Mithridates, but meanwhile Marius led his own troops into Rome in 86 B.C.E., undid Sulla's changes, and killed many of his supporters. Although Marius died shortly after his return to power, the populares who supported him continued to hold Rome. Sulla returned in 83 B.C.E., and after a brief but intense civil war he entered Rome and ordered a ruthless butchery of his opponents. He then attempted to turn back the clock, returning all power to the Senate and restoring the conservative constitution as it had been before the Gracchan reforms. In 81 B.C.E. he was granted the office of dictator and, in sharp contrast to Cincinnatus, used his position as a tool to gain personal power. Dictators were supposed to step down after six months—and many had done so in Roman history—but Sulla held this position for two years. In 79 B.C.E. Sulla abdicated his dictatorship because he was ill and believed his policies would last. Yet civil war was to be the constant lot of Rome for the next forty-eight years, and Sulla's abuse of political office became the blueprint for later leaders.

Civil War

The history of the late republic is the story of power struggles among many famous Roman figures against a background of unrest at home and military campaigns abroad. This led to a series of bloody civil wars that raged from Spain across northern Africa to Egypt.

Sulla's political heirs were Pompey, Crassus, and Julius Caesar, all of them able military leaders and brilliant politicians. Pompey (106–48 B.C.E.) began a meteoric rise to power as a successful commander of troops for Sulla against Marius in Italy, Sicily, and Africa. He then suppressed a rebellion in Spain, led naval forces against pirates in the Mediterranean, and in 67 B.C.E. was sent by the Senate to command Roman forces in the East. He defeated Mithridates and the forces of other rulers as well, transforming their territories into Roman provinces and providing wealth for the Roman treasury.

Crassus (ca. 115–53 B.C.E.) also began his military career under Sulla and became the wealthiest man in Rome through buying and selling land. In 73 B.C.E. a major slave revolt broke out in Italy, led by Spartacus, a former gladiator. The slave armies, which eventually numbered in the tens of thousands, defeated several Roman units sent to quash them. Finally Crassus led a large army against them and put down the revolt. Spartacus was apparently killed on the battlefield, and the slaves who were captured were crucified, with thousands of crosses lining the main road to Rome.

Pompey and Crassus then made an informal agreement with the populares in the Senate. Both were elected consuls in 70 B.C.E. and began to dismantle Sulla's constitution and initiate economic and political reforms once again. They and the Senate moved too slowly for some people, however, who planned an uprising. This plot was discovered, and the forces of the rebels were put down in 63 B.C.E. by an army sent by Cicero (106–43 B.C.E.), a leader of the optimates who was consul at the time. The rebellion and Cicero's skillful handling of it discredited the populares.

The man who cast the longest shadow over these troubled years was Julius Caesar (100–44 B.C.E.). Born of a noble family, he received an excellent education, which he furthered by studying in Greece with some of the most eminent teachers of the day. He had serious intellectual interests and immense literary ability. His account of his military operations in Gaul (present-day France), the *Commentaries on the Gallic Wars*, became a classic of Western literature. Caesar was a superb orator, and his personality and wit made him popular. Military service was an effective stepping-stone to politics, and Caesar was a military

Julius Caesar   In this bust from the first century B.C.E., the sculptor portrays Caesar as a man of power and intensity. Showing individuals as representing certain virtues was common in Roman portraiture. (Museo e Gallerie Nazionali di Capodimonte, Naples, Italy/ The Bridgeman Images)

INDIVIDUALS IN SOCIETY

Queen Cleopatra

Cleopatra VII (69–30 B.C.E.) was a member of the Ptolemy dynasty, the Hellenistic rulers of Egypt who had established power in the third century B.C.E. Although she was a Greek, she was passionately devoted to her Egyptian subjects and was the first in her dynasty who could speak Egyptian in addition to Greek. Just as ancient pharaohs had linked themselves with the gods, she had herself portrayed as the goddess Isis and may have seen herself as a reincarnation of Isis (see Chapter 4).

At the time civil war was raging in the late Roman Republic, Cleopatra and her brother Ptolemy XIII were in a dispute over who would be supreme ruler in Egypt. Julius Caesar captured the Egyptian capital of Alexandria, Cleopatra arranged to meet him, and the two became lovers, although Cleopatra was much younger and Caesar was married. The two apparently had a son, Caesarion, and Caesar's army defeated Ptolemy's army, ending the power struggle. In 46 B.C.E. Cleopatra arrived in Rome, where Caesar put up a statue of her as Isis in one of the city's temples. The Romans hated her because they saw her as a decadent Eastern queen and a threat to what were considered traditional Roman values.

After Caesar's assassination, Cleopatra returned to Alexandria. There she became involved in the continuing Roman civil war that now pitted Octavian, Caesar's grandnephew and heir, against Mark Antony, who commanded the Roman army in the East. When Antony visited Alexandria in 41 B.C.E., he met Cleopatra, and though he was already married to Octavian's sister, he became her lover. He abandoned (and later divorced) his Roman wife, married Cleopatra in 37 B.C.E., and changed his will to favor his children by Cleopatra. Antony's wedding present to Cleopatra was a huge grant of territory, much of it Roman, that greatly increased her power and that of all her children, including Caesarion. Antony also declared Caesarion to be Julius Caesar's rightful heir.

Octavian used the wedding gift as the reason to declare Antony a traitor. He and other Roman leaders described Antony as a romantic fool captivated by the seductive Cleopatra. Roman troops turned against Antony and joined with Octavian, and at the Battle of Actium in 31 B.C.E. Octavian defeated the army and navy of Antony and Cleopatra. Antony committed suicide, as did Cleopatra shortly afterward. Octavian ordered the

The only portraits of Cleopatra that date from her own lifetime are on the coins that she issued. This one, made at the mint of Alexandria, shows her as quite plain, reinforcing the point made by Cicero that her attractiveness was based more on intelligence and wit than on physical beauty. The reverse of the coin shows an eagle, a symbol of rule.
(© The Trustees of the British Museum/Art Resource, NY)

teenage Caesarion killed, but the young children of Antony and Cleopatra were allowed to go back to Rome, where they were raised by Antony's ex-wife. In another consequence of Octavian's victory, Egypt became a Roman province.

Roman sources are viciously hostile to Cleopatra, and she became the model of the alluring woman whose sexual attraction led men to their doom. Stories about her beauty, sophistication, lavish spending, desire for power, and ruthlessness abounded and were retold for centuries. The most dramatic story was that she committed suicide through the bite of a poisonous snake, which may have been true and which has been the subject of countless paintings. Her tumultuous relationships with Caesar and Antony have been portrayed in plays, novels, movies, and television programs.

QUESTIONS FOR ANALYSIS

1. How did Cleopatra benefit from her relationships with Caesar and Antony? How did they benefit from their relationships with her?
2. How did ideas about gender and Roman suspicion of the more sophisticated Greek culture combine to shape Cleopatra's fate and the way she is remembered?
3. In Chapter 1, "Individuals in Society: Hatshepsut and Nefertiti" (see page 31) also focuses on leading female figures in Egypt, but these two women lived more than a thousand years before Cleopatra. How would you compare their situation with hers?

genius who knew how to win battles and turn victories into permanent gains. He was also a shrewd politician of unbridled ambition, who knew how to use the patron-client system to his advantage. He became a protégé of Crassus, who provided cash for Caesar's needs, and at the same time helped the careers of other politicians, who in turn looked to Caesar's interests in Rome when he was away from the city. Caesar launched his military career in Spain, where his courage won the respect and affection of his troops.

In 60 B.C.E. Caesar returned to Rome from Spain and Pompey returned from military victories in the east. Together with Crassus, the three concluded an informal political alliance later termed the **First Triumvirate** (trigh-UHM-veh-ruht), in which they agreed to advance one another's interests. Crassus's money helped Caesar be elected consul, and Pompey married Caesar's daughter Julia. Crassus was appointed governor of Syria, Pompey of Hispania (present-day Spain), and Caesar of Gaul.

Personal ambitions undermined the First Triumvirate. While Caesar was away from Rome fighting in Gaul, his supporters formed gangs that attacked the supporters of Pompey. These were countered by supporters of Pompey, and there were riots in the streets of Rome. The First Triumvirate disintegrated. Crassus died in battle while trying to conquer Parthia, and Caesar and Pompey accused each other of treachery. Fearful of Caesar's popularity and growing power, the Senate sided with Pompey and ordered Caesar to disband his army. He refused, and instead in 49 B.C.E. he crossed the Rubicon River in northern Italy — the boundary of his territorial command — with soldiers. ("Crossing the Rubicon" is still used as an expression for committing to an irreversible course of action.) Although their forces outnumbered Caesar's, Pompey and the Senate fled Rome, and Caesar entered the city without a fight.

Caesar then led his army against those loyal to Pompey and the Senate in Spain and Greece. In 48 B.C.E., despite being outnumbered, he defeated Pompey and his army at the Battle of Pharsalus in central Greece. Pompey fled to Egypt, which was embroiled in a battle for control not between two generals, but between a brother and sister, Ptolemy XIII and Cleopatra VII (69–30 B.C.E.). Caesar followed Pompey to Egypt, Cleopatra allied herself with Caesar, and Caesar's army defeated Ptolemy's army, ending the power struggle. Pompey was assassinated in Egypt, Cleopatra and Caesar became lovers, and Caesar brought Cleopatra to Rome. (See "Individuals in Society: Queen Cleopatra," at left.) Caesar put down a revolt against Roman control by the king of Pontus in northern Turkey, then won a major victory over Pompey's army — now commanded by his sons — in Spain.

In the middle of defeating his enemies in battles all around the Mediterranean (see Map 5.2), Julius Caesar returned to Rome several times and was elected or appointed to various positions, including consul and dictator. He was acclaimed imperator, a title given to victorious military commanders and a term that later gave rise to the word *emperor*. Sometimes these elections happened when Caesar was away fighting; they were often arranged by his chief supporter and client in Rome, Mark Antony (83–30 B.C.E.), who was himself a military commander. Whatever Caesar's official position, after he crossed the Rubicon he simply made changes on his own authority, though often with the approval of the Senate, which he packed with his supporters. The Senate transformed his temporary positions as consul and dictator into ones he would hold for life.

Caesar began to make a number of legal and economic reforms. He issued laws about debt, the collection of taxes, and the distribution of grain and land. Families who had many children were to receive rewards, and Roman allies in Italy were to

First Triumvirate The name later given to an informal political alliance among Caesar, Crassus, and Pompey in which they agreed to advance one another's interests.

Cicero and the Plot to Kill Caesar

Marcus Tullius Cicero was born in January 106 B.C.E. After an excellent education, he settled in Rome to practice law. He held a series of ever-higher public offices, ending with the consulship in 63 B.C.E. By the time of Caesar's return to Rome in 49 B.C.E., Cicero was a senior statesman with great importance as a lawyer and thinker and powerful influence through his skills at oratory. Caesar wrote Cicero a flattering letter stating, "[Y]our approval of my actions elates me beyond words. . . . As for yourself, I hope I shall see you at Rome so that I can avail myself as usual of your advice and resources in all things."* Cicero tended to favor Pompey, however, thinking that Caesar was a greater danger to traditional republican institutions. He was not involved in the plot to assassinate Caesar, perhaps because the conspirators did not trust him to keep the matter quiet. He was involved in the jockeying for power that followed, however, as evidenced by the following letters and speeches.

Trebonius, one of the assassins, wrote to Cicero describing the murder, and on February 2, 43 B.C.E., Cicero gave this frank opinion of the events:

~

Would to heaven you had invited me to that noble feast that you made on the ides of March: no remnants, most assuredly, should have been left behind. Whereas the part you unluckily spared gives us so much perplexity that we find something to regret, even in the godlike service that you and your illustrious associates have lately rendered to the republic. To say the truth, when I reflect that it was owing to the favor of so worthy a man as yourself that Antony now lives to be our general bane, I am sometimes inclined to be a little angry with you for taking him aside when Caesar fell as by this means you have occasioned more trouble to myself in particular than to all the rest of the whole community.†

By the "part you unluckily spared" he meant Mark Antony, Caesar's firm supporter and a fierce enemy of the assassins, whom Cicero feared. Still undecided about what to do after the assassination, Cassius, one of the leaders of the plot, wrote to Cicero asking for advice. Cicero responded, again emphasizing that the conspirators should have killed Antony as well, and clearly miffed that he was not consulted:

~

Where to advise you to begin to restore order I must acknowledge myself at a loss. To say the truth, it is the tyrant alone, and not the tyranny, from which we seem to be delivered: for although the man [Caesar] is destroyed, we still servilely maintain all his despotic ordinances. We do more: and under the pretence of carrying his designs into execution, we approve of measures which even he himself would never have pursued. . . . This outrageous man [Antony] represents me as the principal advisor and promoter of your glorious efforts. Would to heaven the charge were true! For had I been a party in your councils, I should have put it out of his power thus to bother and embarrass our plans. But this was a point that depended on yourselves to decide; and since the opportunity is now over, I can only wish that I were capable of giving you any effective advice. But the truth is that I am utterly at a loss in how to act myself. For what is the purpose of resisting where one cannot oppose force by force?‡

At this stage the young Octavian, Caesar's designated heir, sought Cicero's advice. In a series of letters to his close friend Atticus, Cicero discussed the situation, upset that Decimus Brutus, a general who was one of the conspirators, was not taking charge of the situation:

~

On the second or third of November 44 B.C.E. a letter arrived from Octavian. He has great schemes afoot. He has won the veterans at Casilinum and Calatia over to his

---

* *To Atticus* 9.16.2 in D. R. Shackleton-Bailey, *Cicero's Letters to Atticus*, vol. 4 (Cambridge: Cambridge University Press, 1968), pp. 203–205.

† *To Trebonius* in T. de Quincy, *Cicero: Offices, Essays, and Letters* (New York: Everyman's Library), pp. 328–329.

‡ *To Cassius*, ibid., pp. 324–325.

---

have full citizenship. He reformed the calendar, which had been based on the cycles of the moon, by replacing it with one based on the sun, adapted from the Egyptian calendar. He sponsored celebrations honoring his victories, had coins struck with his portrait, and founded new colonies, which were to be populated by veterans and the poor. He planned even more changes, including transforming elected positions such as consul, tribune, and provincial governor into ones that he appointed.

views, and no wonder since he gives them 500 denarii apiece. He plans to make a round of the other colonies. His object is plain: war with Antony and himself as commander-in-chief. So it looks to me as though in a few days' time we shall be in arms. But whom are we to follow? Consider his name; consider his age. . . . In short, he proffers himself as our leader and expects me to back him up. For my part I have recommended him to go to Rome. I imagine he will have the city rabble behind him, and the honest men too if he convinces them of his sincerity. Ah Brutus, where are you? What a golden opportunity you are losing! I could not foretell *this*, but I thought something of the kind would happen.§

Four days later Cicero records news of the following developments:

~

Two letters for me from Octavian in one day! Now he wants me to return to Rome at once, says he wants to work through the Senate. . . . In short, he presses and I play for time. I don't trust his age and I don't know what he's after. . . . I'm nervous of Antony's power and don't want to leave the coast. But I'm afraid of some star performance during my absence. Varro [an enemy of Antony] doesn't think much of the boy's plan, I take a different view. He has a strong force at his back and *can* have Brutus. And he's going to work quite openly, forming companies at Capua and paying out bounties. War is evidently coming any minute now.**

Even though he contemptuously called him a "boy," Cicero decided to openly side with Octavian. On April 21, 43 B.C.E., he denounced Antony in a speech to the Senate. He reminded his fellow senators how they had earlier opposed Antony:

~

Do you not remember, in the name of the immortal gods, what resolutions you have made against these men

[Antony and his supporters]? You have repealed the acts of Antony. You have taken down his law. You have voted that they were carried by violence and with a disregard of the auspices. You have called out the troops throughout all Italy. You have pronounced that colleague and ally of all wickedness [Antony] a public enemy. What peace can there be with this man? Even if he were a foreign enemy, still, after such actions as have taken place, it would be scarcely possible by any means whatever to have peace. Though seas and mountains and vast regions lay between you, still you would hate such a man without seeing him. But these men will stick to your eyes, and when they can to your very throats; for what fences will be strong enough for us to restrain savage beasts? Oh, but the result of war is uncertain. It is at all events in the power of brave men such as you ought to be to display your valor, for certainly brave men can do that, and not to fear the caprice of fortune.††

Antony and Octavian briefly reconciled and formed the Third Triumvirate. An ill and aging Cicero was declared an enemy of the state and sought to leave Italy, but was intercepted by Antony's men. When Cicero stretched his head out of the window of the litter in which he was being carried, indicating he would surrender, a centurion slit his throat. His head and hands were cut off on Antony's orders and displayed in the Roman Forum. Octavian's opinion about all this as it happened is disputed, but years later he said of Cicero: "A learned man, learned and a lover of his country."‡‡

EVALUATE THE EVIDENCE

1. What can you infer from these letters about how well prepared the conspirators and other leaders in the Senate such as Cicero were to take control of the government after Caesar's death?
2. What do these sources suggest about Cicero's importance and the role of his speeches in the Senate?

§ *To Atticus* 16.8.1–2 in D. R. Shackleton-Bailey, *Cicero's Letters to Atticus*, vol. 6 (Cambridge: Cambridge University Press, 1967), pp. 185–187.

** *To Atticus* 16.9, ibid., p. 189.

†† *The Fourteenth Phillipic* in C. D. Yonge, *Cicero, Select Orations* (New York: Harper and Brothers, 1889), p. 499.

‡‡ Plutarch, *Cicero* 49.15.

Caesar was wildly popular with most people in Rome, and even with many senators. Other senators, led by Brutus and Cassius, two patricians who favored the traditional republic, opposed his rise to what was becoming absolute power. In 44 B.C.E. they conspired to kill him and did so on March 15—a date called the "Ides of March" in the Roman calendar—stabbing him multiple times on the steps of the theater of Pompey, where the Senate was meeting that day.

The conspiring senators called themselves the "Liberators" and said they were defending the liberties of the Roman Republic, but their support for the traditional power of the Senate could do little to save Rome from its pattern of misgovernment. The result of the assassination was another round of civil war. (See "Evaluating the Evidence 5.3: Cicero and the Plot to Kill Caesar," page 148.) Caesar had named his eighteen-year-old grandnephew and adopted son, Octavian, as his heir. In 43 B.C.E. Octavian joined forces with Mark Antony and another of Caesar's lieutenants, Lepidus (LEH-puh-duhs), in a formal pact known later as the **Second Triumvirate**. Together they hunted down Caesar's killers and defeated the military forces loyal to Pompey's sons and to the conspirators. They agreed to divide the provinces into spheres of influence, with Octavian taking most of the west, Antony the east, and Lepidus the Iberian Peninsula and North Africa. The three came into conflict, and Lepidus was forced into exile by Octavian, leaving the other two to confront one another.

Both Octavian and Antony set their sights on gaining more territory. Cleopatra had returned to rule Egypt after Caesar's death, and supported Antony, who became her lover as well as her ally. In 31 B.C.E. Octavian's forces defeated the combined forces of Antony and Cleopatra at the Battle of Actium in Greece, but the two escaped. Octavian pursued them to Egypt, and they committed suicide rather than fall into his hands. Octavian's victory at Actium put an end to an age of civil war. For his success, the Senate in 27 B.C.E. gave Octavian the name Augustus, meaning "revered one." Although the Senate did not mean this to be a decisive break with tradition, that date is generally used to mark the end of the Roman Republic and the start of the Roman Empire.

Second Triumvirate
A formal agreement in 43 B.C.E. among Octavian, Mark Antony, and Lepidus to defeat Caesar's murderers.

LOOKING BACK LOOKING AHEAD

As the Greeks were creating urban culture and spreading it around the Mediterranean, other peoples, including the Etruscans and the people who later became the Romans, built their own societies on the Italian peninsula. The Romans spread their way of life throughout Italy by means of conquest and incorporation. After wars in which they defeated the wealthy city of Carthage, they expanded their political dominance throughout the western Mediterranean basin. Then they conquered in the East until they came to view the entire Mediterranean as *mare nostrum*, "our sea." Yet their successes brought war and civil unrest, and they also brought transformations of Roman society and culture as these became Hellenized.

The final days of the republic were filled with war and chaos, and the republican institutions did not survive. Rome became an empire ruled by one man. The laws and administrative practices of the republic shaped those of the empire, however, as well as those of later states in Europe and beyond. Lyons, Marseilles, Paris, Córdoba, and other modern European cities began as Roman colonies or expanded from small settlements into cities during the period of the republic. When the American Constitution was drafted in 1783, its authors — well read in Roman history and law — favored a balance of powers like those they idealized in the Roman Republic, and they chose to call the smaller and more powerful deliberative assembly the Senate. They, too, were divided into those who favored rule by traditional elites and those who favored broader political power, much like the optimates and populares of the Roman Republic. That division is reflected in the fact that the American Congress has two houses, the House of Representatives, elected directly by voters, and the Senate, originally elected indirectly by state legislatures.

Make Connections

Think about the larger developments and continuities within and across chapters.

1. How would you compare ideals for male and female behavior in republican Rome with those of classical Sparta and classical Athens in Chapter 3? What are some possible reasons for the differences and similarities you have identified?

2. The Phoenicians, the Greeks, and the Romans all established colonies around the Mediterranean. How did these colonies differ, and how were they the same, in terms of their economic functions and political situations?

3. Looking over the long history of the Roman Republic, do interactions with non-Romans or conflicts among Romans themselves appear to be the most significant drivers of change? Explain your answer.

5 REVIEW & EXPLORE

Review the Main Ideas

Answer the focus questions from each section of the chapter.

◆ How did the Romans become the dominant power in Italy? (p. 122)

◆ What were the key institutions of the Roman Republic? (p. 129)

◆ How did the Romans take control of the Mediterranean world? (p. 132)

◆ How did expansion affect Roman society and culture? (p. 135)

◆ What led to the fall of the Roman Republic? (p. 141)

Identify Key Terms

Identify and explain the significance of each item below.

Senate (p. 126)
consuls (p. 126)
patricians (p. 129)
plebeians (p. 129)
Struggle of the Orders (p. 130)
tribunes (p. 131)
patron-client system (p. 132)
Punic Wars (p. 132)
paterfamilias (p. 135)
manumission (p. 138)
latifundia (p. 142)
First Triumvirate (p. 147)
Second Triumvirate (p. 150)

NOTES

1. Aubrey de Sélincourt, trans., *Livy: The Early History of Rome, Books 1–5 of the History of Rome from Its Foundation* (Baltimore: Penguin Books, 1960), p. 58.
2. Plutarch, *Pyrrhos* 21.14. In this chapter, works in Latin with no translator noted were translated by John Buckler.
3. Naphtali Lewis and Meyer Reinhold, eds., *Roman Civilization: Sourcebook I: The Republic* (New York: Harper Torchbooks, 1951), p. 104.

4. Polybius, *The Histories* 38.21.
5. Sallust, *War with Catiline* 10.1–3.
6. Lewis and Reinhold, *Roman Civilization*, p. 489.
7. Ovid, *Fasti* 2.535–539.
8. Horace, *Epistles* 2.1.156.

CHAPTER PREVIEW

Augustus's Reign
How did Augustus create a foundation for the Roman Empire?

Augustus's Successors
How did the Roman state develop after Augustus?

Rome and the Provinces
What was life like in the city of Rome, and what was it like in the provinces?

The Coming of Christianity
How did Christianity grow into a major religious movement?

The Empire in Disarray
What explains the chaos of the third century C.E.?

Life in Imperial Rome
In this terra-cotta relief from the third century C.E., a woman sells fruit in a shop while customers line up in front of her. Shops like this one, where goods were sold and neighbors met each other for conversation, were common in imperial Rome.
(De Agostini Picture Library/A. Dagli Orti/Bridgeman Images)

6

The Roman Empire

27 B.C.E.–284 C.E.

In 27 B.C.E. the civil wars were largely over, at least for a time. With peace came prosperity, stability, and a new vision of Rome's destiny. In his epic poem the *Aeneid* celebrating the founding of Rome, the Roman poet Virgil expressed this vision:

> You, Roman, remember—these are your arts:
> To rule nations, and to impose the ways of peace,
> To spare the humble and to conquer the proud.[1]

This was an ideal, of course, but Augustus, now the ruler of Rome, recognized that ideals and traditions were important to Romans. Instead of creating a new form of government, he left the republic officially intact, but held all real power himself. The rulers that followed him continued to transform Rome into an empire. The boundaries of the Roman Empire expanded in all directions, and the army became an important means of Romanization through its forts, camps, and cities. Gaul, Germany, Britain, and eastern Europe were introduced to Greco-Roman culture. A new religion, Christianity, developed in the eastern Roman province of Judaea, and spread on the roads and sea-lanes used by Roman traders and troops. By the third century C.E. civil wars had returned, however, and it seemed as if Augustus's creation would collapse. ■

Augustus's Reign

FOCUS QUESTION
How did Augustus create a foundation for the Roman Empire?

After Augustus (r. 27 B.C.E.–14 C.E.) ended the civil wars that had raged off and on for decades, he faced the monumental problems of reconstruction. He first had to reconstruct the constitution and the organs of government. Next he had to pay his armies for their services, and care for the welfare of the provinces. Then he had to address the danger of various groups on Rome's European frontiers.

Augustus was highly successful in meeting these challenges. The result of this work was a system of government in which the emperor held all executive power in both the civil government and the military. The Senate remained as a prestigious advisory body whose members functioned at the desire and request of the emperor.

The Principate

Augustus claimed that he was restoring the republic, but he actually transformed the government into one in which all real power was held by a single ruler. As he did this, however, he maintained the illusion that the republic still existed, and he linked his rule with the traditional idea of SPQR (see Chapter 5).

Augustus fit his own position into the republican constitution not by creating a new office for himself but by gradually taking over many of the offices that traditionally had been held by separate people. The Senate named him often as both consul and tribune. As consul, Augustus had the right to call the Senate into session and present legislation to the citizens' assemblies, and as tribune he presided over the *concilium plebis* (see Chapter 5). He was also named **imperator**, a title with which the Senate customarily honored a general after a major victory. He held control of the army, which he made a permanent standing organization. Furthermore, recognizing the importance of religion, he had himself named *pontifex maximus*, or chief priest.

An additional title that Augustus had the Senate bestow on him was *princeps civitatis* (prihn-KEHPS cih-vee-TAH-tees), "first citizen of the state." This title had no official powers attached to it and had been used as an honorific for centuries, so it was inoffensive to Roman ears. One of Augustus's cleverest tactics was to use noninflammatory language for himself and the changes he was making. Only later would *princeps civitatis* become the basis of the word *prince*, meaning "sovereign ruler," although "prince" quite accurately describes what Augustus actually was.

Considering what had happened to Julius Caesar, Augustus wisely wielded all his power in the background, and the government he created is called the **principate**. Although principate leaders were said to be "first among equals," Augustus's tenure clearly marked the end of the republic. Still, for a generation that had known only civil war, the shift away from republican government may have seemed minor compared to the benefits brought by the stability of Augustus's rule.

Augustus curtailed the power of the Senate, but it continued to exist as the chief deliberative body of the state, and it continued to act as a court of law. Under Augustus and his successors, it provided officials to administer

Augustus as Imperator In this marble statue, found in the villa of Augustus's widow, Augustus is depicted in a military uniform and in a pose usually used to show leaders addressing their troops. This portrayal emphasizes his role as imperator, the head of the army. The figures on his breastplate show various peoples the Romans had defeated or with whom they had made treaties, along with assorted deities. Although Augustus did not declare himself a god—as later Roman emperors would—this statue shows him barefoot, just as gods and heroes were in classical Greek statuary, and accompanied by Cupid riding a dolphin, both symbols of the goddess Venus, whom he claimed as an ancestor. (Vatican Museums and Galleries, Vatican State/Bridgeman Images)

Rome and its provinces. The Senate's relations with particular emperors were often hostile, and senators were involved in plots to overthrow various emperors. In general, however, the Senate adapted itself to the new reality and cooperated in running the empire. Governors sent to the provinces were often members of the Senate, and they took the Roman legal system with them.

Without specifically saying so, Augustus created the office of emperor. The English word *emperor* is derived from the Latin word *imperator*, an origin that reflects the fact that Augustus's command of the army was the main source of his power. Augustus governed the provinces where troops were needed for defense and guarded the frontiers from attack. He could declare war, he controlled deployment of the Roman army, and he paid the soldiers' wages. He granted bonuses and gave veterans retirement benefits. Augustus never shared control of the army, and no Roman found it easy to defy him militarily.

Augustus professionalized the military even more than it had been in the late republic, and made the army a recognized institution of government. Soldiers were generally volunteers; they received a salary and training under career officers who advanced in rank according to experience, ability, valor, and length of service. Soldiers served twenty-year terms, plus five in the reserves, and on retiring were to be given a discharge bonus of cash or a piece of land. To pay for this, Augustus ordered a tax on inheritance and on certain types of sales. Those soldiers who were Roman citizens were organized into legions, units of about five thousand men. The legions were backed up by auxiliaries, military forces of noncitizens, some conscripts but mostly volunteers who also served twenty- or twenty-five-year terms. Auxiliaries were paid—though at a lower rate than legionaries—and were granted Roman citizenship when they retired, which gave them legal, social, and economic privileges. Legions were often transferred from place to place as the need arose. Auxiliaries were more likely to stay near the area where they had been recruited, but sometimes they served far away from home as well.

Grants of land to veterans had originally been in Italy, but by Augustus's time there was not enough land for this. Instead he gave veterans land in the frontier provinces that had been taken from the people the Romans conquered, usually near camps with active army units. Some veterans objected, and at Augustus's death they briefly revolted, but these colonies of veterans continued to play an important role in securing the Roman Empire's boundaries and controlling its newly won provinces. Augustus's veterans took abroad with them their Latin language and Roman culture, becoming important agents of Romanization.

The army that Augustus developed was loyal to him as a person, not as the head of the Roman state. This would lead to trouble later, but the basics of the political and military system that Augustus created lasted fairly well for almost three centuries.

Chronology

27 B.C.E.–68 C.E.	Julio-Claudian emperors; expansion into northern and western Europe
ca. 50 B.C.E.–20 C.E.	"Golden age" of Latin literature
ca. 3 B.C.E.–ca. 29 C.E.	Life of Jesus
69–96 C.E.	Flavian emperors; restoration of order
70 C.E.	Rebellion crushed in Judaea
96–180 C.E.	Era of the "five good emperors," with relative peace and prosperity
193–211 C.E.	Emperor Septimius Severus expands Rome's borders in Africa and western Asia
212 C.E.	Edict of Caracalla makes all free males living in Roman Empire citizens
235–284 C.E.	Barracks emperors; civil war; breakdown of the empire; economic decline

imperator Title given to a Roman general after a major victory that came to mean "emperor."

principate Official title of Augustus's form of government, taken from *princeps*, meaning "first citizen."

Roman Expansion

One of the most significant aspects of Augustus's reign was Roman expansion into northern and western Europe (Map 6.1). Augustus began his work in the west and north by completing the conquest of Spain begun by Scipio Africanus in the third century B.C.E. (see Chapter 5). In Gaul he founded twelve new towns, and the Roman road system linked new settlements with one another and with Italy. The German frontier along the Rhine River was the scene of hard fighting. In 12 B.C.E. Augustus ordered a major invasion of Germany beyond the Rhine. Roman legions advanced to the Elbe River, and the area north of the Main River and west of the Elbe

Modern place names of Roman cities

Roman name	Modern name
Aquincum	Budapest
Burdigala	Bordeaux
Camulodunum	Colchester
Colonia Claudia Agrippinensis	Cologne
Corduba	Córdoba
Eburacum	York
Emerita Augusta	Merida
Londinium	London
Lugdunum	Lyons
Lutetia Parisiorum	Paris
Massilia	Marseilles
Mediolanum	Milan
Moguntiacum	Mainz
Nemausus	Nîmes
Singidunum	Belgrade
Vindobona	Vienna

Map legend:
- Roman territory, 44 B.C.E.
- Territory added by death of Augustus, 14 B.C.E.
- Territory added by death of Trajan, 117 C.E.
- Territory added by death of Marcus Aurelius, 180 C.E.
- Territory gained and lost, with dates held
- Parthian Empire, ca. 180 C.E.
- Colony founded under Augustus

MAP 6.1 Roman Expansion Under the Empire, 44 B.C.E.–180 C.E.   Following Roman expansion during the republic, Augustus added vast tracts of Europe to the Roman Empire, which the emperor Trajan later enlarged by assuming control over parts of central Europe, the Near East, and North Africa.

was on the point of becoming Roman. But in 9 C.E. some twenty thousand Roman troops were annihilated at the Battle of the Teutoburg Forest and their general Varus was killed on the battlefield.

Meanwhile Roman troops penetrated the area of modern Austria, southern Bavaria, and western Hungary. Thereafter the Rhine and the Danube remained the Roman frontier in central Europe. The Romans began to build walls, forts, and watchtowers to firm up their defenses, especially in the area between the two rivers, where people could more easily enter Roman territory. The regions of modern Serbia, Bulgaria, and Romania in the Balkans fell, and the Romans created a land-based link between the eastern and western Mediterranean.

Within the area along the empire's northern border the legionaries and auxiliaries built fortified camps. Roads linked the camps with one another, and settlements grew up around the camps. Traders began to frequent the frontier and to do business with the people who lived there. Thus Roman culture—the rough-and-ready kind found in military camps—gradually spread into the north. As a result, for the first time central and northern Europe came into direct and continuous contact with Mediterranean culture. Many Roman camps grew into cities, transforming the economy of the area around them. Roman cities were the first urban developments in most parts of central and northern Europe.

As a political and religious bond between the provinces and Rome, Augustus encouraged the cult of **Roma et Augustus** (Rome and Augustus) as the guardians of the state and the source of all benefits to society. In praying for the good health and welfare of the emperor, Romans and provincials were praying for the empire itself. The cult spread rapidly, especially in the eastern Mediterranean, where it built on the ideas of divine kingship developed in the Hellenistic monarchies (see Chapter 4). Worshipping Roma et Augustus became a symbol of Roman unity, and Roman officials could often judge the degree of loyalty of a province by noting the extent of public temple activities.

Roma et Augustus Patriotic cult encouraged by Augustus and later emperors in which the good of Rome and the good of the emperor were linked.

To make his presence felt further, Augustus had himself portrayed on coins standing alongside the goddess Victory, and on celebratory stone arches built to commemorate military victories. In addition, he had temples, stadiums, marketplaces, and public buildings constructed in Rome and other cities. Later emperors expanded this imperial cult, erecting statues, triumphal arches, columns, temples, and other buildings to honor themselves, their family members, or their predecessors. Many of these were decorated with texts as well as images. Shortly after Augustus's death, for example, an inscription detailing his achievements, known as the *Res Gestae Divi Augusti* (The deeds of the divine Augustus), was carved on monuments throughout the Roman Empire. (See "Evaluating the Evidence 6.1: Augustus, *Res Gestae*," page 158.)

In the late eighteenth century the English historian Edward Gibbon dubbed the stability and relative peace within the empire that Augustus created the **pax Romana**, the "Roman peace," which he saw as lasting about two hundred years, until the end of the reign of Marcus Aurelius in 180 C.E. Those outside the empire might not have agreed that things were so peaceful. The Roman historian Tacitus wrote of a speech delivered by the Scottish chieftain Calcagus before a battle with an invading Roman army in which Calcagus says, "The Romans make a desert and call it peace." The speech may be an invention by Tacitus—this was a common practice for

pax Romana The "Roman peace," a period during the first and second centuries C.E. of political stability and relative peace.

Augustus, *Res Gestae*

During his lifetime Augustus wrote an official account of his long career that began in 44 B.C.E., when he was nineteen years old. He included the work with his will, which told the Senate to set it up as a public inscription. The original document, which no longer survives, was engraved on two bronze columns in front of the Mausoleum of Augustus, a large tomb erected in Rome by Augustus that is still standing. In many other places throughout the Roman Empire copies were carved into monuments, some of which survive, and the text became known as the Res Gestae Divi Augusti (The deeds of the divine Augustus). In this work Augustus offers his readers a firsthand account of his public life. He stresses that he has always acted according to the authority that the Romans bestowed upon him. However, Augustus's publicized opinions of his actions and aims were not always shared by others.

In the opening section Augustus lists his accomplishments and the honors bestowed upon him by the Roman Senate and people.

1. At the age of nineteen, on my own initiative and at my own expense, I raised an army by means of which I restored liberty to the republic, which had been oppressed by the tyranny of a faction. . . .

2. Those who slew my father [Julius Caesar, his adoptive father] I drove into exile, punishing their deed by due process of law, and afterwards when they waged war upon the republic I twice defeated them in battle.

3. Wars, both civil and foreign, I undertook throughout the world, on sea and land, and when victorious I spared all citizens who sued for pardon. The foreign nations which could with safety be pardoned I preferred to save rather than to destroy. The number of Roman citizens who bound themselves to me by military oath was about 500,000. Of

these I settled in colonies or sent back into their own towns, after their term of service, something more than 300,000, and to all I assigned lands, or gave money as a reward for military service. I captured six hundred ships, over and above those which were smaller than triremes.

4. . . . For successful operations on land and sea, conducted either by myself or by my lieutenants under my auspices, the Senate on fifty-five occasions decreed that thanks should be rendered to the immortal gods. The days on which such thanks were rendered by decree of the Senate numbered 890. . . .

6. . . . When the Senate and the Roman people unanimously agreed that I should be elected overseer of laws and morals, without a colleague and with the fullest power, I refused to accept any power offered me which was contrary to the traditions of our ancestors.

In the next section Augustus tells of his personal donations to the republic.

20. The Capitolium and the theatre of Pompey, both works involving great expense, I rebuilt without any inscription of my own name. I restored the channels of the aqueducts which in several places were falling into disrepair through age, and doubled the capacity of the aqueduct called the Marcia by turning a new spring into its channel. . . . I rebuilt in the city eighty-two temples of the gods, omitting none which at that time stood in need of repair. . . .

22. Three times in my own name I gave a show of gladiators, and five times in the name of my sons or grandsons; in these shows there fought about ten thousand men. Twice in my own name I furnished for the people an exhibition of athletes gathered from all parts of the world, and a third time in the name of my grandson.

ancient historians—but it captures the idea that not everyone saw the Roman Empire as a positive force. Gibbon's term has stuck, however, because, especially for those living away from contested frontier areas, this two-hundred-year stretch of Roman history was much more stable and prosperous than what came before or after.

The pax Romana was enforced by troops who remained on active duty or as reserves in the provinces and on the frontier, ready to respond to any resistance to Roman dominance. In general, however, Augustus respected local customs and ordered his

Four times I gave games in my own name; as representing other magistrates twenty-three times. . . . [O]n twenty-six occasions I gave to the people, in the circus, in the forum, or in the amphitheatre, hunts of African wild beasts, in which about three thousand five hundred beasts were slain.

He then discusses his military actions and founding of colonies.

~

25. I freed the sea from pirates. About thirty thousand slaves, captured in that war, who had run away from their masters and had taken up arms against the republic, I delivered to their masters for punishment. The whole of Italy voluntarily took oath of allegiance to me and demanded me as its leader in the war in which I was victorious at Actium. The provinces of the Spains, the Gauls, Africa, Sicily, and Sardinia took the same oath of allegiance. . . .

26. I extended the boundaries of all the provinces which were bordered by races not yet subject to our empire. The provinces of the Gauls, the Spains, and Germany, bounded by the ocean from Gades to the mouth of the Elbe, I reduced to a state of peace. The Alps, from the region such lies nearest to the Adriatic as far as the Tuscan Sea, I brought to a state of peace without waging on any tribe an unjust war. . . . On my order and under my auspices two armies were led, at almost the same time, into Ethiopia and into Arabia, which is called the "Happy," and very large forces of the enemy of both races were cut to pieces in battle and many towns were captured. . . .

28. I settled colonies of soldiers in Africa, Sicily, Macedonia, both Spains, Achaia, Asia, Syria, Gallia Narbonensis, Pisidia. Moreover, Italy has twenty-eight colonies founded under my auspices which have grown to be famous and populous during my lifetime.

Augustus concludes by describing the titles given to him by the Senate.

~

34. In my sixth and seventh consulships, when I had extinguished the flames of civil war, after receiving by universal consent the absolute control of affairs, I transferred the republic from my own control to the will of the Senate and the Roman people. For this service on my part I was given the title of Augustus by decree of the Senate, and the doorposts of my house were covered with laurels by public act, and a civic crown was fixed above my door, and a golden shield was placed in the Curia Julia whose inscription testified that the Senate and the Roman people gave me this in recognition of my valour, my clemency, my justice, and my piety. . . .

35. While I was administering my thirteenth consulship the Senate and the equestrian order and the entire Roman people gave me the title of Father of my Country, and decreed that this title should be inscribed upon the vestibule of my house and in the Senate-house and in the Forum Augustum. . . . At the time of writing this I was in my seventy-sixth year.

EVALUATE THE EVIDENCE

1. What major themes does Augustus address in his account of his career?
2. How does Augustus portray himself in this document?
3. Why do you think Augustus mentions the Senate, the Roman people, and the people of Italy so often?

Source: *Velleius Paterculus*, Loeb Classical Library, Volume 152, translated by Frederick W. Shipley; pp. 345, 347, 349, 351, 355, 377, 379, 381, 383, 385, 387, 389, 393, 399, 401. Cambridge, Mass.: Harvard University Press. First published 1924. The Loeb Classical Library® is a registered trademark of the President and Fellows of Harvard College.

governors to do the same. Roman governors applied Roman law to Romans living in their territories, but they let local people retain their own laws. As long as they provided taxes and did not rebel, they could continue to run their political and social lives as they had before Roman conquest.

While Romans did not force their culture on local people in Roman territories, local elites with aspirations knew that the best way to rise in stature and power was to adopt aspects of Roman culture. Thus, just as ambitious individuals in the Hellenistic world embraced Greek culture and learned to speak Greek, those determined to get

Organist and Horn Player Games, gladiatorial contests, and other events in the cities of the Roman Empire were often accompanied by music. In this floor mosaic from a villa in Nennig, Germany, built in the third century, a horn player plays a large curved instrument known as a *cornu*, which was also used by the military to call troops. The organist plays a water organ (*hydraulis*) in which water stored in the hexagonal podium was pumped through tubes and the force of the water pushed air through the organ pipes. (Museum für Vor und Frühgeschichte, Saarbrücken, Germany/Bridgeman Images)

ahead now learned Latin, and sometimes Greek as well if they wished to be truly well educated.

Especially in cities, Roman culture blended with local traditions. The Roman city of Lugdunum, modern Lyons in southern France, provides an example of this process. The site was originally the capital of a state that had existed before the Roman conquest of Gaul, named for the Gallic god Lug. Julius Caesar made it a Roman military settlement. In 12 B.C.E. Augustus made it a political and religious center, with responsibilities for administering the area and for honoring the gods of both the Romans and Gauls. Physical symbols of this fusion of two cultures can still be seen today. The extensive remains of the amphitheater and other buildings testify to the fact that the city was prosperous enough to afford expensive Roman construction and the style of life that it represented. Many such towns were eventually granted Roman citizenship due to their embrace of Roman culture and government and their importance to the Roman economy. Ambitious young men flocked to provincial capitals such as Lugdunum, for it was here, and not in the countryside, that one could make one's mark.

The Flowering of Latin Literature

Many poets and prose writers were active in the late republic and the principate, and scholars of literature later judged their work to be of such high quality that they called the period from about 50 B.C.E. to 20 C.E. the "golden age" of Latin literature. Roman poets and prose writers celebrated the physical and emotional joys of a comfortable life. Their works were highly polished, elegant in style, and intellectual in conception. Roman poets referred to the gods often and treated mythological themes, but the core subject matter of their work was human, not divine.

Rome's greatest poet was Virgil (70–19 B.C.E.), who drew on earlier traditions, but gave them new twists. The *Georgics*, for example, is a poem about agriculture that used Hellenistic models to capture both the peaceful pleasures and the day-to-day violence of rural life. In vivid language Virgil depicts the death of one of the bulls pulling a plow and the farmer unyoking the remaining animal:

> Look, the bull, shining under the rough plough,
> falls to the ground
> and vomits from his mouth blood mixed with foam,
> and releases his dying groan.
> Sadly moves the ploughman, unharnessing the
> young steer grieving for the death of his brother
> and leaves in the middle of the job
> the plough stuck fast.[2]

Virgil's masterpiece is the *Aeneid* (uh-NEE-ihd), an epic poem that is the Latin equivalent of the Greek *Iliad* and *Odyssey* (see Chapter 3). Virgil's account of the founding of Rome and the early years of the city gave final form to the legend of Aeneas, the Trojan hero (and ancestor of Romulus and Remus) who escaped to Italy at the fall of Troy:

> Arms and the man I sing, who first made way,
> predestined exile, from the Trojan shore
> to Italy, the blest Lavinian strand.
> Smitten of storms he was on land and sea
> by violence of Heaven, to satisfy
> stern Juno's sleepless wrath; and much in war
> he suffered, seeking at the last to found
> the city, and bring o'er his fathers' gods
> to safe abode in Latium; whence arose
> the Latin race, old Alba's reverend lords,
> and from her hills wide-walled, imperial Rome.[3]

As Virgil told it, Aeneas became the lover of Dido, the widowed queen of Carthage, but left her because his destiny called him to found Rome. Swearing the destruction of Rome, Dido committed suicide, and according to Virgil, her enmity helped cause the Punic Wars. In leaving Dido, an "Eastern" queen, Aeneas put duty and the good of the state ahead of marriage or pleasure. The parallels between this story and the very recent real events involving Antony and Cleopatra were not lost on Virgil's audience. Making the public aware of these parallels, and of Virgil's description of Aeneas as an ancestor of Julius Caesar, fit well with Augustus's aims. Therefore, Augustus encouraged Virgil to write the *Aeneid* and made sure it was circulated widely immediately after Virgil died.

The poet Horace (65–8 B.C.E.) rose from humble beginnings to friendship with Augustus. The son of an ex-slave and tax collector, Horace nonetheless received an excellent education, which he finished in Athens. After Augustus's victory Horace returned to Rome and became Virgil's friend. His most important works are a series of odes, short lyric poems often focusing on a single individual or event. One of these commemorated Augustus's victory over Antony and Cleopatra at Actium in 31 B.C.E. Horace depicted Cleopatra as a frenzied queen, drunk with desire to destroy Rome, a view that has influenced opinions about Cleopatra until today.

The historian Livy (59 B.C.E.–17 C.E.) was a friend of Augustus and a supporter of the principate. He especially approved of Augustus's efforts to restore what he saw as republican virtues. Livy's history of Rome, titled simply *Ab Urbe Condita* (From the founding of the city), began with the legend of Aeneas and ended with the reign of Augustus. Livy used the works of earlier Greek and Roman writers, as well as his own experiences, as his source material.

Augustus actively encouraged poets and writers, but he could also turn against them. The poet Ovid (AH-vuhd) (43 B.C.E.–17 C.E.) wrote erotic poetry about absent lovers and the joys of seduction, as well as other works about religious festivals and mythology. His best-known work is *The Art of Love*, a satire of the serious instructional poetry that was common in Rome at the time. *The Art of Love* provides advice to men about how to get and keep women, and for women about how to get and keep men. (See "Evaluating the Evidence 6.2: Ovid, *The Art of Love*," page 162.) This

Ovid, *The Art of Love*

The Art of Love is a humorous guide for lovers written by the Roman poet Ovid. Ovid addresses the first two parts to men, instructing them on how to seduce and keep women — look good, give them compliments, don't be too obvious. The third part is his corresponding advice for women, which in its main points is the same. The section below comes from the beginning of part one, advising men on where and how to meet women.

While you are footloose and free to play the field at your
　　pleasure,
Watch for the one you can tell, "I want no other but
　　you!"
She is not going to come to you floating down from the
　　heavens:
For the right kind of a girl you must keep using your eyes.
Hunters know where to spread their nets for the stag in
　　his cover,
Hunters know where the boar gnashes his teeth in the
　　glade.
Fowlers know brier and bush, and fishermen study the
　　waters
Baiting the hook for the cast just where the fish may be
　　found.
So you too, in your hunt for material worthy of
　　loving,
First will have to find out where the game usually goes.

. . .

. . . The theater's curve is a very good place for your
　　hunting,
More opportunity here, maybe, than anywhere else.
Here you may find one to love, or possibly only to have
　　fun with,
Someone to take for a night, someone to have and to
　　hold.

. . .

Furthermore, don't overlook the meetings when horses are
　　running;
In the crowds at the track opportunity waits.

There is no need for a code of finger-signals or nodding,
Sit as close as you like; no one will stop you at all.
In fact, you will have to sit close — that's one of the rules,
　　at a race track.
Whether she likes it or not, contact is part of the game.
Try to find something in common, to open the
　　conversation;
Don't care too much what you say, just so that every one
　　hears
Ask her, "Whose colors are those?" — that's good for an
　　opening gambit.
Put your own bet down, fast, on whatever she plays.

. . .

Often it happens that dust may fall on the blouse of the
　　lady.
If such dust should fall, carefully brush it away.
Even if there's no dust, brush off whatever there isn't.
Any excuse will do: why do you think you have hands?

. . .

There is another good ground, the gladiatorial shows.
On that sorrowful sand Cupid has often contested,
And the watcher of wounds often has had it himself.
While he is talking, or touching a hand, or studying
　　entries,
Asking which one is ahead after his bet has been laid,
Wounded himself, he groans to feel the shaft of the
　　arrow;
He is victim himself, no more spectator, but show.

EVALUATE THE EVIDENCE

1. What metaphors and symbols does Ovid use to describe finding a lover and falling in love?
2. What does this poem indicate about leisure activities in the Rome of Ovid's day?

Source: Ovid, *The Art of Love*, trans. Rolfe, pp. 106–110. Copyright © 1957 Indiana University Press. Reprinted with permission of Indiana University Press.

Ara Pacis

In the middle years of Augustus's reign, the Roman Senate ordered a huge altar, the Ara Pacis, built to honor him and the peace he had brought to the empire. This was decorated with life-size reliefs of Augustus and members of his family, prominent Romans, and other people and deities. One side, shown here, depicts a goddess figure, most likely the goddess Peace herself, with twin babies on her lap, flanked by nymphs representing land and sea, and surrounded by plants and animals.

(DEA/Gianni Dagli Orti/De Agostini/Getty Images)

EVALUATE THE EVIDENCE

1. What do the elements depicted here most likely symbolize?
2. The Ara Pacis and the *Res Gestae* (see page 158) were both works of public art designed to commemorate the deeds of Augustus. Why might the Senate and Augustus have commissioned such works? Can you think of contemporary parallels?

work was so popular, Ovid relates, that shortly after completing it he felt compelled to write *The Cure for Love*, advising people how to fall out of love and forget their former lovers. Have lots of new lovers, it advises, and don't hang around places, eat foods, or listen to songs that will make you remember your former lover. In 8 B.C.E. Augustus banished Ovid to a city on the Black Sea far from Rome. Why he did so is a mystery, and Ovid himself states only that the reason was "a poem and a mistake." Some scholars argue that Augustus banished Ovid because his poetry celebrated adultery at a time when Augustus was promoting marriage and childbearing, and others say it was because the poet knew about political conspiracies. Whatever its causes, the exile of Ovid became a symbol of misunderstood poetic genius for many later writers.

Marriage and Morality

Augustus's banishing of Ovid may have simply been an excuse to get rid of him, but concern with morality and with what were perceived as traditional Roman virtues was a matter not just for literature in Augustan Rome, but also for law. Augustus promoted marriage and childbearing through legal changes that released free women and freedwomen (female slaves who had been freed) from male guardianship if they had given birth to a certain number of children. Men and women who were unmarried or had no children were restricted in the inheritance of property. Adultery, defined as sex with a married woman or with a woman under male guardianship, was made a crime, not simply the private family matter it had been.

In imperial propaganda, Augustus had his own family depicted as a model of traditional morality, with his wife Livia at his side and dressed in conservative and somewhat old-fashioned clothing rather than the more daring Greek styles that wealthy women were actually wearing in Rome at the time. (See "Evaluating the Evidence 6.3: Ara

Pacis," page 163.) In fact, Augustus's family did not live up to this ideal. Augustus had his daughter Julia arrested and exiled for adultery and treason. Although it is impossible to tell what actually happened, she seems to have had at least one affair after her father forced her to marry a second husband—her stepbrother Tiberius—whom she hated.

Same-sex relationships among men in Rome followed a variety of patterns: some were between social equals and others between men and their slaves. Moralists denounced sexual relationships in which men squandered family money or became subservient to those of lower social status, but no laws were passed against same-sex relationships. We do not know very much about same-sex relationships among women in Rome, though court gossip and criticism of powerful women, including the wives of Augustus's successors, sometimes included charges of such relationships, along with charges of heterosexual promiscuity and other sexual slander.

Augustus's Successors

FOCUS QUESTION
How did the Roman state develop after Augustus?

Augustus's success in creating solid political institutions was tested by the dynasty he created, the Julio-Claudians, whose members schemed against one another trying to win and hold power. The incompetence of one of the Julio-Claudians, Nero, and his failure to deal with the army generals allowed a military commander, Vespasian (veh-SPAY-zhuhn), to claim the throne and establish a new dynasty, the Flavians. The Flavians were followed by the "five good emperors," who were relatively successful militarily and politically. Rome entered a period of political stability, prosperity, and relative peace that lasted until the end of the second century C.E.

The Julio-Claudians and the Flavians

Because the principate was not technically an office, Augustus could not legally hand it to a successor. There were various plots surrounding the succession, including the one for which Ovid was banished. Augustus dealt firmly with plotters, sometimes having them executed, and he also found a way to solve the succession issue. Just as his great-uncle Julius Caesar had adopted him, he adopted his stepson Tiberius (who was also his son-in-law) as his son. Adoption of an heir was a common practice among members of the elite in Rome, who used this method to pass on property to a chosen younger man—often a relative—if they had no sons. Long before Augustus's death he shared his consular and tribunician powers with Tiberius, thus grooming him for the principate. In his will Augustus left most of his vast fortune to Tiberius, and the Senate formally requested Tiberius to assume the burdens of the principate. Formalities apart, by the time of his death in 14 C.E. Augustus had succeeded in creating a dynasty.

For fifty years after Augustus's death the dynasty that he established—known as the Julio-Claudians because all were members of the Julian and Claudian clans—provided the emperors of Rome. Two of the Julio-Claudians who followed Augustus, Tiberius and Claudius, were sound rulers and able administrators. The other two, Caligula and Nero, were weak and frivolous men who exercised their power poorly and to the detriment of the empire.

Praetorians Imperial bodyguard created by Augustus.

Augustus's creation of an imperial bodyguard known as the **Praetorians** (pree-TAWR-ee-uhnz) had repercussions for his successors. In 41 C.E. the Praetorians murdered Caligula and forced the Senate to ratify their choice of Claudius as emperor.

The events were repeated frequently. During the first three centuries of the empire, the Praetorian Guard all too often murdered emperors they were supposed to protect, and raised to emperor men of their own choosing.

In his early years Nero ruled fairly well, but he became increasingly paranoid about the power of those around him. In 68 C.E. his erratic actions and his policies led to a revolt by several generals, which was supported by the Praetorian Guard and members of the Senate. He was declared an enemy of the people and committed suicide. This opened the way to widespread disruption and civil war. In 69 C.E., the "year of the four emperors," four men claimed the position of emperor in quick succession. Roman armies in Gaul, on the Rhine, and in the east marched on Rome to make their commanders emperor. The man who emerged triumphant was Vespasian, commander of the eastern armies.

Vespasian restored the discipline of the armies. To prevent others from claiming the throne, Vespasian designated his sons Titus and Domitian as his successors, thus establishing the Flavian dynasty. Although Roman policy was to rule by peaceful domination whenever possible, he used the army to suppress the rebellions that had begun erupting at the end of Nero's reign. The most famous of these was one that had burst out in Judaea in 66 C.E., sparked by long-standing popular unrest over taxes. Jewish rebels initially defeated the Roman troops stationed in Judaea, but a larger army under the leadership of Vespasian and his son Titus put down the revolt. They destroyed much of the city of Jerusalem, including the Jewish temple, in 70 C.E., and took thousands of Jews as military captives and slaves, dispersing them throughout the empire. The military conquest of Judaea represented a failure of official Roman policy, but it is a good example of the way in which the Romans maintained clear control over their subjects, a control backed by military force if initial attempts at negotiation failed.

The Flavians carried on Augustus's work in Italy and on the frontiers. During the brief reign of Vespasian's son Titus, Mount Vesuvius in southern Italy erupted, destroying Pompeii and other cities and killing thousands of people. (See "Individuals in Society: Pliny the Elder," page 166.) Titus gave money and sent officials to organize the relief effort. His younger brother Domitian, who followed him as emperor, won additional territory in Germany, consolidating it into two new provinces. Later in life he became more autocratic, however, and he was killed in 96 C.E. in a plot that involved his own wife, ending the Flavian dynasty.

The Age of the "Five Good Emperors"

The Flavians were succeeded by a line of relatively competent emperors, whom the political philosopher Niccolò Machiavelli in the sixteenth century termed the **"five good emperors"**—Nerva, Trajan, Hadrian, Antoninus Pius, and Marcus Aurelius. Machiavelli praised them because they all adopted able men as their successors during their lifetimes instead of relying on birth to provide an heir, thus giving Rome stability. None except Marcus Aurelius had a legitimate son, however, so they actually had little choice. They were also following the pattern set by Julius Caesar and Augustus, not breaking new ground. The last four "good emperors" were, in fact, related members of the Antonine family. Historians since Machiavelli have also noted that in some cases their choices were the result of pressure by the army or members of their family, rather than their own political astuteness. Whatever the reasons for the

"five good emperors" The five Roman emperors (Nerva, Trajan, Hadrian, Antoninus Pius, and Marcus Aurelius) of the second century C.E. whose reigns were relatively prosperous and stable.

INDIVIDUALS IN SOCIETY

Pliny the Elder

"My uncle was stationed at Misenum, in active command of the fleet. On 24 August, in the early afternoon, my mother drew his attention to a cloud of unusual size and appearance. . . . My uncle's scholarly acumen saw at once that it was important enough for a closer inspection, and he ordered a boat to be made ready." So begins a letter from the statesman and writer Pliny the Younger to the historian Tacitus, describing what happened when Mount Vesuvius erupted in 79 C.E. Pliny provided terrifying details of clouds of hot ash, raining pumice stones, and sheets of fire, and then sang the praises of his uncle, also named Pliny, whose actions, "begun in a spirit of inquiry, [were] completed as a hero." According to Pliny the Younger's account, his uncle "steer[ed] his course straight for the danger zone with the intention of bringing help to many more people. . . . He was entirely fearless, describing each new movement and phase of the portent to be noted down exactly as he observed them . . . and when his helmsman advised him to turn back he refused, telling him that Fortune stood by the courageous." The elder Pliny (23 C.E.–79 C.E.) died on the beach near Pompeii, most likely from inhaling fumes that aggravated his asthma. His body was discovered several days later when the smoke and ash cleared.

The younger Pliny used this letter to portray his uncle as a model of traditional Roman virtues, but some of what he related was not an exaggeration. Like many young men of his social class — the equestrian — Pliny the Elder studied law and then joined the army as an officer. He was involved in several military campaigns in Germany and also found time to write books, including a volume on military tactics and several biographies. He left military service during Nero's reign and kept out of the limelight, writing noncontroversial books on grammar and rhetoric. After Nero committed suicide and Vespasian came to power, Pliny went back into government service, serving as the procurator (governor) of several different provinces. He again wrote biographies and histories, all of which are now lost, and the work that became his masterpiece, *Natural History*, an encyclopedia in which he sought to cover everything that was known to ancient Romans. In thirty-seven volumes, *Natural History* covers what we would now term biology, geology, astronomy, mineralogy, geography, ethnography, comparative anthropology, medicine, painting, building techniques, and many other subjects. Pliny's "spirit of inquiry" shines through this work, which he researched through the study of hundreds of sources (all carefully cited) and wrote while he was traveling around in government service. It is one of the largest works to have survived from the Roman Empire and served as a source of knowledge into the Renaissance, when it was one of the very first classical books to be published after the invention of the printing press in the fifteenth century. Pliny finished a first draft in about 77 C.E. and was working on revisions when he was appointed fleet commander in the Roman navy and sent to Misenum, near Naples. There the cloud of smoke from the erupting Vesuvius was too interesting for him to ignore, and he set off in a boat to investigate, with deadly results.

No contemporary portrait of Pliny the Elder survives, but his nephew reports that when his body was discovered, it was "still fully clothed and looking more like sleep than death." When Pompeii was excavated, archaeologists used plaster to fill the voids in layers of ash that once held human bodies, allowing us to see the exact position a person was in when he or she died. This plaster cast is not Pliny but is as close to him in death as we can come. (© SZ Photo/Manfred Storck/ Bridgeman Images)

QUESTIONS FOR ANALYSIS

1. What Roman ideals does the younger Pliny portray his uncle as exemplifying through his conduct during the eruption?
2. How did army and government service in the Roman Empire provide opportunities for men of broad interests like Pliny?

Source: Quotations from Pliny the Younger, *Letters* 6.16, translated with an introduction by Betty Radice, vol. 1, pp. 166, 168 (Penguin Classics 1963, reprinted 1969). Reproduced by permission of Penguin Books Ltd.

pattern, however, because all of these emperors were experienced generals and members of the Senate, Rome was provided with a stable series of well-trained political and military leaders for nearly a century, from 96 C.E. to 180 C.E.

Augustus had claimed that his influence arose from the collection of offices the Senate had bestowed on him and that he was merely the first citizen. Already during his rule many recognized that this was a façade, but the Senate continued to exist as a deliberative body and Rome remained officially a republic. Gradually the rulers expanded their individual powers, however, and Rome became in fact an empire, in which increasing amounts of power were held by one man. Although they never adopted the title "king"—this would have been seen as too great a break with Roman traditions—the rulers of Rome are conventionally called emperors. And as emperors took on new tasks and functions, their influence was felt in more areas of life and government.

Hadrian is typical of the emperors of the second century C.E. He received a solid education in Rome and became an ardent admirer of Greek culture. He caught the attention of his elder cousin Trajan, the future emperor, who started him on a military career. At age nineteen Hadrian served on the Danube frontier, where he learned the details of how the Roman army lived and fought and saw for himself the problems of defending the frontiers. When Trajan became emperor in 98 C.E., Hadrian was given important positions in which he learned how to defend and run the empire. Although Trajan did not officially declare Hadrian his successor, at Trajan's death in 117 Hadrian assumed power.

Hadrian built a number of buildings, including the circular Pantheon in Rome and new temples in Athens. He established more formal imperial administrative departments and separated civil service from military service. Men with little talent or taste for the army could instead serve the state as administrators. These innovations made for more efficient running of the empire and increased the authority of the emperor.

Under Trajan the boundaries of the Roman Empire were expanded to their farthest extent, and Hadrian worked to maintain most of these holdings, although he pulled back Roman armies from areas in the East he considered indefensible. No longer a conquering force, the army was expected to defend what had already been won. Forts and watch stations guarded the borders. Outside the forts the Romans built a system of roads that allowed the forts to be quickly supplied and reinforced in times of rebellion or unrest. Trouble for the Romans included two major revolts by Jews in the eastern part of the empire, which resulted in heavy losses on both sides and the exile of many Jews from Judaea.

Roman soldiers also built walls, of which the most famous was one across northern England built primarily during Hadrian's reign. Hadrian's Wall, as it became known, protected Romans from attacks from the north, and also allowed them to regulate immigration and trade through the many gates along the wall. Like all walls around cities or across territory, it served as a symbol and means of power and control as well as a defensive strategy. The later emperor Antoninus Pius built a second wall one hundred miles north, but this was quickly abandoned. Thousands of troops patrolled Hadrian's Wall until the Romans pulled out of the area in the late fourth century.

Roman Britain, ca. 130 C.E.

As the empire expanded, the army grew larger, and more and more troops were auxiliary forces of noncitizens. Because army service could lead to citizenship, men from the provinces and even from beyond the borders of the Roman Empire joined the army willingly to gain this, receive a salary, and learn a trade. The army evolved into a garrison force, with troops guarding specific areas for long periods. Soldiers on active duty had originally been prohibited from marrying, but this restriction was increasingly ignored, and some troops brought their wives and families along on their assignments.

Rome and the Provinces

FOCUS QUESTION
What was life like in the city of Rome, and what was it like in the provinces?

The expansion and stabilization of the empire brought changes to life in the city of Rome and also to life in the provinces in the first two centuries C.E. The city grew to a huge size, bringing the problems that plague any crowded urban area but also opportunities for work and leisure. Roads and secure sea-lanes linked the empire in one vast web, creating a network of commerce and communication. Trade and production flourished in the provinces, and Romans came into indirect contact with China.

Life in Imperial Rome

Rome was truly an extraordinary city, and with a population of over a million it may have been the largest city in the world. Although it boasted stately palaces and beautiful residential areas, most people lived in shoddily constructed houses. They took whatever work was available, producing food, clothing, construction materials, and the many other items needed by the city's residents, or selling these products from small shops or at the city's many marketplaces.

Many residents of the city of Rome were slaves, who ranged from highly educated household tutors or government officials and widely sought sculptors to workers who engaged in hard physical tasks. Slaves sometimes attempted to flee their masters, but those who failed in their escape attempts were returned to their masters and often branded on their foreheads. Others had metal collars fastened around their necks. One collar discovered near Rome read: "I have run away. Capture me. If you take me back to my master Zoninus, you will receive a gold coin."[4]

A story told about the author Plutarch reveals Roman attitudes toward slavery. One of Plutarch's educated slaves had read some of his master's philosophical writings and began to talk back to his master, for which Plutarch had him flogged. The slave accused his master of not acting very philosophically. Plutarch told the man with the whip to continue while he and the slave discussed philosophy. We have no idea whether this actually happened, but it demonstrates the reality of life for most slaves: lofty ideals did not interfere with their actual treatment.

Romans used the possibility of manumission as a means of controlling the behavior of their slaves, and individual Romans did sometimes free their slaves. Often these were house slaves who had virtually become members of the family and who often stayed with their former owner's family after being freed. The example of Helene, the slave of Marcus Aurelius Ammonio, is typical: the master "manumitted in the presence of friends his house-born female Helene, about 34 years old, and ordered her to be free."[5] Ammonio then gave her a gift of money. Manumission was limited by law, however, in part because freeing slaves made them citizens, allowing them to receive public grain and gifts of money, which some Romans thought debased pure Roman citizenship.

A typical day for the Roman family began with a modest breakfast, as in the days of the republic. Afterward came a trip to the outdoor market for the day's provisions. Seafood was a favorite item, as the Romans normally ate meat only at festivals. While poor people ate salt fish, the more prosperous dined on rare fish, oysters, squid, and eels. Wine was the common drink, and the rich often enjoyed rare vintages imported from abroad. Rich or poor, Romans mixed their wine with water, because drinking wine straight was seen as vulgar.

As in the republic, children began their education at home, where parents emphasized moral conduct, especially reverence for the gods and the law and respect for elders. Daughters learned how to manage the house, and sons learned the basics of their future calling from their fathers, who also taught them the use of weapons for military service. Boys boxed, swam, and learned to ride when possible, all to increase their strength, while giving them basic skills. Wealthy boys gained formal education from tutors or schools, generally favoring rhetoric and law for a political career. The lawyer and educator Quintilian (ca. 35–ca. 100 C.E.) expressed a widely held belief that public speaking was the most important academic subject for active citizenship and public life, and that school was the best place to learn this skill:

> The man who can really play his part as a citizen and is capable of meeting the demands both of public and private business, the man who can guide a state by his counsels, give it a firm basis by his legislation and purge its vices by his decisions as a judge, is assuredly no other than the orator. . . . It is above all things necessary that our future orator, who will have to live in the utmost publicity and in the broad daylight of public life, should become accustomed from his childhood to move in society without fear and habituated to a life far removed from that of the pale student, the solitary, and the recluse. His mind requires constant stimulus and excitement, whereas retirement such as has just been mentioned induces languor and the mind becomes mildewed like things that are left in the dark, or else flies to the opposite extreme and becomes puffed up with empty conceit; for he who has no standard of comparison by which to judge his own powers will necessarily rate them too high. . . . Further, at home he can only learn what is taught to himself, while at school he will learn what is taught others as well.[6]

Approaches to Urban Problems

Fire and crime were serious problems in the city, even after Augustus created urban fire and police forces. Streets were narrow, drainage was inadequate, and sanitation was poor. Numerous inscriptions record prohibitions against dumping human refuse and even cadavers on the grounds of sanctuaries and cemeteries. Private houses generally lacked toilets, so people used chamber pots.

In the second century C.E. urban planning and new construction improved the situation. For example, engineers built an elaborate system that collected sewage from public baths, the ground floors of buildings, and public latrines. They also built hundreds of miles of **aqueducts**, sophisticated systems of canals, channels, and pipes,

aqueducts Canals, channels, and pipes that brought freshwater into cities.

Roman Architecture The Pont du Gard at Nîmes in France is a bridge over a river carrying an aqueduct that supplied millions of gallons of water per day to the Roman city of Nîmes in Gaul; the water flowed in a channel at the very top. Although this bridge was built largely without mortar or concrete, many Roman aqueducts and bridges relied on concrete and sometimes iron rods for their strength. (© Masterfile Royalty Free)

most of them underground, that brought freshwater into the city from the surrounding hills. The aqueducts, powered entirely by gravity, required regular maintenance, but they were a great improvement and helped make Rome a very attractive place to live. Building aqueducts required thousands and sometimes tens of thousands of workers, who were generally paid out of the imperial treasury. Aqueducts became a feature of Roman cities in many parts of the empire.

Better disposal of sewage was one way that people living in Rome tried to maintain their health, and they also used a range of treatments to stay healthy and cure illness. This included treatments based on the ideas of the Greek physician Hippocrates; folk remedies; prayers and rituals at the temple of the god of medicine, Asclepius; surgery; and combinations of all of these.

The most important medical researcher and physician working in imperial Rome was Galen (ca. 129–ca. 200 C.E.), a Greek born in modern-day Turkey. Like anyone hoping to rise in stature and wealth, he came to Rome. Building on the work of Hellenistic physicians (see Chapter 4), Galen wrote a huge number of treatises on anatomy and physiology, and became the personal physician of many prominent Romans, including several emperors. He promoted the idea that imbalances among various bodily fluids caused illness, and recommended bloodletting as a cure. This would remain a standard treatment in Western medicine until the eighteenth century. His research into the nervous system and the operation of muscles—most of which he conducted on animals, because the Romans forbade dissections of human cadavers—proved to be more accurate than did his ideas about the circulation of fluids. So did his practical advice on the treatment of wounds, much of which grew out of his and others' experiences with soldiers on the battlefield.

Neither Galen nor any other Roman physician could do much for infectious diseases, and in 165 C.E. troops returning from campaigns in the East brought a new disease with them, which spread quickly in the city and then beyond into other parts of the empire. Modern epidemiologists think this was most likely smallpox, but in the ancient world it became known simply as the Antonine plague, because it occurred during the reigns of emperors from the Antonine family. Whatever it was, it appears to have been extremely virulent in the city of Rome and among the Roman army for a decade or so.

Along with fire and disease, food was an issue in the ever more crowded city. Because of the danger of starvation, the emperor, following republican practice, provided the citizen population with free grain for bread and, later, oil and wine. By feeding the citizenry, the emperor prevented bread riots caused by shortages and high prices. For those who did not enjoy the rights of citizenship, the emperor provided grain at low prices. This measure was designed to prevent speculators from forcing up grain prices in times of crisis. By maintaining the grain supply, the emperor kept the favor of the people and ensured that Rome's poor did not starve.

Popular Entertainment

In addition to supplying grain, the emperor and other wealthy citizens also entertained the Roman populace, often at vast expense. This combination of material support and popular entertainment to keep the masses happy is often termed "bread and circuses." The most popular forms of public entertainment were gladiatorial contests and chariot racing. Gladiatorial combat had begun as a private event during the republic, sponsored by men seeking new ways to honor their ancestors. By the early empire it had grown into a major public spectacle, with sponsors sometimes offering hundreds of gladiator fights along with battles between animals or between animals and humans. Games were advertised on billboards, and spectators were given a program with the names and sometimes the fighting statistics of the pairs, so that they could place bets more easily.

Men came to be gladiators through a variety of ways. Many were soldiers captured in war, sent to Rome or other large cities to be gladiators instead of being killed. Some were criminals, especially slaves found guilty of various crimes. By the imperial period increasing numbers were volunteers, often poor immigrants who saw gladiatorial combat as a way to support themselves. All gladiators were trained in gladiatorial schools and were legally slaves, although they could keep their winnings and a few became quite wealthy. The Hollywood portrayal of gladiatorial combat has men fighting to their death, but this was increasingly rare, as the owners of especially skilled fighters wanted them to continue to compete. Many—perhaps most—did die at a young age from their injuries or later infections, but some fought more than a hundred battles over long careers, retiring to become trainers in gladiatorial schools. Sponsors of matches sought to offer

Gladiator Mosaic   Made in the first half of the fourth century, this mosaic from an estate outside Rome includes the name of each gladiator next to the figure. In the back a gladiator stands in a victory pose, while the fallen gladiator in the front is marked with the symbol Ø, indicating that he has died in combat. Many of the gladiators in this mosaic, such as those at the left, appear less fit and fearsome than the gladiators depicted in movies, more closely reflecting the reality that gladiatorial combat was a job undertaken by a variety of people. (Galleria Borghese, Rome, Italy/Alinari/Bridgeman Images)

viewers ever more unusual spectacles: left-handed gladiators fighting right-handed ones, dwarf gladiators, and for a brief period even female gladiators. For a criminal condemned to die, the arena was preferable to the imperial mines, where convicts worked digging ore and died under wretched conditions. At least in the arena the gladiator might fight well enough to win freedom. Some Romans protested gladiatorial fighting, but the emperors recognized the political value of such spectacles, and most Romans enjoyed them.

The Romans were even more addicted to chariot racing than to gladiatorial shows. Under the empire four permanent teams competed against one another. Each had its own color — red, white, green, or blue. Two-horse and four-horse chariots ran a course of seven laps, about five miles. One charioteer, Gaius Appuleius Diocles, raced for twenty-four years, with over 4,000 starts and nearly 1,500 wins. His admirers honored him with an inscription that proclaimed him champion of all charioteers. Other winning charioteers were also idolized, just as sports stars are today.

Roman spectacles such as gladiator fights and chariot racing are fascinating subjects for movies and computer games, but they were not everyday activities for Romans. As is evident on tombstone inscriptions, ordinary Romans were proud of their work and accomplishments and affectionate toward their families and friends. An impression of them can be gained from their epitaphs.

Prosperity in the Roman Provinces

As the empire grew and stabilized, many Roman provinces grew prosperous. Peace and security opened Britain, Gaul, and the lands of the Danube to settlers from other parts of the Roman Empire (Map 6.2). Veterans were given small parcels of land in the provinces, becoming tenant farmers.

The rural population throughout the empire left few records, but the inscriptions that remain point to a melding of cultures. One sphere where this occurred was language. People used Latin for legal and state religious purposes, but gradually Latin blended with the original language of an area and with languages spoken by those who came into the area later. Slowly what would become the Romance languages of Spanish, Italian, French, Portuguese, and Romanian evolved. Religion was another site of cultural exchange and mixture. Romans moving into an area learned about and began to venerate local gods, and local people learned about Roman ones. Gradually hybrid deities and rituals developed. The process of cultural exchange was at first more urban than rural, but the importance of cities and towns to the life of the wider countryside ensured that its effects spread far afield.

The garrison towns that grew up around provincial military camps became the centers of organized political life, and some grew into major cities, including Eburacum (modern-day York), Lutetia Parisiorum (Paris), and Londinium (London). In order to supply these administrative centers with food, land around them was cultivated more intensively. Roman merchants became early bankers, loaning money to local people and often controlling them financially. Wealthy Roman officials also sometimes built country estates in rural areas near the city, where they did grow crops but also escaped from the stresses of city life.

During the first and second centuries C.E., Roman Gaul became more prosperous than ever before, and prosperity attracted Roman settlers. Roman veterans mingled with the local population and sometimes married into local families. There was not

MAP 6.2 Production and Trade in the Pax Romana, ca. 27 B.C.E.–180 C.E.   This map gives a good idea of the principal products of various parts of the Roman Empire at its height and the trade routes connecting these regions. Map 10.2 on page 302 is a similar map that shows products and trade in roughly the same area nearly a millennium later.

much difference in many parts of the province between the original Celtic villages and their Roman successors.

In Britain, Roman influence was strongest in the south, where more towns developed. Archaeological evidence, such as coins and amphoras that held oil or wine, indicates healthy trading connections with the north, however, as Roman merchandise moved through the gates of Hadrian's Wall in exchange for food and other local products.

Across eastern Europe, Roman influence was weaker than it was in Gaul or southern Britain, and there appears to have been less intermarriage. In Illyria (ih-LIHR-ee-uh) and Dalmatia, regions of modern Albania, Croatia, and Montenegro, the local population never widely embraced either Roman culture or urban life. To a certain extent, however, Romanization occurred simply because the peoples lived in such close proximity.

The Romans were the first to build cities in northern Europe, but in the eastern Mediterranean they ruled cities that had existed before Rome itself was even a village. Here there was much continuity in urban life from the Hellenistic period. There was less construction than in the Roman cities of northern and western Europe because existing buildings could simply be put to new uses.

The well-preserved ruins of the ancient city of Aspendos, at the mouth of the Eurymedon (now Kopru) River on the south coast of modern Turkey (see Map 6.2), give a picture of life in one of these older Eastern cities. Built sometime before 500 B.C.E., the city was an important economic center in the Persian Empire and the site of a major battle in the wars between the Persian Empire and the Greek city-states. It sat among fertile fields, and the resources of the land provided raw materials for industry and trade. Trade along the river and in the port, especially salt, oil, horses, and wool, provided wealth to merchants. Aspendos was one of the earliest cities to mint coins. It was conquered by Alexander the Great and then by the Romans, but it remained prosperous. Romans and indigenous people mixed at the city's central marketplace and in temples and public buildings. The Romans built an aqueduct to bring water into the city, although this was later destroyed in an earthquake. Over the river they also built an arched stone bridge, about thirty feet wide so that carts and chariots could easily travel on it. This may have also collapsed in an earthquake, but its foundations were so sturdy that a thousand years later the area's Turkish rulers used them to build a new bridge, which still stands. In 155 C.E. a local architect built a magnificent theater that probably held seven thousand spectators, who sat under a retractable awning that provided shade. Here men and women enjoyed the great plays of the past and those popular in their own day. They also watched gladiatorial contests, for these were popular in Eastern cities, as was horse racing.

More than just places to live, cities like Aspendos were centers of intellectual and cultural life. Their residents were in touch with the ideas and events of the day, in a network that spanned the entire Mediterranean and reached as far north as Britain. As long as the empire prospered and the revenues reached the imperial coffers, life in provincial cities—at least for the wealthy—could be nearly as pleasant as that in Rome.

Trade and Commerce

The expansion of trade during the pax Romana made the Roman Empire an economic as well as a political force in the provinces (see Map 6.2). Britain and Belgium became prime grain producers, with much of their harvests going to the armies of the Rhine, and Britain's wool industry probably got its start under the Romans. Italy and southern Gaul produced huge quantities of wine, which was shipped in large pottery jugs wherever merchant vessels could carry it. Roman colonists introduced the olive to southern Spain and northern Africa, which soon produced most of the oil consumed in the western part of the empire. In the East the olive oil production of Syrian farmers reached an all-time high, and Egypt produced tons of wheat that fed the Roman populace.

The growth of industry in the provinces was another striking development of this period. Cities in Gaul and Germany eclipsed the old Mediterranean manufacturing centers. Lyons in Gaul and later Cologne in Germany became the new centers of the glassmaking industry, and the cities of Gaul were nearly unrivaled in the manufacture of bronze and brass. The Romans took the manufacture of pottery to an advanced stage by introducing a wider range of vessels and making some of these on an industrial scale in kilns that were large enough to fire tens of thousands of pots at once. The most prized pottery was *terra sigillata*, reddish decorated tableware with a glossy surface. Methods for making terra sigillata spread from Italy northwards into Europe, often introduced by soldiers in the Roman army who had been trained in potterymaking in Italy. These craftsmen set up facilities to make roof tiles, amphoras, and dishes for their units, and local potters began to copy their styles and methods of manufacturing. Terra sigillata often portrayed Greco-Roman gods and heroes, so this pottery spread Mediterranean myths and stories. Local artisans added their own distinctive flourishes and sometimes stamped their names on the pots; these individual touches have allowed archaeologists to trace the pottery trade throughout the Roman Empire in great detail. Aided by all this growth in trade and industry, Europe and western Asia were linked in ways they had not been before.

As the Romans drove farther eastward, they encountered the Parthians, who had established a kingdom in what is now Afghanistan and Iran in the Hellenistic period. In the second century C.E. the Romans tried unsuccessfully to drive out the Parthians, who came to act as a link between Roman and Chinese merchants. Chinese merchants sold their wares to the Parthians, who then carried the goods overland to Mesopotamia or Egypt, from which they were shipped throughout the Roman Empire. Silk was a major commodity traded from the East to the West, along with other luxury goods. In return the Romans traded glassware, precious gems, and slaves.

The pax Romana was also an era of maritime trade, and Roman ships sailed from Egyptian ports to the mouth of the Indus River, where they traded local merchandise and wares imported by the Parthians. In the late first century C.E. the Chinese emperor sent an ambassador, Gan Ying, to make contact with the Roman Empire. Gan Ying made it as far as the Persian Gulf ports, where he heard about the Romans from Parthian sailors and reported back to his emperor that the Romans were wealthy, tall, and strikingly similar to the Chinese. His report became part of a group of accounts about the Romans and other "Western" peoples that circulated widely among scholars and officials in Han China. Educated Romans did not have a corresponding interest in China. For them, China remained more of a mythical than a real place, and they never bothered to learn more about it.

The Coming of Christianity

During the reign of the emperor Tiberius (r. 14–37 C.E.), in the Roman province of Judaea, which had been created out of the Jewish kingdom of Judah, a Jewish man named Jesus of Nazareth preached, attracted a following, and was executed on the order of the Roman prefect Pontius Pilate. At the time this was a minor event, but Christianity, the religion created by Jesus's followers, came to have an enormous impact first in the Roman Empire and later throughout the world.

FOCUS QUESTION
How did Christianity grow into a major religious movement?

Factors Behind the Rise of Christianity

The civil wars that destroyed the Roman Republic left their mark on Judaea, where Jewish leaders had taken sides in the conflict. The turmoil created a climate of violence throughout the area, and among the Jews movements in opposition to the Romans spread. Some of these, such as the Zealots, encouraged armed rebellion against Roman rule, which would, indeed, break out several times in the first and second centuries C.E. Many Jews came to believe that a final struggle was near, and that it would lead to the coming of a savior, or **Messiah**, a descendant of King David who would destroy the Roman legions and inaugurate a period of peace, happiness, and prosperity for Jews. This apocalyptic belief was an old one among Jews, but by the first century C.E. it had become more widespread than ever, with many people prophesying the imminent coming of a Messiah and readying themselves for a cataclysmic battle.

The pagan world also played its part in the story of early Christianity. The term **pagan**, derived from a Latin word meaning "rural dweller," came to refer to those who practiced religions other than Judaism or Christianity. (Christianity was initially an urban religion, and those who lived in the countryside were less likely to be converts.) This included religions devoted to the traditional Roman gods of the hearth, home, and countryside; syncretistic religions that blended Roman and indigenous deities; the cult of the emperor spread through the erection of statues, temples, and monuments; and mystery religions that offered the promise of life after death (see Chapter 4). Many people in the Roman Empire practiced all of these, combining them in whatever way seemed most beneficial or satisfying to them.

The Life and Teachings of Jesus

Into this climate of Messianic hope and Roman religious blending came Jesus of Nazareth (ca. 3 B.C.E.–ca. 29 C.E.). According to Christian Scripture, he was born to deeply religious Jewish parents and raised in Galilee, the stronghold of the Zealots and a trading center where Greeks and Romans interacted with Jews. His ministry began when he was about thirty, and he taught by preaching and telling stories.

Like Socrates, Jesus left no writings. Accounts of his sayings and teachings first circulated orally among his followers and were later written down. The principal evidence for his life and deeds are the four Gospels of the Bible (Matthew, Mark, Luke, and John), books that are part of what Christians later termed the New Testament. These Gospels—the name means "good news"—are records of Jesus's teachings, written to build a community of faith sometime in the late first century C.E. The Gospels were among the most widely copied and circulated early accounts of Jesus's life, and by the fourth century officials in the Christian Church decided that they, along with other types of writing such as letters and prophecies, would form Christian Scripture. The four Gospels included in the Bible are called canonical, from the Greek word that means "the rule" or "the standard." Other early documents also circulated, some of which have been rediscovered in modern times, and their interpretation is often a source of controversy.

The Gospels include certain details of Jesus's life, but they were not meant to be biographies. Their authors had probably heard many different people talk about what Jesus said and did, and there are discrepancies among the four accounts. These differences indicate that early followers had a diversity of beliefs about Jesus's nature

Messiah In Jewish belief, a savior who would bring a period of peace and happiness for Jews.

pagan Originally referring to those who lived in the countryside, it came to mean those who practiced religions other than Judaism or Christianity.

and purpose. This diversity of beliefs about Jesus continues today. Some see him as a moral teacher, some as a prophet, and many as the son of God who rose from the dead and is himself divine.

However, almost all the early sources agree on certain aspects of Jesus's teachings: He preached of a heavenly kingdom of eternal happiness in a life after death, and of the importance of devotion to God and love of others. His teachings were based on Hebrew Scripture and reflected a conception of God and morality that came from Jewish tradition. Jesus's orthodoxy enabled him to preach in the synagogue and the temple, but he deviated from orthodoxy in insisting that he taught in his own name, not in the name of Yahweh (the Hebrew name for God). The Greek translation of the Hebrew word *Messiah* is *Christos*, the origin of the English word *Christ*. Was Jesus the Messiah, the Christ? A small band of followers thought so, and Jesus claimed that he was. Yet Jesus had his own conception of the Messiah. He would establish a spiritual kingdom, not an earthly one. As recounted in one of the Gospels, he commented:

> Do not lay up for yourselves treasures on earth, where moth and rust consume and where thieves break in and steal, but lay up for yourselves treasures in heaven, where neither moth nor rust consumes and where thieves do not break in and steal. For where your treasure is, there will your heart be also.[7]

The Roman official Pontius Pilate, who had authority over much of Judaea, knew little about Jesus's teachings. Like all Roman officials, he was concerned with maintaining peace and order, which was a difficult task in restive Judaea. According to the New Testament, crowds followed Jesus into Jerusalem at the time of Passover, a highly emotional time in the Jewish year that marked the Jewish people's departure from Egypt under the leadership of Moses (see Chapter 2). The prospect that these crowds would spark violence no doubt alarmed Pilate. Some Jews believed that Jesus was the long-awaited Messiah. Others hated and feared him because they thought him religiously dangerous. The four Gospels differ somewhat on exactly what actions Jesus took in the city and what Jesus and Pilate said to each other after Jesus was arrested. They agree that Pilate condemned Jesus to death by crucifixion, and his soldiers carried out the sentence. On the third day after Jesus's crucifixion, some of his followers claimed that he had risen from the dead. For his earliest followers and for generations to come, the resurrection of Jesus became a central element of faith.

The Spread of Christianity

The memory of Jesus and his teachings survived and flourished. Believers in his divinity met in small assemblies or congregations, often in one another's homes, to discuss the meaning of Jesus's message and to celebrate a ritual (later called the Eucharist or Lord's Supper) commemorating his last meal with his disciples before his arrest. Because they expected Jesus to return to the world very soon, they regarded earthly life and institutions as unimportant. Only later did these congregations evolve into what came to be called the religion of Christianity, with a formal organization and set of beliefs.

The catalyst in the spread of Jesus's teachings and the formation of the Christian Church was Paul of Tarsus, a well-educated Hellenized Jew who was comfortable in both the Roman and the Jewish worlds. The New Testament reports that at first he persecuted members of the new sect, but then on the road to the city of Damascus in

Syria he was struck blind by a vision of light and heard Jesus's voice. He converted to belief in Jesus, regained his sight, and became a vigorous promoter of Jesus's ideas. Paul traveled all over the Roman Empire and wrote letters of advice to many groups. These letters were copied and widely circulated, transforming Jesus's ideas into more specific moral teachings. He recognized that Christianity would not grow if it remained within Judaism, and connected it with the non-Jewish world. As a result of his efforts, Paul became the most important figure in changing Christianity from a Jewish sect into a separate religion, and many of his letters became part of Christian Scripture.

The breadth of the Roman Empire was another factor behind the spread of Christianity. If all roads led to Rome, they also led outward to the provinces. This enabled early Christians to spread their faith easily throughout the known world, as Jesus had told his followers to do in the Gospels, thus making his teachings universal. The pagan Romans also considered their secular empire universal, and the early Christians combined the two concepts of universalism.

Though most of the earliest converts seem to have been Jews, or Greeks and Romans who were already interested in Jewish moral teachings, Paul urged that Gentiles, or non-Jews, be accepted on an equal basis. The earliest Christian converts included people from all social classes. These people were reached by missionaries and others who spread the Christian message through family contacts, friendships, and business networks. Many women were active in spreading Christianity. Paul greeted male and female converts by name in his letters and noted that women often provided financial support for his activities. The growing Christian communities differed about the extent to which women should participate in the workings of the religion; some favored giving women a larger role in church affairs, while others were more restrictive, urging women to be silent on religious matters.

People were attracted to Christian teachings for a variety of reasons. It was in many ways a mystery religion, offering its adherents special teachings that would give them immortality. But in contrast to traditional mystery religions, Christianity promised this immortality widely, not only to a select few.

Most early Christians believed that they would rise in body, not simply in spirit, after a final day of judgment, so they favored burial of the dead rather than the more common Roman practice of cremation. They retained the Roman belief that the dead were polluting and so had to be buried outside city walls, however, and in the second century began to dig tunnels in the soft rock around Rome for burials. The bodies were placed in niches along the walls of these underground chambers and then sealed up. Gradually huge complexes of burial passageways called catacombs were dug. Memorial services for martyrs were sometimes held in or near catacombs, but they were not regular places of worship. Many catacombs contain some of the earliest examples of Christian art, and others, dug by Jews or pagans who chose to bury rather than cremate their own dead, contain examples of Jewish and secular Roman art from this period.

Along with the possibility of life after death, Christianity also offered rewards in this world to adherents. One of these was the possibility of forgiveness, for believers accepted that human nature is weak and that even the best Christians could fall into sin. But Jesus loved sinners and forgave those who repented. Christianity was also attractive to many because it gave the Roman world a cause. Instead of passivity, Christians stressed the ideal of striving for a goal. By spreading the word of Christ, Christians played their part in God's plan for the triumph of Christianity on earth. Christianity likewise gave its devotees a sense of community, which was very welcome in the often highly mobile world of the Roman Empire. To stress the spiritual kinship of this new type of community, Christians often called one another "brother" and "sister." Also, many Christians took Jesus's commandment to love one another as a guide and provided support for widows, orphans, and the poor, just as they did for family members. Such material support became increasingly attractive as Roman social welfare programs broke down in the third century.

The Growing Acceptance and Evolution of Christianity

At first most Roman officials largely ignored the followers of Jesus, viewing them simply as one of the many splinter groups within Judaism. Slowly some Roman officials and leaders came to oppose Christian practices and beliefs. They considered Christians to be subversive dissidents because they stopped practicing traditional rituals venerating the hearth and home and they objected—often publicly or in writing—to the cult of the emperor. Some Romans thought that Christianity was one of the worst of the mystery religions, with immoral and indecent rituals. For instance, they thought that the ritual of the Lord's Supper, at which Christians said that they ate and drank the body and blood of Jesus, was an act of cannibalism involving the ritual murder of Roman boys. Many in the Roman Empire also feared that the traditional gods would withdraw their favor from the Roman Empire because of the Christian insistence that these gods either did not exist or were evil spirits. The Christian refusal to worship Roman gods, in their opinion, endangered Roman lives and society. Others worried that Christians were trying to destroy the Roman family with their insistence on a new type of kinship, and they pointed to Jesus's words in the Gospels saying that salvation was far more important than family relationships. A woman who converted, thought many Romans, might use her new faith to oppose her father's choice of marital partner or even renounce marriage itself, an idea supported by the actions of a few female converts.

Persecutions of Christians, including torture and executions, were organized by governors of Roman provinces and sometimes by the emperor, beginning with Nero. Most persecutions were local and sporadic in nature, however, and some of the gory stories about the martyrs are later inventions, designed to strengthen believers with accounts of earlier heroes. Christians differed in their opinions about how to respond to persecution. Some sought out martyrdom, while others thought that doing so went against Christian teachings.

Responses to Christianity on the part of Roman emperors varied. The emperor Trajan forbade his governors to hunt down Christians. Though admitting that he considered Christianity an abomination, he decided it was better policy to leave Christians in peace. Later emperors, including Septimius Severus at the very end of the second century, Decius in the third century, and Diocletian in the fourth century, increased persecutions again, ordering Christians to sacrifice to the emperor and the Roman gods or risk death. Executions followed their edicts, although estimates of how many people were actually martyred in any of these persecutions vary widely.

By the second century C.E. Christianity was also changing. The belief that Jesus was soon coming again gradually waned, and as the number of converts increased,

Christian Oil Lamp
When Christianity spread in the Roman Empire, many believers purchased household goods with Christian symbols. This pottery lamp for an ordinary home, dating from the fourth century, is marked with a common symbol for Jesus, the letters *XP* (chi rho), the first two letters in Greek for *Christos,* "Christ." (Photo by Zev Radovan/© www.BibleLandPictures.com/Alamy Stock Photo)

permanent institutions were established instead of simple house churches. These included buildings and a hierarchy of officials often modeled on those of the Roman Empire. **Bishops**, officials with jurisdiction over a certain area, became especially important. They began to assert that they had the right to determine the correct interpretation of Christian teachings and to choose their successors. Councils of bishops determined which writings would be considered canonical, and lines were increasingly drawn between what was considered correct teaching and what was considered incorrect, or **heresy**.

Christianity also began to attract more highly educated individuals, who developed complex theological interpretations of issues that were not clear in scripture. Often drawing on Greek philosophy and Roman legal traditions, they worked out understandings of such issues as how Jesus could be both divine and human, and how God could be both a father and a son (and later a spirit as well, a Christian doctrine known as the Trinity). Bishops and theologians often modified teachings that seemed upsetting to Romans, such as Jesus's harsh words about wealth and family ties. Given all these changes, Christianity became more formal in the second century, with power more centralized.

bishops Christian Church officials with jurisdiction over certain areas and the power to determine the correct interpretation of Christian teachings.

heresy A religious practice or belief judged unacceptable by church officials.

The Empire in Disarray

FOCUS QUESTION
What explains the chaos of the third century C.E.?

The prosperity and political stability of the second century gave way to a period of domestic upheaval and foreign invasion. The third century saw a long series of able but ambitious military commanders who used their legions to make themselves emperors. Law yielded to the sword, and the office of the emperor lost legitimacy. The nature of the army changed, and the economy weakened because of unsound policies.

Civil Wars and Military Commanders

The reign of Marcus Aurelius (r. 161–180 C.E.), the last of the "five good emperors," was marked by problems. The Tiber River flooded in 162, destroying crops and killing animals, which led to famine. Soldiers returning from wars in the East brought the Antonine plague back to Rome (see page 170) and then carried it northward. Germanic-speaking groups attacked along the Rhine and Danube borders, and the emperor himself took over the campaign against them in 169. He spent most of the rest of his life in military camps along Rome's northern border, where in addition to leading troops he wrote a series of personal reflections in Greek. These *Meditations*, as they later came to be known, are advice to himself about doing one's duty and acting in accordance with nature, ideas that came from Stoic philosophy (see Chapter 4). He wrote:

> Do not act unwillingly nor selfishly nor without self-examination. . . . Take heed not to be transformed into a Caesar, not to be dipped in the purple dye [a color only the emperor could wear]. Keep yourself therefore simple, good, pure, grave, unaffected, the friend of justice, religious, kind, affectionate, strong for your proper work. Wrestle to continue to be the man Philosophy wished to make you. Reverence the gods, save men.[8]

The *Meditations* are a good key to Marcus Aurelius's character, but they appear not to have circulated very much during the centuries immediately after they were written. Certainly very few later emperors took this advice to heart.

After the death of Marcus Aurelius, misrule by his successors led to a long and intense spasm of fighting. Marcus Aurelius's son Commodus was strangled by a conspiracy that included his wife, and in 193 five men claimed the throne in quick succession. Two of them were also assassinated, and Septimius Severus (r. 193–211) emerged as the victor. He restored order, expanded the borders of the Roman Empire in Africa and western Asia, and invaded Scotland. He increased the size of the army significantly and paid the soldiers better. This made him popular with soldiers, though it also increased the taxes on civilians. Some of his policies regarding the army created additional problems in the long run. Changes in recruiting practices that emphasized local recruiting of non-Romans created a Roman army that became less acculturated to Roman values. This army was no longer the vehicle for Romanization that it had been in earlier centuries. In part to increase the tax base, in 212 Septimius Severus's son Caracalla (r. 198–217) issued an edict making all free male residents of the Roman Empire citizens. This made them eligible to serve in the legions—which may have been why Caracalla did this—but also made serving in the army less attractive, and reduced the number of men willing to join.

More than twenty different emperors seized power in the forty-nine years between 235 and 284, a period scholars call the "crisis of the third century." These emperors were generally military commanders from the border provinces, and there were so many that the middle of the third century has become known as the age of the **barracks emperors**. Almost all were either assassinated or died in civil wars, and their concentration on overthrowing the ruling emperor left the borders unguarded. Non-Roman groups on the frontiers took full advantage of the chaos to overrun vast areas. When they reached the Rhine and the Danube, they often found gaping holes in the Roman defenses.

The Emperor Marcus Aurelius   This larger-than-life bronze equestrian statue, sculpted to celebrate his military victories or shortly after his death in 180 C.E., shows the emperor holding up his hand in the conventional imperial greeting. More than twenty equestrian statues could be seen in late imperial Rome, but this is the only one to survive. In the sixteenth century Michelangelo built one of the major plazas of Rome around it, although now the original has been moved to a museum for better preservation and a copy stands outdoors. (Piazza Campodoglio, Rome, Italy/Prisma/UIG via Getty Images)

barracks emperors   The emperors of the middle of the third century, so called because they were military commanders.

Turmoil in Economic Life

This chaos also disrupted areas far away from the borders of the empire. Renegade soldiers and corrupt imperial officials, together with many greedy local agents, preyed on local people. In some places in the countryside, officials requisitioned villagers' livestock and compelled them to do forced labor. Farmers appealed to the government for protection so that they could cultivate the land. Although some of those in authority were unsympathetic and even violent to villagers, many others tried to maintain order. Yet even the best of them also suffered. If officials could not meet their tax quotas, which were rising to support the costs of civil war, they had to pay the deficits from their own pockets. Because the local officials were themselves so hard-pressed, they squeezed what they needed from rural families. Many farmers, unable to pay, were driven off their land, and those remaining faced ruin. As a result, agricultural productivity declined.

In response to the economic crisis, the emperors reduced the amount of silver used in coins, replacing it with less valuable metals such as copper, so that they could continue to pay their troops. This tactic, however, led to crippling inflation, which wiped out savings and sent prices soaring.

The Romans still controlled the Mediterranean, which nurtured commerce. The road system remained largely intact, though often roads were allowed to fall into disrepair. Trade still flowed, but with reduced efficiency and high costs.

By 284 C.E. the empire had reached a crisis that threatened its downfall. The position of emperor was gained no longer by lawful succession but rather by victory in civil war. The empire had failed at the top, and the repercussions of the disaster spread throughout the empire with dire effects.

LOOKING BACK LOOKING AHEAD

The period of the Roman Empire was a rich era in both economic and cultural terms. Roman emperors developed a system of government that ruled over vast areas of diverse people fairly effectively. The resulting stability and peace encouraged agriculture and production. Goods and people moved along roads and sea-lanes, as did ideas, including the new religion of Christianity. All the while, the Romans incorporated indigenous peoples into their way of life as the empire expanded into northern and western Europe. Yet during a long period of internal crisis, civil war, and invasions in the third century, it seemed as if the empire would collapse.

The Roman Empire did not disintegrate in the third century, however. Although emperors came and went in quick and violent succession, the basic institutions and infrastructure of the empire remained intact. Even during the worst of the ordeal, many lower-level officials and ordinary soldiers continued to do their jobs, embodying the principles of duty that Marcus Aurelius advocated. People like this would be key to passing Roman traditions on to institutions that developed later in Europe, including law courts, city governments, and nations.

Make Connections

Think about the larger developments and continuities within and across chapters.

1. What allowed large empires in the ancient world, including the Persians (Chapter 2) and the Romans, to govern vast territories and many different peoples successfully?

2. How was slavery in the Roman Empire different from that of earlier societies? How was it similar? What might account for the continuities and changes in slavery you have identified?

3. If a male resident of Athens during the time of Pericles (Chapter 3) had time-traveled to Rome during the time of Augustus, what might he have found familiar? What might have seemed strange? How might these observations have differed if the time traveler were a female resident of Athens?

6 REVIEW & EXPLORE

Review the Main Ideas

Answer the focus questions from each section of the chapter.

- How did Augustus create a foundation for the Roman Empire? (p. 154)
- How did the Roman state develop after Augustus? (p. 164)
- What was life like in the city of Rome, and what was it like in the provinces? (p. 168)
- How did Christianity grow into a major religious movement? (p. 175)
- What explains the chaos of the third century C.E.? (p. 180)

Identify Key Terms

Identify and explain the significance of each item below.

imperator (p. 154)
principate (p. 154)
Roma et Augustus (p. 157)
pax Romana (p. 157)
Praetorians (p. 164)
"five good emperors" (p. 165)
aqueducts (p. 169)
Messiah (p. 176)
pagan (p. 176)
bishops (p. 180)
heresy (p. 180)
barracks emperors (p. 181)

NOTES

1. Virgil, *Aeneid*, trans. Theodore C. Williams (Boston: Houghton Mifflin, 1910), 6.851–853.
2. Virgil, *Georgics* 3.515–519. In this chapter, works in Latin with no translator noted were translated by John Buckler.
3. Virgil, *Aeneid* 1.1–11.
4. Text in Mary Johnston, *Roman Life* (Chicago: Scott, Foresman, and Co., 1957), p. 172.
5. Napthali Lewis and Meyer Reinhold, *Roman Civilization*, vol. 2 (New York: Harper Torchbooks, 1955), p. 262.
6. H. E. Butler, trans., *The Institutio Oratoria of Quintilian*, vol. 1 (Cambridge, Mass.: Harvard University Press and Loeb Classical Library, 1920), pp. 10–11, 41, 49.
7. Matthew 6:19–21.
8. Marcus Aurelius, *Meditations* 3.5, 6.30, trans. A. S. L. Farquharson (New York: Everyman's Library, 1961), pp. 12, 5.

CHAPTER PREVIEW

Reconstruction Under Diocletian and Constantine
How did Diocletian and Constantine try to reform the empire?

The Growth of the Christian Church
How did the Christian Church become a major force in the Mediterranean and Europe?

Barbarian Society
What were the key characteristics of barbarian society?

Migration, Assimilation, and Conflict
What were some of the causes and consequences of the barbarian migrations?

Christian Missionaries and Conversion
How did the church convert barbarian peoples to Christianity?

The Byzantine Empire
How did the Byzantine Empire preserve the legacy of Rome?

Life in Late Antiquity

In this sixth-century ivory carving, a procession of people carry relics of a saint to a Christian church under construction. New churches often received holy items when they were dedicated, and processions were common ways in which people expressed community devotion.

(Trier Cathedral Treasury, Trier, Germany/akg-images/Newscom)

7

Late Antiquity

250–600

The Roman Empire, with its powerful—and sometimes bizarre— leaders, magnificent buildings, luxurious clothing, and bloody amusements, has long fascinated people. Politicians and historians have closely studied the reasons for its successes and have even more closely analyzed the weaknesses that led to its eventual collapse. From the third century onward, the Western Roman Empire slowly disintegrated. Scholars have long seen this era as one of the great turning points in Western history, a time when the ancient world was transformed into the very different medieval world. During the past several decades, however, focus has shifted to continuities as well as changes, and what is now usually termed "late antiquity" has been recognized as a period of creativity and adaptation, not simply of decline and fall.

The two main agents of continuity in late antiquity were the Christian Church and the Byzantine or Eastern Roman Empire. Missionaries and church officials spread Christianity within and far beyond the borders of the Roman Empire, bringing with them the Latin language and institutions based on Roman models. The Byzantine Empire lasted until 1453, a thousand years longer than the Western Roman Empire, and preserved and transmitted much of ancient Greco-Roman law, philosophy, and institutions. The main agents of change in late antiquity were groups the Romans labeled barbarians migrating into the Roman Empire. They brought different social, political, and economic structures with them, but as they encountered Roman culture and became Christian, their own ways of doing things were also transformed. ■

Reconstruction Under Diocletian and Constantine

FOCUS QUESTION
How did Diocletian and Constantine try to reform the empire?

In the middle of the third century, the Roman Empire faced internal turmoil and external attacks. Civil wars tore the empire apart as emperors rose and fell in quick succession, and barbarian groups migrated and marauded deep within the boundaries of the empire (see Chapter 6). Wars and invasions disrupted normal commerce and agriculture, the primary sources of tax revenues. The barracks emperors of the third century dealt with economic hardship by cutting the silver content of coins until money was virtually worthless. The immediate result was crippling inflation throughout the empire, made worse by the corruption of many officials. Many Romans had become Christian, but the followers of traditional Roman religion were divided in their views of what this meant for the empire. In the early fourth century the emperor Diocletian (r. 284–305), who was born of low-status parents and had risen through the ranks of the military to become emperor, restored order, and the later emperor Constantine (r. 306–337) continued his work. How Diocletian, Constantine, and their successors responded to the problems facing the empire influenced later developments.

tetrarchy Diocletian's four-part division of the Roman Empire.

diocese An administrative unit in the later Roman Empire; adopted by the Christian Church as the territory under the authority of a bishop.

Political Measures

Under Diocletian, Augustus's polite fiction of the emperor as first among equals gave way to the emperor as absolute autocrat. The princeps became *dominus* (lord). The emperor claimed that he was "the elect of god"—that he ruled because of divine favor. To underline the emperor's exalted position, Diocletian and Constantine adopted the gaudy court ceremonies and trappings of the Persian Empire. People entering the emperor's presence prostrated themselves before him and kissed the hem of his robes.

Diocletian recognized that the empire had become too large for one man to handle and divided it into a western half and an eastern half (Map 7.1). Diocletian assumed direct control of the eastern part; he gave the rule of the western part to a colleague, along with the title *augustus*. Around 293 Diocletian further delegated power by appointing two men to assist the augustus and him; each of the four men was given the title *caesar*, and the system was known as the **tetrarchy** (TEH-trahr-kee), meaning "rule of four." He further divided each part of the empire into administrative units called **dioceses**, which were in turn subdivided into small provinces, all governed by an expanded bureaucracy. Although four men ruled the empire, Diocletian was clearly the senior partner and final source of authority.

MAP 7.1 The Division of the Roman World, 293   Under Diocletian, the Roman Empire was first divided into a western and an eastern half, a development that foreshadowed the medieval division between the Latin West and the Byzantine East.

Diocletian's political reforms were a momentous step. The reorganization made the empire easier to administer and placed each of the four central military commands much closer to borders or other trouble spots, so that troops could be sent more quickly when needed. Diocletian hoped that the tetrarchy would supply a clearly defined order of succession and end struggles for power over the emperorship. That did not happen, but much of Diocletian's reorganization remained.

Like Diocletian, Constantine came up through the army, and took control after a series of civil wars. He eventually had authority over the entire empire, but ruled from the East, where he established a new capital for the empire at Byzantium, an old Greek city on the Bosporus, naming it "New Rome," though it was soon called Constantinople. Constantine sponsored a massive building program of palaces, warehouses, public buildings, and even a hippodrome for horse racing, modeling these on Roman buildings. He built defensive works along the borders of the empire, trying hard to keep it together, and used various means to strengthen the army, as did his successors. The emperors ruling from Constantinople could not provide enough military assistance to repel invaders in the western half of the Roman Empire, however, and Roman authority there slowly disintegrated.

Chronology

ca. 293	Diocletian establishes the tetrarchy
313	Edict of Milan, allowing practice of all religions in the Roman Empire
325	Council of Nicaea
354–430	Life of Saint Augustine
378	Visigoths defeat the Roman army at Adrianople
380	Theodosius makes Christianity the official religion of the Roman Empire
410	Visigoths sack Rome
429	Vandals begin their conquest of North Africa
476	Odoacer deposes the last Roman emperor in the West
ca. 481–511	Reign of Clovis
493	Theoderic establishes an Ostrogothic state in Italy
527–565	Reign of Justinian
529	*The Rule of Saint Benedict*
535–572	Byzantines reconquer and rule Italy
597	Pope Gregory I sends missionaries to Britain

Economic Issues

Diocletian and Constantine were faced with a number of economic problems, including inflation and declining tax revenues, and their attempts to solve them illustrate the methods and limitations of absolute monarchy. In a move unprecedented in Roman history, Diocletian issued an edict that fixed maximum prices and wages throughout the empire. He and his assistant emperors dealt with the tax system just as strictly and inflexibly. Taxes became payable in kind, that is, in goods such as grain, sheep, or cloth instead of money, which made them difficult to transport to central authorities. Constantine continued these measures and also made occupations more rigid: all people involved in the growing, preparation, and transportation of food and other essentials were locked into their professions. A baker, for example, could not go into any other business, and his son took up the trade at his death. In this period of severe depression many individuals and communities could not pay their taxes. In such cases local tax collectors, who were also bound to their occupations, had to make up the difference from their own funds. This system soon wiped out a whole class of moderately wealthy people and set the stage for the lack of social mobility that was a key characteristic of European society for many centuries to follow.

The emperors' measures did not really address Rome's central economic problems, however. Because of worsening conditions during the third and fourth centuries, many free farmers and their families were killed by invaders or renegade soldiers, fled the land to escape the barbarians, or abandoned farms ravaged in the fighting. Consequently, large tracts of land lay deserted. Landlords with ample resources began at once to reclaim as much of this land as they could, often hiring back the free farmers who had previously worked the land as paid labor or tenants. The huge villas that resulted were self-sufficient and became islands of stability in an unsettled world.

Free farmers who remained on the land were exposed to the raids of barbarians or robbers and to the tyranny of imperial officials. In return for the protection and security landlords could offer, small landholders gave over their lands and their freedom. To guarantee a supply of labor, landlords denied them freedom to move elsewhere. Henceforth they and their families worked their patrons' land, not their own. Free men and women were becoming tenant farmers bound to the land, what would later be called serfs.

The Acceptance of Christianity

The turmoil of the third century seemed to some emperors, including Diocletian, to be the punishment of the gods. Diocletian stepped up persecution of Christians who would not sacrifice to Rome's traditional deities, portraying them as disloyal to the empire in an attempt to wipe out the faith. These persecutions lasted only a few years, however. Increasing numbers of Romans, including members of prominent families, were converting to Christianity, and many who followed traditional Roman religions no longer saw Christianity as un-Roman (see Chapter 6). Constantine reversed Diocletian's policy and instead ordered toleration of all religions in the Edict of Milan, issued in 313. Whether Constantine was himself a Christian by this point is hotly debated. His later biographer, the Christian bishop Eusebius, reported that he had been converted on a battlefield in 312 after seeing a vision, and other sources attribute his conversion to his Christian mother, Helena. On the other hand, he continued to worship the sun-god, and in 321 proclaimed that Sunday, "the Day of the Sun," would be the official day of rest. He was baptized only shortly before he died, although this was not uncommon for high officials. Whatever his personal beliefs at different stages of his life, there is no debate that he recognized the growing numbers of Christians in the empire and financially supported the church. He freed the clergy from imperial taxation and endowed the building of Christian churches. One of his gifts—the Lateran Palace in Rome—remained the official residence of the popes until the fourteenth century. He allowed others to make gifts to the church as well, decreeing in 321, "Every man, when dying, shall have the right to bequeath as much of his property as he desires to the holy and venerable Catholic Church. And such wills are not to be broken."[1] In return for his support, Constantine expected the assistance of church officials in maintaining order. Helped in part by its favored position in the empire, Christianity slowly became the leading religion (Map 7.2).

Christians disagreed with one another about many issues, which led to schisms (SKIH-zuhms), denunciations, and sometimes violence. In

Gold Coin Showing Constantine
In this gold coin, minted at Ticinum in northern Italy in 316, Constantine is shown with a halo, a symbol of his sacred character and connection to the sun-god. This iconography was later adopted in Christian art to signify divinity or sanctity. (Ashmolean Museum, University of Oxford, UK/Bridgeman Images)

MAP 7.2 The Spread of Christianity, to 600 Originating in Judaea, the southern part of modern Israel and Jordan, Christianity first spread throughout the Roman world and then beyond it in all directions.

the fourth and fifth centuries disputes arose over the nature of Christ. For example, **Arianism** (AI-ree-uh-nih-zuhm), developed by Arius (ca. 250–336), a priest of Alexandria, held that Jesus was created by the will of God the Father and thus was not co-eternal with him. Arian Christians reasoned that Jesus the Son must be inferior to God the Father because the Father was incapable of suffering and did not die. Arianism enjoyed such popularity and provoked such controversy that Constantine, who declared that "internal strife within the Church of God is far more evil and dangerous than any kind of war and conflict," interceded. In 325 he summoned church leaders to a council in Nicaea (nigh-SEE-uh) in Asia Minor and presided over it personally, referring to himself as "your fellow servant of our common Lord and Savior."[2] The council produced the Nicene (nigh-SEEN) Creed, which defined the position that Christ is "eternally begotten of the Father" and of the same substance as the Father. Arius and those who refused to accept Nicene Christianity were banished. Their interpretation of the nature of Christ was declared a heresy, that is, a belief that contradicted the interpretation the church leaders declared was correct,

Arianism A theological belief that originated when Arius, a priest of Alexandria, denied that Christ was co-eternal with God the Father.

which was termed orthodoxy. These actions did not end Arianism, however. Several later emperors were Arian Christian, and Arian missionaries converted many barbarian tribes, who were attracted by the idea that Jesus was God's first-in-command, which fit well with their own warrior hierarchies and was less complicated than the idea of two persons with one substance. The Nicene Creed says little specifically about the Holy Spirit, but in the following centuries the idea that the Father, Son, and Holy Spirit are "one substance in three persons"—the Trinity—became a central doctrine in Christianity, though again there were those who disagreed. Disputes about the nature of Christ also continued, with factions establishing themselves as separate Christian groups. The Nestorians, for example, regarded the divine and human natures in Jesus as distinct from one another, whereas the orthodox opinion was that they were united. The Nestorians split from the rest of the church in the fifth century after their position was outlawed, and settled in Persia. Nestorian Christian missionaries later founded churches in Central Asia, India, and China.

Religious and secular authorities tried in various ways to control this diversity as well as promote Christianity. In 380 the emperor Theodosius (thee-uh-DOH-shee-uhs) made Nicene Christianity the official religion of the empire. Theodosius stripped Roman pagan temples of statues, made the practice of the old Roman state religion a treasonable offense, and persecuted Christians who dissented from orthodox doctrine. Most significant, he allowed the church to establish its own courts and to use its own body of law, called canon law. The church courts, not the Roman government, had jurisdiction over the clergy and ecclesiastical disputes. At the death of Theodosius, the Christian Church was considerably independent of the Roman state. The foundation for later growth in church power had been laid.

Later emperors continued the pattern of active involvement in church affairs. They appointed the highest officials of the church hierarchy; the emperors or their representatives presided at ecumenical councils; and the emperors controlled some of the material resources of the church—land, rents, and dependent peasantry.

The Growth of the Christian Church

FOCUS QUESTION
How did the Christian Church become a major force in the Mediterranean and Europe?

As the emperors changed their policies about Christianity from persecution to promotion, the church grew, gradually becoming the most important institution in the Mediterranean and Europe. The able administrators and creative thinkers of the church developed permanent institutions and complex philosophical concepts that drew on the Greco-Roman tradition, which attracted learned Romans.

The Church and Its Leaders

The early Christian Church benefited from the administrative abilities of church leaders. With the empire in decay, educated people joined and worked for the church in the belief that it was the one institution able to provide some stability. Bishop Ambrose of Milan (339–397) is typical of the Roman aristocrats who held high public office, were converted to Christianity, and subsequently became bishops. Like many bishops, Ambrose had a solid education in classical law and rhetoric, which he used to become an eloquent preacher. He had a strong sense of his authority and even stood up to Emperor Theodosius, who had ordered Ambrose to hand over his major church—called a basilica—to the emperor:

> At length came the command, "Deliver up the Basilica"; I reply, "It is not lawful for us to deliver it up, nor for your Majesty to receive it. By no law can you violate the house of a private man, and do you think that the house of God may be taken away? . . . But do not burden your conscience with the thought that you have any right as Emperor over sacred things. . . . It is written, God's to God and Caesar's to Caesar. The palace is the Emperor's, the churches are the Bishop's. To you is committed jurisdiction over public, not over sacred buildings."[3]

The emperor relented. Ambrose's assertion that the church was supreme in spiritual matters and the state in secular issues was to serve as the cornerstone of the church's position on church-state relations for centuries. Ambrose came to be regarded as one of the fathers of the church, that is, early Christian thinkers whose authority was seen as second only to the Bible in later centuries.

Gradually the church adapted the organizational structure of the Roman Empire begun during the reign of Diocletian. The territory under the authority of a bishop was also called a diocese, with its center a cathedral (from the Latin *cathedra*, meaning "chair"), the church that contained the bishop's official seat of power. A bishop's jurisdiction extended throughout the diocese, and he came to control a large amount of land that was given to or purchased by the church. Bishops generally came from prominent families and had both spiritual and political power; as the Roman Empire disintegrated, they became the most important local authority on many types of issues. They claimed to trace their spiritual ancestry back to Jesus's apostles, a doctrine called **apostolic succession**. Because of the special importance of their dioceses, five bishops—those of Antioch, Alexandria, Jerusalem, Constantinople, and Rome—gained the title of patriarch.

After the capital and the emperor moved to Constantinople, the power of the bishop of Rome grew because he was the only patriarch in the Western Roman Empire. The bishops of Rome stressed that Rome had special significance because of its history as the capital of a worldwide empire. More significantly, they asserted, Rome had a special place in Christian history. According to tradition, Saint Peter, chief of Jesus's disciples, had lived in Rome and been its first bishop. Thus, as successors of Peter, the bishops of Rome—known as popes, from the Latin word *papa*, meaning "father"—claimed a privileged position in the church hierarchy, an idea called the **Petrine Doctrine** that built on the notion of apostolic succession. They stressed their supremacy over other Christian communities and urged other churches to appeal to Rome for the resolution of disputed doctrinal issues. Not surprisingly, the other patriarchs did not agree. They continued to exercise authority in their own regions, and local churches did as well, but the groundwork had been laid for later Roman predominance on religious matters.

In the fifth century the popes also expanded the church's secular authority. Pope Leo I (pontificate 440–461) made treaties with several barbarian leaders who threatened the city of Rome. Gregory I (pontificate 590–604), later called "the Great," made an agreement with the barbarian groups who had cut off Rome's food supply,

Saint Jerome and Saint Ambrose   This wood carving shows Saint Jerome and Saint Ambrose, two of the most important early church fathers, hard at work writing. Divine inspiration appears in the form of an angel and a dove. (Duomo, Modena, Italy/ Photo: Ghigo Roli, 1999. Franco Cosimo Panini Editore © Management Fratelli Alinari/Alinari/Art Resource, NY)

apostolic succession   The doctrine that all bishops can trace their spiritual ancestry back to Jesus's apostles.

Petrine Doctrine   A doctrine stating that the popes (the bishops of Rome) were the successors of Saint Peter and therefore heirs to his highest level of authority as chief of the apostles.

reorganized church lands to increase production, and then distributed the additional food to the poor. He had been an official for the city of Rome before he became a church official, and his administrative and diplomatic talents helped the church expand. He sent missionaries to the British Isles (see page 207) and wrote letters and guides instructing bishops on practical and spiritual matters. He promoted the ideas of Augustine (see page 194), particularly those that defined church rituals as essential for salvation. The Western Christian Church headed by the pope in Rome would become the most enduring nongovernmental institution in world history.

The Development of Christian Monasticism

Christianity began and spread as a city religion. Since the first century, however, some especially pious Christians had felt that the only alternative to the decadence of urban life was complete separation from the world. They believed that the Christian life as set forth in the Gospel could not be lived in the midst of the immorality of Roman society.

This desire to withdraw from ordinary life led to the development of the monastic life. Monasticism began in third-century Egypt, where individuals like Saint Anthony (251?–356) and small groups first withdrew from cities and from organized society to seek God through prayer in desert or mountain caves and shelters, giving up all for Christ. Gradually large colonies of monks gathered in the deserts of Upper Egypt, and Christians came to believe that monks, like the early Christian martyrs executed by Roman authorities before them, could speak to God and that their prayers had special influence. These monks were called hermits, from the Greek word *eremos*, meaning "desert." Many devout women also were attracted to this eremitical (ehr-uh-MIH-tihk-uhl) type of monasticism.

The Egyptian ascetic Pachomius (puh-KOH-mee-uhs) (290–346?) drew thousands of men and women to the monastic life at Tabennisi on the Upper Nile. There were too many for them to live as hermits, so Pachomius organized communities of men and women, creating a new type of monasticism, known as cenobitic (seh-nuh-BIH-tik), that emphasized communal living. Saint Basil (329?–379), an influential bishop from Asia Minor and another of the fathers of the church, encouraged cenobitic monasticism. He and much of the church hierarchy thought that communal living provided an environment for training the aspirant in the virtues of charity, poverty, and freedom from self-deception.

Starting in the fourth century, information about Egyptian monasticism came to the West, and both men and women sought the monastic life. Because of the dangers of living alone in the forests of northern Europe, where wild animals, harsh climate, and barbarian tribes posed ongoing threats, the eremitical form of monasticism did not take root. Most of the monasticism that developed in Gaul, Italy, Spain, England, and Ireland was cenobitic.

Monastery Life

In 529 Benedict of Nursia (480–543), who had experimented with both eremitical and communal forms of monastic life, wrote a brief set of regulations for the monks who had gathered around him at Monte Cassino between Rome and Naples. Benedict's guide for monastic life, known as *The Rule of Saint Benedict*, came to influence all forms of organized religious life in the Western Christian Church. Men and women in monastic houses all followed sets of rules, first those of

Benedict and later those written by other individuals. Because of this, men who lived a communal monastic life came to be called **regular clergy**, from the Latin word *regulus* (rule). Priests and bishops who staffed churches in which people worshipped and who were not cut off from the world were called **secular clergy**. According to official church doctrine, women were not members of the clergy, but this distinction was not clear to most people.

The Rule of Saint Benedict outlined a monastic life of regularity, discipline, and moderation in an atmosphere of silence. Each monk had ample food and adequate sleep. The monk spent part of each day in formal prayer, which consisted of chanting psalms and other prayers from the Bible in the part of the monastery church called the choir. The rest of the day was passed in manual labor, study, and private prayer. The monastic life as conceived by Saint Benedict struck a balance between asceticism (extreme material sacrifice, including fasting and the renunciation of sex) and activity. It thus provided opportunities for men of entirely different abilities and talents—from mechanics to gardeners to literary scholars. The Benedictine form of religious life also appealed to women, because it allowed them to show their devotion and engage in study. Benedict's twin sister Scholastica (480–543) adapted the *Rule* for use by her community of nuns.

Benedictine monasticism also succeeded partly because it was so materially successful. In the seventh and eighth centuries monasteries pushed back forests and wastelands, drained swamps, and experimented with crop rotation. Benedictine houses thus made a significant contribution to the agricultural development of Europe.

Finally, monasteries conducted schools for local young people, and monks and nuns copied manuscripts, preserving classical as well as Christian literature. Local and royal governments drew on the services of the literate men and able administrators the monasteries produced. This was not what Saint Benedict had intended, but perhaps the effectiveness of the institution he designed made it inevitable.

Christianity and Classical Culture

The growth of Christianity was not simply a matter of institutions such as the papacy and monasteries, but also a matter of ideas. The earliest Christian thinkers sometimes rejected Greco-Roman culture, but as Christianity grew from a tiny persecuted group to the official religion of the Roman Empire, its leaders and thinkers gradually came to terms with classical culture (see Chapter 6). They incorporated elements of Greek and Roman philosophy and learning into Christian teachings, modifying them to fit with Christian notions.

Saint Jerome (340–419), for example, a distinguished theologian and linguist regarded as a father of the church, translated the Old and New Testaments from Hebrew and Greek into vernacular Latin. Called the Vulgate, his edition of the Bible served as the official translation until the sixteenth century, and scholars rely on it even today. Familiar with the writings of classical authors, Saint Jerome believed that Christians should study the best of ancient thought because it would direct their minds to God. He maintained that the best ancient literature should be interpreted in light of the Christian faith.

Christian Notions of Gender and Sexuality

Early Christians both adopted and adapted the then-contemporary views of women, marriage, and sexuality. In his plan of salvation, Jesus considered women the equal of men. Women were among the earliest converts to Christianity and took an active

regular clergy Men and women who lived in monastic houses and followed sets of rules, first those of Benedict and later those written by other individuals.

secular clergy Priests and bishops who staffed churches where people worshipped and who were not cut off from the world.

role in its spread, preaching, acting as missionaries, being martyred alongside men, and perhaps even baptizing believers. Because early Christians believed that the Second Coming of Christ was imminent, they devoted their energies to their new spiritual family of co-believers. Early Christians often met in people's homes and called one another "brother" and "sister," a metaphorical use of family terms that was new to the Roman Empire. Women and men joyously accepted the ascetic life, renouncing marriage and procreation to use their bodies for a higher calling. Some women, either singly or in monastic communities, declared themselves "virgins in the service of Christ." All this initially made Christianity seem dangerous to many Romans, who viewed marriage as the foundation of society and the proper patriarchal order.

Not all Christian teachings about gender were radical, however. In the first century C.E. male church leaders began to place restrictions on female believers. Women were forbidden to preach and were gradually excluded from holding official positions in Christianity other than in women's monasteries. Women who chose lives of virginity in the service of God were to be praised; Saint Jerome commented that a woman "who wishes to serve Christ more than the world . . . will cease to be a woman and will be called man," the highest praise he could bestow.[4] Even such women were not to be too independent, however. Both Jewish and classical Mediterranean culture viewed women's subordination as natural and proper, so in limiting the activities of female believers the Christian Church was following well-established patterns, just as it did in modeling its official hierarchy after that of the Roman Empire.

Christian teachings about sexuality built on and challenged classical models. The rejection of sexual activity involved an affirmation of the importance of a spiritual life, but it also incorporated the hostility toward the body found in some Hellenistic philosophies and some of the other religions that had spread in the Roman Empire in this era, such as Manichaeism (MAN-ih-kee-ih-zuhm). Manichaeism, a dualistic religion based on the ideas of the third-century Persian thinker Mani, taught that the spiritual world was good and the material world was evil, so salvation came through education and self-denial. Christian teachings affirmed that God had created the material world and sanctioned marriage, but most Christian thinkers also taught that celibacy was the better life, and that anything that took one's attention from the spiritual world performed an evil function. For most clerical writers (who themselves were male) this temptation came from women, and in some of their writings women themselves are depicted as evil, the "devil's gateway." Thus the writings of many church fathers contain a strong streak of misogyny (hatred of women), which was passed down to later Christian thinkers.

Saint Augustine on Human Nature, Will, and Sin

The most influential church father in the West was Saint Augustine of Hippo (354–430). Saint Augustine was born into an urban family in what is now Algeria in North Africa. His father, a minor civil servant, was a pagan; his mother, Monica, was a devout Christian. He gained an excellent classical education in philosophy and rhetoric and, as was normal for young Roman men, began relations with a concubine, who later had his son. Interested in new religious ideas, he became a Manichaean.

Augustine took teaching positions first in Rome and then in Milan, where he had frequent conversations with Bishop Ambrose. Through his discussions with Ambrose and his own reading, Augustine rejected his Manichaeism and became a Christian. He returned to Africa and later became bishop of the seacoast city of Hippo Regius. He was a renowned preacher to Christians there, a vigorous defender of orthodox Christianity, and the author of more than ninety-three books and treatises.

Augustine's autobiography, *The Confessions*, is a literary masterpiece and one of the most influential books in the history of Europe. Written in the rhetorical style and language of late Roman antiquity, it marks the synthesis of Greco-Roman forms and Christian thought. *The Confessions* describes Augustine's moral struggle, the conflict between his spiritual and intellectual aspirations and his sensual and material self. Many Greek and Roman philosophers had taught that knowledge would lead to virtue. Augustine came to reject this idea, claiming that people do not always act on the basis of rational knowledge. As he notes in *The Confessions*, even before he became a Christian he had decided that chastity was the best possible life, so he prayed to God for "chastity and continency," yet always added "but not yet." His education had not made him strong enough to avoid lust or any other evil; that would come only through God's power and grace.

Augustine's ideas on sin, grace, and redemption became the foundation of all subsequent Western Christian theology, Protestant as well as Catholic. He wrote that the basic force in any individual is the will, which he defined as "the power of the soul to hold on to or to obtain an object without constraint." The end or goal of the will determines the moral character of the individual. When Adam ate the fruit forbidden by God in the Garden of Eden (Genesis 3:6), he committed the "original sin" and corrupted the will. Adam's sin was not simply his own—it was passed on to all later humans through sexual intercourse; even infants were tainted. Original sin thus became a common social stain, in Augustine's opinion, transmitted by sexual desire. Coitus was theoretically good because it was created by God, but it had been corrupted by sin, so every act of intercourse was evil and every child was conceived through a sinful act. By viewing sexual desire as the result of Adam and Eve's disobedience to divine instructions, Augustine linked sexuality even more clearly with sin than had earlier church fathers. Because Adam disobeyed God and fell, all human beings have an innate tendency to sin: their will is weak. But according to Augustine, God restores the strength of the will through grace, which is transmitted in certain rituals that the church defined as **sacraments**. Grace results from God's decisions, not from any merit on the part of the individual.

sacraments Certain rituals defined by the church in which God bestows benefits on the believer through grace.

When Visigothic forces captured the city of Rome in 410, horrified pagans blamed the disaster on the Christians. In response, Augustine wrote *City of God*. This original work contrasts Christianity with the secular society in which it exists. According to Augustine, history is the account of God acting in time. Human history reveals that there are two kinds of people: those who live the life of the flesh, and those who live the life of the spirit in what Augustine called the City of God. The former will endure eternal hellfire; the latter will enjoy eternal bliss.

Augustine maintained that states came into existence as the result of Adam's fall and people's inclination to sin. He believed that the state was a necessary evil with the power to do good by providing the peace, justice, and order that Christians need to pursue their pilgrimage to the City of God. States' legitimate power included the ability to wage war, and Augustine's ideas were later used to develop notions of just warfare.

Barbarian Society

Augustine's *City of God* was written in response to the conquest of Rome by an army of Visigoths, one of the many peoples the Romans—and later historians—labeled "barbarians." The word *barbarian* comes from the Greek *barbaros*, meaning someone who did not speak Greek. (To the Greeks, others seemed to be speaking nonsense syllables; *barbar* is the Greek equivalent of "blah-blah" or "yada-yada.") The Greeks used this word to include people such as the Egyptians, whom the Greeks respected. The Romans usually used the Latin version of *barbarian* to mean the peoples who lived beyond the northeastern boundary of Roman territory, whom they regarded as unruly, savage, and primitive. That value judgment is generally also present when we use "barbarian" in English, but there really is no other word to describe the many different peoples who lived to the north of the Roman Empire. Thus historians of late antiquity use the word *barbarian* to designate these peoples, who spoke a variety of languages but had similarities in their basic social, economic, and political structures. Many of these historians find much to admire in barbarian society.

Scholars have been hampered in investigating barbarian society because most groups did not write and thus kept no written records before Christian missionaries introduced writing. Greek and Roman authors did describe barbarian society, but they were not always objective observers, instead using barbarians to highlight what they thought was right or wrong about their own cultures. Thus written records must be combined with archaeological evidence to gain a more accurate picture. In addition, historians are increasingly deciphering and using the barbarians' own written records that do exist, especially inscriptions carved in stone, bone, and wood and written in the **runic alphabet**. Runic inscriptions come primarily from Scandinavia and the British Isles. Most are short and limited to names, such as inscriptions on tombstones, but some describe the actions of kings and other powerful individuals, and a few of them mention the activities of more ordinary people.

runic alphabet Writing system developed in some barbarian groups that helps give a more accurate picture of barbarian society.

Barbarians included many different ethnic groups with social and political structures, languages, laws, and beliefs that developed in central and northern Europe over many centuries. Among the largest groups were Celts (whom the Romans called Gauls) and Germans; Germans were further subdivided into various groups, such as Ostrogoths, Visigoths, Burgundians, and Franks. *Celt* and *German* are often used as ethnic terms, but they are better understood as linguistic terms, a Celt being a person who spoke a Celtic language, an ancestor of the modern Gaelic or Breton language, and a German

Whalebone Chest   This eighth-century chest made of whalebone, depicting warriors, other human figures, and a horse, tells a story in both pictures and words. The runes along the border are one of the varieties from the British Isles. Contact with the Romans led to the increasing use of the Latin alphabet, though runes and Latin letters were used side by side in some parts of northern Europe for centuries. (Museo Nazionale del Bargello, Florence, Italy/Erich Lessing/Art Resource, NY)

one who spoke a Germanic language, an ancestor of modern German, Dutch, Danish, Swedish, and Norwegian. Celts, Germans, and other barbarians brought their customs and traditions with them when they moved southward, and these gradually combined with classical and Christian patterns to form new types of societies.

Village and Family Life

Barbarian groups usually resided in small villages, and climate and geography determined the basic patterns of how they lived off the land. Many groups lived in small settlements on the edges of clearings where they raised barley, wheat, oats, peas, and beans. Men and women tilled their fields with simple wooden plows and harvested their grains with small iron sickles. The vast majority of people's caloric intake came from grain in some form; the kernels of grain were eaten as porridge, ground up for flour, or fermented into strong, thick beer. (See "Evaluating the Evidence 7.1: Tacitus on Germanic Society," page 198.)

Within the villages, there were great differences in wealth and status. Free men and their families constituted the largest class. The number of cattle a man possessed indicated his wealth and determined his social status. Free men also shared in tribal warfare. Slaves acquired through warfare worked as farm laborers, herdsmen, and household servants.

Ironworking represented the most advanced craft; much of northern Europe had iron deposits, and the dense forests provided wood for charcoal, which was used to provide the clean fire needed to make iron. The typical village had an oven and smiths who produced agricultural tools and instruments of war—one-edged swords, arrowheads, and shields. By the second century C.E. the swords produced by barbarian smiths were superior to the weapons of Roman troops.

In the first two centuries C.E. the quantity and quality of material goods increased dramatically. Goods were used locally and for gift giving, a major social custom. Gift giving conferred status on the giver, whose giving showed his higher (economic) status, cemented friendship, and placed the receiver in his debt. Goods were also traded, though commercial exchange was less important than in the Roman Empire.

Families and kin groups were the basic social units in barbarian society. Families were responsible for the debts and actions of their members and for keeping the peace in general. Barbarian law codes set strict rules of inheritance based on position in the family and often set aside a portion of land that could not be sold or given away by any family member so that the family always retained some land.

Barbarian society was patriarchal: within each household the father had authority over his wife, children, and slaves. Some wealthy and powerful men had more than one wife, a pattern that continued even after they became Christian, but polygamy was not widespread among ordinary people. Women worked alongside men in the fields and forests, and the Roman historian Tacitus reported that at times they joined men on the battlefield, urging them to fight harder. Once women were widowed, they sometimes assumed their husbands' rights over family property and held the guardianship of their children.

Tribes and Hierarchies

The basic social and political unit among barbarian groups was the tribe or confederation, a group whose members believed that they were all descended from a common

Tacitus on Germanic Society

Toward the end of the first century, the Roman historian Tacitus wrote an account of Germanic society based on the works of earlier authors and most likely interviews with Romans who had traveled beyond the northern borders of the empire. His descriptions are not accurate in all respects, but evidence from other written sources and from archaeological excavations has supported a number of them.

Warlike Ardour of the People. When they go into battle, it is a disgrace for the chief to be surpassed in valour, a disgrace for his followers not to equal the valour of the chief. And it is an infamy and a reproach for life to have survived the chief, and returned from the field. . . .

Arrangement of their towns, subterranean dwellings. It is well known that the nations of Germany have not cities, and that they do not even tolerate closely contiguous dwellings. They live scattered and apart, just as a spring, a meadow, or a wood has attracted them. Their village they do not arrange in our fashion, with the buildings connected and joined together, but every person surrounds his dwelling with an open space, either as a precaution against the disasters of fire, or because they do not know how to build. No use is made by them of stone or tile; they employ timber for all purposes, rude masses without ornament or attractiveness. Some parts of their buildings they stain more carefully with a clay so clear and bright that it resembles painting, or a coloured design. They are wont also to dig out subterranean caves, and pile on them great heaps of dung as shelter from winter and as a receptacle for the year's produce. . . .

Their children. In every household the children, naked and filthy, grow up with those stout frames and limbs which we so much admire. Every mother suckles her own offspring and never entrusts it to servants and nurses. The master is not distinguished from the slave by being brought up with greater delicacy. Both live amid the same flocks and lie on the same ground till the freeborn are distinguished by age and recognised by merit. The young men marry late, and their vigour is thus unimpaired. Nor are the maidens hurried into marriage; the same age and a similar stature is required; well-matched and vigorous they wed, and the offspring reproduce the strength of the parents. . . .

Food. A liquor for drinking is made of barley or other grain, and fermented into a certain resemblance to wine. The dwellers on the river-bank also buy wine. Their food is of a simple kind, consisting of wild fruit, fresh game, and curdled milk. They satisfy their hunger without elaborate preparation and without delicacies. In quenching their thirst they are equally moderate. If you indulge their love of drinking by supplying them with as much as they desire, they will be overcome by their own vices as easily as by the arms of an enemy.

EVALUATE THE EVIDENCE

1. What does Tacitus praise, and what does he criticize, about Germanic warriors, food, houses, and child rearing?
2. Tacitus's work was written in part to criticize his fellow Romans, whom he saw as becoming weak from the influx of wealth into the empire. How does this perspective inform his description of Germanic customs? How might such attitudes shape the way Romans responded to the barbarian migrations?

Source: Tacitus, *The Agricola and Germania*, trans. A. J. Church and W. J. Brodribb (London: Macmillan, 1877), pp. 87ff.

---

ancestor and were thus kin. Tribes were led by chieftains. The chief was the member recognized as the strongest and bravest in battle and was elected from among the male members of the most powerful family. He led the group in war, settled disputes among its members, conducted negotiations with outside powers, and offered sacrifices to the gods. The period of migrations and conquests of the Western Roman Empire witnessed the strengthening of the power of chiefs, who often adopted the title of king, though this title implies broader power than they actually had.

Closely associated with the chief in some tribes was the **comitatus**, or war band. These warriors swore loyalty to the chief, fought with him in battle, and were not

comitatus A war band of young men in a barbarian tribe who were closely associated with the chief, swore loyalty to him, and fought with him in battle.

supposed to leave the battlefield without him; to do so implied cowardice, disloyalty, and social disgrace. These oaths of loyalty were later more formalized in the development of feudalism (see Chapter 8).

Although initially a social egalitarianism appears to have existed among members of the comitatus because they regarded each other as kin, during the migrations and warfare of the third and fourth centuries, the war band was transformed into a system of stratified ranks. Among the Ostrogoths, for example, a warrior nobility evolved. Contact with the Romans stimulated demand for goods such as metal armbands, which the Romans produced for trade with barbarian groups. Armbands were of different widths and value, and they became a symbol of hierarchy among warriors, much as the insignia of military rank function today. During the Ostrogothic conquest of Italy, warrior-nobles also began to acquire land as both a mark of prestige and a means to power. As land and wealth came into the hands of a small elite class, social inequalities within the group emerged and gradually grew stronger. These inequalities help explain the origins of the European noble class.

Customary and Written Law

Early barbarian tribes had no written laws. Law was custom, but certain individuals were often given special training in remembering and retelling laws from generation to generation. Beginning in the late fifth century, however, some chieftains and rulers began to collect, write, and publish lists of their customs and laws.

The law code of the Salian Franks, one of the barbarian tribes, included a feature common to many barbarian codes. Any crime that involved a personal injury, such as assault, rape, and murder, was given a particular monetary value, called the **wergeld** (WUHR-gehld) (literally "man-money" or "money to buy off the spear"), that was to be paid by the perpetrator to the victim or the family. The Salic law lists many of these:

> If any person strike another on the head so that the brain appears, and the three bones which lie above the brain shall project, he shall be sentenced to 1200 denars, which make 300 shillings. . . .
>
> If any one have killed a free woman after she has begun bearing children, he shall be sentenced to 2400 denars, which make 600 shillings.[5]

The wergeld varied according to the severity of the crime and also the social status of the victim. The fine for the murder of a woman of childbearing years was the same value as that attached to military officers of the king, to priests, and to boys preparing to become warriors, which suggests the importance of women in Frankish society, at least for their childbearing capacity.

The wergeld system aimed to prevent or reduce violence. If a person accused of a crime agreed to pay the wergeld and if the victim and his or her family accepted the payment, there was peace. If the accused refused to pay the wergeld or if the victim's family refused to accept it, a blood feud ensued. At first, Romans had been subject to Roman law and barbarians to barbarian custom. As barbarian kings accepted Christianity and as Romans and barbarians increasingly intermarried and assimilated culturally, the distinction between the two sets of law blurred and, in the course of the

wergeld Compensatory payment for death or injury set in many barbarian law codes.

seventh and eighth centuries, disappeared. The result would be the new feudal law, to which all who lived in certain areas were subject.

Celtic and Germanic Religion

Like Greeks and Romans, barbarians worshipped hundreds of gods and goddesses with specialized functions. They regarded certain mountains, lakes, rivers, or groves of trees as sacred because these were linked to deities. Rituals to honor the gods were held outdoors rather than in temples or churches, often at certain points in the yearly agricultural cycle. Presided over by a priest or priestess understood to have special abilities to call on the gods' powers, rituals sometimes involved animal (and perhaps human) sacrifice. Among the Celts, religious leaders called druids (DROO-ihds) had legal and educational as well as religious functions, orally passing down laws and traditions from generation to generation. Bards singing poems and ballads also passed down myths and stories of heroes and gods, which were written down much later.

The first written records of barbarian religion came from Greeks and Romans who encountered barbarians or spoke with those who had. They understood barbarian traditions through their own belief systems, often equating barbarian gods with Greco-Roman ones and adapting stories and rituals to blend the two. This assimilation appears to have gone both ways, at least judging by the names of the days of the week. In the Roman Empire the days took their names from Roman deities or astronomical bodies, and in the Germanic languages of central and northern Europe the days acquired the names of corresponding barbarian gods. Jupiter's day, for example, became Thor's day (Thursday); both of these powerful gods were associated with thunder.

Migration, Assimilation, and Conflict

FOCUS QUESTION
What were some of the causes and consequences of the barbarian migrations?

Migrating groups that the Romans labeled barbarians had moved southward and eastward off and on since about 100 B.C.E. (see Chapters 5 and 6). As their movements became more organized in the third and fourth centuries C.E., Roman armies sought to defend the Rhine-Danube border of the Roman Empire, but with troop levels low because Italians were increasingly unwilling to serve in the army, generals were forced to recruit barbarians to fill the ranks. Barbarian refugees and enslaved prisoners of war joined Roman units, and free barbarian units, called *foederati*, allied themselves with Rome. Some barbarian leaders rose to the highest ranks of the Roman army and often assimilated into Roman culture, incorporating their own traditions and intermarrying with Roman families. By the fourth century barbarians made up the majority of those fighting both for and against Rome, and climbed higher and higher in the ranks of the Roman military. Toward the end of the fifth century this barbarian assumption of authority stretched all the way to the top, and the last person with the title of emperor in the Western Roman Empire was deposed by a Gothic general.

Why did the barbarians migrate? In part they were searching for more regular supplies of food, better farmland, and a warmer climate. In part they were pushed by groups living farther eastward, especially by the Huns from Central Asia in the fourth and fifth centuries. Conflicts within and among barbarian groups also led to war and disruption, which motivated groups to move (Map 7.3).

MAP 7.3 The Barbarian Migrations, ca. 340–500   This map shows the migrations of various barbarian groups in late antiquity.

Celtic and Germanic People in Gaul and Britain

The Celts present a good example of both assimilation and conflict. Celtic-speaking peoples had lived in central Europe since at least the fifth century B.C.E. and spread out from there to the Iberian Peninsula in the west, Hungary in the east, and the British Isles in the north. As Julius Caesar advanced northward into what he termed Gaul (present-day France) between 58 and 50 B.C.E. (see Chapter 5), he defeated many Celtic tribes. Celtic peoples conquered by the Romans often assimilated Roman ways, adapting the Latin language and other aspects of Roman culture. In Roman Gaul and then in Roman Britain, towns were planned in the Roman fashion, with temples, public baths, theaters, and amphitheaters. In the countryside large manors controlled the surrounding lands. Roman merchants brought Eastern luxury goods and Eastern religions—including Christianity. The Romans suppressed the Celtic chieftains, and a military aristocracy made up of Romans—some of whom intermarried with Celtic families—governed. In the course of the second and third centuries, many Celts became Roman citizens and joined the Roman army. Celtic culture survived only in areas beyond the borders of the empire. (The modern Welsh, Bretons, Scots, and Irish are all peoples of Celtic descent.)

By the fourth century C.E. Gaul and Britain were under pressure from Germanic groups moving westward, and Rome itself was threatened (see Map 7.3). Imperial troops withdrew from Britain in order to defend Rome, and the Picts from Scotland and the Scots from Ireland (both Celtic-speaking peoples) invaded territory held by the Britons. According to the eighth-century historian Bede (beed), the Briton king Vortigern invited the Saxons from Denmark to help him against his rivals. However, Saxons and other Germanic tribes from the area of modern-day Norway, Sweden, and Denmark turned from assistance to conquest. Their goal was plunder, and at first their invasions led to no permanent settlements. As more Germanic peoples arrived, however, they took over the best lands and eventually conquered most of Britain. Historians have labeled the years 500 to 1066 (the year of the Norman Conquest) the Anglo-Saxon period of English history, after the two largest Germanic groups in England, the Angles and the Saxons.

Anglo-Saxon England was divided along ethnic and political lines. The Germanic kingdoms in the south, east, and center were opposed by the Britons in the west, who wanted to get rid of the invaders. The Anglo-Saxon kingdoms also fought among themselves, causing boundaries to shift constantly. Finally, in the ninth century, under pressure from the Viking invasions, King Alfred of Wessex (r. 871–899) created a more unified state with a reorganized army and system of fortresses for defense.

Anglo-Saxon Helmet   This ceremonial bronze helmet from seventh-century England was found inside a ship buried at Sutton Hoo. The nearly 100-foot-long ship was dragged overland before being buried completely. It held one body and many grave goods, including swords, gold buckles, and silver bowls made in Byzantium. The unidentified person who was buried here was clearly wealthy and powerful. (© The Trustees of the British Museum/Art Resource, NY)

The Anglo-Saxon invasion gave rise to a rich body of Celtic mythology, particularly legends about King Arthur, who first appeared in Welsh poetry in the sixth century and later in histories, epics, and saints' lives. Most scholars see Arthur as a composite figure that evolved over the centuries in songs and stories. In their earliest form as Welsh poems, the Arthurian legends may represent Celtic hostility to Anglo-Saxon invaders, but they later came to be more important as representations of the ideal of medieval knightly chivalry and as compelling stories whose retelling has continued to the present.

Visigoths and Huns

On the European continent, the Germanic peoples included a number of groups with very different cultural traditions. The largest Germanic group was the Goths, who were further subdivided by scholars into Ostrogoths (eastern Goths) and Visigoths (western Goths) based on their migration patterns. Both of these groups played important roles in the political developments of late antiquity.

Pressured by defeat in battle, starvation, and the movement of other groups, the Visigoths moved westward from their homeland north of the Black Sea, and in 376 they petitioned the Roman emperor Valens to admit them to the empire. They offered to fight for Rome in exchange for the province of Thrace in what is now Greece and Bulgaria. Seeing in the hordes of warriors the solution to his manpower problem, Valens agreed. However, the deal fell apart when crop failures led to famine and Roman authorities exploited the Visigoths' hunger by forcing them to sell their own people as slaves in exchange for dog flesh: "the going rate was one dog for one Goth." The Visigoths revolted, joined with other barbarian enemies of Rome, and defeated the Roman army at the Battle of Adrianople in 378, killing Valens and thousands of Roman soldiers in the process. This left a large barbarian army within the borders of the Roman Empire, and not that far from Constantinople.

Valens's successor made peace with the Visigoths, but relations worsened as the Visigoths continued migrating westward (see Map 7.3). The Visigothic king Alaric I, who had also been a general in one of the Roman armies in the east, invaded Italy and sacked Rome in 410. The Visigoths burned and looted the city for three days, which caused many Romans to wonder whether God had deserted them. (See "Evaluating the Evidence 7.2: Battle Between Romans and Goths," page 204.) Seeking to stabilize the situation at home, the imperial government pulled its troops from the British Isles and many areas north of the Alps, leaving these northern areas vulnerable to other migrating groups. A year later Alaric died, and his successor led his people into south-western Gaul, where they established the Visigothic kingdom.

One significant factor in the migration of the Visigoths and other Germanic peoples was pressure from nomadic steppe peoples from Central Asia. They included the Alans, Avars, Bulgars, Khazars, and most prominently the Huns, who attacked the Black Sea area and the Byzantine Empire beginning in the fourth century. The Roman officer and historian Ammianus Marcellinus fought the Huns and later described them with both admiration and scorn:

> They are not at all adapted to battles on foot, but they are almost glued to their horses, which are hardy, it is true, but ugly. From their horses by night or day every one of the nation buys and sells, eats and drinks, and bowed over the narrow neck of the animal relaxes into a sleep so deep as to be accompanied by many dreams. . . . They are subject to no royal restraint, but they are content with the disorderly government of important men, and led by them they force their way through every obstacle. No one in their country ever plows a field or touches a plowhandle. They are all without fixed abode, without hearth, or law, or settled mode of life. . . . In wagons their wives weave for them their hideous garments, in wagons they cohabit with their husbands, bear children, and rear them. . . . Like unreasoning beasts, they are utterly ignorant of the difference between right and wrong.[6]

Under the leadership of their warrior-king Attila, the Huns attacked the Byzantine Empire in 447 and then turned westward. Several Germanic groups allied with them, as did the sister of the Roman emperor, who hoped to take over power from her brother. Their troops combined with those of the Huns, and a huge army took the city of Metz, now in eastern France. A combined army of Romans and Visigoths stopped the advance of the Huns at Châlons, and they retreated. The following year they moved into the Western Roman Empire again, crossing the Alps into Italy, and a papal delegation, including Pope Leo I himself, asked Attila not to attack Rome. Though papal diplomacy was later credited with stopping the advance of the Huns, their dwindling food supplies and a plague that spread among their troops were probably much more important. The Huns retreated from Italy, and within a year Attila was dead. Later leaders were not as effective, and the Huns were never again an important factor in European history. Their conquests had pushed many Germanic groups together, however, transforming smaller bands into larger, more unified peoples who could more easily pick the Roman Empire apart.

Battle Between Romans and Goths

Rome's wars with the Germanic-speaking groups along its northern border come to life in this relief from a Roman sarcophagus of the third century C.E., discovered in a tomb in the city of Rome. The Romans are wearing helmets, and the soldier at the right is wearing iron or bronze chain mail, a defensive technology that the Romans adapted from the Celts.

(Ludovisi sarcophagus from Livia's Villa/Terme Museum, Rome, Italy/Bridgeman Images)

EVALUATE THE EVIDENCE

1. How would you describe this depiction of war? How does the artist show Roman superiority over the barbarians through the placement, dress, and facial features of the soldiers?
2. How does this funeral sculpture reinforce or challenge what you have learned about Roman expansion and the Romans' treatment of the peoples they conquered?

Germanic Kingdoms and the End of the Roman Empire

After they conquered an area, barbarians generally established states ruled by kings. However, the kingdoms did not have definite geographical borders, and their locations shifted as tribes moved. In the fifth century the Burgundians ruled over lands roughly circumscribed by the old Roman army camps in what is now central France and western Switzerland. The Visigoths exercised a weak domination over southern France and much of the Iberian Peninsula (modern Spain) until a Muslim victory at Guadalete in 711 ended Visigothic rule. The Vandals, another Germanic tribe whose destructive ways are commemorated in the word *vandal*, swept across Spain into North Africa in 429 and took over what had been Rome's breadbasket. They established a state that lasted about a century, raided many coastal cities, and even sacked the city of Rome itself in 455.

Barbarian states eventually came to include Italy itself. The Western Roman emperors were generally chosen by the more powerful successors of Constantine in the East, and they increasingly relied on barbarian commanders and their troops to maintain order. In the 470s a series of these commanders took over authority in name as well as in reality, deposing several Roman emperors. In 476 the barbarian chieftain Odoacer (OH-duh-way-suhr) deposed Romulus Augustus, the last person to have the title of Roman emperor in the West. Odoacer did not take on the title of emperor, calling himself instead the king of Italy, so that this date marks the official end of the Roman Empire in the West. Emperor Zeno, the Roman emperor in the East ruling from Constantinople, worried about Odoacer's growing power and promised Theoderic (r. 471–526), the leader of the Ostrogoths who had recently settled in the Balkans, the right to rule Italy if he defeated Odoacer. Theoderic's forces were successful, and in 493 Theoderic established an Ostrogothic state in Italy, with his capital at Ravenna.

For centuries, the end of the Roman Empire in the West was seen as a major turning point in history, the fall of the sophisticated and educated classical world to uncouth and illiterate tribes. This view was further promoted by the English historian and member of Parliament Edward Gibbon, whose six-volume *The History of the Decline and Fall of the Roman Empire*, published in 1776–1788, was required reading for university students well into the twentieth century. Over the last several decades, however, many historians have put greater stress on continuities. The Ostrogoths, for example, maintained many Roman ways. Old Roman families continued to run the law courts and the city governments, and well-educated Italians continued to study the Greek classics. Theoderic's adviser Boethius (ca. 480–524) translated Aristotle's works on logic from Greek into Latin. While imprisoned after falling out of royal favor, Boethius wrote *The Consolation of Philosophy*, which argued that philosophical inquiry was valuable for understanding God. This became one of the most widely read books in the Middle Ages, though its popularity did not prevent Boethius from being executed for treason.

In other barbarian states, as well, aspects of classical culture continued. Barbarian kings relied on officials trained in Roman law, and Latin remained the language of scholarly communication. Greco-Roman art and architecture still adorned the land, and people continued to use Roman roads, aqueducts, and buildings. The Christian Church in barbarian states modeled its organization on that of Rome, and many bishops were from upper-class families that had governed the empire.

Very recently some historians and archaeologists have returned to an emphasis on change. They note that people may have traveled on Roman roads, but the roads were rarely maintained, and travel itself was much less secure than during the Roman Empire. Merchants no longer traded over long distances, so people's access to goods produced outside their local area plummeted. Knowledge about technological processes such as the making of glass and roof tiles declined or disappeared. There was intermarriage and cultural assimilation among Romans and barbarians, but there was also violence and great physical destruction.

The kingdom established by the Franks is a good example of this combination of peaceful assimilation and violent conflict. The Franks were a confederation of Germanic peoples who originated in the marshy lowlands north and east of the northernmost part of the Roman Empire (see Map 7.3). In the fourth and fifth centuries they settled within the empire and allied with the Romans, some attaining high military and civil positions. The Franks believed that Merovech, a man of supernatural origins, founded their ruling dynasty, which was thus called Merovingian (mehr-uh-VIHN-jee-uhn).

The reign of Clovis (KLOH-vis) (r. ca. 481–511) marks the decisive period in the development of the Franks as a unified people. Through military campaigns, Clovis acquired the central provinces of Roman Gaul and began to conquer southern Gaul from the Burgundians and Visigoths. Clovis's conversion to Roman Christianity brought him the crucial support of the bishops of Gaul in his campaigns against tribes that were still pagan or had accepted the Arian version of Christianity. Along with brutal violence, however, the next two centuries witnessed the steady assimilation of Franks and Romans, as many Franks adopted the Latin language and Roman ways, and Romans copied Frankish customs and Frankish personal names.

From Constantinople, Eastern Roman emperors worked to hold the empire together and to reconquer at least some of the West from barbarian tribes. The emperor Justinian (r. 527–565) waged long and hard-fought wars against the Ostrogoths and temporarily regained Italy and North Africa, but his conquests had disastrous consequences. Justinian's wars exhausted the resources of the state, destroyed Italy's economy, and killed a large part of Italy's population. The wars also paved the way for the easy conquest of Italy by another Germanic tribe, the Lombards, shortly after Justinian's death. In the late sixth century the territory of the Western Roman Empire came once again under barbarian sway.

Christian Missionaries and Conversion

FOCUS QUESTION
How did the church convert barbarian peoples to Christianity?

The Mediterranean served as the highway over which Christianity spread to the cities of the Roman Empire. Christian teachings were initially carried by all types of converts, but they were often spread into the countryside and into areas beyond the borders of the empire by those who had dedicated their lives to the church, such as monks. Such missionaries were often sent by popes specifically to convert certain groups. As they preached to barbarian peoples, the missionaries developed new techniques to convert them.

Throughout barbarian Europe, religion was not a private or individual matter; it was a social affair, and the religion of the chieftain or king determined the religion of the people. Thus missionaries concentrated their initial efforts not on ordinary people, but on kings or tribal chieftains and the members of their families, who then ordered their subjects to convert. Because they had more opportunity to spend time with missionaries, queens and other female members of the royal family were often the first converts in an area, and they influenced their husbands and brothers. Germanic kings sometimes accepted Christianity because they came to believe that the Christian God was more powerful than pagan gods and that the Christian God—in either its Arian or Roman version—would deliver victory in battle. They also appreciated that Christianity taught obedience to kingly as well as divine authority. Christian missionaries were generally literate, and they taught reading and writing to young men who became priests or officials in the royal household, a service that kings appreciated.

Missionaries' Actions

During the Roman occupation, small Christian communities were scattered throughout Gaul and Britain. The leaders of some of these, such as Bishop Martin of Tours (ca. 316–397), who founded a monastery and established a rudimentary parish system in his diocese, supported Nicene Christianity (see page 189). Other missionaries were Arian Christians, who also founded dioceses and converted many barbarian groups. Bishop Ulfilas (ca. 310–383), for example, an Ostrogoth himself, translated the Bible from the Greek in which it was normally written into the Gothic language, creating a new Gothic script in order to write it down. The Ostrogoths, Visigoths, Lombards, and Vandals were all originally Arian Christians, though over the sixth and seventh centuries most of them converted to Roman Christianity, sometimes peacefully and sometimes as a result of conquest.

Tradition identifies the conversion of Ireland with Saint Patrick (ca. 385–461). Born in England to a Christian family of Roman citizenship, Patrick was captured and enslaved by Irish raiders and taken to Ireland, where he worked as a herdsman for six years. He escaped and returned to England, where a vision urged him to Christianize Ireland. In preparation, Patrick studied in Gaul and was consecrated a bishop in 432. He returned to Ireland, where he converted the Irish tribe by tribe, first baptizing the chief of each tribe. By the time of Patrick's death, the majority of the Irish people had received Christian baptism.

In his missionary work, Patrick had the strong support of Bridget of Kildare (ca. 450–528), daughter of a wealthy chieftain. Bridget defied parental pressure to marry and became a nun. She and the other nuns at Kildare instructed relatives and friends in basic Christian doctrine, made religious vestments (clothing) for churches, copied books, taught children, and above all set a religious example by their lives of prayer. In this way, in Ireland and later in continental Europe, women like the nuns at Kildare shared in the process of conversion.

The Christianization of the English began in earnest in 597, when Pope Gregory I sent a delegation of monks under the Roman Augustine to Britain. Augustine's approach, like Patrick's, was to concentrate on converting those who held power. When he succeeded in converting Ethelbert, king of Kent, the baptism of Ethelbert's people took place as a matter of course. Augustine established his headquarters, or *see*, at Canterbury, the capital of Kent in southern England.

In the course of the seventh century, two Christian forces competed for the conversion of the pagan Anglo-Saxons: Roman-oriented missionaries traveling north from Canterbury, and Celtic monks from Ireland and northwestern Britain. The Roman and Celtic church organizations, types of monastic life, and methods of arriving at the date of the central feast of the Christian calendar, Easter, differed completely. Through the influence of King Oswiu of Northumbria and the dynamic abbess Hilda of Whitby, the Synod (ecclesiastical council) held at Hilda's convent of Whitby in 664 opted to follow the Roman practices. The conversion of the English and the close attachment of the English Church to Rome had far-reaching consequences because Britain later served as a base for the Christianization of the European continent (see Map 7.2), spreading Roman Christian teachings among both pagans and Arians.

The Process of Conversion

When a ruler marched his people to the waters of baptism, the work of Christianization had only begun. Christian kings could order their subjects to be baptized, married, and buried in Christian ceremonies, and people complied increasingly across Europe. Churches could be built, and people could be required to attend services and belong to parishes, but the process of conversion was a gradual one.

How did missionaries and priests get masses of pagan and illiterate peoples to understand Christian ideals and teachings? They did so through preaching, assimilation, the ritual of penance, and the veneration of saints. Missionaries preached the basic teachings of Christianity in simplified Latin or translated them into the local language. In monasteries and cathedrals, men—and a few women—wrote hymns, prayers, and stories about the lives of Christ and the saints. People heard these and slowly became familiar with Christian notions.

Deeply ingrained pagan customs and practices could not be stamped out by words alone, however, or even by royal edicts. Christian missionaries often pursued a policy of assimilation, easing the conversion of pagan men and women by stressing similarities between their customs and beliefs and those of Christianity. In the same way that classically trained scholars such as Jerome and Augustine blended Greco-Roman

Gregory of Tours on the Veneration of Relics

Accounts of the miracles associated with the relics of saints were an important part of Christian preaching and writing, designed to win converts and strengthen their faith, and to provide spiritual guidance. Gregory of Tours (ca. 539–594), a bishop in the Frankish kingdom, described events surrounding relics in Glory of the Martyrs. *He begins with a discussion of relics associated with the cross on which Jesus had been crucified, the discovery of which was attributed to Emperor Constantine's mother, Helena, who gathered many relics in and around Jerusalem and brought them back to Constantinople. Pieces of this relic were distributed widely throughout Europe, and elaborately decorated reliquaries were made to hold them. As Gregory notes here, some went to the convent in Poitiers (in west-central France) that had been founded by the Merovingian Frankish queen Radegund shortly before Gregory wrote this.*

The cross of the Lord that was found by the empress Helena at Jerusalem is venerated on Wednesday and Friday. Queen Radegund, who is comparable to Helena in both merit and faith, requested relics of this cross and piously placed them in a convent at Poitiers that she founded out of her own zeal. She repeatedly sent servants to Jerusalem and throughout the entire region of the East. These servants visited the tombs of holy martyrs and confessors and brought back relics of them all. After placing them in the silver reliquary with the holy cross itself, she thereafter deserved to see many miracles. . . .

A girl named Chrodigildis was punished by the loss of her eyesight while she was living in the territory of Le Mans after the death of her father. Later, however, while the blessed Queen Radegund was still alive, at the command of King Chilperic she entered the rule of the aforementioned convent. With the most blessed Radegund as a guide, she bowed before the holy reliquary and there kept vigils with the other nuns. When morning came and the others left, she remained in the same place prostrate on the ground. In a vision it seemed to her as if someone had opened her eyes. One eye was restored to health; while she was still concerned about the other, suddenly she was awakened by the sound of a door being unlocked and regained the sight of one eye. There is no doubt that this was accomplished by the power of the cross. The possessed, the lame, and also other ill people are often cured at this place. Enough on this topic. . . .

Through their confession [that is, their not being deterred by persecution] the glorious martyrs have earned the unspeakable benefits of gifts that are always salutary. To petitioners they have revealed themselves by this power that the Lord Creator shared with them. I know that this happened just as my deacon recently told me. This deacon received relics of some martyrs and confessors [heroic believers] from pope Pelagius [II] of Rome [pontificate 579–590]. A large chorus of monks who were chanting psalms and a huge crowd of people escorted him to Ostia. After he boarded a ship the sails were unfurled and hoisted over the rigging of a mast that presented the appearance of a cross. As the wind blew, they set out on the high seas. When they were sailing to reach the port of Marseilles, they began to approach a certain place where a mountain of stone rose from the shore of the sea and, sinking a bit, stretched into the sea to the top of the water. As the wind forced them on, the ship was lifted by a mighty blast into danger. When the ship was shaken as if struck by the rock, the sailors recognized their peril and announced their death. The deacon lifted the reliquary with the holy relics. He groaned and in a loud voice began to invoke the names of the individual saints. He prayed that their power might liberate from danger those who were about to die. The ship, as I said, sailed closer

and Christian ideas, missionaries and converts mixed pagan ideas and practices with Christian ones. Bogs and lakes sacred to Germanic gods became associated with saints, as did various aspects of ordinary life, such as traveling, planting crops, and worrying about a sick child. Aspects of existing midwinter celebrations, which often centered on the return of the sun as the days became longer, were incorporated into celebrations of Christmas. Spring rituals involving eggs and rabbits (both symbols of fertility) were added to Easter.

The ritual of penance was also instrumental in teaching people Christian ideas. Christianity taught that certain actions and thoughts were sins, meaning that they and closer to the rock. Suddenly, out of respect for the holy relics, a wind blew from that spot with great force against the other wind. It crushed the waves and repulsed the opposing wind. By recalling the ship to the deep sea, the wind freed everyone from the danger of death. So they circumvented this impending danger, and by the grace of the Lord and the protection of the saints they arrived at the port they had hoped for. . . .

Because he [Gregory's father] wished himself to be protected by relics of saints, he asked a cleric to grant him something from these relics, so that with their protection he might be kept safe as he set out on this long journey. He put the sacred ashes in a gold medallion and carried it with him. Although he did not even know the names of the blessed men, he was accustomed to recount that he had been rescued from many dangers. He claimed that often, because of the powers of these relics, he had avoided the violence of bandits, the dangers of floods, the threats of turbulent men, and attacks from swords.

I will not be silent about what I witnessed regarding these relics. After the death of my father my mother carried these relics with her. It was the time for harvesting the crops, and huge piles of grain had been collected on the threshing floors. . . . The threshers kindled fires for themselves from the straw. . . . Quickly, fanned by the wind, the fire spread to the piles of grain. The fire became a huge blaze and was accompanied by the shouts of men, the wails of women, and the crying of children. This happened in our field. When my mother, who was wearing these relics around her neck, learned of this, she rushed from the meal and held the sacred relics in front of the balls of flames. In a moment the entire fire so died down that no sparks were found among the piles of burned straw and the seeds. The grain the fire had touched had suffered no harm.

Many years later I received these relics from my mother. While I was travelling from Burgundy to Clermont, a huge storm appeared in my path. The storm frequently flashed with lightning in the sky and rumbled with loud crashes of thunder. Then I took the holy relics from my pocket and raised my hand before the cloud. The cloud immediately divided into two parts and passed by on the right and the left; it threatened neither me nor anyone else. Then, as a presumptuous young man is expected to behave, I began to be inflated by the arrogance of vainglory. I silently thought that this concession had been made especially for me, rather than because of the merits of the saints. I boasted to my travelling companions and insisted that I had deserved that which God had bestowed upon my naïveté. Immediately my horse suddenly slipped beneath me and threw me to the ground. I was so seriously bruised during this accident that I could hardly get up. I understood that this accident had happened because of my pride; and it was sufficient to note that afterwards the urge of vainglory did not bother me. For if it happened that I was worthy to observe some manifestations of the powers of saints, I have proclaimed that they were due to the gift of God through the faith of the saints.

EVALUATE THE EVIDENCE

1. According to Gregory, what gives relics their power, and why should they be venerated?
2. The veneration of relics involved both public display for community devotion and personal ownership for private needs. What examples of each do you see in Gregory's text?
3. Gregory was a historian who wrote chronicles of the Frankish kingdom as well as spiritual works such as this one. How does he use the techniques of a historian, such as identifying his sources, in this work? How do these support his assertions about the power of relics?

Source: Gregory of Tours, *Glory of the Martyrs*, trans. Raymond Van Dam (Liverpool: Liverpool University, 1988), pp. 22, 24, 106–109. Reprinted with permission of Liverpool University Press.

were against God's commands. Only by confessing these sins and asking forgiveness could a sinning believer be reconciled with God. Confession was initially a public ritual, but by the fifth century individual confession to a parish priest was more common. The person knelt before the priest, who questioned him or her about sins he or she might have committed. The priest then set a penance such as fasting or saying specific prayers to allow the person to atone for the sin. The priest and penitent were guided by manuals known as penitentials (peh-nuh-TEHN-shuhlz), which included lists of sins and the appropriate penance. The seventh-century English penitential of Theodore, for example, stipulated that "if a lay Christian vomits because of drunkenness, he shall do penance for fifteen days," while drunken monks were to do penance for thirty days. Those who "commit fornication with a virgin" were to do penance for a year, as were those who perform "divinations according to the custom of the heathens." Penance for killing someone depended on the circumstances. Usually it was seven years, but if the murder was "in revenge for a brother," it was three years; if it was by accident, one year; and if it was "by command of [the killer's] lord" or in "public war," only forty days.[7] Penance gave new Christians a sense of expected behavior, encouraged the private examination of conscience, and offered relief from the burden of sinful deeds.

Most religious observances continued to be community matters, as they had been in the ancient world. People joined with family members, friends, and neighbors at their parish church to attend baptisms, weddings, and funerals presided over by a priest. The parish church often housed the **relics** of a saint, that is, bones, articles of clothing, or other objects associated with a person who had lived (or died) in a way that was spiritually heroic or noteworthy. This patron saint was understood to provide protection and assistance for those who came to worship, and the relics served as a link between the material world and the spiritual. (See "Evaluating the Evidence 7.3: Gregory of Tours on the Veneration of Relics," page 208.)

relics Bones, articles of clothing, or other objects associated with the life of a saint.

Christians came to venerate the saints as powerful and holy. They prayed to saints or to the Virgin Mary to intercede with God, or they simply asked the saints to assist and bless them. The entire village participated in processions marking saints' days or points in the agricultural year, often carrying images of saints or their relics around the houses and fields. The decision to become Christian was often made first by an emperor or king, but actual conversion was a local matter, as people came to feel that the parish priest and the patron saint provided them with benefits in this world and the world to come.

The Byzantine Empire

FOCUS QUESTION

How did the Byzantine Empire preserve the legacy of Rome?

Barbarian migrations and Christian conversions occurred throughout all of Europe in late antiquity, but their impact was not the same in the western and eastern halves of the Roman Empire. The Western Roman Empire gradually disintegrated, but the Roman Empire continued in the East (Map 7.4). The Byzantine or Eastern Roman Empire preserved the forms, institutions, and traditions of the old Roman Empire, and its people even called themselves Romans. Byzantine emperors traced their lines back past Constantine to Augustus, and the Senate in Constantinople carried on the traditions of the old Roman Senate. Most important, however, is how Byzantium protected the intellectual heritage of Greco-Roman civilization and then passed it on to the rest of Europe.

Sources of Byzantine Strength

While the western parts of the Roman Empire gradually succumbed to barbarian invaders, the Byzantine Empire survived Germanic, Persian, and Arab attacks. In 540 the Huns and Bulgars crossed the Danube and raided as far as southern Greece. In 559 a force of Huns and Slavs reached the gates of Constantinople. In 583 the Avars, a mounted Mongol people who had swept across Russia and southeastern Europe,

MAP 7.4 The Byzantine Empire, ca. 600   The strategic position of Constantinople on the waterway between the Black Sea and the Mediterranean was clear to Constantine when he chose the city as the capital of the Eastern Roman Empire. Byzantine territories in Italy were acquired in Emperor Justinian's sixth-century wars and were held for several centuries.

seized Byzantine forts along the Danube and reached the walls of Constantinople. Between 572 and 630 the Sassanid Persians posed a formidable threat, and the Greeks were repeatedly at war with them. Beginning in 632 Muslim forces pressured the Byzantine Empire (see Chapter 8).

Why didn't one or a combination of these enemies capture Constantinople as the Ostrogoths had taken Rome? The answer lies in strong military leadership and even more in the city's location and its excellent fortifications. Justinian's generals were able to reconquer much of Italy and North Africa from barbarian groups, making them part of the Eastern Roman Empire. The Byzantines ruled most of Italy from 535 to 572 and the southern part of the peninsula until the eleventh century; they ruled North Africa until it was conquered by Muslim forces in the late seventh century. Under the skillful command of General Priskos (d. 612), Byzantine armies inflicted a severe defeat on the Avars in 601, and under Emperor Heraclius I (r. 610–641) they crushed the Persians at Nineveh in Iraq. Massive triple walls, built by the emperors Constantine and Theodosius II (r. 408–450) and kept in good repair, protected Constantinople from sea invasion. Within the walls huge cisterns provided water, and vast gardens and grazing areas supplied vegetables and meat, so the defending people could hold out far longer than the besieging army. Attacking Constantinople by land posed greater geographical and logistical problems than a seventh- or eighth-century government could solve. The site was not absolutely impregnable — as the Venetians demonstrated in 1204

Greek Fire   In this illustration from a twelfth-century manuscript, sailors shoot Greek fire toward an attacking ship from a pressurized tube that looks strikingly similar to a modern flamethrower. The exact formula for Greek fire has been lost, but it was probably made from a petroleum product because it continued burning on water. Greek fire was particularly important in Byzantine defenses of Constantinople from Muslim forces in the late seventh century. (Prado, Madrid/Bridgeman Images)

and the Ottoman Turks in 1453—but it was almost so. For centuries the Byzantine Empire served as a bulwark for the West, protecting it against invasions from the East.

The Law Code of Justinian

One of the most splendid achievements of the Byzantine emperors was the preservation of Roman law for the medieval and modern worlds. Roman law had developed from many sources—decisions by judges, edicts of the emperors, legislation passed by the Senate, and the opinions of jurists. By the fourth century it had become a huge, bewildering mass, and its sheer bulk made it almost unusable.

Sweeping and systematic codification took place under the emperor Justinian. He appointed a committee of eminent jurists to sort through and organize the laws. The result was the *Corpus Juris Civilis* (KAWR-puhs JOOR-uhs sih-VIH-luhs) (Body of Civil Law), a multipart collection of laws and legal commentary issued from 529 to 534, and often called simply "Justinian's Code." The first part of this work, the *Codex*, brought together all the existing imperial laws into a coherent whole, eliminated outmoded laws and contradictions, and clarified the law itself. It began with laws ordering the interpretation of Christian doctrine favored by the emperor in opposition to groups such as the Arians and Nestorians, and affirming the power of the emperor in matters of religion, such as this decree first issued by the emperor Theodosius:

> We desire that all peoples subject to Our benign Empire shall live under the same religion that the Divine Peter, the Apostle, gave to the Romans, and which the said religion declares was introduced by himself . . . that is to say, in accordance with the rules of apostolic discipline and the evangelical doctrine, we should believe that the Father, Son, and Holy Spirit constitute a single Deity, endowed with equal majesty, and united in the Holy Trinity.
>
> We order all those who follow this law to assume the name of Catholic Christians, and considering others as demented and insane, We order that they shall bear the infamy of heresy; and when the Divine vengeance which they merit has been appeased, they shall afterwards be punished in accordance with our resentment, which we have acquired from the judgment of Heaven.[8]

The rest of the *Codex* was structured by topic and included provisions on every aspect of life, including economic issues, social concerns, and family life.

The second part of Justinian's Code, the *Digest*, is a collection of the opinions of foremost Roman jurists on complex legal problems, and the third part, the *Institutes*, is a handbook of civil law designed for students and beginning jurists. All three parts were given the force of law and formed the backbone of Byzantine jurisprudence from that point on. Like so much of classical culture, the *Corpus Juris Civilis* was lost in western

Europe with the end of the Roman Empire, but it was rediscovered in the eleventh century and came to form the foundation of law for nearly every modern European nation.

Byzantine Intellectual Life

The Byzantines prized education; because of them, many masterpieces of ancient Greek literature have survived to influence the intellectual life of the modern world. The literature of the Byzantine Empire was predominantly Greek, although politicians, scholars, and lawyers also spoke and used Latin. Justinian's Code was first written in Latin. More people could read in Byzantium than anywhere else in Christian Europe at the time, and history was a favorite topic.

The most remarkable Byzantine historian was Procopius (ca. 500–562), who left a rousing account praising Justinian's reconquest of North Africa and Italy, but also wrote the *Secret History*, a vicious and uproarious attack on Justinian and his wife, the empress Theodora. (See "Individuals in Society: Theodora of Constantinople," page 214.)

Although the Byzantines discovered little that was new in mathematics and geometry, they made advances in terms of military applications. For example, they invented an explosive liquid that came to be known as "Greek fire." The liquid was heated and propelled by a pump through a bronze tube, and as the jet left the tube, it was ignited—somewhat like a modern flamethrower. Greek fire saved Constantinople from Arab assault in 678 and was used in both land and sea battles for centuries, although modern military experts still do not know the exact nature of the compound. In mechanics Byzantine scientists improved and modified artillery and siege machinery.

The Byzantines devoted a great deal of attention to medicine, and the general level of medical competence was far higher in the Byzantine Empire than in western Europe. Yet their physicians could not cope with the terrible disease, often called the "Justinian plague," that swept through the Byzantine Empire and parts of western Europe between 542 and about 560. Probably originating in northwestern India and carried to the Mediterranean region by ships, the disease was similar to what was later identified as the bubonic plague. Characterized by high fever, chills, delirium, and enlarged lymph nodes, or by inflammation of the lungs that caused hemorrhages of black blood, the Justinian plague claimed the lives of tens of thousands of people. The epidemic had profound political as well as social consequences: it weakened Justinian's military resources, thus hampering his efforts to restore unity to the Mediterranean world.

By the ninth or tenth century most major Greek cities had hospitals for the care of the sick. The hospitals might be divided into wards for different illnesses, and hospital staff included surgeons, practitioners, and aids with specialized responsibilities. The imperial Byzantine government bore the costs of these medical facilities.

The Orthodox Church

The continuity of the Roman Empire in the East meant that Christianity developed differently there than it did in the West. The emperors in Constantinople were understood to be Christ's representative on earth; their palace was considered holy and was filled with relics and religious images, called icons. Emperors convened councils, appointed church officials, and regulated the income of the church. As in Rome, there was a patriarch in Constantinople, but he did not develop the same powers that the pope did in the West because there was never a similar power vacuum into which

INDIVIDUALS IN SOCIETY

Theodora of Constantinople

The most powerful woman in Byzantine history was the daughter of a bear trainer for the circus. Theodora (ca. 497–548) grew up in what her contemporaries regarded as an undignified and morally suspect atmosphere, and she worked as a dancer and burlesque actress, both dishonorable occupations in the Roman world. Despite her background, she caught the eye of Justinian, who was then a military leader and whose uncle (and adoptive father) Justin had himself risen from obscurity to become the emperor of the Byzantine Empire. Under Justinian's influence, Justin changed the law to allow an actress who had left her disreputable life to marry whom she liked, and Justinian and Theodora married in 525. When Justinian was proclaimed co-emperor with his uncle Justin on April 1, 527, Theodora received the rare title of *augusta*, or empress. Thereafter her name was linked with Justinian's in the exercise of imperial power.

Most of our knowledge of Theodora's early life comes from the *Secret History*, a tell-all description of the vices of Justinian and his court written around 550 by Procopius (pruh-KOH-pee-uhs), who was the official court historian and thus spent his days praising those same people. In the *Secret History* he portrays Theodora and Justinian as demonic, greedy, and vicious, killing courtiers to steal their property. In scene after detailed scene, Procopius portrays Theodora as particularly evil, sexually insatiable, depraved, and cruel, a temptress who used sorcery to attract men, including the hapless Justinian.

In one of his official histories, *The History of the Wars of Justinian*, Procopius presents a very different Theodora. Riots between the supporters of two teams in chariot races—who formed associations somewhat like both street gangs and political parties—had turned deadly, and Justinian wavered in his handling of the perpetrators. Both sides turned against the emperor, besieging the palace while Justinian was inside it. Shouting "N-I-K-A" (victory), the rioters swept through the city, burning and looting, and destroyed half of Constantinople. Justinian's counselors urged flight, but, according to Procopius, Theodora rose and declared:

> For one who has reigned, it is intolerable to be an exile. . . . If you wish, O Emperor, to save yourself, there is no difficulty: we have ample funds and there are the ships. Yet reflect whether, when you have once escaped to a place of security, you will not prefer death to safety. I agree with an old saying that the purple [that is, the color worn only by emperors] is a fair winding sheet [to be buried in].

Justinian rallied, had the rioters driven into the hippodrome, and ordered between thirty thousand and thirty-five thousand men and women executed. The revolt was

---

Orthodox Church
Eastern Christian Church in the Byzantine Empire.

he needed to step. The **Orthodox Church**, the name generally given to the Eastern Christian Church, was more subject to secular control than the Western Christian Church, although some churchmen did stand up to the emperor. Saint John Chrysostom (ca. 347–407), for example, a bishop and one of the church fathers, thunderously preached against what he saw as the luxury and decadence of the emperor's court and its support of pagan practices, such as erecting statues of rulers. He was banished—twice—but his sermons calling for an ascetic life and support for the poor were copied and recopied for centuries.

Monasticism in the Orthodox world differed in fundamental ways from the monasticism that evolved in western Europe. First, while *The Rule of Saint Benedict* gradually became the universal guide for all western European monasteries, each individual house in the Byzantine world developed its own set of rules for organization and behavior. Second, education never became a central feature of Orthodox monasteries. Monks and nuns had to be literate to perform the appropriate rituals, but no Orthodox monastery assumed responsibility for the general training of the local young.

crushed and Justinian's authority was restored, an outcome approved by Procopius.

Other sources describe or suggest Theodora's influence on imperial policy. Justinian passed a number of laws that improved the legal status of women, such as allowing women to own property the same way that men could and to be guardians over their own children. Justinian is reputed to have consulted her every day about all aspects of state policy, including religious policy regarding the doctrinal disputes that continued throughout his reign. Theodora's influence over her husband and her power in the Byzantine state continued until she died, perhaps of cancer, twenty years before Justinian. Her influence may have even continued after death, for Justinian continued to pass reforms favoring women and, at the end of his life, accepted her interpretation of Christian doctrine. Institutions that she established, including hospitals, orphanages, houses for the rehabilitation of prostitutes, and churches, continued to be reminders of her charity and piety.

Theodora has been viewed as a symbol of the manipulation of beauty and cleverness to attain position and power, and also as a strong and capable co-ruler who held the empire together during riots, revolts, and deadly epidemics. Just as Procopius expressed both views, the debate has continued to today among writers of science fiction and fantasy as well as biographers and historians.

The empress Theodora (center) shown with a halo, symbolizing piety, and a crown, symbolizing power, in an intricate mosaic of thousands of cubes of colored glass and stone, created in Ravenna, Italy, in the sixth century. Like Justinian, Theodora had power over secular and religious institutions, much to the dismay of many at Justinian's court. (San Vitale, Ravenna, Italy/Universal History Archive/UIG via Getty Images)

QUESTIONS FOR ANALYSIS

1. How would you assess the complex legacy of Theodora?
2. Since the official and unofficial views of Procopius are so different regarding the empress, should he be trusted at all as a historical source?

There were also similarities between Western and Eastern monasticism. As in the West, Eastern monasteries became wealthy property owners, with fields, pastures, livestock, and buildings. Since bishops and patriarchs of the Orthodox Church were recruited only from the monasteries, these religious leaders also exercised cultural influence.

Like their counterparts in the West, Byzantine missionaries traveled far beyond the boundaries of the empire in search of converts. In 863 the emperor Michael III sent the brothers Cyril (826–869) and Methodius (815–885) to preach Christianity in Moravia (a region in the modern Czech Republic). Other missionaries succeeded in converting the Russians in the tenth century. Cyril invented a Slavic alphabet using Greek characters, later termed the Cyrillic (suh-RIH-lihk) alphabet in his honor. In the tenth century other missionaries spread Christianity, the Cyrillic alphabet, and Byzantine art and architecture to Russia. The Byzantines were so successful that the Russians would later claim to be the successors of the Byzantine Empire. For a time Moscow was even known as the "Third Rome" (the second Rome being Constantinople).

LOOKING BACK LOOKING AHEAD

The Christian Church and the barbarian states absorbed many aspects of Roman culture, and the Roman Empire continued to thrive in the East as the Byzantine Empire, but western Europe in 600 was very different than it had been in 250. The Western Roman Empire had slowly disintegrated under pressure from barbarian groups. Barbarian kings ruled small states from Italy to Norway, while churches and monasteries rather than emperors and wealthy individuals took on the role of constructing new buildings and providing education. The city of Rome no longer attracted a steady stream of aspiring immigrants and had shrunk significantly, as had many other cities, which were no longer centers of innovation. As the vast network of Roman urban centers dissolved, economies everywhere became more localized. Commentators such as Augustine advised people to put their faith in the eternal City of God rather than in worldly cities, because human history would always bring great change. People who lived with Augustine in Hippo would have certainly understood such counsel, for they watched the Vandals besiege their city in 430, move swiftly across North Africa, and bring an end to Roman rule there. Although Justinian's Byzantine forces reclaimed the area a little over a century later, the culture that survived was as much barbarian as Roman, with smaller cities, less trade, and fewer schools.

Two hundred years after the Vandal attack, the residents of Byzantine North Africa confronted another fast-moving army of conquest, Arabian forces carrying a new religion, Islam. This Arabic expansion dramatically shaped the development of Western civilization. Though the end of the Roman Empire in 476 has long been seen as a dramatic break in European history, the expansion of Islam two centuries later may have been even more significant. Many of the patterns set in late antiquity continued, however. Warrior values such as physical prowess, bravery in battle, and loyalty to one's lord remained central and shaped the development of the political system known as feudalism. The Frankish kingdom established by Clovis continued to expand, becoming the most important state in Europe. The economic and political power of the Christian Church expanded as well, with monasteries and convents providing education for their residents. The vast majority of people continued to live in small villages, trying to raise enough grain to feed themselves and their families, and asking the saints for help to overcome life's difficulties.

Make Connections

Think about the larger developments and continuities within and across chapters.

1. The end of the Roman Empire in the West in 476 has long been viewed as one of the most important turning points in history. Do you agree with this idea? Why or why not?

2. In what ways was the role of the family in barbarian society similar to that of the family in classical Athens (Chapter 3) and republican Rome (Chapter 5)? In what ways was it different? What might account for the similarities and differences that you identify?

3. How did the Christian Church adapt to Roman and barbarian society? How was it different in 600 from how it had been in 100?

7 REVIEW & EXPLORE

Review the Main Ideas

Answer the focus questions from each section of the chapter.

◆ How did Diocletian and Constantine try to reform the empire? (p. 186)

◆ How did the Christian Church become a major force in the Mediterranean and Europe? (p. 190)

◆ What were the key characteristics of barbarian society? (p. 196)

◆ What were some of the causes and consequences of the barbarian migrations? (p. 200)

◆ How did the church convert barbarian peoples to Christianity? (p. 206)

◆ How did the Byzantine Empire preserve the legacy of Rome? (p. 210)

Identify Key Terms

Identify and explain the significance of each item below.

tetrarchy (p. 186)
diocese (p. 186)
Arianism (p. 189)
apostolic succession (p. 191)
Petrine Doctrine (p. 191)
regular clergy (p. 193)
secular clergy (p. 193)
sacraments (p. 195)
runic alphabet (p. 196)
comitatus (p. 198)
wergeld (p. 199)
relics (p. 210)
Orthodox Church (p. 214)

NOTES

1. Maude Aline Huttman, ed. and trans., *The Establishment of Christianity and the Proscription of Paganism* (New York: AMS Press, 1967), p. 164.
2. Eusebius, *Life of Constantine the Great*, trans. Ernest Cushing Richardson (Grand Rapids, Mich.: Eerdmans, 1979), p. 534.
3. R. C. Petry, ed., *A History of Christianity: Readings in the History of Early and Medieval Christianity* (Englewood Cliffs, N.J.: Prentice Hall, 1962), p. 70.
4. Saint Jerome, *Commentaries on the Letter to the Ephesians*, book 16, cited in Vern Bullough, *Sexual Variance in Society and History* (Chicago: University of Chicago Press, 1976), p. 365.
5. E. F. Henderson, ed., *Select Historical Documents of the Middle Ages* (London: G. Bell and Sons, 1912), pp. 176–189.
6. Reprinted by permission of the publishers and the Trustees of the Loeb Classical Library from Ammianus Marcellinus, *The History*, Volume 1, Loeb Classical Library, translated by John C. Rolfe; book 31, pt. 2, pp. 383, 385, 387. Cambridge, Mass.: Harvard University Press. First published 1939. The Loeb Classical Library® is a registered trademark of the President and Fellows of Harvard College.
7. John McNeill and Helena M. Gamer, *Medieval Handbooks of Penance: A Translation of the Principal Libri Poenitentiales and Selections from Related Documents* (New York: Columbia University Press, 1938).
8. Justinian's Code 1.1.1, in S. P. Scott, trans., *The Civil Law*, vol. 12 (Cincinnati: The Central Trust Company, 1932), p. 9.

CHAPTER PREVIEW

The Spread of Islam
What were the origins of Islam, and what impact did it have on Europe as it spread?

Frankish Rulers and Their Territories
How did the Franks build and govern a European empire?

Early Medieval Culture
What were the significant intellectual and cultural changes in Charlemagne's era?

Invasions and Migrations
What were the consequences of the ninth-century invasions and migrations?

Political and Economic Decentralization
How did internal conflict and outside threats shape European political and economic development in this period?

Life in the Early Middle Ages
In this manuscript illumination from Spain, Muslim fishermen take a rich harvest from the sea. Fish were an important part of the diet of all coastal peoples in medieval Europe and were often salted and dried to preserve them for later use.

(From *Cantigas de Santa Maria*, manuscript made under the direction of Alfonso X [1221–1284], King of Castile and Leon/Granger, NYC — All rights reserved)

218

8

Europe in the Early Middle Ages

600–1000

By the fifteenth century, scholars in the growing cities of northern Italy began to think that they were living in a new era, one in which the glories of ancient Greece and Rome were being reborn. What separated their time from classical antiquity, in their opinion, was a long period of darkness, to which a seventeenth-century professor gave the name "Middle Ages." In this conceptualization, Western history was divided into three periods—ancient, medieval, and modern—an organization that is still in use today.

For a long time the end of the Roman Empire in the West was seen as the division between the ancient period and the Middle Ages, but, as we saw in the last chapter, there was continuity as well as change, and the transition from ancient to medieval was a slow process, not a single event. The agents in this process included not only the barbarian migrations that broke the Roman Empire apart but also the new religion of Islam, Slavic and steppe peoples in eastern Europe, and Christian officials and missionaries. The period after the end of antiquity (ca. 600–1000), conventionally known as the "early Middle Ages," was a time of disorder and destruction, but it also marked the creation of a new type of society and a cultural revival that influenced later intellectual and literary traditions. While agrarian life continued to dominate Europe, political and economic structures that would influence later European history began to form, and Christianity continued to spread. People at the time did not know that they were living in an era that would later be labeled "middle" or sometimes even "dark," and we can wonder whether they would have shared this negative view of their own times. ■

The Spread of Islam

FOCUS QUESTION
What were the origins of Islam, and what impact did it have on Europe as it spread?

In the seventh century C.E. two empires dominated the area today called the Middle East: the Byzantine-Greek-Christian empire and the Sassanid-Persian-Zoroastrian empire. Between the two lay the Arabian peninsula, where a merchant called Muhammad began to have religious visions around 610. By the time he died in 632, all Arabia had accepted his creed of Islam. A century later his followers controlled what is now Syria, Palestine, Egypt, North Africa, Spain, and part of France. This Arab expansion profoundly affected the development of Western civilization as well as the history of Africa and Asia.

The Arabs

In Muhammad's time Arabia was inhabited by various tribes, many of them Bedouins (BEH-duh-wuhnz). These nomadic peoples grazed goats and sheep on the sparse patches of grass that dotted the vast semiarid peninsula. The power of the Bedouins came from their fighting skills, toughness, ability to control trade, and possession of horses and camels. Other Arabs lived more settled lives in the southern valleys and coastal towns along the Red Sea, such as Yemen, Mecca, and Medina, supporting themselves by agriculture and trade. Caravan routes crisscrossed Arabia and carried goods to Byzantium, Persia, and Syria. The wealth produced by business transactions led to luxurious living for many residents in the towns.

For all Arabs, the basic social unit was the clan — a group of blood relations connected through the male line. Clans expected loyalty from their members and in turn provided support and protection. Although the nomadic Bedouins condemned the urbanized lifestyle of the cities as immoral and corrupt, Arabs of all types respected certain aspects of one another's customs and had some religious rules and rituals in common. For example, all Arabs kept three months of the year as sacred; during that time any fighting stopped so that everyone could attend holy ceremonies in peace. The city of Mecca was the major religious and economic center of western Arabia. For centuries before the rise of Islam, many Arabs prayed at the Ka'ba (KAH-buh), a temple in Mecca containing a black stone thought to be the dwelling place of a god, as well as objects connected to other gods. Economic links also connected Arab peoples, but what eventually molded the diverse Arab tribes into a powerful political and social unity was a new religion based on the teachings of Muhammad.

The Prophet Muhammad

Qur'an The sacred book of Islam.

Except for a few vague remarks in the **Qur'an** (kuh-RAHN), the sacred book of Islam, Muhammad (ca. 571–632) left no account of his life. Arab tradition accepts some of the sacred stories that developed about him as historically true, but those accounts were not written down until about a century after his death. (Similarly, the earliest accounts of the life of Jesus, the Christian Gospels, were not written until forty to sixty years after his death.) Orphaned at the age of six, Muhammad was raised by his grandfather. As a young man he became a merchant in the caravan trade. Later he entered the service of a wealthy widow, and their subsequent marriage brought him financial independence.

The Qur'an reveals Muhammad to be an extremely devout man, ascetic, self-disciplined, and literate, but not formally educated. He prayed regularly, and when he was about forty he began to experience religious visions. Unsure for a time about what he should do, Muhammad discovered his mission after a vision in which the angel Gabriel instructed him to preach. Muhammad described his visions in a stylized and often rhyming prose and used this literary medium as his *Qur'an*, or "prayer recitation." Muhammad's revelations were written down by his followers during his lifetime and organized into chapters, called *sura*, shortly after his death. In 651 Muhammad's third successor arranged to have an official version published. The Qur'an is regarded by Muslims as the direct words of God to his Prophet Muhammad and is therefore especially revered. (When Muslims around the world use translations of the Qur'an, they do so alongside the original Arabic, the language of Muhammad's revelations.) At the same time, other sayings and accounts of Muhammad, which gave advice on matters that went beyond the Qur'an, were collected into books termed *hadith* (huh-DEETH). Muslim tradition (*Sunna*) consists of both the Qur'an and the hadith.

Muhammad's visions ordered him to preach a message of a single God and to become God's prophet, which he began to do in his hometown of Mecca. He gathered followers slowly, but also provoked a great deal of resistance because he urged people to give up worship of the gods whose sacred objects were in the Ka'ba and also challenged the power of the local elite. In 622 he migrated with his followers to Medina, an event termed the *hijra* (hih-JIGH-ruh) that marks the beginning of the Muslim calendar. At Medina Muhammad was much more successful, gaining converts and working out the basic principles of the faith. That same year, through the Charter of Medina, Muhammad formed the first *umma*, a community that united his followers from different tribes and set religious ties above clan loyalty. The charter also extended rights to non-Muslims living in Medina, including Jews and Christians, which set a precedent for the later treatment of Jews and Christians under Islam.

In 630 Muhammad returned to Mecca at the head of a large army, and he soon united the nomads of the desert and the merchants of the cities into an even larger umma of Muslims, a word meaning "those who comply with God's will." The religion

Chronology

481–752	Merovingian dynasty
ca. 571–632	Life of the Prophet Muhammad
651	Official version of the Qur'an published
711	Muslim forces defeat Visigothic kingdom
711–720	Muslim conquest of Spain
ca. 760–840	Carolingian Renaissance
768–814	Reign of Charlemagne
800	Imperial coronation of Charlemagne
800–900	Free peasants in western Europe increasingly tied to the land as serfs
843	Treaty of Verdun divides Carolingian kingdom
850–1000	Most extensive Viking voyages and conquests
ca. 900	Establishment of Kievan Rus
911	Vikings establish Normandy
950	Muslim Córdoba is Europe's largest and most prosperous city
1000	Stephen crowned first king of Hungary

Dome of the Rock, Jerusalem Completed in 691 and revered by Muslims as the site where Muhammad ascended to Heaven, the Dome of the Rock is the third-holiest place in Islam, after Mecca and Medina. Influenced by Byzantine and Persian architecture, it also has distinctly Arab features, such as Qur'anic inscriptions. (imageBROKER.net/SuperStock)

221

itself came to be called Islam, which means "submission to God." The Ka'ba was re-dedicated as a Muslim holy place, and Mecca became the most holy city in Islam. According to Muslim tradition, the Ka'ba predates the creation of the world and represents the earthly counterpart of God's heavenly throne, to which "pilgrims come dishevelled and dusty on every kind of camel."[1]

By the time Muhammad died in 632, the crescent of Islam, the Muslim symbol, prevailed throughout the Arabian peninsula. During the next century one rich province of the old Roman Empire after another came under Muslim domination — first Syria, then Egypt, and then all of North Africa (Map 8.1). Long and bitter wars (572–591, 606–630) between the Byzantine and Persian Empires left both so weak and exhausted that they easily fell to Muslim attack.

The Teachings and Expansion of Islam

Muhammad's religion eventually attracted great numbers of people, partly because of the straightforward nature of its doctrines. The strictly monotheistic theology outlined in the Qur'an has only a few central tenets: Allah, the Arabic word for God, is all-powerful and all-knowing. Muhammad, Allah's prophet, preached his word and carried his message. Muhammad described himself as the successor both of the Jewish patriarch Abraham and of Christ, and he claimed that his teachings replaced theirs. He invited and won converts from Judaism and Christianity.

Because Allah is all-powerful, believers must submit themselves to him. All Muslims have the obligation of the *jihad* (literally, "self-exertion") to strive or struggle to

MAP 8.1 The Spread of Islam, 622–900 The rapid expansion of Islam in a relatively short span of time testifies to the Arabs' superior fighting skills, religious zeal, and economic organization as well as to their enemies' weakness.

lead a virtuous life and to spread God's rule and law. In some cases striving is an individual struggle against sin; in others it is social and communal and could involve armed conflict, though this is not an essential part of jihad (jee-HAHD). The Islamic belief of "striving in the path of God" is closely related to the central feature of Muslim doctrine, the coming Day of Judgment. Muslims believe with conviction that the Day of Judgment will come; consequently, all of a Muslim's thoughts and actions should be oriented toward the Last Judgment and the rewards of Heaven.

To merit the rewards of Heaven, a person must follow the strict code of moral behavior that Muhammad prescribed. The Muslim must recite a profession of faith in God and in Muhammad as God's prophet: "There is no god but God and Muhammad is his prophet." The believer must pray five times a day, fast and pray during the sacred month of Ramadan, and contribute alms to the poor and needy. If possible, the believer must make a pilgrimage to Mecca once during his or her lifetime. According to the Muslim *shari'a* (shuh-REE-uh), or sacred law, these five practices—the profession of faith, prayer, fasting, giving alms to the poor, and pilgrimage to Mecca—constitute the **Five Pillars of Islam**. The Muslim who faithfully observes the laws of the Qur'an can hope for salvation.

Five Pillars of Islam The five practices Muslims must fulfill according to the shari'a, or sacred law, including the profession of faith, prayer, fasting, giving alms to the poor, and pilgrimage to Mecca.

The Qur'an forbids alcoholic beverages and gambling, as well as a number of foods, such as pork, a dietary regulation adopted from the Mosaic law of the Hebrews. It condemns business usury—that is, lending money at interest rates or taking advantage of market demand for products by charging high prices for them.

Polygyny, the practice of men having more than one wife, was common in Arab society before Muhammad, though for economic reasons the custom was limited to the well-to-do. The Qur'an limited the number of wives a man could have, however: "[Of] women who seem good in your eyes, marry but two, three, or four; and if ye still fear that ye shall not act equitably then only one" (Sura 4:3).

The Qur'an sets forth a strict sexual morality and condemns immoral behavior on the part of men as well as women: "The whore and the fornicator: whip each of them a hundred times. . . . The fornicator shall not marry other than a whore; and the whore shall not marry other than a fornicator" (Sura 24:2–3).

The Qur'an also set out rules for inheritance:

> Men who die and leave wives behind shall bequeath to them a year's maintenance. . . . And your wives shall have a fourth part of what you leave, if you have no issue [offspring]; but if you have issue, then they shall have an eighth part. . . . With regard to your children, God commands you to give the male the portion of two females. (Sura 4:11–12)

With respect to matters of property, Muslim women of the early Middle Ages had more rights than Western women. For example, a Muslim woman retained complete jurisdiction over one-third of her property when she married and could dispose of it in any way she wished. Women in most European countries and the United States did not gain these rights until the nineteenth century.

Sunni and Shi'a Divisions

Every Muslim hoped that by observing the laws of the Qur'an, he or she could achieve salvation, and it was the tenets of Islam preached by Muhammad that bound all Arabs together. Despite the clarity and unifying force of Muslim doctrine, however, divisions developed within the Islamic faith within decades of Muhammad's death. Neither the Qur'an nor the hadith gave clear guidance about how successors to Muhammad were to be chosen, but, according to tradition, in 632 a group of Muhammad's closest followers chose Abu Bakr (uh-BOO BAH-kuhr), who was a close friend of the Prophet and a member of a clan affiliated with the Prophet's clan, as **caliph** (KAY-luhf), a word meaning "successor." He was succeeded by two other caliphs, but these provoked opposition, which coalesced around Ali, Muhammad's cousin and son-in-law. Ali was chosen as the fourth caliph in 656, but was assassinated only five years later by backers of the initial line of caliphs. Ali's supporters began to assert that the Prophet had designated Ali as *imam*, or leader, and that he should rightly have been the first caliph; thus, any caliph who was not a descendant of Ali was a usurper. These supporters of Ali—termed Shi'ites (SHEE-ights) or Shi'a (SHEE-ah) from Arabic terms meaning "supporters" or "partisans" of Ali—saw Ali and subsequent imams as the divinely inspired leaders of the community. The larger body of Muslims who accepted the first elections—termed Sunnis, a word derived from *Sunna*, the practices of the community derived from Muhammad's example—saw the caliphs as political leaders. Since Islam did not have an organized priesthood, the caliphs had an additional function of safeguarding and enforcing the religious law (shari'a) with the advice of scholars (*ulama*), particularly the jurists, judges, and scholastics who were knowledgeable about the Qur'an and hadith. Over the centuries enmity between Sunni and Shi'a Muslims has sometimes erupted into violence, and discord still exists today.

After the assassination of Ali, the caliphate passed to members of the Umayyad (oo-MIGH-uhd) clan, who asserted control and brought stability to the growing Muslim empire. They established their capital at Damascus in Syria, and the Muslim faith continued to expand eastward to India and westward across North Africa. That expansion was facilitated everywhere by three main factors: military strength, trade connections, and tolerance toward non-Muslims. By the early tenth century a Muslim proverb spoke of the Mediterranean Sea as a Muslim lake, though the Greeks at Constantinople contested that notion.

Life in Muslim Spain

In Europe, Muslim political and cultural influence was felt most strongly in the Iberian Peninsula. In 711 a Muslim force crossed the Strait of Gibraltar and easily defeated the weak Visigothic kingdom. (See "Evaluating the Evidence 8.1: The Muslim Conquest of Spain," at right.) A few Christian princes supported by the Frankish rulers held out in northern mountain fortresses, but by 720 the Muslims controlled most of Spain. A member of the Umayyad Dynasty, Abd al-Rahman (r. 756–788) established a kingdom in Spain with its capital at Córdoba (KAWR-doh-buh).

Throughout the Islamic world, Muslims used the term **al-Andalus** to describe the part of the Iberian Peninsula under Muslim control. The name probably derives from the Arabic for "land of the Vandals," the Germanic people who swept across Spain in the fifth century (see Chapter 7). In the eighth century al-Andalus included the entire peninsula from Gibraltar in the south to the Cantabrian Mountains in the north (see Map 8.1). Today we often use the word *Andalusia* (an-duh-LOO-zhuh) to refer especially to southern Spain, but eighth-century Christians throughout Europe called the peninsula "Moorish Spain" because the Muslims who invaded and conquered it were Moors—Berbers from northwest Africa.

caliph A successor, as chosen by a group of Muhammad's closest followers.

al-Andalus The part of the Iberian Peninsula under Muslim control in the eighth century, encompassing most of modern-day Spain.

The Muslim Conquest of Spain

There are no contemporary descriptions from either Muslim or Christian authors of the Muslim conquest of the Iberian Peninsula that began in 711. One of the few existing documents is a treaty from 713 between 'Abd al-'Aziz, the son of the conquering Muslim governor and general Musa ibn Nusair, and Tudmir, the Visigothic Christian ruler of the city of Murcia in southern Spain. Treaties such as this, and military aspects of the conquest, were also described in the earliest surviving account, an anonymous Latin chronicle written by a Christian living in Muslim Spain in 754.

1. A Treaty from 713

In the name of God, the merciful and the compassionate.

This is a document [granted] by 'Abd al-'Aziz ibn Musa ibn Nusair to Tudmir, son of Ghabdush, establishing a treaty of peace and the promise and protection of God and his Prophet (may God bless him and grant him peace). We ['Abd al-'Aziz] will not set special conditions for him or for any among his men, nor harass him, nor remove him from power. His followers will not be killed or taken prisoner, nor will they be separated from their women and children. They will not be coerced in matters of religion, their churches will not be burned, nor will sacred objects be taken from the realm, [so long as] he [Tudmir] remains sincere and fulfills the [following] conditions that we have set for him. He has reached a settlement concerning seven towns: Orihuela, Valentilla, Alicante, Mula, Bigastro, Ello, and Lorca. He will not give shelter to fugitives, nor to our enemies, nor encourage any protected person to fear us, nor conceal news of our enemies. He and [each of] his men shall [also] pay one dinar every year, together with four measures of wheat, four measures of barley, four liquid measures of concentrated fruit juice, four liquid measures of vinegar, four of honey, and four of olive oil. Slaves must each pay half of this amount.

2. Chronicle of 754

In Justinian's time [711], . . . Musa . . . entered the long plundered and godlessly invaded Spain to destroy it. After forcing his way to Toledo, the royal city, he imposed on the adjacent regions an evil and fraudulent peace. He decapitated on a scaffold those noble lords who had remained, arresting them in their flight from Toledo with the help of Oppa, King Egica's son [a Visigothic Christian prince]. With Oppa's support, he killed them all with the sword. Thus he devastated not only [the former Roman province of] Hispania Ulterior, but [the former Roman province of] Hispania Citerior up to and beyond the ancient and once flourishing city of Zaragoza, now, by the judgment of God, openly exposed to the sword, famine, and captivity. He ruined beautiful cities, burning them with fire; condemned lords and powerful men to the cross; and butchered youths and infants with the sword. While he terrorized everyone in this way, some of the cities that remained sued for peace under duress and, after persuading and mocking them with a certain craftiness, the Saracens [Muslims] granted their requests without delay.

EVALUATE THE EVIDENCE

1. What conditions and guarantees are set for Christians living under Muslim rule in the treaty, and how does the author of the chronicle view treaties such as this?
2. What evidence do these documents provide for coexistence between Christians and Muslims in Spain and for hostility between the two groups?

Source: Olivia Remie Constable, ed., *Medieval Iberia: Readings from Christian, Muslim, and Jewish Sources* (Philadelphia: University of Pennsylvania Press, 1997), pp. 37–38, 30–31. Reprinted by permission of the University of Pennsylvania Press.

The ethnic term *Moorish* can be misleading, however, because the peninsula was home to sizable numbers of Jews and Christians as well as Muslim Moors. In business transactions and in much of daily life, all peoples used the Arabic language. With Muslims, Christians, and Jews trading with and learning from one another and occasionally intermarrying, Moorish Spain and Norman Sicily (see Chapter 9) were the only distinctly pluralistic societies in medieval Europe.

Some scholars believe that the eighth and ninth centuries in Andalusia were an era of remarkable interfaith harmony. Jews in Muslim Spain were generally treated well, and Córdoba became a center of Jewish as well as Muslim learning. Many Christians adopted Arab patterns of speech and dress, gave up eating pork, and developed an appreciation for Arab music and poetry. Some Christian women of elite status chose the Muslim practice of veiling their faces in public. Records describe Muslim and Christian youths joining in celebrations and merrymaking.

From the sophisticated centers of Muslim culture in Baghdad, Damascus, and Cairo, al-Andalus seemed a provincial backwater, a frontier outpost with little significance in the wider context of Islamic civilization. On the other hand, "northern barbarians," as Muslims called the European peoples, acknowledged the splendor of Spanish culture. The Saxon nun and writer Hroswitha of Gandersheim (roz-WEETH-uh of GAHN-duhr-shighm) called the city of Córdoba "the ornament of the world." By 950 the city had a population of about a half million, making it Europe's largest and most prosperous city. Many residents lived in large houses and easily purchased the silks and brocades made by the city's thousands of weavers. The streets were well paved and well lit—a sharp contrast to the dark and muddy streets of other cities in Europe—and there was an abundance of freshwater for drinking and bathing. The largest library contained four hundred thousand volumes, a vast collection, particularly when compared with the largest library in northern Europe at the Benedictine abbey of St. Gall in Switzerland, which had only six hundred books.

In Spain, as elsewhere in the Arab world, the Muslims had an enormous impact on agricultural development. They began the cultivation of rice, sugarcane, citrus fruits, dates, figs, eggplants, carrots, and, after the eleventh century, cotton. These crops, together with new methods of field irrigation, provided the population with food products unknown in the rest of Europe. Muslims also brought technological innovations westward, including new kinds of sails and navigational instruments, as well as paper.

Muslim-Christian Relations

What did early Muslims think of Jesus? Jesus is mentioned many times in the Qur'an, which affirms that he was born of Mary the Virgin. He is described as a righteous prophet chosen by God who performed miracles and continued the work of Abraham and Moses, and he was a sign of the coming Day of Judgment. But Muslims held that Jesus was an apostle only, not God, and that people (that is, Christians) who called Jesus divine committed blasphemy (showing contempt for God). The Christian doctrine of the Trinity—that there is one God in three persons (Father, Son, and Holy Spirit)—posed a powerful obstacle to Muslim-Christian understanding because of Islam's emphasis on the absolute oneness of God. Muslims esteemed the Judeo-Christian Scriptures as part of God's revelation, although they believed that the Qur'an superseded them.

Muslims call Jews and Christians *dhimmis*, or "protected people," because they were "people of the book," that is, the Hebrew Scriptures. Christians and Jews in the areas Muslims conquered were allowed to continue practicing their faith, although they did have to pay a special tax. This toleration was sometimes accompanied by suspicion, however. In Spain, Muslim teachers increasingly feared that close contact with Christians and Jews would lead to Muslim contamination and threaten the Islamic faith. Thus, beginning in the late tenth century, Muslim regulations began to officially prescribe what Christians, Jews, and Muslims could do. A Christian or

Jew, however much assimilated, remained an **infidel**. An infidel was an unbeliever, and the word carried a pejorative or disparaging connotation.

By about 950 Caliph Abd al-Rahman III (912–961) of the Umayyad Dynasty of Córdoba ruled most of the Iberian Peninsula from the Mediterranean in the south to the Ebro River in the north. Christian Spain consisted of the tiny kingdoms of Castile, León, Catalonia, Aragon, Navarre, and Portugal. Civil wars among al-Rahman's descendants weakened the caliphate, and the small northern Christian kingdoms began to expand southward, sometimes working together. When Christian forces conquered Muslim territory, Christian rulers regarded their Muslim and Jewish subjects as infidels and enacted restrictive measures similar to those imposed on Christians in Muslim lands. Christian bishops worried that even a knowledge of Islam would lead to ignorance of essential Christian doctrines, and interfaith contacts declined. Christians' perception of Islam as a menace would help inspire the Crusades of the eleventh through thirteenth centuries (see Chapter 9).

infidel A disparaging term used for a person who does not believe in a particular religion.

Cross-Cultural Influences in Science and Medicine

Despite growing suspicions on both sides, the Islamic world profoundly shaped Christian European culture in Spain and elsewhere. Toledo, for example, became an important center of learning through which Arab intellectual achievements entered and influenced western Europe. Arab knowledge of science and mathematics, derived from the Chinese, Greeks, and Hindus, was highly sophisticated. The Muslim mathematician al-Khwarizmi (al-KHWAHR-uhz-mee) (d. 830) wrote the important treatise *Algebra*, the first work in which the word *algebra* is used mathematically. Al-Khwarizmi adopted the Hindu system of numbers (1, 2, 3, 4), used it in his *Algebra*, and applied mathematics to problems of physics and astronomy. (Since our system of numbers is actually Indian in origin, the term *Arabic numerals*, coined about 1847, is a misnomer.) Scholars in Baghdad translated Euclid's *Elements*, the basic text for plane and solid geometry (see Chapter 4). Muslims also instructed Westerners in the use of the zero, which permitted the execution of complicated problems of multiplication and long division.

Middle Eastern Arabs translated and codified the scientific and philosophical learning of Greek and Persian antiquity. In the ninth and tenth centuries that knowledge was brought to Spain, where between 1150 and 1250 it was translated into Latin. Europeans' knowledge of Aristotle (see Chapter 3) changed the entire direction of European philosophy and theology.

Muslim medical knowledge far surpassed that of the West. By the ninth century Arab physicians had translated most of the treatises of the ancient Greek physician Hippocrates and produced a number of important works of their own. Arab science reached its peak in the physician, philologist, philosopher, poet, and scientist ibn-Sina of Bukhara (980–1037), known in the West as Avicenna (ah-vuh-SEH-nuh). His *Canon of Medicine* codified all Greco-Arab medical thought, described the contagious nature of tuberculosis and the spreading of diseases, and listed 760 pharmaceutical drugs.

Astrolabe Made by al-Zarqali
Abu Ishaq Ibrahim al-Zarqali (1029–1087) was an astronomer, inventor, and instrument maker who lived in Toledo, the most important center of learning in Muslim Spain. He wrote works on geography and astronomy that were later translated into Hebrew and Latin, and designed and built instruments, including sophisticated astrolabes, instruments used by astronomers, astrologers, navigators, and surveyors for locating and predicting the positions of the heavenly bodies and determining local time and latitude. (Pictures from History/Bridgeman Images)

Unfortunately, many of these treatises came to the West as translations from Greek to Arabic and then to Latin and inevitably lost a great deal in translation. Nevertheless, in the ninth and tenth centuries Arab knowledge and experience in anatomy and pharmaceutical prescriptions much enriched Western knowledge.

Frankish Rulers and Their Territories

FOCUS QUESTION
How did the Franks build and govern a European empire?

Over two centuries before the Muslim conquest of Spain, the Frankish king Clovis converted to Roman Christianity and established a large kingdom in what had been Roman Gaul (see Chapter 7). Though at that time the Frankish kingdom was simply one barbarian kingdom among many, it grew to become the most important state in Europe, expanding to become an empire. Rulers after Clovis used a variety of tactics to enhance their authority and create a stable system. Charles the Great (r. 768–814), generally known by the French version of his name, Charlemagne (SHAHR-luh-mayne), built on the military and diplomatic foundations of his ancestors and on the administrative machinery of the Merovingian kings. He expanded the Frankish kingdom into what is now Germany and Italy and, late in his long reign, was crowned emperor by the pope.

The Merovingians

Clovis established the Merovingian dynasty in about 481 (see Chapter 7), and under him the Frankish kingdom included much of what is now France and a large section of southwestern Germany. Following Frankish traditions in which property was divided among male heirs, at Clovis's death the kingdom was divided among his four sons. Historians have long described Merovingian Gaul in the sixth and seventh centuries as wracked by civil wars, chronic violence, and political instability as Clovis's descendants fought among themselves. So brutal and destructive were these wars and so violent the conditions of daily life that the term *Dark Ages* was at one time used to designate the entire Merovingian period, although more recently historians have noted that the Merovingians also created new political institutions, so the era was not uniformly bleak.

Merovingian rulers also developed diverse sources of income. These included revenues from the royal estates and the "gifts" of subject peoples, such as plunder and tribute paid by peoples east of the Rhine River. New lands might be conquered and confiscated, and served to replace lands donated as monastic or religious endowments. All free landowners paid a land tax, although some landowners gradually gained immunity from doing so. Fines imposed for criminal offenses and tolls and customs duties on roads, bridges, and waterways (and the goods transported over them) also yielded income. As with the Romans, the minting of coins was a royal monopoly, with drastic penalties for counterfeiting.

The Franks also based some aspects of their government on Roman principles. For example, the basis of the administrative system in the Frankish kingdom was the **civitas** (SIH-vih-tahs)—Latin for a city and surrounding territory—similar to the political organization of the Roman Empire. A **comites** (KOH-meh-tehs)—a senior official or royal companion, later called a count—presided over the civitas, as had governors in Rome. He collected royal revenue, heard lawsuits, enforced justice, and raised troops. Many comites were not conquerors from outside, but came from

civitas The city and surrounding territory that served as a basis of the administrative system in the Frankish kingdoms, based on Roman models.

comites A senior official or royal companion, later called a count, who presided over the civitas.

Saint Radegund and King Clotaire   This eleventh-century manuscript shows the Germanic princess Radegund (ca. 520–586) led before the Merovingian king Clotaire, who became her husband. They had no children, and after Clotaire had Radegund's brother killed, she left him and founded a convent, where she lived the rest of her life. Convents were islands of learning and safety in Merovingian society; from here Radegund corresponded with learned church officials and wrote Latin poems, a few of which have survived. (From the *Life of St. Radegund*/Bibliothèque Municipale, Poitiers, France/ Bridgeman Images)

families that had been administrators in Roman Gaul and were usually native to the regions they administered and knew their areas well. Frankish royal administration involved another official, the *dux* (dooks) or duke. He was a military leader, commanding troops in the territory of several civitas, and thus responsible for all defensive and offensive strategies. Clovis and his descendants also issued capitularies—Roman-style administrative and legislative orders—in an attempt to maintain order in Merovingian society. Some of these laws were designed to protect the clergy and church property from violence, others were meant to define ownership and inheritance, and still others set out to punish crimes such as drunkenness, robbery, arson, rape, and murder.

Within the royal household, Merovingian politics provided women with opportunities, and some queens not only influenced but occasionally also dominated events. Because the finances of the kingdom were merged with those of the royal family, queens often had control of the royal treasury just as more ordinary women controlled household expenditures. The status of a princess or queen also rested on her diplomatic importance, with her marriage sealing or her divorce breaking an alliance with a foreign kingdom or powerful noble family; on her personal relationship with her husband and her ability to give him sons and heirs; and on her role as the mother and guardian of princes who had not reached legal adulthood.

Queen Brunhilda (543?–613), for example, married first one Frankish king and at his death another. When her second husband died, Brunhilda overcame the objections of the nobles and became regent, ruling on behalf of her son until he came of age. Later she governed as regent for her grandsons and, when she was nearly seventy, for her great-grandson. Stories of her ruthlessness spread during her lifetime and were later much embellished by Frankish historians uncomfortable with such a powerful woman. The evil Brunhilda, they alleged, killed ten Frankish kings in pursuit of her political goals, and was finally executed by being torn apart by horses while cheering crowds looked on. How much of this actually happened is impossible to say, but Brunhilda's legend became a model for the wicked queen in European folklore.

Merovingian rulers and their successors led peripatetic lives, traveling constantly to check up on local administrators and peoples. Merovingian kings also relied on the comites and bishops to gather and send local information to them. The court or household of Merovingian kings included scribes who kept records, legal officials who advised the king on matters of law, and treasury agents responsible for aspects of royal finance. These officials could all read and write Latin. Over them all presided the mayor of the palace, the most important secular figure after the king, who governed the palace and the kingdom in the king's absence. Mayors were usually from one of the great aristocratic families, which increasingly through intermarriage blended Frankish and Roman elites. These families possessed landed wealth — villas over which they exercised lordship, dispensing local customary, not royal, law — and they often had rich and lavish lifestyles.

The Rise of the Carolingians

From this aristocracy one family gradually emerged to replace the Merovingian dynasty. The rise of the Carolingians — whose name comes from the Latin *Carolus*, or Charles, the name of several important members of the family — rests on several factors. First, the Carolingian Pippin I (d. 640) acquired the powerful position of mayor of the palace and passed the title on to his heirs. As mayors of the palace and heads of the Frankish bureaucracy, Pippin I and his descendants were entrusted with extraordinary amounts of power and privilege by the Merovingian kings. Although the mayor of the palace was technically employed by the ruling family, the Carolingians would use their influential position to win support for themselves and eventually subvert Merovingian authority. Second, a series of advantageous marriage alliances brought the family estates and influence in different parts of the Frankish world, and provided the Carolingians with landed wealth and treasure with which to reward their allies and followers. Third, military victories over supporters of the Merovingians gave the Carolingians a reputation for strength and ensured their dominance. Pippin I's great-grandson, Charles Martel (r. 714–741), waged war successfully against the Saxons, Frisians, Alamanni, and Bavarians, which further enhanced the family's prestige. In 732 Charles Martel defeated a Muslim force near Poitiers (pwah-tee-AY) in central France. Muslims and Christians have interpreted the battle differently. To the Muslims it was a minor skirmish won by the Franks because of Muslim difficulties in maintaining supply lines over long distances and the distraction of ethnic conflicts and unrest in Islamic Spain. For Christians the Frankish victory was one of the great battles of history, halting Muslim expansion in Europe. Charles Martel and later Carolingians used it to enhance their reputation, portraying themselves as defenders of Christendom against the Muslims.

The Battle of Poitiers helped the Carolingians acquire the support of the church, perhaps their most important asset. Charles Martel and his son Pippin III (r. 751–768) further strengthened their ties to the church by supporting the work of Christian missionaries. The most important of these missionaries was the Englishman Boniface (BAH-nuh-fays) (680–754), who had close ties to the Roman pope. Boniface ordered the oak of Thor, a tree sacred to many pagans, cut down and used the wood to build a church. When the god Thor did not respond by killing him with his lightning bolts, Boniface won many converts. As missionaries preached, baptized, and established churches, they included the Christian duty to obey secular authorities as part of their message, thus extending to Frankish rulers the church's support of secular power that had begun with Constantine (see Chapter 7).

As mayor of the palace, Charles Martel had exercised the power of king of the Franks. His son Pippin III aspired to the title as well as the powers it entailed. Pippin's diplomats were able to convince an embattled Pope Zacharias to rule in his favor against the Merovingians in exchange for military support against the Lombards, who were threatening the papacy. Zacharias invoked his apostolic authority as pope, deposed the Merovingian ruler Chilperic in 752, and declared that Pippin should be king "in order to prevent provoking civil war [between the Merovingians and Carolingians] in Francia."[2] An assembly of Frankish magnates elected Pippin king, and Boniface anointed him. When in 754 Lombard expansion again threatened the papacy, Pope Stephen II journeyed to the Frankish kingdom seeking help. On this occasion, he personally anointed Pippin with the sacred oils and gave him the title "Patrician of the Romans," thus linking him symbolically with the ruling patrician class of ancient Rome. Pippin promised restitution of the papal lands and later made a gift of estates in central Italy.

Because of his anointment, Pippin's kingship took on a special spiritual and moral character. Prior to Pippin only priests and bishops had received anointment. Pippin became the first to be anointed with the sacred oils and acknowledged as *rex et sacerdos* (rehks eht SAHK-ehr-dohse), meaning king and priest. Anointment, not royal blood, set the Christian king apart. By having himself anointed, Pippin cleverly eliminated possible threats to the Frankish throne by other claimants, and the pope promised him support in the future. An important alliance had been struck between the papacy and the Frankish monarchs. When Pippin died, his son Charles, generally known as Charlemagne, succeeded him.

The Warrior-Ruler Charlemagne

Charlemagne's adviser and friend Alcuin (ca. 735–804; see page 236) wrote that "a king should be strong against his enemies, humble to Christians, feared by pagans, loved by the poor and judicious in counsel and maintaining justice."[3] Charlemagne worked to realize that ideal in all its aspects. Through brutal military expeditions that brought wealth—lands, booty, slaves, and tribute—and by peaceful travel, personal appearances, and the sheer force of his personality, Charlemagne sought to awe newly conquered peoples and rebellious domestic enemies.

If an ideal king was "strong against his enemies" and "feared by pagans," Charlemagne more than met the standard. In continuing the expansionist policies of his ancestors, his reign was characterized by constant warfare; according to the chroniclers of the time, only seven years between 714 and 814 were peaceful. Charlemagne fought more than fifty campaigns and became the greatest warrior of the early Middle Ages. He subdued all of the north of modern France, but his greatest successes were in today's Germany, where he fought battles he justified as spreading Christianity to pagan peoples. In the course of a bloody thirty-year war against the Saxons, he added most of the northwestern German peoples to the Frankish kingdom. In his biography of the ruler, Charlemagne's royal secretary Einhard reported that Charlemagne ordered more than four thousand Saxons killed on one day and deported thousands more. Those who surrendered were forced to become Christian, often in mass baptisms. He established bishoprics in areas he had conquered, so church officials and church institutions became important means of imposing Frankish rule.

MAP 8.2 Charlemagne's Conquests, ca. 768–814
Though Charlemagne's hold on much of his territory was relatively weak, the size of his empire was not equaled again until the nineteenth-century conquests of Napoleon.

Charlemagne also achieved spectacular results in the south, incorporating Lombardy into the Frankish kingdom. He ended Bavarian independence and defeated the nomadic Avars, opening eastern Germany for later settlement by Franks. He successfully fought the Byzantine Empire for Venetia, Istria, and Dalmatia and temporarily annexed those areas to his kingdom. Charlemagne's only defeat came at the hands of the Basques of northwestern Spain. By around 805 the Frankish kingdom included all of north-western Europe except Scandinavia and Britain (Map 8.2). Not since the Roman emperors of the third century C.E. had any ruler controlled so much of the Western world. Other than brief periods under Napoleon and Hitler, Europe would never again see as large a unified state as it had under Charlemagne, which is one reason he has become an important symbol of European unity in the twenty-first century.

Carolingian Government and Society

Charlemagne's empire was not a state as people today understand that term; it was a collection of peoples and clans. For administrative purposes, Charlemagne divided his entire kingdom into counties based closely on the old Merovingian *civitas*. Each of the approximately six hundred counties was governed by a count (or in his absence by a viscount), who published royal orders, held courts and resolved legal cases, collected taxes and tolls, raised troops for the army, and supervised maintenance of roads and bridges. (See "Evaluating the Evidence 8.2: The Capitulary de Villis," at right.) Counts were originally sent out from the royal court; later a person native to the region was appointed. As a link between local authorities and the central government, Charlemagne appointed officials called *missi dominici* (mih-see doh-MEH-nee-chee), "agents of the lord king," who checked up on the counts and held courts to handle judicial and financial issues.

Considering the size of Charlemagne's empire, the counts and royal agents were few and far between, and the authority of the central government was weak. The abbots and bishops who served as Charlemagne's advisers envisioned a unified Christian society presided over by a king who was responsible for maintaining peace, law, and order and administering justice. This remained a vision, however, not reality. Instead, society was held together by alliances among powerful families, along with dependent relationships cemented by oaths promising faith and loyalty.

Family alliances were often cemented by sexual relations, including those of Charlemagne himself. Charlemagne had a total of four legal wives, most from other Frankish tribes, and six concubines. Charlemagne's personal desires certainly shaped his complicated relationships—even after the age of sixty-five he continued to sire children—but

The Capitulary de Villis

Charlemagne and other Frankish rulers issued sets of instructions and decisions, called capitularies, to their officials on legal, military, political, and economic matters. Like all instructions or sets of rules, capitularies describe an ideal, not the way things really were, but we can still use them as sources for many aspects of life. The Capitulary de Villis, issued in about 800, describes the wide variety of activities envisioned for royal manors, which were run by individuals called stewards.

We desire that each steward shall make an annual statement of all our income, giving an account of our lands cultivated by the oxen which our own plowmen drive and of our lands which the tenants of farms ought to plow; of the pigs, of the rents, of the obligations and fines; of the game taken in our forests without our permission; of the various compositions [things that have been made]; of the mills, of the forest, of the fields, of the bridges and ships; of the free men and the districts under obligations to our treasury; of markets, vineyards, and those who owe wine to us; of the hay, firewood, torches, planks, and other kinds of lumber; of the waste lands; of the vegetables, millet, panic [a type of millet]; of the wool, flax, and hemp; of the fruits of the trees; of the nut trees, larger and smaller; of the grafted trees of all kinds; of the gardens; of the turnips; of the fish ponds; of the hides, skins, and horns; of the honey and wax; of the fat, tallow [fat used for candles], and soap; of the mulberry wine, cooked wine, mead, vinegar, beer, and wine, new and old; of the new grain and the old; of the hens and eggs; of the geese; of the number of fishermen, workers in metal, sword makers, and shoemakers; of the bins and boxes; of the turners and saddlers; of the forges and mines, — that is, of iron, lead, or other substances; of the colts and fillies. They shall make all these known to us, set forth separately and in order, at Christmas, so that we may know what and how much of each thing we have.

The greatest care must be taken that whatever is prepared or made with the hands, — that is, bacon, smoked meat, sausage, partially salted meat, wine, vinegar, mulberry wine, cooked wine, garum [fermented fish sauce], mustard, cheese, butter, malt, beer, mead, honey, wax, flour, — all should be prepared and made with the greatest cleanliness.

Each steward on each of our domains shall always have, for the sake of ornament, peacocks, pheasants, ducks, pigeons, partridges, and turtle-doves. . . .

For our women's work they are to give at the proper time, as has been ordered, the materials [for cloth-making], — that is, the linen, wool, woad [for making blue dye], vermilion [for making red dye], madder [for making yellow dye], wool combs, teasels, soap, grease, vessels, and the other objects which are necessary. . . .

Each steward shall have in his district good workmen, namely, blacksmiths, a goldsmith, a silversmith, shoemakers, turners, carpenters, sword makers, fishermen, fowlers, soap makers, men who know how to make beer, cider, perry [pear cider], or other kind of liquor good to drink, bakers to make pastry for our table, net makers who know how to make nets for hunting, fishing, and fowling, and other sorts of workmen too numerous to be designated.

EVALUATE THE EVIDENCE

1. What tasks were men expected to do on Charlemagne's estates? What tasks were seen as women's work?

2. How does this listing of the work on medieval estates support the idea that the Carolingian economy was more localized than the economy of the Roman Empire had been (see Chapter 6)?

Source: James Harvey Robinson, ed., *Readings in European History*, vol. 1 (Boston: Ginn and Company, 1904), pp. 137–139.

---

the security and continuation of his dynasty and the need for diplomatic alliances were also important motives. Despite all the women bearing his children, only three of Charlemagne's sons born in wedlock reached adulthood, and only one outlived him. Four surviving legitimate grandsons did ensure perpetuation of the family, however, and the marriages themselves linked Charlemagne with other powerful families even in the absence of sons. Several of his children born out of wedlock became abbots or abbesses of major monasteries, connecting his family with the church as well as the secular hierarchy.

In terms of social changes, the Carolingian period witnessed moderate population growth. The highest aristocrats and church officials lived well, with fine clothing and at least a few rooms heated by firewood. Male nobles hunted and managed their estates, while female nobles generally oversaw the education of their children and sometimes inherited and controlled land on their own. Craftsmen and craftswomen on manorial estates manufactured textiles, weapons, glass, and pottery, primarily for local consumption. Sometimes abbeys and manors served as markets; goods were shipped away to towns and fairs for sale; and a good deal of interregional commerce existed. In the towns, artisans and merchants produced and traded luxury goods for noble and clerical patrons. When compared with earlier Roman cities or with Muslim cities of the time, such as Córdoba and Baghdad, however, Carolingian cities were small; few north of the Alps had more than seven thousand people. Even in Charlemagne's main political center at Aachen, most buildings were made of wood and earth, streets were narrow and muddy, and beggars were a common sight.

The modest economic expansion benefited townspeople and nobles, but it did not significantly alter the lives of most people, who continued to live in a vast rural world dotted with isolated estates and small villages. Here life was precarious. Crops could easily be wiped out by hail, cold, or rain, and transporting food from other areas was impossible. People's diets centered on grain, which was baked into bread, brewed into beer, and especially cooked into gruel. To this were added seasonal vegetables such as peas, cabbage, and onions, and tiny amounts of animal protein, mostly cheese. Clothing and household goods were just as simple, and houses were drafty, smoky, and often shared with animals. Lice, fleas, and other vermin spread disease, and the poor diet led to frequent stomach disorders. Work varied by the season, but at all times of the year it was physically demanding and yielded relatively little. What little there was had to be shared with landowners, who demanded their taxes and rents in the form of crops, animals, or labor.

The Imperial Coronation of Charlemagne

In autumn of the year 800, Charlemagne paid a momentous visit to Rome. Einhard gives this account of what happened:

> His last journey there [to Rome] was due to another factor, namely that the Romans, having inflicted many injuries on Pope Leo — plucking out his eyes and tearing out his tongue, he had been compelled to beg the assistance of the king. Accordingly, coming to Rome in order that he might set in order those things which had exceedingly disturbed the condition of the Church, he remained there the whole winter. It was at the time that he accepted the name of Emperor and Augustus. At first he was so much opposed to this that he insisted that although that day was a great [Christian] feast, he would not have entered the Church if he had known beforehand the pope's intention. But he bore very patiently the jealousy of the Roman Emperors [that is, the Byzantine rulers] who were indignant when he received these titles. He overcame their arrogant haughtiness with magnanimity, . . . by sending frequent ambassadors to them and in his letters addressing them as brothers.[4]

For centuries scholars have debated the reasons for the imperial coronation of Charlemagne. Did Charlemagne plan the ceremony in Saint Peter's on Christmas

Day, or did he merely accept the title of emperor? What did he have to gain from it? If, as Einhard implies, the coronation displeased Charlemagne, was that because it put the pope in the superior position of conferring power on the emperor? What were Pope Leo's motives in arranging the coronation?

Though definitive answers will probably never be found, several things seem certain. First, after the coronation Charlemagne considered himself an emperor ruling a Christian people. Through his motto, *Renovatio romani imperi* (Revival of the Roman Empire), Charlemagne was consciously perpetuating old Roman imperial notions while at the same time identifying with the new Rome of the Christian Church. In this sense, Charlemagne might be considered a precursor of the eventual Holy Roman emperor, although that term didn't come into use for two more centuries. Second, Leo's ideas about gender and rule undoubtedly influenced his decision to crown Charlemagne. In 800 the ruler of the Byzantine Empire was the empress Irene, the first woman to rule Byzantium in her own name, but Leo did not regard her authority as legitimate because she was female. He thus claimed to be placing Charlemagne on a vacant throne. Third, both parties gained: the Carolingian family received official recognition from the leading spiritual power in Europe, and the papacy gained a military protector.

Not surprisingly, the Byzantines regarded the papal acts as rebellious and Charlemagne as a usurper. The imperial coronation thus marks a decisive break between Rome and Constantinople. From Baghdad, however, Harun al-Rashid (r. 786–809), caliph of the Abbasid (uh-BAH-suhd) Empire, congratulated the Frankish ruler with the gift of an elephant. It was named Abu'l Abbas after the founder of the Abbasid Dynasty and may have served as a symbol of the diplomatic link Harun al-Rashid hoped to forge with the Franks against Byzantium. Having plodded its way to Charlemagne's court at Aachen, the elephant survived for nine years, and its death was considered important enough to be mentioned in the Frankish *Royal Annals*, the official chronological record of events, for the year 810. Like everyone else at Aachen, the elephant lived in a city that was far less sophisticated, healthy, and beautiful than the Baghdad of Harun al-Rashid.

The coronation of Charlemagne, whether planned by the Carolingian court or by the papacy, was to have a profound effect on the course of German history and on the later history of Europe. In the centuries that followed, German rulers were eager to gain the imperial title and to associate themselves with the legends of Charlemagne and ancient Rome. Ecclesiastical authorities, on the other hand, continually cited the event as proof that the dignity of the imperial crown could be granted only by the pope.

Early Medieval Culture

As he built an empire through conquest and strategic alliances, Charlemagne also set in motion a cultural revival that had long-lasting consequences. The stimulus he gave to scholarship and learning may, in fact, be his most enduring legacy, although at the time most people continued to live in a world where knowledge was transmitted orally.

FOCUS QUESTION
What were the significant intellectual and cultural changes in Charlemagne's era?

The Carolingian Renaissance

In Roman Gaul through the fifth century, the culture of members of the elite rested on an education that stressed grammar, Greco-Roman works of literature and history, and the legal and medical treatises of the Roman world. Beginning in the seventh and eighth centuries, a new cultural tradition common to Gaul, Italy, the British Isles, and to some extent Spain emerged. This culture was based primarily on Christian sources. Scholars have called the new Christian and ecclesiastical culture of the period from about 760 to 840, and the educational foundation on which it was based, the "Carolingian Renaissance" because Charlemagne was its major patron.

Charlemagne directed that every monastery in his kingdom should cultivate learning and educate the monks and secular clergy so that they would have a better understanding of the Christian writings. He also urged the establishment of cathedral and monastic schools where boys might learn to read and to pray properly. Thus the main purpose of this rebirth of learning was to promote an understanding of the Scriptures and of Christian writers and to instruct people to pray and praise God in the correct manner.

Women shared with men the work of evangelization and the new Christian learning. Rulers, noblemen, and noblewomen founded monasteries for nuns, each governed by an abbess. The abbess oversaw all aspects of life in the monastery. She handled the business affairs, supervised the copying of manuscripts, and directed the daily round of prayer and worship. Women's monasteries housed women who were unmarried, and also often widows, children being taught to read and recite prayers and chants, elderly people seeking a safe place to live, and travelers needing hospitality. Some female houses were, in fact, double monasteries in which the abbess governed two adjoining establishments, one for women and one for men. Monks provided protection from attack and did the heavy work on the land in double monasteries, but nuns handled everything else.

In monasteries and cathedral schools, monks, nuns, and scribes copied books and manuscripts and built up libraries. They developed the beautifully clear handwriting known as "Carolingian minuscule," with both uppercase and lowercase letters, from which modern Roman type is derived. In this era before printed books, works could survive only if they were copied. Almost all of the works of Roman authors that we are now able to read, both Christian and secular, were preserved by the efforts of Carolingian scribes. Some scholars went beyond copying to develop their own ideas, and by the middle years of the ninth century there was a great outpouring of more sophisticated original works. Ecclesiastical writers imbued with the legal ideas of ancient Rome and the theocratic ideals of Saint Augustine instructed the semibarbaric rulers of the West.

The most important scholar at Charlemagne's court was Alcuin (al-KYOO-ihn), who came from Northumbria, one of the kingdoms in England. He was the leader of a palace school at Aachen, where Charlemagne assembled learned men from all over Europe. From 781 until his death, Alcuin was the

Carolingian Minuscule   In the Carolingian period books played a large role in the spread of Christianity and in the promotion of learning. The development of the clearer script known as Carolingian minuscule shown here made books more legible and copying more efficient because more words could fit on the page. (The initial "C" with the Ascension of Christ, book illumination on parchment from the Drogo Sacramentary, Lorraine [Metz], 850–855 A.D./akg-images)

emperor's chief adviser on religious and educational matters. Alcuin's letters to Charlemagne set forth political theories on the authority, power, and responsibilities of a Christian ruler.

Through monastic and cathedral schools, basic literacy in Latin was established among some of the clergy and even among some of the nobility, a change from Merovingian times. By the tenth century the patterns of thought and the lifestyles of educated western Europeans were those of Rome and Latin Christianity. Most people, however, continued to live in an oral world. They spoke local languages, which did not have a written form. Christian services continued to be conducted in Latin, but not all village priests were able to attend a school, and many simply learned the service by rote. Some Latin words and phrases gradually penetrated the various vernacular languages, but the Carolingian Renaissance did not trickle down to ordinary people.

This division between a learned culture of Latin that built on the knowledge of the ancient world and a vernacular culture of local traditions can also be seen in medicine. Christian teaching supported concern for the poor, sick, and downtrodden. Churchmen taught that all knowledge came from God, who had supplied it for people to use for their own benefit. The foundation of a medical school at Salerno in southern Italy in the ninth century gave a tremendous impetus to medical study. The school's location attracted Arab, Greek, and Jewish physicians from all over the Mediterranean region. Students flocked there even from northern Europe.

Despite the advances at Salerno, however, physicians were few in the early Middle Ages, and only the rich could afford them. Local folk medicine practiced by nonprofessionals provided help for commoners, with treatments made from herbs, bark, and other natural ingredients. Infants and children were especially susceptible to a range of illnesses, and about half of the children born died before age five. Although a few people lived into their seventies, most did not, and a forty-year-old was considered old.

Saint Matthew   This manuscript illumination shows Saint Matthew hard at work writing the Gospel that bears his name. He is holding a horn with ink in one hand and a quill in the other. Produced around 800 for Ebbo, the archbishop of the Frankish city of Reims, the illustrations in these Gospels seem strikingly modern in their portrayal of human emotion. (Bibliothèque Municipale, Epernay, France/Erich Lessing/Art Resource, NY)

Northumbrian Learning and Writing

Charlemagne's court at Aachen was not the only center of learning in early medieval Christian Europe. Another was the Anglo-Saxon kingdom of Northumbria, situated at the northernmost tip of the old Roman world. Northumbrian creativity owed a great deal to the intellectual curiosity and collecting zeal of Saint Benet Biscop (ca. 628–689), who brought manuscripts and other treasures back from Italy. These formed the library on which much later study rested.

Northumbrian monasteries produced scores of books: missals (used for the celebration of the Mass); psalters (SAL-tuhrs), which contained the 150 psalms and other prayers used by the monks in their devotions; commentaries on the Scriptures; illuminated manuscripts; law codes; and collections of letters and sermons. (See "Individuals in Society: The Venerable Bede," page 238.) The finest product of Northumbrian art is probably the Gospel book produced at Lindisfarne monastery around 700. The book was produced by a single scribe working steadily over a period of several years, with the expenses involved in the production of such a book—for vellum, coloring, and gold leaf—probably supplied by the monastery's aristocratic patrons.

The finest representative of Northumbrian, and indeed all Anglo-Saxon, scholarship is Bede (ca. 673–735). He was born into a noble family, and when he was seven his parents sent him to Benet Biscop's monastery at Wearmouth as a sign of their religious devotion. Later he was sent to the new monastery at Jarrow five miles away. Surrounded by the hundreds of pagan and Christian books Benet Biscop had brought from Italy, Bede spent the rest of his life there, studying and writing. He wrote textbooks on grammar and writing designed to help students master the intricacies of Latin, commentaries on the Old and New Testaments, historical works relating the lives of abbots and the development of the church, and scientific works on time. His biblical commentaries survive in hundreds of manuscripts, indicating that they were widely studied throughout the Middle Ages. His doctrinal works led him to be honored after his death with the title "Venerable," and centuries after his death to be named a "doctor of the church" by the pope.

Bede's religious writings were actually not that innovative, but his historical writings were, particularly his best-known work, the *Ecclesiastical History of the English People*, written about 720. As the title suggests, Bede's main topic is the growth of Christianity in England. The book begins with a short discussion of Christianity in Roman Britain, then skips to Augustine of Canterbury's mission to the Anglo-Saxons (see Chapter 7). Most of the book tells the story of Christianity's spread from one small kingdom in England to another, with missionaries and the kings who converted as its heroes, and the narrative ends with Bede's own day. Bede searched far and wide for his information, discussed the validity of his evidence, compared various sources, and exercised critical judgment. He includes accounts of miracles, but, like the stories of valiant missionaries, these are primarily related to provide moral lessons, which all medieval writers thought was the chief purpose of history.

One of the lessons that Bede sought to impart with his history is that Christianity should be unified, and one feature of the *Ecclesiastical History of the English People* inadvertently provided a powerful model for this. In his history, Bede adopted a way of reckoning time proposed by an earlier monk that would eventually provide a uniform chronology for all Christians. He dated events from the incarnation of Christ, rather than from the foundation of the city of Rome, as the Romans had done, or from the regnal years of kings, as the Germans did. His history was

A manuscript portrait of Bede, set within the first letter of a copy of his *Life of St. Cuthbert*. This is the letter *d*, with the monster's head forming the upward line and Bede's foot the short downward line. There are no contemporary descriptions of Bede, so the later manuscript illuminator was free to imagine what he looked like. (The Bodleian Library, University of Oxford, Ms Digby 20, folio 194r)

recopied by monks in many parts of Europe, who used this dating method, *anno Domini*, "in the year of the Lord" (later abbreviated A.D.), for their own histories as well. (Though Bede does talk about "before the time of the incarnation of our Lord," the reverse dating system of B.C., "before Christ," does not seem to have been widely used before 1700.) Disputes about whether the year began with the incarnation (that is, the conception) of Christ or his birth, and whether these occurred in 1 B.C. or A.D. 1 (the Christian calendar does not have a year zero), continued after Bede, but his method prevailed.

QUESTIONS FOR ANALYSIS

1. How do the career and accomplishments of Bede fit with the notion of an early medieval "renaissance" of learning?
2. Does Bede's notion that history has a moral purpose still shape the writing of history? Do you agree with him?
3. The Christian calendar dates from a midpoint rather than from a starting point, the way many of the world's calendars do. What advantages does this create in reckoning time? What would you see as the primary reason that the Christian calendar has now been widely adopted worldwide?

The Death of Beowulf

In the long Anglo-Saxon epic poem that bears his name, the hero Beowulf fights and kills the monster Grendel and then Grendel's mother. He then becomes the king of the Geats, one of the Germanic groups that lived in western Sweden, and takes arms late in life against a dragon that was threatening his people.

He ruled it well for fifty winters—that was an aged king, a veteran guardian of his people,—until in the dark nights a certain one began to have power,—a dragon, who on an upland heath kept watch over a hoard. . . .

Then the fiend began to vomit forth flames, to burn the noble dwellings; the gleam of fire blazed forth, a terror to the sons of men; the hateful creature flying in the air would leave there no thing with life. . . .

Beowulf discoursed,—spoke a last time with words of boasting:—"I ventured on many battles in my younger days; once more will I, the aged guardian of the people, seek combat and get renown." . . .

Then rose the doughty champion by his shield; bold under his helmet, he went clad in his war-corslet to beneath the rock cliffs, and trusted in his own strength—not such is the coward's way. Then he who, excellent in virtues, had lived through many wars,—the tumult of battles, when armies dash together,—saw by the rampart a rocky arch whence burst a stream out from the mound; hot was the welling of the flood with deadly fire. He could not any while endure unscorched the hollow near the hoard, by reason of the dragon's flame. . . .

Never a whit [Not in the least] did his comrades, those sons of nobles, stand round him in a body, doing deeds of warlike prowess; but they shrank back into the wood and took care of their lives. . . . [One of Beowulf's warriors assists him, and together they kill the dragon, though Beowulf is mortally wounded in the fight.]

Then the chieftain wise in thought went on until he sat on a seat by the rampart. . . . Beowulf discoursed: despite his hurt, his grievous deadly wound, he spoke,—he knew full well that he had used up his time of earthly joy. . . . "I have ruled over this people fifty winters; there was not one of the kings of the neighbouring tribes who dared encounter me with weapons, or could weigh me down with fear. In my own home I awaited what the times destined for me, kept my own well, did not pick treacherous quarrels, nor have I sworn unjustly any oaths. In all this may I, sick with deadly wounds, have solace; because the Ruler of men may never charge me with the murder of kinsfolk, when my life parts from my body. . . .

"I utter in words my thanks to the Ruler of all, the King of Glory, the everlasting Lord. . . . Bid the war-veterans raise a splendid barrow [mound of earth] after the funeral fire, on a projection by the sea, which shall tower high on Hronesness as a memorial for my people, so that seafarers who urge their tall ships from afar over the spray of ocean shall thereafter call it Beowulf's barrow."

EVALUATE THE EVIDENCE

1. Based on Beowulf's actions and words, what were the qualities of an ideal leader in the early Middle Ages?
2. How do these sections of *Beowulf* provide evidence for the assimilation of Germanic and Christian values discussed in Chapter 7? For the distinctive aspects of early medieval culture discussed in this chapter?

Source: *Beowulf and the Finnesburg Fragment*, trans. John R. Clark Hall, rev. C. L. Wrenn (London: George Allen and Unwin, 1940), pp. 132, 137, 147, 148, 150, 156, 157, 160.

As in Charlemagne's empire, women were important participants in Northumbrian Christian culture. Perhaps the most important abbess of the early medieval period anywhere in Europe was Saint Hilda (d. 680). A noblewoman of considerable learning and administrative ability, she ruled the double monastery of Whitby on the Northumbrian coast, advised kings and princes, and encouraged scholars and poets. Hilda played a key role in the adoption of Roman practices by Anglo-Saxon churches (see Chapter 7).

At about the time the monks at Lindisfarne were producing their Gospel book, another author was probably at work on a nonreligious epic poem, *Beowulf* (BAY-uh-woolf). The poem tells the story of the hero Beowulf's progress from valiant warrior to wise ruler. (See "Evaluating the Evidence 8.3: The Death of Beowulf," above.)

In contrast to most writings of this era, which were in Latin, *Beowulf* was written in the vernacular Anglo-Saxon. The identity of its author (or authors) is unknown, and it survives only in a single copy. The poem includes descriptions of real historical events that took place in fifth- and sixth-century Denmark and Sweden, which have been confirmed by archaeological excavations. These are mixed in with legends, oral traditions, and material from the Bible; though it tells a story set in pagan Denmark and Sweden, it was written in Christian England sometime in the eighth to tenth centuries. *Beowulf* provides evidence of the close relationship between England and the northern European continent in the early Middle Ages, for the North Sea was no barrier to regular contact and cultural exchange. The movements of people and ideas that allowed a work like *Beowulf* to be written only increased in the ninth century, when the North Sea became even more of a highway.

Invasions and Migrations

FOCUS QUESTION

What were the consequences of the ninth-century invasions and migrations?

Charlemagne left his vast empire to his sole surviving son, Louis the Pious (r. 814–840), who attempted to keep the empire intact. This proved to be impossible. Members of the nobility engaged in plots and open warfare against the emperor, often allying themselves with one of Louis's three sons, who were in conflict with their father and with one another. In 843, shortly after Louis's death, his sons agreed to the **Treaty of Verdun** (vehr-DUHN), which divided the empire into three parts: Charles the Bald received the western part; Lothair the middle part and the title of emperor; and Louis the eastern part, from which he acquired the title "the German." Though no one knew it at the time, this treaty set the pattern for political boundaries in Europe that has been maintained until today.

After the Treaty of Verdun, continental Europe was fractured politically. All three kingdoms controlled by the sons of Louis the Pious were torn by domestic dissension and disorder. The frontier and coastal defenses erected by Charlemagne and maintained by Louis the Pious were neglected. No European political power was strong enough to put up effective resistance to external attacks. Beginning around 850 three main groups invaded western Europe: Vikings from Scandinavia, representing the final wave of Germanic migrants; Muslims from the Mediterranean; and Magyars from central Europe forced westward by other peoples (Map 8.3).

The Treaty of Verdun, 843

Treaty of Verdun
Treaty signed in 843 by Charlemagne's grandsons dividing the Carolingian Empire into three parts and setting the pattern for political boundaries in Europe still in use today.

Vikings in Western Europe

From the moors of Scotland to the mountains of Sicily, there arose in the ninth century the prayer, "Save us, O God, from the fury of the Northmen." The feared Northmen were Germanic peoples from the area of modern-day Norway, Sweden, and Denmark who originally lived by farming and fishing. They began to make overseas expeditions, which they themselves called *vikings*, a word that probably derives from a unit of maritime distance. *Viking* came to be used both for the activity ("to go a-viking") and for the people who went on such expeditions. Propelled either by oars or by sails, deckless, and about sixty-five feet long, a Viking ship could carry between forty and sixty men — enough to harass an isolated monastery or village. These ships, navigated by experienced and fearless sailors, moved through complicated rivers, estuaries, and waterways in Europe. Their targets were

MAP 8.3 Invasions and Migrations of the Ninth and Tenth Centuries   This map shows the Viking, Magyar, and Arab invasions and migrations in the ninth and tenth centuries. Compare it with Map 7.3 (page 201) on the barbarian migrations of late antiquity.

initially often isolated monasteries, as these had gold, silver, and other goods that could be easily plundered, but later the Vikings turned to more substantial targets. The Carolingian Empire, with no navy, was helpless. The Vikings moved swiftly, attacked, and escaped to return again.

Scholars disagree about the reasons for Viking attacks and migrations. A very unstable Danish kingship and disputes over the succession led to civil war and disorder, which may have driven warriors abroad in search of booty and supporters. The population of Scandinavia may have grown too large for the available land to support, and cities on the coasts of northern Europe offered targets for plunder. Goods plundered could then be sold, and looting raids turned into trading ventures. Some scholars assert that the Vikings were looking for trade and new commercial contacts from the beginning.

Whatever the motivations, Vikings burned, looted, and did extensive property damage, although there is little evidence that they caused long-term physical destruction—perhaps because, arriving in small bands, they lacked the manpower to do so. They seized nobles and high churchmen and held them for ransom; they also demanded tribute from kings. In 844–845 Charles the Bald had to raise seven thousand pounds of silver, and across the English Channel Anglo-Saxon rulers collected a land tax, the *Danegeld*, to buy off the Vikings. In the Seine and Loire Valleys the frequent presence of Viking war bands seems to have had economic consequences, stimulating the production of food and wine and possibly the manufacture (for sale) of weapons and the breeding of horses.

The slave trade represented an important part of Viking plunder and commerce. Slaves, known as *thralls*, were common in Scandinavian society, and Vikings took people from the British Isles and territories along the Baltic Sea as part of their booty. They sold them as slaves in the markets of Magdeburg and Regensburg, at the fairs of Lyons, and in seaports of the Muslim world. Dublin became a center of the Viking slave trade, with hundreds and sometimes thousands of young men and women bought and sold there in any one year.

In the early tenth century Danish Vikings besieged Paris with fleets of more than a hundred highly maneuverable ships, and the Frankish king Charles the Simple bought them off in 911 by giving them a large part of northern France. There the Vikings established the province of "Northmanland," or Normandy as it was later known, intermarrying with the local population and creating a distinctive Norman culture. From there they sailed around Spain and into the Mediterranean, eventually seizing Sicily from the Muslim Arabs in 1060–1090, while other Normans crossed the English Channel, defeating Anglo-Saxon forces in 1066. Between 850 and 1000 Viking control of northern Europe reached its zenith. Norwegian Vikings moved farther west than any Europeans had before, establishing permanent settlements on Iceland and short-lived settlements in Greenland and Newfoundland in what is now Canada.

The Vikings made positive contributions to the areas they settled. They carried their unrivaled knowledge of shipbuilding and seamanship everywhere. The northeastern and central parts of England where the Vikings settled became known as the *Danelaw* because Danish, not English, laws and customs prevailed there. Scholars believe that some legal institutions, such as the ancestor of the modern grand jury,

Oseberg Ship   This well-preserved and elaborately decorated Viking ship, discovered in a large burial mound in southern Norway, could be powered by sail or oars. Boatbuilders recently constructed a full-scale replica using traditional building methods and materials, and sailed it on the open ocean in 2014, reaching a speed of ten knots. The burial mound contained the skeletons of two older women, one wearing a dress made of fine wool and silk, along with a cart, several sleighs, horses, dogs, and many artifacts, suggesting that this was the grave of a powerful and prominent woman, though her identity is unknown. (Viking Ship Museum, Bygdoy, Norway/Werner Forman Archive/Bridgeman Images)

originated in the Danelaw. Exports from Ireland included iron tools and weapons manufactured there by Viking metal-smiths.

Slavs and Vikings in Eastern Europe

Vikings also brought change in eastern Europe, which was largely populated by Slavs. In antiquity the Slavs lived in central Europe, farming with iron technology, building fortified towns, and worshipping a variety of deities. With the start of the mass migrations of the late Roman Empire, the Slavs moved in different directions and split into what historians later identified as three groups: West, South, and East Slavs.

The group labeled the West Slavs included the Poles, Czechs, Slovaks, and Wends. The South Slavs, comprising peoples who became the Serbs, Croats, Slovenes, Macedonians, and Bosnians, migrated southward into the Balkans. In the seventh century Slavic peoples of the west and south created the state of Moravia along the banks of the Danube River. By the tenth century Moravia's residents were Roman Christian, along with most of the other West and South Slavs. The pattern of conversion was similar to that of the Germanic tribes: first the ruler was baptized, and then missionaries preached, built churches, and spread Christian teachings among the common people. The ruler of Poland was able to convince the pope to establish an independent archbishopric there in 1000, the beginning of a long-lasting connection between Poland and the Roman Church. In the Balkans the Serbs accepted Orthodox Christianity, while the Croats became Roman Christian, a division with a long-standing impact; it was one of the factors in the civil war in this area in the late twentieth century.

Between the fifth and ninth centuries the eastern Slavs moved into the vast areas of present-day European Russia and Ukraine. This enormous area consisted of an immense virgin forest to the north, where most of the eastern Slavs settled, and an endless prairie grassland to the south. In the tenth century Ibrahim Ibn Jakob, a learned Jew from the Muslim caliphate in Córdoba in Spain, traveled in Slavic areas. He found the Slavs to be "violent and inclined to aggression," but far cleaner than Christians in other parts of Europe in which he had traveled, "who wash only once or twice a year." Such filthy habits were unacceptable to someone raised in Muslim Spain, but the Slavs had an ingenious way of both getting clean and staying healthy: "They have no bathhouses as such, but they do make use of wooden huts [for bathing]. They build a stone stove, on which, when it is heated, they pour water. . . . They hold a bunch of grass in their hands, and waft the stream around. Then their pores open, and all excess matter escapes from their bodies."[5]

In the ninth century the Vikings appeared in the lands of the eastern Slavs. Called "Varangians" in the old Russian chronicles, the Vikings were interested primarily in gaining wealth through plunder and trade, and the opportunities were good. Moving up and down the rivers, they soon linked Scandinavia and northern Europe to the Black Sea and to the Byzantine Empire's capital at Constantinople. They raided and looted the cities along the Caspian Sea several times in the tenth century, taking booty and slaves, which they then sold elsewhere; thus raiding turned into trading, and the Scandinavians later established settlements, intermarried, and assimilated with Slavic peoples.

In order to increase and protect their international commerce and growing wealth, the Vikings declared themselves the rulers of the eastern Slavs. According to tradition, the semi-legendary chieftain Ruirik founded a princely dynasty about 860. In any event, the Varangian ruler Oleg (r. 878–912) established his residence at Kiev in modern-day Ukraine. He and his successors ruled over a loosely united confederation of Slavic territories known as Rus, with its capital at Kiev, until 1054. (The word *Russia* comes from *Rus*, though the origins of *Rus* are hotly debated, with some historians linking it with Swedish words and others with Slavic words.)

Oleg and his clansmen quickly became assimilated into the Slavic population, taking local wives and emerging as the noble class. Missionaries of the Byzantine Empire converted the Vikings and local Slavs to Eastern Orthodox Christianity, accelerating the unification of the two groups. Thus the rapidly Slavified Vikings left two important legacies for the future: in about 900 they created a loose unification of Slavic territories, **Kievan Rus**, under a single ruling prince and dynasty, and they imposed a basic religious unity by accepting Orthodox Christianity, as opposed to Roman Catholicism, for themselves and the eastern Slavs.

Even at its height under Great Prince Iaroslav (YAHR-uh-slahv) the Wise (r. 1019–1054), the unity of Kievan Rus was extremely tenuous. Trade, not government, was the main concern of the rulers. Moreover, the Slavified Vikings failed to find a way to peacefully transfer power from one generation to the next. In early Rus there were apparently no fixed rules, and much strife accompanied each succession. Possibly to avoid such chaos, Great Prince Iaroslav, before his death in 1054, divided Kievan Rus among his five sons, who in turn divided their properties when they died. Between 1054 and 1237, Kievan Rus disintegrated into more and more competing units, each ruled by a prince claiming to be a descendant of Ruirik. The princes divided their land like private property because they thought of it as private property. A prince owned a certain number of farms or landed estates and had them worked directly by his people, mainly slaves, called *kholops* in Russian. Outside of these estates, which constituted the princely domain, the prince exercised only limited authority in his principality. Excluding the clergy, two kinds of people lived there: the noble boyars and the commoner peasants.

The **boyars** were descendants of the original Viking warriors, and they also held their lands as free and clear private property. Although the boyars normally fought in princely armies, the customary law declared that they could serve any prince they wished. The ordinary peasants were also truly free. They could move at will wherever opportunities were greatest. In a touching phrase of the times, theirs was "a clean road, without boundaries."[6] In short, fragmented princely power, private property, and personal freedom all went hand in hand.

Magyars and Muslims

Groups of central European steppe peoples known as Magyars also raided villages in the late ninth century, taking plunder and captives, and forcing leaders to pay tribute in an effort to prevent further looting and destruction. Moving westward, small bands of Magyars on horseback reached as far as Spain and the Atlantic coast. They subdued northern Italy, compelled Bavaria and Saxony to pay tribute, and even penetrated into the Rhineland and Burgundy (see Map 8.3). Because of their skill with horses and their Eastern origins, the Magyars were often identified with the earlier Huns by those they conquered, though they are probably unrelated ethnically. This identification, however, may be the origin of the word *Hungarian*.

Magyar forces were defeated by a combined army of Frankish and other Germanic troops at the Battle of Lechfeld near Augsburg in southern Germany in 955, and the

Kievan Rus A confederation of Slavic territories, with its capital at Kiev, ruled by descendants of the Vikings.

Area settled by Varangians, ca. 880
Kievan Rus, 1054

Kievan Rus, ca. 1050

boyars High-ranking nobles in Russia who were descendants of Viking warriors and held their lands as free and clear private property.

Magyars settled in the area that is now Hungary in eastern Europe. Much as Clovis had centuries earlier, the Magyar ruler Géza (GEE-zuh) (r. 970–997), who had been a pagan, became a Roman Christian. This gave him the support of the papacy and offered prospects for alliances with other Roman Christian rulers against the Byzantine Empire, Hungary's southern neighbor. Géza's son Stephen I (r. 997–1038) was officially crowned the king of Hungary by a papal representative on Christmas Day of 1000. He supported the building of churches and monasteries, increased royal power, and encouraged the use of Latin and the Roman alphabet. Hungary's alliance with the papacy shaped the later history of eastern Europe just as Charlemagne's alliance with the papacy shaped western European history. The Hungarians adopted settled agriculture, wrote law codes, and built towns, and Hungary became an important crossroads of trade for German and Muslim merchants.

The ninth century also saw invasions into Europe from the south. In many ways these were a continuation of the earlier Muslim conquests in the Iberian Peninsula, but now they focused on Sicily and mainland Italy. Muslim fleets had attacked Sicily, which was part of the Byzantine Empire, beginning in the seventh century, and by the end of the ninth century they controlled most of the island. The Muslims drove northward, reached Rome in 846 by sailing up the Tiber River and sacked the city, and captured towns along the Adriatic coast almost all the way to Venice. They attacked Mediterranean settlements along the coast of Provence and advanced on land as far as the Alps. In the tenth century Frankish, papal, and Byzantine forces were able to retake much territory, though the Muslims continued to hold Sicily. Under their rule, agricultural innovations from elsewhere in the Muslim world led to new crops such as cotton and sugar, and fortified cities became centers of Muslim learning. Disputes among the Muslim rulers on the island led one faction to ask the Normans for assistance, and between 1060 and 1090 the Normans gradually conquered all of Sicily.

What was the impact of these invasions? From the perspective of those living in what had been Charlemagne's empire, Viking, Magyar, and Muslim attacks contributed to increasing disorder and violence. Italian, French, and English sources often describe this period as one of terror and chaos: "Save us, O God," in the words of the prayer on page 240. People in other parts of Europe might have had a different opinion, however. In Muslim Spain scholars worked in thriving cities, and new crops such as rice enhanced ordinary people's lives. In eastern Europe, states such as Moravia and Hungary became strong kingdoms. A Viking point of view might be the most positive, for by 1100 descendants of the Vikings not only ruled their homelands in Denmark, Norway, and Sweden, but also ruled Normandy, England, Sicily, Iceland, and Kievan Rus, with an outpost in Greenland and occasional voyages to North America.

Political and Economic Decentralization

The large-scale division of Charlemagne's empire into three parts in the ninth century led to a decentralization of power at the local level. Civil wars weakened the power and prestige of kings, who could do little about domestic violence. Likewise, the great invasions, especially those of the Vikings, weakened royal authority. The western Frankish kings were unable to halt the invaders, and the local aristocracy had to assume responsibility for defense. Thus, in the ninth and tenth centuries great aristocratic families increased their authority in the regions of their vested interests.

FOCUS QUESTION
How did internal conflict and outside threats shape European political and economic development in this period?

They built private castles for defense and to live in, and they governed virtually independent territories in which distant and weak kings could not interfere. Common people turned for protection to the strongest power, the local counts, whom they considered their rightful rulers, and free peasants sank to the level of serfs.

Decentralization and the Origins of "Feudalism"

The political power of the Carolingian rulers had long rested on the cooperation of the dominant social class, the Frankish aristocracy. Charlemagne and his predecessors relied on the nobles to help wage wars of expansion and suppress rebellions, and in return these families were given a share of the lands and riches confiscated by the rulers. The most powerful nobles were those able to gain the allegiance of warriors, often symbolized in an oath-swearing ceremony of homage and fealty that grew out of earlier Germanic oaths of loyalty. In this ceremony a warrior (knight) swore his loyalty as a **vassal**—from a Celtic term meaning "servant"—to the more powerful individual, who became his lord. In return for the vassal's loyalty, aid, and military assistance, the lord promised him protection and material support. This support might be a place in the lord's household, but was more likely a piece of land called a *feudum* or **fief** (feef). In the Roman Empire soldiers had been paid for their services with money, but in the cash-poor early Middle Ages their reward was instead a piece of land. Most legal scholars and historians have seen these personal ties of loyalty cemented by grants of land rather than allegiance to an abstract state as a political and social system they term **feudalism**. They have traced its spread from Frankish areas to other parts of Europe.

In the last several decades, increasing numbers of medieval historians have found the idea of a "feudal system" problematic. They note that the word *feudalism* was a later invention, and that vassalage ceremonies, military obligations, and the ownership rights attached to fiefs differed widely from place to place and changed considerably in form and pattern over time. Thus, to these historians, "feudalism" is so varied that it doesn't really have a clear meaning, and it would be better not to use the term at all. The problem is that no one has come up with a better term for the loose arrangements of personal and property ties that developed in the ninth century.

Whether one chooses to use the word *feudalism* or not, these relationships provided some degree of cohesiveness in a society that lacked an adequate government bureaucracy or method of taxation. In fact, because vassals owed administrative as well as military service to their lords, vassalage actually functioned as a way to organize political authority. Vassals were expected to serve as advisers to their lord, and also to pay him fees for important family events, such as the marriage of the vassal's children.

Along with granting land to knights, lords gave land to the clergy for spiritual services or promises of allegiance. In addition, the church held its own lands, and bishops, archbishops, and abbots and abbesses of monasteries sometimes granted fiefs to their own knightly vassals. Thus the "lord" in a feudal relationship was sometimes an institution. Women other than abbesses were generally not granted fiefs, but in most parts of Europe daughters could inherit them if their fathers had no sons. Occasionally, women did go through ceremonies swearing homage and fealty and swore to send fighters when the lord demanded them. More commonly, when their husbands were away women acted as surrogates, defending the territory from attack and carrying out administrative duties.

---

vassal A warrior who swore loyalty and service to a noble in exchange for land, protection, and support.

fief A piece of land granted by a feudal lord to a vassal in return for service and loyalty.

feudalism A term devised by later scholars to describe the political system in which a vassal was generally given a piece of land in return for his loyalty.

Some of the problems associated with the word *feudal* come from the fact that it is sometimes used by nonhistorians as a synonym for "medieval," or to describe relations between landholders and the peasants who lived and worked on their estates. (The latter use comes from Karl Marx, who used "feudalism" to describe a stage of economic development between slavery and capitalism.) Medieval historians on all sides of the debate about feudalism agree, however, that peasants did not swear oaths of vassalage; if there was a feudal system, peasants were not part of it.

Manorialism, Serfdom, and the Slave Trade

In feudal relationships, the "lord" was the individual or institution that had authority over a vassal, but the word *lord* was also used to describe the person or institution that had economic and political authority over peasants who lived in villages and farmed the land. Thus a vassal in one relationship was a slightly different type of lord in another. Most European people in the early Middle Ages were peasants who lived in family groups in villages or small towns and made their living predominantly by raising crops and animals. The village and the land surrounding it were called a manor, from the Latin word for "dwelling" or "homestead." Some fiefs might include only one manor, while great lords or kings might have hundreds of manors under their direct control. Residents of manors worked for the lord in exchange for protection, a system that was later referred to as **manorialism**. Free peasants surrendered themselves and their lands to the lord's jurisdiction. The land was given back, but the peasants became tied to it by various kinds of payments and services. Thus, like vassalage, manorialism involved an exchange. Because the economic power of the warring class rested on landed estates worked by peasants, feudalism and manorialism were linked, but they were not the same system.

manorialism A system in which peasant residents of manors, or farming villages, provided work and goods for their lord in exchange for protection.

Local custom determined precisely what services villagers would provide to their lord, but certain practices became common throughout Europe. The peasant was obliged to give the lord a percentage of the annual harvest, usually in produce, sometimes in cash. The peasant paid a fee to marry someone from outside the lord's estate. To inherit property, the peasant paid a fine, often the best beast the person owned. Above all, the peasant became part of the lord's permanent labor force. With vast stretches of uncultivated virgin land and a tiny labor population, manorial lords encouraged population growth and immigration. The most profitable form of capital was not land but laborers.

In entering into a relationship with a manorial lord, free farmers lost status. Their position became servile, and they became **serfs**. That is, they were bound to the land and could not leave it without the lord's permission. Serfdom was not the same as slavery in that lords did not own the person of the serf, but serfs were subject to the jurisdiction of the lord's court in any dispute over property and in any case of suspected criminal behavior.

serfs Peasants bound to the land by a relationship with a manorial lord.

The transition from freedom to serfdom was slow. In the late eighth century there were still many free peasants. And within the legal category of serfdom there were many economic levels, ranging from the highly prosperous to the desperately poor. Nevertheless, a social and legal revolution was taking place. By the year 800 perhaps 60 percent of the population of western Europe—completely free a century before—had been reduced to serfdom. The ninth-century Viking assaults on Europe created extremely unstable conditions and individual insecurity, increasing the need for protection, accelerating the transition to serfdom, and leading to additional loss of personal freedom.

Though serfdom was not slavery, the Carolingian trade in actual slaves was extensive, generally involving persons captured in war or raids. Merchants in early medieval towns used slaves to pay the suppliers of the luxury goods their noble and clerical customers desired, most of which came into Europe from the East. The Muslim conquest of Spain produced thousands of prisoner-slaves, as did Charlemagne's long wars and the Viking raids. When Frankish conquests declined in the tenth century, German and Viking merchants obtained people on the empire's eastern border who spoke Slavic languages, the origin of our word *slave*. Slaves sold across the Mediterranean fetched three or four times the amounts brought within the Carolingian Empire, so most slaves were sold to Muslims. For Europeans and Arabs alike, selling captives and other slaves was standard procedure. Christian moralists sometimes complained about the sale of Christians to non-Christians, but they did not object to slavery itself.

LOOKING BACK LOOKING AHEAD

The culture that emerged in Europe in the early Middle Ages has justifiably been called the first "European" civilization. While it was by no means "civilized" by modern standards, it had definite characteristics that were shared across a wide region. Other than in Muslim Spain and the pagan areas of northern and eastern Europe, almost all people were baptized Christians.

Everywhere — including Muslim and pagan areas — most people lived in small villages, supporting themselves and paying their obligations to their superiors by raising crops and animals. These villages were on pieces of land increasingly granted to knights in exchange for loyalty and service to a noble lord. The educated elite was infused with Latin ideas and models, for Latin was the common language — written as well as spoken — of educated people in most of Europe.

In the several centuries after 1000, these characteristics — Christianity, village-based agriculture, vassalage, and Latin culture — would not disappear. Historians conventionally term the era from 1000 to about 1300 the "High Middle Ages," but this era was built on a foundation that had already been established. The soaring Gothic cathedrals that were the most glorious architectural feature of the High Middle Ages were often constructed on the footings of early medieval churches, and their walls were built of stones that had once been part of Carolingian walls and castles. Similarly, political structures grew out of the institutions established in the Carolingian period, and later literary and cultural flowerings followed the model of the Carolingian Renaissance in looking to the classical past. Less positive developments also had their roots in the early Middle Ages, including hostilities between Christians and Muslims that would motivate the Crusades, and the continued expansion of serfdom and other forms of unfree labor.

Make Connections

Think about the larger developments and continuities within and across chapters.

1. In both Christianity and Islam, political leaders played an important role in the expansion of the faith into new territory. How would you compare the actions of Constantine and Clovis (both in Chapter 7) with those of the Muslim caliphs and

Charlemagne (in this chapter) in promoting, extending, and establishing their chosen religion?

2. Charlemagne considered himself to be the reviver of the Roman Empire. Thinking about Roman and Carolingian government and society, do you think this is an accurate self-description? Why or why not?

3. How were the ninth-century migrations and invasions of the Vikings, Magyars, and Muslims similar to the earlier barbarian migrations discussed in Chapter 7? How were they different?

8 REVIEW & EXPLORE

Review the Main Ideas

Answer the focus questions from each section of the chapter.

◆ What were the origins of Islam, and what impact did it have on Europe as it spread? (p. 220)

◆ How did the Franks build and govern a European empire? (p. 228)

◆ What were the significant intellectual and cultural changes in Charlemagne's era? (p. 235)

◆ What were the consequences of the ninth-century invasions and migrations? (p. 240)

◆ How did internal conflict and outside threats shape European political and economic development in this period? (p. 245)

Identify Key Terms

Identify and explain the significance of each item below.

Qur'an (p. 220)
Five Pillars of Islam (p. 223)
caliph (p. 224)
al-Andalus (p. 224)
infidel (p. 227)
civitas (p. 228)
comites (p. 228)
Treaty of Verdun (p. 240)
Kievan Rus (p. 244)
boyars (p. 244)
vassal (p. 246)
fief (p. 246)
feudalism (p. 246)
manorialism (p. 247)
serfs (p. 247)

NOTES

1. F. E. Peters, *A Reader on Classical Islam* (Princeton, N.J.: Princeton University Press, 1994), pp. 208–209.
2. Quoted in R. McKitterick, *The Frankish Kingdoms Under the Carolingians, 751–987* (New York: Longman, 1983), p. 34.
3. Quoted ibid., p. 77.
4. Quoted in B. D. Hill, ed., *Church and State in the Middle Ages* (New York: John Wiley & Sons, 1970), pp. 46–47.
5. From Charles Melville and Ahmad Ubaydli, eds. and trans., *Christians and Moors in Spain*, vol. 3 (New York: Oxbow Books, 1992), p. 54.
6. Quoted in R. Pipes, *Russia Under the Old Regime* (New York: Charles Scribner's Sons, 1974), p. 48.

TRAHUNT:CARRUM CUM UINO:ET ARMIS:

CHAPTER PREVIEW

Political Revival and the Origins of the Modern State
How did monarchs try to centralize political power?

Law and Justice
How did the administration of law evolve in this period?

Nobles
What were the roles of nobles, and how did they train for these?

The Papacy
How did the papacy reform the church, and what were the reactions to these efforts?

Monks, Nuns, and Friars
What roles did monks, nuns, and friars play in medieval society?

The Crusades and the Expansion of Christianity
What were the causes, course, and consequences of both the Crusades and the broader expansion of Christianity?

Life in the High Middle Ages
In this detail from the Bayeux tapestry, men pull a cart loaded with wine and spears to the ships with which Duke William of Normandy crossed the English Channel in his invasion of England in 1066. Medieval chronicles, songs, and stories focus on the heroic glories of battle, but logistics and supply were just as important to a medieval army as they are today. Now on display in Bayeux, France, the Bayeux tapestry is actually not a tapestry, but an embroidery panel measuring 231 feet by 19 inches that records the entire conquest.
(Musée de la Tapisserie, Bayeux, France/Bridgeman Images)

9

State and Church in the High Middle Ages

1000–1300

The concept of the state had been one of Rome's great legacies to Western civilization, but for almost five hundred years after the disintegration of the Roman Empire in the West, the state did not exist. Political authority was decentralized, with power spread among many lords, bishops, abbots, and other types of local rulers. The deeply fragmented political units that covered the early medieval European continent did not have the characteristics or provide the services of a modern state.

Beginning in the last half of the tenth century, the invasions and migrations that had contributed to European fragmentation gradually ended, and domestic disorder slowly subsided. Rulers began to develop new institutions of law and government that enabled them to assert their power over lesser lords and the general population. Although nobles remained the dominant class, centralized states slowly crystallized, first in western Europe, and then in eastern and northern Europe. At the same time, energetic popes built their power within the Western Christian Church and tried to assert their superiority over kings and emperors. Monks, nuns, and friars played significant roles in medieval society, both as individuals and as members of institutions. A papal call to retake the holy city of Jerusalem led to nearly two centuries of warfare between Christians and Muslims. Christian warriors, clergy, and settlers moved out from western and central Europe in all directions, so that through conquest and colonization border regions were gradually incorporated into a more uniform Christian realm. ■

Political Revival and the Origins of the Modern State

FOCUS QUESTION
How did monarchs try to centralize political power?

The modern state is an organized territory with definite geographical boundaries, a body of law, and institutions of government. The modern national state provides its citizens with order and protection, supplies a currency that permits financial and commercial transactions, and conducts relations with foreign governments. To accomplish these functions, the state must have officials, bureaucracies, laws, courts of law, soldiers, information, and money. Early medieval governments had few of these elements, but beginning in the eleventh century rulers in some parts of Europe began to manipulate existing institutions to build up their power, becoming kings over growing and slowly centralizing states. As rulers expanded their territories and extended their authority, they developed larger bureaucracies, armies, judicial systems, and other institutions of state to maintain control and ensure order. Because these institutions cost money, rulers also initiated systems for generating revenue and handling financial matters. Some rulers were more successful than others, and the solutions they found to these problems laid the foundations for modern national states.

England

Throughout the ninth century the Vikings had made a concerted effort to conquer and rule all of Anglo-Saxon England. Because of its proximity to Scandinavia and its lack of unity under a single ruler, England probably suffered more from Viking invasions than any other part of Europe. In 878 Alfred, king of the West Saxons (or Wessex), defeated the Vikings, inaugurating a period of recovery and stability in England. Alfred and his immediate successors built a system of local defenses and slowly extended royal rule beyond Wessex to other Anglo-Saxon peoples until one law, royal law, took precedence over local custom. England was divided into local units called shires, or counties, each under the jurisdiction of a shire-reeve (a word that soon evolved into *sheriff*) appointed by the king. Sheriffs were unpaid officials from well-off families responsible for collecting taxes, catching and trying criminals, and raising infantry when the king required it.

The Viking invasions of England resumed, however, and the island eventually came under Viking rule. The Viking Canute (r. 1016–1035) made England the center of his empire while promoting a policy of assimilation and reconciliation between Anglo-Saxons and Vikings. When Canute's heir Edward died childless, there were three claimants to the throne of England—the Anglo-Saxon noble Harold Godwinson (ca. 1022–1066), who had been crowned by English nobles; the Norwegian king Harald III (r. 1045–1066), the grandson of Canute; and Duke William of Normandy, the illegitimate son of Edward's cousin.

In 1066 the forces of Harold Godwinson crushed Harald's invading army in northern England, then quickly marched south when they heard that William had invaded England with his Norman vassals. Harold was decisively defeated by William at the Battle of Hastings—an event now known as the Norman Conquest. In both England and Normandy, William the Conqueror limited the power of the nobles and church officials, and built a unified monarchy. In England he retained the office of sheriffs, but named Normans to the posts. William wanted to determine how much

Chronology

936–973	Reign of Otto I in Germany; facilitates spread of Christianity in the Baltics and eastern Europe	1170	Thomas Becket assassinated in England
1059	Lateran Council restricts election of the pope to the college of cardinals	1180–1223	Reign of Philip II (Philip Augustus) in France; territory of France greatly expanded
1061–1091	Normans defeat Muslims and Byzantines in Sicily	1198–1216	Innocent III; height of the medieval papacy
1066	Norman conquest of England	1215	Magna Carta
1073–1085	Pontificate of Pope Gregory VII, proponent of Gregorian reforms	1216	Papal recognition of Dominican order
1095–1291	Crusades	1221	Papal recognition of Franciscan order
1098	Cistercian order established	1290	Jews expelled from England
1100–1135	Reign of Henry I of England; establishment of the Exchequer, England's bureau of finance	1298	Pope Boniface VIII orders all nuns to be cloistered
1100–1200	Establishment of canon law	1302	Pope Boniface VIII declares all Christians subject to the pope in *Unam Sanctam*
1154–1189	Reign of Henry II of England; revision of legal procedure; beginnings of common law	1306	Jews expelled from France
		1397	Queen Margrete establishes Union of Kalmar

wealth there was in his new kingdom and who held what land. Royal officials were sent to every part of the country, and in every village local men were put under oath to answer the questions of these officials. In the words of a contemporary chronicler:

> So very narrowly did he have it investigated, that there was no single hide [a hide was a measure of land large enough to support one family], nor yard of land, nor indeed . . . one ox nor one cow nor one pig was there left out, and not put down in his record: and all these records were brought to him afterwards.[1]

The resulting record, called the **Domesday Book** (DOOMZ-day) from the Anglo-Saxon word *doom*, meaning "judgment," helped William and his descendants tax land appropriately. The book still survives and is an invaluable source of social and economic information about medieval England. It also helped William and future English kings regard their country as one unit.

Domesday Book A general inquiry about the wealth of his lands ordered by William of Normandy.

William's son Henry I (r. 1100–1135) established a bureau of finance called the Exchequer that became the first institution of the government bureaucracy of England. In addition to various taxes and annual gifts, Henry's income came from money paid to the Crown for settling disputes and as penalties for crimes, as well as money due to him in his private position as landowner and lord. Henry, like other medieval kings, made no distinction between his private income and state revenues, and the officials of the Exchequer began to keep careful records of all monies paid into and out of the royal treasury. (See "Evaluating the Evidence 9.1: Marriage and Wardship in the Norman Exchequer," page 254.)

In 1128 Henry's daughter Matilda was married to Geoffrey of Anjou; their son became Henry II of England and inaugurated the Angevin (AN-juh-vuhn; from Anjou, his father's county) dynasty. Henry II inherited the French provinces of

Marriage and Wardship in the Norman Exchequer

After the Norman Conquest, the kings of England held the right to control the marriages of their vassals, and also held wardship over the widow and children of any vassal who had died. They often sold these rights for cash, which gave the buyer control of the marriage or control over the ward's lands until he or she came of age. The records of the Exchequer include many such payments.

Alice, countess of Warwick, renders account of £1000 and 10 palfreys [the type of horse ridden by women] to be allowed to remain a widow as long as she pleases, and not to be forced to marry by the king. And if perchance she should wish to marry, she shall not marry except with the assent and on the grant of the king, where the king shall be satisfied; and to have the custody of her sons whom she has from the earl of Warwick her late husband.

Hawisa, who was wife of William Fitz Robert, renders account of 130 marks and 4 palfreys that she may have peace from Peter of Borough to whom the king has given permission to marry her; and that she may not be compelled to marry.

Geoffrey de Mandeville owes 20,000 marks to have as his wife Isabella, countess of Gloucester, with all the lands and tenements and fiefs which fall to her.

Thomas de Colville renders an account of 100 marks for having the custody of the sons of Roger Torpel and their land until they come of age.

William, bishop of Ely, owes 220 marks for having the custody of Stephen de Beauchamp with his inheritance and for marrying him where he wishes.

William of St. Mary's church renders an account of 500 marks for having the custody of the heir of Robert Young, son of Robert Fitzharding, with all his inheritance and all its appurtenances and franchises; that is to say with the services of knights and gifts of churches and marriages of women, and to be allowed to marry him to whatever one of his relatives he wishes; and that all his land is to revert to him freely when he comes of age.

Batholomew de Muleton renders an account of 100 marks for having the custody of the land and the heiress of Lambert of Ibtoft, and for marrying the wife of the same Lambert to whomsoever he wishes where she shall not be disparaged and that he may be able to confer her (the heiress) upon whom he wishes.

EVALUATE THE EVIDENCE

1. What types of individuals pay the king for power over marriage or wardship?
2. What do these payments reveal about marriage and family relationships among wealthier groups in medieval society?

Source: Edward P. Cheyney, ed., *Translations and Reprints from the Original Sources of European History*, vol. 4, part 3 (Philadelphia: The Department of History of the University of Pennsylvania, 1897), pp. 26–27.

Anjou, Normandy, Maine, and Touraine in northwestern France, and in 1152 he married Eleanor of Aquitaine, heir to Aquitaine, Poitou (pwah-TOO), and Gascony in southwestern France. As a result, Henry claimed nearly half of today's France, and the histories of England and France became closely intertwined, leading to disputes and conflicts down to the fifteenth century.

France

French kings overcame the Angevin threat to expand and increasingly unify their realm. Following the death of the last Carolingian ruler in 987, an assembly of nobles selected Hugh Capet (kah-PAY) as his successor. Soon after his own coronation, Hugh crowned his oldest surviving son Robert as king to ensure the succession and prevent disputes after his death. This broke with the earlier practices of elective kingship or dividing a kingdom among one's sons, establishing instead the principle of **primogeniture** (prigh-muh-JEH-nuh-choor), in which the king's

primogeniture An inheritance system in which the oldest son inherits all land and noble titles.

eldest son received the Crown as his rightful inheritance. Primogeniture became the standard pattern of succession in medieval western Europe, and also became an increasingly common pattern of inheritance for noble titles as well as land and other forms of wealth among all social classes.

The Capetian (kuh-PEE-shuhn) kings were weak, but they laid the foundation for later political stability. This stability came slowly. In the early twelfth century France still consisted of a number of virtually independent provinces, and the king of France maintained clear jurisdiction over a relatively small area, the Île-de-France. Over time medieval French kings worked to increase the royal domain and extend their authority over the provinces.

The work of unifying France began under Louis VI's grandson Philip II (r. 1180–1223), also known as Philip Augustus. He took Normandy by force from King John of England in 1204, and gained other northern provinces as well. In the thirteenth century Philip Augustus's descendants acquired important holdings in the south. By the end of the thirteenth century most of the provinces of modern France had been added to the royal domain through diplomacy, marriage, war, and inheritance (Map 9.1).

In addition to expanding the royal territory, Philip Augustus devised a method of governing the provinces and providing for communication between the central government in Paris and local communities. Each province retained its own institutions and laws, but royal agents were sent from Paris into the provinces as the king's official representatives with authority to act for him. These agents were never natives of the provinces to which they were assigned, and they could not own land there. This policy reflected the fundamental principle of French administration that officials should gain their power from their connection to the monarchy, not from their own wealth or local alliances.

Philip Augustus and his successors were slower and less effective than were English kings at setting up an efficient bureau of finance. There was no national survey of property like the *Domesday Book* to help determine equitable levels of taxation, and French nobles resisted paying any taxes or fees. Not until the fourteenth century, as a result of the Hundred Years' War, did a national financial bureau emerge — the Chamber of Accounts — and even after that French nobles continued to pay little or no taxes, a problem that would help spark the French Revolution centuries later.

MAP 9.1 The Growth of the Kingdom of France, 1180–1314 The kings of France expanded their holdings through warfare, diplomacy, and strategic marriages, annexing lands that had belonged to independent nobles and taking over territory from the Angevin kings who also ruled England. The province of Toulouse in the south became part of France as a result of the crusade against the Albigensians (see page 267).

Central Europe

Holy Roman Empire The loose confederation of principalities, duchies, cities, bishoprics, and other types of regional governments stretching from Denmark to Rome and from Burgundy to Poland.

In central Europe the German king Otto I (r. 936–973) defeated many other lords to build his power from his original base in Saxony. Some of our knowledge of Otto derives from *The Deeds of Otto*, a history of his reign in heroic verse written by a nun, Hroswitha of Gandersheim (ca. 935–ca. 1003). Hroswitha viewed Otto's victories as part of God's plan: "As often as he set out for war, there was not a people, though haughty because of its strength, that could harm or conquer him, supported as he was by the consolation of the heavenly King."[2]

Otto garnered financial support from church leaders and also asserted the right to control ecclesiastical appointments. Before receiving religious consecration and being invested with the staff and ring symbolic of their offices, bishops and abbots had to perform feudal homage for the lands that accompanied the church office. This practice, later known as "lay investiture," created a grave crisis between the church and the monarchy in the eleventh century (see page 266).

In 955 Otto I inflicted a crushing defeat on the Magyars in the Battle of Lechfeld (see Chapter 8), which made Otto a great hero to the Germans. In 962 he used this victory to have himself crowned emperor by the pope in Aachen, which had been the capital of the Carolingian Empire. He chose this site to symbolize his intention to continue the tradition of Charlemagne and to demonstrate papal support for his rule. Though it was not exactly clear what Otto was the emperor of, by the eleventh century people were increasingly using the term **Holy Roman Empire** to refer to a loose confederation of principalities, duchies, cities, bishoprics, and other types of regional governments stretching from Denmark to Rome and from Burgundy to Poland (Map 9.2).

In this large area of central Europe and northern Italy, the Holy Roman emperors shared power with princes, dukes, archbishops, counts, bishops, abbots, and cities. The office of emperor remained an elected one, though the electors numbered seven—four secular rulers of large territories within the empire and three archbishops.

None of Otto's successors were as forceful as he had been, and by the first half of the twelfth century civil wars wracked the empire. The electors decided the only alternative to continued chaos was the selection of a strong ruler. They chose Frederick Barbarossa of the house of Hohenstaufen (HOH-uhn-shtow-fuhn) (r. 1152–1190). Like William the Conqueror in England and Philip in France, Frederick required

MAP 9.2 The Holy Roman Empire and the Kingdom of Sicily, ca. 1200 Frederick Barbarossa greatly expanded the size of the Holy Roman Empire, but it remained a loose collection of various types of government. The Christian kingdom of Sicily was created when Norman knights overthrew the Muslim rulers, but was later ruled by Frederick II, who was also the Holy Roman emperor.

vassals to take an oath of allegiance to him as emperor and appointed officials to exercise full imperial authority over local communities. He forbade the regional rulers to engage in war with one another and established sworn peace associations with them. These peace associations punished criminals and those who breached the peace.

Between 1154 and 1188 Frederick made six military expeditions into Italy in an effort to assert his imperial rights over the increasingly wealthy towns of northern Italy. While he initially made significant conquests, the Italian cities formed leagues to oppose him, and also allied with the papacy. In 1176 Frederick suffered a crushing defeat at Legnano, where the league armies took massive amounts of booty and many prisoners (see Map 9.2). This battle marked the first time a cavalry of armed knights was decisively defeated by an army largely made of infantrymen from the cities. Frederick was forced to recognize the municipal autonomy of the northern Italian cities and the pope's sovereignty in central Italy. His campaigns in Italy took him away from the parts of the empire north of the Alps, and regional rulers there reasserted their authority toward the end of Frederick's reign and in the reigns of his successors. Thus, in contrast to France and England, Germany did not become a unified state in the Middle Ages, and would not until the nineteenth century.

Italy

The emperor and the pope also came into conflict over Sicily and southern Italy, disputes that eventually involved the kings of France and Spain as well. Between 1061 and 1091 a bold Norman knight, Roger de Hauteville, with papal support and a small band of mercenaries, defeated the Muslims and Byzantines who controlled the island of Sicily. Roger then faced the problem of governing Sicily's heterogeneous population of native Sicilians, Italians, Greeks, Jews, Arabs, and Normans. Roger distributed scattered lands to his followers so no vassal would have a centralized power base. He took an inquest of royal property and forbade his followers to engage in war with one another. To these Norman practices, Roger fused Arab and Greek institutions, such as the bureau for record keeping and administration that had been established by the previous Muslim rulers.

In 1137 Roger's son and heir, Count Roger II, took the city of Naples and much of the surrounding territory in southern Italy. The entire area came to be known as the kingdom of Sicily (or sometimes the Kingdom of the Two Sicilies).

Roger II's grandson Frederick II (r. 1212–1250) was also the grandson of Frederick Barbarossa of Germany. He was crowned king of the Germans at Aachen (1216) and Holy Roman emperor at Rome (1220), but he concentrated all his attention on the southern parts of the

Emperor Frederick II Granting Privileges　A young and handsome Frederick II, with a laurel wreath symbolizing his position as emperor, signs a grant of privileges for a merchant of the Italian city of Asti in this thirteenth-century manuscript. Frederick wears the flamboyant and fashionable clothing of a high noble — long-toed shoes, slit sleeves, and a cape of ermine tails — while the merchant seeking his favor is dressed in more sober and less expensive garb. (Miniature from the *Codex of Astensis*, Archivio Municipale, Asti, Italy/Scala/Art Resource, NY)

empire. Frederick had grown up in multicultural Sicily, knew six languages, wrote poetry, and supported scientists, scholars, and artists, whatever their religion or background. In 1224 he founded the University of Naples to train officials for his growing bureaucracy, sending them out to govern the towns of the kingdom. He tried to administer justice fairly to all his subjects, declaring, "We cannot in the least permit Jews and Saracens [Muslims] to be defrauded of the power of our protection and to be deprived of all other help, just because the difference of their religious practices makes them hateful to Christians," implying a degree of toleration exceedingly rare at the time.[3]

Because of his broad interests and abilities, Frederick's contemporaries called him the "Wonder of the World." But Sicily required constant attention, and Frederick's absences on the Crusades—holy wars sponsored by the papacy for the recovery of Jerusalem from the Muslims (see page 276)—and on campaigns in mainland Italy took their toll. Shortly after he died, the unsupervised bureaucracy fell to pieces. The pope, worried about being encircled by imperial power, called in a French prince to rule the kingdom of Sicily. Like Germany, Italy would remain divided until the nineteenth century.

The Iberian Peninsula

From the eleventh to the thirteenth centuries, power in the Iberian Peninsula shifted from Muslim to Christian rulers. In the eleventh century divisions and civil war in the caliphate of Córdoba allowed Christian armies to conquer an increasingly large part of the Iberian Peninsula. Castile, in the north-central part of the peninsula, became the strongest of the growing Christian kingdoms, and Aragon, in the northeast, the second most powerful. In 1085 King Alfonso VI of Castile and León captured Toledo in central Spain. The following year forces of the Almoravid dynasty that ruled much of northwestern Africa defeated Christian armies and halted Christian advances southward, though they did not retake Toledo. The Almoravids reunified and strengthened the Muslim state for several generations, but the Christians regrouped, and in their North African homeland the Almoravids were overthrown by a rival dynasty, the Almohads, who then laid claim to the remaining Muslim territories in southern Spain.

Alfonso VIII (1158–1214) of Castile, aided by the kings of Aragon, Navarre, and Portugal, crushed the Almohad-led Muslims in 1212, accelerating the Christian push southward. Over the next several centuries, successive popes gave Christian warriors in the Iberian Peninsula the same spiritual benefits that they gave those who traveled to Jerusalem, such as granting them forgiveness for their sins, transforming this advance into a crusade. Christian troops captured the great Muslim cities of Córdoba in 1236 and Seville in 1248. With this, Christians controlled nearly the entire Iberian Peninsula, save for the small state of Granada (Map 9.3). The chief mosques in Muslim cities became cathedrals, and Christian rulers recruited immigrants from western and southern Europe. The cities quickly became overwhelmingly Christian, and gradually rural areas did as well. Fourteenth-century clerical writers would call the movement to expel the Muslims the **reconquista** (reconquest), a sacred and patriotic crusade to wrest the country from "alien" Muslim hands. This idea became part of Spanish political culture and of the national psychology.

reconquista The Christian term for the conquest of Muslim territories in the Iberian Peninsula by Christian forces.

Date of Christian Reconquest

By 814	By 1097	By 1275
By 910	By 1150	By 1492
By 1037	By 1190	✳ Major battle

Maximum extent of Umayyad Caliphate, 750
1236 Date of Christian conquest and establishment of diocese

■ Diocese
✝ Monastery

MAP 9.3 The Reconquista, ca. 750–1492   The Christian conquest of Muslim Spain was followed by ecclesiastical reorganization, with the establishment of dioceses, monasteries, and the Latin liturgy, which gradually tied the peninsula to the heartland of Christian Europe and to the Roman papacy.

Law and Justice

In the early Middle Ages society perceived major crimes as acts against an individual, and such crimes were settled when the accused made a cash payment to the victim or his or her kindred. In the High Middle Ages suspects were pursued and criminals punished for acting against the public interest. Throughout Europe, however, the law was a hodgepodge of local customs and provincial practices. In this period national rulers tried to blend these elements into a uniform system of rules acceptable and applicable to all their peoples, though their success at doing so varied.

FOCUS QUESTION
How did the administration of law evolve in this period?

Local Laws and Royal Courts

In France, this effort to create a royal judicial system was launched by Louis IX (r. 1226–1270). Each French province, even after being made part of the kingdom of France, had retained its unique laws and procedures, but Louis IX published laws for the entire kingdom and sent royal judges to hear complaints of injustice. He established the Parlement of Paris, a kind of supreme court that heard appeals from local administrators and regional courts, and also registered (or announced) royal laws. By the very act of appealing the decisions of local courts to the Parlement of Paris, French people in far-flung provinces were recognizing the superiority of royal justice.

In the Holy Roman Empire, justice was administered at multiple levels. The manorial or seigneurial court, presided over by the local lay or ecclesiastical lord, dealt with such matters as damage to crops and fields, trespass, boundary disputes, and debt. Dukes, counts, bishops, and abbots possessed authority over larger regions, and they dispensed justice in serious criminal cases there. The Holy Roman emperors established a court of appeal similar to that of the French kings, but in their disunited empire it had little power.

England also had a variety of local laws with procedures and penalties that varied from one part of the country to another. Henry I occasionally sent out circuit judges, royal officials who traveled a given circuit or district, to hear civil and criminal cases. Henry II (r. 1154–1189) made this way of extending royal justice an annual practice. Every year royal judges left London and set up court in the counties. These courts regularized procedures in civil cases, gradually developing the idea of a **common law**, one that applied throughout the whole country. Over the next two or three centuries common law became a reality as well as a legal theory. Common law relied on precedent: a decision in an important case served as an authority for deciding similar cases. Thus written codes of law played a less important role in England than they did elsewhere. (This practice has continued to today; in contrast to the United States and most other countries, the United Kingdom does not have a written constitution.)

common law A body of English law established by King Henry II's court that in the next two or three centuries became common to the entire country.

Henry also improved procedure in criminal justice. In 1166 he instructed the sheriffs to summon local juries to conduct inquests and draw up lists of known or suspected criminals. These lists, or indictments, sworn to by the juries, were to be presented to the royal judges when they arrived in the community. This accusing jury is the ancestor of the modern grand jury. Gradually, in the course of the thirteenth century, the king's judges adopted the practice of calling on twelve people (other than the accusing jury) to consider the question of innocence or guilt; this was the forerunner of the trial jury.

One aspect of Henry II's judicial reforms encountered stiff resistance from an unexpected source. In 1164 Henry insisted that everyone, including clerics, be subject to the royal courts. The archbishop of Canterbury Thomas Becket, who was Henry's friend and former chief adviser, vigorously protested that church law required clerics to be subject to church courts.

The disagreement between king and archbishop dragged on for years. Late in December 1170, in a fit of rage, Henry expressed the wish that Becket be destroyed. Four knights took the king at his word. They rode to Canterbury Cathedral and, as the archbishop was leaving evening services, murdered him, slashing off the crown of his head and scattering his brains on the floor of the cathedral. The assassination of an archbishop turned public opinion in England and throughout western Europe against the king, and Henry had to back down. He did public penance for the murder and gave up his attempts to bring clerics under the authority of the royal courts. Miracles were recorded at Becket's tomb; Becket was made a saint; and in a short time Canterbury Cathedral became a major pilgrimage and tourist site.

The Magna Carta

In the later years of Henry's reign, his sons, spurred on by their mother, Eleanor of Aquitaine, fought against their father and one another for power and land. Richard I, known as the Lion-Hearted (r. 1189–1199), won this civil war and acceded to the throne on Henry's death. Soon after, however, he departed on one of the Crusades, and during his reign he spent only six months in England. Richard was captured on his way back from the Crusades and held by the Holy Roman emperor for a very high ransom, paid primarily through loans and high taxes on the English people.

John (r. 1199–1216) inherited his father's and brother's heavy debts, and his efforts to squeeze money out of his subjects created an atmosphere of resentment. In July 1214 John's cavalry suffered a severe defeat at the hands of Philip Augustus of France, which ended English hopes for the recovery of territories from France and strengthened the opposition to John back in England. A rebellion begun by northern barons eventually grew to involve many key members of the English nobility. After lengthy negotiations, John met the barons in 1215 at Runnymede and was forced to approve the charter of rights later called **Magna Carta**.

The charter was simply meant to assert traditional rights enjoyed by certain groups, including the barons, the clergy, and the merchants of London, and thus state limits on the king's power. In time, however, it came to signify the broader principle that everyone, including the king and the government, must obey the law. In the later Middle Ages references to Magna Carta underlined the Augustinian theory that a government, to be legitimate, must promote law, order, and justice (see Chapter 6). The Magna Carta also contains the germ of the idea of "due process of law," meaning that a person has the right to be heard and defended in court and is entitled to the protection of the law. Because later generations referred to Magna Carta as a written statement of English liberties, it gradually came to have an almost sacred symbolic importance.

> **Magna Carta** A peace treaty intended to redress the grievances that particular groups had against King John; it was later viewed as the source of English rights and liberty more generally.

Law in Everyday Life

Statements of legal principles such as the Magna Carta were not how most people experienced the law in medieval Europe. Instead they were involved in or witnessed something judged to be a crime, and then experienced or watched the determination of guilt and the punishment. Judges determined guilt or innocence in a number of ways. In some cases, particularly those in which there was little clear evidence, they ordered a trial by ordeal. An accused person could be tried by fire or water. In the latter case, the accused was tied hand and foot and dropped in a lake or river. People believed that water was a pure substance and would reject anything foul or unclean. Thus a person who sank was considered innocent; a person who floated was found guilty. Trial by ordeal was a ritual that appealed to the supernatural for judgment.

Trials by ordeal are fascinating to modern audiences, but they were relatively rare, and their use declined over the High Middle Ages as judges and courts increasingly favored more

Punishment of Adulterers Preceded by heralds blowing horns and followed by men carrying sticks, a man and a woman found guilty of adultery are led naked through the streets in this thirteenth-century French manuscript. This procession may be driving the couple out of town; banishment was a very common punishment for a number of crimes, including theft and assault. (Bibliothèque Municipale, Agen, France/ Bridgeman Images)

rational procedures. Judges heard testimony, sought witnesses, and read written evidence if it was available. A London case in 1277 provides a good example of how law worked. Around Easter, a man was sent to clean a house that had been abandoned, "but when he came to a dark and narrow place where coals were usually kept, he there found [a] headless body; upon seeing which, he sent word to the chamberlain and sheriffs." These officials went to the house and interviewed the neighbors. The men who lived nearby said that the headless body belonged to Symon de Winten, a tavern owner, whom they had seen quarreling with his servant Roger in early December. That night Roger "seized a knife, and with it cut the throat of Symon quite through, so that the head was entirely severed from the body." He had stuffed the body in the coal room, stolen clothes and a silver cup, and disappeared.[4] The surviving records don't indicate whether Roger was ever caught, but they do indicate that the sheriffs took something as "surety" from the neighbors who testified, that is, cash or goods as a pledge that their testimony was true. Taking sureties from witnesses was a common practice, which may be why the neighbors had not come forward on their own even though they seemed to have detailed knowledge of the murder. People were supposed to report crimes, and they could be fined for not doing so, but it is clear from this case that such community involvement in crime fighting did not always happen.

Had Roger been caught and found guilty, his punishment would have been as public as the investigation. Murder was a capital crime, as were a number of other violent acts, and executions took place outdoors on a scaffold. Hanging was the most common method of execution, although nobles might be beheaded because hanging was seen as demeaning. Minor crimes were punished by fines, corporal punishments such as whipping, or banishment from the area.

Nobles

FOCUS QUESTION
What were the roles of nobles, and how did they train for these?

The expansion of centralized royal power and law involved limiting the power of the nobility, but rulers also worked through nobles, who retained their privileged status and cultural importance. In fact, despite political, scientific, and industrial revolutions, the nobility continued to hold real political and social power in Europe into the nineteenth century. In order to account for this continuing influence, it is important to understand the development of the nobility in the High Middle Ages.

Origins and Status of the Nobility

In the early Middle Ages noble status was generally limited to a very few families who either were descended from officials at the Carolingian court or were leading families among Germanic tribes. Beginning in the eleventh century, knights in the service of higher nobles or kings began to claim noble status. Although nobles were only a small fraction of the total population, the noble class grew larger and more diverse, ranging from poor knights who held tiny pieces of land (or sometimes none at all) to dukes and counts with vast territories.

chivalry Code of conduct in which fighting to defend the Christian faith and protecting one's countrymen were declared to have a sacred purpose.

Originally, most knights focused solely on military skills, but around 1200 there emerged a different ideal of knighthood, usually termed **chivalry** (SHIH-vuhl-ree). Chivalry was a code of conduct in which fighting to defend the Christian faith and protecting one's countrymen were declared to have a sacred purpose. Other qualities gradually became part of chivalry: bravery, generosity, honor, graciousness, mercy, and

Saint Maurice This sandstone statue from Magdeburg Cathedral, carved around 1250, shows the warrior Saint Maurice. Some of the individuals who were held up to young men as models of ideal chivalry were probably real, but their lives were embellished with many stories. One example was Saint Maurice (d. 287), a soldier from Thebes in Egypt apparently executed by the Romans for refusing to renounce his Christian faith. He first emerges in the Carolingian period, and later he was held up as a model knight and declared a patron of the Holy Roman Empire and protector of the imperial army in wars against the pagan Slavs. His image was used on coins, and his cult was promoted by the archbishops of Magdeburg, who moved his relics to their cathedral. This statue is the first surviving portrayal of him as a black man, which became common in Germany until the late sixteenth century, although elsewhere he continued to be depicted as light skinned. He was (and, in some cases, still is) the patron saint of several military orders, including the Order of Saint Maurice of the National Infantry Association in the United States, and so his role as a model soldier lives on. (Markus Hilbich/akg-images)

eventually gallantry toward women, which came to be called "courtly love." The chivalric ideal created a new standard of masculinity for nobles, in which loyalty and honor remained the most important qualities, but graceful dancing and intelligent conversation were not considered unmanly.

Training, Marriage, and Inheritance

For children of aristocratic birth, the years from infancy to around the age of seven or eight were primarily years of play. At about the age of seven, a boy of the noble class who was not intended for the church was placed in the household of one of his father's friends or relatives. There he became a servant to the lord and received formal training in arms. The boy learned to ride and to manage a horse. He had to acquire skill in wielding a sword, hurling a lance, shooting with a bow and arrow, and caring for armor and other equipment. Increasingly, noble youths learned to read and write some Latin. Formal training was concluded around the age of twenty-one, often with the ceremony of knighthood.

The ceremony of knighthood did not necessarily mean attainment of adulthood, power, and responsibility. Sons were completely dependent on their fathers for support. A young man remained a youth until he was in a financial position to marry—that is, until his father died. That might not happen until he was in his late thirties, and marriage at forty was not uncommon. Increasingly, families adopted primogeniture, with property passing to the oldest son. Younger sons might be forced into the clergy or simply forbidden to marry.

Once knighted, the young man traveled for two to three years. His father selected a group of friends to accompany, guide, and protect him. If the young knight and his companions did not depart on a crusade, they hunted, meddled in local conflicts, and did the tournament circuit. The tournament, in which a number of men competed from horseback (in contrast to the joust, which involved only two competitors), gave the young knight experience in pitched battle and a way to show off his masculinity before an audience. Since the horses and equipment of the vanquished were forfeited to the victors, the knight could also gain a profit. Everywhere they went, young knights stirred up trouble, for chivalric ideals of honorable valor and gallant masculinity rarely served as a check on actual behavior.

While noble girls were also trained in preparation for their future tasks, that training was quite different. They were often taught to read the local language and perhaps some Latin and to write and do enough arithmetic to keep household accounts. They also learned music, dancing, and embroidery and how to ride and hunt, both common noble pursuits. Much of this took place in the girl's own home, but, like boys, noble girls were often sent to the homes of relatives or higher nobles to act as servants or ladies in waiting or to learn how to run a household.

Parents often wanted to settle daughters' futures as soon as possible. Men tended to prefer young brides who would have more years to produce children. Therefore, aristocratic girls in the High Middle Ages were married at around the age of sixteen, often to much older men. In the early Middle Ages the custom was for the groom to present a dowry to the bride and her family, but by the late twelfth century the process was reversed because men were in greater demand. Thereafter, the sizes of dowries offered by brides and their families rose higher and higher.

Power and Responsibility

A male member of the nobility became fully adult when he came into the possession of property. He then acquired authority over lands and people, protecting them from attack, maintaining order, and settling disputes. With this authority went responsibility. In the words of Honorius of Autun:

> Soldiers: You are the arm of the Church, because you should defend it against its enemies. Your duty is to aid the oppressed, to restrain yourself from rapine and fornication, to repress those who impugn the Church with evil acts, and to resist those who are rebels against priests. Performing such a service, you will obtain the most splendid of benefices from the greatest of Kings.[5]

Nobles rarely lived up to this ideal, however, and there are countless examples of nobles' stealing church lands instead of defending them, tyrannizing the oppressed rather than aiding them, and regularly engaging in "rapine and fornication" rather than resisting them.

Women played a large and important role in the functioning of the estate. They were responsible for the practical management of the household's "inner economy" — cooking, brewing, spinning, weaving, caring for yard animals. When the lord was

Female Donor in Chartres Cathedral Windows   Nobles and other wealthy people who paid for stained-glass windows often had their portraits included. In the south transept of Chartres Cathedral at the foot of the prophet Isaiah is the portrait of Alix of Thouars, hereditary duchess of Brittany. The windows were made in 1221–1230, right after Alix's death in childbirth, and were donated by her husband, who is also shown in one of the windows; the remaining windows show their son and daughter, though as young adults rather than as the small children they would have been at the time the windows were made. (Chartres Cathedral, Chartres, France/Bridgeman Images) away for long periods, the women frequently managed the herds, barns, granaries, and outlying fields as well. Often the responsibilities of the estate fell to them permanently, as the number of men slain in medieval warfare ran high.

Throughout the High Middle Ages, fighting remained the dominant feature of the noble lifestyle. The church's preaching and condemnations reduced but did not stop violence, and the military values of the nobles' social class encouraged petty warfare and disorder. The nobility thus represented a constant source of trouble for the monarchy.

The Papacy

Kings and emperors were not the only rulers consolidating their power in the High Middle Ages; popes did so as well, through a series of measures that made the church more independent of secular control. In the ninth and tenth centuries secular lords like Otto I controlled the appointment of church officials. Popes and bishops were appointed to advance the political ambitions of their own families rather than for special spiritual qualifications. Under the leadership of a series of reforming popes in the eleventh century, the church tried to end this practice, but the popes' efforts were sometimes challenged by medieval kings and emperors, and the wealth of the church came under sharp criticism.

FOCUS QUESTION
How did the papacy reform the church, and what were the reactions to these efforts?

The Gregorian Reforms

During the ninth and tenth centuries the local church had come under the control of kings and feudal lords, who chose priests and bishops in their territories, granting them land and expecting loyalty and service in return. Church offices from village priest to pope were sources of income as well as positions of authority. Officeholders had the right to collect taxes and fees and often the profits from the land under their control. Church offices were thus sometimes sold outright—a practice called **simony** (SIGH-muh-nee). Not surprisingly, clergy at all levels who had bought their positions or had been granted them for political reasons provided little spiritual guidance, and their personal lives were rarely models of high moral standards. Although the Roman Church officially required men to be unmarried in order to be ordained, there were many married priests and others simply living with women. Popes were chosen by wealthy Roman families from among their members, and after gaining the papal office, they paid more attention to their families' political fortunes than to the health of the church.

simony The buying and selling of church offices, a policy that was officially prohibited but often practiced.

Serious efforts to change all this began under Pope Leo IX (pontificate 1049–1054). Leo ordered clergy in Rome to dismiss their wives and invalidated the ordination of church officials who had purchased their offices. Pope Leo and several of his successors believed that secular or lay control over the church was largely responsible for its lack of moral leadership, so in a radical shift they proclaimed the church independent of secular rulers. The Lateran Council of 1059 decreed that the authority and power to elect the pope rested solely in the **college of cardinals**, a special group of priests from the major churches in and around Rome. The college retains that power today, though the membership has grown and become international.

college of cardinals A special group of high clergy with the authority and power to elect the pope and the responsibility to govern the church when the office of the pope is vacant.

Leo's successor Pope Gregory VII (pontificate 1073–1085) was even more vigorous in his championing of reform and expansion of papal power; for that reason,

excommunication
A penalty used by the Christian Church that meant being cut off from the sacraments and all Christian worship.

the eleventh-century movement is frequently called the "Gregorian reform movement." He denounced clerical marriage and simony in harsh language and ordered **excommunication** (being cut off from the sacraments and all Christian worship) for those who disagreed. He believed that the pope, as the successor of Saint Peter, was the vicar of God on earth and that papal orders were thus the orders of God. Gregory was particularly opposed to lay investiture—the selection and appointment of church officials by secular authority. In February 1075 he held a council at Rome that decreed that clerics who accepted investiture from laymen were to be deposed and laymen who invested clerics were to be excommunicated.

In the late eleventh century and throughout the twelfth and thirteenth, the papacy pressed Gregory's campaign for reform of the church. The popes held a series of councils, known as the Lateran Councils, that ratified decisions ending lay investiture, ordered bishops to live less extravagantly, and ordered married priests to give up their wives and children or face dismissal. Most church officials apparently obeyed, though we have little information on what happened to the families. In other reforms, marriage was defined as a sacrament—a ceremony that provided visible evidence of God's grace—and divorce was forbidden.

Gregory's reforms had a profound effect on nuns and other women in religious orders. The movement built a strict hierarchical church structure with bishops and priests higher in status than nuns, who could not be ordained. The double monasteries of the early Middle Ages were placed under the authority of male abbots. Church councils forbade monks and nuns to sing church services together and ordered priests to limit their visits to convents. The reformers' emphasis on clerical celibacy and chastity led them to portray women as impure and lustful. Thus, in 1298 in the papal decree *Periculoso*, Pope Boniface VIII ordered all nuns to be strictly cloistered, that is, to remain permanently inside the walls of the convent, and for visits with people from outside the house, including family members, to be limited. *Periculoso* was not enforced everywhere, but it did mean that convents became more cut off from medieval society than monasteries were.

Emperor Versus Pope

Gregory thought that the threat of excommunication would compel rulers to abide by his move against lay investiture. Immediately, however, Henry IV in the Holy Roman Empire, William the Conqueror in England, and Philip I in France protested, as the reform would deprive them not only of church income but also of the right to choose which monks and clerics would help them administer their kingdoms. The strongest reaction came from the Holy Roman Empire. Pope Gregory accused Henry IV of lack of respect for the papacy and insisted that disobedience to the pope was disobedience to God. Henry argued that Gregory's type of reform undermined royal authority. Within the empire, religious and secular leaders took sides to pursue their own advantage. In January 1076 many of the German bishops who had been invested by Henry withdrew their allegiance from the pope. Gregory promptly suspended them and excommunicated Henry. The pope told German nobles they no longer owed allegiance to Henry, which obviously delighted them. When powerful nobles invited the pope to come to Germany to settle their dispute with Henry, Gregory traveled to the north. Christmas of 1076 thus witnessed an ironic situation in Germany: the clergy supported the emperor while the great nobility favored the pope.

Henry managed to outwit the pope temporarily. In January 1077 he approached the castle of Countess Matilda of Tuscany (ca. 1046–1115) at Canossa in the Apennines (AH-puh-nighnz), where the pope was staying. According to a letter later sent by Gregory to his German noble allies, Henry stood for three days in the snow, imploring the pope to lift the excommunication. Henry's pleas for forgiveness won him public sympathy, and the pope readmitted the emperor to the Christian community. When the sentence of excommunication was lifted, however, Henry regained the emperorship and authority over his rebellious subjects, but continued his moves against papal power. In 1080 Gregory again excommunicated and deposed the emperor. In return, when Gregory died in 1085, Henry invaded Italy and captured Rome. But Henry won no lasting victory. Gregory's successors encouraged Henry's sons to revolt against their father.

Finally, in 1122 at a conference held at Worms, the issue was settled by compromise. Bishops were to be chosen by the clergy. But since lay rulers were permitted to be present at ecclesiastical elections and to accept or refuse homage from the new prelates, they still possessed an effective veto over ecclesiastical appointments. Papal power was enhanced, but neither side won a clear victory.

The long controversy over lay investiture had tremendous social and political consequences in Germany. The lengthy struggle between papacy and emperor allowed emerging noble dynasties to enhance their position. To control their lands, the great lords built castles, symbolizing their increased power and growing independence. When the papal-imperial conflict ended in 1122, the nobility held the balance of power in Germany, and later German kings, such as Frederick Barbarossa, would fail in their efforts to strengthen the monarchy. For these reasons, division and local independence characterized the Holy Roman Empire in the High Middle Ages.

Criticism and Heresy

The Gregorian reform movement contributed to dissatisfaction with the church among townspeople as well as monarchs. Papal moves against simony, for example, led to widespread concern about the role of money in the church just as papal tax collectors were becoming more efficient and sophisticated. Papal efforts to improve the sexual morality of the clergy led some laypersons to assume they could, and indeed should, remove priests for any type of immorality.

Criticism of the church emerged in many places but found its largest audience in the cities, where the contrast between wealth and poverty could be seen more acutely. In northern Italian towns, the monk Arnold of Brescia (BREH-shah) (ca. 1090–1155), a vigorous advocate of strict clerical poverty, denounced clerical wealth. In France, Peter Waldo (ca. 1140–ca. 1218), a rich merchant of the city of Lyons, gave his money to the poor and preached that only prayers, not sacraments, were needed for salvation. The Waldensians (wawl-DEHN-shuhnz)—as Peter's followers were called—bitterly attacked the sacraments and church hierarchy, and they carried these ideas across Europe. In the towns and cities of southern France, the Albigensians (al-buh-JEHN-see-uhns), also known as the Cathars, used the teachings of Jesus about the evils of material goods to call for the church to give up its property. They asserted that the material world was created not by the good God of the New Testament, but by a different evil God of the Old Testament. People who rejected worldly things, not wealthy bishops or the papacy, should be the religious leaders.

Critical of the clergy and spiritually unfulfilled, townspeople joined the Waldensians and the Albigensians. The papacy denounced supporters of both movements as heretics and began extensive campaigns to wipe them out. In 1208 Pope Innocent III proclaimed a crusade against the Albigensians, and the French monarchy and northern French knights willingly joined in, eager to gain the lands and wealth of southern French cities. After years of fighting, the leaders agreed to terms of peace, which left the French monarchy the primary beneficiary. Later popes sent inquisitors with the power to seek out and eliminate the remaining heretics.

The Popes and Church Law

Pope Urban II laid the foundations for the papal monarchy by reorganizing the papal *curia* (the central government of the Roman Church) and recognizing the college of cardinals as a definite consultative body. The papal curia had its greatest impact as a court of law. As the highest ecclesiastical tribunal, it formulated church law, termed **canon law**. The church developed a system of courts separate from those of secular rulers that handled disputes over church property and ecclesiastical elections and especially questions of marriage and annulment. Most of the popes in the twelfth and thirteenth centuries were canon lawyers who expanded the authority of church courts.

The most famous of the lawyer-popes was Innocent III (pontificate 1198–1216), who became the most powerful pope in history. During his pontificate the church in Rome declared itself to be supreme, united, and "catholic" (worldwide), responsible for the earthly well-being as well as the eternal salvation of Christians everywhere. Innocent pushed the kings of Europe to do his will, compelling King Philip Augustus of France to take back his wife, Ingeborg of Denmark, and King John of England to accept as archbishop of Canterbury a man John did not want.

Innocent called the Fourth Lateran Council in 1215, which affirmed the idea that ordained priests had the power to transform bread and wine during church ceremonies into the body and blood of Christ (a change termed transubstantiation). According to papal doctrine, priests now had the power to mediate for everyone with God, setting the spiritual hierarchy of the church above the secular hierarchies of kings and other rulers. The council affirmed that Christians should confess their sins to a priest at least once a year, and that marriage was a sacrament, and thus indissoluble. It also ordered Jews and Muslims to wear special clothing that set them apart from Christians.

By the early thirteenth century papal efforts at reform begun more than a century earlier had

canon law
Church law, which had its own courts and procedures.

Bishop Ending a Marriage   In this thirteenth-century illumination from a legal manual, a bishop ends a marriage. Marriage was first declared a sacrament by officials in the Catholic Church in the late eleventh century as part of the condemnation of the Cathars, and confirmed as such at the Fourth Lateran Council. Because of this, divorce was prohibited, although marriages could be annulled — that is, declared never to have been valid in the first place — for a variety of reasons, and annulments did occur, particularly for members of the nobility. (Illustration on vellum from *Digeste*, 13th century/Bibliothèque Sainte-Geneviève, Paris, France/Archives Charmet/Bridgeman Images)

Pope Boniface VIII, *Unam Sanctam*

In late 1302, after several years of bitter conflict with King Philip IV of France over control and taxation of the clergy in France, Pope Boniface VIII issued a papal bull declaring the official church position on the proper relationships between church and state. Throughout, the pope uses the "royal we," that is, the plural "we" instead of "I" when talking about himself.

~

We are obliged by the faith to believe and hold—and we do firmly believe and sincerely confess—that there is one Holy Catholic and Apostolic Church, and that outside this Church there is neither salvation nor remission of sins. . . . In which Church there is "one Lord, one faith, one baptism." . . . Of this one and only Church there is one body and one head—not two heads, like a monster—namely Christ, and Christ's vicar is Peter, and Peter's successor, for the Lord said to Peter himself, "Feed my sheep." "My sheep" He said in general, not these or those sheep; wherefore He is understood to have committed them all to him. . . .

And we learn from the words of the Gospel that in this Church and in her power are two swords, the spiritual and the temporal. . . . Truly he who denies that the temporal sword is in the power of Peter, misunderstands the words of the Lord, "Put up thy sword into the sheath." Both are in the power of the Church, the spiritual sword and the material. But the latter is to be used for the Church, the former by her; the former by the priest, the latter by kings and captains but at the will and by the permission of the

priest. The one sword, then, should be under the other, and temporal authority subject to spiritual. . . .

If, therefore, the earthly power err, it shall be judged by the spiritual power; and if a lesser power err, it shall be judged by a greater. But if the supreme power [the papacy] err, it can only be judged by God, not by man. . . . For this authority, although given to a man and exercised by a man, is not human, but rather divine, given at God's mouth to Peter and established on a rock for him and his successors in Him whom he confessed, the Lord saying to Peter himself, "Whatsoever thou shalt bind," etc. Whoever therefore resists this power thus ordained of God, resists the ordinance of God. . . . Furthermore, we declare, state, define, and pronounce that it is altogether necessary to salvation for every human creature to be subject to the Roman pontiff.

EVALUATE THE EVIDENCE

1. According to Pope Boniface, what is the proper relationship between the authority of the pope and the authority of earthly rulers? What is the basis for that relationship?
2. How might the earlier conflicts between popes and secular rulers traced in this chapter have influenced Boniface's declaration?

Source: Henry Bettenson, ed., *Documents of the Christian Church* (Oxford: Oxford University Press, 1963), 385w from pp. 115–116. Used by permission of Oxford University Press.

attained phenomenal success, and the popes ruled a powerful, centralized institution. At the end of the century, however, the papacy again came into a violent dispute with secular rulers. Pope Boniface VIII (pontificate 1294–1303), arguing from precedent, insisted that King Edward I of England and Philip IV of France obtain his consent for taxes they had imposed on the clergy. Edward immediately denied the clergy the protection of the law, and Philip halted the shipment of all ecclesiastical revenue to Rome. Boniface had to back down.

The battle for power between the papacy and the French monarchy became a bitter war of propaganda, with Philip at one point calling the pope a heretic. Finally, in 1302, in a formal written statement known as a papal bull, Boniface insisted that all Christians—including kings—were subject to the pope. (See "Evaluating the Evidence 9.2: Pope Boniface VIII, *Unam Sanctam*," above.) Philip maintained that he was completely sovereign in his kingdom and responsible to God alone. French mercenary troops assaulted and arrested the aged pope at Anagni in Italy. Although Boniface was soon freed, he died shortly afterward. The confrontation at Anagni foreshadowed further difficulties in the Christian Church in the fourteenth century.

Monks, Nuns, and Friars

FOCUS QUESTION
What roles did monks, nuns, and friars play in medieval society?

While the reforming popes transformed the Christian Church into an institution free of lay control at the highest level, leaders of monasteries and convents asserted their independence from secular control on the local level as well. Monks, nuns, and friars played significant roles in medieval society, both as individuals and as members of institutions. Medieval people believed that monks and nuns performed an important social service when they prayed, for their prayers and chants secured God's blessing for society. The friars worked in the cities, teaching and preaching Christian doctrine, but also investigating heretics.

Monastic Revival

In the early Middle Ages many religious houses followed the Benedictine *Rule*, while others developed their own patterns (see Chapter 7). In the High Middle Ages this diversity became more formalized, and **religious orders**, groups of monastic houses following a particular rule, were established. Historians term the foundation, strengthening, and reform of religious orders in the High Middle Ages the "monastic revival."

religious orders Groups of monastic houses following a particular rule.

In Carolingian times, the best Benedictine monasteries had been centers of learning, copying and preserving manuscripts, maintaining schools, and setting high standards of monastic observance. In the period of political disorder that followed the disintegration of the Carolingian Empire, many religious houses fell under the control and domination of local lords. Powerful laymen appointed themselves or their relatives as abbots, took the lands and goods of monasteries, and seized monastic revenues. Accordingly, the level of spiritual observance and intellectual activity in monasteries and convents declined. The local lords also compelled abbots from time to time to provide contingents of soldiers, an obligation stemming from the abbots' judicial authority over knights and peasants on monastic lands. The conflict between an abbot's religious duties on the one hand and his judicial and military obligations on the other posed a serious dilemma.

The first sign of reform came in 909, when William the Pious, duke of Aquitaine, established the abbey of Cluny in Burgundy. Duke William declared that the monastery was to be free from any feudal responsibilities to him or any other lord, its members subordinate only to the pope. The monastery at Cluny, which initially held high standards of religious behavior, came to exert vast religious influence. In the eleventh century Cluny was fortunate in having a series of highly able abbots who ruled for a long time. In a disorderly world, Cluny gradually came to represent stability. Therefore, laypersons placed lands under its custody and monastic priories under its jurisdiction (a priory is a religious house, with generally fewer residents than an abbey, governed by a prior or prioress). In this way, hundreds of religious houses, primarily in France and Spain, came under Cluny's authority.

Deeply impressed laypeople showered gifts on monasteries with good reputations, such as Cluny and its many daughter houses. But as the monasteries became richer, the lifestyle of the monks grew increasingly luxurious. Monastic observance and spiritual fervor declined. Soon fresh demands for reform were heard, resulting in the founding of new religious orders in the late eleventh and early twelfth centuries.

The Cistercians (sihs-TUHR-shuhnz) best represent the new reforming spirit because of their phenomenal expansion and great economic, political, and spiritual influence. In 1098 a group of monks left the rich abbey of Molesmes in Burgundy and founded a new house in the swampy forest of Cîteaux (see-TOH). They planned to avoid all involvement with secular society and decided to accept only uncultivated lands far from regular habitation. The early Cistercians (the word is derived from Cîteaux) determined to keep their services simple and their lives austere, returning to work in the fields and other sorts of manual labor. As with Cluny, their high ideals made them a model, and 525 Cistercian monasteries were founded in the course of the twelfth century all over Europe. The Cistercians' influence on European society was profound, for they used new agricultural methods and technology and spread them throughout Europe. Their improvements in farming and animal raising brought wealth, however, and wealth brought power. By the later twelfth century, as with Cluny earlier, economic prosperity and political power had begun to compromise the original Cistercian ideals.

Life in Convents and Monasteries

Medieval monasteries were religious institutions whose organization and structure fulfilled the social needs of the nobility. The monasteries provided noble boys with education and opportunities for ecclesiastical careers. Although a few men who rose in the ranks of church officials were of humble origins, most were from high-status families. Many had been given to the monastery by their parents. Beginning in the thirteenth century an increasing number of boys and men from professional and merchant families became monks, seeking to take advantage of the opportunities monasteries offered.

Throughout the Middle Ages social class also defined the kinds of religious life open to women. Kings and nobles usually established convents for their daughters, sisters, aunts, or aging mothers, and other women of their class. Like monks, many nuns came into the convent as children, and very often sisters, cousins, aunts, and nieces could all be found in the same place. Thus, though nuns were to some degree cut off from their families by being cloistered, family relationships were maintained within the convent.

The office of abbess or prioress was the most powerful position a woman could hold in medieval society. (See "Individuals in Society: Hildegard of Bingen," page 272.) Abbesses were part of the political structure in the same way that bishops and abbots were, with manors under their financial and legal control. They appointed tax collectors, bailiffs, judges, and often priests in their lands. Some abbesses in the Holy Roman Empire even had the right to name bishops and send representatives to imperial assemblies. Abbesses also opened and supported hospitals, orphanages, and schools and hired builders, sculptors, and painters to construct and decorate residences and churches.

Monasteries for men were headed by an abbot or a prior, who was generally a member of a noble family, often a younger son in a family with several. The main

INDIVIDUALS IN SOCIETY

Hildegard of Bingen

The tenth child of a lesser noble family, Hildegard (1098–1179) was given as a child to an abbey in the Rhineland when she was eight years old; there she learned Latin and received a good education. She spent most of her life in various women's religious communities, two of which she founded herself. When she was a child, she began having mystical visions, often of light in the sky, but told few people about them. In middle age, however, her visions became more dramatic: "And it came to pass . . . when I was 42 years and 7 months old, that the heavens were opened and a blinding light of exceptional brilliance flowed through my entire brain. And so it kindled my whole heart and breast like a flame, not burning but warming . . . and suddenly I understood of the meaning of expositions of the books."* She wanted the church to approve of her visions and wrote first to Bernard of Clairvaux, who answered her briefly and dismissively, and then to Pope Eugenius, who encouraged her to write them down. Her first work was *Scivias* (Know the Ways of the Lord), a record of her mystical visions that incorporates vast theological learning.

Possessed of leadership and administrative talents, Hildegard left her abbey in 1147 to found the convent of Rupertsberg near Bingen. There she produced *Physica* (On the Physical Elements) and *Causa et Curae* (Causes and Cures), scientific works on the curative properties of natural elements, as well as poems, a mystery play, and several more works of mysticism. She carried on a huge correspondence with scholars, prelates, and ordinary people. When she was over fifty, she left her community to preach to audiences of clergy and laity, and she was the only woman of her time whose opinions on religious matters were considered authoritative by the church.

Hildegard's visions have been explored by theologians and also by neurologists, who judge that they may have originated in migraine headaches, as she reports many of the same phenomena that migraine sufferers do: auras of light around objects, areas of blindness, feelings of intense doubt and intense euphoria. The interpretations that she develops come from her theological insight and learning, however, not illness. That same insight also emerges in her music, for which she is best known today. Eighty of her compositions survive—a huge number for a medieval composer—most of them written to be sung by the nuns in her convent, so they have strong lines for female voices. Many of her songs and chants have been recorded and are available on CD, as downloads, and on several Web sites.

Inspired by heavenly fire, Hildegard begins to dictate her visions to her scribe. The original of this elaborately illustrated twelfth-century copy of *Scivias* disappeared from Hildegard's convent during World War II, but fortunately a facsimile copy had already been made. (Private Collection/Bridgeman)

QUESTIONS FOR ANALYSIS

1. Why do you think Hildegard sought church approval for her visions after keeping them secret for so many years?
2. In what ways is Hildegard's life representative of nuns' lives in the High Middle Ages? In what ways were her accomplishments extraordinary?

*From *Scivias*, trans. Mother Columba Hart and Jane Bishop, *The Classics of Western Spirituality* (New York/Mahwah: Paulist Press, 1990), p. 65.

Saint Francis Gives Up His Worldly Possessions

After Francis had given money to a church, his wealthy father ordered Francis to give him back the money. Francis instead took off all his clothes and returned them to his father, signifying his dependence on his father in Heaven rather than his earthly father. The fresco of this event, painted seventy years after Francis's death for the church erected in his honor in Assisi, captures the consternation of Francis's father and the confusion of the local bishop (holding the cloth in front of the naked Francis), who had told the young man to obey his earthly father. By the time the church was built, members of the Franciscan order were in violent disagreement over what Francis would have thought about a huge church built in his honor and other issues of clerical wealth. (Fresco by Giotto di Bondone [ca. 1266–1337]/San Francesco, Upper Church, Assisi, Italy/ Bridgeman Images)

body of monks, known as "choir monks" because one of their primary activities was reciting prayers and services while sitting in the part of the church called the choir, were largely of noble or middle-class background, and they did not till the land themselves. Men from peasant families sometimes became choir monks, but more often they served as lay brothers, doing the manual labor essential to running the monastery. The novice master or novice mistress was responsible for the training of recruits. The efficient operation of a monastic house also required the services of cooks, laundresses, gardeners, seamstresses, mechanics, blacksmiths, pharmacists, and others whose essential work has left, unfortunately, little written trace.

The pattern of life within individual monasteries varied widely from house to house and from region to region. One central activity, however, was performed everywhere. Daily life centered on the liturgy or Divine Office, psalms and other prayers prescribed by Saint Benedict that monks and nuns prayed seven times a day and once during the night. Prayers were offered for peace, rain, good harvests, the civil authorities, and the monks' families and benefactors. Everything connected with prayer was understood as praise of God, so abbeys spent a large percentage of their income on splendid objects to enhance the service, including sacred vessels of embossed silver or gold, altar cloths of the finest silks or velvets, embroideries, and beautiful reliquaries to house the relics of the patron saint.

In some abbeys monks and nuns spent much of their time copying books and manuscripts and then illuminating them, decorating them with human and animal figures or elaborate designs, often painted in bright colors or gold. A few monasteries and convents became centers of learning where talented residents wrote their own works as well as copying those of others.

Monks and nuns also performed a variety of social services in an age when there was no state and no conception of social welfare as a public responsibility. Monasteries often ran schools that gave primary education to young boys; convents did the same for girls. Monasteries served as hotels and resting places for travelers, and frequently operated hospitals and leprosariums, which provided care and attention to the sick, the aged, and the afflicted.

The Friars

friars Men belonging to certain religious orders who lived not in monasteries but out in the world.

Monks and nuns carried out their spiritual and social services largely within the walls of their institutions, but in the thirteenth century new types of religious orders were founded whose members lived out in the world. Members of these new groups were **friars**, not monks. They thought that more contact with ordinary Christians, not less, was a better spiritual path. Friars stressed apostolic poverty, a life based on the teaching of the Gospels in which they would own no property and depend on Christian people for their material needs. Hence they were called mendicants, from the Latin word for begging. The friars' service to the towns and the poor, their ideal of poverty, and their compassion for the human condition made them popular.

One order of friars was started by Domingo de Gúzman (1170?–1221), born in Castile. Domingo (later called Dominic), a well-educated priest, accompanied his bishop in 1206 on an unsuccessful mission to win the Albigensians in southern France back to orthodox teaching. Determined to succeed through ardent preaching, he subsequently returned to France with a few followers. In 1216 the group—officially known as the Preaching Friars, though often called Dominicans—won papal recognition as a new religious order.

Francesco di Bernardone (1181–1226), son of a wealthy Italian cloth merchant of Assisi, had a religious conversion and decided to live and preach the Gospel in absolute poverty. Francis of Assisi, as he came to be known, emphasized not withdrawal from the world, but joyful devotion. In contrast to the Albigensians, who saw the material world as evil, Francis saw all creation as God-given and good. He was widely reported to perform miracles involving animals and birds, and wrote hymns to natural objects. "Be praised, my Lord, through our sister Mother Earth" went one, "who feeds us and rules us and produces various fruits with colored flowers and herbs." This song also praises the sun, wind, air, water, and fire, and it was one of the first religious works ever written in a vernacular dialect. It also provides an example of how Franciscans and other friars used music to convey religious teachings. (See "Evaluating the Evidence 9.3: Brother Henry as Composer and Singer," at right.)

The simplicity, humility, and joyful devotion with which Francis carried out his mission soon attracted others. Although he resisted pressure to establish an order, his followers became so numerous that he was obliged to develop some formal structure. In 1221 the papacy approved the Rule of the Little Brothers of Saint Francis, generally called the Franciscans (frahn-SIHS-kuhnz).

Friars worked among the poor, but also addressed the spiritual and intellectual needs of the middle classes and the wealthy. The Dominicans preferred that their friars be university graduates in order to better preach to a sophisticated urban society. Dominicans soon held professorial chairs at leading universities, and the Franciscans followed suit.

Beginning in 1231 the papacy also used friars to investigate heretics, sometimes under the auspices of a new ecclesiastical court, the Inquisition, in which accused

Brother Henry as Composer and Singer

Toward the end of his life, the Italian Franciscan friar Salimbene of Parma (1221–ca. 1290) wrote a chronicle that includes character sketches of many people he had met. Salimbene traveled widely throughout Italy and France, meeting both important figures such as Emperor Frederick II and less well-known folk such as the fellow Franciscan he describes here.

~

Brother Henry of Pisa was a handsome man, of medium height, generous, amiable, charitable, and merry. He knew how to get along well with everyone, . . . adapting himself to the personality of each one, and he won the love of his own brethren as well as that of the laymen, which is given to few. Moreover, he was a celebrated preacher, beloved by both the clergy and the laity. He knew how to write beautifully, and to paint, which some call illuminate, to write music, and to compose the sweetest and loveliest songs, both in harmony and in plain song. He himself was an excellent singer, and had a strong and sonorous voice, so that it filled the whole choir. And his treble sounded light, very high and clear, but sweet, lovely, and pleasing beyond measure. . . .

That Brother Henry of Pisa was a man of admirable manners, devoted to God and to the Holy Virgin, and to the Blessed Magdalene. No wonder, for the church of his quarter of Pisa bore the name of this saint; the cathedral of the city, in which he had been ordained by the archbishop of Pisa, bore the name of the Blessed Virgin. Brother Henry composed many *cantilena* and many sequences, for example, the words and melody of the following song:

> O Christ, my God,
> O Christ, my Refuge
> O Christ, King and Lord,

[which he patterned] after the song of a maid who was going through the cathedral church of Pisa, singing in the popular tongue:

> If thou carest not for me,
> I'll no longer care for thee.

He made, moreover, the three-part song: "Wretched man, think thou on thy Creator's works!" . . .

He composed a noble melody to the sequence: "He had watered the tree of Jesse," which until then had had a crude one, discordant for singing. Richard of St. Victor wrote the words of this sequence, as well as those of many others.

EVALUATE THE EVIDENCE

1. What qualities of Brother Henry and his songs does Salimbene find worthy of praise?
2. Friars were active out in the world and did not live in monasteries. How did Brother Henry's position as a friar shape the music he created?

people were subjected to lengthy interrogations and torture could be used to extract confessions. It is ironic that groups whose teachings were similar in so many ways to those of heretics were charged with rooting them out. That irony deepened in the case of the Spiritual Franciscans, a group that broke away from the main body of Franciscans to follow Francis's original ideals of absolute poverty. When they denied the pope's right to countermand that ideal, he ordered them tried as heretics.

Women sought to develop similar orders devoted to active service out in the world. Clare of Assisi (1193–1253) became a follower of Francis, who established a place for her to live in a church in Assisi. She was joined by other women, and they attempted to establish a rule that would follow Francis's ideals of absolute poverty and allow them to serve the poor. This rule was accepted by the papacy only after many decades, and then only because she agreed that the order, the Poor Clares, would be cloistered.

In the growing cities of Europe, especially in the Netherlands, groups of lay-women seeking to live religious lives came together as what later came to be known as Beguines (bay-GEENS). They lived communally in small houses called *beguinages*, combining lives of prayer with service to the needy. Beguine spirituality emphasized direct personal communication with God, sometimes through mystical experiences, rather than through the intercession of a saint or official church rituals. Initially some church officials gave guarded approval of the movement, but the church grew increasingly uncomfortable with women who were neither married nor cloistered nuns. By the fourteenth century Beguines were declared heretical, and much of their property was confiscated.

The Crusades and the Expansion of Christianity

FOCUS QUESTION

What were the causes, course, and consequences of both the Crusades and the broader expansion of Christianity?

The Crusades of the eleventh and twelfth centuries were the most obvious manifestation of the papal claim to the leadership of Christian society. The **Crusades** were wars sponsored by the papacy for the recovery of the holy city of Jerusalem from the Muslims. The enormous popular response to papal calls for crusading reveals the influence of the reformed papacy and the depth of religious fervor among many different types of people. The Crusades also reflected the church's new understanding of the noble warrior class, for whom war against the church's enemies was understood as a religious duty. The word *crusade* was not actually used at the time and did not appear in English until the late sixteenth century. It means literally "taking the cross," from the cross that soldiers sewed on their garments as a Christian symbol. At the time people going off to fight simply said they were taking "the way of the cross" or "the road to Jerusalem."

Crusades Wars sponsored by the papacy for the recovery of Jerusalem and surrounding territories from the Muslims in the late eleventh to the late thirteenth centuries.

Background and Motives of the Crusades

The medieval church's attitude toward violence was contradictory. On the one hand, church councils threatened excommunication for anyone who attacked peasants, clerics, or merchants or destroyed crops and unfortified places, a movement termed the Peace of God. Councils also tried to limit the number of days on which fighting was permitted, prohibiting it on Sundays, on special feast days, and in the seasons of Lent and Advent. On the other hand, popes supported armed conflict against kings and emperors if this worked to their advantage, thus encouraging warfare among Christians. After a serious theological disagreement in 1054 split the Orthodox Church of Byzantium and the Roman Church of the West, the pope also contemplated invading the Byzantine Empire, an idea that subsequent popes considered as well.

Although conflicts in which Christians fought Christians were troubling to many thinkers, war against non-Christians was another matter. By the ninth century popes and other church officials encouraged war in defense of Christianity, promising spiritual benefits to those who died fighting. By the eleventh century these benefits were extended to all those who simply joined a campaign: their sins would be remitted without having to do penance, that is, without having to confess to a priest and carry out some action to make up for the sins. Around this time, Christian thinkers were developing the concept of purgatory, a place where those on their way to Heaven stayed for a while to do any penance they had not completed while alive. (Those on their way to Hell went straight there.) Engaging in holy war could shorten one's time in purgatory, or, as many people understood the promise, allow one to head straight to paradise. Popes signified this by providing **indulgences**, grants with the pope's name on them that lessened earthly penance and postmortem purgatory. Popes promised these spiritual benefits, and also provided financial support, for Christian armies in the reconquista in Spain and the Norman campaign against the Muslims in Sicily. Preachers communicated these ideas widely and told stories about warrior-saints who slew hundreds of enemies.

Religious devotion had long been expressed through pilgrimages to holy places, and these were increasingly described in military terms, as battles against the hardships along the way. Pilgrims to Jerusalem were often armed, so the line between pilgrimage and holy war on this particular route was increasingly blurred. In the midst of these developments came a change in possession of Jerusalem. The Arab Muslims who had ruled Jerusalem and the surrounding territory for centuries had generally allowed Christian pilgrims to travel freely, but in the late eleventh century the Seljuk (SEHL-jook) Turks took over Palestine, defeating both Arab and Byzantine armies and pillaging in Christian and Muslim parts of Asia Minor (Map 9.4). They harassed pilgrims and looted churches, and the emperor at Constantinople appealed to the West for support. The emperor's appeal fit well with papal aims, and in 1095 Pope Urban II called for a great Christian holy war against the infidels—a term Christians and Muslims both used to describe the other. Urban offered indulgences to those who would fight for and regain the holy city of Jerusalem.

The Course of the Crusades

Thousands of Western Christians of all classes joined the First Crusade, which began in 1096. Of all the developments of the High Middle Ages, none better reveals Europeans' religious and emotional fervor and the influence of the reformed papacy than the extraordinary outpouring of support for the First Crusade.

The First Crusade was successful, mostly because of the dynamic enthusiasm of the participants. The Crusaders had little more than religious zeal. They knew nothing about the geography or climate of the Middle East. Although there were several nobles with military experience among them, the Crusaders could never agree on a leader, and the entire expedition was marked by disputes among the great lords. Lines of supply were never set up, and starvation and disease wracked the army. Nevertheless, the army pressed on, defeating the Turks in several land battles and besieging a few larger towns, including Antioch. Finally, in 1099, three years after departing Europe, the Crusaders reached Jerusalem. After a month-long siege they got inside the city, where they slaughtered the Muslim defenders.

In the aftermath of the First Crusade, four small "Crusader kingdoms"—Jerusalem, Edessa, Tripoli, and Antioch—were established. Castles and fortified towns were built to defend against Muslim reconquest (see Map 9.4). Between 1096 and 1270 the crusading ideal was expressed in eight papally approved expeditions, though none after the First Crusade accomplished very much. Despite this lack of success, members of European noble families from nearly every generation took up the cross for roughly two hundred years.

The Crusades inspired the establishment of new religious orders, particularly military orders dedicated to protecting the Christian kingdoms. The most important was the Knights Templars, founded in 1119. Many people going off to the Holy Land put their property in Europe under Templar protection, and by the end of

indulgences Grants by the pope that lessened or eliminated the penance that sinners had to pay on earth and in purgatory before ascending to Heaven.

MAP 9.4 The Crusades   This map shows the many different routes that Western Christians took over the centuries to reach Jerusalem.

the thirteenth century the order was extremely wealthy, with secret rituals in which members pledged obedience to their leaders. The Templars began serving as money-lenders and bankers, which further increased their wealth. In 1307 King Philip IV of France sought to grab that wealth for himself; he arrested many Templars, accusing them of heresy, blasphemy, and sodomy. They were tortured, a number were burned at the stake, Philip took much of their money, and the Templars were disbanded.

Women from all walks of life participated in the Crusades. When King Louis IX of France was captured on the Seventh Crusade (1248–1254), his wife, Queen Marguerite, negotiated the surrender of the Egyptian city of Damietta to the Muslims. Some women concealed their sex by donning chain mail and helmets and fought with the knights. Some joined in the besieging of towns and castles by assisting in filling the moats surrounding fortified places with earth so that ladders and war engines could be brought close. More typically, women provided water to fighting men, a service not to be underestimated in the hot, dry climate of the Middle East. They worked as washerwomen, foraged for food, and provided sexual services. There were many more European men than women, however, so marriage and sexual relations between Christian men and Muslim women were not unheard of, although marriages between Western Christian men and Orthodox Christian women who lived in the area were more common.

The Muslim states in the Middle East were politically fragmented when the Crusaders first came, and it took about a century for them to reorganize. They did so dramatically under Saladin (Salah al-Dihn), who first unified Egypt and Syria, and then retook Jerusalem in 1187. Christians immediately attempted to take it back in what was later called the Third Crusade (1189–1192). Frederick Barbarossa of the Holy Roman Empire, Richard the Lion-Hearted of England, and Philip Augustus of France participated, and the Third Crusade was better financed than the previous two. But disputes among the leaders and strategic problems prevented any lasting results. The Crusaders could not retake Jerusalem, though they did keep their hold on port towns, and Saladin allowed pilgrims safe passage to Jerusalem. He also made an agreement with Christian rulers for keeping the peace. From that point on, the Crusader states were more important economically than politically or religiously, giving Italian and French merchants direct access to Eastern products such as perfumes and silk.

In 1202 Innocent III sent out preachers who called on Christian knights to retake Jerusalem. Those who responded—in what would become the Fourth Crusade—negotiated with the Venetians to take them by boat to Cairo, but Venetian interests combined with a succession struggle over the Byzantine throne led the fleet to go to Constantinople instead. Once there, the Crusaders decided to capture and sack Constantinople, destroying its magnificent library and seizing gold, silver, and relics to send home. The Byzantines reasserted their control over the empire in 1261, but it was much smaller and weaker and soon consisted of little more than the city of Constantinople. Moreover, the assault by one Christian people on another helped discredit the entire crusading movement and obviously had no effect on Muslim control of Jerusalem and other areas.

Nonetheless, there were a few more efforts. The Seventh Crusade in 1248, led by King Louis IX of France (r. 1223–1270), tried unsuccessfully to come in through Egypt. Louis also sent monks to the court of the Mongols in Central Asia, who were at this point led by Chinggis Khan, to forge an alliance that would encircle the Muslims. The monks were unsuccessful, but they brought back geographical knowledge of Asia and the peoples they had encountered. In the end, the Mamluk rulers of Egypt conquered the Crusader states, and in 1291 their last stronghold, the port of Acre, fell. Some knights continued their crusading efforts by joining the reconquista in Spain.

Consequences of the Crusades

The Crusades gave kings and the pope opportunities to expand their bureaucracies. They also provided kings with the perfect opportunity to get rid of troublemaking knights, particularly restless younger sons for whom the practice of primogeniture meant few prospects. Some of them were able to carve out lordships in Palestine, Syria, and Greece. Even some members of the middle class who stayed at home profited from the Crusades. Nobles often had to borrow money from city residents to pay for their expeditions, and they put up part of their land as security. If a noble did not return home or could not pay the interest on the loan, the middle-class creditor took over the land.

The Crusades introduced some Europeans to Eastern luxury goods, but their immediate cultural impact on the West remains debatable. Strong economic and intellectual ties with the East had already been developed by the late eleventh century. The Crusades did greatly benefit Italian merchants, who profited from outfitting military expeditions, the opening of new trade routes, and the establishment of trading communities in the Crusader states. Since commerce with the West benefited both Muslims and Europeans, it continued to flourish even after the Crusader states collapsed.

The Crusades proved to be a disaster for Jewish-Christian relations. In many parts of Europe, Jews lent money to peasants, townspeople, and nobles, and indebtedness bred resentment. Inspired by the ideology of holy war and resentment of Jewish economic activities, Christian armies on their way to Jerusalem on the First Crusade joined with local people to attack Jewish families and sometimes entire Jewish communities. In the German cities along the Rhine River, for example, an army of Crusaders under the leadership of a German noble forced Jews to convert through mass baptisms and killed those who resisted; more than eight hundred Jews were killed in Worms and more than a thousand in Mainz. Later Crusades brought similar violence, enhanced by rumors that Jews engaged in the ritual murder of Christians to use their blood in religious rites. As a result of growing hostility, legal restrictions on Jews gradually increased throughout Europe. In 1290 King Edward I of England expelled the Jews from England and confiscated their property and goods; it would be four centuries before they would be allowed back in. King Philip IV of France followed Edward's example in 1306.

The long-term cultural legacy of the Crusades may have been more powerful than their short-term impact. The ideal of a sacred mission to conquer or convert Muslim peoples entered some Europeans' consciousness, and was later used in other situations. When Christopher Columbus sailed west in 1492, he hoped to reach India in part to establish a Christian base from which a new crusade against Islam could be launched. Muslims later looked back on the Crusades as expansionist and imperialist, the beginning of a long trajectory of Western attempts to limit or destroy Islam.

The Expansion of Christianity

The Crusades were not the only example of Christian expansion in the High Middle Ages. As we saw earlier, Christian kingdoms were established in the Iberian Peninsula through the reconquista. This gradual Christian advance was replicated in northern and eastern Europe in the centuries after 1000. People and ideas moved from western France and western Germany into Ireland, Scandinavia, the Baltic lands, and eastern Europe, with significant consequences for those territories. Wars of expansion, the establishment of new Christian bishoprics, and the vast migration of colonists, together with the papal emphasis on a unified Christian world, brought about the gradual Christianization of a larger area. By 1350 Roman Catholic Europe was double the size it had been in 950.

Ireland had been Christian since the days of Saint Patrick (see Chapter 7), but in the twelfth century Norman knights crossed from England, defeated Irish lords, and established bishoprics with defined territorial dioceses. Latin Christian influences also entered the Scandinavian and Baltic regions primarily through the erection of dioceses. Otto I established the first Scandinavian dioceses in Denmark. In Norway Christianity spread in coastal areas beginning in the tenth century, and King Olaf II (r. 1015–1028) brought in clergy and bishops from England and Germany to establish the church more firmly. From Norway Christianity spread to Iceland; from Denmark it spread to Sweden and Finland. In all of these areas, Christian missionaries preached, baptized, and built churches. Royal power advanced institutional Christianity, and traditional Norse religions practiced by the Vikings were outlawed.

In 1397 Queen Margrete I (1353–1412) united the crowns of Denmark, Sweden-Finland, and Norway in the Union of Kalmar. She continued royal support of bishops and worked toward creating a stronger state by checking the power of the nobility and creating a stronger financial base for the monarchy.

In eastern Europe, the German emperor Otto I planted a string of dioceses along his northern and eastern frontiers, hoping to pacify the newly conquered Slavs. German nobles built castles and ruthlessly crushed revolts by Slavic peoples, sometimes using the language of crusade to describe their actions. Albert the Bear, for example, a German noble, proclaimed a crusade against the Slavs and invited German knights to colonize conquered territories, just as earlier the French king had used French knights to crush the Albigensians. A military order of German knights founded in Palestine, the Teutonic (too-TAH-nihk) Knights, moved their operations to eastern Europe and waged wars against the pagan Prussians in the Baltic region, again terming these "crusades." After 1230, from a base in Poland, they established a new Christian territory, Prussia, and gradually the entire eastern shore of the Baltic came under their hegemony.

The church also moved into central Europe, first in Bohemia in the tenth century and from there into Poland and Hungary in the eleventh. In the twelfth and thirteenth centuries, thousands of settlers poured into eastern Europe. These immigrants were German in descent, name, language, and law. Larger towns such as Kraków and Riga engaged in long-distance trade and gradually grew into large urban centers.

Christendom

Through the actions of the Roman emperors Constantine and Theodosius (see Chapter 7), Christianity became in some ways a state as well as a religion. Early medieval writers began to use the word **Christendom** to refer to this Christian realm. Sometimes notions of Christendom were linked directly to specific states, such as Charlemagne's empire and the Holy Roman Empire. More often, however, Christendom was vague, a sort of loose sense of the body of all people who were Christian. When the pope called for holy war against the Muslims, for example, he spoke not only of the retaking of Jerusalem, but also of the defense of Christendom. When missionaries, officials, and soldiers took Christianity into the Iberian Peninsula, Scandinavia, or the Baltic region, they understood their actions as aimed at the expansion of Christendom.

Christendom The term used by early medieval writers to refer to the realm of Christianity.

From the point of view of popes such as Gregory VII and Innocent III, Christendom was a unified hierarchy with the papacy at the top. They pushed for uniformity of religious worship and campaigned continually for use of the same religious service, the Roman liturgy in Latin, in all countries and places. They forbade vernacular Christian rituals or those that differed in their pattern of worship. Under Innocent III papal directives and papal legates flowed to all parts of Europe. Twelve hundred church officials obediently came to Rome from the borderlands as well as the heartland for the Fourth Lateran Council of 1215.

As we have seen in this chapter, however, not everyone had the same view. Kings and emperors may have accepted the Roman liturgy in their lands, but they had their own ideas of the way power should operate in Christendom, even if this brought them into conflict with the papacy. They remained loyal to Christendom as a concept, but they had a profoundly different idea about how it should be structured and who could best defend it. The battles in the High Middle Ages between popes and kings and between Christians and Muslims were signs of how deeply religion had replaced tribal, political, and ethnic structures as the essence of Western culture.

LOOKING BACK LOOKING AHEAD

The High Middle Ages were a time when kings, emperors, and popes expanded their powers and created financial and legal bureaucracies to support those powers. With political expansion and stability came better communication of information, more uniform legal systems, and early financial institutions. Nobles remained the dominant social group, but as monarchs developed new institutions, their kingdoms began to function more like modern states than disorganized territories. Popes made the church more independent of lay control, established the papal curia and a separate system of canon law, approved new religious orders that provided spiritual and social services, and developed new ways of raising revenue. They supported the expansion of Christianity in southern, northern, and eastern Europe and proclaimed a series of Crusades against Muslims to extend still further the boundaries of a Christendom under their control.

Many of the systems of the High Middle Ages expanded in later centuries and are still in existence today: the financial department of the British government remains the Exchequer; the legal systems of Britain and many former British colonies (including the United States) are based on common law; the pope is still elected by the college of cardinals and assisted by the papal curia; the Roman Catholic, Eastern Orthodox, and Anglican Churches still operate law courts that make rulings based on canon law. These systems also contained the seeds of future problems, however, for wealthier nations could sustain longer wars, independent popes could more easily abuse their power, and leaders who espoused crusading ideology could justify the enslavement or extermination of whole peoples.

Despite the long-lived impact of the growth of centralized political and ecclesiastical power — for good or ill — most people who lived during the high medieval period did not have direct experience of centralized institutions. Kings and popes sent tax collectors, judges, and sometimes soldiers, but they themselves remained far away. For most people, what went on closer to home in their families and local communities was far more important.

Make Connections

Think about the larger developments and continuities within and across chapters.

1. What similarities and differences do you see between the institutions and laws established by medieval rulers and those of Roman and Byzantine emperors (Chapters 6 and 7)?

2. What factors over the centuries enabled the Christian Church to become the most powerful and wealthy institution in Europe, and what problems did this create?

3. How would you compare the privileges and roles of medieval nobles with those of earlier hereditary elites, such as those of ancient Mesopotamia and Egypt (Chapter 1) or the patricians of republican Rome (Chapter 5)?

9 REVIEW & EXPLORE

Review the Main Ideas

Answer the focus questions from each section of the chapter.

- How did monarchs try to centralize political power? (p. 252)
- How did the administration of law evolve in this period? (p. 259)
- What were the roles of nobles, and how did they train for these? (p. 262)
- How did the papacy reform the church, and what were the reactions to these efforts? (p. 265)
- What roles did monks, nuns, and friars play in medieval society? (p. 270)
- What were the causes, course, and consequences of both the Crusades and the broader expansion of Christianity? (p. 276)

Identify Key Terms

Identify and explain the significance of each item below.

Domesday Book (p. 253)
primogeniture (p. 254)
Holy Roman Empire (p. 256)
reconquista (p. 258)
common law (p. 260)
Magna Carta (p. 261)
chivalry (p. 262)
simony (p. 265)
college of cardinals (p. 265)
excommunication (p. 266)
canon law (p. 268)
religious orders (p. 270)
friars (p. 274)
Crusades (p. 276)
indulgences (p. 277)
Christendom (p. 281)

NOTES

1. D. C. Douglas and G. E. Greenaway, eds., *English Historical Documents*, vol. 2 (London: Eyre & Spottiswoode, 1961), p. 853.
2. *Hrosvithae Liber Tertius, a Text with Translation*, ed. and trans. Mary Bernardine Bergman (Covington, Ky.: The Sisters of Saint Benedict, 1943), p. 45.
3. J. Johns, *Arabic Administration in Norman Sicily: The Royal Dīwān* (New York: Cambridge University Press, 2002), p. 293.
4. H. T. Riley, ed., *Memorials of London* (London: Longmans Green, 1868).
5. Honorius of Autun, "Elucidarium sive Dialogus," vol. 172, col. 1148.

IAM CRISTI · VI T

CHAPTER PREVIEW

Village Life
What was village life like in medieval Europe?

Popular Religion
How did religion shape everyday life in the High Middle Ages?

Towns and Economic Revival
What led to Europe's economic growth and reurbanization?

Urban Life
What was life like in medieval cities?

Medieval Universities
How did universities serve the needs of medieval society?

Literature and Architecture
How did literature and architecture express medieval values?

Life in the High Middle Ages
In this detail from a magnificent gold mosaic in the ceiling of the Basilica of Saint Clement in Rome, made in the twelfth century, a woman feeds her chickens. Scenes from everyday life often feature in the margins of paintings, mosaics, and books, and provide information about the lives of ordinary people that is unavailable elsewhere.

(Detail from the mosaic *The Triumph of the Cross*, Basilica of St. Clement, Rome, Italy/De Agostini Picture Library/Gianni Dagli Orti/Bridgeman Images)

10

Life in Villages and Cities of the High Middle Ages

1000–1300

Kings, emperors, nobles, and their officials created political and legal institutions that structured many aspects of life in the High Middle Ages, but ordinary people typically worked and lived without paying much attention to the political developments that took place at faraway centers of power. Similarly, the conflicts between popes and secular leaders were dramatic, but for most people religion was primarily a matter of joining with neighbors and family members in rituals to express beliefs, thanks, and hopes.

While the routines of medieval life followed familiar rhythms for centuries, this does not mean that life in the High Middle Ages was unchanging. Agricultural improvements such as better plows and water mills increased the amount and quality of food, and the population grew. Relative security and the increasing food supply allowed for the growth and development of towns and a revival of long-distance trade. Some urban merchants and bankers became as wealthy as great nobles. Trade brought in new ideas as well as merchandise, and cities developed into intellectual and cultural centers. The university, a new type of educational institution, came into being, providing advanced training in theology, medicine, and law. Traditions and values were spread orally and in written form through poems, stories, and songs. Gothic cathedrals, where people saw beautiful stained-glass windows and listened to complex music, were physical manifestations of medieval people's deep faith and pride in their own community. ■

Village Life

The vast majority of people in medieval Europe were peasants who lived in small villages and rarely traveled very far, but since villagers did not perform what were considered "noble" deeds, the aristocratic monks and clerics who wrote the records that serve as historical sources did not spend time or precious writing materials on the peasantry. When common people were mentioned, it was usually with contempt or in terms of the services and obligations they owed. There were exceptions. In the early twelfth century Honorius, a monk and teacher at the monastery of Autun, wrote: "What do you say about the agricultural classes? Most of them will be saved because they live simply and feed God's people by means of their sweat."[1] Today's scholars are far more interested than were their medieval predecessors in the lives of ordinary people, however, and are using archaeological, artistic, and material sources to fill in details that are rarely mentioned in written documents.

Slavery, Serfdom, and Upward Mobility

Honorius lumps together everyone who worked the land, but in fact there were many levels of peasants ranging from outright slaves to free but poor peasants to very rich farmers. The number of slaves who worked the land declined steadily in the High Middle Ages, and those who remained tended to live with wealthier peasant families or with lords. Most rural people in western Europe during this period were serfs rather than slaves, though the distinction between slave and serf was not always clear. Both lacked freedom and both were subject to the will of one person, the manorial lord. Serfs remained bound to the land when their lords died, but unlike slaves they could not be bought and sold outright.

Most serfs worked small plots of land; in addition, all serfs were required to provide a certain number of days of labor a week—more in planting and harvest seasons—on a lord's land. Serfs were also often obliged to pay fees on common occurrences, such as marriage or the inheritance of land from one generation to the next.

Serfdom was a hereditary condition. A person born a serf was likely to die a serf, though many serfs did secure their freedom. As money became more widely available and widely used, some serfs bought their freedom. Some gained it when manorial lords organized groups of villagers to cut down forests or fill in swamps and marshes to make more land available for farming. A serf could clear a patch of fen or forestland, make it productive, and, through prudent saving, buy more land and eventually purchase freedom. Serfs who migrated longer distances, such as German peasants who moved eastward into Slavic lands, were often granted a reduction in labor services as a reward. Thus both internal and external frontier lands in the High Middle Ages provided some opportunities for upward mobility.

The Manor

Most peasants, free and serf, lived in family groups in small villages. One or more villages and the land surrounding them made up a manor controlled by a noble lord or a church official such as a bishop, abbot, or abbess. Peasant dwellings were clumped together, with the fields stretching out beyond. Most villages had a church. In some the lord's large residence was right next to the small peasant houses, while in others the lord lived in a castle or manor house separate from the village. Manors varied greatly in size; some contained a number of villages, and some were very small.

The arable land of the manor was divided between the lord and the peasantry, with the lord's portion known as the demesne (dih-MAYN), or home farm. The manor usually also held pasture or meadowland for the grazing of cattle, sheep, and sometimes goats and often had some forestland as well. Forests were valuable resources, providing wood, ash, and resin for a variety of purposes. Forests were also used for feeding pigs, cattle, and domestic animals on nuts, roots, and wild berries.

Lords generally appointed officials, such as bailiffs, to oversee the legal and business operations of their manors, collect taxes and fees, and handle disputes. Villages in many parts of Europe also developed institutions of self-government to handle issues such as crop rotation, and villagers themselves chose additional officials such as constables, jurors, and ale-tasters. Women had no official voice in running the village, but they did buy, sell, and hold land independently, especially as widows who headed households. In areas of Europe where men left seasonally or more permanently in search of work elsewhere, women played a larger decision-making role, though they generally did not hold official positions.

Manors did not represent the only form of medieval rural economy. In parts of Germany and the Netherlands and in much of southern France, free independent farmers owned land outright, free of rents and service obligations. In Scandinavia the soil was so poor and the climate so harsh that people tended to live on widely scattered farms rather than in villages.

Work

The peasants' work was typically divided according to gender. Men cleared new land, plowed, and cared for large animals; women cared for small animals, spun yarn, and prepared food. Both sexes planted and harvested, though often there were gender-specific tasks within these major undertakings.

Once children were able to walk, they helped their parents in the hundreds of chores that had to be done. Small children collected eggs if the family had chickens

Chronology

1050–1300	Steady rise in population; period of milder climate
ca. 1100	Merchant guilds become rich and powerful in many cities; artisans begin to found craft guilds
1100s	Hospitals and other homes for the sick begin appearing
1100–1300	Height of construction of cathedrals in Europe
1160s	Silver mines opened in Germany, allowing for more coinage
ca. 1200	Founding of first universities
1215	Fourth Lateran Council orders Jews and Muslims to wear distinctive clothing
1225–1274	Life of Thomas Aquinas; *Summa Theologica*
1241	Contract between Lübeck and Hamburg, first in the Hanseatic League
ca. 1300	Bill of exchange becomes most common method of commercial payment in western Europe
1300s	Clocks in general use throughout Europe

or gathered twigs and sticks for firewood. As they grew older, children had more responsible tasks, such as weeding the family's vegetable garden, milking the cows, and helping with the planting or harvesting.

In many parts of Europe, medieval farmers employed the **open-field system**, a pattern that differs sharply from modern farming practices. In the open-field system, the arable land of a manor was divided into two or three fields without hedges or fences to mark the individual holdings of the lord, serfs, and free men. The village as a whole decided what would be planted in each field, rotating the crops according to tradition and need. Some fields would be planted with crops such as wheat, rye, peas, or barley for human consumption, some with oats or other crops for both animals and humans, and some left unworked or fallow to allow the soil to rejuvenate. In addition, legume crops such as peas and beans helped the soil rebuild nutrients and also increased the villagers' protein consumption. In most areas with open-field agriculture, the holdings farmed by any one family did not consist of a whole field but consisted, instead, of strips in many fields. If one strip held by a family yielded little, those in different fields might be more bountiful. Families worked their own land and the lord's, but also cooperated with other families if they needed help, particularly during harvest time. This meant that all shared in any disaster as well as in any large harvest.

Meteorologists think that a slow but steady retreat of polar ice occurred between the ninth and eleventh centuries, and Europe experienced a significant warming trend from 1050 to 1300. The mild winters and dry summers that resulted helped increase agricultural output throughout Europe, particularly in the north.

The tenth and eleventh centuries also witnessed a number of agricultural improvements, especially in the development of mechanisms that replaced or aided human labor. Mills driven by wind and water power dramatically reduced the time and labor required to grind grain, crush seeds for oil, and carry out other tasks. This change had a significant impact on women's productivity. In the ancient world, slaves had been responsible for grinding the grain for bread; as slavery was replaced by serfdom, grinding became women's work. When water- and wind-driven mills were introduced into an area, women were freed from the task of grinding grain and could turn to other tasks, such as raising animals, working in gardens or vineyards, and raising and preparing flax to make linen. They could also devote more time to spinning yarn, which was the bottleneck in cloth production, as each weaver needed at least six spinners. Thus the spread of wind and water power indirectly contributed to an increase in cloth production in medieval Europe.

Another change, which came in the early twelfth century, was a significant increase in the production of iron. Much of this was used for weapons and armor, but it also filled a growing demand in agriculture. Iron was first used for plowshares (the part of the plow that cuts a deep furrow), and then for pitchforks, spades, and axes. Harrows—cultivating instruments with heavy teeth that broke up and smoothed the soil after plowing—began to have iron instead of wooden teeth, making them more effective and less likely to break. Peasants needed money to buy iron implements from village blacksmiths, and they increasingly also needed money to pay their obligations to their lords. To get the cash they needed, they sold whatever surplus they produced in nearby towns, transporting it there in wagons with iron parts.

open-field system System in which the arable land of a manor was divided into two or three fields without hedges or fences to mark individual holdings.

In central and northern Europe, peasants made increasing use of heavy wheeled iron plows pulled by teams of oxen to break up the rich, clay-filled soil common there, and agricultural productivity increased. Further technological improvements allowed horses to be used for plowing as well as oxen. The development of the padded horse collar that rested on the horse's shoulders and was attached to the load by shafts meant that the animal could put its entire weight into the task of pulling. Iron horseshoes prevented horses' hooves from splitting, and better harness systems allowed horses to be hitched together in teams. The use of horses spread in the twelfth century because their greater speed brought greater efficiency to farming and reduced the amount of human labor involved. Horses were also used to haul goods to markets, where peasants sold any excess vegetables, grain, and animals.

By modern standards, medieval agricultural yields were very low, but there was striking improvement between the fifth and the thirteenth centuries. Increased output had a profound impact on society, improving Europeans' health, commerce, industry, and general lifestyle. More food meant that fewer people suffered from hunger and malnourishment and that devastating famines were rarer. Higher yields brought more food for animals as well as people, and the amount of meat that people ate increased slightly. A better diet had an enormous impact on women's lives in particular. More food meant increased body fat, which increased fertility, and more meat—which provided iron—meant that women were less anemic and less subject to disease. Some researchers believe that it was during the High Middle Ages that Western women began to outlive men. Improved opportunities also encouraged people to marry somewhat earlier, which meant larger families and further population growth.

Harvesting Hay A peasant with his socks rolled down to stay cool mows hay with a long scythe, while in the background a mill along a stream stands ready to grind grain or carry out other tasks. This illustration comes from a book of hours made in France in the early fifteenth century, probably for the duke of Bedford. Books of hours were devotional books with psalms, prayers, and calendars of church holidays, sometimes lavishly decorated. They often included cycles of months that linked seasonal rural activities to signs of the zodiac; here Cancer the crab shows that this is June. (From the *Bedford Hours*, 1414–1423, Bedford Master Workshop [fl. ca. 1430–1465]/British Library, London, UK/© British Library Board. All Rights Reserved/Bridgeman Images)

Home Life

In western and central Europe, villages were generally made up of small houses for individual families. Households consisted of a married couple, their children (including stepchildren), and perhaps one or two other relatives. Some homes contained only an unmarried person, a widow, or several unmarried people living together. In southern and eastern Europe, extended families were more likely to live in the same household.

The size and quality of peasants' houses varied according to their relative prosperity, which usually depended on the amount of land held. Poorer peasants lived in windowless cottages built of wood and clay or wattle (poles interwoven with branches or reeds) and thatched with straw. These cottages consisted of one large room that served as both kitchen and living quarters. A shed attached to the house provided storage for tools and shelter for animals. Prosperous peasants added rooms; some wealthy peasants in the early fourteenth century had two-story houses with separate bedrooms for parents and children. For most people, however, living space—especially living space close enough to a fire to feel some warmth in cold weather—was cramped, dark, smoky, and smelly, with animals and people both sharing tight quarters, sometimes with each other.

Every house had a small garden and an outbuilding. Onions, garlic, turnips, and carrots were grown and stored through the winter. Cabbage was shredded, salted, and turned into kraut for storage. The mainstay of the diet for peasants—and for all other classes—was bread. It was a hard, black substance made of barley, millet, and oats, rarely of expensive wheat, which they were more likely to use to pay their taxes and fees to the lord than for their own bread. Most households did not have ovens, which were expensive to build and posed a fire danger; their bread was baked in communal ovens or purchased from households that specialized in bread-baking. The main meal was often bread and a thick soup of vegetables and grains eaten around noon. Peasants ate vegetables not because they appreciated their importance for good health but because there was usually little else available. Animals were too valuable to be used for food on a regular basis, but weaker animals were often slaughtered in the fall so that they did not need to be fed through the winter. Their meat was salted for preservation and eaten on great feast days such as Christmas and Easter.

The diet of people with access to a river, lake, or stream would be supplemented with fish, which could be eaten fresh or preserved by salting. People living close to the sea gathered shellfish. Many places had severe laws against hunting and trapping in the forests. Deer, wild boars, and other game were reserved for the king and nobles. These laws were flagrantly violated, however, and rabbits and wild game often found their way to peasants' tables.

Medieval households were not self-sufficient but bought cloth, metal, leather goods, and even some food in village markets. They also bought ale, the universal drink of the common people in northern Europe. Women dominated in the production of ale. Ale not only provided needed calories but also provided some relief from the difficult, monotonous labor that filled people's lives. Medieval men and women often drank heavily. Brawls and violent fights were frequent at taverns, and English judicial records of the thirteenth century reveal a surprisingly large number of "accidental" deaths in which people drowned, got lost, or fell from horses, often, as the court records say, "coming from an ale," meaning that the victims were probably drunk.

The steady rise in population between the mid-eleventh and fourteenth centuries was primarily the result of warmer climate, increased food supply, and a reduction of violence with growing political stability, rather than dramatic changes in health care. Most treatment of illness was handled by home remedies handed down orally or perhaps through a cherished handwritten family herbal, cookbook, or household guide. Treatments were often mixtures of herbal remedies, sayings, specific foods, prayers, amulets, and ritual healing activities. People suffering from wounds, skin diseases, or broken bones sometimes turned to barber-surgeons. For internal ailments, people consulted apothecaries, who suggested and mixed compounds taken internally or applied orally as a salve or ointment; these were generally mixtures of plants, minerals, and other natural products.

Beginning in the twelfth century in England, France, and Italy, the clergy, noble men and women, and newly rich merchants also established institutions to care for the sick or for those who could not take care of themselves. Within city walls they built hospitals, where care was provided for those with chronic diseases that were not contagious, poor expectant mothers, the handicapped, people recovering from injuries, and foundling children. Outside city walls they built leprosariums or small hospices for people with leprosy and other contagious diseases. Such institutions might be staffed by members of religious orders or by laymen and laywomen who were paid for their work.

Childbirth and Child Abandonment

The most dangerous period of life for any person, peasant or noble, was infancy and early childhood. In normal years perhaps as many as one-third of all children died before age five from illness, malnutrition, and accidents, and this death rate climbed to more than half in years with plagues, droughts, or famines. However, once people reached adulthood, many lived well into their fifties and sixties.

Childbirth was dangerous for mothers as well as infants. Village women helped one another through childbirth, and women who were more capable acquired midwifery skills. In larger towns and cities, such women gradually developed into professional midwives who were paid for their services and who trained younger women as apprentices. For most women, however, childbirth was handled by female friends and family.

Many infants were abandoned by parents or guardians, who left their children somewhere, sold them, or legally gave authority over them to some other person or institution. Sometimes parents believed that someone of greater means or status might find the child and bring him or her up in better circumstances than they could provide. Christian parents gave their children to monasteries as religious acts, donating them to the service of God in the same way they might donate money.

Toward the end of his *Ecclesiastical History*, written when he was well into his sixties, Orderic Vitalis (ca. 1075–ca. 1140), a monk of the Norman abbey of Saint Evroul, explained movingly how he became a monk:

> And so, O glorious God, you didst inspire my father Odeleric to renounce me utterly and submit me in all things to thy governance. So, weeping, he gave me, a weeping child, into the care of the monk Reginald, and sent me away into exile for love of thee, and never saw me again. . . . I crossed the English channel and came into Normandy as an exile, unknown to all, knowing no one. . . . But thou didst suffer me through thy grace to find nothing but kindness among strangers. . . . The name of Vitalis was given me in place of my English name, which sounded harsh to the Normans.[2]

Orderic had no doubt that God wanted him to be a monk, but even half a century later he still remembered his grief. Orderic's father was a Norman priest, and his Anglo-Saxon mother perhaps gave him his "English" name. Qualms of conscience over clerical celibacy may have led Orderic's father to place his son in a monastery.

Donating a child to a monastery was common among the poor until about the year 1000, but less common in the next three hundred years, which saw relative prosperity for peasants. On the other hand, the incidence of noble parents giving their younger sons and daughters to religious houses increased dramatically. This resulted from and also reinforced the system of primogeniture, in which estates were passed intact to the eldest son instead of being divided among heirs (see Chapter 9). Monasteries provided noble younger sons and daughters with career opportunities, and their being thus disposed of removed them as contenders for family land.

Popular Religion

FOCUS QUESTION
How did religion shape everyday life in the High Middle Ages?

Apart from the land, the weather, and local legal and social conditions, religion had the greatest impact on the daily lives of ordinary people in the High Middle Ages. Religious practices varied widely from country to country and even from province to province. But nowhere was religion a one-hour-a-week affair. Most people in medieval Europe were Christian, but there were small Jewish communities scattered in many parts of Europe, and Muslims lived in the Iberian Peninsula, Sicily, and other Mediterranean islands.

Christian Life in Medieval Villages

For Christians the village church was the center of community life—social, political, and economic, as well as religious—with the parish priest in charge of a host of activities. From the side of the church, he read orders and messages from royal and ecclesiastical authorities to his parishioners. The front of the church, typically decorated with scenes of the Last Judgment, was the background against which royal judges traveling on circuit disposed of civil and criminal cases. In busy cities such as London, business agreements were made in the square in front of the church or even inside the church itself.

Although church law placed the priest under the bishop's authority, the manorial lord appointed the priest. Rural priests were peasants and often worked in the fields with the people during the week. On Sundays and holy days, they put on a robe and celebrated mass, or Eucharist, the ceremony in which the priest consecrated bread and wine and distributed it to believers, in a re-enactment of Jesus's Last Supper. They recited the mass in Latin, a language that few commoners, sometimes including the priest himself, could understand. At least once a year villagers were expected to take part in the ceremony and eat the consecrated bread. This usually happened at Easter, after they had confessed their sins to the priest and been assigned a penance.

In everyday life people engaged in rituals and used language heavy with religious symbolism. Before planting, the village priest customarily went out and sprinkled the fields with water, symbolizing refreshment and life. Everyone participated in village processions to honor the saints and ask their protection. The entire calendar was filled with reference to events in the life of Jesus and his disciples, such as Christmas, Easter, and Pentecost. Scriptural references and proverbs dotted everyone's language. The English *good-bye*, the French *adieu*, and the Spanish *adios* all derive from words meaning "God be with you." The signs and symbols of Christianity were visible everywhere, but so, people believed, was the Devil, who lured them to evil deeds. In some medieval images and literature, the Devil is portrayed as black, an identification that shaped Western racial attitudes.

Saints and Sacraments

Along with days marking events in the life of Jesus, the Christian calendar was filled with saints' days. Veneration of the saints had been an important tool of Christian conversion since late antiquity (see Chapter 7), and the cult of the saints was a central feature of popular culture in the Middle Ages. People believed that the saints possessed supernatural powers that enabled them to perform miracles, and the saint became the special property of the locality in which his or her relics rested. In return for the saint's healing and support, peasants offered the saint prayers, loyalty, and gifts.

In the later Middle Ages popular hagiographies (ha-gee-AH-gruh-fees) — biographies of saints based on myths, legends, and popular stories — attributed specialized functions to the saints. Saint Elmo (ca. 300), who supposedly had preached unharmed during a thunder and lightning storm, became the patron of sailors. Saint Agatha (third century), whose breasts were torn with shears because she rejected the attentions of a powerful suitor, became the patron of wet nurses, women with breast difficulties, and bell-ringers (because of the resemblance of breasts to bells). Every occupation had a patron saint, as did cities and even realms.

How were saints chosen? Since the early days of Christianity, individuals whose exemplary virtue was proved by miracles had been venerated by laypeople. Church officials in Rome insisted that they had the exclusive right to determine sainthood, but ordinary people continued to declare people saints. Between 1185 and 1431 only seventy persons were declared saints at Rome, but hundreds of new saints were venerated across Europe. Some clergy preached against the veneration of saints' relics and called it idolatry, but their appeals had little effect.

The Virgin Mary, Christ's mother, was the most important saint. In the eleventh century theologians began to emphasize Mary's spiritual motherhood of all Christians. Special masses commemorated her, churches were built in her honor, and hymns and prayers to her multiplied. Villagers listened intently to sermons telling stories about her life and miracles. One favorite story told of a minstrel and acrobat inspired to perform tumbling feats in Mary's honor:

> [He performed] until from head to heel sweat stood upon him, drop by drop, as blood falls from meat turning on a hearth. . . . [Then] there came down from the heavens a Dame so glorious, that certainly no man had seen one so precious, nor so richly crowned. . . . Then the sweet and courteous Queen herself took a white napkin in her hand, and with it gently fanned her minstrel before the altar. . . . She blesses her minstrel with the sign of God.[3]

People reasoned that if Mary would even bless tumbling (a disreputable form of popular entertainment) as long as it was done with a reverent heart, she would certainly bless their lives of hard work and pious devotion even more.

Along with the veneration of saints, sacraments were an important part of religious practice. Twelfth-century theologians expanded on Saint Augustine's understanding of sacraments (see Chapter 7) and created an entire sacramental system. In 1215 the Fourth Lateran Council formally accepted seven sacraments (baptism, penance, the Eucharist, confirmation, marriage, priestly ordination, anointment of the dying). Medieval Christians believed that these seven sacraments brought God's grace, the divine assistance or help needed to lead a good Christian life and to merit salvation. Most sacraments had to be dispensed by a priest, although spouses officially administered the sacrament of marriage to each other, and laypeople could baptize a dying infant or anoint a dying person if no priest could be found. In this way, the sacramental system enhanced the authority of priests over people's lives, but did not replace strong personal devotion to the saints.

Muslims and Jews

The centrality of Christian ceremonies to daily life for most Europeans meant that those who did not participate were clearly marked as outsiders. Many Muslims left Spain as the Christian "reconquest" proceeded and left Sicily when this became a Christian realm (see Chapter 9), but others converted. In more isolated villages, people simply continued their Muslim rituals and practices, including abstaining from pork, reciting verses from the Qur'an, praying at specified times of the day, and observing Muslim holy days, though they might hide this from the local priest or visiting officials.

Islam was geographically limited in medieval Europe, but by the late tenth century Jews could be found in many areas, often brought in from other areas as clients of rulers to help with finance. There were Jewish communities in Italian and French cities and in the cities along the Rhine. Jewish dietary laws require meat to be handled in a specific way, so Jews had their own butchers; there were Jewish artisans in many other trades as well. Jews held weekly religious services on Saturday, the Sabbath, and celebrated their own annual cycle of holidays. Each of these holidays involved special prayers, services, and often foods, and many of them commemorated events from Jewish history, including various times when Jews had been rescued from captivity.

Jews could supply other Jews with goods and services, but rulers and city leaders increasingly restricted their trade with Christians to banking and money-lending. This enhanced Christian resentment, as did the ideology of holy war that accompanied the Crusades (see Chapter 9). Violence against Jews and restrictions on their activities increased further in much of Europe. Jews were expelled from England and later from France. However, Jews continued to live in the independent cities of the Holy Roman Empire and Italy, and some migrated eastward into new towns that were being established in Slavic areas.

Rituals of Marriage and Birth

Increasing suspicion and hostility marked relations between religious groups throughout the Middle Ages, but there were also important similarities in the ways Christians, Jews, and Muslims understood and experienced their religions. In all three traditions, every major life transition was marked by a ceremony that included religious elements.

Christian weddings might be held in the village church or at the church door, though among well-to-do families the ceremony took place in the house of the bride or bridegroom. A priest's blessing was often sought, though it was not essential to the marriage. Muslim weddings were also finalized by a contract between the bride and groom and were often overseen by a wedding official. Jewish weddings were guided by statements in Talmudic law that weddings were complete when the bride had entered the *chuppah*, which medieval Jewish authorities interpreted to mean a room in the groom's house.

In all three faiths, the wedding ceremony was followed by a wedding party that often included secular rituals. Some rituals symbolized the proper hierarchical relations between the spouses—such as placing the husband's shoe on the bedstead over the couple, symbolizing his authority—or were meant to ensure the couple's fertility—such as untying all the knots in the household, for it was believed that people possessing magical powers could tie knots to inhibit a man's reproductive power. All this came together in what was often the final event of a wedding: the religious official blessed the couple in their marriage bed, often with family and friends standing around or banging on pans, yelling, or otherwise making as much noise as possible to make fun of the couple's first sexual encounter. (Tying cans on the back of the car in which a couple leaves the wedding is a modern remnant of such rituals.)

The friends and family members had generally been part of the discussions, negotiations, and activities leading up to the marriage; marriage united two families and was far too important to leave up to two people alone. Among serfs the manorial lord's permission was often required, with a special fee required to obtain it. (This permission did not, as often alleged, give the lord the right to deflower the bride. Though lords certainly forced sex on female serfs, there is no evidence in any legal sources that lords had the "right of first night," the *jus primae noctis*.) The involvement of family and friends in choosing one's spouse might lead to conflict, but more often the wishes of the couple and their parents, kin, and community were quite similar: all hoped for marriages that provided economic security, honorable standing, and a good number of healthy children. The best marriages offered companionship, emotional support, and even love, but these were understood to grow out of the marriage, not necessarily precede it. Breaking up a marriage meant breaking up the basic production and consumption unit, a very serious matter. The church forbade divorce, and even among non-Christians marital dissolution by any means other than the death of one spouse was rare.

Most brides hoped to be pregnant soon after the wedding. Christian women hoping for children said special prayers to the Virgin Mary or her mother, Anne. Some wore amulets of amber, bone, or mistletoe, thought to increase fertility. Others repeated charms and verses they had learned from other women, or, in desperate cases, went on pilgrimages to make special supplications. Muslim and Jewish women wore small cases with sacred verses or asked for blessings from religious leaders. Women continued these prayers and rituals throughout pregnancy and childbirth, often combining religious traditions with folk beliefs. Women in southern France, for example, offered prayers for easy childbirth and healthy children to Saint Guinefort, a greyhound who had been mistakenly killed by his owner after saving the owner's child from a poisonous snake. The fact that Guinefort was a dog meant he could never become an official saint, but women saw him as a powerful and martyred protector of children.

Judaism, Christianity, and Islam all required women to remain separate from the community for a short time after childbirth and often had special ceremonies welcoming them back once this period was over. These rituals often included prayers, such as this one from the Christian ritual of thanksgiving and purification, called churching, which a woman celebrated six weeks after giving birth: "Almighty and everlasting God, who has freed this woman from the

Wedding Door of the Cathedral in Strasbourg
Medieval cathedrals, such as this one from the thirteenth century, sometimes had a side door depicting a biblical story of ten young women who went to meet a bridegroom. Five of them wisely took extra oil for their lamps, while five foolishly did not (Matthew 25:1–13). In the story, which is a parable about being prepared for the end of the world, the foolish maidens were out of oil when the bridegroom arrived and missed the wedding feast. The "maidens' door" became a popular site for weddings, which were held right in front of it. (Paul M. R. Maeyaert/akg-images)

danger of bearing a child, consider her to be strengthened from every pollution of the flesh so that with a clean heart and pure mind she may deserve to enter into the bosom of our mother, the church, and make her devoted to Your service."[4]

Religious ceremonies also welcomed children into the community. Among Christian families, infants were baptized soon after they were born to ensure that they could enter Heaven. Midwives who delivered children who looked especially weak and sickly often baptized them in an emergency service. In normal baptisms, the women who had assisted the mother in the birth often carried the baby to church, where godparents vowed their support. Godparents were often close friends or relatives, but parents might also choose prominent villagers or even the local lord in the hope that he might later look favorably on the child and provide for him or her in some way.

Within Judaism, a boy was circumcised by a religious official and given his name in a ceremony on his eighth day of life. This *brit milah*, or "covenant of circumcision," was viewed as a reminder of the Covenant between God and Abraham described in Hebrew Scripture. Muslims also circumcised boys in a special ritual, though the timing varied from a few days after birth to adolescence.

Death and the Afterlife

Death was similarly marked by religious ceremonies, and among Europeans of all faiths death did not sever family obligations and connections. Christians called for a priest to perform the sacrament of extreme unction when they thought the hour of death was near. The priest brought holy water, holy oil, a crucifix, and a censer with incense, all objects regarded as having power over death and the sin related to it.

Once the person had died, the body was washed and dressed in special clothing — or a sack of plain cloth — and buried within a day or two. Family and friends joined in a funeral procession, marked by the ringing of church bells; sometimes extra women were hired so that the mourning and wailing were especially loud and intense, a sign of the family's devotion. The wealthy were sometimes buried inside the church — in the walls, under the floor, or under the building itself in a crypt — but most people were buried in the churchyard or a cemetery close by. At the graveside, the priest asked for God's grace for the soul of the deceased and also asked that soul to "rest in peace." This final request was made not only for the benefit of the dead, but also for that of the living. The souls of the dead were widely believed to return to earth: mothers who had died in childbirth might come back seeking to take their children with them; executed criminals might return to gain revenge on those who had brought them to justice (to prevent that return, they were buried at crossroads, permanently under the sign of the cross, or under the gallows itself); ordinary people came seeking help from surviving family members in achieving their final salvation. Priests were hired to say memorial masses on anniversaries of family deaths, especially one week, one month, and one year afterward.

During the High Middle Ages, learned theologians increasingly emphasized the idea of purgatory, the place where souls on their way to Heaven went after death to make amends for their earthly sins. Souls in purgatory did not wander the earth, but they could still benefit from earthly activities; memorial masses, prayers, and donations made in their names could shorten their time in purgatory. So could indulgences (see Chapter 9), those papal grants that relieved a person from earthly penance. Indulgences were initially granted for performing meritorious acts, such as going on a pilgrimage or crusade, but later on they could be obtained by paying a small fee.

The Pilgrim's Guide to Santiago de Compostela

Making pilgrimages to holy shrines is a common practice in many religions. Medieval Christians of all social classes made pilgrimages, often to shrines understood to contain the body of a saint. The shrine of Santiago de Compostela (Saint James at Compostela) in the kingdom of Galicia in the Iberian Peninsula, said to contain the bones of the biblical Saint James, was one of the most popular. In the twelfth century an unknown French author gathered many of the pilgrims' experiences and put these together in a sort of guidebook.

The church, however, was begun in the year 1116 of the Spanish era [1078 C.E.]. . . . From the time when it was begun up to the present day, this church is renewed by the light of the miracles of the blessed James. In it, indeed, health is given to the sick, sight restored to the blind, the tongue of the mute is loosened, hearing is given to the deaf, soundness of limb is granted to cripples, the possessed are delivered, and what is more, the prayers of the faithful are heard, their vows are accepted, the bonds of sin are broken, heaven is opened to those who knock, consolation is given to the grieving, and all the people of foreign nations, flocking from all parts of the world, come together here in crowds bearing with them gifts of praise to the Lord. . . .

The land of Navarre . . . abounds in bread and wine, milk and cattle. . . . The Navarrese wear short black garments extending just down to the knee, like the Scots, and they wear sandals which they call *lavarcas* made of raw hide with the hair on and are bound around the foot with thongs, covering only the soles of the feet and leaving the upper foot bare. In truth, they wear black woollen hooded and fringed capes, reaching to their elbows, which they call *saias*. These people, in truth, are repulsively dressed, and they eat and drink repulsively. For in fact all those who dwell in the household of a Navarrese, servant as well as master, maid as well as mistress, are accustomed to eat all their food mixed together from one pot, not with spoons but with their own hands, and they drink with one cup. If you saw them eat you would think them dogs or pigs. If you heard them speak, you would be reminded of the barking of dogs. For their speech is utterly barbarous. . . .

Then comes Galicia [guh-LIH-shee-uh]. . . . [T]his is wooded and has rivers and is well-provided with meadows and excellent orchards, with equally good fruits and very clear springs; there are few cities, towns or cornfields. It is short of wheaten bread and wine, bountiful in rye bread and cider, well-stocked with cattle and horses, milk and honey, ocean fish both gigantic and small, and wealthy in gold, silver, fabrics, and furs of forest animals and other riches, as well as Saracen [Muslim] treasures. The Galicians, in truth, more than all the other uncultivated Spanish peoples, are those who most closely resemble our French race by their manners, but they are alleged to be irascible and very litigious.

EVALUATE THE EVIDENCE

1. How would you evaluate the author's opinion of the people of Navarre? Of Galicia? How does he compare these people to his own countrymen, the French?

2. Pilgrimages were in many ways the precursors of modern tourism. What similarities do you see between this guide and those for today's travelers?

Source: *The Pilgrim's Guide to Santiago de Compostela*, critical edition and annotated translation by Paula Gerson, Jeanne Krochalis, Annie Shaver-Crandell, and Alison Stones. Copyright © 1997. Reprinted by permission of the authors.

(See "Evaluating the Evidence 10.1: The Pilgrim's Guide to Santiago de Compostela," above.) With this development, their spiritual benefits became transferable, so indulgences could be purchased to shorten the stay in purgatory of one's deceased relatives, as well as to lessen one's own penance or time in purgatory.

The living also had obligations to the dead among Muslims and Jews. In both groups deceased people were buried quickly, and special prayers were said by mourners and family members. Muslims fasted on behalf of the dead and maintained a brief period of official mourning. The Qur'an promises an eternal paradise with flowing rivers to "those who believe and do good deeds" (Qur'an, 4:57) and a Hell of eternal torment to those who do not.

Jews observed specified periods of mourning during which the normal activities of daily life were curtailed. Every day for eleven months after a death and every year after that on the anniversary of the death, a son of the deceased was to recite Kaddish, a special prayer of praise and glorification of God. Judaism emphasized life on earth more than an afterlife, so beliefs about what happens to the soul after death were more varied; the very righteous might go directly to a place of spiritual reward, but most souls went first to a place of punishment and purification generally referred to as *Gehinnom*. After a period that did not exceed twelve months, the soul ascended to the world to come. Those who were completely wicked during their lifetimes might simply go out of existence or continue in an eternal state of remorse.

Towns and Economic Revival

FOCUS QUESTION
What led to Europe's economic growth and reurbanization?

Most people continued to live in villages in the High Middle Ages, but the rise of towns and the growth of a new business and commercial class were a central part of Europe's recovery after the disorders of the tenth century. The growth of towns was made possible by some of the changes already described: a rise in population; increased agricultural output, which provided an adequate food supply for town dwellers; and a degree of peace and political stability, which allowed merchants to transport and sell goods. As towns gained legal and political rights, merchant and craft guilds grew more powerful, and towns became centers of production as well as commerce.

The Rise of Towns

Medieval towns began in many different ways. Some were fortifications erected as a response to ninth-century invasions; the peasants from the surrounding countryside moved within the walls when their area was attacked. Other towns grew up around great cathedrals (see page 318) and monasteries whose schools drew students from distant areas. Many other towns grew from the sites of Roman army camps or cities, which had shrunk in the early Middle Ages but never entirely disappeared. Still others arose where a trade route crossed a river or a natural harbor allowed ships to moor easily.

Regardless of their origins, medieval towns had a few common characteristics. Each town had a marketplace, and most had a mint for the coining of money. The town also had a court to settle disputes. In addition, medieval towns were enclosed by walls. The terms *burgher* (BUHR-guhr) and *bourgeois* derive from the Old English and Old German words *burg, burgh, borg,* and *borough* for "a walled or fortified place." Thus a burgher or bourgeois originally was a person who lived or worked inside the walls. Townspeople supported themselves primarily by exchanging goods and services with one another, becoming artisans, shopkeepers, and merchants. They bought their food from the surrounding countryside, and purchased goods from far away brought by traveling merchants.

No matter where people congregated, they settled on someone's land and had to secure permission to live there from the king, count, abbot, or bishop. Aristocratic nobles and churchmen were sometimes hostile to the towns set up on their land, but they soon realized that these could be a source of profits and benefits.

The growing towns of medieval Europe slowly gained legal and political rights, including the rights to hold municipal courts, select the mayor and other municipal officials, and tax residents and visitors. Lords were often reluctant to grant towns self-government, fearing loss of authority and revenue if they gave the residents full independence. When burghers bargained for a town's political independence, however, they offered sizable amounts of ready cash and sometimes promised payments for years to come. Consequently, lords ultimately agreed to self-government.

In addition to working for the independence of the towns, townspeople tried to acquire liberties for themselves. In the Middle Ages the word *liberties* meant special privileges. The most important privilege a medieval townsperson could gain was personal freedom. It gradually developed that an individual who fled his or her manor and lived in a town for a year and a day was free of servile obligations and status. Thus the growth of towns contributed to a slow decline of serfdom in western Europe, although this took centuries.

Towns developed throughout much of Europe, but the concentration of the textile industry led to the growth of many towns in the Low Countries (present-day Holland, Belgium, and French Flanders): Ghent with about 56,000 people, Bruges (broozh) with 27,000, and Tournai and Brussels with perhaps 20,000 each. In 1300 Paris was the largest city in western Christian Europe, with a population of about 200,000, and Venice, Florence, and Milan each had about 100,000 people (Map 10.1). Constantinople was larger still, with perhaps 300,000 people. Córdoba, the capital of Muslim Spain, may have been the largest city in the world, with a population that might have been nearly half a million, although this declined steeply when the city was conquered by Christian forces in 1236 and many people fled southward, swelling the population of Granada.

Merchant and Craft Guilds

The merchants, who were influential in winning towns' independence from feudal lords, also used their power and wealth to control life within the city walls. The merchants of a town joined together to form a **merchant guild** that prohibited nonmembers from trading in the town. Guild members often made up the earliest town government, serving as mayors and members of the city council, which meant that a town's economic policies were determined by its merchants' self-interest. By the late eleventh century, especially in the towns of the Low Countries and northern Italy, the leaders of the merchant guilds were rich and politically powerful.

merchant guild A band of merchants in a town that prohibited nonmembers from trading in that town.

While most towns were initially established as trading centers, they quickly became centers of production as well. Peasants looking for better opportunities moved to towns—either with their lord's approval or without it—providing both workers and mouths to feed. Some townspeople began to specialize in certain types of food and clothing production: they bought cloth and sewed it into clothing, or purchased and butchered cattle, selling the meat to others who made small meat pies and selling the leather to those who made shoes or bags. Over time some cities specialized in certain items, becoming known for their fine fabrics, their reliable arms and armor, or their elegant gold and silver work.

Like merchants, producers recognized that organizing would bring benefits, and beginning in the twelfth century in many cities they formed **craft guilds** that regulated most aspects of production. Guilds set quality standards for their particular product and regulated the size of workshops and the conduct of members. In most cities individual guilds, such as those of shoemakers or blacksmiths, achieved a monopoly in the production of one particular product, forbidding nonmembers to work. The craft guild then chose some of its members to act as inspectors and set up a court to hear disputes between members, though the city court remained the final arbiter.

craft guild A band of producers in a town that regulated most aspects of production of a good in that town.

MAP 10.1 **European Population Density, ca. 1300** The development of towns and the reinvigoration of trade were directly related in medieval Europe.

Each guild set the pattern by which members were trained and the length of the training period. A boy who wanted to become a weaver, for instance, or whose parents wanted him to, spent four to seven years as an apprentice, often bound by a contract such as the following from thirteenth-century Marseilles in southern France:

April the ninth. I, Peter Borre, in good faith and without guile, place with you, Peter Feissac, weaver, my son Stephen, for the purpose of learning the trade and craft of weaving, to live at your house, and to do work for you from the feast of Easter next for four continuous years, promising you by this agreement to take care that my son does the said work, and that he will be faithful and trustworthy in all that he does, and that he will neither steal nor take anything away from you, nor flee nor depart from you for any reason, until he had completed his apprenticeship.[5]

When the apprenticeship was finished, a young artisan spent several years as a journeyman, working in the shop of a master artisan. He then could make his "masterpiece"—in the case of weavers, a long piece of cloth. If the other masters judged the cloth acceptable, and if they thought the market in their town was large enough to support another weaver, the journeyman could then become a master and start a shop. If the guild decided there were already enough masters, he would need to leave that town and try elsewhere. Many guilds required masters to be married, as they recognized the vital role of the master's wife. She assisted in running the shop, often selling the goods her husband had produced. Their children, both male and female, also worked alongside the apprentices and journeymen. The sons were sometimes formally apprenticed, but the daughters were generally not apprenticed, because many guilds limited formal membership to males.

Most guilds allowed a master's widow to continue operating a shop for a set period of time after her husband's death, for they recognized that she had the necessary skills and experience. Such widows paid all guild dues, but they were not considered full members and could not vote or hold office in the guild. In a handful of cities there were a few all-female guilds, especially in spinning gold thread or weaving silk ribbons for luxury clothing, trades in which girls were formally apprenticed in the same way boys were.

Both craft and merchant guilds were not only economic organizations, but also systems of social support. They took care of elderly masters who could no longer work, and they often supported masters' widows and orphans. They maintained an altar at a city church and provided for the funerals of members and baptisms of their children. Guild members marched together in city parades and reinforced their feelings of solidarity with one another by special ceremonies and distinctive dress. Merchant guilds in some parts of Europe, such as the German cities of Hamburg, Lübeck, and Bremen, had special buildings for celebrations and ceremonies.

The Revival of Long-Distance Trade

The growth of towns went hand in hand with a revival of trade as artisans and craftsmen manufactured goods for both local and foreign consumption (Map 10.2). Most trade centered in towns and was controlled by professional traders. Long-distance trade was risky and required large investments of capital. Robbers and thieves roamed virtually all of the overland trade routes. Pirates infested the sea-lanes, and shipwrecks were common. Since the risks were so great, merchants preferred to share them. A group of people would thus pool their capital to finance an expedition to a distant place. When the ship or caravan returned and the cargo was sold, these investors would share the profits. If disaster struck the caravan, an investor's loss was limited to the amount of that individual's investment.

In the late eleventh century the Italian cities, especially Venice, led the West in trade in general and completely dominated trade with the East. Venetian ships carried salt from the city's own lagoon, pepper and other spices from India and North Africa, silks and carpets from Central Asia, and slaves from many places. In northern Europe, the towns of Bruges, Ghent, and Ypres (EE-pruh) in Flanders built a vast cloth industry, becoming leaders in both the manufacture and trade of textiles.

Two circumstances help explain the lead Venice and these Flemish towns gained in long-distance trade. Both areas enjoyed a high degree of peace and political stability. Geographical factors were equally, if not more, important. Venice, at the northwestern

MAP 10.2 Trade and Manufacturing in Thirteenth-Century Europe   Note the overland and ocean lines of trade and the sources of silver, iron, copper, lead, paper, wool, carpets and rugs, and slaves.

end of the Adriatic Sea, had easy access to transalpine land routes as well as the Adriatic and Mediterranean sea-lanes connected to the markets of North Africa, Byzantium, and Russia. Merchants from Venice and Genoa also seized the commercial opportunities offered by the great fairs (large periodic gatherings that attracted buyers, sellers, and goods) held in the county of Champagne in northern France. Champagne was on the main north-south trade routes, and the counts who ruled the area provided security and enforced contracts. Directly north of Champagne were the towns of Flanders, which also offered unusual possibilities for merchants: just across the Channel from England, Flanders had easy access to English wool. Because the weather in England was colder than in most of Europe, English sheep grew longer and denser wool than sheep elsewhere. With this wool, clothmakers could produce high-quality cloth, which was the most important manufactured product handled by merchants and one of the few European products for which there was a market in the East.

From the late eleventh through the thirteenth centuries, Europe enjoyed a steadily expanding volume of international trade. Trade surged markedly with demand for sugar from the Mediterranean islands to replace honey; spices from Asia to season a bland diet; and fine wines from the Rhineland, Burgundy, and Bordeaux to make life more pleasant. Other consumer goods included luxury woolens from Flanders and Tuscany, furs from Ireland and Russia, brocades and tapestries from Flanders, and silks from Constantinople and even China. Nobles prized fancy household furnishings such as silver plate, as well as swords and armor for their battles. As the trade volume expanded, the use of cash became more widespread. Beginning in the 1160s the opening of new silver mines in Germany, Bohemia, northern Italy, northern France, and western England led to the minting and circulation of vast quantities of silver coins.

Increased trade also led to a higher standard of living. Contact with Eastern civilizations introduced Europeans to eating utensils, and table manners improved. Nobles learned to eat with forks and knives instead of tearing the meat from a roast with their hands. They began to use napkins instead of wiping their greasy fingers on their clothes or on the dogs lying under the table.

Business Procedures

The economic surge of the High Middle Ages led merchants to invent new business procedures. Beginning in Italy, merchants formalized their agreements with new types of contracts, including temporary contracts for land and sea trading ventures and permanent partnerships termed *compagnie* (kahm-pah-NYEE; literally "bread together," that is, sharing bread; the root of the word *company*). Many of these agreements were initially between brothers or other relatives and in-laws, but they quickly grew to include people who were not family members. In addition, they began to involve individuals—including a few women—who invested only their money, leaving the actual running of the business to the active partners. Commercial correspondence, unnecessary when one businessperson oversaw everything and made direct bargains with buyers and sellers, proliferated. Accounting and record keeping became more sophisticated, and credit facilitated business expansion.

The ventures of the German Hanseatic League illustrate these new business procedures. The **Hanseatic League** (often called simply the Hansa) was a mercantile association of towns. It originated in agreements between merchants for mutual security and exclusive trading rights, and it gradually developed into agreements among towns themselves, often sealed with a contract. The first such contract was between the towns of Lübeck and Hamburg in 1241, and during the next century perhaps two hundred cities from Holland to Poland joined the league. From the fourteenth to the sixteenth centuries, the Hanseatic League controlled the trade of northern Europe. In cities such as Bruges and London, Hansa merchants secured special trading concessions, exempting them from all tolls and allowing them to trade at local fairs. These merchants established foreign trading centers, called "factories" because the commercial agents in them were called "factors."

The dramatic increase in trade ran into two serious difficulties in medieval Europe. One was the problem of minting money. Despite investment in mining operations to increase the production of metals, the amount of gold, silver, and

Hanseatic League A mercantile association of towns begun in northern Europe that allowed for mutual protection and trading rights.

The Hanseatic League, 1300–1400

Lübeck   Gabled houses and shops line the river Trave in the old merchants' quarter of Lübeck, the "Queen of the Hanseatic League," while the brick spires of Saint Mary's and Saint Peter's churches, begun in the thirteenth century by prosperous citizens, loom above. Much of the central city and many of the churches were destroyed in World War II, but they have been rebuilt following medieval plans, and this photo provides a good sense of what a Hansa city centered on commerce would have looked like. (Insights/UIG via Getty Images)

copper available for coins was not adequate for the increased flow of commerce. Merchants developed paper bills of exchange, in which coins or goods in one location were exchanged for a sealed letter (much like a modern deposit statement), which could be used in place of metal coinage elsewhere. This made the long, slow, and very dangerous shipment of coins unnecessary, and facilitated the expansion of credit and commerce. By about 1300 the bill of exchange was the normal method of making commercial payments among the cities of western Europe, and it proved to be a decisive factor in their later economic development.

The second problem was a moral and theological one. Church doctrine frowned on lending money at interest, termed *usury* (YOO-zhuh-ree). This doctrine was developed in the early Middle Ages when loans were mainly for consumption, for instance, to tide a farmer over until the next harvest. Theologians reasoned that it was wrong for a Christian to take advantage of the bad luck or need of another Christian. This restriction on Christians' charging interest is one reason why Jews were frequently the moneylenders in early medieval society; it was one of the few occupations not forbidden them. As money-lending became more important to commercial ventures, the church relaxed its position. It declared that some interest was legitimate as a payment for the risk the investor was taking, and that only interest above a certain level would be considered usury. (Even today, governments generally set limits on the rate businesses may charge for loaning money.) The church itself then got into the money-lending business, opening pawnshops in cities.

The stigma attached to lending money was in many ways attached to all the activities of a merchant. Medieval people were uneasy about a person making a profit merely from the investment of money rather than labor, skill, and time. Merchants themselves shared these ideas to some degree, so they gave generous donations to the church and to charities, and took pains not to flaunt their wealth through flashy dress and homes.

The Commercial Revolution

commercial revolution
The transformation of the European economy as a result of changes in business procedures and growth in trade.

Changes in business procedures, combined with the growth in trade, led to a transformation of the European economy often called the **commercial revolution** by historians, who see it as the beginning of the modern capitalist economy. In using this label, historians point not only to increases in the sheer volume of trade and in the complexity and sophistication of business procedures, but also to the development of a new "capitalist spirit" in which making a profit is regarded as a good thing in itself, regardless of the uses to which that profit is put. (See "Individuals in Society: Francesco Datini," at right.) Because capitalism in the Middle Ages primarily involved trade rather than production, it is referred to as mercantile capitalism.

I n 1348, when he was a young teenager, Francesco Datini (1335–1410) lost his father, his mother, a brother, and a sister to the Black Death epidemic that swept through Europe (see Chapter 11). Leaving his hometown of Prato in northern Italy, he apprenticed himself to merchants in nearby Florence for several years to learn accounting and other business skills. At fifteen, he moved to Avignon (ah-veen-YOHN) in southern France. The popes were at this point living in Avignon instead of Rome, and the city offered many opportunities for an energetic and enterprising young man. Datini first became involved in the weapons trade, which offered steady profits, and then became a merchant of spices, wool and silk cloth, and jewels. He was very successful, and at thirty-one he married the young daughter of another merchant in an elaborate wedding that was the talk of Avignon.

In 1378 the papacy returned to Italy, and Datini soon followed, setting up trading companies in Prato, Pisa, and Florence. He focused on cloth and leather and sought to control the trade in products used for the preparation of these materials as well, especially the rare dyes that created the brilliant colors favored by wealthy noblemen and townspeople. He eventually had offices all over Europe and became one of the richest men of his day, opening a mercantile bank and a company that produced cloth.

Datini was more successful than most businessmen, but what makes him particularly stand out was his record keeping. He kept careful account books and ledgers, all of them headed by the phrase "in the name of God and profit." He wrote to the managers of each of his offices every week, providing them with careful advice and blunt criticism: "You cannot see a crow in a bowl of milk." Taking on the son of a friend as an employee, he wrote to the young man: "Do your duty well, and you will acquire honor and profit, and you can count on me as if I were your own father. But if you do not, then do not count on me; it will be as if I had never known you."

When Datini was away from home, which was often, he wrote to his wife every day, and she sometimes responded in ways that were less deferential than we might expect of a woman who was many years younger.

Statue of Francesco Datini located outside the city hall in Prato. (Marble statue by Nicolo Lamberti [ca. 1375–1451], 1409, Piazza del Comune, Prato, Italy/Bridgeman Images)

"I think it is not necessary," she wrote at one point, "to send me a message every Wednesday to say that you will be here on Sunday, for it seems to me that on every Friday you change your mind."

Datini's obsessive record keeping lasted beyond his death, for someone saved all of his records—hundreds of ledgers and contracts, eleven thousand business letters, and over a hundred thousand personal letters—in sacks in his opulent house in Prato, where they were found in the nineteenth century. They provide a detailed picture of medieval business practices and also reveal much about Datini as a person. Ambitious, calculating, luxury loving, and a workaholic, Datini seems similar to a modern CEO. Like many of today's self-made billionaires, at the end of his life Datini began to think a bit more about God and less about profit. In his will, he set up a foundation for the poor in Prato and a home for orphans in Florence, both of which are still in operation. In 1967 scholars established an institute for economic history in Prato, naming it in Datini's honor; the institute now manages the collection of Datini's documents and gathers other relevant materials in its archives.

QUESTIONS FOR ANALYSIS

1. How would you evaluate Datini's motto, "In the name of God and profit"? Is it an honest statement of his aims, a hypocritical justification of greed, a blend of both, or something else?
2. Changes in business procedures in the Middle Ages have been described as a "commercial revolution." Do Datini's business ventures support this assessment? How?

Source: Iris Origo, *The Merchant of Prato: Francesco di Marco Datini, 1335–1410* (New York: Alfred A. Knopf, Inc., 1957).

Part of this capitalist spirit was a new attitude toward time. Country people needed only approximate times—dawn, noon, sunset—for their work. Monasteries needed more precise times to call monks together for the recitation of the Divine Office. In the early Middle Ages monks used a combination of hourglasses, sundials, and water-clocks to determine the time, and then rang bells by hand. In about 1280 new types of mechanical mechanisms seem to have been devised in which weights replaced falling water and bells were rung automatically. Records begin to use the word *clock* (from the Latin word for bell) for these machines, which sometimes indicated the movement of astronomical bodies as well as the hours. The merchants who ran city councils quickly saw clocks as useful, as these devices allowed the opening and closing of markets and shops to be set to certain hours. Through regulations that specified times and bells that marked the day, city people began to develop a mentality that conceived of the universe in quantitative terms. Clocks were also symbols of a city's prosperity. Beautiful and elaborate mechanical clocks, usually installed on the cathedral or town church, were in general use in Italy by the 1320s, in Germany by the 1330s, in England by the 1370s, and in France by the 1380s.

The commercial revolution created a great deal of new wealth, which did not escape the attention of kings and other rulers. Wealth could be taxed, and through taxation kings could create strong and centralized states. The commercial revolution also provided the opportunity for thousands of serfs to improve their social position. The slow but steady transformation of European society from almost completely rural and isolated to urban and relatively more sophisticated constituted the greatest effect of the commercial revolution that began in the eleventh century.

Even so, merchants and business people did not run medieval communities other than in central and northern Italy and in the county of Flanders. Kings and nobles maintained ultimate control over most European cities, such as Paris, London, and Córdoba. Most towns remained small, and urban residents never amounted to more than 10 percent of the total European population. The commercial changes of the eleventh through thirteenth centuries did, however, lay the economic foundations for the development of urban life and culture.

Urban Life

FOCUS QUESTION
What was life like in medieval cities?

In their backgrounds and abilities, townspeople represented diversity and change. Their occupations and their preoccupations were different from those of nobles and peasants. Cities were crowded and polluted, though people flocked into them because they offered the possibility of economic advancement, social mobility, and improvement in legal status. Some urban residents grew spectacularly rich, but the numbers of poor swelled as well.

City Life

Walls surrounded almost all medieval towns and cities, and constant repair of these walls was usually the town's greatest expense. Gates pierced the walls, and visitors waited at the gates to gain entrance to the town. Most streets in a medieval town were marketplaces as much as passages for transit. Poor people selling soap, candles, wooden dishes, and similar cheap products stood next to farmers from the surrounding countryside selling eggs, chickens, or vegetables; people selling firewood or mushrooms they had gathered; and pawnbrokers selling used clothing and household goods. Because there was no way to preserve food easily, people—usually female family members or servants—had to shop every day, and the market was where they met their neighbors, exchanged information, and talked over recent events, as well as purchased needed supplies.

Some selling took place not in the open air but in the craftsman's home. A window or door in the home opened onto the street and displayed the finished products made within to attract passersby. The family lived above the business on the second or third floor. As the business and the family expanded, additional stories were added. Second and third stories jutted out over the ground floor and thus over the street. Since the streets were narrow to begin with, houses lacked fresh air and light. Initially, houses were made of wood and thatched with straw. Fire was a constant danger; because houses were built so close to one another, fires spread rapidly. Municipal governments consequently urged construction in stone or brick.

Most medieval cities developed with little planning. As the population increased, space became increasingly limited. Air and water pollution presented serious problems. Horses and oxen, the chief means of transportation and power, dropped tons of dung on the streets every year. It was universal practice in the early towns to dump household waste, both animal and human, into the road in front of one's house. The stench must have been abominable. In 1298 the citizens of the town of Boutham in Yorkshire, England, received the following order:

> To the bailiffs of the abbot of St. Mary's York, at Boutham. Whereas it is sufficiently evident that the pavement of the said town of Boutham is so very greatly broken up . . . , and in addition the air is so corrupted and infected by the pigsties situated in the king's highways and in the lanes of that town and by the swine feeding and frequently wandering about . . . and by dung and dunghills and many other foul things placed in the streets and lanes, that great repugnance overtakes the king's ministers staying in that town and also others there dwelling and passing through . . . : the king, being unwilling longer to tolerate such great and unbearable defects there, orders the bailiffs to cause the pavement to be suitably repaired . . . before All Saints next, and to cause the pigsties, aforesaid streets and lanes to be cleansed from all dung . . . and to cause them to be kept thus cleansed hereafter.[6]

People of all sorts, from beggars to wealthy merchants, regularly rubbed shoulders in the narrow streets and alleys of crowded medieval cities. This interaction did not mean that people were unaware of social differences, however, for clothing clearly indicated social standing and sometimes occupation. Friars wore black, white, or gray woolen clothing that marked them as members of a particular religious order, while priests and bishops wore layers of specialized clothing, especially when they were officiating at religious services. Military men and servants who lived in noble households dressed in the nobles' distinctive colors known as livery (LIH-vuh-ree). Wealthier urban residents wore bright colors, imported silk or fine woolen fabrics, and fancy headgear, while poorer ones wore darker clothing made of rough linen or linen and wool blends. In university towns, students wore clothing and headgear that marked their status. University graduates—lawyers, physicians, and professors—often wore dark robes, trimmed with fur if they could afford it.

In the later Middle Ages many cities attempted to make clothing distinctions a matter of law as well as of habit. City councils passed **sumptuary laws** that regulated the value of clothing and jewelry that people of different social groups could wear;

sumptuary laws Laws that regulated the value and style of clothing and jewelry that various social groups could wear as well as the amount they could spend on celebrations.

Young Men Playing Stickball   With their tunics hitched up in their belts so that they could move around more easily, young men play a game involving hitting a ball with a stick. Games involving bats and balls were popular, for the equipment needed was made from simple, inexpensive materials. (Playing game of pelota, illuminated page from *Cantigas de Santa Maria*, manuscript made under the direction of Alfonso X [1221–1284], King of Castile and León/DEA/De Agostini/Getty Images)

only members of high social groups could wear velvet, satin, pearls, or fur, for example, or wear clothing embroidered with gold thread or dyed in colors that were especially expensive to produce, such as the purple dye that came from mollusk shells. Along with enforcing social differences, sumptuary laws also attempted to impose moral standards by prohibiting plunging necklines on women or doublets (fitted buttoned jackets) that were too short on men. Their limits on imported fabrics or other materials also served to protect local industries.

Some of these laws called for marking certain individuals as members of groups not fully acceptable in urban society. Many cities ordered prostitutes to wear red or yellow bands on their clothes that were supposed to represent the flames of Hell, and the Fourth Lateran Council required Jews and Muslims to dress in ways that distinguished them from their Christian neighbors. (Many Jewish communities also developed their own sumptuary laws prohibiting extravagant or ostentatious dress.) In some cities, sumptuary laws were expanded to include restrictions on expenditures for parties and family celebrations, again set by social class. Sumptuary laws were frequently broken and were difficult to enforce, but they provide evidence of the many material goods available to urban dwellers as well as the concern of city leaders about the social mobility and extravagance they saw all around them.

Servants and the Poor

Many urban houses were larger than the tiny village dwellings, so families took in domestic servants. A less wealthy household employed one woman who assisted in all aspects of running the household; a wealthier one employed a large staff of male and female servants with specific duties. When there was only one servant, she generally lived and ate with the family, for there was rarely enough space for separate quarters. Even in wealthier households that had many rooms, servants were rarely separated from their employers the way they would be in the nineteenth century, but instead lived on intimate terms with them. In Italian cities, household servants included slaves, usually young women brought in from areas outside of Western Christianity, such as the Balkans.

Along with live-in servants, many households hired outside workers to do specific tasks. These workers laundered clothing and household linens, cared for children or invalids, repaired houses and walls, and carried messages or packages around the city or the surrounding countryside. Urban workers had to buy all their food, so they felt any increase in the price of ale or bread immediately. Their wages were generally low, and children from such families sought work at very young ages.

Illegal activities offered another way for people to support themselves. They stole merchandise from houses, wagons, and storage facilities, fencing it to pawnbrokers or taking it to the next town to sell. They stole goods or money directly from people, cutting the strings of their bags or purses. They sold sex for money, standing on street corners or moving into houses that by the fifteenth century became official brothels. They made and sold mixtures of herbs and drugs claimed to heal all sorts of ailments, perhaps combining this venture with a puppet show, trained animals, magic tricks, or music to draw customers. Or they did all these things and also worked as laundresses, day laborers, porters, peddlers, or street vendors when they could. Cities also drew in orphans, blind people, and the elderly, who resorted to begging for food and money.

Popular Entertainment

Games and sports were common forms of entertainment and relaxation. There were wrestling matches and games akin to modern football, rugby, stickball, and soccer in which balls were kicked, hit, and thrown. People played card and board games of all types. They played with dice carved from stone or bone, or with the knucklebones of animals or wood carved in knucklebone shapes, somewhat like modern jacks. They trained dogs to fight each other or put them in an enclosure to fight a captured bear. In Spain, Muslim knights confronted and killed bulls from horseback as part of religious feast days, developing a highly ritualized cere-mony that would later be further adapted by Spain's Christians. All these sports and games were occasions for wagering and gambling, which preachers sometimes condemned (especially when the games were attached to a holiday or saint's day celebration) but had little power to control.

Religious and family celebrations also meant dancing, which the church also had little success banning or regulating. Men and women danced in lines toward a specific object, such as a tree or a maypole, or in circles, groups, or pairs with specific step patterns. They were accompanied by a variety of instruments: reed pipes such as the chalumeau (an ancestor of the clarinet) and shawm (predecessor to the oboe); woodwinds such as flutes, panpipes, and recorders; stringed instru-ments including dulcimers, harps, lyres, lutes, zithers, and mandolins; brass instruments such as horns and trumpets; and percussion instruments like drums and tambourines. Many of these instruments were simple and were made by their players. Musicians playing string or percussion instruments often sang as well, and people sang without instrumental accompaniment on festive occasions or while working.

Medieval Universities

Just as the first strong secular states emerged in the thirteenth century, so did the first universities. This was no coincidence. The new bureaucratic states and the church needed educated administrators, and universities were a response to this need.

FOCUS QUESTION
How did universities serve the needs of medieval society?

Origins

In the early Middle Ages, monasteries and cathedral schools had offered most of the available formal instruction. Monastery schools were small, but cathedral schools, run by the bishop and his clergy in bustling cities, gradually grew larger. In the eleventh century in Italian cities like Bologna (boh-LOH-nyuh), wealthy businessmen established municipal schools. In the course of the twelfth century, cathedral schools in France and municipal schools in Italy developed into educational institutions that attracted students from a wide area (Map 10.3). These schools were often called *universitas magistrorum et scholarium* (universal society of teachers and students), the origin of the English word *university*. The first European universities appeared in Italy in Bologna, where the specialty was law, and Salerno, where the specialty was medicine.

MAP 10.3 Intellectual Centers of Medieval Europe   Universities provided more sophisticated instruction than did monastery and cathedral schools, but all these institutions served to educate males who had the money to attend.

Legal and Medical Training

The growth of the University of Bologna coincided with a revival of interest in Roman law during the investiture controversy. The study of Roman law as embodied in the Code of Justinian (see Chapter 7) had never completely died out in the West, but in the late eleventh century a complete manuscript of Justinian's Code was discovered in a library in Pisa. This discovery led scholars in nearby Bologna, beginning with Irnerius (ehr-NEH-ree-uhs) (ca. 1055–ca. 1130), to study and teach Roman law intently.

Irnerius and other teachers at Bologna taught law as an organic whole related to the society it regulated, an all-inclusive system based on logical principles that could be applied to difficult practical situations. Thus, as social and economic structures changed, law would change with them. Jurists educated at Bologna—and later at other universities—were hired by rulers and city councils to systematize their law codes and write legal treatises. In the 1260s the English jurist Henry Bracton wrote a comprehensive treatise bringing together the laws and customs of England, and King Alfonso X of Castile had scholars write the *Siete Partidas* (Book in Seven Parts), a detailed plan for administering his whole kingdom according to Roman legal principles.

Canon law (see Chapter 9) was also shaped by the reinvigoration of Roman law, and canon lawyers in ever-greater numbers were hired by church officials or became prominent church officials themselves. In about 1140 the Benedictine monk Gratian put together a collection of nearly 3,800 texts covering all areas of canon law. His collection, known as the *Decretum*, became the standard text on which teachers of canon law lectured and commented.

Jewish scholars also produced elaborate commentaries on law and religious tradition. Medieval universities were closed to Jews, but in some cities in the eleventh century special rabbinic academies opened that concentrated on the study of the Talmud, a compilation of legal arguments, proverbs, sayings, and folklore that had been produced in the fifth century in Babylon (present-day Iraq). Men seeking to become rabbis—highly respected figures within the Jewish community, with authority over economic and social as well as religious matters—spent long periods of time studying the Talmud, which served as the basis for their decisions affecting all areas of life.

Professional medical training began at Salerno. Individuals there, such as Constantine the African (1020?–1087)—who was a convert from Islam and later a Benedictine monk—began to translate medical works out of Arabic. These translations included writings by the ancient Greek physicians and Muslim medical writers, a blending of knowledge that later occurred on the nearby island of Sicily as well. (See "Evaluating the Evidence 10.2: Healthy Living," page 312.) Students of medicine poured into the city.

Medical studies at Salerno were based on classical ideas, particularly those of Hippocrates and Aristotle (see Chapter 3). For the ancient Greeks, ideas about the human body were very closely linked to philosophy and to ideas about the natural world in general. Prime among these was the notion of the four bodily humors—blood, phlegm, black bile, and yellow bile—fluids in the body that influenced bodily health. Each individual was thought to have a characteristic temperament or complexion determined by the balance of these humors, just as today we might describe a person as having a "positive outlook" or a "type A" personality. Disease was generally regarded as an imbalance of humors, which could be diagnosed by taking a

Healthy Living

In this illustration from a very popular fourteenth-century Latin handbook on maintaining health and well-being, women with their sleeves rolled up prepare cloth for medical uses; the woman on the left is trimming small threads off with a one-bladed shear, and the woman on the right is boiling the cloth to bleach it. The men in the background eat a meal and drink wine. The text of this handbook was a translation of an Arabic medical treatise, made in the kingdom of Sicily, the site of much cultural borrowing.

(From *Tacuinum Sanitatis* [vellum]/Österreichische Nationalbibliothek, Vienna, Austria/ Alinari/Bridgeman Images)

EVALUATE THE EVIDENCE

1. Cleanliness and moderation were recommended as essential to healthy living in this handbook. How does the artist convey these values in this scene?
2. Given what you have learned about medieval medical care, why might a handbook like this have been popular with literate urban residents?

---

patient's pulse or examining his or her urine. Treatment was thus an attempt to bring the humors back into balance, which might be accomplished through diet or drugs — mixtures of herbal or mineral substances — or by vomiting, emptying the bowels, or bloodletting. The bodily humors were somewhat gender related — women were regarded as tending toward cold and wet humors and men toward hot and dry — so therapies were also gender distinctive. Men's greater heat, scholars taught, created other gender differences: heat caused men's hair to burn internally so that they went bald, and their shoulders and brains to become larger than those of women (because heat rises and causes things to expand).

These ideas spread throughout Europe from Salerno and became the basis of training for physicians at other universities. University training gave physicians high social status and allowed them to charge high fees. They were generally hired directly by patients as needed, though some had more permanent positions as members of the household staffs of especially wealthy nobles or rulers.

Theology and Philosophy

Law and medicine were important academic disciplines in the Middle Ages, but theology was "the queen of sciences" because it involved the study of God, who made all knowledge possible. Paris became the place to study theology. In the first decades of the twelfth century, students from across Europe crowded into the cathedral school of Notre Dame (NOH-truh DAHM) in Paris.

University professors (a term first used in the fourteenth century) were known as "schoolmen" or **Scholastics**. They developed a method of thinking, reasoning, and

Scholastics University professors in the Middle Ages who developed a method of thinking, reasoning, and writing in which questions were raised and authorities cited on both sides of a question.

writing in which questions were raised and authorities cited on both sides of a question. The goal of this method was to arrive at definitive answers and to provide rational explanations for what was believed on faith.

The Scholastic approach rested on the recovery of classical philosophical texts. Ancient Greek and Arabic texts entered Europe in the early twelfth century by way of Islamic intellectual centers at Baghdad, Córdoba, and Toledo (see Chapter 8). The major contribution of Arab culture to the new currents of Western thought rested in the stimulus Arab philosophers and commentators gave to Europeans' reflections on ancient Greek texts and the ways these texts fit with Christian teachings. One of the young men drawn to Paris was Peter Abelard (1079–1142), the son of a minor Breton knight. Abelard was fascinated by logic, which he believed could be used to solve most problems. He was one of the first Scholastics, and commented, "By doubting we come to questioning, and by questioning we perceive the truth." Abelard was severely censured by a church council, but his cleverness, boldness, and imagination made him a highly popular figure among students.

Abelard's reputation for brilliance drew the attention of one of the cathedral canons, Fulbert, who hired Abelard to tutor his intelligent niece Heloise. The relationship between teacher and pupil passed beyond the intellectual. Heloise became pregnant, and Fulbert pressured the couple to marry. The couple agreed, but wanted the marriage kept secret for the sake of Abelard's career. Furious at Abelard, Fulbert hired men to castrate him. Abelard persuaded Heloise to enter a convent, and he became a monk. Their baby, baptized Astrolabe for a recent Muslim navigational invention, was given to Heloise's family for adoption. The two became leaders of their communities—Abelard an abbot and Heloise a prioress—but they never saw each other again, though they wrote letters, which have become examples of the new self-awareness of the period.

In the thirteenth century Scholastics devoted an enormous amount of time to collecting and organizing knowledge on all topics. Such a collection was published as a *summa* (SOO-muh), or reference book. There were *summae* on law, philosophy, vegetation, animal life, and theology. Saint Thomas Aquinas (1225–1274), a Dominican friar and professor at the University of Paris, produced the most famous of these collections, the *Summa Theologica*, a summation of Christian ideas on a vast number of theological questions, including the nature of God and Christ, moral principles, and the role of the sacraments. In this, and many of his other writings, Aquinas used arguments that drew from ancient Greek philosophers, especially Aristotle, as well as earlier Christian writers. Aquinas was both a theologian and a philosopher: he wrote sermons, prayers, commentaries on books of the Bible, and argumentative works on aspects of Christian theology such as the nature of evil and the power of God, but also commentaries on several of Aristotle's works.

In these, he investigated the branch of philosophy called epistemology, which is concerned with how a person knows something. Aquinas stated that first one knows through sensory perception of the physical world—seeing, hearing, touching, and so on. He maintained that there can be nothing in the mind that is not first in the senses. The second way knowledge comes is through reason, through the mind exercising its natural abilities.

In all these works, Aquinas stressed the power of human reason to demonstrate many basic Christian principles, including the existence of God. To obtain true Christian understanding, he wrote, one needed both reason and faith. His ideas have been extremely influential in both philosophy and theology: in the former through the philosophical school known as Thomism, and in the latter especially through the Catholic Church, which has affirmed many times that they are foundational to Roman Catholic doctrine.

University Students

The influx of students eager for learning, together with dedicated and imaginative teachers, created the atmosphere in which universities grew. By the end of the fifteenth century there were at least eighty universities in Europe. Some universities also offered younger students training in what were termed the seven liberal arts—grammar, rhetoric, logic, mathematics, geometry, music, and astronomy—that could serve as a foundation for more specialized study in all areas.

University students were generally considered to be lower-level members of the clergy—this was termed being in "minor orders"—so any students accused of legal infractions were tried in church, rather than in city, courts. This clerical status, along with widely held ideas about women's lesser intellectual capabilities, meant that university education was restricted to men. Even more than feudal armies—which were often accompanied by women who did laundry, found provisions, cooked meals, and engaged in sex for money—universities were all-male communities. (Most European universities did not admit women until after World War I.)

Though university classes were not especially expensive, the many years that a university education required meant that the sons of peasants or artisans could rarely attend, unless they could find wealthy patrons who would pay their expenses. Most students were the sons of urban merchants or lower-level nobles, especially the younger sons who would not inherit family lands. University degrees were initially designed as licenses to teach at the university, but most students staffed the expanding diocesan, royal, and papal administrations as lawyers and officials.

Students did not spend all their time preparing for their degrees. Much information about medieval students concerns what we might call "extracurricular" activities: university regulations forbidding them to throw rocks at professors; sermons about breaking and entering, raping local women, attacking town residents, and disturbing church services; and court records discussing their drunken brawls, riots, and fights and duels. Students also delayed finishing their studies because life as a student could be pleasant, without the responsibilities that came with becoming fully adult. Student life was described by students in poems, usually anonymous, that celebrated the joys of Venus (the goddess of love) and other gods:

> When we are in the tavern,
> we do not think how we will go to dust,
> but we hurry to gamble,
> which always makes us sweat.
> . . .
> Here no-one fears death,
> but they throw the dice in the name of Bacchus.
> . . .
> To the Pope as to the king
> they all drink without restraint.[7]

Literature and Architecture

The High Middle Ages saw the creation of new types of literature, architecture, and music. Technological advances in such areas as papermaking and stone masonry made some of these innovations possible, as did the growing wealth and sophistication of patrons. Artists and artisans flourished in the more secure environment of the High Middle Ages, producing works that celebrated the glories of love, war, and God.

FOCUS QUESTION
How did literature and architecture express medieval values?

Vernacular Literature and Drama

Latin was the language used in university education, scholarly writing, and works of literature. By the High Middle Ages, however, no one spoke Latin as his or her original mother tongue. The barbarian invasions, the mixture of peoples, and the usual changes in language that occur over time had resulted in a variety of local dialects that blended words and linguistic forms in various ways. As kings increased the size of their holdings, they often ruled people who spoke many different dialects.

In the High Middle Ages, some authors departed from tradition and began to write in their local dialect, that is, in the everyday language of their region, which linguistic historians call the vernacular. This new **vernacular literature** gradually transformed some local dialects into literary languages, such as French, German, Italian, and English, while other local dialects, such as Breton and Bavarian, remained (and remain to this day) means of oral communication.

Facilitating this vernacular writing was a technological advance. By the thirteenth century techniques of making paper from old linen cloth and rags began to spread from Spain, where they had been developed by the Arabs, providing a much cheaper material on which to write than parchment or vellum (see Chapter 8). People started to write down the more mundane and the less serious—personal letters, lists, songs, recipes, rules, instructions—in their dialects, using spellings that were often personal and idiosyncratic. These writings included fables, legends, stories, and myths that had circulated orally for generations, adding to the growing body of written vernacular literature.

Stories and songs in the vernacular were composed and performed at the courts of nobles and rulers. In Germany and most of northern Europe, the audiences favored stories and songs recounting the great deeds of warrior heroes. These epics, known as *chansons de geste* (SHAN-suhn duh JEHST; songs of great deeds), celebrate violence, slaughter, revenge, and physical power. In southern Europe, especially in Provence in southern France, poets who called themselves **troubadours** (TROO-buh-dorz) wrote and sang lyric verses celebrating love, desire, beauty, and gallantry. (See "Evaluating the Evidence 10.3: Courtly Love Poetry," page 316.) Troubadours included a few women, called *trobairitz*, most of whose exact identities are not known.

The songs of the troubadours were widely imitated in Italy, England, and Germany, so they spurred the development of vernacular literature there as well. At the court of his patron, Marie of Champagne, Chrétien de Troyes (ca. 1135–ca. 1190) used the legends of the fifth-century British king Arthur (see Chapter 7) as the basis for innovative tales of battle and forbidden love. His most popular story is that of the noble Lancelot, whose love for Guinevere, the wife of King Arthur, his lord, became physical as well as spiritual. Most of the troubadours came from and wrote for the aristocratic classes, and their poetry suggests the interests and values of noble culture. Their

vernacular literature
Writings in the author's local dialect, that is, in the everyday language of the region.

troubadours Poets who wrote and sang lyric verses celebrating love, desire, beauty, and gallantry.

Courtly Love Poetry

Whether female or male, the troubadour poets celebrated fin'amor, a Provençal word for the pure or perfect love a knight was supposed to feel for his lady, which has in English come to be called "courtly love." In courtly love poetry, the writer praises his or her love object, idealizing the beloved and promising loyalty and great deeds. Most of these songs are written by, or from the perspective of, a male lover who is socially beneath his female beloved; her higher status makes her unattainable, so the lover's devotion can remain chaste and pure, rewarded by her handkerchief, or perhaps a kiss, but nothing more.

Scholars generally agree that poetry praising pure and perfect love originated in the Muslim culture of the Iberian Peninsula, where heterosexual romantic love had long been the subject of poems and songs. Spanish Muslim poets sang at the courts of Christian nobles, and Provençal poets picked up their romantic themes.

Other aspects of courtly love are hotly debated. Was it simply a literary convention, or did it shape actual behavior? Did it celebrate adultery, or was true courtly love pure (and unrequited)? How should we interpret medieval physicians' reports of people (mostly young men) becoming gravely ill from "lovesickness"? Were there actually "courts of love" in which women judged lovers based on a system of rules? Did courtly love lead to greater respect for women or toward greater misogyny, as desire for a beloved so often ended in frustration? It is very difficult to know whether courtly love literature influenced the treatment of real women to any great extent, but it did introduce a new ideal of heterosexual romance into Western literature. Courtly love ideals still shape romantic conventions and often appear in movies, songs, and novels that explore love between people of different social groups.

The following poem was written by Arnaut Daniel, a thirteenth-century troubadour praised by poets from Dante in the thirteenth century to Ezra Pound in the twentieth. Not much is known about him, but his surviving songs capture courtly love conventions perfectly.

~

I only know the grief that comes to me,
to my love-ridden heart, out of over-loving,
since my will is so firm and whole
that it never parted or grew distant from her
whom I craved at first sight, and afterwards:
and now, in her absence, I tell her burning words;
then, when I see her, I don't know, so much I have to,
    what to say.

To the sight of other women I am blind, deaf to hearing
    them
since her only I see, and hear and heed,
and in that I am surely not a false slanderer,
since heart desires her more than mouth may say;
wherever I may roam through fields and valleys, plains
    and mountains
I shan't find in a single person all those qualities
which God wanted to select and place in her.

I have been in many a good court,
but here by her I find much more to praise:
measure and wit and other good virtues,
beauty and youth, worthy deeds and fair disport;
so well kindness taught and instructed her
that it has rooted every ill manner out of her:
I don't think she lacks anything good.

No joy would be brief or short
coming from her whom I endear to guess [my
    intentions],
otherwise she won't know them from me,
if my heart cannot reveal itself without words,
since even the Rhone [River], when rain swells it,

influence extended to all social groups, however, for people who could not read heard the poems and stories from people who could, so that what had originally come from oral culture was recycled back into it.

Drama, derived from the church's liturgy, emerged as a distinct art form during the High Middle Ages. Amateurs and later professional actors performed plays based on biblical themes and on the lives of the saints; these dramas were presented in the towns, first in churches and then at the marketplace. Members of the craft guilds performed "mystery" plays, so called because guilds were sometimes called

has no such rush that my heart doesn't stir
a stronger one, weary of love, when I behold her.

Joy and merriment from another woman seems false and
    ill to me,
since no worthy one can compare with her,
and her company is above the others'.
Ah me, if I don't have her, alas, so badly she has taken me!
But this grief is amusement, laughter and joy,
since in thinking of her, of her am I gluttonous and
    greedy:
ah me, God, could I ever enjoy her otherwise!

And never, I swear, I have liked game or ball so much,
or anything has given my heart so much joy
as did the one thing that no false slanderer
made public, which is a treasure for me only.
Do I tell too much? Not I, unless she is displeased:
beautiful one, by God, speech and voice
I'd lose ere I say something to annoy you.

And I pray my song does not displease you
since, if you like the music and lyrics,
little cares Arnaut whether the unpleasant ones like them
    as well.

*Far fewer poems by female trobairitz have survived than by
male troubadours, but those that have survived express
strong physical and emotional feelings. The following song
was written in the twelfth century by the Countess of Dia. She
was purportedly the wife of a Provençal nobleman, though
biographies of both troubadours and trobairitz were often
made up to fit the conventions of courtly love, so we don't
know for sure. The words to at least four of her songs have
survived, one of them with the melody, which is very rare.*

~

I've suffered great distress
From a knight whom I once owned.
Now, for all time, be it known:
I loved him — yes, to excess. His jilting I've regretted,

Yet his love I never really returned. Now for my sin I can
    only burn:
Dressed, or in my bed.

O if I had that knight to caress
Naked all night in my arms,
He'd be ravished by the charm
Of using, for cushion, my breast. His love I more deeply
    prize
Than Floris did Blancheor's
Take that love, my core, My sense, my life, my eyes!

Lovely lover, gracious, kind,
When will I overcome your fight?
O if I could lie with you one night!
Feel those loving lips on mine! Listen, one thing sets me
    afire:
Here in my husband's place I want you,
If you'll just keep your promise true: Give me everything
    I desire.

EVALUATE THE EVIDENCE

1. Both of these songs focus on a beloved who does not
   return the lover's affection. What similarities and
   differences do you see in them?
2. How does courtly love reinforce other aspects of
   medieval society? Are there aspects of medieval
   society it contradicts?
3. Can you find examples from current popular music that
   parallel the sentiments expressed in these two songs?

Sources: First poem: From "Sol sui qui sai lo sobrafan qu'em sortz" by
Arnaut Daniel, translated by Leonardo Malcovati, www.trobar.org. Used
by permission of Leonardo Malcovati, editor and translator of *Prosody in
England and Elsewhere: A Comparative Approach* (London: Gival Press,
2006), and online at www.trobar.org; second poem: Three verses from
lyrics by the Countess of Dia, often called Beatritz, the Sappho of the
Rhone, in *Lyrics of the Middle Ages: An Anthology*, edited and translated by
James J. Wilhelm. Reproduced with permission of GARLAND PUBLISHING,
INC., in the format Book via Copyright Clearance Center.

"mysteries." By combining comical farce based on ordinary life with serious religious
scenes, plays gave ordinary people an opportunity to identify with religious figures
and think about their faith.

Churches and Cathedrals

The development of secular vernacular literature focusing on human concerns did
not mean any lessening of the importance of religion in medieval people's lives. As we
have seen, religious devotion was expressed through daily rituals, holiday ceremonies,

Notre Dame Cathedral, Paris This view offers a fine example of the twin towers (left), the spire and great rose window over the south portal (center), and the flying buttresses that support the walls and the vaults. Like hundreds of other churches in medieval Europe, it was dedicated to the Virgin Mary. With a spire rising more than 300 feet, Notre Dame was the tallest building in Europe. (David R. Frazier/Science Source)

and the creation of new institutions such as universities and religious orders. People also wanted permanent visible representations of their piety, and both church and city leaders wanted physical symbols of their wealth and power. These aims found their outlet in the building of tens of thousands of churches, chapels, abbeys, and, most spectacularly, **cathedrals** in the twelfth and thirteenth centuries. A cathedral is the church of a bishop and the administrative headquarters of a diocese. The word comes from the Greek word *kathedra*, meaning seat, because the bishop's throne, a symbol of the office, is located in the cathedral.

Most of the churches in the early Middle Ages had been built primarily of wood, which meant they were susceptible to fire. They were often small, with a flat roof, in a rectangular form with a central aisle; this structure, called a basilica, was based on earlier Roman public buildings. With the increasing political stability of the eleventh century, bishops and abbots supported the construction of larger and more fire-resistant churches made almost completely out of stone. As the size of the church grew horizontally, it also grew vertically. Builders adapted Roman-style rounded barrel vaults made of stone for the ceiling; this use of Roman forms led the style to be labeled **Romanesque**.

The next architectural style was **Gothic**, so named by later Renaissance architects who thought that only the uncouth Goths could have invented such a disunified style. In Gothic churches the solid stone barrel-vaulted roof was replaced by a roof made of stone ribs with plaster in between. Because this ceiling was much lighter, side pillars and walls did not need to carry as much weight. Exterior arched stone supports called flying buttresses also carried some of the weight of the roof, so solid walls could be replaced by windows, which let in great amounts of light. Originating in the Île-de-France in the twelfth century, Gothic architecture spread throughout France with the expansion of royal power. From France the new style spread to England, Germany, Italy, Spain, and eastern Europe.

Extraordinary amounts of money were needed to build these houses of worship. The economic growth of the period meant that merchants, nobles, and the church could afford the costs of this unparalleled building boom. Moreover,

cathedral The church of a bishop and the administrative headquarters of a diocese.

Romanesque An architectural style with rounded arches and small windows.

Gothic An architectural style typified by pointed arches and large stained-glass windows.

money was not the only need. A great number of artisans had to be assembled: quarrymen, sculptors, stonecutters, masons, mortar makers, carpenters, blacksmiths, glassmakers, roofers. Each master craftsman had apprentices, and unskilled laborers had to be recruited for the heavy work. Bishops and abbots sketched out what they wanted and set general guidelines, but they left practical needs and aesthetic considerations to the master mason. He held overall responsibility for supervision of the project.

Since cathedrals were symbols of civic pride, towns competed to build the largest and most splendid church. In 1163 the citizens of Paris began Notre Dame Cathedral, planning it to reach the height of 114 feet from the floor to the ceiling at the highest point inside. Many other cathedrals well over 100 feet tall on the inside were built as each bishop and town sought to outdo the neighbors. Towers and spires jutted up another several hundred feet. Medieval people built cathedrals to glorify God—and if mortals were impressed, all the better. Construction of a large cathedral was rarely completed in a lifetime; many were never finished at all. Because generation after generation added to the buildings, many of these churches show the architectural influences of two or even three centuries.

Stained glass beautifully reflects the creative energy of the High Middle Ages. It is both an integral part of Gothic architecture and a distinct form of visual art. From large sheets of colored glass made by glassblowers, artisans cut small pieces, linked them together with narrow strips of lead, and set them in an iron frame prepared to fit the window opening. Windows showed scenes from the Old and New Testaments and the lives of the saints, designed to teach people doctrines of the Christian faith. They also showed scenes from the lives of the artisans and merchants who paid for them.

Once at least part of a cathedral had been built, the building began to be used for religious services. Town residents gathered for masses, baptisms, funerals, and saint's day services, and also used it for guild meetings and other secular purposes. Services became increasingly complex to fit with their new surroundings. Originally, services were chanted by the clergy in unison, in a form of liturgical music termed plainsong or Gregorian chant, but by the eleventh century additional voices singing in different pitches were added, creating what is called polyphony. Church leaders sometimes fumed that polyphony made the text impossible to understand but—along with incense, candles, stained-glass windows, statuary, tapestry wall hangings, and the building itself—music made services in a Gothic cathedral a rich experience.

The frenzy to create the most magnificent Gothic cathedrals eventually came to an end. Begun in 1247, the cathedral in Beauvais reached a height of 157 feet in the interior, exceeding all others. Unfortunately, the weight imposed on the vaults was too great, and the building collapsed in 1284. The collapse was viewed as an aberration, for countless other cathedrals were in various stages of completion at the same time, and none of them fell. In hindsight, however, it can be viewed as a harbinger. Very few cathedrals not yet completed at the time of its collapse were ever finished, and even fewer were started. In the fourteenth century the church itself splintered, and the cities that had so proudly built cathedrals were decimated by famine and disease.

LOOKING BACK LOOKING AHEAD

The High Middle Ages represent one of the most creative periods in the history of Western society. Institutions that are important parts of the modern world, including universities, jury trials, and investment banks, were all developed in this era. Advances were made in the mechanization of labor, business procedures, architectural design, and education. Through the activities of merchants, Europeans again saw products from Africa and Asia in city marketplaces, as they had in Roman times, and wealthier urban residents bought them. Individuals and groups such as craft guilds provided money for building and decorating magnificent Gothic cathedrals, where people heard increasingly complex music and watched plays that celebrated both the lives of the saints and their own daily struggles.

Toward the end of the thirteenth century, however, there were increasing signs of impending problems. The ships and caravans bringing exotic goods also brought new pests. The new vernacular literature created a stronger sense of national identity, which increased hostility toward others. The numbers of poor continued to grow, and efforts to aid their suffering were never enough. As the century ended, villagers and city residents alike continued to gather for worship, but they also wondered whether God was punishing them.

Make Connections

Think about the larger developments and continuities within and across chapters.

1. How was life in a medieval city different from life in a Hellenistic city (Chapter 4), or life in Rome during the time of Augustus (Chapter 6)? In what ways was it similar? What problems did these cities confront that are still issues for cities today?

2. Historians have begun to turn their attention to the history of children and childhood. How were children's lives in the societies you have examined shaped by larger social structures and cultural forces? What commonalities do you see in children's lives across time?

3. Chapter 4 and this chapter both examine ways in which religion and philosophy shaped life for ordinary people and for the educated elite. How would you compare Hellenistic religious practices with those of medieval Europe? How would you compare the ideas of Hellenistic philosophers such as Epicurus or Zeno with those of Scholastic philosophers such as Thomas Aquinas?

10 REVIEW & EXPLORE

Review the Main Ideas

Answer the focus questions from each section of the chapter.

◆ What was village life like in medieval Europe? (p. 286)

◆ How did religion shape everyday life in the High Middle Ages? (p. 292)

◆ What led to Europe's economic growth and reurbanization? (p. 298)

◆ What was life like in medieval cities? (p. 306)

◆ How did universities serve the needs of medieval society? (p. 309)

◆ How did literature and architecture express medieval values? (p. 315)

Identify Key Terms

Identify and explain the significance of each item below.

open-field system (p. 288)
merchant guild (p. 299)
craft guild (p. 299)
Hanseatic League (p. 303)
commercial revolution (p. 304)
sumptuary laws (p. 307)
Scholastics (p. 312)
vernacular literature (p. 315)
troubadours (p. 315)
cathedral (p. 318)
Romanesque (p. 318)
Gothic (p. 318)

NOTES

1. Honorius of Autun, "Elucidarium sive Dialogus de Summa Totius Christianae Theologiae," in *Patrologia Latina*, ed. J. P. Migne (Paris: Garnier Brothers, 1854), vol. 172, col. 1149.
2. M. Chibnall, ed. and trans., *The Ecclesiastical History of Ordericus Vitalis* (Oxford: Oxford University Press, 1972), 2.xiii.
3. Thirteenth-century sermon story, in David Herlihy, ed., *Medieval Culture and Society* (New York: Harper and Row, 1968), pp. 295, 298.
4. Translated and quoted in Susan C. Karant-Nunn, *The Reformation of Ritual: An Interpretation of Early Modern Germany* (London: Routledge, 1997), p. 77.
5. Roy C. Cave and Hervet H. Coulson, *A Source Book for Medieval Economic History* (New York: Biblio and Tannen, 1965), p. 257.
6. H. Rothwell, ed., *English Historical Documents*, vol. 3 (London: Eyre & Spottiswoode, 1975), p. 854.
7. www.classical.net/music/comp.lst/works/orff-cb/carmlyr.php#track14. This verse is from one of the songs known as the Carmina Burana, which are widely available as recordings, downloadable files, and even cell phone ring tones.

CHAPTER PREVIEW

Prelude to Disaster
How did climate change shape the late Middle Ages?

The Black Death
How did the plague reshape European society?

The Hundred Years' War
What were the causes, course, and consequences of the Hundred Years' War?

Challenges to the Church
Why did the church come under increasing criticism?

Social Unrest in a Changing Society
What explains the social unrest of the late Middle Ages?

Life and Death in the Late Middle Ages

In this French manuscript illumination from 1465, armored knights kill peasants while they work in the fields or take refuge in a castle. Aristocratic violence was a common feature of late medieval life, although nobles would generally not have bothered to put on their armor to harass villagers.

(From *Cas de Nobles Hommes et Femmes*, 1465/Musée Condé, Chantilly, France/Bridgeman Images)

11

The Later Middle Ages

1300–1450

During the later Middle Ages the last book of the New Testament, the book of Revelation, inspired thousands of sermons and hundreds of religious tracts. The book of Revelation deals with visions of the end of the world, with disease, war, famine, and death—often called the "Four Horsemen of the Apocalypse"— triumphing everywhere. It is no wonder this part of the Bible was so popular in this period, for between 1300 and 1450 Europeans experienced a frightful series of shocks. The climate turned colder and wetter, leading to poor harvests and famine. People weakened by hunger were more susceptible to disease, and in the middle of the fourteenth century a new disease, probably the bubonic plague, spread throughout Europe. With no effective treatment, the plague killed millions of people. War devastated the countryside, especially in France, leading to widespread discontent and peasant revolts. Workers in cities also revolted against dismal working conditions, and violent crime and ethnic tensions increased as well. Massive deaths and preoccupation with death make the fourteenth century one of the most wrenching periods of Western civilization. Yet, in spite of the pessimism and crises, important institutions and cultural forms, including representative assemblies and national literatures, emerged. Even institutions that experienced severe crisis, such as the Christian Church, saw new types of vitality. ■

Prelude to Disaster

FOCUS QUESTION
How did climate change shape the late Middle Ages?

Toward the end of the thirteenth century the expanding European economy began to slow down, and in the first half of the fourteenth century Europe experienced ongoing climate change that led to lower levels of food production, which had dramatic and disastrous ripple effects. Rulers attempted to find solutions but were unable to deal with the economic and social problems that resulted.

Climate Change and Famine

The period from about 1000 to about 1300 saw a warmer-than-usual climate in Europe, which underlay all the changes and vitality of the High Middle Ages. Around 1300, however, the climate changed for the worse, becoming colder and wetter. Historical geographers refer to the period from 1300 to 1450 as a "little ice age," which they can trace through both natural and human records.

Evidence from nature emerges through the study of Alpine and polar glaciers, tree rings, and pollen left in bogs. Human-produced sources include written reports of rivers freezing and crops never ripening, as well as archaeological evidence such as the collapsed houses and emptied villages of Greenland, where ice floes cut off contact with the rest of the world and the harshening climate meant that the few hardy crops grown in earlier times could no longer survive. The Viking colony on Greenland died out completely, though Inuit people who relied on hunting sea mammals continued to live in the far north, as they had before the arrival of Viking colonists.

Across Europe, an unusual number of storms brought torrential rains, ruining the wheat, oat, and hay crops on which people and animals almost everywhere depended. Since long-distance transportation of food was expensive and difficult, most urban areas depended for grain, produce, and meat on areas no more than a day's journey away. Poor harvests—and one in four was likely to be poor—led to scarcity and starvation. Almost all of northern Europe suffered a **Great Famine** in the years 1315 to 1322, which contemporaries interpreted as a recurrence of the biblical "seven lean years" that afflicted Egypt.

Great Famine A terrible famine in 1315–1322 that hit much of Europe after a period of climate change.

Even in non-famine years, the cost of grain, livestock, and dairy products rose sharply, in part because diseases hit cattle and sheep. Increasing prices meant that

Death from Famine   In this fifteenth-century painting, dead bodies lie in the middle of a path, while a funeral procession at the right includes a man with an adult's coffin and a woman with the coffin of an infant under her arm. People did not simply allow the dead to lie in the street in medieval Europe, though during famines and epidemics it was sometimes difficult to maintain normal burial procedures. (From *Chroniques d'Angleterre,* ca. 1470–1480/British Library, London, UK/© British Library Board. All Rights Reserved/Bridgeman Images)

fewer people could afford to buy food. Reduced caloric intake meant increased susceptibility to disease, especially for infants, children, and the elderly. Workers on reduced diets had less energy, which meant lower productivity, lower output, and higher grain prices.

Social Consequences

The changing climate and resulting agrarian crisis of the fourteenth century had grave social consequences. Poor harvests and famine led to the abandonment of homesteads. In parts of the Low Countries and in the Scottish-English borderlands, entire villages were deserted, and many people became vagabonds, wandering in search of food and work. In Flanders and eastern England, some peasants were forced to mortgage, sublease, or sell their holdings to richer farmers in order to buy food. Throughout the affected areas, young men and women sought work in the towns, delaying marriage. Overall, the population declined because of the deaths caused by famine and disease, though the postponement of marriages and resulting decline in offspring may have also played a part.

As the subsistence crisis deepened, starving people focused their anger on the rich, speculators, and the Jews, who were often targeted as creditors fleecing the poor through pawnbroking. (As explained in Chapter 10, Jews often became moneylenders because Christian authorities restricted their ownership of land and opportunities to engage in other trades.) Rumors spread of a plot by Jews and their agents, the lepers, to kill Christians by poisoning wells. Based on "evidence" collected by torture, many lepers and Jews were killed, beaten, or heavily fined.

Meanwhile, the international character of trade and commerce meant that a disaster in one country had serious implications elsewhere. For example, the infection that attacked English sheep in 1318 caused a sharp decline in wool exports in the following years. Without wool, Flemish weavers could not work, and thousands were laid off. Without woolen cloth, the businesses of Flemish, Hanseatic, and Italian merchants suffered. Unemployment encouraged people to turn to crime.

Government responses to these crises were ineffectual. The three sons of Philip the Fair who sat on the French throne between 1314 and 1328 condemned speculators who held stocks of grain back until conditions were desperate and prices high, and they forbade the sale of grain abroad. These measures had few actual results, however. In England, Edward II (r. 1307–1327) also condemned speculators after his attempts to set price controls on livestock and ale proved futile. He did try to buy grain abroad, but little was available, and such grain as reached southern English ports was stolen by looters and sold on the black market. The king's efforts at famine relief failed.

Chronology

1300–1450	Little ice age
1309–1376	Babylonian Captivity; papacy in Avignon
1310–1320	Dante writes *Divine Comedy*
1315–1322	Great Famine in northern Europe
1320s	First large-scale peasant rebellion in Flanders
1337–1453	Hundred Years' War
1347	Black Death arrives in Europe
1358	Jacquerie peasant uprising in France
1366	Statute of Kilkenny
1378–1417	Great Schism
1381	English Peasants' Revolt
1387–1400	Chaucer writes *Canterbury Tales*

The Black Death

FOCUS QUESTION
How did the plague reshape European society?

Colder weather, failed harvests, and resulting malnourishment left Europe's population susceptible to disease, and unfortunately for the continent, a virulent one appeared in the mid-fourteenth century. Around 1300 improvements in ship design had allowed year-round shipping for the first time. European merchants took advantage of these advances, and ships continually at sea carried all types of cargo. They also carried vermin of all types, especially insects and rats, both of which often harbored pathogens. Rats, fleas, and cockroaches could live for months on the cargo carried along the coasts, disembarking at ports with the grain, cloth, or other merchandise. Just as modern air travel has allowed diseases such as AIDS and the H1N1 virus to spread quickly over very long distances, medieval shipping allowed the diseases of the time to do the same. The most frightful of these diseases, carried on Genoese ships, first emerged in western Europe in 1347; the disease was later called the **Black Death**.

Black Death Plague that first struck Europe in 1347 and killed perhaps one-third of the population.

Pathology

Most historians and microbiologists identify the disease that spread in the fourteenth century as the bubonic plague, which is caused by the bacillus *Yersinia pestis*. The disease normally afflicts rats. Fleas living on the infected rats drink their blood and then pass the bacteria that cause the plague on to the next rat they bite. Usually the disease is limited to rats and other rodents, but at certain points in history—perhaps when most rats have been killed off—the fleas have jumped from their rodent hosts to humans and other animals. One of these instances appears to have occurred in the Eastern Roman Empire in the sixth century, when a plague killed millions of people. Another was in China and India in the 1890s, when millions again died. Doctors and epidemiologists closely studied this outbreak, identified the bacillus as bubonic plague, and learned about the exact cycle of infection for the first time.

The fourteenth-century outbreak showed many similarities to the nineteenth-century one, but also some differences. There are no reports of massive rat die-offs in fourteenth-century records. The medieval plague was often transmitted directly from one person to another through coughing and sneezing (what epidemiologists term *pneumonic* transmission) as well as through flea bites. The fourteenth-century outbreak spread much faster than the nineteenth-century epidemic and was much more deadly, killing as much as one-third of the population when it first reached an area. These differences have led a few historians to speculate that the Black Death was actually not the bubonic plague but a different disease, perhaps something like the Ebola virus. Other scholars counter that the differences could be explained by variant strains of the disease or improvements in sanitation and public health that would have significantly limited the mortality rate of later outbreaks, even in poor countries such as India. These debates fuel continued study of medical aspects of the plague, with scientists using innovative techniques such as studying the tooth pulp of bodies in medieval cemeteries to see if it contains DNA from plague-causing agents.

Though there is some disagreement about exactly what kind of disease the plague was, there is no dispute about its dreadful effects on the body. The classic symptom of the bubonic plague was a growth the size of a nut or an apple in the armpit, in the groin, or on the neck. This was the boil, or *bubo*, that gave the disease its name and caused agonizing pain. If the bubo was lanced and the pus thoroughly drained, the victim had a chance of recovery. If the boil was not lanced, however—and in the fourteenth century, it rarely was—the next stage was the appearance of black spots or blotches caused by bleeding under the skin. (This syndrome did not give the disease its common name; contemporaries did not call the plague the Black Death. Sometime in the fifteenth century the Latin phrase *atra mors*, meaning "dreadful death," was translated as "black death," and the phrase stuck.) Finally, the victim began to cough violently and spit blood. This stage, indicating the presence of millions of bacilli in the bloodstream, signaled the end, and death followed in two or three days. The coughing also released those pathogens into the air, infecting others when they were breathed in and beginning the deadly cycle again on new victims.

Spread of the Disease

Plague symptoms were first described in 1331 in southwestern China, then part of the Mongol Empire. Plague-infested rats accompanied Mongol armies and merchant caravans carrying silk, spices, and gold across Central Asia in the 1330s. The rats then stowed away on ships, carrying the disease to the ports of the Black Sea by the 1340s. One Italian chronicler told of more dramatic means of spreading the disease as well: Mongol armies besieging the city of Kaffa on the shores of the Black Sea catapulted plague-infected corpses over the walls to infect those inside. The city's residents dumped the corpses into the sea as fast as they could, but they were already infected.

In October 1347 Genoese ships brought the plague from Kaffa to Messina, from which it spread across Sicily. Venice and Genoa were hit in January 1348, and from the port of Pisa the disease spread south to Rome and east to Florence and all of Tuscany. By late spring southern Germany was attacked. Frightened French authorities chased a galley bearing plague victims away from the port of Marseilles, but not before plague had infected the city, from which it spread to southern France and Spain. In June 1348 two ships entered the Bristol Channel and introduced it into England, and from there it traveled northeast into Scandinavia. The plague seems to have entered Poland through the Baltic seaports and spread eastward from there (Map 11.1).

Medieval urban conditions were ideal for the spread of disease. Narrow streets were filled with refuse, human excrement, and dead animals. Houses whose upper stories projected over the lower ones blocked light and air. Houses were beginning to be constructed of brick, but many wood, clay, and mud houses remained. A determined rat had little trouble entering such a house. In addition, people were already weakened by famine, standards of personal hygiene remained frightfully low, and the urban populace was crowded together. Fleas and body lice were universal afflictions: everyone from peasants to archbishops had them. One more bite did not cause much alarm, and the association between rats, fleas, and the plague was unknown. Mortality rates can be only educated guesses because population figures for the period before the arrival of the plague do not exist for most countries and cities. Of a total English population of perhaps 4.2 million, probably 1.4 million died of the Black Death. Densely populated Italian cities endured incredible losses. Florence lost between one-half and two-thirds of its population when the plague visited in 1348. Islamic parts of Europe were not spared, nor was the rest of the Muslim world. The most widely accepted estimate for western Europe and the

MAP 11.1 The Course of the Black Death in Fourteenth-Century Europe   The bubonic plague spread across Europe after beginning in the mid-1340s, with the first cases of disease reported in Black Sea ports.

Mediterranean is that the plague killed about one-third of the population in the first wave of infection. (Some areas, including such cities as Milan, Liège, and Nuremberg, were largely spared, primarily because city authorities closed the gates to all outsiders when plague was in the area and enough food had been stored to sustain the city until the danger had passed.)

Nor did central and eastern Europe escape the ravages of the disease. One chronicler records that, in the summer and autumn of 1349, between five hundred and six hundred died every day in Vienna. As the Black Death took its toll on the Holy Roman Empire, waves of emigrants fled to Poland, Bohemia, and Hungary, taking the plague with them. In the Byzantine Empire the plague ravaged the population. The youngest son of Emperor John VI Kantakouzenos died just as his father took over the throne in 1347. "So incurable was the evil," wrote John later in his history of the Byzantine Empire, "that neither any regularity of life, nor any bodily strength could resist it. Strong and weak bodies were all similarly carried away, and those best cared for died in the same manner as the poor."[1]

Across Europe the Black Death recurred intermittently from the 1360s to 1400. It reappeared from time to time over the following centuries as well, though never with the same virulence because by then Europeans had some resistance. Improved standards of hygiene and strictly enforced quarantine measures also lessened the plague's toll, but only in 1721 did it make its last appearance in Europe, in the French port of Marseilles. And only in 1947, six centuries after the arrival of the plague in Europe, did the American microbiologist Selman Waksman discover an effective treatment, streptomycin. Plague continues to infect rodent and human populations sporadically today.

Care of the Sick

Fourteenth-century medical literature indicates that physicians tried many different methods to prevent and treat the plague. People understood that plague and other diseases could be transmitted person to person, and they observed that crowded cities had high death rates, especially when the weather was warm and moist. We now understand that warm, moist conditions make it easier for germs to grow and spread, but fourteenth-century people thought in terms of "poisons" in the air or "corrupted air" coming from swamps, unburied animals, or the positions of the stars. Their treatments thus focused on ridding the air and the body of these poisons and on rebalancing bodily fluids.

People tried anything they thought might help. Perhaps loud sounds like ringing church bells or firing the newly invented cannon would clean poisoned air. Medicines made from plants that were bumpy or that oozed liquid might work, keeping the more dangerous swelling and oozing of the plague away. Magical letter and number combinations, called cryptograms, were especially popular in Muslim areas. They were often the first letters of words in prayers or religious sayings, and they gave people a sense of order when faced with the randomness with which the plague seemed to strike.

It is noteworthy that, in an age of mounting criticism of clerical wealth (see page 340), the behavior of the clergy during the plague was often exemplary. Priests, monks, and nuns cared for the sick and buried the dead. In places like Venice, from which even physicians fled, priests remained to give what ministrations they could. Consequently, their mortality rate was phenomenally high. The German clergy, especially, suffered a severe decline in personnel in the years after 1350.

There were limits to care, however. The Italian writer Giovanni Boccaccio (1313–1375), describing the course of the disease in Florence in the preface to his book of tales, *The Decameron*, identified what many knew — that the disease passed from person to person:

> This pestilence was so powerful that it was transmitted to the healthy by contact with the sick, the way a fire close to dry or oily things will set them aflame. And the evil of the plague went even further: not only did talking to or being around the sick bring infection and a common death, but also touching the clothes of the sick or anything touched or used by them seemed to communicate this very disease to the person involved.[2]

To avoid contagion, wealthier people often fled cities for the countryside, though sometimes this simply spread the plague faster. Some cities tried shutting their gates to prevent infected people and animals from coming in, which worked in a few cities. They also walled up houses in which there was plague, trying to isolate those who were sick from those who were still healthy. In Boccaccio's words, "Almost no one cared for his neighbor . . . brother abandoned brother . . . and—even worse, almost unbelievable—fathers and mothers neglected to tend and care for their children."[3]

Economic, Religious, and Cultural Effects

Economic historians and demographers sharply dispute the impact of the plague on the economy in the late fourteenth century. The traditional view that the plague had a disastrous effect has been greatly modified. By the mid-1300s the population of Europe had grown somewhat beyond what could easily be supported by available agricultural technology, and the dramatic drop in population allowed less fertile land to be abandoned. People turned to more specialized types of agriculture, such as raising sheep or wine grapes, which in the long run proved to be a better use of the land.

The Black Death did bring on a general European inflation. High mortality produced a fall in production, shortages of goods, and a general rise in prices. The price of wheat in most of Europe increased, as did the costs of meat, sausage, and cheese. This inflation continued to the end of the fourteenth century. But labor shortages resulting from the high mortality caused by the plague meant that workers could demand better wages, and the broad mass of people who survived enjoyed a higher standard of living. The greater demand for labor also meant greater mobility for peasants in rural areas and for artisans in towns and cities.

The plague also had effects on religious practices. Despite Boccaccio's comments about family members' coldness, people were saddened by the loss of their loved ones, especially their children. Not surprisingly, some people sought release from the devastating affliction in wild living, but more became more deeply pious. Rather than seeing the plague as a medical issue, they interpreted it as the result of an evil within themselves. God must be punishing them for terrible sins, they thought, so the best remedies were religious ones: asking for forgiveness, praying, trusting in God, making donations to churches, and trying to live better lives. John VI Kantakouzenos reported that in Constantinople, "many of the sick turned to better things in their minds . . . they abstained from all vice during that time and they lived virtuously; many divided their property among the poor, even before they were attacked by the disease."[4] In Muslim areas, religious leaders urged virtuous living in the face of death: give to the poor, reconcile with your enemies, free your slaves, and say a proper good-bye to your friends and family.

Believing that the Black Death was God's punishment for humanity's wickedness, some Christians turned to the severest forms of asceticism and frenzied religious fervor, joining groups of **flagellants** (FLA-juh-luhnts), who whipped and scourged themselves as penance for their and society's sins. Groups of flagellants traveled from town to town, often growing into unruly mobs. Officials worried that they would provoke violence and riots, and ordered groups to disband or forbade them to enter cities.

Along with seeing the plague as a call to reform their own behavior, however, people also searched for scapegoats, and savage cruelty sometimes resulted. As in the decades before the plague, many people believed that the Jews had poisoned the wells of Christian communities and thereby infected the drinking water. Others thought that killing Jews would prevent the plague from spreading to their town, a belief encouraged by flagellant groups. These charges led to the murder of thousands of Jews across Europe, especially in the cities of France and Germany. In Strasbourg, for

flagellants People who believed that the plague was God's punishment for sin and sought to do penance by flagellating (whipping) themselves.

Dance of Death

In this fifteenth-century fresco from a tiny church in Croatia, skeletons lead people from all social classes in a procession.

EVALUATE THE EVIDENCE

1. Based on their clothing and the objects they are carrying, who are the people shown in the fresco? What does this suggest was the artist's message about death?
2. Paintings such as this clearly provide evidence of the preoccupation with death in this era, but does this work highlight other social issues as well? If so, what are they?

(Fresco, 1475, Chapel of Our Lady of the Rocks, Croatia/Stuart Black/© Robert Harding World Imagery/Alamy Stock Photo)

example, several hundred Jews were publicly burned alive. Their houses were looted, their property was confiscated, and the remaining Jews were expelled from the city.

The literature and art of the late Middle Ages reveal a people gripped by morbid concern with death. One highly popular literary and artistic motif, the Dance of Death, depicted a dancing skeleton leading away living people, often in order of their rank. (See "Evaluating the Evidence 11.1: Dance of Death," above.) In the words of one early-fifteenth-century English poem:

> Death spareth not low nor high degree
> Popes, Kings, nor worthy Emperors
> When they shine most in felicity
> He can abate the freshness of their flowers
> Eclipse their bright suns with his showers . . .
> Sir Emperor, lord of all the ground,
> Sovereign Prince, and highest of nobles
> You must forsake your round apples of gold
> Leave behind your treasure and riches
> And with others to my dance obey.[5]

The years of the Black Death witnessed the foundation of new colleges at old universities and of entirely new universities. The foundation charters explain the shortage of priests and the decay of learning as the reasons for their establishment. Whereas older universities such as those at Bologna and Paris had international student bodies, these new institutions established in the wake of the Black Death had more national or local constituencies. Thus the international character of medieval culture weakened, paving the way for schism (SKIH-zuhm) in the Catholic Church even before the Reformation.

As is often true with devastating events, the plague highlighted central qualities of medieval society: deep religious feeling, suspicion of those who were different, and a view of the world shaped largely by oral tradition, with a bit of classical knowledge mixed in among the educated elite.

The Hundred Years' War

FOCUS QUESTION

What were the causes, course, and consequences of the Hundred Years' War?

Hundred Years' War A war between England and France from 1337 to 1453, with political and economic causes and consequences.

The plague ravaged populations in Asia, North Africa, and Europe; in western Europe a long international war that began a decade or so before the plague struck and lasted well into the next century added further misery. England and France had engaged in sporadic military hostilities from the time of the Norman Conquest in 1066, and in the middle of the fourteenth century these became more intense. From 1337 to 1453 the two countries intermittently fought one another in what was the longest war in European history, ultimately dubbed the **Hundred Years' War**, though it actually lasted 116 years.

Causes

The Hundred Years' War had a number of causes, including disagreements over rights to land, a dispute over the succession to the French throne, and economic conflicts. Many of these revolved around the duchy of Aquitaine, a province in southern France that became part of the holdings of the English crown when Eleanor of Aquitaine married King Henry II of England in 1152 (see Chapter 9; a duchy is a territory ruled by a duke). In 1259 Henry III of England had signed the Treaty of Paris with Louis IX of France, affirming English claims to Aquitaine in return for becoming a vassal of the French crown. French policy in the fourteenth century was strongly expansionist, however, and the French kings resolved to absorb the duchy into the kingdom of France. Aquitaine therefore became a disputed territory.

The immediate political cause of the war was a disagreement over who would inherit the French throne after Charles IV of France, the last surviving son of Philip the Fair, died childless in 1328. With him ended the Capetian dynasty of France. Charles IV had a sister — Isabella — but her son was Edward III, king of England. An assembly of French high nobles, meaning to exclude Isabella and Edward from the French throne, proclaimed that "no woman nor her son could succeed to the [French] monarchy." French lawyers defended the position with the claim that the exclusion of women from ruling or passing down the right to rule was part of Salic law, a sixth-century law code of the Franks (see Chapter 7), and that Salic law itself was part of the fundamental law of France. They used this invented tradition to argue that Edward should be barred from the French throne. (The ban on female succession became part of French legal tradition until the end of the monarchy in 1789.) The nobles passed the crown to Philip VI of Valois (r. 1328–1350), a nephew of Philip the Fair.

In 1329 Edward III formally recognized Philip VI's lordship over Aquitaine. Eight years later, Philip, eager to exercise full French jurisdiction there, confiscated the duchy. Edward III interpreted this action as a gross violation of the treaty of 1259 and as a cause for war. Moreover, Edward argued, as the eldest directly surviving male descendant of Philip the Fair, he deserved the title of king of France. Edward III's dynastic argument upset the feudal order in France: to increase their independent power, many French nobles abandoned Philip VI, using the excuse that they had to transfer their loyalty to a different overlord, Edward III. One reason the war lasted so long was that it became a French civil war, with some French nobles, most important the dukes of Burgundy, supporting English monarchs in order to thwart the centralizing goals of the French kings. On the other side, Scotland—resisting English efforts of assimilation—often allied with France; the French supported Scottish raids in northern England, and Scottish troops joined with French armies on the continent.

The governments of both England and France manipulated public opinion to support the war. The English public was convinced that the war was waged for one reason: to secure for King Edward the French crown he had been unjustly denied. Edward III issued letters to the sheriffs describing the evil deeds of the French in graphic terms and listing royal needs. Philip VI sent agents to warn communities about the dangers of invasion. Kings in both countries instructed the clergy to deliver sermons filled with patriotic sentiment. Royal propaganda on both sides fostered a kind of early nationalism, and both sides developed a deep hatred of the other.

Isabella of France and Her Son Edward Enter Oxford   In this illustration for the chronicles of the counts of Flanders (made in 1477 by the artist known as the Master of Mary of Burgundy) Isabella, the sister of Charles IV of France and the wife of Edward II of England, and her son Edward are welcomed by clergy into the city of Oxford in 1326. Isabella and Edward, who was only fourteen at the time, along with her lover Roger Mortimer, had just invaded England with a small army to overthrow her husband and end the influence of his male favorite, Hugh le Despenser. They captured and imprisoned both men, executed Despenser, deposed the king, and may have ordered his murder. Isabella ruled as regent for her son for three years before he assumed personal rule by force and had Mortimer executed. She lived another twenty-eight years in high style as a wealthy woman, watching her son lead successful military ventures in France in the first decades of the Hundred Years' War. These events add further complexity to the complicated dynastic disputes that led to the war and have been the subject of plays, novels, ballets, TV miniseries, and films. (By kind permission of Viscount Coke and the Trustees of Holkham Estate, Norfolk/Bridgeman Images)

Economic factors involving the wool trade and the control of Flemish towns were linked to these political issues. The wool trade between England and Flanders served as the cornerstone of both countries' economies; they were closely interdependent. Flanders technically belonged to the French crown, and the Flemish aristocracy was highly sympathetic to that monarchy. But the wealth of Flemish merchants and cloth manufacturers depended on English wool, and Flemish burghers strongly supported the claims of Edward III. The disruption of commerce with England threatened their prosperity.

The war also presented opportunities for wealth and advancement. Poor and idle knights were promised regular wages. Criminals who enlisted were granted pardons. The great nobles expected to be rewarded with estates. Royal exhortations to the troops before battles repeatedly stressed that, if victorious, the men might keep whatever they seized.

English Successes

The war began with a series of French sea raids on English coastal towns in 1337, but the French fleet was almost completely destroyed when it attempted to land soldiers on English soil, and from that point on the war was fought almost entirely in France and the Low Countries (Map 11.2). It consisted mainly of a series of

MAP 11.2 The Hundred Years' War, 1337–1453   These maps show the change in the land held by the English and French crowns over the course of the Hundred Years' War. Which year marked the greatest extent of English holdings in France?

Siege of the Castle of Mortagne   Medieval warfare usually consisted of small skirmishes and attacks on castles. This miniature shows the 1377 French siege of an English-held castle near Bordeaux that held out for six months. Most of the soldiers use longbows, although at the left two men shoot primitive muskets above a pair of cannon. Painted in the late fifteenth century, the scene reflects the military technology available at the time it was painted, not at the time of the actual siege. (British Library, London, UK/© British Library Board. All Rights Reserved/Bridgeman Images)

random sieges and cavalry raids, fought in fits and starts, with treaties along the way to halt hostilities.

During the war's early stages, England was highly successful. At Crécy in northern France in 1346, English longbowmen scored a great victory over French knights and crossbowmen. Although the aim of longbowmen was not very accurate, the weapon allowed for rapid reloading, and an English archer could send off three arrows to the French crossbowman's one. The result was a blinding shower of arrows that unhorsed the French knights and caused mass confusion. The roar of English cannon—probably the first use of artillery in the Western world—created further panic. This was not war according to the chivalric rules that Edward III would have preferred. Nevertheless, his son, Edward the Black Prince, used the same tactics ten years later to smash the French at Poitiers, where he captured the French king and held him for ransom. Edward was not able to take all of France, but the English held Aquitaine and other provinces, and allied themselves with many of France's nobles. After a brief peace, the French fought back and recovered some territory during the 1370s and 1380s, and then a treaty again halted hostilities as both sides concentrated on conflicts over power at home.

War began again in 1415 when the able English soldier-king Henry V (r. 1413–1422) invaded France. At Agincourt (AH-jihn-kort), Henry's army defeated a much larger French force, again primarily through the skill of English longbowmen. Henry followed up his triumph at Agincourt with the reconquest of Normandy, and by 1419 the English had advanced to the walls of Paris (see Map 11.2). Henry married the daughter of the French king, and a treaty made Henry and any sons the couple would have heir to the French throne. It appeared as if Henry would indeed rule both England and France, but he died unexpectedly in 1422, leaving an infant son as heir. The English continued their victories, however, and besieged the city of Orléans (or-lay-AHN), the only major city in northern France not under their control. But the French cause was not lost.

Joan of Arc and France's Victory

The ultimate French success rests heavily on the actions of Joan, an obscure French peasant girl whose vision and military leadership revived French fortunes and led to victory. (Over the centuries, she acquired the name "of Arc"—*d'Arc* in French—based on her father's name; she never used this name for herself, but called herself "the maiden" — *la Pucelle* in French.) Born in 1412 to well-to-do peasants in the village of Domrémy in Champagne, Joan grew up in a religious household. During adolescence she began to hear voices, which she later said belonged to Saint Michael, Saint Catherine, and Saint Margaret. In 1428 these voices spoke to her with great urgency, telling her that the dauphin (DOH-fuhn), the uncrowned King Charles VII, had to be crowned and the English expelled from France. Joan traveled to the French court wearing male clothing. She had an audience with Charles, who had her questioned about her angelic visions and examined to make sure she was the virgin she said she was. She secured his support to travel with the French army to Orléans dressed as a knight—with borrowed armor and sword. There she dictated a letter to the English ordering them to surrender:

> King of England . . . , do right in the King of Heaven's sight. Surrender to The Maid sent hither by God the King of Heaven, the keys of all the good towns you have taken and laid waste in France. She comes in God's name to establish the Blood Royal, ready to make peace if you agree to abandon France and repay what you have taken. And you, archers, comrades in arms, gentles and others, who are before the town of Orléans, retire in God's name to your own country.[6]

Such words coming from a teenage girl—even one inspired by God—were laughable given the recent course of the conflict, but Joan was amazingly successful. She inspired and led French attacks, forcing the English to retreat from Orléans. The king made Joan co-commander of the entire army, and she led it to a string of victories; other cities simply surrendered without a fight and returned their allegiance to France. In July 1429, two months after the end of the siege of Orléans, Charles VII was crowned king at Reims.

Joan and the French army continued their fight against the English and their Burgundian allies. In 1430 the Burgundians captured Joan. Charles refused to ransom her, and she was sold to the English. A church court headed by a pro-English bishop tried her for heresy, and though nothing she had done was heretical by church doctrine, she was found guilty and burned at the stake in the marketplace at Rouen. (See "Evaluating the Evidence 11.2: The Trial of Joan of Arc," at right.)

The French army continued its victories without her. Sensing a shift in the balance of power, the Burgundians switched their allegiance to the French, who reconquered Normandy and, finally, ejected the English from Aquitaine in the 1440s. As the war dragged on, loss of life mounted, and money appeared to be flowing into a bottom-less pit, demands for an end increased in England. Parliamentary opposition to additional war grants stiffened, fewer soldiers were sent, and more territory passed into French hands. At the war's end in 1453, only the town of Calais (KA-lay) remained in English hands.

What of Joan? A new trial in 1456—requested by Charles VII, who either had second thoughts about his abandonment of Joan or did not wish to be associated with a condemned heretic—was held by the pope. It cleared her of all charges and declared her a martyr. She became a political symbol of France from that point on, and sometimes also a symbol of the Catholic Church in opposition to the government of France. In 1920, for example, she was canonized as a saint shortly after the French government declared separation of church and state in France. Similarly, Joan has been (and

The Trial of Joan of Arc

Joan's interrogation was organized and led by Bishop Pierre Cauchon, one of many French clergy who supported the English. In a number of sessions that took place over several months, she was repeatedly asked about her voices, her decision to wear men's clothing, and other issues. This extract is from the fourth session, on Tuesday, February 27, 1431; Joan is here referred to with the French spelling of her name, Jeanne.

In their presence Jeanne was required by my lord the Bishop of Beauvais to swear and take the oath concerning what touched her trial. To which she answered that she would willingly swear as to what touched her trial, but not as to everything she knew. . . .

Asked whether she had heard her voice since Saturday, she answered: "Yes, indeed, many times." . . . Asked what it said to her when she was back in her room, she replied: "That I should answer you boldly." . . . Questioned as to whether it were the voice of an angel, or of a saint, or directly from God, she answered that the voices were those of Saint Catherine and of Saint Margaret. And their heads are crowned with beautiful crowns, most richly and preciously. And [she said] for [telling you] this I have leave from our Lord. . . .

Asked if the voice ordered her to wear a man's dress, she answered that the dress is but a small matter; and that she had not taken it by the advice of any living man; and that she did not take this dress nor do anything at all save by the command of Our Lord and the angels.

Questioned as to whether it seemed to her that this command to take male dress was a lawful one, she answered that everything she had done was at Our Lord's command, and if He had ordered Jeanne to take a different dress, she would have done so, since it would have been at God's command. . . .

Asked if she had her sword when she was taken prisoner, she said no, but that she had one which was taken from a Burgundian. . . . Asked whether, when she was before the city of Orleans, she had a standard, and of what colour it was, she replied that it had a field sown with fleurs-de-lis, and showed a world with an angel on either side, white in colour, of linen or *boucassin* [a type of fabric], and she thought that the names JESUS MARIA were written on it; and it had a silk fringe. . . . Asked which she preferred, her sword or her standard, she replied that she was forty times fonder of her standard than she was of her sword. . . . She said moreover that she herself bore her standard during an attack, in order to avoid killing anyone. And she added that she had never killed anyone at all. . . .

She also said that during the attack on the fort at the bridge she was wounded in the neck by an arrow, but she was greatly comforted by Saint Catherine, and was well again in a fortnight. . . . Asked whether she knew beforehand that she would be wounded, she said that she well knew it, and had informed her king of it; but that notwithstanding she would not give up her work.

EVALUATE THE EVIDENCE

1. How does Joan explain the way that she chose to answer the interrogators' questions, and her decisions about clothing and actions in battle?
2. Thinking about the structures of power and authority in fifteenth-century France, how do you believe the interrogators would have regarded Joan's answers?

Source: *The Trial of Joan of Arc*, translated with an introduction by W. S. Scott (Westport, Conn.: Associated Booksellers, 1956), 76, 77, 79–80, 82, 83. © 1956, The Folio Society.

continues to be) a symbol of deep religious piety to some, of conservative nationalism to others, and of gender-bending cross-dressing to others. Beneath the pious and popular legends is a teenage girl who saved the French monarchy, the embodiment of France.

Aftermath

In France thousands of soldiers and civilians had been slaughtered and hundreds of thousands of acres of rich farmland ruined, leaving the rural economy of many areas a shambles. These losses exacerbated the dreadful losses caused by the plague. The war had disrupted trade and the great trade fairs, resulting in the drastic reduction of

French participation in international commerce. Defeat in battle and heavy taxation contributed to widespread dissatisfaction and aggravated peasant grievances.

The war had wreaked havoc in England as well, even though only the southern coastal ports saw actual battle. England spent the huge sum of over £5 million on the war effort, and despite the money raised by some victories, the net result was an enormous financial loss. The government attempted to finance the war by raising taxes on the wool crop, which priced wool out of the export market.

In both England and France, men of all social classes had volunteered to serve in the war in the hope of acquiring booty and becoming rich, and some were successful in the early years of the war. As time went on, however, most fortunes seem to have been squandered as fast as they were made. In addition, the social order was disrupted because the knights who ordinarily served as sheriffs, coroners, jurymen, and justices of the peace were abroad.

The war stimulated technological experimentation, especially with artillery. Cannon revolutionized warfare, making the stone castle no longer impregnable. Because only central governments, not private nobles, could afford cannon, their use strengthened the military power of national states.

The long war also had a profound impact on the political and cultural lives of the two countries. Most notably, it stimulated the development of the English Parliament. Between 1250 and 1450 **representative assemblies** flourished in many European countries. In the English Parliament, German *diets*, and Spanish *cortes*, deliberative practices developed that laid the foundations for the representative institutions of modern democratic nations. While representative assemblies declined in most countries after the fifteenth century, the English Parliament endured. Edward III's constant need for money to pay for the war compelled him to summon not only the great barons and bishops, but knights of the shires and citizens from the towns as well. Parliament met in thirty-seven of the fifty years of Edward's reign.

The frequency of the meetings is significant. Representative assemblies were becoming a habit. Knights and wealthy urban residents—or the "Commons," as they came to be called—recognized their mutual interests and began to meet apart from the great lords. The Commons gradually realized that they held the country's purse strings, and a parliamentary statute of 1341 required parliamentary approval of most new taxes. By signing the law, Edward III acknowledged that the king of England could not tax without Parliament's consent.

In England, theoretical consent to taxation and legislation was given in one assembly for the entire country. France had no such single assembly; instead, there were many regional or provincial assemblies. Why did a national representative assembly fail to develop in France? Linguistic, geographical, economic, legal, and political differences remained very strong. People tended to think of themselves as Breton, Norman, Burgundian, and so on, rather than French. In addition, provincial assemblies, highly jealous of their independence, did not want a national assembly. The costs of sending delegates to it would be high, and the result was likely to be increased taxation and a lessening of their own power. Finally, the initiative for convening assemblies rested with the king, but some monarchs lacked the power to call them, and others, including Charles VI, found the very idea of representative assemblies thoroughly distasteful.

In both countries, however, the war did promote the growth of nationalism—the feeling of unity and identity that binds together a people. After victories, each country experienced a surge of pride in its military strength. Just as English patriotism ran

representative assemblies
Deliberative meetings of lords and wealthy urban residents that flourished in many European countries between 1250 and 1450.

strong after Crécy and Poitiers, so French national confidence rose after Orléans. French national feeling demanded the expulsion of the enemy not merely from Normandy and Aquitaine but from all French soil. Perhaps no one expressed this national consciousness better than Joan when she exulted that the enemy had been "driven out of *France*."

Challenges to the Church

In times of crisis or disaster, people of all faiths have sought the consolation of religion. In the fourteenth century, however, the official Christian Church offered little solace. Many priests and friars helped the sick and the hungry, but others paid more attention to worldly matters, and the leaders of the church added to the sorrow and misery of the times. In response to this lack of leadership, members of the clergy challenged the power of the pope, and laypeople challenged the authority of the church itself. Women and men increasingly relied on direct approaches to God, often through mystical encounters, rather than on the institutional church.

FOCUS QUESTION
Why did the church come under increasing criticism?

The Babylonian Captivity and Great Schism

Conflicts between the secular rulers of Europe and the popes were common throughout the High Middle Ages, and in the early fourteenth century the dispute between King Philip the Fair of France and Pope Boniface VIII became particularly bitter (see Chapter 9). After Boniface's death, in order to control the church and its policies, Philip pressured the new pope, Clement V, to settle permanently in Avignon in southeastern France. The popes lived in Avignon from 1309 to 1376, a period in church history often called the **Babylonian Captivity** (referring to the seventy years the ancient Hebrews were held captive in Mesopotamian Babylon).

The Babylonian Captivity badly damaged papal prestige. The seven popes at Avignon concentrated on bureaucratic and financial matters to the exclusion of spiritual objectives, and the general atmosphere was one of luxury and extravagance, which was also the case at many bishops' courts. Raimon de Cornet, a troubadour poet from southern France who was himself a priest, was only one among many criticizing the church. He wrote:

Babylonian Captivity The period from 1309 to 1376 when the popes resided in Avignon rather than in Rome. The phrase refers to the seventy years when the Hebrews were held captive in Babylon.

I see the pope his sacred trust betray,	Our bishops, too, are plunged in similar sin,
For while the rich his grace can gain alway,	For pitilessly they flay the very skin From all their priests who chance to
His favors from the poor are aye with holden.	have fat livings.
He strives to gather wealth as best he may,	For gold their seal official you can win
Forcing Christ's people blindly to obey,	To any writ, no matter what's therein.
So that he may repose in garments golden.	Sure God alone can make them stop
. . .	their thievings.[7]

The leadership of the church was cut off from its historic roots and the source of its ancient authority, the city of Rome. In 1377 Pope Gregory XI brought the papal court back to Rome but died shortly afterward. Roman citizens pressured the cardinals to elect an Italian, and they chose a distinguished administrator, the archbishop of Bari, Bartolomeo Prignano, who took the name Urban VI.

Urban VI (pontificate 1378–1389) had excellent intentions for church reform, but he went about it in a tactless manner. He attacked clerical luxury, denouncing individual cardinals and bishops by name, and even threatened to excommunicate some of them. The cardinals slipped away from Rome and met at Anagni. They declared Urban's election invalid because it had come about under threats from the Roman mob, and excommunicated the pope. The cardinals then elected Cardinal Robert of Geneva, the cousin of King Charles V of France, as pope. Cardinal Robert took the name Clement VII. There were thus two popes in 1378 — Urban at Rome and Clement VII (pontificate 1378–1394) at Avignon. So began the **Great Schism**, which divided Western Christendom until 1417.

Great Schism The division, or split, in church leadership from 1378 to 1417 when there were two, then three, popes.

The powers of Europe aligned themselves with Urban or Clement along strictly political lines. France naturally recognized the French pope, Clement. England, France's long-time enemy, recognized the Italian pope, Urban. Scotland, an ally of France, supported Clement. Aragon, Castile, and Portugal hesitated before deciding for Clement as well. The German emperor, hostile to France, recognized Urban. At first the Italian city-states recognized Urban; later they opted for Clement.

John of Spoleto, a professor at the law school at Bologna, eloquently summed up intellectual opinion of the schism: "The longer this schism lasts, the more it appears to be costing, and the more harm it does; scandal, massacres, ruination, agitations, troubles and disturbances."[8] The schism weakened the religious faith of many Christians and brought church leadership into serious disrepute.

 Avignon · Rome

■ Allegiance to Rome
■ Allegiance to Avignon
■ Official allegiance to Rome but with shifting local allegiances

The Great Schism, 1378–1417

Critiques, Divisions, and Councils

Criticism of the church during the Avignon papacy and the Great Schism often came from the ranks of highly learned clergy and lay professionals. One of these was William of Occam (1289?–1347?), a Franciscan friar and philosopher who predated the Great Schism but saw the papal court at Avignon during the Babylonian Captivity. Occam argued vigorously against the papacy and also wrote philosophical works in which he questioned the connection between reason and faith that had been developed by Thomas Aquinas (see Chapter 10). All governments should have limited powers and be accountable to those they govern, according to Occam, and church and state should be separate.

The Italian lawyer and university official Marsiglio of Padua (ca. 1275–1342) agreed with Occam. In his *Defensor Pacis* (The Defender of the Peace), Marsiglio argued against the medieval idea of a society governed by both church and state, with church supreme. Instead, Marsiglio claimed, the state was the great unifying power in society, and the church should be subordinate to it. Church leadership should rest in a general council made up of laymen as well as priests and superior to the pope. Marsiglio was excommunicated for these radical ideas, and his work was condemned as heresy — as was Occam's — but in the later part of the fourteenth century many thinkers agreed with these two critics of the papacy. They believed that reform of the church could best be achieved through periodic assemblies, or councils, representing all the Christian people. Those who argued this position were called **conciliarists**.

conciliarists People who believed that the authority in the Roman Church should rest in a general council composed of clergy, theologians, and laypeople, rather than in the pope alone.

The English scholar and theologian John Wyclif (WIH-klihf) (ca. 1330–1384) went further than the conciliarists in his argument against medieval church structure.

He wrote that the Scriptures alone should be the standard of Christian belief and practice and that papal claims of secular power had no foundation in the Scriptures. He urged that the church be stripped of its property. He also wanted Christians to read the Bible for themselves and produced the first complete translation of the Bible into English. Wyclif's followers, dubbed Lollards, from a Dutch word for "mumble," by those who ridiculed them, spread his ideas and made many copies of his Bible. Lollard teaching allowed women to preach, and women played a significant role in the movement. Lollards were persecuted in the fifteenth century; some were executed, some recanted, and others continued to meet secretly in houses, barns, and fields to read and discuss the Bible and other religious texts in English. Bohemian students returning from study at the University of Oxford around 1400 brought Wyclif's ideas with them to Prague, the capital of what was then Bohemia and is now the Czech Republic. There another university theologian, Jan Hus (ca. 1372–1415), built on them. He also denied papal authority, called for translations of the Bible into the local Czech language, and declared indulgences—papal offers of remission of penance—useless. Hus gained many followers, who linked his theological ideas with their opposition to the church's wealth and power and with a growing sense of Czech nationalism in opposition to the pope's international power. Hus's followers were successful at defeating the combined armies of the pope and the emperor many times. In the 1430s the emperor finally agreed to recognize the Hussite Church in Bohemia, which survived into the Reformation and then merged with other Protestant churches.

The ongoing schism threatened the church, and in response to continued calls throughout Europe for a council, the cardinals of Rome and Avignon summoned a council at Pisa in 1409. That gathering of prelates and theologians deposed both popes and selected another. Neither the Avignon pope nor the Roman pope would resign, however, and the appalling result was the creation of a threefold schism.

The Hussite Revolution, 1415–1436

The Arrest and Execution of Jan Hus   In this woodcut from Ulrich of Richental's chronicle of the Council of Constance, Hus is arrested by bishops, led away by soldiers while wearing a hat of shame with the word "arch-heretic" on it, and burned at the stake. The final panel shows executioners shoveling his ashes and burned bones into the Rhine. Ulrich of Richental was a merchant in Constance and an eyewitness to Hus's execution and many of the other events of the council. He wrote his chronicle in German shortly after the council ended and paid for it to be illustrated. The original is lost, but many copies were made later in the fifteenth century, and the volume was printed in 1483 with many woodcuts, including this one. Hus became an important symbol of Czech independence, and in 1990 the Czech Republic declared July 6, the date of his execution in 1415, a national holiday. (From *History of the Council of Constance*, 1483/Bibliothèque Polonaise, Paris, France/Archives Charmet/Bridgeman Images)

Finally, under pressure from the German emperor Sigismund, a great council met at the imperial city of Constance (1414–1418). It had three objectives: to wipe out heresy, to end the schism, and to reform the church. Members included cardinals, bishops, abbots, and professors of theology and canon law from across Europe. The council moved first on the first point: despite being granted a safe-conduct to go to Constance by the emperor, Jan Hus was tried, condemned, and burned at the stake as a heretic in 1415. The council also eventually healed the schism. It deposed both the Roman pope and the successor of the pope chosen at Pisa, and it isolated the Avignon pope. A conclave elected a new leader, the Roman cardinal Colonna, who took the name Martin V (pontificate 1417–1431).

Martin proceeded to dissolve the council. Nothing was done about reform, the third objective of the council. In the later part of the fifteenth century the papacy concentrated on Italian problems to the exclusion of universal Christian interests. But the schism and the conciliar movement had exposed the crying need for ecclesiastical reform, thus laying the foundation for the great reform efforts of the sixteenth century.

Lay Piety and Mysticism

The failings of the Avignon papacy followed by the scandal of the Great Schism did much to weaken the spiritual mystique of the clergy in the popular mind. Laypeople had already begun to develop their own forms of piety somewhat separate from the authority of priests and bishops, and these forms of piety became more prominent in the fourteenth century.

confraternities Voluntary lay groups organized by occupation, devotional preference, neighborhood, or charitable activity.

In the thirteenth century lay Christian men and women had formed **confraternities**, voluntary lay groups organized by occupation, devotional preference, neighborhood, or charitable activity. Some confraternities specialized in praying for souls in purgatory, either for specific individuals or for the anonymous mass of all souls. In England they held dances, church festivals, and collections to raise money to clean and repair church buildings and to supply churches with candles and other liturgical objects. Like craft guilds, most confraternities were groups of men, but separate women's confraternities were formed in some towns, often to oversee the production of vestments, altar cloths, and other items made of fabric. All confraternities carried out special devotional practices such as prayers or processions, often without the leadership of a priest. Famine, plague, war, and other crises led to an expansion of confraternities in larger cities and many villages.

In Holland beginning in the late fourteenth century, a group of pious laypeople called the Brethren and Sisters of the Common Life lived in stark simplicity while daily carrying out the Gospel teaching of feeding the hungry, clothing the naked, and visiting the sick. They sought to both ease social problems and make religion a personal inner experience. The spirituality of the Brethren and Sisters of the Common Life found its finest expression in the classic *The Imitation of Christ* by the Dutch monk Thomas à Kempis (1380?–1471), which gained wide appeal among laypeople. It urges Christians to take Christ as their model, seek perfection in a simple way of life, and look to the Scriptures for guidance in living a spiritual life. In the mid-fifteenth century the movement had founded houses in the Netherlands, in central Germany, and in the Rhineland.

For some individuals, both laypeople and clerics, religious devotion included mystical experiences. (See "Individuals in Society: Meister Eckhart," at right.)

INDIVIDUALS IN SOCIETY

Meister Eckhart

Mysticism — the direct experience of the divine — is an aspect of many world religions and has been part of Christianity throughout its history. During the late Middle Ages, however, the pursuit of mystical union became an important part of the piety of many lay-people, especially in the Rhineland area of Germany. In this they were guided by the sermons of the churchman generally known as Meister Eckhart. Born into a German noble family, Eckhart (1260–1329?) joined the Dominican order and studied theology at Paris and Cologne, attaining the academic title of "master" (*Meister* in German). The leaders of the Dominican order appointed him to a series of administrative and teaching positions, and he wrote learned treatises in Latin that reflected his Scholastic training and deep understanding of classical philosophy.

He also began to preach in German, attracting many listeners through his beautiful language and mystical insights. God, he said, was "an oversoaring being and an overbeing nothingness," whose essence was beyond the ability of humans to express: "if the soul is to know God, it must know Him outside time and place, since God is neither in this or that, but One and above them." Only through "unknowing," emptying oneself, could one come to experience the divine. Yet God was also present in individual human souls, and to a degree in every creature, all of which God had called into being before the beginning of time. Within each human soul there was what Eckhart called a "little spark," an innermost essence that allows the soul — with God's grace and Christ's redemptive action — to come to God. "Our salvation depends upon our knowing and recognizing the Chief Good which is God Himself," preached Eckhart; "the Eye with which I see God is the same Eye with which God sees me." "I have a capacity in my soul for taking in God entirely," he went on, a capacity that was shared by all humans, not only members of the clergy or those with special spiritual gifts. Although Eckhart did not reject church sacraments or the hierarchy, he frequently stressed that union with God was best accomplished through quiet detachment and simple prayer rather than pilgrimages, extensive fasts, or other activities: "If the only prayer you said in your whole life was 'thank you,' that would suffice."*

Eckhart's unusual teachings led to charges of heresy in 1327, which he denied. The pope — who was at this point in Avignon — presided over a trial condemning him, but Eckhart appears to have died during the course of the proceedings or shortly thereafter. His writings

A sixteenth-century woodcut of Meister Eckhart teaching.
(Visual Connection Archive)

were ordered destroyed, but his followers preserved many and spread his teachings.

In the last few decades, Meister Eckhart's ideas have been explored and utilized by philosophers and mystics in Buddhism, Hinduism, and neo-paganism, as well as by Christians. His writings sell widely for their spiritual insights, and quotations from them — including the one above about thank-you prayers — can be found on coffee mugs, tote bags, and T-shirts.

QUESTIONS FOR ANALYSIS

1. Why might Meister Eckhart's preaching have been viewed as threatening by the leaders of the church?
2. Given the situation of the church in the late Middle Ages, why might mysticism have been attractive to pious Christians?

*Meister Eckhart's Sermons, trans. Claud Field (London: n.p., 1909).

343

Bridget of Sweden (1303–1373) was a noblewoman who journeyed to Rome after her husband's death. She began to see visions and gave advice based on these visions to both laypeople and church officials. At the end of her life Bridget made a pilgrimage to Jerusalem, where she saw visions of the Virgin Mary, who described to her exactly how she was standing "with [her] knees bent" when she gave birth to Jesus, and how she "showed to the shepherds the nature and male sex of the child."[9] Bridget's visions provide evidence of the ways in which laypeople used their own experiences to enhance their religious understanding; Bridget's own experiences of childbirth shaped the way she viewed the birth of Jesus, and she related to the Virgin Mary in part as one mother to another.

The confraternities and mystics were generally not considered heretical unless they began to challenge the authority of the papacy the way Wyclif, Hus, and some conciliarists did. However, the movement of lay piety did alter many people's perceptions of their own spiritual power.

Social Unrest in a Changing Society

FOCUS QUESTION
What explains the social unrest of the late Middle Ages?

At the beginning of the fourteenth century famine and disease profoundly affected the lives of European peoples. As the century wore on, decades of slaughter and destruction, punctuated by the decimating visits of the Black Death, added further woes. In many parts of France and the Low Countries, fields lay in ruin or untilled for lack of labor. In England, as taxes increased, criticisms of government policy and mismanagement multiplied. Crime and new forms of business organization aggravated economic troubles, and throughout Europe the frustrations of the common people erupted into widespread revolts.

Peasant Revolts

Nobles and clergy lived on the food produced by peasant labor, thinking little of adding taxes to the burden of peasant life. While peasants had endured centuries of exploitation, the difficult conditions of the fourteenth and fifteenth centuries spurred a wave of peasant revolts across Europe. Peasants were sometimes joined by those low on the urban social ladder, resulting in a wider revolution of poor against rich.

The first large-scale rebellion was in the Flanders region of present-day Belgium in the 1320s (Map 11.3). In order to satisfy peace agreements, Flemish peasants were forced to pay taxes to the French, who claimed fiscal rights over the county of Flanders. Monasteries also pressed peasants for additional money above their customary tithes. In retaliation, peasants burned and pillaged castles and aristocratic country houses. A French army crushed the peasant forces, however, and savage repression and the confiscation of peasant property followed in the 1330s.

In the following decades, revolts broke out in many other places. In 1358, when French taxation for the Hundred Years' War fell heavily on the poor, the frustrations of the French peasantry exploded in a massive uprising called the **Jacquerie** (zhah-kuh-REE), after a mythical agricultural laborer, Jacques Bonhomme (Good Fellow). Peasants blamed the nobility for oppressive taxes, for the criminal banditry of the countryside, for losses on the battlefield, and for the general misery. Crowds swept through the countryside, slashing the throats of nobles, burning their castles, raping their wives and daughters, and killing or maiming their horses and cattle. Artisans

Jacquerie A massive uprising by French peasants in 1358 protesting heavy taxation.

MAP 11.3 Fourteenth-Century Revolts   In the later Middle Ages peasant and urban uprisings were endemic, as common as factory strikes in the industrial world. The threat of insurrection served to check unlimited exploitation.

and small merchants in cities and parish priests joined the peasants. Rebels committed terrible destruction, and for several weeks the nobles were on the defensive. Then the upper class united to repress the revolt with merciless ferocity. Thousands of the "Jacques," innocent as well as guilty, were cut down. That forcible suppression of social rebellion, without any effort to alleviate its underlying causes, served to drive protest underground.

In England the Black Death drastically cut the labor supply, and as a result peasants demanded higher wages and fewer manorial obligations. Their lords countered in 1351 with the Statute of Laborers, a law issued by the king that froze wages and bound workers to their manors. This attempt to freeze wages could not be enforced, but a huge gap remained between peasants and their lords, and the peasants sought release for their economic frustrations in revolt. Other factors combined with these economic grievances to fuel the rebellion. The south of England, where the revolt broke out, had been subjected to destructive French raids during the Hundred Years' War. The English government did little to protect the region, and villagers grew increasingly frightened and insecure. Moreover, decades of aristocratic violence against the weak peasantry had bred hostility and bitterness. Social and religious agitation by the popular preacher John Ball fanned the embers of discontent.

The English revolt was ignited by the reimposition of a tax on all adult males to pay for the war with France. Despite widespread opposition to the tax, the royal council ordered sheriffs to collect unpaid taxes by force in 1381. This led to a major uprising later termed the **English Peasants' Revolt**, which involved thousands of people, including artisans and the poor in cities as well as rural residents. Beginning with assaults on the tax collectors, the revolt in England followed a course similar to that of the Jacquerie in France. Castles and manors were sacked. Manorial records were destroyed. Many nobles, including the archbishop of Canterbury who had ordered the collection of the tax, were murdered. The center of the revolt lay in the highly populated and economically advanced south and east, but sections of the north also witnessed rebellions (see Map 11.3).

The boy-king Richard II (r. 1377–1399) met the leaders of the revolt, agreed to charters ensuring peasants' freedom, tricked them with false promises, and then crushed the uprising with terrible ferocity. In the aftermath of the revolt, the nobility tried to restore the labor obligations of serfdom, but they were not successful, and the conversion to money rents continued. The English Peasants' Revolt did not bring social equality to England, but rural serfdom continued to decline, disappearing in England by 1550.

English Peasants' Revolt
Revolt by English peasants in 1381 in response to changing economic conditions.

Urban Conflicts

In Flanders, France, and England, peasant revolts often blended with conflicts involving workers in cities. Unrest also occurred in Italian, Spanish, and German cities. The urban revolts had their roots in the changing conditions of work. In the thirteenth century craft guilds had organized the production of most goods, with masters, journeymen, and apprentices working side by side. In the fourteenth century a new system evolved to make products on a larger scale. Capitalist investors hired many households, with each household performing only one step of the process. Initially these investors were wealthy bankers and merchants, but eventually shop masters themselves embraced the system. This promoted a greater division within guilds between wealthier masters and the poorer masters and journeymen they hired. Some masters became so wealthy from the profits of their workers that they no longer had to work in a shop themselves, nor did their wives and family members, though they still generally belonged to the craft guild.

While capitalism provided opportunities for some artisans to become investors and entrepreneurs, especially in cloth production, for many it led to a decrease in income and status. Guilds sometimes responded to crises by opening up membership, as they did in some places immediately after the Black Death, but they more often responded to competition by limiting membership to existing guild families, which meant that journeymen who were not master's sons or who could not find a master's widow or daughter to marry could never become masters themselves. Remaining journeymen their entire lives, they lost their sense of solidarity with the masters of their craft. Resentment led to rebellion.

Urban uprisings were also sparked by issues involving honor, such as employers' requiring workers to do tasks they regarded as beneath them. As their actual status and economic prospects declined and their work became basically wage labor, journeymen and poorer masters emphasized skill and honor as qualities that set them apart from less skilled workers.

Guilds increasingly came to view the honor of their work as tied to an all-male workplace. When urban economies were expanding in the High Middle Ages, the master's wife and daughters worked alongside him, and female domestic servants also carried out productive tasks. (See "Evaluating the Evidence 11.3: Christine de Pizan, Advice to the Wives of Artisans," page 348.) Masters' widows ran shops after the death of their husbands. But in the fourteenth century women's participation in guilds declined, despite labor shortages caused by the plague. First, masters' widows were limited in the amount of time they could keep operating a shop or were prohibited from hiring journeymen; later, female domestic servants were excluded from any productive tasks; finally, the number of daughters a master craftsman could employ was limited. When women were allowed to work, it was viewed as a substitute for charity.

Sex in the City

Peasant and urban revolts and riots had clear economic bases, but some historians have suggested that late medieval marital patterns may have also played a role. In northwestern Europe, people believed that couples should be economically independent before they married. Thus not only during times of crisis such as the Great Famine, but also in more general circumstances, men and women spent long periods as servants or workers in other households, saving money for married life and learning skills, or they waited until their own parents had died and the family property was distributed.

The most unusual feature of this pattern was the late age of marriage for women. Unlike in earlier time periods and in most other parts of the world, a woman in late medieval northern and western Europe generally entered marriage as an adult in her twenties and took charge of running a household immediately. She was thus not as dependent on her husband or mother-in-law as was a woman who married at a younger age. She also had fewer pregnancies than a woman who married earlier, though not necessarily fewer surviving children.

Men of all social groups had long tended to be older than women when they married. In general, men were in their middle or late twenties at first marriage, with wealthier urban merchants often much older. Journeymen and apprentices were often explicitly prohibited from marrying, as were the students at universities, who were understood to be in "minor orders" and thus like clergy, even if they were not intending to have careers in the church.

The prohibitions on marriage for certain groups of men and the late age of marriage for most men meant that cities and villages were filled with large numbers of young adult men with no family responsibilities who often formed the core of riots and unrest. Not surprisingly, this situation also contributed to a steady market for sexual services outside of marriage, services that in later centuries were termed prostitution. Research on the southern French province of Languedoc in the fourteenth and fifteenth centuries has revealed the establishment of legal houses of prostitution in many cities. Municipal authorities set up houses or districts for prostitution either outside the city walls or away from respectable neighborhoods. For example, authorities in Montpellier set aside Hot Street for prostitution, required women who sold sex to live there, and forbade anyone to molest them. Prostitution thus passed from being

Christine de Pizan, Advice to the Wives of Artisans

Christine de Pizan (1364?–1430) was the daughter and wife of highly educated men who held positions at the court of the king of France. She was widowed at twenty-five with young children and an elderly mother to care for, and she decided to support her family through writing, an unusual choice for anyone in this era and unheard of for a woman. She began to write prose works and poetry, and gained commissions to write a biography of the French king Charles V, several histories, a long poem celebrating Joan of Arc's victory, and a book of military tactics. She became the first woman in Europe to make her living as a writer.

Among Christine's many works were several in which she considered women's nature and proper role in society, a topic of debate since ancient times. Among these was The Treasure of the City of Ladies *(1405, also called* The Book of Three Virtues*), which provides moral suggestions and practical advice on behavior and household management for women of all social classes. Most of the book is directed toward princesses and court ladies, but she also includes shorter sections for more ordinary women. Excerpted here is her advice to the wives of artisans, whose husbands were generally members of urban craft guilds, such as blacksmiths, bakers, or shoemakers.*

All wives of artisans should be very painstaking and diligent if they wish to have the necessities of life. They should encourage their husbands or their workmen to get to work early in the morning and work until late, for mark our words, there is no trade so good that if you neglect your work you will not have difficulty putting bread on the table. And besides encouraging the others, the wife herself should be involved in the work to the extent that she knows all about it, so that she may know how to oversee his workers if her husband is absent, and to reprove them if they do not do well. She ought to oversee them to keep them from idleness, for through careless workers the master is sometimes ruined. And when customers come to her husband and try to drive a hard bargain, she ought to warn him solicitously to take care that he does not make a bad deal. She should advise him to be chary of giving too much credit if he does not know precisely where and to whom it is going, for in this way many come to poverty, although sometimes the greed to earn more or to accept a tempting proposition makes them do it.

In addition, she ought to keep her husband's love as much as she can, to this end: that he will stay at home more willingly and that he may not have any reason to join the foolish crowds of other young men in taverns and indulge in unnecessary and extravagant expense, as many tradesmen do, especially in Paris. By treating him kindly she should protect him as well as she can from this. It is said that three things drive a man from his home: a quarrelsome wife, a smoking fireplace and a leaking roof. She too ought to stay at home gladly and not go every day traipsing hither and yon gossiping with the neighbours and visiting her chums to find out what everyone is doing. That is done by slovenly housewives roaming about the town in groups. Nor should she go off on these pilgrimages got up for no good reason and involving a lot of needless expense. Furthermore, she ought to remind her husband that they should live so frugally that their expenditure does not exceed their income, so that at the end of the year they do not find themselves in debt.

If she has children, she should have them instructed and taught first at school by educated people so that they may know how better to serve God. Afterwards they may be put to some trade by which they may earn a living, for whoever gives a trade or business training to her child gives a great possession. The children should be kept from wantonness and from voluptuousness above all else, for truly it is something that most shames the children of good towns and is a great sin of mothers and fathers, who ought to be the cause of the virtue and good behavior of their children, but they are sometimes the reason (because of bringing them up to be finicky and indulging them too much) for their wickedness and ruin.

EVALUATE THE EVIDENCE

1. How would you describe Christine's view of the ideal artisan's wife?
2. The regulations of craft guilds often required that masters who ran workshops be married. What evidence does Christine's advice provide for why guilds would have stipulated this?
3. How are economic and moral virtues linked for Christine?

Source: Excerpts from pp. 167–168 in Christine de Pisan, *The Treasure of the City of Ladies*, translated with an Introduction by Sarah Lawson (Penguin Classics, 1985). This translation copyright © 1985 by Sarah Lawson. Reproduced by permission of Penguin Books Ltd. For more on Christine, see C. C. Willard, *Christine de Pisan: Her Life and Works* (1984), and S. Bell, *The Lost Tapestries of the City of Ladies: Christine de Pizan's Renaissance Legacy* (2004).

a private concern to being a social matter requiring public supervision. The towns of Languedoc were not unique. Public authorities in Amiens, Dijon, Paris, Venice, Genoa, London, Florence, Rome, most of the larger German towns, and the English port of Sandwich set up brothels.

Young men associated visiting brothels with achieving manhood; for the women themselves, of course, their activities were work. Some women had no choice, for they had been traded to the brothel manager by their parents or some other person as payment for debt, or had quickly become indebted to the manager (most managers were men) for the clothes and other finery regarded as essential to their occupation. The small amount they received from their customers did not equal what they had to pay for their upkeep in a brothel. Poor women—and men—also sold sex illegally outside of city brothels, combining this with other sorts of part-time work such as laundering or sewing. Prostitution was an urban phenomenon because only populous towns had large numbers of unmarried young men, communities of transient merchants, and a culture accustomed to a cash exchange.

Though selling sex for money was legal in the Middle Ages, the position of women who did so was always marginal. In the late fifteenth century cities began to limit brothel residents' freedom of movement and choice of clothing, requiring them to wear distinctive head coverings or bands on their clothing so that they would not be mistaken for "honorable" women. Cities also began to impose harsher penalties on women who did not live in the designated house or section of town. A few women who sold sex did earn enough to donate money to charity or buy property, but most were very poor.

Along with buying sex, young men also took it by force. Unmarried women often found it difficult to avoid sexual contact. Many worked as domestic servants, where their employers or employers' sons or male relatives could easily coerce them, or they worked in proximity to men. Notions of female honor kept upper-class women secluded in their homes, particularly in southern and eastern Europe, but there was little attempt anywhere to protect female servants or day laborers from the risk of seduction or rape. Rape was a capital crime in many parts of Europe, but the actual sentences handed out were more likely to be fines and brief imprisonment, with the severity of the sentence dependent on the social status of the victim and the perpetrator.

Public Bath   In this fanciful scene of a medieval public bath from a 1470 illuminated manuscript, men and women soak in tubs while they eat and drink, entertained by a musician, and a king and church official look on. At the left is a couple about to hop in a bed for sex in what might be a brothel. Normal public baths were far less elaborate, and while they did sometimes offer food, wine, and sex, their main attraction was hot water. This painting is not meant to be realistic but a commentary on declining morals. (Miniature from a manuscript, *Factorum et dictorum memorabilium*, by Valerius Maximus for Antoine of Burgundy, ca. 1470/akg-images)

According to laws regarding rape in most parts of Europe, the victim had to prove that she had cried out and had attempted to repel the attacker, and she had to bring the charge within a short period of time after the attack had happened. Women bringing rape charges were often more interested in getting their own honorable reputations back than in punishing the perpetrators. For this reason, they sometimes asked the judge to force their rapists to marry them.

Same-sex relations—what in the late nineteenth century would be termed "homosexuality"—were another feature of medieval urban life (and of village life, though there are very few sources relating to sexual relations of any type in the rural context). Same-sex relations were of relatively little concern to church or state authorities in the early Middle Ages, but this attitude changed beginning in the late twelfth century. By 1300 most areas had defined such actions as "crimes against nature," with authorities seeing them as particularly reprehensible because they thought they did not occur anywhere else in creation. Same-sex relations, usually termed "sodomy," became a capital crime in most of Europe, with adult offenders threatened with execution by fire. The Italian cities of Venice, Florence, and Lucca created special courts to deal with sodomy, which saw thousands of investigations.

How prevalent were same-sex relations? This is difficult to answer, even in modern society, but the city of Florence provides a provocative case study. In 1432 Florence set up a special board of adult men, the Office of the Night, to "root out . . . the abominable vice of sodomy."[10] Between 1432 and the abolition of the board in 1502, about seventeen thousand men came to its attention, which, even over a seventy-year period, represents a great number in a population of about forty thousand. The men came from all classes of society, but almost all cases involved an adult man and an adolescent boy; they ranged from sex exchanged for money or gifts to long-term affectionate relationships. Florentines believed in a generational model in which different roles were appropriate to different stages in life. In a socially and sexually hierarchical world, the boy in the passive role was identified as subordinate, dependent, and mercenary, words usually applied to women. Florentines, however, never described the dominant partner in feminine terms, for he had not compromised his masculine identity or violated a gender ideal; in fact, the adult partner might be married or have female sexual partners as well as male. Only if an adult male assumed the passive role was his masculinity jeopardized.

Thus in Florence, and no doubt elsewhere in Europe, sodomy was not a marginal practice, which may account for the fact that, despite harsh laws and special courts, actual executions for sodomy were rare. Same-sex relations often developed within the context of all-male environments, such as the army, the craft shop, and the artistic workshop, and were part of the collective male experience. Homoerotic relationships played important roles in defining stages of life, expressing distinctions of status, and shaping masculine gender identity. Same-sex relations involving women almost never came to the attention of legal authorities, so it is difficult to find out how common they were. However, female-female desire was expressed in songs, plays, and stories, as was male-male desire, offering evidence of the way people understood same-sex relations.

Fur-Collar Crime

The Hundred Years' War had provided employment and opportunity for thousands of idle and fortune-seeking knights. But during periods of truce and after the war finally ended, many nobles once again had little to do. Inflation hurt them. Although many were living on fixed incomes, their chivalric code demanded lavish generosity and an aristocratic lifestyle. Many nobles thus turned to crime as a way of raising money. The fourteenth and fifteenth centuries witnessed a great deal of what we might term "fur-collar crime," a medieval version of today's white-collar crime in which those higher up the social scale prey on those who are less well-off.

This "fur-collar crime" involved both violence and fraud. Groups of noble bandits roamed the English countryside, stealing from both rich and poor. Operating like modern urban racketeers, knightly gangs demanded that peasants pay protection money or else have their hovels burned and their fields destroyed. They seized wealthy travelers and held them for ransom. Corrupt landowners, including some churchmen, pushed peasants to pay higher taxes and extra fees. When accused of wrongdoing, fur-collar criminals intimidated witnesses, threatened jurors, and used their influence to persuade judges to support them—or used cash to bribe them outright.

Aristocratic violence led to revolt, and it also shaped popular culture. The ballads of Robin Hood, a collection of folk legends from late medieval England, describe the adventures of the outlaw hero and his merry men as they avenge the common people against fur-collar criminals—grasping landlords, wicked sheriffs, and mercenary churchmen. Robin Hood was a popular figure because he symbolized the deep resentment of aristocratic corruption and abuse; he represented the struggle against tyranny and oppression.

Ethnic Tensions and Restrictions

Large numbers of people in the twelfth and thirteenth centuries migrated from one part of Europe to another in search of land, food, and work: the English into Scotland and Ireland; Germans, French, and Flemings into Poland, Bohemia, and Hungary; Christians into Muslim Spain. Everywhere in Europe, towns recruited people from the countryside as well (see Chapter 10). In frontier regions, townspeople were usually long-distance immigrants and, in eastern Europe, Ireland, and Scotland, ethnically different from the surrounding rural population. In eastern Europe, German was the language of the towns; in Irish towns, French, the tongue of Norman or English settlers, predominated. As a result of this colonization and movement to towns, peoples of different ethnic backgrounds lived side by side.

In the early periods of conquest and colonization, and in all regions with extensive migrations, a legal dualism existed: native peoples remained subject to their traditional laws; newcomers brought and were subject to the laws of the countries from which they came. On the Prussian and Polish frontier, for example, the law was that "men who come there . . . should be judged on account of any crime or contract engaged in there according to Polish custom if they are Poles and according to German custom if they are Germans."[11] Likewise, the conquered Muslim subjects of Christian kings in Spain had the right to be judged under Muslim law by Muslim judges.

The great exception to this broad pattern of legal pluralism was Ireland. From the start, the English practiced an extreme form of discrimination toward the native Irish. The English distinguished between the free and the unfree, and the entire Irish population, simply by the fact of Irish birth, was unfree. When English legal structures were established beginning in 1210, the Irish were denied access to the common-law courts.

In civil (property) disputes, an English defendant did not need to respond to an Irish plaintiff; no Irish person could make a will. In criminal procedures, the murder of an Irishman was not considered a felony. Other than in Ireland, although native peoples commonly held humbler positions, both immigrant and native townspeople prospered during the expanding economy of the thirteenth century. But with the economic turmoil of the fourteenth century, ethnic tensions multiplied.

The later Middle Ages witnessed a movement away from legal pluralism or dualism and toward legal homogeneity and an emphasis on blood descent. The dominant ethnic group in an area tried to bar others from positions of church leadership and guild membership. Marriage laws were instituted that attempted to maintain ethnic purity by prohibiting intermarriage, and some church leaders actively promoted ethnic discrimination. As Germans moved eastward, for example, German bishops refused to appoint non-Germans to any church office, while Czech bishops closed monasteries to Germans.

The most extensive attempt to prevent intermarriage and protect ethnic purity is embodied in the **Statute of Kilkenny** (1366), a law the ruling English imposed on Ireland, which states that "there were to be no marriages between those of immigrant and native stock; that the English inhabitants of Ireland must employ the English language and bear English names; that they must ride in the English way [that is, with saddles] and have English apparel; that no Irishmen were to be granted ecclesiastical benefices or admitted to monasteries in the English parts of Ireland."[12]

Statute of Kilkenny Law issued in 1366 that discriminated against the Irish, forbidding marriage between the English and the Irish, requiring the use of the English language, and denying the Irish access to ecclesiastical offices.

Late medieval chroniclers used words such as *gens* (race or clan) and *natio* (NAH-tee-oh; species, stock, or kind) to refer to different groups. They held that peoples differed according to language, traditions, customs, and laws. None of these were unchangeable, however, and commentators increasingly also described ethnic differences in terms of "blood," which made ethnicity heritable. As national consciousness grew with the Hundred Years' War, for example, people began to speak of "French blood" and "English blood." Religious beliefs came to be conceptualized in terms of blood as well, with people regarded as having Jewish blood, Muslim blood, or Christian blood. The most dramatic expression of this was in Spain, where "purity of blood"—having no Muslim or Jewish ancestors—became an obsession. Blood also came to be used as a way to talk about social differences, especially for nobles. Just as the Irish and English were prohibited from marrying each other, those of "noble blood" were prohibited from marrying commoners in many parts of Europe. As Europeans increasingly came into contact with people from Africa and Asia, and particularly as they developed colonial empires, these notions of blood also became a way of conceptualizing racial categories.

Literacy and Vernacular Literature

The development of ethnic identities had many negative consequences, but a more positive effect was the increasing use of the vernacular, that is, the local language that people actually spoke, rather than Latin (see Chapter 10). Two masterpieces of European culture, Dante's *Divine Comedy* (1310–1320) and Chaucer's *Canterbury Tales* (1387–1400), illustrate a sophisticated use of the rhythms and rhymes of the vernacular.

The *Divine Comedy* of Dante Alighieri (DAHN-tay ah-luh-GYEHR-ee) (1265–1321) is an epic poem of one hundred cantos (verses), each of whose three equal parts describes one of the realms of the next world: Hell, Purgatory, and Paradise. The Roman poet Virgil, representing reason, leads Dante through Hell, where Dante observes the torments of the damned and denounces the disorders of his own time. Passing up into Purgatory, Virgil shows the poet how souls are purified of their disordered inclinations. From Purgatory, Beatrice, a woman Dante once loved and who serves as the symbol of divine revelation in the poem, leads him to Paradise.

The *Divine Comedy* portrays contemporary and historical figures, comments on secular and ecclesiastical affairs, and draws on the Scholastic philosophy of uniting faith and reason. Within the framework of a symbolic pilgrimage, the *Divine Comedy* embodies the psychological tensions of the age. A profoundly Christian poem, it also contains bitter criticism of some church authorities. In its symmetrical structure and use of figures from the ancient world such as Virgil, the poem perpetuates the classical tradition, but as the first major work of literature in the Italian vernacular, it is distinctly modern.

Geoffrey Chaucer (1342–1400) was an official in the administrations of the English kings Edward III and Richard II and wrote poetry as an avocation. His *Canterbury Tales* is a collection of stories in lengthy rhymed narrative. On a pilgrimage to the shrine of Saint Thomas Becket at Canterbury (see Chapter 9), thirty people of various social backgrounds tell tales. In depicting the interests and behavior of all types of people, Chaucer presents a rich panorama of English social life in the fourteenth century. Like the *Divine Comedy*, the *Canterbury Tales* reflects the cultural tensions of the times. Ostensibly Christian, many of the pilgrims are also materialistic, sensual, and worldly, suggesting the ambivalence of the broader society's concern for the next world and frank enjoyment of this one.

Beginning in the fourteenth century, a variety of evidence attests to the increasing literacy of laypeople. Wills and inventories reveal that many people, not just nobles, possessed books—mainly devotional texts, but also romances, manuals on manners and etiquette, histories, and sometimes legal and philosophical texts. In England the number of schools in the diocese of York quadrupled between 1350 and 1500. Information from Flemish and German towns is similar: children were sent to schools and were taught the fundamentals of reading, writing, and arithmetic. Laymen increasingly served as managers or stewards of estates and as clerks to guilds and town governments; such positions obviously required the ability to keep administrative and financial records.

The penetration of laymen into the higher positions of governmental administration, long the preserve of clerics, also illustrates rising lay literacy. With growing frequency, the upper classes sent their daughters to convent schools, where, in addition to instruction in singing, religion, needlework, deportment, and household management, they gained the rudiments of reading and sometimes writing.

The spread of literacy represents a response to the needs of an increasingly complex society. Trade, commerce, and expanding government bureaucracies required an increasing number of literate people. Late medieval culture remained a decidedly oral culture. But by the fifteenth century the evolution toward a more literate culture was already perceptible, and craftsmen would develop the new technology of the printing press in response to the increased demand for reading materials.

LOOKING BACK LOOKING AHEAD

The fourteenth and early fifteenth centuries were certainly times of crisis in western Europe, meriting the label "calamitous" given to them by one popular historian. Famine, disease, and war decimated the European population, and traditional institutions, including secular governments and the church, did little or nothing or, in some cases, made things worse. Trading connections that had been reinvigorated in the High Middle Ages spread the most deadly epidemic ever experienced through western Asia, North Africa, and almost all of Europe. No wonder survivors experienced a sort of shell shock and a fascination with death.

The plague did not destroy the prosperity of the medieval population, however, and it may in fact have indirectly improved the European economy. Wealthy merchants had plenty of money to spend on luxuries and talent. In the century after the plague, Italian artists began to create new styles of painting, writers to pen new literary forms, educators to found new types of schools, and philosophers to develop new ideas about the purpose of human life. These cultural changes eventually spread to the rest of Europe, following the same paths that the plague had traveled.

Make Connections

Think about the larger developments and continuities within and across chapters.

1. The Black Death has often been compared with later pandemics, including the global spread of HIV/AIDS, which began in the 1980s. It is easy to note the differences between these two, but what similarities do you see in the course of the two diseases and their social and cultural consequences?

2. Beginning with Chapter 7, every chapter in this book has discussed the development of the papacy and relations between popes and secular rulers. How were the problems facing the papacy in the fourteenth century the outgrowth of long-term issues? Why had attempts to solve these issues not been successful?

3. In Chapter 3 you learned about the Bronze Age Collapse, and in Chapter 7 about the end of the Roman Empire in the West, both of which have also been seen as "calamitous." What similarities and differences do you see in these earlier times of turmoil and those of the late Middle Ages?

11 REVIEW & EXPLORE

Review the Main Ideas

Answer the focus questions from each section of the chapter.

◆ How did climate change shape the late Middle Ages? (p. 324)

◆ How did the plague reshape European society? (p. 326)

◆ What were the causes, course, and consequences of the Hundred Years' War? (p. 332)

◆ Why did the church come under increasing criticism? (p. 339)

◆ What explains the social unrest of the late Middle Ages? (p. 344)

Identify Key Terms

Identify and explain the significance of each item below.

Great Famine (p. 324)
Black Death (p. 326)
flagellants (p. 330)
Hundred Years' War (p. 332)
representative assemblies (p. 338)
Babylonian Captivity (p. 339)
Great Schism (p. 340)
conciliarists (p. 340)
confraternities (p. 342)
Jacquerie (p. 344)
English Peasants' Revolt (p. 346)
Statute of Kilkenny (p. 352)

NOTES

1. Christos S. Bartsocas, "Two Fourteenth Century Descriptions of the 'Black Death,'" *Journal of the History of Medicine* (October 1966): 395.
2. Giovanni Boccaccio, *The Decameron*, trans. Mark Musa and Peter Bondanella (New York: W. W. Norton, 1982), p. 7.
3. Ibid., p. 9.
4. Bartsocas, "Two Fourteenth Century Descriptions," p. 397.
5. Florence Warren, ed., *The Dance of Death* (Oxford: Early English Text Society, 1931), 10 lines from p. 8. Spelling modernized. Used by permission of the Council of the Early English Text Society.
6. W. P. Barrett, trans., *The Trial of Jeanne d'Arc* (London: George Routledge, 1931), pp. 165–166.
7. James Harvey Robinson, *Readings in European History*, vol. 1 (Boston: Ginn and Company, 1904), pp. 375–376.
8. Quoted in J. H. Smith, *The Great Schism, 1378: The Disintegration of the Medieval Papacy* (New York: Weybright & Talley, 1970), p. 15.
9. Quoted in Katharina M. Wilson, ed., *Medieval Women Writers* (Athens: University of Georgia Press, 1984), p. 245.
10. Michael Rocke, *Forbidden Friendships: Homosexuality and Male Culture in Renaissance Florence* (New York: Oxford University Press, 1996), p. 45.
11. Quoted in R. Bartlett, *The Making of Europe: Conquest, Colonization and Cultural Change, 950–1350* (Princeton, N.J.: Princeton University Press, 1993), p. 205.
12. Quoted ibid., p. 239.

CHAPTER PREVIEW

Wealth and Power in Renaissance Italy
How did politics and economics shape the Renaissance?

Intellectual Change
What new ideas were associated with the Renaissance?

Art and the Artist
How did art reflect new Renaissance ideals?

Social Hierarchies
What were the key social hierarchies in Renaissance Europe?

Politics and the State in Western Europe
How did nation-states develop in this period?

Life in the Renaissance

In this detail from a fresco of the birth of the Virgin Mary in the Church of San Michele al Pozzo Bianco in Bergamo, Italian painter Lorenzo Lotto depicts a birth scene that would have been common among upper-class urban residents in Renaissance Italy. The birth occurs at home, with lots of women bustling about, including servants, dressed simply, and female relatives, in fancier clothing. A professional midwife sits by the side of the bed, and the mother looks quite content, a sign that this has been a successful and fairly easy childbirth, which was not always the case.

(By Lorenzo Lotto [ca. 1480–1556], Church of San Michele al Pozzo Bianco, Bergamo, Italy/Mauro Ranzani Archive/Alinari Archives/Bridgeman Images)

12

European Society in the Age of the Renaissance

1350–1550

While the Hundred Years' War gripped northern Europe, a new culture emerged in southern Europe. The fourteenth century witnessed remarkable changes in Italian intellectual, artistic, and cultural life. Artists and writers thought that they were living in a new golden age, but not until the sixteenth century was this change given the label we use today—the *Renaissance*, derived from the French word for "rebirth." That word was first used by art historian Giorgio Vasari (1511–1574) to describe the art of "rare men of genius" such as his contemporary Michelangelo. Through their works, Vasari judged, the glory of the classical past had been reborn after centuries of darkness. Over time, the word's meaning was broadened to include many aspects of life during that period. The new attitude had a slow diffusion out of Italy, so that the Renaissance "happened" at different times in different parts of Europe. The Renaissance was a movement, not a time period.

Later scholars increasingly saw the cultural and political changes of the Renaissance, along with the religious changes of the Reformation (see Chapter 13) and the European voyages of exploration (see Chapter 14), as ushering in the "modern" world. Some historians view the Renaissance as a bridge between the medieval and modern eras because it corresponded chronologically with the late medieval period and because there were many continuities with that period along with the changes that suggested aspects of the modern world. Others have questioned whether the word *Renaissance* should be used at all to describe an era in which many social groups saw decline rather than advance. The debates remind us that these labels—medieval, Renaissance, modern—are intellectual constructs devised after the fact, and all contain value judgments. ■

Wealth and Power in Renaissance Italy

FOCUS QUESTION
How did politics and economics shape the Renaissance?

Renaissance A French word meaning "rebirth," used to describe the rebirth of the culture of classical antiquity in Italy during the fourteenth to sixteenth centuries.

patronage Financial support of writers and artists by cities, groups, and individuals, often to produce specific works or works in specific styles.

The magnificent art and new ways of thinking in the **Renaissance** rested on economic and political developments in the city-states of northern Italy. Economic growth laid the material basis for the Italian Renaissance, and ambitious merchants gained political power to match their economic power. They then used their money and power to buy luxuries and hire talent in a system of **patronage**, through which cities, groups, and individuals commissioned writers and artists to produce specific works. Political leaders in Italian cities admired the traditions and power of ancient Rome, and this esteem shaped their commissions. Thus economics, politics, and culture were interconnected.

Trade and Prosperity

Northern Italian cities led the way in the great commercial revival of the eleventh century (see Chapter 10). By the middle of the twelfth century Venice, supported by a huge merchant marine, had grown enormously rich through overseas trade, as had Genoa and Milan, which had their own sizable fleets. These cities made important strides in shipbuilding that allowed their ships to sail all year long at accelerated speeds and carrying ever more merchandise.

Another commercial leader, and the city where the Renaissance began, was Florence, situated on fertile soil along the Arno River. Its favorable location on the main road northward from Rome made Florence a commercial hub, and the city grew wealthy buying and selling all types of goods throughout Europe and the Mediterranean—grain, cloth, wool, weapons, armor, spices, glass, and wine.

Florentine merchants also loaned and invested money, and they acquired control of papal banking toward the end of the thirteenth century. Florentine mercantile families began to dominate European banking on both sides of the Alps, setting up offices in major European and North African cities. The profits from loans, investments, and money exchanges that poured back to Florence were pumped into urban industries such as clothmaking, and by the early fourteenth century the city had about eighty thousand people, about twice the population of London at that time. Profits contributed to the city's economic vitality and allowed banking families to control the city's politics and culture.

By the first quarter of the fourteenth century, the economic foundations of Florence were so strong that even severe crises could not destroy the city. In 1344 King Edward III of England repudiated his huge debts to Florentine bankers, forcing some of them into bankruptcy. Soon after, Florence suffered frightfully from the Black Death, losing at least half its population, and serious labor unrest shook the political establishment (see Chapter 11). Nevertheless, the basic Florentine economic structure remained stable, and the city grew again. In the fifteenth century the Florentine merchant and historian Benedetto Dei (DAY-ee) boasted proudly of his city in a letter to an acquaintance from Venice:

> Our beautiful Florence contains within the city in this present year two hundred seventy shops belonging to the wool merchants' guild . . . eighty-three rich and splendid warehouses of the silk merchants' guild. . . . The number of banks amounts to thirty-three; the shops of the cabinet-makers, whose business is carving and inlaid work, to eighty-four . . . there are forty-four goldsmiths' and jewellers' shops.[1]

In Florence and other thriving Italian cities, wealth allowed many people greater material pleasures, a more comfortable life, imported luxuries, and leisure time to appreciate and patronize the arts. Merchants and bankers commissioned public and private buildings from architects, and hired sculptors and painters to decorate their homes and churches. The rich, social-climbing residents of Venice, Florence, Genoa, and Rome came to see life more as an opportunity to be enjoyed than as a painful pilgrimage to the City of God.

Chronology

ca. 1350	Petrarch develops ideas of humanism
1434–1737	Medici family in power in Florence
1440s	Invention of movable metal type
1447–1535	Sforza family in power in Milan
1455–1471	Wars of the Roses in England
1469	Marriage of Isabella of Castile and Ferdinand of Aragon
1477	Louis XI conquers Burgundy
1478	Establishment of the Inquisition in Spain
1492	Spain conquers Granada, ending reconquista; practicing Jews expelled from Spain
1494	Invasion of Italy by Charles VIII of France
1508–1512	Michelangelo paints ceiling of Sistine Chapel
1513	Machiavelli writes *The Prince*
1563	Establishment of first formal academy for artistic training in Florence

Communes and Republics of Northern Italy

The northern Italian cities were **communes**, sworn associations of free men who, like other town residents, began in the twelfth century to seek political and economic independence from local nobles. The merchant guilds that formed the communes built and maintained the city walls and regulated trade, collected taxes, and kept civil order within them. The local nobles frequently moved into the cities, marrying the daughters of rich commercial families and starting their own businesses, often with money they had gained through the dowries provided by their wives. This merger of the northern Italian nobility and the commercial elite created a powerful oligarchy, a small group that ruled the city and surrounding countryside. Yet because of rivalries among competing powerful families within this oligarchy, Italian communes were often politically unstable.

Unrest from below exacerbated the instability. Merchant elites made citizenship in the communes dependent on a property qualification, years of residence within the city, and social connections. Only a tiny percentage of the male population possessed these qualifications and thus could hold political office. The common people, called the **popolo**, were disenfranchised and heavily taxed, and they bitterly resented their exclusion from power. Throughout most of the thirteenth century, in city after city, the popolo used armed force to take over the city governments. At times republican government—in which political power theoretically resides in the people and is exercised by their chosen representatives—was established in numerous Italian cities, including Bologna, Siena, Parma, Florence, Genoa, and other cities. These victories

communes Sworn associations of free men in Italian cities led by merchant guilds that sought political and economic independence from local nobles.

popolo Disenfranchised common people in Italian cities who resented their exclusion from power.

359

A Florentine Bank Scene Originally a "bank" was just a counter; money changers who sat behind the counter became "bankers," exchanging different currencies and holding deposits for merchants and business people. In this scene from fifteenth-century Florence, the bank is covered with an imported Ottoman geometric rug, one of many imported luxury items handled by Florentine merchants. Most cities issued their own coins, but the gold coins of Florence, known as florins, were accepted throughout Europe as a standard currency. (Detail from the fresco *The Story of St. Matthew*, San Francesco, Prato, Italy/Scala/Art Resource, NY)

of the popolo proved temporary, however, because they could not establish civil order within their cities. Merchant oligarchies reasserted their power and sometimes brought in powerful military leaders to establish order. These military leaders, called *condottieri* (kahn-duh-TYER-ee; singular *condottiero*), had their own mercenary armies, and in many cities they took over political power once they had supplanted the existing government.

signori Government by one-man rule in Italian cities such as Milan; also refers to these rulers.

Many cities in Italy became **signori** (seen-YOHR-ee), in which one man—whether condottiero, merchant, or noble—ruled and handed down the right to rule to his son. Some signori (the word is plural in Italian and is used for both persons and forms of government) kept the institutions of communal government in place, but these had no actual power. As a practical matter, there wasn't much difference between oligarchic regimes and signori. Oligarchies maintained a façade of republican government, but the judicial, executive, and legislative functions of government were restricted to a small class of wealthy merchants.

courts Magnificent households and palaces where signori and other rulers lived, conducted business, and supported the arts.

In the fifteenth and sixteenth centuries the signori in many cities and the most powerful merchant oligarchs in others transformed their households into **courts**. Courtly culture afforded signori and oligarchs the opportunity to display and assert their wealth and power. They built magnificent palaces in the centers of cities and required all political business to be done there. Ceremonies connected with family births, baptisms, marriages, and funerals offered occasions for magnificent pageantry and elaborate ritual. Cities welcomed rulers who were visiting with magnificent entrance parades that often included fireworks, colorful banners, mock naval battles, decorated wagons filled with people in costume, and temporary triumphal arches modeled on those of ancient Rome. Rulers of nation-states later copied and adapted all these aspects of Italian courts.

City-States and the Balance of Power

Renaissance Italians had a passionate attachment to their individual city-states: they were politically loyal and felt centered on the city. This intensity of local feeling perpetuated the dozens of small states and hindered the development of one unified state.

In the fifteenth century five powers dominated the Italian peninsula: Venice, Milan, Florence, the Papal States, and the kingdom of Naples (Map 12.1). The major Italian powers controlled the smaller city-states, such as Siena, Mantua, Ferrara, and Modena, and competed furiously among themselves for territory. While the states of northern Europe were moving toward centralization and consolidation, the world of Italian politics resembled a jungle where the powerful dominated the weak. Venice, with its enormous trade empire, ranked as an international power. Though Venice was a republic in name, an oligarchy of merchant-aristocrats actually ran the city. Milan was also called a republic, but the condottieri-turned-signori of the Sforza (SFORT-sah) family ruled harshly and dominated Milan and several smaller cities in the north from 1447 to 1535. Likewise, in Florence the form of government was republican, with authority vested in several councils of state, but the city was effectively ruled by the great Medici (MEH-duh-chee) banking family for three centuries, beginning in 1434. Though not public officials, Cosimo (1389–1464), his son Piero, and his grandson Lorenzo (1449–1492), called Lorenzo the Magnificent by his contemporaries, ruled from behind the scenes from 1434 to 1492. The Medici were then in and out of power for several decades, and in 1569 Florence became no longer a republic but the hereditary Grand Duchy of Tuscany, with the Medici as the Grand

MAP 12.1 The Italian City-States, ca. 1494 In the fifteenth century the Italian city-states represented great wealth and cultural sophistication, though the many political divisions throughout the peninsula invited foreign intervention.

Dukes until 1737. The Medici family produced three popes, and most other Renaissance popes were also members of powerful Italian families, selected for their political skills, not their piety. Along with the Italians was one Spaniard, Pope Alexander VI (pontificate 1492–1503), who was the most ruthless; aided militarily and politically by his illegitimate son Cesare Borgia, he reasserted papal authority in the papal lands. South of the Papal States, the kingdom of Naples was under the control of the king of Aragon.

In one significant respect, however, the Italian city-states anticipated future relations among competing European states after 1500. Whenever one Italian state appeared to gain a predominant position within the peninsula, other states combined against it to establish a balance of power. In the formation of these alliances, Renaissance Italians invented the machinery of modern diplomacy: permanent embassies with resident ambassadors in capitals where political relations and commercial ties needed continual monitoring. The resident ambassador was one of the great political achievements of the Italian Renaissance.

At the end of the fifteenth century Venice, Florence, Milan, and the papacy possessed great wealth and represented high cultural achievement. Wealthy and divided, however, they were also an inviting target for invasion. When Florence and Naples entered into an agreement to acquire Milanese territories, Milan called on France for support, and the French king Charles VIII (r. 1483–1498) invaded Italy in 1494.

Prior to this invasion, the Dominican friar Girolamo Savonarola (1452–1498) had preached to large crowds in Florence a number of fiery sermons predicting that God would punish Italy for its moral vice and corrupt leadership. Florentines interpreted the French invasion as the fulfillment of this prophecy and expelled the Medici dynasty. Savonarola became the political and religious leader of a new Florentine republic and promised Florentines even greater glory in the future if they would reform their ways. (See "Evaluating the Evidence 12.1: A Sermon of Savonarola," at right.) He reorganized the government; convinced it to pass laws against same-sex relations, adultery, and drunkenness; and organized groups of young men to patrol the streets looking for immoral dress and behavior. He held religious processions and what became known as "bonfires of the vanities," huge fires on the main square of Florence in which fancy clothing, cosmetics, pagan books, musical instruments, paintings, and poetry that celebrated human beauty were gathered together and burned.

For a time Savonarola was wildly popular, but eventually people tired of his moral denunciations, and he was excommunicated by the pope, tortured, and burned at the very spot where he had overseen the bonfires. The Medici returned as the rulers of Florence.

The French invasion inaugurated a new period in Italian and European power politics. Italy became the focus of international ambitions and the battleground of foreign armies, particularly those of the Holy Roman Empire and France in a series of conflicts called the Habsburg-Valois wars (named for the German and French dynasties). The Italian cities suffered severely from continual warfare, especially in the frightful sack of Rome in 1527 by imperial forces under the emperor Charles V. Thus the failure of the city-states to consolidate, or at least to establish a common foreign policy, led to centuries of subjection by outside invaders. Italy was not to achieve unification until 1870.

A Sermon of Savonarola

In the autumn of 1494 French armies under Charles VIII surrounded Florence. The Dominican friar Girolamo Savonarola met with the French king and convinced him to spare the city and keep moving his huge army southward. He preached a series of sermons that winter saying that God had chosen Florence to achieve even greater heights under his leadership than it had in the past, provided that it followed his instructions.

O Florence . . . I tell you, do first those two things I told you another time, that is, that everyone go to confession and be purified of sins, and let everyone attend to the common good of the city; and if you will do this, your city will be glorious because in this way she will be reformed spiritually as well as temporally, that is, with regard to her people, and from you will issue the reform of all Italy. Florence will become richer and more powerful than she has ever been, and her empire will expand into many places. But if you will not do what I tell you, God will elect those who, as I said, want to see you divided, and this will be your final destruction. If you would do what I have told you, here is the fire and here is the water: now do it! . . .

But, Florence, if you want your government to be stable and strong and to endure a long time, you must return to God and to living uprightly; otherwise, you will come to ruin. . . . *Furthermore*, it is necessary that the Magnificent Signory [the government of the city] ordain that all those things contrary to godly religion be removed from the city, and in the first place, to act and ordain that the clergy must be good, because priests have to be a mirror to the people wherein everyone beholds and learns righteous living. But let the bad priests and religious be expelled. . . . They should not puff themselves up with so much material wealth, but give it to the very poor for God's sake. . . .

It is necessary that the Signory pass laws against that accursed vice of sodomy [same-sex relations], for which you know that Florence is infamous throughout the whole of Italy; this infamy arises perhaps from your talking and chattering about it so much, so that there is not so much in deeds, perhaps, as in words. Pass a law, I say, and let it be without mercy; that is, let these people be stoned and burned. On the other hand, it is necessary that you remove from among yourselves these poems and games and taverns and the evil fashion of women's clothes, and, likewise, we must throw out everything that is noxious to the health of the soul. Let everyone live for God and not for the world. . . .

The second [resolution]: attend to the common good. O citizens, if you band together and with a good will attend to the common welfare, each shall have more temporal and spiritual goods than if he alone attended to his own particular case. Attend, I say, to the common good of the city, and if anyone would elevate himself, let him be deprived of all his goods.

EVALUATE THE EVIDENCE

1. What does Savonarola tell Florentines they must do, and what will be their reward if they follow his instructions?
2. Savonarola initially had many followers, including well-known writers and artists. Why might his words have found such a ready audience in Florence at that time?

Source: *Selected Writings of Girolamo Savonarola: Religion and Politics, 1490–1498*, trans. and ed. Anne Borelli and Maria Pastore Passaro (New Haven: Yale University Press, 2006), pp. 153, 157, 158. Copyright © 2006 Yale University. Used by permission of Yale University Press.

Intellectual Change

The Renaissance was characterized by self-conscious conviction among educated Italians that they were living in a new era. Somewhat ironically, this idea rested on a deep interest in ancient Latin and Greek literature and philosophy. Through reflecting on the classics, Renaissance thinkers developed new notions of human nature, new plans for education, and new concepts of political rule. The advent of the printing press with movable type would greatly accelerate the spread of these ideas throughout Europe.

FOCUS QUESTION
What new ideas were associated with the Renaissance?

Humanism

Giorgio Vasari was the first to use the word *Renaissance* in print, but he was not the first to feel that something was being reborn. Two centuries earlier the Florentine poet and scholar Francesco Petrarch (1304–1374) spent long hours searching for classical Latin manuscripts in dusty monastery libraries and wandering around the many ruins of the Roman Empire remaining in Italy. He became obsessed with the classical past and felt that the writers and artists of ancient Rome had reached a level of perfection in their work that had not since been duplicated. Writers of his own day should follow these ancient models, thought Petrarch, and ignore the thousand-year period between his own time and that of Rome, which he called the "dark ages" ushered in by the barbarian invasions. Petrarch believed that the recovery of classical texts would bring about a new golden age of intellectual achievement, an idea that many others came to share.

Petrarch clearly thought he was witnessing the dawning of a new era in which writers and artists would recapture the glory of the Roman Republic. Around 1350 he proposed a new kind of education to help them do this, in which young men would study the works of ancient Roman authors, using them as models of how to write clearly, argue effectively, and speak persuasively. The study of Latin classics became known as the *studia humanitates* (STOO-dee-uh oo-mahn-ee-TAH-tayz), usually translated as "liberal studies" or the "liberal arts." People who advocated it were known as *humanists* and their program as **humanism**. Humanism was the main intellectual component of the Renaissance. Like all programs of study, humanism contained an implicit philosophy: that human nature and achievements, evident in the classics, were worthy of contemplation.

humanism A program of study designed by Italians that emphasized the critical study of Latin and Greek literature with the goal of understanding human nature.

The glory of Rome had been brightest, in the opinion of the humanists, in the works of the Roman author and statesman Cicero (106–43 B.C.E.). Cicero had lived during the turbulent era when Julius Caesar and other powerful generals transformed the Roman Republic into an empire (see Chapter 5). In forceful and elegantly worded speeches, letters, and treatises, Cicero supported a return to republican government. Petrarch and other humanists admired Cicero's use of language, literary style, and political ideas. Many humanists saw Caesar's transformation of Rome as a betrayal of the great society, marking the beginning of a long period of decay that the barbarian migrations then accelerated. In his history of Florence written in 1436, the humanist historian and Florentine city official Leonardo Bruni (1374–1444) closely linked the decline of the Latin language after the death of Cicero to the decline of the Roman Republic: "After the liberty of the Roman people had been lost through the rule of the emperors . . . the flourishing condition of studies and of letters perished, together with the welfare of the city of Rome."[2] In this same book, Bruni was also very clear that by the time of his writing, the period of decay had ended and a new era had begun. He was the first to divide history into three eras—ancient, medieval, and modern—though it was another humanist historian who actually invented the term "Middle Ages."

In the fifteenth century Florentine humanists became increasingly interested in Greek philosophy as well as Roman literature, especially in the ideas of Plato. Under the patronage of the Medici, the scholar Marsilio Ficino (1433–1499) began to lecture to an informal group of Florence's cultural elite; his lectures became known as the Platonic Academy, but they were not really a school. Ficino regarded Plato as a divinely inspired precursor to Christ. He translated Plato's dialogues into Latin and wrote commentaries attempting to synthesize Christian and Platonic teachings. Plato's emphasis on the spiritual and eternal over the material and transient fit well with Christian teachings about the immortality of the soul. The Platonic idea that the highest form of love was spiritual desire for pure, perfect beauty uncorrupted by bodily desires could easily be interpreted as Christian desire for the perfection of God.

For Ficino and his most gifted student, Giovanni Pico della Mirandola (1463–1494), both Christian and classical texts taught that the universe was a hierarchy of beings from God down through spiritual beings to material beings, with humanity, right in the middle, as the crucial link that possessed both material and spiritual natures. Pico developed his ideas in a series of 900 theses, or points of argumentation, and offered to defend them against anyone who wanted to come to Rome. The pope declared some of the ideas heretical and arrested Pico, though he was freed through the influence of Lorenzo de' Medici. At Lorenzo's death, Pico became a follower of Savonarola, renounced his former ideas and writings, and died of arsenic poisoning, perhaps at the hands of the recently ousted Medici family.

Man's divinely bestowed nature meant there were no limits to what he could accomplish. Families, religious brotherhoods, neighborhoods, workers' organizations, and other groups continued to have meaning in people's lives, but Renaissance thinkers increasingly viewed these groups as springboards to far greater individual achievement. They were especially interested in individuals who had risen above their background to become brilliant, powerful, or unique. (See "Individuals in Society: Leonardo da Vinci," page 376.) Such individuals had the admirable quality of **virtù** (vihr-TOO), a word that had not the conventional meaning of virtue as moral goodness, but instead the ability to shape the world around according to one's will. Bruni and other historians included biographies of individuals with virtù in their histories of cities and nations, describing ways in which these people had affected the course of history. Through the quality of their works and their influence on others, artists could also exhibit virtù, an idea that Vasari captures in the title of his major work, *The Lives of the Most Excellent Painters, Sculptors, and Architects*. His subjects had achieved not simply excellence but the pinnacle of excellence.

virtù The quality of being able to shape the world according to one's own will.

The last artist included in Vasari's book is Vasari himself, for Renaissance thinkers did not exclude themselves when they searched for models of talent and achievement. Vasari begins his discussion of his own works modestly, saying that these might "not lay claim to excellence and perfection" when compared with those of other artists, but he then goes on for more than thirty pages, clearly feeling he has achieved some level of excellence.

Leon Battista Alberti (1404–1472) had similar views of his own achievements. He had much to be proud of: he wrote novels, plays, legal treatises, a study of the family, and the first scientific analysis of perspective; he designed churches, palaces, and fortifications effective against cannon; he invented codes for sending messages secretly and a machine that could cipher and decipher them. In his autobiography — written late in his life, and in the third person, so that he calls himself "he" instead of "I" — Alberti described his personal qualities and accomplishments:

> Assiduous in the science and skill of dealing with arms and horses and musical instruments, as well as in the pursuit of letters and the fine arts, he was devoted to the knowledge of the most strange and difficult things. . . . He played ball, hurled the javelin, ran, leaped, wrestled. . . . He learned music without teachers . . . and then turned to physics and the mathematical arts. . . . Ambition was alien to him. . . . When his favorite dog died he wrote a funeral oration for him.[3]

His achievements in many fields did make Alberti a "Renaissance man," as we use the term, though it may be hard to believe his assertion that "ambition was alien to him."

Biographies and autobiographies presented individuals that humanist authors thought were worthy models, but sometimes people needed more direct instruction. The ancient Greek philosopher Plato, whom humanists greatly admired, taught that the best way to learn something was to think about its perfect, ideal form. If you wanted to learn about justice, for example, you should imagine what ideal justice would be, rather than look at actual examples of justice in the world around you, for these would never be perfect. Following Plato's ideas, Renaissance authors speculated about perfect examples of many things. Alberti wrote about the ideal country house, which was to be useful, convenient, and elegant. The English humanist Thomas More described a perfect society, which he called Utopia (see page 369).

Education

Humanists thought that their recommended course of study in the classics would provide essential skills for future politicians, diplomats, lawyers, military leaders, and businessmen, as well as writers and artists. It would provide a much broader and more practical type of training than that offered at universities, which at the time focused on theology and philosophy or on theoretical training for lawyers and physicians. Humanists poured out treatises, often in the form of letters, on the structure and goals of education and the training of rulers and leaders.

Humanists put their ideas into practice. Beginning in the early fifteenth century, they opened schools and academies in Italian cities and courts in which pupils began with Latin grammar and rhetoric, went on to study Roman history and political philosophy, and then learned Greek in order to study Greek literature and philosophy. Gradually, humanist education became the basis for intermediate and advanced education for well-to-do urban boys and men. Humanist schools were established in Florence, Venice, and other Italian cities, and by the early sixteenth century across the Alps in Germany, France, and England.

Humanists disagreed about education for women. Many saw the value of exposing women to classical models of moral behavior and reasoning, but they also wondered whether a program of study that emphasized eloquence and action was proper for women, whose sphere was generally understood to be private and domestic. In his book on the family, Alberti stressed that a wife's role should be restricted to the orderliness of the household, food preparation and the serving of meals, the education of children, and the supervision of servants. (Alberti never married, so he never put his ideas into practice in his own household.) Women themselves were bolder in their claims about the value of the new learning. Although humanist academies were not open to women, a few women did become educated in the classics, and wrote and published poetry, fiction, and essays in Latin and vernacular languages.

No book on education had broader influence than Baldassare Castiglione's *The Courtier* (1528). This treatise sought to train, discipline, and fashion the young man into the courtly ideal, the gentleman. According to Castiglione (kahs-teel-YOH-nay), himself a courtier serving several different rulers, the educated man should have a broad background in many academic subjects, and should train his spiritual and physical faculties as well as his intellect. Castiglione envisioned a man who could compose a sonnet, wrestle, sing a song while accompanying himself on an instrument, ride expertly, solve difficult mathematical problems, and, above all, speak and write eloquently. Castiglione also included discussion of the perfect court lady, who, like the courtier, was to be well educated and able to paint, dance, and play a musical instrument. Physical beauty, delicacy, affability, and modesty were also important qualities for court ladies.

In the sixteenth and seventeenth centuries *The Courtier* was translated into most European languages and widely read. It influenced the social mores and patterns of conduct of elite groups in Renaissance and early modern Europe and became a how-to manual for people seeking to improve themselves and rise in the social hierarchy as well. Echoes of its ideal for women have perhaps had an even longer life.

Political Thought

Ideal courtiers should preferably serve an ideal ruler, and biographies written by humanists often described rulers who were just, wise, pious, dignified, learned, brave, kind, and distinguished. In return for such flattering portraits of living rulers or their ancestors, authors sometimes received positions at court, or at least substantial payments. Particularly in Italian cities, however, which often were divided by political factions, taken over by homegrown or regional despots, and attacked by foreign armies, such ideal rulers were hard to find. Humanists thus looked to the classical past for their models. Some, such as Bruni, argued that republicanism was the best form of government. Others used the model of Plato's philosopher-king in the *Republic* to argue that rule by an enlightened individual might be best. Both sides agreed that educated men should be active in the political affairs of their city, a position historians have since termed "civic humanism."

The most famous (or infamous) civic humanist, and ultimately the best-known political theorist of this era, was Niccolò Machiavelli (1469–1527). After the ouster of the Medici with the French invasion of 1494, Machiavelli was secretary to one of the governing bodies in the city of Florence; he was responsible for diplomatic missions and organizing a citizen army. Almost two decades later, power struggles in Florence between rival factions brought the Medici family back to power, and Machiavelli was arrested, tortured, and imprisoned on suspicion of plotting against them. He was released but had no government position, and he spent the rest of his life writing — political theory, poetry, prose works, plays, and a multivolume history of Florence — and making fruitless attempts to regain employment.

The first work Machiavelli finished — though not the first to be published — is his most famous: *The Prince* (1513), which uses the examples of classical and contemporary rulers to argue that the function of a ruler (or any government) is to preserve order and security. Weakness only leads to disorder, which might end in civil war or conquest by an outsider, situations clearly detrimental to any people's well-being. To preserve the state, a ruler should use whatever means he needs — brutality, lying, manipulation — but should not do anything that would make the populace turn against him; stealing or cruel actions done for a ruler's own pleasure would lead to resentment and destroy the popular support needed for a strong, stable realm. "It is much safer for the prince to be feared than loved," Machiavelli advised, "but he ought to avoid making himself hated."[4]

Like the good humanist he was, Machiavelli knew that effective rulers exhibited the quality of virtù. He presented examples from the classical past of just the type of ruler he was describing, but also wrote about contemporary leaders. Cesare Borgia (1475?–1507), Machiavelli's primary example, was the son of Rodrigo Borgia, a Spanish nobleman who later became Pope Alexander VI. Cesare Borgia combined his father's power and his own ruthlessness to build up a state of his own in central Italy. He made good use of new military equipment and tactics, hiring Leonardo da Vinci (1452–1519) as a military engineer, and murdered his political enemies, including the second husband of his sister, Lucrezia. Despite Borgia's efforts, his state fell apart after his father's death, which Machiavelli ascribed not to weakness, but to the operations of fate (*fortuna*, for-TOO-nah, in Italian), whose power even the best-prepared and most merciless ruler could not fully escape, though he should try. Fortuna was personified and portrayed as a goddess in ancient Rome and Renaissance Italy, and Machiavelli's last words about fortune are expressed in gendered terms: "It is better to be impetuous than cautious, for fortune is a woman, and if one wishes to keep her down, it is necessary to beat her and knock her down."[5]

The Prince is often seen as the first modern guide to politics, though Machiavelli was denounced for writing it, and people later came to use the word *Machiavellian* to mean cunning and ruthless. Medieval political philosophers had debated the proper relation between church and state, but they regarded the standards by which all governments were to be judged as emanating from moral principles established by God. Machiavelli argued that governments should instead be judged by how well they provided security, order, and safety to their populace. A ruler's moral code in maintaining these was not the same as a private individual's, for a leader could—indeed, should—use any means necessary. Machiavelli put a new spin on the Renaissance search for perfection, arguing that ideals needed to be measured in the cold light of the real world. This more pragmatic view of the purposes of government, along with Machiavelli's discussion of the role of force and cruelty, was unacceptable to many.

Even today, when Machiavelli's more secular view of the purposes of government is widely shared, scholars debate whether Machiavelli actually meant what he wrote. Most regard him as realistic or even cynical, but some suggest that he was being ironic or satirical, showing princely government in the worst possible light to contrast it with republicanism, which he favored, and also wrote about at length in the *Discourses on Livy*. He dedicated *The Prince* to the new Medici ruler of Florence, however, so any criticism was deeply buried within what was, in that era of patronage, essentially a job application.

Christian Humanism

In the last quarter of the fifteenth century, students from the Low Countries, France, Germany, and England flocked to Italy, absorbed the "new learning," and carried it back to their own countries. Northern humanists shared the ideas of Ficino and Pico about the wisdom of ancient texts, but they went beyond Italian efforts to synthesize the Christian and classical traditions to see humanist learning as a way to bring about reform of the church and deepen people's spiritual lives. These **Christian humanists**, as they were later called, thought that the best elements of classical and Christian cultures should be combined. For example, the classical ideals of calmness, stoical patience, and broad-mindedness should be joined in human conduct with the Christian virtues of love, faith, and hope.

The English humanist Thomas More (1478–1535) began life as a lawyer, studied the classics, and entered government service. Despite his official duties, he had time to

Christian humanists
Northern humanists who interpreted Italian ideas about and attitudes toward classical antiquity and humanism in terms of their own religious traditions.

Thomas More, *Utopia*

Published in 1516, Utopia *is written as a dialogue between Thomas More and Raphael Hythloday, a character More invented who has, in More's telling, recently returned from the newly discovered land of Utopia somewhere in the New World. More and Hythloday first discuss the problems in Europe, and then Hythloday describes how these have been solved in Utopia, ending with a long discussion of the Utopians' ban on private property.*

Well, that's the most accurate account I can give you of the Utopian Republic. To my mind, it's not only the best country in the world, but the only one that has the right to call itself a republic. Elsewhere, people are always talking about the public interest, but all they really care about is private property. In Utopia, where there's no private property, people take their duty to the public seriously. And both attitudes are perfectly reasonable. In other "republics" practically everyone knows that, if he doesn't look out for himself, he'll starve to death, however prosperous his country may be. He's therefore compelled to give his own interests priority over those of the public; that is, of other people. But in Utopia, where everything's under public ownership, no one has any fear of going short, as long as the public storehouses are full. Everyone gets a fair share, so there are never any poor men or beggars. Nobody owns anything, but everyone is rich—for what greater wealth can there be than cheerfulness, peace of mind, and freedom from anxiety? Instead of being worried about his food supply, upset by the plaintive demands of his wife, afraid of poverty for his son, and baffled by the problem of finding a dowry for his daughter, the Utopian can feel absolutely sure that he, his wife, his children, his grandchildren, his great-grandchildren, and as long a line of descendants as the proudest peer could wish to look forward to, will always

have enough to eat and enough to make them happy. There's also the further point that those who are too old to work are just as well provided for as those who are still working.

Now, will anyone venture to compare these fair arrangements in Utopia with the so-called justice of other countries?—in which I'm damned if I can see the slightest trace of justice or fairness. For what sort of justice do you call this? People like aristocrats, goldsmiths, or money-lenders, who either do no work at all, or do work that's really not essential, are rewarded for their laziness or their unnecessary activities by a splendid life of luxury. But labourers, coachmen, carpenters, and farmhands, who never stop working like cart-horses, at jobs so essential that, if they *did* stop working, they'd bring any country to a standstill within twelve months—what happens to them? They get so little to eat, and have such a wretched time, that they'd be almost better off if they *were* cart-horses. Then at least, they wouldn't work quite such long hours, their food wouldn't be very much worse, they'd enjoy it more, and they'd have no fears for the future. As it is, they're not only ground down by unrewarding toil in the present, but also worried to death by the prospect of a poverty-stricken old age.

EVALUATE THE EVIDENCE

1. How does the Utopians' economic system compare with that of Europe, in Hythloday's opinion?
2. Hythloday's comments about wealth have been seen by some scholars as More's criticism of his own society, and by others as proof that More wrote this as a satire, describing a place that could never be. Which view seems most persuasive to you?

Source: Thomas More, *Utopia,* trans. Paul Turner (London: Penguin Books, 1965), pp. 128–129. Reproduced by permission of Penguin Books Ltd.

---

write, and he became most famous for his controversial dialogue *Utopia* (1516), a word More invented from the Greek words for "nowhere." *Utopia* describes a community on an island somewhere beyond Europe where all children receive a good education, primarily in the Greco-Roman classics, and adults divide their days between manual labor or business pursuits and intellectual activities. The problems that plagued More's fellow citizens, such as poverty and hunger, have been solved by a beneficent government. (See "Evaluating the Evidence 12.2: Thomas More, *Utopia*," above.) There is religious toleration, and order and reason prevail. Because Utopian institutions are perfect, however, dissent and disagreement are not acceptable.

More's purposes in writing *Utopia* have been debated just as much as have Machiavelli's in penning *The Prince*. Some view it as a revolutionary critique of More's own hierarchical and violent society, some as a call for an even firmer hierarchy, and others as part of the humanist tradition of satire. It was widely read by learned Europeans in the Latin in which More wrote it, and later in vernacular translations, and its title quickly became the standard word for any imaginary society.

Better known by contemporaries than Thomas More was the Dutch humanist Desiderius Erasmus (dehz-ih-DARE-ee-us ih-RAZ-muhs) (1466?–1536) of Rotterdam. His fame rested on both scholarly editions and translations and popular works. Erasmus's long list of publications includes *The Education of a Christian Prince* (1504), a book combining idealistic and practical suggestions for the formation of a ruler's character through the careful study of the Bible and classical authors; *The Praise of Folly* (1509), a witty satire poking fun at political, social, and especially religious institutions; and, most important, a new Latin translation of the New Testament alongside the first printed edition of the Greek text (1516). In the preface to the New Testament, Erasmus expressed his ideas about Bible translations: "I wish that even the weakest woman should read the Gospel—should read the epistles of Paul. And I wish these were translated into all languages, so that they might be read and understood, not only by Scots and Irishmen, but also by Turks and Saracens."[6]

Two fundamental themes run through all of Erasmus's work. First, education in the Bible and the classics is the means to reform, the key to moral and intellectual improvement. Erasmus called for a renaissance of the ideals of the early church to accompany the renaissance in classical education that was already going on, and criticized the church of his day for having strayed from these ideals. Second, renewal should be based on what he termed "the philosophy of Christ," an emphasis on inner spirituality and personal morality rather than Scholastic theology or outward observances such as pilgrimages or venerating relics. His ideas, and Christian humanism in general, were important roots of the Protestant Reformation, although Erasmus himself denied this and never became a follower of Luther (see Chapter 13).

The Printed Word

The fourteenth-century humanist Petrarch and the sixteenth-century humanist Erasmus had similar ideas on many topics, but the immediate impact of their ideas was very different because of one thing: the invention of the printing press with movable metal type. The ideas of Petrarch were spread slowly from person to person by hand copying. The ideas of Erasmus were spread quickly through print, allowing hundreds or thousands of identical copies to be made in a short time.

Printing with movable metal type developed in Germany in the 1440s as a combination of existing technologies. Several metal-smiths, most prominently Johann Gutenberg, recognized that the metal stamps used to mark signs on jewelry could be covered with ink and used to mark symbols onto a surface in the same way that other craftsmen were using carved wood stamps to print books. (This woodblock printing technique originated in China and Korea centuries earlier.) Gutenberg and his assistants made metal stamps—later called *type*—for every letter of the alphabet and built racks that held the type in rows. This type could be rearranged for every page and so used over and over.

The printing revolution was also made possible by the ready availability of paper, which was also produced using techniques that had originated in China, though, unlike the printing press, this technology had been brought into Europe through Muslim Spain rather than developing independently.

By the fifteenth century the increase in urban literacy, the development of primary schools, and the opening of more universities had created an expanding market for reading materials (see Chapter 11). When Gutenberg developed what he saw at first as a faster way to copy, professional copyists writing by hand and block-book makers, along with monks and nuns, were already churning out reading materials on paper as fast as they could for the growing number of people who could read.

Gutenberg was not the only one to recognize the huge market for books, and his invention was quickly copied. Other craftsmen made their own type, built their own presses, and bought their own paper, setting themselves up in business (Map 12.2). Historians estimate that, within a half century of the publication of Gutenberg's Bible in 1456, somewhere between 8 million and 20 million books were printed in Europe. Whatever the actual figure, the number is far greater than the number of books produced in all of Western history up to that point.

The effects of the invention of movable-type printing were not felt overnight. Nevertheless, movable type radically transformed both the private and the public lives of Europeans by the dawn of the sixteenth century. Print shops became gathering places for people interested in new ideas. Though printers were trained through apprenticeships just like blacksmiths or butchers were, they had connections to the world of politics, art, and scholarship that other craftsmen did not.

Printing gave hundreds or even thousands of people identical books, allowing them to more easily discuss the ideas that the books contained with one another in person or through letters. Printed materials reached an invisible public, allowing silent individuals to join causes and groups of individuals widely separated by geography to form a common identity; this new group consciousness could compete with and transcend older, localized loyalties.

Government and church leaders both used and worried about printing. They printed laws, declarations of war, battle accounts, and propaganda, and they also attempted

Printing Press   In this reproduction of Gutenberg's printing press, metal type sits in a frame (left) ready to be placed in the bottom part of the press, with a leather-covered ink ball for spreading ink on the type ready nearby. Once the type was in place, paper was placed over the frame and a heavy metal plate (right) was lowered onto the paper with a firm pull of the large wooden handle, a technology adapted from winepresses. (Gutenberg Museum, Mainz, Germany/Erich Lessing/Art Resource, NY)

MAP 12.2 The Growth of Printing in Europe, 1448–1552   The speed with which artisans spread printing technology across Europe provides strong evidence for the growing demand for reading material. Presses in the Ottoman Empire were first established by Jewish immigrants who printed works in Hebrew, Greek, and Spanish.

to censor books and authors whose ideas they thought challenged their authority or were incorrect. Officials developed lists of prohibited books and authors, enforcing their prohibitions by confiscating books, arresting printers and booksellers, or destroying the presses of printers who disobeyed. None of this was very effective, and books were printed secretly, with fake title pages, authors, and places of publication, and smuggled all over Europe.

Printing also stimulated the literacy of laypeople and eventually came to have a deep effect on their private lives. Although most of the earliest books and pamphlets dealt with religious subjects, printers produced anything that would sell. They printed professional reference sets for lawyers, doctors, and students, and historical romances, biographies, and how-to manuals for the general public. They discovered that illustrations increased a book's sales, so they published books on a wide range of topics—from history to pornography—full of woodcuts and engravings. Single-page broadsides and fly sheets allowed great public events and "wonders" such as comets and two-headed calves to be experienced vicariously by a stay-at-home readership. Since books and other printed materials were read aloud to illiterate listeners, print bridged the gap between the written and oral cultures.

Art and the Artist

FOCUS QUESTION
How did art reflect new Renaissance ideals?

No feature of the Renaissance evokes greater admiration than its artistic masterpieces. The 1400s (*quattrocento*) and 1500s (*cinquecento*) bore witness to dazzling creativity in painting, architecture, and sculpture. In all the arts, the city of Florence led the way. But Florence was not the only artistic center, for Rome and Venice also became important, and northern Europeans perfected their own styles.

Patronage and Power

In early Renaissance Italy, powerful urban groups often flaunted their wealth by commissioning works of art. The Florentine cloth merchants, for example, delegated Filippo Brunelleschi (broo-nayl-LAYS-kee) to build the magnificent dome on the cathedral of Florence and selected Lorenzo Ghiberti (gee-BEHR-tee) to design the bronze doors of the adjacent Baptistery, a separate building in which baptisms were performed. These works represented the merchants' dominant influence in the community.

Increasingly in the late fifteenth century, wealthy individuals and rulers, rather than corporate groups, sponsored works of art. Patrician merchants and bankers, popes, and princes spent vast sums on the arts to glorify themselves and their families. Writing in about 1470, Florentine ruler Lorenzo de' Medici declared that his family had spent hundreds of thousands of gold florins for artistic and architectural commissions, but commented, "I think it casts a brilliant light on our estate [public reputation] and it seems to me that the monies were well spent and I am very pleased with this."[7]

Patrons varied in their level of involvement as a work progressed; some simply ordered a specific subject or scene, while others oversaw the work of the artist or architect very closely, suggesting themes and styles and demanding changes while the work was in progress. For example, Pope Julius II (pontificate 1503–1513), who commissioned Michelangelo to paint the ceiling of the Vatican's Sistine Chapel in 1508, demanded that the artist work as fast as he could and frequently visited him at his work with suggestions and criticisms. Michelangelo, a Florentine who had spent his young adulthood at the court of Lorenzo de' Medici, complained in person and by letter about the pope's meddling, but his reputation did not match the power of the pope, and he kept working until the chapel was finished in 1512.

In addition to power, art reveals changing patterns of consumption among the wealthy elite in European society. In the rural world of the Middle Ages, society had been organized for war, and men of wealth spent their money on military gear. As Italian nobles settled in towns (see Chapter 10), they adjusted to an urban culture. Rather than employing knights for warfare, cities hired mercenaries. Accordingly, expenditures on military hardware by nobles declined. For the noble recently arrived from the countryside or the rich merchant of the city, a grand urban palace represented the greatest outlay of cash. Wealthy individuals and families ordered gold dishes,

Michelangelo's *David* (1501–1504)
Like all Renaissance artists, Michelangelo worked largely on commissions from patrons. Officials of the city of Florence contracted the young sculptor to produce a statue of the Old Testament hero David to be displayed on the city's main square. Michelangelo portrayed David anticipating his fight against the giant Goliath, and the statue came to symbolize the republic of Florence standing up to its larger and more powerful enemies. (Accademia, Florence, Italy/ Ministero per i Beni e le Attività Culturali/ Scala/Art Resource, NY)

embroidered tablecloths, wall tapestries, paintings on canvas (an innovation), and sculptural decorations to adorn these homes. By the late sixteenth century the Strozzi banking family of Florence spent more on household goods than they did on clothing, jewelry, or food, though these were increasingly elaborate as well.

After the palace itself, the private chapel within the palace symbolized the largest expenditure for the wealthy of the sixteenth century. Decorated with religious scenes and equipped with ecclesiastical furniture, the chapel served as the center of the household's religious life and its cult of remembrance of the dead.

Changing Artistic Styles

Both the content and style of Renaissance art often differed from those of the Middle Ages. Religious topics, such as the Annunciation of the Virgin and the Nativity, remained popular among both patrons and artists, but frequently the patron had himself and his family portrayed in the scene. As the fifteenth century advanced and humanist ideas spread more widely, classical themes and motifs, such as the lives and loves of pagan gods and goddesses, figured increasingly in painting and sculpture, with the facial features of the gods sometimes modeled on living people.

The individual portrait emerged as a distinct artistic genre in this movement. Rather than reflecting a spiritual ideal, as medieval painting and sculpture tended to do, Renaissance portraits showed human ideals, often portrayed in the more realistic style increasingly favored by both artists and patrons. The Florentine painter Giotto (JAH-toh) (1276–1337) led the way in the use of realism; his treatment of the human body and face replaced the formal stiffness and artificiality that had long characterized representation of the human body. Piero della Francesca (frahn-CHAY-skah) (1420–1492) and Andrea Mantegna (mahn-TEHN-yuh) (1430/31–1506) pioneered perspective, the linear representation of distance and space on a flat surface, which enhanced the realism of paintings and differentiated them from the flatter and more stylized images of medieval art. The sculptor Donatello (1386–1466) revived the classical figure, with its balance and self-awareness. In architecture, Filippo Brunelleschi (1377–1446) looked to the classical past for inspiration, designing a hospital for orphans and foundlings in which all proportions—of the windows, height, floor plan, and covered walkway with a series of rounded arches—were carefully thought out to achieve a sense of balance and harmony.

Art produced in northern Europe tended to be more religious in orientation than that produced in Italy. Some Flemish painters, notably Rogier van der Weyden (1399/1400–1464) and Jan van Eyck (1366–1441), were considered the artistic equals of Italian painters and were much admired in Italy. Van Eyck was one of the earliest artists to use oil-based paints successfully, and his religious scenes and portraits all show great realism and remarkable attention to human personality. Albrecht Dürer (1471–1528), from the German city of Nuremberg, studied with artists in Italy, and produced woodcuts, engravings, and etchings that rendered the human form and the natural world in amazing detail. He was fascinated with the theoretical and practical problems of perspective, and designed mechanical devices that could assist artists in solving these. Late in his life he saw the first pieces of Aztec art shipped back to Europe from the New World and commented in his diary about how amazing they were.

In the early sixteenth century the center of the new art shifted from Florence to Rome, where wealthy cardinals and popes wanted visual expression of the church's and their own families' power and piety. Renaissance popes expended enormous enthusiasm and huge sums of money to beautify the city. Pope Julius II tore down the old Saint Peter's Basilica and began work on the present structure in 1506. Michelangelo went to Rome from Florence in about 1500 and began the series of statues, paintings, and architectural projects from which he gained an international reputation: the *Pietà*, *Moses*, the redesigning of the plaza and surrounding palaces on the Capitoline Hill in central Rome, and, most famously, the dome for Saint Peter's and the ceiling and altar wall of the nearby Sistine Chapel.

Raphael Sanzio (1483–1520), another Florentine, got the commission for frescoes in the papal apartments, and in his relatively short life he painted hundreds of portraits and devotional images, becoming the most sought-after artist in Europe. Raphael also oversaw a large workshop with many collaborators and apprentices—who assisted on the less difficult sections of some paintings—and wrote treatises on his philosophy of art in which he emphasized the importance of imitating nature and developing an orderly sequence of design and proportion.

Venice became another artistic center in the sixteenth century. Titian (TIH-shuhn) (1490–1576) produced portraits, religious subjects, and mythological scenes, developing techniques of painting in oil without doing elaborate drawings first, which speeded up the process and pleased patrons eager to display their acquisitions. Titian and other sixteenth-century painters developed an artistic style known in English as "mannerism" (from *maniera* or "style" in Italian) in which artists sometimes distorted figures, exaggerated musculature, and heightened color to express emotion and drama more intently. (A painting by Titian can be found on page 380.)

The Renaissance Artist

Some patrons rewarded certain artists very well, and some artists gained great public acclaim as, in Vasari's words, "rare men of genius." This adulation of the artist has led many historians to view the Renaissance as the beginning of the concept of the artist as having a special talent. In the Middle Ages people believed that only God created, albeit through individuals; the medieval conception recognized no particular value in artistic originality. Renaissance artists and humanists came to think that a work of art was the deliberate creation of a unique personality who transcended traditions, rules, and theories. A genius had a peculiar gift, which ordinary laws should not inhibit. Michelangelo and Leonardo da Vinci perhaps best embody the new concept of the Renaissance artist as genius. (See "Individuals in Society: Leonardo da Vinci," page 376.)

It is important not to overemphasize the Renaissance notion of genius. As certain artists became popular and well known, they could assert their own artistic styles and pay less attention to the wishes of patrons, but even major artists like Raphael generally worked according to the patron's specific guidelines. Whether in Italy or northern Europe, most Renaissance artists trained in the workshops of older artists; Botticelli, Raphael, Titian, and at times even Michelangelo were known for their

What makes a genius? A deep curiosity about an extensive variety of subjects? A divine spark that emerges in talents that far exceed the norm? Or is it just "one percent inspiration and ninety-nine percent perspiration," as Thomas Edison said? However it is defined, Leonardo da Vinci counts as a genius. In fact, Leonardo was one of the individuals whom the Renaissance label "genius" was designed to describe: a special kind of human being with exceptional creative powers. Leonardo (who, despite the title of a popular novel and film, is always called by his first name) was born in Vinci, near Florence, the illegitimate son of Caterina, a local peasant girl, and Ser Piero da Vinci, a notary public. When Ser Piero's marriage to Donna Albrussia produced no children, he and his wife took in Leonardo, whose mother had married another man. Ser Piero secured Leonardo an apprenticeship with the painter and sculptor Andrea del Verrocchio in Florence. In 1472, when Leonardo was just twenty years old, he was already listed as a master in Florence's "Company of Artists."

Leonardo's most famous portrait, *Mona Lisa*, shows a woman with an enigmatic smile that Giorgio Vasari described as "so pleasing that it seemed divine rather than human." The portrait, probably of the young wife of a rich Florentine merchant (her exact identity is hotly debated), may be the best-known painting in the history of art. One of its competitors for that designation would be another work of Leonardo, *The Last Supper*, which has been called "the most revered painting in the world."

Leonardo's reputation as a genius does not rest on his paintings, however, which are actually few in number, but rather on the breadth of his abilities and interests. He is considered by many the first "Renaissance man," a phrase still used for a multitalented individual. Hoping to reproduce what the eye can see, he drew everything he saw around him, including executed criminals hanging on gallows as well as the beauties of nature. Trying to understand how the human body worked, Leonardo studied live and dead bodies, doing autopsies and dissections to investigate muscles and circulation. He carefully analyzed the effects of light, and he experimented with perspective.

Leonardo used his drawings not only as the basis for his paintings but also as a tool of scientific investigation. He drew plans for hundreds of inventions, many of which would become reality centuries later, such as the helicopter, tank, machine gun, and parachute. He was hired by one of the powerful new rulers in Italy, Duke Ludovico Sforza of Milan, to design weapons, fortresses, and water systems, as well as to produce works of art. Leonardo left Milan when Sforza was overthrown, and spent the last years of his life painting, drawing, and designing for the pope and the French king.

large, well-run, and prolific workshops. Though they might be men of genius, artists were still expected to be well trained in proper artistic techniques and stylistic conventions; the notion that artistic genius could show up in the work of an untrained artist did not emerge until the twentieth century. Beginning artists spent years mastering their craft by copying drawings and paintings; learning how to prepare paint and other artistic materials; and, by the sixteenth century, reading books about design and composition. Younger artists gathered together in the evenings for further drawing practice; by the later sixteenth century some of these informal groups had turned into more formal artistic "academies," the first of which was begun in 1563 in Florence by Vasari under the patronage of the Medici.

As Vasari's phrase indicates, the notion of artistic genius that developed in the Renaissance was gendered. All the most famous and most prolific Renaissance artists were male. The types of art in which more women were active, such as textiles, needlework, and painting on porcelain, were regarded not as "major arts," but only as "minor" or "decorative" arts. (The division between "major" and "minor" arts begun

Leonardo experimented with new materials for painting and sculpture, not all of which worked. The experimental method he used to paint *The Last Supper* caused the picture to deteriorate rapidly, and it began to flake off the wall as soon as it was finished. Leonardo regarded it as never quite completed, for he could not find a model for the face of Christ who would evoke the spiritual depth he felt the figure deserved. His gigantic equestrian statue in honor of Ludovico's father, Duke Francesco Sforza, was never made, and the clay model collapsed. He planned to write books on many subjects but never finished any of them, leaving only notebooks. Leonardo once said that "a painter is not admirable unless he is universal." The patrons who supported him—and he was supported very well—perhaps wished that his inspirations would have been a bit less universal in scope, or at least accompanied by more perspiration.

QUESTIONS FOR ANALYSIS

1. In what ways do the notions of a "genius" and of a "Renaissance man" both support and contradict each other? Which better fits Leonardo?
2. Has the idea of artistic genius changed since the Renaissance? How?

Sources: Giorgio Vasari, *Lives of the Artists*, vol. 1, trans. G. Bull (London: Penguin Books, 1965); S. B. Nuland, *Leonardo da Vinci* (New York: Lipper/Viking, 2000).

Vitruvian Man, a drawing by Leonardo showing correlations between the ideal human proportions and the geometric shapes of the circle and square, is based on the ideas of the ancient Roman architect Vitruvius, whose works Leonardo read. (Galleria dell'Accademia, Venice, Italy/Bridgeman Images)

in the Renaissance continues to influence the way museums and collections are organized today.) Like painting, embroidery changed in the Renaissance to become more naturalistic, more visually complex, and more classical in its subject matter. Embroiderers were not trained to view their work as products of individual genius, however, so they rarely included their names on the works, and there is no way to discover their identities.

There are no female architects whose names are known and only one female sculptor, though several women did become well known as painters in their day. Stylistically, their works are different from one another, but their careers show many similarities. The majority of female painters were the daughters of painters or of minor noblemen with ties to artistic circles. Many were eldest daughters or came from families in which there were no sons, so their fathers took unusual interest in their careers. Many women painters began their careers before they were twenty and either produced far fewer paintings after they married or stopped painting entirely. Women were not allowed to study the male nude, a study that was viewed as

Botticelli, *Primavera* (Spring), ca. 1482   Framed by a grove of orange trees, Venus, goddess of love, is flanked on the right by Flora, goddess of flowers and fertility, and on the left by the Three Graces, goddesses of banquets, dance, and social occasions. Above, Venus's son Cupid, the god of love, shoots darts of desire, while at the far right the wind-god Zephyrus chases the nymph Chloris. The entire scene rests on classical mythology, though some art historians claim that Venus is an allegory for the Virgin Mary. Botticelli captured the ideal for female beauty in the Renaissance: slender, with pale skin, a high forehead, red-blond hair, and sloping shoulders. (Galleria degli Uffizi, Florence, Italy/Bridgeman Images)

essential if one wanted to paint large history or biblical paintings with many figures. Women also could not learn the technique of fresco, in which colors are applied directly to wet plaster walls, because such work had to be done in public, which was judged inappropriate for women. Joining a group of male artists for informal practice was also seen as improper, so women had no access to the newly established artistic academies. Like universities, humanist academies, and most craft guild shops, artistic workshops were male-only settings in which men of different ages came together for training and created bonds of friendship, influence, patronage, and sometimes intimacy.

Women were not alone in being excluded from the institutions of Renaissance culture. Though a few rare men of genius such as Leonardo and Michelangelo emerged from artisanal backgrounds, most scholars and artists came from families with at least some money. The ideas of the highly educated humanists did not influence the lives of most people in cities and did not affect life in the villages at all. For rural people and for less well-off town residents, work and play continued much as they had in the High Middle Ages: religious festivals and family celebrations provided people's main amusements, and learning came from one's parents, not through formal schooling (see Chapter 10).

Social Hierarchies

The division between educated and uneducated people was only one of many social hierarchies evident in the Renaissance. Every society has social hierarchies; in ancient Rome, for example, there were patricians and plebeians (see Chapter 5). Such hierarchies are to some degree descriptions of social reality, but they are also idealizations—that is, they describe how people imagined their society to be, without all the messy reality of social-climbing plebeians or groups that did not fit the standard categories. Social hierarchies in the Renaissance were built on those of the Middle Ages that divided nobles from commoners, but they also developed new concepts that contributed to modern social hierarchies, such as those of race, class, and gender.

Race and Slavery

Renaissance people did not use the word *race* the way we do, but often used *race*, *people*, and *nation* interchangeably for ethnic, national, religious, or other groups—the French race, the Jewish nation, the Irish people, "the race of learned gentlemen," and so on. They did make distinctions based on skin color that provide some of the background for later conceptualizations of race, but these distinctions were interwoven with other characteristics when people thought about human differences.

Ever since the time of the Roman Republic, a small number of black Africans had lived in western Europe. They had come, along with white slaves, as the spoils of war. Even after the collapse of the Roman Empire, Muslim and Christian merchants continued to import them. Unstable political conditions in many parts of Africa enabled enterprising merchants to seize people and sell them into slavery. Local authorities afforded these Africans no protection. Long tradition, moreover, sanctioned the practice of slavery. The evidence of medieval art attests to the continued presence of Africans in Europe throughout the Middle Ages and to Europeans' awareness of them.

Beginning in the fifteenth century sizable numbers of black slaves entered Europe. Portuguese sailors brought perhaps a thousand Africans a year to the markets of Seville, Barcelona, Marseilles, and Genoa. In the late fifteenth century this flow increased, with thousands of people taken from the west coast of Africa. By 1530 between four thousand and five thousand were sold to the Portuguese each year. By the mid-sixteenth century blacks, both slave and free, constituted about 10 percent of the population of the Portuguese cities of Lisbon and Évora and roughly 3 percent of the Portuguese population overall. Cities such as Lisbon also had significant numbers of people of mixed African and European descent, as African slaves intermingled with the people they lived among and sometimes intermarried.

Although blacks were concentrated in the Iberian Peninsula, some Africans must have lived in northern Europe as well. In the 1580s, for example, Queen Elizabeth I of England complained that there were too many "blackamoores" competing with needy English people for places as domestic servants. Black servants were much sought after; the medieval interest in curiosities, the exotic, and the marvelous continued in the Renaissance. Italian aristocrats had their portraits painted with their black page boys to indicate their wealth (as in the painting on page 380). Blacks were so greatly in demand at the Renaissance courts of northern Italy, in fact, that

FOCUS QUESTION
What were the key social hierarchies in Renaissance Europe?

Laura de Dianti, **1523**   The Venetian artist Titian portrays a young Italian woman with a gorgeous blue dress and an elaborate pearl and feather head-dress, accompanied by a young black page with a gold earring. Both the African page and the head-dress connect the portrait's subject with the exotic, though slaves from Africa and the Ottoman Empire were actually common in wealthy Venetian house-holds. (Private Collection/© Human Bios International AG)

the Venetians defied papal threats of excommunication to secure them. In 1491 Isabella d'Este, the duchess of Mantua and a major patron of the arts, instructed her agent to secure a black girl between four and eight years old, "shapely and as black as possible." She hoped the girl would become "the best buffoon in the world," and noted, "[W]e shall make her very happy and shall have great fun with her."8 The girl would join musicians, acrobats, and dancers at Isabella's court as a source of entertainment, her status similar to that of the dwarves who could be found at many Renaissance courts.

Africans were not simply amusements at court. In Portugal, Spain, and Italy slaves supplemented the labor force in virtually all occupations—as servants, agricultural laborers, craftsmen, and seamen on ships going to Lisbon and Africa. Agriculture in Europe did not involve large plantations, so large-scale agricultural slavery did not develop there as it would in the late fifteenth century in the New World.

Until the voyages down the African coast in the late fifteenth century, Europeans had little concrete knowledge of Africans and their cultures. They perceived Africa as a remote place, the home of strange people isolated by heresy and Islam from superior European civilization. Africans' contact, even as slaves, with Christian Europeans could only "improve" the blacks, they thought. The expanding slave trade reinforced negative preconceptions about the inferiority of black Africans.

Wealth and the Nobility

The word *class*—as in working class, middle class, and upper class—was not used in the Renaissance to describe social divisions, but by the thirteenth century, and even more so by the fifteenth, the idea of a hierarchy based on wealth was emerging. This was particularly true in cities, where wealthy merchants who oversaw vast trading empires lived in splendor that rivaled the richest nobles. As we saw earlier, in many cities these merchants had gained political power to match their economic might, becoming merchant oligarchs who ruled through city councils. This hierarchy of wealth was more fluid than the older divisions into noble and commoner, allowing individuals and families to rise—and fall—within one generation.

The development of a hierarchy of wealth did not mean an end to the prominence of nobles, however, and even poorer nobility still had higher status than wealthy commoners. Thus wealthy Italian merchants enthusiastically bought noble titles and country villas in the fifteenth century, and wealthy English or Spanish merchants eagerly married their daughters and sons into often-impoverished noble families. The nobility maintained its status in most parts of Europe not by maintaining rigid boundaries, but by taking in and integrating the new social elite of wealth.

Along with being tied to hierarchies of wealth and family standing, social status was linked to considerations of honor. Among the nobility, for example, certain weapons and battle tactics were favored because they were viewed as more honorable. Among urban dwellers, certain occupations, such as city executioner or manager of the municipal brothel, might be well paid but were understood to be dishonorable and so of low status. In cities, sumptuary laws reflected both wealth and honor (see Chapter 10); merchants were specifically allowed fur and jewels, while prostitutes were ordered to wear yellow bands that would remind potential customers of the flames of Hell.

Gender Roles

Renaissance people would not have understood the word *gender* to refer to categories of people, but they would have easily grasped the concept. Toward the end of the fourteenth century, learned men (and a few women) began what was termed the **debate about women** (*querelle des femmes*), a debate about women's character and nature that would last for centuries. Misogynist (muh-SAH-juh-nihst) critiques of women from both clerical and secular authors denounced females as devious, domineering, and demanding. In answer, several authors compiled long lists of famous and praiseworthy women exemplary for their loyalty, bravery, and morality. Christine de Pizan was among the writers who were interested not only in defending women, but also in exploring the reasons behind women's secondary status—that is, why the great philosophers, statesmen, and poets had generally been men. In this they were anticipating discussions about the "social construction of gender" by six hundred years. (See "Evaluating the Evidence 11.3: Christine de Pizan, Advice to the Wives of Artisans," page 348.)

debate about women
Debate among writers and thinkers in the Renaissance about women's qualities and proper role in society.

With the development of the printing press, popular interest in the debate about women grew, and works were translated, reprinted, and shared around Europe. Prints that juxtaposed female virtues and vices were also very popular, with the virtuous women depicted as those of the classical or biblical past and the vice-ridden dressed in contemporary clothes. The favorite metaphor for the virtuous wife was either the snail or the tortoise, both animals that never leave their "houses" and are totally silent, although such images were never as widespread as those depicting wives beating their husbands or hiding their lovers from them.

Beginning in the sixteenth century, the debate about women also became a debate about female rulers, sparked primarily by dynastic accidents in many countries, including Spain, England, Scotland, and France, which led to women's ruling in their own right or serving as advisers to child-kings. The questions were vigorously and at times viciously argued. They directly concerned the social construction of gender: Could a woman's being born into a royal family and educated to rule allow her to overcome the limitations of her sex? Should it? Or stated another way: which was (or should be) the stronger determinant of character and social role, gender or rank? Despite a prevailing sentiment that women were not as fit to rule as men, there were no successful rebellions against female rulers simply because they were women, but in part this was because female rulers, especially Queen Elizabeth I of England, emphasized qualities regarded as masculine—physical bravery, stamina, wisdom, duty—whenever they appeared in public.

Ideas about women's and men's proper roles determined the actions of ordinary men and women even more forcefully. The dominant notion of the "true" man was that of the married head of household, so men whose social status and age would have normally conferred political power but who remained unmarried did not participate in politics at the same level as their married brothers. Unmarried men in Venice, for example, could not be part of the ruling council.

Women were also understood as either "married or to be married," even if the actual marriage patterns in Europe left many women (and men) unmarried until quite late in life (see Chapter 11). This meant that women's work was not viewed as financially supporting a family—even if it did—and was valued less than men's. If they worked for wages, and many women did, women earned about half to two-thirds of what men did, even for the same work. Regulations for vineyard workers in the early sixteenth century, for example, specified:

> Men who work in the vineyards, doing work that is skilled, are to be paid 16 pence per day; in addition, they are to receive soup and wine in the morning, at midday beer, vegetables and meat, and in the evening soup, vegetables and wine. Young boys are to be paid 10 pence per day. Women who work as haymakers are to be given 6 pence a day. If the employer wants to have them doing other work, he may make an agreement with them to pay them 7 or 8 pence. He may also give them soup and vegetables to eat in the morning—but no wine—milk and bread at midday, but nothing in the evening.[9]

The maintenance of appropriate power relationships between men and women, with men dominant and women subordinate, served as a symbol of the proper functioning of society as a whole. Disorder in the proper gender hierarchy was linked with social upheaval and was viewed as threatening. Of all the ways in which Renaissance society was hierarchically arranged—social rank, age, level of education, race, occupation—gender was regarded as the most "natural" and therefore the most important to defend.

Politics and the State in Western Europe

FOCUS QUESTION
How did nation-states develop in this period?

The High Middle Ages had witnessed the origins of many of the basic institutions of the modern state. Sheriffs, inquests, juries, circuit judges, professional bureaucracies, and representative assemblies all trace their origins to the twelfth and thirteenth centuries. The linchpin for the development of states, however, was strong monarchy, and during the period of the Hundred Years' War no ruler in western Europe was able to provide effective leadership. The resurgent power of feudal nobilities weakened the centralizing work begun earlier.

Beginning in the fifteenth century, however, rulers utilized aggressive methods to rebuild their governments. First in the regional states of Italy, then in the expanding monarchies of France, England, and Spain, rulers began the work of reducing violence, curbing unruly nobles, and establishing domestic order. They attempted to secure their borders and enhanced methods of raising revenue. The monarchs of western Europe emphasized royal majesty and royal sovereignty and insisted on the respect and loyalty of all subjects, including the nobility. In central Europe the Holy Roman emperors attempted to do the same, but they were not able to overcome the power of local interests to create a unified state (see Chapter 13).

France

The Black Death and the Hundred Years' War left France drastically depopulated, commercially ruined, and agriculturally weak. Nonetheless, the ruler whom Joan of Arc had seen crowned at Reims, Charles VII (r. 1422–1461), revived the monarchy and France. He seemed an unlikely person to do so. Frail, indecisive, and burdened with questions about his paternity (his father had been deranged; his mother, notoriously promiscuous), Charles VII nevertheless began France's long recovery.

Charles reconciled the Burgundians and Armagnacs (ahr-muhn-YAKZ), who had been waging civil war for thirty years. By 1453 French armies had expelled the English from French soil except in Calais. Charles reorganized the royal council, giving increased influence to lawyers and bankers, and strengthened royal finances through taxes on certain products and on land, which remained the Crown's chief sources of income until the Revolution of 1789.

By establishing regular companies of cavalry and archers—recruited, paid, and inspected by the state—Charles created the first permanent royal army anywhere in Europe. His son Louis XI (r. 1461–1483), called the "Spider King" because of his treacherous character, improved upon Charles's army and used it to control the nobles' separate militias and to curb urban independence. The army was also employed in 1477 when Louis conquered Burgundy upon the death of its ruler Charles the Bold. Three years later, the extinction of the house of Anjou with the death of its last legitimate male heir brought Louis the counties of Anjou, Bar, Maine, and Provence.

Two further developments strengthened the French monarchy. The marriage of Louis XII (r. 1498–1515) and Anne of Brittany added the large western duchy of Brittany to the state. Then King Francis I and Pope Leo X reached a mutually satisfactory agreement about church and state powers in 1516. The new treaty, the Concordat of Bologna, approved the pope's right to receive the first year's income of newly named bishops and abbots in France. In return, Leo X recognized the French ruler's right to select French bishops and abbots. French kings thereafter effectively controlled the appointment and thus the policies of church officials in the kingdom.

Crown lands, ca. 1475

Territory added by 1483

Territory added by 1498

Independent fiefs

— Boundary of France, ca. 1500

The Expansion of France, 1475–1500

England

English society also suffered severely from the disorders of the fifteenth century. The aristocracy dominated the government of Henry IV (r. 1399–1413) and indulged in disruptive violence at the local level, fighting each other, seizing wealthy travelers for ransom, and plundering merchant caravans (see Chapter 11). Population continued to decline. Between 1455 and 1471 adherents of the ducal houses of York and Lancaster contended for control of the Crown in a civil war, commonly called the Wars of the Roses because the symbol of the Yorkists was a white rose and that of the Lancastrians a red one. The chronic disorder hurt trade, agriculture, and domestic industry. Under the pious but mentally disturbed Henry VI (r. 1422–1461), the authority of the monarchy sank lower than it had been in centuries.

The Yorkist Edward IV (r. 1461–1483) began establishing domestic tranquillity. He succeeded in defeating the Lancastrian forces and after 1471 began to reconstruct the monarchy. Edward, his brother Richard III (r. 1483–1485), and Henry VII (r. 1485–1509) of the Welsh house of Tudor worked to restore royal prestige, to crush the power of the nobility, and to establish order and law at the local level. All three rulers used methods that Machiavelli himself would have praised — ruthlessness, efficiency, and secrecy.

Edward IV and subsequently the Tudors, except Henry VIII, conducted foreign policy on the basis of diplomacy, avoiding expensive wars. Thus the English monarchy did not have to depend on Parliament for money, and the Crown undercut that source of aristocratic influence.

Henry VII did summon several meetings of Parliament in the early years of his reign, primarily to confirm laws, but the center of royal authority was the royal council, which governed at the national level. There Henry VII revealed his distrust of the nobility: though not completely excluded, very few great lords were among the king's closest advisers. Instead he chose men from among the smaller landowners and urban residents trained in law. The council conducted negotiations with foreign governments and secured international recognition of the Tudor dynasty through the marriage in 1501 of Henry VII's eldest son, Arthur, to Catherine of Aragon, the daughter of Ferdinand and Isabella of Spain. The council dealt with real or potential aristocratic threats through a judicial offshoot, the Court of Star Chamber, so called because of the stars painted on the ceiling of the room. The court applied methods that were sometimes terrifying: accused persons were not entitled to see evidence against them, sessions were secret, juries were not called, and torture could be applied to extract confessions. These procedures ran directly counter to English common-law precedents, but they effectively reduced aristocratic troublemaking.

When Henry VII died in 1509, he left a country at peace both domestically and internationally, a substantially augmented treasury, an expanding wool trade, and a crown with its dignity and role much enhanced. He was greatly missed after he died "by all his subjects," wrote the historian Polydore Vergil, "who had been able to conduct their lives peaceably, far removed from the assaults and evildoings of scoundrels."[10]

Spain

While England and France laid the foundations of unified nation-states during the Middle Ages, Spain remained a conglomerate of independent kingdoms. By the middle of the fifteenth century, the kingdoms of Castile and Aragon dominated the weaker Navarre, Portugal, and Granada; and the Iberian Peninsula, with the exception of Granada, had been won for Christianity (Map 12.3). The wedding in

MAP 12.3 The Unification of Spain and the Expulsion of the Jews, Fifteenth Century   The marriage of Ferdinand of Aragon and Isabella of Castile in 1469 brought most of the Iberian Peninsula under one monarchy, although different parts of Spain retained distinct cultures, languages, and legal systems. In 1492 Ferdinand and Isabella conquered Granada, where most people were Muslim, and expelled the Jews from all of Spain. Spanish Jews resettled in cities of Europe and the Mediterranean that allowed them in, including Muslim states such as the Ottoman Empire. Muslims were also expelled from Spain over the course of the sixteenth and early seventeenth centuries.

1469 of the dynamic and aggressive Isabella of Castile (r. 1474–1504) and the crafty and persistent Ferdinand of Aragon (r. 1479–1516) did not bring about administrative unity, as each state maintained its own cortes (parliament), laws, courts, and systems of coinage and taxation until about 1700. But the two rulers pursued a common foreign policy, and under their heirs Spain became a more unified realm.

Ferdinand and Isabella were able to exert their authority in ways similar to the rulers of France and England. They curbed aristocratic power by excluding high nobles from the royal council, which had full executive, judicial, and legislative

A Gold Coin of Ferdinand and Isabella

Minting coins provided a way for Renaissance monarchs to enhance their economies and also to show royal might and communicate other messages. This large gold coin, known as the "double excelente," was issued by the Seville mint in 1475, one year after Isabella had become queen in her own right of Castile and Ferdinand had become king because he was her husband. (Ferdinand would become king of Aragon in 1479 when his father died.) The eagle on the reverse holds both their coats of arms.

EVALUATE THE EVIDENCE

1. What symbols of power are shown with the monarchs on the coin? How does the coin convey the fact that their marriage was the union of two rulers?
2. Rulers sometimes stipulated that all major transactions within their realms be carried out with certain coins, much the same way governments today allow only the national currency. What was their aim in doing this, and why might such policies have been hard to enforce?

(photos: Seville mint, 1475/Fitzwilliam Museum, University of Cambridge, UK/Bridgeman Images)

powers under the monarchy, instead appointing lesser landowners. The council and various government boards recruited men trained in Roman law, which exalted the power of the Crown. (See "Evaluating the Evidence 12.3: A Gold Coin of Ferdinand and Isabella," above.) They also secured from the Spanish Borgia pope Alexander VI—Cesare Borgia's father—the right to appoint bishops in Spain and in the Hispanic territories in America, enabling them to establish the equivalent of a national church. With the revenues from ecclesiastical estates, they were able to expand their territories to include the remaining land held by Arabs in southern Spain. The victorious entry of Ferdinand and Isabella into Granada on January 6, 1492, signaled the conclusion of the reconquista (see Map 9.3, page 259). Granada was incorporated into the Spanish kingdom, and after Isabella's death Ferdinand conquered Navarre in the north.

There still remained a sizable and, in the view of the majority of the Spanish people, potentially dangerous minority, the Jews. When the kings of France and England had expelled the Jews from their kingdoms (see Chapter 9), many had sought refuge in Spain. During the long centuries of the reconquista, Christian kings had recognized

Jewish rights and privileges; in fact, Jewish industry, intelligence, and money had supported royal power. While Christians borrowed from Jewish moneylenders and while all who could afford them sought Jewish physicians, a strong undercurrent of resentment of Jewish influence and wealth festered.

In the fourteenth century anti-Semitism in Spain was aggravated by fiery anti-Jewish preaching, by economic dislocation, and by the search for a scapegoat during the Black Death. Anti-Semitic pogroms swept the towns of Spain, and perhaps 40 percent of the Jewish population was killed or forced to convert. Those converted were called *conversos* or **New Christians**. Conversos were often well educated and held prominent positions in government, the church, medicine, law, and business. Numbering perhaps 200,000 in a total Spanish population of about 7.5 million, New Christians and Jews in fifteenth-century Spain exercised influence disproportionate to their numbers.

Such successes bred resentment. Aristocratic grandees resented the conversos' financial independence, the poor hated the converso tax collectors, and churchmen doubted the sincerity of their conversions. Queen Isabella shared these suspicions, and she and Ferdinand had received permission from Pope Sixtus IV in 1478 to establish their own Inquisition to "search out and punish converts from Judaism who had transgressed against Christianity by secretly adhering to Jewish beliefs and performing rites of the Jews."[11] Investigations and trials began immediately, as officials of the Inquisition looked for conversos who showed any sign of incomplete conversion, such as not eating pork.

Recent scholarship has carefully analyzed documents of the Inquisition. Most conversos identified themselves as sincere Christians; many came from families that had received baptism generations before. In response to conversos' statements, officials of the Inquisition developed a new type of anti-Semitism. A person's status as a Jew, they argued, could not be changed by religious conversion, but was in the person's blood and was heritable, so Jews could never be true Christians. In what were known as "purity of blood" laws, having pure Christian blood became a requirement for noble status. Ideas about Jews developed in Spain were important components in European concepts of race, and discussions of "Jewish blood" later expanded into notions of the "Jewish race."

In 1492, shortly after the conquest of Granada, Isabella and Ferdinand issued an edict expelling all practicing Jews from Spain. Of the community of perhaps 200,000 Jews, 150,000 fled. Many Muslims in Granada were forcibly baptized and became another type of New Christian investigated by the Inquisition. Absolute religious orthodoxy and purity of blood served as the theoretical foundation of the Spanish national state.

The Spanish national state rested on marital politics as well as military victories and religious courts. Following their own example, the royal couple made astute marriages for their children with every country that could assist them against France, their most powerful neighbor. In 1496 Ferdinand and Isabella married their second daughter, Joanna, heiress to Castile, to the archduke Philip, heir to the Burgundian Netherlands and the Holy Roman Empire. Philip and Joanna's son Charles V (r. 1519–1556) thus succeeded to a vast inheritance. When Charles's son Philip II joined Portugal to the Spanish crown in 1580, the Iberian Peninsula was at last politically united.

New Christians A term for Jews and Muslims in the Iberian Peninsula who accepted Christianity; in many cases they included Christians whose families had converted centuries earlier.

LOOKING BACK LOOKING AHEAD

The art historian Giorgio Vasari, who first called this era the Renaissance, thought that his contemporaries had both revived the classical past and gone beyond it. Vasari's judgment was echoed for centuries as historians sharply contrasted the art, architecture, educational ideas, social structures, and attitude toward life of the Renaissance with those of the Middle Ages: in this view, whereas the Middle Ages were corporate and religious, the Renaissance was individualistic and secular. More recently, historians and other scholars have stressed continuity as well as change. Families, kin networks, guilds, and other corporate groups remained important in the Renaissance, and religious belief remained firm. This re-evaluation changes our view of the relationship between the Middle Ages and the Renaissance. It may also change our view of the relationship between the Renaissance and the dramatic changes in religion that occurred in Europe in the sixteenth century. Those religious changes, the Reformation, used to be viewed as a rejection of the values of the Renaissance and a return to the intense concern with religion of the Middle Ages. This idea of the Reformation as a sort of counter-Renaissance may be true to some degree, but there are powerful continuities as well. Both movements looked back to a time people regarded as purer and better than their own, and both offered opportunities for strong individuals to shape their world in unexpected ways.

Make Connections

Think about the larger developments and continuities within and across chapters.

1. The word *Renaissance*, invented to describe the cultural flowering in Italy that began in the fifteenth century, has often been used for other periods of advances in learning and the arts, such as the "Carolingian Renaissance" that you read about in Chapter 8. Can you think of other, more recent "Renaissances"? How else is the word used today?

2. Many artists in the Renaissance consciously modeled their works on those of ancient Greece (Chapters 3 and 4) and Rome (Chapters 5 and 6). Comparing the art and architecture shown in those chapters with those in this chapter, what similarities do you see? Are there aspects of classical art and architecture that were *not* emulated in the Renaissance? Why do you think this might be?

3. The Renaissance was clearly a period of cultural change for educated men. Given what you have read about women's lives and ideas about women in this and earlier chapters, did women have a Renaissance? (This question was posed first by the historian Joan Kelly in 1977 and remains a topic of great debate.) Why or why not?

12 REVIEW & EXPLORE

Review the Main Ideas

Answer the focus questions from each section of the chapter.

◆ How did politics and economics shape the Renaissance? (p. 358)

◆ What new ideas were associated with the Renaissance? (p. 363)

◆ How did art reflect new Renaissance ideals? (p. 373)

◆ What were the key social hierarchies in Renaissance Europe? (p. 379)

◆ How did nation-states develop in this period? (p. 382)

Identify Key Terms

Identify and explain the significance of each item below.

Renaissance (p. 358)

patronage (p. 358)

communes (p. 359)

popolo (p. 359)

signori (p. 360)

courts (p. 360)

humanism (p. 364)

virtù (p. 365)

Christian humanists (p. 368)

debate about women (p. 381)

New Christians (p. 387)

NOTES

1. In Gertrude R. B. Richards, *Florentine Merchants in the Age of the Medici* (Cambridge: Harvard University Press, 1932).
2. From *The Portable Renaissance Reader*, p. 27, by James B. Ross and Mary Martin McLaughlin, editors, copyright 1953, 1968, renewed © 1981 by Penguin Random House LLC. Used by permission of Viking Books, an imprint of Penguin Publishing Group, a division of Penguin Random House LLC.
3. Ibid., pp. 480–481, 482, 492.
4. Niccolò Machiavelli, *The Prince*, trans. Leo Paul S. de Alvarez (Prospect Heights, Ill.: Waveland Press, 1980), p. 101.
5. Ibid., p. 149.
6. Quoted in F. Seebohm, *The Oxford Reformers* (London: J. M. Dent & Sons, 1867), p. 256.
7. Quoted in Lauro Martines, *Power and Imagination: City-States in Renaissance Italy* (New York: Vintage Books, 1980), p. 253.
8. Quoted in J. Devisse and M. Mollat, *The Image of the Black in Western Art*, vol. 2, trans. W. G. Ryan (New York: William Morrow, 1979), pt. 2, pp. 187–188.
9. Stuttgart, Württembergische Hauptstaatsarchiv, Generalreskripta, A38, Bü. 2, 1550; trans. Merry Wiesner-Hanks.
10. Denys Hay, ed. and trans., *The Anglia Historia of Polydore Vergil, AD 1485–1537*, book 74 (London: Camden Society, 1950), p. 147.
11. Quoted in Benzion Netanyahu, *The Origins of the Inquisition in Fifteenth Century Spain* (New York: Random House, 1995), p. 921.

CHAPTER PREVIEW

The Early Reformation
What were the central ideas of the reformers, and why were they appealing to different social groups?

The Reformation and German Politics
How did the political situation in Germany shape the course of the Reformation?

The Spread of Protestant Ideas
How did Protestant ideas and institutions spread beyond German-speaking lands?

The Catholic Reformation
What reforms did the Catholic Church make, and how did it respond to Protestant reform movements?

Religious Violence
What were the causes and consequences of religious violence, including riots, wars, and witch-hunts?

Religious Violence in Urban Life

This 1590 painting shows Catholic military forces, including friars in their robes, processing through one of the many towns affected by the French religious wars that followed the Reformation. (*Procession of the Holy League*, 1590/ Musée des Beaux-Arts, Valenciennes, France/Bridgeman Images)

13

Reformations and Religious Wars

1500–1600

Calls for reform of the Christian Church began very early in its history. Throughout the centuries, many Christians believed that the early Christian Church represented a golden age, akin to the golden age of the classical past celebrated by Renaissance humanists. When Christianity became the official religion of the Roman Empire in the fourth century, many believers thought that the church had abandoned its original mission, and they called for a return to a church that was not linked to the state. Throughout the Middle Ages, individuals and groups argued that the church had become too wealthy and powerful and urged monasteries, convents, bishoprics, and the papacy to give up their property and focus on service to the poor. Some asserted that basic teachings of the church were not truly Christian and that changes were needed in theology as well as in institutional structures and practices. The Christian humanists of the late fifteenth and early sixteenth centuries such as Erasmus urged reform, primarily through educational and social change. What was new in the sixteenth century was the breadth of acceptance and the ultimate impact of the calls for reform. This acceptance was due not only to religious issues and problems within the church, but also to political and social factors. In 1500 there was one Christian Church in western Europe to which all Christians at least nominally belonged. One hundred years later there were many, a situation that continues today. ■

The Early Reformation

FOCUS QUESTION

What were the central ideas of the reformers, and why were they appealing to different social groups?

In early-sixteenth-century Europe a wide range of people had grievances with the church. Educated laypeople such as Christian humanists and urban residents, villagers and artisans, and church officials themselves called for reform. This widespread dissatisfaction helps explain why the ideas of Martin Luther, an obscure professor from a new and not very prestigious German university, found a ready audience. Within a decade of his first publishing his ideas (using the new technology of the printing press), much of central Europe and Scandinavia had broken with the Catholic Church, and even more radical concepts of the Christian message were being developed and linked to calls for social change.

The Christian Church in the Early Sixteenth Century

If external religious observances are an indication of conviction, Europeans in the early sixteenth century were deeply pious. Villagers participated in processions honoring the local saints. Merchants and guild members made pilgrimages to the great shrines, such as Saint Peter's in Rome, and paid for altars in local churches. Men and women continued to remember the church in their wills. People of all social groups devoted an enormous amount of their time and income to religious causes and foundations.

Despite—or perhaps because of—the depth of their piety, many people were also highly critical of the Roman Catholic Church and its clergy. The papal conflict with the German emperor Frederick II in the thirteenth century, followed by the Babylonian Captivity and the Great Schism, badly damaged the prestige of church leaders, and the fifteenth-century popes' concentration on artistic patronage and building up family power did not help matters. Papal tax collection methods were attacked orally and in print. Some criticized the papacy itself as an institution, and even the great wealth and powerful courts of the entire church hierarchy. Some groups and individuals argued that certain doctrines taught by the church, such as the veneration of saints and the centrality of the sacraments, were incorrect. They suggested measures to reform institutions, improve clerical education and behavior, and alter basic doctrines. Occasionally these reform efforts had some success, and in at least one area, Bohemia (the modern-day Czech Republic), they led to the formation of a church independent of Rome a century before Luther (see Chapter 11).

In the early sixteenth century, court records, bishops' visitations of parishes, and popular songs and printed images show widespread **anticlericalism**, or opposition to the clergy. The critics concentrated primarily on three problems: clerical immorality, clerical ignorance, and clerical pluralism (the practice of holding more than one church office at a time), with the related problem of absenteeism. Charges of clerical immorality were aimed at a number of priests who were drunkards, neglected the rule of celibacy, gambled, or indulged in fancy dress. Charges of clerical ignorance were motivated by barely literate priests who simply mumbled the Latin words of the Mass by rote without understanding their meaning. Many priests, monks, and nuns lived pious lives of devotion, learning, and service and had strong support from the laypeople in their areas, but everyone also knew (and repeated) stories about lecherous monks, lustful nuns, and greedy priests.

In regard to absenteeism and pluralism, many clerics held several benefices, or offices, simultaneously, but they seldom visited the benefices, let alone performed the

anticlericalism Opposition to the clergy.

Chronology

1517	Martin Luther writes "Ninety-five Theses on the Power of Indulgences"		**1542**	Pope Paul III establishes the Supreme Sacred Congregation of the Roman and Universal Inquisition
1521	Diet of Worms		**1545–1563**	Council of Trent
1521–1559	Habsburg-Valois wars		**1553–1558**	Reign of Mary Tudor and temporary restoration of Catholicism in England
1525	German Peasants' War		**1555**	Peace of Augsburg; official recognition of Lutheranism
1526	Turkish victory at Mohács, which allows spread of Protestantism in Hungary		**1558–1603**	Reign of Elizabeth in England
1530s	Henry VIII ends the authority of the pope in England		**1560–1660**	Height of the European witch-hunt
1535	Angela Merici establishes the Ursulines as first women's teaching order		**1568–1578**	Civil war in the Netherlands
1536	John Calvin publishes *The Institutes of the Christian Religion*		**1572**	Saint Bartholomew's Day massacre
			1588	England defeats Spanish Armada
1540	Papal approval of Society of Jesus (Jesuits)		**1598**	Edict of Nantes

spiritual responsibilities those offices entailed. Instead, they collected revenues from all of them and hired a poor priest, paying him just a fraction of the income to fulfill the spiritual duties of a particular local church. Many Italian officials in the papal curia, the pope's court in Rome, held benefices in England, Spain, and Germany. Revenues from those countries paid the Italian clerics' salaries, provoking not only charges of absenteeism but also nationalistic resentment aimed at the upper levels of the church hierarchy, which was increasingly viewed as foreign. This was particularly the case in Germany, where the lack of a strong central government to negotiate with the papacy meant that demands for revenue were especially high.

There was also local resentment of clerical privileges and immunities. Priests, monks, and nuns were exempt from civic responsibilities, such as defending the city and paying taxes. Yet religious orders frequently held large amounts of urban property, in some cities as much as one-third. City governments were increasingly determined to integrate the clergy into civic life by reducing their privileges and giving them public responsibilities. Urban leaders wanted some say in who would be appointed to high church offices, rather than having this decided far away in Rome. This brought city leaders into opposition with bishops and the papacy, which for centuries had stressed the independence of the church from lay control and the distinction between members of the clergy and laypeople.

Martin Luther

By itself, widespread criticism of the church did not lead to the dramatic changes of the sixteenth century. Instead, the personal religious struggle of a German university professor and priest, Martin Luther (1483–1546), propelled the wave of movements we now call the Reformation. Luther was born at Eisleben in Saxony. At considerable sacrifice, his father sent him to school and then to the University of Erfurt, where he earned a master's degree with distinction. Luther was to proceed to the study of law and a legal career, which for centuries had been the stepping-stone to public office and material success. Instead, however, a sense of religious calling led him to join

Ojhr deutschen merckt mich recht/
Des heiligen Vaters Papstes Knecht/
Bin ich/vnd br in euch jst allein/
Zehn tausent vnd neun hundert carein/
Gnad vnd Ablaß von einer Sünd/
Vor euch/ewer Eltern/Weib vnd Kind/
Sol ein jeder geweyret sein
So viel jhr legt ins Kästelein/
So bald der Gülden im Becken klingt/
Im huy die Seel im Himel springt/

Selling Indulgences A German single-page pamphlet shows a monk offering an indulgence, with the official seals of the pope attached, as people run to put their money in the box in exchange for his promise of heavenly bliss, symbolized by the dove above his head. Indulgences were sold widely in Germany and became the first Catholic practice that Luther criticized openly. This pamphlet also attacks the sale of indulgences, calling this practice devilish and deceitful, a point of view expressed in the woodcut by the peddler's riding on a donkey, an animal that had long been used as a symbol of ignorance. (ullstein bild/ullstein bild via Getty Images)

indulgence A document issued by the Catholic Church lessening penance or time in purgatory, widely believed to bring forgiveness of all sins.

the Augustinian friars, a religious order whose members often preached to, taught, and assisted the poor. (Religious orders were groups whose members took vows and followed a particular set of rules.) Luther was ordained a priest in 1507 and after additional study earned a doctorate of theology. From 1512 until his death in 1546, he served as professor of the Scriptures at the new University of Wittenberg. Throughout his life, he frequently cited his professorship as justification for his reforming work.

Martin Luther was a very conscientious friar, but his scrupulous observance of religious routine, frequent confessions, and fasting gave him only temporary relief from anxieties about sin and his ability to meet God's demands. Through his study of Saint Paul's letters in the New Testament, he gradually arrived at a new understanding of Christian doctrine. His understanding is often summarized as "faith alone, grace alone, Scripture alone." He believed that salvation and justification come through faith. Faith is a free gift of God's grace, not the result of human effort. God's word is revealed only in the Scriptures, not in the traditions of the church.

At the same time that Luther was engaged in scholarly reflections and professorial lecturing, Pope Leo X authorized the sale of a special Saint Peter's indulgence to finance his building plans in Rome. The archbishop who controlled the area in which Wittenberg was located, Albert of Mainz, was an enthusiastic promoter of this indulgence sale. For his efforts, he received a share of the profits so that he could pay off a debt he had incurred in order to purchase a papal dispensation allowing him to become the bishop of several other territories as well.

What exactly was an **indulgence**? According to Catholic theology, individuals who sin could be reconciled to God by confessing their sins to a priest and by doing an assigned penance, such as praying or fasting. But beginning in the twelfth century learned theologians increasingly emphasized the idea of purgatory, a place where souls on their way to Heaven went to make further amends for their earthly sins. Both earthly penance and time in purgatory could be shortened by drawing on what was termed the "treasury of merits." This was a collection of all the virtuous acts that Christ, the apostles, and the saints had done during their lives. People thought of it as a sort of strongbox, like those in which merchants carried coins. An indulgence was a piece of parchment (later, paper), signed by the pope or another church official, that substituted a virtuous act from the treasury of merits for penance or time in purgatory. The papacy and bishops had given Crusaders such indulgences, and by the later Middle Ages they were offered for making pilgrimages or other pious activities and also sold outright (see Chapter 9).

Archbishop Albert's indulgence sale, run by a Dominican friar named Johann Tetzel who mounted an advertising blitz, promised that the purchase of indulgences would bring full forgiveness for one's own sins or release from purgatory for a loved one. One of the slogans—"As soon as coin in coffer rings, the soul from purgatory springs"—brought phenomenal success, and people traveled from miles around to buy indulgences.

Luther was severely troubled that many people believed they had no further need for repentance once they had purchased indulgences. In 1517 he wrote a letter to Archbishop Albert on the subject and enclosed in Latin his "Ninety-five Theses on the Power of Indulgences." His argument was that indulgences undermined the seriousness of the sacrament of penance, competed with the preaching of the Gospel, and downplayed the importance of charity in Christian life. After Luther's death, biographies reported that the theses were also nailed to the door of the church at Wittenberg Castle on October 31, 1517. Such an act would have been very strange—they were in Latin and written for those learned in theology, not for ordinary churchgoers—but it has become a standard part of Luther lore.

Whether the theses were posted or not, they were quickly printed, first in Latin and then in German translation. Luther was ordered to come to Rome, although because of the political situation in the empire, he was able instead to engage in formal scholarly debate with a representative of the church, Johann Eck, at Leipzig in 1519. He refused to take back his ideas and continued to develop his calls for reform, publicizing them in a series of pamphlets in which he moved further and further away from Catholic theology. Both popes and church councils could err, he wrote, and secular leaders should reform the church if the pope and clerical hierarchy did not. There was no distinction between clergy and laypeople, and requiring clergy to be celibate was a fruitless attempt to control a natural human drive. Luther clearly understood the power of the new medium of print, so he authorized the publication of his works.

The papacy responded with a letter condemning some of Luther's propositions, ordering that his books be burned, and giving him two months to recant or be excommunicated. Luther retaliated by publicly burning the letter. By 1521, when the excommunication was supposed to become final, Luther's theological issues had become interwoven with public controversies about the church's wealth, power, and basic structure. The papal legate wrote of the growing furor, "All Germany is in revolution. Nine-tenths shout 'Luther' as their war cry; and the other tenth cares nothing about Luther, and cries 'Death to the court of Rome.'"[1] In this highly charged atmosphere, the twenty-one-year-old emperor Charles V held his first diet (assembly of the nobility, clergy, and cities of the Holy Roman Empire) in the German city of Worms and summoned Luther to appear. Luther refused to give in to demands that he take back his ideas. "Unless I am convinced by the evidence of Scripture or by plain reason," he said, "I cannot and will not recant anything, for it is neither safe nor right to go against conscience."[2] His appearance at the Diet of Worms in 1521 created an even broader audience for reform ideas, and throughout central Europe other individuals began to preach and publish against the existing doctrines and practices of the church, drawing on the long tradition of calls for change as well as on Luther.

Protestant Thought

The most important early reformer other than Luther was the Swiss humanist, priest, and admirer of Erasmus, Ulrich Zwingli (ZWIHNG-lee) (1484–1531). Zwingli

Martin Luther, *On Christian Liberty*

The idea of liberty has played a powerful role in the history of Western society and culture, but the meaning and understanding of liberty have undergone continual change and interpretation. In the Roman world, where slavery was a basic institution, liberty meant the condition of being a free man. In the Middle Ages, possessing liberty meant having special privileges or rights that other persons or institutions did not have. Citizens in London, for example, were said to possess the "freedom of the city," which allowed them to practice trades and own property without interference.

The idea of liberty also has a religious dimension, and the reformer Martin Luther formulated a classic interpretation of liberty in his treatise On Christian Liberty *(sometimes translated as* On the Freedom of a Christian*), arguably his finest piece. Written in Latin for the pope but translated immediately into German and published widely, it contains the main themes of Luther's theology: the importance of faith, the relationship between Christian faith and good works, the dual nature of human beings, and the fundamental importance of the Scriptures. Luther writes that Christians were freed from sin and death through Christ, not through their own actions.*

~

A Christian man is the most free lord of all, and subject to none; a Christian man is the most dutiful servant of all, and subject to everyone. Although these statements appear contradictory, yet, when they are found to agree together, they will do excellently for my purpose. They are both the statements of Paul himself, who says, "Though I be free from all men, yet have I made myself a servant unto all" (I Corinthians 9:19) and "Owe no man anything but to love one another" (Romans 13:8). Now love is by its own nature dutiful and obedient to the beloved object. Thus even Christ, though Lord of all things, was yet made of a woman; made under the law; at once free and a servant; at once in the form of God and in the form of a servant.

Let us examine the subject on a deeper and less simple principle. Man is composed of a twofold nature, a spiritual and a bodily. As regards the spiritual nature, which they name the soul, he is called the spiritual, inward, new man; as regards the bodily nature, which they name the flesh, he is called the fleshly, outward, old man. The Apostle speaks of this: "Though our outward man perish, yet the inward man is renewed day by day" (II Corinthians 4:16). The result of this diversity is that in the Scriptures opposing statements are made concerning the same man, the fact being that in the same man these two men are opposed to one another; the flesh lusting against the spirit, and the spirit against the flesh (Galatians 5:17).

We first approach the subject of the inward man, that we may see by what means a man becomes justified, free, and a true Christian; that is, a spiritual, new, and inward man. It is certain that absolutely none among outward things, under whatever name they may be reckoned, has any influence in producing Christian righteousness or liberty, nor, on the other hand, unrighteousness or slavery. This can be shown by an easy argument. What can it profit to the soul that the body should be in good condition, free, and full of life, that it should eat, drink, and act according to its pleasure, when even the most impious slaves of every kind of vice are prosperous in these matters? Again, what harm can ill health, bondage, hunger, thirst, or any other outward evil, do to the soul, when even the most pious of men, and the freest in the purity of their conscience, are harassed by these things? Neither of these states of things has to do with the liberty or the slavery of the soul.

announced in 1519 that he would not preach from the church's prescribed readings but, relying on Erasmus's New Testament, go right through the New Testament "from A to Z," that is, from Matthew to Revelation. Zwingli was convinced that Christian life rested on the Scriptures, which were the pure words of God and the sole basis of religious truth. He went on to attack indulgences, the Mass, the institution of monasticism, and clerical celibacy. In his gradual reform of the church in Zurich, he had the strong support of the city authorities, who had long resented the privileges of the clergy.

The followers of Luther, Zwingli, and others who called for a break with Rome came to be called Protestants. The word **Protestant** derives from the protest drawn

Protestant The name originally given to followers of Luther, which came to mean all non-Catholic Western Christian groups.

And so it will profit nothing that the body should be adorned with sacred vestment, or dwell in holy places, or be occupied in sacred offices, or pray, fast, and abstain from certain meats, or do whatever works can be done through the body and in the body. Something widely different will be necessary for the justification and liberty of the soul, since the things I have spoken of can be done by an impious person, and only hypocrites are produced by devotion to these things. On the other hand, it will not at all injure the soul that the body should be clothed in profane raiment, should dwell in profane places, should eat and drink in the ordinary fashion, should not pray aloud, and should leave undone all the things above mentioned, which may be done by hypocrites. . . .

One thing, and one alone, is necessary for life, justification, and Christian liberty; and that is the most Holy Word of God, the Gospel of Christ, as He says, "I am the resurrection and the life; he that believeth in me shall not die eternally" (John 9:25), and also, "If the Son shall make you free, ye shall be free indeed" (John 8:36), and "Man shall not live by bread alone, but by every word that proceedeth out of the mouth of God" (Matthew 4:4).

Let us therefore hold it for certain and firmly established that the soul can do without everything except the Word of God, without which none at all of its wants is provided for. But, having the Word, it is rich and wants for nothing, since that is the Word of life, of truth, of light, of peace, of justification, of salvation, of joy, of liberty, of wisdom, of virtue, of grace, of glory, and of every good thing. . . .

But you will ask, "What is this Word, and by what means is it to be used, since there are so many words of God?" I answer, "The Apostle Paul (Romans 1) explains what it is, namely the Gospel of God, concerning His Son, incarnate, suffering, risen, and glorified through the Spirit, the Sanctifier." To preach Christ is to feed the soul, to justify it, to set it free, and to save it, if it believes the preaching. For faith alone, and the efficacious use of the Word of God, bring salvation. "If thou shalt confess with thy mouth the Lord Jesus, and shalt believe in thine heart that God hath raised Him from the dead, thou shalt be saved" (Romans 9:9); . . . and "The just shall live by faith" (Romans 1:17). . . .

But this faith cannot consist of all with works; that is, if you imagine that you can be justified by those works, whatever they are, along with it. . . . Therefore, when you begin to believe, you learn at the same time that all that is in you is utterly guilty, sinful, and damnable, according to that saying, "All have sinned, and come short of the glory of God" (Romans 3:23). . . . When you have learned this, you will know that Christ is necessary for you, since He has suffered and risen again for you, that, believing on Him, you might by this faith become another man, all your sins being remitted, and you being justified by the merits of another, namely Christ alone. . . .

And since it [faith] alone justifies, it is evident that by no outward work or labour can the inward man be at all justified, made free, and saved; and that no works whatever have any relation to him. . . . Therefore the first care of every Christian ought to be to lay aside all reliance on works, and strengthen his faith alone more and more, and by it grow in knowledge, not of works, but of Christ Jesus, who has suffered and risen again for him, as Peter teaches (I Peter 5).

EVALUATE THE EVIDENCE

1. What did Luther mean by liberty?
2. Why, for Luther, were the Scriptures basic to Christian life?

Source: *Luther's Primary Works*, ed. H. Wace and C. A. Buchheim (London: Holder and Stoughton, 1896). Reprinted in *The Portable Renaissance Reader*, ed. James Bruce Ross and Mary Martin McLaughlin (New York: Penguin Books, 1981), pp. 721–726.

up by a small group of reforming German princes at the Diet of Speyer in 1529. The princes "protested" the decisions of the Catholic majority, and the word gradually became a general term applied to all non-Catholic western European Christians.

Luther, Zwingli, and other early Protestants agreed on many things. First, how is a person to be saved? Traditional Catholic teaching held that salvation is achieved by both faith and good works. Protestants held that salvation comes by faith alone, irrespective of good works or the sacraments. God, not people, initiates salvation. (See "Evaluating the Evidence 13.1: Martin Luther, *On Christian Liberty*," above.) Second, where does religious authority reside? Christian doctrine had long maintained that authority rests both in the Bible and in the traditional teaching of the church.

For Protestants, authority rested in the Bible alone. For a doctrine or issue to be valid, it had to have a scriptural basis. Because of this, most Protestants rejected Catholic teachings about the sacraments—the rituals that the church had defined as imparting God's benefits on the believer (see Chapter 10)—holding that only baptism and the Eucharist have scriptural support.

Third, what is the church? Protestants held that the church is a spiritual priesthood of all believers, an invisible fellowship not fixed in any place or person, which differed markedly from the Roman Catholic practice of a hierarchical clerical institution headed by the pope in Rome. Fourth, what is the highest form of Christian life? The medieval church had stressed the superiority of the monastic and religious life over the secular. Protestants disagreed and argued that every person should serve God in his or her individual calling.

Protestants did not agree on everything, and one important area of dispute was the ritual of the Eucharist (also called communion, the Lord's Supper, and, in Catholicism, the Mass). Catholicism holds the dogma of transubstantiation: by the consecrating words of the priest during the Mass, the bread and wine become the actual body and blood of Christ. In opposition, Luther believed that Christ is really present in the consecrated bread and wine, but this is the result of God's mystery, not the actions of a priest. Zwingli understood the Eucharist as a memorial in which Christ was present in spirit among the faithful, but not in the bread and wine. The Colloquy of Marburg, summoned in 1529 to unite Protestants, failed to resolve these differences, though Protestants reached agreement on almost everything else.

The Appeal of Protestant Ideas

Pulpits and printing presses spread the Protestant message all over Germany, and by the middle of the sixteenth century people of all social classes had rejected Catholic teachings and had become Protestant. What was the immense appeal of Luther's religious ideas and those of other Protestants?

Educated people and many humanists were much attracted by Luther's teachings. He advocated a simpler personal religion based on faith, a return to the spirit of the early church, the centrality of the Scriptures in the liturgy and in Christian life, and the abolition of elaborate ceremonies—precisely the reforms the Christian humanists had been calling for. The Protestant insistence that everyone should read and reflect on the Scriptures attracted literate and thoughtful city residents. This included many priests and monks who left the Catholic Church to become clergy in the new Protestant churches. In addition, townspeople who envied the church's wealth and resented paying for it were attracted by the notion that the clergy should also pay taxes and should not have special legal privileges. After Zurich became Protestant, the city council taxed the clergy and placed them under the jurisdiction of civil courts.

Scholars in many disciplines have attributed Luther's fame and success to the invention of the printing press, which rapidly reproduced and made known his ideas. Many printed works included woodcuts and other illustrations, so that even those who could not read could grasp the main ideas. Equally important was Luther's incredible skill with language, as seen in his two catechisms (compendiums of basic religious knowledge) and in hymns that he wrote for congregations to sing. Luther's linguistic skill, together with his translation of the New Testament into German in 1523, led to the acceptance of his dialect of German as the standard written version of the German language.

Both Luther and Zwingli recognized that for reforms to be permanent, political authorities as well as concerned individuals and religious leaders would have to accept them. Zwingli worked closely with the city council of Zurich, and city councils themselves took the lead in other cities and towns of Switzerland and south Germany. They appointed pastors who they knew had accepted Protestant ideas, required them to swear an oath of loyalty to the council, and oversaw their preaching and teaching.

Luther lived in a territory ruled by a noble—the elector of Saxony—and he also worked closely with political authorities, viewing them as fully justified in asserting control over the church in their territories. Indeed, he demanded that German rulers reform the papacy and its institutions, and he instructed all Christians to obey their secular rulers, whom he saw as divinely ordained to maintain order. Individuals may have been convinced of the truth of Protestant teachings by hearing sermons, listening to hymns, or reading pamphlets, but a territory became Protestant when its ruler, whether a noble or a city council, brought in a reformer or two to re-educate the territory's clergy, sponsored public sermons, and confiscated church property. This happened in many of the states of the Holy Roman Empire during the 1520s.

The Radical Reformation and the German Peasants' War

While Luther and Zwingli worked with political authorities, some individuals and groups rejected the idea that church and state needed to be united. Beginning in the 1520s, groups in Switzerland, Germany, and the Netherlands sought instead to create a voluntary community of believers separate from the state, as they understood it to have existed in New Testament times. In terms of theology and spiritual practices, these individuals and groups varied widely, though they are generally termed "radicals" for their insistence on a more extensive break with prevailing ideas. Some adopted the baptism of adult believers, for which they were called by their enemies "Anabaptists," which means "rebaptizers." (Early Christians had practiced adult baptism, but infant baptism became the norm, which meant that adults undergoing baptism were repeating the ritual.) Some groups attempted communal ownership of property, living very simply and rejecting anything they thought unbiblical. Some reacted harshly to members who deviated, but others argued for complete religious toleration and individualism.

Some religious radicals thought the end of the world was coming soon, and in the 1530s a group took over the German city of Münster, which they predicted would be the site of a New Jerusalem that would survive God's final judgment. They called for communal ownership of property and expelled those who refused to be rebaptized. Combined armies of Catholics and Protestants besieged the city and executed its leaders. The insurrection at Münster and the radicals' unwillingness to accept a state church marked them as societal outcasts and invited hatred and persecution, for both Protestant and Catholic authorities saw a state church as key to maintaining order. Anabaptists and other radicals were banished or cruelly executed by burning, beating, or drowning. (See "Individuals in Society: Anna Jansz of Rotterdam," page 400.) Their community spirit and heroism in the face of martyrdom, however, contributed to the survival of radical ideas. Later, the Quakers, with their pacifism; the Baptists, with their emphasis on inner spiritual light; the Congregationalists, with their democratic church organization; and in 1787 the authors of the U.S. Constitution, with their opposition

Anna Jansz (1509–1539) was born into a well-to-do family in the small city of Briel in the Netherlands. She married, and when she was in her early twenties she and her husband came to accept Anabaptism after listening to a traveling preacher. They were baptized in 1534 and became part of a group who believed that God would soon come to bring judgment on the wicked and deliver his true followers. Jansz wrote a hymn conveying these apocalyptic beliefs and foretelling vengeance on those who persecuted Anabaptists: "I hear the Trumpet sounding, From far off I hear her blast! . . . O murderous seed, what will you do? Offspring of Cain, you put to death The lambs of the Lord, without just cause — It will be doubly repaid to you! Death now comes riding on horseback, We have seen your fate! The sword is passing over the land, With which you will be killed and slain, And you will not escape from Hell!"

Jansz and her husband traveled to England, where she had a child, but in November 1538 she and her infant son, Isaiah, returned to the Netherlands, along with another woman. As the story was later told, the two women were recognized as Anabaptists by another traveler because of songs they were singing, perhaps her "Trumpet Song" among them. They were arrested and interrogated in the city of Rotterdam, and sentenced to death by drowning. The day she was executed — January 24, 1539 — Anna Jansz wrote a long testament to her son, providing him with spiritual advice: "My son, hear the instruction of your mother, and open your ears to hear the words of my mouth. Watch, today I am travelling the path of the Prophets, Apostles, and Martyrs, and drink from the cup from which they have all tasted. . . . But if you hear of the existence of a poor, lowly, cast-out little company, that has been despised and rejected by the World, go join it. . . . Honor the Lord through the works of your hands. Let the light of Scripture shine in you. Love your Neighbor; with an effusive, passionate heart deal your bread to the hungry."

Anabaptists later compiled accounts of trials and executions, along with letters and other records, into martyrologies designed to inspire deeper faith. One of the most widely read of these describes Jansz on her way

An etching of Anna Jansz on the way to her execution, from a 1685 Anabaptist martyrology. (Used by permission of the Mennonite Historical Library, Goshen College, Indiana)

to the execution. She offered a certain amount of money to anyone who would care for her son; a poor baker with six children agreed, and she passed the child to him. The martyrology reports that the baker later became quite wealthy, and that her son, Isaiah, became mayor of the city of Rotterdam. As such, he would have easily been able to read the court records of his mother's trial.

Anna Jansz was one of thousands of people executed for their religious beliefs in sixteenth-century Europe. A few of these were high-profile individuals such as Thomas More, the Catholic former chancellor of England executed by King Henry VIII, but most were quite ordinary people. Many were women. Women's and men's experiences of martyrdom were similar in many ways, but women also confronted additional challenges. Some were pregnant while in prison — execution was delayed until the baby was born — or, like Jansz, had infants with them. They faced procedures of questioning, torture, and execution that brought dishonor as well as pain. Eventually many Anabaptists, as well as others whose religion put them in opposition to their rulers, migrated to parts of Europe that were more tolerant. By the seventeenth century the Netherlands had become one of the most tolerant places in Europe, and Rotterdam was no longer the site of executions for religious reasons.

QUESTIONS FOR ANALYSIS

1. How did religion, gender, and social class all shape Jansz's experiences and the writings that she left behind?
2. Why might Jansz's hymn and her Anabaptist beliefs have seemed threatening to those who did not share her beliefs?

Source: Quotations from *Elisabeth's Manly Courage: Testimonials and Songs of Martyred Anabaptist Women in the Low Countries*, ed. and trans. Hermina Joldersma and Louis Peter Grijp (Milwaukee: Marquette University Press, 2001).

to the "establishment of religion" (state churches), would all trace their origins, in part, to the radicals of the sixteenth century.

Radical reformers sometimes called for social as well as religious change, a message that resonated with the increasingly struggling German peasantry. In the early sixteenth century the economic condition of the peasantry varied from place to place but was generally worse than it had been in the fifteenth century and was deteriorating. Crop failures in 1523 and 1524 aggravated an explosive situation. Nobles had aggrieved peasants by seizing village common lands, by imposing new rents and requiring additional services, and by taking the peasants' best horses or cows whenever a head of household died. The peasants made demands that they believed conformed to the Scriptures, and they cited radical thinkers as well as Luther as proof that they did.

Luther wanted to prevent rebellion. Initially he sided with the peasants, blasting the lords for robbing their subjects. But when rebellion broke out, peasants who expected Luther's support were soon disillusioned. Freedom for Luther meant independence from the authority of the Roman Church; it did not mean opposition to legally established secular powers. As for biblical support for the peasants' demands, he maintained that the Scriptures had nothing to do with earthly justice or material gain, a position that Zwingli supported. Firmly convinced that rebellion would hasten the end of civilized society, Luther wrote the tract *Against the Murderous, Thieving Hordes of the Peasants*: "Let everyone who can smite, slay, and stab [the peasants], secretly and openly, remembering that nothing can be more poisonous, hurtful or devilish than a rebel."[3] The nobility ferociously crushed the revolt. Historians estimate that more than seventy-five thousand peasants were killed in 1525.

The German Peasants' War of 1525 greatly strengthened the authority of lay rulers. Not surprisingly, the Reformation lost much of its popular appeal after 1525, though peasants and urban rebels sometimes found a place for their social and religious ideas in radical groups. Peasants' economic conditions did moderately improve, however. For example, in many parts of Germany, enclosed fields, meadows, and forests were returned to common use.

Marriage, Sexuality, and the Role of Women

Luther and Zwingli both believed that a priest's or nun's vows of celibacy went against human nature and God's commandments, and that marriage brought spiritual advantages and so was the ideal state for nearly all human beings. Luther married a former nun, Katharina von Bora (1499–1532), and Zwingli married a Zurich widow, Anna Reinhart (1491–1538). Both women quickly had several children. Most other Protestant reformers also married, and their wives had to create a new and respectable role for themselves — pastor's wife — to overcome being viewed as simply a new type of priest's concubine. They were living demonstrations of their husband's convictions about the superiority of marriage to celibacy, and they were expected to be models of wifely obedience and Christian charity.

Though they denied that marriage was a sacrament, Protestant reformers stressed that it had been ordained by God when he presented Eve to Adam, served as a "remedy" for the unavoidable sin of lust, provided a site for the pious rearing of the next generation of God-fearing Christians, and offered husbands and wives companionship and consolation. (See "Evaluating the Evidence 13.2: Domestic Scene," page 402.)

Domestic Scene

The Protestant notion that the best form of Christian life was marriage and a family helps explain the appeal of Protestantism to middle-class urban men and women, such as those shown in this domestic scene. The engraving, titled Concordia *(Harmony), includes the biblical inscription of what Jesus called the greatest commandment —* "You shall love the Lord your God with all your heart and all your soul and your neighbor as yourself" *(Deuteronomy 6; Matthew 22) — on tablets at the back. The large covered bed at the back was both a standard piece of furniture in urban homes and a symbol of proper marital sexual relations.*

(Mary Evans Picture Library/The Images Works)

EVALUATE THE EVIDENCE

1. What are the different family members doing? What elements of this image suggest that this is a pious, Christian family?
2. How do the various family roles shown here support the Protestant ideal of marriage and family?

A proper marriage was one that reflected both the spiritual equality of men and women and the proper social hierarchy of husbandly authority and wifely obedience.

Protestants did not break with medieval scholastic theologians in their idea that women were to be subject to men. Women were advised to be cheerful rather than grudging in their obedience, for in doing so they demonstrated their willingness to follow God's plan. Men were urged to treat their wives kindly and considerately, but also to enforce their authority, through physical coercion if necessary. European marriage manuals used the metaphor of breaking a horse for teaching a wife obedience, though laws did set limits on the husband's power to do so.

Protestants saw marriage as a contract in which each partner promised the other support, companionship, and the sharing of mutual goods. Because, in Protestant eyes, marriage was created by God as a remedy for human weakness, marriages in which spouses did not comfort or support one another physically, materially, or emotionally endangered their own souls and the surrounding community. The only solution might be divorce and remarriage, which most Protestants came to allow. Protestant allowance of divorce differed markedly from Catholic doctrine, which viewed marriage as a sacramental union that, if validly entered into, could not be dissolved (Catholic canon law allowed only separation with no remarriage). Although permitting divorce was a dramatic legal change, it did not have a dramatic impact on newly Protestant areas. Because marriage was the cornerstone of society socially and economically, divorce was a desperate last resort. In many Protestant jurisdictions the annual divorce rate hovered around 0.02 to 0.06 per thousand people. (By contrast, in 2010 the U.S. divorce rate was 3.6 per thousand people.)

As Protestants believed marriage was the only proper remedy for lust, they uniformly condemned prostitution. The licensed brothels that were a common feature of late medieval urban life (see Chapter 11) were closed in Protestant cities, and harsh punishments were set for prostitution. Many Catholic cities soon closed their brothels as well, although Italian cities favored stricter regulations rather than closure. Selling sex was couched in moral rather than economic terms, as simply one type of "whoredom," a term that also included premarital sex, adultery, and other unacceptable sexual activities. "Whore" was also a term that reformers used for their theological opponents; Protestants compared the pope to the biblical whore of Babylon, a symbol of the end of the world, while Catholics called Luther's wife a whore because she had first been married to Christ as a nun before her marriage to Luther. Closing brothels did not end the exchange of sex for money, of course, but simply reshaped it. Smaller illegal brothels were established, or women selling sex moved to areas right outside city walls.

Martin Luther and Katharina von Bora   Lucas Cranach the Elder painted this double marriage portrait to celebrate Luther's wedding in 1525 to Katharina von Bora, a former nun. The artist was one of the witnesses at the wedding and, in fact, had presented Luther's marriage proposal to Katharina. Using a go-between for proposals was very common, as was having a double wedding portrait painted. This particular couple quickly became a model of the ideal marriage, and many churches wanted their portraits. More than sixty similar paintings, with slight variations, were produced by Cranach's workshop and hung in churches and wealthy homes. (Galleria degli Uffizi, Florence, Italy/Alinari/Bridgeman Images)

The Protestant Reformation clearly had a positive impact on marriage, but its impact on women was more mixed. Many nuns were in convents not out of a strong sense of religious calling, but because their parents placed them there. Convents nevertheless provided women of the upper classes with an opportunity to use their literary, artistic, medical, or administrative talents if they could not or would not marry. The Reformation generally brought the closing of monasteries and convents, and marriage became virtually the only occupation for upper-class Protestant women. Women in some convents recognized this and fought the Reformation, or argued that they could still be pious Protestants within convent walls. Most nuns left, however, and we do not know what happened to them. The Protestant emphasis on marriage made unmarried women (and men) suspect, for they did not belong to the type of household regarded as the cornerstone of a proper, godly society.

A few women took Luther's idea about the priesthood of all believers to heart and wrote religious works. Argula von Grumbach, a German noblewoman, supported Protestant ideas in print, asserting, "I am not unfamiliar with Paul's words that women should be silent in church but when I see that no man will or can speak, I am driven by the word of God when he said, he who confesses me on earth, him will I confess, and he who denies me, him will I deny."[4] No sixteenth-century Protestants allowed women to be members of the clergy, however, though monarchs such as Elizabeth I of England and female territorial rulers of the states of the Holy Roman Empire did determine religious policies just as male rulers did.

The Reformation and German Politics

FOCUS QUESTION

How did the political situation in Germany shape the course of the Reformation?

Although criticism of the church was widespread in Europe in the early sixteenth century, reform movements could be more easily squelched by the strong central governments that had evolved in Spain and France. England, too, had a strong monarchy, but the king broke from the Catholic Church for other reasons (see page 408). The Holy Roman Empire, in contrast, included hundreds of largely independent states. Against this background of decentralization and strong local power, Martin Luther had launched a movement to reform the church. Two years after he published the "Ninety-five Theses," the electors of the Holy Roman Empire chose as emperor a nineteen-year-old Habsburg prince who ruled as Charles V (r. 1519–1556). The course of the Reformation was shaped by this election and by the political relationships surrounding it.

The Rise of the Habsburg Dynasty

War and diplomacy were important ways that states increased their power in sixteenth-century Europe, but so was marriage. Royal and noble sons and daughters were important tools of state policy. The benefits of an advantageous marriage stretched across generations, a process that can be seen most dramatically with the Habsburgs. The Holy Roman emperor Frederick III, a Habsburg who was the ruler of most of Austria, acquired only a small amount of territory—but a great deal of money—with his marriage to Princess Eleonore of Portugal in 1452. He arranged for his son Maximilian to marry Europe's most prominent heiress, Mary of Burgundy, in 1477; she inherited the Netherlands, Luxembourg, and the County of Burgundy in what is now eastern France. Through this union with the rich and powerful duchy of Burgundy, the Austrian house of Habsburg, already the strongest ruling family in the empire, became an international power. The marriage of Maximilian and Mary angered the French, however, who considered Burgundy French territory, and inaugurated centuries of conflict between the Austrian house of Habsburg and the kings of France.

Maximilian learned the lesson of marital politics well, marrying his son and daughter to the children of Ferdinand and Isabella, the rulers of Spain, much of southern Italy, and eventually the Spanish New World empire. His grandson Charles V fell heir to a vast and incredibly diverse collection of states and peoples, each governed in a different manner and held together only by the person of the emperor (Map 13.1). Charles's Italian adviser, the grand chancellor Gattinara, told the young ruler, "God has set you on the path toward world monarchy." Charles, a Catholic, not only believed this but also was convinced that it was his duty to maintain the political and religious unity of Western Christendom.

Religious Wars in Switzerland and Germany

In the sixteenth century the practice of religion remained a public matter. The ruler determined the official form of religious practice in his (or occasionally her) jurisdiction. Almost everyone believed that the presence of a faith different from that of the majority represented a political threat to the security of the state, and few believed in religious liberty.

Luther's ideas appealed to German rulers for a variety of reasons. Though Germany was not a nation, people did have an understanding of being German because of their language and traditions. Luther frequently used the phrase "we Germans" in his

MAP 13.1 **The Global Empire of Charles V, ca. 1556**   Charles V exercised theoretical jurisdiction over more European territory than anyone since Charlemagne. He also claimed authority over large parts of North and South America (see Map 14.2, page 436), though actual Spanish control was weak in much of the area.

attacks on the papacy. Luther's appeal to national feeling influenced many rulers otherwise confused by or indifferent to the complexities of the religious matters of the time. Some German rulers were sincerely attracted to Lutheran ideas, but material considerations swayed many others to embrace the new faith. The rejection of Roman Catholicism and adoption of Protestantism would mean the legal confiscation of lush farmlands, rich monasteries, and wealthy shrines. Thus many political authorities in the empire became Protestant in part to extend their financial and political power and to enhance their independence from the emperor.

Charles V was a vigorous defender of Catholicism, so it is not surprising that the Reformation led to religious wars. The first battleground was Switzerland, which was officially part of the Holy Roman Empire, though it was really a loose confederation of thirteen largely autonomous territories called cantons. Some cantons remained Catholic, and some became Protestant, and in the late 1520s the two sides went to war. Zwingli was killed on the battlefield in 1531, and both sides quickly decided that a treaty was preferable to further fighting. The treaty basically allowed each canton to determine its own religion and ordered each side to give up its foreign alliances, a policy of neutrality that has been characteristic of modern Switzerland.

Trying to halt the spread of religious division, Charles V called an Imperial Diet in 1530, to meet at Augsburg. The Lutherans developed a statement of faith, later called the Augsburg Confession, and the Protestant princes presented this to the emperor. (The Augsburg Confession remains an authoritative statement of belief for many Lutheran churches.) Charles refused to accept it and ordered all Protestants to return to the Catholic Church and give up any confiscated church property. This demand backfired, and Protestant territories in the empire—mostly northern German principalities and southern German cities—formed a military alliance. The emperor could not respond militarily, as he was in the midst of a series of wars with the French: the Habsburg-Valois wars (1521–1559), fought in Italy along the eastern and southern borders of France and eventually in Germany. The Ottoman Turks had also taken much of Hungary and in 1529 were besieging Vienna.

The 1530s and early 1540s saw complicated political maneuvering among many of the powers of Europe. Various attempts were made to heal the religious split with a church council, but stubbornness on both sides made it increasingly clear that this would not be possible and that war was inevitable. Charles V realized that he was fighting not only for religious unity, but also for a more unified state, against territorial rulers who wanted to maintain their independence. He was thus defending both church and empire.

Fighting began in 1546, and initially the emperor was very successful. This success alarmed both France and the pope, however, who did not want Charles to become even more powerful. The pope withdrew papal troops, and the Catholic king of France sent money and troops to the Lutheran princes. Finally, in 1555 Charles agreed to the Peace of Augsburg, which, "in order to bring peace into the holy empire," officially recognized Lutheranism. The political authority in each territory was permitted to decide whether the territory would be Catholic or Lutheran and was ordered to let other territories "enjoy their religious beliefs, liturgy, and ceremonies as well as their estates in peace." Most of northern and central Germany became Lutheran, while the south remained Roman Catholic. There was no freedom of religion within the territories, however. Princes or town councils established state churches to which all subjects of the area had to belong. Dissidents had to convert or leave, although the treaty did order that "they shall neither be hindered in the sale of their estates after due payment of the local taxes nor injured in their honor."[5] Religious refugees became a common feature on the roads of the empire, though rulers did not always let their subjects leave as easily as the treaty stipulated.

The Peace of Augsburg ended religious war in Germany for many decades. His hope of uniting his empire under a single church dashed, Charles V abdicated in 1556 and moved to a monastery, transferring power over his holdings in Spain and the Netherlands to his son Philip and his imperial power to his brother Ferdinand.

The Spread of Protestant Ideas

States within the Holy Roman Empire were the earliest territories to accept the Protestant Reformation, but by the later 1520s and 1530s religious change came to Denmark-Norway, Sweden, England, France, and eastern Europe. In most of these areas, a second generation of reformers built on Lutheran and Zwinglian ideas to develop their own theology and plans for institutional change. The most important of the second-generation reformers was John Calvin, whose ideas would profoundly influence the social thought and attitudes of European peoples and their descendants all over the world.

FOCUS QUESTION
How did Protestant ideas and institutions spread beyond German-speaking lands?

Scandinavia

The first area outside the empire to officially accept the Reformation was the kingdom of Denmark-Norway under King Christian III (r. 1536–1559). Danish scholars studied at the University of Wittenberg, and Lutheran ideas spread into Denmark very quickly. In the 1530s the king officially broke with the Catholic Church, and most clergy followed. The process went smoothly in Denmark, but in northern Norway and Iceland (which Christian also ruled) there were violent reactions, and Lutheranism was only gradually imposed on a largely unwilling populace.

In Sweden, Gustavus Vasa (r. 1523–1560), who came to the throne during a civil war with Denmark, also took over control of church personnel and income. Protestant ideas spread, though the Swedish Church did not officially accept Lutheran theology until later in the century.

Henry VIII and the Reformation in England

As on the continent, the Reformation in England had economic and political as well as religious causes. The impetus for England's break with Rome was the desire of King Henry VIII (r. 1509–1547) for a new wife, though his own motives also included political, social, and economic elements.

Henry VIII was married to Catherine of Aragon, the daughter of Ferdinand and Isabella and widow of Henry's older brother, Arthur. Marriage to a brother's widow went against canon law, and Henry had been required to obtain a special papal dispensation to marry Catherine. The marriage had produced only one living heir, a daughter, Mary. By 1527 Henry decided that God was showing his displeasure with the marriage by denying him a son, and he appealed to the pope to have the marriage annulled. He was also in love with a court lady in waiting, Anne Boleyn, and assumed that she would give him the son he wanted. Normally an annulment would not have been a problem, but the troops of Emperor Charles V were in Rome at that point, and Pope Clement VII was essentially their prisoner. Charles V was the nephew of Catherine of Aragon and thus was vigorously opposed to an annulment, which would

Allegory of the Tudor Dynasty   The unknown creator of this work intended to glorify the virtues of the Protestant succession; the painting has no historical reality. Henry VIII (seated) hands the sword of justice to his Protestant son Edward VI. The Catholic queen Mary and her husband, Philip of Spain (left), are followed by Mars, god of war, signifying violence and civil disorder. At right the figures of Peace and Plenty accompany the Protestant Elizabeth I, symbolizing England's happy fate under her rule. (Yale Center for British Art, Paul Mellon Collection, USA/Bridgeman Images)

have declared his aunt a fornicator and his cousin Mary a bastard. The pope stalled.

With Rome thwarting his matrimonial plans, Henry decided to remove the English Church from papal jurisdiction. In a series of measures during the 1530s, Henry used Parliament to end the authority of the pope and make himself the supreme head of the church in England. Some opposed the king and were beheaded, among them Thomas More, the king's chancellor and author of *Utopia* (see Chapter 12). When Anne Boleyn failed twice to produce a male child, Henry VIII charged her with adulterous incest and in 1536 had her beheaded. His third wife, Jane Seymour, gave Henry the desired son, Edward, but she died a few days after childbirth. Henry went on to three more wives.

Theologically, Henry was conservative, and the English Church retained such traditional Catholic practices and doctrines as confession, clerical celibacy, and transubstantiation. Under the influence of his chief minister, Thomas Cromwell, and the man he had appointed archbishop of Canterbury, Thomas Cranmer, he did agree to place an English Bible in every church. He also decided to dissolve the English monasteries, primarily because he wanted their wealth. Working through Parliament, between 1535 and 1539 the king ended nine hundred years of English monastic life, dispersing the monks and nuns and confiscating their lands. Their proceeds enriched the royal treasury, and hundreds of properties were sold to the middle and upper classes, the very groups represented in Parliament. The dissolution of the monasteries did not achieve a more equitable distribution of land and wealth; rather, the redistribution of land strengthened the upper classes and tied them to both the Tudor dynasty and the new Protestant Church.

The nationalization of the church and the dissolution of the monasteries led to important changes in government administration. Vast tracts of formerly monastic land came temporarily under the Crown's jurisdiction, and new bureaucratic machinery had to be developed to manage those properties. Cromwell reformed and centralized the king's household, the council, the secretariats, and the Exchequer. New departments of state were set up. Surplus funds from all departments went into a liquid fund to be applied to areas where there were deficits. This balancing resulted in greater efficiency and economy, and Henry VIII's reign saw the growth of the modern centralized bureaucratic state.

Did the religious changes under Henry VIII have broad popular support? Historians disagree about this. Some English people had been dissatisfied with the existing Christian Church before Henry's measures, and Protestant literature circulated. Traditional Catholicism exerted an enormously strong and vigorous hold over the imagination and loyalty of the people, however. Most clergy and officials accepted Henry's moves, but all did not quietly acquiesce. In 1536 popular opposition in the north to the religious changes led to the Pilgrimage of Grace, a massive rebellion that proved the largest in English history. The "pilgrims" accepted a truce, but their leaders were arrested, tried, and executed. Recent scholarship points out that people rarely "converted" from Catholicism to Protestantism overnight. People responded to an action of the Crown that was played out in their own neighborhood—the closing of a monastery, the ending of Masses for the dead—with a combination of resistance, acceptance, and collaboration. Some enthusiastically changed to Protestant forms of prayer, for example, while others recited Protestant prayers in church while keeping pictures of the Catholic saints at home.

Loyalty to the Catholic Church was particularly strong in Ireland. Ireland had been claimed by English kings since the twelfth century, but in reality the English had firm control of only the area around Dublin, known as the Pale. In 1536, on orders from London, the Irish Parliament, which represented only the English landlords and the people of the Pale, approved the English laws severing the church from Rome. The Church of Ireland was established on the English pattern, and the (English) ruling class adopted the new reformed faith. Most of the Irish people remained Roman Catholic, thus adding religious antagonism to the ethnic hostility that had been a feature of English policy toward Ireland for centuries (see Chapter 11). Irish armed opposition to the Reformation led to harsh repression by the English. Catholic property was confiscated and sold, and the profits were shipped to England. The Roman Church was essentially driven underground, and the Catholic clergy acted as national as well as religious leaders.

Upholding Protestantism in England

In the short reign of Henry's sickly son, Edward VI (r. 1547–1553), Protestant ideas exerted a significant influence on the religious life of the country. Archbishop Thomas Cranmer simplified the liturgy, invited Protestant theologians to England, and prepared the first *Book of Common Prayer* (1549), which was later approved by Parliament. In stately and dignified English, the *Book of Common Prayer* included the order for all services and prayers of the Church of England.

The equally brief reign of Mary Tudor (r. 1553–1558) witnessed a sharp move back to Catholicism. The devoutly Catholic daughter of Catherine of Aragon, Mary rescinded the Reformation legislation of her father's reign and restored Roman Catholicism. Mary's marriage to her cousin Philip II of Spain (r. 1556–1598), son of the emperor Charles V, proved highly unpopular in England, and her execution of several hundred Protestants further alienated her subjects. During her reign, about a thousand Protestants fled to the continent. Mary's death raised to the throne her half-sister Elizabeth, Henry's daughter with Anne Boleyn, who had been raised a Protestant. Elizabeth's reign from 1558 to 1603 inaugurated the beginnings of religious stability.

At the start of Elizabeth's reign, sharp differences existed in England. On the one hand, Catholics wanted a Roman Catholic ruler. On the other hand, a vocal number of returning exiles wanted all Catholic elements in the Church of England eliminated. The latter, because they wanted to "purify" the church, were called "Puritans."

Shrewdly, Elizabeth chose a middle course between Catholic and Puritan extremes. Working through Parliament, she ordered church and government officials to swear that she was supreme in matters of religion as well as politics, required her subjects to attend services in the Church of England or risk a fine, and called for frequent preaching of Protestant ideas. (See "Evaluating the Evidence 13.3: Elizabethan Injunctions About Religion," page 410.) She did not interfere with people's privately

Elizabethan Injunctions About Religion

In 1559, acting through Parliament, Queen Elizabeth issued a series of rules governing many aspects of religious life. These prohibited clergy and laypeople from engaging in certain religious practices, and required them to do others.

The first is that all deans, archdeacons, parsons, vicars, and other ecclesiastical persons shall faithfully keep and observe, and as far as in them may be, shall cause to be observed and kept of others, all and singular laws and statutes made for the restoring to the crown the ancient jurisdiction over the state ecclesiastical, and abolishing of all foreign power repugnant to the same. And furthermore, all ecclesiastical persons having cure of soul [that is, clergy who preach], shall to the uttermost of their wit, knowledge, and learning, purely and sincerely, and without any color or dissimulation, declare, manifest and open, four times every year at the least, in their sermons and other collations, that all usurped and foreign power, having no establishment nor ground by the law of God, was of most just causes taken away and abolished, and that therefore no manner of obedience or subjection within her Highness's realms and dominions is due unto any such foreign power. And that the queen's power within her realms and dominions is the highest power under God, to whom all men within the same realms and dominions, by God's laws owe most loyalty and obedience, afore and above all other powers and potentates in earth. . . .

That they, the persons above rehearsed, shall preach in their churches, and every other cure they have, one sermon, every quarter of the year at the least, wherein they shall purely and sincerely declare the Word of God, and in the same, exhort their hearers to the works of faith, mercy, and charity specially prescribed and commanded in Scripture, and that works devised by men's fantasies, besides Scripture, as wandering to pilgrimages, offering of money, candles, or tapers to relics or images, or kissing and licking

of the same, praying upon beads, or such like superstition, have not only no promise of reward in Scripture, for doing of them, but contrariwise, great threats and malediction of God, for that they be things tending to idolatry and superstition, which of all other offenses God almighty doth most detest and abhor, for that the same diminish his honor and glory. . . .

Every parson, vicar, and curate shall upon every holy day and every second Sunday in the year, hear and instruct all the youth of the parish for half an hour at the least, before Evening Prayer, in the Ten Commandments, the Articles of the Belief, and in the Lord's Prayer. . . .

Because in all alterations and specially in rites and ceremonies, there happeneth discord among the people, and thereupon slanderous words and railings whereby charity, the knot of all Christian society, is loosed. The queen's Majesty being most desirous of all other earthly things, that her people should live in charity both towards God and man, and therein abound in good works, willeth and straightly commandeth all manner of her subjects to forbear all vain and contentious disputations in matters of religion.

EVALUATE THE EVIDENCE

1. Whose authority in matters of religion do these rules reject, and whose do they declare to be supreme? What religious activities are required, and what religious activities are prohibited?
2. Given what you have read in this chapter, would you expect that the queen's order to end "disputations in matters of religion" was followed?

Source: Denis R. Janz, ed., *A Reformation Reader: Primary Texts with Introductions* (Minneapolis: Fortress Press, 1999), pp. 315, 316.

held beliefs, however. As she put it, she did not "want to make windows into men's souls." The Anglican Church, as the Church of England was called, moved in a moderately Protestant direction. Services were conducted in English, monasteries were not re-established, and clergymen were allowed to marry. But the church remained hierarchical, with archbishops and bishops, and services continued to be elaborate, with the clergy in distinctive robes, in contrast to the simpler services favored by many continental Protestants.

Toward the end of the sixteenth century Elizabeth's reign was threatened by European powers attempting to re-establish Catholicism. Philip II of Spain had hoped that his marriage to Mary Tudor would reunite England with Catholic Europe, but Mary's death ended those plans. Another Mary—Mary, Queen of Scots (r. 1560–1567)—provided a new opportunity. Mary was Elizabeth's cousin, but she was Catholic. Mary was next in line to the English throne, and Elizabeth imprisoned her because she worried—quite rightly—that Mary would become the center of Catholic plots to overthrow her. In 1587 Mary became implicated in a plot to assassinate Elizabeth, a conspiracy that had Philip II's full backing. When the English executed Mary, the Catholic pope urged Philip to retaliate.

Philip prepared a vast fleet to sail from Lisbon to Flanders, where a large army of Spanish troops was stationed because of religious wars in the Netherlands (see page 420). The Spanish ships were to escort barges carrying some of the troops across the English Channel to attack England. On May 9, 1588, *la felicíssima armada*—"the most fortunate fleet," as it was ironically called in official documents—composed of more than 130 vessels, sailed from Lisbon harbor. The **Spanish Armada** met an English fleet in the Channel before it reached Flanders. The English ships were smaller, faster, and more maneuverable, and many of them had greater firing power than their Spanish counterparts. A combination of storms and squalls, spoiled food and rank water, inadequate Spanish ammunition, and, to a lesser extent, English fire ships that caused the Spanish to scatter gave England the victory. On the journey home many Spanish ships went down in the rough seas around Ireland; perhaps sixty-five ships managed to reach home ports.

The battle in the English Channel has frequently been described as one of the decisive battles in world history. In fact, it had mixed consequences. Spain soon rebuilt its navy, and after 1588 the quality of the Spanish fleet improved. The war between England and Spain dragged on for years. Yet the defeat of the Spanish Armada prevented Philip II from reimposing Catholicism on England by force. In England the victory contributed to a David and Goliath legend that enhanced English national sentiment.

The Route of the Spanish Armada, 1588

Spanish Armada The fleet sent by Philip II of Spain in 1588 against England as a religious crusade against Protestantism. Weather and the English fleet defeated it.

Calvinism

In 1509, while Luther was preparing for a doctorate at Wittenberg, John Calvin (1509–1564) was born in Noyon in northwestern France. As a young man he studied law, which had a decisive impact on his mind and later his thought. In 1533 he experienced a religious crisis, as a result of which he converted to Protestantism.

Calvin believed that God had specifically selected him to reform the church. Accordingly, he accepted an invitation to assist in the reformation of the city of Geneva. There, beginning in 1541, Calvin worked assiduously to establish a well-disciplined Christian society in which church and state acted together.

To understand Calvin's Geneva, it is necessary to understand Calvin's ideas. These he embodied in **The Institutes of the Christian Religion**, published first in 1536 and in its final form in 1559. The cornerstone of Calvin's theology was his belief in the absolute sovereignty and omnipotence of God and the total weakness of humanity. Before the infinite power of God, he asserted, men and women are as insignificant as grains of sand.

Calvin did not ascribe free will to human beings because that would detract from the sovereignty of God. Men and women cannot actively work to achieve salvation; rather,

The Institutes of the Christian Religion Calvin's formulation of Christian doctrine, which became a systematic theology for Protestantism.

predestination The teaching that God has determined the salvation or damnation of individuals based on his will and purpose, not on their merit or works.

God in his infinite wisdom decided at the beginning of time who would be saved and who damned. This viewpoint constitutes the theological principle called **predestination**. Calvin explained his view:

> Predestination we call the eternal decree of God, by which he has determined in himself, what he would have become of every individual. . . . For they are not all created with a similar destiny; but eternal life is foreordained for some, and eternal damnation for others. . . . To those whom he devotes to condemnation, the gate of life is closed by a just and irreprehensible, but incomprehensible, judgment. How exceedingly presumptuous it is only to inquire into the causes of the Divine will; which is in fact, and is justly entitled to be, the cause of everything that exists. . . . For the will of God is the highest justice; so that what he wills must be considered just, for this very reason, because he wills it.[6]

Many people consider the doctrine of predestination, which dates back to Saint Augustine and Saint Paul, to be a pessimistic view of the nature of God. But "this terrible decree," as even Calvin called it, did not lead to pessimism or fatalism. Instead, many Calvinists came to believe that although one's own actions could do nothing to change one's fate, hard work, thrift, and proper moral conduct could serve as signs that one was among the "elect" chosen for salvation.

Calvin transformed Geneva into a community based on his religious principles. The most powerful organization in the city became the Consistory, a group of laymen and pastors charged with investigating and disciplining deviations from proper doctrine and conduct.

Serious crimes and heresy were handled by the civil authorities, which, with the Consistory's approval, sometimes used torture to extract confessions. Between 1542 and 1546 alone seventy-six persons were banished from Geneva, and fifty-eight were executed for heresy, adultery, blasphemy, and witchcraft (see page 421). Among them was the Spanish humanist and refugee Michael Servetus, who was burned at the stake for denying the scriptural basis for the Trinity, rejecting child baptism, and insisting that a person under twenty cannot commit a mortal sin, all of which were viewed as threats to society.

Geneva became the model of a Christian community for many Protestant reformers. Religious refugees from France, England, Spain, Scotland, and Italy visited Calvin's Geneva, and many of the most prominent exiles from Mary Tudor's England stayed. Subsequently, the church of Calvin — often termed "Reformed" — served as the model for the Presbyterian Church in Scotland, the Huguenot Church in France (see page 418), and the Puritan churches in England and New England.

Calvinism became the compelling force in international Protestantism. Calvinists believed that any occupation could be a God-given "calling," and should be carried out with diligence and dedication. This doctrine encouraged an aggressive, vigorous activism in both work and religious life, and Calvinism became the most dynamic force in sixteenth- and seventeenth-century Protestantism.

Calvinism spread on the continent of Europe, and also found a ready audience in Scotland. There, as elsewhere, political authority was the decisive influence in reform. The monarchy was weak, and factions of virtually independent nobles competed for power. King James V and his daughter Mary, Queen of Scots, staunch Catholics and close allies of Catholic France, opposed reform, but the Scottish nobles supported it. One man, John Knox (1505?–1572), dominated the reform movement, which led to the establishment of a state church.

Knox was determined to structure the Scottish Church after the model of Geneva, where he had studied and worked with Calvin. In 1560 Knox persuaded the Scottish Parliament, which was dominated by reform-minded barons, to end papal authority and rule by bishops, substituting governance by presbyters, or councils of ministers. The Presbyterian Church of Scotland was strictly Calvinist in doctrine, adopted a simple and dignified service of worship, and laid great emphasis on preaching.

The Reformation in Eastern Europe

While political and economic issues determined the course of the Reformation in western and northern Europe, ethnic factors often proved decisive in eastern Europe, where people of diverse backgrounds had settled in the later Middle Ages. In Bohemia in the fifteenth century, a Czech majority was ruled by Germans. Most Czechs had adopted the ideas of Jan Hus, and the emperor had been forced to recognize a separate Hussite Church (see Chapter 11). Yet Lutheranism appealed to Germans in Bohemia in the 1520s and 1530s, and the nobility embraced Lutheranism in opposition to the Catholic Habsburgs. The forces of the Catholic Reformation promoted a Catholic spiritual revival in Bohemia, and some areas reconverted. This complicated situation would be one of the causes of the Thirty Years' War in the early seventeenth century.

By 1500 Poland and the Grand Duchy of Lithuania were jointly governed by king, senate, and diet (parliament), but the two territories retained separate officials, judicial systems, armies, and forms of citizenship. The combined realms covered almost five hundred thousand square miles, making Poland-Lithuania the largest European polity, but a population of only about 7.5 million people was very thinly scattered over that land.

The population of Poland-Lithuania was also very diverse; Germans, Italians, Tartars, and Jews lived among Poles and Lithuanians. Such peoples had come as merchants, invited by medieval rulers because of their wealth or to make agricultural improvements. Each group spoke its native language, though all educated people spoke Latin. Luther's ideas took root in Germanized towns but were opposed by King Sigismund I (r. 1506–1548) as well as by ordinary Poles, who held strong anti-German feeling. The Reformed tradition of John Calvin, with its stress on the power of church elders, appealed to the Polish nobility, however. The fact that Calvinism originated in France, not in Germany, also made it more attractive than Lutheranism. But doctrinal differences among Calvinists, Lutherans, and other groups prevented united opposition to Catholicism, and a Counter-Reformation gained momentum. By 1650, due largely to the efforts of the Jesuits (see page 417), Poland was again staunchly Roman Catholic.

Hungary's experience with the Reformation was even more complex. Lutheranism was spread by Hungarian students who had studied at Wittenberg, and sympathy for it developed at the royal court of King Louis II in Buda. But concern about "the German heresy" by the Catholic hierarchy and among the high nobles found expression in a decree of the Hungarian Diet in 1523 that "all Lutherans and those favoring them . . . should have their property confiscated and themselves punished with death as heretics."[7]

Before such measures could be acted on, a military event on August 26, 1526, had profound consequences for both the Hungarian state and the Protestant Reformation there. On the plain of Mohács in southern Hungary, the Ottoman sultan Suleiman the Magnificent inflicted a crushing defeat on the Hungarians, killing King Louis II, many of the nobles, and more than sixteen thousand ordinary soldiers. The Hungarian kingdom was then divided into three parts: the Ottoman Turks absorbed the great plains, including the capital, Buda; the Habsburgs ruled the north and west; and Ottoman-supported Janos Zapolya held eastern Hungary and Transylvania.

The Turks were indifferent to the religious conflicts of Christians, whom they regarded as infidels. Christians of all types paid extra taxes to the sultan, but kept their faith. Many Magyar (Hungarian) nobles accepted Lutheranism; Lutheran schools and parishes headed by men educated at Wittenberg multiplied; and peasants welcomed the new faith. The majority of Hungarian people were Protestant until the late seventeenth century, when Hungarian nobles recognized Habsburg (Catholic) rule and Ottoman Turkish withdrawal in 1699 led to Catholic restoration.

The Catholic Reformation

FOCUS QUESTION
What reforms did the Catholic Church make, and how did it respond to Protestant reform movements?

Between 1517 and 1547 Protestantism made remarkable advances. Nevertheless, the Roman Catholic Church made a significant comeback. After about 1540 no new large areas of Europe, other than the Netherlands, accepted Protestant beliefs (Map 13.2). Many historians see the developments within the Catholic Church after the Protestant Reformation as two interrelated movements: one a drive for internal reform linked to earlier reform efforts, the other a Counter-Reformation that opposed Protestants intellectually, politically, militarily, and institutionally. In both movements, the papacy, new religious orders, and the Council of Trent that met from 1545 to 1563 were important agents.

Papal Reform and the Council of Trent

Renaissance popes and their advisers were not blind to the need for church reforms, but they resisted calls for a general council representing the entire church, and feared that any transformation would mean a loss of power, revenue, and prestige. This changed beginning with Pope Paul III (pontificate 1534–1549), when the papal court became the center of the reform movement rather than its chief opponent. The lives of the pope and his reform-minded cardinals, abbots, and bishops were models of decorum and piety, in contrast to Renaissance popes who concentrated on building churches and enhancing the power of their own families. Paul III and his successors supported improvements in education for the clergy, the end of simony (the selling of church offices), and stricter control of clerical life.

Holy Office The official Roman Catholic agency founded in 1542 to combat international doctrinal heresy.

In 1542 Pope Paul III established the Supreme Sacred Congregation of the Roman and Universal Inquisition, often called the **Holy Office**, with jurisdiction over the Roman Inquisition, a powerful instrument of the Catholic Reformation. The Roman

MAP 13.2 Religious Divisions in Europe, ca. 1555   The Reformations shattered the religious unity of Western Christendom. The situation was even more complicated than a map of this scale can show. Many cities within the Holy Roman Empire, for example, accepted a different faith than the surrounding countryside; Augsburg, Basel, and Strasbourg were all Protestant, though surrounded by territory ruled by Catholic nobles.

Inquisition was a committee of six cardinals with judicial authority over all Catholics and the power to arrest, imprison, and execute suspected heretics. The Holy Office published the *Index of Prohibited Books*, a catalogue of forbidden reading that included works by Christian humanists such as Erasmus as well as by Protestants. Within the Papal States the Inquisition effectively destroyed heresy, but outside the papal territories its influence was slight.

Pope Paul III also called a general council, which met intermittently from 1545 to 1563 at Trent, an imperial city close to Italy. It was called not only to reform the Catholic Church but also to secure reconciliation with the Protestants. Lutherans and Calvinists were invited to participate, but their insistence that the Scriptures be the sole basis for discussion made reconciliation impossible. In addition, the political objectives of Charles V and France both worked against reconciliation: Charles wanted to avoid alienating the Lutheran nobility in the empire, and France wanted the Catholics and Lutherans to remain divided in order to keep Germany decentralized and weak.

Nonetheless, the decrees of the Council of Trent laid a solid basis for the spiritual renewal of the Catholic Church. It gave equal validity to the Scriptures and to tradition as sources of religious truth and authority. It reaffirmed the seven sacraments and the traditional Catholic teaching on transubstantiation. It tackled the disciplinary matters that had disillusioned the faithful, requiring bishops to reside in their own dioceses, suppressing pluralism and simony, and forbidding the sale of indulgences. Clerics who kept concubines were to give them up, and bishops were given greater authority. The council required every diocese to establish a seminary for the education and training of the clergy. Seminary professors were to determine whether candidates for ordination had vocations, genuine callings to the priesthood. This was a novel idea, since from the time of the early church, parents had determined their sons' (and daughters') religious careers. For the first time, great emphasis was laid on preaching and instructing the laity, especially the uneducated.

One decision had especially important social consequences for laypeople. The Council of Trent stipulated that for a marriage to be valid, the marriage vows had to be made publicly before a priest and witnesses. Trent thereby ended the widespread practice of private marriages in Catholic countries, curtailing the number of denials and conflicts that inevitably resulted from marriages that took place in secret.

Although it did not achieve all of its goals, the Council of Trent composed decrees that laid a solid basis for the spiritual renewal of the church. The doctrinal and disciplinary legislation of Trent served as the basis for Roman Catholic faith, organization, and practice through the middle of the twentieth century.

New and Reformed Religious Orders

Just as seminaries provided education, so did religious orders, which aimed at raising the moral and intellectual level of the clergy and people. The monasteries and convents of many existing religious orders were reformed so that they followed more rigorous standards. In Spain, for example, the Carmelite nun Teresa of Ávila (1515–1582) traveled around the country reforming her Carmelite order to bring it back to stricter standards of asceticism and poverty, a task she understood God had set for her in mystical visions, which she described in her own writings. Some officials in the church criticized her as a "restless gadabout, a disobedient and obstinate woman" who had gone against St. Paul's commands that women were not to teach. At one point she was even investigated by the Spanish Inquisition in an effort to make sure her inspiration came from God and not the Devil. The process was dropped, however, and she founded many new convents, which she saw as answers to the Protestant takeover of Catholic churches elsewhere in Europe. "We shall fight for Him [God]," she wrote, "even though we are very cloistered."[8]

New religious orders were founded, some of which focused on education. The Ursuline order of nuns, for example, founded by Angela Merici (1474–1540), focused on the education of women. The daughter of a country gentleman, Angela Merici worked for many years among the poor, sick, and uneducated around her native Brescia in northern Italy. In 1535 she established the first women's religious order concentrating exclusively on teaching young girls, with the goal of re-Christianizing society by training future wives and mothers. After receiving papal approval in 1565, the Ursulines rapidly spread to France and the New World.

The most significant new order was the Society of Jesus, or **Jesuits**. Founded by Ignatius Loyola (1491–1556), the Jesuits played a powerful international role in strengthening Catholicism in Europe and spreading the faith around the world. While recuperating from a severe battle wound in his legs, Loyola studied books about Christ and the saints and decided to give up his military career and become a soldier of Christ. During a year spent in seclusion, prayer, and asceticism, he gained insights that went into his great classic, *Spiritual Exercises* (1548). This work, intended for study during a four-week period of retreat, set out a training program of structured meditation designed to develop spiritual discipline and allow one to meld one's will with that of God. Loyola introduces his program:

> By the term "Spiritual Exercises" is meant every method of examination of conscience, of meditation, of contemplation, of vocal and mental prayer, and of other spiritual activities. For just as taking a walk, journeying on foot, and running are bodily exercises, so we call Spiritual Exercises every way of preparing and disposing the soul to rid itself of all inordinate attachments, and, after their removal, of seeking and finding the will of God in the disposition of our life for the salvation of our soul.[9]

Just like today's physical trainers, Loyola provides daily exercises that build in intensity over the four weeks of the program, and charts on which the exerciser can track his progress.

Loyola was a man of considerable personal magnetism. After study at universities in Salamanca and Paris, he gathered a group of six companions and in 1540 secured papal approval of the new Society of Jesus. The first Jesuits, recruited primarily from wealthy merchant and professional families, saw their mission as improving people's spiritual condition rather than altering doctrine. Their goal was not to reform the church, but "to help souls."

The Society of Jesus developed into a highly centralized, tightly knit organization. In addition to the traditional vows of poverty, chastity, and obedience, professed members vowed special obedience to the pope. Flexibility and the willingness to respond to the needs of time and circumstance formed the Jesuit tradition, which proved attractive to many young men. The Jesuits achieved phenomenal success for the papacy and the reformed Catholic Church, carrying Christianity to India and Japan before 1550 and to Brazil, North America, and the Congo in the seventeenth century. Within Europe the Jesuits brought southern Germany and much of eastern Europe back to Catholicism. Jesuit schools adopted the modern humanist curricula and methods, educating the sons of the nobility as well as the poor. As confessors and spiritual directors to kings, Jesuits exerted great political influence.

Jesuits Members of the Society of Jesus, founded by Ignatius Loyola, whose goal was the spread of the Roman Catholic faith.

Religious Violence

FOCUS QUESTION

What were the causes and consequences of religious violence, including riots, wars, and witch-hunts?

In 1559 France and Spain signed the Treaty of Cateau-Cambrésis (CAH-toh kam-BRAY-sees), which ended the long conflict known as the Habsburg-Valois wars. Spain was the victor. France, exhausted by the struggle, had to acknowledge Spanish dominance in Italy, where much of the fighting had taken place. However, true peace was elusive, and over the next century religious differences led to riots, civil wars, and international conflicts. Especially in France and the Netherlands, Protestants and Catholics used violent actions as well as preaching and teaching against each other, for each side regarded the other as a poison in the community that would provoke the wrath of God. Catholics continued to believe that Calvinists and Lutherans could be reconverted; Protestants persisted in thinking that the Roman Church should be destroyed. Catholics and Protestants alike feared people of other faiths, whom they often saw as agents of Satan. Even more, they feared those who were explicitly identified with Satan: witches living in their midst. This era was the time of the most virulent witch persecutions in European history, as both Protestants and Catholics tried to make their cities and states more godly.

French Religious Wars

The costs of the Habsburg-Valois wars, waged intermittently through the first half of the sixteenth century, forced the French to increase taxes and borrow heavily. King Francis I (r. 1515–1547) also tried two new devices to raise revenue: the sale of public offices and a treaty with the papacy. The former proved to be only a temporary source of money: once a man bought an office, he and his heirs were exempt from taxation. But the latter, known as the Concordat of Bologna (see Chapter 12), gave the French crown the right to appoint all French bishops and abbots, ensuring a rich supplement of money and offices. Because French rulers possessed control over appointments and had a vested financial interest in Catholicism, they had no need to revolt against Rome.

Significant numbers of those ruled, however, were attracted to the Reformed religion of Calvinism. Initially, Calvinism drew converts from among reform-minded members of the Catholic clergy, industrious city dwellers, and artisan groups. Most French Calvinists, called **Huguenots**, lived in major cities, such as Paris, Lyons, and Rouen. By the time King Henry II (r. 1547–1559) died in 1559—accidentally shot in the face at a tournament celebrating the Treaty of Cateau-Cambrésis—perhaps one-tenth of the population had become Calvinist.

The feebleness of the French monarchy was the seed from which the weeds of civil violence sprang. The three weak sons of Henry II who occupied the throne could not provide the necessary leadership, and they were often dominated by their mother, Catherine de' Medici. The French nobility took advantage of this monarchical weakness. Just as German princes in the Holy Roman Empire had adopted Lutheranism as a means of opposition to Emperor Charles V, so French nobles frequently adopted Protestantism as a religious cloak for their independence. Armed clashes between Catholic royalist lords and Calvinist antimonarchical lords occurred in many parts of France. Both Calvinists and Catholics believed that the other's books, services, and

Huguenots French Calvinists.

ministers polluted the community. Preachers incited violence, and religious ceremonies such as baptisms, marriages, and funerals triggered it.

Calvinist teachings called the power of sacred images into question, and mobs in many cities took down and smashed statues, stained-glass windows, and paintings, viewing this as a way to purify the church. Though it was often inspired by fiery Protestant sermons, this iconoclasm, or destruction of religious images, is an example of ordinary men and women carrying out the Reformation themselves. Catholic mobs responded by defending images, and crowds on both sides killed their opponents, often in gruesome ways.

A savage Catholic attack on Calvinists in Paris on Saint Bartholomew's Day, August 24, 1572, followed the usual pattern. The occasion was the marriage ceremony of the king's sister Margaret of Valois to the Protestant Henry of Navarre, which was intended to help reconcile Catholics and Huguenots. Instead, Huguenot wedding guests in Paris were massacred, and other Protestants were slaughtered by mobs. Religious violence spread to the provinces, where thousands were killed. This Saint Bartholomew's Day massacre led to a civil war that dragged on for fifteen years. Agriculture in many areas was destroyed; commercial life declined severely; and starvation and death haunted the land.

What ultimately saved France was a small group of moderates of both faiths, called **politiques**, who believed that only the restoration of strong monarchy could reverse the trend toward collapse. The politiques also favored accepting the Huguenots as an officially recognized and organized group. The death of Catherine de' Medici, followed by the assassination of King Henry III, paved the way for the accession of Henry of Navarre (the unfortunate bridegroom of the Saint Bartholomew's Day massacre), a politique who became Henry IV (r. 1589–1610).

Henry's willingness to sacrifice religious principles to political necessity saved France. He converted to Catholicism but also issued the **Edict of Nantes** in 1598, which granted liberty of conscience and liberty of public worship to Huguenots in 150 fortified towns. The reign of Henry IV and the Edict of Nantes prepared the way for French absolutism in the seventeenth century by helping restore internal peace in France.

politiques Catholic and Protestant moderates who held that only a strong monarchy could save France from total collapse.

Edict of Nantes A document issued by Henry IV of France in 1598, granting liberty of conscience and of public worship to Calvinists, which helped restore peace in France.

The Netherlands Under Charles V

In the Netherlands, what began as a movement for the reformation of the church developed into a struggle for Dutch independence. Emperor Charles V had inherited the seventeen provinces that compose present-day Belgium and the Netherlands (see page 404). Each was self-governing and enjoyed the right to make its own laws and collect its own taxes. The provinces were united politically only in recognition of a common ruler, the emperor. The cities of the Netherlands made their living by trade and industry.

In the Low Countries, as elsewhere, corruption in the Roman Church and the critical spirit of the Renaissance provoked pressure for reform, and Lutheran ideas took root. Charles V had grown up in the Netherlands, however, and he was able to limit their impact. But Charles V abdicated in 1556 and transferred power over the Netherlands to his son Philip II, who had grown up in Spain. Protestant ideas spread.

Spanish Soldiers Killing Protestants in Haarlem In this engraving by the Calvinist artist Franz Hogenberg, Spanish soldiers accompanied by priests kill residents of the Dutch city of Haarlem by hanging or beheading, and then dump their bodies in the river. Haarlem had withstood a seven-month siege by Spanish troops in 1572–1573, and after the starving city surrendered, the garrison of troops and forty citizens judged guilty of sedition were executed. Images such as this were part of the propaganda battle that accompanied the wars of religion, but in many cases there were actual atrocities, on both sides. (Color engraving, ca. 1567/Private Collection/Bridgeman Images)

The Netherlands, 1609

Union of Utrecht The alliance of seven northern provinces (led by Holland) that declared its independence from Spain and formed the United Provinces of the Netherlands.

By the 1560s Protestants in the Netherlands were primarily Calvinists. Calvinism's intellectual seriousness, moral gravity, and emphasis on any form of labor well done appealed to urban merchants, financiers, and artisans. Whereas Lutherans taught respect for the powers that be, Calvinists tended to encourage opposition to political authorities who were judged to be ungodly.

When Spanish authorities attempted to suppress Calvinist worship and raised taxes in the 1560s, rioting ensued. Calvinists sacked thirty Catholic churches in Antwerp, destroying the religious images in them in a wave of iconoclasm. From Antwerp the destruction spread. Philip II sent twenty thousand Spanish troops under the duke of Alva to pacify the Low Countries. Alva interpreted "pacification" to mean ruthless extermination of religious and political dissidents. On top of the Inquisition, he opened his own tribunal, soon called the "Council of Blood." On March 3, 1568, fifteen hundred men were executed. To Calvinists, all this was clear indication that Spanish rule was ungodly and should be overthrown.

Between 1568 and 1578 civil war raged in the Netherlands between Catholics and Protestants and between the seventeen provinces and Spain. Eventually the ten southern provinces, the Spanish Netherlands (the future Belgium), came under the control of the Spanish Habsburg forces. The seven northern provinces, led by Holland, formed the **Union of Utrecht** and in 1581 declared their independence from Spain. The north was Protestant; the south remained Catholic. Philip did not accept this, and war continued. England was even drawn into the conflict, supplying money and troops to the northern United Provinces. (Spain launched an unsuccessful invasion of England in response; see page 411.) Hostilities ended in 1609 when Spain agreed to a truce that recognized the independence of the United Provinces.

The Great European Witch-Hunt

The relationship between the Reformation and the upsurge in trials for witchcraft that occurred at roughly the same time is complex. Increasing persecution for witchcraft actually began before the Reformation in the 1480s, but it became especially common about 1560, and the mania continued until roughly 1660. Religious reformers' extreme notions of the Devil's powers and the insecurity created by the religious wars contributed to this increase. Both Protestants and Catholics tried and executed witches, with church officials and secular authorities acting together.

The heightened sense of God's power and divine wrath in the Reformation era was an important factor in the witch-hunts, but so was a change in the idea of what a witch was. Nearly all premodern societies believe in witchcraft and make some attempts to control witches, who are understood to be people who use magical forces. In the later Middle Ages, however, many educated Christian theologians, canon lawyers, and officials added a demonological component to this notion of what a witch was. For them, the essence of witchcraft was making a pact with the Devil. Witches were no longer simply people who used magical power to get what they wanted, but rather people used by the Devil to do what he wanted. Witches were thought to engage in wild sexual orgies with the Devil, fly through the night to meetings called sabbats that parodied Christian services, and steal communion wafers and unbaptized babies to use in their rituals. Some demonological theorists also claimed that witches were organized in an international conspiracy to overthrow Christianity. Witchcraft was thus spiritualized, and witches became the ultimate heretics, enemies of God.

Trials involving this new notion of witchcraft as diabolical heresy began in Switzerland and southern Germany in the late fifteenth century, became less numerous in the early decades of the Reformation when Protestants and Catholics were busy fighting each other, and then picked up again in about 1560. Scholars estimate that during the sixteenth and seventeenth centuries between 100,000 and 200,000 people were officially tried for witchcraft and between 40,000 and 60,000 were executed.

Though the gender balance varied widely in different parts of Europe, between 75 and 85 percent of those tried and executed were women. Ideas about women and the roles women actually played in society were thus important factors shaping the witch-hunts. Some demonologists expressed virulent misogyny, or hatred of women, and particularly emphasized women's powerful sexual desire, which could be satisfied only by a demonic lover. Most people viewed women as weaker than men and so more likely to give in to an offer by the Devil. In both classical and Christian traditions, women were associated with nature, disorder, and the body, all of which were linked with the demonic. Women's actual lack of power in society and gender norms about the use of violence meant that they were more likely to use scolding and cursing to get what they wanted instead of taking people to court or beating them up. Curses were generally expressed (as they often are today) in religious terms; "go to Hell" was calling on the powers of Satan.

Legal changes also played a role in causing, or at least allowing for, massive witch trials. One of these was a change from an accusatorial legal procedure to an

Witch Pamphlet This printed pamphlet presents the confession of "Mother Waterhouse," a woman convicted of witchcraft in England in 1566, who describes her "many abominable deeds" and "execrable sorcery" committed over fifteen years, and asks for forgiveness right before her execution. Enterprising printers often produced cheap, short pamphlets during witch trials, knowing they would sell, sometimes based on the actual trial proceedings and sometimes just made up. They both reflected and helped create stereotypes about what witches were and did. (Private Collection/Bridgeman Images)

inquisitorial procedure. In the former, a suspect knew the accusers and the charges they had brought, and an accuser could in turn be liable for trial if the charges were not proven. In the latter, legal authorities themselves brought the case. This change made people much more willing to accuse others, for they never had to take personal responsibility for the accusation or face the accused person's relatives. Areas in Europe that did not make this legal change saw very few trials. Inquisitorial procedure involved intense questioning of the suspect, often with torture. Torture was also used to get the names of additional suspects, as most lawyers firmly believed that no witch could act alone.

The use of inquisitorial procedure did not always lead to witch-hunts. The most famous inquisitions in early modern Europe, those in Spain, Portugal, and Italy, were in fact very lenient in their treatment of people accused of witchcraft. The Inquisition in Spain executed only a handful of witches, the Portuguese Inquisition only one, and the Roman Inquisition none, though in each of these there were hundreds of cases. Inquisitors believed in the power of the Devil and were no less misogynist than other judges, but they doubted very much whether the people accused of witchcraft had actually made pacts with the Devil that gave them special powers. They viewed such people not as diabolical Devil worshippers but as superstitious and ignorant peasants who should be educated rather than executed. Thus most people brought up before the Inquisition for witchcraft were sent home with a warning and a penance.

Most witch trials began with a single accusation in a village or town. Individuals accused someone they knew of using magic to spoil food, make children ill, kill animals, raise a hailstorm, or do other types of harm. Tensions within families, households, and neighborhoods often played a role in these accusations. Women number very prominently among accusers and witnesses as well as among those accused of witchcraft because the actions witches were initially charged with, such as harming children or curdling milk, were generally part of women's sphere. A woman also gained economic and social security by conforming to the standard of the good wife and mother and by confronting women who deviated from it.

Once a charge was made, the suspect was brought in for questioning. One German witch pamphlet from 1587 described a typical case:

> Walpurga Hausmännin . . . upon kindly questioning and also torture . . . confessed . . . that the Evil One indulged in fornication with her . . . and made her many promises to help her in her poverty and need. . . . She promised herself body and soul to him and disowned God in heaven. . . . She destroyed a number of cattle, pigs, and geese . . . and dug up [the bodies] of one or two innocent children. With her devil-paramour and other playfellows she has eaten these and used their hair and their little bones for witchcraft.

Confession was generally followed by execution. In this case, Hausmännin was "dispatched from life to death by burning at the stake . . . her body first to be torn five times with red-hot irons."[10]

Detailed records of witch trials survive for many parts of Europe. They have been used by historians to study many aspects of witchcraft, but they cannot directly answer what seems to us an important question: did people really practice witchcraft and think they were witches? They certainly confessed to evil deeds and demonic practices, sometimes without torture, but where would we draw the line between reality and fantasy? Clearly people were not riding through the air on pitchforks, but did they think they did? Did they actually invoke the Devil when they were angry at a neighbor, or was this simply in the minds of their accusers? Trial records cannot tell us, and historians have answered these questions very differently, often using insights from psychoanalysis or the study of more recent victims of torture in their explanations.

After the initial suspect had been questioned, and particularly if he or she had been tortured, the people who had been implicated were brought in for questioning. This might lead to a small hunt, involving from five to ten suspects, and it sometimes grew into a much larger hunt, which historians have called a "witch panic." Panics were most common in the part of Europe that saw the most witch accusations in general: the Holy Roman Empire, Switzerland, and parts of France. Most of this area consisted of very small governmental units that were jealous of each other and, after the Reformation, were divided by religion. The rulers of these small territories often felt more threatened than did the monarchs of western Europe, and they saw persecuting witches as a way to demonstrate their piety and concern for order. Moreover, witch panics often occurred after some type of climatic disaster, such as an unusually cold and wet summer, and they came in waves.

In large-scale panics a wider variety of suspects were taken in — wealthier people, children, a greater proportion of men. Mass panics tended to end when it became clear to legal authorities, or to the community itself, that the people being questioned or executed were not what they understood witches to be, or that the scope of accusations was beyond belief.

As the seventeenth century ushered in new ideas about science and reason, many began to question whether witches could make pacts with the Devil or engage in the wild activities attributed to them. Doubts about whether secret denunciations were valid or whether torture would ever yield truthful confessions gradually spread among the same type of religious and legal authorities who had so vigorously persecuted witches. Prosecutions for witchcraft became less common and were gradually outlawed. The last official execution for witchcraft in England was in 1682, though the last one in the Holy Roman Empire was not until 1775.

LOOKING BACK LOOKING AHEAD

The Renaissance and the Reformation are often seen as two of the key elements in the creation of the "modern" world. The radical changes brought by the Reformation contained many aspects of continuity, however. Sixteenth-century reformers looked back to the early Christian Church for their inspiration, and many of their reforming ideas had been advocated for centuries. Most Protestant reformers worked with political leaders to make religious changes, just as early church officials had worked with Emperor Constantine and his successors as Christianity became the official religion of the Roman Empire in the fourth century. The spread of Christianity and the spread of Protestantism were accomplished not only by preaching, persuasion, and teaching, but also by force and violence. The Catholic Reformation was carried out by activist popes, a church council, and new religious orders, like earlier reforms of the church had been.

Just as they linked with earlier developments, the events of the Reformation were also closely connected with what is often seen as the third element in the "modern" world: European exploration and colonization. Only a week after Martin Luther stood in front of Charles V at the Diet of Worms declaring his independence in matters of religion, Ferdinand Magellan, a Portuguese sea captain with Spanish ships, was killed in a group of islands off the coast of Southeast Asia. Charles V had provided the backing for Magellan's voyage, the first to circumnavigate the globe. Magellan viewed the spread of Christianity as one of the purposes of his trip, and later in the sixteenth century institutions created as part of the Catholic Reformation, including the Jesuit order and the Inquisition, would operate in European colonies overseas as well as in Europe itself. The islands where Magellan was killed were later named the Philippines, in honor of Charles's son Philip, who sent the ill-fated Spanish Armada against England. Philip's opponent Queen Elizabeth was similarly honored when English explorers named a huge chunk of territory in North America "Virginia" as a tribute to their "Virgin Queen." The desire for wealth and power was an important motivation in the European voyages and colonial ventures, but so was religious zeal.

Make Connections

Think about the larger developments and continuities within and across chapters.

1. Martin Luther is always on every list of the one hundred most influential people of all time. Should he be? Why or why not? Who else from this chapter should be on such a list, and why?

2. How did Protestant ideas about gender, marriage, and the role of women break with those developed earlier in the history of the Christian Church (Chapters 6, 7, 9)? What continuities do you see? What factors account for the pattern that you have found?

3. In what ways was the Catholic Reformation of the sixteenth century similar to earlier efforts to reform the church, including the Gregorian reforms of the twelfth century (Chapter 9) and late medieval reform efforts (Chapter 11)? In what ways was it different?

13 REVIEW & EXPLORE

Review the Main Ideas

Answer the focus questions from each section of the chapter.

◆ What were the central ideas of the reformers, and why were they appealing to different social groups? (p. 392)

◆ How did the political situation in Germany shape the course of the Reformation? (p. 404)

◆ How did Protestant ideas and institutions spread beyond German-speaking lands? (p. 407)

◆ What reforms did the Catholic Church make, and how did it respond to Protestant reform movements? (p. 414)

◆ What were the causes and consequences of religious violence, including riots, wars, and witch-hunts? (p. 418)

Identify Key Terms

Identify and explain the significance of each item below.

anticlericalism (p. 392)

indulgence (p. 394)

Protestant (p. 396)

Spanish Armada (p. 411)

The Institutes of the Christian Religion (p. 411)

predestination (p. 412)

Holy Office (p. 414)

Jesuits (p. 417)

Huguenots (p. 418)

politiques (p. 419)

Edict of Nantes (p. 419)

Union of Utrecht (p. 420)

NOTES

1. Quoted in Owen Chadwick, *The Reformation* (Baltimore: Penguin Books, 1976), p. 55.

2. Quoted in E. H. Harbison, *The Age of Reformation* (Ithaca, N.Y.: Cornell University Press, 1963), p. 52.

3. Quoted in S. E. Ozment, *The Age of Reform, 1250–1550: An Intellectual and Religious History of Late Medieval and Reformation Europe* (New Haven, Conn.: Yale University Press, 1980), p. 284.

4. Ludwig Rabus, *Historien der heyligen Außerwolten Gottes Zeugen, Bekennern und Martyrern* (n.p., 1557), fol. 41. Trans. Merry Wiesner-Hanks.

5. From Henry Bettenson, ed., *Documents of the Christian Church*, 2d ed. (London: Oxford University Press, 1963), pp. 301–302. Used by permission of Oxford University Press.

6. J. Allen, trans., *John Calvin: The Institutes of the Christian Religion* (Philadelphia: Westminster Press, 1930), bk. 3, chap. 21, para. 5, 7.

7. Quoted in David P. Daniel, "Hungary," in *The Oxford Encyclopedia of the Reformation*, vol. 2, ed. H. J. Hillerbrand (New York: Oxford University Press, 1996), p. 273.

8. Teresa of Avila, *The Way of Perfection*, translated and quoted in Jodi Bilinkoff, *The Avila of St. Teresa: Religious Reform in a Sixteenth-Century City* (Ithaca: Cornell University Press, 1989), p. 136.

9. *The Spiritual Exercises of St. Ignatius of Loyola*, trans. Louis J. Puhl, S.J. (Chicago: Loyola University, 1951), p. 1.

10. From *The Fugger News-Letters*, ed. Victor von Klarwell, trans. P. de Chary (London: John Lane, The Bodley Head Ltd., 1924), quoted in James Bruce Ross and Mary Martin McLaughlin, *The Portable Renaissance Reader* (New York: Penguin, 1968), pp. 258, 260, 262.

CHAPTER PREVIEW

World Contacts Before Columbus

What was the Afroeurasian trading world prior to the era of European exploration?

The European Voyages of Discovery

How and why did Europeans undertake ambitious voyages of expansion?

Conquest and Settlement

How did European powers acquire colonies in the Americas, and how were they governed?

The Era of Global Contact

How was the era of global contact shaped by new forms of exploitation, commercial exchange, and forced migration?

Changing Attitudes and Beliefs

How did new encounters shape cultural attitudes and beliefs in Europe and the rest of the world?

Life in the Age of Discovery
The arrival of the Portuguese in Japan in 1453 inspired a series of artworks depicting the *namban-jin*, or southern barbarians, as they were known. This detail from an early-seventeenth-century painted screen shows Portuguese sailors unloading trade goods from a merchant ship.

(Detail from a Namban Byobu Japanese painted screen/Museu Nacional de Soares dos Reis, Porto, Portugal/Bridgeman Images)

14

European Exploration and Conquest

1450–1650

In 1450 Europeans were relatively marginal players in a centuries-old trading system that linked Africa, Asia, and Europe. The Indian Ocean was the locus of a vibrant cosmopolitan Afroeurasian trade world in which Arab, Persian, Turkish, Indian, African, Chinese, and European merchants and adventurers competed for trade in spices, silks, and other goods. Elites everywhere prized Chinese porcelains and silks, while wealthy members of the Celestial Kingdom, as China called itself, wanted gold, ivory, and rhinoceros horn from Africa, and exotic goods and peacocks from India. African people wanted textiles from India and cowrie shells from the Maldives in the Indian Ocean. Europeans craved Asian silks and spices, but they had few desirable goods to offer their trading partners.

By 1550 the European search for better access to Asian trade goods had led to a new overseas empire in the Indian Ocean and the accidental discovery of the Western Hemisphere. South and North America were soon drawn into a global network of trade centers and political empires, which Europeans came to dominate. The era of globalization had begun, creating new political systems and forms of economic exchange as well as cultural assimilation, conversion, and resistance. Europeans sought to impose their values on the peoples they encountered while struggling to comprehend these peoples' societies. The Age of Discovery (1450–1650), as the time of these encounters is known, laid the foundations for the modern world. ■

World Contacts Before Columbus

FOCUS QUESTION

What was the Afroeurasian trading world prior to the era of European exploration?

In the fifteenth century a type of world economy, known as the Afroeurasian trade world, linked the products and people of Asia, Africa, and Europe. Before Christopher Columbus began his voyages to the New World in 1492, the West was not the dominant player in world trade. Nevertheless, wealthy Europeans were eager consumers of luxury goods from the East, which they received through Venetian and Genoese middlemen.

The Trade World of the Indian Ocean

The Indian Ocean was the center of the Afroeurasian trade world, serving as a crossroads for exchange among China, India, the Middle East, Africa, and Europe (Map 14.1). From the seventh through the fourteenth centuries, the volume of this trade steadily increased, declining only during the catastrophic years of the Black Death.

Merchants congregated in a series of cosmopolitan port cities strung around the Indian Ocean. Most of these cities had some form of autonomous self-government. Mutual self-interest largely limited violence and prevented attempts to monopolize trade. The most developed area of this commercial web was the South China Sea. In

MAP 14.1 The Fifteenth-Century Afroeurasian Trading World   After a period of decline following the Black Death and the Mongol invasions, trade revived in the fifteenth century. Muslim merchants dominated trade, linking ports in East Africa and the Red Sea with those in India and the Malay Archipelago. Chinese admiral Zheng He's voyages (1405–1433) followed the most important Indian Ocean trade routes, in the hope of imposing Ming dominance of trade and tribute.

the fifteenth century the port of Malacca became a great commercial entrepôt (AHN-truh-poh), a trading post to which goods were shipped for storage while awaiting redistribution. To Malacca came Chinese porcelains, silks, and camphor (used in the manufacture of many medications); pepper, cloves, nutmeg, and raw materials such as sandalwood from the Moluccas; sugar from the Philippines; and Indian textiles, copper weapons, incense, dyes, and opium.

The Mongol emperors opened the doors of China to the West, encouraging Europeans like the Venetian trader and explorer Marco Polo to do business there. Marco Polo's tales of his travels from 1271 to 1295 and his encounter with the Great Khan fueled Western fantasies about the exotic Orient. Polo vividly recounted the splendors of the khan's court and the city of Hangzhou, which he described as "the finest and noblest in the world" in which "the number and wealth of the merchants, and the amount of goods that passed through their hands, was so enormous that no man could form a just estimate thereof."[1] After the Mongols fell to the Ming Dynasty in 1368, China entered a period of economic expansion, population growth, and urbanization. By the end of the dynasty in 1644, the Chinese population had tripled to between 150 million and 200 million people. The city of Nanjing had 1 million inhabitants, making it the largest city in the world, while the new capital, Beijing, had more than 600,000 inhabitants, more than any European city. Historians agree that China had the most advanced economy in the world until at least the start of the eighteenth century.

China also took the lead in exploration, sending Admiral Zheng He's fleet along the trade web as far west as Egypt. From 1405 to 1433 each of his seven expeditions involved hundreds of ships and tens of thousands of men. In one voyage alone, Zheng He (JEHNG HUH) sailed more than 12,000 miles, compared to Columbus's 2,400 miles on his first voyage some sixty years later.[2] Although the ships brought back many wonders, such as giraffes and zebras, the purpose of the voyages was primarily diplomatic, to enhance China's prestige and seek tribute-paying alliances. The high expense of the voyages in a period of renewed Mongol encroachment led to the abandonment of the maritime expeditions after the deaths of Zheng He and the emperor. China's turning away from external trade opened new opportunities for European states to expand their role in Asian trade.

Another center of trade in the Indian Ocean was India. The subcontinent had ancient links with its neighbors to the northwest: trade between South Asia and Mesopotamia dates back to the origins of human civilization. The Roman Empire acquired cotton textiles, exotic animals, and other luxury goods from India. Arab merchants who circumnavigated India on their way to trade in the South China Sea established trading posts along the southern coast of India, where the cities of Calicut and Quilon became thriving commercial centers. India was an important contributor of goods to the world trading system. Most of the world's pepper was grown in India, and Indian cotton and silk textiles, mainly from the Gujarat region, were also highly prized.

Chronology

1271–1295	Marco Polo travels to China
1443	Portuguese establish first African trading post at Arguin
1492	Columbus lands in the Americas
1511	Portuguese capture Malacca from Muslims
1518	Spanish king authorizes slave trade to New World colonies
1519–1522	Magellan's expedition circumnavigates the world
1521	Cortés conquers the Mexica Empire
1533	Pizarro conquers the Inca Empire
1602	Dutch East India Company established

The Port of Calicut in India
The port of Calicut, located on the west coast of India, was a center of the Indian Ocean spice trade during the Middle Ages. Vasco da Gama arrived in Calicut in 1498 and obtained permission to trade there, leading to hostilities between the Portuguese and the Arab traders who had previously dominated the port. (From *Civitates Orbis Terrarum*, ca. 1572/Private Collection/The Stapleton Collection/Bridgeman Images)

The Trading States of Africa

By 1450 Africa had a few large empires along with hundreds of smaller states. From 1250 until its defeat by the Ottomans in 1517, the Mamluk Egyptian empire was one of the most powerful on the continent. Its capital, Cairo, was a center of Islamic learning and religious authority as well as a hub for Indian Ocean trade goods. Sharing in Cairo's prosperity was the African highland state of Ethiopia, a Christian kingdom with scattered contacts with European rulers. On the east coast of Africa, Swahili-speaking city-states engaged in the Indian Ocean trade, exchanging ivory, rhinoceros horn, tortoise shells, and slaves for textiles, spices, cowrie shells, porcelain, and other goods. Peopled by confident and urbane merchants, cities like Kilwa, Malindi, Mogadishu, and Mombasa were known for their prosperity and culture.

In the fifteenth century most of the gold that reached Europe came from the western part of the Sudan region in West Africa and from the Akan (AH-kahn) peoples living near present-day Ghana. Transported across the Sahara by Arab and African traders on camels, the gold was sold in the ports of North Africa. Other trading routes led to the Egyptian cities of Alexandria and Cairo, where the Venetians held commercial privileges.

Inland nations that sat astride the north-south caravan routes grew wealthy from this trade. In the mid-thirteenth century the kingdom of Mali emerged as an important player on the overland trade route, gaining prestige from its ruler Mansa Musa's fabulous pilgrimage to Mecca in 1324/25. Mansa Musa reportedly came to the throne after the previous king failed to return from a naval expedition he led to explore the Atlantic Ocean. A document by a contemporary scholar, al-Umari, quoted Mansa Musa's description of his predecessor as a man who "did not believe that the ocean was impossible to cross. He wished to reach the other side and was passionately interested in doing so."[3] After only one ship returned from an earlier expedition, the king set out himself at the head of a fleet of two thousand vessels, a voyage from which no one returned. Corroboration of these early expeditions is lacking, but this report underlines the wealth and ambition of Mali in this period. In later centuries the diversion of gold away from the trans-Sahara routes would weaken the inland states of Africa politically and economically.

Gold was one important object of trade; slaves were another. Slavery was practiced in Africa, as it was virtually everywhere else in the world, long before the arrival of Europeans. Arab and African merchants took West African slaves to the Mediterranean to be sold in European, Egyptian, and Middle Eastern markets and also brought eastern Europeans—a major element of European slavery—to West Africa as slaves. In addition, Indian and Arab merchants traded slaves in the coastal regions of East Africa.

Legends about Africa played an important role in Europeans' imagination of the outside world. They long cherished the belief in a powerful Christian nation in Africa ruled by a mythical king, Prester John, who was believed to be a descendant of one of the three kings who visited Jesus after his birth.

The Ottoman and Persian Empires

The Middle East served as an intermediary for trade between Asia, Africa, and Europe and was also an important supplier of goods for foreign exchange, especially silk and cotton. Two great rival Muslim empires, the Persian Safavids (sah-FAH-vidz) and the Turkish Ottomans, dominated the region. Persian merchants could be found in trading communities as far away as the Indian Ocean. Persia was also a major producer and exporter of silk.

The Persians' Shi'ite Muslim faith clashed with the Ottomans' adherence to Sunnism. Economically, the two competed for control over western trade routes to the East. Under Sultan Mohammed II (r. 1451–1481), the Ottomans captured Europe's largest city, Constantinople, in May 1453. Renamed Istanbul, the city became the capital of the Ottoman Empire. By the mid-sixteenth century the Ottomans controlled the sea trade in the eastern Mediterranean, Syria, Palestine, Egypt, and the rest of North Africa, and their power extended into Europe as far west as Vienna.

Ottoman expansion frightened Europeans. The Ottoman armies seemed invincible and the empire's desire for expansion limitless. In France in the sixteenth century, only forty books were published on the American discoveries compared to eighty on Turkey and the Turks.[4] The strength of the Ottomans helps explain some of the missionary fervor Christians brought to new territories. It also raised economic concerns. With trade routes to the East dominated by the Ottomans, Europeans wished to find new trade routes free of Ottoman control.

Genoese and Venetian Middlemen

Compared to the riches and vibrancy of the East, Europe constituted a minor outpost of the world trading system. European craftsmen produced few products to rival the fine wares and coveted spices of Asia. In the late Middle Ages, the Italian city-states of Venice and Genoa controlled the European luxury trade with the East.

In 1304 Venice established formal relations with the sultan of Mamluk Egypt, opening operations in Cairo, a gateway to Asian trade. Venetian merchants specialized in goods like spices, silks, and carpets, which they obtained from middlemen in the eastern Mediterranean and Asia Minor. A little went a long way. Venetians purchased no more than five hundred tons of spices a year around 1400, with a profit of about 40 percent. The most important spice was pepper, grown in India and Indonesia, which constituted 60 percent of the spices they purchased in 1400.[5]

The Venetians exchanged Eastern luxury goods for European products they could trade abroad, including Spanish and English wool, German metal goods, Flemish textiles, and silk cloth made in their own manufactures with imported raw materials. Eastern demand for such items, however, was low, leading Venetians to fund their purchases through shipping and trade in firearms and slaves. At least half of what they traded with the East took the form of precious metal, much of it acquired in

Egypt and North Africa. When the Portuguese arrived in Asia in the late fifteenth century, they found Venetian coins everywhere.

Venice's ancient rival was Genoa. In the wake of the Crusades, Genoa dominated the northern route to Asia through the Black Sea. Expansion in the thirteenth and fourteenth centuries took the Genoese as far as Persia and the Far East. In 1291 they sponsored an expedition into the Atlantic in search of India. The ships were lost, and their exact destination and motivations remain unknown. This voyage reveals the long roots of Genoese interest in Atlantic exploration.

In the fifteenth century, with Venice claiming victory in the spice trade, the Genoese shifted focus from trade to finance and from the Black Sea to the western Mediterranean. Located on the northwestern coast of Italy, Genoa had always been active in the western Mediterranean, trading with North African ports, southern France, Spain, and even England and Flanders through the Strait of Gibraltar. When Spanish and Portuguese voyages began to explore the western Atlantic, Genoese merchants, navigators, and financiers provided their skills and capital to the Iberian monarchs. The Genoese, for example, ran many of the sugar plantations established on the Atlantic islands colonized by the Portuguese. Genoese merchants would eventually help finance Spanish colonization of the New World.

A major element of Italian trade was slavery. Merchants purchased slaves, many of whom were fellow Christians, in the Balkans. The men were sold to Egypt for the sultan's army or sent to work as agricultural laborers in the Mediterranean. Young girls, who constituted the majority of the trade, were sold in western Mediterranean ports as servants or concubines. After the loss of the Black Sea—and thus the source of slaves—to the Ottomans, the Genoese sought new supplies of slaves in the West, taking the Guanches (indigenous peoples from the Canary Islands), Muslim prisoners, Jewish refugees from Spain, and by the early 1500s both black and Berber Africans. With the growth of Spanish colonies in the New World, Genoese and Venetian merchants would become important players in the Atlantic slave trade.

Italian experience in colonial administration, slaving, and international trade served as a model for the Iberian states as they pushed European expansion to new heights. Mariners, merchants, and financiers from Venice and Genoa—most notably Christopher Columbus—played a crucial role in bringing the fruits of this experience to the Iberian Peninsula and to the New World.

The European Voyages of Discovery

FOCUS QUESTION
How and why did Europeans undertake ambitious voyages of expansion?

As we have seen, Europe was by no means isolated before the voyages of exploration and its "discovery" of the New World. But because they did not produce many products desired by Eastern elites, Europeans played only a small role in the Indian Ocean trading world. As Europe recovered from the Black Death, new European players entered the scene with novel technology, eager to spread Christianity and to undo Italian and Ottoman domination of trade with the East. A century after the plague, Iberian explorers began the overseas voyages that helped create the modern world, with staggering consequences for their own continent and the rest of the planet.

Causes of European Expansion

European expansion had multiple causes. The first was economic. By the middle of the fifteenth century, Europe was experiencing a revival of population and economic activity after the lows of the Black Death. This revival created demand for luxuries, especially spices, from the East. The fall of Constantinople and subsequent Ottoman control of trade routes created obstacles to fulfilling these demands. Europeans needed to find new sources of precious metal to trade with the Ottomans or trade routes that bypassed the Ottomans.

Why were spices so desirable? Introduced into western Europe by the Crusaders in the twelfth century, pepper, nutmeg, ginger, mace, cinnamon, and cloves added flavor and variety to the monotonous European diet. Not only did spices serve as flavorings for food, but they were also used in anointing oil and as incense for religious rituals, and as perfumes, medicines, and dyes in daily life. Apart from their utility, the expense and exotic origins of spices meant that they were a high-status good, which European elites could use to demonstrate their social status.

Religious fervor and the crusading spirit were another important catalyst for expansion. Just seven months separated Isabella and Ferdinand's conquest of the emirate of Granada, the last remaining Muslim state on the Iberian Peninsula, and Columbus's departure across the Atlantic. Overseas exploration thus transferred the militarist religious fervor of the reconquista (reconquest) to new non-Christian territories. As they conquered indigenous empires, Iberians brought the attitudes and administrative practices developed during the reconquista to the Americas. Conquistadors fully expected to be rewarded with land, titles, and power over conquered peoples, just as the leaders of the reconquista had been.

Like other men of the Renaissance era, explorers sought to win glory for their amazing exploits and demonstrated a genuine interest in learning more about unknown waters. The European discoveries thus constituted one manifestation of Renaissance curiosity about the physical universe. The detailed journals many voyagers kept attest to their wonder and fascination with the new peoples and places they visited.

Individual explorers often manifested all of these desires at once. Christopher Columbus, a devout Christian, aimed to discover new territories where Christianity could be spread while seeking a direct trade route to Asia. The motives of the Portuguese explorer Bartholomew Diaz were, in his own words, "to serve God and His Majesty, to give light to those who were in darkness and to grow rich as all men desire to do." When the Portuguese explorer Vasco da Gama reached the port of Calicut, India, in 1498 and a native asked what he wanted, he replied, "Christians and spices."[6]

The bluntest of the Spanish **conquistadors** (kohn-KEES-tuh-dorz), Hernán Cortés, announced as he prepared to conquer Mexico, "I have come to win gold, not to plow the fields like a peasant."[7] Eagerness for exploration was heightened by a lack of opportunity at home. After the reconquista, young men of the Spanish upper classes found their economic and political opportunities greatly limited. The ambitious turned to the sea to seek their fortunes.

Ordinary sailors were ill paid, and life at sea meant danger, overcrowding, and hunger. For months at a time, 100 to 120 people lived and worked in a space of 1,600 to 2,000 square feet. A lucky sailor would find enough space on deck to unroll his sleeping mat. Horses, cows, pigs, chickens, rats, and lice accompanied sailors on the voyages. As one scholar concluded, "traveling on a ship must have been one of the most uncomfortable and oppressive experiences in the world."[8]

Men chose to join these miserable crews to escape poverty at home, to continue a family trade, or to find better lives as illegal immigrants in the colonies. Many orphans and poor boys were placed on board as apprentices and had little say in the

conquistador Spanish for "conqueror"; Spanish soldier-explorers, such as Hernán Cortés and Francisco Pizarro, who sought to conquer the New World for the Spanish crown.

decision. Women also paid a price for the voyages of exploration. Left alone for months or years at a time, and frequently widowed, sailors' wives struggled to feed their families. The widow of a sailor lost on a voyage in 1519 had to wait almost thirty years to collect her husband's salary from the Spanish crown.[9]

The people who stayed at home had a powerful impact on the process. Merchants provided the capital for many early voyages and had a strong say in their course. To gain authorization and financial support for their expeditions, they sought official sponsorship from the Crown. Competition among European monarchs for the prestige and profit of overseas exploration was a crucial factor in encouraging the steady stream of expeditions that began in the late fifteenth century.

The small number of Europeans who could read provided a rapt audience for tales of fantastic places and unknown peoples. Cosmography, natural history, and geography aroused enormous interest among educated people in the fifteenth and sixteenth centuries. One of the most popular books of the time was the fourteenth-century text *The Travels of Sir John Mandeville*, which purported to be a firsthand account of the author's travels in the Middle East, India, and China. Although we now know the stories were fictional, these fantastic tales of cannibals, one-eyed giants, men with the heads of dogs, and other marvels convinced audiences through their vividly and persuasively described details. Christopher Columbus took a copy of Mandeville and the equally popular and more reliable *The Travels of Marco Polo* on his voyage in 1492.

Technology and the Rise of Exploration

The Iberian powers actively sought technological improvements in shipbuilding, weaponry, and navigation in order to undertake successful voyages of exploration and trade. Medieval European seagoing vessels consisted of single-masted sailing ships or narrow, open galleys propelled by oars, which were common in Mediterranean trade. Though adequate for short journeys that hugged the shoreline, such vessels were incapable of long-distance journeys or high-volume trade. To sail to the Indian Ocean or cross the Atlantic, larger and sturdier craft were necessary. In the course of the fifteenth century, the Portuguese developed the **caravel**, a three-mast sailing ship. Its multiple sails and sternpost rudder made the caravel a more maneuverable vessel that required fewer crewmen to operate. It could carry more cargo than a galley, which meant it could sail farther without stopping for supplies and return with a larger cache of profitable goods. When fitted with cannon, it could dominate larger vessels and bombard port cities.[10]

caravel A small, maneuverable, three-mast sailing ship developed by the Portuguese in the fifteenth century that gave the Portuguese a distinct advantage in exploration and trade.

Great strides in cartography and navigational aids were also made during this period. Around 1410 Arab scholars reintroduced Europeans to **Ptolemy's Geography**. Written in the second century C.E. by a Hellenized Egyptian, the work synthesized the geographical knowledge of the classical world. Ptolemy's work provided significant improvements over medieval cartography, clearly depicting the world as round and introducing the idea of latitude and longitude to plot position accurately. It also contained crucial errors. Unaware of the Americas, Ptolemy showed the world as much smaller than it is, so that Asia appeared not very distant from Europe to the west. Both the assets and the flaws of Ptolemy's work shaped the geographical knowledge that explorers like Christopher Columbus brought to their voyages.

Ptolemy's *Geography* A second-century-C.E. work that synthesized the classical knowledge of geography and introduced the concepts of longitude and latitude. Reintroduced to Europeans about 1410 by Arab scholars, its ideas allowed cartographers to create more accurate maps.

Originating in China, the compass was brought to the West in the late Middle Ages; by using the compass to determine their direction and estimating their speed of travel over a set length of time, mariners could determine the course of a ship's voyage, a system of navigation known as "dead reckoning." In the late fifteenth century Portuguese scholars devised a new technique of "celestial reckoning," which involved using the astrolabe, an instrument invented by the ancient Greeks to determine the position of the stars and other celestial bodies. Commissioned by Portuguese king John II, a group of astronomers in the 1480s showed that mariners could determine their latitude at sea by using a specially designed astrolabe to determine the altitude of the polestar or the sun, and consulting tables of these bodies' movements. This was a crucial step forward in maritime navigational techniques.

Brass Astrolabe   Between 1500 and 1635 over nine hundred ships sailed from Portugal to ports on the Indian Ocean, in annual fleets composed of five to ten ships. Portuguese sailors used astrolabes, such as the one shown here, to accurately plot their position. (British Museum, London, UK/Werner Forman/Universal Images Group/Getty Images)

Much of the new technology that Europeans used on their voyages was borrowed from the East. Gunpowder, the compass, and the sternpost rudder were Chinese inventions. The triangular lateen sail, which allowed caravels to tack against the wind, was a product of the Indian Ocean trade world. Advances in navigational techniques and cartography, including the maritime astrolabe, drew on a rich Iberian tradition of Jewish and Arab mathematics and astronomy. Sometimes assistance to Europeans came from humans rather than instruments. The famed explorer Vasco da Gama employed a local Indian pilot to guide his expedition from the East African coast to India. In exploring new territories, European sailors thus called on techniques and knowledge developed over centuries in China, the Muslim world, and the Indian Ocean.

The Portuguese Overseas Empire

For centuries Portugal was a small, poor nation on the margins of European life whose principal activities were fishing and subsistence farming. It would have been hard for a European to predict Portugal's phenomenal success overseas after 1450. Yet Portugal had a long history of seafaring and navigation. Blocked from access to western Europe by Spain, the Portuguese turned to the Atlantic and North Africa, whose waters they knew better than other Europeans did. Nature favored the Portuguese: winds blowing along their coast offered passage to Africa, its Atlantic islands, and, ultimately, Brazil. Once they had mastered the secret to sailing against the wind to return to Europe (by sailing further west to catch winds from the southwest), they were ideally poised to lead Atlantic exploration.

In the early phases of Portuguese exploration, Prince Henry (1394–1460), a younger son of the king, played a leading role. A nineteenth-century scholar dubbed Henry "the Navigator" because of his support for the study of geography and navigation and for the annual expeditions he sponsored down the western coast of Africa. Although he never personally participated in voyages of exploration, Henry's involvement ensured that Portugal did not abandon the effort despite early disappointments.

MAP 14.2 Overseas Exploration and Conquest in the Fifteenth and Sixteenth Centuries   The voyages of discovery marked a dramatic new phase in the centuries-old migrations of European peoples. This world map depicts the voyages of the most significant European explorers of this period, while the inset map shows Spanish and Portuguese colonies of the eighteenth century.

The objectives of Portuguese exploration included military glory; the conversion of Muslims; and a quest to find gold, slaves, and an overseas route to the spice markets of India. Portugal's conquest of Ceuta, an Arab city in northern Morocco, in 1415 marked the beginning of European overseas expansion. In the 1420s, under Henry's direction, the Portuguese began to settle the Atlantic islands of Madeira (ca. 1420) and the Azores (1427). In 1443 they founded their first African commercial settlement at Arguin in North Africa. By the time of Henry's death in 1460, his support for exploration was vindicated—from the Portuguese point of view—by thriving sugar plantations on the Atlantic islands, the first arrival of enslaved Africans in Portugal (see page 451), and new access to African gold.

The Portuguese next established fortified trading posts, called factories, on the gold-rich Guinea coast and penetrated into the African continent all the way to Timbuktu (Map 14.2). By 1500 Portugal controlled the flow of African gold to Europe. In contrast to the Spanish conquest of the Americas (see pages 442–444), the Portuguese did not establish large settlements in West Africa or seek to control the political or cultural lives of those with whom they traded. Instead, they sought easier and faster profits by inserting themselves into pre-existing trading systems. For the first century of their relations, African rulers were equal partners with the Portuguese, benefiting from their experienced armies and European vulnerability to tropical diseases.

The Portuguese then pushed farther south down the west coast of Africa. In 1487 Bartholomew Diaz rounded the Cape of Good Hope at the southern tip of Africa, but storms and a threatened mutiny forced him to turn back. A decade later Vasco da Gama succeeded in rounding the Cape while commanding a fleet of four ships in search of a sea route to India. With the help of an Indian guide, da Gama reached the port of Calicut in India. He returned to Lisbon loaded with spices and samples of Indian cloth, having proved the possibility of lucrative trade with the East via the Cape route. Thereafter, a Portuguese convoy set out for passage around the Cape every March.

Lisbon became the entrance port for Asian goods into Europe, but this was not accomplished without a fight. Muslim-controlled port city-states had long controlled the rich trade of the Indian Ocean, and they did not surrender their dominance willingly. From 1500 to 1515 the Portuguese used a combination of bombardment and diplomatic treaties to establish trading forts at Goa, Malacca, Calicut, and Hormuz, thereby laying the foundation for a Portuguese trading empire in the sixteenth and seventeenth centuries. The acquisition of port cities and their trade routes brought riches to Portugal, but, as in Africa, the Portuguese had limited impact on the lives and religious faith of peoples beyond their coastal holdings. Moreover, despite their advances in shipbuilding, weaponry, and navigation, the Portuguese were never able to enforce a total monopoly on trading in the Indian Ocean.

Inspired by the Portuguese, the Spanish had also begun the quest for empire. Theirs was to be a second, entirely different, mode of colonization, leading to the conquest of existing empires, large-scale settlement, and the assimilation of a subjugated indigenous population.

Spain's Voyages to the Americas

We now know that Christopher Columbus was not the first to explore the Atlantic. Ninth-century Vikings established short-lived settlements in Newfoundland, and it is probable that others made the voyage, either on purpose or accidentally, carried by westward currents off the coast of Africa. In the late fifteenth century the achievements of Portugal's decades of exploration made the moment right for Christopher Columbus's attempt to find a westward route across the Atlantic to Asia.

A native of the port city of Genoa, Christopher Columbus was early on drawn to the life of the sea. He became an experienced seaman and navigator and worked as a mapmaker in Lisbon. He was familiar with *portolans*—written descriptions of the courses along which ships sailed—and the use of the compass for dead reckoning. (He carried an astrolabe on his first voyage, but did not use it for navigation.) As he asserted in his journal: "I have spent twenty-three years at sea and have not left it for any length of time worth mentioning, and I have seen every thing from east to west [meaning he had been to England] and I have been to Guinea [North and West Africa]."[11]

Columbus was also a deeply religious man. He had witnessed the Spanish conquest of Granada and shared fully in the religious and nationalistic fervor surrounding that event. Like the Spanish rulers and most Europeans of his age, Columbus understood Christianity as a missionary religion that should be carried to all places of the earth. He viewed himself as a divine agent: "God made me the messenger of the new heaven and the new earth of which he spoke in the Apocalypse of St. John . . . and he showed me the post where to find it."[12]

Rejected for funding by the Portuguese in 1483 and by Ferdinand and Isabella in 1486, Columbus's project to find a westward passage to the Indies finally won the backing of the Spanish monarchy in 1492. Buoyed by the success of the reconquista and eager to earn profits from trade, the Spanish crown named Columbus viceroy over any territory he might discover and promised him one-tenth of the material rewards of the journey.

Columbus and his small fleet left Spain on August 3, 1492. Inspired by the stories of Mandeville and Marco Polo, Columbus dreamed of reaching the court of the Mongol emperor, the Great Khan (not realizing that the Ming Dynasty had overthrown the Mongols in 1368). Based on Ptolemy's *Geography* and other texts, he expected to pass the islands of Japan and then land on the east coast of China.

After a brief stop in the Canary Islands, he landed in the Bahamas, which he christened San Salvador, on October 12, 1492. In a letter he wrote to Ferdinand and Isabella on his return to Spain, Columbus described the natives as handsome, peaceful, and primitive people whose body painting reminded him of that of the Canary Islands natives. Believing he was somewhere off the east coast of Japan, in what he considered the Indies, he called them "Indians," a name later applied to all inhabitants of the Americas. Columbus concluded that they would make good slaves and could easily be converted to Christianity. (See "Evaluating the Evidence 14.1: Columbus Describes His First Voyage," page 440.)

Columbus's First Voyage to the New World, 1492–1493

Scholars have identified the inhabitants of the islands as the Taino people, speakers of the Arawak language, who inhabited Hispaniola (modern-day Haiti and Dominican Republic) and other islands in the Caribbean. From San Salvador, Columbus sailed southwest, landing on Cuba on October 28. Deciding that he must be on the mainland near the coastal city of Quinsay (now Hangzhou), he sent a small embassy inland with letters from Ferdinand and Isabella and instructions to locate the grand city. Although they found no large settlement or any evidence of a great kingdom, the sight of Taino people wearing gold ornaments on Hispaniola suggested that gold was available in the region. In January, confident that its source would soon be found, he headed back to Spain to report on his discovery. News of his voyage spread rapidly across Europe.[13]

On his second voyage, Columbus forcibly subjugated the island of Hispaniola and enslaved its indigenous peoples. On this and subsequent voyages, Columbus brought with him settlers for the new Spanish territories, along with agricultural seed and livestock. Columbus himself, however, had limited skills in governing. Revolt soon broke out against him and his brother on Hispaniola. A royal expedition sent to investigate returned the brothers to Spain in chains, and a royal governor assumed control of the colony.

Columbus was very much a man of his times. To the end of his life in 1506, he believed that he had found small islands off the coast of Asia. He never realized the scope of his achievement: he had found a vast continent unknown to Europeans, except for a fleeting Viking presence centuries earlier. He could not know that the scale of his discoveries would revolutionize world power and set in motion a new era of trade, empire, and human migration.

Spain "Discovers" the Pacific

The Florentine navigator Amerigo Vespucci (veh-SPOO-chee) (1454–1512) realized what Columbus had not. Writing about his discoveries on the coast of modern-day Venezuela, Vespucci stated: "Those new regions which we found and explored with the fleet . . . we may rightly call a New World." This letter, titled *Mundus Novus* (The New World), was the first document to describe America as a continent separate from Asia. In recognition of Amerigo's bold claim, the continent was named for him.

To settle competing claims to the Atlantic discoveries, Spain and Portugal turned to Pope Alexander VI. The resulting **Treaty of Tordesillas** (tor-duh-SEE-yuhs) in 1494 gave Spain everything to the west of an imaginary line drawn down the Atlantic, and Portugal everything to the east. This arbitrary division worked in Portugal's favor when in 1500 an expedition led by Pedro Álvares Cabral, en route to India, landed on the coast of Brazil, which Cabral claimed as Portuguese territory.

The search for profits determined the direction of Spanish exploration. Because its profits from Hispaniola and other Caribbean islands were insignificant compared to the enormous riches that the Portuguese were reaping in Asia, Spain renewed the search for a western passage to Asia. In 1519 Charles V of Spain sent the Portuguese mariner Ferdinand Magellan (1480–1521) to find a sea route to the spices of the Moluccas off the southeast coast of Asia. Magellan sailed southwest across the Atlantic to Brazil, and after a long search along the coast he located the treacherous straits that now bear his name (see Map 14.2). The new ocean he sailed into after a rough passage through the straits seemed so calm that Magellan dubbed it the Pacific, from the Latin word for peaceful. His fleet sailed north up the west coast of South America and then headed west into the immense expanse of the Pacific toward the Malay Archipelago. (Some of these islands were conquered later, in the 1560s, and named the "Philippines" for Philip II of Spain.)

Magellan's first impressions of the Pacific were terribly mistaken. Terrible storms, disease, starvation, and violence devastated the expedition. Magellan had set out with a fleet of five ships and around 270 men. Sailors on two of the ships attempted mutiny on the South American coast; one ship was lost, and another ship deserted and returned to Spain before even traversing the straits. The trip across the Pacific took ninety-eight days, and the men survived on rats and sawdust. Magellan himself died in a skirmish in the Malay Archipelago. Only one ship, with eighteen men aboard, returned to Spain from the east by way of the Indian Ocean, the Cape of Good Hope, and the Atlantic in 1522. The voyage—the first to circumnavigate the globe—had taken close to three years.

Despite the losses, this voyage revolutionized Europeans' understanding of the world by demonstrating the vastness of the Pacific. The earth was clearly much larger than Ptolemy's map had shown. Although the voyage made a small profit in spices, it also demonstrated that the westward passage to the Indies was too long and dangerous for commercial purposes. Spain soon abandoned the attempt to oust Portugal from the Eastern spice trade and concentrated on exploiting her New World territories.

Early Exploration by Northern European Powers

Spain's northern European rivals also set sail across the Atlantic during the early days of exploration in search of a northwest passage to the Indies. In 1497 John Cabot, a Genoese merchant living in London, undertook a voyage to Brazil, but

Treaty of Tordesillas The 1494 agreement giving Spain everything to the west of an imaginary line drawn down the Atlantic and giving Portugal everything to the east.

Columbus Describes His First Voyage

On his return voyage to Spain in February 1493, Christopher Columbus composed a letter intended for wide circulation and had copies of it sent ahead to Queen Isabella and King Ferdinand. Because the letter sums up Columbus's understanding of his achievements, it is considered the most important document of his first voyage. Remember that his knowledge of Asia rested heavily on Marco Polo's Travels, *published around 1298.*

Since I know that you will be pleased at the great success with which the Lord has crowned my voyage, I write to inform you how in thirty-three days I crossed from the Canary Islands to the Indies, with the fleet which our most illustrious sovereigns gave me. I found very many islands with large populations and took possession of them all for their Highnesses; this I did by proclamation and unfurled the royal standard. No opposition was offered.

I named the first island that I found "San Salvador," in honour of our Lord and Saviour who has granted me this miracle. . . . When I reached Cuba, I followed its north coast westwards, and found it so extensive that I thought this must be the mainland, the province of Cathay. . . .*
From there I saw another island eighteen leagues eastwards which I then named "Hispaniola." . . .†

Hispaniola is a wonder. The mountains and hills, the plains and meadow lands are both fertile and beautiful. They are most suitable for planting crops and for raising cattle of all kinds, and there are good sites for building towns and villages. The harbours are incredibly fine and there are many great rivers with broad channels and the majority contain gold.‡ The trees, fruits and plants are very different from those of Cuba. In Hispaniola there are many spices and large mines of gold and other metals. . . .§

The inhabitants of this island, and all the rest that I discovered or heard of, go naked, as their mothers bore them, men and women alike. A few of the women, however, cover a single place with a leaf of a plant or piece of cotton which they weave for the purpose. They have no iron or steel or arms and are not capable of using them, not because they are not strong and well built but because they are amazingly timid. All the weapons they have are canes cut at seeding time, at the end of which they fix a sharpened stick, but they have not the courage to make use of these, for very often when I have sent two or three men to a village to have conversation with them a great number of them have come out. But as soon as they saw my men all fled immediately, a father not even waiting for his son. And this is not because we have harmed any of them; on the contrary, wherever I have gone and been able to have conversation with them, I have given them some of the various things I had, a cloth and other articles, and received nothing in exchange. But they have still remained incurably timid.

---

* Cathay is the old name for China. In the logbook and later in this letter, Columbus accepts the native story that Cuba is an island that can be circumnavigated in something more than twenty-one days, yet he insists here and during the second voyage that it is part of the Asiatic mainland.

† Hispaniola is the second-largest island of the West Indies. Haiti occupies the western third of the island, the Dominican Republic the rest.

‡ This did not prove to be true.
§ These statements are also inaccurate.

---

landed on Newfoundland instead. The next year he returned and reconnoitered the New England coast. These forays proved futile, and the English established no permanent colonies in the territories they explored. News of the riches of Mexico and Peru later inspired the English to renew their efforts, this time in the extreme north. Between 1576 and 1578 Martin Frobisher made three voyages in and around the Canadian bay that now bears his name. Frobisher hopefully brought a quantity of ore back to England with him, but it proved to be worthless.

Early French exploration of the Atlantic was equally frustrating. Between 1534 and 1541 Frenchman Jacques Cartier made several voyages and explored the St. Lawrence River of Canada, searching for a passage to the wealth of Asia. His

True, when they have been reassured and lost their fear, they are so ingenuous and so liberal with all their possessions that no one who has not seen them would believe it. If one asks for anything they have they never say no. On the contrary, they offer a share to anyone with demonstrations of heartfelt affection, and they are immediately content with any small thing, valuable or valueless, that is given them. I forbade the men to give them bits of broken crockery, fragments of glass or tags of laces, though if they could get them they fancied them the finest jewels in the world. . . .

I hoped to win them to the love and service of their Highnesses and of the whole Spanish nation and to persuade them to collect and give us of the things which they possessed in abundance and which we needed. They have no religion and are not idolaters; but all believe that power and goodness dwell in the sky and they are firmly convinced that I have come from the sky with these ships and people. In this belief they gave me a good reception everywhere, once they had overcome their fear; and this is not because they are stupid—far from it, they are men of great intelligence, for they navigate all those seas, and give a marvellously good account of every thing—but because they have never before seen men clothed or ships like these. . . .

In all these islands the men are seemingly content with one woman, but their chief or king is allowed more than twenty. The women appear to work more than the men and I have not been able to find out if they have private property. As far as I could see whatever a man had was shared among all the rest and this particularly applies to food. . . . In another island, which I am told is larger than Hispaniola, the people have no hair. Here there is a vast quantity of gold, and from here and the other islands I bring Indians as evidence.

In conclusion, to speak only of the results of this very hasty voyage, their Highnesses can see that I will give them as much gold as they require, if they will render me some very slight assistance; also I will give them all the spices and cotton they want. . . . I will also bring them as much aloes as they ask and as many slaves, who will be taken from the idolaters. I believe also that I have found rhubarb and cinnamon and there will be countless other things in addition. . . .

So all Christendom will be delighted that our Redeemer has given victory to our most illustrious King and Queen and their renowned kingdoms, in this great matter. They should hold great celebrations and render solemn thanks to the Holy Trinity with many solemn prayers, for the great triumph which they will have, by the conversion of so many peoples to our holy faith and for the temporal benefits which will follow, for not only Spain, but all Christendom will receive encouragement and profit.

This is a brief account of the facts. Written in the caravel off the Canary Islands.**

15 February 1493

At your orders   THE ADMIRAL

EVALUATE THE EVIDENCE

1. How did Columbus explain the success of his voyage?
2. What was Columbus's view of the Native Americans he met?
3. In what ways does he exaggerate about the Caribbean islands' possessing gold, cotton, and spices?

Source: Approximately 1,109 words from *The Four Voyages of Christopher Columbus*, pp. 115–123, ed. and trans. J. M. Cohen (Penguin Classics, 1969). Reproduced by permission of Penguin Books Ltd.

**Actually, Columbus was off Santa Maria in the Azores.

exploration of the St. Lawrence was halted at the great rapids west of the present-day island of Montreal; he named the rapids "La Chine" in the optimistic belief that China lay just beyond. When this hope proved vain, the French turned to a new source of profit within Canada itself: trade in beavers and other furs. As had the Portuguese in Asia, French traders bartered with local peoples, who maintained control over their trade goods. French fishermen also competed with Spanish and English ships for the teeming schools of cod they found in the Atlantic waters around Newfoundland. Fishing vessels salted the catch on board and brought it back to Europe, where a thriving market for fish was created by the Catholic prohibition on eating meat on Fridays and during Lent.

Conquest and Settlement

FOCUS QUESTION
How did European powers acquire colonies in the Americas, and how were they governed?

Before Columbus's arrival, the Americas were inhabited by thousands of groups of indigenous peoples with different languages and cultures. These groups ranged from hunter-gatherer tribes organized into tribal confederations to settled agriculturalists to large-scale empires containing bustling cities and towns. The best estimate is that the peoples of the Americas numbered between 35 and 50 million in 1492. Their lives were radically transformed by the arrival of Europeans.

The growing European presence in the New World transformed its land and its peoples forever. While Iberian powers conquered enormous territories in Central and South America, incorporating pre-existing peoples and empires, the northern European powers came later to colonization and established scattered settlements hugging the North American coastline.

Spanish Conquest of the Aztec and Inca Empires

The first two decades after Columbus's arrival in the New World saw Spanish settlement of Hispaniola, Cuba, Puerto Rico, and other Caribbean islands. Based on rumors of a wealthy mainland civilization, the Spanish governor in Cuba sponsored expeditions to the Yucatán coast of the Gulf of Mexico, including one in 1519 under the command of the conquistador Hernán Cortés (1485–1547). Alarmed by Cortés's ambition, the governor decided to withdraw his support, but Cortés quickly set sail before being removed from command. Accompanied by 11 ships, 450 men, 16 horses, and 10 cannon, Cortés landed on the Mexican coast on April 21, 1519. His camp soon received visits by delegations of unarmed Aztec leaders bearing gifts and news of their great emperor.

Aztec Empire A large and complex Native American civilization in modern Mexico and Central America that possessed advanced mathematical, astronomical, and engineering technology.

The **Aztec Empire**, an alliance between the Mexica people and their conquered allies, had risen rapidly in size and power in the early fifteenth century. At the time of the Spanish arrival, the empire was ruled by Moctezuma II (r. 1502–1520), from his capital at Tenochtitlan (tay-nawch-teet-LAHN), now Mexico City. The Aztecs were a sophisticated civilization with an advanced understanding of mathematics, astronomy, and engineering; and with oral poetry and historical traditions. As in European nations at the time, a hereditary nobility dominated the army, the priesthood, and the state bureaucracy, living from the proceeds of the agricultural labor of the common people.

Within weeks of his arrival, Cortés acquired translators who provided vital information on the empire and its weaknesses. To legitimize his authority, Cortés founded the settlement of Veracruz and had himself named its military commander. He then burned his ships to prevent any disloyal or frightened followers from returning to Cuba.

The vulnerability Cortés discovered was local resentment against the Aztec Empire. The Aztec state practiced warfare against neighboring peoples to secure captives for religious sacrifices and laborers for agricultural and building projects. Once conquered, subject tribes paid continual tribute to the empire through their local chiefs. Realizing that he could exploit dissensions within the empire to his own advantage, Cortés forged an alliance with Tlaxcala (tlah-SKAH-lah) and other subject kingdoms. In October a combined Spanish-Tlaxcalan force occupied the city of Cholula, second largest in the empire, and massacred many thousand inhabitants. Strengthened by this display of ruthless power, Cortés made alliances with other native kingdoms. In November 1519, with a few hundred Spanish men and some six thousand indigenous warriors, Cortés marched on Tenochtitlan.

Invasion of Tenochtitlan, 1519–1521

The Mexica Capital of Tenochtitlan   This wood-cut map was published in 1524 along with Cortés's letters describing the conquest of the Mexica. Tenochtitlan occupied an island and was laid out in concentric circles. The administrative and religious buildings were at the heart of the city, which was surrounded by residential quarters. Cortés marveled at the city: "The city is as large as Seville or Cordoba. . . . The city has many squares where markets are held. . . . There is one square . . . where there are daily more than sixty thousand souls, buying and selling. In the service and manners of its people, their fashion of living was almost the same as in Spain, with just as much harmony and order." (Newberry Library, Chicago, Illinois, USA/Bridgeman Images)

Historians have long debated Moctezuma's response to the arrival of the Spanish. Unlike other native leaders, he refrained from attacking the Spaniards but instead welcomed Cortés and his men into Tenochtitlan. Moctezuma was apparently deeply impressed by Spanish victories and believed the Spanish were invincible. Sources written after the conquest claimed that the emperor believed Cortés was an embodiment of the god Quetzalcoatl, whose return was promised in Aztec myth.

While it is impossible to verify those claims, it is clear that Moctezuma's long hesitation proved disastrous. When Cortés—with incredible boldness—took Moctezuma hostage, the emperor's influence crumbled. During the ensuing attacks and counterattacks, Moctezuma was killed. The Spaniards and their allies escaped from the city, suffering heavy losses. Cortés quickly began gathering forces and making new alliances against the Aztecs. In May 1521 he conducted a second assault on Tenochtitlan, leading an army of approximately one thousand Spanish and seventy-five thousand native warriors.[14]

Spanish victory in late summer 1521 was hard-won and greatly aided by the effects of smallpox, which had devastated the besieged population of the city. After establishing a new capital in the ruins of Tenochtitlan, Cortés and other conquistadors began the systematic conquest of Mexico.

More surprising than the defeat of the Aztecs was the fall of the remote **Inca Empire**. Perched more than 9,800 feet above sea level, the Incas were isolated from North American indigenous cultures and knew nothing of the Aztec Empire or its collapse. Like the Mexica, the Incas had created a polity that rivaled that of the Europeans in population and complexity. The Incas' strength lay largely in their bureaucratic efficiency. They divided their empire into four major regions containing eighty provinces and twice as many districts. Officials at each level used an extensive network of roads to transmit information and orders back and forth through the empire. While the Aztecs used a system of glyphs for writing, the Incas had devised a complex system of colored and knotted cords, called *khipus*, for administrative bookkeeping. The empire also benefited from the use of llamas as pack animals (by contrast, no beasts of burden existed in Mesoamerica).

By the time of the Spanish invasion, however, the Inca Empire had been weakened by a civil war over succession and an epidemic of disease, possibly smallpox,

Inca Empire   The vast and sophisticated Peruvian empire centered at the capital city of Cuzco that was at its peak from 1438 until 1532.

443

which may have spread through trade with groups in contact with Europeans. Francisco Pizarro (ca. 1475–1541), a conquistador of modest Spanish origins, landed on the northern coast of Peru on May 13, 1532, the very day the Inca leader Atahualpa (ah-tuh-WAHL-puh) won control of the empire after five years of fighting. As Pizarro advanced across the steep Andes toward Cuzco, the capital of the Inca Empire, Atahualpa was also heading there for his coronation.

Like Moctezuma in Mexico, Atahualpa was aware of the Spaniards' movements. He sent envoys to invite the Spanish to meet him in the provincial town of Cajamarca. His plan was to lure the Spanish into a trap, seize their horses and ablest men for his army, and execute the rest. With an army of some forty thousand men stationed nearby, Atahualpa felt he had little to fear. Instead, the Spaniards ambushed and captured him, collected an enormous ransom in gold, and then executed him in 1533 on trumped-up charges. The Spanish then marched on to Cuzco, profiting once again from internal conflicts to form alliances with local peoples. When Cuzco fell in 1533, the Spanish plundered immense riches in gold and silver.

How was it possible for several hundred Spanish conquistadors to defeat powerful empires commanding large armies, vast wealth, and millions of inhabitants? Historians seeking answers to this question have emphasized a combination of factors: the boldness and audacity of conquistadors like Cortés and Pizarro; the military superiority provided by Spanish firepower and horses; divisions within the Aztec and Inca Empires, which produced many native allies for the Spanish; and, of course, the devastating impact of contagious diseases among the indigenous population. Ironically, the well-organized, urban-based Aztec and Inca Empires were more vulnerable to wholesale takeover than more decentralized and fragmented groups like the Maya in the Yucatán peninsula, whose independence was not wholly crushed until the end of the seventeenth century.

Portuguese Brazil

Unlike Mesoamerica or the Andes, the territory of Brazil contained no urban empires, but instead roughly 2.5 million nomadic and settled people divided into small tribes and many different language groups. In 1500 the Portuguese crown named Pedro Álvares Cabral commander of a fleet headed for the spice trade of the Indies. En route the fleet sailed far to the west, accidentally landing on the coast of Brazil, which Cabral claimed for Portugal under the terms of the Treaty of Tordesillas (see page 439). The Portuguese soon undertook a profitable trade with local people in brazil-wood, a valued source of red dye.

In the 1520s Portuguese settlers brought sugarcane production to Brazil. They initially used enslaved indigenous laborers on sugar plantations, but the rapid decline in the indigenous population soon led to the use of forcibly transported Africans (see pages 451–454). In Brazil the Portuguese thus created a new form of colonization in the Americas: large plantations worked by enslaved people. This model would spread throughout the Caribbean along with sugar production in the seventeenth century.

Colonial Empires of England and France

For almost a century after the fall of the Aztec capital of Tenochtitlan, the Spanish and Portuguese dominated European overseas trade and colonization. In the early seventeenth century, however, northern European powers profited from Spanish weakness to challenge its monopoly over the seas. They eventually succeeded in creating multisited overseas empires, consisting of settler colonies in North America, plantations with slaves in the Caribbean, and scattered trading posts in West Africa and Asia. Competition among them was encouraged by mercantilist economic doctrine, which dictated that foreign trade was a zero-sum game in which one country's gains necessarily entailed another's loss (see Chapter 15).

Unlike the Iberian powers, whose royal governments financed exploration and directly ruled the colonies, England, France, and the Netherlands conducted the initial phase of colonization via chartered companies endowed with monopolies over settlement and trade in a given area. These corporate bodies were granted extensive powers over faraway colonies, including exclusive rights to conduct trade, wage war, raise taxes, and administer justice.

The first English colony was founded at Roanoke (in what is now North Carolina) in 1585. After a three-year loss of contact with England, the settlers were found to have disappeared; their fate remains a mystery. The colony of Virginia, founded at Jamestown in 1607, initially struggled to grow sufficient food and faced hostility from the Powhatan Confederacy. Eventually it thrived by producing tobacco for a growing European market. Indentured servants obtained free passage to the colony in exchange for several years of work and the promise of greater opportunity for economic and social advancement than in England. In the 1670s English colonists from the Caribbean island of Barbados settled Carolina, where conditions were suitable for large rice plantations. During the late seventeenth century enslaved Africans replaced indentured servants as laborers on tobacco and rice plantations, and a harsh racial divide was imposed.

For the first settlers on the coast of New England, the reasons for seeking a new life in the colonies were more religious than economic. Many of these colonists were radical Protestants escaping Anglican repression. The small and struggling outpost of Plymouth Colony (1620) was followed by Massachusetts Bay Colony (1630), which grew into a prosperous settlement. Religious disputes in Massachusetts led to the dispersion of settlers into the new communities of Providence, Connecticut, Rhode Island, and New Haven. Because New England lacked the conditions for plantation agriculture, slavery was always a minor element of life there.

Whereas the Spanish established wholesale dominance over Mexico and Peru and its indigenous inhabitants, English settlements hugged the Atlantic coastline and excluded indigenous people from their territories rather than incorporating them. In place of the unified rule exerted by the Spanish crown, England's colonization was haphazard and decentralized in nature, leading to greater autonomy and diversity among its colonies. As the English crown grew more interested in colonial expansion, efforts were made to acquire the territory between New England in the north and Virginia in the south. The goal was to unify English holdings and minimize French and Dutch competition on the Atlantic seaboard. The results of these efforts were the mid-Atlantic colonies: the Catholic settlement of Maryland (1632); New York, captured from the Dutch in 1664; and the Quaker colony of Pennsylvania (1681).

Whereas English settlements were largely agricultural, the French established trading factories in present-day Canada, much like those of the Portuguese in Asia and Africa. In 1608 Samuel de Champlain founded the first permanent French settlement at Quebec as a post for trading beaver pelts with local Algonquin and Huron peoples. The settlement of Ville-Marie, later named Montreal, followed in 1642.

Louis XIV's capable economic minister, Jean-Baptiste Colbert, established direct royal control over New France (Canada) and tried to enlarge its population by sending colonists. French immigration to New Canada was always minuscule compared with the stream of settlers who came to British North America; nevertheless, the French were energetic and industrious traders and explorers. Following the waterways of the St. Lawrence River, the Great Lakes, and the Mississippi River, they ventured into much of North America in the 1670s and 1680s. In 1673 the Jesuit Jacques Marquette and the merchant Louis Joliet sailed down the Mississippi and claimed possession of the land on both sides of the river as far south as present-day Arkansas. In 1682 Robert de La Salle traveled the Mississippi to the Gulf of Mexico, opening the way for French occupation of Louisiana.

In the first decades of the seventeenth century, English and French naval captains also defied Spain's hold over the Caribbean Sea (see Map 14.2). The English seized control of Bermuda (1612), Barbados (1627), and a succession of other islands. The French took Cayenne (1604), St. Christophe (1625), Martinique and Guadeloupe (1635), and, finally, Saint-Domingue (1697) on the western half of Spanish-occupied Hispaniola. These islands acquired new importance after 1640, when the Portuguese brought sugar plantations to Brazil. Sugar and slaves quickly followed in the West Indies (see pages 451–454), making the Caribbean plantations the most lucrative of all colonial possessions.

Northern European expansion also occurred in the Old World. In the seventeenth century France and England—along with Denmark and other northern European powers—established fortified trading posts in West Africa as bases for purchasing slaves and in India and the Indian Ocean as bases for purchasing spices and other luxury goods. Thus, by the end of the seventeenth century, a handful of European powers possessed overseas empires that truly spanned the globe.

Colonial Administration

While the earliest exploration and conquest were undertaken by private initiatives (authorized and sponsored by the state), the Spanish and Portuguese governments quickly assumed direct control of overseas territories. In 1503 the Spanish granted the port of Seville a monopoly over all traffic to the New World and established the House of Trade, or *Casa de la Contratación*, to oversee economic matters. In 1523 Spain added to this body the Royal and Supreme Council of the Indies, with authority over all colonial affairs, subject to approval by the king. Spanish territories themselves were divided initially into two **viceroyalties**, or administrative divisions: New Spain, created in 1535, with its capital at Mexico City; and Peru, created in 1542, with its capital at Lima. In the eighteenth century two additional viceroyalties were added: New Granada, with Bogotá as its administrative center; and La Plata, with Buenos Aires as its capital (see Map 14.2).

Within each territory the viceroy, or imperial governor, exercised broad military and civil authority as the direct representative of Spain. The viceroy presided over the *audiencia* (ow-dee-EHN-see-ah), a board of twelve to fifteen judges that served as his advisory council and the highest judicial body. As in Spain, settlement in the Americas was centered on cities and towns. In each city, the municipal council, or *cabildo*, exercised local authority. Women were denied participation in public life, a familiar pattern from both Spain and precolonial indigenous society.

viceroyalties The name for the four administrative units of Spanish possessions in the Americas: New Spain, Peru, New Granada, and La Plata.

Portugal adopted similar patterns of rule, with India House in Lisbon functioning much like the Spanish House of Trade and royal representatives overseeing Portuguese possessions in West Africa and Asia. To secure the vast expanse of Brazil, in the 1530s the Portuguese implemented the system of captaincies, hereditary grants of land given to nobles and loyal officials who bore the costs of settling and administering their territories. Over time, the Crown secured greater power over the captaincies, appointing royal governors to act as administrators. The captaincy of Bahia was the site of the capital, Salvador, home to the governor general and other royal officials.

Throughout the Americas, the Catholic Church played an integral role in Iberian rule. Churches and cathedrals were consecrated, often on precolonial sacred sites, and bishoprics were established. The papacy allowed Portuguese and Spanish officials greater control over the church than was the case at home, allowing them to appoint clerics and collect tithes. This control allowed colonial powers to use the church as an instrument to indoctrinate indigenous people in European ways of life (see page 457).

By the end of the seventeenth century the French crown had followed the Iberian example and imposed direct rule over its North American colonies. The king appointed military governors to rule alongside intendants, royal officials possessed of broad administrative and financial authority within their intendancies. In the mid-eighteenth century reform-minded Spanish king Charles III (r. 1759–1788) adopted the intendant system for the Spanish colonies.

England's colonies followed a distinctive path. Drawing on English traditions of representative government (see Chapter 15), its colonists established their own proudly autonomous assemblies to regulate local affairs. Wealthy merchants and landowners dominated the assemblies, yet common men had more say in politics than was the case in England. Up to the mid-eighteenth century, the Crown found little reason to dispute colonial liberties in the north, but it did acquire greater control over the wealthy plantation colonies of the Caribbean and tobacco-rich Virginia.

The Era of Global Contact

The New and Old Worlds were brought into contact and forever changed by the European voyages of discovery and their aftermath. For the first time, a truly global economy emerged in the sixteenth and seventeenth centuries, and it forged new links among far-flung peoples, cultures, and societies. The ancient civilizations of Europe, Africa, the Americas, and Asia confronted each other in new and rapidly evolving ways. Those confrontations led to conquest, forced migration, devastating population losses, and brutal exploitation. The exchange of goods and people between Europe and the New World brought highly destructive diseases to the Americas, but it also gave both the New and Old Worlds new crops that eventually altered consumption patterns across the globe.

Indigenous Population Loss and Economic Exploitation

From the time of Christopher Columbus in Hispaniola, the Spanish made use of the **encomienda system** to profit from the peoples and territories they subjugated in the Americas. This system was a legacy of the methods used to reward military leaders in the time of the reconquista, when victorious officers received feudal privileges over

FOCUS QUESTION
How was the era of global contact shaped by new forms of exploitation, commercial exchange, and forced migration?

encomienda system A system whereby the Spanish crown granted the conquerors the right to forcibly employ groups of Indians in exchange for providing food, shelter, and Christian teaching.

conquered areas in return for their service. First in the Caribbean and then on the mainland, conquistadors granted their followers the right to employ groups of indigenous people as laborers and to demand tribute payments from them in exchange for providing food, shelter, and instruction in the Christian faith. Commonly, an individual conquistador was assigned a tribal chieftain along with all of the people belonging to his kin group. This system was first used in Hispaniola to work gold fields and then in Mexico for agricultural labor and, when silver was discovered in the 1540s, for silver mining.

A 1512 Spanish law authorizing the use of encomiendas called for indigenous people to be treated fairly, but in practice the system led to terrible abuses, including overwork, beatings, and sexual violence. Spanish missionaries publicized these abuses, leading to debates in Spain about the nature and proper treatment of indigenous people (see pages 457–459). King Charles I responded to such complaints in 1542 with the New Laws, which set limits on the authority of encomienda holders, including their ability to transmit their privileges to heirs.

The New Laws provoked a revolt in Peru and were little enforced throughout Spanish territories. Nonetheless, the Crown gradually gained control over encomiendas in central areas of the empire and required indigenous people to pay tributes in cash, rather than in labor. To respond to a growing shortage of indigenous workers, royal officials established a new government-run system of forced labor, called *repartimiento* in New Spain and *mita* in Peru. Administrators assigned a certain percentage of the inhabitants of native communities to labor for a set period each year in public works, mining, agriculture, and other tasks. Laborers received modest wages in exchange, which they could use to fulfill tribute obligations. In the seventeenth century, as land became a more important source of wealth than labor, elite settlers purchased *haciendas*, enormous tracts of farmland worked by dependent indigenous laborers and slaves.

Spanish systems for exploiting the labor of indigenous peoples were both a cause of and a response to the disastrous decline in their numbers that began soon after the arrival of Europeans. Some indigenous people died as a direct result of the violence of conquest and the disruption of agriculture and trade caused by warfare. The most important cause of death, however, was infectious disease, a tragic consequence of the Europeans' arrival (see page 451).

Indigenous people's ability to survive infectious disease was reduced by overwork and exhaustion. Moreover, labor obligations diverted local people from tending to their own crops and thus contributed to malnutrition, reduced fertility rates, and starvation. Women were separated from their babies, producing high infant mortality rates. Malnutrition and hunger in turn lowered resistance to disease.

The pattern of devastating disease and population loss established in the Spanish colonies was repeated everywhere Europeans settled. (See "Evaluating the Evidence 14.2: Interpreting the Spread of Disease Among Natives," at right.) Overall, population declined by as much as 90 percent or more across the Americas after European contact, but with important regional variations. In general, densely populated urban centers were worse hit than rural areas, and tropical, low-lying regions suffered more than cooler, higher-altitude ones. Some scholars have claimed that losses may have been overreported, since many indigenous people fled their communities—or listed themselves as mixed race (and thus immune from forced labor)—to escape Spanish exploitation. By the mid-seventeenth century the worst losses had occurred and a slight recovery began.

Interpreting the Spread of Disease Among Natives

Thomas Hariot participated in the 1585 expedition to Roanoke, the short-lived English colony. After his return, he wrote A Briefe and True Report of the New Found Land of Virginia, *which describes the natural environment and the indigenous peoples he encountered. Although biased by his Christian faith and European way of life, Hariot strove to present an accurate, detailed, and balanced viewpoint, making his work a precious source on Native American life and early contacts with Europeans. In this passage, he describes the disastrous effects on the Carolina Algonquins of contagious disease, perhaps measles, smallpox, or influenza.*

There was no town where we had any subtle device [cunning maneuvers] practiced against us, we leaving it unpunished or not revenged (because we sought by all means possible to win them by gentleness) but that within a few days after our departure from every such town, the people began to die very fast, and many in short space; in some towns about twenty, in some forty, in some sixty, & in one six score, which in truth was very many in respect of their numbers. This happened in no place that we could learn but where we had been, where they used some practice against us, and after such time; The disease also so strange, that they neither knew what it was, nor how to cure it; the like by report of the oldest men in the country never happened before, time out of mind. A thing specially observed by us as also by the natural inhabitants themselves.

Insomuch that when some of the inhabitants which were our friends . . . had observed such effects in four or five towns to follow their wicked practices [of harming the Englishmen], they were persuaded that it was the work of our God through our means, and that we by him might kill and slay whom we would without weapons and not come near them.

And thereupon when it had happened that they had understanding that any of their enemies had abused us in our journeys, hearing that we had wrought no revenge with our weapons, . . . [they] did come and entreat us that we would be a means to our God that [their enemies] as others that had dealt with us might in like sort die; alleging how much it would be for our credit and profit, as also theirs; and hoping furthermore that we would do so much at their requests in respect of the friendship we profess them.

Whose entreaties although we showed that they were ungodly, affirming that our God would not subject himself to any such prayers and requests of me: that indeed all things have been and were to be done according to his good pleasure as he had ordained: and that we to show ourselves his true servants ought rather to make petition for the contrary, that they with them might live together with us, be made partakers of his truth & serve him in righteousness; but notwithstanding in such sort, that we refer that as all other things, to be done according to his divine will & pleasure, and as by his wisdom he had ordained to be best.

EVALUATE THE EVIDENCE

1. According to Hariot, how did the Native Americans allied with the English interpret the epidemics of disease that struck indigenous villages? How do they seem to have viewed their relations with the English?

2. This document sheds light on how one group of indigenous people experienced the suffering and death brought by European diseases. Based on your reading in this chapter, could you imagine differing responses among other groups?

Source: Thomas Hariot, *A Briefe and True Report of the New Found Land of Virginia* (1590; New York: J. Sabin & Sons, 1871), p. 28. Spelling modernized.

Colonial administrators responded to native population decline by forcibly combining dwindling indigenous communities into new settlements and imposing the rigors of the encomienda and the repartimiento. By the end of the sixteenth century the search for fresh sources of labor had given birth to the new tragedy of the Atlantic slave trade (see page 451).

Life in the Colonies

Many factors helped shape life in European colonies, including geographical location, pre-existing indigenous cultures, patterns of European settlement, and the policies and cultural values of the European nations that claimed them as empire. Throughout the New World, colonial settlements were hedged by immense borderlands where European power was weak and Europeans and non-Europeans interacted on a more equal basis.

Women played a crucial role in the emergence of colonial societies. The first explorers formed unions with native women, through coercion or choice, and relied on them as translators and guides and to form alliances with indigenous powers. As settlement developed, the character of each colony was influenced by the presence or absence of European women. Where women and children accompanied men, as in the British colonies and the Spanish mainland colonies, new settlements took on European languages, religion, and ways of life that have endured, with input from local cultures, to this day. Where European women did not accompany men, as on the west coast of Africa and most European outposts in Asia, local populations largely retained their own cultures, to which male Europeans acclimatized themselves. The scarcity of women in all colonies, at least initially, opened up opportunities for those who did arrive, leading one cynic to comment that even "a whore, if handsome, makes a wife for some rich planter."[15]

It was not just the availability of Englishwomen that prevented Englishmen from forming unions with indigenous women. English cultural attitudes drew strict boundaries between "civilized" and "savage," and even settlements of Christianized native peoples were segregated from the English. This was in strong contrast with the situation in New France, where royal officials initially encouraged French traders to form ties with indigenous people, including marrying local women. Assimilation of the native population was seen as one solution to the low levels of immigration from France.

The vast majority of women who crossed the Atlantic were captive Africans, constituting four-fifths of the female newcomers before 1800.[16] Wherever slavery existed, masters profited from their power to engage in sexual relations with enslaved women. One important difference among European colonies was in the status of children born from such unions. In some colonies, mostly those dominated by the Portuguese, Spanish, or French, substantial populations of free people of color descended from the freed children of such unions. In English colonies, masters were less likely to free children they fathered with female slaves.

The mixing of indigenous peoples with Europeans and Africans created whole new populations and ethnicities and complex forms of identity (see Chapter 17). In Spanish America the word *mestizo*—*métis* in French—described people of mixed Native American and European descent. The blanket terms "mulatto" and "people of color" were used for those of mixed African and European origin. With its immense slave-based plantation agriculture system, large indigenous population, and relatively low Portuguese immigration, Brazil developed a particularly complex racial and ethnic mosaic.

A Mixed-Race Procession   The Incas used drinking vessels, known as *keros*, for the ritual consumption of maize beer at feasts. This kero from the early colonial period depicts a multiracial procession: an Inca dignitary is preceded by a Spanish trumpet player and an African drummer. This is believed to be one of the earliest visual representations of an African in the Americas. (British Museum, London, UK/ Werner Forman/Universal Images Group/Getty Images)

The Columbian Exchange

The travel of people and goods between the Old and New Worlds led to an exchange of animals, plants, and diseases, a complex process known as the **Columbian exchange**. As we have seen, the introduction of new diseases to the Americas had devastating consequences. But other results of the exchange brought benefits not only to the Europeans but also to indigenous peoples.

European immigrants to the Americas wanted a familiar diet, so they searched for climatic zones favorable to familiar crops. Everywhere they settled, the Spanish and Portuguese brought and raised wheat with labor provided by the encomienda system. Grapes and olives brought over from Spain did well in parts of Peru and Chile. Europeans also introduced domestic livestock and horses, which allowed for faster travel and easier transport of heavy loads. In turn, Europeans returned home with many food crops that became central elements of their diet, such as potatoes, maize (corn), and tomatoes.

While the exchange of foods was a great benefit to both cultures, the introduction of European pathogens to the New World had a disastrous impact on the native population. In Europe, infectious diseases like smallpox, measles, and influenza—originally passed on from domestic animals living among the population—killed many people each year. Given the size of the population and the frequency of outbreaks, in most of Europe these diseases were experienced in childhood, and survivors carried immunity or resistance. Over centuries of dealing with these diseases, the European population had had time to adapt. Prior to contact with Europeans, indigenous peoples of the New World suffered from insect-borne diseases and some infectious ones, but their lack of domestic livestock spared them the host of highly infectious diseases known in the Old World. The arrival of Europeans spread these microbes among a completely unprepared population, and they fell victim in vast numbers (see pages 447–448.) The wave of catastrophic epidemic disease that swept the Western Hemisphere after 1492 can be seen as an extension of the swath of devastation wreaked by the Black Death in the fourteenth century, first on Asia and then on Europe. The world after Columbus was thus unified by disease as well as by trade and colonization.

Sugar and Slavery

Two crucial and interrelated elements of the Columbian exchange were the transatlantic trade in sugar and slaves. Throughout the Middle Ages slavery was deeply entrenched in the Mediterranean, but it was not based on race; many slaves were European in origin. How, then, did black African slavery enter the European picture and take root in the Americas? In 1453 the Ottoman capture of Constantinople halted the flow of slaves from the eastern Mediterranean to western Europe. Additionally, the successes of the Iberian reconquista drastically diminished the supply of Muslim captives. Cut off from its traditional sources of slaves, Mediterranean Europe turned to sub-Saharan Africa, which had a long history of internal slave trading. (See "Individuals in Society: Juan de Pareja," page 452.)

As Portuguese explorers began their voyages along the western coast of Africa, one of the first commodities they sought was slaves. In 1444 the first ship returned to Lisbon with a cargo of enslaved Africans. While the first slaves were simply seized by small raiding parties, Portuguese merchants soon found that it was easier to trade with local leaders, who were accustomed to dealing in slaves captured through warfare with neighboring powers. In 1483 the Portuguese established an alliance with

Columbian exchange The exchange of animals, plants, and diseases between the Old and the New Worlds.

During the long wars of the reconquista, Muslims and Christians captured each other in battle and used the defeated as slaves. As the Muslims were gradually eliminated from Iberia in the fifteenth and sixteenth centuries, the Spanish and Portuguese turned to the west coast of Africa for a new supply of slaves. Most slaves worked as domestic servants, rather than in the fields. Some received specialized training as artisans.

Not all people of African descent were slaves, and some experienced both freedom and slavery in a single lifetime. The life and career of Juan de Pareja (pah-REH-huh) illustrates the complexities of the Iberian slave system and the heights of achievement possible for those who gained freedom.

Pareja was born in Antequera, an agricultural region and the old center of Muslim culture near Seville in southern Spain. Of his parents we know nothing. Because a rare surviving document calls him a "mulatto," one of his parents must have been white and the other must have had some African blood. In 1630 Pareja applied to the mayor of Seville for permission to travel to Madrid to visit his brother and "to perfect his art." The document lists his occupation as "a painter in Seville." Since it mentions no other name, it is reasonable to assume that Pareja arrived in Madrid a free man. Sometime between 1630 and 1648, however, he came into the possession of the artist Diego Velázquez (1599–1660); Pareja became a slave.

How did Velázquez acquire Pareja? By purchase? As a gift? Had Pareja fallen into debt or committed some crime and thereby lost his freedom? We do not know. Velázquez, the greatest Spanish painter of the seventeenth century, had a large studio with many assistants. Pareja was set to grinding powders to make colors and to preparing canvases. He must have demonstrated ability because when Velázquez went to Rome in 1648, he chose Pareja to accompany him.

In 1650, as practice for a portrait of Pope Innocent X, Velázquez painted Pareja. The portrait shows Pareja dressed in fine clothing and gazing self-confidently at the viewer. Displayed in Rome in a public exhibition of Velázquez's work, the painting won acclaim from his contemporaries. That same year, Velázquez signed the document that gave Pareja his freedom, to become effective in 1654. Pareja lived out the rest of his life as an independent painter.

What does the public career of Pareja tell us about the man and his world? Pareja's career suggests that a person

Velázquez, *Juan de Pareja*, 1650. (Metropolitan Museum of Art, New York, USA/photo © Christie's Images/Bridgeman Images)

of African descent might fall into slavery and yet still acquire professional training and work alongside his master in a position of confidence. Moreover, if lucky enough to be freed, a former slave could exercise a profession and live his own life in Madrid. Pareja's experience was far from typical for a slave in the seventeenth century, but it reminds us of the myriad forms that slavery took in this period.

QUESTIONS FOR ANALYSIS

1. Since slavery was an established institution in Spain, speculate on Velázquez's possible reasons for giving Pareja his freedom.
2. In what ways does Pareja represent Europe's increasing participation in global commerce and exploration?

Sources: Jonathan Brown, *Velázquez: Painter and Courtier* (New Haven, Conn.: Yale University Press, 1986); *Grove Dictionary of Art* (New York: Macmillan, 2000); Sister Wendy Beckett, *Sister Wendy's American Collection* (New York: Harper Collins Publishers, 2000), p. 15.

MAP 14.3 Seaborne Trading Empires in the Sixteenth and Seventeenth Centuries   By the mid-seventeenth century trade linked all parts of the world except for Australia. Notice that trade in slaves was not confined to the Atlantic but involved almost all parts of the world.

the kingdom of Kongo. The royal family eventually converted to Christianity, and Portuguese merchants intermarried with Kongolese women, creating a permanent Afro-Portuguese community. From 1490 to 1530 Portuguese traders brought hundreds of enslaved Africans to Lisbon each year (Map 14.3), where they eventually constituted 10 percent of the city's population.

In this stage of European expansion, the history of slavery became intertwined with the history of sugar. Originally sugar was an expensive luxury, but population increases and monetary expansion in the fifteenth century led to increasing demand. Native to the South Pacific, sugar was taken in ancient times to India, where farmers learned to preserve cane juice as granules that could be stored and shipped. From there, sugar crops traveled to China and the Mediterranean, where islands like Crete and Sicily had the warm and wet climate needed for growing sugarcane. When Genoese and other Italians colonized the Canary Islands and the Portuguese settled on the Madeira Islands, sugar plantations came to the Atlantic.

Sugar was a particularly difficult crop to produce for profit. Seed-stems were planted by hand, thousands to the acre. When mature, the cane had to be harvested and processed rapidly to avoid spoiling. Moreover, sugar has a virtually constant growing season, meaning that there was no fallow period when workers could recuperate from the arduous labor. The invention of roller mills to crush the cane more efficiently meant that yields could be significantly augmented, but only if a sufficient labor force was found to supply the mills. Europeans solved the labor problem by forcing first native islanders and then enslaved Africans to provide the backbreaking work.

The transatlantic slave trade began in 1518 when the Spanish emperor Charles V authorized traders to bring enslaved Africans to the Americas. The Portuguese brought the first slaves to Brazil around 1550; by 1600 four thousand were being imported annually. After its founding in 1621, the Dutch West India Company, with the full support of the United Provinces, transported thousands of Africans to Brazil and the Caribbean, mostly to work on sugar plantations. In the mid-seventeenth century the English got involved. From 1660 to 1698 the Royal African Company held a monopoly over the slave trade from the English crown.

Before 1700, when slavers decided it was better business to improve conditions, some 20 percent of slaves died on the voyage.[17] The most common cause of death was from dysentery induced by poor-quality food and water, crowding, and lack of sanitation. Men were often kept in irons during the passage, while women and girls were considered fair game for sailors. To increase profits, slave traders packed several hundred captives on each ship. One slaver explained that he removed his boots before entering the slave hold because he had to crawl over the slaves' packed bodies.[18] On sugar plantations, death rates from the brutal pace of labor were extremely high, leading to a constant stream of new shipments of slaves from Africa.

In total, scholars estimate that European traders embarked over 12 million enslaved Africans across the Atlantic from 1500 to 1875 (of whom roughly 10.7 million disembarked), with the peak of the trade occurring in the eighteenth century.[19] By comparison, only 2 to 2.5 million Europeans migrated to the New World during the same period. Slaves worked in an infinite variety of occupations: as miners, soldiers, sailors, servants, and artisans and in the production of sugar, cotton, rum, indigo, tobacco, wheat, and corn.

Spanish Silver and Its Economic Effects

The sixteenth century has often been called Spain's golden century, but silver mined in the Americas was the true source of Spain's wealth. In 1545, at an altitude of fifteen thousand feet, the Spanish discovered an extraordinary source of silver at Potosí (poh-toh-SEE) (in present-day Bolivia) in territory conquered from the Inca Empire. The frigid place where nothing grew had been unsettled. A half century later 160,000 people lived there, making it about as populous as the city of London. By 1550 Potosí yielded perhaps 60 percent of all the silver mined in the world. From Potosí and the mines at Zacatecas (za-kuh-TAY-kuhhs) and Guanajuato (gwah-nah-HWAH-toh) in Mexico, huge quantities of precious metals poured forth. To protect this treasure from French and English pirates, armed convoys transported it to Spain each year. Between 1503 and 1650, 35 million pounds of silver and over 600,000 pounds of gold entered Seville's port. Spanish predominance, however, proved temporary.

In the sixteenth century Spain experienced a steady population increase, creating a sharp rise in the demand for food and goods. Spanish colonies in the Americas also demanded consumer goods, such as cloth and luxury goods. Since Spain had expelled some of its best farmers and businessmen—the Muslims and Jews—in the fifteenth century, the Spanish economy was suffering and could not meet the new demands. The excess of demand over supply led to widespread inflation. The result was a rise in production costs and a further decline in Spain's productive capacity.

Did the flood of silver bullion from America cause the inflation? Prices rose most steeply before 1565, but bullion imports reached their peak between 1580 and 1620. Thus silver did not cause the initial inflation. It did, however, greatly exacerbate the situation, and, along with the ensuing rise in population, the influx of silver significantly contributed to the upward spiral of prices. Inflation severely strained government budgets. Several times between 1557 and 1647, Spain's King Philip II and his successors wrote off the state debt, thereby undermining confidence in the government and leaving the economy in shambles. After 1600, when the population declined, prices gradually stabilized.

As Philip II paid his armies and foreign debts with silver bullion, Spanish inflation was transmitted to the rest of Europe. Between 1560 and 1600 much of Europe experienced large price increases. Prices doubled and in some cases quadrupled. Spain suffered most severely, but all European countries were affected. Because money bought less, people who lived on fixed incomes, such as nobles, were badly hurt. Those who owed fixed sums of money, such as the middle class, prospered because in a time of rising prices, debts lessened in value each year. Food costs rose most sharply, and the poor fared worst of all.

In many ways, though, it was not Spain but China that controlled the world trade in silver. The Chinese demanded silver for their products and for the payment of imperial taxes. China was thus the main buyer of world silver, absorbing half the world's production. The silver market drove world trade, with New Spain and Japan being mainstays on the supply side and China dominating the demand side. The world trade in silver is one of the best examples of the new global economy that emerged in this period.

The Birth of the Global Economy

With the Europeans' discovery of the Americas and their exploration of the Pacific, the entire world was linked for the first time in history by seaborne trade. The opening of that trade brought into being three successive commercial empires: the Portuguese, the Spanish, and the Dutch.

The Portuguese were the first worldwide traders. In the sixteenth century they controlled the sea route to India (see Map 14.3). From their fortified bases at Goa on the Arabian Sea and at Malacca on the Malay Peninsula, ships carried goods to the Portuguese settlement at Macao, founded in 1557, in the South China Sea. From Macao Portuguese ships loaded with Chinese silks and porcelains sailed to the Japanese port of Nagasaki and to the Philippine port of Manila, where Chinese goods were exchanged for Spanish silver from New Spain. Throughout Asia the Portuguese traded in slaves—sub-Saharan Africans, Chinese, and Japanese. The Portuguese exported horses from Mesopotamia and copper from Arabia to India; from India they exported hawks and peacocks for the Chinese and Japanese markets. Back to Portugal they brought Asian spices that had been purchased with textiles produced in India and with gold and ivory from East Africa. They also shipped back sugar from their colony in Brazil, produced by enslaved Africans whom they had transported across the Atlantic.

Goods from the Global Economy Spices from Southeast Asia were a driving force behind the new global economy and among the most treasured European luxury goods. They were used not only for cooking but also as medicines and health tonics. This fresco shows a fifteenth-century Italian pharmacist measuring out spices for a customer. (Issogne Castle, Val d'Aosta, Italy, Alfredo Dagli Orti/The Art Archive at Art Resource, NY)

Coming to empire a few decades later than the Portuguese, the Spanish were determined to claim their place in world trade. The Spanish Empire in the New World was basically a land empire, but across the Pacific the Spaniards built a seaborne empire centered at Manila in the Philippines. The city of Manila served as the transpacific bridge between Spanish America and China. In Manila, Spanish traders used silver from American mines to purchase Chinese silk for European markets. The European demand for silk was so huge that in 1597, for example, 12 million pesos of silver, almost the total value of the transatlantic trade, moved from Acapulco in New Spain to Manila (see Map 14.3).

In the final years of the sixteenth century the Dutch challenged the Spanish and Portuguese Empires. During this period the Protestant Dutch were engaged in a long war of independence from their Spanish Catholic overlords. The joining of the Portuguese crown to Spain in 1580 meant that the Dutch had both strategic and commercial reasons to attack Portugal's commercial empire. In 1599 a Dutch fleet returned to Amsterdam carrying 600,000 pounds of pepper and 250,000 pounds of cloves and nutmeg. Those who had invested in the expedition received a 100 percent profit. The voyage led to the establishment in 1602 of the Dutch East India Company, founded with the stated intention of capturing the Asian spice trade from the Portuguese.

In return for assisting Indonesian princes in local squabbles and disputes with the Portuguese, the Dutch won broad commercial concessions. Through agreements, seizures, and outright military aggression, they gained control of the western access to the Indonesian archipelago in the first half of the seventeenth century. Gradually, they acquired political domination over the archipelago itself. The Dutch were willing to use force more ruthlessly than the Portuguese and had superior organizational efficiency. These factors allowed them to expel the Portuguese from Ceylon and other East Indian islands in 1660 and henceforth control the immensely lucrative production and trade of spices. The company also established the colony of Cape Town on the southern tip of Africa as a provisioning point for its Asian fleets.

Not content with challenging the Portuguese in the Indian Ocean, the Dutch also aspired to a role in the Americas. Founded in 1621, during their war with Spain, the Dutch West India Company aggressively sought to open trade with North and South America and capture Spanish territories there. The company captured or destroyed hundreds of Spanish ships, seized the Spanish silver fleet in 1628, and captured portions of Brazil and the Caribbean. The Dutch also successfully interceded in the transatlantic slave trade, establishing a large number of trading stations on the west coast of Africa. Ironically, the nation that was known throughout Europe as a bastion of tolerance and freedom came to be one of the principal operators of the slave trade starting in the 1640s.

Changing Attitudes and Beliefs

The age of overseas expansion heightened Europeans' contacts with the rest of the world. Religion was one of the most important arenas of cultural contact, as European missionaries aimed to spread Christianity in both the New World and East Asia, with mixed results. While Christianity was embraced in parts of the New World, it was met largely with suspicion in China and Japan. However, the East-West contacts did lead to exchanges of influential cultural and scientific ideas.

These contacts also gave birth to new ideas about the inherent superiority or inferiority of different races, sparking vociferous debate about the status of Africans and indigenous peoples of the Americas. The essays of Michel de Montaigne epitomized a new spirit of skepticism and cultural relativism, while the plays of William Shakespeare reflected the efforts of one great writer to come to terms with the cultural complexity of his day.

FOCUS QUESTION
How did new encounters shape cultural attitudes and beliefs in Europe and the rest of the world?

Religious Conversion

Converting indigenous people to Christianity was one of the most important justifications for European expansion. Jesuit missionaries were active in Japan and China in the sixteenth and seventeenth centuries, until authorities banned their teachings. The first missionaries to the New World accompanied Columbus on his second voyage, and more than 2,500 Franciscans, Dominicans, Jesuits, and other friars crossed the Atlantic in the following century. Later French explorers were also accompanied by missionaries who preached to the Native American tribes with whom the French traded.

Catholic friars were among the first Europeans to seek an understanding of native cultures and languages as part of their effort to render Christianity comprehensible to indigenous people. In Mexico they not only learned the Nahuatl language, but also taught it to non-Nahuatl-speaking groups to create a shared language for Christian teaching. They were also the most vociferous opponents of abuses committed by Spanish settlers (see the next section).

Religion had been a central element of pre-Columbian societies, and many—if not all—indigenous people were receptive to the new religion that accompanied the victorious Iberians. (See "Evaluating the Evidence 14.3: Tenochtitlan Leaders Respond to Spanish Missionaries," page 458.) It is estimated that missionaries had baptized between 4 and 9 million indigenous people in New Spain by the mid-1530s.[20] In addition to spreading Christianity, missionaries taught indigenous peoples European methods of agriculture and instilled loyalty to colonial masters.

Despite the success of initial conversion efforts, authorities became suspicious about the thoroughness of native peoples' conversion and their lingering belief in the old gods. They could not prevent the melding together of Catholic teachings with elements of pagan beliefs and practices. For example, a sixteenth-century apparition of the Virgin Mary in Mexico City, known as the Virgin of Guadalupe, which became a central icon of New World Catholicism, seems to have been based on veneration of the Aztec Mother Earth goddess, Tonantzin.

European Debates About Indigenous Peoples

Iberian exploitation of the native population of the Americas began from the moment of Columbus's arrival in 1492. Denunciations of this abuse by Catholic missionaries,

Tenochtitlan Leaders Respond to Spanish Missionaries

For the conquered peoples of the New World, the imposition of Christianity and repression of their pre-existing religions represented yet another form of loss. This document describes the response of the vanquished leaders of Tenochtitlan to Franciscan missionaries seeking to convert them in 1524. The account was written down in the 1560s by or for Bernardino de Sahagún, a Franciscan missionary. Sahagún is well known for his General History of the Things of New Spain *(also known as the* Florentine Codex*), a multivolume account of Mexica history, culture, and society he produced in collaboration with indigenous artists and informants.*

~

You have told us that we do not know the One who gives us life and being, who is Lord of the heavens and of the earth. You also say that those we worship are not gods. This way of speaking is entirely new to us, and very scandalous. We are frightened by this way of speaking because our forebears who engendered and governed us never said anything like this. On the contrary, they left us this our custom of worshiping our gods, in which they believed and which they worshiped all the time that they lived here on earth. They taught us how to honor them. And they taught us all the ceremonies and sacrifices that we make. They told us that through them [our gods] we live and are, and that we were beholden to them, to be theirs and to serve countless centuries before the sun began to shine and before there was daytime. They said that these gods that we worship give us everything we need for our physical existence: maize, beans, chia seeds, etc. We appeal to them for the rain to make the things of the earth grow.

These our gods are the source of great riches and delights, all of which belong to them. They live in very delightful places where there are always flowers, vegetation, and great freshness, a place unknown to mere mortals, called Tlalocan, where there is never hunger, poverty, or illness. It is they who bestow honors, property, titles, and kingdoms, gold and silver, precious feathers, and gemstones.

There has never been a time remembered when they were not worshiped, honored, and esteemed. Perhaps it is a century or two since this began; it is a time beyond counting. . . .

It is best, our lords, to act on this matter very slowly, with great deliberation. We are not satisfied or convinced by what you have told us, nor do we understand or give credit to what has been said of our gods. . . . All of us together feel that it is enough to have lost, enough that the power and royal jurisdiction have been taken from us. As for our gods, we will die before giving up serving and worshiping them.

EVALUATE THE EVIDENCE

1. What reasons do the leaders of Tenochtitlan offer for rejecting the missionaries' teachings? In their view, what elements of their lives will be affected by abandoning the worship of their gods?
2. What insight does this document provide into the mind-set of Mexica people shortly following conquest?

Source: *Coloquios y doctrina Cristiana,* ed. Miguel León-Portilla, in *Colonial Spanish America: A Documentary History,* ed. Kenneth Mills and William B. Taylor (Wilmington, Del.: SR Books, 1998), pp. 21–22. Used by permission of Rowman & Littlefield.

however, quickly followed, inspiring vociferous debates both in Europe and in the colonies about the nature of indigenous peoples and how they should be treated. Bartolomé de Las Casas (1474–1566), a Dominican friar and former encomienda holder, was one of the earliest and most outspoken critics of the brutal treatment inflicted on indigenous peoples. He wrote:

To these quiet Lambs . . . came the Spaniards like most c(r)uel Tygres, Wolves and Lions, enrag'd with a sharp and tedious hunger; for these forty years past, minding nothing else but the slaughter of these unfortunate wretches, whom with divers kinds of torments neither seen nor heard of before, they have so cruelly and inhumanely butchered, that of three millions of people which Hispaniola itself did contain, there are left remaining alive scarce three hundred persons.[21]

Mounting criticism in Spain led King Charles I to assemble a group of churchmen and lawyers to debate the issue in 1550 in the city of Valladolid. One side, led by Juan Ginés de Sepúlveda, argued that conquest and forcible conversion were both necessary and justified to save indigenous people from the horrors of human sacrifice, cannibalism, and idolatry. He described them as barbarians who belonged to a category of inferior beings identified by the ancient Greek philosopher Aristotle as naturally destined for slavery. Against these arguments, Las Casas and his supporters depicted indigenous people as rational and innocent children, who deserved protection and tutelage from more advanced civilizations. Both sides claimed victory in the debate, but it had little effect on the situation in the Americas.

Eagerly reading denunciations of Spanish abuses by critics like Las Casas, northern Europeans derived the **"Black Legend"** of Spanish colonialism, the notion that the Spanish were uniquely brutal and cruel in their conquest and settlement of the Americas.

Spanish Atrocities in the New World   The illustrations provided by Theodor de Bry to accompany Bartolomé de Las Casas's *Short Account of the Destruction of the Indies* depict atrocities committed by the Spanish in their conquest and settlement of the Americas. De Bry, a converted Protestant, thereby contributed to the "Black Legend" of Spanish colonization. (Engraving by Theodor de Bry, from a work by Bartolomé de Las Casas, 1598/Photo 12/UIG via Getty Images)

However, the legend also helped northern European powers, like France and England, overlook their own record of colonial violence and exploitation.

> **"Black Legend"** The notion that the Spanish were particularly ruthless and cruel in their conquest and domination of the Americas, an idea often propagated by Spain's rivals.

New Ideas About Race

At the beginning of the transatlantic slave trade, most Europeans would have thought of Africans, if they thought of them at all, as savages in their social customs, religious practices, language, and methods of war. They grouped Africans into the despised categories of pagan heathens and Muslim infidels.

As Europeans turned to Africa for new sources of slaves, they drew on beliefs about Africans' supposed primitiveness and barbarity to defend slavery and even argue, like Sepúlveda with regard to indigenous Americans, that enslavement benefited Africans by bringing them the light of Christianity. In 1444 an observer defended the enslavement of the first Africans by Portuguese explorers as necessary for their salvation "because they lived like beasts, without any of the customs of rational creatures, since they did not even know what were bread and wine, nor garments of cloth, nor life in the shelter of a house; and worse still was their ignorance, which deprived them of knowledge of good, and permitted them only a life of brutish idleness."[22]

Over time, the institution of slavery fostered unprecedented ideas about racial inequality. Africans gradually became seen as utterly distinct from and wholly inferior to Europeans. From rather vague assumptions about Africans' non-Christian religious beliefs and general lack of civilization, Europeans developed increasingly rigid ideas of racial superiority and inferiority to safeguard the growing profits gained from plantation slavery. Black skin became equated with slavery itself as Europeans at home and in the colonies convinced themselves that blacks were destined by God to serve them as slaves in perpetuity.

Support for this belief went back to the Greek philosopher Aristotle's argument that some people are naturally destined for slavery and to biblical associations between darkness and sin. A more explicit justification was found in the story of Noah's curse upon the descendants of his disobedient son Ham to be the "servant[s] of servants." Biblical genealogies listing Ham's sons as those who peopled North Africa and Cush (which includes parts of modern Egypt and Sudan) were read to mean that all inhabitants of those regions bore Noah's curse. From the sixteenth century onward, many defenders of slavery cited this story as justification for their actions.

After 1700 the emergence of new methods of observing and describing nature led to the use of science to define race. Although the term originally referred to a nation or an ethnic group, henceforth "race" would be used to describe supposedly biologically distinct groups of people, whose physical differences produced differences in culture, character, and intelligence. Biblical justifications for inequality thereby gave way to supposedly scientific ones (see pages 527–529).

Michel de Montaigne and Cultural Curiosity

Racism was not the only possible reaction to the new worlds emerging in the sixteenth century. Decades of religious fanaticism, bringing civil anarchy and war, led some Catholics and Protestants to doubt that any one faith contained absolute truth. Added to these doubts was the discovery of peoples in the New World who had radically different ways of life. These shocks helped produce ideas of skepticism and cultural relativism. Skepticism is a school of thought founded on doubt that total certainty or definitive knowledge is ever attainable. The skeptic is cautious and critical and suspends judgment. Cultural relativism suggests that one culture is not necessarily superior to another, just different. Both notions found expression in the work of Frenchman Michel de Montaigne (duh mahn-TAYN) (1533–1592).

Montaigne developed a new literary genre, the essay—from the French *essayer*, meaning "to test or try"—to express his ideas. Published in 1580, Montaigne's *Essays* consisted of short reflections drawing on his extensive reading in ancient texts, his experience as a government official, and his own moral judgment. Intending his works to be accessible to ordinary people, Montaigne wrote in French rather than Latin and in an engaging conversational style. His essays were quickly translated into other European languages and became some of the most widely read texts of the early modern period.

Montaigne's essay "Of Cannibals" reveals the impact of overseas discoveries on one thoughtful European. In contrast to the prevailing views of his day, he rejected the notion that one culture is superior to another. Speaking of native Brazilians, he wrote:

> I find that there is nothing barbarous and savage in this nation [Brazil], . . . except, that everyone gives the title of barbarism to everything that is not according to his usage; as, indeed, we have no other criterion of truth and reason, than the example and pattern of the opinions and customs of the place wherein we live. . . . They are savages in the same way that we say fruits are wild, which nature produces of herself and by her ordinary course; whereas, in truth, we ought rather to call those wild whose natures we have changed by our artifice and diverted from the common order.[23]

In his own time, few would have agreed with Montaigne's challenge to ideas of European superiority or his even more radical questioning of the superiority of humans over animals. Nevertheless, his popular essays contributed to a basic shift in attitudes. "Wonder," he said, "is the foundation of all philosophy, research is the means of all learning, and ignorance is the end."[24] Montaigne thus inaugurated an era of doubt.

William Shakespeare and His Influence

In addition to the essay as a literary genre, the period fostered remarkable creativity in other branches of literature. England—especially in the latter part of Queen Elizabeth I's reign and in the first years of her successor, James I (r. 1603–1625)—witnessed remarkable literary expression. The undisputed master of the period was the dramatist William Shakespeare, whose genius lay in the originality of his characterizations, the diversity of his plots, his understanding of human psychology, and his unsurpassed gift for language. Born in 1564 to a successful glove manufacturer in Stratford-upon-Avon, Shakespeare grew into a Renaissance man with a deep appreciation of classical culture, individualism, and humanism. Although he wrote sparkling comedies and stirring historical plays, his greatest masterpieces were his later tragedies, including *Hamlet*, *Othello*, and *Macbeth*, which explore an enormous range of human problems and are open to an almost infinite variety of interpretations.

Like Montaigne's essays, Shakespeare's work reveals the impact of the new discoveries and contacts of his day. The title character of *Othello* is described as a "Moor of Venice." In Shakespeare's day, the term "Moor" referred to Muslims of North African origin, including those who had migrated to the Iberian Peninsula. It could also be applied, though, to natives of the Iberian Peninsula who converted to Islam or to non-Muslim Berbers in North Africa. To complicate things even more, references in the play to Othello as "black" in skin color have led many to believe that Shakespeare intended him to be a sub-Saharan African. This confusion in the play aptly reflects the uncertainty in Shakespeare's own time about racial and religious classifications. In contrast to the prevailing view of Moors as inferior, Shakespeare presents Othello as a complex human figure, whose only crime is to have "loved [his wife] not wisely, but too well."

Shakespeare's last play, *The Tempest*, also highlights the issue of race and race relations. The plot involves the stranding on an island of sorcerer Prospero and his daughter Miranda. There Prospero finds and raises Caliban, a native of the island, whom he instructs in his own language and religion. After Caliban's attempted rape of Miranda, Prospero enslaves him, earning the hatred of his erstwhile pupil. Modern scholars often note the echoes between this play and the realities of imperial conquest and settlement in Shakespeare's day. It is no accident, they argue, that the poet portrayed Caliban as a monstrous dark-skinned island native who was best suited for slavery. Shakespeare himself borrows words from Montaigne's essay "Of Cannibals," suggesting that he may have intended to criticize, rather than endorse, racial intolerance. Shakespeare's work shows us one of the finest minds of the age grasping to come to terms with the racial and religious complexities around him.

LOOKING BACK LOOKING AHEAD

In 1517 Martin Luther issued his "Ninety-five Theses," launching the Protestant Reformation; just five years later, Ferdinand Magellan's expedition sailed around the globe, shattering European notions of terrestrial geography. Within a few short years, old medieval certainties about Heaven and earth began to collapse. In the ensuing decades, Europeans struggled to come to terms with religious difference at home and the multitudes of new peoples and places they encountered abroad. While some Europeans were fascinated and inspired by this new diversity, too often the result was violence. Europeans endured decades of civil war between Protestants and Catholics, and indigenous peoples suffered massive population losses as a result of European warfare, disease, and exploitation. Tragically, both Catholic and Protestant religious leaders condoned the African slave trade that brought suffering and death to millions of people.

Even as the voyages of discovery coincided with the fragmentation of European culture, they also played a role in longer-term processes of state centralization and consolidation. The new monarchies of the Renaissance produced stronger and wealthier governments capable of financing the huge expenses of exploration and colonization. Competition to gain overseas colonies became an integral part of European politics. Spain's investment in conquest proved spectacularly profitable and yet, as we will see in Chapter 15, the ultimate result was a weakening of its power. Over time the Netherlands, England, and France also reaped tremendous profits from colonial trade, which helped them build modernized, centralized states. The path from medieval Christendom to modern nation-states led through religious warfare and global encounter.

Make Connections

Think about the larger developments and continuities within and across chapters.

1. Michel de Montaigne argued that people's assessments of what was "barbaric" merely drew on their own habits and customs; based on the earlier sections of this chapter, how widespread was this openness to cultural difference? Was he alone or did others share this view?

2. To what extent did the European voyages of expansion and conquest inaugurate an era of global history? Is it correct to date the beginning of "globalization" from the late fifteenth century? Why or why not?

14 REVIEW & EXPLORE

Review the Main Ideas

Answer the focus questions from each section of the chapter.

- ◆ What was the Afroeurasian trading world prior to the era of European exploration? (p. 428)
- ◆ How and why did Europeans undertake ambitious voyages of expansion? (p. 432)
- ◆ How did European powers acquire colonies in the Americas, and how were they governed? (p. 442)
- ◆ How was the era of global contact shaped by new forms of exploitation, commercial exchange, and forced migration? (p. 447)
- ◆ How did new encounters shape cultural attitudes and beliefs in Europe and the rest of the world? (p. 457)

Identify Key Terms

Identify and explain the significance of each item below.

conquistador (p. 433)
caravel (p. 434)
Ptolemy's *Geography* (p. 434)
Treaty of Tordesillas (p. 439)
Aztec Empire (p. 442)
Inca Empire (p. 443)
viceroyalties (p. 446)
encomienda system (p. 447)
Columbian exchange (p. 451)
"Black Legend" (p. 459)

NOTES

1. Marco Polo, *The Book of Ser Marco Polo, the Venetian: Concerning the Kingdoms and Marvels of the East*, vol. 2, trans. and ed. Colonel Sir Henry Yule (London: John Murray, 1903), pp. 185–186.

2. Thomas Benjamin, *The Atlantic World: Europeans, Africans, Indians and Their Shared History, 1400–1900* (Cambridge: Cambridge University Press, 2009), p. 56.

3. Quoted in J. Devisse, "Africa in Inter-Continental Relations," in *General History of Africa*, vol. 4, *Africa from the Twelfth to the Sixteenth Century*, ed. D. T. Niane (Berkeley, Calif.: Heinemann Educational Books, 1984), p. 664.

4. Geoffrey Atkinson, *Les nouveaux horizons de la Renaissance française* (Paris: Droz, 1935), pp. 10–12.

5. G. V. Scammell, *The World Encompassed: The First European Maritime Empires, c. 800–1650* (Berkeley: University of California Press, 1981), p. 101.

6. Quoted in C. M. Cipolla, *Guns, Sails, and Empires: Technological Innovation and the Early Phases of European Expansion, 1400–1700* (New York: Minerva Press, 1965), p. 132.

7. Quoted in F. H. Littell, *The Macmillan Atlas: History of Christianity* (New York: Macmillan, 1976), p. 75.

8. Pablo E. Pérez-Mallaína, *Spain's Men of the Sea: Daily Life on the Indies Fleet in the Sixteenth Century* (Baltimore: Johns Hopkins University Press, 1998), p. 133.

9. Ibid., p. 19.

10. John Law, "On the Methods of Long Distance Control: Vessels, Navigation, and the Portuguese Route to India," in *Power, Action and Belief: A New Sociology of Knowledge?* ed. John Law, Sociological Review Monograph 32 (London: Routledge & Kegan Paul, 1986), pp. 234–263.

11. Quoted in F. Maddison, "Tradition and Innovation: Columbus' First Voyage and Portuguese Navigation in the Fifteenth Century," in *Circa 1492: Art in the Age of Exploration*, ed. J. A. Levenson (Washington, D.C.: National Gallery of Art, 1991), p. 69.

12. Quoted in R. L. Kagan, "The Spain of Ferdinand and Isabella," in *Circa 1492: Art in the Age of Exploration*, ed. J. A. Levenson (Washington, D.C.: National Gallery of Art, 1991), p. 60.

13. Peter Hulme, *Colonial Encounters: Europe and the Native Caribbean, 1492–1797* (London: Methuen, 1986), pp. 22–31.

14. Benjamin, *The Atlantic World*, p. 141.

15. Cited in Geoffrey Vaughn Scammell, *The First Imperial Age: European Overseas Expansion, c. 1400–1715* (London: Routledge, 2002), p. 62.

16. Ibid., p. 432.

17. Herbert S. Klein, "Profits and the Causes of Mortality," in *The Atlantic Slave Trade*, ed. David Northrup (Lexington, Mass.: D. C. Heath and Co., 1994), p. 116.

18. Malcolm Cowley and Daniel P. Mannix, "The Middle Passage," in *The Atlantic Slave Trade*, ed. David Northrup (Lexington, Mass.: D. C. Heath and Co., 1994), p. 101.

19. Voyages: The Trans-Atlantic Slave Trade Database, http://www.slavevoyages.org/tast/assessment/estimates.

20. David Carrasco, *The Oxford Encyclopedia of Mesoamerican Cultures* (Oxford: Oxford University Press, 2001), p. 208.

21. Quoted in C. Gibson, ed., *The Black Legend: Anti-Spanish Attitudes in the Old World and the New* (New York: Knopf, 1971), pp. 74–75.

22. Quoted in James H. Sweet, "The Iberian Roots of American Racist Thought," *The William and Mary Quarterly* 54 (1997): 155.

23. C. Cotton, trans., *The Essays of Michel de Montaigne* (New York: A. L. Burt, 1893), pp. 207, 210.

24. Ibid., p. 523.

CHAPTER PREVIEW

Seventeenth-Century Crisis and Rebuilding
What were the common crises and achievements of seventeenth-century European states?

Absolutism in France and Spain
What factors led to the rise of the French absolutist state under Louis XIV, and why did absolutist Spain experience decline in the same period?

Absolutism in Austria and Prussia
What were the social conditions of eastern Europe, and how did the rulers of Austria and Prussia transform their nations into powerful absolutist monarchies?

The Development of Russia and the Ottoman Empire
What were the distinctive features of Russian and Ottoman absolutism?

Constitutional Rule in England and the Dutch Republic
Why and how did the constitutional state triumph in the Dutch Republic and England?

Life at the French Royal Court

King Louis XIV receives foreign ambassadors to celebrate a peace treaty. The king grandly occupied the center of his court, which in turn served as the pinnacle for the French people and, at the height of his glory, for all of Europe.

(By Charles Le Brun [1619–1690], 1678/Museum of Fine Arts, Budapest, Hungary/Erich Lessing/Art Resource, NY)

15

Absolutism and Constitutionalism

ca. 1589–1725

The seventeenth century was a period of crisis and transformation in Europe. Agricultural and manufacturing slumps led to food shortages and shrinking population rates. Religious and dynastic conflicts led to almost constant war, visiting violence and destruction on ordinary people and reshaping European states. With Louis XIV of France taking the lead, armies grew larger than they had been since the time of the Roman Empire, resulting in new government bureaucracies and higher taxes. Yet even with these obstacles, European states succeeded in gathering more power, and by 1680 much of the unrest that originated with the Reformation was resolved.

These crises were not limited to western Europe. Central and eastern Europe experienced even more catastrophic dislocation, with German lands serving as the battleground of the Thirty Years' War and borders constantly vulnerable to attack from the east. In Prussia and in Habsburg Austria absolutist states emerged in the aftermath of this conflict. Russia and the Ottoman Turks also experienced turmoil in the mid-seventeenth century, but maintained their distinctive styles of absolutist government. The Russian and Ottoman Empires seemed foreign and exotic to western Europeans, who saw them as far removed from their political, religious, and cultural values.

While absolutism emerged as the solution to crisis in many European states, a small minority adopted a different path, placing sovereignty in the hands of privileged groups rather than the Crown. Historians refer to states where executive power was limited by law as "constitutional." The two most important seventeenth-century constitutionalist states were England and the Dutch Republic. Constitutionalism should not be confused with democracy. The elite rulers of England and the Dutch Republic pursued the same policies as absolute monarchs: increased taxation, government authority, and social control. Nonetheless, they served as influential models to onlookers across Europe as forms of government that checked the power of a single ruler. ■

Seventeenth-Century Crisis and Rebuilding

FOCUS QUESTION
What were the common crises and achievements of seventeenth-century European states?

Historians often refer to the seventeenth century as an "age of crisis," when Europe was challenged by population losses, economic decline, and social and political unrest. These difficulties were partially due to climate changes that reduced agricultural productivity, but they also resulted from bitter religious divides, war, and increased governmental pressures. Peasants and the urban poor were hit especially hard by the economic problems, and they frequently rose in riot against high food prices.

The atmosphere of crisis encouraged governments to take emergency measures to restore order, measures that they successfully turned into long-term reforms that strengthened the power of the state. These included a spectacular growth in army size as well as increased taxation, the expansion of government bureaucracies, and the acquisition of land or maritime empires. In the long run, European states proved increasingly able to impose their will on the populace.

The Social Order and Peasant Life

Peasants occupied the lower tiers of a society organized in hierarchical levels. At the top, the monarch was celebrated as a semidivine being, chosen by God to embody the state. In Catholic countries, the clergy occupied the second level, due to their sacred role interceding with God and the saints on behalf of their flocks. Next came nobles, whose privileged status derived from their ancient bloodlines and centuries of leadership on the battlefield. Traditional Christian prejudices against commerce and money meant that merchants could never lay claim to the highest honors. However, many prosperous mercantile families had bought their way into the nobility through service to the rising monarchies of the fifteenth and sixteenth centuries and constituted a second tier of nobles. Those lower on the social scale, the peasants and artisans who constituted the vast majority of the population, were expected to defer to their betters with humble obedience. This was the "Great Chain of Being" that linked God to his creation in a series of ranked social groups.

In addition to being rigidly hierarchical, European societies were patriarchal in nature, with men assuming authority over women as a God-given prerogative. The family thus represented a microcosm of the social order. The father ruled his family like a king ruled his domains. Religious and secular law commanded a man's wife, children, servants, and apprentices to defer to his will. Fathers did not possess the power of life and death, like Roman patriarchs, but they were entitled to use physical violence, imprisonment, and other forceful measures to impose their authority. These

Chronology

ca. 1500–1650	Consolidation of serfdom in eastern Europe	1665–1683	Jean-Baptiste Colbert applies mercantilism to France
1533–1584	Reign of Ivan the Terrible in Russia	1670	Charles II agrees to re-Catholicize England in secret agreement with Louis XIV
1589–1610	Reign of Henry IV in France	1670–1671	Cossack revolt led by Stenka Razin
1598–1613	Time of Troubles in Russia	ca. 1680–1750	Construction of absolutist palaces
1620–1740	Growth of absolutism in Austria and Prussia	1682	Louis XIV moves court to Versailles
1642–1649	English civil war, which ends with execution of Charles I	1682–1725	Reign of Peter the Great in Russia
1643–1715	Reign of Louis XIV in France	1683–1718	Habsburgs push the Ottoman Turks from Hungary
1653–1658	Military rule in England under Oliver Cromwell (the Protectorate)	1685	Edict of Nantes revoked in France
1660	Restoration of English monarchy under Charles II	1688–1689	Glorious Revolution in England
		1701–1713	War of the Spanish Succession

powers were balanced by expectations that a good father would provide and care for his dependents.

In the seventeenth century most Europeans lived in the countryside. The hub of the rural world was the small peasant village centered on a church and a manor. Life was in many ways circumscribed by the village, although we should not underestimate the mobility induced by war, food shortage, and the desire to seek one's fortune or embark on religious pilgrimage.

In western Europe, a small number of peasants in each village owned enough land to feed themselves and had the livestock and plows necessary to work their land. These independent farmers were leaders of the peasant village. They employed the landless poor, rented out livestock and tools, and served as agents for the noble lord. Below them were small landowners and tenant farmers who did not have enough land to be self-sufficient. These families sold their best produce on the market to earn cash for taxes, rent, and food. At the bottom were villagers who worked as dependent laborers and servants. In eastern Europe, the vast majority of peasants toiled as serfs for noble landowners and did not own land in their own right (see page 480).

Rich or poor, east or west, bread was the primary element of the diet. The richest ate a white loaf, leaving brown bread to those who could not afford better. Peasants paid stiff fees to the local miller for grinding grain into flour and sometimes to the lord for the right to bake bread in his oven. Bread was most often accompanied by a soup made of roots,

Peasants Working the Land Working the land was harsh toil for seventeenth-century peasants, but strong family and community bonds gave life meaning and made survival possible. The rich and colorful clothing of the peasants shown here reflects an idealized vision of the peasants' material circumstances. (*The Month of March*, by the Studio of Pieter de Witte [ca. 1548–1628], [oil on canvas], undated/© Sotheby's/akg-images)

herbs, beans, and perhaps a small piece of salt pork. An important annual festival in many villages was the killing of the family pig. The whole family gathered to help, sharing a rare abundance of meat with neighbors and carefully salting the extra and putting down the lard. In some areas, menstruating women were careful to stay away from the kitchen because of superstitious fears that they would cause the lard to spoil.

Famine and Economic Crisis

European rural society lived on the edge of subsistence. Because of the crude technology and low crop yield, peasants were constantly threatened by scarcity and famine. In the seventeenth century a period of colder and wetter climate throughout Europe, dubbed the "little ice age" by historians, meant a shorter farming season with lower yields. A bad harvest created food shortages; a series of bad harvests could lead to famine. Recurrent famines significantly reduced the population of early modern Europe. Most people did not die of outright starvation but perished through the spread of diseases like smallpox and typhoid, which were facilitated by malnutrition and exhaustion. Outbreaks of bubonic plague continued in Europe until the 1720s.

The Estates of Normandy, a provincial assembly, reported on the dire conditions in northern France during an outbreak of plague:

> Of the 450 sick persons whom the inhabitants were unable to relieve, 200 were turned out, and these we saw die one by one as they lay on the roadside. A large number still remain, and to each of them it is only possible to dole out the least scrap of bread. We only give bread to those who would otherwise die. The staple dish here consists of mice, which the inhabitants hunt, so desperate are they from hunger. They devour roots which the animals cannot eat; one can, in fact, not put into words the things one sees. . . . We certify to having ourselves seen herds, not of cattle, but of men and women, wandering about the fields between Rheims and Rhétel, turning up the earth like pigs to find a few roots; and as they can only find rotten ones, and not half enough of them, they become so weak that they have not strength left to seek food.[1]

Industry also suffered. The output of woolen textiles, one of the most important European manufactures, declined sharply in the first half of the seventeenth century. Food prices were high, wages stagnated, and unemployment soared. This economic crisis was not universal: it struck various regions at different times and to different degrees. In the middle decades of the century, for example, Spain, France, Germany, and England all experienced great economic difficulties, but these years were the golden age of the Netherlands.

The urban poor and peasants were the hardest hit. When the price of bread rose beyond their capacity to pay, they frequently expressed their anger by rioting. In towns they invaded bakers' shops to seize bread and resell it at a "just price." In rural areas they attacked convoys taking grain to the cities. Women often led these actions, since their role as mothers gave them some impunity in authorities' eyes. Historians have used the term "moral economy" for this vision of a world in which community needs predominate over competition and profit.

The Thirty Years' War

Harsh economic conditions in the seventeenth century were greatly exacerbated by the decades-long conflict known as the Thirty Years' War (1618–1648). The Holy Roman Empire was a confederation of hundreds of principalities, independent cities, duchies, and other polities loosely united under an elected emperor. The uneasy truce between Catholics and Protestants created by the Peace of Augsburg in 1555 deteriorated as the faiths of various areas shifted. Lutheran princes felt compelled to form the Protestant Union (1608), and Catholics retaliated with the Catholic League (1609). Each alliance was determined that the other should make no religious or territorial advance. Dynastic interests were also involved; the Spanish Habsburgs strongly supported the goals of their Austrian relatives: the unity of the empire and the preservation of Catholicism within it.

The war is traditionally divided into four phases. The first, or Bohemian, phase (1618–1625) was characterized by civil war in Bohemia between the Catholic League and the Protestant Union. In 1620 Catholic forces defeated Protestants at the Battle of the White Mountain. The second, or Danish, phase of the war (1625–1629)—so called because of the leadership of the Protestant king Christian IV of Denmark (r. 1588–1648)—witnessed additional Catholic victories. The Catholic imperial army led by Albert of Wallenstein swept through Silesia, north to the Baltic, and east into Pomerania, scoring smashing victories. Under Charles I, England briefly and unsuccessfully intervened in this phase of the conflict by entering alliances against France and Spain. Habsburg power peaked in 1629. The emperor issued the Edict of Restitution, whereby all Catholic properties lost to Protestantism since 1552 were restored, and only Catholics and Lutherans were allowed to practice their faiths.

The third, or Swedish, phase of the war (1630–1635) began with the arrival in Germany of the Swedish king Gustavus Adolphus (r. 1594–1632) and his army. The ablest administrator of his day and a devout Lutheran, he intervened to support the empire's Protestants. The French chief minister, Cardinal Richelieu, subsidized the Swedes, hoping to weaken Habsburg power in Europe. Gustavus Adolphus won two important battles but was fatally wounded in combat. The final, or French, phase of the war (1635–1648) was prompted by Richelieu's concern that the Habsburgs would rebound after the death of Gustavus Adolphus. Richelieu declared war on Spain and sent military as well as financial assistance. Finally, in October 1648 peace was achieved.

The 1648 **Peace of Westphalia** that ended the Thirty Years' War marked a turning point in European history. For the most part, conflicts fought over religious faith receded. The treaties recognized the independent authority of more than three hundred German princes (Map 15.1), reconfirming the emperor's severely limited authority. The Augsburg agreement of 1555 became permanent, adding Calvinism to Catholicism and Lutheranism as legally permissible creeds. The north German states remained Protestant, the south German states Catholic.

The Thirty Years' War was the most destructive event for the central European economy and society prior to the world wars of the twentieth century. Perhaps one-third of urban residents and two-fifths of the rural population died, leaving entire areas depopulated. Trade in southern German cities, such as Augsburg, was virtually destroyed. Agricultural areas suffered catastrophically. Many small farmers lost their land, allowing nobles to enlarge their estates and consolidate their control.[2]

Peace of Westphalia The name of a series of treaties that concluded the Thirty Years' War in 1648 and marked the end of large-scale religious violence in Europe.

Achievements in State-Building

In the context of warfare, economic crisis, and demographic decline, seventeenth-century monarchs took urgent measures to restore order and rebuild their states. Traditionally, historians have distinguished between the absolutist governments of France, Spain, central Europe, and Russia and the constitutionalist governments of England and the Dutch Republic. Whereas absolutist monarchs gathered all power under their

MAP 15.1 Europe After the Thirty Years' War   This map shows the political division of Europe after the Treaty of Westphalia (1648) ended the war. France emerged as the strongest power in Europe at the end of the Thirty Years' War. Based on this map, what challenges did the French state still face in dominating Europe after 1648? How does the map represent Swedish gains and Spanish losses in the Treaty of Westphalia?

personal control, English and Dutch rulers were obliged to respect laws passed by representative institutions. More recently, historians have emphasized commonalities among these powers. Despite their political differences, all these states shared common projects of protecting and expanding their frontiers, raising new taxes, consolidating central control, and competing for the new colonies opening up in the New and Old Worlds. In so doing, they followed a broad pattern of state-building and consolidation of power found across Eurasia in this period.

Rulers encountered formidable obstacles in achieving these goals. Without paved roads, telephones, or other modern technology, it took weeks to convey orders from the central government to the provinces and even longer to distant colonies. Rulers also suffered from lack of reliable information about their realms, making it impossible to police and tax the population effectively. Local power structures presented another serious obstacle. Nobles, the church, provincial and national assemblies, town councils, guilds, and other bodies held legal privileges, which could not easily be rescinded. Many kingdoms were composed of groups of people of different ethnicities who spoke a language different from that of the ruling dynasty, which further diminished their willingness to obey.

Nonetheless, over the course of the seventeenth century both absolutist and constitutional governments achieved new levels of power and national unity. They did so by transforming emergency measures of wartime into permanent structures of government and by subduing privileged groups through the use of force and through economic and social incentives. Increased state authority may be seen in four areas in particular: greater taxation, growth in armed forces, larger and more efficient bureaucracies, and territorial expansion both within Europe and overseas.

Over time, centralized power added up to something close to sovereignty. A state may be termed sovereign when it possesses a monopoly over the instruments of justice and the use of force within clearly defined boundaries. In a sovereign state, no system of courts, such as church tribunals, competes with state courts in the dispensation of justice; and private armies, such as those of feudal lords, present no threat to central authority. While seventeenth-century states did not acquire total sovereignty, they made important strides toward that goal.

Warfare and the Growth of Army Size

The driving force of seventeenth-century state-building was warfare. In medieval times, feudal lords had raised armies only for particular wars or campaigns; now monarchs began to recruit their own forces and maintain permanent standing armies. Instead of serving their own interests, army officers were required to be loyal and obedient to state officials. New techniques for training and deploying soldiers meant a rise in the professional standards of the army.

Along with professionalization came an explosive growth in army size. The French took the lead, with the army growing from roughly 125,000 men in the Thirty Years' War to 340,000 at the end of the seventeenth century.[3] Changes in the style of armies encouraged this growth. Mustering a royal army took longer than simply hiring a mercenary band, giving enemies time to form coalitions. For example, the large coalitions Louis XIV confronted (see pages 477–478) required him to fight on multiple fronts with huge armies. In turn, the relative size and wealth of France among European nations allowed Louis to field enormous armies and thereby to pursue the ambitious foreign policies that caused his alarmed neighbors to form coalitions against him.

Noble values of glory and honor outshone concerns for safety or material benefit. Because they personally led their men in battle, noble officers experienced high death rates on the battlefield. Nobles also fell into debt because they had to purchase their positions in the army and the units they commanded, which meant that they were obliged to assume many of the costs involved in creating and maintaining their units. It was not until the 1760s that the French government assumed the full cost of equipping troops.

Other European powers were quick to follow the French example. The rise of absolutism in central and eastern Europe was thus accompanied by a vast expansion in the size of armies. Great Britain followed a similar, albeit distinctive pattern. Instead of building a land army, the island nation focused on naval forces and eventually built the largest navy in the world.

Popular Political Action

As governments continuously raised taxes to meet the costs of war, neighborhood riots over the cost of bread turned into armed uprisings. Popular revolts were extremely common in England, France, Spain, Portugal, and Italy during the Thirty Years' War. In 1640 Philip IV of Spain faced revolt in Catalonia, the economic center of his realm. At the same time he struggled to put down uprisings in Portugal and in the northern provinces of the Netherlands. In 1647 the city of Palermo, in Spanish-occupied Sicily, exploded in protest over food shortages caused by a series of bad harvests. Fearing public unrest, the city government subsidized the price of bread, attracting even more starving peasants from the countryside. When Madrid ordered an end to subsidies, municipal leaders decided to lighten the loaf rather than raise prices. Not fooled by this change, local women led a bread riot, shouting "Long live the king and down with the taxes and the bad government!" Insurgency spread to the rest of the island and eventually to Naples on the mainland. Apart from affordable food, rebels demanded the suppression of extraordinary taxes and participation in municipal government. Some dreamed of a republic that would abolish noble tax exemptions. Despite initial successes, the revolt lacked unity and strong leadership and could not withstand the forces of the state.

In France urban uprisings became a frequent aspect of the social and political landscape. Beginning in 1630 and continuing intermittently through the early 1700s, major insurrections occurred at Dijon, Bordeaux (bor-DOH), Montpellier, Lyons, and Amiens. All were characterized by deep popular anger and violence directed at outside officials sent to collect taxes. These officials were sometimes seized, beaten, and hacked to death. For example, in 1673 Louis XIV's imposition of new taxes on legal transactions, tobacco, and pewter ware provoked an uprising in Bordeaux.

Municipal and royal authorities often struggled to overcome popular revolt. They feared that stern repressive measures, such as sending in troops to fire on crowds, would create martyrs and further inflame the situation, while full-scale occupation of a city would be very expensive and detract from military efforts elsewhere. The limitations of royal authority gave some leverage to rebels. To quell riots, royal edicts were sometimes suspended, prisoners released, and discussions initiated.

By the beginning of the eighteenth century this leverage had largely disappeared. Municipal governments were better integrated into the national structure, and local authorities had prompt military support from the central government. People who publicly opposed royal policies and taxes received swift and severe punishment.

Absolutism in France and Spain

FOCUS QUESTION

What factors led to the rise of the French absolutist state under Louis XIV, and why did absolutist Spain experience decline in the same period?

In the Middle Ages jurists held that as a consequence of monarchs' coronation and anointment with sacred oil, they ruled "by the grace of God." Law was given by God; kings "found" the law and acknowledged that they must respect and obey it. Kings in absolutist states amplified these claims, asserting that they were responsible to God alone. They claimed exclusive power to make and enforce laws, denying any other institution or group the authority to check their power. In France the founder of the Bourbon monarchy, Henry IV, established foundations upon which his successors Louis XIII and Louis XIV built a stronger, more centralized French state. Louis XIV is often seen as the epitome of an "absolute" monarch, with his endless wars, increased taxes and economic regulation, and glorious palace at Versailles. In truth, his success relied on collaboration with nobles, and thus his example illustrates both the achievements and the compromises of absolutist rule.

As French power rose in the seventeenth century, the glory of Spain faded. Once the fabulous revenue from American silver declined, Spain's economic stagnation could no longer be disguised, and the country faltered under weak leadership.

The Foundations of French Absolutism

At the beginning of the seventeenth century France's position appeared extremely weak. Struggling to recover from decades of religious civil war, France posed little threat to Spain's predominance in Europe. Yet by the end of the century the countries' positions were reversed.

Henry IV (r. 1589–1610) inaugurated a remarkable recovery by defusing religious tensions and rebuilding France's economy. He issued the Edict of Nantes, allowing Huguenots (French Protestants) the right to worship in 150 traditionally Protestant towns throughout France. He built new roads and canals to repair the ravages of years of civil war and raised revenue by selling royal offices instead of charging high taxes. Despite his efforts at peace, Henry was murdered in 1610 by a Catholic zealot.

Cardinal Richelieu (1585–1642) became first minister of the French crown on behalf of Henry's young son, Louis XIII (r. 1610–1643). Richelieu's domestic policies were designed to strengthen royal control. He acted to repress Protestantism, which he viewed as a divisive force in the realm. He also extended the use of intendants, commissioners for each of France's thirty-two districts who were appointed directly by the monarch, to whom they were solely responsible. These officials recruited men for the army, supervised tax collection, presided over the administration of local law, checked up on the local nobility, and regulated economic activities in their districts. As the intendants' power increased under Richelieu, so did the power of the centralized French state.

Richelieu's main foreign policy goal was to destroy the Habsburgs' grip on territories that surrounded France. Consequently, Richelieu supported Habsburg enemies, including Protestants during the Thirty Years' War (see page 469). For the French cardinal, interests of state outweighed religious considerations.

Cardinal Jules Mazarin (1602–1661) succeeded Richelieu as chief minister for the next child-king, the four-year-old Louis XIV, who inherited the throne from his father in 1643. Along with the regent, Queen Mother Anne of Austria, Mazarin continued Richelieu's centralizing policies. His struggle to increase royal revenues to meet the costs of war led to the uprisings of 1648–1653 known as the **Fronde**. In Paris, magistrates of the Parlement of Paris, the nation's most important law court, were outraged by the Crown's autocratic measures. These so-called robe nobles (named for the robes they wore in court) encouraged violent protest by the common people. As rebellion spread outside Paris and to the sword nobles (the traditional warrior nobility), civil order broke down completely, and young Louis XIV had to flee Paris for his safety.

Fronde A series of violent uprisings during the early reign of Louis XIV triggered by growing royal control and increased taxation.

Much of the rebellion died away, however, when Louis XIV was declared king in his own right in 1651, ending the regency of his mother Anne of Austria. (French law prohibited a woman from inheriting the throne, so periods when a queen mother acted as regent for a child-king were always vulnerable moments.) The French people were desperate for peace and stability after the disorders of the Fronde and were willing to accept a strong monarch who could reimpose order. Louis pledged to do just that when he assumed personal rule of his realm at Mazarin's death in 1661.

Louis XIV and Absolutism

In the reign of Louis XIV (r. 1643–1715), the longest in European history, the French monarchy reached the peak of absolutist development. Louis believed in the doctrine of the divine right of kings: God had established kings as his rulers on earth, and they were answerable ultimately to him alone. To symbolize his central role in the divine order, when he was fifteen years old Louis danced at a court ballet dressed as the sun, thereby acquiring the title "Sun King."

In addition to parading his power before the court, Louis worked very hard at the business of governing. He ruled his realm through several councils of state and insisted on taking a personal role in many of their decisions. He selected councilors from the recently ennobled or the upper middle class and offered this explanation: "[T]he public should know, from the rank of those whom I chose to serve me, that I had no intention of sharing power with them."[4] Despite increasing financial problems, Louis never called a meeting of the Estates General, thereby depriving nobles of united expression or action. Nor did Louis have a first minister. In this way he avoided the inordinate power of a Richelieu.

Although personally tolerant, Louis hated division within the realm and insisted that religious unity was essential to his royal dignity and to the security of the state. He thus pursued the policy of Protestant repression launched by Richelieu. In 1685 Louis revoked the Edict of Nantes. The new law ordered the Catholic baptism of Huguenots (French Calvinists), the destruction of Huguenot churches, the closing of schools, and the exile of Huguenot pastors who refused to renounce their faith. Around two hundred thousand Protestants, including some of the king's most highly skilled artisans, fled into exile.

Despite his claims to absolute authority, multiple constraints existed on Louis's power. As a representative of divine power, he was obliged to rule in a manner consistent with virtue and benevolence. He had to uphold the laws issued by his royal predecessors. Moreover, he also relied on the collaboration of nobles, who maintained tremendous prestige and authority in their ancestral lands. Without their cooperation, it would have been impossible to extend his power throughout France or wage his many foreign wars. Louis's efforts to elicit noble cooperation can be witnessed in the court life he created at his spectacular palace at Versailles.

Hyacinthe Rigaud, Portrait of Louis XIV, 1701 This was one of Louis XIV's favorite portraits of himself. He liked it so much that he had many copies of the portrait made; his successors had their own portraits painted in the same posture with the same clothing and accoutrements. (*Louis XIV in Royal Costume*, 1701, by Hyacinthe François Rigaud [1659–1743] [oil on canvas])/Musée du Louvre, Paris, France/Bridgeman Images)

Life at Versailles

Through most of the seventeenth century the French court had no fixed home, following the monarch to his numerous palaces and country residences. In 1682 Louis moved his court and government to the newly renovated palace at Versailles, a former

Letter from Versailles

Born in 1652, the German princess Elisabeth-Charlotte was the daughter of the elector of the Palatinate, one of the many small states of the Holy Roman Empire. In 1671 she married the duke of Orléans, brother of Louis XIV. When Louis's wife died in 1683, Elisabeth-Charlotte became the highest-ranked woman at the French court. Despite the considerable pride she took in her position, her correspondence reveals her unhappiness and boredom with court life and her longing for home, as shown in the letter to her sister excerpted below.

I have nothing new to tell you; I walk and read and write; sometimes the king drives me to the hunt in his calèche. There are hunts every day; Sundays and Wednesdays are my son's days; the king hunts Mondays and Thursdays; Wednesdays and Saturdays Monseigneur [heir to the throne] hunts the wolf; M. le Comte de Toulouse, Mondays and Wednesdays; the Duc du Maine, Tuesdays; and M. le Duc, Fridays. They say if all the hunting kennels were united there would be from 900 to 1000 dogs. Twice a week there is a comedy. But you know, of course, that I go nowhere [due to mourning for her recently deceased husband]; which vexes me, for I must own that the theatre is the greatest amusement I have in the world, and the only pleasure that remains to me. . . .

If the Court of France was what it used to be one might learn here how to behave in society; but— excepting the king and Monsieur [the king's brother, her deceased husband]— no one any longer knows what politeness is. The young men think only of horrible debauchery. I do not advise any one to send their children here; for instead of learning good things, they will only take lessons in misconduct. You are right in blaming Germans who send their sons to France; how I wish that you and I were men and could go to the wars!—but that's a completely useless wish to have. . . . If I could with propriety return to Germany you would see me there quickly. I love that country; I think it more agreeable than all others, because there is less of luxury that I do not care for, and more of the frankness and integrity which I seek. But, be it said between ourselves, I was placed here against my will, and here I must stay till I die. There is no likelihood that we shall see each other again in this life; and what will become of us after that God only knows.

EVALUATE THE EVIDENCE

1. What are the principal amusements of court life, according to Elisabeth-Charlotte? What comparison does she draw between life in Germany and France?
2. How does the image of Versailles conveyed by Elisabeth-Charlotte contrast with the images of the palace found elsewhere in this chapter? How do you explain this contrast? If courtiers like her found life so dreary at court, why would they stay?

Source: *The Correspondence of Madame, Princess Palatine, Marie-Adélaïde de Savoie, and Madame de Maintenon*, ed. and trans. Katharine Prescott Wormeley (Boston: Hardy, Pratt, 1902), pp. 50–52.

hunting lodge. The palace quickly became the center of political, social, and cultural life. The king required all great nobles to spend at least part of the year in attendance on him there, so he could keep an eye on their activities. Since he controlled the distribution of state power and wealth, nobles had no choice but to obey and compete with each other for his favor at Versailles.

The glorious palace, with its sumptuous interiors and extensive formal gardens, was a mirror to the world of French glory, soon copied by would-be absolutist monarchs across Europe. The reality of daily life in the palace was less glamorous. Versailles served as government offices for royal bureaucrats, as living quarters for the royal family and nobles, and as a place of work for hundreds of domestic servants. It was also open to the public at certain hours of the day. As a result, it was crowded with three thousand to ten thousand people every day. Even high nobles had to put up with cramped living space, and many visitors complained of the noise, smell, and crowds. (See "Evaluating the Evidence 15.1: Letter from Versailles," above.)

Louis further revolutionized court life by establishing an elaborate set of etiquette rituals to mark every moment of his day, from waking up and dressing in the morning to removing his clothing and retiring at night. Courtiers vied for the honor of participating in these ceremonies, with the highest in rank claiming the privilege of handing the king his shirt. Endless squabbles broke out over what type of chair one could sit on at court and the order in which great nobles entered and were seated in the chapel for Mass.

These rituals may seem absurd, but they were far from trivial. The king controlled immense resources and privileges; access to him meant favored treatment for government offices, military and religious posts, state pensions, honorary titles, and a host of other benefits. Courtiers sought these rewards for themselves and their family members and followers. A system of patronage—in which a higher-ranked individual protected a lower-ranked one in return for loyalty and services—flowed from the court to the provinces. Through this mechanism Louis gained cooperation from powerful nobles.

Although they could not hold public offices or posts, women played a central role in the patronage system. At court the king's wife, mistresses, and other female relatives recommended individuals for honors, advocated policy decisions, and brokered alliances between factions. Noblewomen played a similar role, bringing their family connections to marriage to form powerful social networks. Onlookers sometimes resented the influence of powerful women at court. The duke of Saint-Simon said of Madame de Maintenon, Louis XIV's mistress and secret second wife, "Many people have been ruined by her, without having been able to discover the author of the ruin, search as they might."

Louis XIV was also an enthusiastic patron of the arts, commissioning many sculptures and paintings for Versailles as well as performances of dance and music. Scholars characterize the art and literature of the age of Louis XIV as French classicism. By this they mean that the artists and writers of the late seventeenth century imitated the subject matter and style of classical antiquity, that their work resembled that of Renaissance Italy, and that French art possessed the classical qualities of discipline, balance, and restraint. Louis XIV also loved the stage, and in the plays of Molière and Racine his court witnessed the finest achievements in the history of French theater. In this period aristocratic ladies wrote many genres of literature and held salons in their Parisian mansions where they engaged in witty and cultured discussions of poetry, art, theater, and the latest worldly events. Their refined conversational style led Molière and other observers to mock them as "*précieuses*" (PREH-see-ooz; literally "precious"), or affected and pretentious. Despite this mockery, the précieuses represented an important cultural force ruled by elite women.

With Versailles as the center of European politics, French culture grew in international prestige. French became the language of polite society and international diplomacy, gradually replacing Latin as the language of scholarship and learning. Royal courts across Europe spoke French, and the great aristocrats of Russia, Sweden, Germany, and elsewhere were often more fluent in French than in the tongues of their homelands. France inspired a cosmopolitan European culture in the late seventeenth century that looked to Versailles as its center.

The French Economic Policy of Mercantilism

France's ability to build armies and fight wars depended on a strong economy. Fortunately for Louis, his controller general, Jean-Baptiste Colbert (1619–1683), proved to be a financial genius. Colbert's central principle was that the wealth and the economy of France should serve the state. To this end, from 1665 to his death in 1683, Colbert rigorously applied mercantilist policies to France.

Mercantilism is a collection of governmental policies for the regulation of economic activities by and for the state. It derives from the idea that a nation's international power is based on its wealth, specifically its supply of gold and silver. To accumulate wealth, a country always had to sell more goods abroad than it bought. To decrease French purchases of goods from outside the country, Colbert insisted that French industry should produce everything needed by the French people.

To increase exports, Colbert supported old industries and created new ones, focusing especially on textiles, which were the most important sector of manufacturing. He enacted new production regulations, created guilds to boost quality standards, and encouraged foreign craftsmen to immigrate to France. To encourage the purchase of French goods, he abolished many domestic tariffs and raised tariffs on foreign products. In 1664 Colbert founded the Company of the East Indies with (unfulfilled) hopes of competing with the Dutch for Asian trade.

Colbert also hoped to make Canada — rich in untapped minerals and some of the best agricultural land in the world — part of a vast French empire. He sent four thousand colonists to Quebec, whose capital had been founded in 1608 under Henry IV. Subsequently, the Jesuit Jacques Marquette and the merchant Louis Joliet sailed down the Mississippi River, which they named Colbert in honor of their sponsor (the name soon reverted to the original Native American one). Marquette and Joliet claimed possession of the land on both sides of the river as far south as present-day Arkansas. In 1684 French explorers continued down the Mississippi to its mouth and claimed vast territories for Louis XIV. The area was called, naturally, "Louisiana."

During Colbert's tenure as controller general, Louis was able to pursue his goals without massive tax increases and without creating a stream of new offices. The constant pressure of warfare after Colbert's death, however, undid many of his economic achievements.

Louis XIV's Wars

Louis XIV wrote that "the character of a conqueror is regarded as the noblest and highest of titles." In pursuit of the title of conqueror, he kept France at war for thirty-three of the fifty-four years of his personal rule. François le Tellier, marquis de Louvois, Louis's secretary of state for war, equaled Colbert's achievements in the economic realm. Louvois created a professional army in which the French state, rather than private nobles, employed the soldiers. Uniforms and weapons were standardized, and a rational system of training and promotion was devised. Many historians believe that the new loyalty, professionalism, and growth of the French army represented the peak of Louis's success in reforming government. As in so many other matters, his model was followed across Europe.

mercantilism A system of economic regulations aimed at increasing the power of the state based on the belief that a nation's international power was based on its wealth, specifically its supply of gold and silver.

The Acquisitions of Louis XIV, 1668–1713

Paris

FRANCHE-COMTÉ

FRANCE

Territory gained
◻ 1668　◻ 1678　◻ 1713

Louis's goal was to expand France to what he considered its natural borders. His armies managed to extend French borders to include important commercial centers in the Spanish Netherlands and Flanders as well as the entire province of Franche-Comté between 1667 and 1678. In 1681 Louis seized the city of Strasbourg, and three years later he sent his armies into the province of Lorraine. At that moment the king seemed invincible. In fact, Louis had reached the limit of his expansion. The wars of the 1680s and 1690s brought no additional territories but placed unbearable strains on French resources. Colbert's successors resorted to desperate measures to finance these wars, including devaluation of the currency and new taxes.

Louis's last war was endured by a French people suffering high taxes, crop failure, and widespread malnutrition and death. In 1700 the childless Spanish king Charles II (r. 1665–1700) died, opening a struggle for control of Spain and its colonies. His will bequeathed the Spanish crown and its empire to Philip of Anjou, Louis XIV's grandson (Louis's wife, Maria-Theresa, was Charles's sister). The will violated a prior treaty by which the European powers had agreed to divide the Spanish possessions between the king of France and the Holy Roman emperor, both brothers-in-law of Charles II. Claiming that he was following both Spanish and French interests, Louis broke with the treaty and accepted the will, thereby triggering the War of the Spanish Succession (1701–1713).

In 1701 the English, Dutch, Austrians, and Prussians formed the Grand Alliance against Louis XIV. War dragged on until 1713. The **Peace of Utrecht**, which ended the war, allowed Louis's grandson Philip to remain king of Spain on the understanding that the French and Spanish crowns would never be united. France surrendered Nova Scotia, Newfoundland, and the Hudson Bay territory to England, which also acquired Gibraltar, Minorca, and control of the African slave trade from Spain (Map 15.2).

Peace of Utrecht A series of treaties, from 1713 to 1715, that ended the War of the Spanish Succession, ended French expansion in Europe, and marked the rise of the British Empire.

The Peace of Utrecht represented the balance-of-power principle in operation, setting limits on the extent to which any one power—in this case, France—could expand. It also marked the end of French expansion. Thirty-five years of war had given France the rights to all of Alsace and some commercial centers in the north. But at what price? In 1714 an exhausted France hovered on the brink of bankruptcy. It is no wonder that when Louis XIV died on September 1, 1715, many subjects felt as much relief as they did sorrow.

The Decline of Absolutist Spain in the Seventeenth Century

At the beginning of the seventeenth century France's position appeared extremely weak. Struggling to recover from decades of religious civil war that had destroyed its infrastructure and economy, France could not dare to compete with Spain's empire or its mighty military. Yet by the end of the century their positions were reversed, and France had surpassed all expectations to attain European dominance.

By the early seventeenth century the seeds of Spanish disaster were sprouting. Between 1610 and 1650 Spanish trade with the colonies in the New World fell 60 percent due to competition from local industries in the colonies and from Dutch and English traders. At the same time, the native Indian and African slaves who toiled in the South American silver mines suffered frightful epidemics of disease. Ultimately, the mines that filled the empire's treasury started to run dry, and the quantity of metal produced steadily declined after 1620.

MAP 15.2 Europe After the Peace of Utrecht, 1715   The series of treaties commonly called the Peace of Utrecht ended the War of the Spanish Succession and redrew the map of Europe. A French Bourbon king succeeded to the Spanish throne. France surrendered the Spanish Netherlands (later Belgium), then in French hands, to Austria, and recognized the Hohenzollern rulers of Prussia. Spain ceded Gibraltar to Great Britain, for which it has been a strategic naval station ever since. Spain also granted Britain the *asiento*, the contract for supplying African slaves to the Americas.

In Madrid, however, royal expenditures constantly exceeded income. To meet mountainous state debt, the Crown repeatedly devalued the coinage and declared bankruptcy, which resulted in the collapse of national credit. Meanwhile, manufacturing and commerce shrank. In contrast to the other countries of western Europe, Spain had a tiny middle class. The elite condemned moneymaking as vulgar and undignified. Thousands entered economically unproductive professions: there were said to be nine thousand monasteries in the province of Castile alone. To make matters worse, the Crown expelled some three hundred thousand *Moriscos*, or former Muslims, in 1609, significantly reducing the pool of skilled workers and merchants. Those working in the textile industry were forced out of business by steep inflation that pushed their production costs to the point where they could not compete in colonial and international markets.[5]

Spanish aristocrats, attempting to maintain an extravagant lifestyle they could no longer afford, increased the rents on their estates. High rents and heavy taxes in turn drove the peasants from the land, leading to a decline in agricultural productivity. In cities wages and production stagnated. Spain also ignored new scientific methods that might have improved agricultural or manufacturing techniques because they came from the heretical nations of Holland and England.

The Spanish crown had no solutions to these dire problems. Philip III (r. 1598–1621), a melancholy and deeply pious man, handed the running of the government over to the duke of Lerma, who used it to advance his personal and familial wealth. Philip IV (r. 1621–1665) left the management of his several kingdoms to Gaspar de Guzmán, Count-Duke of Olivares. Olivares was an able administrator who has often been compared to Richelieu. He did not lack energy and ideas, and he succeeded in devising new sources of revenue. But he clung to the grandiose belief that the solution to Spain's difficulties rested in a return to the imperial tradition of the sixteenth century. Unfortunately, the imperial tradition demanded the revival of war with the Dutch at the expiration of a twelve-year truce in 1622 and a long war with France over Mantua (1628–1659). Spain thus became embroiled in the Thirty Years' War. These conflicts, on top of an empty treasury, brought disaster.

Spain's situation worsened with internal conflicts and fresh military defeats through the remainder of the seventeenth century. In 1640 Spain faced serious revolts in Catalonia and Portugal. In 1643 the French inflicted a crushing defeat on a Spanish army at Rocroi in what is now Belgium. By the Treaty of the Pyrenees of 1659, which ended the French-Spanish conflict, Spain was compelled to surrender extensive territories to France. In 1688 the Spanish crown reluctantly recognized the independence of Portugal, almost a century after the two crowns were joined. The era of Spanish dominance in Europe had ended.

Absolutism in Austria and Prussia

FOCUS QUESTION
What were the social conditions of eastern Europe, and how did the rulers of Austria and Prussia transform their nations into powerful absolutist monarchies?

The rulers of eastern Europe also labored to build strong absolutist states in the seventeenth century. But they built on social and economic foundations far different from those in western Europe, namely serfdom and the strong nobility who benefited from it. The endless wars of the seventeenth century allowed monarchs to increase their power by building large armies, increasing taxation, and suppressing representative institutions. In exchange for their growing political authority, monarchs allowed nobles to remain as unchallenged masters of their peasants, a deal that appeased both king and nobility, but left serfs at the mercy of the lords. The most successful states were Austria and Prussia, which witnessed the rise of absolutism between 1620 and 1740.

The Return of Serfdom in the East

While economic and social hardship was common across Europe, important differences existed between east and west. In the west the demographic losses of the Black Death allowed peasants to escape from serfdom as they acquired enough land to feed themselves. In eastern Europe seventeenth-century peasants had largely lost their ability to own land independently. Eastern lords dealt with the labor shortages caused by the Black Death by restricting the right of their peasants to move to take advantage of better opportunities elsewhere. In Prussian territories by 1500 the law required that runaway peasants be hunted down and returned to their lords. Moreover, lords steadily took more and more of their peasants' land and arbitrarily imposed heavier labor obligations. By the early 1500s lords in many eastern territories could command their peasants to work for them without pay for as many as six days a week.

The gradual erosion of the peasantry's economic position was bound up with manipulation of the legal system. The local lord was also the local prosecutor, judge, and jailer. There were no independent royal officials to provide justice or uphold the common law. The power of the lord reached far into serfs' everyday lives. Not only was their freedom of movement restricted, but they also required permission to marry or could be forced to marry. Lords could reallocate the lands worked by their serfs at will or sell serfs apart from their families. These conditions applied even on lands owned by the church.

Between 1500 and 1650 the consolidation of serfdom in eastern Europe was accompanied by the growth of commercial agriculture, particularly in Poland and eastern Germany. As economic expansion and population growth resumed after 1500, eastern lords increased the production of their estates by squeezing sizable surpluses out of the impoverished peasants. They then sold these surpluses to foreign merchants, who exported them to the growing cities of wealthier western Europe. The Netherlands and England benefited the most from inexpensive grain from the east.

It was not only the peasants who suffered in eastern Europe. With the approval of kings, landlords systematically undermined the medieval privileges of the towns and the power of the urban classes. Instead of selling products to local merchants, landlords sold directly to foreigners, bypassing local towns. Eastern towns also lost their medieval right of refuge and were compelled to return runaways to their lords. The population of the towns and the urban middle classes declined greatly. This development both reflected and promoted the supremacy of noble landlords in most of eastern Europe in the sixteenth century.

The Austrian Habsburgs

Like all the people of central Europe, the Habsburgs emerged from the Thirty Years' War impoverished and exhausted. Their efforts to destroy Protestantism in the German lands and to turn the weak Holy Roman Empire into a real state had failed. Although the Habsburgs remained the hereditary emperors, real power lay in the hands of a bewildering variety of separate political jurisdictions. Defeat in central Europe encouraged the Habsburgs to turn away from a quest for imperial dominance and to focus inward and eastward in an attempt to unify their diverse holdings. If they could not impose Catholicism in the empire, at least they could do so in their own domains.

Habsburg victory over Bohemia during the Thirty Years' War was an important step in this direction. Ferdinand II (r. 1619–1637) drastically reduced the power of the Bohemian Estates, the largely Protestant representative assembly. He also confiscated the landholdings of Protestant nobles and gave them to loyal Catholic nobles and to the foreign aristocratic mercenaries who led his armies. After 1650 a large portion of the Bohemian nobility was of recent origin and owed its success to the Habsburgs.

With the support of this new nobility, the Habsburgs established direct rule over Bohemia. Under their rule the condition of the enserfed peasantry worsened substantially: three days per week of unpaid labor became the norm. Protestantism was also stamped out. These changes were significant advances in creating absolutist rule in Bohemia.

Ferdinand III (r. 1637–1657) continued to build state power. He centralized the government in the empire's German-speaking provinces, which formed the core Habsburg holdings. For the first time, a permanent standing army was ready to put down any internal opposition. The Habsburg monarchy then turned east toward the plains of Hungary, which had been divided between the Ottomans and the Habsburgs in the early sixteenth century. Between 1683 and 1699 the Habsburgs pushed the Ottomans from most of Hungary and Transylvania. The recovery of all the former kingdom of Hungary was completed in 1718.

The Hungarian nobility, despite its reduced strength, effectively thwarted the full development of Habsburg absolutism. Throughout the seventeenth century Hungarian nobles rose in revolt against attempts to impose absolute rule. They never triumphed decisively, but neither were they crushed the way the nobility in Bohemia had been in 1620. In 1703, with the Habsburgs bogged down in the War of the Spanish Succession, the Hungarians rose in one last patriotic rebellion under Prince Francis Rákóczy. The prince and his forces were eventually defeated, but the Habsburgs agreed to restore many of the traditional privileges of the aristocracy in return for Hungarian acceptance of hereditary Habsburg rule. Thus Hungary, unlike Austria and Bohemia, was never fully integrated into a centralized, absolute Habsburg state.

Despite checks on their ambitions in Hungary, the Habsburgs made significant achievements in state-building elsewhere by forging consensus with the church and the nobility. A sense of common identity and loyalty to the monarchy grew among elites in Habsburg lands, even to a certain extent in Hungary. German became the language of the state, and zealous Catholicism helped fuse a collective identity.

Vienna became the political and cultural center of the empire. By 1700 it was a thriving city with a population of one hundred thousand and its own version of Versailles, the royal palace of Schönbrunn.

Prussia in the Seventeenth Century

In the fifteenth and sixteenth centuries the Hohenzollern family had ruled parts of eastern Germany as the imperial electors of Brandenburg and the dukes of Prussia. The title of "elector" gave its holder the privilege of being one of only seven princes or archbishops entitled to elect the Holy Roman emperor, but the electors had little real power. When he came to power in 1640, the twenty-year-old Frederick William, later known as the "Great Elector," was determined to unify his three provinces and enlarge his holdings. These provinces were Brandenburg; Prussia, inherited in 1618; and scattered territories along the Rhine inherited in 1614 (Map 15.3). Each was inhabited by German-speakers, but each had its own estates. Although the estates had not met regularly during the chaotic Thirty Years' War, taxes could not be levied without their consent. The estates of Brandenburg and Prussia were dominated by the nobility and the landowning classes, known as the **Junkers**.

Frederick William profited from ongoing European war and the threat of invasion from Russia when he argued for the need for a permanent standing army. In 1660 he

Junkers The nobility of Brandenburg and Prussia, they were reluctant allies of Frederick William in his consolidation of the Prussian state.

MAP 15.3 **The Growth of Austria and Brandenburg-Prussia to 1748**   Austria expanded to the southwest into Hungary and Transylvania at the expense of the Ottoman Empire. It was unable to hold the rich German province of Silesia, however, which was conquered by Brandenburg-Prussia.

persuaded Junkers in the estates to accept taxation without consent in order to fund an army. They agreed to do so in exchange for reconfirmation of their own privileges, including authority over the serfs. Having won over the Junkers, the king crushed potential opposition to his power from the towns. One by one, Prussian cities were eliminated from the estates and subjected to new taxes on goods and services.

Thereafter, the estates' power declined rapidly, for the Great Elector had both financial independence and superior force. He revealed his strategy toward managing the estates in the written instructions he left his son:

> Always regulate the expenditures according to the revenues, and have officials diligently render receipts every year. When the finances are in a good state again, then you will have enough means, and you will not have to request money from the estates or address them. Then it is also not necessary to hold the many and expensive parliaments, because the more parliaments you hold, the more authority is taken from you, because the estates always try something that is detrimental to the majesty of the ruler.[6]

A Prussian Giant Grenadier
Frederick William I wanted tall, handsome soldiers. He dressed them in tight, bright uniforms to distinguish them from the peasant population from which most soldiers came. He also ordered several portraits of his favorites, such as this one, from his court painter, J. C. Merk. Grenadiers (greh-nuh-DEERZ) wore the miter cap instead of an ordinary hat so that they could hurl their heavy grenades unimpeded by a broad brim. (Deutsches Historisches Museum, Berlin, Germany/© DHM/The Bridgeman Art Library)

By following his own advice, Frederick William tripled state revenue during his reign and expanded the army drastically. In 1688 a population of 1 million supported a peacetime standing army of 30,000. In 1701 the elector's son, Frederick I, received the elevated title of king of Prussia (instead of elector) as a reward for aiding the Holy Roman emperor in the War of the Spanish Succession.

The Consolidation of Prussian Absolutism

Frederick William I, "the Soldiers' King" (r. 1713–1740), completed his grandfather's work, eliminating the last traces of parliamentary estates and local self-government. It was he who truly established Prussian absolutism and transformed Prussia into a military state. Frederick William was intensely attached to military life. He always wore an army uniform, and he lived the highly disciplined life of the professional soldier. Years later he followed the family tradition by leaving his own written instructions to his son: "A formidable army and a war chest large enough to make this army mobile in times of need can create great respect for you in the world, so that you can speak a word like the other powers."[7]

Penny-pinching and hard-working, Frederick William achieved results. The king and his ministers built an exceptionally honest and conscientious bureaucracy to administer the country and foster economic development. Twelfth in Europe in population, Prussia had the fourth-largest army by 1740. The Prussian army was the best in Europe, astonishing foreign observers with its precision, skill, and discipline. As one Western traveler put it: "There is no theatre in Berlin whatsoever, diversion is understood to be the handsome troops who parade daily. A special attraction is the great Potsdam Grenadier Regiment . . . when they practice drill, when they fire and when they parade up and down, it is as if they form a single body."[8]

Nevertheless, Prussians paid a heavy and lasting price for the obsessions of their royal drillmaster. Army expansion was achieved in part through forced conscription, which was declared lifelong in 1713. Desperate draftees fled the country or injured themselves to avoid service. Finally, in 1733 Frederick William I ordered that all Prussian men would undergo military training and serve as reservists in the army, allowing him to preserve both agricultural production and army size. To appease the Junkers, the king enlisted them to lead his growing army. The proud nobility thus commanded the peasantry in the army as well as on the estates.

With all men harnessed to the war machine, Prussian civil society became rigid and highly disciplined. As a Prussian minister later summed up, "To keep quiet is the first civic duty."[9] Thus the policies of Frederick William I, combined with harsh peasant bondage and Junker tyranny, laid the foundations for a highly militaristic country.

The Development of Russia and the Ottoman Empire

FOCUS QUESTION
What were the distinctive features of Russian and Ottoman absolutism?

Russia occupied a unique position among Eurasian states. With borders straddling eastern Europe and northwestern Asia, its development into a strong imperial state drew on elements from both continents. Like the growth of the Muslim empires in Central and South Asia and the Ming Dynasty in China, the expansion of Russia was a result of the weakening of the great Mongol Empire. After declaring independence from the Mongols, the Russian tsars conquered a vast empire, extending through North Asia all the way to the Pacific Ocean. State-building and territorial expansion culminated during the reign of Peter the Great, who forcibly introduced elements of Western culture and society.

While Europeans debated, and continued to debate, whether or not Russia was a Western society, there was no question in their minds that the Ottomans were outsiders. Even absolutist rulers disdained Ottoman sultans as cruel and tyrannical despots. Despite stereotypes, however, the Ottoman Empire was in many ways more tolerant than its Western counterparts, providing protection and security to other religions while steadfastly maintaining the Muslim faith. The Ottoman state combined the Byzantine heritage of the territory it had conquered with Persian and Arab traditions. Flexibility and openness to other ideas and practices were sources of strength for the empire.

Mongol Rule in Russia and the Rise of Moscow

In the thirteenth century the Mongols had conquered Kievan Rus, the medieval Slavic state centered first at Novgorod and then at Kiev, a city on the Dnieper River; this state included most of present-day Ukraine, Belarus, and part of northwest Russia. For two hundred years, the Mongols forced the Slavic princes to submit to their rule and to render tribute and slaves. The princes of the Grand Duchy of Moscow, a principality within Kievan Rus, became particularly adept at serving the Mongols. They loyally put down uprisings and collected the khan's taxes. Eventually the Muscovite princes were able to destroy the other princes who were their rivals for power. Ivan III (r. 1462–1505), known as Ivan the Great, successfully expanded the principality of Moscow eastward toward the Baltic Sea and westward to the Ural Mountains and the Siberian frontier.

By 1480 Ivan III was strong enough to refuse to pay tribute to the Mongols and declare the autonomy of Moscow. To legitimize their new position, Ivan and his successors borrowed elements of Mongol rule. They forced weaker Slavic principalities to render tribute previously paid to Mongols and borrowed Mongol institutions such as the tax system, postal routes, and census. Loyalty from the highest-ranking nobles, or **boyars**, helped the Muscovite princes consolidate their power.

Another source of legitimacy for Moscow was its claim to the political and religious legacy of the Byzantine Empire. After the fall of Constantinople to the Turks in 1453, the princes of Moscow saw themselves as the heirs of both the Byzantine caesars (or emperors) and the empire's Orthodox Christianity. The title "tsar," first taken by Ivan IV in 1547, is in fact a contraction of *caesar*. The tsars considered themselves rightful and holy rulers, an idea promoted by Orthodox churchmen who spoke of "holy Russia" as the "Third Rome." The marriage of Ivan III to the daughter of the last Byzantine emperor further enhanced Moscow's assertion of imperial authority.

boyars The highest-ranking members of the Russian nobility.

Building the Russian Empire

Developments in Russia took a chaotic turn with the reign of Ivan IV (r. 1533–1584), the famous "Ivan the Terrible," who rose to the throne at age three. His mother died, possibly poisoned, when he was eight, leaving Ivan to suffer insults and neglect from the boyars at court. At age sixteen Ivan pushed aside his advisers, and in an awe-inspiring ceremony, with gold coins pouring down on his head, he majestically crowned himself tsar.

Russian Peasant An eighteenth-century French artist visiting Russia recorded his impressions of the daily life of the Russian people in this etching of a fish merchant pulling his wares through a snowy village on a sleigh. Two caviar vendors behind him make a sale to a young mother standing at her doorstep with her baby in her arms. (Pierson: Les Amis de Paris–Saint Pétersbourgh)

After the sudden death of his wife, however, Ivan began a campaign of persecution against those he suspected of opposing him. He executed members of leading boyar families, along with their families, friends, servants, and peasants. To replace them, Ivan created a new service nobility, whose loyalty was guaranteed by their dependence on the state for land and titles.

Cossacks Free groups and outlaw armies originally comprising runaway peasants living on the borders of Russian territory from the fourteenth century onward. By the end of the sixteenth century they had formed an alliance with the Russian state.

As landlords demanded more from the serfs who survived the persecutions, growing numbers of peasants fled toward wild, recently conquered territories to the east and south. There they joined free groups and warrior bands known as **Cossacks**. Ivan responded by tying peasants ever more firmly to the land and to noble landholders. Simultaneously, he ordered that urban dwellers be bound to their towns and jobs so that he could tax them more heavily. The urban classes had no security in their property, and even the wealthiest merchants were dependent agents of the tsar. These restrictions checked the growth of the Russian middle classes and stood in sharp contrast to economic and social developments in western Europe.

Ivan combined domestic oppression with external aggression. His reign was successful in defeating the remnants of Mongol power, adding vast new territories to the realm, and laying the foundations for the huge, multiethnic Russian empire. In the 1550s, strengthened by an alliance with Cossack bands, Ivan conquered the Muslim khanates of Kazan and Astrakhan and brought the fertile steppe region around the Volga River under Russian control. In the 1580s Cossacks fighting for the Russian state crossed the Ural Mountains and began the long conquest of Siberia. Because of the size of the new territories and their distance from Moscow, the Russian state did not initially seek to impose the Orthodox religion and maintained local elites in positions of honor and leadership, buying their loyalty with grants of land. In relying on cooperation from local elites and ruthlessly exploiting the common people, the Russians followed the pattern of the Spanish and other early modern European imperial states.

■	Moscow, ca. 1300
■	Gains by 1505
■	Gains by 1584
■	Gains by 1725
✳	Major battle

The Expansion of Russia to 1725

Following Ivan's death, Russia entered a chaotic period known as the "Time of Troubles" (1598–1613). While Ivan's relatives struggled for power, Cossacks and peasants rebelled against nobles and officials. This social explosion from below brought the nobles together. They crushed the Cossack rebellion and brought Ivan's sixteen-year-old grandnephew, Michael Romanov, to the throne (r. 1613–1645). The Romanov dynasty would endure as one of the most successful European absolutist dynasties until the Russian Revolution of 1917.

Like their Western counterparts, the Romanov tsars made several important achievements in state-building during the second half of the seventeenth century. After a long war, Russia gained land in Ukraine from Poland in 1667 and completed the conquest of Siberia by the end of the century. Territorial expansion was accompanied by growth of the bureaucracy and the army. The tsars employed foreign experts to reform the Russian army, and enlisted Cossack warriors to fight Siberian campaigns. The great profits from Siberia's natural resources, especially furs, funded the Romanovs' bid for Great Power status. Russian imperialist expansion to the east paralleled the Western powers' exploration and conquest of the Atlantic world in the same period.

The growth of state power did nothing to improve the lot of the common people. In 1649 a new law code extended serfdom to all peasants in the realm, giving lords unrestricted rights over their serfs and establishing penalties for harboring runaways. The new code also removed the privileges that non-Russian elites had enjoyed within the empire and required conversion to Russian Orthodoxy. Henceforth, Moscow maintained strict control of trade and administration throughout the empire.

The peace imposed by harsh Russian rule was disrupted in 1670 by a rebellion led by the Cossack Stenka Razin, who attracted a great army of urban poor and peasants. He and his followers killed landlords and government officials and proclaimed freedom from oppression, but their rebellion was defeated in 1671. The ease with which Moscow crushed the rebellion testifies to the success of the Russian state in unifying and consolidating its empire.

The Reforms of Peter the Great

Heir to Romanov efforts at state-building, Peter the Great (r. 1682–1725) embarked on a tremendous campaign to accelerate and complete these processes. A giant for his time at six feet seven inches, and possessing enormous energy and willpower, Peter built on the service obligations of Ivan the Terrible and his successors and continued their tradition of territorial expansion. In particular, he was determined to gain access to the sea for his virtually landlocked state.

Peter realized a first step toward this goal by conquering the Ottoman fort of Azov in 1696 and quickly built Russia's first navy base. In 1697 the tsar led a group of 250 Russian officials and young nobles on an eighteen-month tour of western European capitals. Peter was fascinated by foreign technology, and he hoped to forge an anti-Ottoman alliance to strengthen his claims on the Black Sea. Traveling unofficially to avoid lengthy diplomatic ceremonies, Peter met with foreign kings, master shipbuilders, gunners, and other specialists. He failed to secure a military alliance, but he did learn his lessons from the growing power of the Dutch and the English. He also engaged more than a hundred foreign experts to return with him to Russia to help build the navy and improve Russian infrastructure. (See "Evaluating the Evidence 15.2: Peter the Great and Foreign Experts," page 488.)

Having failed to gain support for an anti-Ottoman alliance and suffering a reversal of fortune at Azov, Peter switched tactics and entered into a secret agreement with Denmark and Poland to wage a sudden war of aggression against Sweden with the goal of securing access to the Baltic Sea. Peter and his allies believed that their combined forces could win easy victories because Sweden was in the hands of a new and inexperienced king.

Peter the Great and Foreign Experts

John Deane, an eminent shipbuilder, was one of the many foreign artisans and experts brought to Russia by Peter the Great after the latter's foreign tour of 1697. Several months after his arrival in Russia, Deane sent a glowing account of the tsar's technical prowess to his patron in England, the marquess of Carmarthen, admiral of the English fleet.

~

At my arrival in Moscow, I fell very ill of the Bloody-Flux, which made me be in Moscow when his Majesty came home: About the latter end of October I was somewhat recovered, his Majesty then carried me down to Voronize* with him. Voronize is about 400 English Miles South-East from Moscow. There the Czar immediately set up a ship of 60 guns, where he is both Foreman and Master-Builder; and not to flatter him, I'll assure your Lordship it will be the best ship among them, and 'tis all from his own Draught; How he fram'd her together and how he made the Mould, and in so short a time as he did is really wonderful: But he is able at this day to put his own notions into practice, and laugh at his Dutch and Italian builders for their ignorance. There are several pieces of workmanship, as in the keel, stem, and post, which are all purely his own invention, and sound good work, and would be approved of by all the shipwrights of England if they saw it. . . .

* Size of the naval shipyard.

After some time [I] fell sick again; and at Christmas, when his Majesty came to Moscow, he brought me back again for recovery of my health, where I am at present. . . . The whole place is inhabited by the Dutch; I believe there may be 400 families. Last Sunday and Monday the strangers were invited to the consecration of General La Fort's house, which is the noblest building in Russia, and finely furnisht. There were all the envoys, and as near as I could guess 200 gentlemen, English, French, and Dutch, and about as many ladies; each day were dancing and musick. All the envoys, and all the lords (but three in Moscow) are going to Voronize to see the fleet, I suppose. His majesty went last Sunday to Voronize with Prince Alexander and I am to go down (being something recovered) with the Vice-Admiral about six days hence.

EVALUATE THE EVIDENCE

1. According to Deane, what evidence did Peter give of his skills in shipbuilding? Based on this document, how would you characterize the relationship between Peter the Great and his foreign experts?
2. What other evidence does Deane provide of the impact of foreigners on life in Russia?

Source: John Deane, *A Letter from Moscow to the Marquess of Carmarthen, Relating to the Czar of Muscovy's Forwardness in His Great Navy, & c. Since His Return Home*, London, 1699.

Eighteen-year-old Charles XII of Sweden (1697–1718) surprised Peter. He defeated Denmark quickly in 1700, then turned on Russia. In a blinding snowstorm, his well-trained professional army attacked and routed unsuspecting Russians besieging the Swedish fortress of Narva on the Baltic coast. It was, for the Russians, a grim beginning to the long and brutal Great Northern War, which lasted from 1700 to 1721.

Peter responded to this defeat with new measures to increase state power, strengthen his military forces, and gain victory. He required all nobles to serve in the army or in the civil administration—for life. Since a more modern army and government required skilled experts, Peter created new schools and universities and required every young nobleman to spend five years in education away from home. Peter established an interlocking military-civilian bureaucracy with fourteen ranks, and he decreed that all had to start at the bottom and work toward the top. The system allowed some people of non-noble origins to rise to high positions, a rarity in Europe at the time. These measures gradually combined to make the army and government more powerful and efficient.

Peter also greatly increased the service requirements of commoners. In the wake of the Narva disaster, he established a regular standing army of more than two hundred thousand peasant-soldiers, drafted for life and commanded by noble officers. He added an additional hundred thousand men in special regiments of Cossacks and foreign mercenaries. To fund the army, taxes on peasants increased threefold during Peter's reign. Serfs were also arbitrarily assigned to work in the growing number of factories and mines that supplied the military. Under Peter, Russia's techniques for governing its territories — including the policing of borders and individual identity documents — were far ahead of those of most other imperial powers.

In 1709 Peter's new war machine was able to crush the small army of Sweden in Ukraine at Poltava, one of the most significant battles in Russian history. Russia's victory against Sweden was conclusive in 1721, and Estonia and present-day Latvia came under Russian rule for the first time. The cost was high: warfare consumed 80 to 85 percent of all revenues. But Russia became the dominant power in the Baltic and very much a great European power.

After his victory at Poltava, Peter channeled enormous resources into building a new Western-style capital on the Baltic to rival the great cities of Europe. Originally a desolate and swampy Swedish outpost, the magnificent city of St. Petersburg was designed to reflect modern urban planning, with wide, straight avenues, buildings set in a uniform line, and large parks. Each summer, twenty-five thousand to forty thousand peasants were sent to provide construction labor in St. Petersburg without pay.

There were other important consequences of Peter's reign. For Peter, modernization meant westernization, and he encouraged the spread of Western culture along with technology and urban planning. Peter required nobles to shave their heavy beards and wear Western clothing, previously banned in Russia. He also ordered them to attend parties where young men and women would mix together and freely choose their own spouses. From these efforts a new elite class of Western-oriented Russians began to emerge.

Peter's reforms were unpopular with many Russians. For nobles, one of Peter's most detested reforms was the imposition of unigeniture — inheritance of land by one son alone — cutting daughters and other sons from family property. For peasants, the reign of the tsar saw a significant increase in the bonds of serfdom, and the gulf between the enserfed peasantry and the educated nobility increased. Despite the unpopularity of Peter's reforms, his modernizing and westernizing of Russia paved the way for it to move somewhat closer to the European mainstream in its thought and institutions during the Enlightenment, especially under Catherine the Great.

Peter the Great Cutting a Boyar's Beard
As part of his westernization program, Peter the Great obliged Russian men to shave their long beards, a shock to traditional Orthodox notions of masculinity. Like many of his reforms, these were aimed primarily at the noble boyars; many peasants continued to wear beards in the countryside. (Universal History Archive/Getty Images)

The Ottoman Empire

Most Christian Europeans perceived the Ottomans as the antithesis of their own values and traditions and viewed the empire as driven by an insatiable lust for warfare and conquest. In their view the fall of Constantinople was a historic catastrophe and the taking of the Balkans a form of despotic imprisonment. To Ottoman eyes, the world looked very different. The siege of Constantinople liberated a glorious city from its long decline under the Byzantines. Rather than being a despoiled captive,

MAP 15.4 The Ottoman Empire at Its Height, 1566 The Ottomans, like their great rivals the Habsburgs, rose to rule a vast dynastic empire encompassing many different peoples and ethnic groups. The army and the bureaucracy served to unite the disparate territories into a single state under an absolutist ruler.

the Balkans were a haven for refugees fleeing the growing intolerance of Western Christian powers. The Ottoman Empire provided a safe haven for Jews, Muslims, and even some Christians from the Inquisition and religious war.

The Ottomans came out of Central Asia as conquering warriors, settled in Anatolia (present-day Turkey), and, at their peak in the mid-sixteenth century, ruled one of the most powerful empires in the world (see Chapter 14). Their possessions stretched from western Persia across North Africa and into the heart of central Europe (Map 15.4).

The Ottoman Empire was built on a unique model of state and society. Agricultural land was the personal hereditary property of the **sultan**, and peasants paid taxes to use the land. There was therefore an almost complete absence of private landed property and no hereditary nobility. The Ottomans also employed a distinctive form of government administration. The top ranks of the bureaucracy were staffed by the sultan's slave corps. Because Muslim law prohibited enslaving other Muslims, the sultan's agents purchased slaves along the borders of the empire. Within the realm, the sultan levied a "tax" of one thousand to three thousand male children on the conquered Christian populations in the Balkans every year. These young slaves were raised in Turkey as Muslims and were trained to fight and to administer. Unlike enslaved Africans in European colonies, who faced a dire fate, the most talented

sultan The ruler of the Ottoman Empire; he owned all the agricultural land of the empire and was served by an army and bureaucracy composed of highly trained slaves.

Ottoman slaves rose to the top of the bureaucracy, where they might acquire wealth and power. The less fortunate formed the core of the sultan's army, the **janissary corps**. These highly organized and efficient troops gave the Ottomans a formidable advantage in war with western Europeans. By 1683 service in the janissary corps had become so prestigious that the sultan ceased recruitment by force, and it became a volunteer army open to Christians and Muslims.

The Ottomans divided their subjects into religious communities, and each *millet*, or "nation," enjoyed autonomous self-government under its religious leaders. The Ottoman Empire recognized Orthodox Christians, Jews, Armenian Christians, and Muslims as distinct millets, but despite its tolerance, the empire was an explicitly Islamic state. The **millet system** created a powerful bond between the Ottoman ruling class and religious leaders, who supported the sultan's rule in return for extensive authority over their own communities. Each millet collected taxes for the state, regulated group behavior, and maintained law courts, schools, houses of worship, and hospitals for its people.

Istanbul (known outside the empire by its original name, Constantinople) was the capital of the empire. The "old palace" was for the sultan's female family members, who lived in isolation under the care of eunuchs, men who were castrated to prevent sexual relations with women. The newer Topkapi palace was where officials worked and young slaves trained for future administrative or military careers. Sultans married women of the highest social standing, while keeping many concubines of low rank. To prevent the elite families into which they married from acquiring influence over the government, sultans procreated only with their concubines and not with official wives. They also adopted a policy of allowing each concubine to produce only one male heir. At a young age, each son went to govern a province of the empire accompanied by his mother. These practices were intended to stabilize power and prevent a recurrence of the civil wars of the late fourteenth and early fifteenth centuries.

Sultan Suleiman undid these policies when he boldly married his concubine, a former slave of Polish origin named Hürrem, and had several children with her. (See "Individuals in Society: Hürrem," page 492.) Starting with Suleiman, imperial wives began to take on more power. Marriages were arranged between sultans' daughters and high-ranking servants, creating powerful new members of the imperial household. Over time, the sultan's exclusive authority waned in favor of a more bureaucratic administration.

Like European states, the Ottoman Empire suffered significant crises in the late sixteenth and early seventeenth centuries. Raised in the harem rather than taking on provincial governorships, the sultans who followed Suleiman were inexperienced and faced numerous political revolts. Ottoman finances suffered from the loss of international trade to the Portuguese and the Dutch, and the empire—like Spain—suffered from rising prices and a shrinking population. While the Bourbon monarchy was modernizing and enlarging the French army, the Ottomans failed to adopt new military technologies and training methods. As a result, its military strength, long feared throughout Europe, declined, leading ultimately to the ceding of Hungary and Transylvania to the Austrian Habsburgs in 1699 (see page 482). The Ottoman state adapted to these challenges with some measure of success, but did not recover the glory it held under Suleiman.

janissary corps The core of the sultan's army, composed of slave conscripts from non-Muslim parts of the empire; after 1683 it became a volunteer force.

millet system A system used by the Ottomans whereby subjects were divided into religious communities, with each millet (nation) enjoying autonomous self-government under its religious leaders.

INDIVIDUALS IN SOCIETY
Hürrem

In Muslim culture, *harem* means a sacred place or a sanctuary. The term was applied to the part of the household occupied by women and children and forbidden to men outside the family. The most famous harem member in Ottoman history was Hürrem, wife of Suleiman the Magnificent.

Like many of the sultan's concubines, Hürrem (1505?–1558) was of foreign birth. Tradition holds that she was born Aleksandra Lisowska in the kingdom of Poland (present-day Ukraine). Captured during a Tartar raid and enslaved, she entered the imperial harem between 1517 and 1520, when she was about fifteen years old. Reports from Venetian visitors claimed that she was not outstandingly beautiful, but was possessed of wonderful grace, charm, and good humor, earning her the Turkish nickname Hürrem, or "joyful one." Soon after her arrival, Hürrem became the imperial favorite.

Suleiman's love for Hürrem led him to set aside all precedents for the role of a concubine, including the rule that concubines must cease having children once they gave birth to a male heir. By 1531 Hürrem had given Suleiman one daughter and five sons. In 1533 or 1534 Suleiman entered formal marriage with his consort — an unprecedented and scandalous honor for a concubine. Suleiman reportedly lavished attention on his wife and defied convention by allowing her to remain in the palace throughout her life instead of accompanying her son to a provincial governorship.

Contemporaries were shocked by Hürrem's influence over the sultan and resentful of the apparent role she played in politics and diplomacy. The Venetian ambassador Bassano wrote that "the Janissaries and the entire court hate her and her children likewise, but because the Sultan loves her, no one dares to speak."* Court rumors circulated that Hürrem used witchcraft to control the sultan and ordered the sultan's execution of his first-born son by another mother.

The correspondence between Suleiman and Hürrem, unavailable until the nineteenth century, along with Suleiman's own diaries, confirms her status as the sultan's most trusted confidant and adviser. During his frequent absences, the pair exchanged passionate love letters. Hürrem included political information and warned of potential uprisings. She also intervened in affairs between the empire and her former home, apparently helping Poland attain its privileged diplomatic status. She brought a feminine touch to diplomatic relations, sending personally embroidered articles to foreign leaders.

Hürrem used her enormous pension to contribute a mosque, two schools, a hospital, a fountain, and two public baths to Istanbul. In Jerusalem, Mecca, and Istanbul, she provided soup kitchens and hospices for pilgrims and the poor. She died in 1558, eight years before her husband. Her son Selim II (r. 1566–1574) inherited the throne.

*Quoted in Galina Yermolenko, "Roxolana: The Greatest Empresse of the East," *The Muslim World* 95 (2005): 235.

Constitutional Rule in England and the Dutch Republic

FOCUS QUESTION

Why and how did the constitutional state triumph in the Dutch Republic and England?

While France, Prussia, Russia, and Austria developed absolutist states, England and the Netherlands evolved toward **constitutionalism**, which is the limitation of government by law. Constitutionalism also implies a balance between the authority and power of the government, on the one hand, and the rights and liberties of the subjects, on the other. By definition, all constitutionalist governments have a constitution, be it written or unwritten. A nation's constitution may be embodied in one basic document and occasionally revised by amendment, like the Constitution of the United States. Or it may be only partly formalized and include parliamentary statutes, judicial decisions, and a body of traditional procedures and practices, like the English and Dutch constitutions.

Despite their common commitment to constitutional government, England and the Dutch Republic represented significantly different alternatives to absolute rule. After

Relying on Western observers' reports, historians traditionally depicted Hürrem as a manipulative and power-hungry social climber. They portrayed her career as the beginning of a "sultanate of women" in which strong imperial leadership gave way to court intrigue and debauchery. More recent historians have emphasized the intelligence and courage Hürrem demonstrated in navigating the ruthlessly competitive world of the harem.

Hürrem's journey from Ukrainian maiden to concubine to sultan's wife captured enormous public attention. She is the subject of numerous paintings, plays, and novels, as well as an opera, a ballet, and a symphony by the composer Haydn. Interest in and suspicion of Hürrem continues. In 2003 a Turkish miniseries once more depicted her as a scheming intriguer.

This portrait emphasizes the beauty and sensual allure of Hürrem, who journeyed from slave to harem favorite to wife of the sultan and mother of his successor. (Pictures from History/akg-images)

QUESTIONS FOR ANALYSIS

1. What types of power did Hürrem exercise during her lifetime? How did her gender enable her to attain certain kinds of power and also constrain her ability to exercise it?
2. What can an exceptional woman like Hürrem reveal about the broader political and social world in which she lived?

Source: Leslie P. Pierce, *The Imperial Harem: Women and Sovereignty in the Ottoman Empire* (New York: Oxford University Press, 1993).

decades of civil war and an experiment with **republicanism**, the English opted for a constitutional monarchy in 1688. This settlement, which has endured to this day, retained a monarch as the titular head of government but vested sovereignty in an elected parliament. Upon gaining independence from Spain in 1648, the Dutch rejected monarchical rule, adopting a republican form of government in which elected estates held supreme power. Neither was democratic by any standard, but to frustrated inhabitants of absolutist states they were shining examples of the restraint of arbitrary power and the rule of law.

Religious Divides and Civil War

In 1588 Queen Elizabeth I of England (r. 1558–1603) exercised very great personal power; by 1689 the English monarchy was severely circumscribed. A rare female monarch, Elizabeth was able to maintain control over her realm in part by refusing to marry and submit to a husband. She was immensely popular with her people, but left no immediate heir to continue her legacy.

constitutionalism A form of government in which power is limited by law and balanced between the authority and power of the government, on the one hand, and the rights and liberties of the subjects or citizens on the other hand; could include constitutional monarchies or republics.

republicanism A form of government in which there is no monarch and power rests in the hands of the people as exercised through elected representatives.

493

In 1603 Elizabeth's Scottish cousin James Stuart succeeded her as James I (r. 1603–1625). Like Louis XIV, James believed that a monarch has a divine right to his authority and is responsible only to God. James went so far as to lecture the House of Commons: "There are no privileges and immunities which can stand against a divinely appointed King." Such a view ran directly counter to the long-standing English tradition that a person's property could not be taken away without due process of law. James I and his son Charles I (r. 1625–1649) considered such constraints intolerable and a threat to their divine-right prerogative. Consequently, bitter squabbles erupted between the Crown and the House of Commons. The expenses of England's intervention in the Thirty Years' War, through hostilities with Spain (1625–1630) and France (1627–1629), only exacerbated tensions. Charles I's response was to refuse to summon Parliament from 1629 onward.

Religious issues also embittered relations between the king and the House of Commons. In the early seventeenth century many English people felt dissatisfied with the Church of England established by Henry VIII (r. 1509–1547). Calvinist **Puritans** wanted to take the Reformation further by "purifying" the Anglican Church of Roman Catholic elements—elaborate vestments and ceremonials, bishops, and even the giving and wearing of wedding rings.

James I responded to such ideas by declaring, "No bishop, no king." For James, bishops were among the chief supporters of the throne. His son and successor, Charles I, further antagonized religious sentiments by marrying a French princess and supporting the heavy-handed policies of the archbishop of Canterbury William Laud (1573–1645). Laud provoked outrage by imposing two new elements on church organization in Scotland: a new prayer book, modeled on the Anglican *Book of Common Prayer*, and bishoprics.

Charles avoided addressing grievances against him by refusing to call Parliament into session from 1629 to 1640. Instead, he financed his government through extraordinary stopgap levies considered illegal by most English people. However, when Scottish Calvinists revolted against his religious policies, Charles was forced to summon Parliament to obtain funds for an army to put down the revolt. Accordingly, this Parliament, called the "Long Parliament" because it sat from 1640 to 1660, enacted legislation that limited the power of the monarch, and made government without Parliament impossible.

In 1641 the Parliament passed the Triennial Act, which compelled the king to summon Parliament every three years. The Commons impeached Archbishop Laud and then threatened to abolish bishops. King Charles, fearful of a Scottish invasion—the original reason for summoning Parliament—reluctantly accepted these measures.

The next act in the conflict was precipitated by the outbreak of rebellion in Ireland, where English governors and landlords had long exploited the people. In 1641 the Catholic gentry of Ireland led an uprising in response to a feared invasion by anti-Catholic forces of the British Long Parliament.

Without an army, Charles I could neither come to terms with the Scots nor respond to the Irish rebellion. After a failed attempt to arrest parliamentary leaders, Charles left London for the north of England, where he began to raise an army. In response, Parliament formed its own army, the New Model Army, composed of the

Puritans Members of a sixteenth- and seventeenth-century reform movement within the Church of England that advocated purifying it of Roman Catholic elements, like bishops, elaborate ceremonials, and wedding rings.

militia of the city of London and country squires with business connections. During the spring of 1642 both sides prepared for war. In July a linen weaver became the first casualty of the civil war during a skirmish between royal and parliamentary forces in Manchester.

The English civil war (1642–1649) pitted the power of the king against that of the Parliament. After three years of fighting, Parliament's New Model Army defeated the king's armies at the Battles of Naseby and Langport in the summer of 1645. Charles, though, refused to concede defeat. Both sides jockeyed for position, waiting for a decisive event. This arrived in the form of the army under the leadership of Oliver Cromwell, a member of the House of Commons and a devout Puritan. In 1647 Cromwell's forces captured the king and dismissed anti-Cromwell members of the Parliament. In 1649 the remaining representatives, known as the "Rump Parliament," put Charles on trial for high treason. Charles was found guilty and beheaded on January 30, 1649, an act that sent shock waves around Europe.

The English Civil War, 1642–1649

The Puritan Protectorate

With the execution of Charles, kingship was abolished. The question remained of how the country would be governed. One answer was provided by philosopher Thomas Hobbes (1588–1679). Hobbes held a pessimistic view of human nature and believed that, left to themselves, humans would compete violently for power and wealth. The only solution, as he outlined in his 1651 treatise *Leviathan*, was a social contract in which all members of society placed themselves under the absolute rule of the sovereign, who would maintain peace and order. Hobbes imagined society as a human body in which the monarch served as head and individual subjects together made up the body. Just as the body cannot sever its own head, so Hobbes believed that society could not, having accepted the contract, rise up against its king.

Hobbes's longing for a benevolent absolute monarch was not widely shared in England. Instead, Oliver Cromwell and his supporters enshrined a commonwealth, or republican government, known as the **Protectorate**. Theoretically, legislative power rested in the surviving members of Parliament, and executive power was lodged in a council of state. In fact, the army controlled the government, and Oliver Cromwell controlled the army, ruling what was essentially a military dictatorship.

The army prepared a constitution, the Instrument of Government (1653), that invested executive power in a lord protector (Cromwell) and a council of state. It provided for triennial parliaments and gave Parliament the sole power to raise taxes. But after repeated disputes, Cromwell dismissed Parliament in 1655, and the instrument was never formally endorsed. Cromwell continued the standing army and proclaimed quasi-martial law. He divided England into twelve military districts, each governed by a major general. Reflecting Puritan ideas of morality, Cromwell's state forbade sports, closed the theaters, and rigorously censored the press.

On the issue of religion, Cromwell favored some degree of toleration, and the Instrument of Government gave all Christians except Roman Catholics the right to practice their faith. Cromwell had long associated Catholicism in Ireland with sedition and heresy, and led an army there to reconquer the country

Protectorate The English military dictatorship (1653–1658) established by Oliver Cromwell following the execution of Charles I.

Puritan Occupations
These twelve engravings depict typical Puritan occupations and show that the Puritans came primarily from the artisan and lower middle classes. The governing classes and peasants made up a much smaller percentage of the Puritans and generally adhered to the traditions of the Church of England. (Private Collection/© Look and Learn/Peter Jackson Collection/Bridgeman Images)

in August 1649. One month later, his forces crushed a rebellion at Drogheda and massacred the garrison. After Cromwell's departure for England, atrocities worsened. The English banned Catholicism in Ireland, executed priests, and confiscated land from Catholics for English and Scottish settlers. These brutal acts left a legacy of Irish hatred for England.

Cromwell adopted mercantilist policies similar to those of absolutist France. He enforced a Navigation Act (1651) requiring that English goods be transported on English ships. The act was a great boost to the development of an English merchant marine and brought about a short but successful war with the commercially threatened Dutch. While mercantilist legislation ultimately benefited English commerce, for ordinary people the turmoil of foreign war only added to the harsh conditions of life induced by years of civil war. Cromwell also welcomed the immigration of Jews because of their skills in business, and they began to return to England after four centuries of absence.

The Protectorate collapsed when Cromwell died in 1658 and his ineffectual son succeeded him. Fed up with military rule, the English longed for a return to civilian government and, with it, common law and social stability. By 1660 they were ready to restore the monarchy.

The Restoration of the English Monarchy

The Restoration of 1660 brought to the throne Charles II (r. 1660–1685), eldest son of Charles I, who had been living on the continent. Both houses of Parliament were also restored, together with the established Anglican Church. The Restoration failed to resolve two serious problems, however. What was to be the attitude of the state toward Puritans, Catholics, and dissenters from the established church? And what was to be the relationship between the king and Parliament?

To answer the first question, Parliament enacted the **Test Act** of 1673 against those outside the Church of England, denying them the right to vote, hold public office, preach, teach, attend the universities, or even assemble for meetings. But these restrictions could not be enforced. When the Quaker William Penn held a meeting of his Friends and was arrested, the jury refused to convict him.

In politics, Charles II's initial determination to work well with Parliament did not last long. Finding that Parliament did not grant him an adequate income, in 1670 Charles entered into a secret agreement with his cousin Louis XIV. The French king would give Charles £200,000 annually, and in return Charles would relax the laws against Catholics, gradually re-Catholicize England, and convert to Catholicism himself. When the details of this treaty leaked out, a great wave of anti-Catholic sentiment swept England.

When Charles died and his Catholic brother James became king, the worst English anti-Catholic fears were realized. In violation of the Test Act, James II (r. 1685–1688) appointed Roman Catholics to positions in the army, the universities, and local government. When these actions were challenged in the courts, the judges, whom James had appointed, decided in favor of the king. James and his supporters opened new Catholic churches and schools and issued tracts promoting Catholicism. Attempting to broaden his base of support with Protestant dissenters and nonconformists, James granted religious freedom to all.

James's opponents, a powerful coalition of eminent persons in Parliament and the Church of England, bitterly resisted James's ambitions. They offered the English throne to James's heir, his Protestant daughter Mary, and her Dutch husband, Prince William of Orange. In December 1688 James II, his queen, and their infant son fled to France and became pensioners of Louis XIV. Early in 1689 William and Mary were crowned king and queen of England.

Constitutional Monarchy

The English call the events of 1688 and 1689 the "Glorious Revolution" because they believe it replaced one king with another with barely any bloodshed. In truth, William's arrival sparked revolutionary riots and violence across the British Isles and in North American cities such as Boston and New York. Uprisings by supporters of James, known as Jacobites, occurred in 1689 in Scotland. In Ireland, the two sides waged outright war from 1689 to 1691. William's victory at the Battle of the Boyne (1690) and the subsequent Treaty of Limerick (1691) sealed his accession to power.

In England, the revolution represented the final destruction of the idea of divine-right monarchy. The men who brought about the revolution framed their intentions in the Bill of Rights, which was formulated in direct response to Stuart absolutism. Law was to be made in Parliament; once made, it could not be suspended by the Crown. Parliament had to be called at least once every three years. The independence of the judiciary was established, and there was to be no standing army in peacetime. Protestants could

Test Act Legislation, passed by the English Parliament in 1673, to secure the position of the Anglican Church by stripping Puritans, Catholics, and other dissenters of the right to vote, preach, assemble, hold public office, and teach at or attend the universities.

John Locke, *Two Treatises of Government*

In 1688 opponents of King James II invited his daughter Mary and her husband, the Dutch prince William of Orange, to take the throne of England. James fled for the safety of France. One of the most outspoken proponents of the "Glorious Revolution" that brought William and Mary to the throne was philosopher John Locke. In this passage, Locke argues that sovereign power resides in the people, who may reject a monarch who does not obey the law.

But government into whosesoever hands it is put, being as I have before shown, entrusted with this condition, and for this end, that men might have and secure their properties, the prince or senate, however it may have power to make laws for the regulation of property between the subjects one amongst another, yet can never have a power to take to themselves the whole, or any part of the subjects' property, without their own consent. For this would be in effect to leave them no property at all. . . .

'Tis true, governments cannot be supported without great charge, and 'tis fit every one who enjoys his share of the protection, should pay, out of this estate, his proportion for the maintenance of it. But still it must be with his own consent, i.e., the consent of the majority, giving it either by themselves, or their representatives chosen by them; for if any one shall claim a power to lay and levy taxes on the people, by his own authority, and without such consent of the people, he thereby invades the fundamental law of property, and subverts the end of government. For what property have I in

that which another may be right to take when he pleases to himself. . . .

The constitution of the legislative is the first and fundamental act of society, whereby provision is made for the continuation of their union, under the direction of persons, and bonds of laws, made by persons authorized thereunto, by the consent and appointment of the people, without which no one man, or number of men, amongst them, can have authority of making laws that shall be binding to the rest. When any one, or more, shall take upon them to make laws, whom the people have not appointed so to do, they make laws without authority, which the people are not therefore bound to obey; by which means they come again to be out of subjection, and may constitute to themselves a new legislative, as they think best, being in full liberty to resist the force of those, who, without authority, would impose any thing upon them.

EVALUATE THE EVIDENCE

1. For what reason do people form a government, according to Locke? What would be the justification for disobeying laws and rejecting the authority of government?
2. In what ways does this document legitimize the events of the Glorious Revolution?

Source: John Locke, *Two Treatises of Government*. Reprinted in *England's Glorious Revolution, 1688–1689*, ed. Steven C. A. Pincus (Boston: Bedford/St. Martin's, 2006), pp. 161–162, 164.

possess arms, but the Catholic minority could not. A Catholic could not inherit the throne. Additional legislation granted freedom of worship to Protestant dissenters, but not to Catholics. William and Mary accepted these principles when they took the throne, and the House of Parliament passed the Bill of Rights in December 1689.

The Glorious Revolution and the concept of representative government found its best defense in political philosopher John Locke's *Two Treatises of Government* (1690). Locke (1632–1704) maintained that a government that oversteps its proper function—protecting the natural rights of life, liberty, and property—becomes a tyranny. (See "Evaluating the Evidence 15.3: John Locke, *Two Treatises of Government*," above.) By "natural" rights Locke meant rights basic to all men because all have the ability to reason. Under a tyrannical government, the people have the natural right to rebellion. On the basis of this link, he justified limiting the vote to property owners. Locke's idea that there are natural or universal rights equally valid for all peoples and societies was especially popular in colonial America. American colonists also appreciated his arguments that

Jan Steen, *The Merry Family*, 1668
In this painting from the Dutch golden age, a happy family enjoys a boisterous song while seated around the dining table. Despite its carefree appearance, the painting was intended to teach a moral lesson. The children are shown drinking wine and smoking, bad habits they have learned from their parents. The inscription hanging over the mantelpiece (upper right) spells out the message clearly: "As the Old Sing, so Pipe the Young." (Oil on canvas/ Rijksmuseum, Amsterdam, The Netherlands/ Album/Art Resource, NY)

Native Americans had no property rights since they did not cultivate the land and, by extension, no political rights because they possessed no property.

Although the events of 1688 and 1689 brought England closer to Locke's ideal, they did not constitute a democratic revolution. The revolution placed sovereignty in Parliament, and Parliament represented the upper classes. The age of aristocratic government lasted at least until 1832 and in many ways until 1928, when women received full voting rights.

The Dutch Republic in the Seventeenth Century

In the late sixteenth century the seven northern provinces of the Netherlands fought for and won their independence from Spain. The independence of the Republic of the United Provinces of the Netherlands was recognized in 1648 in the treaty that ended the Thirty Years' War. In this period, often called the "golden age" of the Netherlands, Dutch ideas and attitudes played a profound role in shaping a new and modern worldview. At the same time, the United Provinces developed its own distinctive model of a constitutional state.

Rejecting the rule of a monarch, the Dutch established a republic, a state in which power rested in the hands of the people and was exercised through elected representatives. Other examples of republics in early modern Europe included the Swiss Confederation and several autonomous city-states of Italy and the Holy Roman Empire. Among the Dutch, an oligarchy of wealthy businessmen called regents handled domestic affairs in each province's Estates (assemblies). The provincial Estates held virtually all the power. A federal assembly, or States General, handled foreign affairs and war, but it did not possess sovereign authority. All issues had to be referred back to the local Estates for approval, and each of the seven provinces could veto any proposed legislation. Holland, the province with the largest navy and the most wealth, usually dominated the republic and the States General.

stadholder The executive officer in each of the United Provinces of the Netherlands, a position often held by the princes of Orange.

In each province, the Estates appointed an executive officer, known as the **stadholder**, who carried out ceremonial functions and was responsible for military defense. Although in theory the stadholder was freely chosen by the Estates and was answerable to them, in practice the strong and influential House of Orange usually held the office of stadholder in several of the seven provinces of the republic. This meant that tensions always lingered between supporters of the House of Orange and those of the staunchly republican Estates, who suspected that the princes of Orange harbored monarchical ambitions. When one of them, William III, took the English throne in 1688 with his wife, Mary, the republic simply continued without stadholders for several decades.

The political success of the Dutch rested on their phenomenal commercial prosperity. The Dutch originally came to dominate European shipping by putting profits from their original industry—herring fishing—into shipbuilding. They boasted the lowest shipping rates and largest merchant marine in Europe, allowing them to undersell foreign competitors (see Chapter 14). In the seventeenth century global trade and commerce brought the Dutch the highest standard of living in Europe, perhaps in the world. Salaries were high, and all classes of society ate well. A scholar has described the Netherlands as "an island of plenty in a sea of want." Consequently, the Netherlands experienced very few of the food riots that characterized the rest of Europe.[10]

The moral and ethical bases of Dutch commercial wealth were thrift, frugality, and religious toleration. Although there is scattered evidence of anti-Semitism, Jews enjoyed a level of acceptance and assimilation in business and general culture unique in early modern Europe. In the Dutch Republic, toleration paid off: it attracted a great deal of foreign capital and investment. After Louis XIV revoked the Edict of Nantes, many Huguenots fled France for the Dutch Republic. They brought with them a high level of artisanal skill and business experience as well as a loathing for state repression that would inspire the political views of the Enlightenment (see page 520).

Baroque Art and Music

Throughout European history, the cultural tastes of one age have often seemed unsatisfactory to the next. So it was with the baroque. The term *baroque* may have come from the Portuguese word for an "odd-shaped, imperfect pearl" and was commonly used by late-eighteenth-century art critics as an expression of scorn for what they considered an overblown, unbalanced style. Specialists now agree that the baroque style marked one of the high points in the history of European culture.

Rome and the revitalized Catholic Church of the late sixteenth century spurred the early development of the baroque. The papacy and the Jesuits encouraged the growth of an intensely emotional, exuberant art. These patrons wanted artists to go beyond the Renaissance focus on pleasing a small, wealthy cultural elite. They wanted artists to appeal to the senses and thereby touch the souls and kindle the faith of ordinary churchgoers while proclaiming the power and confidence of the reformed Catholic Church. In addition to this underlying religious emotionalism, the baroque drew its sense of drama, motion, and ceaseless striving from the Catholic Reformation. The interior of the famous Jesuit Church of Jesus in Rome—the Gesù—combined all these characteristics in its lavish, wildly active decorations and frescoes.

Rubens, *Garden of Love*, 1633–1634 This painting is an outstanding example of the lavishness and richness of baroque art. Born and raised in northern Europe, Peter Paul Rubens trained as a painter in Italy. Upon his return to the Spanish Netherlands, he became a renowned and amazingly prolific artist, patronized by rulers across Europe. Rubens was a devout Catholic, and his work conveys the emotional fervor of the Catholic Reformation. (Oil on canvas/Prado, Madrid, Spain/Giraudon/Bridgeman Images)

Taking definite shape in Italy after 1600, the baroque style in the visual arts developed with exceptional vigor in Catholic countries—in Spain and Latin America, Austria, southern Germany, and Poland. Yet baroque art was more than just "Catholic art" in the seventeenth century and the first half of the eighteenth. True, neither Protestant England nor the Netherlands ever came fully under the spell of the baroque, but neither did Catholic France. And Protestants accounted for some of the finest examples of baroque style, especially in music. The baroque style spread partly because its tension and bombast spoke to an agitated age that was experiencing great violence and controversy in politics and religion.

In painting, the baroque reached maturity early with Peter Paul Rubens (1577–1640), the most outstanding and most representative of baroque painters. Studying in his native Flanders and in Italy, where he was influenced by masters of the High Renaissance such as Michelangelo, Rubens developed his own rich, sensuous, colorful style, which was characterized by animated figures, melodramatic contrasts, and monumental size. Rubens excelled in glorifying monarchs such as Queen Mother Marie de' Medici of France. He was also a devout Catholic; nearly half of his pictures treat Christian subjects. Yet one of Rubens's trademarks was the fleshy, sensual nudes who populate his canvases as Roman goddesses, water nymphs, and remarkably voluptuous saints and angels.

In music, the baroque style reached its culmination almost a century later in the dynamic, soaring lines of the endlessly inventive Johann Sebastian Bach (1685–1750). Organist and choirmaster of several Lutheran churches across Germany, Bach was equally at home writing secular concertos and sublime religious cantatas. Bach's organ music combined the baroque spirit of invention, tension, and emotion in an unforgettable striving toward the infinite. Unlike Rubens, Bach was not fully appreciated in his lifetime, but since the early nineteenth century his reputation has grown steadily.

LOOKING BACK LOOKING AHEAD

The seventeenth century represented a difficult passage between two centuries of dynamism and growth. On one side lay the sixteenth century of religious enthusiasm and strife, overseas expansion, rising population, and vigorous commerce. On the other side stretched the eighteenth-century era of renewed population growth, economic development, and cultural flourishing. The first half of the seventeenth century was marked by the spread of religious and dynastic warfare across Europe, resulting in the death and dislocation of many millions. This catastrophe was compounded by recurrent episodes of crop failure, famine, and epidemic disease, all of which contributed to a stagnant economy and population loss. In the middle decades of the seventeenth century, the very survival of the European monarchies established in the Renaissance appeared in doubt.

With the re-establishment of order in the second half of the century, maintaining political and social stability was of paramount importance to European rulers and elites. In western and eastern Europe, a host of monarchs proclaimed their God-given and "absolute" authority to rule in the name of peace, unity, and good order. Rulers' ability to impose such claims in reality depended a great deal on compromise with local elites, who acquiesced to state power in exchange for privileges and payoffs. In this way, absolutism and constitutionalism did not always differ as much as they claimed. Both systems relied on political compromises forged from decades of strife.

The eighteenth century was to see this status quo thrown into question by new Enlightenment aspirations for human society, which themselves derived from the inquisitive and self-confident spirit of the Scientific Revolution. By the end of the century, demands for real popular sovereignty would challenge the foundations of the political order so painfully achieved in the seventeenth century.

Make Connections

Think about the larger developments and continuities within and across chapters.

1. This chapter has argued that, despite their political differences, rulers in absolutist and constitutionalist nations faced similar obstacles in the mid-seventeenth century and achieved many of the same goals. What evidence for this argument do you find in the chapter? Do you think that absolutist and constitutionalist rulers were, on the whole, more similar or more different?

2. Proponents of absolutism in western Europe believed that their form of monarchical rule was fundamentally different from and superior to what they saw as the "despotism" of Russia and the Ottoman Empire. What was the basis of this belief, and how accurate do you think it was?

15 REVIEW & EXPLORE

Review the Main Ideas

Answer the focus questions from each section of the chapter.

◆ What were the common crises and achievements of seventeenth-century European states? (p. 466)

◆ What factors led to the rise of the French absolutist state under Louis XIV, and why did absolutist Spain experience decline in the same period? (p. 472)

◆ What were the social conditions of eastern Europe, and how did the rulers of Austria and Prussia transform their nations into powerful absolutist monarchies? (p. 480)

◆ What were the distinctive features of Russian and Ottoman absolutism? (p. 484)

◆ Why and how did the constitutional state triumph in the Dutch Republic and England? (p. 492)

Identify Key Terms

Identify and explain the significance of each item below.

Peace of Westphalia (p. 469)
Fronde (p. 473)
mercantilism (p. 477)
Peace of Utrecht (p. 478)
Junkers (p. 482)
boyars (p. 485)
Cossacks (p. 486)
sultan (p. 490)
janissary corps (p. 491)
millet system (p. 491)
constitutionalism (p. 492)
republicanism (p. 493)
Puritans (p. 494)
Protectorate (p. 495)
Test Act (p. 497)
stadholder (p. 500)

NOTES

1. Quoted in Cecile Hugon, *Social France in the XVII Century* (London: McMilland, 1911), p. 189.
2. H. Kamen, "The Economic and Social Consequences of the Thirty Years' War," *Past and Present* 39 (1968): 44–61.
3. John A. Lynn, "Recalculating French Army Growth," in *The Military Revolution Debate: Readings on the Military Transformation of Early Modern Europe*, ed. Clifford J. Rogers (Boulder, Colo.: Westview Press, 1995), p. 125.
4. Quoted in John A. Lynn, *Giant of the Grand Siècle: The French Army, 1610–1715* (Cambridge: Cambridge University Press, 1997), p. 74.
5. J. H. Elliott, *Imperial Spain, 1469–1716* (New York: Mentor Books, 1963), pp. 306–308.
6. German History Documents, http://germanhistorydocs.ghi-dc.org/docpage.cfm?docpage_id=3733.
7. H. Rosenberg, *Bureaucracy, Aristocracy, and Autocracy: The Prussian Experience, 1660–1815* (Boston: Beacon Press, 1966), p. 43.
8. Cited in Giles MacDonogh, *Frederick the Great: A Life in Deed and Letters* (New York: St. Martin's, 2001), p. 23.
9. Rosenberg, *Bureaucracy, Aristocracy, and Autocracy*, p. 40.
10. S. Schama, *The Embarrassment of Riches: An Interpretation of Dutch Culture in the Golden Age* (New York: Alfred A. Knopf, 1987), pp. 165–170; quotation is on p. 167.

CHAPTER PREVIEW

The Scientific Revolution
What revolutionary discoveries were made in the sixteenth and seventeenth centuries, and why did they occur in Europe?

Important Changes in Scientific Thinking and Practice
What intellectual and social changes occurred as a result of the Scientific Revolution?

The Rise and Spread of Enlightenment Thought
How did the Enlightenment emerge, and what were major currents of Enlightenment thought?

The Social Life of the Enlightenment
How did Enlightenment thinkers address issues of racial and social difference, and how did new institutions and social practices diffuse Enlightenment thought?

Enlightened Absolutism
What impact did new ways of thinking have on political developments and monarchical absolutism?

Life During the Scientific Revolution
This 1768 painting by Joseph Wright captures the popularization of science and experimentation during the Enlightenment. Here, a scientist demonstrates the creation of a vacuum by withdrawing air from a flask, with the suffocating cockatoo serving as shocking proof of the experiment.
(An *Experiment on a Bird in the Air Pump*, 1768/National Gallery, London/ Bridgeman Images)

16

Toward a New Worldview

1540–1789

The intellectual developments of the sixteenth and seventeenth centuries created the modern worldview that the West continues to hold—and debate—to this day. In this period, fundamentally new ways of understanding the natural world emerged. Those leading the changes saw themselves as philosophers and referred to their field of study as "natural philosophy." Whereas medieval scholars looked to authoritative texts like the Bible or the classics, early modern natural philosophers performed experiments and relied on increasingly complex mathematical calculations. The resulting conception of the universe and its laws remained in force until Albert Einstein's discoveries at the beginning of the twentieth century. Along with new discoveries in botany, zoology, chemistry, and other domains, these developments constituted a fundamental shift in the basic framework for understanding the natural world and the methods for examining it known collectively as the "Scientific Revolution."

In the eighteenth century philosophers extended the use of reason from the study of nature to human society. They sought to bring the light of reason to bear on the darkness of prejudice, outmoded traditions, and ignorance. Self-proclaimed members of an "Enlightenment" movement, they wished to bring the same progress to human affairs as their predecessors had brought to the understanding of the natural world. While the Scientific Revolution ushered in modern science, the Enlightenment created concepts of human rights, equality, progress, universalism, and tolerance that still guide Western societies today. At the same time, some people used their new understanding of nature and reason to proclaim their own superiority, thus rationalizing attitudes now regarded as racist and sexist. Transformations in science and philosophy were enabled and encouraged by European overseas expansion, which challenged traditional ways of thinking by introducing an enormous variety of new peoples, plants, and animals. ■

The Scientific Revolution

FOCUS QUESTION
What revolutionary discoveries were made in the sixteenth and seventeenth centuries, and why did they occur in Europe?

Until the middle of the sixteenth century, Europeans relied on an understanding of motion and matter drawn from the ancient Greek philosopher Aristotle and adapted to Christian theology. The rise of the university, along with the intellectual vitality of the Renaissance and technological advancements, inspired European scholars to seek better explanations. From the sun-centered universe proposed by the Polish astronomer Nicolaus Copernicus to the great synthesis of physics and astronomy accomplished by the English scientist Isaac Newton, a revolutionary new understanding of the universe had emerged by the end of the seventeenth century. Collectively known as the "Scientific Revolution," the work of these scientists constituted highly significant milestones in the creation of modern science.

Hailed today as pioneers of a modern worldview, the major figures of the Scientific Revolution were for the most part devout Christians who saw their work as heralding the glory of creation and who combined older traditions of magic, astrology, and alchemy with their pathbreaking experimentation. Their discoveries took place in a broader context of international trade, imperial expansion, and cultural exchange. Alongside developments in modern science and natural philosophy, the growth of natural history in this period is now recognized by historians as a major achievement of the Scientific Revolution.

Why Europe?

In 1500 scientific activity flourished in many parts of the world. With the expansion of Islam into the lands of the Byzantine Empire in the seventh and eighth centuries, Muslim scholars inherited ancient Greek learning, which itself was built on centuries of borrowing from older civilizations in Egypt, Babylonia, and India. The interaction of peoples and cultures across the vast Muslim world, facilitated by religious tolerance and the common scholarly language of Arabic, was highly favorable to advances in learning.

In a great period of cultural and intellectual flourishing from 1000 to 1500, Muslim scholars thrived in cultural centers such as Baghdad and Córdoba, the capital of Islamic Spain. They established the world's first universities in Constantinople, Fez (Morocco), and Cairo. In this fertile atmosphere, scholars surpassed the texts they had inherited in areas such as mathematics, physics, astronomy, and medicine. Arab and Persian mathematicians, for example, invented algebra, the concept of the algorithm, and decimal point notation, while Arab astronomers improved on measurements recorded in ancient works.

China was also a vital center of scientific activity, which reached a peak in the mid-fourteenth century. Among its many achievements, papermaking, gunpowder, and the use of the compass in navigation were the most influential for the West. In Mesoamerica, civilizations such as the Maya and the Aztecs devised complex calendar systems based on astronomical observations and developed mathematics and writing.

Given the multiple world sites of learning and scholarship, it was by no means inevitable that Europe would take the lead in scientific thought or that "modern science" as we know it would emerge. In world history, periods of advancement produced by intense cultural interaction, such as those that occurred after the spread of Islam, are often followed by stagnation and decline during times of conflict and loss of authority. This is what happened in western Europe after the fall of the Western Roman Empire in the fifth century and in the Maya civilization after the collapse of its cultural and political centers around 900. The Muslim world successfully resisted a similar threat after the Mongol invasions.

The re-establishment of stronger monarchies and the growth of trade in the High Middle Ages contributed to a renewal of learning in western Europe. As Europeans began to encroach on Islamic lands in Iberia, Sicily, and the eastern Mediterranean, they became aware of the rich heritage of ancient Greek learning in these regions and the ways scholars had improved upon received knowledge. In the twelfth century many Greek texts—including works of Aristotle, Ptolemy, Galen, and Euclid previously unknown in the West—were translated into Latin, along with the commentaries of Arab scholars. A number of European cities created universities in which Aristotle's works dominated the curriculum.

As Europe recovered from the ravages of the Black Death in the late fourteenth and fifteenth centuries, the intellectual and cultural movement known as the Renaissance provided a crucial foundation for the Scientific Revolution (see Chapter 12). Scholars called humanists, working in the bustling mercantile city-states of Italy, emphasized the value of acquiring knowledge for the practical purposes of life. The quest to restore the glories of the ancient past led to the rediscovery of other classical texts such as Ptolemy's *Geography*, which was translated into Latin around 1410. An encyclopedic treatise on botany by Theophrastus was rediscovered in the 1450s moldering on the shelves of the Vatican library. The fall of Constantinople to the Ottomans in 1453 resulted in a great influx of little-known Greek works, as Christian scholars fled to Italy with their precious texts.

In this period, western European universities established new professorships of mathematics, astronomy, and natural philosophy. The prestige of the new fields was low, especially mathematics, which was reserved for practical problems such as accounting, surveying, and computing planetary tables, but not used as a tool to understand the functioning of the physical world itself. Nevertheless, these professorships

Chronology

ca. 1540–1700	Scientific Revolution
ca. 1690–1789	Enlightenment
ca. 1700–1800	Growth of book publishing
1720–1780	Rococo style in art and decoration
1740–1748	War of the Austrian Succession
1740–1780	Reign of the empress Maria Theresa of Austria
1740–1786	Reign of Frederick the Great of Prussia
ca. 1740–1789	Salons led by Parisian elites
1751–1772	Philosophes publish *Encyclopedia: The Rational Dictionary of the Sciences, the Arts, and the Crafts*
1756–1763	Seven Years' War
1762–1796	Reign of Catherine the Great of Russia
1780–1790	Reign of Joseph II of Austria
1791	Establishment of the Pale of Settlement

eventually enabled the union of mathematics with natural philosophy that was to be a hallmark of the Scientific Revolution.

European overseas expansion in the fifteenth and sixteenth centuries provided another catalyst for new thought about the natural world. In particular, the navigational problems of long oceanic voyages in the age of expansion stimulated scientific research and invention. To help solve these problems, inventors developed many new scientific instruments, such as the telescope, barometer, thermometer, pendulum clock, microscope, and air pump. Better instruments, which permitted more accurate observations, often led to important new knowledge. Another crucial technology in this period was printing, which provided a faster and less expensive way to circulate knowledge.

Political and social conflicts were widespread in Eurasia in the sixteenth and early seventeenth centuries, but they had different results. The three large empires of the Muslim world—the Ottomans, Safavid Persians, and Mughals—that arose in the wake of the Mongol Empire sought to restore order and assert legitimacy in part by imposing Islamic orthodoxy. Their failure to adopt the printing press can be seen as part of a wider reaction against earlier traditions of innovation. Similarly, in China, under the Qing Dynasty, political newcomers legitimized their authority through stricter adherence to traditional ways. In contrast, western Europe remained politically fragmented into smaller competitive nations, divisions that were augmented by the religious fracturing of the Protestant Reformation. These conditions made it impossible for authorities to impose one orthodox set of ideas and thus allowed individuals to question dominant patterns of thinking.

Scientific Thought to 1500

The term *science* as we use it today came into use only in the nineteenth century. For medieval scholars, philosophy was the path to true knowledge about the world, and its proofs consisted of the authority of ancients (as interpreted by Christian theologians) and their techniques of logical argumentation. Questions about the physical nature of the universe and how it functioned belonged to a minor branch of philosophy, called **natural philosophy**. Natural philosophy was based primarily on the ideas of Aristotle, the great Greek philosopher of the fourth century B.C.E. Medieval theologians such as Thomas Aquinas brought Aristotelian philosophy into harmony with Christian doctrines. According to the Christianized view of Aristotle, a motionless earth stood at the center of the universe and was encompassed by ten separate concentric crystal spheres in which were embedded the moon, the sun, planets, and stars. Beyond the spheres was Heaven, with the throne of God and the souls of the saved. Angels kept the spheres moving in perfect circles.

Aristotle's views also dominated thinking about physics and motion on earth. Aristotle had distinguished between the world of the celestial spheres and that of the earth—the sublunar world. The spheres consisted of a perfect, incorruptible "quintessence," or fifth essence. The sublunar world, however, was made up of four imperfect, changeable elements: air, fire, water, and earth. Aristotle and his followers also believed that a uniform force moved an object at a constant speed and that the object would stop as soon as that force was removed.

Aristotle's cosmology made intellectual sense, but it could not account for the observed motions of the stars and planets and, in particular, provided no explanation for the apparent backward motion of the planets (which we now know occurs as

natural philosophy An early modern term for the study of the nature of the universe, its purpose, and how it functioned; it encompassed what we would call "science" today.

planets closer to the sun periodically overtake the earth on their faster orbits). The great second-century scholar Ptolemy, a Hellenized Egyptian, offered a theory for this phenomenon. According to Ptolemy, the planets moved in small circles, called epicycles, each of which moved in turn along a larger circle, or deferent. Ptolemaic astronomy was less elegant than Aristotle's neat nested circles and required complex calculations, but it provided a surprisingly accurate model for predicting planetary motion.

The work of Ptolemy also provided the basic foundation of knowledge about the earth. Rediscovered around 1410, his *Geography* presented crucial advances on medieval cartography by representing a round earth divided into 360 degrees with the major latitude marks. Ptolemy's work reintroduced the idea of using coordinates of latitude and longitude to plot points on the earth's surface, a major advantage for long-distance navigation. However, Ptolemy's map reflected the limits of ancient knowledge, showing only the continents of Europe, Africa, and Asia, with land covering three-quarters of the world. Lacking awareness of the Pacific Ocean and the Americas, Ptolemy vastly underestimated the distance west from Europe to Asia.

The Aristotelian Universe as Imagined in the Sixteenth Century A round earth is at the center, surrounded by spheres of water, air, and fire. Beyond this small nucleus, the moon, the sun, and the five planets were embedded in their own rotating crystal spheres, with the stars sharing the surface of one enormous sphere. Beyond, the heavens were composed of unchanging ether. (From *Cosmographia*, by Peter Apian, 1630/Universal History Archive/UIG/Bridgeman Images)

These two frameworks reveal the strengths and limitations of European knowledge on the eve of the Scientific Revolution. Overcoming the authority of the ancients to develop a new understanding of the natural world, derived from precise techniques of observation and experimentation, was a monumental achievement. Europeans were not the first to use experimental methods—of which there was a long tradition in the Muslim world and elsewhere—but they were the first to separate scientific knowledge decisively from philosophical and religious beliefs and to accord mathematics a fundamental role in understanding the natural world.

The Copernican Hypothesis

The first great departure from the medieval system was the work of the Polish cleric Nicolaus Copernicus (1473–1543). Copernicus studied astronomy, medicine, and church law at the famed universities of Bologna, Padua, and Ferrara before taking up a church position in East Prussia. Copernicus came to believe that Ptolemy's cumbersome rules detracted from the majesty of a perfect creator. He preferred an idea espoused by some ancient Greek and Arab scholars: that the sun, rather than the earth, was at the center of the universe. Without questioning the Aristotelian belief in crystal spheres or the idea that circular motion was divine, Copernicus theorized that the stars and planets, including the earth, revolved around a fixed sun. Copernicus worked on his hypothesis from 1506 to 1530, but, fearing the ridicule of other scholars, he did not publish his *On the Revolutions of the Heavenly Spheres* until 1543, the year of his death.

Copernican hypothesis
The idea that the sun, not the earth, was the center of the universe.

The **Copernican hypothesis** had enormous scientific and religious implications, many of which the conservative Copernicus did not anticipate. First, it put the stars at rest, their apparent nightly movement simply a result of the earth's rotation. Thus it destroyed the main reason for believing in crystal spheres capable of moving the stars around the earth. Second, Copernicus's theory suggested a universe of staggering size. If in the course of a year the earth moved around the sun and yet the stars appeared to remain in the same place, then the universe was unthinkably large. Third, by using mathematics, instead of philosophy, to justify his theories, Copernicus challenged the traditional hierarchy of the disciplines. Finally, by characterizing the earth as just another planet, Copernicus destroyed the basic idea of Aristotelian physics — that the earthly sphere was quite different from the heavenly one. Where then were Heaven and the throne of God?

Religious leaders varied in their response to Copernicus's theories. A few Protestant scholars became avid Copernicans, while others accepted some elements of his criticism of Ptolemy, but firmly rejected the notion that the earth moved, a doctrine that contradicted the literal reading of some passages of the Bible. Among Catholics, Copernicus's ideas drew little attention prior to 1600. Because the Catholic Church had never held to literal interpretations of the Bible, it did not officially declare the Copernican hypothesis false until 1616.

Other events were almost as influential in creating doubts about traditional astronomy. In 1572 a new star appeared and shone very brightly for almost two years. The new star, which was actually a distant exploding star, made an enormous impression on people. It seemed to contradict the idea that the heavenly spheres were unchanging and therefore perfect. In 1577 a new comet suddenly moved through the sky, cutting a straight path across the supposedly impenetrable crystal spheres. It was time, as a sixteenth-century scientific writer put it, for "the radical renovation of astronomy."[1]

Brahe, Kepler, and Galileo: Proving Copernicus Right

One astronomer who agreed with the Copernican hypothesis was the Danish astronomer Tycho Brahe (TEE-koh BRAH-hee) (1546–1601). Brahe established himself as Europe's leading astronomer with his detailed observations of the new star that appeared in 1572. Impressed by his work, the king of Denmark provided funds for Brahe to build the most sophisticated observatory of his day.

Upon the king's death, Brahe acquired a new patron in the Holy Roman emperor Rudolph II and built a new observatory in Prague. For twenty years Brahe observed the stars and planets with the naked eye in order to create new and improved tables of planetary motions, dubbed the *Rudolphine Tables* in honor of his patron. His limited understanding of mathematics and his sudden death in 1601, however, prevented him from making much sense out of his mass of data. Part Ptolemaic, part Copernican, he believed that all the planets except the earth revolved around the sun and that the entire group of sun and planets revolved in turn around the earth-moon system.

Brahe's assistant, Johannes Kepler (1571–1630), carefully re-examined his predecessor's notations and came to believe that they could not be explained by Ptolemy's astronomy. Abandoning the notion of epicycles and deferents — which even Copernicus had retained in part — Kepler developed three revolutionary laws of planetary motion. First, largely through observations of the planet Mars, he demonstrated that the orbits of the planets around the sun are elliptical rather than circular. Second, he demonstrated that the planets do not move at a uniform speed in their orbits. When a planet is close to the sun it moves more rapidly, and it slows as it moves farther away from the sun. Finally, Kepler's third law stated that the time a planet takes to make its complete orbit is precisely related to its distance from the sun.

Kepler's contribution was monumental. Whereas Copernicus had used mathematics to describe planetary movement, Kepler proved mathematically the precise relations of a sun-centered (solar) system. He thus united for the first time the theoretical cosmology of natural philosophy with mathematics. His work demolished the old system of Aristotle and Ptolemy, and with his third law he came close to formulating the idea of universal gravitation (see the next section). In 1627 he also completed Brahe's *Rudolphine Tables*, which were used by astronomers for many years.

While Kepler was unraveling planetary motion, a young Florentine named Galileo Galilei (1564–1642) was challenging Aristotelian ideas about motion on earth. Like Kepler and so many early scientists, Galileo was a poor nobleman first marked for a religious career. Instead, his fascination with mathematics led to a professorship in which he examined motion and mechanics in a new way. Galileo focused on deficiencies in Aristotle's theories of motion. He measured the movement of a rolling ball across a surface, repeating the action again and again to verify his results. In his famous acceleration experiment, he showed that a uniform force—in this case, gravity—produced a uniform acceleration. Through another experiment, he formulated the **law of inertia**. He found that rest was not the natural state of objects. Rather, an object continues in motion forever unless stopped by some external force. His discoveries proved Aristotelian physics wrong.

On hearing details about the invention of the telescope in Holland, Galileo made one for himself and trained it on the heavens. He quickly discovered the first four moons of Jupiter, which clearly suggested that Jupiter could not possibly be embedded in an impenetrable crystal sphere as Aristotle and Ptolemy maintained. This discovery provided new evidence for the Copernican theory, in which Galileo already believed. Galileo then pointed his telescope at the moon. He wrote in 1610 in *The Sidereal Messenger*: "By the aid of a telescope anyone may behold

law of inertia A law formulated by Galileo that states that motion, not rest, is the natural state of an object, and that an object continues in motion forever unless stopped by some external force.

Galileo's Telescopic Observations of the Moon   Among the many mechanical devices Galileo invented was a telescope that could magnify objects thirty times (other contemporary telescopes could magnify objects only three times). Using this telescope, he obtained the empirical evidence that proved the Copernican system. He sketched many illustrations of his observations, including the six phases of the moon shown here. (telescope: Museo delle Scienze, Florence, Italy/akg-images; moon: Biblioteca Nazionale Centrale, Florence, Italy/Eric Vandeville/Gamma Rapho via Getty Images)

Galileo Galilei, *The Sidereal Messenger*

In this passage from The Sidereal Messenger *(1610), Galileo Galilei recounts his experiments to build a telescope and his observations of the moon. By discovering the irregularity of the moon's surface, Galileo disproved a central tenet of medieval cosmography: that the heavens were composed of perfect, unblemished spheres essentially different from the base matter of earth.*

About ten months ago a report reached my ears that a Dutchman had constructed a telescope, by the aid of which visible objects, although at a great distance from the eye of the observer, were seen distinctly as if near. . . . A few days after, I received confirmation of the report in a letter written from Paris . . . , which finally determined me to give myself up first to inquire into the principle of the telescope, and then to consider the means by which I might compass [achieve] the invention of a similar instrument, which a little while after I succeeded in doing, through deep study of the theory of refraction; and I prepared a tube, at first of lead, in the ends of which I fitted two glass lenses, both plane on one side, but on the other side one spherically convex, and the other concave. . . . At length, by sparing neither labour nor expense, I succeeded in constructing for myself an instrument so superior that objects seen through it appear magnified nearly a thousand times, and more than thirty times nearer than if viewed by the natural powers of sight alone. . . .

Let me speak first of the surface of the moon, which is turned towards us. For the sake of being understood more easily, I distinguish two parts in it, which I call respectively the brighter and the darker. The brighter part seems to surround and pervade the whole hemisphere, but the darker part, like a sort of cloud, discolours the moon's surface and makes it appear covered with spots. Now these spots . . . are plain to every one, and every age has seen them, wherefore I shall call them *great* or *ancient* spots, to distinguish them from other spots, smaller in size, but so thickly scattered that they sprinkle the whole surface of the moon, but especially the brighter portion of it. These spots have never been observed by any one before me, and from my observations of them, often repeated, I have been led to that opinion which I have expressed, namely, that I feel sure that the surface of the moon is not perfectly smooth, free from inequalities and exactly spherical, as a large school of philosophers considers with regard to the moon and the other heavenly bodies, but that, on the contrary, it is full of inequalities, uneven, full of hollows and protuberances, just like the surface of the earth itself, which is varied everywhere by lofty mountains and deep valleys.

EVALUATE THE EVIDENCE

1. What did the telescope permit Galileo to see on the moon that was not visible to the naked eye, and how did he interpret his observations?
2. Why were Galileo's observations so important to the destruction of the Ptolemaic universe?

Source: Galileo Galilei, *The Sidereal Messenger* (London: Rivingtons, 1880), pp. 10–11, 14–15.

[the Milky Way] in a manner which so distinctly appeals to the senses that all the disputes which have tormented philosophers through so many ages are exploded by the irrefutable evidence of our eyes, and we are freed from wordy disputes upon the subject."[2] (See "Evaluating the Evidence 16.1: Galileo Galilei, *The Sidereal Messenger*," above.)

Reading these famous lines, one feels a crucial corner in Western civilization being turned. No longer should one rely on established authority. A new method of learning and investigating was being developed, one that proved useful in any field of inquiry. A historian investigating documents of the past, for example, is not so different from a Galileo studying stars and rolling balls.

Newton's Synthesis

By about 1640 the work of Brahe, Kepler, and Galileo had been largely accepted by the scientific community despite opposition from religious leaders. The old Aristotelian astronomy and physics were in ruins, and several fundamental breakthroughs had been made. But the new findings failed to explain what forces controlled the movement of the planets and objects on earth. That challenge was taken up by English scientist Isaac Newton (1642–1727), a genius who spectacularly united the experimental and theoretical-mathematical sides of modern science.

Newton was born into the lower English gentry, and he enrolled at Cambridge University in 1661. He arrived at some of his most basic ideas about physics in 1666 at age twenty-four, but was unable to prove them mathematically. In 1684, after years of studying optics, Newton returned to physics for eighteen intensive months. The result was his towering accomplishment, a single explanatory system that could integrate the astronomy of Copernicus, as corrected by Kepler's laws, with the physics of Galileo and his predecessors. Newton did this through a set of mathematical laws that explain motion and mechanics. These laws were published in 1687 in Newton's *Mathematical Principles of Natural Philosophy* (also known as the *Principia*). Because of their complexity, it took scientists and engineers two hundred years to work out all their implications.

The key feature of the Newtonian synthesis was the **law of universal gravitation**. According to this law, every body in the universe attracts every other body in the universe in a precise mathematical relationship, whereby the force of attraction is proportional to the quantity of matter of the objects and inversely proportional to the square of the distance between them. The whole universe—from Kepler's elliptical orbits to Galileo's rolling balls—was unified in one majestic system. Newton's synthesis of mathematics with physics and astronomy prevailed until the twentieth century and established him as one of the most important figures in the history of science. Yet, near the end of his life, this acclaimed figure declared: "I do not know what I may appear to the world; but to myself I seem to have been only like a boy, playing on the seashore, and diverting myself, in now and then finding a smoother pebble or a prettier shell than ordinary, whilst the great ocean of truth lay all undiscovered before me."[3]

law of universal gravitation Newton's law that all objects are attracted to one another and that the force of attraction is proportional to the objects' quantity of matter and inversely proportional to the square of the distance between them.

Natural History and Empire

At the same time that they made advances in astronomy and physics, Europeans embarked on the pursuit of knowledge about unknown geographical regions and the useful and valuable resources they contained. Because they were the first to acquire a large overseas empire, the Spanish pioneered these efforts. Following the conquest of the Aztec and Inca Empires (see Chapter 14), they sought to learn about and profit from their New World holdings. The Spanish crown sponsored many scientific expeditions to gather information and specimens, out of which emerged new discoveries that reshaped the fields of botany, zoology, cartography, and metallurgy, among others. These accomplishments have attracted less attention from historians in part because the strict policy of secrecy imposed on scientific discoveries by the Spanish crown limits the number of available documents about them.

Plants were a particular source of interest because they offered tremendous profits in the form of spices, medicines, dyes, and cash crops. King Philip II of Spain sent his personal physician, Francisco Hernández, to New Spain for seven years in the 1560s. Hernández filled fifteen volumes with illustrations of three thousand plants previously unknown in Europe. He extensively interviewed local healers about the plants' medicinal properties, thereby benefiting from centuries of Mesoamerican botanical knowledge. In the seventeenth century, for example, the Spanish obtained

"An Account of a Particular Species of Cocoon"

To disseminate its members' work, the Royal Society of England published the results of its meetings in the Philosophical Transactions of the Royal Society. The passage below is excerpted from a presentation made to the society in the mid-eighteenth century by the Reverend Samuel Pullein, a graduate of Trinity College in Dublin. A relative of the governor of Jamaica, Pullein became fascinated by the idea of introducing silkworm cultivation to the American colonies. His presentation exemplifies the contribution of many minor enthusiasts to the progress of science in this period and the importance of colonialism to the new knowledge.

Having lately seen the aurelia of a particular species of caterpillar, I judged, from its texture and consistence, that there might be procured from it a silk not inferior to that of the common silk-worm in its quality, and in its quantity much superior. I have made some experiments on this new species of silk-pod, which strengthen this opinion.

This pod is about three inches and a quarter in length, and above one inch in diameter; its outward form not so regular an oval as that of the common silk-worm; its consistence somewhat like that of a dried bladder, when not fully blown; its colour of a reddish brown; its whole weight 21 grains.

Upon cutting open this outer integument, there appeared in the inside a pod completely oval, as that of the silk-worm. It was covered with some floss-silk, by which it was connected to the outer coat, being of the same colour. Its length was two inches; its diameter nearly one inch; and its weight nine grains.

The pod could not be easily unwinded, because it was perforated by the moth: but, upon putting it in hot water, I reeled off so much as sufficed to form a judgment of the strength and staple of its silk.

The single thread winded off the pod in the same manner as that of the common silk-worm; seeming in all respects as fine, and as tough. I doubled this thread so often as to contain twenty in thickness; and the compound thread was as smooth, as elastic, and as glossy, as that of the common silk-worm. I tried what weight it would bear; and it bore fifteen ounces and a half, and broke with somewhat less than sixteen, upon several trials. . . .

The caterpillar which produces this pod is a native of America. It was found in Pennsylvania: the pod was fixed to the small branch of a tree, which seemed to be either of the crab or hawthorn species. . . .

I do not conceive that it will be at all difficult to find out the caterpillar, or the tree it feeds on; or to reel such a quantity of the silk as shall, when woven into ribband, more fully demonstrate whether it be of that value which I judge it. For by comparing it with the *cocoon* of the wild Chinese silk-worm, from which an excellent species of silk is made, I have no doubt of its being the same species; and would be glad if, by this memorial, I could induce the people of America to make trial of it.

EVALUATE THE EVIDENCE

1. What is Pullein's aim in presenting his research to the Royal Society? How does he try to establish the credibility of his claims about the silkworm?
2. In what ways does this document belong to the "Scientific Revolution" as discussed in this chapter? What does Pullein's presentation tell us about the nature of "science" presented to the Royal Society in the mid-eighteenth century?

Source: "An Account of a Particular Species of Cocoon, or Silk-Pod, from America," Reverend Samuel Pullein, M.A., *Philosophical Transactions of the Royal Society* 15 (1759): 54–57.

a monopoly on the world's supply of cinchona bark, which comes from a tree native to the high altitudes of the Andes and was the first effective treatment for malaria.

Other countries followed the Spanish example as their global empires expanded, relying on both official expeditions and the private initiative of merchants, missionaries, and settlers. (See "Evaluating the Evidence 16.2: 'An Account of a Particular Species of Cocoon,'" above.) Royal botanical gardens served as living laboratories for cultivating valuable foreign plants. Over time, the stream of new information about plant and animal species overwhelmed existing intellectual frameworks. Carl

Linnaeus (1707–1778) of Sweden sent his students on exploratory voyages around the world and, based on their observations and the specimens they collected, devised a formal system of naming and classifying living organisms still used today (with substantial revisions).

New encyclopedias of natural history popularized this knowledge with realistic drawings and descriptions emphasizing the usefulness of animals and plants. Audiences at home eagerly read the accounts of naturalists who braved the heat, insects, and diseases of tropical jungles to bring home exotic animal, vegetable, and mineral specimens (along with indigenous human subjects). They heard much less about the many local guides, translators, and practitioners of medicine and science who made these expeditions possible and who contributed rich knowledge about the natural world.

Magic and Alchemy

Recent historical research on the Scientific Revolution has focused on the contribution of ideas and practices that no longer belong to the realm of science, such as astrology and alchemy. For most of human history, interest in astronomy was inspired by the belief that the movement of heavenly bodies influenced events on earth. Many of the most celebrated astronomers also worked as astrologers. Used as a diagnostic tool in medicine, astrology formed a regular part of the curriculum of medical schools.

Centuries-old practices of magic and alchemy also remained important traditions for natural philosophers. Early modern practitioners of magic strove to understand and control hidden connections they perceived among different elements of the natural world, such as that between a magnet and iron. The idea that objects possessed hidden or "occult" qualities that allowed them to affect other objects was a particularly important legacy of the magical tradition. Belief in occult qualities—or numerology or cosmic harmony—was not antithetical to belief in God. On the contrary, adherents believed that only a divine creator could infuse the universe with such meaningful mystery.

Johannes Kepler exemplifies the interaction among these different strands of interest in the natural world. His duties as court mathematician included casting horoscopes for the royal family, and he guided his own life by astrological principles. He also wrote at length on cosmic harmonies and explained elliptical motion through ideas about the beautiful music created by the combined motion of the planets. Kepler's fictional account of travel to the moon, written partly to illustrate the idea of a non-earth-centered universe, caused controversy and may have contributed to the arrest and trial of his mother as a witch in 1620. Kepler also suffered because of his unorthodox brand of Lutheranism, which led to his condemnation by both Lutherans and Catholics.

Another example of the interweaving of ideas and beliefs is Sir Isaac Newton, who was both intensely religious and fascinated by alchemy, whose practitioners believed (among other things) that base metals could be turned into gold. Critics complained that his idea of universal gravitation was merely a restatement of old magical ideas about the innate sympathies between bodies; Newton himself believed that the attraction of gravity resulted from God's actions in the universe.

Important Changes in Scientific Thinking and Practice

FOCUS QUESTION

What intellectual and social changes occurred as a result of the Scientific Revolution?

The Scientific Revolution was not accomplished by a handful of brilliant individuals working alone. Advancements occurred in many fields—medicine, chemistry, and botany, among others—as scholars developed new methods to seek answers to long-standing problems. They did so in collaboration with skilled craftsmen who invented new instruments and helped conduct experiments. These results circulated in an intellectual community from which women were usually excluded.

The Methods of Science: Bacon and Descartes

One of the keys to the achievement of a new worldview in the seventeenth century was the development of better ways of obtaining knowledge. Two important thinkers, Francis Bacon (1561–1626) and René Descartes (day-KAHRT) (1596–1650), were influential in describing and advocating for improved scientific methods based, respectively, on experimentation and mathematical reasoning.

The English politician and writer Francis Bacon was the greatest early propagandist for the experimental method. Rejecting the Aristotelian and medieval method of using speculative reasoning to build general theories, Bacon argued that new knowledge had to be pursued through empirical research. The researcher who wants to learn more about leaves or rocks, for example, should not speculate about the subject but rather collect a multitude of specimens and then compare and analyze them to derive general principles. Bacon formalized the empirical method, which had already been used by Brahe and Galileo, into the general theory of inductive reasoning known as **empiricism**. Bacon's work, and his prestige as lord chancellor under James I, led to the widespread adoption of what was called "experimental philosophy" in England after his death. In 1660 followers of Bacon created the Royal Society (still in existence), which met weekly to conduct experiments and discuss the latest findings of scholars across Europe.

empiricism A theory of inductive reasoning that calls for acquiring evidence through observation and experimentation rather than deductive reason and speculation.

On the continent, more speculative methods retained support. In 1619, as a twenty-three-year-old soldier serving in the Thirty Years' War, the French philosopher René Descartes experienced a life-changing intellectual vision. Descartes saw that there was a perfect correspondence between geometry and algebra and that geometrical spatial figures could be expressed as algebraic equations and vice versa. A major step forward in the history of mathematics, Descartes's discovery of analytic geometry provided scientists with an important new tool.

Descartes used mathematics to elaborate a highly influential vision of the workings of the cosmos. Accepting Galileo's claim that all elements of the universe are composed of the same matter, Descartes began to investigate the basic nature of matter. Drawing on ancient Greek atomist philosophies, Descartes developed the idea that matter was made up of identical "corpuscles" (tiny particles) that collided together in an endless series of motions, akin to the workings of a machine. All occurrences in nature could be analyzed as matter in motion and, according to Descartes, the total "quantity of motion" in the universe was constant. Descartes's mechanistic view of the universe depended on the idea that a vacuum was impossible, which meant that every action had an equal reaction, continuing in an eternal chain reaction.

Although Descartes's hypothesis about the vacuum was proved wrong, his notion of a mechanistic universe intelligible through the physics of motion proved inspirational. Decades later, Newton rejected Descartes's idea of a full universe and several of his other ideas, but retained the notion of a mechanistic universe as a key element of his own system.

Descartes's greatest achievement was to develop his initial vision into a whole philosophy of knowledge and science. The Aristotelian cosmos was appealing in part because it corresponded with the evidence of the human senses. When experiments proved that sensory impressions could be wrong, Descartes decided it was necessary to doubt them and everything that could reasonably be doubted, and to then, as in geometry, use deductive reasoning from self-evident truths, which he called "first principles," to ascertain scientific laws. Descartes's reasoning ultimately reduced all substances to "matter" and "mind"—that is, to the physical and the spiritual. The devout Descartes believed that God had endowed man with reason for a purpose and that rational speculation could provide a path to the truths of creation. His view of the world as consisting of two fundamental entities is known as **Cartesian dualism**. Descartes's thought was highly influential in France and the Netherlands, but less so in England, where experimental philosophy won the day.

Both Bacon's inductive experimentalism and Descartes's deductive mathematical reasoning had flaws. Bacon's inability to appreciate the importance of mathematics and his obsession with practical results clearly showed the limitations of antitheoretical empiricism. Likewise, some of Descartes's positions demonstrated the inadequacy of rigid, dogmatic rationalism. For example, he believed that it was possible to deduce the whole science of medicine from first principles. Although insufficient on their own, Bacon's and Descartes's extreme approaches are combined in the modern scientific method, which began to crystallize in the late seventeenth century.

Cartesian dualism
Descartes's view that all of reality could ultimately be reduced to mind and matter.

Medicine, the Body, and Chemistry

The Scientific Revolution, which began with the study of the cosmos, soon transformed the understanding of the microcosm of the human body. For many centuries the ancient Greek physician Galen's explanation of the body carried the same authority as Aristotle's account of the universe. According to Galen, the body contained four humors: blood, phlegm, black bile, and yellow bile. Illness was believed to result from an imbalance of humors, which is why doctors frequently prescribed bloodletting to expel excess blood.

Swiss physician and alchemist Paracelsus (1493–1541) was an early proponent of the experimental method in medicine and pioneered the use of chemicals and drugs to address what he saw as chemical, rather than humoral, imbalances. Another experimentalist, Flemish physician Andreas Vesalius (1516–1564), studied anatomy by dissecting human bodies, often those of executed criminals. In 1543, the same year Copernicus published *On the Revolutions*, Vesalius issued his masterpiece, *On the Structure of the Human Body*. Its two hundred precise drawings revolutionized the understanding of human anatomy, disproving Galen, just as Copernicus and his successors had disproved Aristotle and Ptolemy. The experimental approach also led English royal physician William Harvey (1578–1657) to discover the circulation of blood through the veins and arteries in 1628. Harvey

ANDREÆ VESALII.

was the first to explain that the heart worked like a pump and to explain the function of its muscles and valves.

Robert Boyle (1627–1691) was a key figure in the victory of experimental methods in England and helped create the Royal Society in 1660. Boyle's scientific work led to the development of modern chemistry. Following Paracelsus's lead, he undertook experiments to discover the basic elements of nature, which he believed was composed of infinitely small atoms. Boyle was the first to create a vacuum, thus disproving Descartes's belief that a vacuum could not exist in nature, and he discovered Boyle's law (1662), which states that the pressure of a gas varies inversely with volume.

Science and Religion

It is sometimes assumed that the relationship between science and religion is fundamentally hostile and that the pursuit of knowledge based on reason and proof is incompatible with faith. Yet during the Scientific Revolution most practitioners were devoutly religious and saw their work as contributing to the celebration of God's glory rather than undermining it. However, the concept of heliocentrism, which displaced the earth from the center of the universe, threatened the understanding of the place of mankind in creation as stated in Genesis. All religions derived from the Old Testament—Catholic, Protestant, Jewish, and Muslim—thus faced difficulties accepting the Copernican system. The leaders of the Catholic Church were initially less hostile than Protestant and Jewish religious leaders, but in the first decades of the sixteenth century the Catholic attitude changed. In 1616 the Holy Office placed the works of Copernicus and his supporters, including Kepler, on a list of books Catholics were forbidden to read.

Out of caution, Galileo Galilei silenced his views on heliocentrism for several years, until 1623 saw the ascension of Pope Urban VIII, a man sympathetic to the new science. However, Galileo's 1632 *Dialogue on the Two Chief Systems of the World* went too far. Published in Italian and widely read, it openly lampooned the Aristotelian view and defended Copernicus. In 1633 Galileo was tried for heresy by the papal Inquisition.

Imprisoned and threatened with torture, the aging Galileo recanted, "renouncing and cursing" his Copernican errors.

Thereafter, the Catholic Church became more hostile to science, a change that helped account for the decline of science in Italy (but not in Catholic France) after 1640. At the same time, some Protestant countries, including the Netherlands, Denmark, and England, became quite "pro-science." This was especially true in countries without a strong religious authority capable of imposing religious orthodoxy on scientific questions.

Science and Society

The rise of modern science had many consequences. First, it created a new social group—the international scientific community. Members of this community were linked together by common interests and values as well as by scholarly journals and associations. The personal success of scientists and scholars depended on making new discoveries, and science became competitive. Second, as governments intervened to support and sometimes direct research, the new scientific community became closely tied to the state and its agendas. National academies of science were created under state sponsorship in London in 1660, Paris in 1666, Berlin in 1700, and later across Europe.

It was long believed that the Scientific Revolution had little relationship to practical concerns and the life of the masses until the late-eighteenth-century Industrial Revolution (see Chapter 20). More recently, historians have emphasized the importance of skilled craftsmen in the rise of science, particularly in the development of the experimental method. Many artisans developed a strong interest in emerging scientific ideas, and, in turn, the practice of science in the seventeenth century often relied on artisans' expertise in making instruments and conducting precise experiments.

Some things did not change in the Scientific Revolution. For example, scholars willing to challenge received ideas about the natural universe did not question the seemingly natural inequalities between the sexes. Instead, the emergence of professional science may have worsened them in some ways. When Renaissance courts served as centers of learning, talented noblewomen could find niches in study and research. But the rise of a scientific community raised new barriers for women because the universities and academies that furnished professional credentials refused them entry.

There were, however, a number of noteworthy exceptions. In Italy, universities and academies did offer posts to women. Across Europe, women worked as makers of wax anatomical models and as botanical and zoological illustrators, like Maria Sibylla Merian. They were also very much involved in informal scientific communities, attending salons (see page 530), participating in scientific experiments, and writing learned treatises. Some female intellectuals became full-fledged members of the philosophical dialogue. In England, Margaret Cavendish, Anne Conway, and Mary Astell all contributed to debates about Descartes's mind-body dualism, among other issues. Descartes himself conducted an intellectual correspondence with the princess Elizabeth of Bohemia, of whom he stated: "I attach more weight to her judgment than to those messieurs the Doctors, who take for a rule of truth the opinions of Aristotle rather than the evidence of reason."[4]

The Rise and Spread of Enlightenment Thought

FOCUS QUESTION
How did the Enlightenment emerge, and what were major currents of Enlightenment thought?

Enlightenment The influential intellectual and cultural movement of the late seventeenth and eighteenth centuries that introduced a new worldview based on the use of reason, the scientific method, and progress.

rationalism A secular, critical way of thinking in which nothing was to be accepted on faith, and everything was to be submitted to reason.

The political, intellectual, and religious developments of the early modern period that gave rise to the Scientific Revolution further contributed to a series of debates about key issues in eighteenth-century Europe and the wider world that came to be known as the **Enlightenment**. The conflicts of the Reformation that led to the devastating violence of the Thirty Years' War brought old religious certainties into question; the strong states that emerged to quell the disorder soon inspired questions about political sovereignty and its limits. Increased movement of peoples, goods, and ideas within and among the continents of Asia, Africa, Europe, and America offered examples of surprisingly different ways of life and values. Finally, the tremendous achievements of the Scientific Revolution inspired intellectuals to believe that answers to all the questions being asked could be found through observation and the use of reason.

Intellectual turmoil in the late seventeenth century thus gave rise to the new worldview of the eighteenth-century Enlightenment. This worldview, which has played a large role in shaping the modern mind, grew out of a rich mix of diverse and often conflicting ideas that were debated in international networks. Despite the diversity, three central concepts stand at the core of Enlightenment thinking. The first and foremost idea was that the methods of natural science could and should be used to examine and understand all aspects of life. This was what intellectuals meant by *reason*, a favorite word of Enlightenment thinkers. Nothing was to be accepted on faith; everything was to be submitted to **rationalism**, a secular, critical way of thinking. A second important Enlightenment concept was that the scientific method was capable of discovering the laws of human society as well as those of nature. These tenets led to the third key idea, that of progress. Enlightenment thinkers believed that, armed with the proper method of discovering the laws of human existence, human beings could create better societies and better people.

The Early Enlightenment

Loosely united by certain key ideas, the European Enlightenment (ca. 1690–1789) was a broad intellectual and cultural movement that gained strength gradually and did not reach its maturity until about 1750. Its origins in the late seventeenth century lie in a combination of developments, including political opposition to absolutist rule; religious conflicts between Protestants and Catholics and within Protestantism; European contacts with other cultures; and the attempt to apply principles and practices from the Scientific Revolution to human society. The generation that came of age between the publication of Newton's *Principia* in 1687 and the death of Louis XIV in 1715 thus tied the knot between the Scientific Revolution and a new outlook on life. Whereas medieval and Reformation thinkers had been concerned primarily with abstract concepts of sin and salvation, and Renaissance humanists had drawn their inspiration from the classical past, Enlightenment thinkers believed that their era had gone far beyond antiquity and that intellectual progress was within their reach.

A key crucible for Enlightenment thought was the Dutch Republic, with its proud commitment to religious tolerance and republican rule. When Louis XIV demanded that all Protestants convert to Catholicism, around two hundred thousand French

Protestants, or Huguenots, fled the country, many destined for the Dutch Republic. From this haven of tolerance, Huguenots and their supporters began to publish tracts denouncing religious intolerance and suggesting that only a despotic monarch, not a legitimate ruler, would deny religious freedom. Their challenge to authority thus combined religious and political issues.

These dual concerns drove the career of one important early Enlightenment writer, Pierre Bayle (1647–1706), a Huguenot who took refuge in the Dutch Republic. Bayle critically examined the religious beliefs and persecutions of the past in his *Historical and Critical Dictionary* (1697). Demonstrating that human beliefs had been extremely varied and very often mistaken, he concluded that nothing can ever be known beyond all doubt, a view known as skepticism. His influential *Dictionary* was found in more private libraries of eighteenth-century France than any other book.

The Dutch Jewish philosopher Baruch Spinoza (1632–1677) was another key figure in the transition from the Scientific Revolution to the Enlightenment. Deeply inspired by advances in science—in particular by debates about Descartes's thought—Spinoza sought to apply natural philosophy to thinking about human society. He borrowed Descartes's emphasis on rationalism and his methods of deductive reasoning, but rejected the French thinker's mind-body dualism. Instead, Spinoza came to espouse monism, the idea that mind and body were united in one substance and that God and nature were merely two names for the same thing. He envisioned a deterministic universe in which good and evil were merely relative values and human actions were shaped by outside circumstances, not free will. Spinoza was excommunicated by the relatively large Jewish community of Amsterdam for his controversial religious ideas, but he was heralded by his Enlightenment successors as a model of personal virtue and courageous intellectual autonomy.

The German philosopher and mathematician Gottfried Wilhelm von Leibniz (1646–1716), who had developed calculus independently of Isaac Newton, refuted both Cartesian dualism and Spinoza's monism. Instead, he adopted the idea of an infinite number of substances, or "monads," from which all matter is composed. His *Theodicy* (1710) declared that ours must be "the best of all possible worlds" because it was created by an omnipotent and benevolent God. Leibniz's optimism was later ridiculed by the French philosopher Voltaire in *Candide or Optimism* (1759).

Out of this period of intellectual turmoil came John Locke's *Essay Concerning Human Understanding* (1690). In this work Locke (1632–1704), a physician and member of the Royal Society, brilliantly set forth a new theory about how human beings learn and form their ideas. Whereas Descartes based his deductive logic on the conviction that certain first principles, or innate ideas, are imbued in humans by God, Locke insisted that all ideas are derived from experience. The human mind at birth is like a blank tablet, or tabula rasa, on which understanding and beliefs are inscribed by experience. Human development is therefore determined by external forces, like education and social institutions, not innate characteristics. Locke's essay contributed to the theory of **sensationalism**, the idea that all human ideas and thoughts are produced as a result of sensory impressions.

sensationalism The idea that all human ideas and thoughts are produced as a result of sensory impressions.

Along with Newton's *Principia*, the *Essay Concerning Human Understanding* was one of the great intellectual inspirations of the Enlightenment. Locke's equally

Philosophes' Dinner Party This engraving depicts one of the famous dinners hosted by Voltaire at Ferney, the estate on the French-Swiss border where he spent the last twenty years of his life. A visit to the great philosophe (pictured in the center with arm raised) became a cherished pilgrimage for Enlightenment writers. (Engraving by Jean Huber [1721–1786]/Album/Art Resource, NY)

important contribution to political theory, *Two Treatises of Government* (1690), insisted on the sovereignty of the Parliament against the authority of the Crown (see Chapter 15).

The Influence of the Philosophes

Divergences among the early thinkers of the Enlightenment show that, while they shared many of the same premises and questions, the answers they found differed widely. The spread of this spirit of inquiry owed a great deal to the work of the **philosophes** (fee-luh-ZAWFZ), a group of intellectuals in France who proudly proclaimed that they, at long last, were bringing the light of reason to their ignorant fellow humans.

Philosophe is the French word for "philosopher," and in the mid-eighteenth century France became a hub of Enlightenment thought. There were at least three reasons for this. First, French was the international language of the educated classes, and France was the wealthiest and most populous country in Europe. Second, the rising unpopularity of King Louis XV and his mistresses generated growing discontent and calls for reform among the educated elite. Third, the French philosophes made it their goal to reach a larger audience of elites, many of whom were joined together in a concept inherited from the Renaissance known as the Republic of Letters—an imaginary transnational realm of the critical thinkers and writers.

To appeal to the public and get around the censors, the philosophes wrote novels and plays, histories and philosophies, and dictionaries and encyclopedias, all filled with satire and double meanings to spread their message. One of the greatest philosophes, the baron de Montesquieu (mahn-tuhs-KYOO) (1689–1755), pioneered this approach in *The Persian Letters*, an extremely influential social satire published in 1721 and considered the first major work of the French Enlightenment. It consisted of amusing letters supposedly written by two Persian travelers who as outsiders saw European customs in unique ways, thereby allowing Montesquieu a vantage point for criticizing existing practices and beliefs.

Disturbed by the growth in absolutism under Louis XIV and inspired by the example of the physical sciences, he set out to apply the critical method to the problem

philosophes A group of French intellectuals who proclaimed that they were bringing the light of knowledge to their fellow humans in the Age of Enlightenment.

of government in *The Spirit of Laws* (1748). Arguing that forms of government were shaped by history and geography, Montesquieu identified three main types: monarchies, republics, and despotisms. A great admirer of the English parliamentary system, Montesquieu argued for a separation of powers, with political power divided among different classes and legal estates holding unequal rights and privileges. Montesquieu was no democrat; he was apprehensive about the uneducated poor and he did not question the sovereignty of the French monarchy. But he was concerned that absolutism in France was drifting into tyranny and believed that strengthening the influence of intermediary powers was the best way to prevent it. Decades later, his theory of separation of powers had a great impact on the constitutions of the young United States in 1789 and of France in 1791.

The most famous philosophe was François Marie Arouet, known by the pen name Voltaire (vohl-TAIR) (1694–1778). In his long career, Voltaire wrote more than seventy witty volumes, hobnobbed with royalty, and died a millionaire through shrewd speculations. His early career, however, was turbulent, and he was twice arrested for insulting noblemen. To avoid a prison term, Voltaire moved to England for three years, and there he came to share Montesquieu's enthusiasm for English liberties and institutions.

Returning to France, Voltaire met Gabrielle-Emilie Le Tonnelier de Breteuil, marquise du Châtelet (SHAH-tuh-lay) (1706–1749), a gifted noblewoman. Madame du Châtelet invited Voltaire to live in her country house at Cirey in Lorraine and became his longtime companion, under the eyes of her tolerant husband. Passionate about science, she studied physics and mathematics and published scientific articles and translations, including the first translation of Newton's *Principia* into French, still in use today. Excluded from the Royal Academy of Sciences because she was a woman, Madame du Châtelet had no doubt that women's limited role in science was due to their unequal education. Discussing what she would do if she were a ruler, she wrote, "I would reform an abuse which cuts off, so to speak, half the human race. I would make women participate in all the rights of humankind, and above all in those of the intellect."[5]

While living at Cirey, Voltaire wrote works praising England and popularizing English science. Yet, like almost all of the philosophes, Voltaire was a reformer, not a revolutionary, in politics. He pessimistically concluded that the best one could hope for in the way of government was a good monarch, since human beings "are very rarely worthy to govern themselves." Nor did Voltaire believe in social and economic equality. The only realizable equality, Voltaire thought, was that "by which the citizen only depends on the laws which protect the freedom of the feeble against the ambitions of the strong."[6]

Voltaire's philosophical and religious positions were much more radical. Voltaire believed in God, but he rejected Catholicism in favor of **deism**, belief in a distant noninterventionist deity. Drawing on mechanistic philosophy, he envisioned a universe in which God acted like a great clockmaker who built an orderly system and then stepped aside to let it run. Above all, Voltaire and most of the philosophes hated all forms of religious intolerance, which they believed led to fanaticism and cruelty.

The strength of the philosophes lay in their dedication and organization. Their greatest achievement was a group effort—the seventeen-volume *Encyclopedia: The Rational Dictionary of the Sciences, the Arts, and the Crafts*, edited by Denis Diderot (DEE-duh-roh) (1713–1784) and Jean le Rond d'Alembert (dah-luhm-BEHR) (1717–1783). The two men set out in 1751 to find coauthors who would examine

deism Belief in a distant, noninterventionist deity; common among Enlightenment thinkers.

the rapidly expanding whole of human knowledge and teach people how to think critically and objectively about all matters. As Diderot said, he wanted the *Encyclopedia* to "change the general way of thinking."[7]

Completed in 1765 despite opposition from the French state and the Catholic Church, the *Encyclopedia* contained seventy-two thousand articles by leading scientists, writers, skilled workers, and progressive priests. Science and the industrial arts were exalted, religion and immortality questioned. Intolerance, legal injustice, and out-of-date social institutions were openly criticized. The *Encyclopedia* also included many articles describing non-European cultures and societies, including acknowledgment of Muslim scholars' contribution to the development of Western science. Summing up the new worldview of the Enlightenment, the *Encyclopedia* was widely read, especially in less expensive reprint editions, and it was extremely influential.

After about 1770 a number of thinkers and writers began to attack the philosophes' faith in reason and progress. The most famous of these was Jean-Jacques Rousseau (1712–1778). The son of a poor Swiss watchmaker, Rousseau made his way into the Parisian Enlightenment through his brilliant intellect. Rousseau was both one of the most influential voices of the Enlightenment and, in his ultimate rejection of rationalism and civilized sociability, a harbinger of reaction against Enlightenment ideals.

Like other Enlightenment thinkers, Rousseau was passionately committed to individual freedom. Unlike them, however, he attacked rationalism and civilization as destroying, rather than liberating, the individual. Warm, spontaneous feeling, Rousseau believed, had to complement and correct cold intellect. Moreover, he asserted, the basic goodness of the individual and the unspoiled child had to be protected from the cruel refinements of civilization. Rousseau's ideals greatly influenced the early Romantic movement, which rebelled against the culture of the Enlightenment in the late eighteenth century.

Rousseau's contribution to political theory in *The Social Contract* (1762) was based on two fundamental concepts: the general will and popular sovereignty. According to Rousseau, the general will is sacred and absolute, reflecting the common interests of all the people, who have displaced the monarch as the holder of sovereign power. The general will is not necessarily the will of the majority, however. At times the general will may be the authentic, long-term needs of the people as correctly interpreted by a farsighted minority. Little noticed before the French Revolution, Rousseau's concept of the general will appealed greatly to democrats and nationalists after 1789.

Enlightenment Movements Across Europe

The Enlightenment was a movement of international dimensions, with thinkers traversing borders in a constant exchange of visits, letters, and printed materials. Voltaire alone wrote almost eighteen thousand letters to correspondents in France and across Europe. The Republic of Letters, as this international group of scholars and writers was called, was a truly cosmopolitan set of networks stretching from western Europe to its colonies in the Americas, to Russia and eastern Europe, and along the routes of trade and empire to Africa and Asia.

Within this broad international conversation, scholars have identified numerous regional and national particularities. Outside of France, many strains of Enlightenment — Protestant, Catholic, and Jewish — sought to reconcile reason with faith, rather than emphasizing the errors of religious fanaticism and intolerance. Some scholars point to a distinctive "Catholic Enlightenment" that aimed to renew and reform the church from within, looking to divine grace rather than human will as the source of progress.

The Scottish Enlightenment, which was centered in Edinburgh, was marked by an emphasis on common sense and scientific reasoning. After the Act of Union with England in 1707, Scotland was freed from political crisis to experience a vigorous period of intellectual growth. Advances in philosophy were also stimulated by the creation of the first public educational system in Europe.

A central figure in Edinburgh was David Hume (1711–1776), whose emphasis on civic morality and religious skepticism had a powerful impact at home and abroad. Hume strove to apply Newton's experimental methods to what he called the "science of man." Building on Locke's writings on learning, Hume argued that the human mind is really nothing but a bundle of impressions. These impressions originate only in sensory experiences and our habits of mentally joining these experiences together. Therefore, reason cannot tell us anything about questions that cannot be verified by sensory experience (in the form of controlled experiments or mathematics), such as the origin of the universe or the existence of God. Hume further argued, in opposition to Descartes, that reason alone could not supply moral principles and that they derived instead from emotions and desires, such as feelings of approval or shame. Hume's rationalistic inquiry thus ended up undermining the Enlightenment's faith in the power of reason by emphasizing the superiority of the senses and the passions over reason in driving human thought and behavior.

Hume's emphasis on human experience, rather than abstract principle, had a formative influence on another major figure of the Scottish Enlightenment, Adam Smith (1723–1790). Smith argued that social interaction produced feelings of mutual sympathy that led people to behave in ethical ways, despite inherent tendencies toward self-interest. By observing others and witnessing their feelings, individuals imaginatively experienced such feelings and learned to act in ways that would elicit positive sentiments and avoid negative ones. Smith believed that the thriving commercial life of the eighteenth century was likely to produce civic virtue through the values of competition, fair play, and individual autonomy. In *An Inquiry into the Nature and Causes of the Wealth of Nations* (1776), Smith attacked the laws and regulations created by mercantilist governments that, he argued, prevented commerce from reaching its full capacity (see Chapter 17).

Inspired by philosophers of moral sentiments, like Hume and Smith, as well as by physiological studies of the role of the nervous system in human perception, the celebration of sensibility became an important element of eighteenth-century culture. *Sensibility* referred to an acute sensitivity of the nerves and brains to outside stimuli, which produced strong emotional and physical reactions. Novels, plays, and other literary genres depicted moral and aesthetic sensibility as a particular characteristic of women and the upper classes. The proper relationship between reason and the emotions (or between *Sense and Sensibility*, as Jane Austen put it in the title of her 1811 novel) became a key question.

After 1760 Enlightenment ideas were hotly debated in the German-speaking states, often in dialogue with Christian theology. Immanuel Kant (1724–1804), a professor in East Prussia, was the greatest German philosopher of his day. Kant posed the question of the age when he published a pamphlet in 1784 titled *What Is Enlightenment?* He answered, "*Sapere Aude* [dare to know]! 'Have the courage to use your own understanding' is therefore the motto of enlightenment." He argued that if intellectuals were granted the freedom to exercise their reason publicly in print, enlightenment would almost surely follow. Kant was no revolutionary; he also insisted that in their private lives, individuals must obey all laws, no matter how unreasonable, and should be punished for "impertinent" criticism. Like other Enlightenment figures in central and east-central Europe, Kant thus tried to reconcile absolute monarchical authority and religious faith with a critical public sphere.

Northern Europeans often regarded the Italian states as culturally backward, yet important developments in Enlightenment thought took place in the Italian peninsula. After achieving independence from Habsburg rule (1734), the kingdom of Naples entered a period of intellectual flourishing as reformers struggled to lift the heavy weight of church and noble power. In northern Italy a central figure was Cesare Beccaria (1738–1794), a nobleman educated at Jesuit schools and the University of Pavia. His *On Crimes and Punishments* (1764) was a passionate plea for reform of the penal system that decried the use of torture, arbitrary imprisonment, and capital punishment, and advocated the prevention of crime over the reliance on punishment. The text was quickly translated into French and English and made an impact throughout Europe and its colonies.

The Social Life of the Enlightenment

FOCUS QUESTION

How did Enlightenment thinkers address issues of racial and social difference, and how did new institutions and social practices diffuse Enlightenment thought?

The Scientific Revolution and the political and religious conflicts of the late seventeenth century were not the only developments that influenced European thinkers. Europeans' increased interactions with non-European peoples and cultures also helped produce the Enlightenment spirit.

Global Contacts

In the wake of the great discoveries of the fifteenth and sixteenth centuries, the rapidly growing travel literature taught Europeans that the peoples of China, India, Africa, and the Americas had very different beliefs and customs. Europeans shaved their faces and let their hair grow. Ottomans shaved their heads and let their beards grow. In Europe a man bowed before a woman to show respect. In Siam a man turned his back on a woman when he met her because it was disrespectful to look directly at her. Countless similar examples discussed in travel accounts helped change the perspective of educated Europeans. They began to look at truth and morality in relative, rather than absolute, terms. If anything was possible, who could say what was right or wrong?

The powerful and advanced nations of Asia were obvious sources of comparison with the West. Seventeenth-century Jesuit missionaries served as a conduit for transmission of knowledge to the West about Chinese history and culture. The philosopher and mathematician Leibniz corresponded with Jesuits stationed in China, coming to believe that Chinese ethics and political philosophy were superior but that Europeans had equaled China in science and technology; some scholars believe his concept of monads was influenced by Confucian teaching on the inherent harmony between the cosmic order and human society.[8]

During the eighteenth-century Enlightenment, opinion on China was divided. Voltaire and some other philosophes revered China—without ever visiting or seriously studying it—as an ancient culture replete with wisdom and learning, ruled by benevolent absolutist monarchs. They enthusiastically embraced Confucianism as a natural religion in which universal moral truths were uncovered by reason. By contrast, Montesquieu and Diderot criticized China as a despotic land ruled by fear.

Attitudes toward Islam and the Muslim world were similarly mixed. As the Ottoman military threat receded at the end of the seventeenth century, some Enlightenment thinkers assessed Islam favorably. Some deists praised Islam as superior to Christianity and Judaism in its rationality, compassion, and tolerance. Others, including Spinoza, saw Islamic culture as superstitious and favorable to despotism. In most cases, writing about Islam and Muslim cultures served primarily as a means to reflect on Western values and practices. Thus Montesquieu's *Persian Letters* used the Persian harem as a symbol of despotic rule that he feared his own country was adopting. Voltaire's play about the life of the Prophet portrayed Muhammad as the epitome of the religious fanaticism the philosophes opposed.

One writer with considerable personal experience in a Muslim country was Lady Mary Wortley Montagu, wife of the English ambassador to the Ottoman Empire. Her letters challenged prevailing ideas by depicting Turkish people as sympathetic and civilized. Montagu also disputed the notion that women were oppressed in Ottoman society.

Apart from debates about Asian and Muslim lands, the "discovery" of the New World and subsequent explorations in the Pacific Ocean also destabilized existing norms and values in Europe. One popular idea, among Rousseau and others, was that indigenous peoples of the Americas were living examples of "natural man," who embodied the essential goodness of humanity uncorrupted by decadent society. Other popular candidates for utopian natural men were the Pacific Island societies explored by Captain James Cook and others from the 1770s on.

Enlightenment Debates About Race

As scientists developed taxonomies of plant and animal species in response to discoveries in the Americas, they also began to classify humans into hierarchically ordered "races" and to speculate on the origins of such races. In *The System of Nature* (1735), Swedish botanist Carl von Linné argued that nature was organized into a God-given hierarchy. The comte de Buffon (komt duh buh-FOHN) argued that humans originated with one species that then developed into distinct races due largely to climatic conditions.

Enlightenment thinkers such as David Hume and Immanuel Kant helped popularize these ideas. In *Of Natural Characters* (1748), Hume wrote:

> I am apt to suspect the negroes and in general all other species of men (for there are four or five different kinds) to be naturally inferior to the whites. There never was a civilized nation of any other complexion than white, nor even any individual eminent amongst them, no arts, no sciences. . . . Such a uniform and constant difference could not happen, in so many countries and ages if nature had not made an original distinction between these breeds of men.[9]

Denis Diderot, "Supplement to Bougainville's Voyage"

Denis Diderot was born in a provincial town in eastern France and educated in Paris. Rejecting careers in the church and the law, he devoted himself to literature and philosophy. In 1749, sixty years before Charles Darwin's birth, Diderot was jailed by Parisian authorities for publishing an essay questioning God's role in creation and suggesting the autonomous evolution of species. Following these difficult beginnings, Diderot's editorial work and writing on the Encyclopedia *were the crowning intellectual achievements of his life and, according to some, of the Enlightenment itself.*

Like other philosophes, Diderot employed numerous genres to disseminate Enlightenment thought, ranging from scholarly articles in the Encyclopedia *to philosophical treatises, novels, plays, book reviews, and erotic stories. His "Supplement to Bougainville's Voyage" (1772) was a fictional account of a European voyage to Tahiti inspired by the writings of traveler Louis-Antoine de Bougainville. In this passage, Diderot expresses his own loathing of colonial conquest and exploitation through the voice of an elderly Tahitian man. The character's praise for his own culture allows Diderot to express his Enlightenment idealization of "natural man," free from the vices of civilized societies.*

He was the father of a large family. When the Europeans arrived he looked upon them with scorn, showing neither astonishment, nor fear, nor curiosity. On their approach he turned his back and retired into his hut. Yet his silence and anxiety revealed his thoughts only too well; he was inwardly lamenting the eclipse of his countrymen's happiness. When Bougainville was leaving the island, as the natives swarmed on the shore, clutching his clothes, clasping his companions in their arms and weeping, the old man made his way forward and proclaimed solemnly, "Weep, wretched natives of Tahiti, weep. But let it be for the coming and not the leaving of these ambitious, wicked men. One day you will know them better. One day they will come back, bearing in one hand the piece of wood you see in that man's belt, and, in the other, the sword hanging by the side of that one, to enslave you, slaughter you, or make you captive to their follies and vices. One day you will be subject to them, as corrupt, vile and miserable as they are. . . ."

Then turning to Bougainville, he continued, "And you, leader of the ruffians who obey you, pull your ship away swiftly from these shores. We are innocent, we are content, and you can only spoil that happiness. We follow the pure instincts of nature, and you have tried to erase its impression from our hearts. Here, everything belongs to everyone, and you have preached I can't tell what distinction between 'yours' and 'mine.' . . . If a Tahitian should one day land on your shores and engrave

Kant taught and wrote as much about "anthropology" and "geography" as he did about standard philosophical themes such as logic, metaphysics, and moral philosophy. He elaborated his views about race in *On the Different Races of Man* (1775), claiming that there were four human races, each of which had derived from an original race. According to Kant, the closest descendants of the original race were the white inhabitants of northern Germany. (Scientists now know the human race originated in Africa.)

Using the word *race* to designate biologically distinct groups of humans, akin to distinct animal species, was new. Previously, Europeans had grouped other peoples into "nations" based on their historical, political, and cultural affiliations, rather than on supposedly innate physical differences. Unsurprisingly, when European thinkers drew up a hierarchical classification of human species, their own "race" was placed at the top. Europeans had long believed they were culturally superior to "barbaric" peoples in Africa and, since 1492, the New World. Now emerging ideas about racial difference taught them they were biologically superior as well. In turn, scientific racism helped legitimate and justify the tremendous growth of slavery that occurred during the eighteenth century. If one "race" of humans was fundamentally different on one of your stones or on the bark of one of your trees, *This land belongs to the people of Tahiti*, what would you think then? You are stronger than we are, and what does that mean? When one of the miserable trinkets with which your ship is filled was taken away, what an uproar you made, what revenge you exacted! At that moment, in the depths of your heart, you were plotting the theft of an entire country! You are not a slave, you would rather die than be one, and yet you wish to make slaves of us. Do you suppose, then, that a Tahitian cannot defend his own liberty and die for it as well? This inhabitant of Tahiti, whom you wish to ensnare like an animal, is your brother. You are both children of Nature. What right do you have over him that he does not have over you? You came; did we attack you? Have we plundered your ship? Did we seize you and expose you to the arrows of our enemies? Did we harness you to work with our animals in the fields? We respected our own image in you.

"Leave us our ways; they are wiser and more decent than yours. We have no wish to exchange what you call our ignorance for your useless knowledge. Everything that we need and is good for us we already possess. Do we merit contempt because we have not learnt how to acquire superfluous needs? When we are hungry, we have enough to eat. When we are cold, we have enough to wear. You have entered our huts; what do you suppose we lack? Pursue as far as you wish what you call the comforts of life, but let sensible beings stop when they have no more to gain from their labours than imaginary benefits. If you persuade us to go beyond the strict bounds of necessity, when will we finish our work? When will we enjoy ourselves? We have kept our annual and daily labours within the smallest possible limits, because in our eyes nothing is better than rest. Go back to your own country to agitate and torment yourselves as much as you like. But leave us in peace. Do not fill our heads with your factitious needs and illusory virtues. . . ."

EVALUATE THE EVIDENCE

1. On what grounds does the speaker argue for the Tahitians' basic equality with the Europeans?
2. What is the good life according to the speaker, and how does it contrast with the European way of life? Which do you think is the better path?
3. In what ways could Diderot's thoughts here be seen as representative of Enlightenment ideas? Are there ways in which they are not?
4. How realistic do you think this account is? How might defenders of expansion respond?

Source: Edited excerpts from pp. 41–43 in Denis Diderot, *Political Writings*, translated and edited by John Hope Mason and Robert Wokler. Copyright © 1992 by Cambridge University Press. Reprinted by permission of Cambridge University Press.

and inferior, its members could be seen as particularly fit for enslavement and liable to benefit from tutelage by the superior race.

Racist ideas did not go unchallenged. The abbé Raynal's *History of the Two Indies* (1770) fiercely attacked slavery and the abuses of European colonization. *Encyclopedia* editor Denis Diderot adopted Montesquieu's technique of criticizing European attitudes through the voice of outsiders in his dialogue between Tahitian villagers and their European visitors. (See "Evaluating the Evidence 16.3: Denis Diderot, 'Supplement to Bougainville's Voyage,'" above.) Scottish philosopher James Beattie (1735–1803) responded directly to claims of white superiority by pointing out that Europeans had started out as savage as nonwhites supposedly were and that many non-European peoples in the Americas, Asia, and Africa had achieved high levels of civilization. Former slaves, like Olaudah Equiano (see Chapter 17) and Ottobah Cugoana, published eloquent memoirs testifying to the horrors of slavery and the innate equality of all humans. These challenges to racism, however, were in the minority. Many other Enlightenment voices supporting racial inequality—Thomas Jefferson among them—may be found.

Women and the Enlightenment

Dating back to the Renaissance *querelle des dames*, the debate over women's proper role in society and the nature of gender differences continued to fascinate Enlightenment thinkers. Some philosophes championed greater rights and expanded education for women, claiming that the position and treatment of women were the best indicators of a society's level of civilization and decency.[10] In *Persian Letters*, Montesquieu used the oppression of women in the harem, described in letters from the wives of Usbek—one of the Persian voyagers—as a potent symbol of the political tyranny he identified with the Persian Empire. At the end of the book, the rebellion of the harem against the cruel eunuchs Usbek left in charge serves to make Montesquieu's point that despotism must ultimately fail.

In the 1780s the marquis de Condorcet, a celebrated mathematician and contributor to the *Encyclopedia*, went so far as to urge that women should share equal rights with men. This was an extremely rare position. Most philosophes accepted that women were inferior to men intellectually as well as physically. They sought moderate reform at best, particularly in the arena of female education, and had no desire to upend men's traditional dominance over women.

From the first years of the Enlightenment, women writers made crucial contributions both to debates about women's rights and to the broader Enlightenment discussion. In 1694 Mary Astell published *A Serious Proposal to the Ladies*, which encouraged women to aspire to the life of the mind and proposed the creation of a women's college. Astell also harshly criticized the institution of marriage. Echoing arguments made against the absolute authority of kings during the Glorious Revolution (see Chapter 15), she argued that husbands should not exercise absolute control over their wives in marriage. Yet Astell, like most female authors of the period, was careful to acknowledge women's God-given duties to be good wives and mothers.

The explosion of printed literature over the eighteenth century (see the next section) brought significant numbers of women writers into print, but they remained a small proportion of published authors. In the second half of the eighteenth century, women produced some 15 percent of published novels, the genre in which they enjoyed the greatest success. They represented a much tinier proportion of nonfiction authors.[11]

salon Regular social gathering held by talented and rich Parisians in their homes, where philosophes and their followers met to discuss literature, science, and philosophy.

If they remained marginal in the world of publishing, women played a much more active role in the informal dimensions of the Enlightenment: conversation, letter writing, travel, and patronage. A key element of their informal participation was as salon hostesses, or *salonnières* (sah-lahn-ee-EHRZ). **Salons** were weekly meetings held in wealthy households, which brought together writers, aristocrats, financiers, and noteworthy foreigners for meals and witty discussions of the latest trends in literature, science, and philosophy. One prominent salonnière was Madame du Deffand, whose weekly Parisian salon included such guests as Montesquieu, d'Alembert, and Benjamin Franklin, then serving as the first U.S. ambassador to France. Invitations to salons were highly coveted; introductions to the rich and powerful could make the career of an ambitious writer, and, in turn, the social elite found amusement and cultural prestige in their ties to up-and-coming artists and men of letters.

Madame de Pompadour, Mistress to French King Louis XV Madame de Pompadour used the wealth at her command to patronize many highly skilled artists and craftsmen. She helped popularize the ornate, lightly colored, and highly decorative rococo style, epitomized by the sumptuous trimmings of her dress. (By François Boucher [1703–1770], [oil on canvas]/© Scottish National Gallery, Edinburgh/Bridgeman Images)

Elite women also exercised great influence on artistic taste. Soft pastels, ornate interiors, sentimental portraits, and starry-eyed lovers protected by hovering cupids were all hallmarks of the style they favored. This style, known as **rococo** (ruh-KOH-koh), was popular throughout Europe in the period from 1720 to 1780. It was particularly associated with the mistress of Louis XV, Madame de Pompadour, who used her position to commission paintings, furniture, and other luxury objects in the rococo style.

Women's prominent role as society hostesses and patrons of the arts and letters outraged some Enlightenment thinkers. According to Jean-Jacques Rousseau, women and men were radically different by nature and should play diametrically opposed roles in life. Destined by nature to assume the active role in sexual relations, men were naturally suited for the rough-and-tumble of politics and public life. Women's role was to attract male sexual desire in order to marry and create families and then to care for their homes and children in private. For Rousseau, wealthy Parisian women's love for attending social gatherings and pulling the strings of power was unnatural and had a corrupting effect on both politics and society. Some women eagerly accepted Rousseau's idealized view of their domestic role, but others—such as the English writer Mary Wollstonecraft—vigorously rejected his notion of women's limitations.

Rousseau's emphasis on the natural laws governing women echoed a wider shift in ideas about gender during this period, as doctors, scientists, and philosophers increasingly agreed that women's essential characteristics were determined by their sexual organs and reproductive functions. This turn to nature, rather than tradition or scripture, as a means to understand human society had parallels in contemporary views on racial difference. Just as writers like Rousseau used women's "natural" passivity to argue for their subordinate role in society, so Kant and others used ideas about non-Europeans' "natural" inferiority to defend slavery and colonial domination. The new powers of science and reason were thus marshaled to imbue traditional stereotypes with the force of natural law. Scholars continue to debate the apparent paradox between Enlightenment thinkers' ideals of equality, progress, and reason and their acceptance of racial and gender inequality.

rococo A popular style in Europe in the eighteenth century, known for its soft pastels, ornate interiors, sentimental portraits, and starry-eyed lovers protected by hovering cupids.

Urban Culture and Life in the Public Sphere

Enlightenment ideas did not float on thin air. A series of new institutions and practices encouraged the spread of enlightened ideas. From about 1700 to 1789, the production and consumption of books grew significantly and the types of books people read changed dramatically. For example, the proportion of religious and devotional books published in Paris declined after 1750; history and law held constant; the arts and sciences surged.

Reading more books on many more subjects, the educated public approached reading in a new way. The old style of reading in Europe had been centered on a core of sacred texts read aloud by the father to his assembled family. Now reading involved a broader field of books that constantly changed. Reading became individual and silent, and texts could be questioned.

For those who could not afford to purchase books, lending libraries offered access to the new ideas of the Enlightenment. Coffeehouses, which first appeared in the late seventeenth century, became meccas of philosophical discussion. In addition to these institutions, book clubs, debating societies, Masonic lodges (groups of Freemasons, a secret society that accepted craftsmen and shopkeepers as well as middle-class men and nobles), salons, and newspapers all played roles in the creation of a new **public sphere** that celebrated open debate informed by critical reason. The public sphere was an idealized space where members of society came together as individuals to discuss issues relevant to the society, economics, and politics of the day.

What of the common people? Did they participate in the Enlightenment? Enlightenment philosophes did not direct their message to peasants or urban laborers. They believed that the masses had no time or talent for philosophical speculation and that elevating them would be a long and potentially dangerous process. Deluded by superstitions and driven by violent passions, the people, they thought, were like children in need of firm parental guidance. D'Alembert characteristically made a sharp distinction between "the truly enlightened public" and "the blind and noisy multitude."[12]

Despite these prejudices, the ideas of the philosophes did find an audience among some members of the common people. At a time of rising literacy, book prices were dropping and many philosophical ideas were popularized in cheap pamphlets and through public reading. Although they were barred from salons and academies, ordinary people were not immune to the new ideas in circulation.

public sphere An idealized intellectual space that emerged in Europe during the Enlightenment, where the public came together to discuss important issues relating to society, economics, and politics.

Enlightened Absolutism

FOCUS QUESTION

What impact did new ways of thinking have on political developments and monarchical absolutism?

How did the Enlightenment influence political developments? To this important question there is no easy answer. Most Enlightenment thinkers outside of England and the Netherlands, especially in central and eastern Europe, believed that political change could best come from above—from the ruler—rather than from below. Royal absolutism was a fact of life, and the monarchs of Europe's leading states clearly had no intention of giving up their great power. Therefore, the philosophes and their sympathizers realistically concluded that a benevolent absolutism offered the best opportunities for improving society.

Many government officials were interested in philosophical ideas. They were among the best-educated members of society, and their daily involvement in complex affairs of state made them naturally attracted to ideas for improving human society. Encouraged and instructed by these officials, some absolutist rulers tried to reform their governments in accordance with Enlightenment ideals—what historians have called the **enlightened absolutism** of the later eighteenth century. In both Catholic and Protestant lands, rulers typically fused Enlightenment principles with religion, drawing support for their innovations from reform-minded religious thinkers. The most influential of the new-style monarchs were in Prussia, Russia, and Austria, and their example illustrates both the achievements and the great limitations of enlightened absolutism. France experienced its own brand of enlightened absolutism in the contentious decades prior to the French Revolution (see Chapter 19).

enlightened absolutism
Term coined by historians to describe the rule of eighteenth-century monarchs who, without renouncing their own absolute authority, adopted Enlightenment ideals of rationalism, progress, and tolerance.

Frederick the Great of Prussia

Frederick II (r. 1740–1786), commonly known as Frederick the Great, built masterfully on the work of his father, Frederick William I (see Chapter 15). Although in his youth he embraced culture and literature rather than the militarism championed by his father, by the time he came to the throne Frederick was determined to use the splendid army he had inherited.

Therefore, when the young empress Maria Theresa of Austria inherited the Habsburg dominions upon the death of her father, Charles VI, Frederick pounced. He invaded her rich province of Silesia (sigh-LEE-zhuh), defying solemn Prussian promises to respect the Pragmatic Sanction, a diplomatic agreement that had guaranteed Maria Theresa's succession. In 1742, as other greedy powers vied for her lands in the European War of the Austrian Succession (1740–1748), Maria Theresa was forced to cede almost all of Silesia to Prussia. In one stroke Prussia had doubled its population to 6 million people. Now Prussia unquestionably stood as a European Great Power.

Though successful in 1742, Frederick had to fight against great odds to save Prussia from total destruction after the ongoing competition between Britain and France for colonial empire brought another great conflict in 1756. Maria Theresa, seeking to regain Silesia, formed an alliance with the leaders of France and Russia. The aim of the alliance during the resulting Seven Years' War (1756–1763) was to conquer Prussia and divide up its territory. Despite invasions from all sides, Frederick fought on with stoic courage. In the end he was miraculously saved: Peter III came to the Russian throne in 1762 and called off the attack against Frederick, whom he greatly admired.

The terrible struggle of the Seven Years' War tempered Frederick's interest in territorial expansion and brought him to consider how more humane policies for his subjects might also strengthen the state. Thus Frederick went beyond a superficial commitment to Enlightenment culture for himself and his circle. He tolerantly allowed his subjects to believe as they wished in religious and philosophical matters. He promoted the advancement of knowledge, improving his country's schools and permitting scholars to publish their findings. Moreover, Frederick tried to improve the lives of his subjects more directly. As he wrote to his friend Voltaire, "I must enlighten my people, cultivate their manners and morals, and make them as happy as human beings can be, or as happy as the means at my disposal permit."

The War of the Austrian Succession, 1740–1748

The legal system and the bureaucracy were Frederick's primary tools. Prussia's laws were simplified, torture was abolished, and judges decided cases quickly and impartially. Prussian officials became famous for their hard work and honesty. After the Seven Years' War ended in 1763, Frederick's government energetically promoted the reconstruction of agriculture and industry. Frederick himself set a good example. He worked hard and lived modestly, claiming that he was "only the first servant of the state." Thus Frederick justified monarchy in terms of practical results and said nothing of the divine right of kings.

Frederick's dedication to high-minded government went only so far, however. While he condemned serfdom in the abstract, he accepted it in practice and did not free the serfs on his own estates. He accepted and extended the privileges of the nobility, who remained the backbone of the army and the entire Prussian state.

cameralism View that monarchy was the best form of government, that all elements of society should serve the monarch, and that, in turn, the state should use its resources and authority to increase the public good.

In reforming Prussia's bureaucracy, Frederick drew on the principles of **cameralism**, the German science of public administration that emerged in the decades following the Thirty Years' War. Influential throughout the German lands, cameralism held that monarchy was the best of all forms of government, that all elements of society should be placed at the service of the state, and that, in turn, the state should make use of its resources and authority to improve society. Predating the Enlightenment, cameralist interest in the public good was usually inspired by the needs of war. Cameralism shared with the Enlightenment an emphasis on rationality, progress, and utilitarianism.

Catherine the Great of Russia

Catherine the Great of Russia (r. 1762–1796) was one of the most remarkable rulers of her age, and the French philosophes adored her. Catherine was a German princess from Anhalt-Zerbst, an insignificant principality sandwiched between Prussia and Saxony. Her father commanded a regiment of the Prussian army, but her mother was related to the Romanovs of Russia, and that proved to be Catherine's opening to power.

Catherine's Romanov connection made her a suitable bride at the age of fifteen for the heir to the Russian throne. It was a mismatch from the beginning, but her *Memoirs* made her ambitions clear: "I did not care about Peter, but I did care about the crown." When her husband, Peter III, came to power during the Seven Years' War, his decision to withdraw Russian troops from the coalition against Prussia alienated the army. Catherine profited from his unpopularity to form a conspiracy to depose her husband. In 1762 Catherine's lover Gregory Orlov and his three brothers, all army officers, murdered Peter, and the German princess became empress of Russia.

Catherine had drunk deeply at the Enlightenment well. Never questioning that absolute monarchy was the best form of government, she set out to rule in an enlightened manner. She had three main goals. First, she worked hard to continue Peter the Great's effort to bring the culture of western Europe to Russia (see Chapter 15). To do so, she imported Western architects, musicians, and intellectuals. She bought masterpieces of Western art and patronized the philosophes. An enthusiastic letter writer, she corresponded extensively with Voltaire and praised him as the "champion of the human race." When the French government banned the *Encyclopedia*, she

Catherine the Great and Denis Diderot　　Self-proclaimed adherent of Enlightenment ideals, Russian empress Catherine the Great enthusiastically corresponded with philosophes like Voltaire and Denis Diderot. When Diderot put his library on sale to raise much-needed funds, Catherine sent him the money but allowed him to keep his books. Historians have long debated the "enlightened despotism" represented by Catherine and other absolutist rulers. (Catherine: Based on a work by Alexander Roslin [1718–1793], [oil on canvas]/Museum of Art, Serpukhov, Russia/Bridgeman Images; Diderot: By Louis Michel van Loo [1707–1771]/ Musée du Louvre, Paris, France/Fine Art Images/Heritage Images/Getty Images)

offered to publish it in St. Petersburg, and she sent money to Diderot when he needed it. With these actions, Catherine won good press in the West for herself and for her country. Moreover, this intellectual ruler, who wrote plays and loved good talk, set the tone for the entire Russian nobility. Peter the Great westernized Russian armies, but it was Catherine who westernized the imagination of the Russian nobility.

Catherine's second goal was domestic reform, and she began her reign with sincere and ambitious projects. In 1767 she appointed a legislative commission to prepare a new law code. This project was never completed, but Catherine did restrict the practice of torture and allowed limited religious toleration. She also tried to improve education and strengthen local government. The philosophes applauded these measures and hoped more would follow.

Such was not the case. In 1773 a common Cossack soldier named Emelian Pugachev sparked a gigantic uprising of serfs, very much as Stenka Razin had done a century earlier (see Chapter 15). Proclaiming himself the true tsar, Pugachev issued orders abolishing serfdom, taxes, and army service. Thousands joined his cause, slaughtering landlords and officials over a vast area of southwestern Russia. Pugachev's untrained forces eventually proved no match for Catherine's noble-led army. Betrayed by his own company, Pugachev was captured and savagely executed.

Pugachev's rebellion put an end to any intentions Catherine had about reforming the system. The peasants were clearly dangerous, and her empire rested on the support of the nobility. After 1775 Catherine gave the nobles absolute control of their serfs, and she extended serfdom into new areas, such as Ukraine. In 1785 she freed nobles forever from taxes and state service. Under Catherine the Russian nobility attained its most exalted position, and serfdom entered its most oppressive phase.

Catherine's third goal was territorial expansion, and in this respect she was extremely successful. Her armies subjugated the last descendants of the Mongols and the Crimean Tartars, and began the conquest of the Caucasus (KAW-kuh-suhs). Her greatest coup by far was the partition of Poland (Map 16.1). When, between 1768

MAP 16.1 The Partition of Poland, 1772–1795   In 1772 war between Russia and Austria threatened over Russian gains from the Ottoman Empire. To satisfy desires for expansion without fighting, Prussia's Frederick the Great proposed that parts of Poland be divided among Austria, Prussia, and Russia. In 1793 and 1795 the three powers partitioned the remainder, and the republic of Poland ceased to exist.

and 1772, Catherine's armies scored unprecedented victories against the Ottomans and thereby threatened to disturb the balance of power between Russia and Austria in eastern Europe, Frederick of Prussia obligingly came forward with a deal. He proposed that Turkey be let off easily and that Prussia, Austria, and Russia each compensate itself by taking a gigantic slice of the weakly ruled Polish territory. Catherine jumped at the chance. The first partition of Poland took place in 1772. Subsequent partitions in 1793 and 1795 gave away the rest of Polish territory, and the ancient republic of Poland vanished from the map.

The Austrian Habsburgs

Another female monarch, Maria Theresa (r. 1740–1780) of Austria, set out to reform her nation, although traditional power politics was a more important motivation for her than were Enlightenment teachings. A devoutly Catholic mother and wife who inherited power from her father, Charles VI, Maria Theresa was a remarkable but old-fashioned absolutist. Her more radical son, Joseph II (r. 1780–1790), drew on Enlightenment ideals, earning the title of "revolutionary emperor."

Emerging from the long War of the Austrian Succession in 1748 with the serious loss of Silesia, Maria Theresa was determined to introduce reforms that would make the state stronger and more efficient. First, she initiated church reform, with measures aimed at limiting the papacy's influence, eliminating many religious holidays, and reducing the number of monasteries. Second, a whole series of administrative renovations strengthened the central bureaucracy, smoothed out some provincial differences, and revamped the tax system, taxing even the lands of nobles, previously exempt from taxation. Third, the government sought to improve the lot of the agricultural population, cautiously reducing the power of lords over their hereditary serfs and their partially free peasant tenants.

Coregent with his mother from 1765 onward and a strong supporter of change from above, Joseph II moved forward rapidly when he came to the throne in 1780. Most notably, Joseph abolished serfdom in 1781, and in 1789 he decreed that peasants could pay landlords in cash rather than through labor on their land. This measure was violently rejected not only by the nobility but also by the peasants it was intended to help, because they lacked the necessary cash. When a disillusioned Joseph died prematurely at forty-nine, the entire Habsburg empire was in turmoil. His brother Leopold II (r. 1790–1792) canceled Joseph's radical edicts in order to re-establish order. Peasants once again were required to do forced labor for their lords.

Despite differences in their policies, Joseph II and the other absolutists of the later eighteenth century combined old-fashioned state-building with the culture and critical thinking of the Enlightenment. In doing so, they succeeded in expanding the role of the state in the life of society. They perfected bureaucratic machines that were to prove surprisingly adaptive and enduring. Their failure to implement policies we would recognize as humane and enlightened—such as abolishing serfdom—may reveal inherent limitations in Enlightenment thinking about equality and social justice, rather than deficiencies in their execution of Enlightenment programs. The fact that leading philosophes supported rather than criticized eastern rulers' policies exposes the blind spots of the era.

In 1743 a small, humpbacked Jewish boy with a stammer left his poor parents in Dessau in central Germany and walked eighty miles to Berlin, the capital of Frederick the Great's Prussia. According to one story, when the boy reached the Rosenthaler (ROH-zuhn-taw-lehr) Gate, the only one through which Jews could pass, he told the inquiring watchman that his name was Moses and that he had come to Berlin "to learn." The watchman laughed and waved him through. "Go Moses, the sea has opened before you."*

In Berlin the young Mendelssohn studied Jewish law and eked out a living copying Hebrew manuscripts in a beautiful hand. But he was soon fascinated by an intellectual world that had been closed to him in the Dessau ghetto. There, like most Jews throughout central Europe, he had spoken Yiddish—a mixture of German, Polish, and Hebrew. Now, working mainly on his own, he mastered German; learned Latin, Greek, French, and English; and studied mathematics and Enlightenment philosophy. Word of his exceptional abilities spread in Berlin's Jewish community (the dwelling of 1,500 of the city's 100,000 inhabitants). He began tutoring the children of a wealthy Jewish silk merchant, and he soon became the merchant's clerk and later his partner. But his great passion remained the life of the mind and the spirit, which he avidly pursued in his off-hours.

Gentle and unassuming in his personal life, Mendelssohn was a bold thinker. Reading eagerly in Western philosophy since antiquity, he was, as a pious Jew, soon convinced that Enlightenment teachings need not be opposed to Jewish thought and religion. He concluded that reason could complement and strengthen religion, although each would retain its integrity as a separate sphere.† Developing his idea in his first great work, *On the Immortality of the Soul* (1767), Mendelssohn used the neutral setting of a philosophical dialogue between Socrates and his followers in ancient Greece to argue that the human soul lived forever. In refusing to bring religion and critical thinking into conflict, he was strongly influenced by contemporary German philosophers who argued similarly on behalf of Christianity. He reflected the way the German Enlightenment generally supported established religion, in contrast to the French Enlightenment, which attacked it.

*H. Kupferberg, *The Mendelssohns: Three Generations of Genius* (New York: Charles Scribner's Sons, 1972), p. 3.
†David Sorkin, *Moses Mendelssohn and the Religious Enlightenment* (Berkeley: University of California Press, 1996), pp. 8ff.

Lavater (right) attempts to convert Mendelssohn, in a painting by Moritz Oppenheim of an imaginary encounter. (By Moritz Daniel Oppenheim [1800–1882], [oil on canvas]/akg-images)

Mendelssohn's treatise on the human soul captivated the educated German public, which marveled that a Jew could have written a philosophical masterpiece. In the excitement, a Christian zealot named Johann Casper Lavater challenged Mendelssohn in a pamphlet to demonstrate how the Christian faith was not "reasonable" or to accept Christianity. Replying politely but passionately, the Jewish philosopher affirmed that his studies had only strengthened him in his faith, although he did not seek to convert anyone not born into Judaism. Rather, he urged toleration in religious matters and spoke up courageously against Jewish oppression.

Orthodox Jew and German philosophe, Moses Mendelssohn serenely combined two very different worlds. He built a bridge from the ghetto to the dominant culture over which many Jews would pass, including his novelist daughter Dorothea and his famous grandson, the composer Felix Mendelssohn.

QUESTIONS FOR ANALYSIS

1. How did Mendelssohn seek to influence Jewish religious thought in his time?
2. How do Mendelssohn's ideas compare with those of the French Enlightenment?

Jewish Life and the Limits of Enlightened Absolutism

Perhaps the best example of the limitations of enlightened absolutism are the debates surrounding the emancipation of the Jews. Europe's small Jewish populations lived under highly discriminatory laws. For the most part, Jews were confined to tiny, overcrowded ghettos, were excluded by law from most professions, and could be ordered out of a kingdom at a moment's notice. Still, a very few did manage to succeed and to obtain the right of permanent settlement, usually by performing some special service for the state. Many rulers relied on Jewish bankers for loans to raise armies and run their kingdoms. Jewish merchants prospered in international trade because they could rely on contacts with colleagues in Jewish communities scattered across Europe.

In the eighteenth century an Enlightenment movement known as the **Haskalah** emerged from within the European Jewish community, led by the Prussian philosopher Moses Mendelssohn (1729–1786). (See "Individuals in Society: Moses Mendelssohn and the Jewish Enlightenment," at left.) Christian and Jewish Enlightenment philosophers, including Mendelssohn, began to advocate for freedom and civil rights for European Jews. In an era of reason and progress, they argued, restrictions on religious grounds could not stand. The Haskalah accompanied a period of controversial social change within Jewish communities, in which rabbinic controls loosened and heightened interaction with Christians took place.

Arguments for tolerance won some ground. The British Parliament passed a law allowing naturalization of Jews in 1753, but later repealed the law due to public outrage. The most progressive reforms took place under Austrian emperor Joseph II. Among his liberal edicts of the 1780s were measures intended to integrate Jews more fully into society, including eligibility for military service, admission to higher education and artisanal trades, and removal of requirements for special clothing or emblems. Welcomed by many Jews, these reforms raised fears among traditionalists of assimilation into the general population.

Many monarchs rejected all ideas of emancipation. Although he permitted freedom of religion to his Christian subjects, Frederick the Great of Prussia firmly opposed any general emancipation for the Jews, as he did for the serfs. Catherine the Great, who acquired most of Poland's large Jewish population when she annexed part of that country in the late eighteenth century, similarly refused. In 1791 she established the Pale of Settlement, a territory including parts of modern-day Poland, Latvia, Lithuania, Ukraine, and Belarus, in which most Jews were required to live. Jewish habitation was restricted to the Pale until the Russian Revolution in 1917.

The first European state to remove all restrictions on the Jews was France under the French Revolution. Over the next hundred years, Jews gradually won full legal and civil rights throughout the rest of western Europe. Emancipation in eastern Europe took even longer and aroused more conflict and violence.

Haskalah The Jewish Enlightenment of the second half of the eighteenth century, led by the Prussian philosopher Moses Mendelssohn.

The Pale of Settlement, 1791

LOOKING BACK LOOKING AHEAD

Hailed as the origin of modern thought, the Scientific Revolution must also be seen as a product of its past. Medieval universities gave rise to important new scholarship, and the ambition and wealth of Renaissance patrons nurtured intellectual curiosity. Religious faith also influenced the Scientific Revolution, inspiring thinkers to understand the glory of God's creation, while bringing censure and personal tragedy to others. Natural philosophers following Copernicus pioneered new methods of observing and explaining nature while drawing on centuries-old traditions of mysticism, astrology, alchemy, and magic.

The Enlightenment ideas of the eighteenth century were a similar blend of past and present; they could serve as much to bolster absolutist monarchical regimes as to inspire revolutionaries to fight for individual rights and liberties. Although the Enlightenment fostered critical thinking about everything from science to religion, the majority of Europeans, including many prominent thinkers, remained devout Christians.

The achievements of the Scientific Revolution and the Enlightenment are undeniable. Key Western values of rationalism, human rights, and open-mindedness were born from these movements. With their new notions of progress and social improvement, Europeans would embark on important revolutions in industry and politics in the centuries that followed. Nonetheless, others have seen a darker side. For these critics, the mastery over nature permitted by the Scientific Revolution now threatens to overwhelm the earth's fragile equilibrium, and the Enlightenment belief in the universal application of reason can lead to arrogance and intolerance of other people's spiritual, cultural, and political values. Such vivid debates about the legacy of these intellectual and scientific developments testify to their continuing importance in today's world.

Make Connections

Think about the larger developments and continuities within and across chapters.

1. How did the era of European exploration and discovery (Chapter 14) affect the ideas of scientists and philosophers discussed in this chapter? In what ways did contact with new peoples and places stimulate new forms of thought among Europeans?

2. What was the relationship between the Scientific Revolution and the Enlightenment? How did new ways of understanding the natural world influence thinking about human society?

3. Compare the policies and actions of seventeenth-century absolutist rulers (Chapter 15) with their "enlightened" descendants described in this chapter. How accurate is the term *enlightened absolutism*?

16 REVIEW & EXPLORE

Review the Main Ideas

Answer the focus questions from each section of the chapter.

◆ What revolutionary discoveries were made in the sixteenth and seventeenth centuries, and why did they occur in Europe? (p. 506)

◆ What intellectual and social changes occurred as a result of the Scientific Revolution? (p. 516)

◆ How did the Enlightenment emerge, and what were major currents of Enlightenment thought? (p. 520)

◆ How did Enlightenment thinkers address issues of racial and social difference, and how did new institutions and social practices diffuse Enlightenment thought? (p. 526)

◆ What impact did new ways of thinking have on political developments and monarchical absolutism? (p. 532)

Identify Key Terms

Identify and explain the significance of each item below.

natural philosophy (p. 508)
Copernican hypothesis (p. 510)
law of inertia (p. 511)
law of universal gravitation (p. 513)
empiricism (p. 516)
Cartesian dualism (p. 517)
Enlightenment (p. 520)
rationalism (p. 520)
sensationalism (p. 521)
philosophes (p. 522)
deism (p. 523)
salon (p. 530)
rococo (p. 531)
public sphere (p. 532)
enlightened absolutism (p. 533)
cameralism (p. 534)
Haskalah (p. 539)

NOTES

1. Quoted in H. Butterfield, *The Origins of Modern Science* (New York: Macmillan, 1951), p. 47.
2. Ibid., p. 120.
3. Quoted in John Freely, *Aladdin's Lamp: How Greek Science Came to Europe Through the Islamic World* (New York: Knopf, 2009), p. 225.
4. Jacqueline Broad, *Women Philosophers of the Seventeenth Century* (Cambridge: Cambridge University Press, 2003), p. 17.
5. L. Schiebinger, *The Mind Has No Sex? Women in the Origins of Modern Science* (Cambridge, Mass.: Harvard University Press, 1989), p. 64.
6. Quoted in G. L. Mosse et al., eds., *Europe in Review* (Chicago: Rand McNally, 1964), p. 156.
7. Quoted in P. Gay, "The Unity of the Enlightenment," *History* 3 (1960): 25.
8. D. E. Mungello, *The Great Encounter of China and the West, 1500–1800,* 2d ed. (Lanham, Md.: Rowman & Littlefield, 2005), p. 98.
9. Quoted in Emmanuel Chukwudi Eze, ed., *Race and the Enlightenment: A Reader* (Oxford: Blackwell, 1997), p. 33.
10. See E. Fox-Genovese, "Women in the Enlightenment," in *Becoming Visible: Women in European History*, 2d ed., ed. R. Bridenthal, C. Koonz, and S. Stuard (Boston: Houghton Mifflin, 1987), esp. pp. 252–259, 263–265.
11. Aurora Wolfgang, *Gender and Voice in the French Novel, 1730–1782* (Aldershot, U.K.: Ashgate, 2004), p. 8.
12. Jean Le Rond d'Alembert, *Eloges lus dans les séances publiques de l'Académie française* (Paris, 1779), p. ix, quoted in Mona Ozouf, "'Public Opinion' at the End of the Old Regime," *The Journal of Modern History* 60, Supplement: Rethinking French Politics in 1788 (September 1988): S9.

CHAPTER PREVIEW

Working the Land
What important developments led to increased agricultural production, and how did these changes affect peasants?

The Beginning of the Population Explosion
Why did the European population rise dramatically in the eighteenth century?

The Growth of Rural Industry
How and why did rural industry intensify in the eighteenth century?

The Debate over Urban Guilds
What were guilds, and why did they become controversial in the eighteenth century?

The Atlantic World and Global Trade
How did colonial markets boost Europe's economic and social development, and what conflicts and adversity did world trade entail?

The Port of Bristol
Starting in the late seventeenth century the English port of Bristol prospered through colonial trade with the West Indies and North America. In the eighteenth century it became a major hub of the slave trade, shipping finished goods to Africa to purchase captives, who were in turn transported to the Americas in exchange for sugar, rum, and tobacco for English markets.
(*Bristol Docks and Quay*, ca. 1760 [oil on canvas]/© Bristol Museum and Art Gallery, UK/Bridgeman Images)

17

The Expansion of Europe

1650–1800

Absolutism and aristocracy, a combination of raw power and elegant refinement, were a world apart from the common people. For most people in the eighteenth century, life remained a struggle with poverty and uncertainty, with the landlord and the tax collector. In 1700 peasants on the land and artisans in their shops lived little better than had their ancestors in the Middle Ages, primarily because European societies still could not produce very much as measured by modern standards. Despite the hard work of ordinary men, women, and children, there was seldom enough good food, warm clothing, and decent housing. The idea of progress, of substantial improvement in the lives of great numbers of people, was still the dream of only a small elite in fashionable salons.

Yet the economic basis of European life was beginning to change. In the course of the eighteenth century, the European economy emerged from the long crisis of the seventeenth century, responded to challenges, and began to expand once again. Population resumed its growth, while colonial empires extended and developed. Some areas were more fortunate than others. The rising Atlantic powers—the Dutch Republic, France, and above all England—and their colonies led the way. The expansion of agriculture, industry, trade, and population marked the beginning of a surge comparable to that of the eleventh- and twelfth-century springtime of European civilization. But this time, broadly based expansion was not cut short by plague and famine. This time the response to new challenges led toward one of the most influential developments in human history, the Industrial Revolution, considered in Chapter 20. ■

Working the Land

FOCUS QUESTION

What important developments led to increased agricultural production, and how did these changes affect peasants?

At the end of the seventeenth century the economy of Europe was agrarian. With the exception of the Dutch Republic and England, at least 80 percent of the people of western Europe drew their livelihoods from agriculture. In eastern Europe the percentage was considerably higher. Men and women were tied to the land, plowing fields and sowing seed, reaping harvests and storing grain. Yet even in a rich agricultural region such as the Po Valley in northern Italy, every bushel of wheat seed sown yielded on average only five or six bushels of grain at harvest. By modern standards, output was distressingly low.

In most regions of Europe, climatic conditions produced poor or disastrous harvests every eight or nine years. In famine years the number of deaths soared far above normal. A third of a village's population might disappear in a year or two. But new developments in agricultural technology and methods gradually brought an end to the ravages of hunger in western Europe.

The Legacy of the Open-Field System

Why, in the late seventeenth century, did many areas of Europe produce barely enough food to survive? The answer lies in patterns of farming inherited from the Middle Ages, which sustained fairly large numbers of people, but did not produce material abundance. From the Middle Ages up to the seventeenth century, much of Europe was farmed through the open-field system. The land to be cultivated was divided into several large fields, which were in turn cut up into long, narrow strips. The fields were open, and the strips were not enclosed into small plots by fences or hedges. The whole peasant village followed the same pattern of plowing, sowing, and harvesting in accordance with long-standing traditions.

The ever-present problem was soil exhaustion. Wheat planted year after year in a field will deplete nitrogen in the soil. Since the supply of manure for fertilizer was limited, the only way for the land to recover was to lie fallow for a period of time. Clover and other annual grasses that sprang up in unplanted fields restored nutrients to the soil and also provided food for livestock. In the early Middle Ages a year of fallow was alternated with a year of cropping; then three-year rotations were introduced. On each strip of land, a year of wheat or rye was followed by a year of oats or beans and only then by a year of fallow. Peasants staggered the rotation of crops, so some wheat, legumes, and pastureland were always available. The three-year system was an important achievement because cash crops could be grown two years out of three, rather than only one year in two.

Traditional village rights reinforced communal patterns of farming. In addition to rotating field crops in a uniform way, villages maintained open meadows for hay and natural pasture. After the harvest villagers also pastured their animals on the wheat or rye stubble. In many places such pasturing followed a brief period, also established by tradition, for the gleaning of grain. In this process, poor women would go through the fields picking up the few single grains that had fallen to the ground in the course of the harvest. Many villages were surrounded by woodlands, also held in common, which provided essential firewood, building materials, and nutritional roots and berries.

The state and landlords continued to levy heavy taxes and high rents, thereby stripping peasants of much of their meager earnings. The level of exploitation varied.

Generally speaking, the peasants of eastern Europe were worst off. As we saw in Chapter 15, they were serfs bound to their lords in hereditary service. In much of eastern Europe, working several days per week on the lord's land was not uncommon. Well into the nineteenth century, individual Russian serfs and serf families were regularly bought and sold.

Social conditions were better in western Europe, where peasants were generally free from serfdom. In France, western Germany, England, and the Low Countries (modern-day Belgium and the Netherlands), peasants could own land and could pass it on to their children. In years with normal harvests, most people had enough food to fill their bellies. Yet life in the village was hard, and poverty was the reality for most people.

New Methods of Agriculture

The seventeenth century saw important gains in productivity in some regions that would slowly extend to the rest of Europe. By 1700 less than half of the population of Britain and the Dutch Republic worked in agriculture, producing enough to feed the remainder of the population. Many elements combined in this production growth, but the key was new ways of rotating crops that allowed farmers to forgo the unproductive fallow period altogether and maintain their land in continuous cultivation. The secret to eliminating the fallow lay in deliberately alternating grain with crops that restored nutrients to the soil, such as peas and beans, root crops like turnips and potatoes, and clover and other grasses.

Clover was one of the most important crops, because it restores nitrogen directly to the soil through its roots. Other crops produced additional benefits. Potatoes and many types of beans came to Europe as part of the sixteenth-century Columbian exchange between the New and the Old Worlds (see Chapter 14). Originally perceived by Europeans as fit only for animal feed, potatoes eventually made their way to the human table, where they provided a nutritious supplement to the peasant's meager diet. With more fodder, hay, and root vegetables for the winter months, peasants and larger farmers could build up their herds of cattle and sheep. More animals meant more manure to fertilize and restore the soil. More animals also meant more meat and dairy products as well as more power to pull plows in the fields and bring carts to market.

Over time, crop rotation spread to other parts of Europe, and farmers developed increasingly specialized patterns of crop rotation to suit different kinds of soils. For example, in the late eighteenth century farmers in French Flanders near Lille alternated a number of grain, root, and hay crops in a given field on a ten-year schedule. Ongoing experimentation, fueled by developments in the Scientific Revolution (see Chapter 16), led to more methodical farming.

Chronology

1600–1850	Growth in agriculture, pioneered by the Dutch Republic and England
1651–1663	British Navigation Acts
1652–1674	Anglo-Dutch wars
1700–1790	Height of Atlantic slave trade; expansion of rural industry in Europe
1701–1763	British and French mercantilist wars of empire
1720–1722	Last outbreak of bubonic plague in Europe
1720–1789	Growth of European population
1756–1763	Seven Years' War
1760–1815	Height of parliamentary enclosure in England
1763	Treaty of Paris; France cedes its possessions in India and North America
1770	James Cook claims the east coast of Australia for England
1776	Adam Smith publishes *An Inquiry into the Nature and Causes of the Wealth of Nations*
1805	British takeover of India complete
1807	British slave trade abolished

The Seed Drill   The seed drill had a metal plow in front (depicted behind the horse's back feet) to dig channels in the earth and a container behind it that distributed seed evenly into the channels. The drill allowed farmers to plant seeds at consistent depths and in straight lines, a much more efficient system than the old method of simply scattering seed across the field. (Prisma/UIG via Getty Images)

Advocates of the new crop rotations, who included an emerging group of experimental scientists, some government officials, and a few big landowners, believed that new methods were scarcely possible within the traditional framework of open fields and common rights. A farmer who wanted to experiment with new methods would have to get all the landholders in the village to agree to the plan. Advocates of improvement argued that innovating agriculturalists needed to enclose and consolidate their scattered holdings into compact, fenced-in fields in order to farm more effectively. In doing so, the innovators also needed to enclose the village's natural pastureland, or common, into individual shares. According to proponents of this movement, known as **enclosure**, the upheaval of village life was the necessary price of technical progress.

That price seemed too high to many rural people who had small, inadequate holdings or very little land at all. Traditional rights were precious to these poor peasants, who used commonly held pastureland to graze livestock, and marshlands or forest outside the village as a source for foraged goods that could make the difference between survival and famine in harsh times. Thus, when the small landholders and the village poor could effectively oppose the enclosure of the open fields and the common lands, they did so. In many countries they found allies among the larger, predominantly noble landowners who were also wary of enclosure because it required large investments in purchasing and fencing land and thus posed risks for them as well.

The old system of unenclosed open fields and the new system of continuous rotation coexisted in Europe for a long time. Open fields could still be found in much of France and Germany as late as the nineteenth century because peasants there had successfully opposed eighteenth-century efforts to introduce the new techniques. Through the end of the eighteenth century, the new system of enclosure was extensively adopted only in the Low Countries and England.

enclosure The movement to fence in fields in order to farm more effectively, at the expense of poor peasants who relied on common fields for farming and pasture.

The Leadership of the Low Countries and England

The seventeenth-century Dutch Republic, already the most advanced country in Europe in many areas of human endeavor (see Chapter 15), pioneered advancements in agriculture. By the middle of the seventeenth century intensive farming was well established, and the innovations of enclosed fields, continuous rotation, heavy manuring, and a wide variety of crops were all present. Agriculture was highly specialized and commercialized, especially in the province of Holland.

One reason for early Dutch leadership in farming was that the area was one of the most densely populated in Europe. In order to feed themselves and provide employment, the Dutch were forced at an early date to seek maximum yields from their land and to increase the cultivated area through the steady draining of marshes and swamps. The pressure of population was connected with the second cause: the growth of towns and cities. Stimulated by commerce and overseas trade, Amsterdam grew from thirty thousand to two hundred thousand inhabitants in its golden seventeenth century. The growing urban population provided Dutch peasants with markets for all they could produce and allowed each region to specialize in what it did best. Thus the Dutch could develop their potential, and the Low Countries became, as one historian wrote, "the Mecca of foreign agricultural experts who came . . . to see Flemish agriculture with their own eyes, to write about it and to propagate its methods in their home lands."[1]

The English were among their best students. In the mid-seventeenth century English farmers borrowed the system of continuous crop rotation from the Dutch. They also drew on Dutch expertise in drainage and water control. Large parts of seventeenth-century Holland had once been sea and sea marsh, and the efforts of centuries had made the Dutch the world's leaders in drainage. In the first half of the seventeenth century, Dutch experts made a great contribution to draining the extensive marshes, or fens, of wet and rainy England. The most famous of these Dutch engineers, Cornelius Vermuyden, directed one large drainage project in Yorkshire and another in Cambridgeshire. In the Cambridge fens, Vermuyden and his Dutch workers eventually reclaimed forty thousand acres, which were then farmed intensively in the Dutch manner. Swampy wilderness was converted into thousands of acres of some of the best land in England.

Based on the seventeenth-century achievements, English agriculture continued to progress during the eighteenth century, growing enough food to satisfy a rapidly growing population. Jethro Tull (1674–1741), part crank and part genius, was an important English innovator. A true son of the early Enlightenment, Tull adopted a critical attitude toward accepted ideas about farming and tried to develop better methods through empirical research. He was especially enthusiastic about using horses, rather than slower-moving oxen, for plowing. He also advocated sowing seed with drilling equipment rather than scattering it by hand. Drilling distributed seed in an even manner and at the proper depth. There were also improvements in livestock, inspired in part by the earlier successes of English country gentlemen in breeding ever-faster horses for the races and fox hunts that were their passions. Selective breeding of ordinary livestock was a marked improvement over the haphazard breeding of the past.

One of the most important—and bitterly contested—aspects of English agricultural development was the enclosure of open fields and commons. More than half the farmland in England was enclosed through private initiatives prior to 1700; Parliament completed this work in the eighteenth century. From the 1760s to 1815 a series of acts of Parliament enclosed most of the remaining common land. Arthur Young, another agricultural experimentalist, celebrated large-scale enclosure as a necessary means to achieve progress. (See "Evaluating the Evidence 17.1: Arthur Young on the Benefits of Enclosure," page 548.) Many of his contemporaries, as well as the historians that followed him, echoed that conviction. More recent research, however, has shown that regions that maintained open-field farming were still able to adopt crop rotation and other innovations, suggesting that enclosures were not a prerequisite for increased production.

Arthur Young on the Benefits of Enclosure

In the 1760s Arthur Young farmed his family property in Essex, England, devoting himself to experiments in the latest techniques of agriculture and animal husbandry. He traveled through the British Isles and France meeting with farmers and collecting information on their crop yields and methods of cultivation. His published observations — and his optimistic views on progress in agriculture — were widely read and acclaimed in his day. In the passage below, Young expounds on the benefits of enclosing open fields.

Respecting open field lands, the quantity of labour in them is not comparable to that of enclosures; for, not to speak of the great numbers of men that in enclosed countries are constantly employed in winter in hedging and ditching, what comparison can there be between the open field system of one half or a third of the lands being in fallow, receiving only three ploughings; and the same portion now tilled four, five, or six times by Midsummer, then sown with turnips, those hand-hoed twice, and then drawn by hand, and carted to stalls for beasts; or else hurdled out in portions for fatting sheep! What a scarcity of employment in one case, what a variety in the other! And consider the vast tracts of land in the kingdom (no less than the whole upon which turnips are cultivated) that have undergone this change since the last century. I should also remind the reader of other systems of management; beans and peas hand-hoed for a fallow — the culture of potatoes — of carrots, of coleseed, &c. — the hoeing of white corn — with the minuter improvements in every part of the culture of all crops — every article of which is an increase of labour. Then he should remember the vast tracts of country uncultivated in the last century, which have been enclosed and converted into new farms, a much greater tract in 80 years than these

writers dream of: all this is the effect of enclosures, and consequently they also have yielded a great increase of employment. . . .

The fact is this; in the central counties of the kingdom, particularly Northamptonshire, Leicestershire, and parts of Warwick, Huntingdon and Buckinghamshires, there have been within 30 years large tracts of the open field arable under that vile course, 1 fallow, 2 wheat, 3 spring corn, enclosed and laid down to grass, being much more suited to the wetness of the soil than corn; and yields in beef, mutton, hides and wool, beyond comparison a greater neat produce than when under corn. . . . Thus the land yields a greater neat produce in food for mankind — the landlord doubles his income, which enables him to employ so many more manufacturers and artisans — the farmer increases his income, by means of which he also does the same — the hides and wool are a creation of so much employment for other manufacturers.

EVALUATE THE EVIDENCE

1. What are the various improvements in agriculture described by Young in this passage? How do they relate to one another?
2. Why does Young think that enclosures produce more employment opportunities than open fields do? Based on your reading in the chapter, did everyone perceive the benefits produced by enclosure in the same way as Young?

Source: Arthur Young, *Political Arithmetic: Containing Observations on the Present State of Great Britain; and the Principles of Her Policy in the Encouragement of Agriculture* (London: W. Nicoll, 1774), pp. 72–73, 148.

Many critics of Arthur Young's day emphasized the social upheaval caused by enclosure. By eliminating common rights and greatly reducing the access of poor men and women to the land, the eighteenth-century enclosure movement marked the completion of two major historical developments in England — the rise of capitalist market-oriented estate agriculture and the emergence of a landless rural proletariat. By the early nineteenth century a tiny minority of wealthy English and Scottish landowners held most of the land and pursued profits aggressively, leasing their holdings through agents at competitive prices to middle-size farmers, who relied on landless laborers for their workforce. These landless laborers worked very long hours, usually following a dawn-to-dusk schedule six days a week all year long. Not only was the small landholder deprived of his land, but improvements in technology meant that fewer laborers were needed to work the large farms, and unemployment spread throughout the countryside. As one observer commented:

> It is no uncommon thing for four or five wealthy graziers to engross a large inclosed lordship, which was before in the hands of twenty or thirty farmers, and as many smaller tenants or proprietors. All these are thereby thrown out of their livings, and many other families, who were chiefly employed and supported by them, such as blacksmiths, carpenters, wheelwrights and other artificers and tradesmen, besides their own labourers and servants.[2]

In no other European country had this **proletarianization**—this transformation of large numbers of small peasant farmers into landless rural wage earners—gone so far. England's village poor found the cost of change heavy and unjust.

proletarianization The transformation of large numbers of small peasant farmers into landless rural wage earners.

The Beginning of the Population Explosion

Another factor that affected the existing order of life and drove economic changes in the eighteenth century was the beginning of the population explosion. Explosive growth continued in Europe until the twentieth century, by which time it was affecting non-Western areas of the globe. In this section we examine the background and causes of the population growth; the following section considers how the challenge of more mouths to feed and more hands to employ affected the European economy.

FOCUS QUESTION
Why did the European population rise dramatically in the eighteenth century?

Long-Standing Obstacles to Population Growth

Until 1700 the total population of Europe grew slowly much of the time, and it followed an irregular cyclical pattern (Figure 17.1). This cyclical pattern had a great influence on many aspects of social and economic life. The terrible ravages of the Black Death of 1348–1350 caused a sharp drop in population and food prices after 1350 and also created a labor shortage throughout Europe. Some economic historians calculate that for common people in western Europe who managed to steer clear of warfare and of power struggles within the ruling class, the later Middle Ages was an era of exceptional well-being.

By the mid-sixteenth century much of Europe had returned to its pre-plague population levels. In this buoyant period, farmers brought new land into cultivation and urban settlements grew significantly. But this well-being eroded in the course of the sixteenth century. Population growth outstripped the growth of production after about 1500. There was less food, housing, fuel, and other resources per person, and prices rose more rapidly than wages, a development intensified by the inflow of precious metals from the Americas (see Chapter 14). The century-long period of general, if uneven, inflation that followed, known as the European price revolution, substantially lowered

FIGURE 17.1 The Growth of Population in England, 1550–1850 England is a good example of both the uneven increase of European population before 1700 and the third great surge of growth that began in the eighteenth century. (Source: Data from E. A. Wrigley et al., *English Population History from Family Reconstitution, 1580–1837* [Cambridge: Cambridge University Press, 1997], p. 614.)

living standards. Population figures stagnated or declined across much of Europe, and widespread poverty was an undeniable reality.

During the seventeenth century births and deaths, fertility and mortality, returned to a crude but effective balance. The population grew modestly in normal years at a rate of perhaps 0.5 to 1 percent, or enough to double the population in 70 to 140 years. This is, of course, a generalization encompassing many different patterns. In areas such as Russia and colonial New England, where there was a great deal of frontier to be settled, the annual rate of natural increase, not counting immigration, might well have exceeded 1 percent. In a country such as France, where the land had long been densely settled, the rate of increase might have been less than 0.5 percent.

Although population growth of even 1 percent per year seems fairly modest, it will produce a very large increase over a long period: in three hundred years it will result in sixteen times as many people. Yet such significant increases did not occur in agrarian Europe. In certain abnormal years and tragic periods—the Black Death was only the most extreme example—many more people died than were born, and total population fell sharply, even catastrophically. A number of years of modest growth would then be necessary to make up for those who had died in an abnormal year. Such savage increases in deaths occurred periodically in the seventeenth century on a local and regional scale, and these demographic crises combined to check the growth of population until after 1700.

The grim reapers of demographic crisis were famine, epidemic disease, and war. Episodes of famine were inevitable in all eras of premodern Europe, given low crop yields and unpredictable climatic conditions. In the seventeenth century much of Europe experienced unusually cold and wet weather, which produced even more severe harvest failures and food shortages than usual. Contagious diseases, like typhus, smallpox, syphilis, and the ever-recurring bubonic plague, also continued to ravage Europe's population on a periodic basis. War was another scourge, and its indirect effects were even more harmful than the purposeful killing during military campaigns. Soldiers and camp followers passed all manner of contagious diseases throughout the countryside. Armies requisitioned scarce food supplies and disrupted the agricultural cycle while battles destroyed precious crops, livestock, and farmlands. The Thirty Years' War (1618–1648) witnessed all possible combinations of distress (see Chapter 15). The number of inhabitants in the German states alone declined by more than two-thirds in some large areas and by at least one-third almost everywhere else.

The New Pattern of the Eighteenth Century

In the eighteenth century the traditional demographic pattern of Europe was transformed. Growth took place unevenly, with Russia growing very quickly after 1700 and France much more slowly. Nonetheless, the explosion of population was a major phenomenon in all European countries. Europeans grew in numbers steadily from 1720 to 1789, with especially dramatic increases after about 1750 (Figure 17.2). Between 1700 and 1835 the population of Europe doubled in size.

What caused this population growth? In some areas, especially England, women had more babies than before because new opportunities for employment in rural industry (see page 552) allowed them to marry at an earlier age. But the basic cause of European population increase as a whole was a decline in mortality—fewer deaths.

One of the primary reasons behind this decline was the still-unexplained disappearance of the bubonic plague. Following the Black Death in the fourteenth century, plague had remained part of the European experience, striking again and again with savage force, particularly in towns. In 1720 a ship from Syria and the Levant brought the disease to Marseilles. As a contemporary account described it, "The Porters employ'd in unloading the Vessel, were immediately seiz'd with violent Pains in the Head . . . soon after they broke out in Blotches and Buboes, and died in three Days."[3] Plague quickly spread within and beyond Marseilles, killing up to one hundred thousand. By 1722 the epidemic had passed, and that was the last time plague fell on western and central Europe. Exactly why plague disappeared is unknown. Stricter measures of quarantine in Mediterranean ports and along the Austrian border with the Ottoman Empire helped by carefully isolating human carriers of plague. Chance and plain good luck were probably just as important.

Advances in medical knowledge did not contribute much to reducing the death rate in the eighteenth century. The most important advance in preventive medicine in this period was inoculation against smallpox, a disease that killed approximately four hundred thousand people each year in Europe. Widely practiced in the Ottoman Empire, inoculation was popularized in England in the 1720s by the wife of the former English ambassador, but did not spread to the rest of the continent for decades. Improvements in the water supply and sewage, which were frequently promoted by strong absolutist monarchies, did contribute to somewhat better public health and helped reduce such diseases as typhoid and typhus in urban areas of western Europe. Improvements in water supply and the drainage of swamps also reduced Europe's large insect population. Flies and mosquitoes played a major role in spreading diseases, especially those striking children and young adults. Thus early public health measures contributed to the decline in mortality that began with the disappearance of plague and continued into the early nineteenth century.

Human beings also became more successful in their efforts to safeguard the supply of food. The eighteenth century was a time of considerable canal and road building in western Europe. These advances in transportation, which were also among the more positive aspects of strong absolutist states, lessened the impact of local crop failure and famine. Emergency supplies could be brought in, and localized starvation became less frequent. Wars became less destructive than in the seventeenth century and spread fewer epidemics.

None of the population growth would have been possible if not for the advances in agricultural production in the seventeenth and eighteenth centuries, which increased the

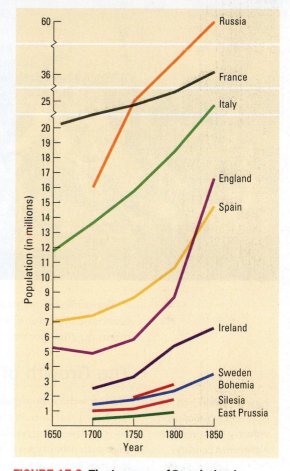

FIGURE 17.2 The Increase of Population in Europe, 1650–1850 Population grew across Europe in the eighteenth century, though the most dramatic increases occurred after 1750. Russia experienced the largest increase and emerged as Europe's most populous state, as natural increase was complemented by growth from territorial expansion. (Source: Data from Massimo Livi Bacci, *The Population of Europe* [Wiley-Blackwell, 2000], p. 8.)

The Plague at Marseilles The bishop of Marseilles blesses victims of the plague that overwhelmed Marseilles in 1720. Some one hundred thousand people died in the outbreak, which was the last great episode of plague in western Europe. (By Nicolas-André Monsiau [1754–1837], [oil on canvas]/Photo: Christian Jean/Musée du Louvre, Paris, France/© RMN–Grand Palais/Art Resource, NY)

food supply and contributed nutritious new foods, particularly the potato from South America. In short, population grew in the eighteenth century primarily because years of higher-than-average death rates were less catastrophic. Famines, epidemics, and wars continued to occur and to affect population growth, but their severity moderated.

Population growth intensified the imbalance between the number of people and the economic opportunities available to them. Deprived of land by the enclosure movement, the rural poor were forced to look for new ways to make a living.

The Growth of Rural Industry

FOCUS QUESTION
How and why did rural industry intensify in the eighteenth century?

cottage industry A stage of industrial development in which rural workers used hand tools in their homes to manufacture goods on a large scale for sale in a market.

The growth of population increased the number of rural workers with little or no land, and this in turn contributed to the development of industry in rural areas. The poor in the countryside increasingly needed to supplement their agricultural earnings with other types of work, and urban capitalists were eager to employ them, often at lower wages than urban workers received. **Cottage industry**, which consisted of manufacturing with hand tools in peasant cottages and work sheds, grew markedly in the eighteenth century and became a crucial feature of the European economy.

To be sure, peasant communities had always made clothing, processed food, and constructed housing for their own use. But medieval peasants did not produce manufactured goods on a large scale for sale in a market. By the eighteenth century, however, the pressures of rural poverty led many poor villagers to seek additional work, and far-reaching changes for daily rural life were set in motion.

The Putting-Out System

putting-out system The eighteenth-century system of rural industry in which a merchant loaned raw materials to cottage workers, who processed them and returned the finished products to the merchant.

Cottage industry was often organized through the **putting-out system**. The two main participants in the putting-out system were the merchant capitalist and the rural worker. In this system, the merchant loaned, or "put out," raw materials to cottage workers, who processed the raw materials in their own homes and returned the finished products to the merchant. There were endless variations on this basic relationship. Sometimes rural workers bought their own raw materials and produced goods that they sold to the merchant. Sometimes whole families were involved in domestic industry; at other times the tasks were closely associated with one gender or age group. Sometimes several workers toiled together to perform a complicated process in a workshop outside the home. The relative importance of earnings from the land and from industry varied greatly for handicraft workers, although industrial wages usually became more important for a given family with time.

As industries grew in scale and complexity, production was often broken into many stages. For example, a merchant would provide raw wool to one group of workers for spinning into thread. He would then pass the thread to another group of workers to be bleached, to another for dyeing, and to another for weaving into cloth. The merchant paid outworkers by the piece and proceeded to sell the finished product to regional, national, or international markets.

The putting-out system grew because it had competitive advantages. Underemployed labor was abundant, and poor peasants and landless laborers would work for low wages. Since production in the countryside was unregulated, workers and merchants could change procedures and experiment as they saw fit. Because workers did not need to meet rigid guild standards, cottage industry became capable of producing many kinds of goods. Textiles; all manner of knives, forks, and housewares; buttons and gloves; and clocks could be produced quite satisfactorily in the countryside. Although luxury goods for the rich, such as exquisite tapestries and fine porcelain, demanded special training, close supervision, and centralized workshops, the limited skills of rural industry were sufficient for everyday articles.

Rural manufacturing did not spread across Europe at an even rate. It developed most successfully in England, particularly for the spinning and weaving of woolen cloth. By 1500 half of England's textiles were being produced in the countryside. By 1700 English industry was generally more rural than urban and heavily reliant on the putting-out system. Most continental countries, with the exception of Flanders and the Dutch Republic, developed rural industry more slowly. The latter part of the eighteenth century witnessed a remarkable expansion of rural industry in certain densely populated regions of continental Europe (Map 17.1).

The Lives of Rural Textile Workers

Until the nineteenth century the industry that employed the most people in Europe was textiles. The making of linen, woolen, and eventually cotton cloth was the typical activity of cottage workers engaged in the putting-out system. A look inside the cottage of the English weaver illustrates a way of life as well as an economic system. The rural worker lived in a small cottage with tiny windows and little space. The cottage was often a single room that served as workshop, kitchen, and bedroom. There were only a few pieces of furniture, of which the weaver's loom was by far the largest and most important. That loom changed somewhat in the early eighteenth century when John Kay's invention of the flying shuttle enabled the weaver to throw the shuttle back and forth between the threads with one hand. Aside from that improvement, however, the loom was as it had been for much of history and as it would remain until the arrival of mechanized looms in the first decades of the nineteenth century.

Handloom weaving was a family enterprise. All members of the family helped in the work, so that "every person from seven to eighty (who retained their sight and who could move their hands) could earn their bread," as one eighteenth-century English observer put it.[4] Operating the loom was usually considered a man's job, reserved for the male head of the family. Women and children worked at auxiliary tasks; they prepared the warp (vertical) threads and mounted them on the loom, wound threads on bobbins

Persons per square mile
- More than 100
- 50 to 100
- Fewer than 50

- Textile production
- Metal production
- *Wool* Main textile product

MAP 17.1 Industry and Population in Eighteenth-Century Europe The growth of cottage manufacturing in rural areas helped country people increase their income and contributed to population growth. The putting-out system began in England, and much of the work was in the textile industry. Cottage industry was also strong in the Low Countries — modern-day Belgium and the Netherlands.

for the weft (horizontal) threads, and sometimes operated the warp frame while the father passed the shuttle.

The work of four or five spinners was needed to keep one weaver steadily employed. Since the weaver's family usually could not produce enough thread, merchants hired the wives and daughters of agricultural workers, who took on spinning work in their spare time. In England, many widows and single women also became "spinsters," so many in fact that the word became a synonym for an unmarried woman. In parts of Germany, spinning employed whole families and was not reserved for women.

Relations between workers and employers were often marked by sharp conflict. There were constant disputes over the weights of materials and the quality of finished work. Merchants accused workers of stealing raw materials, and weavers complained that merchants delivered underweight bales. Suspicion abounded.

Conditions were particularly hard for female workers. While men could earn decent wages through long hours of arduous labor, women's wages were usually much lower because they were not considered the family's primary wage earner. In England's Yorkshire wool industry, a male wool comber earned a good wage of 12 shillings or more a week, while a female spinner could hope for only 3½ shillings.[5]

A single or widowed spinner faced a desperate struggle with poverty. Any period of illness or unemployment could spell disaster for her and any children she might have. In 1788 one English writer condemned the low wages of spinners in Norwich: "The suffering of thousands of wretched individuals, willing to work, but starving from their ill requited labour; of whole families of honest industrious children offering their little hands to the wheel, and asking bread of the helpless mother, unable through this well regulated manufacture to give it to them."[6]

From the merchant capitalist's point of view, the problem was not low wages but maintaining control over the labor force. Cottage workers were scattered across the countryside and their work depended on the agricultural calendar. In spring and late summer, planting and haymaking occupied all hands in the rural village, leading to shortages in the supply of thread. Merchants bitterly resented their lack of control over rural labor because their own livelihood depended on their ability to meet orders on time. They accused workers—especially female spinners—of laziness, drunkenness, and immorality. If workers failed to produce enough thread, they reasoned, it must be because their wages were too high and they had little incentive to work.

Merchants thus insisted on maintaining the lowest possible wages to force the "idle" poor into productive labor. They also lobbied for, and obtained, new police powers over workers. Imprisonment and public whipping became common punishments for pilfering small amounts of yarn or cloth. For poor workers, their right to hold on to the bits and pieces left over in the production process was akin to the traditional peasant right of gleaning in common lands. With progress came the loss of traditional safeguards for the poor.

The Industrious Revolution

One scholar has used the term **industrious revolution** to summarize the social and economic changes taking place in northwestern Europe in the late seventeenth and early eighteenth centuries.[7] This occurred as households reduced leisure time, stepped up the pace of work, and, most important, redirected the labor of women and children away from the production of goods for household consumption and toward wage work. In the countryside the spread of cottage industry can be seen as one manifestation of the industrious revolution, while in the cities there was a rise in female employment outside the home (see page 557). By working harder and increasing the number of wageworkers, rural and urban households could purchase more goods, even in a time of stagnant or falling wages.

The effect of these changes is still debated. While some scholars lament the encroachment of longer work hours and stricter discipline on traditional family life, others insist that poor families made decisions based on their own self-interests. With more finished goods becoming available at lower prices, households sought cash income to participate in an emerging consumer economy.

The role of women and girls in this new economy is particularly controversial. When women entered the labor market, they almost always worked at menial, tedious jobs for very low wages. Yet when women earned their own wages, they also seem to have exercised more independence in marriage choices and household decision making. Most of their scant earnings went for household necessities, items of food and clothing they could no longer produce now that they worked full-time, but sometimes a few shillings were left for a ribbon or a new pair of stockings. Women's

industrious revolution The shift that occurred as families in northwestern Europe focused on earning wages instead of producing goods for household consumption; this reduced their economic self-sufficiency but increased their ability to purchase consumer goods.

use of their surplus income thus helped spur the rapid growth of the textile industries in which they labored so hard.

These new sources and patterns of labor established important foundations for the Industrial Revolution of the late eighteenth and nineteenth centuries (see Chapter 20). They created households in which all members worked for wages rather than in a family business and in which consumption relied on market-produced rather than homemade goods. It was not until the mid-nineteenth century, with rising industrial wages, that a new model emerged in which the male "breadwinner" was expected to earn enough to support the whole family and women and children were relegated back to the domestic sphere. With women estimated to compose more than 40 percent of the global workforce, today's world is experiencing a second industrious revolution in a similar climate of stagnant wages and increased demand for consumer goods.[8]

The Debate over Urban Guilds

FOCUS QUESTION
What were guilds, and why did they become controversial in the eighteenth century?

One consequence of the growth of rural industry was an undermining of the traditional **guild system** that protected urban artisans. Guilds continued to dominate production in towns and cities, providing their masters with economic privileges as well as a proud social identity, but they increasingly struggled against competition from rural workers. Meanwhile, those excluded from guild membership—women, day laborers, Jews, and foreigners—worked on the margins of the urban economy.

In the second half of the eighteenth century, critics like Adam Smith attacked the guilds as outmoded institutions that obstructed technical progress and innovation. Until recently, most historians repeated that view. An ongoing reassessment of guilds now emphasizes their ability to adapt to changing economic circumstances.

guild system The organization of artisanal production into trade-based associations, or guilds, each of which received a monopoly over its trade and the right to train apprentices and hire workers.

Urban Guilds

Originating around 1200 during the economic boom of the Middle Ages, the guild system reached its peak in most of Europe in the seventeenth and eighteenth centuries. During this period, urban guilds increased dramatically in cities and towns across Europe. In Louis XIV's France, for example, finance minister Jean-Baptiste Colbert revived the urban guilds and used them

Guild Procession in Seventeenth-Century Brussels   Guilds played an important role in the civic life of the early modern city. They collected taxes from their members, imposed quality standards and order on the trades, and represented the interests of commerce and industry to the government. In return, they claimed exclusive monopolies over their trades and the right to govern their own affairs. Guilds marched in processions, like the one shown here, at important city events, proudly displaying their corporate insignia. (*The Senior Guilds*, 1616, by Denis van Alsloot [fl. 1599–1628]/Victoria and Albert Museum, London, UK/V & A Images, London/Art Resource, NY)

to encourage high-quality production and to collect taxes (see Chapter 15). The number of guilds in the city of Paris grew from 60 in 1672 to 129 in 1691.

Guild masters occupied the summit of the world of work. Each guild possessed a detailed set of privileges, including exclusive rights to produce and sell certain goods, access to restricted markets in raw materials, and the rights to train apprentices, hire workers, and open shops. Any individual who violated these monopolies could be prosecuted. Guilds also served social and religious functions, providing a locus of sociability and group identity to the middling classes of European cities.

To ensure there was enough work to go around, guilds restricted their membership to men who were Christians, had several years of work experience, paid membership fees, and successfully completed a masterpiece. Masters' sons enjoyed automatic access to their fathers' guilds, while outsiders—including Jews and Protestants in Catholic countries—were barred from entering. Most urban men and women worked in non-guild trades as domestic servants, manual laborers, and vendors of food, used clothing, and other goods.

The guilds' ability to enforce their barriers varied a great deal across Europe. In England, national regulations superseded guild rules, sapping their importance. In France, the Crown developed an ambiguous attitude toward guilds, relying on them for taxes and enforcement of quality standards, yet allowing non-guild production to flourish in the countryside in the 1760s, and even in some urban neighborhoods. The German guilds were perhaps the most powerful in Europe, and the most conservative. Journeymen in German cities, with their masters' support, violently protested the encroachment of non-guild workers.

While most were hostile to women, a small number of guilds did accept women. Most involved needlework and textile production, occupations that were considered appropriate for women. In 1675 seamstresses gained a new all-female guild in Paris, and soon seamstresses joined tailors' guilds in parts of France, England, and the Dutch Republic. By the mid-eighteenth century male masters began to hire more female workers, often in defiance of their own guild statutes.

Adam Smith and Economic Liberalism

At the same time that cottage industry began to infringe on the livelihoods of urban artisans, new Enlightenment ideals called into question the very existence of the guild system. Eighteenth-century critics derided guilds as outmoded and exclusionary institutions that obstructed technical innovation and progress. One of the best-known critics of government regulation of trade and industry was Adam Smith (1723–1790), a leading figure of the Scottish Enlightenment (see Chapter 16). Smith developed the general idea of freedom of enterprise and established the basis for modern economics in his groundbreaking work *Inquiry into the Nature and Causes of the Wealth of Nations* (1776). Smith criticized guilds for their stifling restrictions, a critique he extended to all state monopolies and privileged companies. Far preferable, in his view, was free competition, which would protect consumers from price gouging and give all citizens an equal right to do what they did best. Smith advocated a more highly developed "division of labor," which entailed separating craft production into individual tasks to increase workers' speed and efficiency. (See "Evaluating the Evidence 17.2: Adam Smith on the Division of Labor," page 558.)

Adam Smith on the Division of Labor

In An Inquiry into the Nature and Causes of the Wealth of Nations *(1776), Scottish philosopher Adam Smith argued that commercial society — his term for the early capitalism of his age — was finally freeing the individual from the constraints of tradition, superstition, and cumbersome regulations. The passage below contains Smith's famous description of the division of labor, which permits a small number of men to do the work of many more. Although Smith lauded the gains in efficiency, skilled artisans bitterly resented the loss of control and specialized knowledge imposed by dividing production into isolated, repetitive steps.*

To take an example, therefore, from a very trifling manufacture; but one in which the division of labor has been very often taken notice of, the trade of the pin-maker; a workman not educated to this business . . . nor acquainted with the use of the machinery employed in it . . . could scarce, perhaps, with his utmost industry, make one pin in a day, and certainly could not make twenty. But in the way in which this business is now carried on, not only the whole work is a peculiar trade, but it is divided into a number of branches, of which the greater part are likewise peculiar trades. One man draws out the wire, another straightens it, a third cuts it, a fourth points it, a fifth grinds it at the top for receiving the head; to make the head requires two or three distinct operations; to put it on, is a peculiar business, to whiten the pins is another; it is even a trade by itself to put them into the paper; and the important business of making a pin is, in this manner, divided into about eighteen distinct operations, which, in some manufactories, are all performed by distinct hands, though in others the same man will sometimes perform two or three of them. I have seen a small manufactory of this kind where ten men only were employed, and where some of them consequently performed two or three distinct operations. But though they were very poor, and therefore but indifferently accommodated with the necessary machinery, they could, when they exerted themselves, make among them about twelve pounds of pins in a day. There are in a pound upward of four thousand pins of a middling size. Those ten persons, therefore, could make among them upward of forty-eight thousand pins in a day. Each person, therefore, making a tenth part of forty-eight thousand pins, might be considered as making four thousand eight hundred pins in a day. But if they had all wrought separately and independently, and without any of them having been educated to this peculiar business, they certainly could not each of them have made twenty, perhaps not one pin in a day; that is, certainly not the two hundred and fortieth, perhaps not the four thousand eight hundredth part of what they are at present capable of performing, in consequence of a proper division and combination of their different operations.

EVALUATE THE EVIDENCE

1. Into what steps — what Smith calls "peculiar trades" — is pin making divided? How do these steps make it possible for ten men to do the work of hundreds?
2. Why would skilled craftsmen oppose the division of labor described by Smith? What disadvantages did it create for them? For their guilds?

Source: Adam Smith, *The Wealth of Nations*, part 1 (New York: P. F. Collier & Son, 1902), pp. 44–45.

In keeping with his fear of political oppression and with the "system of natural liberty" that he championed, Smith argued that government should limit itself to "only three duties": it should provide a defense against foreign invasion, maintain civil order with courts and police protection, and sponsor certain indispensable public works and institutions that could never adequately profit private investors. He believed that the pursuit of self-interest in a competitive market would be sufficient to improve the living conditions of citizens, a view that quickly emerged as the classic argument for **economic liberalism**.

However, Smith did not advocate unbridled capitalism. Unlike many disgruntled merchant capitalists, he applauded the modest rise in real wages of British workers in the eighteenth century, stating: "No society can surely be flourishing

economic liberalism
A belief in free trade and competition based on Adam Smith's argument that the invisible hand of free competition would benefit all individuals, rich and poor.

and happy, of which the far greater part of the members are poor and miserable." Smith also acknowledged that employers were "always and everywhere in a sort of tacit, but constant and uniform combination, not to raise the wages of labor above their actual rate" and sometimes entered "into particular combinations to sink the wages even below this rate." While he celebrated the rise in productivity allowed by the division of labor, he also acknowledged its demoralizing effects on workers and called for government intervention to raise workers' living standards.[9]

Many educated people in France, including government officials, shared Smith's ideas. In 1774, the reform-minded economics minister Anne-Robert-Jacques Turgot issued a law in the name of Louis XV, ordering the grain trade to be freed from state regulation. Two years later, another edict abolished all French guilds. The law stated:

> We wish to abolish these arbitrary institutions, which do not allow the poor man to earn his living; which reject a sex whose weakness has given it more needs and fewer resources . . . ; which destroy emulation and industry and nullify the talents of those whose circumstances have excluded them from membership of a guild; which deprive the state and the arts of all the knowledge brought to them by foreigners; which retard the progress of these arts . . . ; [and which] burden industry with an oppressive tax, which bears heavily on the people.[10]

Vociferous popular protest against these measures led to Turgot's disgrace shortly afterward and the cancellation of his reforms, but the legislators of the French Revolution (see Chapter 19) returned to a liberal economic agenda in 1789. The National Assembly definitively abolished guilds in 1791. Other European countries followed suit more slowly, with guilds surviving in central Europe and Italy into the second half of the nineteenth century. By the middle of the nineteenth century economic liberalism was championed by most European governments and elites.

Some artisans welcomed the deregulation espoused by Smith and Turgot, but many continued to uphold the ideals of the guilds. In the late eighteenth and early nineteenth centuries, skilled artisans across Europe espoused the values of high-quality hand craftsmanship and limited competition in contrast to the proletarianization and loss of skills they endured in mechanized production. Recent scholarship has challenged wholly negative views of the guilds, emphasizing the flexibility and adaptability of the guild system and the role it played in fostering confidence in quality standards.

The Atlantic World and Global Trade

In addition to agricultural improvement, population pressure, and growing cottage industry, the expansion of Europe in the eighteenth century was characterized by the increase of world trade. Adam Smith himself declared that "the discovery of America and that of a passage to the East Indies by the Cape of Good Hope, are the two greatest and most important events recorded in the history of mankind."[11] In the eighteenth century Spain and Portugal revitalized their empires and began drawing more wealth from renewed colonial development. Yet once again the countries of northwestern Europe—the Dutch Republic, France, and above all Great Britain—benefited most.

FOCUS QUESTION
How did colonial markets boost Europe's economic and social development, and what conflicts and adversity did world trade entail?

The Atlantic economy that these countries developed from 1650 to 1790 would prove crucial in the building of a global economy. Great Britain, which was formed in 1707 by the union of England and Scotland into a single kingdom, gradually became the leading maritime power. Thus the British played the critical role in building a fairly unified Atlantic economy that provided remarkable opportunities for them and their colonists. They also competed ruthlessly with France and the Netherlands for trade and territory in the Americas and Asia.

Mercantilism and Colonial Competition

Britain's commercial leadership in the eighteenth century had its origins in the mercantilism of the seventeenth century (see Chapter 15). Eventually eliciting criticism from Enlightenment thinker Adam Smith and other proponents of free trade in the late eighteenth century, European mercantilism was a system of economic regulations aimed at increasing the power of the state. As practiced by a leading figure such as Colbert under Louis XIV, mercantilism aimed particularly at creating a favorable balance of foreign trade in order to increase a country's stock of gold. A country's gold holdings served as an all-important treasure chest that could be opened periodically to pay for war in a violent age.

Navigation Acts A series of English laws that controlled the import of goods to Britain and British colonies.

In England, the desire to increase both military power and private wealth resulted in the mercantile system of the **Navigation Acts**. Oliver Cromwell established the first of these laws in 1651, and the restored monarchy of Charles II extended them in 1660 and 1663. The acts required that most goods imported from Europe into England and Scotland (Great Britain after 1707) be carried on British-owned ships with British crews or on ships of the country producing the articles. Moreover, these laws gave British merchants and shipowners a virtual monopoly on trade with British colonies. The colonists were required to ship their products on British (or American) ships and to buy almost all European goods from Britain. It was believed that these economic regulations would eliminate foreign competition, thereby helping British merchants and workers as well as colonial plantation owners and farmers. It was hoped, too, that the emerging British Empire would develop a shipping industry with a large number of experienced seamen who could serve during wartime in the Royal Navy.

The Navigation Acts were a form of economic warfare. Their initial target was the Dutch, who were far ahead of the English in shipping and foreign trade in the mid-seventeenth century (see Chapter 15). In conjunction with three Anglo-Dutch wars between 1652 and 1674, the Navigation Acts seriously damaged Dutch shipping and commerce. The British seized the thriving Dutch colony of New Amsterdam in 1664 and renamed it New York. By the late seventeenth century the Dutch Republic was falling behind England in shipping, trade, and colonies.

Thereafter France stood clearly as England's most serious rival in the competition for overseas empire. Rich in natural resources, with a population three or four times that of England, and allied with Spain, continental Europe's leading military power was already building a powerful fleet and a worldwide system of rigidly monopolized colonial trade. Thus from 1701 to 1763 Britain and France were locked in a series of wars to decide, in part, which nation would become the leading maritime power and claim the profits of Europe's overseas expansion (Map 17.2).

The first round was the War of the Spanish Succession (see Chapter 15), which started in 1701 when Louis XIV accepted the Spanish crown willed to his grandson.

MAP 17.2 The Atlantic Economy in 1701   The growth of trade encouraged both economic development and military conflict in the Atlantic basin. Four continents were linked together by the exchange of goods and people.

Colonel James Tod of the East India Company Traveling by Elephant Through Rajasthan, India   By the end of the eighteenth century agents of the British East India Company exercised growing military and political authority in India, in addition to monopolizing Britain's lucrative economic trade with the subcontinent. (Victoria and Albert Museum, London, UK/Bridgeman Images)

Besides upsetting the continental balance of power, a union of France and Spain threatened to encircle and destroy the British colonies in North America (see Map 17.2). Defeated by a great coalition of states after twelve years of fighting, Louis XIV was forced in the Peace of Utrecht (YOO-trehkt) in 1713 to cede his North American holdings in Newfoundland, Nova Scotia, and the Hudson Bay territory to Britain. Spain was compelled to give Britain control of its West African slave trade—the so-called *asiento* (ah-SYEHN-toh)—and to let Britain send one ship of merchandise into the Spanish colonies annually.

Conflict continued among the European powers over both domestic and colonial affairs. The War of the Austrian Succession (1740–1748), which started when Frederick the Great of Prussia seized Silesia from Austria's Maria Theresa (see Chapter 16), gradually became a world war that included Anglo-French conflicts in India and North America. The war ended with no change in the territorial situation in North America. This inconclusive standoff helped set the stage for the Seven Years' War (1756–1763; see Chapter 19). In central Europe, France aided Austria's Maria Theresa in her quest to win back Silesia from the Prussians, who had formed an alliance with England. In North America, French and British settlers engaged in territorial skirmishes that eventually resulted in all-out war that drew in Native American allies on both sides of the conflict (see Map 19.1, page 614). By 1763 Prussia had held off the Austrians, and British victory on all colonial fronts was ratified in the **Treaty of Paris**. British naval power, built in large part on the rapid growth of the British shipping industry after the passage of the Navigation Acts, had triumphed decisively: Britain had realized its goal of monopolizing a vast trading and colonial empire.

Treaty of Paris The treaty that ended the Seven Years' War in Europe and the colonies in 1763, and ratified British victory on all colonial fronts.

The Atlantic Economy

As the volume of transatlantic trade increased, the regions bordering the ocean were increasingly drawn into an integrated economic system. Commercial exchange in the Atlantic has often been referred to as the "triangle trade," designating a three-way transport of goods: European commodities, like guns and textiles, to Africa; enslaved Africans to the colonies; and colonial goods, such as cotton, tobacco, and sugar, back to Europe (see Map 17.2).

Over the course of the eighteenth century, the economies of European nations bordering the Atlantic Ocean, especially England, relied more and more on colonial exports. In England, sales to the mainland colonies of North America and the West Indian sugar islands—with an important assist from West Africa and Latin America—soared from £500,000 to £4 million (Figure 17.3). Exports to England's colonies in Ireland and India also rose substantially from 1700 to 1800. By 1800 sales to European countries—England's traditional trading partners—represented only one-third of exports, down from two-thirds a century earlier. England also benefited from importing colonial products. Colonial monopolies allowed the English to obtain a steady supply of such goods at beneficial prices and to re-export them to other nations at high profits. Moreover, many colonial goods, like sugar and tobacco, required processing before consumption and thus contributed new manufacturing jobs in England. In the eighteenth century, stimulated by trade and empire building, England's capital city, London, grew into the West's largest and richest city. Thus the mercantilist system achieved remarkable success for England, and by the 1770s the country stood on the threshold of the epoch-making changes that would become known as the Industrial Revolution (see Chapter 20).

Although they lost many possessions to the English in the Seven Years' War, the French still profited enormously from colonial trade. The colonies of Saint-Domingue (modern-day Haiti), Martinique, and Guadeloupe remained in French hands and provided immense fortunes in plantation agriculture and slave trading during the second half of the eighteenth century. By 1789 the population of Saint-Domingue included five hundred thousand slaves whose labor had allowed the colony to become the world's leading producer of coffee and sugar and the most profitable plantation colony in the New World.[12] The wealth generated from colonial trade fostered the confidence of the merchant classes in Paris, Bordeaux, and other large cities, and merchants soon joined other elite groups clamoring for political reforms.

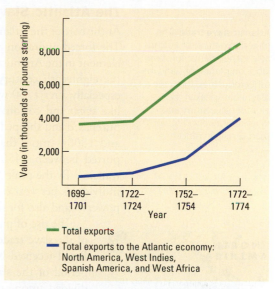

FIGURE 17.3 Exports of English Manufactured Goods, 1700–1774 While trade between England and Europe stagnated after 1700, English exports to Africa and the Americas boomed and greatly stimulated English economic development. (Source: Data from R. Davis, "English Foreign Trade, 1700–1774," *Economic History Review*, 2d ser., 15 [1962]: 302–303.)

The third major player in the Atlantic economy, Spain, also saw its colonial fortunes improve during the eighteenth century. Not only did it gain Louisiana from France in 1763, but its influence expanded westward all the way to northern California through the efforts of Spanish missionaries and ranchers. Its mercantilist goals were boosted by a recovery in silver production, which had dropped significantly in the seventeenth century.

Silver mining also stimulated food production for the mining camps, and wealthy Spanish landowners developed a system of **debt peonage** to keep indigenous workers on their estates. Under this system, which was similar to serfdom, a planter or rancher would keep workers in perpetual debt bondage by advancing them food, shelter, and a little money.

Although the "triangle trade" model highlights some of the most important flows of commerce across the Atlantic, it significantly oversimplifies the picture. For example, a brisk intercolonial trade also existed, with the Caribbean slave colonies importing food in the form of fish, flour, and livestock from the northern colonies and rice from the south, in exchange for sugar and slaves (see Map 17.2). Many colonial traders violated imperial monopolies to trade with the most profitable partners, regardless of nationality. Moreover, the Atlantic economy was inextricably linked to trade with the Indian and Pacific Oceans (see pages 570–571).

debt peonage A form of serfdom that allowed a planter or rancher to keep his workers or slaves in perpetual debt bondage by periodically advancing food, shelter, and a little money.

The Atlantic Slave Trade

Atlantic slave trade The forced migration of Africans across the Atlantic for slave labor on plantations and in other industries; the trade reached its peak in the eighteenth century and ultimately involved more than 12 million Africans.

At the core of the Atlantic world were the misery and profit of the **Atlantic slave trade**. The forced migration of millions of Africans—cruel, unjust, and tragic—was a key element in the Atlantic system and western European economic expansion throughout the eighteenth century. The brutal practice intensified dramatically after 1700 and especially after 1750 with the growth of trade and demand for slave-produced goods like sugar and cotton. According to the most authoritative source, European traders purchased and shipped 6.5 million enslaved Africans across the Atlantic between 1701 and 1800—more than half of the estimated total of 12.5 million Africans transported between 1450 and 1900, of whom 15 percent died in procurement and transit.[13] By the peak decade of the 1780s, shipments averaged about eighty thousand individuals per year in an attempt to satisfy the constantly rising demand for labor power—and also for slave owners' profits—in the Americas.

The rise of plantation agriculture was responsible for the tremendous growth of the slave trade. Among all European colonies, the plantations of Portuguese Brazil received by far the largest number of enslaved Africans over the entire period of the slave trade—45 percent of the total. Another 45 percent were divided among the many Caribbean colonies. The colonies of mainland North America took only 3 percent of slaves arriving from Africa, a little under four hundred thousand, relying mostly on natural growth of the enslaved population.

Eighteenth-century intensification of the slave trade resulted in fundamental changes in its organization. After 1700, as Britain became the undisputed leader in shipping slaves across the Atlantic, European governments and ship captains cut back on fighting among themselves and concentrated on commerce. They generally adopted the shore method of trading, which was less expensive than maintaining fortified trading posts. Under this system, European ships sent boats ashore to trade with African dealers or invited dealers to bring traders and slaves out to their ships. This method allowed ships to move easily along the coast from market to market and to depart more quickly for the Americas.

Plantation Zones, ca. 1700

Some African merchants and rulers who controlled exports profited from the greater demand for slaves. With their newfound wealth, some Africans gained access to European and colonial goods, including firearms. But generally such economic returns did not spread very far, and the negative consequences of the expanding slave trade predominated. Wars among African states to obtain salable captives increased, and leaders used slave profits to purchase more arms than textiles and consumer goods. While the populations of Europe and Asia grew substantially in the eighteenth century, the population of Africa stagnated or possibly declined. As one contemporary critic observed:

> I do not know if coffee and sugar are essential to the happiness of Europe, but I know that these two products have accounted for the unhappiness of two great regions of the world: America has been depopulated so as to have land on which to plant them; Africa has been depopulated so as to have the people to cultivate them.[14]

Most Europeans did not personally witness the horrors of the slave trade between Africa and the Americas, and until the early part of the eighteenth century they considered the African slave trade a legitimate business. But as details of the plight of

The Atlantic Slave Trade   This engraving from 1814 shows traders leading a group of slaves to the West African coast, where they will board ships to cross the Atlantic. Many slaves died en route or arrived greatly weakened and ill. (Bibliothèque de l'Arsenal, Paris/Archives Charmet/Bridgeman Images)

enslaved people became known, a campaign to abolish slavery developed in Britain. (See "Evaluating the Evidence 17.3: Olaudah Equiano's Economic Arguments for Ending Slavery," page 566.) In the late 1780s the abolition campaign grew into a mass movement of public opinion, the first in British history. British women were prominent in this movement, denouncing the immorality of human bondage and stressing the cruel and sadistic treatment of enslaved women and families. These attacks put the defenders of slavery on the defensive. In 1807 Parliament abolished the British slave trade, although slavery continued in British colonies and the Americas for decades.

Identities and Communities of the Atlantic World

As contacts between the Atlantic coasts of the Americas, Africa, and Europe became more frequent, and as European settlements grew into well-established colonies, new identities and communities emerged. The term *Creole* referred to people of Spanish ancestry born in the Americas. Wealthy Creoles and their counterparts throughout the Atlantic colonies prided themselves on following European ways of life. In addition to their lavish plantation estates, they maintained townhouses in colonial cities built on the European model, with theaters, central squares, churches, and coffeehouses. They purchased luxury goods made in Europe, and their children were often sent to be educated in the home country.

Over time, however, the colonial elite came to feel that their circumstances gave them different interests and characteristics from those of their home population. As one observer explained, "A turn of mind peculiar to the planter, occasioned by a physical difference of constitution, climate, customs, and education, tends . . . to repress the remains of his former attachment to his native soil."[15] Colonial elites became "Americanized" by adopting native foods, like chocolate and potatoes, and sought relief from tropical disease in native remedies. Creole traders and planters, along with their counterparts in English colonies, increasingly resented the regulations and taxes imposed by colonial bureaucrats. Such resentment would eventually lead to revolution against colonial powers (see Chapter 19).

Not all Europeans in the colonies were wealthy; indeed, many arrived as indentured servants and had to labor for several years before acquiring freedom. Numerous poor or middling whites worked as clerks, shopkeepers, craftsmen, and, in North America, farmers and laborers. With the exception of British North America, white Europeans made up a minority of the population; they were outnumbered in Spanish

Olaudah Equiano's Economic Arguments for Ending Slavery

According to his autobiography, first published in 1789, Olaudah Equiano was born in Benin (modern Nigeria) of Ibo ethnicity and was abducted and transported across the Atlantic as a child. Equiano served a British Royal Navy officer, who educated the boy, but then sold him to a Quaker merchant. Equiano eventually bought his freedom from his master and returned to England, where he worked as a hairdresser and merchant seaman. Having won fame by publishing his life story, Equiano campaigned ardently to end slavery, as documented in the excerpt below.

Tortures, murder, and every other imaginable barbarity and iniquity, are practised upon the poor slaves with impunity. I hope the great slave trade will be abolished. I pray it may be an event at hand. The great body of manufacturers, uniting in the cause, will considerably facilitate and expedite it; and, as I have already stated, it is most substantially their interest and advantage, and as such the nation's at large (except those persons concerned in the manufacturing [of] neck-yokes, collars, chains, hand-cuffs, leg-bolts, drags, thumbscrews, iron muzzles, and coffins; cats, scourges, and other instruments of torture used in the slave trade). In a short time one sentiment alone will prevail, from motives of interest as well as justice and humanity. Europe contains one hundred and twenty million of inhabitants. Query — How many millions doth Africa contain? Supposing the Africans, collectively and individually, to expend 5£ a head in raiment and furniture yearly when civilized, &c. an immensity beyond the reach of imagination!

This I conceive to be a theory founded upon facts, and therefore an infallible one. If the blacks were permitted to remain in their own country, they would double themselves every fifteen years. In proportion to such increase will be the demand for manufactures. Cotton and indigo grow spontaneously in most parts of Africa; a consideration this of no small consequence to the manufacturing towns of Great Britain. It opens a most immense, glorious, and happy prospect — the clothing, &c. of a continent ten thousand miles in circumference, and immensely rich in productions of every denomination in return for manufactures.

EVALUATE THE EVIDENCE

1. Why does Equiano believe England will profit more by trading with free Africans than by enslaving them? Who do you think the audience for this document was, and how might the audience have affected the message?
2. What broader economic and cultural developments in eighteenth-century England does Equiano's plea reflect?

Source: Olaudah Equiano, *The Interesting Narrative of the Life of Olaudah Equiano*, ed. Robert J. Allison, 2d ed. (Boston: Bedford/St. Martin's, 2007), p. 213.

America by indigenous peoples and in the Caribbean by the growing numbers of enslaved people of African descent. Since European migrants were disproportionately male, much of the population of the Atlantic world descended from unions — forced or through choice — of European men and indigenous or African women. Colonial attempts to identify and control racial categories greatly influenced developing Enlightenment thought on racial difference (see Chapter 16).

Mixed-race populations sometimes rose to the colonial elite. The Spanish conquistadors often consolidated their power through marriage to the daughters of local rulers, and their descendants were among the most powerful inhabitants of Spanish America. In the Spanish and French Caribbean, as in Brazil, many masters acknowledged and freed their mixed-race children, leading to sizable populations of free people of color. Advantaged by their fathers, some became wealthy land and slave owners in their own right. In the second half of the eighteenth century, the prosperity of some free people of color brought a backlash from the white population of Saint-Domingue in the form of new race laws prohibiting nonwhites from marrying whites and forcing them to adopt distinctive attire.

British colonies followed a distinctive pattern. There, whole families, rather than individual men, migrated, resulting in a rapid increase in the white population. This development was favored by British colonial law, which forbade marriage between English men and women and Africans or Native Americans. In the British colonies of the Caribbean and the southern mainland, masters tended to leave their mixed-race progeny in slavery rather than freeing them, maintaining a stark discrepancy between free whites and enslaved people of color.[16] The identities inspired by the Atlantic world were equally complex. In some ways, the colonial encounter helped create new and more fixed forms of identity. Inhabitants of distinct regions of European nations came to see themselves as "Spanish" or "English" when they crossed the Atlantic; similarly, their colonial governments imposed the identity of "Indian" and "African" on peoples with vastly different linguistic, cultural, and political origins. The result was the creation of new Creole communities that melded cultural and social elements of various groups of origin with the new European cultures.[17]

The status of mixed-race people, known as mestizos in Spanish America and métis in New France, was ambiguous. Spanish administrators applied purity of blood (*limpieza de sangre*) laws—originally used to exclude Jews and Muslims during the reconquista—to indigenous and African peoples. Some mixed-race people sought to enter Creole society and obtain its many official and unofficial privileges by passing as white. Over time, where they existed in any number, mestizos and free people of color established their own communities and social hierarchies based on wealth, family connections, occupation, and skin color.

Converting indigenous people to Christianity was a key ambition for all European powers in the New World. Galvanized by the Protestant Reformation and the perceived need to protect and spread Catholicism, Catholic powers actively sponsored missionary efforts. Jesuits, Franciscans, Dominicans, and other religious orders established missions throughout Spanish, Portuguese, and French colonies (see Chapter 14). In Central and South America, large-scale conversion forged enduring Catholic cultures in Portuguese and Spanish colonies. Conversion efforts in North America were less effective because indigenous settlements were more scattered and native people were less integrated into colonial communities. On the whole, Protestants were less active as missionaries in this period, although some dissenters, like Moravians, Quakers, and Methodists, did seek converts among indigenous and enslaved people. (See "Individuals in Society: Rebecca Protten," page 568.)

The practice of slavery reveals important limitations on efforts to spread Christianity. Slave owners often refused to baptize their slaves, fearing that enslaved people would use their Christian status to claim additional rights. In some areas, particularly among the mostly African-born slaves of the Caribbean, elements of African religious belief and practice endured, often incorporated with Christian traditions.

Restricted from owning land and holding many occupations in Europe, Jews were eager participants in the new Atlantic economy and established a network of mercantile communities along its trade routes. As in the Old World, Jews in European colonies faced discrimination; for example, restrictions existed on the number of slaves they could own in Barbados in the early eighteenth century.[18] Jews were considered to be white Europeans and thus ineligible to be slaves, but they did not enjoy equal status with Christians. The status of Jews adds one more element to the complexity of Atlantic identities.

In the mid-1720s a young English-speaking girl who came to be known as Rebecca traveled by ship from Antigua to the small Danish sugar colony of St. Thomas, today part of the U.S. Virgin Islands. Eighty-five percent of St. Thomas's four thousand inhabitants were of African descent, almost all enslaved. Sugar plantations demanded backbreaking work, and slave owners used extremely brutal methods to maintain control, including amputations and beheadings for runaways.

Surviving documents refer to Rebecca as a "mulatto," indicating a mixed European and African ancestry. A wealthy Dutch-speaking planter named van Beverhout purchased the girl for his household staff, sparing her a position in the grueling and deadly sugar fields. Rebecca won the family's favor, and they taught her to read, write, and speak Dutch. They also shared with her their Protestant faith and took the unusual step of freeing her.

As a free woman, she continued to work as a servant for the van Beverhouts and to study the Bible and spread its message of spiritual freedom. In 1736 she met some missionaries for the Moravian Church, a German-Protestant sect that emphasized emotion and communal worship and devoted its mission work to the enslaved peoples of the Caribbean. The missionaries were struck by Rebecca's piety and her potential to assist their work. As one wrote: "She researches diligently in the Scriptures, loves the Savior, and does much good for other Negro women because she does not simply walk alone with her good ways but instructs them in the Scriptures as well." A letter Rebecca sent to Moravian women in Germany declared: "Oh how good is the Lord. My heart melts when I think of it. His name is wonderful. Oh! Help me to praise him, who has pulled me out of the darkness. I will take up his cross with all my heart and follow the example of his poor life."*

Rebecca soon took charge of the Moravians' female missionary work. Every Sunday and every evening after work, she would walk for miles to lead meetings with enslaved and free black women. The meetings consisted of reading and writing lessons, prayers, hymns, a sermon, and individual discussions in which she encouraged her new sisters in their spiritual growth.

In 1738 Rebecca married a German Moravian missionary, Matthaus Freundlich, a rare but not illegal case of mixed marriage. The same year, her husband bought a plantation, with slaves, to serve as the headquarters of their mission work. The Moravians—and presumably Rebecca herself—wished to spread Christian faith

*Quotations from Jon F. Sensbach, *Rebecca's Revival: Creating Black Christianity in the Atlantic World* (Cambridge, Mass.: Harvard University Press, 2006), pp. 61, 63.

The Atlantic Enlightenment

Enlightenment ideas thrived in the colonies, although with as much diversity and disagreement as in Europe (see Chapter 16). The colonies of British North America were deeply influenced by the Scottish Enlightenment, with its emphasis on pragmatic approaches to the problems of life. Following the Scottish model, leaders in the colonies adopted a moderate, "commonsense" version of the Enlightenment that emphasized self-improvement and ethical conduct. In most cases, this version of the Enlightenment was perfectly compatible with religion and was chiefly spread through the growing colleges and universities of the colonies, which remained church-based institutions.

Some thinkers went even further in their admiration for Enlightenment ideas. Benjamin Franklin's writings and political career provide an outstanding example of the combination of the pragmatism and economic interests of the Scottish Enlightenment with the constitutional theories of John Locke, Jean-Jacques Rousseau, and the baron de Montesquieu. Franklin was privately a lifelong deist, meaning that he believed in God but not in organized religion. Nonetheless, he continued to attend among slaves and improve their treatment, but did not oppose the institution of slavery itself.

Authorities nonetheless feared that baptized and literate slaves would agitate for freedom, and they imprisoned Rebecca and Matthaus and tried to shut down the mission. Only the unexpected arrival on St. Thomas of German aristocrat and Moravian leader Count Zinzendorf saved the couple. Exhausted by their ordeal, they left for Germany in 1741 accompanied by their small daughter, but both father and daughter died soon after their arrival.

In Marienborn, a German center of the Moravian faith, Rebecca encountered other black Moravians, who lived in equality alongside their European brethren. In 1746 she married another missionary, Christian Jacob Protten, son of a Danish sailor and, on his mother's side, grandson of a West African king. She and another female missionary from St. Thomas were ordained as deaconesses, probably making them the first women of color to be ordained in the Western Christian Church.

In 1763 Rebecca and her husband set out for her husband's birthplace, the Danish slave fort at Christiansborg (in what is now Accra, Ghana) to establish a school for mixed-race children. Her husband died in 1769, leaving Rebecca a widow once more. After declining the offer of passage back to the West Indies in 1776, she died in obscurity near Christiansborg in 1780.

A portrait of Rebecca Protten with her second husband and their daughter, Anna-Maria. (Courtesy of Jon F. Sensbach. Used by permission of the Moravian Archives [Unity Archives, Herrnhut, Germany], GS-393)

QUESTIONS FOR ANALYSIS

1. Why did Moravian missionaries assign such an important leadership role to Rebecca? What particular attributes did she offer?
2. Why did Moravians, including Rebecca, accept the institution of slavery instead of fighting to end it?
3. What does Rebecca's story teach us about the Atlantic world of the mid-eighteenth century?

church and respect religious proprieties, a cautious pattern followed by fellow deist Thomas Jefferson and other leading thinkers of the American Enlightenment.

Northern Enlightenment thinkers often depicted Spain and its American colonies as the epitome of the superstition and barbarity they contested. The Catholic Church strictly controlled the publication of books on the Iberian Peninsula and in Spanish America. Nonetheless, the Bourbon dynasty that took power in Spain in the early eighteenth century followed its own course of enlightened absolutism, just like its counterparts in the rest of Europe (see Chapter 16). Under King Carlos III (r. 1759–1788) and his son Carlos IV (r. 1788–1808), Spanish administrators attempted to strengthen colonial rule by posting a standing army in the colonies and increasing royal monopolies and taxes to pay for it. They also ordered officials to gather more accurate information about the colonies as a basis for improving the government. Enlightened administrators debated the status of indigenous peoples and whether it would be better for these peoples (and for the prosperity of Spanish America) if they maintained their distinct legal status or were integrated into Spanish society.

The British in India, ca. 1785 This Indian miniature shows the wife (center) of a British officer attended by many Indian servants. A British merchant (left) awaits her attention. The picture reflects the luxurious lifestyle of British elites in India, many of whom returned home with colossal fortunes. (The British Library, London, UK/ Werner Forman Archive/Art Resource, NY)

Educated Creoles were well aware of the new currents of thought, and the universities, newspapers, and salons of Spanish America produced their own reform ideas. The establishment of a mining school in Mexico City in 1792, the first in the Spanish colonies, illuminates the practical achievements of reformers. As in other European colonies, one effect of Enlightenment thought was to encourage Creoles to criticize the policies of the mother country and aspire toward greater autonomy.

Trade and Empire in Asia and the Pacific

As the Atlantic economy took shape, Europeans continued to vie for dominance in the Asian trade. Between 1500 and 1600 the Portuguese had become major players in the Indian Ocean trading world, eliminating Venice as Europe's chief supplier of spices and other Asian luxury goods. The Portuguese dominated but did not fundamentally alter the age-old pattern of Indian Ocean trade, which involved merchants from many areas as more or less autonomous players. This situation changed radically with the intervention of the Dutch and then the English (see Chapter 14).

Formed in 1602, the Dutch East India Company had taken control of the Portuguese spice trade in the Indian Ocean, with the port of Batavia (Jakarta) in Java as its center of operations. Within a few decades it had expelled the Portuguese from Ceylon and other East Indian islands. Unlike the Portuguese, the Dutch transformed the Indian Ocean trading world. Whereas East Indian states and peoples maintained independence under the Portuguese, who treated them as autonomous business partners, the Dutch established outright control and reduced them to dependents.

After these successes, the Dutch hold in Asia faltered in the eighteenth century due to the company's failure to diversify to meet changing consumption patterns. Spices continued to compose much of its shipping, despite their declining importance in the European diet, probably due to changing fashions in food and luxury consumption. Fierce competition from its main rival, the English East India Company (established 1600), also severely undercut Dutch trade.

Britain initially struggled for a foothold in Asia. With the Dutch monopolizing the Indian Ocean, the British turned to India, the source of lucrative trade in silks, textiles, and pepper. Throughout the seventeenth century the English East India Company relied on trade concessions from the powerful Mughal emperor, who granted only piecemeal access to the subcontinent. Finally, in 1716 the Mughals conceded empire-wide trading privileges. As Mughal power waned, British East India Company agents increasingly intervened in local affairs and made alliances or waged war against Indian princes.

Britain's great rival for influence in India was France. During the War of the Austrian Succession, British and French forces in India supported opposing rulers in local power struggles. In 1757 East India Company forces under Robert Clive conquered the rich northeastern province of Bengal at the Battle of Plassey. French-English rivalry was finally resolved by the Treaty of Paris, which granted all of France's possessions in India to the British with the exception of Pondicherry, an Indian Ocean port city. With the elimination of their rival, British ascendancy in India accelerated. In 1765 the Mughal shah granted the East India Company *diwani*, the right to civil administration and tax collection, in Bengal and neighboring provinces. By the early nineteenth century the company had overcome vigorous Indian resistance to gain economic and political dominance of much of the subcontinent; direct administration by the British government replaced East India Company rule after a large-scale rebellion in 1857.

India, 1805

The late eighteenth century also witnessed the beginning of British settlement of the continent of Australia. The continent was first sighted by Europeans in the early seventeenth century, and thereafter parts of the coast were charted by European ships. Captain James Cook claimed the east coast of Australia for England in 1770, naming it New South Wales. The first colony was established there in the late 1780s, relying on the labor of convicted prisoners forcibly transported from Britain. Settlement of the western portion of the continent followed in the 1790s. The first colonies struggled for survival and, after an initial period of friendly relations, soon aroused the hostility and resistance of aboriginal peoples. Cook himself was killed by islanders in Hawaii in 1779, having charted much of the Pacific Ocean for the first time.

The rising economic and political power of Europeans in this period drew on the connections they established between the Asian and Atlantic trade worlds. An outstanding example is the trade in cowrie shells. These seashells, originating in the Maldive Islands in the Indian Ocean, were used as a form of currency in West Africa. European traders obtained them in Asia, packing them alongside porcelains, spices, and silks for the journey home. The cowries were then brought from European ports to the West African coast to be traded for slaves. Indian textiles were also prized in Africa and played a similar role in exchange. Thus the trade of the Atlantic was inseparable from Asian commerce, and Europeans were increasingly found dominating commerce in both worlds.

LOOKING BACK LOOKING AHEAD

By the turn of the eighteenth century, western Europe had begun to shake off the effects of a century of famine, disease, warfare, economic depression, and demographic stagnation. The eighteenth century witnessed a breakthrough in agricultural production that, along with improved infrastructure and the retreat of epidemic disease, contributed to a substantial increase in population. One crucial catalyst for agricultural innovation was the Scientific Revolution, which provided new tools of empirical observation and experimentation. The Enlightenment as well, with its emphasis on progress and public welfare, convinced government officials, scientists, and informed landowners to seek better solutions to old problems. By the end of the century, industry and trade had also attracted enlightened commentators who advocated free markets and less government control. Modern ideas of political economy thus constitute one more legacy of the Enlightenment, but — like the Enlightenment itself — they drew criticism from nineteenth- and twentieth-century thinkers.

As the era of European exploration and conquest gave way to colonial empire building, the eighteenth century witnessed increased consolidation of global markets and bitter competition among Europeans for the spoils of empire. From its slow inception in the mid-fifteenth century, the African slave trade reached brutal heights in the second half of the eighteenth century. The eighteenth-century Atlantic world thus tied the shores of Europe, the Americas, and Africa in a web of commercial and human exchange that also had strong ties with the Pacific and the Indian Oceans.

The new dynamics of the eighteenth century prepared the way for world-shaking changes. Population growth and rural industry began to undermine long-standing traditions of daily life in western Europe. The transformed families of the industrious revolution developed not only new habits of work, but also a new sense of confidence in their abilities. By the 1770s England was approaching an economic transformation fully as significant as the great political upheaval destined to develop shortly in neighboring France. In the same period, the first wave of resistance to European domination rose up in the colonies. The great revolutions of the late eighteenth century would change the world forever.

Make Connections

Think about the larger developments and continuities within and across chapters.

1. How did agriculture, industry, and population affect each other in the eighteenth century? How and why did developments in one area affect the other areas?

2. Compare the economic and social situation of western Europe in the mid-eighteenth century with that of the seventeenth century (Chapter 15). What were the achievements of the eighteenth century, and what factors allowed for such progress to be made?

3. The eighteenth century was the period of the European Enlightenment, which celebrated tolerance and human liberty (Chapter 16). Paradoxically, it was also the era of a tremendous increase in slavery, which brought suffering and death to millions. How can you explain this paradox?

17 REVIEW & EXPLORE

Review the Main Ideas

Answer the focus questions from each section of the chapter.

◆ What important developments led to increased agricultural production, and how did these changes affect peasants? (p. 544)

◆ Why did the European population rise dramatically in the eighteenth century? (p. 549)

◆ How and why did rural industry intensify in the eighteenth century? (p. 552)

◆ What were guilds, and why did they become controversial in the eighteenth century? (p. 556)

◆ How did colonial markets boost Europe's economic and social development, and what conflicts and adversity did world trade entail? (p. 559)

Identify Key Terms

Identify and explain the significance of each item below.

enclosure (p. 546)
proletarianization (p. 549)
cottage industry (p. 552)
putting-out system (p. 552)
industrious revolution (p. 555)
guild system (p. 556)
economic liberalism (p. 558)
Navigation Acts (p. 560)
Treaty of Paris (p. 562)
debt peonage (p. 563)
Atlantic slave trade (p. 564)

NOTES

1. B. H. Slicher van Bath, *The Agrarian History of Western Europe, A.D. 500–1850* (New York: St. Martin's Press, 1963), p. 240.

2. Quoted in Paul Mantoux, *The Industrial Revolution in the Eighteenth Century: An Outline of the Beginnings of the Modern Factory System* (1961; Abingdon, U.K.: Routledge, 2005), p. 175.

3. Thomas Salmon, *Modern History: Or the Present State of All Nations* (London, 1730), p. 406.

4. Quoted in I. Pinchbeck, *Women Workers and the Industrial Revolution, 1750–1850* (1930; Abingdon, U.K.: Frank Cass, 1977), p. 113.

5. Richard J. Soderlund, "'Intended as a Terror to the Idle and Profligate': Embezzlement and the Origins of Policing in the Yorkshire Worsted Industry, c. 1750–1777," *Journal of Social History* 31 (Spring 1998): 658.

6. Quoted in Maxine Berg, *The Age of Manufactures, 1700–1820: Industry, Innovation, and Work in Britain* (London: Routledge, 1994), p. 124.

7. Jan de Vries, *The Industrious Revolution: Consumer Behavior and the Household Economy, 1650 to the Present* (Cambridge: Cambridge University Press, 2008).

8. Jan de Vries, "The Industrial Revolution and the Industrious Revolution," *The Journal of Economic History* 54, no. 2 (June 1994): 249–270; discusses the industrious revolution of the second half of the twentieth century.

9. R. Heilbroner, *The Essential Adam Smith* (New York: W. W. Norton, 1986), p. 196.

10. S. Pollard and C. Holmes, eds., *Documents of European Economic History*, vol. 1, *The Process of Industrialization, 1750–1870* (New York: St. Martin's Press, 1968), p. 53.

11. Ibid., p. 281.

12. Laurent Dubois and John D. Garrigus, *Slave Revolution in the Caribbean, 1789–1904* (New York: Palgrave, 2006), p. 8.

13. Figures obtained from Voyages: The Trans-Atlantic Slave Trade Database, http://www.slavevoyages.org/assessment/estimates (accessed January 17, 2016).

14. Quoted in Thomas Benjamin, *The Atlantic World: Europeans, Africans, Indians and Their Shared History, 1400–1900* (Cambridge: Cambridge University Press, 2009), p. 211.

15. Pierre Marie François Paget, *Travels Round the World in the Years 1767, 1768, 1769, 1770, 1771*, vol. 1 (London, 1793), p. 262.

16. Orlando Patterson, *Slavery and Social Death* (Cambridge, Mass.: Harvard University Press, 1982), p. 255.

17. Tamar Herzog, "Identities and Processes of Identification in the Atlantic World," in *The Oxford Handbook of the Atlantic World, 1450–1850*, ed. Nicholas Canny and Philip Morgan (Oxford: Oxford University Press, 2011), pp. 480–491.

18. Erik R. Seeman, "Jews in the Early Modern Atlantic: Crossing Boundaries, Keeping Faith," in *The Atlantic in Global History, 1500–2000*, ed. Jorge Cañizares-Esguerra and Erik R. Seeman (Upper Saddle River, N.J.: Pearson Prentice Hall, 2007), p. 43.

CHAPTER PREVIEW

Marriage and the Family
What changes occurred in marriage and the family in the course of the eighteenth century?

Children and Education
What was life like for children, and how did attitudes toward childhood evolve?

Popular Culture and Consumerism
How did increasing literacy and new patterns of consumption affect people's lives?

Religious Authority and Beliefs
What were the patterns of popular religion, and how did they interact with the worldview of the educated public and their Enlightenment ideals?

Medical Practice
How did the practice of medicine evolve in the eighteenth century?

Market Day
Open-air markets provided city dwellers with fresh produce, meat, and dairy products. They were also a lively site for meeting friends, catching up on the latest news, and enjoying the passing spectacle of urban life. In European cities, this tradition has continued to the present day.
(*A Market Day*, 1765, Central European School [oil on canvas]/© Sotheby's/akg-images)

Life in the Era of Expansion

1650–1800

The discussion of agriculture and industry in the last chapter showed the common people at work, straining to make ends meet within the larger context of population growth, gradual economic expansion, and ferocious competition at home and overseas. This chapter shows us how that world of work was embedded in a rich complex of family organization, community practices, everyday experiences, and collective attitudes. As with the economy, traditional habits and practices of daily life changed considerably over the eighteenth century. Change was particularly dramatic in the growing cities of northwestern Europe, where traditional social controls were undermined by the anonymity and increased social interaction of the urban setting.

Historians have studied many aspects of popular life, including marriage patterns and family size, childhood and education, nutrition, health care, and religious worship. Uncovering the life of the common people is a formidable challenge because they left few written records and regional variations abounded. Yet imaginative research has resulted in major findings and much greater knowledge. It is now possible to follow the common people into their homes, workshops, churches, and taverns and to ask, "What were the everyday experiences and attitudes of ordinary people, and how did they change over the eighteenth century?" ■

Marriage and the Family

FOCUS QUESTION

What changes occurred in marriage and the family in the course of the eighteenth century?

The basic unit of social organization is the family. Within the structure of the family, human beings love, mate, and reproduce. The family bears primary responsibility to teach the child, imparting values and customs that condition an individual's behavior for a lifetime. The family is also an institution woven into the web of history. It evolves and changes, assuming different forms in different times and places. The eighteenth century was an important moment of change in family life, as patterns of marriage shifted and individuals adapted and conformed to the new and changing realities of the family unit.

Late Marriage and Nuclear Families

Because census data before the modern period are rare, historians have turned to parish registers of births, deaths, and marriages to uncover details of European family life before the nineteenth century. These registers reveal that the three-generation extended family was a rarity in western and central Europe. When young European couples married, they normally established their own households and lived apart from their parents, much like the nuclear families (a family group consisting of parents and their children with no other relatives) common in the United States today. If a three-generation household came into existence, it was usually because a widowed parent moved into the home of a married child.

Most people did not marry young in the seventeenth and eighteenth centuries. The average person married surprisingly late, many years after reaching adulthood and many more after beginning to work. Studies of western Europe in the seventeenth and eighteenth centuries show that both men and women married for the first time at an average age of twenty-five to twenty-seven. Furthermore, 10 to 20 percent of men and women in western Europe never married at all. Matters were different in eastern Europe, where the multigeneration household was the norm, marriage occurred around age twenty, and permanent celibacy was much less common.

Why did young people in western Europe delay marriage? The main reason was that couples normally did not marry until they could start an independent household and support themselves and their future children. Peasants often needed to wait until their father's death to inherit land and marry. In the towns, men and women worked to accumulate enough savings to start a small business and establish their own home. As one father stated in an advice book written for his son: "Money is the sinew of love, as well as war; you can do nothing happily in wedlock without it; the other [virtue and beauty] are court-cards, but they are not of the trump-suit and are foiled by every sneaking misadventure."[1]

Laws and tradition also discouraged early marriage. In some areas couples needed permission from the local lord or landowner in order to marry. Poor couples had particular difficulty securing the approval of local officials, who believed that freedom to marry for the lower classes would result in more landless paupers, more abandoned children, and more money for welfare. Village elders often agreed.

The custom of late marriage combined with the nuclear-family household distinguished western European society from other areas of the world. Historians have argued that this late-marriage pattern was responsible for at least part of the economic advantage western Europeans acquired relative to other world regions. Late marriage joined a mature man and a mature woman—two adults who had already accumulated social and economic capital and could transmit self-reliance and skills to the next generation. The relative closeness in age between husband and wife favored a greater degree of gender equality than existed in areas where older men married much younger women.

Work Away from Home

Many young people worked within their families until they could start their own households. Boys plowed and wove; girls spun and tended the cows. Many others left home to work elsewhere. Around age fifteen, an apprentice from a rural village would typically move to a city or town to learn a trade, earning little and working hard. If he was lucky and had connections, he might eventually be admitted to a guild and establish his economic independence. Many poor families could not afford apprenticeships for their sons. Without craft skills, these youths drifted from one tough job to another: hired hand for a small farmer, wage laborer on a new road, carrier of water or domestic servant in a nearby town.

Many adolescent girls also left their families to work. The range of opportunities open to them was more limited, however. Apprenticeship was sometimes available with mistresses in traditionally female occupations like seamstress, linen draper, or midwife. With the growth in production of finished goods for the emerging consumer economy during the eighteenth century (see Chapter 17), demand rose for skilled female labor and, with it, a wider range of jobs became available for women. Nevertheless, women still continued to earn much lower wages for their work than men.

Service in another family's household was by far the most common job for girls, and even middle-class families often sent their daughters into service. The legions of young servant girls worked hard but had little independence. Constantly under the eye of her mistress, the servant girl had many tasks—cleaning, shopping, cooking, and child care. Often the work was endless, for there were few laws to limit exploitation. Court records are full of servant girls' complaints of physical mistreatment by their mistresses. There were many like the fifteen-year-old English girl in the early eighteenth century who told the judge that her mistress had not only called her "very opprobrious names, as Bitch, Whore and the like," but also "beat her without provocation and beyond measure."[2]

Male apprentices told similar tales of abuse and they shared the legal status of "servants" with housemaids, but they were far less vulnerable to the sexual exploitation that threatened young girls. In theory, domestic service offered a girl protection and security in a new family. But in practice, she was often the easy prey of a lecherous master or his sons or friends. If the girl became pregnant, she could be fired and thrown out in disgrace. Many families could not or would not accept such a girl back into the home. Forced to make their own way, these girls had no choice but to turn to a harsh life of prostitution (see page 580) and petty thievery. "What are we?"

Chronology

1684	Jean-Baptiste de la Salle founds Brothers of the Christian Schools
1717	Elementary school attendance mandatory in Prussia
1750–1790	John Wesley preaches revival in England
1750–1850	Illegitimacy explosion
1757	Madame du Coudray publishes *Manual on the Art of Childbirth*
1762	Jean-Jacques Rousseau advocates more attentive child care in *Emile*
1763	Louis XV orders Jesuits out of France
1774	Elementary school attendance mandatory in Austria
1776	Thomas Paine publishes *Common Sense*
1796	Edward Jenner performs first smallpox vaccination

exclaimed a bitter Parisian prostitute. "Most of us are unfortunate women, without origins, without education, servants and maids for the most part."[3] Adult women who remained in service, at least in large towns and cities, could gain more autonomy and distressed their employers by changing jobs frequently.

Premarital Sex and Community Controls

Ten years between puberty and marriage was a long time for sexually mature young people to wait. Many unmarried couples satisfied their sexual desires with fondling and petting. Others went further and engaged in premarital intercourse. Those who did so risked pregnancy and the stigma of illegitimate birth. Birth control was not unknown in Europe before the nineteenth century, but it was primitive and unreliable. Condoms, made from sheep intestines, became available in the mid-seventeenth century, replacing uncomfortable earlier versions made from cloth. They were expensive and mainly used by aristocratic libertines and prostitutes. The most common method of contraception was coitus interruptus—withdrawal by the male before ejaculation. The French, who were early leaders in contraception, were using this method extensively by the end of the eighteenth century.

Despite the lack of reliable contraception, premarital sex did not result in a large proportion of illegitimate births in most parts of Europe until 1750. English parish registers seldom listed more than one illegitimate child out of every twenty children baptized. Some French parishes in the seventeenth century had extraordinarily low rates of illegitimacy, with less than 1 percent of babies born out of wedlock. Illegitimate babies were apparently a rarity, at least as far as the official records are concerned.

Where collective control over sexual behavior among youths failed, community pressure to marry often prevailed. A comparison of marriage and birth dates of seven representative parishes in seventeenth-century England shows that around 20 percent of children must have been conceived before the couple was married, but only 2 percent were born out of wedlock.[4] Figures for the French village of Auffay in Normandy in the eighteenth century were remarkably similar. No doubt many of these French and English couples were already engaged, or at least in a committed relationship, before they entered into intimate relations, and pregnancy simply set the marriage date once and for all.

The combination of low rates of illegitimate birth with large numbers of pregnant brides reflects the powerful **community controls** of the traditional village, particularly the open-field village, with its pattern of cooperation and common action. An unwed mother with an illegitimate child was inevitably viewed as a grave threat to the economic, social, and moral stability of the community. Irate parents, anxious village elders, indignant priests, and stern landlords all combined to pressure young people who wavered about marriage in the face of unexpected pregnancies. In the countryside these controls meant that premarital sex was not entered into lightly and that it was generally limited to those contemplating marriage.

The concerns of the village and the family weighed heavily on couples' lives after marriage as well. Whereas uninvolved individuals today try to stay out of the domestic disputes of their neighbors, the people in peasant communities gave such affairs loud and unfavorable publicity either at the time or during the carnival season (see page 589). Relying on degrading public rituals, known as **charivari**, the young

community controls
A pattern of cooperation and common action in a traditional village that sought to uphold the economic, social, and moral stability of the closely knit community.

charivari Degrading public rituals used by village communities to police personal behavior and maintain moral standards.

men of the village would typically gang up on their victim and force him or her to sit astride a donkey facing backward and holding up the donkey's tail. They would parade the overly brutal spouse-beater or the adulterous couple around the village, loudly proclaiming the offenders' misdeeds. The donkey ride and other colorful humiliations ranging from rotten vegetables splattered on the doorstep to obscene and insulting midnight serenades were common punishments throughout much of Europe. They epitomized the community's effort to police personal behavior and maintain moral standards.

New Patterns of Marriage and Illegitimacy

In the second half of the eighteenth century, long-standing patterns of marriage and illegitimacy shifted dramatically. One important change was an increased ability for young people to make decisions about marriage for themselves, rather than following the interests of their families. This change occurred because social and economic transformations made it harder for families and communities to supervise their behavior. More youths in the countryside worked for their own wages, rather than on a family farm, and their economic autonomy translated into increased freedom of action. Moreover, many youths joined the flood of migrants to the cities, either with their families or in search of work on their own. Urban life provided young people with more social contacts and less social control.

A less positive outcome of loosening social control was an **illegitimacy explosion**, concentrated in England, France, Germany, and Scandinavia. In Frankfurt, Germany, for example, births out of wedlock rose steadily from about 2 percent of all births in the early eighteenth century to a peak of about 25 percent around 1850. In Bordeaux, France, 36 percent of all babies were being born out of wedlock by 1840. Small towns and villages experienced less startling climbs, but between 1750 and 1850 increases from an initial range of 1 to 3 percent to a range of 10 to 20 percent were commonplace. Given the meager economic opportunities open to single mothers, their circumstances were desperate.

illegitimacy explosion The sharp increase in out-of-wedlock births that occurred in Europe between 1750 and 1850, caused by low wages and the breakdown of community controls.

Why did the number of illegitimate births skyrocket? One reason was a rise in sexual activity among young people. The loosened social controls that gave young people more choice in marriage also provided them with more opportunities to yield to sexual desire. As in previous

The Village Wedding   The spirited merry-making of a peasant wedding was a popular theme of European artists in the eighteenth century. Given the harsh conditions of life, a wedding provided a treasured moment of feasting, dancing, and revelry. With the future of the village at stake, the celebration of marriage was a public event. (Private Collection/Bridgeman Images)

generations, many of the young couples who engaged in sexual activity intended to marry. In one medium-size French city in 1787–1788, the great majority of unwed mothers stated that sexual intimacy had followed promises of marriage. Their sisters in rural Normandy frequently reported that they had been "seduced in anticipation of marriage."[5]

The problem for young women who became pregnant was that fewer men followed through on their promises. The second half of the eighteenth century witnessed sharply rising prices for food, homes, and other necessities of life. Many soldiers, day laborers, and male servants were no doubt sincere in their proposals, but their lives were insecure, and they hesitated to take on the burden of a wife and child.

The romantic yet practical dreams and aspirations of young people were thus frustrated by low wages, inequality, and changing economic and social conditions. Old patterns of marriage and family were breaking down. Only in the late nineteenth century would more stable patterns reappear.

Sex on the Margins of Society

Not all sex acts took place between men and women hopeful of marriage. Prostitution offered both single and married men an outlet for sexual desire. After a long period of relative tolerance, prostitutes encountered increasingly harsh and repressive laws in the sixteenth and early seventeenth centuries as officials across Europe closed licensed brothels and declared prostitution illegal.

Despite this repression, prostitution continued to flourish in the eighteenth century. Most prostitutes were working women who turned to the sex trade when confronted with paltry wages and unemployment. Such women did not become social pariahs, but retained ties with the communities of laboring poor to which they belonged. If caught by the police, however, they were liable to imprisonment or banishment. Venereal disease was also a constant threat. Prostitutes were subjected to humiliating police examinations for disease, although medical treatments were at best rudimentary. Farther up the social scale were courtesans whose wealthy protectors provided apartments, servants, fashionable clothing, and cash allowances. After a brilliant but brief career, an aging courtesan faced with the loss of her wealthy client could descend once more to streetwalking.

Relations between individuals of the same sex attracted even more condemnation than did prostitution, since they defied the Bible's limitation of sex to the purposes of procreation. Male same-sex relations, described as "sodomy" or "buggery," were prohibited by law in most European states, under pain of death. Such laws, however, were enforced unevenly, most strictly in Spain and far less so in the Scandinavian countries and Russia.[6]

Protected by their status, nobles and royals sometimes openly indulged their same-sex desires, which were accepted as long as they married and produced legitimate heirs. It was common knowledge that King James I, sponsor of the first translation of the Bible into English, had male lovers, but these relationships were tolerated because they did not prevent him from having seven children with his wife, Anne of Denmark. The duchess of Orléans, sister-in-law of French king Louis XIV, complained in her letters about her husband's male lovers, one of whom was appointed tutor to the couple's son. She also repeated rumors about the homosexual inclinations of King William of England, hero of the Glorious Revolution (see Chapter 15).

In the late seventeenth century homosexual subcultures began to emerge in Paris, Amsterdam, and London, with their own slang, meeting places, and styles of dress. Unlike the relations described above, which involved men who took both wives and male lovers, these groups included men exclusively oriented toward other men. In London, they called themselves "mollies," a term originally applied to prostitutes, and some began to wear women's clothing and adopt effeminate behavior. A new self-identity began to form among homosexual men: a belief that their same-sex desire made them fundamentally different from other men. As a character in one late-eighteenth-century fiction declared, he was in "a category of men different from the other, a class Nature has created in order to diminish or minimize propagation."[7]

Same-sex relations existed among women as well, but they attracted less anxiety and condemnation than those among men. Some women were prosecuted for "unnatural" relations; others attempted to escape the narrow confines imposed on them by dressing as men. Cross-dressing women occasionally snuck into the armed forces, such as Ulrika Elenora Stålhammar, who served as a man in the Swedish army for thirteen years and married a woman. After confessing her transgressions, she was sentenced to a lenient one-month imprisonment.[8] The beginnings of a distinctive lesbian subculture appeared in London and other large cities at the end of the eighteenth century.

Across the early modern period, traditional tolerance for sexual activities outside of heterosexual marriage—be they sex with prostitutes or same-sex relations among male courtiers—faded. This process accelerated in the eighteenth century as Enlightenment critics attacked court immorality and preached virtue and morality for middle-class men, who were expected to prove their worthiness to claim the reins of political power.

Children and Education

On the whole, western European women married late, but then began bearing children rapidly. If a woman married before she was thirty, and if both she and her husband lived to fifty, she would most likely give birth to six or more children. Infant mortality varied across Europe, but was very high by modern standards, and many women died in childbirth due to limited medical knowledge and technology.

For those children who did survive, Enlightenment ideals that emerged in the latter half of the century stressed the importance of parental nurturing. The new worldview also led to an increase in elementary schools throughout Europe. Despite the efforts of enlightened absolutists and religious institutions, however, formal education reached only a minority of ordinary children.

FOCUS QUESTION
What was life like for children, and how did attitudes toward childhood evolve?

Child Care and Nursing

Newborns entered a dangerous world. They were vulnerable to infectious diseases, and many babies died of dehydration brought about by bad bouts of ordinary diarrhea. Of those who survived infancy, many more died in childhood. Even in a rich family, little could be done for an ailing child. Childbirth was also dangerous. Women who bore six children faced a cumulative risk of dying in childbirth of 5 to 10 percent, a thousand times as great as the risk in Europe today.[9] They died from blood loss and shock during delivery and from infections caused by unsanitary conditions. The joy of pregnancy was thus shadowed by fear of loss of the mother or her child.

In the countryside, women of the lower classes generally breast-fed their infants for two years or more. Although not a foolproof means of birth control, breast-feeding decreases the likelihood of pregnancy by delaying the resumption of ovulation. By nursing their babies, women limited their fertility and spaced their children two or three years apart. Nursing also saved lives: breast-fed infants received precious immunity-producing substances and were more likely to survive than those who were fed other food.

Areas where babies were not breast-fed — typically in northern France, Scandinavia, and central and eastern Europe — experienced the highest infant mortality rates. In these areas, many people believed that breast-feeding was bad for a woman's health or appearance. Across Europe, women of the aristocracy and upper middle class seldom nursed their own children because they found breast-feeding undignified and it interfered with their social responsibilities. The alternatives to breast-feeding consisted of feeding babies cow's or goat's milk or paying lactating women to provide their milk.

Wealthy women hired live-in wet nurses to suckle their babies (which usually meant sending the nurse's own infant away to be nursed by someone else). Working women in the cities also relied on wet nurses because they needed to earn a living. Unable to afford live-in wet nurses, they often turned to the cheaper services of women in the countryside. Rural **wet-nursing** was a widespread business in the eighteenth century, conducted within the framework of the putting-out system. The traffic was in babies rather than in yarn or cloth, and two or three years often passed before the wet-nurse worker in the countryside finished her task.

wet-nursing A widespread and flourishing business in the eighteenth century in which women were paid to breast-feed other women's babies.

Wet-nursing was particularly common in northern France. Toward the end of the century, roughly twenty thousand babies were born in Paris each year. Almost half were placed with rural wet nurses through a government-supervised distribution network; 20 to 25 percent were placed in the homes of Parisian nurses personally selected by their parents; and another 20 to 25 percent were abandoned to foundling hospitals, which would send them to wet nurses in the countryside. The remainder (perhaps 10 percent) were nursed at home by their mothers or live-in nurses.[10]

Reliance on wet nurses raised levels of infant mortality because of the dangers of travel, the lack of supervision of conditions in wet nurses' homes, and the need to share milk between a wet nurse's own baby and the one or more babies she was hired to feed. A study of mortality rates in mid-eighteenth-century France shows that 25 percent of babies died before their first birthday, and another 30 percent before age ten.[11] In England, where more mothers nursed, only some 30 percent of children did not reach their tenth birthday.

Within each country and across Europe, tremendous regional variation existed. Mortality rates were higher in overcrowded and dirty cities; in low-lying, marshy regions; and during summer months when rural women were busy in agricultural work and had less time to tend to infants. The corollary of high infant mortality was high fertility. Women who did not breast-feed their babies or whose children died in infancy became pregnant more quickly and bore more children. Thus, on balance, the number of children who survived to adulthood tended to be the same across Europe, with higher births balancing the greater loss of life in areas that relied on wet-nursing.

In the second half of the eighteenth century, critics mounted a harsh attack against wet-nursing. Enlightenment thinkers proclaimed that wet-nursing was robbing European society of reaching its full potential. They were convinced, incorrectly, that the population was declining (in fact it was rising, but they lacked accurate population data) and blamed this decline on women's failure to nurture their children properly. Some also railed against practices of contraception and masturbation, which they believed were robbing their nations of potential children. Despite these complaints, many women continued to rely on wet nurses for convenience or from necessity.

Foundlings and Infanticide

The young woman who could not provide for an unwanted child had few choices, especially if she had no prospect of marriage. Abortions were illegal, dangerous, and apparently rare. In desperation, some women, particularly in the countryside, hid unwanted pregnancies, delivered in secret, and smothered their newborn infants. The punishment for infanticide was death. Yet across Europe, convictions for infanticide dropped in the second half of the eighteenth century, testimony, perhaps, to growing social awareness of the crushing pressures caused by unwanted pregnancies.

Another sign of this awareness was the spread of homes for abandoned children in cities across Europe. Homes for abandoned children first took hold in Italy, Spain, and Portugal in the sixteenth century, spreading to France in 1670 and the rest of Europe thereafter. In eighteenth-century England the government acted on a petition calling for a foundling hospital "to prevent the frequent murders of poor, miserable infants at birth" and "to suppress the inhuman custom of exposing newborn children to perish in the streets."

By the end of the eighteenth century, European foundling hospitals were admitting annually about one hundred thousand abandoned children, nearly all of them infants. One-third of all babies born in Paris in the 1770s were immediately abandoned to foundling homes. There appears to have been no differentiation by sex in the numbers of children sent to foundling hospitals. Many of the children were the offspring of single women, the result of the illegitimacy explosion of the second half of the eighteenth century. But fully one-third of all the foundlings were abandoned by married couples too poor to feed another child.[12]

At their best, foundling homes were a good example of Christian charity and social concern in an age of great poverty and inequality. They provided the rudiments of an education and sought to place the children in apprenticeship or domestic service once they reached an appropriate age. Philosopher Jean-Jacques Rousseau defended his decision to place his five illegitimate children in a foundling home — despite their mother's opposition — on the grounds of "poverty and misfortune." He also claimed that the hospital would shield them from the stigma of illegitimacy and provide a home that was "better, or at least more secure, than what [he] would have been able to provide."[13]

Yet the foundling home was no panacea. Even in the best of these homes, 50 percent of the babies normally died within a year. In the worst, fully 90 percent did not survive, falling victim to infectious disease, malnutrition, and neglect.[14] None of Rousseau's children are known to have survived.

Attitudes Toward Children

What were the typical circumstances of children's lives? Some scholars have claimed that high mortality rates prevented parents from forming emotional attachments to young children. With a reasonable expectation that a child might die, some scholars believe, parents maintained an attitude of indifference, if not downright negligence. Most historians now believe, however, that seventeenth- and eighteenth-century parents did love their children, suffered anxiously when they fell ill, and experienced extreme anguish when they died.

Parents were well aware of the dangers of infancy and childhood. The great eighteenth-century English historian Edward Gibbon (1737–1794) wrote, with some exaggeration, that "the death of a new born child before that of its parents may seem unnatural but it is a strictly probable event, since of any given number the greater part are extinguished before the ninth year, before they possess the faculties of the mind and the body." Gibbon's father named all his boys Edward after himself, hoping that at least one of them would survive to carry his name. His prudence was not misplaced. Edward the future historian and eldest survived. Five brothers and sisters who followed him all died in infancy.

Emotional prudence could lead to emotional distance. The French essayist Michel de Montaigne, who lost five of his six daughters in infancy, wrote, "I cannot abide that passion for caressing new-born children, which have neither mental activities nor recognisable bodily shape by which to make themselves loveable and I have never willingly suffered them to be fed in my presence."[15] In contrast to this harsh picture, however, historians have drawn ample evidence from diaries, letters, and family portraits that parents of all social classes did cherish their children. This was equally true of mothers and fathers and of attitudes toward sons and daughters. The English poet Ben Jonson wrote movingly in "On My First Son" of the death of his six-year-old son Benjamin, which occurred during a London plague outbreak in 1603:

> Farewell, thou child of my right hand, and joy;
> My sin was too much hope of thee, loved boy.
> Seven years thou wert lent to me, and I thee pay,
> Exacted by thy fate, on the just day.

In a society characterized by much violence and brutality, discipline of children was often severe. The axiom "Spare the rod and spoil the child" seems to have been coined in the mid-seventeenth century. Susannah Wesley (1669–1742), mother of John Wesley, the founder of Methodism (see page 598), agreed. According to her, the first task of a parent toward her children was "to conquer the will, and bring them to an obedient temper." She reported that her babies were "taught to fear the rod, and to cry softly; by which means they escaped the abundance of correction they might otherwise have had, and that most odious noise of the crying of children was

The First Step of Childhood This tender snapshot of a baby's first steps toward an adoring mother exemplifies new attitudes toward children and raising them ushered in by the Enlightenment. Authors like Jean-Jacques Rousseau encouraged elite mothers like the one pictured here to take a more personal interest in raising their children, instead of leaving them in the hands of indifferent wet nurses and nannies. Many women responded eagerly to this call, and the period saw a more sentimentalized view of childhood and family life. (By François Gerard [1770–1837]/Fogg Art Museum, Harvard Art Museums, Cambridge, Massachusetts, USA/ Erich Lessing/Art Resource, NY)

rarely heard in the house."[16] They were beaten for lying, stealing, disobeying, and quarreling, and forbidden from playing with other neighbor children. Susannah's methods of disciplining her children were probably extreme even in her own day, but they do reflect a broad consensus that children were born with an innately sinful will that parents must overcome. (See "Evaluating the Evidence 18.1: Parisian Boyhood," page 586.)

The Enlightenment produced an enthusiastic new discourse about childhood and child rearing. Starting around 1760 critics called for greater tenderness toward children and proposed imaginative new teaching methods. In addition to supporting foundling homes and urging women to nurse their babies, these new voices ridiculed the practice of swaddling babies and using whaleboned corsets to mold children's bones. Rejecting the custom of dressing children in miniature versions of adult clothing, critics called for comfortable clothing to allow freedom of movement. Rather than emphasizing original sin, these enlightened voices celebrated the child as an innocent product of nature. Since they viewed nature as inherently positive, Enlightenment educators advocated safeguarding and developing children's innate qualities rather than thwarting and suppressing them. Accordingly, they believed the best hopes for a new society, untrammeled by the prejudices of the past, lay in a radical reform of child-rearing techniques.

One of the century's most influential works on child rearing was Jean-Jacques Rousseau's *Emile, or On Education* (1762), inspired in part, Rousseau claimed, by remorse for the abandonment of his own children. In *Emile*, Rousseau argued that boys' education should include plenty of fresh air and exercise and that boys should be taught practical craft skills in addition to book learning. Reacting to what he perceived as the vanity and frivolity of upper-class Parisian women, Rousseau insisted that girls' education focus on their future domestic responsibilities. For Rousseau, women's "nature" destined them solely for a life of marriage and child rearing. The sentimental ideas of Rousseau and other reformers were enthusiastically adopted by elite women, some of whom began to nurse their own children.

Parisian Boyhood

The life of Jacques-Louis Ménétra, a Parisian glazier, exemplified many of the social patterns of his day. He lost his mother in infancy, was educated at a parish school, married late, and had four children, two of whom died. Ménétra distinguished himself from other workingmen, however, by writing an autobiography describing his tumultuous childhood, his travels around France as a journeyman, and his settled life as a guild master. Ménétra's father was often violent, but he fiercely defended his son against rumored child abductions in Paris (in reality the police had over-stepped orders to arrest children loitering in the streets).

I was born on 13 July 1738 a native of this great city. My father belonged to the class usually called artisans. His profession was that of glazier. Hence it is with him that I begin my family tree and I shall say nothing about my ancestors. My father married and set himself up at the same time and wed a virtuous girl who gave him four children, three daughters and one boy, myself, all of whose little pranks I'm going to write about.

My father became a widower when I was two years old. I had been put out to nurse. My grandmother who always loved me a great deal and even idolized me, knowing that the nurse I was with had her milk gone bad, came to get me and after curing me put me back out to nurse [where] I ended up with a pretty good woman who taught me early on the pro-fession of begging. My [grand]mother and my godfather when they came to see me . . . found me in a church begging charity. They took me home and from then until the age of eleven I lived with my good grandmother. My father wanted me back, afraid that he would have to pay my board. He put me to work in his trade even though several people tried to talk him out of it [but] he wouldn't listen to them. . . .

When I felt a little better, I went back to my usual ways which is to say that my father was always angry with me.

One night when I was lighting the way in a staircase where he was installing a casement and not mounting it the way he wanted with an angry kick [he] knocked out all my teeth. When I got back home my (step)mother took me to a dentist by the name of Ricie who put back the teeth that weren't broken and I went three weeks eating nothing but bouillon and soup.

In those days it was rumored that they were taking young boys and bleeding them and that they were lost forever and that their blood was used to bathe a princess suffering from a disease that could only be cured with human blood. There was plenty of talk about that in Paris. My father came to get me at school as many other fathers did along with seven big coopers armed with crowbars. The rumor was so strong that the windows of the police station were broken and several poor guys were assaulted and one was even burned in the place de Grève because he looked like a police informer. Children weren't allowed to go outside; three poor wretches were hanged in the place de Grève to settle the matter and restore calm in Paris.

EVALUATE THE EVIDENCE

1. What hardships did the young Ménétra face in his childhood? What attitude did he display toward his childhood experiences?
2. What characteristic elements of eighteenth-century family life does Ménétra's childhood reflect? Does his story provide evidence for or against the thesis that parents deeply loved their children?

Source: Jacques-Louis Ménétra, *Journal of My Life*, ed. Daniel Roche, trans. Arthur Goldhammer, pp. 18, 21–22. Copyright © 1986 Columbia University Press. Reprinted with permission of the publisher.

The Spread of Elementary Schools

The availability of education outside the home gradually increased over the early modern period. The wealthy led the way in the sixteenth century with special col-leges, often run by Jesuits in Catholic areas. Schools charged specifically with edu-cating children of the common people began to appear in the second half of the seventeenth century. They taught six- to twelve-year-old children basic literacy, reli-gion, and perhaps some arithmetic for the boys and needlework for the girls. The number of such schools expanded in the eighteenth century, although they were never sufficient to educate the majority of the population.

Religion played an important role in the spread of education. From the middle of the seventeenth century, Presbyterian Scotland was convinced that the path to salvation lay in careful study of the Scriptures, and it established an effective network of parish schools for rich and poor alike. The Church of England and the dissenting congregations—Puritans, Presbyterians, Quakers, and so on—established "charity schools" to instruct poor children. The first proponents of universal education, in Prussia, were inspired by the Protestant idea that every believer should be able to read the Bible and by the new idea of raising a population capable of effectively serving the state. As early as 1717 Prussia made attendance at elementary schools compulsory for boys and girls in areas where schools existed.[17] More Protestant German states, such as Saxony and Württemberg (VUHR-tuhm-burg), followed suit in the eighteenth century.

Catholic states pursued their own programs of popular education. In the 1660s France began setting up charity schools to teach poor children their catechism and prayers as well as reading and writing. These were run by parish priests or by new educational teaching orders. One of the most famous orders was Jean-Baptiste de la Salle's Brothers of the Christian Schools. Founded in 1684, the schools had thirty-five thousand students across France by the 1780s. Enthusiasm for popular education was even greater in the Habsburg empire. Inspired by the expansion of schools in rival Protestant German states, Maria Theresa issued her own compulsory education edict in 1774, imposing five hours of school, five days a week, for all children aged six to twelve.[18] Across Europe some elementary education was becoming a reality, and schools became increasingly significant in the life of the child.

Popular Culture and Consumerism

Because of the new efforts in education, basic literacy expanded among the popular classes, whose reading habits centered primarily on religious material, but who also began to incorporate more practical and entertaining literature. In addition to reading, people of all classes enjoyed a range of leisure activities including storytelling, fairs, festivals, and sports.

One of the most important developments in European society in the eighteenth century was the emergence of a fledgling consumer culture. Much of the expansion took place among the upper and upper-middle classes, but a boom in cheap reproductions of luxury items also opened doors for people of modest means. From food to ribbons and from coal stoves to umbrellas, the material worlds of city dwellers grew richer and more diverse. This "consumer revolution," as it has been called, created new expectations for comfort, hygiene, and self-expression, thus dramatically changing European daily life in the eighteenth century.

FOCUS QUESTION
How did increasing literacy and new patterns of consumption affect people's lives?

Popular Literature

The surge in childhood education in the eighteenth century led to a remarkable growth in literacy between 1600 and 1800. Whereas in 1600 only one male in six was barely literate in France and Scotland, and one in four in England, by 1800 almost nine out of ten Scottish males, two out of three French males (Map 18.1),

Percentage of bridegrooms able to sign their names to marriage register

- 80–100
- 50–79
- 20–49
- 0–19
- Unknown

Bay of Biscay

Paris

Mediterranean Sea

MAP 18.1 Literacy in France, ca. 1789 Literacy rates increased but still varied widely between and within states in eighteenth-century Europe.

and more than half of English males were literate. In all three countries, most of the gains occurred in the eighteenth century. Women were also increasingly literate, although they lagged behind men.

The growth in literacy promoted growth in reading, and historians have carefully examined what the common people read. While the Bible remained the overwhelming favorite, especially in Protestant countries, short pamphlets known as chapbooks were the staple of popular literature. Printed on the cheapest paper, many chapbooks featured Bible stories, prayers, and the lives of saints and exemplary Christians. This pious literature gave believers moral teachings and a faith that helped them endure their daily struggles.

Entertaining, often humorous stories formed a second element of popular literature. Fairy tales, medieval romances, true crime stories, and fantastic adventures were some of the delights that filled the peddler's pack as he approached a village. These tales presented a world of danger and magic, of supernatural powers, fairy godmothers, and evil trolls, that provided a temporary flight from harsh everyday reality. They also contained nuggets of ancient folk wisdom, counseling prudence in a world full of danger and injustice, where wolves dress like grandmothers and eat Little Red Riding Hoods.

Finally, some popular literature was highly practical, dealing with rural crafts, household repairs, useful plants, and similar matters. Much lore was stored in almanacs, where calendars listing secular, religious, and astrological events were mixed with agricultural schedules, arcane facts, and jokes. The almanac was highly appreciated even by many in the comfortable classes. In this way, elites shared some elements of a common culture with the masses.

While it is safe to say that the vast majority of ordinary people—particularly peasants in isolated villages—did not read the great works of the Enlightenment, they were not immune from the new ideas. Urban working people were exposed to Enlightenment thought through the news and gossip that spread across city streets, workshops, markets, and taverns. They also had access to cheap pamphlets that helped translate Enlightenment critiques into ordinary language. Servants, who usually came from rural areas and traveled home periodically, were well situated to transmit ideas from educated employers to the village.

Certainly some ordinary people did assimilate Enlightenment ideals. Thomas Paine, author of some of the most influential texts of the American Revolution, was an English corset-maker's son who left school at age twelve and carried on his father's trade before emigrating to the colonies. His 1776 pamphlet *Common Sense* attacked the weight of custom and the evils of government against the natural society of men. This text, which sold 120,000 copies in its first months of publication, is vivid proof of working people's reception of Enlightenment ideas. Paine's stirring mastery of such ideas was perhaps unique, but his access to them was certainly not.

Leisure and Recreation

Despite the spread of literacy, the culture of the village remained largely oral rather than written. In the cold, dark winter months, peasant families gathered around the fireplace to sing, tell stories, do craftwork, and keep warm. In some parts of Europe, women would gather together in someone's cottage to chat, sew, spin, and laugh. Sometimes a few young men would be invited so that the daughters (and mothers) could size up potential suitors in a supervised atmosphere. A favorite recreation of men was drinking and talking with buddies in public places, and it was a sorry village that had no tavern. In addition to old favorites such as beer and wine, the common people turned with gusto to cheap and potent hard liquor, which fell in price because of improved techniques for distilling grain in the eighteenth century.

Towns and cities offered a wider range of amusements, including pleasure gardens, theaters, and lending libraries. Urban fairs featured prepared foods, acrobats, and conjuring acts. Leisure activities were another form of consumption marked by growing commercialization. For example, commercial, profit-making spectator sports emerged in this period, including horse races, boxing matches, and bullfights. Modern sports heroes, such as brain-bashing heavyweight champions and haughty bullfighting matadors, made their appearance on the historical scene.

Blood sports, such as bullbaiting and cockfighting, also remained popular with the masses. In bullbaiting, the bull, usually staked on a chain in the courtyard of an inn, was attacked by ferocious dogs for the amusement of the innkeeper's clients. Eventually the maimed and tortured animal was slaughtered by a butcher and sold as meat. In cockfighting, two roosters, carefully trained by their owners and armed with razor-sharp steel spurs, slashed and clawed each other in a small ring until the victor won—and the loser died. An added attraction of cockfighting was that the screaming spectators could bet on the lightning-fast combat.

Popular recreation merged with religious celebration in a variety of festivals and processions throughout the year. The most striking display of these religiously inspired events was **carnival**, a time of reveling and excess in Catholic Europe, especially in Mediterranean countries. Carnival preceded Lent—the forty days of fasting and penitence before Easter—and for a few exceptional days in February or March, a wild release of drinking, masquerading, and dancing reigned. Moreover, a combination of plays, processions, and raucous spectacles turned the established order upside down. Peasants dressed as nobles and men as women, and rich masters waited on their servants at the table. This annual holiday gave people a much-appreciated chance to release their pent-up frustrations and aggressions before life returned to the usual pattern of hierarchy and hard work.

The rowdy pastimes of the populace attracted criticism from clerical and lay elites in the second half of the eighteenth century. In 1772 the Spanish crown banned dragons and giants from the Corpus Christi parade, and the vibrant carnival of Venice was outlawed under Napoleon's rule in 1797. In the same period English newspapers publicly denounced boxing, gambling, blood sports, and other uncouth activities;

blood sports Events such as bullbaiting and cockfighting that involved inflicting violence and bloodshed on animals and that were popular with the eighteenth-century European masses.

carnival The few days of revelry in Catholic countries that preceded Lent and that included drinking, masquerading, dancing, and rowdy spectacles that upset the established order.

one described bullbaiting in 1791 as "a disgrace to a civilized people."[19] However, historians have tended to overstate claims for a "culture war" between elites and the populace in the eighteenth century. Certainly, many wealthy and educated Europeans continued to enjoy the folktales of the chapbooks and they shared the love of gambling, theater, and sport. Moreover, both peasants and patricians—even most enlightened thinkers—shared a deep religiosity. In turn, as we have seen, common people were by no means cut off from the new currents of thought. Thus cultural elements continued to be shared across social divides.

New Foods and Appetites

At the beginning of the eighteenth century, ordinary men and women depended on grain as fully as they had in the past. Bread was quite literally the staff of life. Peasants in the Beauvais region of France ate two pounds of bread a day, washing it down with water, wine, or beer. Their dark bread was made from roughly ground wheat and rye—the standard flour of the common people. Even peasants normally needed to buy some grain for food, and, in full accord with landless laborers and urban workers, they believed in the moral economy and the **just price**. That is, they believed that prices should be "fair," protecting both consumers and producers, and that just prices should be imposed by government decree if necessary. When prices rose above this level, they often took action in the form of bread riots (see Chapter 15).

just price The idea that prices should be fair, protecting both consumers and producers, and that they should be imposed by government decree if necessary.

The rural poor also ate a quantity of vegetables. Peas and beans were probably the most common. Grown as field crops in much of Europe since the Middle Ages, they were eaten fresh in late spring and summer. Dried, they became the basic ingredients in the soups and stews of the long winter months. In most regions other vegetables appeared on the tables of the poor in season, primarily cabbages, carrots, and wild greens. Fruit was mostly limited to the summer months. Too precious to drink, milk was used to make cheese and butter, which peasants sold in the market to earn cash for taxes and land rents.

Chocolate Drinking   These Spanish tiles from 1710 illustrate the new practice of preparing and drinking hot chocolate. Originating in the New World, chocolate was one of the many new foods imported to Europe in the wake of the voyages of discovery. The first Spanish chocolate mills opened in the mid-seventeenth century, and consumption of chocolate rapidly increased. The inclusion of these tiles in the decoration of a nobleman's house testifies to public interest in the new drink. (Detail of ceiling tile, from Teia, Spain/Museu de Ceramica, Barcelona, Spain/Album/Art Resource, NY)

The common people of Europe ate less meat in 1700 than in 1500 because their general standard of living had declined and meat was more expensive. Moreover, harsh laws in most European countries reserved the right to hunt and eat game, such as rabbits, deer, and partridges, to nobles and large landowners. Few laws were more bitterly resented—or more frequently broken—by ordinary people than those governing hunting.

The diet of small traders and artisans—the people of the towns and cities—was less monotonous than that of the peasantry. Bustling markets provided a substantial variety of meats, vegetables, and fruits, although bread and beans still formed the bulk of such families' diets. Not surprisingly, the diet of the rich was quite different from that of the poor. The upper classes were rapacious carnivores, and a truly elegant dinner consisted of an abundance of rich meat and fish dishes laced with piquant sauces and complemented with sweets, cheeses, and wine in great quantities. During such dinners, it was common to spend five or more hours at table, eating and drinking and enjoying the witty banter of polite society.

Patterns of food consumption changed markedly as the century progressed. Because of a growth of market gardening, a greater variety of vegetables appeared in towns and cities. This was particularly the case in the Low Countries and England, which pioneered new methods of farming. Introduced into Europe from the Americas—along with corn, squash, tomatoes, and many other useful plants—the humble potato provided an excellent new food source. Containing a good supply of carbohydrates, calories, and vitamins A and C, the potato offset the lack of vitamins in the poor person's winter and early-spring diet, and it provided a much higher caloric yield than grain for a given piece of land. After initial resistance, the potato became an important dietary supplement in much of Europe by the end of the century.

The most remarkable dietary change in the eighteenth century was in the consumption of commodities imported from abroad. Originally expensive and rare luxury items, goods like tea, sugar, coffee, chocolate, and tobacco became staples for people of all social classes. With the exception of tea—which originated in China—most of the new consumables were produced in European colonies in the Americas. In many cases, the labor of enslaved peoples enabled the expansion in production and drop in prices that allowed such items to spread to the masses.

Why were colonial products so popular? Part of the motivation for consuming these products was a desire to emulate the luxurious lifestyles of the elite. Having seen pictures of or read about the fine lady's habit of "teatime" or the gentleman's appreciation for a pipe, common Europeans sought to experience these pleasures for themselves. Moreover, the quickened pace of work in the eighteenth century created new needs for stimulants among working people. (See "Evaluating the Evidence 18.2: A Day in the Life of Paris," page 592.) Whereas the gentry took tea as a leisurely and genteel ritual, the lower classes drank tea or coffee at work to fight monotony and fatigue. With the widespread adoption of these products (which turned out to be mildly to extremely addictive), working people in Europe became increasingly dependent on faraway colonial economies and enslaved labor. Their understanding of daily necessities and how to procure those necessities shifted definitively, linking them to global trade networks they could not comprehend or control.

A Day in the Life of Paris

Louis-Sébastien Mercier (1740–1814) was the best chronicler of everyday life in eighteenth-century Paris. His masterpiece was the Tableau de Paris *(1781–1788), a multivolume work composed of 1,049 chapters that covered subjects ranging from convents to cafés, bankruptcy to booksellers, the latest fashions to royal laws. As this excerpt demonstrates, he aimed to convey the infinite diversity of people, places, and things he saw around him, and in so doing he left future generations a precious record of the changing dynamics of Parisian society in the second half of the eighteenth century.*

Mercier's family belonged to the respectable artisan classes. This middling position ideally situated Mercier to observe the extremes of wealth and poverty around him. Although these volumes contain many wonderful glimpses of daily life, they should not be taken for an objective account. Mercier brought his own moral and political sensibilities, influenced by Jean-Jacques Rousseau, to the task of description.

~

Chapter 39: How the Day Goes

It is curious to see how, amid what seems perpetual life and movement, certain hours keep their own characteristics, whether of bustle or of leisure. Every round of the clock-hand sets another scene in motion, each different from the last, though all about equal in length. Seven o'clock in the morning sees all the gardeners, mounted on their nags and with their baskets empty, heading back out of town again. No carriages are about, and not a presentable soul, except a few neat clerks hurrying to their offices. Nine o'clock sets all the barbers in motion, covered from head to foot with flour—hence their soubriquet of "whitings"*—wig in one hand, tongs in the other. Waiters from the lemonade-shops are busy with trays of coffee and rolls, breakfast for those who live in furnished rooms. . . . An hour later the Law comes into action; a black cloud of legal practitioners and hangers-on descend

upon the Châtelet,† and the other courts; a procession of wigs and gowns and briefbags, with plaintiffs and defendants at their heels. Midday is the stockbrokers' hour, and the idlers'; the former hurry off to the Exchange, the latter to the Palais-Royal.‡ The Saint-Honoré§ quarter, where all the financiers live, is at its busiest now, its streets are crowded with the customers and clients of the great.

At two o'clock those who have invitations to dine set out, dressed in their best, powdered, adjusted, and walking on tiptoe not to soil their stockings. All the cabs are engaged, not one is to be found on the rank; there is a good deal of competition for these vehicles, and you may see two would-be passengers jumping into a cab together from different sides, and furiously disputing which was first. . . .

Three o'clock and the streets are not so full; everyone is at dinner; there is a momentary calm, soon to be broken, for at five fifteen the din is as though the gates of hell were opened, the streets are impassable with traffic going all ways at once, towards the playhouses or the public gardens. Cafés are at their busiest.

Towards seven the din dies down, everywhere and all at once. You can hear the cab-horses' hoofs pawing the stones as they wait—in vain. It is as though the whole town were gagged and bound, suddenly, by an invisible hand. This is the most dangerous time of the whole day for thieves and such, especially towards autumn when the days begin to draw in; for the watch is not yet about, and violence takes its opportunity.

Night falls; and, while scene-shifters set to work at the playhouses, swarms of other workmen, carpenters, masons and the like, make their way towards the poorer quarters. They leave white footprints from the plaster on their shoes, a trail that any eye can follow. They are off home, and to

---

* Small fish typically rolled in flour and fried.

† The main criminal court of Paris.
‡ A garden surrounded by arcades with shops and cafés.
§ A fashionable quarter for the wealthy.

---

consumer revolution
The wide-ranging growth in consumption and new attitudes toward consumer goods that emerged in the cities of northwestern Europe in the second half of the eighteenth century.

Toward a Consumer Society

Along with foodstuffs, all manner of other goods increased in variety and number in the eighteenth century. This proliferation led to a growth in consumption and new attitudes toward consumer goods so wide-ranging that some historians have referred to an eighteenth-century **consumer revolution**.[20] The result of this revolution was the birth of a new type of society in which people derived their self-identity as much from bed, at the hour which finds elegant ladies sitting down to their dressing-tables to prepare for the business of the night.

At nine this begins; they all set off for the play. Houses tremble as the coaches rattle by, but soon the noise ceases; all the fine ladies are making their evening visits, short ones, before supper. Now the prostitutes begin their night parade, breasts uncovered, heads tossing, colour high on their cheeks, and eyes as bold as their hands. These creatures, careless of the light from shop-windows and street lamps, follow and accost you, trailing through the mud in their silk stockings and low shoes, with words and gestures well matched for obscenity. . . .

By eleven, renewed silence. People are at supper, private people, that is; for the cafés begin at this hour to turn out their patrons, and to send the various idlers and workless and poets back to their garrets for the night. A few prostitutes still linger, but they have to use more circum-spection, for the watch is about, patrolling the streets, and this is the hour when they "gather 'em in"; that is the traditional expression.

A quarter after midnight, a few carriages make their way home, taking the non–card players back to bed. These lend the town a sort of transitory life; the tradesman wakes out of his first sleep at the sound of them, and turns to his wife, by no means unwilling. More than one young Parisian must owe his existence to this sudden passing rattle of wheels. . . .

At one in the morning six thousand peasants arrive, bringing the town's provision of vegetables and fruits and flowers, and make straight for the Halles.** . . . As for the market itself, it never sleeps. . . . Perpetual noise, perpetual motion, the curtain never rings down on the enormous stage; first come the fishmongers, and after these the egg-dealers, and after these the retail buyers; for the Halles keep all the other markets of Paris going; they are the warehouses whence these draw their supplies. The food of the whole city is shifted and sorted in high-piled baskets;

you may see eggs, pyramids of eggs, moved here and there, up steps and down, in and out of the throngs, miraculous; not one is ever broken. . . .

This impenetrable din contrasts oddly with the sleeping streets, for at that hour none but thieves and poets are awake.

Twice a week, at six, those distributors of the staff of life, the bakers of Gonesse,†† bring in an enormous quantity of loaves to the town, and may take none back through the barriers. And at this same hour workmen take up their tools, and trudge off to their day's labour. Coffee with milk is, unbelievably, the favoured drink among these stalwarts nowadays. . . .

So coffee-drinking has become a habit, and one so deep-rooted that the working classes will start the day on nothing else. It is not costly, and has more flavour to it, and more nourishment too, than anything else they can afford to drink; so they consume immense quantities, and say that if a man can only have coffee for breakfast it will keep him going till nightfall.

EVALUATE THE EVIDENCE

1. What different social groups does Mercier describe? Does he approve or disapprove of Parisian society as he describes it?
2. How do the social classes described by Mercier differ in their use of time, and why? Do you think the same distinctions exist today?
3. What evidence of the consumer revolution can you find in Mercier's account? How do the goods used by eighteenth-century Parisians compare to the ones you use in your life today?

Source: Excerpt from *Panorama of Paris: Selections from "Le Tableau de Paris,"* by Louis-Sébastien Mercier, based on the translation by Helen Simpson, edited with a new preface and translations by Jeremy D. Popkin. Copyright © 1999 The Pennsylvania State University. Reprinted by permission of Penn State Press.

** The city's central wholesale food market.

†† A suburb of Paris, famous for the excellent bread baked there.

their consuming practices as from their working lives and place in the production process. As people gained the opportunity to pick and choose among a wide variety of consumer goods, new notions of individuality and self-expression developed. A shop-girl could stand out from her peers by her choice of a striped jacket, a colored parasol, or simply a new ribbon for her hair. The full emergence of a consumer society did not take place until much later, but its roots lie in the eighteenth century.

Increased demand for consumer goods was not merely an innate response to increased supply. Eighteenth-century merchants cleverly pioneered new techniques to incite demand: they initiated marketing campaigns, opened fancy boutiques with large windows, and advertised the patronage of royal princes and princesses. By diversifying their product lines and greatly accelerating the turnover of styles, they seized the reins of fashion from the courtiers who had earlier controlled it. Instead of setting new styles, duchesses and marquises now bowed to the dictates of fashion merchants. (See "Individuals in Society: Rose Bertin, 'Minister of Fashion,'" at right.) Fashion also extended beyond court circles to touch many more items and social groups.

Clothing was one of the chief indicators of the growth of consumerism. Shrewd entrepreneurs made fashionable clothing seem more desirable, while legions of women entering the textile and needle trades made it ever cheaper. As a result, eighteenth-century western Europe witnessed a dramatic rise in the consumption of clothing, particularly in large cities. One historian has documented an enormous growth in the size and value of Parisians' wardrobes from 1700 to 1789, as well as a new level of diversity in garments and accessories, colors, and fabrics.[21] Colonial economies again played an important role in lowering the cost of materials, such as cotton cloth and vegetable dyes, largely due to the unpaid toil of enslaved Africans. Cheaper copies of elite styles made it possible for working people to aspire to follow fashion for the first time.

Elite onlookers were sometimes shocked by the sight of lower-class people in stylish outfits. In 1784 Mrs. Fanny Cradock described encountering her milkman during an evening stroll "dressed in a fashionable suit, with an embroidered waistcoat, silk knee-breeches and lace cuffs."[22] The spread of fashion challenged the traditional social order of Europe by blurring the boundaries between social groups and making it harder to distinguish between noble and commoner on the bustling city streets.

Mrs. Cradock's milkman notwithstanding, women took the lead in the spread of fashion. Parisian women significantly outconsumed men, acquiring larger and more expensive wardrobes than those of their husbands, brothers, and fathers. This was true across the social spectrum; in ribbons, shoes, gloves, and lace, European working women reaped in the consumer revolution what they had sown in the industrious revolution (see Chapter 17). There were also new gender distinctions in dress. Previously, noblemen had vied with noblewomen in the magnificence of their apparel; by the end of the eighteenth century men had renounced brilliant colors and voluptuous fabrics to don early versions of the plain dark suit that remains standard male formal wear in the West. This was one more aspect of the increasingly rigid boundaries drawn between appropriate male and female behavior.

Changes in outward appearances were reflected in inner spaces, as new attitudes about privacy, individualism, and intimate life also emerged. Historians have used notaries' probate inventories to peer into ordinary people's homes. In 1700 the cramped home of a

First Hot-Air Balloon Flight, 1783 This engraving depicts the world's first free hot-air balloon flight as seen from the Parisian residence of Benjamin Franklin, who was then serving as American ambassador to France. The balloon, invented by the Montgolfier brothers, traveled over five miles in a twenty-minute flight to great public acclaim. (Bibliothèque Nationale, Paris, France/ Bridgeman Images)

One day in 1779, as the French royal family rode in a carriage through the streets of Paris, Queen Marie Antoinette noticed her fashion merchant, Rose Bertin, observing the royal procession. "Ah! there is mademoiselle Bertin," the queen exclaimed, waving her hand. Bertin responded with a curtsy. The king then stood and greeted Bertin, followed by the royal family and their entourage.* The incident shocked the public, for no common merchant had ever received such homage from royalty.

Bertin had come a long way from her humble beginnings. Born in 1747 to a poor family in northern France, she moved to Paris in the 1760s to work as a shop assistant. Bertin eventually opened her own boutique on the fashionable rue Saint-Honoré. In 1775 Bertin received the highest honor of her profession when she was selected by Marie Antoinette as one of her official purveyors.

Based on the queen's patronage, and riding the wave of the new consumer revolution, Bertin became one of the most successful entrepreneurs in Europe. Bertin established not only a large clientele, but also a reputation for pride and arrogance. She refused to work for non-noble customers, claiming that the orders of the queen and the court required all her attention. She astounded courtiers by referring to her "work" with the queen, as though the two were collaborators rather than absolute monarch and lowly subject. Bertin's close relationship with Marie Antoinette and the fortune the queen spent on her wardrobe hurt the royal family's image. One journalist derided Bertin as a "minister of fashion," whose influence outstripped that of all the others in royal government.

In January 1787 rumors spread through Paris that Bertin had filed for bankruptcy with debts of 2 to 3 million livres (a garment worker's annual salary was around 200 livres). Despite her notoriously high prices and rich clients, this news did not shock Parisians,

In this 1746 painting by François Boucher, a leisured lady has just been coiffed by her hairdresser. Wearing the cape she donned to protect her clothing from the hair powder, she receives a fashion merchant, who displays an array of ribbons and other finery. (*The Milliner*/DEA Picture Library/Getty Images)

because the nobility's reluctance to pay its debts was equally well known. Bertin somehow held on to her business. Some said she had spread the bankruptcy rumors herself to shame the court into paying her bills.

Bertin remained loyal to the Crown during the tumult of the French Revolution (see Chapter 19) and sent dresses to the queen even after the arrest of the royal family. Fearing for her life, she left France for Germany in 1792 and continued to ply her profession in exile. She returned to France in 1800 and died in 1813, one year before the restoration of the Bourbon monarchy might have renewed her acclaim.†

Rose Bertin scandalized public opinion with her self-aggrandizement and ambition, yet history was on her side. She was the first celebrity fashion stylist and one of the first self-made career women to rise from obscurity to fame and fortune based on her talent, taste, and hard work. Her legacy remains in the exalted status of today's top fashion designers and in the dreams of small-town girls to make it in the big city.

QUESTIONS FOR ANALYSIS

1. Why was the relationship between Queen Marie Antoinette and Rose Bertin so troubling to the public? Why would relations between a queen and a fashion merchant have political implications?
2. Why would someone who sold fashionable clothing and accessories rise to such a prominent position in business and society? What makes fashion so important in the social world?

---

*Mémoires secrets pour servir à l'histoire de la république des lettres en France, vol. 13, 299, 5 mars 1779 (London: John Adamson, 1785).

†On Rose Bertin, see Clare Haru Crowston, "The Queen and Her 'Minister of Fashion': Gender, Credit and Politics in Pre-Revolutionary France," *Gender and History* 14, no. 1 (April 2002): 92–116.

modest family consisted of a few rooms, each of which had multiple functions. The same room was used for sleeping, receiving friends, and working. In the eighteenth century rents rose sharply, making it impossible to gain more space, but families began attributing specific functions to specific rooms. They also began to erect inner barriers within the home to provide small niches in which individuals could seek privacy.

New levels of comfort and convenience accompanied this trend toward more individualized ways of life. In 1700 a meal might be served in a common dish, with each person dipping his or her spoon into the pot. By the end of the eighteenth century even humble households contained a much greater variety of cutlery and dishes, making it possible for each person to eat from his or her own plate. More books and prints, which also proliferated at lower prices, decorated the shelves and walls. Improvements in glassmaking provided more transparent glass, which allowed daylight to penetrate into gloomy rooms. Cold and smoky hearths were increasingly replaced by more efficient and cleaner coal stoves, which also eliminated the backache of cooking over an open fire. Rooms were warmer, better lit, more comfortable, and more personalized, and the spread of street lighting made it safer to travel in cities at night.

Standards of bodily and public hygiene also improved. Public bathhouses, popular across Europe in the Middle Ages, had gradually closed in the early modern period due to concerns over sexual promiscuity and infectious disease. Many Europeans came to fear that immersing the body in hot water would allow harmful elements to enter the skin. Carefully watched by his physician, Louis XIII of France took his first bath at age seven, while James I of England refused to wash more than his hands. Personal cleanliness consisted of wearing fresh linen and using perfume to mask odors, both expensive practices that bespoke wealth and social status. From the mid-eighteenth century on, enlightened doctors revised their views and began to urge more frequent bathing. Spa towns, like Bath, England, became popular sites for the wealthy to see each other and be seen. Officials also took measures to improve the cleaning of city streets in which trash, human soil, and animal carcasses were often left to rot.

The scope of the new consumer economy should not be exaggerated. These developments were concentrated in large cities in northwestern Europe and North America. Even in these centers the elite benefited the most from new modes of life. This was not yet the society of mass consumption that emerged toward the end of the nineteenth century with the full expansion of the Industrial Revolution. The eighteenth century did, however, lay the foundations for one of the most distinctive features of modern Western life: societies based on the consumption of goods and services obtained through the market in which individuals form their identities and self-worth through the goods they consume.

Religious Authority and Beliefs

FOCUS QUESTION

What were the patterns of popular religion, and how did they interact with the worldview of the educated public and their Enlightenment ideals?

Though the critical spirit of the Enlightenment made great inroads in the eighteenth century, the majority of ordinary men and women, especially those in rural areas, retained strong religious faith. The church promised salvation, and it gave comfort in the face of sorrow and death. Religion also remained strong because it was embedded in local traditions and everyday social experience.

Yet the popular religion of village Europe was also enmeshed in a larger world of church hierarchies and state power. These powerful outside forces sought to regulate religious life at the local level. Their efforts created tensions that helped set the scene for vigorous religious revivals in Protestant Germany and England as well as in Catholic France.

Church Hierarchy

In the eighteenth century religious faith not only endured, but grew more fervent in many parts of Europe. The local parish church remained the focal point of religious devotion and community cohesion. Congregants gossiped and swapped stories after services, and neighbors came together in church for baptisms, marriages, funerals, and special events. Priests and parsons kept the community records of births, deaths, and marriages; distributed charity; looked after orphans; and provided primary education to the common people. Thus the parish church was woven into the very fabric of community life.

While the parish church remained central to the community, it was also subject to greater control from the state. In Protestant areas, princes and monarchs headed the official church, and they regulated their "territorial churches" strictly, selecting personnel and imposing detailed rules. Clergy of the official church dominated education, and followers of other faiths suffered religious and civil discrimination. By the eighteenth century the radical ideas of the Reformation had resulted in another version of church bureaucracy.

Catholic monarchs in this period also took greater control of religious matters in their kingdoms, weakening papal authority. In both Spain and Portugal, the Catholic Church was closely associated with the state, a legacy of the long internal reconquista and sixteenth-century imperial conquests overseas. In the eighteenth century the Spanish crown took firm control of ecclesiastical appointments. Papal proclamations could not even be read in Spanish churches without prior approval from the government. In Portugal, religious enthusiasm led to a burst of new churches and monasteries in the early eighteenth century.

France went even further in establishing a national Catholic Church, known as the Gallican Church. Louis XIV's expulsion of Protestants in 1685 was accompanied by an insistence on the king's prerogative to choose and control bishops and issue laws regarding church affairs. Catholicism gained new ground in the Holy Roman Empire with the conversion of a number of Protestant princes and successful missionary work by Catholic orders among the populace. While it could not eradicate Protestantism altogether, the Habsburg monarchy successfully consolidated Catholicism as a pillar of its political control.

The Jesuit order played a key role in fostering the Catholic faith, providing extraordinary teachers, missionaries, and agents of the papacy. In many Catholic countries they exercised tremendous political influence, holding high government positions and educating the nobility in their colleges. By playing politics so effectively, however, the Jesuits elicited a broad coalition of enemies. Bitter controversies led Louis XV to order the Jesuits out of France in 1763 and to confiscate their property. France and Spain then pressured Rome to dissolve the Jesuits completely. In 1773 a reluctant pope caved in, although the order was revived after the French Revolution.

The Jesuit order was not the only Christian group to come under attack in the middle of the eighteenth century. The dominance of the larger Catholic Church and established Protestant churches was also challenged, both by enlightened reformers from above and by the faithful from below. Influenced by Enlightenment ideals, some Catholic rulers believed that the clergy in monasteries and convents should make a more practical contribution to social and religious life. Austria, a leader in controlling the church (see Chapter 16) and promoting primary education, showed how far the process could go. Maria Theresa began by sharply restricting entry into what she termed "unproductive" orders. In his Edict on Idle Institutions, her successor, Joseph II, abolished contemplative orders, henceforth permitting only orders that were engaged in teaching, nursing, or other practical work. The state expropriated the dissolved monasteries and convents and used their wealth to create more parishes throughout Austria. This edict had a disproportionate effect on women because most of their orders were cloistered from the outside world and thus were not seen as "useful." Joseph II also issued edicts of religious tolerance, including for Jews, making Austria one of the first European states to lift centuries-old restrictions on its Jewish population.

Protestant Revival

Official efforts to reform state churches in the eighteenth century were confronted by a wave of religious enthusiasm from below. By the late seventeenth century the vast transformations of the Protestant Reformation were complete and had been widely adopted in most Protestant churches. Medieval practices of idolatry, saint worship, and pageantry were abolished; stained-glass windows were smashed and murals whitewashed. Yet many official Protestant churches had settled into a smug complacency. This, along with the growth of state power and bureaucracy in local parishes, threatened to eclipse one of the Reformation's main goals—to bring all believers closer to God.

In the Reformation heartland, one concerned German minister wrote that the Lutheran Church "had become paralyzed in forms of dead doctrinal conformity" and badly needed a return to its original inspiration.[23] His voice was one of many that prepared and then guided a Protestant revival that succeeded because it answered the intense but increasingly unsatisfied needs of common people.

The Protestant revival began in Germany in the late seventeenth century. It was known as **Pietism** (PIGH- uh-tih-zum), and three aspects helped explain its powerful appeal. First, Pietism called for a warm, emotional religion that everyone could experience. Enthusiasm—in prayer, in worship, in preaching, in life itself—was the key concept. "Just as a drunkard becomes full of wine, so must the congregation become filled with spirit," declared one exuberant writer.[24]

Second, Pietism reasserted the earlier radical stress on the priesthood of all believers, thereby reducing the gulf between official clergy and Lutheran laity. Bible reading and study were enthusiastically extended to all classes, and this provided a powerful spur for popular literacy as well as individual religious development. Pietists were largely responsible for the educational reforms implemented by Prussia in the early eighteenth century (see page 587). Third and finally, Pietists believed in the practical power of Christian rebirth in everyday affairs. Reborn Christians were expected to lead good, moral lives and to come from all social classes.

Pietism soon spread through the German-speaking lands and to Scandinavia. It also had a major impact on John Wesley (1703–1791), who served as the catalyst for popular religious revival in England. (See "Evaluating the Evidence 18.3: Advice to Methodists," at right.) Wesley came from a long line of ministers, and when he went to Oxford University to prepare for the clergy, he mapped a fanatically earnest

Pietism A Protestant revival movement in early-eighteenth-century Germany and Scandinavia that emphasized a warm and emotional religion, the priesthood of all believers, and the power of Christian rebirth in everyday affairs.

Advice to Methodists

John Wesley (1703–1791) was the fifteenth child of an Anglican rector and a strict mother. As a small child, he was rescued from certain death in a house fire; in later years, he saw this moment as a sign of providential grace. Along with his brother Charles, John Wesley is recognized as the founder of Methodism, an evangelical movement that began within the Church of England and was influenced by German Pietism. In the passage below, Wesley offers his advice to followers of the new religious movement he had inspired, who had been dubbed "Methodists" for their scrupulous and methodical approach to religious worship.

By *Methodists* I mean, a People who profess to pursue (in whatsoever Measure they have attained) Holiness of Heart and Life, inward and outward Conformity in all Things to the revealed Will of God: Who place Religion in an uniform Resemblance of the great Object of it; in a steady Imitation of Him they worship, in all his inimitable Perfections; more particularly, in Justice, Mercy, and Truth, or universal Love filling the Heart, and governing the Life. . . .

Your *Name* is new (at least, as used in a religious Sense), not heard of, till a few Years ago, either in our own, or any other Nation. Your *Principles* are new, in this respect, That there is no other Set of People among us (and, possibly, not in the Christian World) who hold them all, in the same Degree and Connection; who so strenuously and continually insist on the absolute Necessity of universal Holiness both in Heart and Life; of a peaceful, joyous Love of God; of a supernatural Evidence of Things not seen; of an inward Witness that we are the Children of God, and of the Inspiration of the Holy Ghost, in order to any good

Thought, or Word, or Work. And perhaps there is no other Set of People (at least not visibly united together), who lay *so much*, and yet *no more* Stress than you do, on Rectitude of *Opinions*, on outward *Modes of Worship*, and the Use of those *Ordinances* which you acknowledge to be of God. . . .

Your *Strictness* of Life, taking the whole of it together, may likewise be accounted new. I mean, your making it a Rule, to abstain from fashionable *Diversions*, from *reading* Plays, Romances, or Books of Humour, from *singing* innocent Songs, or *talking* in a merry, gay, diverting Manner; your *Plainness* of Dress; your *Manner of Dealing* in Trade; your Exactness in observing the *Lord's Day*; your Scrupulosity as to Things that have *not paid Custom*; your total Abstinence from *spirituous Liquors* (unless in Cases of Extreme Necessity); your Rule, "not to mention the Fault of an absent Person, in Particular, of *Ministers*, or of *those in Authority*," may justly be termed new.

EVALUATE THE EVIDENCE

1. What elements of the Methodist faith does Wesley identify as "new" in this document? To what or whom is he comparing Methodists?
2. To what changes under way in English society does this document appear to be responding? What social practices do Methodists oppose, according to Wesley?

Source: John Wesley, *Advice to the People Call'd Methodists* (Bristol: Felix Farley, 1745), pp. 3, 5–6.

"scheme of religion." After becoming a teaching fellow at Oxford, Wesley organized a Holy Club for similarly minded students, who were soon known contemptuously as **Methodists** because they were so methodical in their devotion. Yet like the young Martin Luther, Wesley remained intensely troubled about his own salvation even after his ordination as an Anglican priest in 1728.

Wesley's anxieties related to grave problems of the faith in England. The government shamelessly used the Church of England to provide favorites with high-paying jobs. Both church and state officials failed to respond to the spiritual needs of the people, and services and sermons had settled into an uninspiring routine. The separation of religion from local customs and social life was symbolized by church doors that were customarily locked on weekdays. Moreover, Enlightenment skepticism was making inroads among the educated classes, and deism—a belief in God but not in

Methodists Members of a Protestant revival movement started by John Wesley, so called because they were so methodical in their devotion.

Hogarth's Satirical View of the Church   William Hogarth (1697–1764) was one of the foremost satirical artists of his day. This image mocks a London Methodist meeting, where the congregation swoons in enthusiasm over the preacher's sermon. The woman in the foreground giving birth to rabbits is an allusion to a hoax perpetrated in 1726 by a servant named Mary Tofts; the gullibility of those who believed Tofts is likened to that of the Methodist congregation. (From *Hogarth Restored: The Whole Works of the Celebrated William Hogarth*, 1812/Private Collection/The Stapleton Collection/Bridgeman Images)

organized religion—was becoming popular. Some bishops and church leaders seemed to believe that doctrines such as the virgin birth were little more than elegant superstitions.

Wesley's inner search in the 1730s was deeply affected by his encounter with Moravian Pietists, whom he first met on a ship as he traveled across the Atlantic to take up a position in Savannah, Georgia. The small Moravian community in Georgia impressed him as a productive, peaceful, and pious world, reflecting the values of the first apostles. (For more on the Moravian Church, see "Individuals in Society: Rebecca Protten," in Chapter 17 on page 568.) After returning to London, following a disastrous failed engagement and the disappointment of his hopes to convert Native Americans, he sought spiritual counseling from a Pietist minister from Germany. Their conversations prepared Wesley for a mystical, emotional "conversion" in 1738. He described this critical turning point in his *Journal*:

> In the evening I went to a [Christian] society in Aldersgate Street where one was reading Luther's preface to the Epistle to the Romans. About a quarter before nine, while he was describing the change which God works in the heart through faith in Christ, I felt my heart strangely warmed. I felt I did trust in Christ, Christ alone for salvation; and an assurance was given me that he had taken away my sins, even mine, and saved me from the law of sin and death.[25]

Wesley's emotional experience resolved his intellectual doubts about the possibility of his own salvation. Moreover, he was convinced that any person, no matter how poor or uneducated, might have a similarly heartfelt conversion and gain the same blessed assurance. He took the good news to the people, traveling some 225,000 miles by horseback and preaching more than forty thousand sermons between 1750 and 1790. Since existing churches were often overcrowded and the church-state establishment was hostile, Wesley preached in open fields. People came in large numbers. Of critical importance was Wesley's rejection of Calvinist predestination—the doctrine of salvation granted to only a select few. Instead, he preached that all men and women who earnestly sought salvation might be saved. It was a message of hope and joy, of free will and universal salvation.

Wesley's ministry used lay preachers to reach new converts, formed Methodist cells, and eventually resulted in a new denomination. And just as Wesley had been inspired by the Pietist revival in Germany, so evangelicals in the Church of England and the old dissenting groups now followed Wesley's example of preaching to all people, giving impetus to an even broader awakening among the lower classes. Thus in Protestant countries religion continued to be a vital force in the lives of the people.

Catholic Piety

Religion also flourished in Catholic Europe around 1700, but there were important differences from Protestant practice. First, the visual contrast was striking; baroque art still lavished rich and emotionally exhilarating figures and images on Catholic churches, whereas most Protestant churches had removed their art during the Reformation. Moreover, people in Catholic Europe on the whole participated more actively in formal worship than did Protestants. More than 95 percent of the population probably attended church for Easter communion, the climax of the religious year.

The tremendous popular strength of religion in Catholic countries can in part be explained by the church's integral role in community life and popular culture. Thus, although Catholics reluctantly confessed their sins to priests, they enthusiastically came together in religious festivals to celebrate the passage of the liturgical year. In addition to the great processional days—such as Palm Sunday, the joyful re-enactment of Jesus's triumphal entry into Jerusalem—each parish had its own saints' days, processions, and pilgrimages. Led by its priest, a congregation might march around the village or across the countryside to a local shrine. Millions of Catholic men and women also joined religious associations, known as confraternities, where they participated in prayer and religious services and collected funds for poor relief and members' funerals. The Reformation had largely eliminated such activities in Protestant areas.

Catholicism had its own version of the Pietist revivals that shook Protestant Europe. **Jansenism** has been described by one historian as the "illegitimate off-spring of the Protestant Reformation and the Catholic Counter-Reformation."[26] It originated with Cornelius Jansen (1585–1638), bishop of Ypres in the Spanish Netherlands, who called for a return to the austere early Christianity of Saint Augustine. In contrast to the worldly Jesuits, Jansen emphasized the heavy weight of original sin and accepted the doctrine of predestination. Although outlawed by papal and royal edicts as Calvinist heresy, Jansenism attracted Catholic followers eager for religious renewal, particularly among the French. Many members of France's urban elite, especially judicial nobles and some parish priests, became known for their Jansenist piety and spiritual devotion. Such stern religious values encouraged the judiciary's increasing opposition to the French monarchy in the second half of the eighteenth century.

Among the urban poor, a different strain of Jansenism took hold. Prayer meetings brought men and women together in ecstatic worship, and some participants fell into convulsions and spoke in tongues. The police of Paris posted spies to report on such gatherings and conducted mass raids and arrests.

Jansenism A sect of Catholicism originating with Cornelius Jansen that emphasized the heavy weight of original sin and accepted the doctrine of predestination; it was out-lawed as heresy by the pope.

Marginal Beliefs and Practices

In the countryside, many peasants continued to hold religious beliefs that were marginal to the Christian faith altogether, often of obscure or even pagan origin. On the Feast of Saint Anthony, for example, priests were expected to bless salt and bread for farm animals to protect them from disease. Catholics believed that saints' relics could bring fortune or attract lovers, and there were healing springs for many ailments. In 1796 the Lutheran villagers of Beutelsbach in southern Germany incurred the ire of local officials when they buried a live bull at a crossroads to ward off an epidemic of hoof-and-mouth disease.[27] The ordinary person combined strong Christian faith with a wealth of time-honored superstitions.

Inspired initially by the fervor of the Reformation era, then by the critical rationalism of the Enlightenment, religious and secular authorities sought increasingly to "purify" popular spirituality. Thus one parish priest in France lashed out at his parishioners, claiming that they were "more superstitious than devout . . . and sometimes appear as baptized idolaters."[28] French priests particularly denounced the "various remnants of paganism" found in popular bonfire ceremonies during Lent, in which young men, "yelling and screaming like madmen," tried to jump over the bonfires in order to help the crops grow and to protect themselves from illness. One priest saw rational Christians regressing into pagan animals—"the triumph of Hell and the shame of Christianity."[29]

The severity of the attack on popular belief varied widely by country and region. Where authorities pursued purification vigorously, as in Austria under Joseph II, pious peasants saw only an incomprehensible attack on age-old faith and drew back in anger. It was in this era of rationalism and disdain for superstition that the persecution of witches slowly came to an end across Europe. Common people in the countryside continued to fear the Devil and his helpers, but the elite increasingly dismissed such fears and refused to prosecute suspected witches. The last witch was executed in England in 1682, the same year France prohibited witchcraft trials. By the late eighteenth century the witchcraft hunts had ended across Europe.

Medical Practice

FOCUS QUESTION

How did the practice of medicine evolve in the eighteenth century?

Although significant breakthroughs in medical science would not come until the middle and late nineteenth century, the Enlightenment's inherent optimism and its focus on improving human life through understanding of the laws of nature produced a great deal of research and experimentation in the eighteenth century. Medical practitioners greatly increased in number, although their techniques did not differ much from those of previous generations. Care of the sick in this era was the domain of several competing groups: traditional healers, apothecaries (pharmacists), physicians, surgeons, and midwives. From the Middle Ages through the seventeenth century, both men and women were medical practitioners. However, since women were generally denied admission to medical colleges and lacked the diplomas necessary to practice, the range of medical activities open to them was restricted. In the eighteenth century women's traditional roles as midwives and healers eroded even further.

Faith Healing and General Practice

In the course of the eighteenth century, traditional healers remained active, drawing on centuries of folk knowledge about the curative properties of roots, herbs, and other plants. Faith healing also remained popular, especially in the countryside. Faith healers and their patients believed that evil spirits caused illness by lodging in people and that the proper treatment was to exorcise, or drive out, the offending devil. Religious and secular officials did their best to stamp out such practices, but with little success.

In the larger towns and cities, apothecaries sold a vast number of herbs, drugs, and patent medicines for every conceivable "temperament and distemper." By the eighteenth century many of these medicines were derived from imported plants. The Asian spices prized since medieval times often had medicinal uses; from the sixteenth century onward, the Portuguese and then the Dutch dominated the Indian Ocean trade in these spices (see Chapter 14). As Europeans expanded to the New World, they brought a keen interest in potentially effective and highly profitable medicinal plants. Botanists accompanied European administrators and explorers to the Americas, where they profited from the healing traditions of indigenous peoples and, in the plantation societies of the Caribbean, enslaved Africans. They returned to Europe with a host of medicinal plants such as ipecacuanha, sarsaparilla, opium, and cinchona, the first effective treatment for fever. Over the course of the seventeenth century, imports of medicinal plants boomed. By the late eighteenth century, England was importing annually £100,000 worth of drugs, compared to only £1,000 or £2,000 in 1600.[30]

Like all varieties of medical practitioners, apothecaries advertised their wares, their high-class customers, and their miraculous cures in newspapers and commercial circulars. Medicine, like food and fashionable clothing, thus joined the era's new and loosely regulated commercial culture.

Physicians, who were invariably men, were apprenticed in their teens to practicing physicians for several years of on-the-job training. This training was then rounded out with hospital work or some university courses. Seen as gentlemen who did not labor with their hands, many physicians diagnosed and treated patients by correspondence or through oral dialogue, without conducting a physical examination. Because their training was expensive, physicians came mainly from prosperous families and they usually concentrated on urban patients from similar social backgrounds. Nevertheless, even poor people spent hard-won resources to seek treatment for their loved ones.

Physicians in the eighteenth century were increasingly willing to experiment with new methods, but time-honored practices lay heavily on them. They laid great stress on purging, and bloodletting was still considered a medical cure-all. It was the way "bad blood," the cause of illness, was removed and the balance of humors necessary for good health was restored.

Improvements in Surgery

Long considered to be craftsmen comparable to butchers and barbers, surgeons began studying anatomy seriously and improved their art in the eighteenth century. With endless opportunities to practice, army surgeons on gory battlefields led the way. They learned that a soldier with an extensive wound, such as a shattered leg or arm, could perhaps be saved if the surgeon could obtain a flat surface above the wound that could be cauterized with fire. Thus, if a soldier had a broken limb and the bone stuck out, the surgeon amputated so that the remaining stump could be cauterized and the likelihood of death reduced.

The eighteenth-century surgeon (and patient) labored in the face of incredible difficulties. Almost all operations were performed without painkillers, for the anesthesia of the day was hard to control and too dangerous for general use. Many patients died from the agony and shock of such operations. Surgery was also performed in utterly unsanitary conditions, for there was no knowledge of bacteriology and the nature of infection. The simplest wound treated by a surgeon could fester and lead to death.

Midwifery

Midwives continued to deliver the overwhelming majority of babies throughout the eighteenth century. Trained initially by another woman practitioner—and regulated by a guild in many cities—the midwife primarily assisted in labor and delivering babies. She also treated female problems, such as irregular menstrual cycles, breast-feeding difficulties, infertility, and venereal disease, and ministered to small children.

The midwife orchestrated labor and birth in a woman's world, where friends and relatives assisted the pregnant woman in the familiar surroundings of her own home. The male surgeon (and the husband) rarely entered this female world, because most births, then as now, were normal and spontaneous. After the invention of forceps became publicized in 1734, surgeon-physicians used their monopoly over this and other instruments to seek lucrative new business. Attacking midwives as ignorant and dangerous, they sought to undermine faith in midwives and persuaded growing numbers of wealthy women of the superiority of their services. As one male expert proclaimed:

> A midwife is usually a creature of the lowest class of human beings, and of course utterly destitute of education, who from indigence, and that she is incapable of everything else, has been compelled to follow, as the last and sole resources a profession which people fondly imagine no very difficult one, never dreaming that the least glimpse of previous instruction is required for that purpose. . . . Midwives are universally ignorant. For where or how should she come by any thing deserving the name of knowledge.[31]

Research suggests that women practitioners successfully defended much but not all of their practice in the eighteenth century. One enterprising French midwife, Madame du Coudray, wrote a widely used textbook, *Manual on the Art of Childbirth* (1757), in order to address complaints about incompetent midwives. She then secured royal financing for her campaign to teach birthing techniques. Du Coudray traveled all over France using a life-size model of the female torso and fetus to help teach illiterate women. Despite criticism, it appears that midwives generally lost no more babies than did male doctors, who were still summoned to treat non-elite women only when life-threatening situations required surgery.

Women also continued to perform almost all nursing. Female religious orders ran many hospitals, and at-home nursing was almost exclusively the province of women. Thus, although they were excluded from the growing ranks of formally trained and authorized practitioners, women continued to perform the bulk of informal medical care. Nursing as a secular profession did not emerge until the nineteenth century.

The Conquest of Smallpox

Experimentation and the intensified search for solutions to human problems led to some real advances in medicine after 1750. The eighteenth century's greatest medical triumph was the eradication of smallpox. With the progressive decline of bubonic plague, smallpox became the most terrible of the infectious diseases, and it is estimated that 60 million Europeans died of it in the eighteenth century.

The first step in the conquest of this killer in Europe came in the early eighteenth century. An English aristocrat whose beauty had been marred by the pox, Lady Mary Wortley Montagu, learned about the long-established practice of smallpox inoculation in the Muslim lands of western Asia while her husband was serving as British

The Wonderful Effects of the New Inoculation!
The talented caricaturist James Gillray satirized widespread anxieties about the smallpox vaccination in this lively image. The discoveries of Edward Jenner a few years prior to Gillray's caricature had led to the adoption of a safer vaccine derived from cowpox. The artist mocks this breakthrough by showing cows bursting from the boils supposedly brought on by the vaccine. (Private Collection/Bridgeman Images)

ambassador to the Ottoman Empire. She had her own son successfully inoculated with the pus from a smallpox victim and was instrumental in spreading the practice in England after her return in 1722. But inoculation was risky and was widely condemned because about one person in fifty died from it. In addition, people who had been inoculated were infectious and often spread the disease.

While the practice of inoculation with the smallpox virus was refined over the century, the crucial breakthrough was made by Edward Jenner (1749–1823), a talented country doctor. His starting point was the countryside belief that dairymaids who had contracted cowpox did not get smallpox. Cowpox produces sores that resemble those of smallpox, but the disease is mild and is not contagious.

For eighteen years Jenner practiced a kind of Baconian science, carefully collecting data. Finally, in 1796 he performed his first vaccination on a young boy using matter taken from a milkmaid with cowpox. After performing more successful vaccinations, Jenner published his findings in 1798. The new method of treatment spread rapidly, and smallpox soon declined to the point of disappearance in Europe and then throughout the world.

LOOKING BACK LOOKING AHEAD

The fundamental patterns of life in early modern Europe remained very much the same up to the eighteenth century. The vast majority of people lived in the countryside and followed age-old rhythms of seasonal labor in the fields and farmyard. Community ties were close in small villages, where the struggle to prevail over harsh conditions called on all hands to work together and to pray together. The daily life of a peasant in 1700 would have been familiar to his ancestors in the fifteenth century. Indeed, the three orders of society enshrined in the medieval social hierarchy — clergy, nobility, peasantry — were binding legal categories in France up to 1789.

And yet, the economic changes inaugurated in the late seventeenth century — intensive agriculture, cottage industry, the industrious revolution, and colonial expansion — contributed to the profound social and cultural transformation of daily life in eighteenth-century Europe. Men and women of the laboring classes, especially in the cities, experienced change in many facets of their daily lives: in loosened community controls over sex and marriage, rising literacy rates, new goods and new forms of self-expression, and a wave of religious piety that challenged traditional orthodoxies. Lay and secular elites attacked some forms of popular life, but considerable overlap continued between popular and elite culture.

Economic, social, and cultural change would culminate in the late eighteenth century with the outbreak of revolution in the Americas and Europe. Initially led by the elite, political upheavals relied on the enthusiastic participation of the poor and their desire for greater inclusion in the life of the nation. Such movements also encountered resistance from the common people when revolutionaries trampled on their religious faith. For many observers, contemporaries and historians alike, the transformations of the eighteenth century constituted a fulcrum between the old world of hierarchy and tradition and the modern world with its claims to equality and freedom.

Make Connections

Think about the larger developments and continuities within and across chapters.

1. How did the expansion of agriculture and trade (Chapter 17) contribute to changes in daily life in the eighteenth century?

2. What were the main areas of improvement in the lives of the common people in the eighteenth century, and what aspects of life remained unchanged or even deteriorated?

3. How did Enlightenment thought (Chapter 16) affect education, child care, medicine, and religion in the eighteenth century?

18 REVIEW & EXPLORE

Review the Main Ideas

Answer the focus questions from each section of the chapter.

♦ What changes occurred in marriage and the family in the course of the eighteenth century? (p. 576)

♦ What was life like for children, and how did attitudes toward childhood evolve? (p. 581)

♦ How did increasing literacy and new patterns of consumption affect people's lives? (p. 587)

♦ What were the patterns of popular religion, and how did they interact with the worldview of the educated public and their Enlightenment ideals? (p. 596)

♦ How did the practice of medicine evolve in the eighteenth century? (p. 602)

Identify Key Terms

Identify and explain the significance of each item below.

community controls (p. 578)
charivari (p. 578)
illegitimacy explosion (p. 579)
wet-nursing (p. 582)
blood sports (p. 589)
carnival (p. 589)
just price (p. 590)
consumer revolution (p. 592)
Pietism (p. 598)
Methodists (p. 599)
Jansenism (p. 601)

NOTES

1. Archibald Campbell, Marquis of Argyll, *Instructions to a Son, Containing Rules of Conduct in Publick and Private Life* (Glasgow: E. Foulis, 1743), p. 33.

2. Quoted in J. M. Beattie, "The Criminality of Women in Eighteenth-Century England," *Journal of Social History* 8 (Summer 1975): 86.

3. Quoted in R. Cobb, *The Police and the People: French Popular Protest, 1789–1820* (Oxford: Clarendon Press, 1970), p. 238.

4. Peter Laslett, *Family Life and Illicit Love: Essays in Historical Sociology* (Cambridge: Cambridge University Press, 1977).

5. G. Gullickson, *Spinners and Weavers of Auffay: Rural Industry and the Sexual Division of Labor in a French Village, 1750–1850* (Cambridge: Cambridge University Press, 1986), p. 186.

6. Louis Crompton, *Homosexuality and Civilization* (Cambridge, Mass.: Belknap Press, 2003), p. 321.

7. D. S. Neff, "Bitches, Mollies, and Tommies: Byron, Masculinity and the History of Sexualities," *Journal of the History of Sexuality* 11, no. 3 (July 2002): 404.

8. George E. Haggerty, ed., *Encyclopedia of Gay Histories and Cultures* (New York: Garland Publishing, 2000), pp. 1311–1312.

9. Pier Paolo Viazzo, "Mortality, Fertility, and Family," in *Family Life in Early Modern Times, 1500–1789*, ed. David I. Kertzer and Marzio Barbagli (New Haven, Conn.: Yale University Press, 2001), p. 180.

10. George Sussman, *Selling Mother's Milk: The Wet-Nursing Business in France, 1715–1914* (Urbana: University of Illinois Press, 1982), p. 22.

11. Yves Blayo, "La Mortalité en France de 1740 à 1820," *Population*, special issue 30 (1975): 135.

12. Viazzo, "Mortality, Fertility, and Family," pp. 176–178.

13. Quoted in Matthew Gerber, *Bastards: Politics, Family, and Law in Early Modern France* (Oxford: Oxford University Press, 2012), p. 125.

14. Alysa Levene, "The Estimation of Mortality at the London Foundling Hospital, 1741–99," *Population Studies* 59, no. 1 (2005): 87–97.

15. Quoted in Robert Woods, "Did Montaigne Love His Children? Demography and the Hypothesis of Parental Indifference," *Journal of Interdisciplinary History* 33, no. 3 (2003): 421.

16. Quoted in Gay Ochiltree and Don Edgar, *The Changing Face of Childhood* (Melbourne: Institute of Family Studies, 1981), p. 11.

17. James Van Horn Melton, *Absolutism and the Eighteenth-Century Origins of Compulsory Schooling in Prussia and Austria* (Cambridge: Cambridge University Press, 2003), p. 46.

18. James Van Horn Melton, "The Theresian School Reform of 1774," in *Early Modern Europe*, ed. James B. Collins and Karen L. Taylor (Oxford: Blackwell, 2006).

19. Jeremy Black, *The English Press in the Eighteenth Century* (Philadelphia: University of Pennsylvania Press, 1987), p. 262.

20. Neil McKendrik, John Brewer, and J. H. Plumb, *The Birth of a Consumer Society: The Commercialization of Eighteenth-Century England* (Bloomington: Indiana University Press, 1982).

21. Daniel Roche, *The Culture of Clothing: Dress and Fashion in the Ancien Regime*, trans. Jean Birrell (Cambridge: Cambridge University Press, 1996).

22. Quoted in Cissie Fairchilds, "The Production and Marketing of Populuxe Goods in Eighteenth-Century Paris," in *Consumption and the World of Goods*, ed. John Brewer and Roy Porter (London: Routledge, 1993), p. 228.

23. Quoted in K. Pinson, *Pietism as a Factor in the Rise of German Nationalism* (New York: Columbia University Press, 1934), p. 13.

24. Ibid., pp. 43–44.

25. Quoted in S. Andrews, *Methodism and Society* (London: Longmans, Green, 1970), p. 327.

26. Dale Van Kley, "The Rejuvenation and Rejection of Jansenism in History and Historiography," *French Historical Studies* 29 (Fall 2006): 649–684.

27. David Sabean, *The Power in the Blood: Popular Culture and Village Discourse in Early Modern Germany* (Cambridge: Cambridge University Press, 1984), p. 174.

28. Quoted in I. Woloch, *Eighteenth-Century Europe: Tradition and Progress, 1715–1789* (New York: W. W. Norton, 1982), p. 292.

29. Quoted in T. Tackett, *Priest and Parish in Eighteenth-Century France* (Princeton, N.J.: Princeton University Press, 1977), p. 214.

30. Patrick Wallis, "Exotic Drugs and English Medicine: England's Drug Trade, c. 1550–c. 1800," *Social History of Medicine* 2, no. 1 (2012): 26.

31. Louis Lapeyre, *An Enquiry into the Merits of These Two Important Questions: I. Whether Women with Child Ought to Prefer the Assistance of Their Own Sex to That of Men-Midwives? II. Whether the Assistance of Men-Midwives Is Contrary to Decency?* (London: S. Bladon, 1772), p. 29.

CHAPTER PREVIEW

Background to Revolution
What were the factors leading to the revolutions of the late eighteenth century?

The American Revolutionary Era, 1775–1789
Why and how did American colonists forge a new, independent nation?

Revolution in France, 1789–1791
How did the events of 1789 result in a constitutional monarchy in France, and what were the consequences?

World War and Republican France, 1791–1799
Why and how did the French Revolution take a radical turn entailing terror at home and war with European powers?

The Napoleonic Era, 1799–1815
How did Napoleon Bonaparte assume control of France and much of Europe, and what factors led to his downfall?

The Haitian Revolution, 1791–1804
How did slave revolt on colonial Saint-Domingue lead to the creation of the independent nation of Haiti in 1804?

The Taking of the Bastille, July 14, 1789
The French Revolution began on July 14, 1789, when a group of angry Parisians attacked a royal prison on the east side of the city, known as the Bastille. Although only seven prisoners were being held at the time, the prison had become a symbol of despotic rule.

(*The Taking of the Bastille, 14 July 1789/* French School/Château de Versailles, France/Bridgeman Images)

19
Revolutions in Politics

1775–1815

A great wave of revolution rocked both sides of the Atlantic Ocean in the last decades of the eighteenth century. As trade goods, individuals, and ideas circulated in ever-greater numbers across the Atlantic Ocean, debates and events in one locale soon influenced those in another. As changing social realities challenged the old order of life and Enlightenment ideals of freedom and equality flourished, reformers in many places demanded fundamental changes in politics and government. At the same time, wars fought for dominance of the Atlantic economy left European states weakened by crushing debts, making them vulnerable to calls for reform.

The revolutionary era began in North America in 1775, and the United States of America won freedom from Britain in 1783. Then in 1789, France, the most populous country in western Europe and a center of culture and intellectual life, became the leading revolutionary nation. It established first a constitutional monarchy, then a radical republic, and finally a new empire under Napoleon that would last until 1815. During this period of constant domestic turmoil, French armies brought revolution to much of Europe. Inspired both by the ideals of the Revolution on the continent and by their own experiences and desires, the slaves of Saint-Domingue rose up in 1791. Their rebellion would eventually lead to the creation of the new independent nation of Haiti in 1804. In Europe and its colonies abroad, the age of modern politics was born. ■

Background to Revolution

FOCUS QUESTION

What were the factors leading to the revolutions of the late eighteenth century?

The origins of the late-eighteenth-century revolutions in British North America, France, and Haiti were complex. No one cause lay behind them, nor was revolution inevitable or certain of success. However, a set of shared factors helped set the stage for revolt. Among them were fundamental social and economic changes and political crises that eroded state authority. Another significant cause of revolutionary fervor was the impact of political ideas derived from the Enlightenment. Even though most Enlightenment writers were cautious about political reform, their confidence in reason and progress helped inspire a new generation to fight for greater freedom from repressive governments. Perhaps most important, financial crises generated by the expenses of imperial warfare brought European states to their knees and allowed abstract discussions of reform to become pressing realities.

Social Change

Eighteenth-century European society was legally divided into groups with special privileges, such as the nobility and the clergy, and groups with special burdens, such as the peasantry. Nobles were the largest landowners, possessing one-quarter of the agricultural land of France, while constituting less than 2 percent of the population. They enjoyed exemption from direct taxation as well as exclusive rights to hunt game, bear swords, and use gold thread in their clothing. In most countries, various middle-class groups—professionals, merchants, and guild masters—enjoyed privileges that allowed them to monopolize all sorts of economic activity. Poor peasants and urban laborers, who constituted the vast majority of the population, bore the brunt of taxation and were excluded from the world of privilege.

Traditional prerogatives persisted in societies undergoing dramatic and destabilizing change. Europe's population rose rapidly after 1750, and its cities and towns swelled in size. Inflation kept pace with population growth, making it ever more difficult to find affordable food and living space. One way the poor kept up, and even managed to participate in the new consumer revolution (see Chapter 18), was by working harder and for longer hours. More women and children entered the paid labor force, challenging the traditional hierarchies and customs of village life.

Economic growth created new inequalities between rich and poor. While the poor struggled with rising prices, investors grew rich from the spread of rural manufacture and overseas trade, including the trade in enslaved Africans and in the products of slave labor. Old distinctions between landed aristocracy and city merchants began to fade as enterprising nobles put money into trade and rising middle-class bureaucrats and merchants purchased landed estates and noble titles. Marriages between proud nobles and wealthy, educated commoners (called the *bourgeoisie* [boor-ZHWAH-zee] in France) served both groups' interests, and a mixed-caste elite began to take shape. In the context of these changes, ancient privileges seemed to pose an intolerable burden to many observers.

Another social change involved the racial regimes established in European colonies to legitimize and protect slavery. By the late eighteenth century European law accepted that only Africans and people of African descent were subject to slavery. Even free people of color—a term for nonslaves of African or mixed African-European descent—were subject to special laws restricting the property they could own, whom they could marry, and what clothes they could wear. Racial privilege conferred a new dimension of entitlement on European settlers in the colonies, and they used extremely brutal methods to enforce it. The contradiction between slavery and the Enlightenment ideals of liberty and equality was all too evident to the enslaved and the free people of color.

Growing Demands for Liberty and Equality

In addition to destabilizing social changes, the ideals of liberty and equality helped fuel revolutions in the Atlantic world. What did these concepts mean to eighteenth-century politicians and other people, and why were they so radical and revolutionary in their day?

The call for liberty was first of all a call for individual human rights. Before the revolutionary period, even the most enlightened monarchs believed they needed to regulate what people wrote and believed. Opposing this long-standing practice, supporters of the cause of individual liberty (who became known as "liberals" in the early nineteenth century) demanded freedom to worship according to the dictates of their consciences, an end to censorship, and freedom from arbitrary laws and from judges who simply obeyed orders from the government. The Declaration of the Rights of Man and of the Citizen, issued at the beginning of the French Revolution, proclaimed that "liberty consists in being able to do anything that does not harm another person." In the context of the monarchical and absolutist forms of government then dominating Europe, this was a truly radical idea.

The call for liberty was also a call for a new kind of government. Reformers believed that the people had sovereignty—that is, that the people alone had the authority to make laws limiting an individual's freedom of action. In practice, this system of government meant choosing legislators who represented the people and were accountable to them. Monarchs might retain their thrones, but their rule should be constrained by the will of the people.

Equality was a more ambiguous idea. Eighteenth-century liberals argued that, in theory, all citizens should have identical rights and liberties and that the nobility had no right to special privileges based on birth. However, they accepted a number of distinctions. First, most eighteenth-century liberals were men of their times, and they generally believed that equality between men and women was neither practical nor desirable. Women played an important political role in the revolutionary movements at several points, but the men who wrote constitutions for the new republics limited formal political rights—the right to vote, to run for office, and to participate in government—to men. Second, few questioned the superiority of people of European

Chronology

1775–1783	American Revolution
1786–1789	Height of French monarchy's financial crisis
1789	Ratification of U.S. Constitution; storming of the Bastille; feudalism abolished in France
1789–1799	French Revolution
1790	Burke publishes *Reflections on the Revolution in France*
1791	Slave insurrection in Saint-Domingue
1792	Wollstonecraft publishes *A Vindication of the Rights of Woman*
1793	Execution of Louis XVI
1793–1794	Robespierre's Reign of Terror
1794	Robespierre deposed and executed; France abolishes slavery in all territories
1794–1799	Thermidorian reaction
1799–1815	Napoleonic era
1804	Haitian republic declares independence
1812	Napoleon invades Russia
1814–1815	Napoleon defeated and exiled

descent over those of indigenous or African origin. Even those who believed that the slave trade was unjust and should be abolished usually felt that emancipation was so dangerous that it needed to be an extremely gradual process.

Third, liberals never believed that everyone should be equal economically. Although Thomas Jefferson wrote in an early draft of the American Declaration of Independence that everyone was equal in "the pursuit of property," liberals certainly did not expect equal success in that pursuit. (Jefferson later changed "property" to the more noble-sounding "happiness.") Great differences in fortune between rich and poor were perfectly acceptable. The essential point was that every free white male should have a legally equal chance at economic gain. However limited they appear to modern eyes, these demands for liberty and equality were revolutionary, given that a privileged elite had long existed with little opposition.

The two most important Enlightenment references for late-eighteenth-century liberals were John Locke and the baron de Montesquieu (see Chapter 16). Locke maintained that England's long political tradition rested on "the rights of Englishmen" and on representative government through Parliament. He argued that if a government oversteps its proper function of protecting the natural rights of life, liberty, and private property, it becomes a tyranny. Montesquieu was also inspired by English constitutional history and the Glorious Revolution of 1688–1689, which placed sovereignty in Parliament (see Chapter 15). He, too, believed that powerful "intermediary groups"—such as the judicial nobility of which he was a proud member—offered the best defense of liberty against despotism.

The belief that representative institutions could defend their liberty and interests appealed powerfully to the educated middle classes. Yet liberal ideas about individual rights and political freedom also appealed to members of the hereditary nobility, at least in western Europe and as formulated by Montesquieu. Representative government did not mean democracy, which liberal thinkers tended to equate with mob rule. Rather, they envisioned voting for representatives as being restricted to men who owned property—those with "a stake in society." The blurring of practical distinctions between landed aristocrats and wealthy commoners meant that there was no clear-cut opposition between nobles and non-nobles on political issues.

Revolutions thus began with aspirations for equality and liberty among the social elite. Soon, however, dissenting voices emerged as some revolutionaries became frustrated with the limitations of liberal notions of equality and liberty and clamored for a fuller realization of these concepts. Depending on location, their demands included universal male suffrage, political rights for women and free people of color, the emancipation of slaves, and government regulations to reduce economic inequality. The age of revolution was thus marked by bitter conflicts over how far reform should go and to whom it should apply.

The Seven Years' War

The roots of revolutionary ideas could be found in Enlightenment texts, but it was by no means inevitable that their ideas would result in revolution. Many members of the educated elite were satisfied with the status quo or too intimidated to challenge it. Instead, events—political, economic, and military—created crises that opened the door for the development of radical thought and action. One of the most important was the global conflict known as the Seven Years' War (1756–1763).

The war's battlefields stretched from central Europe to India to North America (where the conflict was known as the French and Indian War), pitting a new alliance of England and Prussia against the French, Austrians, and, later, Spanish. Its origins were in conflicts left unresolved at the end of the War of the Austrian Succession in 1748 (see Chapter 16), during which Prussia seized the Austrian territory of Silesia. In central Europe, Austria's Maria Theresa vowed to win back Silesia and to crush Prussia, thereby re-establishing the Habsburgs' traditional leadership in German affairs. By the end of the Seven Years' War, Maria Theresa had almost succeeded, but Prussia survived with its boundaries intact.

Unresolved tensions also lingered in North America, particularly regarding the border between the French and British colonies. The encroachment of English settlers into territory claimed by the French in the Ohio Valley resulted in skirmishes that soon became war. Although the inhabitants of New France were greatly outnumbered—Canada counted 55,000 inhabitants, compared to 1.2 million in the thirteen English colonies—French forces achieved major victories until 1758. Both sides relied on the participation of Native American tribes with whom they had long-standing trading contacts and actively sought new indigenous allies during the conflict. The tide of the conflict turned when the British diverted resources from the war in Europe, using superior sea power to destroy France's fleet and choke its commerce around the world. In 1759 the British laid siege to Quebec for four long months, finally defeating the French in a battle that sealed the nation's fate in North America.

British victory on all colonial fronts was ratified in the 1763 Treaty of Paris. Canada and all French territory east of the Mississippi River passed to Britain, and France ceded Louisiana to Spain as compensation for Spain's loss of Florida to Britain. France also gave up most of its holdings in India, opening the way to British dominance on the subcontinent (Map 19.1).

By 1763 Britain had realized its goal of monopolizing a vast trading and colonial empire, but at a tremendous cost in war debt. France emerged from the conflict humiliated and broke, but with its profitable Caribbean colonies intact. In the aftermath of war, both British and French governments had to raise taxes to repay loans, raising a storm of protest and demands for fundamental reform. Since the Caribbean colony of Saint-Domingue remained French, political turmoil in the mother country would directly affect its population. The seeds of revolutionary conflict in the Atlantic world were thus sown.

The American Revolutionary Era, 1775–1789

Increased taxes and government control were a crucial factor behind colonial protests in the New World, where the era of liberal political revolution began. After revolting against their home country, the thirteen mainland colonies of British North America succeeded in establishing a new unified government. Participants in the revolution believed they were demanding only the traditional rights of English men and women. But those traditional rights were liberal rights, and in the American context they had strong democratic and popular overtones. Thus the American Revolution was fought in the name of ideals that were still quite radical for their time. In founding a

FOCUS QUESTION
Why and how did American colonists forge a new, independent nation?

MAP 19.1 The Seven Years' War in Europe, North America, and India, 1755–1763   As a result of the war, France lost its vast territories in North America and India. In an effort to avoid costly conflicts with Native Americans living in the newly conquered territory, the British government in 1763 prohibited colonists from settling west of the Appalachian Mountains. One of the few remaining French colonies in the Americas, Saint-Domingue (on the island of Hispaniola) was the most profitable plantation colony in the New World.

government based on liberal principles, the Americans set an example that would have a forceful impact on France and its colonies. Yet the revolution did not resolve the question of social and political equality, which eluded the enslaved, women, free blacks, and indigenous people.

The Origins of the Revolution

The high cost of the Seven Years' War doubled the British national debt. Anticipating further expenses to defend the half a billion acres in new territory granted by the Treaty of Paris, the government in London imposed bold new administrative measures. Breaking with a tradition of loose colonial oversight, the British announced that they would maintain a large army in North America and tax the colonies directly.

In 1765 Parliament passed the Stamp Act, which levied taxes on a long list of commercial and legal documents, diplomas, newspapers, almanacs, and playing cards. A stamp glued to each article indicated that the tax had been paid.

These measures seemed perfectly reasonable to the British, for a much heavier stamp tax already existed in Britain, and proceeds from the tax were to fund the defense of the colonies. Nonetheless, the colonists vigorously protested the Stamp Act by rioting and by boycotting British goods. Thus Parliament reluctantly repealed it.

Another area of contention was settlement of the new territory acquired by the Treaty of Paris. At the end of the Seven Years' War, land-squeezed settlers quickly moved west across the Appalachian Mountains into the Ohio Valley, sparking conflict with the Ottawa and other tribes already present in the region as well as remaining French settlers. To prevent costly wars in distant territory, the British government in 1763 issued a royal proclamation prohibiting

Commemorative Teapot   Manufacturers were quick to bring products to the market celebrating weighty political events, like this British teapot heralding "Stamp Act Repeal'd." By purchasing such items, ordinary people could champion political causes of the day and bring public affairs into their private lives. (Made by the Cockhill Pit Factory, 1766/© Peabody Essex Museum, Salem, Massachusetts, USA/ Bridgeman Images)

colonists to settle west of the Appalachian Mountains. The so-called Proclamation Line did little to stem land speculation and the flow of migrants, but it did exacerbate suspicion and tensions between Britain and its colony. These disputes raised important political questions. To what extent could the British government reassert its power while limiting the authority of elected colonial bodies? Who had the right to make laws for Americans? The British government replied that Americans were represented in Parliament, albeit indirectly (like most British people), and that Parliament ruled throughout the empire. Many Americans felt otherwise. In the words of John Adams, a major proponent of colonial independence, "A Parliament of Great Britain can have no more rights to tax the colonies than a Parliament of Paris." Thus British colonial administration and parliamentary supremacy came to appear as unacceptable threats to existing American liberties.

Americans' resistance to these threats was fed by the great degree of independence they had long enjoyed. In British North America, unlike in England and Europe, no powerful established church existed, and religious freedom was taken for granted. Colonial assemblies made the important laws, which were seldom overturned by the British government. Also, the right to vote was much more widespread than in England. In many parts of colonial Massachusetts, for example, as many as 95 percent of adult males could vote.

Moreover, greater political equality was matched by greater social and economic equality, at least for the free white population. No hereditary nobility exercised privileges over peasants and other social groups. Instead, independent farmers dominated colonial society. This was particularly true in the northern colonies, where the revolution originated.

In 1773 disputes over taxes and representation flared up again. Under the Tea Act of that year, the British government permitted the financially hard-pressed East India Company to ship tea from China directly to its agents in the colonies, rather than through London middlemen, who sold to independent merchants in the colonies. Thus the company secured a profitable monopoly on the tea trade, and colonial merchants were excluded. The price on tea was actually lowered for colonists, but the act generated a great deal of opposition because of its impact on local merchants.

In protest, Boston men disguised as Native Americans staged a rowdy protest (later called the "Tea Party") by boarding East India Company ships and throwing tea from them into the harbor. In response, the so-called Coercive Acts of 1774 closed the port of Boston, curtailed local elections, and expanded the royal governor's power. County conventions in Massachusetts urged that the acts be "rejected as the attempts of a wicked administration to enslave America." Other colonial assemblies joined in the denunciations. In September 1774 the First Continental Congress—consisting of colonial delegates who sought at first to peacefully resolve conflicts with Britain—met in Philadelphia. The more radical members of this assembly argued successfully against concessions to the English crown. The British Parliament also rejected compromise, and in April 1775 fighting between colonial and British troops began at Lexington and Concord.

Independence from Britain

As fighting spread, the colonists moved slowly toward open calls for independence. The uncompromising attitude of the British government and its use of German mercenaries did much to dissolve loyalties to the home country and to unite the separate colonies. *Common Sense* (1775), a brilliant attack by the recently arrived English radical Thomas Paine (1737–1809), also mobilized public opinion in favor of independence. A runaway bestseller with sales of 120,000 copies in a few months, Paine's tract ridiculed the idea of a small island ruling a great continent. In his call for freedom and republican government, Paine expressed Americans' growing sense of separateness and moral superiority.

On July 4, 1776, the Second Continental Congress adopted the Declaration of Independence. Written by Thomas Jefferson and others, this document boldly listed the tyrannical acts committed by George III (r. 1760–1820) and confidently proclaimed the natural rights of mankind and the sovereignty of the American states. The Declaration of Independence in effect universalized the traditional rights of English people and made them the rights of all mankind. It stated that "all Men are created equal, that they are endowed by their Creator with certain unalienable Rights, that among these are Life, Liberty, and the Pursuit of Happiness." No other American political document has ever caused such excitement, either at home or abroad.

After the Declaration of Independence, the conflict often took the form of a civil war pitting patriots against Loyalists, those who maintained an allegiance to the Crown. The Loyalists, who numbered up to 20 percent of the total white population, tended to be wealthy and politically moderate. They were small in number in New England and Virginia, but more common in the Deep South and on the western frontier. British commanders also recruited Loyalists from enslaved people by promising freedom to any slave who left his master to fight for the mother country.

Many wealthy patriots—such as John Hancock and George Washington—willingly allied themselves with farmers and artisans in a broad coalition. This coalition harassed the Loyalists and confiscated their property to help pay for the war, causing 60,000 to 80,000 of them to flee, mostly to Canada. The broad social base of the revolutionaries tended to make the revolution democratic. State governments extended the right to vote to many more men, including free African American men in many cases, but not to women.

On the international scene, the French wanted revenge against the British for the humiliating defeats of the Seven Years' War. Thus they sympathized with the rebels and supplied guns and gunpowder from the beginning of the conflict. By 1777 French volunteers were arriving in Virginia, and a dashing young nobleman, the marquis de Lafayette (1757–1834), quickly became one of the most trusted generals of George Washington, who was commanding American troops. In 1778 the French government offered a formal alliance to the American ambassador in Paris, Benjamin Franklin, and in 1779 and 1780 the Spanish and Dutch declared war on Britain. Catherine the Great of Russia helped organize the League of Armed Neutrality to protect neutral shipping rights and succeeded in hampering Britain's naval power.

Thus by 1780 Britain was engaged in a war against most of Europe as well as the thirteen colonies. In these circumstances, and in the face of severe reverses in India, in the West Indies, and at Yorktown in Virginia, a new British government decided to cut its losses and end the war. American officials in Paris were receptive to negotiating a deal with England alone, for they feared that France wanted a treaty that would bottle up the new nation east of the Appalachian Mountains and give British holdings west of the Appalachians to France's ally, Spain. Thus the American negotiators deserted their French allies and accepted the extraordinarily favorable terms Britain offered.

Under the Treaty of Paris of 1783, Britain recognized the independence of the thirteen colonies and ceded all its territory between the Allegheny Mountains and the Mississippi River to the Americans. Out of the bitter rivalries of the Old World, the Americans snatched dominion over a vast territory.

Framing the Constitution

The liberal program of the American Revolution was consolidated by the federal Constitution, the Bill of Rights, and the creation of a national republic. Assembling in Philadelphia in the summer of 1787, the delegates to the Constitutional Convention were determined to end the period of economic depression, social uncertainty, and leadership under a weak central government that had followed independence. The delegates thus decided to grant the federal, or central, government important powers: regulation of domestic and foreign trade, the right to tax, and the means to enforce its laws.

Strong rule would be placed squarely in the context of representative self-government. Senators and congressmen would be the lawmaking delegates of the voters, and the president of the republic would be an elected official. The central government would operate in Montesquieu's framework of checks and balances, under which authority was distributed across three different branches—the executive, legislative, and judicial branches—that would prevent one interest from gaining too much power. The power of the federal government would in turn be checked by that of the individual states.

When the results of the Constitutional Convention were presented to the states for ratification, a great public debate began. The opponents of the proposed Constitution—the Antifederalists—charged that the framers of the new document had taken too much power from the individual states and made the federal government too strong. Moreover, many Antifederalists feared for the individual freedoms for which they had fought. To overcome these objections, the Federalists promised to spell out these basic freedoms as soon as the new Constitution was adopted. The result was the first ten amendments to the Constitution, which the first Congress passed shortly after it met in New York in March 1789. These amendments, ratified in 1791, formed an effective Bill of Rights to safeguard the individual. Most of them—trial by jury, due process of law, the right to assemble, freedom from unreasonable search—had their origins in English law and the English Bill of Rights of 1689. Other rights—the freedoms of speech, the press, and religion—reflected natural-law theory and the strong value colonists had placed on independence from the start.

Limitations of Liberty and Equality

The American Constitution and the Bill of Rights exemplified the strengths and the limits of what came to be called classical liberalism. Liberty meant individual freedoms and political safeguards. Liberty also meant representative government, but it did not mean democracy, with its principle of one person, one vote. Equality meant equality before the law, not equality of political participation or wealth. It did not mean equal rights for slaves, indigenous peoples, or women.

A vigorous abolitionist movement during the 1780s led to the passage of emancipation laws in all northern states, but slavery remained prevalent in the South, and discord between pro- and antislavery delegates roiled the Constitutional Convention of 1787. The result was a compromise stipulating that an enslaved person would count as three-fifths of a person in tallying population numbers for taxation and proportional representation in the House of Representatives. This solution levied higher taxes on the South, but also guaranteed slaveholding states greater representation in Congress, which they used to oppose emancipation. Congress did ban slavery in federal territory in 1789, then the export of slaves from any state, and finally, in 1808, the import of slaves to any state.

The new republic also failed to protect the Native American tribes whose lands fell within or alongside the territory ceded by Britain at the Treaty of Paris. The 1787 Constitution promised protection to Native Americans and guaranteed that their land would not be taken without consent. Nonetheless, the federal government forced tribes to concede their land for meager returns; state governments and the rapidly expanding population paid even less heed to the Constitution and often simply seized Native American land for new settlements.

Although lacking the voting rights enjoyed by so many of their husbands and fathers in the relatively democratic colonial assemblies, women played a vital role in the American Revolution. As household provisioners, women were essential

Abigail Adams, "Remember the Ladies"

Abigail Adams wrote many letters to her husband, John Adams, during the long years of separation imposed by his political career. In March 1776 he was serving in the Continental Congress in Philadelphia as Abigail and their children experienced the British siege of Boston and a smallpox epidemic. This letter, written from the family farm in Braintree, Massachusetts, combines news from home with pressing questions about the military and political situation, and a call to "Remember the Ladies" when drafting a new constitution.

March 31, 1776

I wish you would ever write me a Letter half as long as I write you; and tell me if you may where your Fleet are gone? What sort of Defence Virginia can make against our common Enemy? Whether it is so situated as to make an able Defence? . . .

Do not you want to see Boston; I am fearful of the smallpox, or I should have been in before this time. I got Mr. Crane to go to our House and see what state it was in. I find it has been occupied by one of the Doctors of a Regiment, very dirty, but no other damage has been done to it. The few things which were left in it are all gone. . . .

I feel very differently at the approach of spring to what I did a month ago. We knew not then whether we could plant or sow with safety, whether when we had toiled we could reap the fruits of our own industry, whether we could rest in our own Cottages, or whether we should not be driven from the sea coasts to seek shelter in the wilderness, but now we feel as if we might sit under our own vine and eat the good of the land. . . .

I long to hear that you have declared an independency — and by the way in the new Code of Laws which I suppose it will be necessary for you to make I desire you would

Remember the Ladies, and be more generous and favorable to them than your ancestors. Do not put such unlimited power in the hands of the Husbands. Remember all men would be tyrants if they could. If particular care and attention is not paid to the Ladies we are determined to foment a Rebellion, and will not hold ourselves bound by any Laws in which we have no voice, or Representation.

That your Sex are Naturally Tyrannical is a Truth so thoroughly established as to admit of no dispute, but such of you as wish to be happy willingly give up the harsh title of Master for the more tender and endearing one of Friend. Why then, not put it out of the power of the vicious and the Lawless to use us with cruelty and indignity with impunity. Men of Sense in all Ages abhor those customs which treat us only as the vassals of your Sex. Regard us then as beings placed by providence under your protection and in imitation of the Supreme Being make use of that power only for our happiness.

EVALUATE THE EVIDENCE

1. What does Adams's letter suggest about her relationship with her husband and the role of women in the family in this period?
2. What does Adams's letter tell us about what it was like to live through the American Revolution and how a woman might perceive the new liberties demanded by colonists?

Source: Letter from Abigail Adams to John Adams, 31 March–5 April 1776 (electronic edition), *Adams Family Papers: An Electronic Archive*, Massachusetts Historical Society, http://www.masshist.org/digitaladams/. Used by permission.

participants in boycotts of British goods, like tea, which squeezed profits from British merchants and fostered the revolutionary spirit. After the outbreak of war, women raised funds for the Continental Army and took care of homesteads, workshops, and other businesses when their men went off to fight. Yet despite Abigail Adams's plea to her husband, John Adams, that the framers of the Declaration of Independence should "remember the ladies," women did not receive the right to vote in the new Constitution, an omission confirmed by a clause added in 1844. (See "Evaluating the Evidence 19.1: Abigail Adams, 'Remember the Ladies,'" above.)

Revolution in France, 1789–1791

FOCUS QUESTION

How did the events of 1789 result in a constitutional monarchy in France, and what were the consequences?

No country felt the consequences of the American Revolution more deeply than France. Hundreds of French officers served in America and were inspired by the experience. The most famous of these, the young and impressionable marquis de Lafayette, left home as a great aristocrat determined to fight France's traditional foe, England. He returned with a love of liberty and firm republican convictions. French intellectuals engaged in passionate analysis of the federal Constitution as well as the constitutions of the various states of the new United States. The American Revolution undeniably fueled dissatisfaction with the old monarchical order in France. Yet the French Revolution did not mirror the American example. It was more radical and more complex, more influential and more controversial, more loved and more hated. For Europeans and most of the rest of the world, it was the great revolution of the eighteenth century, the revolution that opened the modern era in politics.

Breakdown of the Old Order

As did the American Revolution, the French Revolution had its immediate origins in the government's financial difficulties. The efforts of the ministers of King Louis XV (r. 1715–1774) to raise taxes to meet the expenses of the War of the Austrian Succession and the Seven Years' War were thwarted by the high courts, known as the parlements. The noble judges of the parlements resented the Crown's threat to their exemption from taxation and decried the government's actions as a form of royal despotism.

When renewed efforts to reform the tax system similarly failed in 1776, the government was forced to finance its enormous expenditures during the American war with borrowed money. As a result, the national debt soared. In 1786 the finance minister informed the timid king Louis XVI that the nation was on the verge of bankruptcy. Fully 50 percent of France's annual budget went to interest payments on the ever-increasing debt. Another 25 percent went to maintain the military, while 6 percent was absorbed by the royal family and the court at Versailles. Less than 20 percent of the national budget served the productive functions of the state, such as transportation and general administration.

Unlike England, which had a far larger national debt relative to its population, France had no central bank and no paper currency. Therefore, when a depressed economy and a lack of public confidence made it increasingly difficult for the government to obtain new loans, the government could not respond simply by printing more money. It had no alternative but to try increasing taxes. Because France's tax system was unfair and out-of-date, increased revenues were possible only through fundamental reforms. Such reforms, which would affect all groups in France's complex and fragmented society, were guaranteed to create social and political unrest.

Financial crisis struck a monarchy that had lost much of its mantle of royal authority. Louis XV scandalized the country with a series of mistresses of low social origins. To make things worse, he refused to take communion because his adultery placed him in a state of sin. The king was being stripped of the sacred aura of God's anointed on earth (a process called desacralization) and was being reinvented in the popular imagination as a degenerate. Maneuverings among political factions at court further distracted the king and prevented decisive action from his government.

Despite the progressive desacralization of the monarchy, Louis XV would probably have prevailed had he lived longer, but he died in 1774. The new king, Louis XVI (r. 1774–1792), was a shy twenty-year-old with good intentions. Taking the throne, he is reported to have said, "What I should like most is to be loved."[1] The eager-to-please monarch Louis waffled on political reform and the economy, and proved unable to quell the rising storm of opposition.

The Formation of the National Assembly

Spurred by a depressed economy and falling tax receipts, Louis XVI's minister of finance revived old proposals to impose a general tax on all landed property as well as to form provincial assemblies to help administer the tax, and he convinced the king to call an assembly of notables in 1787 to gain support for the idea. The assembled notables, mainly aristocrats and high-ranking clergy, declared that such sweeping tax changes required the approval of the **Estates General**, the representative body of all three estates, which had not met since 1614.

Facing imminent bankruptcy, the king tried to reassert his authority. He dismissed the notables and established new taxes by decree. The judges of the Parlement of Paris promptly declared the royal initiative null and void. When the king tried to exile the judges, a tremendous wave of protest swept the country. Frightened investors refused to advance more loans to the state. Finally in July 1788, a beaten Louis XVI bowed to public opinion and called for the Estates General. Absolute monarchy was collapsing.

As its name indicates, the Estates General was a legislative body with representatives from the three orders, or **estates**, of society: the clergy, nobility, and everyone else. Following centuries-old tradition, each estate met separately to elect delegates, first at a local and then at a regional level. Results of the elections reveal the mind-set of each estate on the eve of the Revolution. The local assemblies of the clergy, representing the first estate, elected mostly parish priests rather than church leaders, demonstrating their dissatisfaction with the church hierarchy. The nobility, or second estate, voted in a majority of conservatives, primarily from the provinces, where nobles were less wealthy, more devout, and more numerous. Nonetheless, fully one-third of noble representatives were liberals committed to major changes. Commoners

Estates General A legislative body in prerevolutionary France made up of representatives of each of the three classes, or estates. It was called into session in 1789 for the first time since 1614.

estates The three legal categories, or orders, of France's inhabitants: the clergy, the nobility, and everyone else.

The Awakening of the Third Estate
This cartoon from July 1789 represents the third estate as a common man throwing off his chains and rising up against his oppression, as the first estate (the clergy) and the second estate (the nobility) look on in fear. (*The Awakening of the Third Estate, July 1789*/French School/colored engraving/Musée de la Ville de Paris, Musée Carnavalet, Paris, France/Bridgeman Images)

Abbé Sieyès, *What Is the Third Estate?*

In the flood of pamphlets that appeared after Louis XVI's call for a meeting of the Estates General, the most influential was written in 1789 by a Catholic priest named Emmanuel Joseph Sieyès. In "What Is the Third Estate?" the abbé Sieyès vigorously condemned the system of privilege that lay at the heart of French society. The term privilege *combined the Latin words for "private" and "law." In Old Regime France, no one set of laws applied to all; over time, the monarchy had issued a series of particular laws, or privileges, that enshrined special rights and entitlements for select individuals and groups. Noble privileges were among the weightiest.*

Sieyès rejected this entire system of legal and social inequality. Deriding the nobility as a foreign parasite, he argued that the common people of the third estate, who did most of the work and paid most of the taxes, constituted the true nation. His pamphlet galvanized public opinion and played an important role in convincing representatives of the third estate to proclaim themselves a "National Assembly" in June 1789. Sieyès later helped bring Napoleon Bonaparte to power, abandoning the radicalism of 1789 for an authoritarian regime.

1. What is the Third Estate? Everything.
2. What has it been until now in the political order? Nothing.
3. What does it want? To become something.
   . . . What is a Nation? A body of associates living under a *common* law and represented by the same *legislature*.

Is it not more than certain that the noble order has privileges, exemptions, and even rights that are distinct from the rights of the great body of citizens? Because of this, it [the noble order] does not belong to the common order, it is not covered by the law common to the rest. Thus its civil rights already make it a people apart inside the great Nation. It is truly *imperium in imperio* [a law unto itself].

As for its *political* rights, the nobility also exercises them separately. It has its own representatives who have no mandate from the people. Its deputies sit separately, and even when they assemble in the same room with the deputies of the ordinary citizens, the nobility's representation still remains essentially distinct and separate: it is foreign to the Nation by its very principle, for its mission does not emanate from the people, and by its purpose, since it consists in defending, not the general interest, but the private interests of the nobility.

The Third Estate therefore contains everything that pertains to the Nation and nobody outside of the Third Estate can claim to be part of the Nation. What is the Third Estate? EVERYTHING. . . .

By Third Estate is meant the collectivity of citizens who belong to the common order. Anybody who holds a legal privilege of any kind leaves that common order, stands as an exception to the common law, and in consequence does not belong to the Third Estate. . . . It is certain that the moment a citizen acquires privileges contrary to common law, he no longer belongs to the common order. His new interest is opposed to the general interest; he has no right to vote in the name of the people. . . .

In vain can anyone's eyes be closed to the revolution that time and the force of things have brought to pass; it is none

of the third estate, who constituted over 95 percent of the population, elected primarily lawyers and government officials to represent them, with few delegates representing business and the poor.

The petitions for change drafted by the assemblies showed a surprising degree of consensus about the key issues confronting the realm. In all three estates, voices spoke in favor of replacing absolutism with a constitutional monarchy in which laws and taxes would require the consent of the Estates General in regular meetings. There was also the strong feeling that individual liberties would have to be guaranteed by law and that economic regulations should be loosened.

On May 5, 1789, the twelve hundred delegates of the three estates gathered in Versailles for the opening session of the Estates General. Despite widespread hopes for serious reform, the Estates General quickly deadlocked over the issue of voting procedures. Controversy had begun during the electoral process itself, the less real. Once upon a time the Third Estate was in bondage and the noble order was everything that mattered. Today the Third is everything and nobility but a word. Yet under the cover of this word a new and intolerable aristocracy has slipped in, and the people has every reason to no longer want aristocrats. . . .

What is the will of a Nation? It is the result of individual wills, just as the Nation is the aggregate of the individuals who compose it. It is impossible to conceive of a legitimate association that does not have for its goal the common security, the common liberty, in short, the public good. No doubt each individual also has his own personal aims. He says to himself, "protected by the common security, I will be able to peacefully pursue my own personal projects, I will seek my happiness where I will, assured of encountering only those legal obstacles that society will prescribe for the common interest, in which I have a part, and with which my own personal interest is so usefully allied." . . .

Advantages which differentiate citizens from one another lie outside the purview of citizenship. Inequalities of wealth or ability are like the inequalities of age, sex, size, etc. In no way do they detract from the *equality* of citizenship. These individual advantages no doubt benefit from the protection of the law; but it is not the legislator's task to create them, to give privileges to some and refuse them to others. The law grants nothing; it protects what already exists until such time that what exists begins to harm the common interest. These are the only limits on individual freedom. I imagine the law as being at the center of a large globe; we the citizens without exception, stand equidistant from it on the surface and occupy equal places; all are equally dependent on the law, all present it with their liberty and their property to be protected; and this is what I call the *common rights of citizens*, by which they are all alike. All these individuals communicate with each other, enter into contracts, negotiate, always under the common guarantee of the law. If in this general activity somebody wishes to get control over the person of his neighbor or usurp his property, the common law goes into action to repress this criminal attempt and puts everyone back in their place at the same distance from the law. . . .

It is impossible to say what place the two privileged orders [the clergy and the nobility] ought to occupy in the social order: this is the equivalent of asking what place one wishes to assign to a malignant tumor that torments and undermines the strength of the body of a sick person. It must be *neutralized*. We must re-establish the health and working of all organs so thoroughly that they are no longer susceptible to these fatal schemes that are capable of sapping the most essential principles of vitality.

EVALUATE THE EVIDENCE

1. What criticism of noble privileges does Sieyès offer? Why does he believe nobles are "foreign" to the nation?
2. How does Sieyès define the nation, and why does he believe that the third estate constitutes the nation?
3. What relationship between citizens and the law does Sieyès envision? What limitations on the law does he propose?

Source: Excerpt from pp. 65–70 in *The French Revolution and Human Rights: A Brief Documentary History*, edited, translated, and with an introduction by Lynn Hunt. Copyright © 1996 by Bedford Books of St. Martin's Press. Used by permission of the publisher.

when the government confirmed that, following precedent, each estate should meet and vote separately. During the lead-up to the Estates General, critics had demanded a single assembly dominated by the third estate. In his famous pamphlet *What Is the Third Estate?* the abbé Emmanuel Joseph Sieyès (himself a member of the first estate) argued that the nobility was a tiny, overprivileged minority and that the third estate constituted the true strength of the French nation. (See "Evaluating the Evidence 19.2: Abbé Sieyès, *What Is the Third Estate?*" above.) The government granted the third estate as many delegates as the clergy and the nobility combined, but then nullified the reform by granting one vote per estate instead of one vote per person. This meant that the two privileged estates could always outvote the third.

In angry response, in June 1789 delegates of the third estate refused to meet until the king ordered the clergy and nobility to sit with them in a single body. On June 17 the third estate, which had been joined by a few parish priests, voted to call itself the **National Assembly**. On June 20, excluded from their hall because of "repairs," the delegates moved to a large indoor tennis court where they swore the famous Tennis Court Oath, pledging not to disband until they had been recognized as a national assembly and had written a new constitution.

The king's response was disastrously ambivalent. On June 23 he made a conciliatory speech urging reforms, and four days later he ordered the three estates to meet together. At the same time, Louis apparently followed the advice of relatives and court nobles who urged him to dissolve the Assembly by force. The king called an army of eighteen thousand troops toward the capital to bring the delegates under control, and on July 11 he dismissed his finance minister and other more liberal ministers. It appeared that the monarchy was prepared to use violence to restore its control.

Popular Uprising and the Rights of Man

While delegates at Versailles were pressing for political rights, economic hardship gripped the common people. Conditions were already tough, due to the government's disastrous financial situation. A poor grain harvest in 1788 caused the price of bread to soar, and inflation spread quickly through the economy. As a result, demand for manufactured goods collapsed, and many artisans and small traders lost work. In Paris perhaps 150,000 of the city's 600,000 people were unemployed by July 1789.

Against this background of poverty and political crisis, the people of Paris entered decisively onto the revolutionary stage. They believed that, to survive, they should have steady work and enough bread at fair prices. They also feared that the dismissal of the king's liberal finance minister would put them at the mercy of aristocratic landowners and grain speculators. At the beginning of July, knowledge spread of the massing of troops near Paris. On July 14, 1789, several hundred people stormed the Bastille (ba-STEEL), a royal prison, to obtain weapons for the city's defense. Faced with popular violence, Louis soon announced the reinstatement of his finance minister and the withdrawal of troops from Paris. The National Assembly was now free to continue its work.

Just as the laboring poor of Paris had decisively intervened in the Revolution, the struggling French peasantry also took matters into their own hands. Peasants bore the brunt of state taxation, church tithes, and noble privileges. Since most did not own enough land to be self-sufficient, they were hard-hit by the rising price of bread. In the summer of 1789, throughout France peasants began to rise in insurrection against their lords, ransacking manor houses and burning feudal documents that recorded their obligations. In some areas peasants reoccupied common lands enclosed by landowners and seized forests. Fear of marauders and vagabonds hired by vengeful landlords—called the **Great Fear** by contemporaries—seized the rural poor and fanned the flames of rebellion.

Faced with chaos, the National Assembly responded to the swell of popular uprising with a surprise maneuver on the night of August 4, 1789. By a decree of the Assembly, all the old noble privileges—peasant serfdom where it still existed,

National Assembly The first French revolutionary legislature, made up primarily of representatives of the third estate and a few from the nobility and clergy, in session from 1789 to 1791.

The Great Fear, 1789

Great Fear The fear of noble reprisals against peasant uprisings that seized the French countryside and led to further revolt.

exclusive hunting rights, fees for having legal cases judged in the lord's court, the right to make peasants work on the roads, and a host of other dues — were abolished along with the tithes paid to the church. From this point on, French peasants would seek mainly to protect and consolidate this victory.

On August 27, 1789, the Assembly further issued the Declaration of the Rights of Man and of the Citizen. This clarion call of the liberal revolutionary ideal guaranteed equality before the law, representative government for a sovereign people, and individual freedom. This revolutionary credo, only two pages long, was disseminated throughout France and the rest of Europe and around the world.

The National Assembly's declaration had little practical effect for the poor and hungry people of France. The economic crisis worsened after the fall of the Bastille, as aristocrats fled the country and the luxury market collapsed. Foreign markets also shrank, and unemployment among the urban working classes grew. In addition, women — the traditional managers of food and resources in poor homes — could no longer look to the church, which had been stripped of its tithes, for aid.

On October 5 some seven thousand women marched the twelve miles from Paris to Versailles to demand action. This great crowd, "armed with scythes, sticks and pikes," invaded the National Assembly. Interrupting a delegate's speech, an old woman defiantly shouted into the debate, "Who's that talking down there? Make the chatterbox shut up. That's not the point: the point is that we want bread."[2] Hers was the genuine voice of the people, essential to any understanding of the French Revolution. The women invaded the royal apartments, killed some of the royal bodyguards, and searched for the queen, Marie Antoinette, who was widely despised for her frivolous and supposedly immoral behavior. It seems likely that only the intervention of Lafayette and the National Guard saved the royal family. But the only way to calm the disorder was for the king to live closer to his people in Paris, as the crowd demanded.

The Women of Paris March to Versailles
On October 5, 1789, thousands of poor Parisian women marched to Versailles to protest the price of bread. For the common people, the king was the baker of last resort, responsible for feeding his people during times of scarcity. The image of a set of scales one woman holds aloft (along with a loaf of bread stuck on the tip of her pike) symbolizes the crowd's desire for justice and for bread to be sold at the same price per pound as it always had been. The women forced the royal family to return with them to live in Paris, rather than remain isolated from their subjects at court. (*The Women's March on Versailles in October 1789*, 18th-century French print/DEA/Gianni Dagli Orti/Getty Images)

Liberal elites brought the Revolution into being and continued to lead politics. Yet the people of France were now roused and would henceforth play a crucial role in the unfolding of events.

A Constitutional Monarchy and Its Challenges

The day after the women's march on Versailles, the National Assembly followed the king to Paris, and the next two years, until September 1791, saw the consolidation of the liberal revolution. In June 1790 the National Assembly abolished the nobility, and in July the king swore to uphold the as-yet-unwritten constitution, effectively enshrining a constitutional monarchy. The king remained the head of state, but all lawmaking power now resided in the National Assembly, elected by French males who possessed a set amount of property, comprising roughly half the male population. The constitution passed in September 1791 was the first in French history. It legalized divorce and broadened women's rights to inherit property and to obtain financial support for illegitimate children from fathers, but excluded women from political office and voting.

This decision was attacked by a small number of men and women who believed that the rights of man should be extended to all French citizens. Politically active women wrote pamphlets, formed clubs, and petitioned the assembly on behalf of women's right to participate in the life of the nation. Olympe de Gouges (1748–1793), a self-taught writer and woman of the people, protested the evils of slavery as well as the injustices done to women. In September 1791 she published her *Declaration of the Rights of Woman*. This pamphlet echoed its famous predecessor, the Declaration of the Rights of Man and of the Citizen, proclaiming, "Woman is born free and remains equal to man in rights." De Gouges's position found little sympathy among leaders of the Revolution, however.

In addition to ruling on women's rights, the National Assembly replaced the complicated patchwork of historic provinces with eighty-three departments of approximately equal size, a move toward more rational and systematic methods of administration. In the name of economic liberty, the deputies prohibited guilds and workers' associations, and abolished internal customs fees. Thus the National Assembly applied the spirit of the Enlightenment in a thorough reform of France's laws and institutions.

The National Assembly also imposed a radical reorganization on religious life. The Assembly granted religious freedom to the small minority of French Protestants and Jews. In November 1789 it nationalized the property of the Catholic Church and abolished monasteries. The government used all former church property as collateral to guarantee a new paper currency, the assignats (A-sihg-nat), and then sold the property in an attempt to put the state's finances on a solid footing.

Imbued with the rationalism and skepticism of the eighteenth-century Enlightenment, many delegates distrusted popular piety and "superstitious religion." Thus in July 1790, with the Civil Constitution of the Clergy, they established a national church with priests chosen by voters. The National Assembly then forced the Catholic clergy to take an oath of loyalty to the new government. The pope formally condemned this measure, and only half the priests of France swore the oath. Many sincere Christians, especially those in the countryside, were appalled by these changes in the religious order.

World War and Republican France, 1791–1799

When Louis XVI accepted the National Assembly's constitution in September 1791, a young provincial lawyer and delegate named Maximilien Robespierre (1758–1794) concluded that "the Revolution is over." Robespierre was right in the sense that the most constructive and lasting reforms were in place. Yet he was wrong in suggesting that turmoil had ended, for a much more radical stage lay ahead, one that would bring war with foreign powers, the declaration of terror at home, and a transformation in France's government.

FOCUS QUESTION

Why and how did the French Revolution take a radical turn entailing terror at home and war with European powers?

The International Response

The outbreak of revolution in France produced great excitement and a sharp division of opinion in Europe and the United States. On the one hand, liberals and radicals saw a mighty triumph of liberty over despotism. On the other hand, conservative leaders such as British statesman Edmund Burke (1729–1797) were intensely troubled. In 1790 Burke published *Reflections on the Revolution in France*, in which he defended inherited privileges. He glorified Britain's unrepresentative Parliament and predicted that reform like that occurring in France would lead only to chaos and tyranny.

One passionate rebuttal came from a young writer in London, Mary Wollstonecraft (1759–1797). Incensed by Burke's book, Wollstonecraft (WOOL-stuhn-kraft) wrote a blistering attack, *A Vindication of the Rights of Man* (1790). Two years later, she published her masterpiece, *A Vindication of the Rights of Woman* (1792). Like de Gouges in France, Wollstonecraft demanded equal rights for women. She also advocated coeducation out of the belief that it would make women better wives and mothers, good citizens, and economically independent. Considered very radical for the time, the book became a founding text of the feminist movement.

The kings and nobles of continental Europe, who had at first welcomed the Revolution in France as weakening a competing power, now feared its impact. In June 1791 the royal family was arrested after a failed attempt to escape France. To supporters of the Revolution, the attempted flight was proof that the king was treacherously seeking foreign support for an invasion of France. To the monarchs of Austria and Prussia, the arrest of a crowned monarch was unacceptable. Two months later they issued the Declaration of Pillnitz, proclaiming their willingness to intervene in France to restore Louis XVI's rule if necessary. But the crowned heads of Europe misjudged the situation. The new French representative body, called the Legislative Assembly, that convened in October 1791 had new delegates and a different character. Although the delegates were still prosperous, well-educated middle-class men, they were younger and less cautious than their predecessors. Since the National Assembly had declared sitting deputies ineligible for re-election, none of them had previously served as national representatives. Many of them belonged to the political **Jacobin Club**. Such clubs had proliferated in Parisian neighborhoods since the beginning of the Revolution, drawing men and women to debate the political issues of the day.

Jacobins and other deputies reacted with patriotic fury to the Declaration of Pillnitz. They said that if the kings of Europe were attempting to incite war against

Jacobin Club A political club in revolutionary France whose members were well-educated radical republicans.

France, then "we will incite a war of people against kings. . . . Ten million Frenchmen, kindled by the fire of liberty, armed with the sword, with reason, with eloquence would be able to change the face of the world and make the tyrants tremble on their thrones."[3] In April 1792 France declared war on Francis II of Austria, the Habsburg monarch.

France's crusade against tyranny went poorly at first. Prussia joined Austria against the French, who broke and fled at their first military encounter with this First Coalition of foreign powers united against the Revolution. On behalf of the crowns of Austria and Prussia, the duke of Brunswick, commander of the coalition armies, issued a declaration threatening to destroy Paris if harm came to the royal family. The Legislative Assembly declared the country in danger, and volunteers rallied to the capital. The Brunswick manifesto heightened suspicion of treason on the part of the French king and queen. On August 10, 1792, a revolutionary crowd attacked the royal palace at the Tuileries (TWEE-luh-reez), while the royal family fled to the Legislative Assembly. Rather than offering refuge, the Assembly suspended the king from all his functions, imprisoned him, and called for a constitutional assembly to be elected by universal male suffrage.

The Second Revolution and the New Republic

The fall of the monarchy marked a radicalization of the Revolution, a phase that historians often call the **second revolution**. Louis's imprisonment was followed by the September Massacres. Fearing invasion by the Prussians and riled up by rumors that counter-revolutionaries would aid the invaders, angry crowds stormed the prisons and killed jailed priests and aristocrats. In late September 1792 the new, popularly elected National Convention, which replaced the Legislative Assembly, proclaimed France a republic, a nation in which the people, instead of a monarch, held sovereign power.

As with the Legislative Assembly, many members of the new National Convention belonged to the Jacobin Club of Paris. But the Jacobins themselves were increasingly divided into two bitterly opposed groups — the **Girondists** (juh-RAHN-dihsts) and **the Mountain**, led by Robespierre and another young lawyer, Georges Jacques Danton.

This division emerged clearly after the National Convention overwhelmingly convicted Louis XVI of treason. The Girondists accepted his guilt but did not wish to put the king to death. By a narrow majority, the Mountain carried the day, and Louis was executed on January 21, 1793, by guillotine, which the French had recently perfected. Marie Antoinette suffered the same fate later that year. But both the Girondists and the Mountain were determined to continue the "war against tyranny." The Prussians had been stopped at the Battle of Valmy on September 20, 1792, one day before the republic was proclaimed. French armies then invaded Savoy and captured Nice, moved into the German Rhineland, and by November 1792 were occupying the entire Austrian Netherlands (modern Belgium).

Everywhere they went, French armies of occupation chased princes, abolished feudalism, and found support among some peasants and middle-class people. But French armies also lived off the land, requisitioning food and supplies and plundering local treasures. The liberators therefore looked increasingly like foreign

second revolution From 1792 to 1795, the second phase of the French Revolution, during which the fall of the French monarchy introduced a rapid radicalization of politics.

Girondists A moderate group that fought for control of the French National Convention in 1793.

the Mountain Led by Robespierre, the French National Convention's radical faction, which seized legislative power in 1793.

invaders. Meanwhile, international tensions mounted. In February 1793 the National Convention, at war with Austria and Prussia, declared war on Britain, the Dutch Republic, and Spain as well. Republican France was now at war with almost all of Europe.

Groups within France added to the turmoil. Peasants in western France revolted against being drafted into the army, with the Vendée region of Brittany emerging as the epicenter of revolt. Devout Catholics, royalists, and foreign agents encouraged their rebellion, and the counter-revolutionaries recruited veritable armies to fight for their cause.

In March 1793 the National Convention was locked in a life-and-death political struggle between members of the Mountain and the more moderate Girondists. With the middle-class delegates so bitterly divided, the people of Paris once again emerged as the decisive political factor. The laboring poor and the petty traders were often known as the **sans-culottes** because their men wore trousers instead of the knee breeches of the aristocracy and the solid middle class. (See "Evaluating the Evidence 19.3: Contrasting Visions of the Sans-Culottes," page 630.) They demanded radical political action to defend the Revolution. The Mountain, sensing an opportunity to outmaneuver the Girondists, joined with sans-culottes activists to engineer a popular uprising. On June 2, 1793, armed sans-culottes invaded the Convention and forced its deputies to arrest twenty-nine Girondist deputies for treason. All power passed to the Mountain.

The Convention also formed the Committee of Public Safety in April 1793 to deal with threats from within and outside France. The Committee, led by Robespierre, held dictatorial power, allowing it to use whatever force necessary to defend the Revolution. Moderates in leading provincial cities revolted against the Committee's power and demanded a decentralized government. Counter-revolutionary forces in the Vendée won significant victories, and the republic's armies were driven back on all fronts. By July 1793 only the areas around Paris and on the eastern frontier were firmly held by the central government. Defeat seemed imminent.

Areas of Insurrection, 1793

sans-culottes The laboring poor of Paris, so called because the men wore trousers instead of the knee breeches of the aristocracy and middle class; the word came to refer to the militant radicals of the city.

Total War and the Terror

A year later, in July 1794, the central government had reasserted control over the provinces, and the Austrian Netherlands and the Rhineland were once again in French hands. This remarkable change of fortune was due to the revolutionary government's success in harnessing the explosive forces of a planned economy, revolutionary terror, and modern nationalism in a total war effort.

Robespierre and the Committee of Public Safety advanced on several fronts in 1793 and 1794, seeking to impose republican unity across the nation. First, they collaborated with the sans-culottes, who continued pressing the common people's case for fair prices and a moral economic order. Thus in September 1793 Robespierre and his coworkers established a planned economy with egalitarian social overtones. Rather than let supply and demand determine prices, the government set maximum prices for key products. Though the state was too weak to enforce all its price regulations, it did fix the price of bread in Paris at levels the poor could afford.

The people were also put to work, producing arms, munitions, uniforms, boots, saddles, and other necessary supplies for the war effort. The government told craftsmen

Contrasting Visions of the Sans-Culottes

These two images offer profoundly different representations of a sans-culotte woman. The image on the left was created by a French artist, while the image on the right is English. The French words above the image on the right read in part, "Heads! Blood! Death! . . . I am the Goddess of Liberty! . . . Long Live the Guillotine!"

(Musée de la Ville de Paris, Musée Carnavalet, Paris, France/Bridgeman Images)

(© Courtesy of the Warden and Scholars of New College, Oxford, UK/Bridgeman Images)

EVALUATE THE EVIDENCE

1. How would you describe the woman on the left? What qualities does the artist seem to ascribe to her, and how do you think these qualities relate to the sans-culottes and the Revolution? How would you characterize the facial expression and attire of the woman on the right? How does the inclusion of the text contribute to your impressions of her?
2. What does the contrast between these two images suggest about differences between French and English perceptions of the sans-culottes and of the French Revolution? Why do you think the artists have chosen to depict women?

Reign of Terror The period from 1793 to 1794 during which Robespierre's Committee of Public Safety tried and executed thousands suspected of treason and a new revolutionary culture was imposed.

what to produce, nationalized many small workshops, and requisitioned raw materials and grain. These reforms amounted to an emergency form of socialism, which thoroughly frightened Europe's propertied classes and greatly influenced the subsequent development of socialist ideology.

Second, while radical economic measures furnished the poor with bread and the armies with supplies, the **Reign of Terror** (1793–1794) enforced compliance with republican beliefs and practices. The Constitution of 1793, which had been completed in June 1793 and approved by a national referendum, was indefinitely suspended in favor of a "revolutionary government." Special courts responsible only to

Robespierre's Committee of Public Safety tried "enemies of the nation" for political crimes. Some forty thousand French men and women were executed or died in prison and around three hundred thousand were arrested, making Robespierre's Reign of Terror one of the most controversial phases of the Revolution. Presented as a necessary measure to save the republic, the Terror was a weapon directed against all suspected of opposing the revolutionary government. As Robespierre himself put it, "Terror is nothing more than prompt, severe inflexible justice."[4] For many Europeans of the time, however, the Reign of Terror represented a frightening perversion of the ideals of 1789.

In their efforts to impose unity, the Jacobins also took actions to suppress women's participation in political debate, which they perceived as disorderly and a distraction from women's proper place in the home. On October 30, 1793, the National Convention declared that "the clubs and popular societies of women, under whatever denomination are prohibited." Among those convicted of sedition was writer Olympe de Gouges, who was sent to the guillotine in November 1793.

The third element of the Committee's program was to bring about a cultural revolution that would transform former royal subjects into republican citizens. The government sponsored revolutionary art and songs as well as a new series of secular festivals to celebrate republican virtue and patriotism. It also attempted to rationalize French daily life by adopting the decimal system for weights and measures and a new calendar based on ten-day weeks. Another important element of this cultural revolution was the campaign of de-Christianization, which aimed to eliminate Catholic symbols and beliefs. Fearful of the hostility aroused in rural France, however, Robespierre called for a halt to de-Christianization measures in mid-1794.

The final element in the program of the Committee of Public Safety was its appeal to a new sense of national identity and patriotism. With a common language and a common tradition newly reinforced by the revolutionary ideals of popular sovereignty and democracy, many French people developed an intense emotional commitment to the defense of the nation, and they saw the war against foreign opponents as a life-and-death struggle between good and evil. This was the birth of modern nationalism, which would have a profound effect on subsequent European history.

The all-out mobilization of French resources under the Terror combined with the fervor of nationalism to create an awesome fighting machine. A decree of August 1793 imposed the draft on all unmarried young men, and by January 1794 French armed forces outnumbered those of their enemies almost four to one.[5] Well trained, well equipped, and constantly indoctrinated, the enormous armies of the republic were led by young, impetuous generals. These generals often had risen from the ranks, and they personified the opportunities the Revolution offered gifted sons of the people. By spring 1794 French armies were victorious on all fronts and domestic revolt was largely suppressed. The republic was saved.

The Thermidorian Reaction and the Directory

The success of French armies led the Committee of Public Safety to relax the emergency economic controls, but the Committee extended the political Reign of Terror. In March 1794 the revolutionary tribunal sentenced many of its critics to death. Two weeks later Robespierre sent long-standing collaborators who he believed had turned against him, including Danton, to the guillotine. In June 1794 a new law removed defendants' right of legal counsel and criminalized criticism of the Revolution. A group of radicals and moderates in the Convention, knowing that they might be next, organized a conspiracy. They howled down Robespierre when he tried to speak to the National Convention on July 27, 1794—a date known as 9 Thermidor according to France's newly adopted republican calendar. The next day it was Robespierre's turn to be guillotined.

As Robespierre's closest supporters followed their leader to the guillotine, the respectable middle-class lawyers and professionals who had led the liberal Revolution of 1789 reasserted their authority. This period of **Thermidorian reaction**, as it was called, hearkened back to the ideals of the early Revolution; the new leaders of government proclaimed an end to the revolutionary expediency of the Terror and the return of representative government, the rule of law, and liberal economic policies. In 1795 the National Convention abolished many economic controls, let prices rise sharply, and severely restricted the local political organizations through which the sans-culottes exerted their strength.

Thermidorian reaction
A reaction to the violence of the Reign of Terror in 1794, resulting in the execution of Robespierre and the loosening of economic controls.

In the same year, members of the National Convention wrote a new constitution to guarantee their economic position and political supremacy. As in previous elections, the mass of the population could vote only for electors who would in turn elect the legislators, but the new constitution greatly reduced the number of men eligible to become electors by instating a substantial property requirement. It also inaugurated a bicameral legislative system for the first time in the Revolution, with a Council of 500 serving as the lower house that initiated legislation and a Council of Elders (composed of about 250 members aged forty years or older) acting as the upper house that approved new laws. To prevent a new Robespierre from monopolizing power, the new Assembly granted executive power to a five-man body, called the Directory.

The Directory continued to support French military expansion abroad. War was no longer so much a crusade as a response to economic problems. Large, victorious French armies reduced unemployment at home. However, the French people quickly grew weary of the corruption and ineffectiveness that characterized the Directory. The trauma of years of military and political violence had alienated the public, and the Directory's heavy-handed and opportunistic policies did not reverse the situation. This general dissatisfaction revealed itself clearly in the national elections of 1797, which returned a large number of conservative and even monarchist deputies who favored peace at almost any price. Two years later Napoleon Bonaparte ended the Directory in a coup d'état (koo day-TAH) and substituted a strong dictatorship for a weak one.

The Execution of Robespierre After overseeing the Terror, during which thousands of men and women accused of being enemies of the Revolution faced speedy trial and execution, it was Maximilien Robespierre's turn to face the guillotine on 9 Thermidor Year II (July 28, 1794). (Musée de la Ville de Paris, Musée Carnavalet, Paris, France/Bridgeman Images)

The Napoleonic Era, 1799–1815

For almost fifteen years, from 1799 to 1814, France was in the hands of a keen-minded military dictator of exceptional ability. One of history's most fascinating leaders, Napoleon Bonaparte (1769–1821) realized that he needed to put an end to civil strife in France in order to create unity and consolidate his rule. And he did. But Napoleon saw himself as a man of destiny, and the glory of war and the dream of universal empire proved irresistible. For years he spiraled from victory to victory, but in the end he was destroyed by a mighty coalition united in fear of his restless ambition.

FOCUS QUESTION
How did Napoleon Bonaparte assume control of France and much of Europe, and what factors led to his downfall?

Napoleon's Rule of France

Born in Corsica into an impoverished noble family in 1769, Napoleon left home and became a lieutenant in the French artillery in 1785. Converted to the revolutionary cause and rising rapidly in the republican army, Napoleon was placed in command of French forces in Italy and won brilliant victories there in 1796 and 1797. His next campaign, in Egypt, was a failure, but Napoleon returned to France before the fiasco was generally known, and his reputation remained intact. French aggression in Egypt and elsewhere provoked the British to organize a new alliance in 1798, the Second Coalition, that also included Austria and Russia.

Napoleon soon learned that some prominent members of the legislature were plotting against the Directory. The plotters' dissatisfaction stemmed not so much from the Directory's ruling dictatorially as from the fact that it was a weak dictatorship. Ten years of upheaval and uncertainty had made firm rule much more appealing than liberty and popular politics to these disillusioned revolutionaries. The abbé Sieyès personified this evolution in thinking. In 1789 he had written that the nobility was grossly overprivileged and that the entire people should rule the French nation. Now Sieyès's motto was "Confidence from below, authority from above."

The flamboyant thirty-year-old Napoleon, nationally revered for his heroism, was an ideal figure of authority. On November 9, 1799, Napoleon and his conspirators ousted the Directors, and the following day soldiers disbanded the legislature at bayonet point. Napoleon was named first consul of the republic, and a new constitution consolidating his position was overwhelmingly approved by a nationwide vote in December 1799. Republican appearances were maintained, but Napoleon became the real ruler of France.

Napoleon's domestic policy centered on using his popularity and charisma to maintain order and end civil strife. He did so by appeasing powerful groups in France by according them favors in return for loyal service. Napoleon's bargain with the solid middle class was codified in the famous Civil Code of March 1804, also known as the **Napoleonic Code**, which reasserted two of the fundamental principles of the Revolution of 1789: equality of all male citizens before the law, and security of wealth and private property. Napoleon and the leading bankers of Paris established the privately owned Bank of France in 1800, which served the interests of both the state and the financial oligarchy. Napoleon won over peasants by defending the gains in land and status they had won during the Revolution.

At the same time, Napoleon consolidated his rule by recruiting disillusioned revolutionaries to form a network of ministers, prefects, and centrally appointed mayors. Nor were members of the old nobility slighted. In 1800 and again in 1802

Napoleonic Code French civil code promulgated in 1804 that reasserted the 1789 principles of the equality of all male citizens before the law and the absolute security of wealth and private property, as well as restricting rights accorded to women by previous revolutionary laws.

Napoleon granted amnesty to one hundred thousand émigrés on the condition that they return to France and take a loyalty oath. Members of this returning elite soon ably occupied many high posts in the expanding centralized state. Napoleon also created a new imperial nobility in order to reward his most talented generals and officials.

Napoleon applied his diplomatic skills to healing the Catholic Church in France so that it could serve as a bulwark of social stability. After arduous negotiations, Napoleon and Pope Pius VII (pontificate 1800–1823) signed the Concordat (kuhn-KOHR-dat) of 1801. The pope obtained the right for French Catholics to practice their religion freely, but Napoleon gained political power: his government now nominated bishops, paid the clergy, and exerted great influence over the church.

The domestic reforms of Napoleon's early years were his greatest achievement. Much of his legal and administrative reorganization has survived in France to this day, but order and unity had a price: authoritarian rule. Women lost many of the gains they had made in the 1790s. Under the Napoleonic Code, women were dependents of either their fathers or their husbands, and they could not make contracts or have bank accounts in their own names. Napoleon and his advisers aimed at re-establishing a family monarchy, where the power of the husband and father was as absolute over the wife and the children as that of Napoleon was over his subjects. He also curtailed free speech and freedom of the press and manipulated voting in the occasional elections. After 1810 political suspects were held in state prisons, as they had been during the Terror.

Napoleon's Expansion in Europe

Napoleon was above all a great military man. After coming to power in 1799, he sent peace feelers to Austria and Great Britain, the two remaining members of the Second Coalition that had been formed against France in 1798. When they rejected his overtures, Napoleon's armies decisively defeated the Austrians. In the Treaty of Lunéville (1801), Austria accepted the loss of almost all its Italian possessions, and German territory on the west bank of the Rhine was incorporated into France. The British agreed to the Treaty of Amiens in 1802, allowing France to control the former Dutch Republic (known as the Batavian Republic since 1795), the Austrian Netherlands, the west bank of the Rhine, and most of the Italian peninsula. The Treaty of Amiens was a diplomatic triumph for Napoleon, and peace with honor and profit increased his popularity at home.

In 1802 Napoleon was secure but driven to expand his power. Aggressively redrawing the map of German-speaking lands so as to weaken Austria and encourage the secondary states of southwestern Germany to side with France, Napoleon tried to restrict British trade with all of Europe. He then plotted to attack Great Britain, but his Mediterranean fleet was destroyed by Lord Nelson at the Battle of Trafalgar on October 21, 1805. Invasion of England was henceforth impossible. Renewed fighting had its advantages, however, for the first consul used the wartime atmosphere to have himself proclaimed emperor in late 1804.

Austria, Russia, and Sweden joined with Britain to form the Third Coalition against France shortly before the Battle of Trafalgar. Actions such as Napoleon's assumption of the Italian crown had convinced both Alexander I of Russia and

Francis II of Austria that Napoleon was a threat to the European balance of power. Yet they were no match for Napoleon, who scored a brilliant victory over them at the Battle of Austerlitz in December 1805. Alexander I decided to pull back, and Austria accepted large territorial losses in return for peace as the Third Coalition collapsed.

Napoleon then reorganized the German states to his liking. In 1806 he abolished many of the tiny German states as well as the ancient Holy Roman Empire and established by decree the German Confederation of the Rhine, a union of fifteen German states minus Austria, Prussia, and Saxony. Naming himself "protector" of the confederation, Napoleon firmly controlled western Germany.

Napoleon's intervention in German affairs alarmed the Prussians, who mobilized their armies after more than a decade of peace with France. Napoleon attacked and won two more brilliant victories in October 1806 at Jena and Auerstädt, where the Prussians were outnumbered two to one. The war with Prussia, now joined by Russia, continued into the following spring. After Napoleon's larger armies won another victory, Alexander I of Russia was ready to negotiate the peace. In the subsequent treaties of Tilsit in 1807, Prussia lost half of its population, while Russia accepted Napoleon's reorganization of western and central Europe and promised to enforce Napoleon's economic blockade against British goods.

German Confederation of the Rhine, 1806

The Grand Empire and Its End

Increasingly, Napoleon saw himself as the emperor of Europe, not just of France. The so-called **Grand Empire** he built had three parts. The core, or first part, was an ever-expanding France, which by 1810 included today's Belgium and the Netherlands, parts of northern Italy, and German territories on the east bank of the Rhine. The second part consisted of a number of dependent satellite kingdoms, on the thrones of which Napoleon placed members of his large family. The third part comprised the independent but allied states of Austria, Prussia, and Russia. After 1806 Napoleon expected both satellites and allies to support his **Continental System**, a blockade in which no ship coming from Britain or her colonies could dock at a port controlled by the French. It was intended to halt all trade between Britain and continental Europe, thereby destroying the British economy and its military force.

The impact of the Grand Empire on the peoples of Europe was considerable. In the areas incorporated into France and in the satellites (Map 19.2), Napoleon abolished feudal dues and serfdom to the benefit of the peasants and middle class. Yet Napoleon had to put the prosperity and special interests of France first in order to safeguard his power base. Levying heavy taxes in money and men for his armies, he came to be regarded more as a conquering tyrant than as an enlightened liberator. Thus French rule sparked patriotic upheavals and encouraged the growth of reactive nationalism, for individuals in different lands learned to identify emotionally with their own embattled national families as the French had done earlier.

The first great revolt occurred in Spain. In 1808 Napoleon deposed Spanish king Ferdinand VII and placed his own brother Joseph on the throne. However, a coalition of Catholics, monarchists, and patriots rebelled against Napoleon's attempts

Grand Empire The empire over which Napoleon and his allies ruled, encompassing virtually all of Europe except Great Britain and Russia.

Continental System A blockade imposed by Napoleon to halt all trade between continental Europe and Britain, thereby weakening the British economy and military.

MAP 19.2 Napoleonic Europe in 1812   At the height of the Grand Empire in 1810, Napoleon had conquered or allied with every major European power except Britain. But in 1812, angered by Russian repudiation of his ban on trade with Britain, Napoleon invaded Russia with disastrous results. Compare this map with Map 15.2 (page 479), which shows the division of Europe in 1715.

to make Spain a French satellite. French armies occupied Madrid, but the foes of Napoleon fled to the hills and waged uncompromising guerrilla warfare. Spain was a clear warning: resistance to French imperialism was growing.

Yet Napoleon pushed on. In 1810, when the Grand Empire was at its height, Britain still remained at war with France, helping the guerrillas in Spain and Portugal. The Continental System was a failure. Instead of harming Britain, the system provoked the British to set up a counter-blockade, which created hard times in France. Perhaps looking for a scapegoat, Napoleon turned on Alexander I of Russia, who in 1811 openly repudiated Napoleon's war of prohibitions against British goods.

Francisco Goya, *The Third of May 1808*
Spanish master Francisco Goya created a passionate and moving indictment of the brutality
of war in this painting from 1814, which depicts
the close-range execution of Spanish rebels by
Napoleon's forces in May 1808. Goya's painting
evoked the bitterness and despair of many
Europeans who suffered through Napoleon's
invasions. (Prado, Madrid, Spain/Bridgeman Images)

Napoleon's invasion of Russia began in
June 1812 with a force that eventually numbered 600,000, probably the largest force
yet assembled in a single army. Only one-
third of this army was French, however;
nationals of all the satellites and allies were
drafted into the operation. Originally plan-
ning to winter in the Russian city of Smolensk, Napoleon recklessly pressed on toward
Moscow. The great Battle of Borodino that followed was a draw. Alexander ordered the
evacuation of Moscow, which the Russians then burned in part, and he refused to negotiate. Finally, after five weeks in the scorched and abandoned city, Napoleon ordered a
retreat, one of the greatest military disasters in history. The Russian army, the Russian
winter, and starvation cut Napoleon's army to pieces. When the frozen remnants
staggered into Poland and Prussia in December, 370,000 men had died and another
200,000 had been taken prisoner.[6]

Leaving his troops to their fate, Napoleon raced to Paris to raise yet another army.
Possibly he might still have saved his throne if he had been willing to accept a France
reduced to its historical size—the proposal offered by Austria's foreign minister,
Prince Klemens von Metternich. But Napoleon refused. Austria and Prussia deserted
Napoleon and joined Russia and Great Britain in the Treaty of Chaumont in
March 1814, by which the four powers formed the Quadruple Alliance to defeat the
French emperor.

All across Europe patriots called for a "war of liberation" against Napoleon's oppression. Less than a month later, on April 4, 1814, a defeated Napoleon abdicated his
throne. After this unconditional abdication, the victorious allies granted Napoleon
the island of Elba off the coast of Italy as his own tiny state. Napoleon was allowed to
keep his imperial title, and France was required to pay him a yearly income of 2 million francs.

The allies also agreed to the restoration of the Bourbon dynasty under Louis XVIII
(r. 1814–1824) and promised to treat France with leniency in a peace settlement.
The new monarch sought support among the people by issuing the Constitutional
Charter, which accepted many of France's revolutionary changes and guaranteed civil
liberties.

Yet Louis XVIII lacked the magnetism of Napoleon. Hearing of political unrest in
France and diplomatic tensions in Vienna, Napoleon staged a daring escape from Elba

in February 1815 and marched on Paris with a small band of followers. French officers and soldiers who had fought so long for their emperor responded to the call. Louis XVIII fled, and once more Napoleon took command. But Napoleon's gamble was a desperate long shot, for the allies were united against him. At the end of a frantic period known as the Hundred Days, they crushed his forces at Waterloo on June 18, 1815, and imprisoned him on the rocky island of St. Helena, off the western coast of Africa. Louis XVIII returned to the throne, and the allies dealt more harshly with the French. As for Napoleon, he took revenge by writing his memoirs, nurturing the myth that he had been Europe's revolutionary liberator, a romantic hero whose lofty work had been undone by oppressive reactionaries.

The Haitian Revolution, 1791–1804

FOCUS QUESTION

How did slave revolt on colonial Saint-Domingue lead to the creation of the independent nation of Haiti in 1804?

The events that led to the creation of the independent nation of Haiti constitute the third, and perhaps most extraordinary, chapter of the revolutionary era in the late eighteenth century. Prior to 1789 Saint-Domingue, the French colony that was to become Haiti, reaped huge profits through a ruthless system of slave-based plantation agriculture. News of revolution in France lit a powder keg of contradictory aspirations among white planters, free people of color, and slaves. While revolutionary authorities debated how far to extend the rights of man on Saint-Domingue, first free people of color and then enslaved people took matters into their own hands, rising up to claim their freedom. They succeeded, despite invasion by the British and Spanish and Napoleon Bonaparte's bid to reimpose French control. In 1804 Haiti became the only nation in history to claim its freedom through slave revolt.

Revolutionary Aspirations in Saint-Domingue

On the eve of the French Revolution, Saint-Domingue—the most profitable of all Caribbean colonies—was even more rife with social tensions than France itself. The colony, which occupied the western third of the island of Hispaniola, was inhabited by a variety of social groups who resented and mistrusted one another. The European population included French colonial officials, wealthy plantation owners and merchants, and poor artisans and clerks. Individuals of French or European descent born in the colonies were called "Creoles," and over time they had developed their own interests, at times distinct from those of metropolitan France. Vastly outnumbering the white population were the colony's five hundred thousand enslaved people alongside a sizable population of some forty thousand free people of African and mixed African and European descent. Members of this last group referred to themselves as free people of color.

Legal and economic conditions on Saint-Domingue vastly favored the white population. Most of the island's enslaved population performed grueling toil in the island's sugar plantations. The highly outnumbered planters used extremely brutal methods, such as beating, maiming, and executing slaves, to maintain their control. The 1685 Code Noir (Black Code) that set the parameters of slavery was intended to provide minimal standards of humane treatment, but its tenets were rarely enforced. Masters calculated that they could earn more by working slaves ruthlessly and purchasing new ones when they died, than by providing the food, rest, and medical care needed to allow the enslaved population to reproduce naturally. This meant a constant inflow of newly enslaved people from Africa was necessary to work the plantations.

Despite their brutality, slaveholders on Saint-Domingue freed a surprising number of their slaves, mostly their own mixed-race children, thereby producing one of the largest populations of free people of color in any slaveholding colony. The Code Noir had originally granted free people of color the same legal status as whites: they could own property, live where they wished, and pursue any education or career they desired. From the 1760s on, however, the rising prosperity and visibility of this group provoked resentment from the white population. In response, colonial administrators began rescinding the rights of free people of color, and by the time of the French Revolution myriad aspects of their lives were subject to discriminatory laws.

The political and intellectual turmoil of the 1780s, with its growing rhetoric of liberty, equality, and fraternity, raised new challenges and possibilities for each of Saint-Domingue's social groups. For enslaved people, who constituted approximately 90 percent of the population, news of abolitionist movements in France led to hopes that the mother country might grant them freedom. Free people of color looked to reforms in Paris as a means of gaining political enfranchisement and reasserting equal status with whites. The Creole elite, not surprisingly, saw matters very differently. Infuriated by talk of abolition and determined to protect their way of life, they looked to revolutionary ideals of representative government for the chance to gain control of their own affairs, as had the American colonists before them.

The National Assembly frustrated the hopes of all these groups. Cowed by colonial representatives who claimed that support for free people of color would result in slave insurrection and independence, the Assembly refused to extend French

Slave Revolt on Saint-Domingue   This illustration, from the proslavery perspective, emphasizes the violence and destructiveness of the slave rebellion in Saint-Domingue. Many white settlers fled to the United States and other Caribbean islands with as much of their property, including slaves, as they could take with them. (The Library Company of Philadelphia)

constitutional safeguards to the colonies. After dealing this blow to the aspirations of slaves and free people of color, the Assembly also reaffirmed French monopolies over colonial trade, thereby angering Creole planters as well. Like the American settlers before them, the colonists chafed under the rule of the mother country.

In July 1790 Vincent Ogé (aw-ZHAY) (ca. 1750–1791), a free man of color, returned to Saint-Domingue from Paris determined to win rights for his people. He raised an army of several hundred and sent letters to the new Provincial Assembly of Saint-Domingue demanding political rights for all free citizens. But Ogé's demands were refused, so he and his followers turned to armed insurrection. After initial victories, his army was defeated, and Ogé was tortured and executed by colonial officials. Revolutionary leaders in Paris were more sympathetic to Ogé's cause. In May 1791, responding to what it perceived as partly justified grievances, the National Assembly granted political rights to free people of color born to two free parents who possessed sufficient property. When news of this legislation arrived in Saint-Domingue, the white elite was furious, and the colonial governor refused to enact it. Violence now erupted between groups of whites and free people of color in parts of the colony.

The Outbreak of Revolt

Just as the sans-culottes helped push forward more radical reforms in France, the second stage of revolution in Saint-Domingue also resulted from decisive action from below. In August 1791 slaves, who had witnessed the confrontation between whites and free people of color for over a year, took events into their own hands. Groups of slaves held a series of nighttime meetings to plan a mass insurrection. In doing so, they drew on their own considerable military experience; the majority of slaves had been born in Africa, and many had served in the civil wars of the kingdom of Kongo and other conflicts before being taken into slavery.[7] They also drew on a long tradition of slave resistance prior to 1791, which had ranged from work slow-downs, to running away, to taking part in African-derived religious rituals and dances known as *vodou* (or voodoo). According to some sources, the August 1791 pact to take up arms was sealed by such a voodoo ritual.[8]

Revolts began on a few plantations on the night of August 22. Within a few days the uprising had swept much of the northern plain, creating a slave army estimated at around 2,000 individuals. By August 27 it was described by one observer as "10,000 strong, divided into 3 armies, of whom 700 or 800 are on horseback, and tolerably well-armed."[9] During the next month enslaved combatants attacked and destroyed hundreds of sugar and coffee plantations.

On April 4, 1792, as war loomed with the European states, the National Assembly issued a decree extending full citizenship rights to free people of color, including the right to vote. As in France, voting rights and the ability to hold public office applied to men only. The Assembly hoped this measure would win the loyalty of free people of color and their aid in defeating the slave rebellion.

Warfare in Europe soon spread to Saint-Domingue (Map 19.3). Since the beginning of the slave insurrection, the Spanish colony of Santo Domingo, on the eastern side of the island of Hispaniola, had supported rebel slaves. In early 1793 the Spanish began to bring slave leaders and their soldiers into the Spanish army. Toussaint L'Ouverture (TOO-sahn LOO-vair-toor) (1743–1803), a freed slave who had joined

MAP 19.3 The War of Haitian Independence, 1791–1804   Neighbored by the Spanish colony of Santo Domingo, Saint-Domingue was the most profitable European colony in the Caribbean. In 1770 the French transferred the capital from Le Cap to Port-au-Prince. Slave revolts erupted in the north near Le Cap in 1791. Port-au-Prince became the capital of the newly independent Haiti in 1804.

the revolt, was named a Spanish officer. In September the British navy blockaded the colony, and invading British troops captured French territory on the island. For the Spanish and British, revolutionary chaos provided a tempting opportunity to capture a profitable colony.

Desperate for forces to oppose France's enemies, commissioners sent by the newly elected National Convention promised to emancipate all those who fought for France. By October 1793 they had abolished slavery throughout the colony. On February 4, 1794, the Convention ratified the abolition of slavery and extended it to all French territories, including the Caribbean colonies of Martinique and Guadeloupe. In some ways this act merely acknowledged the achievements already won by the slave insurrection itself.

The tide of battle began to turn when Toussaint L'Ouverture switched sides, bringing his military and political skills, along with four thousand well-trained soldiers, to support the French war effort. By 1796 the French had regained control of the colony, and L'Ouverture had emerged as a key military leader. (See "Individuals in Society: Toussaint L'Ouverture," page 642.) In May 1796 he was named commander of the western province of Saint-Domingue (see Map 19.3).

L ittle is known of the early life of Saint-Domingue's brilliant military and political leader Toussaint L'Ouverture. He was born in 1743 on a plantation outside Le Cap owned by the Count de Bréda. According to tradition, L'Ouverture was the eldest son of a captured African prince from modern-day Benin. Toussaint Bréda, as he was then called, occupied a privileged position among slaves. Instead of performing backbreaking labor in the fields, he served his master as a coachman and livestock keeper. He also learned to read and write French and some Latin, but he was always more comfortable with the Creole dialect.

During the 1770s the plantation manager emancipated L'Ouverture, who subsequently leased his own small coffee plantation and slaves. He married Suzanne Simone, who already had one son, and the couple had another son during their marriage. In 1791 he joined the slave uprisings that swept Saint-Domingue, and he took on the *nom de guerre* (war name) "L'Ouverture," meaning "the opening." L'Ouverture rose to prominence among rebel slaves allied with Spain and by early 1794 controlled his own army. A devout Catholic who led a frugal and ascetic life, L'Ouverture impressed others with his enormous physical energy, intellectual acumen, and air of mystery. In 1794 he defected to the French side and led his troops to a series of victories against the Spanish. In 1795 the National Convention promoted L'Ouverture to brigadier general.

Over the next three years L'Ouverture successively eliminated rivals for authority on the island. First he freed himself of the French commissioners sent to govern the colony. With a firm grip on power in the northern province, L'Ouverture defeated General André Rigaud in 1800 to gain control in the south. His army then marched on the capital of Spanish Santo Domingo on the eastern half of the island, meeting little resistance. The entire island of Hispaniola was now under his command.

With control of Saint-Domingue in his hands, L'Ouverture was confronted with the challenge of building a post-emancipation society, the first of its kind. The task was made even more difficult by the chaos wreaked by war, the destruction of plantations, and bitter social and racial tensions. For L'Ouverture the most pressing concern was to re-establish the plantation economy. Without revenue to pay his army, the gains of the rebellion could be lost. He therefore encouraged white

Equestrian portrait of Toussaint L'Ouverture.
(© Photos 12/Alamy Stock Photo)

planters to return to reclaim their property. He also adopted harsh policies toward former slaves, forcing them back to their plantations and restricting their ability to acquire land. When they resisted, he sent troops across the island to enforce submission. L'Ouverture's 1801 constitution reaffirmed his draconian labor policies and named L'Ouverture governor for life, leaving Saint-Domingue as a colony in name alone. In June 1802 French forces arrested L'Ouverture and jailed him at Fort de Joux in France's Jura Mountains near the Swiss border. L'Ouverture died of pneumonia on April 7, 1803. It was left to his lieutenant, Jean Jacques Dessalines, to win independence for the new Haitian nation.

QUESTIONS FOR ANALYSIS

1. Toussaint L'Ouverture was both slave and slave owner. How did each experience shape his life and actions?
2. What did Toussaint L'Ouverture and Napoleon Bonaparte have in common? How did they differ?

The increasingly conservative nature of the French government during the Thermidorian reaction, however, threatened to undo the gains made by former slaves and free people of color.

The War of Haitian Independence

With Toussaint L'Ouverture acting increasingly as an independent ruler of the western province of Saint-Domingue, another general, André Rigaud (1761–1811), set up his own government in the southern peninsula. Tensions mounted between L'Ouverture and Rigaud. While L'Ouverture was a freed slave of African descent, Rigaud belonged to the free colored elite. This elite resented the growing power of former slaves like L'Ouverture, who in turn accused them of adopting the racism of white settlers. Civil war broke out between the two sides in 1799, when L'Ouverture's forces, led by his lieutenant, Jean Jacques Dessalines (1758–1806), invaded the south. Victory over Rigaud in 1800 gave L'Ouverture control of the entire colony.

This victory was soon challenged by Napoleon, who had his own plans for re-establishing slavery and using the profits as a basis for expanding French power. Napoleon ordered his brother-in-law, General Charles-Victor-Emmanuel Leclerc (1772–1802), to lead an expedition to the island to crush the new regime. In 1802 Leclerc landed in Saint-Domingue and ordered the arrest of Toussaint L'Ouverture. The rebel leader, along with his family, was deported to France, where he died in 1803.

It was left to L'Ouverture's lieutenant, Jean Jacques Dessalines, to unite the resistance, and he led it to a crushing victory over French forces. On January 1, 1804, Dessalines formally declared the independence of Saint-Domingue and the creation of the new sovereign nation of Haiti, the name used by the pre-Columbian inhabitants of the island. The Haitian constitution was ratified in 1805.

Haiti, the second independent state in the Americas and the first in Latin America, was born from the first successful large-scale slave revolt in history. This event spread shock and fear through slaveholding societies in the Caribbean and the United States, bringing to life their worst nightmares of the utter reversal of their power and privilege. Fearing the spread of rebellion to the United States, President Thomas Jefferson refused to recognize Haiti as an independent nation. The liberal proponents of American revolution thus chose to protect slavery at the expense of revolutionary ideals of universal human rights. The French government imposed crushing indemnity charges on Haiti to recompense the loss of French property, dealing a harsh blow to the fledgling nation's economy.

Yet Haitian independence had fundamental repercussions for world history, helping spread the idea that liberty, equality, and fraternity must apply to all people. The next phase of Atlantic revolution soon opened in the Spanish American colonies.

LOOKING BACK LOOKING AHEAD

A great revolutionary wave swept both sides of the Atlantic Ocean in the late eighteenth century. The revolutions in British North America, France, and Haiti were individual and unique, but they had common origins and consequences for Western and, indeed, world history. Despite the French monarchy's ongoing claims to the absolutist rule imposed by Louis XIV, the eighteenth century had inaugurated monumental changes, as population grew, urbanization spread, and literacy increased. Enlightenment ideals, especially those of John Locke and the baron de Montesquieu, influenced all orders of society, and reformers increasingly championed limiting monarchical authority in the name of popular sovereignty.

The Atlantic world was the essential context for this age of revolutions. The movement of peoples, commodities, and ideas across the Atlantic Ocean in the eighteenth century created a world of common debates, conflicts, and aspirations. Moreover, the high stakes of colonial empire heightened competition among European states, leading to a series of wars that generated crushing costs for overburdened treasuries. For both the British in their North American colonies and the French at home, the desperate need for new taxes weakened government authority and opened the door to revolution. In turn, the ideals of the French Revolution inspired slaves and free people of color in Saint-Domingue, thus opening the promise of liberty, equality, and fraternity to people of all races.

The chain reaction did not end with the birth of an independent Haiti in 1804. On the European continent throughout the nineteenth and early twentieth centuries, periodic convulsions occurred as successive generations struggled over political rights first proclaimed by the generation of 1789. Meanwhile, as dramatic political events unfolded, a parallel economic revolution was gathering steam. This was the Industrial Revolution, originating around 1780 and accelerating through the end of the eighteenth century (see Chapter 20). After 1815 the twin forces of industrialization and democratization would combine to transform Europe and the world.

Make Connections

Think about the larger developments and continuities within and across chapters.

1. What were major differences and similarities among the American, French, and Haitian Revolutions?

2. How did the increased circulation of goods, people, and ideas across the Atlantic in the eighteenth century (Chapter 17) contribute to the outbreak of revolution on both sides of the ocean?

3. To what extent would you characterize the revolutions discussed in this chapter as Enlightenment movements (Chapter 16)?

19 REVIEW & EXPLORE

Review the Main Ideas

Answer the focus questions from each section of the chapter.

◆ What were the factors leading to the revolutions of the late eighteenth century? (p. 610)

◆ Why and how did American colonists forge a new, independent nation? (p. 613)

◆ How did the events of 1789 result in a constitutional monarchy in France, and what were the consequences? (p. 620)

◆ Why and how did the French Revolution take a radical turn entailing terror at home and war with European powers? (p. 627)

◆ How did Napoleon Bonaparte assume control of France and much of Europe, and what factors led to his downfall? (p. 633)

◆ How did slave revolt on colonial Saint-Domingue lead to the creation of the independent nation of Haiti in 1804? (p. 638)

Identify Key Terms

Identify and explain the significance of each item below.

Estates General (p. 621)
estates (p. 621)
National Assembly (p. 624)
Great Fear (p. 624)
Jacobin Club (p. 627)
second revolution (p. 628)
Girondists (p. 628)
the Mountain (p. 628)
sans-culottes (p. 629)
Reign of Terror (p. 630)
Thermidorian reaction (p. 632)
Napoleonic Code (p. 633)
Grand Empire (p. 635)
Continental System (p.635)

NOTES

1. Quoted in G. Wright, *France in Modern Times*, 4th ed. (New York: W. W. Norton, 1987), p. 34.
2. G. Pernoud and S. Flaisser, eds., *The French Revolution* (Greenwich, Conn.: Fawcett, 1960), p. 61.
3. Quoted in L. Gershoy, *The Era of the French Revolution, 1789–1799* (New York: Van Nostrand, 1957), p. 150.
4. Quoted in Wim Klooster, *Revolutions in the Atlantic World: A Comprehensive History* (New York: New York University Press, 2009), p. 74.
5. T. Blanning, *The French Revolutionary Wars, 1787–1802* (London: Arnold, 1996), pp. 116–128.

6. D. Sutherland, *France, 1789–1815: Revolution and Counterrevolution* (New York: Oxford University Press, 1986), p. 420.
7. John K. Thornton, "'I Am the Subject of the King of Congo': African Political Ideology and the Haitian Revolution," *Journal of World History* 4, no. 2 (Fall 1993): 181–214.
8. Laurent Dubois, *Avengers of the New World: The Story of the Haitian Revolution* (Cambridge, Mass.: Belknap Press, 2004), pp. 43–45, 99–100.
9. Quoted ibid., p. 97.

CHAPTER PREVIEW

The Industrial Revolution in Britain
Why did the Industrial Revolution begin in Britain, and how did it develop between 1780 and 1850?

Industrialization in Europe and the World
How did countries in Europe and around the world respond to the challenge of industrialization?

New Patterns of Working and Living
How did work evolve during the Industrial Revolution, and how did daily life change for working people?

Relations Between Capital and Labor
How did the changes brought about by the Industrial Revolution lead to new social classes, and how did people respond to the new structure?

Life in the Industrial Revolution

Daily life for industrial workers was harsh, especially for the many child laborers who worked in the new factories and in other industries, like the glassworks pictured here. Long hours of work, strict discipline, and low wages were the lot of most industrial workers, whose living standards did not improve until the 1840s.

(*The Falcon Glassworks*, c. 1840, [oil on canvas]/© Museum of London/HIP/The Image Works)

20

The Revolution in Energy and Industry

ca. 1780–1850

While revolutions in France and across the Atlantic were opening a new political era, another revolution was beginning to transform economic and social life. The Industrial Revolution took off around 1780 in Great Britain and soon began to influence continental Europe and the United States. Non-European nations began to industrialize after 1860.

Industrialization profoundly modified much of human experience. It changed patterns of work, transformed the social class structure and the way people thought about class, and eventually altered the international balance of political power. Quite possibly only the development of agriculture during Neolithic times had a comparable impact and significance.

What was revolutionary about the Industrial Revolution was not its pace or that it represented a sharp break with the previous period. On the contrary, the Industrial Revolution built on earlier developments, and the rate of progress was slow. What was remarkable about the Industrial Revolution was that it inaugurated a period of sustained economic and demographic growth that has continued to the present day. Although it took time, the Industrial Revolution eventually helped ordinary people in the West gain a higher standard of living as the widespread poverty of preindustrial Europe gradually receded.

Such fundamental transitions did not occur overnight. National wealth rose much more quickly than improvements in the European standard of living until about 1850. This was because, even in Britain, only a few key industries experienced a technological revolution. Many more industries continued to use old methods. In addition, wage increases were modest until the mid-nineteenth century, and the gradual withdrawal of children and married women from paid work meant that the household as a whole earned the same or less. ■

The Industrial Revolution in Britain

FOCUS QUESTION

Why did the Industrial Revolution begin in Britain, and how did it develop between 1780 and 1850?

The Industrial Revolution began in Great Britain, the nation created in 1707 by the formal union of Scotland, Wales, and England. The transformation in industry was something new in history, and it was unplanned. With no models to copy and no idea of what to expect, Britain pioneered not only in industrial technology but also in social relations and urban living. Just as France was a trailblazer in political change, Britain was the leader in economic development, and it must therefore command special attention.

Why Britain?

Perhaps the most important debate in economic history focuses on why the Industrial Revolution originated in western Europe, and Britain in particular, rather than in other parts of the world, such as Asia. Historians continue to debate this issue, but the best answer seems to be that Britain possessed a unique set of possibilities and constraints—abundant coal, high wages, a relatively peaceful and centralized government, well-developed financial systems, innovative culture, highly skilled craftsmen, and a strong position in empire and global trade—that spurred its people to adopt a capital-intensive, machine-powered system of production. The long-term economic advantages of this system were not immediately apparent, and its adoption by the British was more a matter of circumstance than a planned strategy.

Thus a number of factors came together over the long term to give rise to the Industrial Revolution in Britain. The Scientific Revolution and the Enlightenment fostered a new worldview that embraced progress and the role of research and experimentation in understanding and mastering the natural world. Britain's intellectual culture emphasized the public sharing of knowledge, including that of scientists and technicians from other countries. The British Royal Society of Arts, for example, sponsored prizes for innovations in machinery and agriculture and played a pivotal part in the circulation of "useful knowledge."

In the economic realm, the seventeenth-century expansion of rural industry produced a surplus of English woolen cloth. Exported throughout Europe, English cloth brought commercial profits and high wages to the detriment of traditional producers in Flanders and Italy. By the eighteenth century the expanding Atlantic economy and trade with India and China were also serving Britain well. The mercantilist colonial empire Britain aggressively built, augmented by a strong position in Latin America and in the transatlantic slave trade, provided raw materials like cotton and a growing market for British manufactured goods (see Chapter 17). Strong demand for British manufacturing meant that British workers earned high wages compared to the rest of Europe.

Agriculture also played an important role in bringing about the Industrial Revolution in Britain. English farmers were second only to the Dutch in

Industrial areas ■ Woolen cloth
■ Coal deposit — Canals, 1800
○ Metal goods — Navigable rivers

Cottage Industry and Transportation in Eighteenth-Century Great Britain

Chronology

ca. 1765	Hargreaves invents spinning jenny; Arkwright creates water frame	**1829**	Stephenson's *Rocket*, an early locomotive
1769	Watt patents modern steam engine	**1830s**	Industrial banks in Belgium
ca. 1780–1850	Industrial Revolution; population boom in Britain	**1834**	*Zollverein* erected among most German states
1799	Combination Acts passed in England	**1842**	Mines Act passed in Britain
1802–1833	Series of Factory Acts passed by British government to limit the workday of child laborers and set minimum hygiene and safety requirements	**1844**	Engels, *The Condition of the Working Class in England*
		1850s	Japan begins to adopt Western technologies; industrial gap widens between the West and the rest of the world
1805	Egypt begins process of modernization		
1810	Strike of Manchester cotton spinners	**1851**	Great Exhibition held at Crystal Palace in London
ca. 1815	Western European countries seek to adopt British industrial methods		
		1860s	Germany and the United States begin to rapidly industrialize
1824	Combination Acts repealed		

productivity in 1700, and they were continually adopting new methods of farming. The result, especially before 1760, was a period of bountiful crops and low food prices. Because of increasing efficiency, landowners were able to produce more food with a smaller workforce. By the mid-eighteenth century, on the eve of the Industrial Revolution, less than half of Britain's population worked in agriculture. The enclosure movement had deprived many small landowners of their land, leaving the landless poor to work as hired agricultural laborers or in cottage industry. These groups created a large pool of potential laborers for the new factories.

Abundant food and high wages in turn meant that the ordinary English family no longer had to spend almost everything it earned just to buy bread. Thus the family could spend more on manufactured goods — a razor for the man or a shawl for the woman. They could also pay to send their children to school. Britain's populace enjoyed high levels of literacy and numeracy (knowledge of mathematics) compared to the rest of Europe. Moreover, in the eighteenth century the members of the average British family were redirecting their labor away from unpaid work for household consumption and toward work for wages that they could spend on goods, a trend reflecting the increasing commercialization of the entire European economy.

Britain also benefited from rich natural resources and a well-developed infrastructure. In an age when it was much cheaper to ship goods by water than by land, no part of England was more than fifty miles from navigable water. Beginning in the 1770s a canal-building boom enhanced this advantage. Rivers and canals provided easy movement of England's and Wales's enormous deposits of iron and coal, resources that would be critical raw materials in Europe's early industrial age. The abundance of coal combined with high wages in manufacturing placed Britain in a unique position among European nations: its manufacturers had extremely strong incentives to develop technologies to draw on the power of coal to increase workmen's productivity. In parts of the world with lower wages, such as India and China, the costs of mechanization at first outweighed potential gains in productivity.

A final factor favoring British industrialization was the heavy hand of the British state and its policies, especially in the formative decades of industrial change. Despite its rhetoric in favor of "liberty," Britain's parliamentary system taxed its population aggressively. The British state collected twice as much per capita as the supposedly "absolutist" French monarchy and spent the money on a navy to protect imperial commerce and on an army that could be used to quell uprisings by disgruntled workers. Starting with the Navigation Acts under Oliver Cromwell (see Chapter 15), the British state also adopted aggressive tariffs, or duties, on imported goods to protect its industries.

Industrial Revolution
A term first coined in 1799 to describe the burst of major inventions and economic expansion that began in Britain in the late eighteenth century.

All these factors combined to initiate the **Industrial Revolution**, a term first coined by awed contemporaries in the 1820s to describe the burst of major inventions and technical changes under way. This technical revolution went hand in hand with an impressive quickening in the annual rate of industrial growth in Britain. Whereas industry had grown at only 0.7 percent between 1700 and 1760 (before the Industrial Revolution), it grew at the much higher rate of 3 percent between 1801 and 1831 (when industrial transformation was in full swing).[1]

Technological Innovations and Early Factories

The pressure to produce more goods for a growing market and to reduce the labor costs of manufacturing was directly related to the first decisive breakthrough of the Industrial Revolution: the creation of the world's first machine-powered factories in the British cotton textile industry. Technological innovations in the manufacture of cotton cloth led to a new system of production and social relationships. This was not the first time in European history that large numbers of people were systematically put to work in a single locale; the military arsenals of late medieval Venice are one example of a much older form of "factory." The crucial innovation in Britain was the introduction of machine power into the factory and the organization of labor around the functioning of highly productive machines.

The putting-out system that developed in the seventeenth-century textile industry involved a merchant who loaned, or "put out," raw materials to cottage workers who processed the raw materials in their own homes and returned the finished products to the merchant. There was always a serious imbalance in textile production based on cottage industry: the work of four or five spinners was needed to keep one weaver steadily employed. Cloth weavers constantly had to find more thread and more spinners. During the eighteenth century the putting-out system grew across Europe, but most extensively in Britain. There, pressured

Woman Working a Spinning Jenny The loose cotton strands on the slanted bobbins shown in this illustration of Hargreaves's spinning jenny passed up to the sliding carriage and then on to the spindles in back for fine spinning. The worker, almost always a woman, regulated the sliding carriage with one hand, and with the other she turned the crank on the wheel to supply power. By 1783 one woman could spin by hand a hundred threads at a time. (© Mary Evans Picture Library/The Image Works)

by growing demand, the system's limitations began to outweigh its advantages around 1760.

Many a tinkering worker knew that a better spinning wheel promised rich rewards. It proved hard to spin the traditional raw materials—wool and flax—with improved machines, but cotton was different. Cotton textiles had first been imported into Britain from India by the East India Company as a rare and delicate luxury for the upper classes. In the eighteenth century a lively market for cotton cloth emerged in West Africa, where the English and other Europeans traded it in exchange for slaves. By 1760 a tiny domestic cotton industry had emerged in northern England, but it could not compete with cloth produced in India and other parts of Asia. At this time, Indian cotton textiles dominated the world market, due to their workers' mastery over design and dyeing techniques, easy access to raw materials, and relatively low wages. International competition thus drove English entrepreneurs to invent new technologies to bring down labor costs.

After many experiments over a generation, a gifted carpenter and jack-of-all-trades, James Hargreaves, invented his cotton-spinning jenny about 1765. At almost the same moment, a barber-turned-manufacturer named Richard Arkwright invented (or possibly pirated) another kind of spinning machine, the water frame. These breakthroughs produced an explosion in the infant cotton textile industry in the 1780s, when it was increasing the value of its output at an unprecedented rate of about 13 percent each year. By 1790 the new machines were producing ten times as much cotton yarn as had been made in 1770.

Hargreaves's **spinning jenny** was simple, inexpensive, and powered by hand. In early models from six to twenty-four spindles were mounted on a sliding carriage, and each spindle spun a fine, slender thread. The machines were usually worked by women, who moved the carriage back and forth with one hand and turned a wheel to supply power with the other. Now it was the male weaver who could not keep up with the vastly more efficient female spinner.

Arkwright's spinning frame employed a different principle, using a series of rollers to stretch the yarn. It quickly acquired a capacity of several hundred spindles and demanded much more power than a single operator could provide. A solution was found in waterpower. The **water frame** required large specialized mills located beside rivers in factories that employed as many as one thousand workers. The water frame did not completely replace cottage industry, however, for it could spin only a coarse, strong thread, which was then put out for respinning on hand-operated cottage jennies. Around 1780 a hybrid machine—called a mule—invented by Samuel Crompton proved capable of spinning very fine and strong thread in large quantities. (See "Individuals in Society: Samuel Crompton," page 652.) Gradually, all cotton spinning was concentrated in large-scale water-powered factories.

These revolutionary developments in the textile industry allowed British manufacturers to compete successfully in international markets in both fine and coarse cotton thread. At first, the machines were too expensive to build and did not provide enough savings in labor to be adopted in continental Europe or elsewhere. Where wages were low and investment capital was scarce, there was little point in adopting mechanized production until significant increases in the machines' productivity, and a drop in the cost of manufacturing them, occurred in the first decades of the nineteenth century.[2]

spinning jenny A simple, inexpensive, hand-powered spinning machine created by James Hargreaves in 1765.

water frame A spinning machine created by Richard Arkwright that had a capacity of several hundred spindles and used waterpower; it therefore required a larger and more specialized mill—a factory.

INDIVIDUALS IN SOCIETY
Samuel Crompton

Samuel Crompton's life story illustrates the remarkable ingenuity and determination of the first generation of inventors of the Industrial Revolution as well as the struggles they faced in controlling and profiting from their inventions. Crompton was born in 1753 in Bolton-in-the Moors, a Lancashire village active in the domestic production of cotton thread and cloth. Crompton descended from small landowners and weavers, but his grandfather had lost the family land and his father died shortly after his birth.

Crompton's mother was a pious and energetic woman who supported the family by tenant farming and spinning and weaving cotton. Crompton spent years spinning in childhood until he was old enough to begin weaving. His mother ensured that he was well educated at the local school, and as a teenager he attended night classes, studying algebra, mathematics, and trigonometry.

This was the period when John Kay's invention of the flying shuttle doubled the speed of handloom weaving, leading to a drastic increase in the demand for thread (see Chapter 17). Crompton's family acquired one of the new spinning jennies — invented by James Hargreaves — and he saw for himself how they advanced production. He was also acquainted with Richard Arkwright, inventor of the water frame, who then operated a barbershop in Bolton.

In 1774 Crompton began work on the spinning machine that would consume what little free time, and spare money, he possessed over the next five years.

Solitary by nature, and fearful of competition and the violence of machine breakers, Crompton worked alone and in secret. He earned a little extra money playing violin in the Bolton theater orchestra, and he possessed a set of tools left over from his father's own mechanical experiments.

The result of all this effort was the spinning mule, so called because it combined the rollers of Arkwright's water frame with the moving carriage of Hargreaves's spinning jenny. With the mule, spinners could produce very fine and strong thread in large quantities, something no previous machine had permitted. The mule effectively ended England's reliance on India for the finest muslin cloth.

In 1780, possessed of a spectacular technological breakthrough and a beloved bride, Crompton seemed poised for a prosperous and happy life. Demand surged for the products of his machine, and manufacturers were desperate to learn its secrets. Too poor and naïve to purchase a patent for his invention, Crompton shared it with manufacturers through a subscription agreement. Unfortunately, he received little of the promised money in return.

Once exposed to the public, the spinning mule quickly spread across Great Britain. Crompton continued to make high-quality yarn, but had to compete with all the other workshops using his machine. Moreover, he could not keep skilled workers, since they were constantly lured away by his competitors' higher wages.

Families using cotton in cottage industry were freed from their constant search for adequate yarn from scattered part-time spinners, since all the thread needed could be spun in the cottage on the jenny or obtained from a nearby factory. The income of weavers, now hard-pressed to keep up with the spinners, rose markedly until about 1792. They were among the highest-earning workers in England. As a result, large numbers of agricultural laborers became handloom weavers, while mechanics and capitalists sought to invent a power loom to save on labor costs. This Edmund Cartwright achieved in 1785. But the power looms of the factories worked poorly at first and did not replace handlooms until the 1820s.

Working conditions in the early cotton factories were so poor that adult weavers and spinners were reluctant to work in them. Factory owners often turned to young orphans and children instead. By placing them in "apprenticeship" with factory owners, parish officers charged with caring for such children saved money. At the same time, the factory owners gained workers over whom they exercised

As others earned great wealth with the mule, Crompton grew frustrated by his relative poverty. In 1811 he toured Great Britain to document his invention's impact. He estimated that 4,600,000 mules were then in operation that directly employed 70,000 people. Crompton's supporters took these figures to Parliament, which granted him a modest reward of £5,000. However, this boost did little to improve his fortunes, and his subsequent business ventures failed. In 1824 local benefactors took up a small subscription to provide for his needs, but he died in poverty in 1827 at the age of seventy-four.

Samuel Crompton, inventor of the spinning mule.
(Engraving by Thomas Barlow [1824–1889], based on a painting by Charles Allingham/SSPL/Getty Images)

QUESTIONS FOR ANALYSIS

1. What factors in Crompton's life enabled him to succeed as an inventor?
2. Why did Crompton fail to profit from his inventions?
3. What does the contrast between Richard Arkwright's fantastic success and Crompton's relative failure tell us about innovation and commercial enterprise in the Industrial Revolution?

Source: Gilbert James France, *The Life and Times of Samuel Crompton, Inventor of the Spinning Machine Called the Mule* (London: Simpkin Marshall, 1859).

Replica of the spinning mule, a hybrid machine that combined features from Hargreaves's spinning jenny and Arkwright's water frame. (SSPL/Getty Images)

almost the authority of slave owners. Apprenticed as young as five or six years of age, boy and girl workers were forced by law to labor for their masters for as many as fourteen years. Housed, fed, and locked up nightly in factory dormitories, the young workers labored thirteen or fourteen hours a day for little or no pay. Harsh physical punishment maintained brutal discipline. To be sure, poor children typically worked long hours in many types of demanding jobs, but this wholesale coercion of orphans as factory apprentices constituted exploitation on a truly unprecedented scale.

The creation of the world's first machine-powered factories in the British cotton textile industry in the 1770s and 1780s, which grew out of the putting-out system of cottage production, was a major historical development. Both symbolically and substantially, the big new cotton mills marked the beginning of the Industrial Revolution in Britain. By 1831 the largely mechanized cotton textile industry accounted for fully 22 percent of the country's entire industrial production.

The Steam Engine Breakthrough

Human beings have long used their toolmaking abilities to construct machines that convert one form of energy into another for their own benefit. In the medieval period, Europeans began to adopt water mills to grind their grain and windmills to pump water and drain swamps. More efficient use of water and wind in the sixteenth and seventeenth centuries enabled them to accomplish more. Nevertheless, even into the eighteenth century Europe, like other areas of the world, continued to rely mainly on wood for energy, and human beings and animals continued to perform most work. This dependence meant that Europe and the rest of the world remained poor in energy and power.

By the eighteenth century wood was in ever-shorter supply in Britain. Processed wood (charcoal) was the fuel that was mixed with iron ore in the blast furnace to produce pig iron, crude iron molded into ingots called "pigs" that could be processed into steel, cast iron, or wrought iron. The iron industry's appetite for wood was enormous, and by 1740 the British iron industry was stagnating. Vast forests enabled Russia in the eighteenth century to become the world's leading producer of iron, much of which was exported to Britain. As wood became ever more scarce, the British looked to coal (combustible rock composed of fossilized organic matter) as an alternative. They had first used coal in the late Middle Ages as a source of heat. By 1640 most homes in London were heated with coal, and it was also used in industry to provide heat for making beer, glass, soap, and other products. The breakthrough came when industrialists began to use coal to produce mechanical energy and to power machinery.

To produce more coal, mines had to be dug deeper and deeper and, as a result, were constantly filling with water. Mechanical pumps, usually powered by animals walking in circles at the surface, had to be installed. Animal power was expensive and bothersome. In an attempt to overcome these disadvantages, Thomas Savery in 1698 and Thomas Newcomen in 1705 invented the first primitive **steam engines**. Both engines burned coal to produce steam, which was then used to operate a pump. Although both models were extremely inefficient, by the early 1770s many of the Savery engines and hundreds of the Newcomen engines were operating successfully in English and Scottish mines.

In 1763 a gifted young Scot named James Watt (1736–1819) was drawn to a critical study of the steam engine. Watt was employed at the time by the University of Glasgow as a skilled craftsman making scientific instruments. Scotland's Enlightenment emphasis on practicality and social progress had caused its universities to become pioneers in technical education. In 1763 Watt was called on to repair a Newcomen engine being used in a physics course. After a series of observations, Watt saw that the Newcomen engine's waste of energy could be reduced by adding a separate condenser. This splendid invention, patented in 1769, greatly increased the efficiency of the steam engine.

To invent something is one thing; to make it a practical success is quite another. Watt needed skilled workers, precision parts, and capital, and the relatively advanced nature of the British economy proved essential. A partnership in 1775 with Matthew Boulton, a wealthy English industrialist, provided Watt with adequate capital and exceptional skills in salesmanship. Among Britain's highly skilled locksmiths,

steam engines A breakthrough invention by Thomas Savery in 1698 and Thomas Newcomen in 1705 that burned coal to produce steam, which was then used to operate a pump; the early models were superseded by James Watt's more efficient steam engine, patented in 1769.

James Nasmyth's Mighty Steam Hammer   Nasmyth's invention was the forerunner of the modern pile driver, and its successful introduction in 1832 epitomized the rapid development of steam-power technology in Britain. In this painting by the inventor himself, workers manipulate a massive iron shaft being hammered into shape at Nasmyth's foundry near Manchester. (Ann Ronan Pictures/Print Collector/Getty Images)

tinsmiths, and millwrights, Watt found mechanics who could install, regulate, and repair his sophisticated engines. From ingenious manufacturers such as the cannonmaker John Wilkinson, Watt was gradually able to purchase precision parts. This support allowed him to create an effective vacuum in the condenser and regulate a complex engine. In more than twenty years of constant effort, Watt made many further improvements. By the late 1780s the firm of Boulton and Watt had made the steam engine a practical and commercial success in Britain.

The coal-burning steam engine of Watt and his followers was the Industrial Revolution's most fundamental advance in technology. For the first time in history, humanity had, at least for a few generations, almost unlimited power at its disposal. For the first time, inventors and engineers could devise and implement all kinds of power equipment to aid people in their work. The steam-power plant began to replace waterpower in cotton-spinning factories during the 1780s, contributing greatly to that industry's phenomenal rise. Steam also took the place of waterpower in flour mills, in the malt mills used in breweries, in the flint mills supplying the pottery industry, and in the mills exported by Britain to the West Indies to crush sugarcane.

The British iron industry was radically transformed. Originally, the smoke and fumes resulting from coal burning meant that coal could not be substituted for charcoal in smelting iron. Starting around 1710, ironmakers began to use coke—a smokeless and hot-burning fuel produced by heating coal to rid it of water and other impurities—to smelt pig iron. After 1770 the adoption of steam-driven bellows in blast furnaces allowed for great increases in the quantity of pig iron produced by British ironmakers. In the 1780s Henry Cort developed the puddling furnace, which allowed pig iron to be refined in turn with coke.

Strong, skilled ironworkers—the puddlers—"cooked" molten pig iron in a great vat, raking off globs of refined iron for further processing. Cort also developed steam-powered rolling mills, which were capable of turning out finished iron in every shape and form. The economic consequence of these technical innovations was a great boom in the British iron industry. In 1740 annual British iron production was only 17,000 tons. With the spread of coke smelting and the impact of Cort's inventions, production had reached 260,000 tons by 1806. In 1844 Britain produced 3 million tons of iron. Once expensive, iron became the cheap, basic, indispensable building block of the British economy.

Steam-Powered Transportation

The coal industry had long used plank roads and rails to move coal wagons within mines and at the surface. Rails reduced friction and allowed a horse or a human being to pull a much heavier load. Thus, once a rail capable of supporting a heavy locomotive was developed in 1816, all sorts of experiments with steam engines on rails went forward.

The first steam locomotive was built by Richard Trevithick after much experimentation. George Stephenson acquired glory for his locomotive named ***Rocket***, which sped down the track of the just-completed Liverpool and Manchester Railway at a maximum speed of 35 miles per hour, without a load, in 1829. The line from Liverpool to Manchester was a financial as well as a technical success, and many private companies quickly began to build more rail lines. Within twenty years they had completed the main trunk lines of Great Britain (Map 20.1). Other countries were quick to follow, with the first steam-powered trains operating in the United States in the 1830s and in Brazil, Chile, Argentina, and the British colonies of Canada, Australia, and India in the 1850s.

Rocket The name given to George Stephenson's effective locomotive that was first tested in 1829 on the Liverpool and Manchester Railway at 35 miles per hour.

The arrival of the railroad had many significant consequences. It dramatically reduced the cost and uncertainty of shipping freight over land. Previously, markets had tended to be small and local; as the barrier of high transportation costs was lowered, markets became larger and even nationwide. Larger markets encouraged larger factories with more sophisticated machinery in a growing number of industries. Such factories could make goods more cheaply and gradually subjected most cottage workers and many urban artisans to severe competitive pressures. In all countries, the construction of railroads created a strong demand for unskilled labor and contributed to the growth of a class of urban workers.

The steam engine also transformed water travel. French engineers completed the first steamships in the 1770s, and the first commercial steamships came into use in North America several decades later. The *Clermont* began to travel the waters of the Hudson River in New York State in 1807, shortly followed by ships belonging to brewer John Molson on the St. Lawrence River. The steamship brought the advantages of the railroad—speed, reliability, efficiency—to water travel.

MAP 20.1 The Industrial Revolution in Great Britain, ca. 1850 Industry concentrated in the rapidly growing cities of the north and the center of England, where rich coal and iron deposits were close to one another.

Industry and Population

In 1851 London hosted an industrial fair called the Great Exhibition in the newly built **Crystal Palace**. More than 6 million visitors from all over Europe marveled at the gigantic new exhibition hall set in the middle of a large, centrally located park. The building was made entirely of glass and iron, both of which were now cheap and abundant. Sponsored by the British royal family, the exhibition celebrated the new era of industrial technology and the kingdom's role as world economic leader.

Britain's claim to be the "workshop of the world" was no idle boast, for it produced two-thirds of the world's coal and more than half of all iron and cotton cloth. More generally, in 1860 Britain produced a remarkable 20 percent of the entire world's output of industrial goods, whereas it had produced only about 2 percent of the total in 1750.[3] As the British economy significantly increased its production of manufactured goods, the gross national product (GNP) rose roughly fourfold at constant prices between 1780 and 1851. At the same time, the population of Britain boomed, growing from about 9 million in 1780 to almost 21 million in 1851. Thus growing numbers consumed much of the increase in total production.

Rapid population growth in Britain was key to industrial development. More people meant a more mobile labor force, with many young workers in need of employment and ready to go where the jobs were. Sustaining the dramatic increase in population, in turn, was only possible through advances in production in agriculture and industry. Based on the lessons of history, many contemporaries feared that the rapid growth in population would inevitably lead to disaster. In his *Essay on the Principle of Population* (1798), Thomas Malthus (1766–1834) examined the dynamics of human populations. He argued:

> There are few states in which there is not a constant effort in the population to increase beyond the means of subsistence. This constant effort as constantly tends to subject the lower classes of society to distress, and to prevent any great permanent melioration of these conditions.[4]

Given the limited resources available, Malthus concluded that the only hope of warding off such "positive checks" to population growth as famine and disease was "prudential restraint." That is, young men and women had to limit the growth of population by marrying late in life. But Malthus was not optimistic about this possibility. The powerful attraction of the sexes, he feared, would cause most people to marry early and have many children.

Economist David Ricardo (1772–1823) spelled out the pessimistic implications of Malthus's thought. Ricardo's depressing **iron law of wages** posited that over an extended period of time, because of the pressure of population growth, wages would always sink to subsistence level. That is, wages would be just high enough to keep workers from starving.

Malthus, Ricardo, and their followers were proved wrong in the long run, largely because industrialization improved productivity beyond what they could imagine. However, until the 1820s, or even the 1840s, contemporary observers might reasonably have concluded that the economy and the total population were racing neck and neck, with the outcome very much in doubt. There was another problem as well.

Crystal Palace The location of the Great Exhibition in 1851 in London; an architectural masterpiece made entirely of glass and iron.

iron law of wages Theory proposed by English economist David Ricardo suggesting that the pressure of population growth prevents wages from rising above the subsistence level.

Perhaps workers, farmers, and ordinary people did not get their rightful share of the new wealth. Perhaps only the rich got richer, while the poor got poorer or made no progress. We will turn to this great issue after situating the process of industrialization in its European and global context.

Industrialization in Europe and the World

FOCUS QUESTION

How did countries in Europe and around the world respond to the challenge of industrialization?

As new technologies and a new organization of labor began to revolutionize production in Britain, other countries took notice and began to emulate its example. With the end of the Napoleonic Wars, the nations of the European continent quickly adopted British inventions and achieved their own pattern of technological innovation and economic growth. By the last decades of the nineteenth century, western European countries as well as the United States and Japan had industrialized their economies to a considerable, albeit variable, degree.

Industrialization in other parts of the world proceeded more gradually, with uneven jerks and national and regional variations. Scholars are still struggling to explain these variations as well as the dramatic gap that emerged for the first time in history between Western and non-Western levels of economic production. These questions are especially important because they may offer valuable lessons for poor countries that today are seeking to improve their material condition through industrialization and economic development. The latest findings on the nineteenth-century experience are encouraging. They suggest that there were alternative paths to the industrial world and that there was and is no need to follow a rigid, predetermined British model.

National and International Variations

Comparative data on industrial production in different countries over time help give us an overview of what happened. One set of data, the work of a Swiss scholar, compares the level of industrialization on a per capita basis in several countries from 1750 to 1913. These data are far from perfect, but they reflect basic trends and are presented in Table 20.1 for closer study.

Table 20.1 presents a comparison of how much industrial product was produced, on average, for each person in a given country in a given year. All the numbers are expressed in terms of a single index number of 100, which equals the per capita level of industrial goods in Great Britain in 1900. Every number in the table is thus a percentage of the 1900 level in Britain and is directly comparable with other numbers. The countries are listed in roughly the order that they began to use large-scale, power-driven technology.

What does this overview tell us? First, one sees in the first column that in 1750 all countries were fairly close together, including non-Western nations such as China and India. Both China and India had been extremely important players in early modern world trade; both were sophisticated, technologically advanced, and economically powerful up to 1800 (see Chapter 14). However, the column headed 1800 shows that Britain had opened up a noticeable lead over all countries by 1800, and that gap progressively widened as the Industrial Revolution accelerated through 1830 and reached full maturity by 1860.

Second, the table shows that Western countries began to emulate the British model successfully over the course of the nineteenth century, with significant variations in the timing and in the extent of industrialization. Belgium, achieving independence from the Netherlands in 1831 and rich in iron and coal, led in adopting Britain's new technology, and it experienced a great surge between 1830 and 1860. France developed factory production more gradually and did not experience "revolutionary" growth in overall industrial output.

Slow but steady growth in France was overshadowed by the spectacular rise of the German lands and the United States after 1860 in what has been termed the "second industrial revolution." In general, eastern and southern Europe began the process of modern industrialization later than northwestern and central Europe. Nevertheless, these regions made real progress in the late nineteenth century, as growth after 1880 in Austria-Hungary, Italy, and Russia suggests. This meant that all European states as well as the United States managed to raise per capita industrial levels in the nineteenth century.

These increases stood in stark contrast to the decreases that occurred at the same time in many non-Western countries, most notably in China and India, as Table 20.1 shows. European countries industrialized to a greater or lesser extent even as most of the non-Western world stagnated. Japan, which is not included in this table, stands out as an exceptional area of non-Western industrial growth in the second half of the nineteenth century. After the forced opening of the country to the West in the 1850s, Japanese entrepreneurs began to adopt Western technology and manufacturing methods, resulting in a production boom by the late nineteenth century. Different rates of wealth- and power-creating industrial development, which heightened disparities within Europe, also greatly magnified existing inequalities between Europe and the rest of the world.

TABLE 20.1 Per Capita Levels of Industrialization, 1750–1913

	1750	1800	1830	1860	1880	1900	1913
Great Britain	10	16	25	64	87	100	115
Belgium	9	10	14	28	43	56	88
United States	4	9	14	21	38	69	126
France	9	9	12	20	28	39	59
Germany	8	8	9	15	25	52	85
Austria-Hungary	7	7	8	11	15	23	32
Italy	8	8	8	10	12	17	26
Russia	6	6	7	8	10	15	20
China	8	6	6	4	4	3	3
India	7	6	6	3	2	1	2

Note: All entries are based on an index value of 100, equal to the per capita level of industrialization in Great Britain in 1900. Data for Great Britain includes Ireland, England, Wales, and Scotland.

Source: P. Bairoch, "International Industrialization Levels from 1750 to 1980," *Journal of European Economic History* 11 (Spring 1982): 294, U.S. Journals at Cambridge University Press.

Industrialization in Continental Europe

Throughout Europe the eighteenth century was an era of agricultural improvement, population increase, expanding foreign trade, and growing cottage industry. Thus, when the pace of British industry began to accelerate in the 1780s, continental businesses began to emulate the new methods. British industry enjoyed clear superiority, but the European continent was close behind. During the period of the revolutionary and Napoleonic wars, from 1793 to 1815, however, western Europe experienced tremendous political and social upheaval that temporarily halted economic development. With the return of peace in 1815, western European countries again began to play catch-up.

They faced significant challenges. In the newly mechanized industries, British goods were being produced very economically, and these goods had come to dominate

MAP 20.2 Continental Industrialization, ca. 1850   Although continental countries were beginning to make progress by 1850, they still lagged far behind Great Britain. For example, continental railroad building was still in an early stage, whereas the British rail system was essentially complete (see Map 20.1). Coal played a critical role in nineteenth-century industrialization both as a power source for steam engines and as a raw material for making iron and steel.

world markets. In addition, British technology had become so advanced that few engineers or skilled technicians outside England understood it. Moreover, the technology of steam power had grown much more expensive. It involved large investments in the iron and coal industries and, after 1830, in railroads. Continental business people had difficulty amassing the large sums of money the new methods demanded, and laborers bitterly resisted the move to working in factories. All these factors slowed the spread of machine-powered industry (Map 20.2).

Nevertheless, western European nations possessed a number of advantages that helped them respond to these challenges. First, most had rich traditions of putting-out enterprise, merchant capitalists, and skilled urban artisans. These assets gave their firms the ability to adapt and survive in the face of new market conditions. Second, continental capitalists did not need to develop their own advanced technology. Instead, they could simply "borrow" the new methods developed in Great Britain. European countries also had a third asset that many non-Western areas lacked in the nineteenth century: they had strong, independent governments that did not fall under foreign political control. These governments would use the power of the state to promote industry and catch up with Britain.

Most continental businesses adopted factory technology slowly, and handicraft methods lived on. Indeed, continental industrialization usually brought substantial but uneven expansion of handicraft industry in both rural and urban areas for a time. Artisan production of luxury items grew in France as the rising income of the international middle class created increased foreign demand for silk scarves, embroidered needlework, perfumes, and fine wines. Focusing on artisanal luxury production made sense for French entrepreneurs given their long history of dominance in that sector. Rather than being a "backward" refusal to modernize, it represented a sound strategic choice that allowed the French to capitalize on their know-how and international reputation for high-quality goods.

Agents of Industrialization

Western European success in adopting British methods took place despite the best efforts of the British to prevent it. The British realized the great value of their technical discoveries and tried to keep their secrets to themselves. Until 1825 it was illegal for artisans and skilled mechanics to leave Britain; until 1843 the export of textile machinery and other equipment was forbidden. Many talented, ambitious workers, however, slipped out of the country illegally and introduced the new methods abroad.

One such man was William Cockerill, a Lancashire carpenter. He and his sons began building cotton-spinning equipment in French-occupied Belgium in 1799. In 1817 the most famous son, John Cockerill, built a large industrial enterprise in Liège in southern Belgium, which produced machinery, steam engines, and then railway locomotives. He also established modern ironworks and coal mines. Cockerill's plants in the Liège area became a center for the gathering and transmitting of industrial information across Europe. Many skilled British workers came to work for Cockerill, and some went on to found their own companies throughout Europe.

Thus British technicians and skilled workers were a powerful force in the spread of early industrialization. A second agent of industrialization consisted of talented entrepreneurs such as Fritz Harkort (1793–1880), a pioneer in the German machinery industry. Serving in England as a Prussian army officer during the Napoleonic Wars, Harkort was impressed with what he saw. Harkort set up shop building steam engines in the Ruhr Valley, on the western border with France. In spite of problems obtaining skilled workers and machinery, Harkort succeeded in building and selling engines. However, his ambitious efforts also resulted in large financial losses for himself and his partners. His career illustrates both the great efforts of a few important business leaders to duplicate the British achievement and the difficulty of the task.

National governments played an even more important role in supporting industrialization in continental Europe than in Britain. **Tariff protection** was one such support, and it proved to be important. The French, for example, responded to a flood of cheap British goods in 1815 after the Napoleonic Wars by laying high taxes on imported goods. Customs agreements emerged among some German states starting in 1818, and in 1834 a number of states signed a treaty creating a customs union, or *Zollverein*. The treaty allowed goods to move between member states without tariffs, while erecting a single uniform tariff against other nations.

tariff protection
A government's way of supporting and aiding its own economy by laying high taxes on imported goods from other countries, as when the French responded to cheaper British goods flooding their country by imposing high tariffs on some imported products.

After 1815 continental governments also bore the cost of building roads, canals, and railroads to improve transportation. Belgium led the way in the 1830s and 1840s. Built rapidly as a unified network, Belgium's state-owned railroads stimulated the development of heavy industry and made the country an early industrial leader. In France, the state shouldered all the expense of acquiring and laying roadbed, including bridges and tunnels. In short, governments helped pay for railroads, the all-important leading sector in continental industrialization.

Finally, banks also played a larger and more creative role on the continent than in Britain. Previously, almost all banks in Europe had been private. Because of the possibility of unlimited financial loss, the partners of private banks tended to be conservative and were content to deal with a few rich clients and a few big merchants. They generally avoided industrial investment as being too risky.

In the 1830s two important Belgian banks pioneered in a new direction. They received permission from the growth-oriented government to establish themselves as corporations enjoying limited liability. That is, if the bank went bankrupt, stockholders could now lose only their original investments in the bank's common stock, and they could not be forced by the courts to pay for any additional losses out of other property they owned. Limited liability helped these Belgian banks attract investors. They mobilized impressive resources for investment in big companies, became industrial banks, and successfully promoted industrial development.

Similar corporate banks became important in France and the German lands in the 1850s and 1860s. Usually working in collaboration with governments, corporate banks established and developed many railroads and many companies working in heavy industry, which were also increasingly organized as limited liability corporations.

The combined efforts of governments, skilled workers, entrepreneurs, and industrial banks meshed successfully after 1850 and the financial crash of 1873. In Belgium, France, and the German states, key indicators of modern industrial development—such as railway mileage, iron and coal production, and steam engine capacity—increased at average annual rates of 5 to 10 percent. As a result, rail

The Circle of the Rue Royale, Paris, 1868   The Circle of the Rue Royale was an exclusive club of aristocrats, bankers, railway owners, and other members of Parisian high society. This group portrait projects the wealth and elegance of the club's members, who are gathered on the balcony of a hotel. (*The Circle of the Rue Royale, Paris, 1868*, by James Jacques Joseph Tissot [1836–1902], [oil on canvas]/Fine Art Images/Heritage Images/Getty Images)

networks were completed in western and much of central Europe, and the leading continental countries mastered the industrial technologies that had first been developed by the British. In the early 1870s Britain was still Europe's most industrial nation, but a select handful of nations had closed the gap.

The Global Picture

The Industrial Revolution did not have a transformative impact beyond Europe prior to the 1860s, with the exception of the United States and Japan, both early adopters of British practices. In many countries, national governments and pioneering entrepreneurs did make efforts to adopt the technologies and methods of production that had proved so successful in Britain, but they fell short of transitioning to an industrial economy. For example, in Russia the imperial government brought steamships to the Volga River and a railroad to the capital, St. Petersburg, in the first decades of the nineteenth century. By midcentury ambitious entrepreneurs had established steam-powered cotton factories using imported British machines. However, these advances did not lead to overall industrialization of the country, most of whose people remained mired in rural servitude. Instead, Russia confirmed its role as provider of raw materials, especially timber and grain, to the hungry West.

Egypt, a territory of the Ottoman Empire, similarly began an ambitious program of modernization after a reform-minded viceroy took power in 1805. This program included the use of imported British technology and experts in textile manufacture and other industries. These industries, however, could not compete with lower-priced European imports. Like Russia, Egypt fell back on agricultural exports to European markets, like sugar and cotton.

Such examples of faltering efforts at industrialization could be found in many other regions of the Middle East, Asia, and Latin America. Where European governments maintained direct or indirect political control, they acted to monopolize colonial markets as both sources of raw materials and consumers for their own products, rather than encouraging the spread of industrialization. Such regions could not respond to low-cost imports by raising tariffs, as the United States and western European nations had done, because they were controlled by imperial powers that did not allow them to do so. In India, millions of poor textile workers lost their livelihood because they could not compete with industrially produced British cottons. The British charged stiff import duties on Indian cottons entering the kingdom, but prohibited the Indians from doing the same to British imports. As a British trade encyclopedia boasted in 1844:

> The British manufacturer brings the cotton of India from a distance of 12,000 miles, commits it to his spinning jennies and power-looms, carries back their products to the East, making them again to travel 12,000 miles; and in spite of the loss of time, and of the enormous expense incurred by this voyage of 24,000 miles, the cotton manufactured by his machinery becomes less costly than the cotton of India spun and woven by the hand near the field that produced it.[5]

Latin American economies were disrupted by the early-nineteenth-century wars of independence. As these countries' economies recovered in the mid-nineteenth century, they increasingly adopted steam power for sugar and coffee processing and for transportation. Like elsewhere, this technology first supported increased agricultural production for export and only later drove domestic industrial production. As in India, the arrival of cheap British cottons destroyed the pre-existing textile industry that had employed many people.

The rise of industrialization in Britain, western Europe, and the United States thus caused other regions of the world to become increasingly economically dependent. Instead of industrializing, many territories underwent a process of deindustrialization due to imperialism and economic competition. In turn, relative economic weakness made them vulnerable to the new wave of imperialism undertaken by industrialized nations in the second half of the nineteenth century (see Chapter 24).

As for China, it did not adopt mechanized production until the end of the nineteenth century, but continued as a market-based, commercial society with a massive rural sector and industrial production based on traditional methods. Some regions of China experienced slow economic growth, while others were stagnant. In the 1860s and 1870s, when Japan was successfully adopting industrial methods, the Chinese government showed similar interest in Western technology and science. However, China faced widespread uprisings in the mid-nineteenth century, which drained attention and resources to the military. With China poised to surpass the United States in economic production by 2020, scholars now wonder whether the ascension of Europe and the West from 1800 was merely a brief interruption in a much longer pattern of Asian dominance.

New Patterns of Working and Living

FOCUS QUESTION
How did work evolve during the Industrial Revolution, and how did daily life change for working people?

Having first emerged in the British countryside in the late eighteenth century, factories and industrial labor began migrating to cities by the early nineteenth century. As factories moved from rural to urban areas, their workforce evolved as well, from pauper children to families to men and women uprooted from their traditional rural communities. Many women, especially young single women and poor women, continued to work, but married women began to limit their participation in the workforce when possible. For some people, the Industrial Revolution brought improvements, but living and working conditions for the poor stagnated or even deteriorated until around 1850, especially in overcrowded industrial cities.

Work in Early Factories

The first factories of the Industrial Revolution were cotton mills, which began functioning in the 1770s along fast-running rivers and streams and were often located in sparsely populated areas. Cottage workers, accustomed to the putting-out system, were reluctant to work in the new factories even when they received relatively good wages. In a factory, workers had to keep up with the machine and follow its relentless tempo. Moreover, they had to show up every day, on time, and work long, monotonous hours under the constant supervision of demanding overseers, and they were punished systematically if they broke the work rules. For example, if a worker was late to work, or accidentally spoiled material, the employer deducted fines from the weekly pay. Employers frequently beat children and adolescents for their infractions.

Cottage workers were not used to that way of life. All members of the family worked hard and long, but in spurts, setting their own pace. They could interrupt their work when they wished. Women and children could break up their long hours of spinning with other tasks. On Saturday afternoon the head of the family delivered the week's work to the merchant manufacturer and got paid. Saturday night was a time of relaxation and drinking, especially for the men.

Also, early factories resembled English poorhouses, where destitute people went to live at public expense. Some poorhouses were industrial prisons, where the inmates had to work in order to receive food and lodging. The similarity between large brick factories and large stone poorhouses increased the cottage workers' fear of factories and their hatred of factory discipline. It was cottage workers' reluctance to work in factories that prompted early cotton mill owners to turn to pauper children. Mill owners contracted with local officials to employ large numbers of such children, who had no say in the matter. Attitudes began to change in the last decade of the eighteenth century, as middle-class reformers publicized the brutal toil imposed on society's most vulnerable members.

Working Families and Children

By the 1790s the early pattern had begun to change. The use of pauper apprentices was in decline, and in 1802 it was forbidden by Parliament. Many more textile factories were being built, mainly in urban areas, where they could use steam power rather than waterpower and attract a workforce more easily than in the countryside. People came from near and far to work in the cities, as factory workers and as porters, builders, and domestic servants. Collectively, these wage laborers came to be known as the "working class," a term first used in the late 1830s.

In some cases, workers accommodated to the system by carrying over familiar working traditions. Some came to the mills and the mines in the family units in which they had labored on farms and in the putting-out system. The mill or mine owner bargained with the head of the family and paid him or her for the efforts of the whole family. In the cotton mills, children worked for their mothers or fathers, collecting scraps and "piecing" broken threads together. In the mines, children sorted coal and worked the ventilation equipment. Their mothers hauled coal in the tunnels below the surface, while their fathers hewed with pick and shovel at the face of the seam.

Ties of kinship were particularly important for newcomers, who often traveled great distances to find work. Many urban workers in Great Britain were from Ireland. They were forced out of rural Ireland by population growth and deteriorating economic conditions from 1817 on, and their numbers increased dramatically in the desperate years of the potato famine, from 1845 to 1851 (see Chapter 21). As early as 1824 most of the workers in the Glasgow cotton mills were Irish; in 1851 one-sixth of the population of Liverpool was Irish. Like many other immigrant groups held together by ethnic and religious ties, however, the Irish worked together, formed their own neighborhoods, and preserved their cultural traditions.

In the early decades of the nineteenth century, however, technical changes made it less and less likely that workers could continue to labor in family groups. As control and discipline passed into the hands of impersonal managers and overseers, adult workers began to protest against inhuman conditions on behalf of their children. Some enlightened employers and social reformers in Parliament argued that more humane standards were necessary, and they used widely circulated parliamentary reports to influence public opinion. For example, Robert Owen (1771–1858), a successful manufacturer in Scotland, testified in 1816 before an investigating committee on the basis of his experience. He argued that employing children under ten years of age as factory workers was "injurious to the children, and not beneficial to the proprietors."[6] Workers also provided graphic testimony at such hearings as reformers pressed Parliament to pass corrective laws. These efforts resulted in a series of British **Factory Acts** from 1802 to 1833 that progressively limited the workday of child laborers and set minimum hygiene and safety requirements. (See "Evaluating the Evidence 20.1: Debate over Child Labor Laws," at right.) The Factory Act of 1833 installed a system of full-time professional inspectors to enforce the provisions of previous acts. Children between ages nine and thirteen could work a maximum of eight hours per day, not including two hours for education. Teenagers aged fourteen to eighteen could work up to twelve hours, while those under nine were banned from employment. The Factory Acts constituted significant progress in preventing the exploitation of children. One unintended drawback of restrictions on child labor, however, was that they broke the pattern of whole families working together in the factory because efficiency required standardized shifts for all workers. After 1833 the number of children employed in industry declined rapidly.

Factory Acts English laws passed from 1802 to 1833 that limited the workday of child laborers and set minimum hygiene and safety requirements.

The New Sexual Division of Labor

With the restriction of child labor and the collapse of the family work pattern in the 1830s came a new sexual division of labor. By 1850 the man was emerging as the family's primary wage earner, while the married woman found only limited job opportunities. Generally denied good jobs at high wages in the growing urban economy, wives were expected to concentrate on their duties at home.

separate spheres A gender division of labor with the wife at home as mother and homemaker and the husband as wage earner.

This new pattern of **separate spheres** had several aspects. First, all studies agree that married women from the working classes were much less likely to work full-time for wages outside the house after the first child arrived, although they often earned small amounts doing putting-out handicrafts at home and taking in boarders. Second, when married women did work for wages outside the house, they usually came from the poorest families, where the husbands were poorly paid, sick, unemployed, or missing. Third, these poor married or widowed women were joined by legions of young unmarried women, who worked full-time but only in certain jobs, of which textile factory work, laundering, and domestic service were particularly important. Fourth, all women were generally confined to low-paying, dead-end jobs. Evolving gradually, but largely in place by 1850, the new sexual division of labor constituted a major development in the history of women and of the family.

Several factors combined to create this new sexual division of labor. First, the new and unfamiliar discipline of the clock and the machine was especially hard on married women of the laboring classes. Relentless factory discipline conflicted with child care in a way that labor on the farm or in the cottage had not. A woman operating earsplitting spinning machinery could mind a child of seven or eight working beside her (until such work was outlawed), but she could no longer pace herself through pregnancy or breast-feed her baby on the job. Thus a working-class woman had strong incentives to stay home, if she could afford it. Caring for babies was a less important factor in areas of continental Europe, such as northern France and

Debate over Child Labor Laws

The Cotton Mills and Factories Act of 1819 was one of a series of acts intended to prevent the exploitation of child laborers in Britain, largely by restricting their working hours. Debate in the House of Commons over the legislation pitted those arguing for humanitarian considerations against defenders of economic freedom. A passionate proponent of the bill was Sir Robert Peel, himself a factory owner and father of a future British prime minister.

19 February 1818

Sir Robert Peel. . . . About fifteen years ago he had brought in a Bill for the Regulation of Apprentices in Cotton Manufactories. At that time they were the description of persons most employed in those manufactories. He himself had a thousand of them. . . . Since that time, however, the business had been much extended. Manufactories were established in large towns, and the proprietors availed themselves of all the poor population of those towns. In Manchester alone 20,000 persons were employed in the cotton manufactories, and in the whole of England about three times that number. . . . It was notorious that children of a very tender age were dragged from their beds some hours before day light, and confined in the factories not less than fifteen hours; and it was also notoriously the opinion of the faculty, that no children of eight or nine years of age could bear that degree of hardship with impunity to their health and constitution. It had been urged by the humane, that there might be two sets of young labourers for one set of adults. He was afraid this would produce more harm than good. The better way would be to shorten the time of working for adults as well as for children; and to prevent the introduction of the latter at a very early age. . . . The children . . . were prevented from growing to their full size. In consequence, Manchester, which used to furnish numerous recruits for the army, was now wholly unproductive in that respect. . . .

Lord Lascelles. . . . The individuals who were the objects of the hon. gentleman's proposition were free labourers. This excited his jealousy; for, were the principle of interference with free labourers once admitted, it was difficult to say how far it might not be carried. . . .

Mr. Philips strongly objected to the adoption of any measure of this description, and denied that the employment of children in the cotton factories operated, as had been described, to stint their growth, impair their comfort, or scatter disease amongst them. . . . Small factories were often ill ventilated, and from that circumstance the health of a person might suffer more in six hours in one of these factories, than in fifteen hours in a factory which was well ventilated and properly constructed in other respects. But how could this evil be cured by any bill? The small factories generally went to ruin, and that was the cure for the evil. From the returns made to the House, out of 31,117, the number of persons employed in these returns, 1717, or 5½ per cent, were of the age of 10 and under, 13,203 from 10 to 18, and 16,197 of the age of 18 and upwards. Out of 27,827 persons, there were 1,830 only who could not read.

EVALUATE THE EVIDENCE

1. What arguments for and against labor regulation do the two sides offer? What rhetorical strategies do they use to strengthen their arguments?
2. In what ways do these arguments reflect the changes in working and living patterns described in the text?

Source: Commons Sitting of 19 February 1818, series 1, vol. 37, Cotton Factories Bill, cc559-66, http://hansard.millbanksystems.com/commons/1818/feb/19/cotton-factories-bill.

Scandinavia, where women relied on paid wet nurses instead of breast-feeding their babies (see Chapter 18).

Second, running a household in conditions of primitive urban poverty was an extremely demanding job in its own right. There were no supermarkets or public transportation. Shopping, washing clothes, and feeding the family constituted a never-ending challenge. Taking on a brutal job outside the house—a "second shift"—had limited appeal for the average married woman from the working class. Thus many women might well have accepted the emerging division of labor as the best available strategy for family survival in the industrializing society.[7]

Third, to a large degree the young, generally unmarried women who did work for wages outside the home were segregated from men and confined to certain "women's jobs" because the new sexual division of labor replicated long-standing patterns of gender segregation and inequality. In the preindustrial economy, a small sector of the labor market had always been defined as "women's work," especially tasks involving needlework, spinning, food preparation, child care, and nursing. This traditional sexual division of labor took on new overtones, however, in response to the factory system. Previously, at least in theory, young people worked under a watchful parental eye. The growth of factories and mines brought unheard-of opportunities for girls and boys to mix on the job, free of familial supervision. Such opportunities led to more unplanned pregnancies and fueled the illegitimacy explosion that had begun in the late eighteenth century and that gathered force until at least 1850. Thus segregation of jobs by gender was partly an effort by older people to control the sexuality of working-class youths.

Investigations into the British coal industry before 1842 provide a graphic example of this concern. (See "Evaluating the Evidence 20.2: The Testimony of Young Mine Workers," page 670.) The middle-class men leading the inquiry professed horror at the sight of girls and women working without shirts, which was a common practice because of the heat, and they quickly assumed the prevalence of licentious sex with the male miners, who also wore very little clothing. In fact, many girls and married women worked for related males in a family unit that provided considerable protection and restraint. Yet many witnesses from the working class also believed that the mines were inappropriate and dangerous places for women and girls. Some miners stressed particularly the danger of sexual aggression for girls working past puberty. As one explained, "I consider it a scandal for girls to work in the pits. Till they are 12 or 14 they may work very well but after that it's an abomination. . . . The work of the pit does not hurt them, it is the effect on their morals that I complain of."[8] The **Mines Act of 1842** prohibited underground work for all women and girls as well as for boys under ten.

Mines Act of 1842 English law prohibiting underground work for all women and girls as well as for boys under ten.

Some women who had to support themselves protested against being excluded from coal mining, which paid higher wages than most other jobs open to working-class women. But provided they were part of families that could manage economically, the girls and the women who had worked underground were generally pleased with the law. In explaining her satisfaction in 1844, one mother of four provided real insight into why many married working women accepted the emerging sexual division of labor:

While working in the pit I was worth to my [miner] husband seven shillings a week, out of which we had to pay 2½ shillings to a woman for looking after the younger children. I used to take them to her house at 4 o'clock in the morning, out of their own beds, to put them into hers. Then there was one shilling a week for washing; besides, there was mending to pay for, and other things. The house was not guided. The other children broke things; they did not go to school when they were sent; they would be playing about, and get ill-used by other children, and their clothes torn. Then when I came home in the evening, everything was to do after the day's labor, and I was so tired I had no heart for it; no fire lit, nothing cooked, no water fetched, the house dirty, and nothing comfortable for my husband. It is all far better now, and I wouldn't go down again.[9]

Child Labor in Coal Mines
Public sentiment against child labor in coal mines was provoked by the publication of dramatic images of the harsh working conditions children endured. The Mines Act of 1842 prohibited the employment underground of women and girls, and boys under the age of ten. (*Child Labour in an English Coal Mine*, 1844, colored lithograph/akg-images)

A final factor encouraging working-class women to withdraw from paid labor was the domestic ideals emanating from middle-class women, who had largely embraced the "separate spheres" ideology. Middle-class reformers published tracts and formed societies to urge poor women to devote more care and attention to their homes and families.

Living Standards for the Working Class

Despite the best efforts of hard-working men and women, living conditions for the industrialized poor were often abysmal. Although the evidence is complex and sometimes contradictory, most historians of the Industrial Revolution now agree that overall living standards for the working class did not rise substantially until the 1840s at the earliest. British wages were always high compared to those in the rest of Europe, but the stresses of war with France from 1792 to 1815 led to a decline in the average British worker's real wages and standard of living. These difficult war years, with high unemployment and inflation, lent a grim color to the new industrial system. Factory wages began to rise after 1815, but these gains were modest and were offset by a decline in the labor of children and married women, meaning that many households had less total income than before. Moreover, many people still worked outside the factories as cottage workers or rural laborers, and in those sectors wages declined. Thus the increase in the productivity of industry did not lead to an increase in the purchasing power of the British working classes. Only after 1830, and especially after 1840, did real wages rise substantially, so that the average worker earned roughly 30 percent more in real terms in 1850 than in 1770.[10]

Up to that point, the demands of labor in the new industries probably outweighed their benefits as far as working people were concerned. Many landless poor people in the late eighteenth century were self-employed cottage workers living in close-knit rural communities; with industrialization they worked longer and harder at jobs that

The Testimony of Young Mine Workers

The use of child labor in British industrialization quickly attracted the attention of humanitarians and social reformers. This interest led to investigations by parliamentary commissions, which resulted in laws limiting the hours and the ages of children working in large factories. Designed to build a case for remedial legislation, parliamentary inquiries gave large numbers of workers a rare chance to speak directly to contemporaries and to historians.

The moving passages that follow are taken from testimony gathered in 1841 and 1842 by the Ashley Mines Commission. Interviewing employers and many male and female workers, the commissioners focused on the physical condition of the youth and on the sexual behavior of workers far underground. The subsequent Mines Act of 1842 sought to reduce immoral behavior and sexual bullying by prohibiting underground work for all women and girls (and for boys younger than ten).

Mr. Payne, coal master

That children are employed generally at nine years old in the coal pits and sometimes at eight. In fact, the smaller the vein of coal is in height, the younger and smaller are the children required; the work occupies from six to seven hours per day in the pits; they are not ill-used or worked beyond their strength; a good deal of depravity exists but they are certainly not worse in morals than in other branches of the Sheffield trade, but upon the whole superior; the morals of this district are materially improving; Mr. Bruce, the clergyman, has been zealous and active in endeavoring to ameliorate their moral and religious education.

Ann Eggley, hurrier, 18 years old

I'm sure I don't know how to spell my name. We go at four in the morning, and sometimes at half-past four. We begin to work as soon as we get down. We get out after four, sometimes at five, in the evening. We work the whole time except an hour for dinner, and sometimes we haven't time to eat. I hurry [move coal wagons underground] by myself, and have done so for long. I know the corves [small coal wagons] are very heavy, they are the biggest corves anywhere about. The work is far too hard for me; the sweat runs off me all over sometimes. I am very tired at night. Sometimes when we get home at night we have not power to wash us, and then we go to bed. Sometimes we fall asleep in the chair. Father said last night it was both a shame and a disgrace for girls to work as we do, but there was naught else for us to do. I began to hurry when I was seven and I have been hurrying ever since. I have been 11 years in the pits. The girls are always tired.

I was poorly twice this winter; it was with headache. I hurry for Robert Wiggins; he is not akin to me. . . . We don't always get enough to eat and drink, but we get a good supper. I have known my father go at two in the morning to work . . . and he didn't come out till four. I am quite sure that we work constantly 12 hours except on Saturdays. We wear trousers and our shifts in the pit and great big shoes clinkered and nailed. The girls never work naked to the waist in our pit. The men don't insult us in the pit. The conduct of the girls in the pit is good enough sometimes and sometimes bad enough. I never went to a day-school. I went a little to a Sunday-school, but I soon gave it over.

I thought it too bad to be confined both Sundays and week-days. I walk about and get the fresh air on Sundays. I have not learnt to read. I don't know my letters. I never learnt naught. I never go to church or chapel; there is no church or chapel at Gawber, there is none nearer than a mile. . . . I have never heard that a good man came into the

were often more grueling and more dangerous. In England nonagricultural workers labored about 250 days per year in 1760 as compared to 300 per year in 1830, while the normal workday remained an exhausting eleven hours throughout the entire period. In 1760 nonagricultural workers still observed many religious and public holidays by not working, and many workers took Monday off. These days of leisure and relaxation declined rapidly after 1760, and by 1830 nonagricultural workers had joined landless agricultural laborers in toiling six rather than five days a week.[11]

world who was God's son to save sinners. I never heard of Christ at all. Nobody has ever told me about him, nor have my father and mother ever taught me to pray. I know no prayer; I never pray.

Patience Kershaw, aged 17

My father has been dead about a year; my mother is living and has ten children, five lads and five lasses; the oldest is about thirty, the youngest is four; three lasses go to mill; all the lads are colliers, two getters and three hurriers; one lives at home and does nothing; mother does nought but look after home.

All my sisters have been hurriers, but three went to the mill. Alice went because her legs swelled from hurrying in cold water when she was hot. I never went to day-school; I go to Sunday-school, but I cannot read or write; I go to pit at five o'clock in the morning and come out at five in the evening; I get my breakfast of porridge and milk first; I take my dinner with me, a cake, and eat it as I go; I do not stop or rest any time for the purpose; I get nothing else until I get home, and then have potatoes and meat, not every day meat. I hurry in the clothes I have now got on, trousers and ragged jacket; the bald place upon my head is made by thrusting the corves; my legs have never swelled, but sisters' did when they went to mill; I hurry the corves a mile and more under ground and back; they weigh 300 cwt.;* I hurry 11 a day; I wear a belt and chain at the workings to get the corves out; the putters [miners] that I work for are *naked* except their caps; they pull off all their clothes; I see them at work when I go up; sometimes they beat me, if I am not quick enough, with their hands; they strike me upon my back; the boys take liberties with me, sometimes, they pull me about; I am

the only girl in the pit; there are about 20 boys and 15 men; all the men are naked; I would rather work in mill than in coal-pit.

Isabel Wilson, 38 years old, coal putter

When women have children thick [fast] they are compelled to take them down early. I have been married 19 years and have had 10 bairns [children]; seven are in life. When on Sir John's work was a carrier of coals, which caused me to miscarry five times from the strains, and was gal [very] ill after each. Putting is no so oppressive; last child was born on Saturday morning, and I was at work on the Friday night.

Once met with an accident; a coal brake my cheek-bone, which kept me idle some weeks. I have wrought below 30 years, and so has the guid man; he is getting touched in the breath now.

None of the children read, as the work is no regular. I did read once, but no able to attend to it now; when I go below lassie 10 years of age keeps house and makes the broth or stir-about.

EVALUATE THE EVIDENCE

1. How does Payne's testimony compare with that of Ann Eggley and Patience Kershaw?
2. Describe the work of Eggley, Kershaw, and Wilson. What strikes you most about the testimonies of these workers?
3. The witnesses were responding to questions from middle-class commissioners. What did the commissioners seem interested in? Why?

Source: *Voices of the Industrial Revolution: Selected Readings from the Liberal Economists and Their Critics*, pp. 87–90, edited by J. Bowditch and C. Ramsland (Ann Arbor: The University of Michigan Press, 1961). Reprinted by permission of the publisher.

* An old English unit of weight equaling 112 pounds.

As the factories moved to urban areas, workers followed them in large numbers, leading to an explosion in the size of cities, especially in the north of England. Life in the new industrial cities, such as Manchester and Glasgow, was grim. Migrants to the booming cities found expensive, hastily constructed, overcrowded apartments and inadequate sanitary systems. Infant mortality, disease, malnutrition, and accidents took such a high toll in human life that life expectancy was only around twenty-five to twenty-seven years, some fifteen years less than the national average.[12] Perhaps the most shocking evidence of the impact of the Industrial Revolution on living standards is the finding that child mortality levels rose after 1825, especially in industrial areas.

Another way to consider the workers' standard of living is to look at the goods they purchased. Such evidence is somewhat contradictory, but generally suggestive of stagnant or declining living standards until the middle of the nineteenth century. One important area of improvement was in the consumption of cotton goods, which became much cheaper and could be enjoyed by all classes. Now millions of poor people could afford to wear cotton slips and underpants as well as cotton dresses and shirts. However, in other areas, food in particular, the modest growth in factory wages was not enough to compensate for rising prices.

From the 1840s onward, matters improved considerably as wages made substantial gains and the prices of many goods dropped. A greater variety of foods became available, including the first canned goods. Some of the most important advances were in medicine. Smallpox vaccination became routine, and surgeons began to use anesthesia in the late 1840s. By 1850 trains had revolutionized transportation for the masses, while the telegraph made instant communication possible for the first time in human history. In addition, gaslights greatly expanded the possibilities of nighttime activity. Gas lighting is one of the most important examples of a direct relationship between the scientific advances of the eighteenth century—in this case, chemistry—and the development of new technologies of the Industrial Revolution.

More difficult to measure than real wages or life expectancy was the impact of the Industrial Revolution on community and social values. As young men and women migrated away from their villages to seek employment in urban factories, many close-knit rural communities were destroyed. Village social and cultural traditions disappeared without new generations to carry them on. Although many young people formed new friendships and appreciated the freedoms of urban life, they also suffered from the loneliness of life in the anonymous city. The loss of skills and work autonomy, along with the loss of community, must be included in the assessment of the Industrial Revolution's effect on the living conditions of workers.

Relations Between Capital and Labor

FOCUS QUESTION

How did the changes brought about by the Industrial Revolution lead to new social classes, and how did people respond to the new structure?

In Great Britain, industrial development led to the creation of new social groups and intensified long-standing conflicts between capital and labor. A new class of factory owners and industrial capitalists arose. These men and women and their families strengthened the wealth and size of the middle class, which had previously been made up mainly of merchants and professional people. The demands of modern industry regularly brought the interests of the middle-class industrialists into conflict with those of the people who worked for them—the working class. As observers took notice of these changes, they raised new questions about how industrialization affected social relationships. Meanwhile, enslaved labor in European colonies contributed to the industrialization process in multiple ways.

The New Class of Factory Owners

Early industrialists operated in a highly competitive economic system. As the careers of James Watt and Fritz Harkort illustrate, there were countless production problems, and success and large profits were by no means certain. Manufacturers therefore waged a constant battle to cut their production costs and stay afloat. Much of the profit had to go back into the business for new and better machinery.

Most early industrialists drew upon their families and friends for labor and capital, but they came from a variety of backgrounds. Many, such as Harkort, were from well-established families with rich networks of contacts and support. Others, such as Watt and Cockerill, were of modest means, especially in the early days. Artisans and skilled workers of exceptional ability had unparalleled opportunities. Members of ethnic and religious groups who had been discriminated against jumped at the new chances and often helped each other. Scots, Quakers, and other Protestant dissenters were tremendously important in Britain; Protestants and Jews dominated banking in Catholic France. Many of the industrialists were newly rich, and, not surprisingly, they were very proud and self-satisfied.

As factories and firms grew larger, opportunities declined, at least in well-developed industries. It became considerably harder for a gifted but poor young mechanic to start a small enterprise and end up as a wealthy manufacturer. Formal education became more important for young men as a means of success and advancement, but studies at the advanced level were expensive. In Britain by 1830 and in France and Germany by 1860, leading industrialists were more likely to have inherited their well-established enterprises, and they were financially much more secure than their struggling parents had been. They also had a greater sense of class-consciousness; they were fully aware that ongoing industrial development had widened the gap between themselves and their workers.

Just like working-class women, the wives and daughters of successful businessmen found fewer opportunities for active participation in Europe's increasingly complex business world. Rather than contributing as vital partners in a family-owned enterprise, as so many middle-class women had done, these women were increasingly valued for their ladylike gentility. By 1850 some influential women writers and most businessmen assumed that middle-class wives and daughters should avoid work in offices and factories. Rather, a middle-class lady was expected to concentrate on her proper role as wife and mother, preferably in an elegant residential area far removed from ruthless commerce and the volatile working class. (See "Evaluating the Evidence 20.3: Advice for Middle-Class Women," page 675.)

Responses to Industrialization

From the beginning, the British Industrial Revolution had its critics. Among the first were the Romantic poets. William Blake (1757–1827) called the early factories "satanic mills" and protested against the hard life of the London poor. William Wordsworth (1770–1850) lamented the destruction of the rural way of life and the pollution of the land and water. Some handicraft workers—notably the **Luddites**, who attacked factories in northern England in 1811 and later—smashed the new machines, which they believed were putting them out of work. Doctors and reformers wrote of problems in the factories and new towns, while Malthus and Ricardo concluded that workers would earn only enough to stay alive.

Luddites Group of handicraft workers who attacked factories in northern England in 1811 and later, smashing the new machines that they believed were putting them out of work.

Luddite Rioters   Named after a mythic leader, "General Ludd," the Luddite riots began in 1811 in Nottinghamshire and quickly spread to manufacturing districts throughout England. Their target was the mechanized looms that led to lower wages and unemployment among hand-weavers. Machine breaking was quickly declared a capital crime, and a number of Luddites were executed. (*Luddite Rioters*, 19th century English engraving/Private Collection/Bridgeman Images)

This pessimistic view was accepted and reinforced by Friedrich Engels (1820–1895), the future revolutionary and colleague of Karl Marx (see Chapter 21). After studying conditions in northern England, this young son of a wealthy Prussian cotton manufacturer published in 1844 *The Condition of the Working Class in England*, a blistering indictment of the capitalist classes. "At the bar of world opinion," he wrote, "I charge the English middle classes with mass murder, wholesale robbery, and all the other crimes in the calendar." The new poverty of industrial workers was worse than the old poverty of cottage workers and agricultural laborers, according to Engels. The culprit was industrial capitalism, with its relentless competition and constant technical change. Engels's extremely influential charge of capitalist exploitation and increasing worker poverty was embellished by Marx and later socialists (see Chapter 21).

Analysis of industrial capitalism, often combined with reflections on the French Revolution, led to the development of a new overarching interpretation—a new paradigm—regarding social relationships. Briefly, this paradigm argued that individuals were members of separate classes based on their relationship to the means of production, that is, the machines and factories that dominated the new economy. As owners of expensive industrial machinery and as dependent laborers in their factories, the two main groups of society had separate and conflicting interests. Accordingly, the comfortable, well-educated "public" of the eighteenth century came increasingly to be defined as the middle class ("middle" because they were beneath the small group of aristocracy at the top of society who claimed to be above industrial activity), and the "people" gradually began to perceive themselves as composing a modern working class. And if the new class interpretation was more of a simplification than a fundamental truth for some critics, it appealed to many because it seemed to explain what was happening. Therefore, conflicting classes existed, in part, because many individuals came to believe they existed and developed an awareness that they belonged to a particular social class—what Karl Marx called **class-consciousness**.

class-consciousness
Awareness of belonging to a distinct social and economic class whose interests might conflict with those of other classes.

Advice for Middle-Class Women

The adoption of steam-powered machines generated tremendous profits during the Industrial Revolution. Factory owners and managers enjoyed new wealth, and skilled male workers eventually began to hope for wages high enough to keep their wives and children at home. These social changes encouraged the nineteenth-century "separate spheres" ideology, which emphasized the importance of women's role as caretakers of the domestic realm. Sarah Stickney Ellis's The Women of England: Their Social Duties and Domestic Habits, *excerpted below, was one of a flood of publications offering middle-class women advice on shopping, housekeeping, and supervising servants.*

"What shall I do to gratify myself—to be admired—or to vary the tenor of my existence?" are not the questions which a woman of right feelings asks awaking to the avocations of the day. Much more congenial to the highest attributes of woman's character, are inquiries such as these: "How shall I endeavor through this day to turn the time, the health, and the means permitted me to enjoy, to the best account? Is any one sick, I must visit their chamber without delay, and try to give their apartment an air of comfort, by arranging such things as the wearied nurse may not have thought of. Is any one about to set off on a journey, I must see that the early meal is spread, to prepare it with my own hands, in order that the servant,

who was working late last night, may profit by unbroken rest. Did I fail in what was kind or considerate to any of the family yesterday; I will meet her this morning with a cordial welcome, and show, in the most delicate way I can, that I am anxious to atone for the past. Was any one exhausted by the last day's exertion, I will be an hour before them this morning, and let them see that their labor is so much in advance. Or, if nothing extraordinary occurs to claim my attention, I will meet the family with a consciousness that, being the least engaged of any member of it, I am consequently the most at liberty to devote myself to the general good of the whole, by cultivating cheerful conversation, adapting myself to the prevailing tone of feeling, and leading those who are least happy, to think and speak of what will make them more so."

EVALUATE THE EVIDENCE

1. What daily tasks and duties does Sarah Stickney Ellis prescribe for the mother of the family?
2. How does this document exemplify the changes in the sexual division of labor and ideals of domesticity described in the text?

Source: Sarah Stickney Ellis, *The Women of England: Their Social Duties and Domestic Habits*, in *The Past Speaks*, 2d ed., ed. Walter Arnstein (Lexington, Mass.: D. C. Heath, 1993), 2:173.

Meanwhile, other observers believed that conditions were improving for the working people. In his 1835 study of the cotton industry, Andrew Ure (yoo-RAY) wrote that conditions in most factories were not harsh and were even quite good. Edwin Chadwick, a government official well acquainted with the problems of the working population, concluded that the "whole mass of the laboring community" was increasingly able "to buy more of the necessities and minor luxuries of life."[13] Nevertheless, those who thought—correctly—that conditions were getting worse for working people were probably in the majority.

The Early British Labor Movement

Not everyone worked in large factories and coal mines during the Industrial Revolution. In 1850 more British people still worked on farms than in any other single occupation, although rural communities were suffering from outward migration. The second-largest occupation was domestic service, with more than

1 million household servants, 90 percent of whom were women. Thus many old, familiar jobs outside industry lived on and provided alternatives to industrial labor.

Within industry itself, the pattern of artisans working with hand tools in small shops remained unchanged in many trades, even as others were revolutionized by technological change. For example, the British iron industry was completely dominated by large-scale capitalist firms by 1850. Many large ironworks had more than one thousand people on their payrolls. Yet the firms that fashioned iron into small metal goods, such as tools, tableware, and toys, employed on average fewer than ten wage workers who used handicraft skills. The survival of small workshops gave many workers an alternative to factory employment.

Working-class solidarity and class-consciousness developed both in small workshops and in large factories. In the northern factory districts, anticapitalist sentiments were frequent by the 1820s. Commenting in 1825 on a strike in the woolen center of Bradford and the support it had gathered from other regions, one newspaper claimed with pride that "it is all the workers of England against a few masters of Bradford."[14] Even in trades that did not undergo mechanization, unemployment and stagnant wages contributed to class awareness.

Such sentiments ran contrary to the liberal tenets of economic freedom championed by eighteenth-century thinkers like Adam Smith. Liberal economic principles were embraced by statesmen and middle-class business owners in the late eighteenth century and continued to gather strength in the early nineteenth century. In 1799 Parliament passed the **Combination Acts**, which outlawed unions and strikes. In 1813 and 1814 Parliament repealed an old law regulating the wages of artisans and the conditions of apprenticeship. As a result of these and other measures, certain skilled artisan workers, such as bootmakers and high-quality tailors, found aggressive capitalists ignoring traditional work rules and trying to flood their trades with unorganized women workers and children to beat down wages.

The capitalist attack on artisan guilds and work rules was bitterly resented by many craftworkers, who subsequently played an important part in Great Britain and in other countries in gradually building a modern labor movement. The Combination Acts were widely disregarded by workers. Printers, papermakers, carpenters, tailors, and other such craftsmen continued to take collective action, and societies of skilled factory workers also organized unions in defiance of the law. Unions sought to control the number of skilled workers, to limit apprenticeship to members' own children, and to bargain with owners over wages.

They were not afraid to strike; there was, for example, a general strike of adult cotton spinners in Manchester in 1810. In the face of widespread union activity, Parliament repealed the Combination Acts in 1824, and unions were tolerated, though not fully accepted, after 1825.

The next stage in the development of the British trade-union movement was the attempt to create a single large national union. This effort was led not so much by working people as by social reformers such as Robert Owen. Owen, a self-made cotton manufacturer, had pioneered in industrial relations by combining firm discipline with concern for the health, safety, and hours of his workers. After 1815 he experimented

Combination Acts British laws passed in 1799 that outlawed unions and strikes, favoring capitalist business people over skilled artisans. Bitterly resented and widely disregarded by many craft guilds, the acts were repealed by Parliament in 1824.

with cooperative and socialist communities, including one at New Harmony, Indiana. Then in 1834 Owen was involved in the organization of one of the largest and most visionary of the early national unions, the Grand National Consolidated Trades Union.

When Owen's and other ambitious schemes collapsed, the British labor movement moved once again after 1851 in the direction of craft unions. The most famous of these was the Amalgamated Society of Engineers, which represented skilled machinists. These unions won real benefits for members by fairly conservative means and thus became an accepted part of the industrial scene.

British workers also engaged in direct political activity in defense of their interests. After the collapse of Owen's national trade union, many working people went into the Chartist movement, which sought political democracy. The key Chartist demand—that all men be given the right to vote—became the great hope of millions of common people. Workers were also active in campaigns to limit the workday in factories to ten hours and to permit duty-free importation of wheat into Great Britain to secure cheap bread. Thus working people developed a sense of their own identity and played an active role in shaping the new industrial system. They were neither helpless victims nor passive beneficiaries.

The Impact of Slavery

Another mass labor force of the Industrial Revolution was composed of the millions of enslaved men, women, and children who toiled in European colonies in the Caribbean and in North and South America. Historians have long debated the extent to which revenue from slavery contributed to Britain's achievements in the Industrial Revolution.

Most now agree that profits from colonial plantations and slave trading were a small portion of British national income in the eighteenth century and were probably more often invested in land than in industry. Nevertheless, the impact of slavery on Britain's economy was much broader than its direct profits alone. In the mid-eighteenth century the need for items to exchange for colonial cotton, sugar, tobacco, and slaves stimulated demand for British manufactured goods in the Caribbean, North America, and West Africa. Britain's dominance in the slave trade also led to the development of finance and credit institutions that helped early industrialists obtain capital for their businesses. Investments in canals, roads, and railroads made possible by profits from colonial trade provided the necessary infrastructure to move raw materials and products of the factory system.

The British Parliament abolished the slave trade in 1807 and freed all slaves in British territories in 1833, but by 1850 most of the cotton processed by British mills was supplied by the labor of enslaved people in the southern United States. Thus the Industrial Revolution was deeply entangled with the Atlantic world and the misery of slavery.

LOOKING BACK LOOKING AHEAD

The Industrial Revolution was a long process of economic innovation and growth occurring first in Britain around 1780 and spreading to the European continent after 1815. The development of machines powered first by water and then by steam allowed for a tremendous growth in productivity, which enabled Britain to assume the lead in the world's production of industrial goods. Industrialization fundamentally changed the social landscape of European countries, creating a new elite of wealthy manufacturers and a vast working class of urban wage laborers whose living conditions remained grim until the mid-nineteenth century.

One popular idea in the 1830s, first developed by a French economist, was that Britain's late-eighteenth-century "industrial revolution" paralleled the political events in France during the French Revolution. One revolution was economic, while the other was political; one was ongoing and successful, while the other had failed and come to a definite end in 1815, when Europe's conservative monarchs defeated Napoleon and restored the French kings of the Old Regime.

In fact, in 1815 the French Revolution, like the Industrial Revolution, was an unfinished revolution. Just as Britain was in the midst of its economic transformation and the states of northwestern Europe had only begun industrialization, so too after 1815 were the political conflicts and ideologies of revolutionary France still very much alive. The French Revolution had opened the era of modern political life not just in France but across Europe. It had brought into existence many of the political ideologies that would interact with the social and economic forces of industrialization to refashion Europe and create a new urban society. Moreover, in 1815 the unfinished French Revolution carried the very real possibility of renewed political upheaval. This possibility, which conservatives feared and radicals longed for, would become dramatic reality in 1848, when political revolutions swept across Europe like a whirlwind.

Make Connections

Think about the larger developments and continuities within and across chapters.

1. Why did Great Britain take the lead in industrialization, and when did other countries begin to adopt the new techniques and organization of production?

2. How did the achievements in agriculture and rural industry of the late seventeenth and eighteenth centuries (Chapter 17) pave the way for the Industrial Revolution of the late eighteenth century?

3. How would you compare the legacy of the political revolutions of the late eighteenth century (Chapter 19) with that of the Industrial Revolution? Which seems to you to have created the most important changes, and why?

20 REVIEW & EXPLORE

Review the Main Ideas

Answer the focus questions from each section of the chapter.

◆ Why did the Industrial Revolution begin in Britain, and how did it develop between 1780 and 1850? (p. 648)

◆ How did countries in Europe and around the world respond to the challenge of industrialization? (p. 658)

◆ How did work evolve during the Industrial Revolution, and how did daily life change for working people? (p. 664)

◆ How did the changes brought about by the Industrial Revolution lead to new social classes, and how did people respond to the new structure? (p. 672)

Identify Key Terms

Identify and explain the significance of each item below.

Industrial Revolution (p. 650)
spinning jenny (p. 651)
water frame (p. 651)
steam engines (p. 654)
Rocket (p. 656)
Crystal Palace (p. 657)
iron law of wages (p. 657)
tariff protection (p. 661)
Factory Acts (p. 666)
separate spheres (p. 666)
Mines Act of 1842 (p. 668)
Luddites (p. 673)
class-consciousness (p. 674)
Combination Acts (p. 676)

NOTES

1. N. F. R. Crafts, *British Economic Growth During the Industrial Revolution* (Oxford: Oxford University Press, 1985), p. 32.
2. Robert C. Allen, *The British Industrial Revolution in Global Perspective* (Cambridge: Cambridge University Press, 2009), pp. 1–2.
3. P. Bairoch, "International Industrialization Levels from 1750 to 1980," *Journal of European Economic History* 11 (Spring 1982): 269–333.
4. Quoted in J. Bowditch and C. Ramsland, eds., *Voices of the Industrial Revolution* (Ann Arbor: University of Michigan Press, 1961), p. 55, from the fourth edition of Thomas Malthus, *Essay on the Principle of Population* (1807).
5. Quoted in Emma Griffin, *A Short History of the British Industrial Revolution* (Basingstoke, U.K.: Palgrave Macmillan, 2010), p. 126.
6. Quoted in E. R. Pike, *"Hard Times": Human Documents of the Industrial Revolution* (New York: Praeger, 1966), p. 109.
7. See especially J. Brenner and M. Rama, "Rethinking Women's Oppression," *New Left Review* 144 (March–April 1984): 33–71, and sources cited there.

8. J. Humphries, ". . . 'The Most Free from Objection' . . . The Sexual Division of Labor and Women's Work in Nineteenth-Century England," *Journal of Economic History* 47 (December 1987): 941; Pike, "*Hard Times*," p. 266.
9. Quoted in Pike, "*Hard Times*," p. 208.
10. Joel Mokyr, *The Enlightened Economy: An Economic History of Britain, 1700–1850* (New Haven, Conn.: Yale University Press, 2009), pp. 460–461.
11. Hans-Joachim Voth, *Time and Work in England, 1750–1830* (Oxford: Oxford University Press, 2000), pp. 118–133, 268–270.
12. Mokyr, *The Enlightened Economy*, p. 455.
13. Quoted in W. A. Hayek, ed., *Capitalism and the Historians* (Chicago: University of Chicago Press, 1954), p. 126.
14. Quoted in D. Geary, ed., *Labour and Socialist Movements in Europe Before 1914* (Oxford: Berg, 1989), p. 29.

CHAPTER PREVIEW

The Aftermath of the Napoleonic Wars
How was peace restored and maintained after 1815?

The Spread of Radical Ideas
What new ideologies emerged to challenge conservatism?

The Romantic Movement
What were the characteristics of the Romantic movement?

Reforms and Revolutions Before 1848
How and where was conservatism challenged after 1815?

The Revolutions of 1848
What were the main causes and results of the revolutions of 1848?

Life in the Revolutionary Era
Between 1830 and 1848 crowds stormed public areas to force political change in many parts of Europe. In this dramatic scene from the revolutions of 1830, rioters in Brussels demand Belgian national independence from the Netherlands. At the top right, a patriot clutches the Belgian tricolor flag while another brandishes a list of revolutionary demands; at the center, a youth has died in the fight for the nation, inspiring fellow citizens to join the cause.
(By Gustave Wappers [1803–1874], [oil on canvas]/Musée Royaux des Beaux-Arts de Belgique, Brussels, Belgium/© Leemage/Bridgeman Images)

21

Ideologies and Upheavals

1815–1850

The momentous economic and political transformation of modern times that began in the late eighteenth century with the "unfinished" revolutions—the Industrial Revolution in England and the political revolution in France—would play out with unpredictable consequences in the first half of the nineteenth century. Attempts to halt the spread of the progressive forces associated with the French Revolution led first to a reassertion of conservative political control in continental Europe. Following the leadership of Austrian foreign minister Klemens von Metternich, the aristocratic leaders of the Great Powers sought to stamp out the spread of liberal and democratic reforms.

The political and cultural innovations made possible by the unfinished revolutions, however, proved difficult to contain. In politics, powerful new ideologies—liberalism, nationalism, and socialism—emerged to oppose Metternich's revitalized conservatism. In literature, art, and music, Romanticism—an intellectual and artistic movement that challenged the certainties of the Enlightenment and fed the growth of popular nationalism—captured the intensity of the era. A successful revolution in Greece, liberal reform in Great Britain, and popular unrest in France gave voice to ordinary people's desire for political and social change. All these movements helped launch the great wave of revolutions that swept across Europe in 1848, and the dramatic results would have a lasting impact on the shape of Western civilization. ■

The Aftermath of the Napoleonic Wars

FOCUS QUESTION

How was peace restored and maintained after 1815?

The eventual eruption of revolutionary political forces in 1848 was by no means predictable as the Napoleonic era ended. Quite the contrary. After finally defeating Napoleon, the conservative, aristocratic monarchies of Russia, Prussia, Austria, and Great Britain — known as the Quadruple Alliance — reaffirmed their determination to hold France in line. Even before Napoleon's final defeat, the allies had agreed to meet to fashion a general peace accord in 1814 at the Congress of Vienna, where they faced a great challenge: how could they construct a lasting settlement that would not sow the seeds of another war? By carefully managing the balance of power, redrawing the boundaries of formerly French-held territories, and embracing conservative restoration, they brokered an agreement that contributed to fifty years of peace in Europe (Map 21.1).

MAP 21.1 Europe in 1815   In 1815 Europe contained many different states, but after the defeat of Napoleon international politics was dominated by the five Great Powers: Russia, Prussia, Austria, Great Britain, and France. (The number rises to six if one includes the Ottoman Empire.) At the Congress of Vienna, the Great Powers redrew the map of Europe.

Chronology

1790s–1840s	Romantic movement in literature and the arts	**1830**	Greece wins independence from Ottomans
1809–1848	Metternich serves as Austrian foreign minister		France invades Algeria
1810	Germaine de Staël publishes *On Germany*		Charles X repudiates the Constitutional Charter; insurrection and collapse of the government follow
1814–1815	Congress of Vienna		
1815	Revision of Corn Laws in Great Britain; Holy Alliance formed		Louis Philippe succeeds to the throne and maintains a narrowly liberal regime
June 18, 1815	Napoleon defeated at the Battle of Waterloo	**1832**	Reform Bill in Britain
		1839	Socialist Louis Blanc publishes *The Organization of Work*
1819	Karlsbad Decrees issued by German Confederation	**1840**	Anarchist Pierre-Joseph Proudhon publishes *What Is Property?*
1820	Congress of Troppau proclaims the principle of intervention to maintain autocratic regimes	**1845–1851**	Great Famine in Ireland
		1847	Ten Hours Act in Britain
1821	Austria crushes a liberal revolution in Naples and restores the Sicilian autocracy	**1848**	Revolutions in France, Austria, and Prussia; Marx and Engels publish *The Communist Manifesto*
1823	French armies restore the Spanish crown		

The European Balance of Power

Elite representatives of the Quadruple Alliance (plus a representative of the restored Bourbon monarch of France) — including Tsar Alexander I of Russia, King Friedrich Wilhelm III of Prussia, Emperor Franz II of Austria, and their foreign ministers — met to fashion the peace at the **Congress of Vienna** from September 1814 to June 1815. A host of delegates from the smaller European states also attended the conference and offered minor assistance.

Such a face-to-face meeting of kings and emperors was very rare at the time. Professional ambassadors and court representatives had typically conducted state-to-state negotiations; now national leaders engaged in what we would today call "summit diplomacy." Participants at the congress enjoyed any number of festivities associated with aristocratic court culture, including formal receptions, military parades and reviews, sumptuous dinner parties, fancy ballroom dances, fireworks displays, and operatic and theatrical productions. Participation in Vienna's vibrant salon culture offered further opportunities to socialize, discuss current issues, and make informal deals that could be confirmed at the conference table. All the while, newspapers, pamphlets, periodicals, and satiric cartoons kept readers across Europe up-to-date on social events as well as the latest political developments and agreements. The conference thus marked an important transitional moment in Western history. The salon society and public sphere of the seventeenth-century Enlightenment (see Chapter 16) gradually shifted toward nineteenth-century cultures of publicity and public opinion informed by more modern mass-media campaigns.[1]

The allied powers were concerned first and foremost with the defeated enemy, France. Self-interest and traditional ideas about the balance of power motivated allied moderation toward the former foe. To Klemens von Metternich (MEH-tuhr-nihk)

Congress of Vienna A meeting of the Quadruple Alliance (Russia, Prussia, Austria, and Great Britain), restoration France, and smaller European states to fashion a general peace settlement that began after the defeat of Napoleon's France in 1814.

Congress of Vienna The Congress of Vienna was renowned for its intense diplomatic deal making, resulting in the Treaty of Vienna. The congress won additional notoriety for its ostentatious parades, parties, and dance balls. The painting here portrays a mounted group of European royalty, led by the Prussian emperor and the Russian tsar, in a flamboyant parade designed to celebrate Napoleon's defeat the year before. Onlookers toast the victorious monarchs. The display of flags, weapons, and heraldic emblems symbolizes the unity of Europe's Great Powers, while the long tables in the background suggest the extent of the festivities. Such images were widely distributed to engender popular support for the conservative program. (*The Celebration of the Prater in the Presence of the Reigning Monarchs*, 1815/Collection of the Palaces Artstetten and Luberegg/akg-image)

and Robert Castlereagh (KA-suhl-ray), the foreign ministers of Austria and Great Britain, the balance of power meant an international equilibrium of political and military forces that would discourage aggression by any combination of states or, worse, the domination of Europe by any single state. Their French negotiating partner, the skillful and cynical diplomat Charles Talleyrand, concurred.

The allies offered France lenient terms after Napoleon's abdication. They agreed to restore the Bourbon king to the French throne. The first Treaty of Paris, signed before the conference (and before Napoleon escaped from Elba and attacked the Bourbon regime), gave France the boundaries it had possessed in 1792, which were larger than those of 1789. In addition, France did not have to pay war reparations. Thus the victorious powers avoided provoking a spirit of victimization and desire for revenge in the defeated country.

The Quadruple Alliance combined leniency with strong defensive measures designed to raise barriers against the possibility of renewed French aggression. Belgium and Holland—incorporated into the French empire under Napoleon—were united under an enlarged and independent "Kingdom of the Netherlands" capable of opposing French expansion to the north. The German-speaking lands on France's eastern border, also taken by Napoleon (see Chapter 19), were returned to Prussia. As a famous German anthem put it, the expanded Prussia would now stand as the "watch on the Rhine" against French attack. In addition, the allies reorganized the German-speaking territories of central Europe. A new German Confederation, a loose association of German-speaking states based on Napoleon's reorganization of the territory dominated by Prussia and Austria, replaced the roughly three hundred principalities, free cities, and dynastic states of the Holy Roman Empire with just thirty-eight German states (see Map 21.1).

Austria, Britain, Prussia, and Russia furthermore used the balance of power to settle their own potentially dangerous disputes. The victors generally agreed that each of them should receive compensation in the form of territory for their victory over the French. Great Britain had already won colonies and strategic outposts during the long wars. Austria gave up territories in Belgium and southern Germany but expanded greatly elsewhere, taking the rich provinces of Venetia and Lombardy in northern Italy as well as former Polish possessions and new lands on the eastern coast of the Adriatic.

Russian and Prussian claims for territorial expansion were more contentious. When Russia had pushed Napoleon out of central Europe, its armies had expanded its control over Polish territories. Tsar Alexander I wished to make Russian rule permanent. But when France, Austria, and Great Britain all argued for limits on Russian gains, the tsar ceded territories back to Prussia and accepted a smaller Polish kingdom. Prussian claims on the state of Saxony, a wealthy kingdom in the German Confederation, were particularly contentious. The Saxon king had supported Napoleon to the bitter end; now Wilhelm III wanted to incorporate Saxony into Prussia. Under pressure, he agreed to partition the state, leaving an independent Saxony in place, a change that posed no real threat to its Great Power neighbors but soothed their fears of Prussian expansionism. These territorial changes and compromises fell very much within the framework of balance-of-power ideology.

Unfortunately for France, in February 1815 Napoleon suddenly escaped from his "comic kingdom" on the island of Elba and re-ignited his wars of expansion for a brief time (see Chapter 19). Yet the second Treaty of Paris, concluded in November 1815 after Napoleon's final defeat at Waterloo, was still relatively moderate toward France. The elderly Louis XVIII was restored to his throne for a second time. France lost only a little territory, had to pay an indemnity of 700 million francs, and was required to support a large army of occupation for five years. The rest of the settlement concluded at the Congress of Vienna was left intact. The members of the Quadruple Alliance, however, did agree to meet periodically to discuss their common interests and to consider appropriate measures for the maintenance of peace in Europe. This agreement marked the beginning of the European "Congress System," which lasted long into the nineteenth century and settled many international crises peacefully, through international conferences or "congresses" and balance-of-power diplomacy.

Metternich and Conservatism

The political ideals of conservatism, often associated with Austrian foreign minister Prince Klemens von Metternich (1773–1859), dominated Great Power discussions at the Congress of Vienna. Metternich's determined defense of the monarchical status quo made him a villain in the eyes of most progressive, liberal thinkers of the nineteenth century. Yet rather than denounce his politics, we can try to understand the general conservatism he represented. Born into the landed nobility of the Rhineland, Metternich was an internationally oriented aristocrat who made a brilliant diplomatic career. Austrian foreign minister from 1809 to 1848, the cosmopolitan and conservative Metternich had a pessimistic view of human nature, which he believed was ever prone to error, excess, and self-serving behavior. The disruptive events of the French Revolution and the

Prince Klemens von Metternich This portrait by Sir Thomas Lawrence reveals much about Metternich, the foreign minister of the Austrian Empire. Handsome, refined, and intelligent, this grand aristocrat passionately defended his class and its interests. (Royal Collection Trust © Her Majesty Queen Elizabeth II, 2015/Bridgeman Images)

Napoleonic Wars confirmed these views, and Metternich's conservatism would emerge as a powerful new political ideological force in response to the revolutionary age.

Metternich firmly believed that liberalism, as embodied in revolutionary America and France, bore the responsibility for the untold bloodshed and suffering caused by twenty-five years of war. Like Edmund Burke (see Chapter 19) and other conservatives, Metternich blamed liberal middle-class revolutionaries for stirring up the lower classes. Authoritarian, aristocratic government, he concluded, was necessary to protect society from the baser elements of human behavior, which were easily released in a democratic system. Organized religion was another pillar of strong government. Metternich despised the anticlericalism of the Enlightenment and the French Revolution and maintained that Christian morality was a vital bulwark against radical change.

Metternich defended his elite class and its rights and privileges with a clear conscience. The church and nobility were among Europe's most ancient and valuable institutions, and conservatives regarded tradition as the basic foundation of human society.

The threat of liberalism appeared doubly dangerous to Metternich because it generally went with aspirations for national independence. Liberals believed that each people, each national group, had a right to establish its own independent government and fulfill its own destiny. Though Metternich and other conservatives might accept some form of constitutional monarchy, the idea of national self-determination under liberal constitutional government was repellent because it threatened to revolutionize central Europe and destroy the Austrian Empire.

After centuries of war, royal intermarriage, and territorial expansion, the vast Austrian Empire of the Habsburgs included many regions and peoples within its borders (Map 21.2). The numerous kingdoms, duchies, and principalities under Habsburg rule included the lands of the Austrian crown, the Kingdom of Hungary, the Kingdom of Bohemia, and the Kingdom of Lombardy-Venetia, to name just the largest. Noble houses in these territories maintained some control, but ultimate authority rested with the Habsburg emperor. The peoples of the Austrian Empire spoke at least eleven different languages and observed vastly different customs; an astonishing variety of different ethnic groups mingled in the same provinces and the same villages. They included about 8 million Germans, about one-fourth of the population. Some 5.5 million Magyars (Hungarians), 5 million Italians, 4 million Czechs, and 2 million Poles lived alongside each other in the imperial state, as did smaller groups of Slovenes, Croats, Serbs, Romanians, Jews, and Armenians.[2] The various Slavic groups, together with the Italians and the Romanians, lived in widely scattered regions, yet they outnumbered the politically dominant Germans and Hungarians (see Map 21.2).

The multiethnic empire Metternich served had strengths and weaknesses. A large population and vast territories gave the empire economic and military clout, but its potentially dissatisfied ethnicities and nationalities undermined political unity. In these circumstances, Metternich and the Habsburg dynasty virtually had to oppose liberalism and nationalism—if Austria was to remain intact and powerful, it could hardly accommodate ideologies that demanded national independence.

On the Austrian Empire's borders, the Russian Empire and, to a lesser extent, the Ottoman Empire supported and echoed Metternich's efforts to hold back liberalism

MAP 21.2 Peoples of the Habsburg Monarchy, 1815   The old dynastic state ruled by the Habsburg monarchy was a patchwork of nationalities and ethnic groups, in which territorial borders barely reflected the diversity of where different peoples actually lived. Note especially the widely scattered pockets of Germans and Hungarians. How do you think this ethnic diversity might have led to the rise of national independence movements in the Austrian Empire?

and nationalism. Bitter enemies, the far-flung Russian and Ottoman Empires were both absolutist states with powerful armies and long traditions of expansion and conquest. Because of those conquests, both were also multinational empires with many peoples, languages, and religions, but in each case most of the ruling elite came from the dominant ethnic group—the Orthodox Christian Russians of central and northern Russia and the Muslim Ottoman Turks of Anatolia (much of modern Turkey). After 1815 both of these multinational absolutist states worked to preserve their respective traditional conservative orders. Only after 1840 did each in turn experience a profound crisis and embark on a program of fundamental reform and modernization, as we shall see in Chapter 23.

Repressing the Revolutionary Spirit

Conservative political ideologies had important practical consequences. Under Metternich's leadership, Austria, Prussia, and Russia embarked on a decades-long crusade against the liberties and civil rights associated with the French and American Revolutions. The first step was the formation in September 1815 of the **Holy Alliance** by Austria, Prussia, and Russia. First proposed by Russia's Alexander I, the alliance worked to repress reformist and revolutionary movements and stifle desires for national independence across Europe.

Holy Alliance An alliance formed by the conservative rulers of Austria, Prussia, and Russia in September 1815 that became a symbol of the repression of liberal and revolutionary movements all over Europe.

The conservative restoration first brought its collective power to bear on southern Europe. In 1820 revolutionaries successfully forced the kings of Spain and the southern Italian Kingdom of the Two Sicilies to establish constitutional monarchies, with press freedoms, universal male suffrage, and other liberal reforms. Metternich was horrified; revolution was rising once again. Calling a conference at Troppau in Austria, he and Alexander I proclaimed the principle of active intervention to maintain all autocratic regimes whenever they were threatened. Austrian forces then marched into Naples in 1821 and restored the autocratic power of Ferdinand I in the Two Sicilies. A French invasion of Spain in 1823 likewise returned power to the king there.

The conservative policies of Metternich and the Holy Alliance limited reform not only in Austria and the Italian peninsula but also in the entire German Confederation. The states in the German Confederation retained independence, and though ambassadors from each met in a Confederation Diet, or assembly, it had little real political power. When liberal reformers and university students began to protest for the national unification of the German states, the Austrian and Prussian leadership used the diet to issue and enforce the infamous **Karlsbad Decrees** in 1819. These decrees required the German states to outlaw liberal political organizations, police their universities and newspapers, and establish a permanent committee with spies and informers to clamp down on liberal or radical reformers. (See "Evaluating the Evidence 21.1: The Karlsbad Decrees: Conservative Reaction in the German Confederation," at right.)

The forces of reaction squelched reform in Russia as well. In St. Petersburg in December 1825, a group of about three thousand army officers inspired by liberal ideals staged a protest against the new tsar, Nicholas I. Troops loyal to Nicholas I surrounded and assaulted the group with gunfire, cavalry, and cannon, leaving some sixty men dead; the surviving leaders were publicly hanged, and the rest sent to exile in Siberia. Through censorship, military might, secret police, imprisonment, and execution, conservative regimes in central Europe used the powers of the state to repress liberal reform wherever possible.

Karlsbad Decrees Issued in 1819, these repressive regulations were designed to uphold Metternich's conservatism, requiring the German states to root out subversive ideas and squelch any liberal organizations.

Limits to Conservative Power and Revolution in South America

Metternich liked to call himself "the chief Minister of Police in Europe," and the members of the Holy Alliance continually battled liberal political change.[3] Metternich's system proved quite effective in central Europe, at least until 1848, but the monarchists failed to stop dynastic change in France in 1830 or prevent Belgium from winning independence from the Netherlands in 1831.

The most dramatic challenge to conservative power occurred not in Europe, but overseas in South America. In the 1820s South American elites rose up and broke away from the Spanish crown and established a number of new republics based at first on liberal Enlightenment ideals. The leaders of the revolutions were primarily wealthy Creoles, direct descendants of Spanish parents born in the Americas. The well-established and powerful Creoles—only about 5 percent of the population—resented the political and economic control of an even smaller elite minority of *peninsulares*, people born in Spain who lived in and ruled the colonies. The vast majority of the population, composed of "mestizos" and "mulattos" (people of ethnically mixed heritage), enslaved and freed Africans, and native indigenous peoples, languished at the bottom of the social pyramid.

By the late 1700s the Creoles had begun to question Spanish policy and even the necessity of further colonial rule. The spark for revolt came during the Napoleonic Wars, when the French occupation of Spain in 1808 weakened the power of the

The Karlsbad Decrees:
Conservative Reaction in the German Confederation

In 1819 a member of a radical student fraternity at the German University of Jena assassinated the conservative author and diplomat August von Kotzebue. Metternich used the murder as an excuse to promulgate the repressive Karlsbad Decrees, which clamped down on liberal nationalists in the universities and the press throughout the German Confederation.

Law on Universities

1. A special representative of the ruler of each state shall be appointed for each university, with appropriate instructions and extended powers, and shall reside in the place where the university is situated. . . .

The function of this agent shall be to see to the strictest enforcement of existing laws and disciplinary regulations; to observe carefully the spirit which is shown by the instructors in the university in their public lectures and regular courses, and, without directly interfering in scientific matters or in the methods of teaching, to give a salutary direction to the instruction, having in view the future attitude of the students. Lastly, he shall devote unceasing attention to everything that may promote morality, good order, and outward propriety among the students. . . .

2. The confederated governments mutually pledge themselves to remove from the universities or other public educational institutions all teachers who, by obvious deviation from their duty, or by exceeding the limits of their functions, or by the abuse of their legitimate influence over the youthful minds, or by propagating harmful doctrines hostile to public order or subversive of existing governmental institutions, shall have unmistakably proved their unfitness for the important office intrusted to them. . . .

[Articles 3 and 4 ordered the universities to enforce laws against secret student societies.]

Press Law

1. So long as this decree shall remain in force no publication which appears in the form of daily issues, or as a serial not exceeding twenty sheets of printed matter, shall go to press in any state of the union without the previous knowledge and approval of the state officials. . . .

6. The Diet shall have the right, moreover, to suppress on its own authority, without being petitioned, such writings included in Article 1, in whatever German state they may appear, as, in the opinion of a commission appointed by it, are inimical to the honor of the union, the safety of individual states, or the maintenance of peace and quiet in Germany. There shall be no appeal from such decisions. . . .

Establishment of an Investigative Committee

1. Within a fortnight, reckoned from the passage of this decree, there shall convene, under the auspices of the Confederation . . . an extraordinary commission of investigation to consist of seven members, including the chairman.

2. The object of the commission shall be a joint investigation, as thorough and extensive as possible, of the facts relating to the origin and manifold ramifications of the revolutionary plots and demagogical associations directed against the existing constitution and the internal peace both of the union and of the individual states.

EVALUATE THE EVIDENCE

1. How do these regulations express the spirit of reactionary politics after the Napoleonic Wars? Why were university professors and students singled out as special targets?

2. The Karlsbad Decrees were periodically renewed until finally overturned during the revolutions of 1848. Do you think they were effective in checking the growth of liberal politics?

Source: James Harvey Robinson, *Readings in European History*, vol. 2 (Boston: Ginn and Company, 1906), pp. 547–550.

---

autocratic Spanish crown and the Napoleonic rhetoric of rights inspired revolutionaries. Yet the Creoles hesitated, worried that open revolt might upend the social pyramid or even lead to a slave revolution as in Haiti (see Chapter 19).

The South American revolutions thus began from below, with spontaneous uprisings by subordinated peoples of color. Creole leaders quickly took control of a struggle that would prove to be more prolonged and violent than the American Revolution, with outcomes less clear. In the north, the competent general Simón Bolívar—the Latin American equivalent of George Washington—defeated Spanish forces and established a short-lived "Gran Colombia," which lasted from 1819 to 1830. Bolívar, the "people's liberator," dreamed of establishing a federation of South American states, modeled on the United States. To the south, José de San Martín, a liberal-minded military commander, successfully threw off Spanish control by 1825.

Dreams of South American federation and unity proved difficult to realize. By 1830 the large northern state established by Bolívar had fractured, and by 1840 the borders of the new nations looked much like the map of Latin America today. Most of the new states initially received liberal constitutions, but these were difficult to implement in lands where the vast majority of people had no experience with constitutional rule and women and the great underclass of non-Creoles were not allowed to vote. Experiments with liberal constitutions soon gave way to a new political system controlled by *caudillos* (cow-DEE-yohs), or strong men, sometimes labeled warlords. Often former Creoles, the caudillos ruled limited territories on the basis of military strength, family patronage, and populist politics. The South American revolutions had failed to establish lasting constitutional republics, but they did demonstrate the revolutionary potential of liberal ideals and the limits on conservative control.

The Spread of Radical Ideas

FOCUS QUESTION
What new ideologies emerged to challenge conservatism?

In the years following the peace settlement of 1815, intellectuals and social observers sought to harness the radical ideas of the revolutionary age to new political movements. Many rejected conservatism, with its stress on tradition, a hereditary monarchy, a privileged landowning aristocracy, and an official state church. Often inspired by liberties championed during the French Revolution, radical thinkers developed and refined alternative ideologies—or political philosophies—and tried to convince people to follow them. In so doing, they helped articulate the basic political ideals that continue to shape Western society today.

Liberalism and the Middle Class

liberalism The principal ideas of this movement were equality and liberty; liberals demanded representative government and equality before the law as well as individual freedoms such as freedom of the press, freedom of speech, freedom of assembly, freedom of worship, and freedom from arbitrary arrest.

The principal ideas of **liberalism**—liberty and equality—were by no means defeated in 1815. First realized successfully in the American Revolution and then achieved in part in the French Revolution, liberalism demanded representative government as opposed to autocratic monarchy, and equality before the law for all as opposed to separate classes with separate legal rights. Liberty also meant specific individual freedoms: freedom of the press, freedom of speech, freedom of assembly, freedom of worship, and freedom from arbitrary arrest. Such ideas are still the guiding beliefs in modern democratic states, but in Europe in 1815 only France with Louis XVIII's Constitutional Charter and Great Britain with its Parliament had realized any of the liberal program. Even in those countries, liberalism had only begun to succeed.

laissez faire A doctrine of economic liberalism that calls for unrestricted private enterprise and no government interference in the economy.

Although conservatives still saw liberalism as a profound threat, it had gained a group of powerful adherents: the new upper classes made wealthy through growing industrialization and global commerce. This group promoted the liberal economic doctrine of **laissez faire** (lay-say FEHR), which called for free trade (including relaxation of import/export duties), unrestricted private enterprise, and no government interference in the economy.

As we saw in Chapter 17, Adam Smith posited the idea of economic liberalism and free-market capitalism in 1776 in opposition to mercantilism and its attempt to regulate trade. Smith argued that freely competitive private enterprise would give all citizens a fair and equal opportunity to do what they did best and would result in greater income for everyone, not just the rich. (Smith's form of liberalism is often called "classical liberalism" in the United States, in order to distinguish it sharply from modern American liberalism, which generally favors more government programs to meet social needs and regulate the economy.)

In the first half of the nineteenth century, liberal political ideals became closely associated with narrow class interests. Starting in the 1820s in Britain, business elites enthusiastically embraced laissez-faire policies because they proved immensely profitable, and used liberal ideas to defend their right to do as they wished in their factories. Labor unions were outlawed because, these elites argued, unions restricted free competition and the individual's "right to work." Early-nineteenth-century liberals favored representative government, but they generally wanted property qualifications attached to the right to vote. In practice, this meant limiting the vote to very small numbers of the well-to-do. Workers, peasants, and women, as well as middle-class shopkeepers, clerks, and artisans, did not own the necessary property and thus could not vote.

As liberalism became increasingly identified with upper-class business interests, some opponents of conservatism felt that liberalism did not go nearly far enough. Inspired by memories of the French Revolution and the example of Jacksonian democracy in the young American republic, this group embraced republicanism: an expanded liberal ideology that endorsed universal democratic voting rights, at least for males, and radical equality for all. Republicans were more willing than most liberals to endorse violent upheaval to achieve goals. In addition, republicans might advocate government action to create jobs, redistribute income, and level social differences. As the results of the revolutions of 1830 and 1848 suggest, liberals and radical republicans could join forces against conservatives only up to a point.

The Growing Appeal of Nationalism

Nationalism—destined to have an enormous influence in the modern world—was another radical idea that gained popularity in the years after 1815. The nascent power of nationalism was revealed in the success of the French armies in the revolutionary and Napoleonic wars, when soldiers inspired by patriotic loyalty to the French nation achieved victory after victory (see Chapter 19). Early nationalists found inspiration in the vision of a people united by a common language, a common history and culture, and a common territory. In German-speaking central Europe, defeat by Napoleon's armies had made the vision of a national people united in defense of their "fatherland" particularly attractive.

In the early nineteenth century such national unity was more a dream than a reality as far as most ethnic groups or nationalities were concerned. Local dialects abounded, even in relatively cohesive countries like France, where peasants from nearby villages often failed to understand each other. Moreover, a variety of ethnic groups shared the territory of most states, not just the Austrian, Russian, and Ottoman Empires discussed earlier. Over the course of the nineteenth century, nationalism nonetheless gathered force as a political philosophy. Advancing literacy rates, the establishment of a mass press, the growth of large state bureaucracies, compulsory education, and conscription armies all created a common culture that encouraged ordinary people to take pride in their national heritage.

nationalism The idea that each people had its own genius and specific identity that manifested itself especially in a common language and history, and often led to the desire for an independent political state.

In multiethnic states, however, nationalism could promote disintegration. Recognizing the power of the "national idea," European nationalists—generally educated, middle-class liberals and intellectuals—sought to turn the cultural unity that they desired into political reality. They believed that every nation, like every citizen, had the right to exist in freedom and to develop its unique character and spirit, and they hoped to make the territory of each people coincide with well-defined borders in an independent nation-state.

This political goal made nationalism explosive, particularly in central and eastern Europe, where different peoples overlapped and intermingled. As discussed, the Austrian, Russian, and Ottoman central states refused to allow national minorities independence. This suppression fomented widespread discontent among nationalists who wanted freedom from oppressive imperial rule. In the many different principalities of the Italian peninsula and the German Confederation, to the contrary, nationalists yearned for national unification across what they saw as divisive and obsolete state borders. Whether they sought independence or unification, before 1850 nationalist movements were fresh, idealistic, and progressive, if not revolutionary.

In recent years historians have tried to understand why the nationalist vision, which typically fit poorly with existing conditions and promised much upheaval, was so successful in the long run. Of fundamental importance in the rise of nationalism was the development of a complex industrial and urban society, which required more sophisticated forms of communication between individuals and groups.[4] The need for improved communication promoted the use of a standardized national language in many areas, creating at least a superficial cultural unity as a standard tongue spread through mass education and the emergence of the popular press. When a minority population was large and concentrated, the nationalist campaign for a standardized language often led the minority group to push for a separate nation-state.

Scholars generally argue that nations are recent creations, the product of a new, self-conscious nationalist ideology. Thus nation-states emerged in the nineteenth century as "imagined communities" that sought to bind millions of strangers together around the abstract concept of an all-embracing national identity. This meant bringing citizens together with emotionally charged symbols and ceremonies, such as independence holidays and patriotic parades. On these occasions the imagined nation of equals might celebrate its most hallowed traditions, which were often recent inventions.[5]

Between 1815 and 1850 most people who believed in nationalism also believed in either liberalism or radical republicanism. They typically shared a deep belief in the creativity and nobility of the people. Liberals and especially republicans, for example, saw the people as the ultimate source of all government. Yet nationally minded liberals and republicans agreed that the benefits of self-government would be possible only if individuals were bonded together by common traditions that transcended local interests and even class differences. Thus in the early nineteenth century the liberty of the individual and the love of a free nation overlapped greatly.

Despite some confidence that a world system based on independent nation-states would promote global harmony, early nationalists eagerly emphasized the differences between peoples and developed a strong sense of "us" versus "them." To this "us-them" outlook, nationalists could all too easily add two highly volatile ingredients: a sense of national mission and a sense of national superiority. As Europe entered an age of increased global interaction, these powerful ideas would lead to aggression and conflict, as powerful nation-states backed by patriotic citizens competed with each other on the international stage.

The Foundations of Modern Socialism

More radical than liberalism or nationalism was **socialism**. Early socialist thinkers were a diverse group with wide-ranging ideas. Yet they shared a sense that the political revolution in France, the growth of industrialization in Britain, and the rise of laissez faire had created a profound spiritual and moral crisis. Modern capitalism, they believed, fomented a selfish individualism that encouraged inequality and split the community into isolated fragments. Society urgently required fundamental change to re-establish cooperation and a new sense of community.

Early socialists felt an intense desire to help the poor, and they preached that the rich and the poor should be more nearly equal economically. To this end, they believed that private property should be strictly regulated by the government, or abolished outright and replaced by state or community ownership. Economic planning, greater social equality, and state regulation of property were the key ideas of early socialism — and have remained central to all socialism since.

One influential group of early socialist advocates became known as the "utopian socialists" because their grand schemes for social improvement ultimately proved unworkable. The Frenchmen Count Henri de Saint-Simon (awn-REE duh san-see-MOHN) (1760–1825) and Charles Fourier (sharl FAWR-ee-ay) (1772–1837), as well as the British industrialist Robert Owen, all founded movements intended to establish model communities that would usher in a new age of happiness and equality.

Saint-Simon's "positivism" optimistically proclaimed the tremendous possibilities of industrial development: "The golden age of the human species . . . is before us!"[6] The key to progress was proper social organization that required the "parasites" — the court, the aristocracy, lawyers, and churchmen — to give way, once and for all, to the "doers" — the leading scientists, engineers, and industrialists. The doers would carefully plan the economy and guide it forward by undertaking vast public works projects and establishing investment banks. Saint-Simon also stressed in highly moralistic terms that every social institution ought to have as its main goal improved conditions for the poor.

After 1830 the utopian critique of capitalism became sharper. Charles Fourier called for the construction of mathematically precise, self-sufficient communities called "phalanxes," each made up of 1,620 people. In the phalanx, all property was owned by the community and used for the common good. Fourier was an early proponent of the total emancipation of women. According to Fourier, under capitalism young single women were shamelessly "sold" to their future husbands for dowries and other financial considerations. Therefore, he called for the abolition of marriage and for sexual freedom and free unions based only on love. The great British utopian Robert Owen, an early promoter of labor unions, likewise envisaged a society organized into socialistic industrial-agricultural communities. Saint-Simon, Fourier, and Owen all had followers who tried to put their ideas into practice. Though these attempts had mostly collapsed by the 1850s, utopian socialist ideas remained an inspiration for future reformers and revolutionaries.

Some socialist thinkers embraced the even more radical ideas of anarchism. In his 1840 pamphlet *What Is Property?* Pierre-Joseph Proudhon (1809–1865), a self-educated printer, famously argued "property is theft!" Property, he claimed, was profit that was stolen from the worker, the source of all wealth. Distrustful of all authority and political systems, Proudhon believed that states should be abolished and that society should be organized in loose associations of working people.

socialism A backlash against the emergence of individualism and the fragmentation of industrial society, and a move toward cooperation and a sense of community; the key ideas were economic planning, greater social equality, and state regulation of property.

Other early socialists, like Louis Blanc (1811–1882), a sharp-eyed, intelligent journalist, focused on more practical reforms. In his *Organization of Work* (1839), he urged workers to agitate for universal voting rights and take control of the state peacefully. Blanc believed that the government should set up publicly funded workshops and factories to guarantee full employment. The right to work had to become as sacred as any other right.

As industrialization advanced in European cities, working people began to embrace the socialist message. This happened first in France, where workers cherished the memory of the radical phase of the French Revolution and became violently opposed to laissez-faire laws that denied their right to organize in guilds and unions. Developing a sense of class in the process of their protests, workers favored collective action and government intervention in economic life. Thus the aspirations of workers and radical theorists reinforced each other, and a genuine socialist movement emerged in Paris in the 1830s and 1840s.

Marxism An influential political program based on the socialist ideas of German radical Karl Marx, which called for a working-class revolution to overthrow capitalist society and establish a Communist state.

The Birth of Marxist Socialism

In the 1840s France was the center of socialism, but in the following decades the German intellectual Karl Marx (1818–1883) would weave the diffuse strands of socialist thought into a distinctly modern ideology. Marxist socialism—or **Marxism**—would have a lasting impact on political thought and practice.

The son of a Jewish lawyer who had converted to Lutheranism, the young Marx was a brilliant student. After earning a Ph.D. in philosophy at Humboldt University in Berlin in 1841, he turned to journalism, and his critical articles about the laboring poor caught the attention of the Prussian police. Forced to flee Prussia in 1843, Marx traveled around Europe, promoting socialism and avoiding the authorities. He lived a modest, middle-class life with his wife, Jenny, and their children, often relying on his friend and colleague Friedrich Engels (see Chapter 20) for financial support. After the revolutions of 1848, Marx settled in London, where he spent the rest of his life as an advocate of working-class revolution. *Capital*, his magnum opus, appeared in 1867.

Marx was a dedicated scholar, and his work united sociology, economics, philosophy, and history in an impressive synthesis. From Scottish and English political economists like Adam Smith and David Ricardo, Marx learned to apply social-scientific analysis to economic problems, though he pushed these liberal ideas in radical directions. Deeply influenced by the utopian socialists, Marx championed ideals of social equality and community. He criticized his socialist predecessors, however, for their fanciful utopian schemes, claiming that his version of "scientific" socialism was rooted in historic law, and therefore realistic. Following German philosophies of idealism associated with Georg Hegel (1770–1831), Marx came to believe that history had patterns and purpose and moved forward in stages toward an ultimate goal.

Bringing these ideas together, Marx argued that class struggle over economic wealth was the great engine of human history. In his view, one class had always exploited the other, and with the advent of modern industry, society was split more clearly than ever before: between

Karl Marx and His Family Active in the revolutions of 1848, Marx fled Germany and eventually settled in London, where he wrote *Capital*, the weighty exposition of his socialist theories. Despite his advocacy of radical revolution, Marx and his wife, Jenny, pictured here with two of their daughters, lived a respectable though modest middle-class life. Standing on the left is Friedrich Engels, an accomplished writer and political theorist who was Marx's long-time friend, financial supporter, and intellectual collaborator. (© Mary Evans Picture Library/Marx Memorial Library/The Image Works)

the upper class—the **bourgeoisie** (boor-ZHWAH-zee)—and the working class—the **proletariat**. The bourgeoisie, a tiny minority, owned the means of production and grew rich by exploiting the labor of workers. Over time, Marx argued, the proletariat would grow ever larger and ever poorer, and their increasing alienation would lead them to develop a sense of revolutionary class-consciousness. Then, just as the bourgeoisie had triumphed over the feudal aristocracy in the French Revolution, the proletariat would overthrow the bourgeoisie in a violent revolutionary cataclysm. The result would be the end of class struggle and the arrival of communism, a system of radical equality.

Fascinated by the rapid expansion of modern capitalism, Marx based his revolutionary program on an insightful yet critical analysis of economic history. Under feudalism, he wrote, labor had been organized according to long-term contracts of rights and privileges. Under capitalism, to the contrary, labor was a commodity like any other, bought and sold for wages in the free market. The goods workers produced were always worth more than what those workers were paid, and the difference—"surplus value," in Marx's terms—was pocketed by the bourgeoisie in the form of profit.

According to Marx, capitalism was immensely productive but highly exploitative. In a never-ending search for profit, the bourgeoisie would squeeze workers dry and then expand across the globe, until all parts of the world were trapped in capitalist relations of production. Contemporary ideals, such as free trade, private property, and even marriage and Christian morality, were myths that masked and legitimized class exploitation. To many people, Marx's argument that the contradictions inherent in this unequal system would eventually be overcome in a working-class revolution appeared to be the irrefutable capstone of a brilliant interpretation of historical trends.

When Marx and Engels published *The Communist Manifesto* on the eve of the revolutions of 1848, their opening claim that "a spectre is haunting Europe—the spectre of Communism" was highly exaggerated. The Communist movement was in its infancy. Scattered groups of socialists, anarchists, and labor leaders were hardly united around Marxist ideas. But by the time Marx died in 1883, Marxist socialism had profoundly reshaped left-wing radicalism in ways that would inspire revolutionaries around the world for the next one hundred years.

The Romantic Movement

The early nineteenth century brought changes to literature and the other arts as well as political ideas. Followers of the new Romantic movement, or Romanticism, revolted against the emphasis on rationality, order, and restraint that characterized the Enlightenment and the controlled style of classicism. Forerunners appeared from about 1750 on, but the movement crystallized fully in the 1790s, primarily in England and Germany. Romanticism gained strength and swept across Europe until the 1840s, when it gradually gave way to Realism.

The Tenets of Romanticism

Like other cultural movements, **Romanticism** was characterized by intellectual diversity. Nonetheless, common parameters stand out. Artists inspired by Romanticism repudiated the emphasis on reason associated with well-known Enlightenment philosophes like Voltaire or Montesquieu (see Chapter 16). Romantics championed instead emotional exuberance, unrestrained imagination, and spontaneity in both art and

bourgeoisie The middle-class minority who owned the means of production and, according to Marx, exploited the working-class proletariat.

proletariat The industrial working class who, according to Marx, were unfairly exploited by the profit-seeking bourgeoisie.

FOCUS QUESTION
What were the characteristics of the Romantic movement?

Romanticism An artistic movement at its height from about 1790 to the 1840s that was in part a revolt against classicism and the Enlightenment, characterized by a belief in emotional exuberance, unrestrained imagination, and spontaneity in both art and personal life.

personal life. Preoccupied with emotional excess, Romantic works explored the awesome power of love and desire and of hatred, guilt, and despair.

Where Enlightenment thinkers applied the scientific method to social issues and cast rosy predictions for future progress, Romantics valued intuition and nostalgia for the past. Where Enlightenment thinkers embraced secularization, Romantics sought the inspiration of religious ecstasy. Where Enlightenment thinkers valued public life and civic affairs, Romantics delved into the supernatural and turned inward, to the hidden recesses of the self. As the Austrian composer Franz Schubert exclaimed in 1824:

> Oh imagination, thou supreme jewel of mankind, thou inexhaustible source from which artists and scholars drink! Oh, rest with us—despite the fact that thou art recognized only by a few—so as to preserve us from that so-called Enlightenment, that ugly skeleton without flesh or blood![7]

Nowhere was the break with Enlightenment classicism more apparent than in Romanticism's general conception of nature. Classicists were not particularly interested in nature. The Romantics, in contrast, were enchanted by stormy seas, untouched forests, and icy arctic wastelands. Nature could be awesome and tempestuous, a source of beauty or spiritual inspiration. Most Romantics saw the growth of modern industry as an ugly, brutal attack on their beloved nature and on venerable traditions. They sought escape—in the unspoiled Lake District of northern England, in exotic North Africa, in an imaginary and idealized Middle Ages.

The study of history became a Romantic obsession. History held the key to a universe now perceived to be organic and dynamic, not mechanical and static, as Enlightenment thinkers had believed. Historical novels like Sir Walter Scott's *Ivanhoe* (1820), a passionate romance set in twelfth-century England, found eager readers among the literate middle classes. Professional historians influenced by Romanticism, such as Jules Michelet, went beyond the standard accounts of great men or famous battles. Michelet's many books on the history of France consciously promoted the growth of national aspirations; by fanning the embers of memory, Michelet encouraged the French people to search the past for their special national destiny.

Romanticism was a lifestyle as well as an intellectual movement. Many early-nineteenth-century Romantics lived lives of tremendous emotional intensity. Obsessive love affairs, duels to the death, madness, strange illnesses, and suicide were not uncommon. Romantic artists typically led bohemian lives, wearing their hair long and uncombed in preference to donning powdered wigs, and rejecting the manners and morals of refined society. Great individualists, the Romantics believed that the full development of one's unique human potential was the supreme purpose in life.

Romantic Literature

Romanticism found its distinctive voice in poetry, as the Enlightenment had in prose. Though Romantic poetry had important forerunners in the German "Storm and Stress" movement of the 1770s and 1780s, its first great poets were English: William Blake, William Wordsworth, Samuel Taylor Coleridge, and Sir Walter Scott

English Romantic Poets

These poems by Percy Bysshe Shelley and John Keats stand as sublime examples of literary Romanticism.

OZYMANDIAS
Percy Bysshe Shelley, 1818

I met a traveller from an antique land
Who said: "Two vast and trunkless legs of stone
Stand in the desert. Near them, on the sand,
Half sunk, a shattered visage lies, whose frown,
And wrinkled lip, and sneer of cold command,
Tell that its sculptor well those passions read
Which yet survive, stamped on these lifeless things,
The hand that mocked them and the heart that fed.
And on the pedestal these words appear—
'My name is Ozymandias, king of kings:
Look on my works, ye Mighty, and despair!'
Nothing beside remains. Round the decay
Of that colossal wreck, boundless and bare,
The lone and level sands stretch far away."

BRIGHT STAR
John Keats, 1819

Bright star, would I were stedfast as thou art—
    Not in lone splendour hung aloft the night

And watching, with eternal lids apart,
    Like nature's patient, sleepless Eremite,
The moving waters at their priestlike task
    Of pure ablution round earth's human shores,
Or gazing on the new soft-fallen mask
    Of snow upon the mountains and the moors—
No—yet still stedfast, still unchangeable,
    Pillow'd upon my fair love's ripening breast,
To feel for ever its soft fall and swell,
    Awake for ever in a sweet unrest,
Still, still to hear her tender-taken breath,
And so live ever—or else swoon to death.

EVALUATE THE EVIDENCE

1. How do these poems express some of the basic tenets of Romanticism? How, for example, do they explore notions of decline and death?
2. Are the powerful emotions described in and evoked by these poems incompatible with Enlightenment rationalism?

Source: George Edward Woodberry, ed., *The Complete Poetical Works of Percy Bysshe Shelley* (Boston: Houghton, Mifflin, and Company, 1892), p. 201; H. Buxton Forman, ed., *The Complete Works of John Keats*, vol. 3 (Glasgow: Gowars and Gray, 1901), p. 224.

were all active by 1800, followed shortly by Lord Byron, Percy Bysshe Shelley, and John Keats. (See "Evaluating the Evidence 21.2: English Romantic Poets," above.)

A towering leader of English Romanticism, William Wordsworth was deeply influenced by Rousseau and the spirit of the early French Revolution. Wordsworth settled in the rural Lake District of England with his sister, Dorothy, and Samuel Taylor Coleridge (1772–1834). In 1798 Wordsworth and Coleridge published their *Lyrical Ballads*, which abandoned flowery classical conventions for the language of ordinary speech and endowed simple subjects with the loftiest majesty. Wordsworth believed that all natural things were sacred, and his poetry often expressed a mystical appreciation of nature:

To every natural form, rock, fruit or flower
Even the loose stones that cover the high-way
I gave a moral life, I saw them feel,
Or link'd them to some feeling: the great mass
Lay bedded in a quickening soul, and all
That I beheld, respired with inward meaning.[8]

Here Wordsworth expressed his love of nature in commonplace forms that a variety of readers could appreciate. The short stanza well illustrates his famous conception of poetry as the "spontaneous overflow of powerful feeling [which] takes its origin from emotion recollected in tranquility."[9]

In France under Napoleon, classicism remained strong and at first inhibited the growth of Romanticism. An early French champion of the new movement, Germaine de Staël (duh STAHL) (1766–1817) urged the French to throw away their worn-out classical models. Her study *On Germany* (1810) extolled the spontaneity and enthusiasm of German writers and thinkers, and it had a powerful impact on the post-1815 generation in France. (See "Individuals in Society: Germaine de Staël," at right.) Between 1820 and 1850 the Romantic impulse broke through in the poetry and prose of Alphonse de Lamartine, Victor Hugo, and George Sand (pseudonym of the woman writer Amandine-Aurore-Lucile Dudevant). Of these, Victor Hugo (1802–1885) became the most well known.

Son of a Napoleonic general, Hugo achieved an amazing range of rhythm, language, and image in his lyric poetry. His powerful novels exemplified the Romantic fascination with fantastic characters, exotic historical settings, and extreme emotions. The hero of Hugo's famous *The Hunchback of Notre Dame* (1831) is the great cathedral's deformed bell-ringer, a "human gargoyle" overlooking the teeming life of fifteenth-century Paris. Renouncing his early conservatism, Hugo equated freedom in literature with liberty in politics and society. His political evolution was thus exactly the opposite of Wordsworth's, in whom youthful radicalism gave way to middle-aged caution. As the contrast between the two artists suggests, Romanticism was compatible with many political beliefs.

In central and eastern Europe, literary Romanticism and early nationalism often reinforced one another. Well-educated Romantics championed their own people's histories, cultures, and unique greatness. Like modern anthropologists, they studied peasant life and transcribed the folk songs, tales, and proverbs that the cosmopolitan Enlightenment had disdained. The brothers Jacob and Wilhelm Grimm were particularly successful at rescuing German fairy tales from oblivion. (See "Evaluating the Evidence 21.3: Jacob and Wilhelm Grimm, *Children's Stories and Household Tales*," page 700.) In the Slavic lands, Romantics played a decisive role in converting spoken peasant languages into modern written languages. In the vast Austrian, Russian, and Ottoman Empires, with their many ethnic minorities, the combination of Romanticism and nationalism was particularly potent. Ethnic groups dreaming of independence could find revolutionary inspiration in Romantic visions of a historic national destiny.

Romanticism in Art and Music

Romantic concerns with nature, history, and the imagination extended well beyond literature, into the realms of art and music. France's Eugène Delacroix (oo-ZHEHN deh-luh-KWAH) (1798–1863), one of Romanticism's greatest artists, painted dramatic, colorful scenes that stirred the emotions. Delacroix was fascinated with remote and exotic subjects, whether lion hunts in Morocco or dreams of languishing, sensuous women in a sultan's harem. The famous German painter Casper David Friedrich (1774–1840) preferred somber landscapes of

INDIVIDUALS IN SOCIETY
Germaine de Staël

Rich, intellectual, passionate, and assertive, Germaine Necker de Staël (1766–1817) astonished contemporaries and still fascinates historians. She was strongly influenced by her parents, poor Swiss Protestants who soared to the top of prerevolutionary Parisian society. Her brilliant but rigid mother filled Germaine's head with knowledge, and each week the precocious child listened, wide-eyed and attentive, to illustrious writers and philosophers debating ideas at her mother's salon. At age twelve, she suffered a physical and mental breakdown. Only then was she allowed to have a playmate to romp about with on the family estate. Her adoring father was Jacques Necker, a banker who made an enormous fortune and became France's reform-minded minister of finance before the Revolution. Worshipping her father in adolescence, Germaine also came to love politics.

Germaine de Staël. (Portrait by Marie Eleomore Godefroid [1778–1849], copy of a painting by François Gerard/Château de Versailles, France/Bridgeman Images)

Accepting at nineteen an arranged marriage with Baron de Staël-Holstein, a womanizing Swedish diplomat bewitched by her dowry, Germaine began her life's work. She opened her own intellectual salon and began to write and publish. Her wit and exuberance attracted foreigners and liberal French aristocrats, one of whom became the first of many lovers as her marriage soured and she searched unsuccessfully for the happiness of her parents' union. Fleeing Paris in 1792 and returning after the Thermidorian reaction (see Chapter 19), she subsequently angered Napoleon by criticizing his dictatorial rule. In 1803 he permanently banished her from Paris.

Retiring again to her isolated estate in Switzerland and skillfully managing her inherited wealth, Staël fought insomnia with opium and boredom with parties that attracted luminaries from all over Europe. Always seeking stimulation for her restless mind, she traveled widely in Italy and Germany and drew upon these experiences in her novel *Corinne* (1807) and her study *On Germany* (1810). Both works summed up her Romantic faith and enjoyed enormous success.

Staël urged creative individuals to abandon traditional rules and classical models. She encouraged them to embrace experimentation, emotion, and enthusiasm. Enthusiasm, which she had in abundance, was the key,

the royal road to creativity, personal fulfillment, and human improvement. Thrilling to music, for example, she felt that only an enthusiastic person could really appreciate this gift of God, this wordless message that "unifies our dual nature and blends senses and spirit in a common rapture."*

Yet a profound sadness runs through her writing. This sadness, so characteristic of the Romantic temperament, grew in part out of disappointments in love and prolonged exile. But it also grew out of the insoluble predicament of being an enormously gifted woman in an age of intense male sexism. Little wonder that uneasy male competitors and literary critics took delight in ridiculing and defaming her as a neurotic and masculine woman, a mediocre and unnatural talent who had foolishly dared to enter the male world of serious thought and action. Even her supporters could not accept her for what she was. Poet Lord Byron recognized her genius and called her "the most eminent woman author of this, or perhaps of any century" but quickly added that "she should have been born a man."†

Buffeted and saddened by this scorn and condescension, Staël advocated equal rights for women throughout her life. Only with equal rights and duties—in education and careers, in love and marital relations—could a woman ever hope to realize her intellectual and emotional potential. Practicing what she preached as best she could, Germaine de Staël was a trailblazer in the struggle for women's rights.

QUESTIONS FOR ANALYSIS

1. In what ways did Germaine de Staël's life and thought reflect basic elements of the Romantic movement?
2. Why did male critics often attack Staël? What do these criticisms tell us about gender relations in the early nineteenth century?

*Quoted in G. R. Besser, *Germaine de Staël Revisited* (New York: Twayne Publishers, 1994), p. 106. Enhanced by a feminist perspective, this fine study is highly recommended.
†Quoted ibid., p. 139.

Jacob and Wilhelm Grimm, *Children's Stories and Household Tales*

Familiar fairy tales such as "Snow White" and "Little Red Riding Hood" are the legacy of the Brothers Grimm — Jacob (1785–1863) and Wilhelm (1768–1859) — university-trained linguists who traveled through rural Germany recording folktales in the first decades of the nineteenth century. Determined to preserve what Wilhelm called "a world of magic" in a time of rapid change, their work uncovered a popular oral culture that worked mythic, pagan, and Christian themes into folktales and legends about the trials and joys of everyday life. In 1812 the brothers published the first volume of Children's Stories and Household Tales, *which marked the start of a collaborative, scholarly study of German myth and history. The Grimms brought together the Romantic idealization of simple rural virtues and the growing appreciation of national character and difference. Collecting German folktales at the height of the Napoleonic Wars and the French occupation of German territories helped popularize a specifically national tradition, which set the Germans apart from the French and offered at least passive resistance to the foreign invaders. In the passages below, Wilhelm eloquently describes the importance of uncovering lost tales and emphasizes the unique "riches of German poetry" found in folktales.*

~

From *Children's Stories and Household Tales*, Volume 1, 1812

When a storm of some other calamity from the heavens destroys an entire crop, it is reassuring to find that a small spot on a path lined by hedges or bushes has been spared and that a few stalks, at least, remain standing. If the sun favors them with light, they continue to grow, alone and unobserved, and no scythe comes along to cut them down prematurely for vast storage bins. But near the end of the summer, once they have ripened and become full, poor devout hands seek them out; ear upon ear, carefully bound and esteemed more highly than entire sheaves, they are brought home, and for the entire winter they provide nourishment, perhaps the only seed for the future. That is how it all seems to us when we review the riches of German poetry from earlier times and discover that nothing of it has been kept alive. Even the memory of it is lost — folk songs and these innocent household tales are all that remain. . . .

We know them and we love them just because we happen to have heard them in a certain way, and we like them without reflecting on why. . . . [O]ne quickly discovers that the custom [of telling these tales] persists only in places where there is a warm openness to poetry or where there are imaginations not yet deformed by the perversities of modern life. . . .

We have tried to collect these tales in as pure a form as possible. In many, the narrative flow is interrupted by rhymes and lines of verse, which sometimes clearly alliterate but are never sung during the telling of a tale. Precisely these are the oldest and best tales. No details have been added or embellished or changed, for we would have been reluctant

ruined churches or remote arctic shipwrecks, which captured the divine presence in natural forces.

In England the Romantic painters Joseph M. W. Turner (1775–1851) and John Constable (1776–1837) were fascinated by nature, but their interpretations of it contrasted sharply, aptly symbolizing the tremendous emotional range of the Romantic movement. Turner depicted nature's power and terror; wild storms and sinking ships were favorite subjects. Constable painted gentle Wordsworthian landscapes in which human beings lived peacefully with their environment, the comforting countryside of unspoiled rural England.

Musicians and composers likewise explored the Romantic sensibility. Abandoning well-defined musical structures, the great Romantic composers used a wide range of forms to create profound musical landscapes that evoked powerful emotions. They transformed the small classical orchestra, tripling its size by adding wind instruments, percussion, and more brass and strings. The crashing to expand stories already so rich by adding analogies and allusions. They cannot be invented. A collection of this kind has never existed in Germany.

From *Children's Stories and Household Tales, Volume 2, 1815*

The true value of these tales must really be set quite high: they put our ancient heroic poetry in a new light that could not have been produced in any other way. Briar Rose [or Sleeping Beauty], who is put to sleep after being pricked by a spindle, is really Brunhilde, put to sleep after being pricked by a thorn. . . . Snow White sleeps peacefully with the same glowing red colors of life on her cheeks as Snaefrid, the most beautiful woman of all, at whose coffin sits Harald the Fair-Haired [Brunhilde, Snaefrid, and Harald are characters from ancient Germanic myths]. . . . These folktales have kept intact German myths that were thought to be lost, and we are firmly convinced that if a search were conducted in all the hallowed regions of our fatherland, long neglected treasures would transform themselves into fabulous treasures and help to found the study of the origins of our poetry. It works the same way with the many dialects of our language. In them a large part of the words and peculiarities that we had long held to be defunct live on undetected.

The aim of our collection was not just to serve the cause of the history of poetry. It was also our intention that the poetry living in it be effective, bringing pleasure when it could, and that it therefore become a manual of manners. . . .

We have published variant forms, along with relevant notes, in the appendix. Those who feel indifferent to such things will find it easier to skip over them than we would have found to omit them. They belong to the book, since it is a contribution to the history of German folk poetry. These different versions seem more noteworthy to us than they do to those who see in them nothing more than variants or corrupt forms of a once extant archetypal form. For us, they are more likely to be attempts to capture, through numerous approaches, an inexhaustibly rich ideal type.

EVALUATE THE EVIDENCE

1. How does the view of German history promoted by the Grimms bring together Romanticism and nationalism? How do the folktales lend authenticity to ideas about the historical roots of the German nation?

2. In the selections above, Wilhelm claims that the stories were collected in "as pure a form as possible" without added details or embellishments, and he later underscores the importance of including "variant forms" of each story. Why does he make these appeals to the scientific method? Would it matter if the Grimm brothers had embellished the tales?

Source: Maria Tatar, ed., *The Annotated Brothers Grimm*, bicentennial ed. (New York: Norton, 2012), pp. 435–436; 440; 443–445.

chords evoking the surge of the masses in Chopin's "Revolutionary Etude" and the bottomless despair of the funeral march in Beethoven's Third Symphony— such were the modern orchestra's musical paintings that plumbed the depths of human feeling.

This range and intensity gave music and musicians much greater prestige and publicity than in the past. Music no longer simply complemented a church service or helped a nobleman digest his dinner. It became a sublime end in itself, most perfectly realizing the endless yearning of the soul. The unbelievable one-in-a-million performer—the great virtuoso who could transport the listener to ecstasy and hysteria—became a cultural hero. People swooned, for example, for Franz Liszt (1811–1886), the greatest pianist of his age, as they scream for rock stars today.

The first great Romantic composer is also the most famous today. Ludwig van Beethoven (1770–1827) used contrasting themes and tones to produce dramatic conflict and inspiring resolutions. As one contemporary admirer wrote, "Beethoven's

Delacroix, *Massacre at Chios*, 1824 This moving masterpiece by Romantic artist Eugène Delacroix portrays an Ottoman massacre of ethnic Greeks on the island of Chios during the struggle for national independence in Greece. The Greek revolt won the enthusiastic support of European liberals, nationalists, and Romantics, and this massive oil painting (ca. 13 feet by 11 feet) portrays the Ottomans as cruel and violent oppressors holding back the course of history. (Musée du Louvre, Paris, France/Bridgeman Images)

music sets in motion the lever of fear, of awe, of horror, of suffering, and awakens just that infinite longing which is the essence of Romanticism."[10] Beethoven's range and output were tremendous. At the peak of his fame, he began to lose his hearing. He considered suicide but eventually overcame despair: "I will take fate by the throat; it will not bend me completely to its will."[11] Beethoven continued to pour out immortal music, although his last years were silent, spent in total deafness.

Reforms and Revolutions Before 1848

FOCUS QUESTION
How and where was conservatism challenged after 1815?

While the Romantics enacted a revolution in the arts, liberal, national, and socialist forces battered against the conservative restoration of 1815. Political change could result from gradual and peaceful reform or from violent insurrection, but everywhere it took the determination of ordinary people standing up to the prerogatives of the powerful. Between 1815 and 1848 three important countries—Greece, Great Britain, and France—experienced variations on this basic theme.

National Liberation in Greece

Though conservative statesmen had maintained the autocratic status quo despite revolts in Spain and the Two Sicilies, a national revolution succeeded in Greece in the 1820s. Since the fifteenth century the Greeks had lived under the domination of the Ottoman Turks. In spite of centuries of foreign rule, the Greeks had survived as a people, united by their language and the Greek Orthodox religion. In the early nineteenth century the general growth of national aspirations inspired a desire for independence. This rising national movement led to the formation of secret societies and then to open revolt in 1821, led by Alexander Ypsilanti (ihp-suh-LAN-tee), a Greek patriot and a general in the Russian army.

At first, the Great Powers, particularly Metternich, opposed the revolution and refused to back Ypsilanti, primarily because they sought a stable Ottoman Empire as a bulwark against Russian interests in southeast Europe. Yet the Greek cause had powerful defenders. Educated Europeans and Americans cherished the culture of classical Greece; Russians admired the piety of their Orthodox brethren. Writers and artists, moved by the Romantic impulse, responded enthusiastically to the Greek national struggle. The famous English Romantic poet Lord Byron even joined the Greek revolutionaries to fight (as he wrote in a famous poem) "that Greece might yet be free."

The Greeks, though often quarreling among themselves, battled the Ottomans while hoping for the support of European governments. In 1827 Britain, France, and Russia yielded to popular demands at home and directed Ottoman leaders to accept an armistice. When they refused, the navies of these three powers trapped the Ottoman fleet at Navarino. Russia then declared another of its periodic wars of expansion against the Ottomans. This led to the establishment of a Russian protectorate over much of present-day Romania, which had also been under Ottoman rule. Great Britain, France, and Russia finally declared Greece independent in 1830 and installed a German prince as king of the new country in 1832. Despite this imposed regime, which left the Greek people restive, they had won their independence in a heroic war of liberation against a foreign empire.

Greek Independence, 1830

Liberal Reform in Great Britain

Pressure from below also reshaped politics in Great Britain, but through a process of gradual reform rather than revolution. Eighteenth-century Britain had been remarkably stable. The landowning aristocracy dominated society, but that class was neither closed nor rigidly defined. Successful business and professional people could buy land and become gentlefolk, while the common people enjoyed limited civil rights. Yet the constitutional monarchy was hardly democratic. With only about 8 percent of the population allowed to vote, the British Parliament, easily manipulated by the king, remained in the hands of the upper classes. Government policies supported the aristocracy and the new industrial capitalists at the expense of the laboring classes.

By the 1780s there was growing interest in some kind of political reform, and organized union activity began to emerge in force during the Napoleonic Wars (see Chapter 19). Yet the radical aspects of the French Revolution threw the British aristocracy into a panic for a generation, making it extremely hostile to any attempts to change the status quo.

In 1815 open conflict between the ruling class and laborers emerged when the aristocracy rammed far-reaching changes in the **Corn Laws** through Parliament. Britain had been unable to import cheap grain from eastern Europe during the war years, leading to high prices and large profits for the landed aristocracy. With the war over, grain (which the British generically called "corn") could be imported again, allowing the price of wheat and bread to go down and benefiting almost everyone—except aristocratic landlords. The new Corn Laws placed high tariffs (or fees) on imported grain. Its cost rose to improbable levels, ensuring artificially high bread prices for working people and handsome revenues for aristocrats. Seldom has a class legislated more selfishly for its own narrow economic advantage or done more to promote a class-based view of political action.

The change in the Corn Laws, coming as it did at a time of widespread unemployment and postwar economic distress, triggered protests and demonstrations by urban laborers, who enjoyed the support of radical intellectuals. In 1817 the Tory government, controlled completely by the landed aristocracy, responded by temporarily

Corn Laws British laws governing the import and export of grain, which were revised in 1815 to prohibit the importation of foreign grain unless the price at home rose to improbable levels, thus benefiting the aristocracy but making food prices high for working people.

Anti–Corn Law League   This line drawing, printed on silk fabric, graced the interior crown of a top hat sold as the "Corn Law Repeal Hat." The Anti–Corn Law League, a forerunner of today's political pressure groups, successfully used a number of propaganda techniques to mobilize a broad urban coalition dedicated to free trade and the end of tariffs on imported grain. For example, each league supporter was encouraged to join the national organization and receive a membership card. How do the various texts and scenes on the hat lining evoke arguments against the Corn Laws? Why would these arguments win popular support? (Universal History Archive/UIG/Bridgeman Images)

Battle of Peterloo   The army's violent suppression of a protest that took place at Saint Peter's Fields in Manchester in reaction to the revision of the Corn Laws.

Reform Bill of 1832   A major British political reform that increased the number of male voters by about 50 percent and gave political representation to new industrial areas.

suspending the traditional rights of peaceable assembly and habeas corpus, which gives a person under arrest the right to a trial. Two years later, Parliament passed the infamous Six Acts, which, among other things, placed controls on a heavily taxed press and practically eliminated all mass meetings. These acts followed an enormous but orderly protest, at Saint Peter's Fields in Manchester, which was savagely broken up by armed cavalry. Nicknamed the **Battle of Peterloo**, in scornful reference to the British victory at Waterloo, this incident demonstrated the government's determination to repress dissenters.

Strengthened by ongoing industrial development, emerging manufacturing and commercial groups insisted on a place for their new wealth alongside the landed wealth of the aristocracy in the framework of political power and social prestige. They called for many kinds of liberal reform: changes in town government, organization of a new police force, more rights for Catholics and dissenters, and reform of the Poor Laws to provide aid to some low-paid workers. In the 1820s a less frightened Tory government moved in the direction of better urban administration, greater economic liberalism, civil equality for Catholics, and limited imports of foreign grain. These actions encouraged the middle classes to press on for reform of Parliament so they could have a larger say in government.

The Whig Party, though led like the Tories by elite aristocrats, had by tradition been more responsive to middle-class commercial and manufacturing interests. In 1830 a Whig ministry introduced "an act to amend the representation of the people of England and Wales." After a series of setbacks, the Whigs' **Reform Bill of 1832** was propelled into law by a mighty surge of popular support. Significantly, the bill moved British politics in a democratic direction and allowed the House of Commons to emerge as the all-important legislative body, at the expense of the aristocrat-dominated House of Lords. The new industrial areas of the country gained representation in the Commons, and many old "rotten boroughs"—electoral districts that had very few voters and that the landed aristocracy had bought and sold—were eliminated. The number of voters increased by about 50 percent, to include about 12 percent of adult men in Britain and Ireland. Comfortable middle-class groups in the urban population, as well as some substantial farmers who leased their land, received the vote. Thus the conflicts building in Great Britain were successfully—though only temporarily—resolved. Continued peaceful reform within the system appeared difficult but not impossible.

The "People's Charter" of 1838 and the Chartist movement it inspired pressed British elites for yet more radical reform (see Chapter 20). Inspired by the economic distress of the working class in the 1830s and 1840s, the Chartists demanded universal male (but not female) suffrage. They saw complete political democracy and rule by the common people—the great majority of the population—as the means to a good and just society. Hundreds of thousands of people signed gigantic petitions calling on Parliament to grant all men the right to vote, first in 1839, again in 1842, and yet again in 1848. Parliament rejected all three petitions. In the short run, the working poor failed with their Chartist demands, but they learned a valuable lesson in mass politics.

While calling for universal male suffrage, many working-class people joined with middle-class manufacturers in the Anti–Corn Law League, founded in Manchester in 1839. Mass participation made possible a popular crusade led by fighting liberals, who argued that lower food prices and more jobs in industry depended on repeal of the Corn Laws. Much of the working class agreed. When Ireland's potato crop failed in 1845 and famine prices for food seemed likely in England, Tory prime minister Robert Peel joined with the Whigs and a minority of his own party to repeal the Corn Laws in 1846 and allow free imports of grain. England escaped famine. Thereafter the liberal doctrine of free trade became almost sacred dogma in Great Britain.

The following year, the Tories passed a bill designed to help the working classes, but in a different way. The Ten Hours Act of 1847 limited the workday for women and young people in factories to ten hours. In competition with the middle class for the support of the working class, Tory legislators continued to support legislation regulating factory conditions. This competition between a still-powerful aristocracy and a strong middle class was a crucial factor in Great Britain's peaceful political evolution. The working classes could make temporary alliances with either competitor to better their own conditions.

Ireland and the Great Famine

The people of Ireland did not benefit from the political competition in England. In the mid-nineteenth century, Ireland was an agricultural nation, and the great majority of the rural population (outside of the northern counties of Ulster, which were partly Presbyterian) were Irish Catholics. They typically rented their land from a tiny minority of Church of England Protestant landowners, who often resided in England. Using a middleman system, these absentee landlords leased land for short periods only, set rents at will, and easily evicted their tenants. In short, landlords used their power to grab as much profit as possible.

Trapped in an exploitative tenant system driven by a pernicious combination of religion and class, Irish peasants lived in abominable conditions. Wretched one-room mud cabins dotted the Irish countryside; the typical tenant farmer could afford neither shoes nor stockings. Hundreds of shocking accounts described hopeless poverty. The novelist Sir Walter Scott wrote:

> The poverty of the Irish peasantry is on the extreme verge of human misery; their cottages would scarce serve for pig styes even in Scotland; and their rags seem the very refuse of a sheep, and are spread over their bodies with such an ingenious variety of wretchedness that you would think nothing but some sort of perverted taste could have assembled so many shreds together.[12]

A compassionate French traveler agreed, writing that Ireland was "pure misery, naked and hungry. . . . I saw the American Indian in his forests and the black slave in his chains, and I believed that I was seeing the most extreme form of human misery; but that was before I knew the lot of poor Ireland."[13]

Despite the terrible conditions, population growth sped upward, part of Europe's general growth trend begun in the early eighteenth century (see Chapter 17). Between 1780 and 1840 the Irish population doubled from 4 million to 8 million. Extensive cultivation of the humble potato was largely responsible for this rapid growth. A single acre of land planted with the nutritious potato could feed a family of six for a year, and the hardy tuber thrived on Ireland's boggy wastelands. About one-half of the Irish population subsisted on potatoes and little else. Needing only a big potato patch to survive, the rural poor married early. To be sure, a young couple faced a life of extreme poverty. They would literally live on potatoes, supplemented perhaps with a bit of grain or milk. Yet the decision to marry and have large families made sense. A couple could manage rural poverty better than someone living alone, and children meant extra hands in the fields.

As population and potato dependency grew, however, conditions became more precarious. From 1820 onward, deficiencies and diseases in the potato crop occurred with disturbing frequency. Then in 1845 and 1846, and again in 1848 and 1851, the potato crop failed in Ireland. Blight attacked the young plants, and leaves and tubers rotted. Unmitigated disaster—the **Great Famine**—followed, as already impoverished peasants experienced widespread sickness and starvation.

The British government, committed to rigid free-trade ideology, reacted slowly. Relief efforts were tragically inadequate. Moreover, the government continued to collect taxes, landlords demanded their rents, and tenants who could not pay were evicted and their homes destroyed. Famine or no, Ireland remained the conquered jewel of foreign landowners.

The Great Famine shattered the pattern of Irish population growth. Fully 1 million emigrants fled the famine between 1845 and 1851, mostly to the United States and Canada, and up to 1.5 million people died. The elderly and the very young were hardest hit. Alone among the countries of Europe, Ireland experienced a declining population in the second half of the nineteenth century, as it became a land of continuous out-migration, early death, late marriage, and widespread celibacy.

Great Famine The result of four years of potato crop failure in the late 1840s in Ireland, a country that had grown dependent on potatoes as a dietary staple.

Devoués à la mort.   Fabrique de balles Patriotiques.

The Great Famine intensified anti-British feeling and promoted Irish nationalism, for the bitter memory of starvation, exile, and British inaction burned deeply into the popular consciousness. Patriots of the later nineteenth and early twentieth centuries could call on powerful collective emotions in their campaigns for land reform, home rule, and, eventually, Irish independence.

The Revolution of 1830 in France

Like Greece and the British Isles, France experienced dramatic political change in the first half of the nineteenth century, and the French experience especially illustrates the disruptive potential of popular liberal politics. The Constitutional Charter granted by Louis XVIII in the Bourbon restoration of 1814 was a limited liberal constitution (see Chapter 19). The charter protected economic and social gains made by sections of the middle class and the peasantry in the French Revolution, permitted some intellectual and artistic freedom, and created a parliament with upper and lower houses. Immediately after Napoleon's abortive Hundred Days, the moderate, worldly king refused to bow to the wishes of die-hard aristocrats who wanted to sweep away all the revolutionary changes. Instead, Louis appointed as his ministers moderate royalists, who sought and obtained the support of a majority of the representatives elected to the lower Chamber of Deputies between 1816 and Louis's death in 1824.

Louis XVIII's charter was liberal but hardly democratic. Only about 100,000 of the wealthiest males out of a total population of 30 million had the right to vote for the deputies who, with the king and his ministers, made the laws of the nation. Nonetheless, the "notable people" who did vote came from very different backgrounds. There were wealthy businessmen, war profiteers, successful professionals, ex-revolutionaries, large landowners from the old aristocracy and the middle class, Bourbons, and Bonapartists. The old aristocracy, with its pre-1789 mentality, was a minority within the voting population.

Louis's conservative successor, Charles X (r. 1824–1830), a true reactionary, wanted to re-establish the old order in France. Increasingly blocked by the opposition of the deputies, Charles's government turned in 1830 to military adventure in an effort to rally French nationalism and gain popular support. A long-standing

Scenes from the Revolution of 1830 in Paris   Titled "Game of the Heroes of the Memorable Days of July," these hand-colored playing cards portray incidents from the uprising in Paris in July 1830. The captions at the bottom read, from left, "Duty unto Death"; "Making the Bullets of Patriotism"; "Aid to the Ill-Fated Brave One"; and "The Amazon of 1830." These fanciful yet moving scenes idealize the revolutionary zeal of the ordinary men and women who fought government troops and helped overthrow the rule of King Charles X. In reality, though, their efforts replaced the king but not the system. (Musée de la Ville de Paris, Musée Carnavalet, Paris, France/Bridgeman Images)

economic and diplomatic dispute with Muslim Algeria, a vassal state of the Ottoman Empire, provided the opportunity.

In June 1830 a French force of thirty-seven thousand crossed the Mediterranean, landed to the west of Algiers, and took the capital city in three short weeks. Victory seemed complete, but in 1831 Algerians in the interior revolted and waged a fearsome war that lasted until 1847, when French armies finally subdued the country. The conquest of Algeria marked the rebirth of French imperial expansion, and the colonial government encouraged French, Spanish, and Italian immigrants to move to Algeria and settle on large tracts of land expropriated from the region's Muslim inhabitants.

Emboldened by the initial good news from Algeria, Charles repudiated the Constitutional Charter in an attempted coup in July 1830. He censored the press and issued decrees stripping much of the wealthy middle class of its voting rights. The immediate reaction, encouraged by liberal lawyers, journalists, and middle-class businessmen, was an insurrection in the capital. Printers, other artisans, and small traders fired up by popular republicanism rioted in the streets of Paris, and three days of vicious street fighting brought down the government. Charles fled. Then the upper middle class, which had fomented the revolt, abandoned the more radical workers and skillfully seated Charles's cousin, Louis Philippe, duke of Orléans, on the vacant throne.

Events in Paris reverberated across Europe. In the Netherlands, Belgian Catholics revolted against the Dutch king and established the independent kingdom of Belgium. In Switzerland, regional liberal assemblies forced cantonal governments to amend their constitutions, leading to two decades of political conflict. And in partitioned Poland, an armed nationalist rebellion against the tsarist government was crushed by the Russian Imperial Army.

Despite the abdication of Charles X, in France the political situation remained fundamentally unchanged. The new king, Louis Philippe (r. 1830–1848), accepted the Constitutional Charter of 1814 and adopted the red, white, and blue flag of the French Revolution. Beyond these symbolic actions, however, popular demands for more thorough reform went unanswered. The upper middle class had effected a change in dynasty that maintained the status quo and the narrowly liberal institutions of 1815. Republicans, democrats, social reformers, and the poor of Paris were bitterly disappointed. They had made a revolution, but it seemed for naught.

The Revolutions of 1848

FOCUS QUESTION

What were the main causes and results of the revolutions of 1848?

In the late 1840s Europe entered a period of tense economic and political crisis. Bad harvests across the continent caused widespread distress. Uneven industrial development failed to provide jobs or raise incomes, and boosted the popularity of radical ideologies. As a result, limited revolts broke out across Europe: a rebellion in the northern part of Austria in 1846, a civil war in Switzerland in 1847, and an uprising in Naples, Italy, in January 1848.

Full-scale revolution broke out in France in February 1848, and its shock waves rippled across the continent. Only the most developed countries—Great Britain, Belgium, and the Netherlands—and the least developed—the Ottoman and Russian Empires—escaped untouched. Elsewhere governments toppled, as monarchs and ministers bowed or fled. National independence, liberal democratic constitutions, and social reform: the lofty aspirations of a generation seemed at hand. Yet in the end, the revolutions failed.

A Democratic Republic in France

By the late 1840s revolution in Europe was almost universally expected, but it took events in Paris—once again—to turn expectations into realities. For eighteen years Louis Philippe's reign, labeled the "bourgeois monarchy" because it served the selfish interests of France's wealthy elites, had been characterized by stubborn inaction and complacency. Corrupt politicians refused to approve social legislation or consider electoral reform. Frustrated desires for change, high-level financial scandals, and a general sense of stagnation dovetailed with a severe depression that began with crop failures in 1846 to 1847. The government did little to prevent the agrarian crisis from dragging down the entire economy.

The government's failures united a diverse group of opponents against the king. Bourgeois merchants, opposition deputies, and liberal intellectuals shared a sense of outrage with middle-class shopkeepers, skilled artisans, and unskilled working people. Widespread discontent eventually touched off a popular revolt in Paris. On the night of February 22, 1848, workers joined by some students began tearing up cobblestones and building barricades. Armed with guns and dug in behind their makeshift fortresses, the workers and students demanded a new government. On February 24 the National Guard broke ranks and joined the revolutionaries. Louis Philippe refused to call in the army and abdicated in favor of his grandson. But the common people in arms would tolerate no more monarchy. This refusal led to the proclamation of a provisional republic, headed by a ten-man executive committee and certified by cries of approval from the revolutionary crowd.

The revolutionaries immediately set about drafting a democratic, republican constitution for France's Second Republic. Building such a republic meant giving the right to vote to every adult male, and this was quickly done. Bold decrees issued by the provisional republican government expressed sympathy for revolutionary freedoms by calling for liberty, fraternity, and equality. The revolutionary government guaranteed workplace reforms, freed all slaves in French colonies, and abolished the death penalty. Yet there were profound differences within the revolutionary coalition. On the one hand, the moderate liberal republicans of the middle class viewed universal male suffrage as the ultimate concession to dangerous popular forces, and they strongly opposed any further radical social measures. On the other hand, radical republicans, influenced by a generation of utopian socialists and appalled by the poverty and misery of the urban poor, were committed to some kind of socialism. Hard-pressed urban artisans, who hated the unrestrained competition of cutthroat capitalism, advocated a combination of strong craft unions and worker-owned businesses.

Worsening depression and rising unemployment brought these conflicting goals to the fore in 1848. Louis Blanc (see page 694), who along with a worker named Albert represented the republican socialists in the provisional government, pressed for recognition of a socialist right to work. Blanc urged the creation of the permanent government-sponsored cooperative workshops he had advocated in *The Organization of Work*. Such workshops would be an alternative to capitalist employment and a decisive step toward a new, noncompetitive social order.

The moderate republicans, willing to provide only temporary relief, wanted no such thing. The resulting compromise set up national workshops—soon to become little more than a vast program of pick-and-shovel public works—and established a special commission under Blanc to "study the question." This satisfied no one. The national workshops were, however, better than nothing. An army of desperate poor from the French provinces and even from foreign countries streamed into Paris to sign up for the workshops. As the economic crisis worsened, the number enrolled in the workshops soared from 10,000 in March to 120,000 by June, and another 80,000 tried unsuccessfully to join.

While the Paris workshops grew, the French people went to the election polls in late April. The result was a bitter loss for the republicans. Voting in most cases for the first time, the people of France elected to the new 900-person Constituent Assembly 500 monarchists and conservatives, only about 270 moderate republicans, and just 80 radicals or socialists.

One of the moderate republicans was the author of *Democracy in America*, Alexis de Tocqueville (1805–1859), who had predicted the overthrow of Louis Philippe's government. He explained the election results by observing that the socialist movement in Paris aroused the fierce hostility of France's peasants as well as the middle and upper classes. The French peasants owned land, and according to Tocqueville, "private property had become with all those who owned it a sort of bond of fraternity."[14] Tocqueville saw that a majority of the members of the new Constituent Assembly was firmly committed to centrist moderation and strongly opposed to the socialists and their artisan allies, a view he shared.

This clash of ideologies — of liberal moderation and radical socialism — became a clash of classes and arms after the elections. The new government's executive committee dropped Blanc and thereafter included no representative of the Parisian working class. Fearing that their socialist hopes were about to be dashed, artisans and unskilled workers invaded the Constituent Assembly on May 15 and tried to proclaim a new revolutionary state. The government used the middle-class National Guard to squelch this uprising. As the workshops continued to fill and grow more radical, the fearful but powerful propertied classes in the Assembly took the offensive. On June 22 the government dissolved the workshops in Paris, giving the workers the choice of joining the army or going to workshops in the provinces.

A spontaneous and violent uprising followed. Frustrated in their thwarted attempt to create a socialist society, masses of desperate people were now losing even their life-sustaining relief. Barricades sprang up again in the narrow streets of Paris, and a terrible class war began. Working people fought with the courage of utter desperation, but this time the government had the army and the support of peasant France. After three terrible "June Days" of street fighting and the death or injury of more than ten thousand people, the republican army under General Louis Cavaignac stood triumphant in a sea of working-class blood and hatred.

The revolution in France thus ended in spectacular failure. The February coalition of the middle and working classes had in four short months become locked in mortal combat. In place of a generous democratic republic, the Constituent Assembly completed a constitution featuring a strong executive. This allowed Louis Napoleon, nephew of Napoleon Bonaparte, to win a landslide victory in the election of December 1848. The appeal of his great name as well as the desire of the propertied classes for order at any cost had led to what would become a semi-authoritarian regime.

Revolution and Reaction in the Austrian Empire

Throughout central Europe, the first news of the upheaval in France evoked feverish excitement and then popular revolution, lending credence to Metternich's famous quip "When France sneezes, all Europe catches cold." Across the Austrian Empire and the German Confederation, liberals demanded written constitutions, representative government, and greater civil liberties from authoritarian regimes (Map 21.3). When governments hesitated, popular revolts broke out. Urban workers and students served as the shock troops, but they were allied with middle-class liberals and peasants. In the face of this united front, monarchs made quick concessions. The revolutionary coalition, having secured great and easy victories, then broke down as it had in France. The traditional forces—the monarchy, the aristocracy, the regular army—recovered their nerve, reasserted their authority, and revoked many, though not all, of the reforms. Reaction was everywhere victorious.

The revolution in the Austrian Empire began in Hungary in March 1848, when nationalistic Hungarians demanded national autonomy, full civil liberties, and universal suffrage. Anti-imperial insurrection broke out in the northern Italian territories of Lombardy-Venetia the same month, and Austrian forces retreated after five days of street fighting. As the monarchy in Vienna hesitated, radicalized Viennese students and workers took to the streets of the imperial capital and raised barricades in defiance of the government. Meanwhile, peasant disturbances broke out across the empire. The Habsburg emperor Ferdinand I (r. 1835–1848) capitulated and promised reforms and a liberal constitution. When Metternich refused to compromise, the aging conservative was forced to resign and fled to London. The old absolutist order seemed to be collapsing with unbelievable rapidity.

Yet the revolutionary coalition lacked stability. When the monarchy abolished serfdom, with its degrading forced labor and feudal services, the newly free peasants lost interest in the political and social questions agitating the cities. Meanwhile, the

MAP 21.3 The Revolutions of 1848 In February and March 1848 revolutions broke out in the European heartlands: France, the Austrian Empire, and the German Confederation. In contrast, relative stability reigned in Great Britain, Belgium, the Netherlands, and the Russian and Ottoman Empires. Why did some regions descend into revolution, and not others? Can a study of geography help explain the difference?

coalition of urban revolutionaries broke down along class lines over the issue of socialist workshops and universal voting rights for men.

Conflicting national aspirations further weakened and ultimately destroyed the revolutionary coalition. In March the Hungarian revolutionary leaders pushed through an extremely liberal, almost democratic, constitution for the Kingdom of Hungary. But the Hungarian revolutionaries also sought to transform the mosaic of provinces and peoples in their territories into a unified, centralized Hungarian nation. The minority groups that formed half of the population — the Croats, Serbs, and Romanians — rejected such unification (see Map 21.2). Each group felt entitled to political autonomy and cultural independence. In a similar way, Czech nationalists based in Prague and other parts of Bohemia came into conflict with German nationalists living in the same region. Thus desires for national autonomy within the Austrian Empire enabled the monarchy to play off one ethnic group against the other.

Finally, conservative aristocratic forces rallied under the leadership of the archduchess Sophia, a Bavarian princess married to the Habsburg emperor's brother. Deeply ashamed of the emperor's collapse before a "mess of students," she insisted that Ferdinand I, who had no heir, abdicate in favor of her son, Franz Joseph.[15] Powerful nobles organized around Sophia in a secret conspiracy to reverse and crush the revolution.

The first conservative breakthrough came when the army bombarded Prague and savagely crushed a working-class revolt there on June 17, 1848. By August the Austrians had crushed the Italian insurrection. At the end of October, the well-equipped, predominantly peasant troops of the regular Austrian army bombarded the student and working-class radicals dug in behind barricades in Vienna with heavy artillery. They retook the city at the cost of more than four thousand casualties. The determination of the Austrian aristocracy and the loyalty of its army sealed the triumph of reaction and the defeat of revolution.

When Franz Joseph (r. 1848–1916) was crowned emperor of Austria immediately after his eighteenth birthday in December 1848, only the Hungarians had yet to be brought under control. Another determined conservative, Nicholas I of Russia (r. 1825–1855), obligingly lent his iron hand. On June 6, 1849, 130,000 Russian troops poured into Hungary and subdued the country after bitter fighting. For a number of years, the Habsburgs ruled the Kingdom of Hungary as a conquered territory.

Prussia, the German Confederation, and the Frankfurt National Parliament

After Austria, Prussia was the largest and most influential kingdom in the German Confederation. Since the Napoleonic Wars, liberal German reformers had sought to transform absolutist Prussia into a constitutional monarchy, hoping it would then lead the thirty-eight states of the German Confederation into a unified nation-state. The agitation that followed the fall of Louis Philippe, on top of several years of crop failure and economic crises, encouraged liberals to press their demands. In March 1848 excited crowds in urban centers across the German Confederation called for liberal reforms and a national parliament, and many regional rulers quickly gave in to their demands.

When artisans and factory workers rioted in Berlin, the capital of Prussia, and joined temporarily with the middle-class liberals in the struggle against the monarchy, the autocratic yet compassionate Prussian king, Friedrich Wilhelm IV (r. 1840–1861), vacillated and then caved in. On March 21 he promised to grant Prussia a liberal constitution and to merge Prussia into a new national German state.

But urban workers wanted much more—and the Prussian aristocracy wanted much less—than the moderate constitutional liberalism conceded by the king. The workers issued a series of democratic and vaguely socialist demands that troubled their middle-class allies. An elected Prussian Constituent Assembly met in Berlin to write a constitution for the Prussian state, and a conservative clique gathered around the king to urge counter-revolution.

At the same time, elections were held across the German Confederation for a national parliament, which convened to write a federal constitution that would lead to national unification. When they met in Frankfurt that May, the state officials, lawyers, professors, and businessmen elected to parliament represented the interests of the social elite. Their calls for constitutional monarchy, free speech, religious tolerance, and abolition of aristocratic privilege were typical of moderate national liberalism. The deputies essentially ignored calls for more radical action from industrial workers, peasants, republicans, and socialists.

In October 1848 the Frankfurt parliament turned to the question of national unification and borders. At first, the deputies proposed unification around a **Greater Germany** that would include the German-speaking lands of the Austrian Empire in a national state—but not non-German territories in Italy and central Europe. This proposal foundered on Austrian determination to maintain its empire, and some parliamentarians advocated a Lesser Germany that would unify Prussia and other German states without Austria. Even as the deputies debated Germany's future in the autumn of 1848, the forces of counter-revolution pushed back reformists and revolutionaries in Prussia and the other German states.

Greater Germany A liberal plan for German national unification that included the German-speaking parts of the Austrian Empire, put forth at the national parliament in 1848 but rejected by Austrian rulers.

Despite Austrian intransigence, in March 1849 the national parliament finally completed its draft of a liberal constitution and requested Friedrich Wilhelm IV of Prussia to serve as emperor of a "lesser" German national state (minus Austria). By early 1849, however, reaction had rolled back liberal reforms across the German Confederation. Prussian troops had already crushed popular movements across the German Confederation, and Friedrich Wilhelm had reasserted his royal authority and disbanded the Prussian Constituent Assembly. He contemptuously refused to accept the "crown from the gutter" offered by the parliament in Frankfurt. Bogged down by their preoccupation with nationalist issues, the reluctant revolutionaries in Frankfurt had waited too long and acted too timidly. By May 1849 all but the most radical deputies had resigned from the parliament, and in June Prussian troops forcibly dissolved what remained of the assembly.

Friedrich Wilhelm in fact wanted to be emperor of a unified Germany, but only on his own authoritarian terms. With the liberal threat successfully squelched, he tried to get the small monarchies of Germany to elect him emperor. Austria balked. Supported by Russia, the Austrians forced Prussia to renounce all schemes of unification in late 1850. The German Confederation was re-established in 1851, and a decade of reaction followed. In an echo of the Karlsbad Decrees, state security forces monitored universities, civic organizations, and the press throughout the confederation. Former revolutionaries fled into exile, and German liberals gave up demands for national unification. In the various German states, reactionary monarchs, aided by ever-growing state bureaucracies, granted their subjects conservative constitutions and weak parliaments that maintained aristocratic control. Attempts to unite the Germans—first in a liberal national state and then in a conservative Prussian empire—had failed completely.

LOOKING BACK LOOKING AHEAD

Viewed from a broad historical perspective, Europe's economic and social foundations in 1750 remained agricultural and rural. Although Enlightenment thought was beginning to question the status quo, authoritarian absolutism dominated political life. One hundred years later, the unfinished effects of the Industrial and French Revolutions had brought fundamental changes to the social fabric of daily life and politics across Europe. The liberal ideals of representative government and legal equality realized briefly in revolutionary France inspired intellectuals and social reformers, who adopted ideologies of liberalism, nationalism, Romanticism, and socialism to challenge the conservative order. The uneven spread of industrial technologies and factory organization into developed areas across Europe spurred the growth of an urban working class, but did little to raise the living standards of most workers, peasants, and artisans. Living on the edge of subsistence, the laboring poor in rural and urban areas alike remained subject to economic misfortune, mass unemployment, and food shortages, and they turned repeatedly to protest, riots, and violent insurrection in pursuit of economic and political rights.

In 1848 the poor joined middle- and upper-class reformers in a great wave of revolution that forced conservative monarchs across the continent to grant liberal and national concessions — at least for a moment. Divisions in the revolutionary coalition and the power of the autocratic state forced back the wave of reform, and the revolutions ended in failure. Conservative monarchies revived, nationalist movements collapsed, and hopes for German unification withered. Yet protest on the barricades and debate in liberal parliaments had given a generation a wealth of experience with new forms of participatory politics, and the ideologies associated with the French Revolution would continue to invigorate reformers and revolutionaries after 1850. Nationalism, with its commitment to the imagined community of a great national family and the nation-state, would become a dominant political force, particularly as European empires extended their reach after 1875. At the same time, as agriculture and rural life gradually declined in economic importance, the consolidation of industrialization would raise living standards, sustain a growing urban society, and reshape family and class relationships. Diverse, complicated, and fascinating, pockets of this new urban society already existed in 1850. By 1900 it dominated northwestern Europe and was making steady inroads to the east and south.

Make Connections

Think about the larger developments and continuities within and across chapters.

1. Why did the ideas of the Romantic movement so easily support reformist and radical political ideas, including liberalism, republicanism, and nationalism? What does this reveal about the general connections between art and politics?

2. How did the spread of radical ideas and the movements for reform and revolution explored in this chapter draw on the "unfinished" political and industrial revolutions (Chapters 19 and 20) of the late eighteenth century?

3. The years between 1815 and 1850 witnessed the invention of a number of new political ideologies and the application of these ideologies in a variety of struggles for political power. What impact would these ideologies and struggles have later in the nineteenth and twentieth centuries? Do they still have an impact today?

21 REVIEW & EXPLORE

Review the Main Ideas

Answer the focus questions from each section of the chapter.

- How was peace restored and maintained after 1815? (p. 682)
- What new ideologies emerged to challenge conservatism? (p. 690)
- What were the characteristics of the Romantic movement? (p. 695)
- How and where was conservatism challenged after 1815? (p. 702)
- What were the main causes and results of the revolutions of 1848? (p. 708)

Identify Key Terms

Identify and explain the significance of each item below.

Congress of Vienna (p. 683)
Holy Alliance (p. 687)
Karlsbad Decrees (p. 688)
liberalism (p. 690)
laissez faire (p. 690)
nationalism (p. 691)
socialism (p. 693)
Marxism (p. 694)
bourgeoisie (p. 695)
proletariat (p. 695)
Romanticism (p. 695)
Corn Laws (p. 703)
Battle of Peterloo (p. 704)
Reform Bill of 1832 (p. 704)
Great Famine (p. 706)
Greater Germany (p. 713)

NOTES

1. See B. E. Vick, *The Congress of Vienna: Power and Politics After Napoleon* (Cambridge, Mass.: Harvard University Press, 2014), pp. 11–14.
2. A. Sked, *The Decline and Fall of the Habsburg Empire, 1815–1918* (London: Longman, 1989), pp. 1–2.
3. Quoted in D. Blackbourn, *The Long Nineteenth Century: A History of Germany, 1780–1918* (New York: Oxford University Press, 1998), p. 122.
4. E. Gellner, *Nations and Nationalism* (Oxford: Basil Blackwell, 1983), especially pp. 19–39.
5. This paragraph draws on the influential views of B. Anderson, *Imagined Communities: Reflections on the Origins and Spread of Nationalism*, rev. ed. (London: Verso, 1991), and E. J. Hobsbawm and T. Ranger, eds., *The Invention of Tradition* (Cambridge: Cambridge University Press, 1983).
6. Quoted in F. E. Manuel and F. P. Manuel, *Utopian Thought in the Western World* (Cambridge, Mass.: Harvard University Press, 1979), p. 589.
7. Quoted in H. G. Schenk, *The Mind of the European Romantics* (New York: Oxford University Press, 1979), p. 5.

8. Quoted ibid., p. 169.
9. Quoted in O. Frey, *Emotions Recollected in Tranquility—Wordsworth's Concept of Poetry in "I Wandered Lonely as a Cloud"* (Munich: GRIN Verlag, 2008), p. 5.
10. Quoted in A. Comini, *The Changing Image of Beethoven: A Study in Mythmaking* (Santa Fe, N.M.: Sunstone Press, 2008), p. 79.
11. Quoted in F. B. Artz, *From the Renaissance to Romanticism: Trends in Style in Art, Literature, and Music, 1300–1830* (Chicago: University of Chicago Press, 1962), pp. 276, 278.
12. Quoted in G. O'Brien, *The Economic History of Ireland from the Union to the Famine* (London: Longmans, Green, 1921), p. 21.
13. Quoted ibid., pp. 23–24.
14. A. de Tocqueville, *Recollections* (New York: Columbia University Press, 1949), p. 94.
15. W. L. Langer, *Political and Social Upheaval, 1832–1852* (New York: Harper & Row, 1969), p. 361.

CHAPTER PREVIEW

Taming the City
How did urban life change in the nineteenth century?

Rich and Poor and Those in Between
What did the emergence of urban industrial society mean for rich and poor and those in between?

Changing Family Lifestyles
How did urbanization affect family life and gender roles?

Science and Thought
How and why did intellectual life change in this period?

Life in the Nineteenth-Century City

The excitement and variety of urban life sparkle in this depiction of a public entertainment gala in 1860, sponsored by London's Royal Dramatic College and held in the city's fabulous Crystal Palace.
(By Alexander Blaikley [1816–1903]/© Fine Art Photographic Library/Corbis)

22

Life in the Emerging Urban Society

1840–1914

When Londoners gathered in 1860 at the Grand Fete in the Crystal Palace (see painting at left), they enjoyed the pleasures of an established urban society that would have been unthinkable just sixty years earlier. Across the nineteenth century, as industrialization expanded exponentially, Europeans left their farms and country villages to find work in the ever-growing towns and cities. By 1900, in much of developed western Europe, more than half the population lived in urban conglomerations, a trend of rural-to-urban migration that would spread and continue across the twentieth century.

Despite the happy faces in the London crowd pictured here, the emerging urban society brought costs as well as benefits. On the whole, living standards rose in the nineteenth century, but wages and living conditions varied greatly, and many city dwellers were still poor. Advances in public health and urban planning brought some relief to the squalid working-class slums, yet vast differences in income, education, and occupation still divided people into socially stratified groups. As a result, rather than discuss "the working class" or "the middle class," it is more accurate to speak of "working classes" and "middle classes" and consider the blurred boundaries between the two. Major changes in family life and gender roles accompanied this diversified class system. Dramatic breakthroughs in chemistry, medicine, and electrical engineering further transformed urban society after 1880, and a new generation of artists, writers, and professional social scientists struggled to explain and portray the vast changes wrought by urbanization. ◼

Taming the City

FOCUS QUESTION
How did urban life change in the nineteenth century?

Since the Middle Ages, European cities had been centers of government, culture, and large-scale commerce. They had also been congested, dirty, and unhealthy. Beginning in the early nineteenth century, the Industrial Revolution took these unfortunate realities of urban life to unprecedented levels. While historians may debate whether the overall social impact of industrialization was generally positive or negative, there is little doubt that rapid urban growth worsened long-standing overcrowding, pollution, and unhealthy living conditions. Taming the city posed a frightening challenge for society. Only the full-scale efforts of government leaders, city planners, reformers, scientists, and civic-minded citizens would ameliorate the ferocious savagery of the industrial metropolis.

Industry and the Growth of Cities

The main causes of the poor quality of urban life — dense overcrowding, pervasive poverty, and lack of medical knowledge — had existed for centuries. Because the typical city had always been a "walking city," with no public transportation, great masses of people needed to live in close proximity to shops, markets, and workplaces. Packed together almost as tightly as possible, people in cities suffered and died from the spread of infectious disease in far greater numbers than their rural counterparts. In the larger towns, more people died each year than were born, on average, and urban populations maintained their numbers only because newcomers continually arrived from rural areas.

The Industrial Revolution exacerbated these deplorable conditions. The steam engine freed industrialists from dependence on the energy of fast-flowing streams and rivers so that by 1800 there was every incentive to build new factories in urban areas, which had many advantages. Cities had better transportation facilities than the countryside and thus better supplies of coal and raw materials. Cities had many hands wanting work, for they drew people like a magnet, and as a result concentrated demand for manufactured goods. And it was a great advantage for a producer to have other factories nearby to supply the business's needs and buy its products. Therefore, as industry grew, already overcrowded and unhealthy cities expanded rapidly.

Great Britain, the first country in the world to go through the early stages of the Industrial Revolution (see Chapter 20), was forced to face the acute challenges of a changing urban environment early on. In the 1820s and 1830s the populations of a number of British cities increased by 40 to 70 percent each decade. The number of people living in cities of 20,000 or more in England and Wales jumped from 1.5 million in 1801 to 6.3 million in 1851 and reached 15.6 million in 1891. Such cities accounted for 17 percent of the total English population in 1801, 35 percent as early as 1851, and fully 54 percent in 1891. Other countries duplicated the English pattern as they industrialized (Map 22.1). (See "Evaluating the Evidence 22.1: First Impressions of the World's Biggest City," page 720.)

Except on the outskirts, early-nineteenth-century cities in Britain used every scrap of available land to the fullest extent. Parks and open areas were almost nonexistent. Developers erected buildings on the smallest possible lots in order to pack the maximum number of people into a given space. Narrow houses were built attached to one another in long rows. These row houses had neither front nor back yards, and only a narrow alley in back separated one row from the next. Other buildings were built

Chronology

ca. 1840s–1890s	Realism dominant in Western arts and literature	1859	Darwin publishes *On the Origin of Species by the Means of Natural Selection*
1848	Cholera epidemic and first public health law in Britain	1865	Completion of London sewer system
ca. 1850–1870	Modernization of Paris	1869	Mendeleev creates periodic table
1850–1914	Condition of working classes improves	1880–1913	Second Industrial Revolution; birthrate steadily declines in Europe
1854	Pasteur begins studying fermentation and in 1863 develops pasteurization	1890	Max Weber publishes *The Protestant Ethic and the Spirit of Capitalism*
1854–1870	Development of germ theory	1890s	Electric streetcars introduced in Europe

around courtyards completely enclosed on all four sides. Many people lived in tiny apartments or small, overcrowded cellars or attics. "Six, eight, and even ten occupying one room is anything but uncommon," wrote a Scottish doctor for a government investigation in 1842.

These highly concentrated urban populations lived in extremely unsanitary and unhealthy conditions. Open drains and sewers flowed alongside or down the middle of unpaved streets. Toilet facilities were primitive and inadequate. In parts of Manchester, as many as two hundred people shared a single outhouse. Such privies filled up rapidly, and since they were infrequently emptied, sewage often overflowed and seeped into cellar dwellings. Moreover, some courtyards in poorer neighborhoods

MAP 22.1 **European Cities of 100,000 or More, 1800–1900**
There were more large cities in Great Britain in 1900 than in all of Europe in 1800.

First Impressions of the World's Biggest City

In this anonymous, tongue-in-cheek passage, first published as a humorous sketch around 1870, a country man describes his first impressions of urban life. At that time London, with over 4 million inhabitants, was the largest city in the world.

A man's first residence in London is a revolution in his life and feelings. He loses at once no small part of his individuality. He was a man before, now he is a "party." No longer known as Mr. Brown, but as (say) No. XXI., he feels as one of many cogs in one of the many wheels of an incessantly wearing, tearing, grinding, system of machinery. His country notions must be modified, and all his life-long ways and takings-for-granted prove crude and questionable. He is hourly reminded "This is not the way in London; that this won't work here," or, "people always expect," and "you'll soon find the difference." . . .

Competition in London is very rife. The cheap five-shilling hatter was soon surprised by a four-and-nine-penny shop opposite. Few London men could live but by a degree of energy which the country dealer little knows. The wear and tear of nerve-power and the discharge of brain-power in London are enormous. The London man lives fast. . . .

Many other things contribute to make our new Londoner feel smaller in his own eyes. The living stream flows by him in the streets; he never saw so many utter strangers to him and to each other before; their very pace and destination are different; there is a walk and business determination distinctly London. In other towns men saunter they know not whither, but nearly every passer-by in London has his point, and is making so

resolutely towards it that it seems not more his way than his destination as he is carried on with the current; and of street currents there are two, to the City and from the City, so distinct and persistent, that our friend can't get out of one without being jostled by the other. . . .

Self-dependence is another habit peculiarly of London growth. Men soon discover they have no longer the friend, the relative or the neighbour of their own small town to fall back upon. . . .

No doubt there are warm friendships and intimacies in London as well as in the country, but few and far between. People associate more at arm's length, and give their hand more readily than their heart, and hug themselves within their own domestic circles. You know too little of people to be deeply interested either in them or their fortunes, so you expect nothing and are surprised at nothing. An acquaintance may depart London life, and even this life, or be sold up and disappear, without the same surprise or making the same gap as in a village circle.

EVALUATE THE EVIDENCE

1. Why does the author assert, "The London man lives fast"?
2. Does this account of modern city life support or contradict the arguments of the new sociologists, discussed later in the chapter?
3. Is this a realistic portrait of city life? How does the author use humor to engage the reader?

Source: Henry Mayhew et al., "Life in London," in *London Characters and the Humorous Side of London Life* (London: Chatto and Windus, 1881), pp. 277–281.

---

became dunghills, collecting excrement that was sometimes sold as fertilizer and sometimes simply continued to accumulate. As one historian put it, by the 1840s the better-off classes had come to the "shocking realization that millions of English men, women, and children were living in shit."[1]

The environmental costs of rapid urbanization and industrialization were enormous as well. Black soot from coal-fired factories and train engines fouled city air, and by 1850 the River Thames was little better than an open sewer.

Who or what bore responsibility for these awful conditions? The crucial factors included the tremendous pressure of more people and the total absence of public transportation. People simply had to jam themselves together to get to shops and factories on foot. In addition, government in Great Britain, both local and national, only slowly established sanitary facilities and adequate building codes. Scientific understanding of the causes and consequences of urban crowding advanced slowly, and some elites rigidly opposed government action. Certainly, Great Britain had no monopoly on overcrowded and unhealthy urban conditions. Many continental cities were every bit as bad.

Most responsible of all was the sad legacy of rural housing conditions in preindustrial society combined with an appalling ignorance of germs and basic hygiene. When ordinary people moved to the city, housing was far down on their list of priorities, and they generally took dirt for granted. One English miner told an investigator, "I do not think it usual for the lasses [in the coal mines] to wash their bodies; my sisters never wash themselves." As for the men, "their legs and bodies are as black as your hat."[2]

The Advent of the Public Health Movement

Around the middle of the nineteenth century, people's fatalistic acceptance of their overcrowded, unsanitary surroundings began to give way to a growing interest in reform and improvement. Edwin Chadwick, one of the commissioners charged with the administration of relief to paupers under Britain's revised Poor Law of 1834, emerged as a powerful voice for reform. Chadwick found inspiration in the ideas of radical philosopher Jeremy Bentham (1748–1832), whose approach to social issues, called **utilitarianism**, had taught that public problems ought to be dealt with on a rational, scientific basis to advance the "greatest good for the greatest number." Applying these principles, Chadwick soon became convinced that disease and death actually caused poverty, because a sick worker was an unemployed worker and orphaned children were poor children. Most important, Chadwick believed that government could help prevent disease by cleaning up the urban environment.

utilitarianism The idea of Jeremy Bentham that social policies should promote the "greatest good for the greatest number."

Chadwick collected detailed reports from local Poor Law officials on the "sanitary conditions of the laboring population" and published his hard-hitting findings in 1842. This mass of widely publicized evidence proved that disease was related to filthy environmental conditions, which were in turn caused largely by lack of drainage, sewers, and garbage collection.

Chadwick correctly believed that the stinking excrement of communal outhouses could be dependably carried off by water through sewers at less than one-twentieth the cost of removing it by hand. The inexpensive iron pipes and tile drains of the industrial age would provide running water and sewerage for all sections of town, not just the wealthy ones. In 1848, with the cause strengthened by a cholera epidemic that raged across Britain, Chadwick's report became the basis of Great Britain's first public health law, which created a national health board and gave cities broad authority to build modern sanitation systems.

The public health movement won dedicated supporters in the United States, France, and Germany from the late 1840s on. Governments accepted at least limited responsibility for the health of all citizens, and their programs broke decisively with the age-old fatalism of urban populations. By the 1860s and 1870s European cities were making real progress toward adequate water supplies and sewer systems. Though factories and coal stoves continued to pump black smoke into the air, and pollution remained a serious problem, city dwellers started to reap the reward of better health, and death rates began to decline (Figure 22.1).

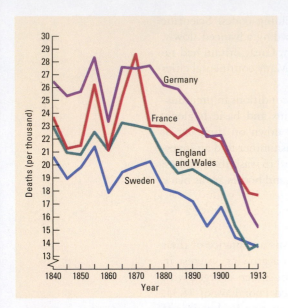

FIGURE 22.1 **The Decline of Death Rates in England and Wales, Germany, France, and Sweden, 1840–1913** A rising standard of living, improvements in public health, and better medical knowledge all contributed to the dramatic decline of death rates in the nineteenth century.

germ theory The idea that disease was caused by the spread of living organisms that could be controlled.

The Bacterial Revolution

Although improved sanitation in cities promoted a better quality of life and some improvements in health care, effective control of communicable disease required a great leap forward in medical knowledge and biological theory. Early reformers, including Chadwick, were seriously handicapped by their adherence to the prevailing miasmatic theory of disease — the belief that people contracted disease when they inhaled the bad odors of decay and putrefying excrement. In the 1840s and 1850s keen observation by doctors and public health officials pinpointed the role of bad drinking water in the transmission of disease and suggested that contagion was spread through physical contact with filth, not by its odors, thus weakening the miasmatic idea.

The breakthrough in understanding how bad drinking water and filth actually made people sick arrived when the French chemist Louis Pasteur developed the **germ theory** of disease. Pasteur (pas-TUHR) (1822–1895), who began studying fermentation for brewers in 1854, used a microscope to develop a simple test that brewers could use to monitor the fermentation process and avoid spoilage. He found that fermentation depended on the growth of living organisms and that the activity of these organisms could be suppressed by heating the beverage — a process that came to be called pasteurization, which he first implemented in the early 1860s. The breathtaking implication of this discovery was that specific diseases were caused by specific living organisms — germs — and that those organisms could be controlled.

By 1870 the work of Pasteur and others had demonstrated the general connection between germs and disease. When, in the middle of the 1870s, German country doctor Robert Koch (kawkh) and his coworkers developed pure cultures of harmful bacteria and described their life cycles, the dam broke. Over the next twenty years, researchers — mainly Germans — identified the organisms responsible for disease after disease. These discoveries led to the development of a number of effective vaccines, though some infections resisted treatment until scientists developed antibiotics in the middle of the next century.

Acceptance of germ theory brought about dramatic improvements in the deadly environment of hospitals and operating rooms (see Chapter 18). In 1865, when Pasteur showed that the air was full of bacteria, English surgeon Joseph Lister (1827–1912) immediately grasped the connection between aerial bacteria and the problem of wound infection. He reasoned that a chemical disinfectant applied to a wound dressing would "destroy the life of the floating particles" (or germs). Lister's antiseptic principle worked wonders. In the 1880s German surgeons developed the more sophisticated practice of sterilizing not only the wound but also everything — hands, instruments, clothing — that entered the operating room.

The achievements of the bacterial revolution coupled with the public health movement saved millions of lives, particularly after about 1880. Mortality rates began to decline dramatically in European countries (see Figure 22.1) as the awful death sentences of the past—diphtheria, typhoid, typhus, cholera, yellow fever—became vanishing diseases. City dwellers especially benefited from these developments. By 1910 a great silent revolution had occurred: the death rates for people of all ages in urban areas were generally no greater than those for people in rural areas, and sometimes they were lower.

Improvements in Urban Planning

In addition to public health improvements, more effective urban planning was an important key to unlocking a better quality of urban life in the nineteenth century. France took the lead in this area during the rule of Napoleon III (r. 1848–1870), who used government action to promote the welfare of his subjects. Napoleon III believed that rebuilding much of Paris would provide employment, improve living conditions, limit the outbreak of cholera epidemics—and testify to the power and glory of his empire. He hired Baron Georges Haussmann (HOWS-muhn) (1809–1884), an aggressive, impatient Alsatian, to modernize the city. An authoritarian manager and capable city planner, Haussmann bulldozed both buildings and opposition. In twenty years Paris was completely transformed (Map 22.2).

MAP 22.2 The Modernization of Paris, ca. 1850–1870 The addition of broad boulevards, large parks, and grand train stations transformed Paris. The cutting of the new north-south axis — known as the Boulevard Saint-Michel — was one of Haussmann's most controversial projects. His plan razed much of Paris's medieval core and filled the Île de la Cité with massive government buildings. Note the addition of new streets and light rail systems (the basis of the current Parisian subway system, the "metro") that encircle the city core, emblematic of the public transportation revolution that enhanced living conditions in nineteenth-century European cities.

Paris before 1860

Expanded city limits established in 1860

Public park opened during Second Empire

Wall of Philippe Auguste (1180–1210)

Tollhouse Wall (1784–1791), razed by Haussmann to rebuild as boulevards

Fortress Wall (1841–1845)

Street constructed by Haussmann

Other street

Railway system created by Haussmann

Major railroad station

The Paris of 1850 was a labyrinth of narrow, dark streets, the results of desperate overcrowding and a lack of effective planning. More than one-third of the city's 1 million inhabitants lived in a central district not twice the size of New York's Central Park. Residents faced terrible conditions and extremely high death rates. The entire metropolis had few open spaces and only two public parks.

For two decades Haussmann and his fellow planners proceeded on many interrelated fronts. With a bold energy that often shocked their contemporaries, they razed old buildings in order to cut broad, straight, tree-lined boulevards through the center of the city as well as in new quarters rising on the outskirts (see Map 22.2). These boulevards, designed in part to prevent the easy construction and defense of barricades by revolutionary crowds, permitted traffic to flow freely and afforded impressive vistas. Their creation demolished some of the worst slums. New streets stimulated the construction of better housing, especially for the middle classes. Planners created small neighborhood parks and open spaces throughout the city and developed two very large parks suitable for all kinds of holiday activities — one on the affluent west side and one on the poor east side of the city. The city improved its sewers, and a system of aqueducts more than doubled the city's supply of clean, fresh water.

Rebuilding Paris provided a new model for urban planning and stimulated urban reform throughout Europe, particularly after 1870. In city after city, public authorities mounted a coordinated attack on many of the interrelated problems of the urban environment. As in Paris, improvements in public health through better water supply and waste disposal often went hand in hand with new boulevard construction. Urban planners in cities such as Vienna and Cologne followed the Parisian example of tearing down old walled fortifications and replacing them with broad, circular boulevards on which they erected office buildings, town halls, theaters, opera houses, and museums. These ring roads and the new boulevards that radiated outward from the city center eased movement and encouraged urban expansion (see Map 22.2). Zoning expropriation laws, which allowed a majority of the owners of land in a given quarter of the city to impose major street or sanitation improvements on a reluctant minority, were an important mechanism of the urban reform movement.

Urban Poverty Nineteenth-century London was notorious for its urban squalor, captured in this 1895 photo of Kensington High Street. For the families that lived in these ramshackle apartments, this small, unsanitary courtyard served as a cramped recreation, market, and working space. (*Market Court, Kensington High Street, London*, c. 1895/English Heritage/Heritage Images/Getty Images)

Public Transportation

The development of mass public transportation often accompanied urban planning, further enhancing living conditions. In the 1870s many European cities authorized private companies to operate horse-drawn streetcars, which had been developed in the United States, to carry riders along the growing number of major thoroughfares. Then in the 1890s the real revolution occurred: European countries adopted another American transit innovation, a streetcar that ran on the newly harnessed power of electricity.

Electric streetcars were cheaper, faster, more dependable, cleaner, and more comfortable than their horse-drawn counterparts. Workers, shoppers, and schoolchildren hopped on board during the workweek. On weekends and holidays, streetcars carried urban dwellers on happy outings to parks and the countryside, to racetracks and music halls. In 1886 the horse-drawn streetcars of Austria-Hungary, France, Germany, and Great Britain carried about 900 million riders per year. By 1910 electric streetcar systems in those four countries were carrying 6.7 billion riders.[3]

Mass transit helped greatly in the struggle for decent housing. The new boulevards and horse-drawn streetcars facilitated a middle-class move to better and more spacious housing in the 1860s and 1870s; after 1890 electric streetcars meant people of even modest means could access new, improved housing. Though still densely populated, cities expanded and became less congested. In England in 1901, only 9 percent of the urban population was overcrowded in terms of the official definition of more than two persons per room. On the continent, many city governments in the early twentieth century built electric streetcar and light rail systems to provide transportation to the growing number of workers who lived in the new public and private housing developments built beyond the city limits. Suburban commuting was born.

Rich and Poor and Those in Between

As the quality of urban life improved across Europe, the class structure became more complex and diverse. Urban society featured many distinct social groups, all of which existed in a state of constant flux and competition. The gap between rich and poor remained enormous and quite traditional, but there were numerous gradations between the extremes.

The Distribution of Income

By 1850 at the latest, real wages—that is, wages received by workers adjusted for changes in the prices they paid—were rising for the mass of the population, and they continued to do so until 1914. The real wages of British workers, for example, almost doubled between 1850 and 1906. Similar increases occurred in continental countries as industrial development quickened after 1850. Ordinary people took a major step forward in the centuries-old battle against poverty, reinforcing efforts to improve many aspects of human existence.

Greater economic rewards for the average person did not, however, eliminate hardship and poverty. Nor did they make the wealth and income of the rich and the poor significantly more equal, as contemporary critics argued and economic historians have

FOCUS QUESTION
What did the emergence of urban industrial society mean for rich and poor and those in between?

clearly demonstrated. The aristocracy—with imposing wealth, unrivaled social prestige, and substantial political influence—retained its position at the very top of the social ladder, followed closely by a new rich elite, composed mainly of the most successful business families from banking, industry, and large-scale commerce. In fact, the prominent families of the commercial elite tended to marry into the old aristocracy, to form a new upper class of at most 5 percent of the population. Much of the aristocracy welcomed this development. Having experienced a sharp decline in its relative income in the course of industrialization, the landed aristocracy had met big business coming up the staircase and was often delighted to trade titles, country homes, and snobbish elegance for good, hard cash. Some of the best bargains were made through marriages to American heiresses. Correspondingly, wealthy aristocrats tended increasingly to exploit their agricultural and mineral resources as if they were business people.

Income inequality reflected social status. In almost every advanced country around 1900, the richest 5 percent of all households in the population received about a third of all national income, and the richest 20 percent of households received from 50 to 60 percent of it. As a result, the lower 80 percent received only 40 to 50 percent of all income—far less per household than the two richest classes. Moreover, the bottom 30 percent of all households received 10 percent or less of all income.

To understand the full significance of these statistics, one must realize that the middle classes were much smaller than they are today. In the nineteenth century they accounted for less than 20 percent of the population (that is, only about one in five families earned enough to be labeled "middle class"). Moreover, in the nineteenth century (and for centuries before as well) income taxes on the wealthy were light or nonexistent. Thus the gap between rich and poor remained enormous at the beginning of the twentieth century. Indeed, it was probably almost as great as it had been in the late eighteenth century, in the age of agriculture and aristocracy.

The great gap between rich and poor endured, in part, because industrial and urban development made society more diverse and classes less unified; the effects were serious. Society had not split into two sharply defined opposing classes, as Karl Marx had predicted (see Chapter 21). Instead, the economic specialization that enabled society to produce goods more effectively had created a remarkable variety of new social groups. There developed an almost unlimited range of jobs, skills, and earnings; one group or subclass blended into another in a complex, confusing hierarchy. Between the tiny elite of the very rich and the sizable mass of the dreadfully poor lived a range of subclasses, each filled with individuals struggling to rise or at least to hold their own in the social order. In this atmosphere of competition and hierarchy, neither the "middle class" nor the "working class" actually acted as a single unified force. Rather, the social and occupational hierarchy developed enormous variations, though the age-old pattern of great economic inequality remained firmly intact.

The People and Occupations of the Middle Classes

By the beginning of the twentieth century, the diversity and range within the urban middle class were striking. Indeed, it makes sense to replace the idea of a single "middle class" with a group of "middle classes" whose members engaged in occupations requiring mental, rather than physical, skill.

Below the wealthy top tier, the much larger, much less wealthy, and increasingly diversified middle class included moderately successful industrialists and merchants as well as professionals in law, business, and medicine. As industry and technology expanded in the nineteenth century, a growing demand developed for experts with specialized knowledge, and advanced education soared in importance among the middle classes. Engineering, for example, emerged from the world of skilled labor as a full-fledged profession with considerable prestige. Architects, chemists, accountants, and surveyors, to name only a few, first achieved professional standing in this period. They established criteria for advanced training and certification and banded together in organizations to promote and defend their interests. As governments grew and provided more services, and very large corporations (such as railroads or arms manufacturers) controlled ever-larger numbers of human and physical resources, middle-class professionals also found jobs as managers in large public and private institutions. Government officials and private executives had specialized knowledge and the capacity to earn a good living.

Industrialization expanded and diversified the lower middle class as well. The number of independent, property-owning shopkeepers and small business people grew, and so did the number of white-collar employees—a mixed group of traveling salesmen, bookkeepers, store managers, and clerks who staffed the offices and branch stores of large corporations. White-collar employees owned little property and often earned no more than better-paid skilled or semiskilled workers. Yet white-collar workers were fiercely committed to the middle-class ideal of upward social mobility. The suit, the tie, the soft, clean hands that accompanied low-level retail and managerial work became important status symbols that set this group above those who earned a living through manual labor.

Relatively well educated but without complex technical skills, many white-collar occupational groups strove to achieve professional standing and higher social status. Elementary school teachers largely succeeded in this effort. Miserably paid part-time workers in the early nineteenth century, teachers rode the wave of mass education to respectable middle-class status and income. Nurses also rose from the lower ranks of unskilled labor to precarious middle-class standing. Dentistry was taken out of the hands of working-class barbers and placed in the hands of highly trained (and middle-class) professionals.

Middle-Class Culture and Values

Despite growing occupational diversity and conflicting interests, lifestyle preferences loosely united the European middle classes. Food, housing, clothes, and behavior all expressed middle-class values and testified to the superior social standing of this group over the working classes.

Unlike the working classes, the middle classes had the money to eat well, and spent a substantial portion of their household budget on food and entertainment. They consumed meat in abundance: a well-off family might spend 10 percent of its annual income on meat and fully 25 percent on food and drink. The dinner party— a favored social occasion—boosted spending. A wealthy middle-class family might give a lavish party for eight to twelve almost every week, and such parties were especially common on holidays.

The middle-class wife could cope with this endless procession of meals, courses, and dishes because she had servants as well as money at her disposal. Indeed, the employment of at least one full-time maid to cook and clean was the clearest sign that a family had crossed the cultural divide separating the working classes from what some contemporary observers called the "servant-keeping classes." The greater a family's income, the greater the number of servants it employed. Servants absorbed about another 25 percent of income at all levels of the middle class.

Well fed and well served, the middle classes were also well housed by 1900. Many prosperous families rented, rather than owned, their homes, complete with tiny rooms for servants in the basement or under the eaves of the top floor. And, just as the aristocracy had long divided the year between palatial country estates and lavish townhouses during "the season," so the upper middle class purchased country places or built beach houses for weekend and summer use.

The middle classes paid great attention to outward appearances, especially their clothes. The factory, the sewing machine, and the department store had all helped reduce the cost and expand the variety of clothing. Middle-class women were particularly attentive to the dictates of fashion, though men also wore the now-appropriate business suit. Ownership of private coaches and carriages, expensive items in the city, further testified to rising social status.

Rich Europeans could devote more time to "culture" and leisure pursuits than less wealthy or well-established families could. The keystones of culture and leisure were books, music, and travel. The long Realist novel, the heroic operas of composers Wagner and Verdi, the diligent striving of the dutiful daughter at the piano, and the packaged tour to a foreign country were all sources of middle-class pleasure.

In addition to their material tastes, the middle classes generally agreed upon a strict code of behavior, manners, and morality. They stressed hard work, self-discipline, and personal achievement. Middle-class social reformers denounced drunkenness and gambling as vices and celebrated sexual purity and fidelity as virtues, especially for women. Men and women who fell into vice, crime, or poverty were held responsible for their own circumstances. A stern sense of Christian morals, preached tirelessly by religious leaders, educators, and politicians, reaffirmed these values. The middle-class individual was supposed to know right from wrong and act accordingly.

The People and Occupations of the Working Classes

At the beginning of the twentieth century, about four out of five people belonged to the working classes—that is, people whose livelihoods depended primarily on physical labor and who did not employ domestic servants. Many of them were still small landowning peasants and hired farm hands, and this was especially the case in eastern Europe. In western and central Europe, however, the typical worker had left the land. By 1900 less than 8 percent of the people in Great Britain worked in agriculture, and in rapidly industrializing Germany only 25 percent were employed in agriculture and forestry. Even in less industrialized France, under 50 percent of the population worked the land.

The urban working classes were even less unified and homogeneous than the middle classes. First, economic development and increased specialization expanded the traditional range of working-class skills, earnings, and experiences. Meanwhile, the old sharp distinction between highly skilled artisans and unskilled manual workers gradually broke down. To be sure, highly skilled printers and masons as well as unskilled dockworkers and common laborers continued to exist. But between these extremes there appeared ever more semiskilled groups, including trained factory

Rat Catching   Although antivivisectionist reform groups successfully pressured city and state authorities to ban many forms of cruelty to animals, the sport of "ratting" continued to attract working- and middle-class crowds well into the nineteenth century. In this 1852 painting, an all-male crowd at the Blue Anchor Tavern on the outskirts of London lays bets on the trained Manchester terrier Tiny as he tries to kill two hundred rats in a single hour. Because they saw rats as verminous pests that brought filth and disease into Europe's rapidly growing cities, the authorities tolerated rat killing for sport, a pastime that was a throwback to the inhumane bullbaiting and cockfighting popular in the early modern era (see Chapter 18). (© Museum of London, UK/Bridgeman Images)

workers. Skilled, semiskilled, and unskilled workers developed divergent lifestyles and cultural values. These differences contributed to a keen sense of social status and hierarchy within the working classes, creating great diversity and undermining the class unity predicted by Marx.

Highly skilled workers—about 15 percent of the working classes—became known as the **labor aristocracy**. They earned only about two-thirds of the income of the bottom ranks of the servant-keeping classes, but that was fully double the earnings of unskilled workers. The most "aristocratic" of these highly skilled workers were construction bosses and factory foremen, who had risen from the ranks and were fiercely proud of their achievement. The labor aristocracy also included members of the traditional highly skilled handicraft trades that had not been mechanized or placed in factories, like cabinetmakers, jewelers, and printers.

While the labor aristocracy enjoyed its exalted position, maintaining that status was by no means certain. Gradually, as factory production eliminated more and more crafts, lower-paid, semiskilled factory workers replaced many skilled artisans. Traditional wood-carvers and watchmakers virtually disappeared, for example, as the making of furniture and timepieces now took place in factories. At the same time, industrialization opened new opportunities for new kinds of highly skilled workers, such as shipbuilders and railway locomotive engineers. Thus the labor elite remained in a state of flux, as individuals and whole crafts moved up and down the social scale.

To maintain their precarious standing, the upper working class adopted distinctive values and straitlaced, almost puritanical behavior. Like the middle classes, the labor aristocracy believed firmly in middle-class morality and economic improvement. Families in the upper working class saved money regularly, worried about their children's education, and valued good housing. Wives seldom sought employment outside the home. Despite these similarities, skilled workers viewed themselves not as aspirants to the middle class but as the pacesetters and natural model for the rest of the working classes. Well aware of the degradation not so far below them, they practiced self-discipline and stern morality and generally frowned on

labor aristocracy   The highly skilled workers, such as factory foremen and construction bosses, who made up about 15 percent of the working classes from about 1850 to 1914.

heavy drinking and sexual permissiveness. As one German skilled worker somberly warned, "The path to the brothel leads through the tavern" and from there to drastic decline or total ruin.[4]

Below the labor aristocracy stood the enormously complex world of hard work, composed of both semiskilled and unskilled workers. Established construction workers—carpenters, bricklayers, pipe fitters—stood near the top of the semiskilled hierarchy, often flirting with (or sliding back from) the labor elite. A large number of the semiskilled were factory workers, who earned highly variable but relatively good wages. These workers included substantial numbers of unmarried women, who began to play an increasingly important role in the industrial labor force.

Below the semiskilled workers, a larger group of unskilled workers included day laborers such as longshoremen, wagon-driving teamsters, and "helpers" of all kinds. Many of these people had real skills and performed valuable services, but they were unorganized and divided, united only by the common fate of meager earnings and poor living conditions. The same lack of unity characterized street vendors and market people—these self-employed members of the lower working classes competed savagely with each other and with established shopkeepers of the lower middle class.

One of the largest components of the unskilled group was domestic servants, whose numbers grew steadily in the nineteenth century. In Great Britain, for example, one out of every seven employed persons in 1911 was a domestic servant. The great majority were women; indeed, one out of every three girls in Britain between the ages of fifteen and twenty worked as a domestic servant. Throughout Europe, many female domestics in the cities were recent migrants from rural areas. As in earlier times, domestic service meant hard work at low pay with limited personal independence and the danger of sexual exploitation. For the full-time general maid in a lower-middle-class family, an unending routine of babysitting, shopping, cooking, and cleaning defined a lengthy working day. In the wealthiest households, the serving girl was at the bottom of a rigid hierarchy of status-conscious butlers and housekeepers.

Nonetheless, domestic service had real attractions for young women from rural areas who had few specialized skills. Marriage prospects were better, or at least more varied, in the city than back home. And though wages were low, they were higher and more regular than in hard agricultural work—which was being replaced by mechanization, at any rate. Finally, as one London observer noted, young girls and other migrants from the countryside were drawn to the city by "the contagion of numbers, the sense of something going on, the theaters and the music halls, the brightly lighted streets and busy crowds—all, in short, that makes the difference between the Mile End fair on a Saturday night, and a dark and muddy country lane, with no glimmer of gas and with nothing to do."[5]

Many young domestics made the successful transition to working-class wife and mother. Yet with an unskilled or unemployed husband, a growing family, and limited household income, many working-class wives had to join the broad ranks of working women in the **sweated industries**. These industries expanded rapidly after 1850 and resembled the old putting-out and cottage industries of earlier times (see Chapter 17). The women normally worked at home and were paid by the piece, not by the hour. They and their young children who helped them earned pitiful wages and lacked any job security. Women decorated dishes or embroidered linens, took in

sweated industries Poorly paid handicraft production, often carried out by married women paid by the piece and working at home.

laundry for washing and ironing, or made clothing, especially after the advent of the sewing machine. An army of poor women, usually working at home, accounted for many of the inexpensive ready-made clothes displayed on department store racks and in tiny shops.

Working-Class Leisure and Religion

Notwithstanding hard physical labor and lack of wealth, the urban working classes sought fun and recreation, and they found both. Across Europe, drinking remained unquestionably the favorite leisure-time activity of working people. For many middle-class moralists, as well as moralizing historians since, love of drink was the curse of the modern age—a sign of social dislocation and popular suffering. Certainly, drinking was deadly serious business. One English slum dweller recalled that "drunkenness was by far the commonest cause of dispute and misery in working class homes. On account of it one saw many a decent family drift down through poverty into total want."[6]

Generally, however, heavy problem drinking declined in the late nineteenth century as it became less socially acceptable. This decline reflected in part the moral leadership of the labor aristocracy. At the same time, drinking became more publicly acceptable. Cafés and pubs became increasingly bright, friendly places. Working-class political activities, both moderate and radical, were also concentrated in taverns and pubs. Moreover, social drinking in public places by married couples and sweethearts became an accepted and widespread practice for the first time. This greater participation by women undoubtedly helped civilize the world of drink and hard liquor.

The two other leisure-time passions of working-class culture were sports and music halls. "Cruel sports," such as bullbaiting and cockfighting, still popular in the middle of the century, had greatly declined throughout Europe by the 1880s. Commercialized spectator sports filled their place; horse racing and soccer were the most popular. Working people gambled on sports events, and for many a working person a desire to decipher racing forms provided a powerful incentive toward literacy. Music halls and vaudeville theaters, the working-class counterparts of middle-class opera and classical theater, were enormously popular throughout Europe. In 1900 London had more than fifty

Moulin Rouge   A group of barmaids perform the French cancan in 1895 at the Moulin Rouge, a famous Parisian cabaret/nightclub, while a live orchestra plays in the balcony above. The cancan was a fast and provocative dance that involved rapid dips and turns, and high kicks that revealed the performers' legs and frilly underwear. The new industrial society made leisure time available to more and more people of all classes, and mixed-couple entertainment including dance balls, theater performance, and dining out became increasingly popular. (Photo © Dazy René/Bridgeman Images)

such halls and theaters. Music hall audiences included men and women, which may account for the fact that drunkenness, premarital sex, marital difficulties, and mothers-in-law were all favorite themes of broad jokes and bittersweet songs.

In more serious moments, religion continued to provide working people with solace and meaning. The eighteenth-century vitality of popular religion in Catholic countries and the Protestant rejuvenation exemplified by German Pietism and English Methodism (see Chapter 18) carried over into the nineteenth century. Indeed, many historians see the early nineteenth century as an age of religious revival. Yet historians recognize that by the last few decades of the nineteenth century, a considerable decline in both church attendance and church donations had occurred in most European countries. And it seems clear that this decline was greater for the urban working classes than for their rural counterparts or for the middle classes.

Why did working-class church attendance decline? On one hand, the construction of churches failed to keep up with the rapid growth of urban population, especially in new working-class neighborhoods. On the other, throughout the nineteenth century workers saw Catholic and Protestant churches as conservative institutions that defended status quo politics, hierarchical social order, and middle-class morality. Socialist political parties, in particular, attacked organized religion as a pillar of bourgeois society; and as the working classes became more politically conscious, they tended to see established churches as allied with their political opponents. In addition, religion underwent a process historians call "feminization": in the working and middle classes alike, women were more pious and attended service more regularly than men. Urban workingmen in particular developed vaguely antichurch attitudes, even though they might remain neutral or positive toward religion itself.

The pattern was different in the United States, where most nineteenth-century churches also preached social conservatism. But because church and state had always been separate and because a host of denominations and even different religions competed for members, working people identified churches much less with the political and social status quo. Instead, individual churches in the United States were often closely identified with an ethnic group rather than a social class, and churches thrived, in part, as a means of asserting ethnic identity. This same process occurred in Europe if the church or synagogue had never been linked to the state and served as a focus for ethnic cohesion. Irish Catholic churches in Protestant Britain, Catholic churches in partitioned Polish lands, and Jewish synagogues in Russia were outstanding examples.

Changing Family Lifestyles

FOCUS QUESTION
How did urbanization affect family life and gender roles?

By the 1850s the family had stabilized considerably after the disruption of the late eighteenth and early nineteenth centuries. With the consolidation caused by industrialization and urbanization, the growing middle classes created a distinctive middle-class lifestyle, which set them off from peasants, workers, and the aristocracy. New ideas about courtship and marriage, family and gender roles, and homemaking and child rearing expressed middle-class norms and values in ways that would have a profound impact on family life in the century to come. Changes in family life affected both men and women and all social classes, but to varying degrees. Leading a middle-class lifestyle was prohibitively expensive for workers and peasants, and middle-class family values at first had little relevance for their lives. Yet as the nineteenth century drew to a close, the middle-class lifestyle increasingly became the norm for all classes.

Middle-Class Marriage and Courtship Rituals

Rather than marry for convenience, or for economic or social reasons—as was still common among workers, peasants, and aristocrats—by the 1850s the middle-class couple was supposed to follow an idealized model: they met, courted, fell deeply in love, and joined for life because of a shared emotional bond. Of course, economic considerations in marriage by no means disappeared. But an entire culture of romantic love—popularized in advice manuals, popular fiction, and art, and practiced in courtship rituals, weddings, and married life—now surrounded the middle-class couple with a tender emotional charge. The growing popularity among all classes toward the end of the nineteenth century of what historians call **companionate marriage** underscores the impact of historical change on human emotions and behaviors.

Strict rules for courtship and engagement enshrined in the concept of falling in love ensured that middle-class individuals would make an appropriate match. Parents, chaperones, and the general public closely guarded the boundary between courtship and sex, between the proper and the improper. Young couples were seldom alone before they became engaged, and individuals rarely paired off with someone from an inappropriate class background. Premarital sex was taboo for women, though men might experiment, a double standard that revealed the value the middle classes placed on sexual morality and especially women's virginity before marriage.

Engagement also followed a complicated set of rules and rituals. Secret engagements led to public announcements, and then the couple could appear together, though only escorted by chaperones in potentially delicate situations. Couples might walk arm in arm, but custom placed strict limits on physical intimacy. A couple might find ways to experiment with sexual behaviors, but only in secret—secrecy that confirmed the special feelings of "true love" between the couple.

Marriage had its own set of rules. Usually a middle-class man could marry only if he could support a wife, children, and a servant, which meant he had to be well established in his career and fairly prosperous. As a result, some middle-class men never married, because they could not afford it. These customs created special difficulties for young middle-class women, who could rarely pursue an independent career or acquire a home without a husband. The system encouraged mixed-age marriages. A new husband was typically much older than his young wife, who usually had no career and entered marriage directly out of her parents' home or perhaps a girl's finishing school. She would have had little experience with the realities of adult life.

Love meant something different to men and women. Trained to fall passionately in love with "Mr. Right," young women equated marriage with emotional intensity. Men, on the other hand, were supposed to "find a wife": they took a more active but dispassionate role in courtship. Since women generally were quite young, the

companionate marriage
Marriage based on romantic love and middle-class family values that became increasingly dominant in the second half of the nineteenth century.

Stephan Zweig on Middle-Class Youth and Sexuality

Growing up in Vienna in a prosperous Jewish family, Stephan Zweig (1881–1942) became an influential voice calling for humanitarian values and international culture in early-twentieth-century Europe. Passionately opposed to the First World War, Zweig wrote poetry, plays, and novels. But he was most famous for his biographies: shrewd psychological portraits of historical figures such as Magellan and Marie Antoinette. After Hitler came to power in 1933, Zweig lived in exile until his death in 1942. Zweig's last work was The World of Yesterday *(1943), one of the truly fascinating autobiographies of the twentieth century. In the following passage, Zweig recalls the romantic experiences and sexual separation of middle-class youth before the First World War.*

During the eight years of our higher schooling [beyond grade school], something had occurred which was of great importance to each one of us: we ten-year-olds had grown into virile young men of sixteen, seventeen, and eighteen, and Nature began to assert its rights. . . . It did not take us long to discover that those authorities in whom we had previously confided—school, family, and public morals—manifested an astonishing insincerity in this matter of sex. But what is more, they also demanded secrecy and reserve from us in this connection. . . .

This "social morality," which on the one hand privately presupposed the existence of sexuality and its natural course, but on the other would not recognize it openly at any price, was doubly deceitful. While it winked one eye at a young man and even encouraged him with the other "to sow his wild oats," as the kindly language of the home put it, in the case of a woman it studiously shut both eyes and acted as if it

were blind. That a man could experience desires, and was permitted to experience them, was silently admitted by custom. But to admit frankly that a woman could be subject to similar desires, or that creation for its eternal purposes also required a female polarity, would have transgressed the conception of the "sanctity of womanhood." In the pre-Freudian era, therefore, the axiom was agreed upon that a female person could have no physical desires as long as they had not been awakened by man, and that, obviously, was officially permitted only in marriage. But even in those moral times, in Vienna in particular, the air was full of dangerous erotic infection, and a girl of good family had to live in a completely sterilized atmosphere, from the day of her birth until the day when she left the altar on her husband's arm. In order to protect young girls, they were not left alone for a single moment. . . . Every book which they read was inspected, and above all else, young girls were constantly kept busy to divert their attention from any possible dangerous thoughts. They had to practise the piano, learn singing and drawing, foreign languages, and the history of literature and art. They were educated and overeducated. But while the aim was to make them as educated and as socially correct as possible, at the same time society anxiously took great pains that they should remain innocent of all natural things to a degree unthinkable today. A young girl of good family was not allowed to have any idea of how the male body was formed, or to know how children came into the world, for the angel was to enter into matrimony not only physically untouched, but completely "pure" spiritually as well. "Good breeding," for a young girl of that time, was identical with ignorance of life; and this ignorance ofttimes lasted for the rest of their lives. . . .

man was encouraged to see himself as the protector of a young and fragile creature. In short, the typical middle-class marriage was more similar to a child-parent relationship than a partnership of equals, a situation finely portrayed in Henrik Ibsen's famous play *A Doll's House* (1879). The inequality of marriage was codified in European legal systems that, with rare exceptions, placed property ownership in the hands of the husband.

Middle- and Working-Class Sexuality

A double standard in sexual relations paralleled the gender inequalities built into middle-class standards of love and marriage. Middle-class moralists of all stripes cast men as aggressively sexual creatures, while women—the "angel in the house"—were supposed to be pure and chaste and act as a brake on male desire. Contemporary

What possibilities actually existed for a young man of the middle-class world? In all the others, in the so-called lower classes, the problem was no problem at all. . . . In most of our Alpine villages the number of natural children greatly exceeded the legitimate ones. Among the proletariat, the worker, before he could get married, lived with another worker in free love. . . . It was only in our middle-class society that such a remedy as an early marriage was scorned. . . . And so there was an artificial interval of six, eight, or ten years between actual manhood and manhood as society accepted it; and in this interval the young man had to take care of his own "affairs" or adventures.

Those days did not give him too many opportunities. Only a very few particularly rich young men could afford the luxury of keeping a mistress, that is, taking an apartment and paying her expenses. And only a very few fortunate young men achieved the literary ideal of love of the times—the only one which it was permitted to describe in novels—an affair with a married woman. The others helped themselves for the most part with shopgirls and waitresses, and this offered little inner satisfaction. . . . But, generally speaking, prostitution was still the foundation of the erotic life outside of marriage; in a certain sense it constituted a dark underground vault over which rose the gorgeous structure of middle-class society with its faultless, radiant façade.

The present generation has hardly any idea of the gigantic extent of prostitution in Europe before the [First] World War. Whereas today it is as rare to meet a prostitute on the streets of a big city as it is to meet a wagon in the road, then the sidewalks were so sprinkled with women for sale that it was more difficult to avoid than to find them. To this was added the countless number of "closed houses," the night clubs, the cabarets, the dance parlours with their dancers and singers, and the bars with their "comeon" girls. At that time female wares were offered for sale at every hour and at every price. . . . And this was the same city, the same society, the same morality, that was indignant when young girls rode bicycles, and declared it a disgrace to the dignity of science when Freud in his calm, clear, and penetrating manner established truths that they did not wish to be true. The same world that so pathetically defended the purity of womanhood allowed this cruel sale of women, organized it, and even profited thereby.

We should not permit ourselves to be misled by sentimental novels or stories of that epoch. It was a bad time for youth. The young girls were hermetically locked up under the control of the family, hindered in their free bodily as well as intellectual development. The young men were forced to secrecy and reticence by a morality which fundamentally no one believed or obeyed. Unhampered, honest relationships—in other words, all that could have made youth happy and joyous according to the laws of Nature—were permitted only to the very few.

EVALUATE THE EVIDENCE

1. According to Zweig, how did the sex lives of young middle-class women and young middle-class men differ? What accounted for these differences?
2. What were the differences between the sex lives of the middle class and those of the "so-called lower classes"? What was Zweig's opinion of these differences?
3. Zweig ends with a value judgment: "It was a bad time for youth." Do you agree or disagree? Why?

Source: Excerpts from pp. 67, 76–78, 81–83, 88 in *The World of Yesterday* by Stephan Zweig, translated by Helmut Ripperger. Translation copyright 1943, renewed © 1971 by the Viking Press, Inc. Used by permission of Viking Books, an imprint of Penguin Publishing Group, a division of Penguin Random House LLC.

science legitimized this double standard. According to late-nineteenth-century physicians, men, easily aroused by the sight of a wrist or ankle, fell prey to their raging biological drives, while respectable women were supposedly uninterested in sex by nature.

Middle-class moralists assumed that men would enter marriage with some sexual experience, though this was unthinkable for a middle-class woman. When middle-class men did seek premarital sex, middle-class women were off limits. Instead, bourgeois men took advantage of their class status and sought lower-class women, domestic servants, or prostitutes. If a young middle-class woman had experimented with or even was suspected of having had premarital sex, her chances for an acceptable marriage fell dramatically. (See "Evaluating the Evidence 22.2: Stephan Zweig on Middle-Class Youth and Sexuality," above.)

The sexual standards of the working classes stood in marked contrast to these norms in the early nineteenth century, but that changed over time. Premarital sex for both men and women was common and more acceptable among workers. In the first half of the nineteenth century, among the lower classes, about one-third of the births in many large European cities occurred outside of wedlock. The second half of the century saw the reversal of this high rate of illegitimacy: in western, northern, and central Europe, more babies were born to married mothers. Young, unmarried workers were probably engaging in just as much sexual activity as their parents and grandparents who had created the illegitimacy explosion of 1750 to 1850 (see Chapter 18). But in the later part of the nineteenth century, pregnancy for a young single woman, which a couple might see as the natural consequence of a serious relationship, led increasingly to marriage and the establishment of a two-parent household. Indeed, one in three working-class women was pregnant when she married. This important development reflected the spread of middle-class ideals of family respectability among the working classes, as well as their gradual economic improvement. Romantic love held working-class families together, and marriage was less of an economic challenge. The urban working-class couple of the late nineteenth century thus became more stable, and that stability strengthened the family as an institution.

Prostitution

In the late nineteenth century prostitution was legal in much of Europe. In Italy, France, Great Britain, and much of Germany, the state licensed brothels and registered individual prostitutes. In Paris, 155,000 women were registered as prostitutes between 1871 and 1903, and 750,000 others were suspected of prostitution in the same years. In Berlin, in 1909 alone, the authorities registered over 40,000 prostitutes. The totals are probably low, since most women in the sex trade tried to avoid government registration.

In streets, dance halls, and pubs across Europe, young working-class women used prostitution as a source of second income or as a way to weather a period of unemployment. Their clients were generally lower-class men, soldiers, and sailors, though middle- and upper-class men looking to "sow wild oats" also paid for sexual encounters. Streetwalking offered women some measure of financial independence, but the work was dangerous. Violence and rape, police harassment, and venereal disease were commonplace hazards.

Prostitutes clearly violated middle-class ideals of feminine respectability, but among the working classes prostitution was tolerated as more-or-less acceptable work of a temporary nature. Like domestic service, prostitution was a stage of life, not permanent employment. After working as prostitutes in their youth, many women went on to marry (or live with) men of their own class and establish homes and families.

As middle-class family values became increasingly prominent after the 1860s, prostitution generated great concern among social reformers. The prostitute—immoral, lascivious, and unhealthy in middle-class eyes—served as the dark mirror image of the respectable middle-class woman. Authorities blamed prostitutes for spreading crime and disease, particularly syphilis. Before the discovery of penicillin, syphilis was indeed a terrifying and widespread affliction. Its painful symptoms led to physical and mental decline and often death; medical treatment was embarrassing and for the most part ineffective.

As general concerns with public health gained recognition, state and city authorities across Europe subjected prostitutes—in their eyes the vector of contagious disease—to increased surveillance. The British Contagious Diseases Acts, in force between 1864 and 1886, exemplified the trend. Under these acts, special plainclothes policemen required women identified as "common prostitutes" to undergo biweekly medical exams. If they showed signs of venereal disease, they were interned in a "lock hospital" and forced to undergo treatment; when the outward signs of disease went away, they were released.

The Contagious Diseases Acts were controversial from the start. A determined middle-class feminist campaign against the policy, led by feminist Josephine Butler and the Ladies National Association, loudly proclaimed that the acts physically abused poor women, violated their constitutional rights, and legitimized male vice. Under pressure, Parliament repealed the laws in 1886. Yet heavy-handed government regulation had devastated the informality of working-class prostitution. Now branded as "registered girls," prostitutes experienced new forms of public humiliation, and the trade was increasingly controlled by male pimps rather than by the women themselves. Prostitution had never been safe, but it had been accepted, at least among the working classes. Prostitutes were now stigmatized as social and sexual outsiders.

Separate Spheres and the Importance of Homemaking

After 1850 the work of wives became increasingly distinct and separate from that of their husbands in all classes. The preindustrial pattern among both peasants and cottage workers, in which husbands and wives both worked and shared basic household duties, became less common. In wealthier homes, this change was particularly dramatic. The good middle-class family man earned the wages to support the household; the public world of work, education, and politics was male space. Respectable middle-class women did not work outside the home and rarely even traveled alone in public. Working-class women, including servants and prostitutes, were more visible in public places, but if a middle-class woman went out without a male escort, she might be accused of low morals or character. Thus many historians have stressed that the societal ideal in nineteenth-century Europe became a strict division of labor by gender within rigidly constructed **separate spheres**: the "private sphere," where the woman acted as wife, mother, and homemaker, and the "public sphere," where the husband acted as wage earner and family provider.

separate spheres The nineteenth-century gendered division of labor and lifestyles that cast men as breadwinners and women as homemakers.

For the middle classes, the private single-family home, a symbol of middle-class status and a sanctuary from the callous outside world of competitive capitalism, was central to the notion of separate spheres. At the heart of the middle-class home stood the woman: notions of femininity, motherhood, and family life came together in the ideal of domestic space. Middle-class floor plans grew to include separate sleeping rooms for parents and each family member—unheard of among the lower classes—as well as a special drawing room (or parlor), used to entertain guests. Plump sofas, bric-a-brac, and souvenirs graced domestic interiors; curtains of heavy red velvet and colorful silks draped doors and windows. Such ostentatious displays were far too expensive for the working classes, who made up 80 percent of the population.

Middle-class women were spared the masculine burdens of the outside working world, and lower-class servants ensured that they had free time to turn the private sphere into a domestic refuge of love and privacy. Numerous middle-class housekeeping manuals made the wife's responsibilities quite clear, as this Swedish handbook

Christmas and the Sentimental Pleasures of the Middle-Class Home
Victorian Christmas celebrated the family values and lifestyles of the middle classes at their most expressive. This clichéd portrait of a wealthy middle-class family holiday — with holly adorning the walls, mistletoe hanging above the fireplace, children singing carols with their parents, and contented grand-parents sitting by a warm fire — captures the intimacy and love that increasingly bound together middle-class and working-class families alike during the nineteenth century. Titled *Home Sweet Home* and released for commercial reproduction and sale around 1900, prints of this image of domestic bliss no doubt adorned the walls of many middle-class parlors like the one shown in the painting. (Private Collection/Photo © Christie's Images/ Bridgeman Images)

from 1889 suggests: "A man who spends most of his day away from the family, who has to work outside the home, counts on finding a restful and refreshing atmosphere when he returns home, and sometimes even a little merriment or a surprise. . . . It is his wife's duty to ensure that he is not disappointed in his expectation. She must do her utmost to make his stay at home as pleasant as possible; she can thus continue to keep her influence over him and retain his affection undiminished."[7]

By 1900 working-class families had adopted many middle-class values, but they did not have the means to fully realize the ideal of separate spheres. Women were the primary homemakers, and, as in the upper classes, men did little or no domestic labor. But many working-class women also made a monetary contribution to family income by taking in a boarder, doing piecework at home in the sweated industries (see page 730), or getting an outside job. While middle-class family life centered on an ample daily meal, working-class women struggled to put sufficient food on the table. Working women worked to create a homelike environment that at least resembled that of the middle class — cleaning house, collecting trinkets, and decorating domestic interiors — but working men often preferred to spend time in the local pub with workmates, rather than come home. Indeed, alcoholism and domestic violence afflicted many working-class families, even as they worked to build a relationship based on romantic love.

Feminist historians have often criticized the middle-class ideal of separate spheres because it restricted women's educational and employment opportunities, and the women's rights movement that emerged in the late nineteenth century certainly challenged the limitations of the model. In recent years, however, some scholars have been rethinking gender roles within the long-term development of consumer behavior and household economies. In the era of industrialization, these scholars suggest, the "breadwinner-homemaker" household that developed from about 1850 onward was rational consumer behavior that improved the lives of all family members, especially in the working classes.[8]

According to this view, when husbands specialized in earning an adequate cash income—the "family wage" that labor unions demanded—and wives specialized in managing the home, the working-class wife could produce desirable benefits that could not be bought in a market, such as improved health, better eating habits, and better behavior. For example, higher wages from the breadwinner could buy more raw food, but only the homemaker's careful selection, processing, and cooking would allow the family to benefit from increased spending on food. Running an urban household was a complicated, demanding, and valuable task. Twice-a-day food shopping, careful economizing, and fighting the growing crusade against dirt—not to mention child rearing—constituted a full-time occupation. Working yet another job for wages outside the home had limited appeal for most married women unless the earnings were essential for family survival. The homemaker's managerial skills, however, enabled the working-class couple to maximize their personal well-being.

The woman's guidance of the household went hand in hand with the increased pride in the home and family and the emotional importance attached to them in working- and middle-class families alike. According to one historian, by 1900 the English song "Home, Sweet Home" had become "almost a second national anthem."[9] Domesticity and family ties were now central to the lives of millions of people of all classes.

Child Rearing

Another striking sign of deepening emotional ties within the family was a growing emphasis on the love and concern that mothers gave their infants. Early emotional bonding and a willingness to make real sacrifices for the welfare of the infant became increasingly important among the comfortable classes by the end of the eighteenth century, though the ordinary mother of modest means adopted new attitudes only as the nineteenth century progressed. The baby became more important, and women became better mothers.

The surge of maternal feeling was shaped by and reflected in a wave of specialized books on child rearing and infant hygiene, such as French family reformer Gustav Droz's phenomenally successful book *Papa, Mama, and Baby*, which went through 121 editions between 1866 and 1884. Droz urged fathers to become affectionate toward their children and pitied those "who do not know how to roll around on the carpet, play at being a horse and a great wolf, and undress their baby."[10] Following expert advice, mothers increasingly breast-fed their infants, rather than paying wet nurses to do so. Breast-feeding involved sacrifice—a temporary loss of freedom, if nothing else. Yet when there was no good alternative to mother's milk, it saved lives. Another sign, from France, of increased parental affection is that fewer illegitimate babies were abandoned as foundlings after about 1850. Moreover, the practice of swaddling disappeared completely. Instead, ordinary mothers allowed their babies freedom of movement and delighted in their spontaneity.

The loving care lavished on infants was matched by greater concern for older children and adolescents. They, too, were bound in the strong emotional ties of a more intimate and protective family. For one thing, European women began to limit the number of children they bore in order to care adequately for those they had (Figure 22.2). By the end of the nineteenth century, the birthrate was declining across Europe, and it continued to do so until after World War II. The Englishwoman who married in the 1860s, for example, had an average of about six children; her

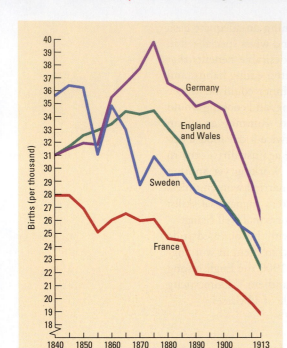

FIGURE 22.2 The Decline of Birthrates in England and Wales, France, Germany, and Sweden, 1840–1913   Women had fewer babies for a variety of reasons, including the fact that their children were increasingly less likely to die before reaching adulthood. How do these numbers compare with those in Figure 22.1?

daughter marrying in the 1890s had only four; and her granddaughter marrying in the 1920s had only two or possibly three.

The most important reason for this revolutionary reduction in family size, in which the comfortable and well-educated classes took the lead, was parents' desire to improve their economic and social position and that of their children. Children were no longer an economic asset in the late nineteenth century. By having fewer youngsters, parents could give those they had valuable advantages, from music lessons and summer vacations to long, expensive university educations and suitable dowries. A young German skilled worker with only one child spoke for many in his class when he said, "We want to get ahead, and our daughter should have things better than my wife and sisters did."[11] Thus the growing tendency of couples in the late nineteenth century to use a variety of contraceptive methods—the rhythm method, the withdrawal method, and mechanical devices, including after the 1840s condoms and diaphragms made of vulcanized rubber—reflected increased concern for children.

In middle-class households, parents expended considerable effort to ensure that they raised their children according to prevailing family values. Indeed, many parents, especially in the middle classes, probably became too concerned about their children, unwittingly subjecting them to an emotional pressure cooker of almost unbearable intensity. Professional family experts, including teachers, doctors, and reformers like Droz, produced a vast popular literature on child rearing that encouraged parents to focus on developing their children's self-control, self-fulfillment, and sense of Christian morality. Family specialists recommended against corporal punishment—still common in worker and peasant households—but even though they typically escaped beatings, the children of the wealthy grew up under constant observation and discipline, a style of parenting designed to teach the self-control necessary for adult success. Parents carefully monitored their children's sexual behavior, and masturbation—according to one expert "the most shameful and terrible of all vices"—was of particular concern.[12] (See "Evaluating the Evidence 22.2: Stephan Zweig on Middle-Class Youth and Sexuality," page 734.)

Attempts to repress the child's sexuality generated unhealthy tension, often made worse by the rigid division of gender roles within the family. While family experts lauded parental love, and especially love between mother and child, they believed that relations between father and child were troubled by a lack of emotional bonding. At work all day, the father came home a stranger to his offspring; his world of business was far removed from the maternal world of spontaneous affection. Moreover, the father set demanding rules, often expecting the child to succeed where he himself had failed and making his approval conditional on achievement. This kind of distance was especially the case in the wealthiest families, in which domestic servants, nannies, and tutors did much of the work of child rearing. Wealthy parents saw their children only over dinner, or on special occasions like birthdays or holidays.

The children of the working classes probably had more avenues of escape from such tensions than did those of the middle classes. Unlike their middle-class counterparts, who remained economically dependent on their families until a long education was finished or a proper marriage secured, working-class boys and girls went to work when they reached adolescence. Earning wages on their own, they could bargain with their parents by the time they were sixteen or seventeen for greater independence within the household. If they were unsuccessful in these negotiations, they could and did leave home to live cheaply as paying lodgers in other working-class homes. Not until the twentieth century would middle-class youths be equally free to break away from the family when emotional ties became oppressive.

The Feminist Movement

The ideal of separate spheres and the rigid gender division of labor meant that middle-class women faced great obstacles when they needed—or wanted—to move into the man's world of paid employment outside the home. Married women were subordinated to their husbands by law and lacked many basic legal rights. In England, a wife had no legal identity and hence no right to own property in her own name. Even the wages she might earn belonged to her husband. In France, the Napoleonic Code (see Chapter 19) enshrined the principle of female subordination and gave the wife few legal rights regarding property, divorce, and custody of the children.

Facing discrimination in education and employment and suffering from a lack of legal rights, some women rebelled and began the long-continuing fight for equality of the sexes and the rights of women. Their struggle proceeded on two main paths. First, following in the steps of women such as Mary Wollstonecraft (see Chapter 19), organizations founded by middle-class feminists campaigned for equal legal rights for women as well as access to higher education, professional employment, and the vote. Middle-class feminists argued that unmarried women and middle-class widows with inadequate incomes simply had to have more opportunities to support themselves. Second, feminists argued that paid (as opposed to unpaid) work could relieve the monotony that some women found in their sheltered middle-class existence and add greater meaning to their lives. In the late nineteenth century women's organizations scored some significant victories, such as the 1882 law giving English married women full property rights. More women gradually found professional and white-collar employment, especially after 1880, in fields such as teaching, nursing, and social work.

First-Wave Feminists in Action   In May 1914 suffragette leader Emily Pankhurst was arrested by a police superintendent when she tried to present a petition to the king at Buckingham Palace. The British suffragettes often engaged in provocative public acts of civic disobedience in their campaign for women's right to vote. How do you account for the reaction of the male onlookers? (© Museum of London, UK/Bridgeman Images)

Progress toward women's rights was slow and hard-won. In Britain, the women's **suffrage movement** mounted a militant struggle for the right to vote, particularly in the decade before World War I. Inspired by the slogan "Deeds Not Words," women "suffragettes" marched in public demonstrations, heckled members of Parliament, and slashed paintings in London's National Gallery. Jailed for political activities, they

suffrage movement
A militant movement for women's right to vote led by middle-class British women around 1900.

INDIVIDUALS IN SOCIETY

Franziska Tiburtius

Why did a small number of women in the late nineteenth century brave great odds and embark on professional careers? And how did a few of them manage to reach their objectives? The career and personal reflections of Franziska Tiburtius (tigh-bur-TEE-uhs), a pioneer in German medicine, suggest that talent, determination, and economic necessity were critical ingredients to both the attempt and the success.*

Like many women of her time who studied and pursued professional careers, Franziska Tiburtius (1843–1927) was born into a property-owning family of modest means. The youngest of nine children growing up on a small estate in northeastern Germany, the sensitive child wilted under a harsh governess but flowered with a caring teacher and became an excellent student. Graduating at sixteen and needing to support herself, Tiburtius had few opportunities. A young woman from a "proper" background could work as a governess or teacher without losing her respectability and spoiling her matrimonial prospects, but that was about it. She tried both avenues. Working for six years as a governess in a noble family and no doubt learning that poverty was often one's fate in this genteel profession, she then turned to teaching.

*This portrait draws on Conradine Lück, *Frauen: Neun Lebensschicksale* (Reutlingen: Ensslin & Laiblin, n.d.), pp. 153–185.

Called home from her studies in Britain in 1871 to care for her brother, who had contracted typhus as a field doctor in the Franco-Prussian War, she found her calling. She decided to become a medical doctor.

Supported by her family, Tiburtius's decision was truly audacious. In all Europe, only the University of Zurich accepted female students. Moreover, if it became known that she had studied medicine and failed, she would probably never get a job as a teacher. No parent would entrust a daughter to an emancipated radical who had carved up dead bodies. Although the male students at the university sometimes harassed the female ones with crude pranks, Tiburtius thrived. The revolution of the microscope and the discovery of microorganisms thrilled Tiburtius, and she was fascinated by her studies. She became close friends with a fellow female student from Germany, Emilie Lehmus, with whom she would form a lifelong partnership in medicine.

Graduating at age thirty-three in 1876, Tiburtius went to stay with her doctor brother in Berlin. Though well qualified to practice, she was blocked by pervasive discrimination. Not permitted to take the state medical exams, she could practice only as an unregulated (and unprofessional) "natural healer." But after persistent fighting with the bureaucrats, she was able to display her diploma and practice as "Franziska Tiburtius, M.D., University of Zurich."

went on highly publicized hunger strikes. Yet conservatives dismissed what they called "the shrieking sisterhood," and British women received the vote only in 1919.

In Germany before 1900, women were not admitted as fully registered students at a single university. Determined pioneers had to fight with tremendous fortitude to break through sexist barriers to advanced education and subsequent professional employment. (See "Individuals in Society: Franziska Tiburtius," above.) By 1913 the Federation of German Women's Association, an umbrella organization for regional feminist groups, had some 470,000 members. Their protests had a direct impact on the revised German Civil Code of 1906, which granted women substantial gains in family law and property rights.

Women inspired by utopian and especially Marxist socialism (see Chapter 21) blazed an alternative path. Often scorning the reform programs of middle-class feminists, socialist women leaders argued that the liberation of working-class women would come only with the liberation of the entire working class through revolution. In the meantime, they championed the cause of working women and won some

Soon Tiburtius and Lehmus realized their dream and opened a clinic. Subsidized by a wealthy industrialist, they focused on treating women factory workers. The clinic filled a great need and was soon treating many patients. A room with beds for extremely sick women was later expanded into a second clinic.

Tiburtius and Lehmus became famous. For fifteen years, they were the only women doctors in all of Berlin and inspired a new generation of women. Though they added the wealthy to their thriving practice, they always concentrated on the poor, providing them with subsidized and up-to-date treatment. Talented, determined, and working with her partner, Tiburtius experienced fully the joys of personal achievement and useful service. Above all, Tiburtius overcame the tremendous barriers raised up against women seeking higher education and professional careers, providing an inspiring model for those who dared to follow.

QUESTIONS FOR ANALYSIS

1. Analyze Franziska Tiburtius's life. What lessons do you draw from it? How do you account for her bold action and success?
2. In what ways was Tiburtius's career related to improvements in health in urban society and to the expansion of the professions?

Franziska Tiburtius, pioneering woman physician in Berlin. (1915 photograph/akg-images)

practical improvements, especially in Germany, where the socialist movement was most effectively organized. In a general way, these different approaches to women's issues reflected the diversity of classes in urban society.

Science and Thought

Major changes in Western science and thought accompanied the emergence of urban society. Two aspects of these complex intellectual developments stand out as especially significant. First, scientific knowledge in many areas expanded rapidly. Breakthroughs in chemistry, physics, and electricity profoundly influenced the Western worldview and spurred the creation of new products and whole industries. The natural and social sciences were also established as highly respected fields of study. Second, between about the 1840s and the 1890s Western arts and literature underwent a shift from soaring Romanticism to tough-minded Realism.

FOCUS QUESTION
How and why did intellectual life change in this period?

The Triumph of Science in Industry

The quickening pace of scientific advancements in the last third of the nineteenth century resulted in many practical benefits. The intellectual achievements of the Scientific Revolution (see Chapter 16) had resulted in few such benefits, and theoretical knowledge had also played a relatively small role in the Industrial Revolution in England (see Chapter 20). But breakthroughs in industrial technology in the late eighteenth century enormously stimulated basic scientific inquiry as researchers sought to explain theoretically how such things as steam engines and blast furnaces actually worked. The result was an explosive growth of fundamental scientific discoveries from the 1830s onward. In contrast to earlier periods, these theoretical discoveries were increasingly transformed into material improvements for the general population.

A perfect example of the translation of better scientific knowledge into practical human benefits was the work of Louis Pasteur and his followers in biology and the medical sciences (see page 722). Another was the development of the branch of physics known as **thermodynamics**. Building on Isaac Newton's laws of mechanics and on studies of steam engines, thermodynamics investigated the relationship between heat and mechanical energy. The law of conservation of energy held that different forms of energy—such as heat, electricity, and magnetism—could be converted but neither created nor destroyed. By midcentury, physicists had formulated the fundamental laws of thermodynamics, which were then applied to mechanical engineering, chemical processes, and many other fields.

> **thermodynamics** A branch of physics built on Newton's laws of mechanics that investigated the relationship between heat and mechanical energy.

Chemistry and electricity were two other fields characterized by extremely rapid scientific progress. And in both fields, "science was put in the service of industry," as the influential economist Alfred Marshall (1842–1924) argued at the time. Chemists devised ways of measuring the atomic weight of different elements, and in 1869 the Russian chemist Dmitri Mendeleev (mehn-duh-LAY-uhf) (1834–1907) codified the rules of chemistry in the periodic law and the periodic table. Chemistry was subdivided into many specialized branches, including organic chemistry—the study of the compounds of carbon. Applying theoretical insights gleaned from this new field, researchers in large German chemical companies discovered ways of transforming the dirty, useless coal tar that accumulated in coke ovens into beautiful, expensive synthetic dyes for the world of fashion. German production of synthetic dyes soared, and by 1900 German chemical companies controlled 90 percent of world production.

Electricity, a scientific curiosity in 1800, was totally transformed by a century of tremendous technological advancement. It became a commercial form of energy, first used in communications (the telegraph, which spurred quick international communication with the laying of underwater cables), then in electrochemistry (refining aluminum, for example), and finally in central power generation (for lighting, transportation, and industrial motors). And by 1890 the internal combustion engine fueled by petroleum was an emerging competitor to steam and electricity alike.

> **Second Industrial Revolution** The burst of industrial creativity and technological innovation that promoted strong economic growth in the last third of the nineteenth century.

The successful application of scientific research in the fast-growing electrical and organic chemical industries between 1880 and 1913 provided a model for other industries. Systematic "R&D"—research and development—was born in the late nineteenth century. Above all, the burst of industrial creativity and technological innovation, often called the **Second Industrial Revolution**, promoted the strong economic growth in the last third of the nineteenth century that drove the urban reforms and the rising standard of living considered in this chapter.

The triumph of science and technology had three other significant consequences. First, though ordinary citizens continued to lack detailed scientific knowledge, everyday experience and innumerable articles in newspapers and magazines impressed the importance of science on the popular mind. Second, as science became more prominent in popular thinking, the philosophical implications of science formulated in the Enlightenment spread to broad sections of the population. Natural processes appeared to be determined by rigid laws, leaving little room for either divine intervention or human will. Yet scientific and technical advances had also fed the Enlightenment's optimistic faith in human progress, which now appeared endless and automatic to growing numbers of people. Third, the methods of science acquired unrivaled prestige after 1850. For many, the union of careful experiment and abstract theory was the only reliable route to truth and objective reality. The "unscientific" intuitions of poets and the revelations of saints seemed hopelessly inferior.

Darwin and Natural Selection

Scientific research also progressed rapidly outside of the world of industry and technology, sometimes putting forth direct challenges to traditional beliefs. In geology, for example, Charles Lyell (1797–1875) effectively discredited the long-standing view that the earth's surface had been formed by short-lived cataclysms, such as biblical floods and earthquakes. Instead, according to Lyell's principle of uniformitarianism, the same geological processes that are at work today slowly formed the earth's surface over an immensely long time. The vast timescale required for the processes that Lyell described to have these effects undermined traditional beliefs about the age of the earth based on religious teachings. Similarly, the evolutionary view of biological development, first proposed by the Greek Anaximander in the sixth century B.C.E., re-emerged in a more modern form in the work of French naturalist Jean-Baptiste Lamarck (1744–1829). Lamarck asserted that all forms of life had arisen through a long process of continuous adjustment to the environment, a dramatic challenge to the belief in divine creation of species.

Lamarck's work was flawed — he believed that the characteristics parents acquired in the course of their lives could be inherited by their children — and was not accepted, but it helped prepare the way for Charles Darwin (1809–1882), the most influential of all nineteenth-century evolutionary thinkers. As the official naturalist on a five-year scientific cruise to Latin America and the South Pacific beginning in 1831, Darwin carefully collected specimens of the different animal species he encountered on the voyage. Back in England, convinced by fossil evidence and by his friend Lyell that the earth and life on it were immensely ancient, Darwin came to doubt the general belief in a special divine creation of each species of animal. Instead, he concluded, all life had gradually evolved from a common ancestral origin in an unending "struggle for survival." After long hesitation, Darwin published his research, which immediately attracted wide attention.

Darwin's great originality lay in suggesting precisely how biological evolution might have occurred. His theory of **evolution** is summarized in the title of his work *On the Origin of Species by the Means of Natural Selection* (1859). Decisively influenced by the gloomy assertions of Thomas Malthus (MAL-thuhs) that populations naturally

evolution The idea, applied by thinkers in many fields, that stresses gradual change and continuous adjustment.

grow faster than their food supplies (see Chapter 20), Darwin argued that chance differences among the individual members of a given species help some survive while others die. Thus the variations that prove useful in the struggle for survival are selected naturally, and they gradually spread to the entire species through reproduction.

Darwin's controversial theory had a powerful and many-sided influence on European thought and the European middle classes. Because his ideas seemed to suggest that evolution moved along without God's intervention, and that humans were simply one species among many others, some conservatives accused Darwin of anti-Christian beliefs and mocked him for suggesting that humans descended from apes. Others hailed Darwin as the great scientist par excellence, the "Newton of biology," who had revealed once again the powers of objective science.

Some thinkers went a step further and applied Darwin's theory of biological evolution to human affairs. English philosopher Herbert Spencer (1820–1903) saw the human race as driven forward to ever-greater specialization and progress by a brutal economic struggle that determined the "survival of the fittest." The poor were the ill-fated weak; the prosperous were the chosen strong. Spencer's **Social Darwinism** gained adherents among nationalists, who viewed global competition between countries as a grand struggle for survival, as well as among imperialists, who used Social Darwinist ideas to justify the "natural" rule of the supposedly more civilized West over their colonial subjects and territories.

Social Darwinism A body of thought drawn from the ideas of Charles Darwin that applied the theory of biological evolution to human affairs and saw the human race as driven by an unending economic struggle that would determine the survival of the fittest.

The Modern University and the Social Sciences

By the 1880s major universities across Europe had been modernized and professionalized. Education now emphasized controlled research projects in newly established clinics and laboratories; advanced students conducted independent research in seminar settings. An increasingly diversified professoriate established many of the academic departments still found in today's universities, from anthropology to zoology. In a striking development, faculty devoted to the newly instituted human or social sciences took their place alongside the hard sciences. Using critical methods often borrowed from natural science, social scientists studied massive sets of numerical data that governments had begun to collect on everything from birthrates to crime and from population to prostitution. Like Karl Marx, they were fascinated by the rise of capitalism and modernity; unlike Marx, they preferred to understand rather than revolutionize society.

Sociology, the critical analysis of contemporary or historical social groups, emerged as a leading social science. Perhaps the most prominent and influential late-nineteenth-century sociologist was the German Max Weber (1864–1920). In his most famous book, *The Protestant Ethic and the Spirit of Capitalism* (1890), Weber argued that the rise of capitalism was directly linked to Protestantism in northern Europe. Pointing to the early and successful modernization of countries like the Netherlands and England, he concluded that Protestantism gave religious approval to hard work, saving, and investing—the foundations for capitalist development—because worldly success was a sign of God's approval. This famous argument seriously challenged the basic ideas of Marxism: ideas, for Weber, were just as important as economics or class struggle in the rise of capitalism. Yet like Marx, Weber held a critical view of the rationalization of the human spirit, trapped in what he called the "iron cage" of capitalist relations. Modern industrial society, according to Weber, had turned people into "specialists without spirit, hedonists without heart." An ambitious scholar, Weber wrote extensively on capitalist ratio-nalization, modern bureaucracy, industrialization and agriculture, and the forms of political leadership.

In France, the prolific sociologist Émile Durkheim (1858–1917) earned an inter-national reputation for his wide-ranging work. His study of the psychic and social basis of religion, *The Elementary Forms of Religious Life* (1912), remains a classic of social-scientific thought. In his pioneering work of quantitative sociology, *Suicide* (1897), Durkheim concluded that ever-higher suicide rates were caused by wide-spread feelings of "anomie," or rootlessness. Because modern society had stripped life of all sense of tradition, purpose, and belonging, Durkheim believed, anomie was inescapable; only an entirely new moral order might offer some relief.

Other sociologists contributed to the critique of modern society. The German Ferdinand Tönnies (1855–1936) argued that with industrialization Western civiliza-tion had undergone a fundamental transformation from "community" to "society." Rationalized self-interest had replaced traditional values, leading to intensified alien-ation and a cold bureaucratic age. In *The Crowd* (1895), French sociologist Gustav Le Bon (1841–1931) wrote that the alienated masses were prone to gathering in mass crowds, in which individuals lost control over their emotions and actions. According to the deeply conservative Le Bon, a strong, charismatic leader could easily manipu-late the crowd's collective psyche and turn the servile mass into a violent and danger-ous revolutionary mob.

The new sociologists cast a bleak light on urban industrial society. While they acknowledged some benefits of rationalization and modernization, they bemoaned the accompanying loss of community and tradition. In some ways, their diagnosis of the modern individual as an isolated atom suffering from anomie and desperately seeking human connection was chillingly prescient: the powerful Communist and Fascist movements that swept through Europe after World War I seemed to win pop-ular support precisely by offering ordinary people a renewed sense of social belonging.

Realism in Art and Literature

In art and literature, the key themes of **Realism** emerged in the 1840s and continued to dominate Western culture until the 1890s. Realist artists and writers believed that artistic works should depict life exactly as it was. Forsaking the personal, emotional viewpoint of the Romantics for strict, supposedly factual objectivity, the Realists observed and recorded the world around them—often to expose the sordid reality of modern life.

Emphatically rejecting the Romantic search for the exotic and the sublime, Real-ism (or "Naturalism," as it was often called) energetically pursued the typical and the commonplace. Beginning with a dissection of the middle classes, from which most of them sprang, many Realists eventually focused on the working classes, especially the urban working classes, which had been neglected in imaginative literature before this time. The Realists put a microscope to many unexplored and taboo subjects, including sex, labor strikes, violence, and alcoholism, and hastened to report that slums and factories teemed with savage behavior. Shocked middle-class critics denounced Realism as ugly sensationalism wrapped provocatively in pseudoscientific declarations and crude language—even as the movement attracted a growing middle-class audience, fascinated by the sensationalist view "from below."

Realism A literary movement that, in contrast to Romanticism, stressed the depiction of life as it actually was.

Realism in the Arts   Realist depictions of gritty everyday life challenged the Romantic emphasis on nature and the emotions, as well as the Neoclassical focus on famous men and grand events. French painter Honoré Daumier's *The Third-Class Carriage*, completed in 1864, is a famous example of Realism in the arts that portrays the effects of industrialization in the mid-nineteenth century. In muted colors, Daumier's painting captures the grinding poverty and weariness of the poor but also lends a sense of dignity to their humble lives. (Metropolitan Museum of Art, New York, USA/Bridgeman Images)

The Realist movement began in France, where Romanticism had never been completely dominant. Artists like Gustave Courbet, Jean-François Millet, and Honoré Daumier painted scenes of laboring workers and peasants in somber colors and simple compositions, exemplified in Daumier's 1864 painting *The Third-Class Carriage* (above). Daumier's art championed the simple virtues of the working class and lampooned the greed and ill will of the rich bourgeoisie; a caricature of King Louis Philippe earned him six months in prison.

Literary Realism also began in France, where Honoré de Balzac, Gustave Flaubert, and Émile Zola became internationally famous novelists. Balzac (1799–1850) spent thirty years writing a vastly ambitious panorama of postrevolutionary French life. Known collectively as *The Human Comedy*, this series of nearly one hundred stories, novels, and essays vividly portrays more than two thousand characters from virtually all sectors of French society. Balzac pictured urban society as grasping, amoral, and brutal. In his novel *Father Goriot* (1835), the hero, a poor student from the provinces, eventually surrenders his idealistic integrity to feverish ambition and society's pervasive greed.

Madame Bovary (1857), the masterpiece of Flaubert (floh-BEHR) (1821–1880), is far narrower in scope than Balzac's work but is still famous for its depth of psychological insight and critique of middle-class values. Unsuccessfully prosecuted as an outrage against public morality and religion, Flaubert's carefully crafted novel tells the ordinary, even banal, story of a frustrated middle-class housewife who has an adulterous love affair and is betrayed by her lover. Without moralizing, Flaubert portrays the provincial middle class as petty, smug, and hypocritical.

Émile Zola (1840–1902) was most famous for his seamy, animalistic view of working-class life. But he also wrote gripping, carefully researched stories featuring the stock exchange, the big department store, and the army, as well as urban slums and bloody battles between police and sturdy coal strikers. Like many later Realists, Zola sympathized with socialism, a view evident in his overpowering novel *Germinal* (1885). (See "Evaluating the Evidence 22.3: Émile Zola and Realism in Literature," at right.)

Realism quickly spread beyond France. In England, Mary Ann Evans (1819–1880), who wrote under the pen name George Eliot, brilliantly achieved a more deeply felt, less sensational kind of Realism in her great novel *Middlemarch: A Study of Provincial*

Émile Zola and Realism in Literature

"There should no longer be any school, no more formulas, no standards of any sort; there is only life itself, an immense field where each may study and create as he likes," wrote Émile Zola in 1867. The great Realist author applied these precepts in the opening lines of his 1885 masterpiece novel, Germinal, *which championed the rights of French coal miners in the late nineteenth century.*

Over the open plain, beneath a starless sky as dark and thick as ink, a man walked alone along the highway from Marchiennes to Montsou, a straight paved road ten kilometres in length, intersecting the beetroot-fields. He could not even see the black soil before him, and only felt the immense flat horizon by the gusts of March wind, squalls as strong as on the sea, and frozen from sweeping leagues of marsh and naked earth. No tree could be seen against the sky, and the road unrolled as straight as a pier in the midst of the blinding spray of darkness.

The man had set out from Marchiennes about two o'clock. He walked with long strides, shivering beneath his worn cotton jacket and corduroy breeches. A small parcel tied in a check handkerchief troubled him much, and he pressed it against his side, sometimes with one elbow, sometimes with the other, so that he could slip to the bottom of his pockets both the benumbed hands that bled beneath the lashes of the wind. A single idea occupied his head — the empty head of a workman without work and without lodging — the hope that the cold would be less keen after sunrise. For an hour he went on thus, when on the left, two kilometres from Montsou, he saw red flames, three fires burning in the open air and apparently suspended. At first he hesitated, half afraid. Then he could not resist the painful need to warm his hands for a moment. . . .

Suddenly, at a bend in the road, the fires reappeared close to him, though he could not understand how they burnt so high in the dead sky, like smoky moons. But on the level soil another sight had struck him. It was a heavy mass, a low pile of buildings from which rose the silhouette of a factory chimney; occasional gleams appeared from dirty windows, five or six melancholy lanterns were hung outside to frames of blackened wood, which vaguely outlined the profiles of gigantic stages; and from this fantastic apparition, drowned in night and smoke, a single voice arose, the thick, long breathing of a steam escapement that could not be seen.

Then the man recognized a [mine] pit. His despair returned. What was the good? There would be no work. Instead of turning towards the buildings he decided at last to ascend the pit bank, on which burnt in iron baskets the three coal fires which gave light and warmth for work. The labourers in the cutting must have been working late; they were still throwing out the useless rubbish. . . . He could distinguish living shadows tipping over the trains or tubs near each fire.

EVALUATE THE EVIDENCE

1. Zola claimed to represent "only life itself," but the vivid description in his prose often creates heavily dramatized effects, as in this selection. Why does Zola use such deeply poetic imagery?
2. How do the style and subject matter of Realism compare and contrast with those of Romanticism?

Source: Émile Zola, *Germinal,* trans. Havelock Ellis (London: Everyman's Library, 1894).

Life (1871–1872). The novels of Thomas Hardy (1840–1928), such as *Tess of the D'Urbervilles* (1891) and *The Return of the Native* (1878), depict ordinary men and women frustrated and crushed by social prejudice, sexual puritanism, and bad luck. The greatest Russian Realist, Count Leo Tolstoy (1828–1910), combined Realism in description and character development with an atypical moralizing, especially in his later work. In *War and Peace* (1864–1869), a monumental novel set against the background of Napoleon's invasion of Russia in 1812, Tolstoy developed his fatalistic theory of human history, which regards free will as an illusion and the achievements of even the greatest leaders as only the channeling of historical necessity. Yet Tolstoy's central message is one that most of the people discussed in this chapter would have readily accepted: human love, trust, and everyday family ties are life's enduring values.

LOOKING BACK LOOKING AHEAD

When the peoples of northwestern Europe looked out at the economic and social landscape in the early twentieth century, they had good reason to feel that the promise of the Industrial Revolution was being realized. The dark days of urban squalor and brutal working hours had given way after 1850 to a gradual rise in the standard of living for all classes. Scientific discoveries were combining with the applied technology of public health and industrial production to save lives and drive continued economic growth.

Moreover, social and economic advances seemed to be matched by progress in the political sphere. The years following the dramatic failure of the revolutions of 1848 saw the creation of unified nation-states in Italy and Germany, and after 1870, as we shall see in the following chapters, nationalism and the nation-state reigned in Europe. Although the rise of nationalism created tensions among the European countries, these tensions would not explode until 1914 and the outbreak of the First World War. Instead, the most aggressive and destructive aspects of European nationalism found their initial outlet in the final and most powerful surge of Western overseas expansion. Thus Europe, transformed by industrialization and nationalism, rushed after 1875 to seize territory and build new or greatly expanded authoritarian empires in Asia and Africa.

Make Connections

Think about the larger developments and continuities within and across chapters.

1. What were the most important changes in everyday life from the eighteenth century (Chapter 18) to the nineteenth century? What main causes or agents drove these changes?

2. Did the life of ordinary people improve, stay the same, or even deteriorate over the nineteenth century when compared to the previous century? What role did developments in science, medicine, and urban planning play in this process?

3. How did the emergence of a society divided into working and middle classes affect the workplace, homemaking, and family values and gender roles?

22 REVIEW & EXPLORE

Review the Main Ideas

Answer the focus questions from each section of the chapter.

◆ How did urban life change in the nineteenth century? (p. 718)

◆ What did the emergence of urban industrial society mean for rich and poor and those in between? (p. 725)

◆ How did urbanization affect family life and gender roles? (p. 732)

◆ How and why did intellectual life change in this period? (p. 743)

Identify Key Terms

Identify and explain the significance of each item below.

utilitarianism (p. 721)

germ theory (p. 722)

labor aristocracy (p. 729)

sweated industries (p. 730)

companionate marriage (p. 733)

separate spheres (p. 737)

suffrage movement (p. 741)

thermodynamics (p. 744)

Second Industrial Revolution (p. 744)

evolution (p. 745)

Social Darwinism (p. 746)

Realism (p. 747)

NOTES

1. S. Marcus, "Reading the Illegible," in *The Victorian City: Images and Realities*, ed. H. J. Dyos and Michael Wolff, vol. 1 (London: Routledge & Kegan Paul, 1973), p. 266.

2. Quoted in E. Chadwick, *Report on the Sanitary Condition of the Labouring Population of Great Britain*, ed. M. W. Flinn (Edinburgh: University of Edinburgh Press, 1965; original publication, 1842), pp. 315–316.

3. J. McKay, *Tramways and Trolleys: The Rise of Urban Mass Transport in Europe* (Princeton, N.J.: Princeton University Press, 1976), p. 81.

4. Quoted in R. P. Neuman, "The Sexual Question and Social Democracy in Imperial Germany," *Journal of Social History* 7 (Winter 1974): 276.

5. Quoted in J. A. Banks, "The Contagion of Numbers," in *The Victorian City: Images and Realities*, ed. H. J. Dyos and Michael Wolff, vol. 1 (London: Routledge & Kegan Paul, 1973), p. 112.

6. Quoted in R. Roberts, *The Classic Slum: Salford Life in the First Quarter of the Century* (Manchester, U.K.: University of Manchester Press, 1971), p. 95.

7. J. Frykman and O. Löfgren, *Culture Builders: A Historical Anthropology of Middle-Class Life* (New Brunswick, N.J.: Rutgers University Press, 1987), p. 134.

8. See the pioneering work of J. de Vries, *The Industrious Revolution: Consumer Behavior and the Household Economy* (Cambridge: Cambridge University Press, 2008), especially pp. 186–237.

9. Roberts, *The Classic Slum*, p. 35.

10. Quoted in T. Zeldin, *France, 1848–1945*, vol. 1 (Oxford: Clarendon Press, 1973), p. 328.

11. Quoted in Neuman, "The Sexual Question," p. 281.

12. Frykman and Löfgren, *Culture Builders*, p. 114.

CHAPTER PREVIEW

Napoleon III in France
How did Napoleon III seek to reconcile popular and conservative forces in an authoritarian nation-state?

Nation Building in Italy, Germany, and the United States
How did conflict and war lead to the construction of strong nation-states in Italy, Germany, and the United States?

The Modernization of Russia and the Ottoman Empire
What steps did Russia and the Ottoman Turks take toward modernization, and how successful were they?

The Responsive National State, 1871–1914
What general domestic political trends emerged after 1871?

The Nation and the People
How did popular nationalism evolve in the last decades of the nineteenth century?

Marxism and the Socialist Movement
Why did the socialist movement grow, and how revolutionary was it?

Life in the Age of Nationalism

Conscripts in an Italian village cheer a speech by a local dignitary as a soldier bids farewell to his family before joining the army in the field. This portrait pays homage to the Italian peasant, willing to fight for his newborn country. This idealized scene depicts the changing relationship between state and citizen, as nationalism came to predominate at all levels of society.

(By Gerolamo Induno [1825–1890], [oil on canvas]/Civico Museo del Risorgimento, Milano, Italy/De Agostini Picture Library/Alfredo Dagli Orti/Bridgeman Images)

23

The Age of Nationalism

1850–1914

In the years that followed the revolutions of 1848, Western society progressively developed, for better or worse, an effective organizing principle capable of coping with the many-sided challenges of the unfinished industrial and political revolutions and the emerging urban society. That principle was nationalism—mass identification with the nation-state. Just as industrialization and urbanization had brought vast changes to class relations, family lifestyles, and science and culture, the triumph of nationalism remade territorial boundaries and forged new relations between the nation-state and its citizens.

The rise of nationalism and the nation-state, enormously significant historical developments, was by no means completely predictable. Nationalism had been a powerful force since at least 1789, but the goal of creating independent nation-states, inhabited by people sharing a common ethnicity, language, history, and territory, had repeatedly failed, most spectacularly in the revolutions of 1848. By 1914, however, most Europeans lived in nation-states, and the ideology of nationalism had become an almost universal faith in the Western world. The governments of the new nation-states took various forms, from conservative authoritarianism to parliamentary monarchy to liberal republicanism. Whatever the political system, in most cases the nation-state became increasingly responsive to the needs of its people, opening the political franchise and offering citizens at least rudimentary social and economic benefits. At the same time, the nation-state demanded more from its citizens, most obviously in the form of rising income taxes and universal military service. Nationalism, which before 1848 appealed primarily to liberals seeking political reform or national independence, became an ever more conservative ideology. At its worst, populists and fanatics eagerly manipulated and sometimes abused the growing patriotism of ordinary people to justify exclusionary policies against Jews and other ethnic minorities, and to promote expansionary projects in overseas colonies. ■

Napoleon III in France

FOCUS QUESTION
How did Napoleon III seek to reconcile popular and conservative forces in an authoritarian nation-state?

Early nationalism was generally liberal and idealistic and could be democratic and radical (see Chapter 21). Yet nationalism also flourished in authoritarian states, which imposed social and economic changes from above. Napoleon Bonaparte's France had already combined national feeling with authoritarian rule. Napoleon's nephew, Louis Napoleon, revived and extended this combination.

France's Second Republic

Although Louis Napoleon Bonaparte had played no part in French politics before 1848, universal male suffrage and widespread popular support gave him three times as many votes as the four other presidential candidates combined in the French presidential election of December 1848. This outcome occurred for several reasons. First, he had the great name of his uncle, whom romantics had transformed into a demigod after 1820. Second, as Karl Marx stressed at the time, middle-class and peasant property owners feared the socialist challenge of urban workers and the chaos of the revolution of 1848, and they wanted a tough ruler to protect their property and provide stability. Third, Louis Napoleon enunciated a positive program for France in pamphlets widely circulated before the election.

Paris in the Second Empire   The flash and glitter of unprecedented prosperity in the Second Empire come alive in this vibrant contemporary painting. Writers and intellectuals chat with elegant women and trade witticisms with financiers and government officials at the Café Tortoni, a favorite rendezvous for fashionable society. Horse-drawn omnibuses with open top decks mingle with cabs and private carriages on the broad new boulevard. (Musée de la Ville de Paris, Musée Carnavalet, Paris, France/Bridgeman Images)

Chronology

1839–1876	Western-style Tanzimat reforms in Ottoman Empire	**1880s**	Educational reforms in France create a secular public school system
1852–1870	Reign of Napoleon III in France	**1880s–1890s**	Widespread return to protectionism among European states
1859–1870	Unification of Italy		
1861	Freeing of Russian serfs	**1883**	First social security laws to help workers in Germany
1861–1865	U.S. Civil War		
1866	Austro-Prussian War	**1890–1900**	Witte initiates second surge of Russian industrialization
1870–1871	Franco-Prussian War; unification of Germany	**1905**	Revolution in Russia
1870–1878	Kulturkampf, Bismarck's attack on Catholic Church	**1906–1914**	Social reform in Great Britain
1873	Stock market crash spurs renewed anti-Semitism, beginning in central and eastern Europe	**1908**	Young Turks seize power in Ottoman Empire

Above all, Louis Napoleon promoted a vision of national unity and social progress. He believed that the government should represent the people and help them economically. But how could these tasks be accomplished? Corrupt parliaments and political parties were not the answer, according to Louis Napoleon. French politicians represented special-interest groups, particularly middle-class ones. The answer was a strong, even authoritarian, national leader, like the first Napoleon, whose efforts to provide jobs and stimulate the economy would serve all people, rich and poor. This leader would be linked to each citizen by direct democracy, his sovereignty uncorrupted by politicians and legislative bodies. To the many common people who voted for him, Louis Napoleon appeared to be a strong leader and a forward-looking champion of popular interests.

Elected to a four-year term by an overwhelming majority, Louis Napoleon was required by the constitution to share power with the National Assembly, which was overwhelmingly conservative. With some misgivings, he signed conservative-sponsored bills that increased greatly the role of the Catholic Church in primary and secondary education and deprived many poor people of the right to vote. He took these steps in hopes that the Assembly would vote funds to pay his personal debts and change the constitution so he could run for a second term.

But in 1851, after the Assembly failed to cooperate with that last aim, Louis Napoleon began to conspire with key army officers. On December 2, 1851, he illegally dismissed the legislature and seized power in a coup d'état. There was some armed resistance in Paris and widespread insurrection in the countryside in southern France, but the army crushed these popular protests. Restoring universal male suffrage and claiming to stand above political bickering, Louis Napoleon called on the French people, as the first Napoleon had done, to legalize his actions. They did: 92 percent voted to make him president for ten years. A year later, in a plebiscite, 97 percent voted to make him hereditary emperor.

Napoleon III's Second Empire

Louis Napoleon—now proclaimed Emperor Napoleon III—experienced both success and failure between 1852 and 1870, when he fell from power. In the 1850s his policies led to economic growth. His government promoted the new investment banks and massive railroad construction that were at the heart of the Industrial Revolution on the continent (see Chapter 20). It fostered general economic expansion through an ambitious program of public works, which included rebuilding Paris to improve the urban environment (see Chapter 22). The profits of business owners soared, rising wages of workers outpaced inflation, and unemployment declined greatly.

Initially, Louis Napoleon's hope that economic progress would reduce social and political tensions was at least partially realized. Until the mid-1860s he enjoyed support from France's most dissatisfied group, the urban workers. Government regulation of pawnshops and support for credit unions and better working-class housing were evidence of helpful reform in the 1850s. In the 1860s Louis Napoleon granted workers the right to form unions and the right to strike—important economic rights denied by earlier governments.

At first, political power remained in the hands of the emperor. He alone chose his ministers, who had great freedom of action. At the same time, Louis Napoleon restricted but did not abolish the newly reformed Assembly. Members were elected by universal male suffrage every six years, and Louis Napoleon and his government took these elections very seriously. They tried to entice notable people, even those who had opposed the regime, to stand as government candidates in order to expand the base of support. Moreover, the government used its officials and appointed mayors to spread the word that election of the government's candidates—and defeat of the opposition—would provide roads, tax rebates, and a thousand other local benefits.

In 1857 and again in 1863, Louis Napoleon's system worked brilliantly and produced overwhelming electoral victories for government-backed candidates. In the 1860s, however, this electoral system gradually disintegrated. A sincere nationalist, Napoleon had wanted to reorganize Europe on the principle of nationality and gain influence and territory for France and himself in the process. Instead, problems in Italy and the rising power of Prussia led to increasing criticism at home from his Catholic and nationalist supporters. With increasing effectiveness, the middle-class liberals who had always wanted a less authoritarian regime denounced his rule.

Napoleon was always sensitive to the public mood. Public opinion, he once said, always wins the last victory, and he responded to critics with progressive liberalization. He gave the Assembly greater powers and opposition candidates greater freedom, which they used to good advantage. In 1869 the opposition, consisting of republicans, monarchists, and liberals, polled almost 45 percent of the vote.

The next year, a sick and weary Louis Napoleon again granted France a new constitution, which combined a basically parliamentary regime with a hereditary emperor as chief of state. In a final plebiscite on the eve of the disastrous war with Prussia (see page 763), 7.5 million Frenchmen approved the new constitution—only 1.5 million opposed it. Napoleon III's successful attempt to reconcile a strong central state with universal male suffrage showed that nationalism was compatible with authoritarian government, even as France moved in an increasingly democratic direction.

Nation Building in Italy, Germany, and the United States

Louis Napoleon's triumph in 1848 and his authoritarian rule in the 1850s provided the old ruling classes of Europe with a new model in politics. Would the expanding urban middle classes and even portions of the working classes rally to a strong, conservative national state that promised economic growth, social benefits, and national unity, as in France? This was one of the great political questions in the 1850s and 1860s. In Europe, the national unification of Italy and Germany offered a resounding answer. In the United States, nation building marked by sectional differences over slavery offered another.

FOCUS QUESTION
How did conflict and war lead to the construction of strong nation-states in Italy, Germany, and the United States?

Italy to 1850

Before 1850 Italy had never been united. The Italian peninsula was divided in the Middle Ages into competing city-states. A battleground for the Great Powers after 1494, Italy was reorganized in 1815 at the Congress of Vienna into a hodgepodge of different states. Austrian foreign minister Prince Klemens von Metternich captured the essence of the situation when he dismissed Italy as only "a geographical expression" (Map 23.1).

Between 1815 and 1848 the goal of a unified Italian nation captured the imaginations of many Italians. There were three basic approaches. First, the radical and idealistic patriot Giuseppe Mazzini called for a centralized democratic republic based on universal male suffrage and the will of the people. (See "Evaluating the Evidence 23.1: The Struggle for the Italian Nation," page 759.) Second, Vincenzo Gioberti, a Catholic priest, sought a federation of existing states under the presidency of a progressive pope. The third approach centered on Victor Emmanuel II, the autocratic king of Sardinia-Piedmont. Many Italians sought a federation under this prominent king, much as Germans looked to Prussia for national leadership. It helped that Piedmont was one of the most industrialized, modern territories in the Italian peninsula.

The third alternative was strengthened by the failures of 1848, when Austria smashed Mazzini's republicanism. Victor Emmanuel II, crowned in 1849, retained the liberal constitution granted by his father under duress the previous year. This constitution combined a strong monarchy with a fair degree of civil liberties and parliamentary government, though deputies were elected by a limited franchise based on income. To some of the Italian middle classes, the Kingdom of Sardinia-Piedmont appeared to be a liberal, progressive state ideally suited to drive Austria out of northern Italy and lead a united Italy. By contrast, Mazzini's brand of democratic republicanism seemed quixotic and too radical.

As for the papacy, the initial cautious support for unification under Pope Pius IX (pontificate 1846–1878) had given way to hostility after he was temporarily driven from Rome during the upheavals of 1848. For a long generation, the papacy opposed not only national unification but also most modern trends. In 1864 in the *Syllabus of Errors*, Pius IX denounced rationalism, socialism, separation of church and state, and religious liberty. The Catholic Church would be a bulwark against liberalism and progressive reform for the next two decades.

MAP 23.1 **The Unification of Italy, 1859–1870** The leadership of Sardinia-Piedmont, nationalist fervor, and Garibaldi's attack on the Kingdom of the Two Sicilies were decisive factors in the unification of Italy.

Cavour and Garibaldi in Italy

The struggle for Italian unification under Emmanuel II was supported by a brilliant statesman, Count Camillo Benso di Cavour (kuh-VOOR), who served as prime minister of Sardinia-Piedmont from 1852 until his death in 1861. A nobleman who made a substantial fortune in business before entering politics, Cavour had limited and realistic national goals. Until 1859 he sought unity only with the states of northern and perhaps central Italy, which would nonetheless greatly expand the existing kingdom.

In the 1850s Cavour worked to consolidate Sardinia-Piedmont as a liberal constitutional state capable of leading northern Italy. His program of building highways and railroads, expanding civil liberties, and opposing clerical privilege increased support for his efforts throughout northern Italy. Yet Cavour realized that Sardinia-Piedmont could not drive Austria out of the north without the help of a powerful ally. Accordingly, he established a secret alliance with Napoleon III against Austria in July 1858.

Cavour then goaded Austria into attacking Piedmont in 1859, and Louis Napoleon came to Italy's defense. After defeating the Austrians at the Battles of Magenta and

The Struggle for the Italian Nation

The leading prophet of Italian nationalism and unification before 1848, Giuseppe Mazzini founded a secret society called Young Italy to fight for the unification of the Italian states in a democratic republic. This selection, from the chapter "Duties Towards Your Country" in Mazzini's best-known work, The Duties of Man (1858), was addressed to Italian workingmen.

Your first Duties . . . are to Humanity. . . . But what can each of you, with his isolated powers, do for the moral improvement, for the progress of Humanity? . . .

God gave you the means of multiplying your forces and your powers of action indefinitely when he gave you a Country, when, like a wise overseer of labor, who distributes the different parts of the work according to the capacity of the workmen, he divided Humanity into distinct groups upon the face of our globe, and thus planted the seeds of nations. Evil governments have disfigured the design of God, which you may see clearly marked out, as far, at least, as regards Europe, by the courses of the great rivers, by the lines of the lofty mountains, and by other geographical conditions; they have disfigured it by conquest, by greed, by jealousy of the just sovereignty of others; disfigured it so much that today there is perhaps no nation except England and France whose confines correspond to this design.

[These evil governments] did not, and they do not, recognize any country except their own families and dynasties, the egoism of caste. But the divine design will infallibly be fulfilled. Natural divisions, the innate spontaneous tendencies of the peoples will replace the arbitrary divisions sanctioned by evil governments. The map of Europe will be remade. The Countries of the People will rise, defined by the voice of the free, upon the ruins of the Countries of Kings and privileged castes. Between these

Countries there will be harmony and brotherhood. And then the work of Humanity for the general amelioration, for the discovery and application of the real law of life, carried on in association and distributed according to local capacities, will be accomplished by peaceful and progressive development.

Then each of you, strong in the affections and in the aid of many millions of men speaking the same language, endowed with the same tendencies, and educated by the same historic tradition, may hope by your personal effort to benefit the whole of Humanity.

Without Country you have neither name, voice, nor rights, no admission as brothers into the fellowship of the Peoples. You are the bastards of Humanity. Soldiers without a banner, . . . you will find neither faith nor protection. . . . Do not beguile yourselves with the hope of emancipation from unjust social conditions if you do not first conquer a Country for yourselves; where there is no Country there is no common agreement to which you can appeal; the egoism of self-interest rules alone, and he who has the upper hand keeps it, since there is no common safeguard for the interests of all.

EVALUATE THE EVIDENCE

1. What, according to Mazzini, are the sources of national belonging? What role does religion play in his account? Would you label Mazzini a liberal nationalist?

2. How do Mazzini's ideas on Italian nationhood compare to the other two approaches at the time (see page 757)?

Source: G. Mazzini, *The Duties of Man and Other Essays* (London: J. M. Dent and Sons, 1907), pp. 51–54.

Solferino, however, Napoleon did a sudden about-face. Worried by criticism from French Catholics for supporting the pope's declared enemy, he abandoned Cavour and made a compromise peace with the Austrians in July 1859. The Kingdom of Sardinia-Piedmont received only Lombardy, the area around Milan, from Austria. The rest of Italy remained essentially unchanged.

Yet the skillful maneuvers of Cavour's allies in the moderate nationalist movement salvaged his plans for Italian unification. While the war against Austria raged in the north, pro-unification nationalists in Tuscany and elsewhere in central Italy encouraged popular revolts that easily toppled their ruling princes. Using and controlling this popular enthusiasm, middle-class nationalist leaders in central Italy called for fusion with Sardinia-Piedmont. This was not at all what the Great Powers wanted, but the nationalists held firm. In early 1860, Cavour regained Napoleon III's support by ceding Savoy and Nice to France. The people of central Italy then voted overwhelmingly to join a greatly enlarged kingdom under Victor Emmanuel. Cavour had achieved his original goal, a united northern Italian state (see Map 23.1).

For superpatriots such as Giuseppe Garibaldi (1807–1882), however, the job of unification was only half done. The son of a poor sailor, Garibaldi personified the romantic, revolutionary nationalism and republicanism of Mazzini and 1848. Leading a corps of volunteers against Austria in 1859, Garibaldi emerged in 1860 as an independent force in Italian politics.

Partly to use him and partly to get rid of him, Cavour secretly supported Garibaldi's bold plan to "liberate" the Kingdom of the Two Sicilies. Landing in Sicily in May 1860, Garibaldi's guerrilla band of a thousand **Red Shirts** captured the imagination of the peasantry, who rose in bloody rebellion against their landlords. Outwitting the twenty-thousand-man royal army, the guerrilla leader won battles, gained volunteers, and took Palermo. Then Garibaldi and his men crossed to the mainland, marched triumphantly toward Naples, and prepared to attack Rome and the pope. The wily Cavour quickly sent Sardinian forces to occupy most of the Papal States (but not Rome) and to intercept Garibaldi.

Red Shirts The guerrilla army of Giuseppe Garibaldi, who invaded Sicily in 1860 in an attempt to liberate it, winning the hearts of the Sicilian peasantry.

Cavour realized that an attack on Rome would bring war with France, and he feared Garibaldi's radicalism and popular appeal. He immediately organized a plebiscite in the conquered territories. Despite the urging of some radical supporters, the patriotic Garibaldi did not oppose Cavour, and the people of the south voted to join the kingdom of Sardinia. When Garibaldi and Victor Emmanuel II rode together through Naples to cheering crowds in October 1860, they symbolically sealed the union of north and south, of monarch and nation-state.

Cavour had successfully controlled Garibaldi and turned popular nationalism in a conservative direction. The new kingdom of Italy, which expanded to include Venice in 1866 and Rome in 1870, was a parliamentary monarchy under Victor Emmanuel II, neither radical nor fully democratic. Only a half million out of 22 million Italians had the right to vote, and the propertied classes and the common people remained divided. A great and growing social and cultural gap also separated the progressive, industrializing north from the stagnant, agrarian south. The new Italy was united on paper, but profound divisions remained.

Growing Austro-Prussian Rivalry

In the aftermath of 1848 the German states were locked in a political stalemate. After Austria and Russia blocked Prussian king Friedrich Wilhelm IV's attempt in 1850 to unify Germany, tension grew between Austria and Prussia as they struggled to dominate the German Confederation (see Chapter 21).

Economic differences exacerbated this rivalry. Austria had not been included in the German Customs Union, or *Zollverein* (TZOLE-fur-ayne), when it was founded in 1834 to stimulate trade and increase state revenues. By the end of 1853 Austria was the only state in the German Confederation outside the union. As middle-class and business groups profited from participation in the Zollverein, Prussia's leading role within the customs union gave it a valuable advantage in its struggle against Austria.

Prussia had emerged from the upheavals of 1848 with a weak parliament, which was in the hands of the wealthy liberal middle class by 1859. Longing for national unification, these middle-class representatives wanted to establish once and for all that the parliament, not the king, held ultimate political power, including control of the army. At the same time, the national uprising in Italy in 1859 made a profound impression on Prussia's tough-minded Wilhelm I (r. 1861–1888). Convinced that great political change and war—perhaps with Austria, perhaps with France—were quite possible, Wilhelm I and his top military advisers pushed to raise taxes and increase the defense budget in order to double the size of the army. The Prussian parliament rejected the military budget in 1862, and the liberals triumphed completely in new elections. Wilhelm I then appointed Count Otto von Bismarck as Prussian prime minister and encouraged him to defy the parliament. This was a momentous choice.

Bismarck and the Austro-Prussian War

The most important figure in German history between Martin Luther and Adolf Hitler, Otto von Bismarck (1815–1898) has been the object of enormous interest and debate. A great hero to some and a great villain to others, Bismarck was above all a master of practical politics who first honed his political skills as a high-ranking diplomat for the Prussian government. Born into the Prussian landowning aristocracy and devoted to his sovereign, Bismarck had a strong personality and an unbounded desire for power. Yet in his drive to secure power for himself and for Prussia, Bismarck remained extraordinarily flexible and pragmatic. Keeping his options open, Bismarck moved with determination and cunning toward his goal.

When he took office as prime minister in 1862, in the midst of the constitutional crisis caused by the deadlock on the military budget, Bismarck made a strong but unfavorable impression. Declaring that Wilhelm's government would rule without parliamentary consent, he lashed out at the liberal middle-class opposition: "The great questions of the day will not be decided by speeches and resolutions—that was the blunder of 1848 and 1849—but by blood and iron."

Denounced by liberals for his view that "might makes right," Bismarck had the Prussian bureaucracy go right on collecting taxes, even though the parliament refused to approve the budget. Bismarck also reorganized the army. And for four years, from 1862 to 1866, voters continued to express their opposition by sending large liberal majorities to the parliament.

Opposition at home spurred Bismarck to search for success abroad. The extremely complicated question of Schleswig-Holstein—two provinces that belonged to Denmark but were members of the German Confederation (Map 23.2)—provided a welcome opportunity. In 1864, when the Danish king tried, as he had in 1848, to bring these two provinces into a more centralized Danish state against the will of the German Confederation, Prussia enlisted Austria in a short and successful war against Denmark.

Bismarck, however, was convinced that Prussia had to control completely the northern, predominantly Protestant part of the confederation, which meant expelling Austria from German affairs. After the victory over Denmark, Bismarck's clever maneuvering left Prussia in a position to force Austria out by war. Recognizing that such a war would have to be localized to avoid provoking a larger European alliance against Prussia, Bismarck skillfully neutralized Russia and France.

MAP 23.2 The Unification of Germany, 1864–1871 This map shows how Prussia expanded and a new German Empire was created through the Austro-Prussian War of 1866 and the Franco-Prussian War of 1870–1871.

The Austro-Prussian War of 1866 that followed lasted only seven weeks. Using railroads to quickly mobilize troops, who were armed with new and more efficient breech-loading rifles, the Prussian army defeated Austria decisively at the Battle of Sadowa (SAH-daw-vah) in Bohemia on July 3. Anticipating Prussia's future needs, Bismarck offered Austria generous peace terms. Austria paid no reparations and lost no territory to Prussia, although Venetia was ceded to Italy. But the existing German Confederation was dissolved, and Austria agreed to withdraw from German affairs. Prussia conquered and annexed several small states north of the Main River and completely dominated the remaining principalities in the newly formed North German Confederation. The mainly Catholic states of the south remained independent but allied with Prussia. Bismarck's fundamental goal of Prussian expansion was partially realized (see Map 23.2).

Taming the German Parliament

Bismarck had long been convinced that the old order he so ardently defended would have to make peace, on its own terms, with the liberal middle class and nationalists. Impressed with Napoleon III's example in France, he realized that nationalists were not necessarily hostile to conservative, authoritarian government. Moreover, the events of 1848 convinced Bismarck that the German middle class could be led to prefer national unity under conservative leadership rather than a long, uncertain battle for a truly liberal state. Thus during the Austrian war, he increasingly identified Prussia's fate with the "national development of Germany."

To consolidate Prussian control, Bismarck fashioned a federal constitution for the new North German Confederation. Each state retained its own local government, but the king of Prussia became president of the confederation, and the chancellor—Bismarck—was responsible only to the president. The federal bureaucracy—under Wilhelm I and Bismarck—controlled the army and foreign affairs. A weak federal legislature, with members of the lower house elected by universal male suffrage, gave some voice to popular opinion. With this radical innovation, Bismarck opened the door to the possibility of going over the head of the middle class directly to the people, as Napoleon III had done in France. All the while, however, ultimate power rested in the hands of the Prussian king and army.

In Prussia itself, Bismarck held out an olive branch to the parliamentary opposition. Marshaling all his diplomatic skill, Bismarck asked the parliament to pass a special indemnity bill to approve, after the fact, all the government's spending between 1862 and 1866. With German unity in sight, most of the liberals eagerly cooperated. The constitutional struggle in Prussia ended, and the German middle class came to accept the monarchical authority that Bismarck represented.

The Franco-Prussian War

The final act in the drama of German unification followed quickly. Bismarck calculated that a patriotic war with France would drive the south German states into his arms. Taking advantage of a diplomatic issue—whether a distant relative of Prussia's Wilhelm I might become king of Spain—Bismarck pressed France. By 1870 the French leaders of the Second Empire, goaded by Bismarck and alarmed by their powerful new neighbor, declared war to teach Prussia a lesson.

As soon as war began, Bismarck enlisted support of the south German states. While other governments maintained their neutrality—Bismarck's generosity to Austria in 1866 paid big dividends—combined German forces under Prussian leadership decisively defeated the main French army at Sedan on September 1, 1870. Louis Napoleon himself was captured and humiliated. Three days later, French patriots in Paris proclaimed yet another French republic and vowed to continue fighting. But after five months, in January 1871, a besieged and starving Paris surrendered, and France accepted Bismarck's harsh peace terms.

By this time, the south German states had agreed to join a new German Empire. With Bismarck by his side, Wilhelm I was proclaimed emperor of Germany in the Hall of Mirrors in the palace of Versailles. As in the 1866 constitution, the king of Prussia and his ministers had ultimate power in the new German Empire, and the lower house of the legislature was elected by universal male suffrage.

Bismarck imposed a severe penalty on France: payment of a colossal indemnity of 5 billion francs and loss of the rich eastern province of Alsace and part of Lorraine to

Proclaiming the German Empire, January 1871 This commemorative painting by Anton von Werner testifies to the nationalistic intoxication in Germany after the victory over France at Sedan. Wilhelm I of Prussia stands on a platform surrounded by princes and generals in the famous Hall of Mirrors in the palace of Versailles, while officers from all the units around a besieged Paris cheer and salute him with uplifted swords as emperor of a unified Germany. Bismarck, in white (center), stands between king and army. (By Anton Alexander von Werner [1843–1915]/Schloss Friedrichsruhe, Germany/Bridgeman Images)

Germany. French men and women of all classes viewed these territorial losses as a terrible crime (see Map 23.2). They could never forget and never forgive, poisoning relations between France and Germany after 1871.

The Franco-Prussian War, which many Europeans saw as a test of nations in a pitiless Darwinian struggle for existence, released an enormous surge of patriotic feeling in the German Empire. Bismarck's genius, the invincible Prussian army, the solidarity of king and people in a unified nation—such themes grew immensely popular with many German citizens during and after the war. The weakest of the Great Powers in 1862, Prussia with united Germany had become the most powerful state in Europe in less than a decade, and most Germans were enormously proud. Semi-authoritarian nationalism and a new conservatism, based on an alliance of the landed nobles and middle classes, had triumphed in Germany.

Slavery and Nation Building in the United States

The United States also experienced a process of bloody nation building. Nominally united, the country was divided by the slavery question, and economic development in the young republic carried free and slaveholding states in very different directions. Northerners extended family farms westward and began building English-model factories in the northeast. By 1850 an industrializing, urbanizing North was also building canals and railroads and attracting most of the European immigrants arriving in the nation.

In sharp contrast, industry and cities developed more slowly in the South, and European immigrants largely avoided the region. Even though three-quarters of all Southern white families were small farmers and owned no slaves, plantation owners holding twenty or more slaves dominated the economy and society. These profit-minded slave owners used gangs of enslaved Africans to establish a vast plantation economy

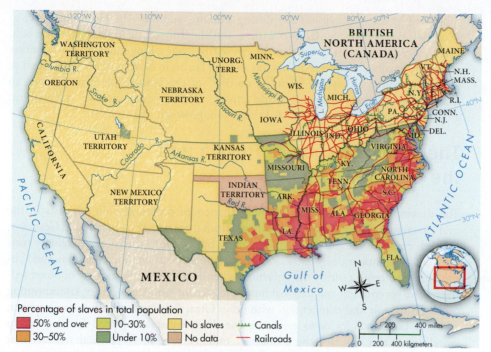

MAP 23.3 Slavery in the United States, 1860   This map shows the United States on the eve of the Civil War. Although many issues contributed to the developing opposition between North and South, slavery was the fundamental, enduring issue that underlay all others. Lincoln's prediction, "I believe this government cannot endure permanently half slave and half free," tragically proved correct.

across the Deep South, where cotton was king (Map 23.3). By 1850 the region produced 5 million bales a year, supplying textile mills in Europe and New England.

The rise of the cotton empire greatly expanded slave-based agriculture in the South, spurred exports, and played a key role in igniting rapid U.S. economic growth. The large profits flowing from cotton led influential Southerners to defend slavery. In doing so, Southern whites developed a strong cultural identity and came to see themselves as a closely knit "we" distinct from the Northern "they." Because Northern whites viewed their free-labor system as more just, and economically and morally superior to slavery, North-South antagonisms intensified.

Tensions reached a climax after 1848 when the United States won the Mexican-American War (1846–1848) and gained a vast area stretching from west Texas to the Pacific Ocean. Debate over the extension of slavery in this new territory hardened attitudes on both sides. Abraham Lincoln's election as president in 1860 gave Southern secessionists the chance they had been waiting for. Determined to win independence, eleven states left the Union and formed the Confederate States of America.

The resulting Civil War (1861–1865), the bloodiest conflict in American history, ended with the South decisively defeated and the Union preserved. In the aftermath of the war, certain dominant characteristics of American life and national culture took shape. Powerful business corporations emerged, steadfastly

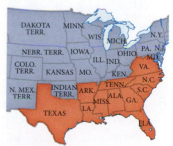

U.S. Secession, 1860–1861

Homestead Act An American law enacted during the Civil War that gave western land to settlers, reinforcing the concept of free labor in a market economy.

supported by the Republican Party during and after the war. The **Homestead Act** of 1862, which gave western land to settlers, and the Thirteenth Amendment of 1865, which ended slavery, reinforced the concept of free labor taking its chances in a market economy. Finally, the success of Lincoln and the North in holding the Union together seemed to confirm that the "manifest destiny" of the United States was indeed to straddle a continent as a great world power. Thus a new American nationalism, grounded in economic and territorial expansion, grew out of a civil war.

The Modernization of Russia and the Ottoman Empire

FOCUS QUESTION

What steps did Russia and the Ottoman Turks take toward modernization, and how successful were they?

The Russian and the Ottoman Empires experienced profound political crises in the mid-nineteenth century. These crises differed from those occurring in Italy and Germany, for both empires were vast multinational states built on long traditions of military conquest and absolutist rule by elites from the dominant Russians and Ottoman Turks. In the early nineteenth century the governing elites in both empires strongly opposed representative government and national independence for ethnic minorities, concentrating on absolutist rule and competition with other Great Powers. For both states, however, relentless power politics led to serious trouble. Their leaders recognized that they had to "modernize" and embrace the economic, military, and social-political reforms that might enable a country to compete effectively with leading European nations.

The "Great Reforms" in Russia

In the 1850s Russia was a poor agrarian society with a rapidly growing population. Almost 90 percent of the people lived off the land, and industrialization developed slowly. Bound to the lord from birth, the peasant serf was little more than a slave, and by the 1840s serfdom had become a central moral and political issue for the government. The slow pace of modernization encouraged the growth of protest movements, from radical Marxists clamoring for socialist revolution to middle-class intellectuals who sought a liberal constitutional state. Then a humiliating Russian defeat in the Crimean War underscored the need for modernizing reforms.

Crimean War A conflict fought between 1853 and 1856 over Russian desires to expand into Ottoman territory; Russia was defeated by France, Britain, and the Ottomans, underscoring the need for reform in the Russian Empire.

The **Crimean War** (1853–1856) grew out of the breakdown of the European balance of power established at the Congress of Vienna (see Chapter 21), general Great Power competition over the Middle East, and Russian desires to expand into the European territories of the Ottoman Empire. A Russian-French dispute over the protection of Christian shrines in Jerusalem sparked the conflict. Famous for incompetent leadership on all sides, the war revealed the awesome power of modern weaponry, particularly artillery, in ways that anticipated the U.S. Civil War. Massive naval engagements, doomed cavalry charges, and staggering casualties—Russia alone lost about 450,000 soldiers—captured the imagination of home-front audiences, who followed events in the national press. By 1856 France and Great Britain, aided by the Ottoman Empire and Sardinia, had joined forces in an effort to limit Russian territorial expansion. This alliance decisively defeated Russia.

The war convinced Russia's leaders that they had fallen behind the industrializing nations of western Europe. At the very least, Russia needed railroads, better armaments, and military reform to remain a Great Power. Moreover, the

The Crimean War, 1853–1856

disastrous war raised the specter of massive peasant rebellion, making reform of serfdom imperative. Military disaster forced liberal-leaning Tsar Alexander II (r. 1855–1881) and his ministers along the path of rapid social change and modernization.

In a bold move, Alexander II abolished serfdom in 1861. About 22 million emancipated peasants received citizenship rights and the chance to purchase, on average, about half of the land they cultivated. Yet they had to pay fairly high prices, and because the land was to be owned collectively, each peasant village was jointly responsible for the payments of all the families in the village. Collective ownership made it difficult for individual peasants to improve agricultural methods or leave their villages. Thus old patterns of behavior predominated, limiting the effects of reform.

Most of Alexander II's later reforms were also halfway measures. In 1864 the government established a new institution of local government, the zemstvo. Members of this local assembly were elected by a three-class system of townspeople, peasant villagers, and noble landowners. A zemstvo executive council dealt with local problems. Russian liberals hoped that this reform would lead to an elected national parliament, but it did not. The zemstvos remained subordinate to the traditional bureaucracy and the local nobility. In addition, changes to the legal system established independent courts and equality before the law. The government relaxed but did not remove censorship, and somewhat liberalized policies toward Russian Jews.

Russian efforts to promote economic modernization proved more successful. Transportation and industry, both vital to the military, were transformed in two industrial surges. The first came after 1860, when the government encouraged and subsidized private railway companies. The railroads linked important cities in the western territories of the empire and enabled Russia to export grain and thus earn money to finance further development. The jewel in the crown of the Russian rail system was the 5,700-mile-long Trans-Siberian Railway. Passing through seven time zones from Moscow to Vladivostok, this crucial rail line brought millions of immigrant peasants from western Russia into the lightly populated areas to the east. The grain they grew was moved west along the line, to help feed the growing cities in Russia's heartland (Map 23.4). Industrial suburbs grew up around Moscow and St. Petersburg, and a class of modern factory workers began to take shape. Industrial development and the growing proletariat class helped spread Marxist thought and spurred the transformation of the Russian revolutionary movement after 1890.

Strengthened by industrial development, Russia began to expand by seizing lands on the borders of the empire. Russia took control of territory in far eastern Siberia, on the border with China, and in Central Asia, north of Afghanistan. The imperial state also encroached upon the Islamic lands of the Caucasus, along the northeast border of the Ottoman Empire. Russian peasants, always hungry for land, used the new rail systems to move to and settle in the newly colonized areas, at times displacing local residents (see Map 23.4). The rapid expansion of the Russian Empire to the south and east excited ardent Russian nationalists and superpatriots, who became some of the government's most enthusiastic supporters. Alexander II consolidated imperial control by suppressing nationalist movements among Poles, Ukrainians, and Baltic peoples in the western lands of the Russian Empire. By 1900 the Russian Empire commanded a vast and diverse array of peoples and places.

Alexander II's political reforms outraged reactionaries but never went far enough for liberals and radicals. In 1881 a member of the "People's Will," a small anarchist group, assassinated the tsar, and the era of reform came to an abrupt end. The new

MAP 23.4 Russian Expansion, 1856–1900
The impressive expansion of the Russian railroad system in the second half of the nineteenth century, capped by the completion of the Trans-Siberian Railroad around 1910, helped Russia integrate territories along its southern and eastern Asian borders into the imperial state.

tsar, Alexander III (r. 1881–1894), was a determined reactionary. Nevertheless, from 1890 to 1900 economic modernization and industrialization surged ahead for the second time, led by Sergei Witte (suhr-GAY VIH-tuh), finance minister from 1892 to 1903. The tough, competent Witte believed that industrial backwardness threatened Russia's greatness. Under his leadership, the government doubled the network of state-owned railways to thirty-five thousand miles. Witte established high protective tariffs to support Russian industry, and he put the country on the gold standard to strengthen Russian finances.

Witte's greatest innovation was to use Westerners to catch up with the West. He encouraged foreigners to build factories in Russia, believing that "the inflow of foreign capital is . . . the only way by which our industry will be able to supply our country quickly with abundant and cheap products."[1] His efforts to entice western Europeans to locate their factories in Russia were especially successful in southern Russia. There, in eastern Ukraine, foreign entrepreneurs and engineers built an enormous and very modern steel and coal industry. In 1900 peasants still constituted the great majority of the population, but Russia was catching up with the more industrialized West.

The Russian Revolution of 1905

Catching up partly meant further territorial expansion, for this was the age of Western imperialism. By 1903 Russia had established a sphere of influence in Chinese Manchuria and was eyeing northern Korea, which put Russia in conflict with the goals of an equally imperialistic Japan. Tsar Nicholas II (r. 1894–1917), who replaced his father in 1894, ignored their diplomatic protests. In response, the Japanese launched a surprise attack on Port Arthur, a Russian naval base in northern China, in February 1904. The resulting Russo-Japanese war lasted less than a year. After Japan scored repeated victories, which included annihilating a Russian fleet, the humiliated Russians surrendered in September 1905.

Once again, military disaster abroad brought political upheaval at home. The business and professional classes had long wanted a liberal, representative government. Urban factory workers were organized in a radical and still-illegal labor movement. Peasants had gained little from the era of reforms and suffered from poverty and overpopulation. At the same time, the empire's minorities and subject nationalities, such as the Poles, the Ukrainians, and the Latvians, continued to call for self-rule. With the army pinned down in Manchuria, all these currents of discontent converged in the revolution of 1905.

On a Sunday in January 1905, a massive crowd of workers and their families converged peacefully on the Winter Palace in St. Petersburg to present a petition to Nicholas II. Suddenly troops opened fire, killing and wounding hundreds. The **Bloody Sunday** massacre produced a wave of general indignation that turned many Russians against the tsar. (See "Evaluating the Evidence 23.2: Eyewitness Accounts of Bloody Sunday," page 770.)

By the summer of 1905 strikes and political rallies, peasant uprisings, revolts among minority nationalities, and mutinies by troops were sweeping the country. The revolutionary surge culminated in October 1905 in a paralyzing general strike that forced the government to capitulate. The tsar then issued the October Manifesto, which granted full civil rights and promised a popularly elected **Duma** (or parliament) with real legislative power. The manifesto split the opposition. Frightened middle-class leaders embraced it, which helped the government repress the popular uprising and survive as a constitutional monarchy.

On the eve of the opening of the first Duma in May 1906, the government issued the new constitution, the Fundamental Laws. The tsar retained great powers. The Duma, elected indirectly by universal male suffrage with a largely appointive upper house, could debate and pass laws, but the tsar had an absolute veto. As in Bismarck's Germany, the tsar appointed his ministers, who did not need to command a majority in the Duma.

The predominantly middle-class liberals, the largest group in the newly elected Duma, saw the Fundamental Laws as a step backward. Cooperation with Nicholas II's ministers soon broke down, and after months of deadlock the tsar dismissed the Duma. Thereupon he and his advisers, including the talented Pyotr Stolypin, who served as prime minister, unilaterally rewrote the electoral law. These revisions greatly increased the electoral weight of the conservative propertied classes. When new elections were held, the tsar could count on a legislative majority loyal to the monarchy. His government then pushed through important agrarian reforms designed to break down collective village ownership of land and encourage the more enterprising peasants—Stolypin's "wager on the strong and sober," meant to encourage economic growth. The government reformed the education and banking systems, but these acts were accompanied by harsh repression of dissidents and radicals. About three thousand suspected revolutionaries were executed by the state, and the hangman's noose became known as "Stolypin's necktie." In 1914, on the eve of the First World War, Russia was partially modernized, a conservative constitutional monarchy with a peasant-based but industrializing economy and significant pockets of discontent.

Reform and Readjustment in the Ottoman Empire

By the early nineteenth century the economic and political changes reshaping Europe were also at play in the Ottoman Empire, which stretched around the northeastern, eastern, and southern shores of the Mediterranean Sea. The borderlands of this vast

Bloody Sunday A massacre of peaceful protesters at the Winter Palace in St. Petersburg in 1905, triggering a revolution that overturned absolute tsarist rule and made Russia into a conservative constitutional monarchy.

Duma The Russian parliament that opened in 1906, elected indirectly by universal male suffrage but controlled after 1907 by the tsar and the conservative classes.

Eyewitness Accounts of Bloody Sunday

Newspaper reporters for the Times *(London) and* Le Matin *(Paris) expressed shock at the rapid outbreak of deadly violence on Bloody Sunday (January 22, 1905), one of the events that sparked the Russian Revolution of 1905. The Cossacks referred to in the* Times *account were soldiers recruited from Russia's southern steppes. Father Gapon, also mentioned in that report, was an Orthodox priest who led the march.*

From the *Times* (London)

Event has succeeded event with such bewildering rapidity that the public is staggered and shocked beyond measure. The first trouble began at 11 o'clock, when the military tried to turn back some thousands of strikers at one of the bridges . . . where the constant flow of workmen pressing forward refused to be denied access to the common rendezvous in the Palace Square. The Cossacks at first used their knouts [whips], then the flat of their sabers, and finally they fired. The strikers in the front ranks fell on their knees and implored the Cossacks to let them pass, protesting that they had no hostile intentions. They refused, however, to be intimidated by blank cartridges, and orders were given to load with ball.

The passions of the mob broke loose like a bursting dam. The people, seeing the dead and dying carried away in all directions, the snow on the streets and pavements soaked with blood, cried aloud for vengeance. Meanwhile the situation at the Palace was becoming momentarily worse. The troops were reported to be unable to control the vast masses which were constantly surging forward. Re-enforcements were sent, and at 2 o'clock here also the order was given to fire. Men, women, and children fell at each volley, and were carried away in ambulances, sledges, and carts. The indignation and fury of every class were aroused. Students, merchants, all classes of the population alike were inflamed. At the moment of writing, firing is going on in every quarter of the city.

Father Gapon, marching at the head of a large body of workmen, carrying a cross and other religious emblems, was wounded in the arm and shoulder. The two forces of workmen are now separated. Those on the other side of the river are arming with swords, knives, and smiths' and carpenters' tools, and are busy erecting barricades. The troops are apparently reckless, firing right and left, with or without reason. The rioters continue to appeal to them, saying, "You are Russians! Why play the part of bloodthirsty butchers?" . . .

A night of terror is in prospect.

From *Le Matin* (Paris)

The soldiers of the Preobrazhensky regiment, without any summons to disperse, shoot down the unfortunate people as if they were playing at bloodshed. Several hundred fall; more than a hundred and fifty are killed. They are almost all children, women, and young people. It is terrible. Blood flows on all sides. At 5 o'clock the crowd is driven back, cut down and repelled on all sides. The people, terror-stricken, fly in every direction. Scared women and children slip, fall, rise to their feet, only to fall again farther on. At this moment a sharp word of command is heard and the victims fall en masse. There had been no disturbances to speak of. The whole crowd is unarmed and has not uttered a single threat.

EVALUATE THE EVIDENCE

1. Can you begin to reconstruct the events of Bloody Sunday from these reports? Who seems to be responsible for the violence?
2. Did popular protest help ordinary people win rights from the Russian state?

Source: James Harvey Robinson and Charles Beard, eds., *Readings in Modern European History*, vol. 2 (Boston: Ginn and Company, 1909), pp. 373–374.

---

empire experienced constant flux and conflict. Russia had occupied Ottoman provinces on the Danube River in the last decades of the eighteenth century and grabbed more during the Napoleonic Wars. In 1816 the Ottomans were forced to grant Serbia local autonomy. In 1830 the Greeks won independence, and French armies began their long and bloody takeover of Ottoman Algeria. Yet the Ottomans achieved important victories during the same decades. Egyptian forces under the leadership of Muhammad Ali, the Ottoman governor in Egypt, restored order in the Islamic holy lands and conquered significant portions of Sudan, south of Egypt.

Muhammad Ali, a ruthless and intelligent soldier-politician, ruled Egypt in the name of the Ottoman sultan from 1805 to 1848. His modernizing reforms of agriculture, industry, and the military (see Chapter 24) helped turn Egypt into the most powerful state in the eastern Mediterranean. In time, his growing strength directly challenged the Ottoman sultan and Istanbul's ruling elite. From 1831 to 1840 Egyptian troops under the leadership of Muhammad Ali's son Ibrahim occupied and governed the Ottoman province of Syria and Palestine, and threatened to depose the Ottoman sultan Mahmud II (r. 1808–1839).

This conflict forced the Ottomans to seek European support. Mahmud II's dynasty survived, but only because the European powers, led by Britain, allied with the Ottomans to discipline Muhammad Ali. The European powers preferred a weak and dependent Ottoman Empire to a strong, economically independent state under a dynamic leader such as Muhammad Ali.

Pasha Hilim Receiving Archduke Maximilian of Austria   As this painting suggests, Ottoman leaders became well versed in European languages and culture. They also mastered the game of power politics, playing one European state against another to secure the Ottoman Empire's survival. (By Peter Johann Nepomuk Geiger [1805–1880]/Miramare Palace, Trieste, Italy/Alfredo Dagli Orti/The Art Archive at Art Resource, NY)

Faced with growing European military and economic competition, liberal Ottoman statesmen in 1839 launched an era of radical reforms known as the **Tanzimat**, or "Reorganization." The Tanzimat reforms, borrowed from western European models, were designed to modernize the empire. The high point of reform came when the new liberal-minded sultan, Abdul Mejid (r. 1839–1861), issued the Imperial Rescript of 1856, just after the Crimean War. Articles in the decree called for equality before the law regardless of religious faith, a modernized administration and army, and private ownership of land. As part of the reform policy, and under economic pressure from the European powers that had paid for the empire's war against Russia in Crimea, Ottoman leaders adopted free-trade policies. New commercial laws removed tariffs on foreign imports and permitted foreign merchants to operate freely throughout the empire.

The turn to nineteenth-century liberal capitalism had mixed effects. On one hand, with the growth of Western-style banking and insurance systems, elite Christian and Jewish businessmen in the empire prospered. Yet the bulk of the profits went to foreign investors rather than Ottoman subjects. More important, the elimination of traditional state-controlled monopolies sharply cut imperial revenues. In 1851 Sultan Mejid was forced to borrow 55 million francs from British and French bankers to cover state deficits. Other loans followed, and intractable indebtedness led to the bankruptcy of the Ottoman state two decades later.

Intended to bring revolutionary modernization, the Tanzimat permitted partial recovery but fell short of its goals. The Ottoman initiatives did not curtail the appetite of Western imperialists, who secured a stranglehold on the imperial economy via

Tanzimat   A set of reforms designed to remake the Ottoman Empire on a western European model.

issuing loans. The reforms also failed to halt the growth of nationalism among some Christian subjects in the Balkans, which resulted in crises and increased pressure from neighboring Austria and Russia, eager to gain access to the Balkans and the eastern Mediterranean.

Finally, equality before the law for all citizens, regardless of religious affiliation, actually increased religious disputes, which were often encouraged and manipulated by the European powers eager to seize any pretext for intervention. This development embittered relations between religious conservatives and social liberals, a struggle that ultimately distracted the government from its reform mission. Religious conservatives in both the Muslim and Greek Orthodox communities detested the religious reforms, which they viewed as an impious departure from tradition. These conservatives became dependable supporters of Sultan Abdülhamid II (ahb-dool-hah-MEED) (r. 1876–1909), who in 1876 halted the reform movement and turned away from European liberalism in his long and repressive reign.

Abdülhamid II's government failed to halt foreign efforts to fragment and ultimately take control over key Ottoman territories. Defeat in the Russo-Turkish War (1877–1878) meant the loss to Russia of Ottoman districts in the Caucasus; formal declarations of independence for Romania, Montenegro, and Serbia, all former Ottoman territories in the Balkans; and the establishment of an autonomous Bulgaria, still nominally under the Ottoman sultan's control. By the 1890s the government's failures had encouraged a powerful resurgence of the modernizing impulse under the banner of the Committee of Union and Progress (CUP), an umbrella organization that united multiethnic reformist groups from across the empire. These fervent patriots, unofficially called the **Young Turks**, seized power in a 1908 coup and forced the sultan to implement new reforms. Although they failed to stop the rising tide of anti-Ottoman nationalism in the Balkans, the Young Turks helped prepare the way for the rise of modern secular Turkey after the defeat and collapse of the Ottoman Empire in World War I.

Young Turks Fervent patriots who seized power in a 1908 coup in the Ottoman Empire, forcing the conservative sultan to implement reforms.

The Responsive National State, 1871–1914

FOCUS QUESTION

What general domestic political trends emerged after 1871?

The decades after 1870 brought rapid change to the structures and ideas of European politics. Despite some major differences between countries, European domestic politics had a new common framework, the nation-state. The common themes within that framework were the emergence of mass politics and growing popular loyalty toward the nation. Traditional elites hardly disappeared, but they were forced into new arrangements in order to exercise power, and a group of new, pragmatic politicians took leading roles. The major states of western Europe adopted constitutions of some sort, and universal male suffrage was granted in Britain, France, and Germany and elsewhere, at least in voting for the lower houses of parliament. New political parties representing a broad spectrum of interests and groups, from workers and liberals to Catholics and conservatives, engaged in hard-fought election campaigns to provide benefits to their constituencies.

Powerful bureaucracies emerged to govern growing populations and manage modern economies, and the growth of the state spurred a growth in the social responsibilities of government. The new responsive national state offered its citizens free education and some welfare and public health benefits, and for good reason many ordinary people felt increasing loyalty to their governments and their nations.

Building popular support for strong nation-states had a less positive side. Conservative and moderate leaders both found that workers who voted socialist—whose potential revolutionary power they feared—would rally around the flag in a diplomatic crisis or cheer when colonial interests seized a distant territory of doubtful value. Therefore, after 1871 governing elites frequently used antiliberal militarist and imperialist policies in attempts to unite national populations and overcome or mask intractable domestic conflicts. In the end, the manipulation of foreign policy to manage domestic issues inflamed the international tensions that erupted in the cataclysms of World War I and the Russian Revolution.

The German Empire

The history of Germany after 1871 exemplified many of these general political developments. Like the United States, the new German Empire adopted a federal system: a union of Prussia and twenty-four smaller states, each with separate legislatures. Much of the everyday business of government was conducted by the individual states, but there was a strong national government with a chancellor—until 1890, Bismarck—and a popularly elected national parliament called the **Reichstag** (RIKES-tahg). Although Bismarck repeatedly ignored the wishes of the parliamentary majority, he nonetheless preferred to win the support of the Reichstag to lend legitimacy to his policy goals. This situation gave the political parties opportunities to influence national policy. Until 1878 Bismarck relied mainly on the National Liberals, who had rallied to him after 1866. They supported legislation useful for economic growth and unification of the country.

Less wisely, the National Liberals backed Bismarck's attack on the Catholic Church, the so-called **Kulturkampf** (kool-TOOR-kahmpf), or "culture struggle." Like Bismarck, the middle-class National Liberals were alarmed by Pius IX's declaration of papal infallibility in 1870. That dogma seemed to ask German Catholics to put loyalty to their church, a foreign power, above their loyalty to their newly unified nation. Kulturkampf initiatives aimed at making the Catholic Church subject to government control. However, only in Protestant Prussia did the Kulturkampf have even limited success, because elsewhere Catholics generally voted for the Center Party, which blocked passage of laws hostile to the church.

In 1878 Bismarck abandoned his attack on the church and instead courted the Catholic Center Party, whose supporters included many Catholic small farmers in western and southern Germany. By revoking free-trade policy and enacting high tariffs on cheap grain from the United States, Canada, and Russia, he won over both the Catholic Center and the conservative Protestant Junkers, nobles with large landholdings in East Prussia.

Other governments followed Bismarck's lead, and the 1880s and 1890s saw a widespread return to protectionism in Europe. France, in particular, established very high tariffs to protect agriculture and industry. By raising tariffs, European governments offered an effective response to a major domestic economic problem—foreign competition—in a way that won greater popular loyalty. At the same time, the rise of protectionism exemplified the dangers of self-centered nationalism: new tariffs led to international name-calling and nasty trade wars.

After the failure of the Kulturkampf, Bismarck's government tried to stop the growth of the **German Social Democratic Party (SPD)**, Germany's Marxist, working-class political party, which was established in the 1870s. Both conservative elites and

Reichstag The popularly elected lower house of government of the new German Empire after 1871.

Kulturkampf Bismarck's attack on the Catholic Church within Germany from 1870 to 1878, resulting from Pius IX's declaration of papal infallibility.

German Social Democratic Party (SPD) A German working-class political party founded in the 1870s, the SPD championed Marxism but in practice turned away from Marxist revolution and worked instead in the German parliament for social and workplace reforms.

middle-class liberals genuinely feared the SPD's revolutionary language and allegiance to a Marxist movement that transcended the nation-state. In 1878 Bismarck pushed through the Reichstag the Anti-Socialist Laws, which banned Social Democratic associations, meetings, and publications. The Social Democratic Party was driven underground, but it maintained substantial influence, and Bismarck decided to try another tack.

In an attempt to win working-class support, Bismarck urged the Reichstag to enact a variety of state-supported social welfare measures. Big business and some conservatives accused him of creating "state socialism," but Bismarck ably pressed his program in many lively speeches, as the following excerpt suggests:

> Give the working-man the right to work as long as he is healthy; assure him care when he is sick; assure him maintenance when he is old. If you do that, and do not fear the [financial] sacrifice, or cry out at State Socialism as soon as the words "provision for old age" are uttered, — if the state would show a little more Christian solicitude for the working-man, then I believe the gentlemen of the Wyden [Social Democratic] program will sound their bird-call in vain, and that the thronging toward them will cease as soon as working-men see that the Government and legislative bodies are earnestly concerned with their welfare.[2]

Bismarck and his supporters carried the day, and his essentially conservative nation-state pioneered in providing social welfare programs. In 1883 he pushed through the Reichstag the first of several social security laws to help wage earners by providing national sickness insurance. An 1884 law created accident insurance; one from 1889 established old-age pensions and retirement benefits. Henceforth sick, injured, and retired workers could look forward to some regular benefits from the state. This national social security system, paid for through compulsory contributions by wage earners and employers as well as grants from the state, was the first of its kind anywhere. Bismarck's social security system did not wean workers from voting socialist, but it did give them a small stake in the system and protect them from some of the uncertainties of the competitive industrial economy. This enormously significant development was a product of political competition, as well as government efforts to win popular support by defusing the SPD's radical appeal.

Increasingly, the key issue in German domestic politics was socialism and, specifically, the rapid growth of the SPD. In 1890 the new emperor, the young, idealistic, and unstable Wilhelm II (r. 1888–1918), opposed Bismarck's attempt to renew the Anti-Socialist Laws. Eager to rule in his own right and to earn the support of the workers, Wilhelm II forced Bismarck to resign. Afterward, German foreign policy changed profoundly and mostly for the worse, but the government did pass new laws to aid workers and legalize socialist political activity.

Yet Wilhelm II was no more successful than Bismarck in getting workers to renounce socialism. Indeed, Social Democrats won more and more seats in the Reichstag, becoming Germany's largest single party in 1912. Though this electoral victory shocked aristocrats and their wealthy, conservative allies, who held exaggerated fears of an impending socialist upheaval, the revolutionary socialists had actually become less radical in Germany. In the years before World War I, the SPD broadened its base by adopting a more patriotic tone, allowing for greater military spending and imperialist expansion. German socialists abandoned revolutionary aims to concentrate instead on gradual social and political reform (see pages 783–787).

Republican France

Although Napoleon III's reign made some progress in reducing antagonisms between classes, the Franco-Prussian War undid these efforts. In 1871 France seemed hopelessly divided once again. The patriotic republicans who proclaimed the Third Republic in Paris after the military disaster at Sedan refused to admit defeat by the Germans. They defended Paris with great heroism for weeks, living off rats and zoo animals until they were starved into submission by German armies in January 1871.

When the next national elections sent a large majority of conservatives and monarchists to the National Assembly and France's new leaders decided they had no choice but to surrender Alsace (al-SAS) and Lorraine to Germany, the traumatized Parisians exploded in patriotic frustration and proclaimed the Paris Commune in March 1871. Avowedly radical, the leaders of the Commune wanted to establish a revolutionary government in Paris and rule without interference from the conservative French countryside. Their program included workplace reforms, the separation of church and state, press censorship, and radical feminism. The National Assembly, led by aging politician Adolphe Thiers (TEE-ehr), ordered the French army into Paris and brutally crushed the Commune. Twenty thousand people died in the fighting. As in June 1848, it was Paris against the provinces, French against French.

Out of this tragedy, France slowly formed a new national unity, achieving considerable stability before 1914. How do we account for this? Luck played a part. Until 1875 the monarchists in the ostensibly republican National Assembly had a majority but could not agree on who should be king. The compromise Bourbon candidate refused to rule except under the white flag of his absolutist ancestors—a completely unacceptable condition for many supporters of a constitutional monarchy. In the meantime, Thiers's destruction of the radical Commune and his other firm measures showed the fearful provinces and the middle classes that the Third Republic could be politically moderate and socially conservative. France therefore reluctantly retained republican government. As President Thiers cautiously said, this was "the government which divides us least."

Another stabilizing factor was the skill and determination of moderate republican leaders in the early years. The most famous was Léon Gambetta (gam-BEH-tuh), the son of an Italian grocer, a warm, easygoing, unsuccessful lawyer turned professional politician. By 1879 the great majority of members of both the upper and the lower houses of the National Assembly were republicans, and the Third Republic had firm foundations after almost a decade.

The moderate republicans sought to preserve their creation by winning the allegiance of the next generation. The Assembly legalized trade unions, and France worked to expand its colonial empire. More important, a series of laws between 1879 and 1886 greatly expanded the state system of public, tax-supported schools and established free compulsory elementary education for both girls and boys. In the past, most elementary and much secondary education had occurred in Catholic schools, which had long been hostile to republics and much of secular life. Free compulsory elementary education became secular republican education. Not only in France, but throughout the Western world, the expansion of public education served as a critical nation-building tool in the late nineteenth century.

Although the educational reforms of the 1880s disturbed French Catholics, many of them rallied to the republic in the 1890s. The limited acceptance of the modern world by the more liberal Pope Leo XIII (pontificate 1878–1903) eased conflicts between church and state. Unfortunately, the **Dreyfus affair** renewed church-state tensions.

In 1894 Alfred Dreyfus, a Jewish captain in the French army, was falsely accused and convicted of treason. His family never doubted his innocence and fought to reopen the case, enlisting the support of prominent republicans and intellectuals, including novelist Émile Zola. In 1898 and 1899 the case split France apart. On one side was the army, which had manufactured evidence against Dreyfus, joined by anti-Semites, conservative nationalists, and most of the Catholic establishment. On the other side stood liberals and most of the more radical republicans.

Dreyfus was eventually declared innocent, but the battle revived republican animosity toward the Catholic Church. Between 1901 and 1905 the government severed all ties between the state and the church. The government stopped paying priests' and bishops' salaries and placed committees of lay Catholics in control of all churches. Suddenly on their own financially, Catholic schools soon lost a third of their students, greatly increasing the state school system's reach and thus its power of indoctrination. Thus deep religious and political divisions, as well as a growing socialist movement (see page 787), challenged the apparent stability of the Third Republic.

Great Britain and Ireland

Historians often cast late-nineteenth-century Britain as a shining example of peaceful and successful political evolution, where an effective two-party Parliament skillfully guided the country from classical liberalism to full-fledged democracy with hardly a misstep. This "Whig view" of Great Britain is not so much wrong as it is incomplete. After the right to vote was granted to males of the wealthy middle class in 1832, opinion leaders and politicians wrestled for some time with further expansion of the franchise. In 1867 the Second Reform Bill of Benjamin Disraeli and the Conservative Party extended the vote to all middle-class males and the best-paid workers in order to broaden their own base of support beyond the landowning class. After 1867 English political parties and electoral campaigns became more modern, and the "lower orders" appeared to vote as responsibly as their "betters." Hence the Third Reform Bill of 1884 gave the vote to almost every adult male.

While the House of Commons drifted toward democracy, the House of Lords was content to slumber nobly. Between 1901 and 1910, however, the Lords tried to reassert itself. Acting as supreme court of the land, it ruled against labor unions in two important decisions. And after the Liberal Party came to power in 1906, the Lords vetoed several measures passed by the Commons, including the so-called **People's Budget**, designed to increase spending on social welfare services. When the king threatened to create enough new peers to pass the bill, the Lords finally capitulated, as they had with the Reform Bill of 1832 (see Chapter 21). Aristocratic conservatism yielded to popular democracy.

Extensive social welfare measures, previously slow to come to Great Britain, were passed in a spectacular rush between 1906 and 1914. During those years the Liberal Party, inspired by the fiery Welshman David Lloyd George (1863–1945), enacted the People's Budget and substantially raised taxes on the rich. This income helped the government pay for national health insurance, unemployment benefits, old-age pensions, and a host of other social measures. The state tried to integrate the urban masses socially as well as politically, though the refusal to grant women the right to vote encouraged a

Dreyfus affair A divisive case in which Alfred Dreyfus, a Jewish captain in the French army, was falsely accused and convicted of treason. The Catholic Church sided with the anti-Semites against Dreyfus; after Dreyfus was declared innocent, the French government severed all ties between the state and the church.

People's Budget A bill proposed after the Liberal Party came to power in Britain in 1906, it was designed to increase spending on social welfare services, but was initially vetoed in the House of Lords.

determined and increasingly militant suffrage movement (see Chapter 22).

This record of accomplishment was only part of the story, however. On the eve of World War I, the unanswered question of Ireland brought Great Britain to the brink of civil war. The terrible Irish famine of the 1840s and early 1850s had fueled an Irish revolutionary movement. The Irish Republican Brotherhood, established in 1858 and known as the "Fenians," engaged in violent campaigns against British rule. The British responded with repression and arrests (see image at right). Seeking a way out of the conflict, the English slowly granted concessions, such as rights for Irish peasants and the abolition of the privileges of the Anglican Church. Liberal prime minister William Gladstone (1809–1898), who twenty years earlier had proclaimed, "My mission is to pacify Ireland," introduced bills to give Ireland self-government, or home rule, in 1886 and in 1893. They failed to pass, but in 1913 Irish nationalists finally gained such a bill for Ireland.

Irish Home Rule   In December 1867 members of the "Fenians," an underground group dedicated to Irish independence from British rule, detonated a bomb outside Clerkenwell Prison in London. Their attempt to liberate Irish Republican activists failed. Though the bomb blew a hole in the prison walls, damaged nearby buildings, and killed twelve innocent bystanders, no Fenians were freed. The British labeled the event the "Clerkenwell Outrage," and its violence evokes revealing parallels with the radical terrorist attacks of today. (From *Illustrierte Zeitung*, Leipzig, Germany, 4 January 1868/akg-images)

Thus Ireland, the Emerald Isle, was on the brink of achieving self-government. Yet to the same extent that the Catholic majority in the southern counties wanted home rule, the Protestants of the northern counties of Ulster came to oppose it. Motivated by the accumulated fears and hostilities of generations, the Ulster Protestants refused to submerge themselves in a majority-Catholic Ireland, just as Irish Catholics had refused to submit to a Protestant Britain.

The Ulsterites vowed to resist home rule. By December 1913 they had raised one hundred thousand armed volunteers, and much of English public opinion supported their cause. In response, in 1914 the Liberals in the House of Lords introduced a compromise home-rule bill that did not apply to the northern counties. This bill, which openly betrayed promises made to Irish nationalists, was rejected in the Commons, and in September the original home-rule bill passed but with its implementation delayed. The Irish question had been overtaken by the earth-shattering world war that began in August 1914, and final resolution was suspended for the duration of the hostilities.

Irish developments illustrated once again the power of national feeling and national movements in the nineteenth century. Moreover, they demonstrated that central governments could not elicit greater loyalty unless they could capture and control that elemental current of national feeling. Though Great Britain had much going for it—power, parliamentary rule, prosperity—none of these availed in the face of the conflicting nationalisms created by Irish Catholics and Protestants. Similarly, progressive Sweden was powerless to stop a Norwegian national movement, which culminated in Norway's leaving Sweden and becoming fully independent in 1905. In this light, one can also understand the difficulties faced by the Ottoman Empire in the Balkans in the late nineteenth century. It was only a matter of time before the Serbs, Bulgarians, and Romanians would break away.

The Austro-Hungarian Empire

The dilemma of conflicting nationalisms in Ireland or the Ottoman Empire helps one appreciate how desperate the situation in the Austro-Hungarian Empire had become by the early twentieth century. In 1848 Magyar nationalism had driven Hungarian patriots to declare an independent Hungarian republic, which Russian and Austrian armies savagely crushed in the summer of 1849 (see Chapter 21). Throughout the 1850s Hungary was ruled as a conquered territory, and Emperor Franz Joseph and his bureaucracy tried hard to centralize the state and Germanize the language and culture of the different ethnic groups there.

Then, in the wake of its defeat by Prussia in 1866 and the loss of northern Italy, a weakened Austria agreed to a compromise and in 1867 established the so-called dual monarchy. The Austrian Empire was divided in two, and the Magyars gained virtual independence for Hungary. Henceforth each half of the empire dealt with its own ethnic minorities. The two states still shared the same monarch and common ministries for finance, defense, and foreign affairs.

In Austria, ethnic Germans were only one-third of the population, and many Germans saw their traditional dominance threatened by Czechs, Poles, and other Slavs. The language used in government and elementary education at the local level became a particularly emotional issue in the Austrian parliament. From 1900 to 1914 the legislature was so divided that ministries generally could not obtain a majority and ruled instead by decree. Efforts by both conservatives and socialists to defuse national antagonisms by stressing economic issues that cut across ethnic lines were largely unsuccessful.

In Hungary, the Magyar nobility in 1867 restored the constitution of 1848 and used it to dominate both the Magyar peasantry and the minority populations until 1914. Only the wealthiest one-fourth of adult males had the right to vote, making the parliament the creature of the Magyar elite. Laws promoting the use of the Magyar language in schools and government were bitterly resented, especially by Croatians and Romanians. While Magyar extremists campaigned loudly for total separation from Austria, the radical leaders of their subject nationalities dreamed of independence from Hungary. Unlike most major countries, which harnessed nationalism to strengthen the state after 1871, the Austro-Hungarian Empire was progressively weakened by it.

The Nation and the People

FOCUS QUESTION
How did popular nationalism evolve in the last decades of the nineteenth century?

In the first two-thirds of the nineteenth century, nationalism convulsed the autocratic states of Europe. Liberal constitutionalists and radical republicans championed the national idea as a way to challenge authoritarian monarchs, liberate minority groups from imperial rule, and unify diverse territories into a single state. Yet in the decades after 1870 — corresponding to the rise of the responsive national state — nationalist ideology evolved in a different direction. Nationalism began to appeal more to those on the right wing of the political spectrum than the left. In these same years the "us-them" outlook associated with nationalism gained force, bolstered by modern scientific racism. Some fanatics and demagogic political leaders sought to build extreme nationalist movements by whipping up racist animosity toward imaginary enemies, especially Jews. The growth of modern anti-Semitism after 1880 epitomized the most negative aspects of European nationalism before the First World War.

Making National Citizens

Responding to national unification, an Italian statesman famously remarked, "We have made Italy. Now we must make Italians." His comment captured the dilemma faced by political leaders in the last third of the nineteenth century. As the nation-state extended voting rights and welfare benefits to more and more people, the question of national loyalty became more and more pressing. Politicians and nationalist ideologues made forceful attempts to ensure the people's conformity to their laws, but how could they ensure that national governments would win their citizens' heartfelt allegiance?

The issue was pressing. The recent unification of Italy and Germany, for example, had brought together a patchwork of previously independent states with different customs, loyalties, and in some cases languages. In Italy, only about 2 percent of the population spoke the language that would become official Italian. In Germany, regional and religious differences and strong traditions of local political autonomy undermined collective feeling. In Great Britain, deep class differences still dampened national unity, and across the territories of central and eastern Europe, overlapping ethnic groups with distinct languages and cultures challenged the logic of nation building. Even in France, where national boundaries had been fairly stable for several centuries, only about 50 percent of the people spoke proper French. The 60 percent of the population that still lived in rural areas often felt stronger allegiance to their village or region than to the distant nation headquartered in Paris.

Yet by the 1890s most ordinary people had accepted, if not embraced, the notion of national belonging. There were various reasons for nationalism's growing popularity. For one, modern nation-states imposed centralized institutions across their entire territories, which reached even the lowliest citizen. Universal military conscription, introduced in most of Europe after the Franco-Prussian War (Britain was an exception), yanked peasants off their land and workers out of their factories and exposed young male conscripts to patriotic values. Free compulsory education leveled out language differences and taught children about glorious national traditions. In Italy and Germany, the introduction of a common currency, standard weights and measurements, and a national post office eroded regional differences. Boasting images of grand historical events or prominent leaders, even postage stamps and banknotes could impart a sense of national solidarity.

Improved transportation and communication networks broke down regional differences and reinforced the national idea as well. The extension of railroad service into hinterlands and the improvement of local roads shattered rural isolation, boosted the growth of national markets for commercial agriculture, and helped turn "peasants into Frenchmen."[3] Literacy rates and compulsory schooling advanced rapidly in the late nineteenth century, and more and more people read about national history or the latest political events in growing numbers of newspapers, magazines, and books.

A diverse group of intellectuals, politicians, and ideologues of all stripes eagerly promoted national pride. At Humboldt University in Berlin, for example, the prominent history professor Heinrich von Treitschke championed German superiority, especially over archrival Great Britain. Scholars like Treitschke uncovered the deep roots of national identity in ancient folk traditions; in shared language, customs, race, and religion; and in historic attachments to national territory. Such accounts, often based on flimsy historical evidence, were popularized in the classroom and the press. Few nationalist thinkers sympathized with French philosopher Ernest Renan, who suggested that national identity was based more on a people's current desire for a "common life" and an invented, heroic past than on actual, true-to-life historical experiences.

A variety of new symbols and rituals brought nationalism into the lives of ordinary people. Each nation had its own unique capital city, flag, military uniform, and national anthem. New symbols, such as Britain's doughty John Bull, France's republican Marianne, America's stern Uncle Sam, and Germany's solid Michel, supposedly embodied shared national characteristics. All citizens could participate in newly invented national holidays, such as Bastille Day in France, first held in 1880 to commemorate the French Revolution, or Sedan Day in Germany, created to celebrate Germany's victory over France in 1871. Royal weddings, coronations, jubilees, and funerals brought citizens into the streets to celebrate the nation's leaders—Queen Victoria's 1887 Golden Jubilee set a high standard. Public squares and parks received prominent commemorative statues and monuments, such as the grand memorial to Victor Emmanuel II in central Rome, or the ostentatious Monument to the Battle of Nations built in Leipzig to honor German victory in the Napoleonic Wars. Surrounded by these inescapable elements of everyday nationalism, most ordinary people grew to see themselves as members of their national communities.[4]

Nationalism and Racism

Where nationalism in the first two-thirds of the nineteenth century had often been a force for liberal reform and peaceful brotherhood, expressed in its most optimistic form by thinkers like Giuseppe Mazzini (see "Evaluating the Evidence 23.1: The Struggle for the Italian Nation," page 759), it now took on more populist and exclusionary tones. The ideal of national belonging had from the start created an "us-them" outlook (see Chapter 21). After the 1870s the growing popularity of supposedly scientific understandings of racial difference added additional layers of meaning to this dichotomy. Though we now understand that there is no genetic evidence that divides humanity into distinct races, most people in the late nineteenth century believed that race was a product of heredity. Many felt pride in their own national racial characteristics—French, English, German, Jewish, Slavic, and many others—that were supposedly passed down from generation to generation. Unfortunately, pride in one's own heritage easily led to denigration of someone else's.

Modern attempts to use race to categorize distinct groups of people had their roots in Enlightenment thought (see Chapter 16). Now a new group of intellectuals, including race theorists such as Count Arthur de Gobineau and Houston Stewart Chamberlain, claimed that their ideas about racial difference were scientific, based on hard biological "facts" about bloodlines and heredity. In his early book *On the Inequality of the Human Races* (1854), Gobineau divided humanity into the white, black, and yellow races based on geographical location and championed the white "Aryan race" for its supposedly superior qualities. Social Darwinist ideas about the "survival of the fittest," when applied to the "contest" between nations and races, drew on such ideas to further popularize stereotypes about inferior and superior races.

The close links between nationalism and scientific racism helped justify imperial expansion, as we shall see in the next chapter. Nationalist racism also fostered domestic persecution and exclusion, as witnessed by Bismarck's Kulturkampf and the Dreyfus affair. According to race theorists, the nation was supposed to be racially pure, and ethnic minorities were viewed as outsiders and targets for reform, repression, and relocation.

Thus the ethnic Russian leaders of the Russian Empire targeted minority Poles and Czechs for "Russification," a process by which they might learn the Russian language and assimilate into Russian society. Germans likewise viewed the large number of ethnic Poles living in East Prussia as a "national threat" that required "Germanization" before they could be seen as equals to the supposedly superior Germans. For many nationalists, driven by ugly currents of race hatred, Jews were the ultimate outsiders, the stereotypical "inferior race" that posed the greatest challenge to national purity.

Jewish Emancipation and Modern Anti-Semitism

Changing political principles and the triumph of the nation-state had revolutionized Jewish life in western and central Europe. The decisive turning point came in 1848, when Jews formed part of the revolutionary vanguard in Vienna and Berlin and the Frankfurt Assembly endorsed full rights for German Jews. In 1871 the constitution of the new German Empire consolidated the process of Jewish emancipation in that nation. It abolished all restrictions on Jewish marriage, choice of occupation, place of residence, and property ownership. However, even with this change, exclusion from government employment and discrimination in social relations remained.

The trend toward legal emancipation presented Jews with challenges and opportunities. Traditional Jewish occupations, such as court financial agent, village moneylender, and peddler, were undermined by free-market reforms, but careers in business, the professions, and the arts opened. European Jews excelled in wholesale and retail trade, banking and finance, consumer industries, journalism, medicine, and law, as well as the fine arts. By 1871 a majority of Jewish people in western and central Europe had improved their economic situation enough to enter the middle classes. Middle-class Jews came to identify strongly with their respective nation-states and, with good reason, saw themselves as patriotic citizens.

Vicious anti-Semitism reappeared with force in central and eastern Europe after the stock market crash of 1873. Drawing on long traditions of religious intolerance, segregation into ghettos, and periodic anti-Jewish riots and expulsions (or pogroms), late-nineteenth-century anti-Semitism now drew on the exclusionary

"The Expulsion of the Jews from Russia" So reads this postcard, correctly suggesting that Russian government officials often encouraged the popular anti-Semitism that helped drive many Jews out of Russia in the late nineteenth century. The road signs indicate that these poor Jews are crossing into Germany, where they will find a grudging welcome and a meager meal at the Jolly Onion Inn. Other Jews from eastern Europe settled in France and Britain, thereby creating small but significant Jewish populations in both of these countries for the first time since they had expelled most of their Jews in the Middle Ages. (Alliance Israélite Universelle, Paris, France/Archives Charmet/Bridgeman Images)

INDIVIDUALS IN SOCIETY
Theodor Herzl

Theodor Herzl in Palestine, 1898. (David Wolffsohn/Imagno/Getty Images)

In September 1897, only days after his vision and energy had called into being the First Zionist Congress in Basel, Switzerland, Theodor Herzl (1860–1904) assessed the results in his diary: "If I were to sum up the Congress in a word—which I shall take care not to publish—it would be this: At Basel I founded the Jewish state. If I said this out loud today I would be greeted by universal laughter. In five years perhaps, and certainly in fifty years, everyone will perceive it."* Herzl's buoyant optimism, which so often carried him forward, was prophetic. Leading the Zionist movement until his death in 1904, at age forty-four, Herzl guided the first historic steps toward modern Jewish political nationhood and the creation of Israel in 1948.

Theodor Herzl was born in Budapest, Hungary, into an upper-middle-class, German-speaking Jewish family. When he was eighteen, his family moved to Vienna, where he studied law. As a university student, he soaked up the liberal beliefs of most well-to-do Viennese Jews, which included the assimilation of German culture. Wrestling with his nonreligious Jewishness and his strong pro-German feeling, Herzl embraced German nationalism and joined a German dueling fraternity. There he discovered that full acceptance required openly anti-Semitic attitudes and a repudiation of all things Jewish. Herzl resigned.

After receiving his law degree, Herzl embarked on a literary career. In 1889 he married into a wealthy Viennese Jewish family, but he and his socialite wife were mismatched and never happy together. Herzl achieved considerable success as both a journalist and a playwright. His witty comedies focused on the bourgeoisie, including Jewish millionaires trying to live like aristocrats. Accepting many German stereotypes, Herzl sometimes depicted eastern Jews as uneducated and grasping. But he believed that the Jewish shortcomings he perceived were the results of age-old persecution and would disappear through education and assimilation. Herzl also took a growing pride in Jewish steadfastness in the face of victimization and suffering.

The emergence of modern anti-Semitism (see page 781) shocked Herzl, as it did many acculturated Jewish Germans. Moving to Paris in 1891 as the correspondent for Vienna's leading liberal newspaper, Herzl studied contemporary politics and pondered recent historical developments. He came to a bold conclusion, published in 1896 as *The Jewish State: An Attempt at a Modern Solution to the Jewish Question.*

*Quotes are from Theodor Herzl, *The Diaries of Theodor Herzl*, trans. and ed. with an introduction by Marvin Lowenthal (New York: Grosset & Dunlap, 1962), pp. 224, 22, xxi.

According to Herzl, Jewish assimilation had failed, and attempts to combat European anti-Semitism would never succeed. Only by building an independent Jewish state could the Jewish people flourish.

Herzl developed his Zionism before the anti-Jewish agitation accompanying the Dreyfus affair, which only served to strengthen his faith in his analysis. Generally rebuffed by skeptical Jewish elites in western and central Europe, Herzl turned for support to youthful idealists and the poor Jewish masses. He became an inspiring man of action, rallying the delegates to the annual Zionist congresses, directing the growth of the worldwide Zionist organization, and working himself to death. Herzl also understood that national consciousness required powerful emotions and symbols, such as a Jewish flag. Flags build nations, he said, because people "live and die for a flag."

Putting the Zionist vision before non-Jews and world public opinion, Herzl believed in international diplomacy and political agreements. He traveled constantly to negotiate with European rulers and top officials, seeking their support in securing territory for a Jewish state, usually suggesting that it take form in Palestine, a territory in the Ottoman Empire. Aptly described by an admiring contemporary as "the first Jewish statesman since the destruction of Jerusalem," Herzl proved most successful in Britain. His work paved the way for the 1917 Balfour Declaration, which solemnly pledged British support for a "Jewish homeland" in Palestine.

QUESTIONS FOR ANALYSIS

1. Describe Herzl's background and early beliefs. Do you see a link between Herzl's early German nationalism and his later Zionism?
2. Why did Herzl believe an independent Jewish state with its own national flag was necessary?
3. How did Herzl work as a leader to turn his Zionist vision into a reality?

aspects of modern popular nationalism and the pseudoscience of race. Fanatic anti-Semites whipped up resentment against Jewish achievement and Jewish "financial control" and claimed that the Jewish race or "blood" (beyond the Jewish religion) posed a biological threat to Christian peoples. Such ideas were popularized by the repeated publication of the notorious forgery "The Protocols of the Elders of Zion," a falsified account of a secret meeting supposedly held at the First Zionist Congress in Basel in 1897. The "Protocols," actually written by the Russian secret police, suggested that Jewish elders planned to dominate the globe. Such anti-Semitic beliefs were particularly popular among conservatives, extreme nationalists, and people who felt threatened by Jewish competition, such as small shopkeepers, officeworkers, and professionals.

Anti-Semites created nationalist political parties that attacked and insulted Jews to win popular support. Anti-Semitism helped Karl Lueger and his Christian Socialist Party, for example, win striking electoral victories in Vienna in the 1890s. Lueger, mayor of Vienna from 1897 to 1910, combined fierce anti-Semitic rhetoric with municipal ownership of basic services, and he appealed especially to the German-speaking lower middle class—and an unsuccessful young artist named Adolf Hitler.

Before 1914 anti-Semitism was most oppressive in eastern Europe, where Jews suffered from social prejudice and rampant poverty. In the western borderlands of the Russian Empire, where 4 million of Europe's 7 million Jewish people lived in 1880 with few legal rights, officials used anti-Semitism to channel popular discontent away from the government and onto the Jewish minority. Russian Jews were regularly denounced as foreign exploiters who corrupted national traditions, and in 1881 to 1882 a wave of violent pogroms commenced in southern Russia. The police and the army stood aside for days while peasants looted and destroyed Jewish property, and official harassment continued in the following decades.

The growth of radical anti-Semitism spurred the emergence of **Zionism**, a Jewish political movement whose adherents believed that Christian Europeans would never overcome their anti-Semitic hatred. To escape the burdens of anti-Semitism, leading Zionists such as Theodor Herzl advocated the creation of a Jewish state in Palestine—a homeland where European Jews could settle and live free of social oppression. (See "Individuals in Society: Theodor Herzl," at left.) Zionism was particularly popular among Jews living in Russia. Many embraced self-emancipation and the vision of a Zionist settlement in Palestine, or emigrated to western or central Europe and the United States. About 2.75 million Jews left central and eastern Europe between 1881 and 1914.

Zionism A movement dedicated to building a Jewish national homeland in Palestine, started by Theodor Herzl.

Marxism and the Socialist Movement

Nationalism served, for better or worse, as a new unifying principle. But what about socialism? Socialist parties, generally Marxist groups dedicated to international proletarian revolution, grew rapidly in these years. Did this mean that national states had failed to gain the support of workers?

FOCUS QUESTION
Why did the socialist movement grow, and how revolutionary was it?

The Socialist International

The growth of socialist parties after 1871 was phenomenal. (See "Evaluating the Evidence 23.3: Adelheid Popp, the Making of a Socialist," page 784.) Neither Bismarck's Anti-Socialist Laws nor his extensive social security system checked the growth of the

Adelheid Popp, the Making of a Socialist

Nationalism and socialism appeared locked in bitter competition in Europe before 1914, but they actually complemented each other in many ways. Both faiths were secular as opposed to religious, and both fostered political awareness. A working person who became interested in politics and developed nationalist beliefs might well convert to socialism at a later date.

This was the case for Adelheid Popp (1869–1939), a self-taught working woman who became an influential socialist leader. Born into a desperately poor working-class family in Vienna, in what she remembered as a "hard and gloomy childhood," she was forced by her parents to quit school at age ten to begin full-time work. She struggled with low-paying piecework for years before she landed a solid factory job, as she recounts in the following selection from her widely read autobiography. Always an avid reader, Popp became the editor of a major socialist newspaper for German working women. She then told her life story so that all working women might share her truth: "Socialism could change and strengthen others, as it did me."

~

[Finally] I found work again; I took everything that was offered me in order to show my willingness to work, and I passed through much. But at last things became better. [At age fifteen] I was recommended to a great factory which stood in the best repute. Three hundred girls and about fifty men were employed. I was put in a big room where sixty women and girls were at work.

Against the windows stood twelve tables, and at each sat four girls. We had to sort the goods which had been manufactured, others had to count them, and a third set had to brand on them the mark of the firm. We worked from 7 A.M. to 7 P.M. We had an hour's rest at noon, half-an-hour in the afternoon. . . . I had never yet been paid so much. . . .

I seemed to myself to be almost rich. . . . [Yet] from the women of this factory one can judge how sad and full of deprivation is the lot of a factory worker. In none of the neighbouring factories were the wages so high; we were envied everywhere. Parents considered themselves fortunate if they could get their daughters of fourteen in there on leaving school. . . . And even here, in this paradise, all were badly nourished. Those who stayed at the factory for the dinner hour would buy themselves for a few pennies a sausage or the leavings of a cheese shop. . . . In spite of all the diligence and economy, every one was poor, and trembled at the thought of losing her work. All humbled themselves, and suffered the worst injustice from the foremen, not to risk losing this good work, not to be without food. . . .

I did not only read novels and tales; I had begun . . . to read the classics and other good books. I also began to take an interest in public events. . . . I was not democratically inclined. I was full of enthusiasm then for emperors, and kings and highly placed personages played no small part in my fancies. . . . I bought myself a strict Catholic paper, that criticised very adversely the workers' movement, which was attracting notice. Its aim was to educate in a patriotic and religious direction. . . . I took the warmest interest in the events that occurred in the royal families, and I took the

German Social Democratic Party, which espoused radical Marxism even though it sought reform through legal parliamentary politics. By 1912 the SPD had millions of followers—mostly people from the working classes—and was the largest party in the Reichstag. Socialist parties grew in other countries as well, though nowhere else with such success. In 1883 Russian exiles in Switzerland founded the Russian Social Democratic Party, and various socialist groups were unified in 1905 in the French Section of the Workers International. Belgium and Austria-Hungary also had strong socialist parties.

As the name of the French party suggests, Marxist socialist parties strove to join together in an international organization, and in 1864 Marx himself helped found the socialist International Working Men's Association, also known as the First International. In the following years, Marx battled successfully to control the organization and used its annual international meetings as a means of spreading his doctrines of socialist revolution. He enthusiastically endorsed the radical patriotism of the Paris Commune death of the Crown Prince of Austria so much to heart that I wept a whole day. . . . Political events [also] held me in suspense. The possibility of a war with Russia roused my patriotic enthusiasm. I saw my brother already returning from the battlefield covered with glory. . . .

When a particularly strong anti-Semitic feeling was noticeable in political life, I sympathised with it for a time. A broad sheet, "How Israel Attained Power and Sovereignty over all the Nations of the Earth," fascinated me. . . .

About this time an Anarchist group was active. Some mysterious murders which had taken place were ascribed to the Anarchists, and the police made use of them to oppress the rising workmen's movement. . . . I followed the trial of the Anarchists with passionate sympathy. I read all the speeches, and because, as always happens, Social Democrats, whom the authorities really wanted to attack, were among the accused, I learned their views. I became full of enthusiasm. Every single Social Democrat . . . seemed to me a hero. . . . There was unrest among the workers . . . and demonstrations of protest followed. When these were repeated the military entered the "threatened" streets. . . . In the evenings I rushed in the greatest excitement from the factory to the scene of the disturbance. The military did not frighten me; I only left the place when it was "cleared."

Later on my mother and I lived with one of my brothers who had married. Friends came to him, among them some intelligent workmen. One of these workmen was particularly intelligent, and . . . could talk on many subjects. He was the first Social Democrat I knew. He brought me many books, and explained to me the difference between Anarchism and Socialism. I heard from him, also for the first time, what a republic was, and in spite of my former enthusiasm for royal dynasties, I also declared myself in favour of a republican form of government. I saw everything so near and so clearly, that I actually counted the weeks which must still elapse before the revolution of state and society would take place. From this workman I received the first Social Democratic party organ. . . . I first learned from it to understand and judge of my own lot. I learned to see that all I had suffered was the result not of a divine ordinance, but of an unjust organization of society. . . .

In the factory I became another woman. . . . I told my [female] comrades all that I had read of the workers' movement. Formerly I had often told stories when they had begged me for them. But instead of narrating . . . the fate of some queen, I now held forth on oppression and exploitation. I told of accumulated wealth in the hands of a few, and introduced as a contrast the shoemakers who had no shoes and the tailors who had no clothes. On breaks I read aloud the articles in the Social Democratic paper and explained what Socialism was as far as I understood it. . . . [While I was reading] it often happened that one of the clerks passing by shook his head and said to another clerk: "The girl speaks like a man."

EVALUATE THE EVIDENCE

1. How did Popp describe and interpret work in the factory?
2. According to her autobiography, what accounts for Popp's nationalist sentiments early on? How and why did she become a Social Democrat?
3. Was Popp likely to lead other working women to socialism by reading them articles from socialist newspapers? Why or why not?

Source: Slightly adapted from A. Popp, *The Autobiography of a Working Woman*, trans. E. C. Harvey (Chicago: F. G. Browne, 1913), pp. 29, 34–35, 39, 66–69, 71, 74, 82–90.

and its terrible struggle against the French state as a giant step toward socialist revolution. Marx's fervent embrace of working-class violence frightened many of his early supporters, especially the more moderate British labor leaders. Internal tensions led to the collapse of the First International in 1876.

Yet international proletarian solidarity remained an important objective for Marxists. In 1889, as the individual parties in different countries grew stronger, socialist leaders came together to form the Second International, which lasted until 1914. Though only a federation of national socialist parties, the Second International had a great psychological impact. It had a permanent executive, and every three years delegates from the different parties met to interpret Marxist doctrines and plan coordinated action. May 1 (May Day) was declared an annual international one-day strike, a day of marches and demonstrations. Prosperous elites and conservative middle-class citizens feared the growing power of socialism and the Second International, but many workers joined the cause.

"Greetings from the May Day Festival" Workers participated enthusiastically in the annual one-day strike on May 1 in Stuttgart, Germany, to honor international socialist solidarity, as this postcard suggests. Speeches, picnics, and parades were the order of the day, and workers celebrated their respectability and independent culture. Picture postcards like this one and the one on page 781 developed with railroads, mass travel, and high-speed printing. (Published by August Henning, Nürnberg, Germany, 1899/akg-images)

Labor Unions and Marxist Revisionism

Was socialism really radical and revolutionary in these years? On the whole, it was not. As socialist parties grew and attracted large numbers of members, they looked less and less toward revolution, and more and more toward gradual change and steady improvement for the working class. The mainstream of European socialism became militantly moderate. Socialists still liked to alarm mainstream politicians with revolutionary rhetoric. But they increasingly worked within the system, often joining labor unions to win practical workplace reforms.

Workers themselves grew less inclined to follow radical programs for several reasons. As they gained the right to vote and to participate politically in the nation-state, workers focused their attention more on elections than on revolutions. As workers won real, tangible benefits, this furthered the process. And workers were not immune to patriotic education and indoctrination during military service. Many responded positively to drum-beating parades and aggressive foreign policy as they loyally voted for socialists. Nor were workers by any means a unified group with shared social and political interests—as we saw in Chapter 22.

Perhaps most important of all, workers' standard of living rose gradually but substantially after 1850. The quality of life in urban areas improved dramatically as well. For all these reasons, workers became more moderate: they demanded gains, but they were less likely to take to the barricades in pursuit of them.

The growth of labor unions reinforced the trend toward moderation. In the early stages of industrialization, unions were generally prohibited by law. A famous law of the French Revolution had declared all guilds and unions illegal in the name of "liberty" in 1791. In Great Britain, attempts by workers to unite were made criminal conspiracies in 1799. Other countries had similar laws that hampered union development. Unions were considered subversive bodies to be hounded and crushed.

From this sad position workers struggled to escape. Great Britain led the way in 1824 and 1825 when it granted unions the right to exist—though generally not the right to strike. After the collapse of Robert Owen's attempt to form one big national union in the 1830s (see Chapter 20), new and more practical kinds of unions appeared. Limited primarily to highly skilled workers such as machinists and carpenters, these "new model unions" concentrated on winning better wages and hours through collective bargaining and compromise. This approach helped pave the way to the full acceptance of unions in Britain in the 1870s, and after 1890 unions for unskilled workers developed.

Developments in Germany, the most industrialized and unionized continental country by 1914, were particularly instructive. German unions did not receive basic rights until 1869, and until the Anti-Socialist Laws were repealed in 1890, they were frequently harassed by the government as socialist fronts. As a result, in 1895 Germany had only about 270,000 union members in a male industrial workforce of nearly 8 million. Then, with almost all legal harassment eliminated, union membership skyrocketed, reaching roughly 3 million in 1912.

This great expansion both reflected and influenced the changing character of German unions. Increasingly, union activists focused on bread-and-butter issues — wages, hours, working conditions — rather than on fomenting socialist revolution. Genuine collective bargaining, long opposed by socialist intellectuals as a sellout, was officially recognized as desirable by the German Trade Union Congress in 1899. When employers proved unwilling to bargain, a series of strikes forced them to change their minds. In 1913 alone, over ten thousand collective bargaining agreements benefiting 1.25 million workers were signed.

The German trade unions and their leaders were in fact, if not in name, thoroughgoing revisionists. **Revisionism** was an effort by various socialists to update Marx's doctrines to reflect the realities of the time. Thus the socialist Eduard Bernstein (1850–1932) argued in 1899 in his *Evolutionary Socialism* that many of Marx's predictions had been proved false.

> Social conditions have not developed to such an acute opposition of things and classes as is depicted in the Communist Manifesto. . . . The number of members of the possessing classes to-day is not smaller but larger. . . .
>
> In all advanced countries we see the privileges of the capitalist bourgeoisie yielding step by step to democratic organizations. Under the influence of this, and driven by the movement of the working classes which is daily becoming stronger, a social reaction has set in against the exploiting tendencies of capital.[5]

revisionism An effort by moderate socialists to update Marxist doctrines to reflect the realities of the late nineteenth century.

Socialists, according to thinkers like Bernstein, should reform their doctrines and tactics to meet these changed conditions. They should combine with other progressive forces to win continued evolutionary gains for workers through legislation, unions, and further economic development. These views were denounced as heresy by the SPD and later by the Second International. Yet the revisionist, gradualist approach continued to gain the tacit acceptance of many German socialists, particularly in the trade unions.

Moderation found followers elsewhere. In France, the great socialist leader Jean Jaurès (1859–1914) formally repudiated revisionism in order to establish a unified socialist party, but he remained at heart a gradualist and optimistic secular humanist. Questions of revolution or revisionism also divided Russian Marxists.

By the early twentieth century socialist parties had clear-cut national characteristics. Russians and socialists in the Austro-Hungarian Empire tended to be the most radical. The German party talked revolution and practiced reformism, greatly influenced by its enormous trade-union movement. The French party talked revolution and tried to practice it, unrestrained by a trade-union movement that was both very weak and very radical. In Britain, the socialist but non-Marxist Labour Party, reflecting the well-established union movement, was formally committed to gradual reform. In Spain and Italy, Marxist socialism was very weak. There anarchism, seeking to smash the state rather than the bourgeoisie, dominated radical thought and action.

In short, socialist policies and doctrines varied from country to country. Socialism itself was to a large extent "nationalized" behind the façade of international unity. This helps explain why when war came in 1914, almost all socialist leaders and most workers supported their national governments and turned away from international solidarity.

LOOKING BACK LOOKING AHEAD

In 1900 the triumph of the national state in Europe seemed almost complete. In the aging Austro-Hungarian, Russian, and Ottoman Empires, ethnic minorities continued to fight for national independence, and class, region, religion, and ethnicity still generated social and political differences across Europe. Nonetheless, the politically unified nation-state, resting solidly upon ongoing industrialization and the emerging urban society, governed with the consent and even the devotion of many of its citizens. Ordinary people developed a sense of patriotic allegiance to the nation and saw themselves as members of a national group — for instance, Swedes, Germans, Italians, or Americans. This newfound sense of national identity often eroded or leveled out other social differences.

Responsive and capable of tackling many practical problems, the European nation-state of 1900 was in part the realization of ideologues and patriots like Mazzini and the middle-class liberals active in the unsuccessful revolutions of 1848. Yet whereas early nationalists had envisioned a Europe of free peoples and international peace, the nationalists of 1900 had been nurtured in an atmosphere of competition between European states and the wars of unification in the 1850s and 1860s. This new generation of nationalists reveled in the strength of their unity, and the nation-state became the foundation stone of a new system of global power.

Thus after 1870, even as the responsive nation-state improved city life and brought social benefits to ordinary people, Europe's leading countries extended their imperial control around the globe. In Asia and Africa, the European powers seized territory, fought brutal colonial wars, and built authoritarian empires. Moreover, in Europe itself the universal faith in nationalism, which usually reduced social tensions within states, promoted a bitter, almost Darwinian, competition between states. Thus European nationalism threatened the very progress and unity it had helped to build. In 1914 the power of unified nation-states would turn on itself, unleashing the First World War and doling out self-inflicted wounds of enormous proportions to all of Europe's peoples.

Make Connections

Think about the larger developments and continuities within and across chapters.

1. By 1900 most countries in Europe and North America had established modern nation-states, but the road to nation building varied dramatically from place to place. Which countries were most successful in building viable nation-states? What accounts for the variation?

2. How and why did the relationship between the state and its citizens change in the last decades of the nineteenth century?

3. Liberalism, socialism, and nationalism first emerged as coherent ideologies in the decades around 1800 (Chapter 21). How had they changed by 1900?

23 REVIEW & EXPLORE

Review the Main Ideas

Answer the focus questions from each section of the chapter.

◆ How did Napoleon III seek to reconcile popular and conservative forces in an authoritarian nation-state? (p. 754)

◆ How did conflict and war lead to the construction of strong nation-states in Italy, Germany, and the United States? (p. 757)

◆ What steps did Russia and the Ottoman Turks take toward modernization, and how successful were they? (p. 766)

◆ What general domestic political trends emerged after 1871? (p. 772)

◆ How did popular nationalism evolve in the last decades of the nineteenth century? (p. 778)

◆ Why did the socialist movement grow, and how revolutionary was it? (p. 783)

Identify Key Terms

Identify and explain the significance of each item below.

Red Shirts (p. 760)
Homestead Act (p. 766)
Crimean War (p. 766)
Bloody Sunday (p. 769)
Duma (p. 769)
Tanzimat (p. 771)
Young Turks (p. 772)
Reichstag (p. 773)
Kulturkampf (p. 773)
German Social Democratic Party (SPD) (p. 773)
Dreyfus affair (p. 776)
People's Budget (p. 776)
Zionism (p. 783)
revisionism (p. 787)

NOTES

1. Quoted by J. McKay in *Pioneers for Profit: Foreign Entrepreneurship and Russian Industrialization, 1885–1913* (Chicago: University of Chicago Press, 1970), p. 11.

2. W. Dawson, *Bismarck and State Socialism* (London: Swan Sonnenschein & Co., 1890), pp. 63–64.

3. E. Weber, *Peasants into Frenchmen: The Modernization of Rural France, 1870–1914* (Stanford: Stanford University Press, 1976).

4. See E. Hobsbawm, "Mass Producing Traditions: Europe, 1870–1914," in *The Invention of Tradition*, ed. E. Hobsbawm and T. Ranger (New York: Cambridge University Press, 1992), pp. 263–307.

5. E. Bernstein, *Evolutionary Socialism: A Criticism and Affirmation*, trans. E. Harvey (New York: B. W. Huebsch, 1909), pp. x–xvi, quoted in J. H. Hexter et al., *The Traditions of the Western World* (Chicago: Rand McNally, 1967), pp. 797–798.

CHAPTER PREVIEW

Industrialization and the World Economy
What were some of the global consequences of European industrialization between 1815 and 1914?

Global Migration Around 1900
How was massive migration an integral part of Western expansion?

Western Imperialism, 1880–1914
How did Western imperialism change after 1880?

Responding to Western Imperialism
What was the general pattern of non-Western responses to Western expansion?

Life on the Imperial Frontier
Colonialism entangled the lives of Europeans, natives, and immigrants, as seen in this 1886 painting of the city of Durban in the British colony of South Africa, the site of a minor gold rush. Here European settlers view an exhibit of gold nuggets found in local mines, as a South Asian migrant laborer and an African Zulu, both dressed in their traditional clothing, pass by.
(From *The Spanish and American Illustration*, 1886/Photo © Tarker/Bridgeman Images)

24

The West and the World

1815–1914

While industrialization and nationalism were transforming urban and rural life throughout Europe, western Europeans were reshaping the world. At the peak of its power and pride, the West entered the third and most dynamic phase of the aggressive expansion that had begun with the Crusades and continued with the rise of seaborne colonial empires. At the same time, millions of Europeans picked up stakes and emigrated abroad, primarily to North and South America but also to Australia, North and South Africa, and Asiatic Russia. An ever-growing stream of people, products, and ideas flowed into and out of Europe in the nineteenth century. Hardly any corner of the globe was left untouched.

The most spectacular manifestations of Western expansion came in the late nineteenth century when the leading European nations established or enlarged their far-flung colonial empires. This political annexation of territory in the 1880s—the "New Imperialism," as it is often called by historians—was the capstone of Europe's underlying economic and technological transformation. More directly, Europe's New Imperialism rested on a formidable combination of superior military might and strong authoritarian rule, and it posed a brutal challenge to African and Asian peoples. Different societies met this Western challenge in different ways. By 1914 non-Western elites in many lands were rallying their peoples and leading an anti-imperialist struggle for dignity and genuine independence that would eventually triumph after 1945. ■

Industrialization and the World Economy

FOCUS QUESTION

What were some of the global consequences of European industrialization between 1815 and 1914?

The Industrial Revolution created, first in Great Britain and then in continental Europe and North America, a tremendously dynamic economic system. In the course of the nineteenth century, that system expanded across the face of the earth. Some of this extension into non-Western areas was peaceful and beneficial, for the West had many products and techniques the rest of the world desired. If peaceful methods failed, however, Europeans used their superior military power to force non-Western nations to open their doors to Western economic interests. In general, Europeans fashioned the global economic system so that the largest share of the ever-increasing gains from trade, technology, and migration flowed to the West and its propertied classes.

The Rise of Global Inequality

The Industrial Revolution in Europe marked a momentous turning point in human history. Those regions of the world that industrialized in the nineteenth century (mainly Europe and North America) increased their wealth and power enormously in comparison to those that did not. A gap between the core industrializing regions and the soon-to-be colonized or semi-colonized regions outside the European–North American core (mainly in Africa, Asia, the Middle East, and Latin America) emerged and widened throughout the nineteenth century. Moreover, this pattern of uneven global development became institutionalized, or built into the structure of the world economy. Thus a "lopsided world" evolved, a world with a rich north and a poor south (albeit with regional variations).

In recent years economic historians have charted the long-term evolution of this gap, and Figure 24.1 summarizes the findings of one important study. Three main points stand out. First, in 1750 the average standard of living was no higher in Europe as a whole than in the rest of the world. Second, it was industrialization that opened the gaps in average wealth and well-being among countries and regions. Third, income per person stagnated in the colonized world before 1913, in striking contrast to the industrializing regions. Only after 1945, in the era of decolonization and political independence, did former colonies make real economic progress, beginning in their turn the critical process of industrialization.

The rise of these enormous income disparities, which indicate similar and striking disparities in food and clothing, health and education, and life expectancy and general material well-being, has generated a great deal of debate. One school of interpretation stresses that the West used science, technology, capitalist organization, and even its rational worldview to create massive wealth, and then used that wealth and power to its advantage. Another school argues that the West used its political and economic power to steal much of the world's riches, continuing in the nineteenth and twentieth centuries the rapacious colonialism born of

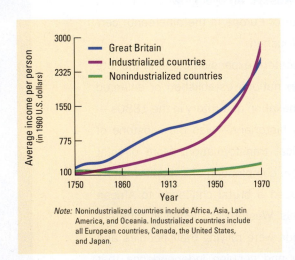

FIGURE 24.1 The Growth of Average Income per Person in Industrialized Countries, Nonindustrialized Countries, and Great Britain, 1750–1970 Growth is given in 1960 U.S. dollars and prices.

Note: Nonindustrialized countries include Africa, Asia, Latin America, and Oceania. Industrialized countries include all European countries, Canada, the United States, and Japan.

Chronology

1805–1848	Muhammad Ali modernizes Egypt	1885	Russian expansion reaches borders of Afghanistan
1839–1842	First Opium War; Treaty of Nanking	1898	United States takes over Philippines; hundred days of reform in China; Battle of Omdurman
1853	Perry "opens" Japan for trade		
1856–1860	Second Opium War	1899	Kipling writes "The White Man's Burden"
1857–1858	Britain crushes Great Rebellion in India		
1863–1879	Reign of Ismail in Egypt	1899–1902	South African War
1867	Meiji Restoration in Japan	1902	Conrad publishes *Heart of Darkness*; Hobson publishes *Imperialism*
1869	Suez Canal opens		
1880–1900	Most of Africa falls under European rule	1912	Western-style republic replaces China's Qing Dynasty
1884–1885	Berlin Conference	1914	Panama Canal opens

the era of expansion. Because these issues are complex and there are few simple answers, it is helpful to consider them in the context of world trade in the nineteenth century.

The World Market

Commerce between nations has always stimulated economic development. In the nineteenth century Europe directed an enormous increase in international commerce. Great Britain took the lead in cultivating export markets for its booming industrial output, as British manufacturers looked first to Europe and then around the world, seeking consumers for Britain's growing numbers of mass-produced goods.

Take the case of cotton textiles. By 1820 Britain was exporting 50 percent of its production. Europe bought 50 percent of these cotton textile exports, while India bought only 6 percent and had its own well-established textile industry. Then as European nations and the United States erected protective tariff barriers to promote domestic industry, British cotton textile manufacturers aggressively sought other foreign markets in non-Western areas. By 1850 India was buying 25 percent and Europe only 16 percent of a much larger volume of production. As a British colony, India could not raise tariffs to protect its ancient, indigenous cotton textile industry, which collapsed, leaving thousands of Indian weavers unemployed.

In addition to its dominance in the export market, Britain was also the world's largest importer of goods. From the repeal of the Corn Laws in 1846 (see Chapter 21) to the outbreak of World War I in 1914, Britain remained the world's emporium, the globe's largest trader of agricultural products, raw materials, and manufactured goods. Under free-trade policies, open access to Britain's market stimulated the development of mines and plantations in many non-Western areas.

Improved transportation systems fostered international trade. Wherever railroads were built, they drastically reduced transportation costs, opened new economic opportunities, and called forth new skills and attitudes. European investors funded much of the railroad construction undertaken in Latin America, Asia, and Africa, which connected seaports with resource-rich inland cities and regions, as opposed to linking and developing cities and regions within a given country. Thus railroads dovetailed effectively with Western economic interests, facilitating the inflow and sale of Western manufactured goods and the export and the development of local raw materials.

The power of steam revolutionized transportation by sea as well as by land. Steam power began to supplant sails on the oceans of the world in the late 1860s. Passenger and freight rates tumbled as ship design became more sophisticated, and the intercontinental shipment of low-priced raw materials became feasible. The time needed to cross the Atlantic dropped from three weeks in 1870 to about ten days in 1900, and the opening of the Suez and Panama Canals (in 1869 and 1914, respectively) shortened transport time to other areas of the globe considerably. In addition, improved port facilities made loading and unloading cargo less expensive, faster, and more dependable.

The revolution in land and sea transportation encouraged European entrepreneurs to open up and exploit vast new territories around the world. Improved transportation enabled Asia, Africa, and Latin America to ship not only familiar agricultural products—spices, tea, sugar, coffee—but also new raw materials for industry, such as jute, rubber, cotton, and coconut oil. The export of raw materials supplied by these "primary producers" to Western manufacturers boosted economic growth in core countries but did little to establish independent industry in the nonindustrialized periphery.

New communications systems were used to direct the flow of goods across global networks. Transoceanic telegraph cables, firmly in place by the 1880s, enabled rapid communications among the financial centers of the world. While a British tramp freighter steamed from Calcutta to New York, a broker in London could arrange by telegram for it to carry American cargo to Australia. The same communications network conveyed world commodity prices instantaneously.

As their economies grew, Europeans began to make massive foreign investments beginning about 1840. By the outbreak of World War I in 1914, Europeans had invested more than $40 billion abroad. Great Britain, France, and Germany were the principal investing countries (Map 24.1). The great gap between rich and poor within Europe meant that the wealthy and moderately well-to-do could and did send great sums abroad in search of interest and dividends.

Most of the capital exported did not go to European colonies or protectorates in Asia and Africa. About three-quarters of total European investment went to other European countries, or to settler colonies—so-called **neo-Europes**, a term coined by historian Alfred Crosby to describe regions where the climate and topography resembled the European homeland, including the United States, Canada, Australia, New Zealand, Latin America, and parts of Siberia. In these relatively advanced regions, which had already attracted significant settler populations of ethnic Europeans, Europe found its most profitable opportunities for investment in construction of railroads, ports, and utilities. By lending money to construct foreign railroads, Europeans enabled white settlers to buy European rails and locomotives and develop sources of cheap food and raw materials.

Much of this investment was peaceful and mutually beneficial for lenders and borrowers. The extension of Western economic power and the construction of neo-Europes, however, were disastrous for indigenous peoples. Native Americans and Australian Aborigines especially were decimated by the diseases, liquor, and weapons of an aggressively expanding Western society.

neo-Europes Settler colonies with established populations of Europeans, such as North America, Australia, New Zealand, and Latin America, where Europe found outlets for population growth and its most profitable investment opportunities in the nineteenth century.

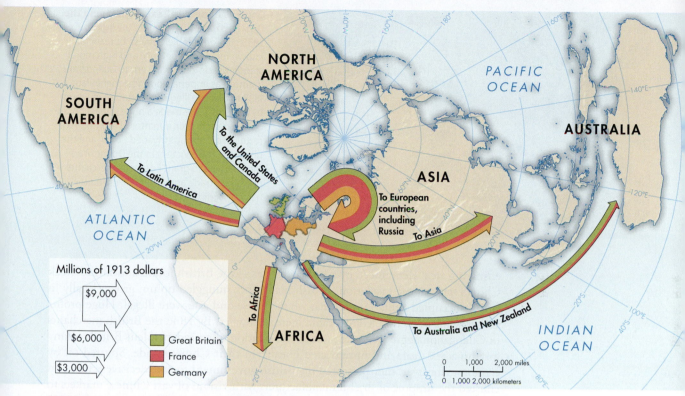

MAP 24.1 European Investment to 1914 Foreign investment grew rapidly after 1850, and Britain, France, and Germany were the major investing nations. As this map suggests, most European investment was not directed to the African and Asian areas seized in the New Imperialism after 1880.

The Opening of China

Europe's development of robust offshoots in sparsely populated North America, Australia, and much of Latin America absorbed huge quantities of goods, investments, and migrants. Yet Europe's economic and cultural penetration of old, densely populated civilizations was also profoundly significant. Interaction with such civilizations increased the Europeans' trade and profit, and they were prepared to use force, if necessary, to attain their desires. This was what happened in China, a striking example of the pattern of European intrusion into non-Western lands.

For centuries China had sent more goods and inventions to Europe than it had received, and such was still the case in the early nineteenth century. Trade with Europe was carefully regulated by the Chinese imperial government, ruled by the Qing (ching), or Manchu, Dynasty in the nineteenth century. Qing officials required all foreign merchants to live in the southern port of Guangzhou (Canton) and to buy and sell only to licensed Chinese merchants. Practices considered harmful to Chinese interests were strictly forbidden.

For years the little community of foreign merchants in Guangzhou had to accept this Chinese system. By the 1820s, however, the dominant group of these merchants, the British, were flexing their muscles. Moreover, in opium—that "destructive and

Commissioner Lin Zexu Overseeing the Destruction of Opium at Guangzhou, 1839 A formidable Chinese bureaucrat known for his competence and high moral standards, Lin Zexu was sent to Guangzhou (Canton) as imperial commissioner in late 1838 to halt the illegal importation of opium by the British. He made a huge impact on the opium trade within a matter of months. As a result, British troops invaded China, and the ultimate British victory in the Opium Wars forced China to grant European merchants one-sided trade agreements. (Pictures from History/Bridgeman Images)

ensnaring vice" denounced by Chinese decrees—the British found a means to break China's self-imposed isolation. British merchants smuggled opium grown legally in British-occupied India into China, where its use and sale were illegal. Huge profits and growing addiction led to a rapid increase in sales. By 1836 the British merchants in Guangzhou aggressively demanded the creation of an independent British colony in China and "safe and unrestricted liberty" in their Chinese trade. Spurred on by economic motives, they pressured the British government to take decisive action and enlisted the support of British manufacturers with visions of vast Chinese markets to be opened to their goods as well.

At the same time, the Qing government decided that the opium trade had to be stamped out. It was ruining the people and stripping the empire of its silver, which went to British merchants to pay for the drug. The government began to vigorously prosecute Chinese drug dealers. In 1839 it sent special envoy Lin Zexu to Guangzhou to deal with the crisis. Lin Zexu punished Chinese who purchased opium and seized the opium supplies of the British merchants, who then withdrew to the barren island of Hong Kong. He sent a famous letter justifying his policy to Queen Victoria in London.

The wealthy, well-connected British merchants appealed to their allies in London for support, and the British government responded. It also wanted free, unregulated trade with China, as well as the establishment of diplomatic relations on the European model, complete with ambassadors, embassies, and published treaties. Using troops from India and taking advantage of its control of the seas, Britain occupied several coastal cities and in the first of two **Opium Wars** forced China to give in to British demands. In the Treaty of Nanking in 1842, the imperial government was required to cede the island of Hong Kong to Britain forever, pay an indemnity of $100 million, and open up four large cities to unlimited foreign trade with low tariffs.

With Britain's new power over Chinese commerce, the opium trade flourished, and Hong Kong developed rapidly as an Anglo-Chinese enclave. But disputes over trade between China and the Western powers continued. Finally, the second Opium War (1856–1860) culminated in the occupation of Beijing by seventeen thousand British and French troops, who intentionally burned down the emperor's summer

Opium Wars Two mid-nineteenth-century conflicts between China and Great Britain over the British trade in opium, which were designed to "open" China to European free trade. In defeat, China gave European traders and missionaries increased protection and concessions.

palace. Another round of one-sided treaties gave European merchants and missionaries greater privileges and protection and forced the Chinese to accept trade and investment on unfavorable terms in several more cities. Thus did Europeans use opium addiction and military aggression to blow a hole in the wall of Chinese seclusion and open the country to foreign trade and foreign ideas.

Japan and the United States

China's neighbor Japan had its own highly distinctive civilization and even less use for Westerners. European traders and missionaries first arrived in Japan, an archipelago nation slightly smaller than California, in the sixteenth century. By 1640 Japanese leaders had reacted quite negatively to their presence. The government decided to expel all foreigners and seal off the country from all European influences in order to preserve traditional Japanese culture and society. When American and British whaling ships began to appear off Japanese coasts almost two hundred years later, the policy of exclusion was still in effect. An order of 1825 commanded Japanese officials to "drive away foreign vessels without second thought."[1]

Japan's unbending isolation seemed hostile and barbaric to the West, particularly to the United States. It complicated the practical problems of ensuring the safety of shipwrecked American sailors and the provisioning of whaling ships and China traders sailing in the eastern Pacific. It also thwarted American business leaders' hope of trade and profit. Moreover, Americans shared the self-confidence and dynamism of expanding Western society, and they felt destined to play a great role in the Pacific. To Americans it seemed the duty of the United States to force the Japanese to open their ports and behave as a "civilized" nation.

After several unsuccessful American attempts to establish commercial relations with Japan, Commodore Matthew Perry steamed into Edo (now Tokyo) Bay in 1853. Relying on **gunboat diplomacy** by threatening to attack, Perry demanded diplomatic negotiations with the emperor. Japan entered a grave crisis. Some Japanese military leaders urged resistance, but senior officials realized how defenseless their cities were against naval bombardment. Shocked and humiliated, they reluctantly signed a treaty with the United States that opened two ports and permitted trade. Over the next five years, more treaties spelled out the rights and privileges of the Western nations and their merchants in Japan. Japan was "opened." What the British had done in China with two wars, the Americans had achieved in Japan with the threat of one.

Western Penetration of Egypt

Egypt's experience illustrates not only the explosive power of the expanding European economy and society but also their seductive appeal. European involvement in Egypt also led to a new model of formal political control, which European powers applied widely in Africa and Asia after 1882.

Of great importance in African and Middle Eastern history, the ancient land of the pharaohs had since 525 B.C.E. been ruled by a succession of foreigners, most recently by the Ottoman sultans. In 1798 French armies under young General Napoleon Bonaparte invaded the Egyptian part of the Ottoman Empire and occupied the territory for three years. Into the power vacuum left by the French withdrawal stepped an extraordinary Albanian-born, Turkish-speaking general, Muhammad Ali (1769–1849).

gunboat diplomacy The use or threat of military force to coerce a government into economic or political agreements.

First appointed governor of Egypt in 1805 by the Ottoman sultan, Muhammad Ali set out to build his own state on the strength of a large, powerful army organized along European lines. He drafted for the first time the illiterate peasant masses of Egypt, and he hired French and Italian army officers to train both these raw recruits and their Turkish officers in modern military methods. He reformed the government bureaucracy, cultivated new lands, and improved communication networks. By the end of his reign in 1848, Muhammad Ali had established a strong and virtually independent Egyptian state, to be ruled by his family on a hereditary basis within the Ottoman Empire (see Chapter 23).

Muhammad Ali's modernization program attracted large numbers of Europeans to the banks of the Nile. The port city of Alexandria had more than fifty thousand Europeans by 1864. Europeans served not only as army officers but also as engineers, doctors, government officials, and police officers. Others turned to trade, finance, and shipping.

To pay for his ambitious plans, Muhammad Ali encouraged the development of commercial agriculture. This move had profound implications. Egyptian peasants were poor but largely self-sufficient, growing food for their own consumption on state-owned lands allotted to them by tradition. Faced with the possibility of export agriculture, high-ranking officials and members of Muhammad Ali's family began carving large private landholdings out of the state domain. These new landlords made the peasants their tenants and forced them to grow cash crops such as cotton and rice geared to European markets. Egyptian landowners "modernized" agriculture, but to the detriment of peasant living standards.

These trends continued under Muhammad Ali's grandson Ismail (ihs-MAH-eel), who in 1863 began his sixteen-year rule as Egypt's khedive (kuh-DEEV), or prince. Educated at France's leading military academy, Ismail was a westernizing autocrat. The large irrigation networks he promoted boosted cotton production and exports to Europe, and with his support a French company completed the Suez Canal in 1869. The Arabic of the Egyptian masses replaced the Turkish spoken by Ottoman rulers as the official language. Young Egyptians educated in Europe spread new skills, and Cairo acquired modern boulevards and Western hotels. As Ismail proudly declared, "My country is no longer in Africa, we now form part of Europe."[2]

Yet Ismail was too impatient and reckless. His projects were enormously expensive, and by 1876 Egypt owed foreign bondholders a colossal debt that it could not pay. France and Great Britain intervened and forced Ismail to appoint French and British commissioners to oversee Egyptian finances and ensure payment of the Egyptian debt in full. This momentous decision marked a sharp break with the past. Throughout most of the nineteenth century, Europeans had used military might and political force primarily to make sure that non-Western lands would accept European trade and investment. Now Europeans were going to effectively rule Egypt.

The Suez Canal, 1869

Foreign financial control evoked a violent nationalistic reaction among Egyptian religious leaders, young intellectuals, and army officers. In 1879, under the leadership of Colonel Ahmed Arabi, they formed the Egyptian Nationalist Party. Continuing diplomatic pressure on the government, which forced Ismail to abdicate in favor of his ineffectual son, Tewfiq (r. 1879–1892), resulted in bloody anti-European riots in Alexandria in 1882. A number of Europeans were killed, and Tewfiq and his court had to flee to British ships for safety. When the British fleet bombarded Alexandria, more riots swept the country, and Colonel Arabi led a revolt. But a British expeditionary force put down the rebellion and occupied all of Egypt that year.

The British said their occupation was temporary, but British armies remained in Egypt until 1956. Before the First World War (1914–1918), they maintained the façade of Egypt as an autonomous province of the Ottoman Empire, but the khedive was a mere puppet. British rule did result in tax reforms and somewhat better conditions for peasants, while foreign bondholders received their interest and Egyptian nationalists nursed their injured pride.

The British takeover in Egypt provided a new model for European expansion in densely populated lands. Such expansion was based on military force, political domination, and a self-justifying ideology of beneficial reform. This model predominated until 1914. Thus did Europe's Industrial Revolution lead to tremendous political as well as economic expansion throughout the world after 1880.

Global Migration Around 1900

A poignant human drama accompanied economic expansion: millions of people pulled up stakes and left their ancestral lands in the course of history's greatest migration. To millions of ordinary people for whom the opening of China and the interest on the Egyptian debt had not the slightest significance, this great movement was the central experience in the saga of Western expansion. It was, in part, because of this **global mass migration** that the West's impact on the world in the nineteenth century was so powerful and many-sided.

A note on vocabulary may be in order here: *migration* refers to general human movement; *emigrants* (or *emigration*) refers to people leaving one country for another; *immigrants* (or *immigration*) refers to people entering one country from another. When people migrate, they emigrate from and immigrate to.

The Pressure of Population

In the early eighteenth century European population growth entered its third and decisive stage, which continued unabated until the early twentieth century. Birthrates eventually declined in the nineteenth century, but so did death rates, mainly because of the rising standard of living and the revolution in public health (see Chapter 22). During the hundred years before 1900 the population of Europe (including Asiatic Russia) more than doubled, from approximately 188 million to roughly 432 million.

These figures actually understate Europe's population explosion, for between 1815 and 1932 more than 60 million Europeans left the subcontinent. These emigrants went primarily to the rapidly growing neo-Europes—North and South America, Australia, New Zealand, and Siberia. Since the population of native Africans, Asians, and Americans grew more slowly than that of Europeans, the number of Europeans and people of predominantly European origin jumped from about 24 percent of the world's total in 1800 to about 38 percent on the eve of World War I.

The growth of the European population provided further impetus for Western expansion, and it drove more and more people to emigrate. As in the eighteenth

FOCUS QUESTION
How was massive migration an integral part of Western expansion?

global mass migration The mass movement of people from Europe in the nineteenth century; one reason that the West's impact on the world was so powerful and many-sided.

century, the rapid increase in numbers in Europe proper led to land hunger and relative overpopulation in area after area. In most countries, emigration increased twenty years after a rapid growth in population, as children grew up, saw little available land and few opportunities, and departed. This pattern was especially prevalent when rapid population increase predated extensive industrial development, which offered the best long-term hope of creating jobs and reducing poverty. Thus millions of country folk in industrialized parts of Europe moved to cities in search of work, while those in more slowly industrializing regions went abroad.

Before looking more closely at the people who emigrated, consider these three facts. First, the number of men and women who left Europe increased rapidly at the end of the nineteenth century and leading up to World War I. As Figure 24.2 shows, more than 11 million left in the first decade of the twentieth century, over five times the number departing in the 1850s. Thus large-scale emigration was a defining characteristic of European society at the turn of the century.

Second, different countries had very different patterns of migration. People left Britain and Ireland in large numbers from the 1840s on. This outflow reflected not only rural poverty but also the movement of skilled industrial technicians and the preferences shown to British migrants in the overseas British Empire. Ultimately, about one-third of all European emigrants between 1840 and 1920 came from the British Isles. German emigration was quite different. It grew irregularly after about 1830, reaching a first peak in the early 1850s and another peak in the early 1880s. Thereafter it declined rapidly, for at that point Germany's rapid industrialization provided adequate jobs at home. This pattern contrasted sharply with that of Italy. More and more Italians left the country right up to 1914, forced out by relatively slow industrial growth and poor living standards in Italian villages. In short, migration patterns mirrored social and economic conditions in the various European countries and provinces.

Third, although the United States did absorb the largest overall number of European emigrants, fewer than half of all these emigrants went to the United States. Asiatic Russia, Canada, Argentina, Brazil, Australia, and New Zealand also attracted large numbers, as Figure 24.3 shows. Moreover, immigrants accounted for a larger proportion of the total population in Argentina, Brazil, and Canada than in the United States. The common American assumption that European emigration meant immigration to the United States is quite inaccurate.

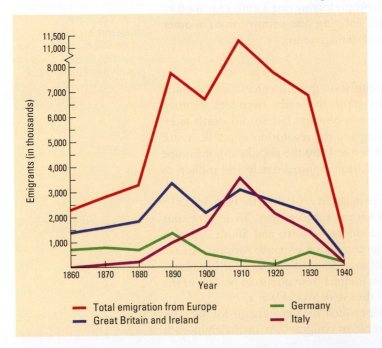

FIGURE 24.2 Emigration from Europe by Decade, 1860–1940 Emigration from Europe followed regional economic trends, as the comparison in this chart suggests. Overall, emigration from Europe grew quickly until the outbreak of World War I in 1914, after which it declined rapidly.

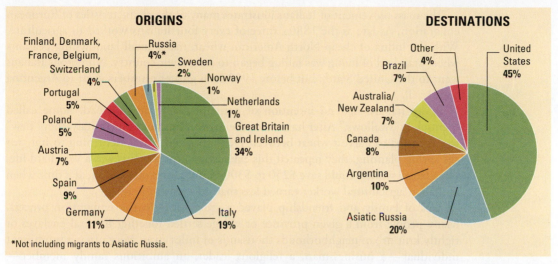

FIGURE 24.3 Origins and Destinations of European Emigrants, 1851–1960   European emigrants came from many countries; almost half of them went to the United States.

European Emigration

What kind of people left Europe, and what were their reasons for doing so? The European emigrant was generally an energetic small farmer or skilled artisan trying hard to stay ahead of poverty, not a desperately impoverished landless peasant or urban proletarian. Small peasant landowners and village craftsmen typically left Europe because of the lack of available land and the growing availability of inexpensive factory-made goods, which threatened their traditional livelihoods.

Determined to maintain or improve their status, immigrants brought great benefits to the countries that received them, in large part because the vast majority were young, typically unmarried, and ready to work hard in the new land, at least for a time. Many Europeans moved but remained within Europe, settling temporarily or permanently in another European country. Jews from central Europe and peasants from Ireland moved to Great Britain; Russians and Poles sought work in Germany; and Spaniards, Portuguese, and Italians went to France. A substantial number of Europeans were actually migrants as opposed to immigrants who settled in new lands—that is, they returned home after some time abroad. One in two immigrants to Argentina and probably one in three to the United States eventually returned to their native lands.

The likelihood of repatriation varied greatly by nationality. People who emigrated from the Balkans, for instance, were much more likely to return to their countries than people from Ireland or eastern European Jews. For those who returned, the possibility of buying land in the old country was of central importance. In Ireland (as well as in England and Scotland), large, often-absentee landowners owned most land; little was up for sale. In Russia, most Jews faced discrimination and were forced to live in the Pale of Settlement (see Chapter 16), and non-Jews owned most property. Therefore, when Irish farmers and Russian Jewish artisans emigrated in search of opportunity, or, for Jews, to escape pogroms (see Chapter 23), it was basically a once-and-for-all departure.

The mass movement of Italians illustrates many of the characteristics of European emigration. As late as the 1880s, three of every four Italians worked in agriculture. With the influx of cheap North American wheat, many small landowning peasants whose standard of living was falling began to leave their country. Numerous Italians went to the United States, but before 1900 even greater numbers went to Argentina and Brazil.

Many Italians had no intention of permanently settling abroad. Some called themselves "swallows." After harvesting their own wheat and flax in Italy, they "flew" to Argentina to harvest wheat between December and April. Returning to Italy for the spring planting, they repeated this exhausting process. This was a very hard life, but a frugal worker could save $250 to $300 in the course of a season, at a time when an Italian agricultural worker earned less than $1 a day in Italy.

Ties of family and friendship played a crucial role in the emigration process. Many people from a given province or village settled together in rural enclaves or tightly knit urban neighborhoods thousands of miles away. Very often a prominent individual—a businessman, a religious leader, an ambitious family member— would blaze the way, and others would follow, forming a "migration chain."

Many landless young European men and women were spurred to leave by a spirit of revolt and independence. In Sweden and in Norway, in Jewish Russia and in Italy, these young people felt frustrated by the power of the small minority in the privileged classes, which often controlled both church and government and resisted demands for liberal reform and greater opportunity. Many a young Norwegian seconded the passionate cry of Norway's national poet, Martinius Bjørnson (BYURN-sawn): "Forth will I! Forth! I will be crushed and consumed if I stay."[3] Many young Jews wholeheartedly agreed with a spokesman of Kiev's Jewish community in 1882, who summed up his congregation's growing defiance in the face of brutal persecution: "Our human dignity is being trampled upon, our wives and daughters are being dishonored, we are looted and pillaged; either we get decent human rights or else let us go wherever our eyes may lead us."[4]

Thus for many, emigration was a radical way to gain basic human rights. Emigration rates slowed in countries where the people won basic political and social reforms, such as the right to vote, equality before the law, and social security.

Asian Emigration

Not all emigration was from Europe. A substantial number of Chinese, Japanese, Indians, and Filipinos—to name only four key groups—also responded to rural hardship with temporary or permanent emigration. At least 3 million Asians moved abroad before 1920. Most went as indentured laborers to work under incredibly difficult conditions on the plantations or in the gold mines of Latin America, southern Asia, Africa, California, Hawaii, and Australia. This marked the rise of a new global trend: white estate owners very often used Asian immigrants to replace or supplement black workers after the suppression of the slave trade.

In the 1840s, for example, the Spanish government actively recruited Chinese laborers to meet the strong demand for field hands in Cuba. Between 1853 and 1873, when such immigration was stopped, more than 130,000 Chinese laborers went to Cuba. The majority spent their lives as virtual slaves. The great landlords of Peru also brought in more than 100,000 workers from China in the nineteenth century, and there were similar movements of Asians elsewhere.

Emigration from Asia would undoubtedly have grown to much greater proportions if planters and mine owners in search of cheap labor had been able to hire as many Asian workers as they wished. But they could not. Many Asians fled the plantations and gold mines as soon as possible, seeking greater opportunities in trade and towns. There they came into conflict with local populations, whether in Malaya, southern Africa, or areas settled by Europeans. When that took place in neo-Europes, European settlers demanded a halt to Asian immigration. By the 1880s the American and Australian governments had instituted exclusionary acts—discriminatory laws designed to keep Asians from entering the country.

In fact, the explosion of mass mobility in the late nineteenth century, combined with the growing appeal of nationalism and scientific racism (see Chapter 23), encouraged a variety of attempts to control immigration flows and seal off national borders. National governments established strict rules for granting citizenship and asylum to foreigners. Passports and customs posts monitored movement across increasingly tight national boundaries. Such attempts were often inspired by **nativism**, beliefs that led to policies giving preferential treatment to established inhabitants above immigrants. Thus French nativists tried to limit the influx of Italian migrant workers, German nativists stopped Poles from crossing eastern borders, and American nativists (in the 1920s) restricted immigration from southern and eastern Europe and banned it outright from much of Asia. (See "Evaluating the Evidence 24.1: Nativism in the United States," page 804.)

A crucial factor in migration patterns before 1914 was, therefore, immigration policies that offered preferred status to "acceptable" racial and ethnic groups in the open lands of possible permanent settlement. This, too, was part of Western dominance in the increasingly lopsided world. Largely successful in monopolizing the best overseas opportunities, Europeans and people of European ancestry reaped the main benefits from the mass migration. By 1913 people in Australia, Canada, and the United States had joined the British in having the highest average incomes in the world, while incomes in Asia and Africa lagged far behind.

Vaccinating Migrants Bound for Hawaii, 1904   First Chinese, then Japanese, and finally Koreans and Filipinos went across the Pacific in large numbers to labor in Hawaii on American-owned sugar plantations in the late nineteenth century. The native Hawaiians had been decimated by disease, creating a severe labor shortage for Hawaii's plantation economy. U.S. plantation owners filled the shortage with East Asian immigrant workers. (© Corbis)

nativism Policies and beliefs, often influenced by nationalism, scientific racism, and mass migration, that give preferential treatment to established inhabitants over immigrants.

Western Imperialism, 1880–1914

The expansion of Western society reached its apex between about 1880 and 1914. In those years, the leading European nations not only continued to send massive streams of migrants, money, and manufactured goods around the world, but also rushed to create or enlarge vast empires. This political empire building, under direct European rule, contrasted sharply with the economic penetration of non-Western territories between 1816 and 1880, which had left a China or a Japan "opened" but politically independent. By contrast, the empires of the late nineteenth century recalled the old

FOCUS QUESTION
How did Western imperialism change after 1880?

Nativism in the United States

In this 1896 Senate speech, the dynamic and well-respected Republican senator Henry Cabot Lodge expressed nativist anxieties about "race mixing" in the United States and called for rigid immigration restrictions. Most Europeans who immigrated to the United States in the late nineteenth century were Roman Catholics from Italy and central Europe and Jews and Slavs from Poland and Russia — "races" that nativists considered superior to Asians and Africans but far below the Anglo-Saxon Protestants from northern Europe, who constituted the majority of U.S. immigrants until the 1870s.

Restricting Immigration

This bill is intended to amend the existing law so as to restrict still further immigration to the United States. Paupers, diseased persons, convicts, and contract laborers are now excluded. By this bill it is proposed to make a new class of excluded immigrants, and to add to those which have just been named the totally ignorant. . . .

[We propose] to exclude all immigrants who could neither read nor write, and this is the plan which was adopted by the committee. . . . In their report the committee have shown by statistics, which have been collected and tabulated with great care, the emigrants who would be affected by this illiteracy test. . . . It is found . . . that the illiteracy test will bear most heavily upon the Italians, Russians, Poles, Hungarians, Greeks, and Asiatics, and very lightly, or not at all, upon English-speaking emigrants, or Germans, Scandinavians, and French. In other words, the races most affected by the illiteracy test are those whose emigration to this country has begun within the last twenty years and swelled rapidly to enormous proportions, races with which the English-speaking people have never hitherto assimilated, and who are most alien to the great body of the people of the United States. . . .

Immigration and the Economy

There is no one thing which does so much to bring about a reduction of wages and to injure the American wage earner as the unlimited introduction of cheap foreign labor through unrestricted immigration. Statistics show that the change in the race character of our immigration has been accompanied by a corresponding decline in its quality. . . .

Immigration and Citizenship

When we speak of a race, . . . we mean the moral and intellectual characters, which in their association make the soul of a race, and which represent the product of all its past, the inheritance of all its ancestors. . . .

[I]t is on the moral qualities of the English-speaking race that our history, our victories, and all our future rest. There is only one way in which you can lower those qualities or weaken those characteristics, and that is by breeding them out. If a lower race mixes with a higher in sufficient numbers, history teaches us that the lower race will prevail. . . . The lowering of a great race means not only its own decline, but that of civilization. . . .

Mr. President, more precious even than forms of government are the mental and moral qualities which make what we call our race. While those stand unimpaired all is safe. When those decline all is imperiled. . . . The time has certainly come, if not to stop, at least to check, to sift, and to restrict those immigrants. . . . The gates which admit men to the United States and to citizenship in the great republic should no longer be left unguarded.

EVALUATE THE EVIDENCE

1. How does Lodge's understanding of race drive his enthusiasm for immigration restrictions?
2. Why would nativist arguments win popular support in the late nineteenth century?

Source: Henry Cabot Lodge, *Speeches and Addresses, 1884–1909* (Boston: Houghton Mifflin Company, 1909), pp. 245, 247, 249–250, 262, 264–266.

New Imperialism The late-nineteenth-century drive by European countries to create vast political empires abroad.

European colonial empires of the sixteenth to eighteenth centuries. Because this renewed imperial push came after a long pause in European expansionism, contemporaries termed it the **New Imperialism**.

Characterized by a frantic rush to plant the flag over as many people and as much territory as possible, the New Imperialism had momentous consequences. By the early twentieth century almost 84 percent of the globe was dominated by European nations, and Britain alone controlled one-quarter of the earth's territory and one-third of its population. The New Imperialism created tensions among competing European states and led to wars and threats of war with non-European powers. Aimed primarily at Africa and Asia, the New Imperialism put millions of non-Western peoples directly under European rule.

The European Presence in Africa Before 1880

Prior to 1880, European nations controlled only about 10 percent of Africa. The French had begun conquering Algeria in 1830, and by 1880 substantial numbers of French, Italian, and Spanish colonists had settled among the overwhelming Arab majority there. Yet the overall effect on Africa was minor.

At the southern tip of the continent, Britain had taken possession of the Dutch settlements in and around Cape Town during the wars with Napoleon I. This take-over of the Cape Colony had led disgruntled Dutch cattle ranchers and farmers in 1835 to make their so-called Great Trek into the interior, where they fought the Zulu and Xhosa (KO-sah) peoples for land. After 1853 the Boers, or **Afrikaners** (a-frih-KAH-nuhrz), as the descendants of the Dutch in the Cape Colony were beginning to call themselves, proclaimed their independence and defended it against British armies. By 1880 Afrikaner and British settlers, who detested each other and lived in separate areas, had wrested control of much of South Africa from the Zulu, Xhosa, and other African peoples.

Afrikaners Descendants of the Dutch settlers in the Cape Colony in southern Africa.

In addition to the French in the north and the British and Afrikaners in the south, European trading posts and forts dating back to the Age of Discovery and the slave trade dotted the coast of West Africa, and the Portuguese maintained a loose hold on their old possessions in Angola and Mozambique. Elsewhere, over the great mass of the continent, Europeans did not rule.

After 1880 the situation changed drastically. In a spectacular manifestation of the New Imperialism, European countries jockeyed for territory in Africa, breaking sharply with previous patterns of colonization and diplomacy.

The Scramble for Africa After 1880

Between 1880 and 1900 Britain, France, Belgium, Germany, and Italy scrambled for African possessions as if their national livelihoods depended on it (Map 24.2). By 1900 nearly the whole continent had been carved up and placed under European rule: only Ethiopia, which fought off Italian invaders, and Liberia, which had been settled by freed slaves from the United States, remained independent. In all other African territories, European powers tightened their control and established colonial governments in the years before 1914.

In the complex story of the European seizure of Africa, certain events and individuals stand out. Of enormous importance was the British occupation of Egypt in 1882, which established the new model of formal political control (see page 798). King Leopold II of Belgium (r. 1865–1909), an energetic, strong-willed monarch of a tiny country with a lust for distant territory, also played a crucial role. As early as 1861, he had laid out his vision of expansion: "The sea bathes our coast, the world lies before us. Steam and electricity have annihilated distance, and all the nonappropriated lands on the surface of the globe can become the field of our operations and of our success."[5]

Colonial presence, 1914

British	Belgian
French	Spanish
German	Independent African states
Italian	Afrikaner republic
Portuguese	

MAP 24.2 The Partition of Africa   The European powers carved up Africa after 1880 and built vast political empires. European states also seized territory in Asia in the nineteenth century, although some Asian states and peoples managed to maintain their political independence (see Map 24.3, page 810). Compare the patterns of European imperialism in Africa and Asia, using this map and Map 24.3.

By 1876 Leopold's expansionism focused on central Africa. He formed a financial syndicate under his personal control to send Henry M. Stanley, a sensation-seeking journalist and part-time explorer, to the Congo basin. Stanley established trading stations, signed unfair treaties with African chiefs, and planted the Belgian flag. Leopold's actions alarmed the French, who quickly sent out an expedition under Pierre de Brazza. In 1880 de Brazza signed a treaty of protection with the chief of the large Teke tribe and began to establish a French protectorate on the north bank of the Congo River.

Leopold's intrusion into the Congo area called attention to the possibilities of African colonization, and by 1882 Europe had caught "African fever." A gold-rush mentality led to a determined race for territory, and rampant greed threatened the balance of power in Europe. To lay down some basic rules for this new and dangerous global competition, Jules Ferry of France and Otto von Bismarck of Germany arranged an international conference on Africa in Berlin in 1884 and 1885. The **Berlin Conference**, attended by over ten Western powers including the United States, established the principle that European claims to African territory had to rest on "effective occupation" (a strong presence on the ground) to be recognized by other states. This meant that Europeans would push relentlessly into interior regions from all sides and that no single European power would be able to claim the entire continent. The conference recognized Leopold's personal rule over a neutral Congo Free State and agreed to work to stop slavery and the slave trade in Africa.

The Berlin Conference coincided with Germany's sudden emergence as an imperial power. Prior to about 1880, Bismarck, like many other European leaders at the time, had seen little value in colonies. In 1884 and 1885, as political agitation for expansion increased, Bismarck did an abrupt about-face, and Germany established protectorates over a number of small African kingdoms and tribes in Togo, the Cameroons region, southwest Africa, and, later, East Africa. In acquiring colonies, Bismarck cooperated against the British with France's Jules Ferry, an ardent republican who also embraced imperialism. With Bismarck's tacit approval, the French pressed southward from Algeria, eastward from their old forts on the Senegal coast, and northward from their protectorate on the Congo River to take control of parts of West and Central Africa.

Meanwhile, the British began to enlarge their own African colonies, beginning at the southern tip of the African continent. Led by Cecil Rhodes (1853–1902), prime minister of Britain's Cape Colony, British colonists leapfrogged over the two Afrikaner states — the Orange Free State and the Transvaal (see Map 24.2) — in the early 1890s and established protectorates over Bechuanaland (bech-WAH-nuh-land; now Botswana) and Rhodesia (now Zimbabwe and Zambia), named in honor of its founder. (See "Individuals in Society: Cecil Rhodes," page 808.)

English-speaking capitalists like Rhodes developed fabulously rich gold mines in the Transvaal, and this unilateral territorial and economic expansion heightened tensions between the British and Afrikaner (Dutch Boer) settlers. In 1899 the conflict erupted in the bloody South African War, or Boer War (1899–1902). After a series of defeats at the hands of the determined Boers, the British shipped some 180,000 troops to southern Africa. Overwhelming British forces put the Boers on the defensive,

Berlin Conference A meeting of European leaders held in 1884 and 1885 in order to lay down some basic rules for imperialist competition in sub-Saharan Africa.

INDIVIDUALS IN SOCIETY
Cecil Rhodes

Cecil Rhodes epitomized the dynamism and the ruthlessness of the New Imperialism. He built a corporate monopoly, claimed vast tracts in Africa, and established the famous Rhodes scholarships to develop colonial (and American) leaders who would love and strengthen the British Empire. But to Africans, he left a bitter legacy.

Rhodes came from a large middle-class family and at seventeen went to southern Africa to seek his fortune. He soon turned to diamonds, newly discovered at Kimberley, picked good business partners, and was wealthy by 1876. But Rhodes, often called a dreamer, wanted more. He entered Oxford University, where he studied while returning periodically to Africa. His musings crystallized in a Social Darwinist belief in progress through racial competition and territorial expansion. "I contend," he wrote, "that we [English] are the finest race in the world and the more of the world we inhabit the better it is for the human race."*

Rhodes's belief in British expansion never wavered. In 1880 he formed the De Beers Mining Company, and by 1888 his firm had monopolized southern Africa's diamond production and earned fabulous profits. Rhodes also entered the Cape Colony's legislature and became the colony's all-powerful prime minister from 1890 to 1896.

His main objective was to annex the Afrikaner republics and impose British rule on as much land as possible beyond their northern borders. Working through a state-approved private company financed in part by De Beers, Rhodes's agents forced and cajoled African kings to accept British "protection," and then put down rebellions with machine guns. Britain thus obtained a great swath of empire on the cheap.

But Rhodes, like many high achievers obsessed with power and personal aggrandizement, went too far. He backed, and then declined to call back, the 1896 Jameson Raid, a failed British invasion of the Afrikaner Transvaal, which was designed to topple the Dutch-speaking republic. Repudiated by top British leaders who had encouraged his plan, Rhodes had to resign as prime minister. In declining health, he continued to agitate against the Afrikaner republics. He died at age forty-nine as the South African War (1899–1902) ended.

In accounting for Rhodes's remarkable but flawed achievements, both sympathetic and critical biographers

Cecil Rhodes, after crushing the last African revolt in Rhodesia in 1896. (© Baldwin H. Ward. Ward & Kathryn C. Ward/ Corbis)

stress his imposing physical size, enormous energy, and charismatic personality. His ideas were commonplace, but he believed in them passionately, and he could persuade and inspire others to follow his lead. Rhodes the idealist was nonetheless a born negotiator, a crafty deal maker who believed that everyone could be had for a price. According to his most insightful biographer, Rhodes's homosexuality — discreet, partially repressed, but undeniable — was also "a major component of his magnetism and his success."† Never comfortable with women, he loved male companionship. He drew together a "band of brothers," both gay and straight, who shared in his pursuit of power.

Rhodes cared nothing for the rights of Africans and blacks. Both a visionary and an opportunist, he looked forward to an eventual reconciliation of Afrikaners and British in a united white front. Therefore, as prime minister of the Cape Colony, he broke with the colony's liberal tradition and supported Afrikaner demands to reduce drastically the number of black voters and limit black freedoms. This helped lay the foundation for the Union of South Africa's brutal policy of racial segregation known as apartheid after 1948.

QUESTIONS FOR ANALYSIS

1. In what ways did Rhodes's career epitomize the New Imperialism in Africa?
2. How did Rhodes relate to Afrikaners and to black Africans? How do you account for the differences and the similarities?

*Robert I. Rotberg, *The Founder: Cecil Rhodes and the Pursuit of Power* (New York: Oxford University Press, 1988), p. 150.
†Ibid., p. 408.

and they responded with an intensive guerrilla war that took two years to put down. During the fighting, both sides enlisted the support of indigenous African troops. The British forces resorted to "scorched earth" policies, burning crops and villages in Boer regions, and, most notoriously, placed Boers and native Africans in rudimentary concentration camps in an attempt to halt the guerrilla campaign. News of these tactics provoked liberal outrage at home in Britain.

The war ended with a British victory in 1902, and in 1910 the Afrikaner territories were united with the old Cape Colony and the eastern province of Natal in a new Union of South Africa, established as a largely "self-governing" colony but still under British control. Gradually, however, the defeated Afrikaners used their numerical superiority over the British settlers to take political power, as even the most educated nonwhites lost the right to vote, except in the Cape Colony.

The British also fought to enlarge their colonies in West Africa, impatiently pushing northward from the Cape Colony, westward from Zanzibar, and southward from Egypt. In 1885 British troops stationed in the Sudanese city of Khartoum, an outpost on the Nile that protected imperial interests in Egypt, were massacred by fiercely independent Muslim Sudanese. A decade later the British sought to establish permanent rule in the disputed territory. Under the command of General Sir Herbert Kitchener (who would serve Britain as secretary of state for war during World War I), a well-armed force moved cautiously and more successfully up the Nile River, building a railroad to supply arms and reinforcements as it went. Finally, in 1898 these British troops confronted the poorly armed Sudanese army at the Battle of Omdurman (ahm-duhr-MAHN) (see Map 24.2). Sudanese soldiers charged the British lines time and time again, only to be cut down by the recently invented Maxim machine gun. In the solemn words of one English observer, "It was not a battle but an execution. The bodies were . . . spread evenly over acres and acres." In the end, about 10,000 Sudanese soldiers lay dead, while 28 Britons had been killed and 145 wounded.[6]

Continuing up the Nile after the battle, Kitchener's armies found that a small French force had already occupied the village of Fashoda (fuh-SHOH-duh). Locked in imperial competition with Britain ever since the British occupation of Egypt, France had tried to be first to reach one of Africa's last unclaimed areas—the upper reaches of the Nile. The result was a serious diplomatic crisis and the threat of war between two major European powers. Wracked by the Dreyfus affair (see Chapter 23) and unwilling to fight, France eventually backed down and withdrew its forces, allowing the British to take over.

The British conquest of Sudan exemplifies the general process of empire building in Africa. The fate of the Muslim-Sudanese force at Omdurman was inflicted on native peoples who openly resisted European control: they were blown away by vastly superior military force. The violent German suppression of armed rebellions in the colonies of German East Africa and German Southwest Africa, where revolt led to full-scale warfare and the deaths of some one hundred thousand Herero and Nama Africans, confirmed the rule. But as the Fashoda incident showed, however much the European powers squabbled for territory around the world, they had the sense to stop short of actually fighting each other. Imperial ambitions were not worth a great European war.

Imperialism in Asia

Although their sudden division of Africa was more spectacular, Europeans also exerted political control over much of Asia. Here the Dutch were a major player. In 1815 the Dutch ruled little more than the island of Java in the East Indies. Thereafter they gradually brought almost all of the three-thousand-mile Malay Archipelago under their political authority, though—in good imperialist fashion—they had to share some of the spoils with Britain and Germany. In the critical decade of the 1880s, the French under the leadership of Ferry took Indochina. India, Japan, and China also experienced a profound imperialist impact (Map 24.3).

Two other great imperialist powers, Russia and the United States, also acquired territories in Asia. Russia moved steadily forward on two fronts throughout the

MAP 24.3 Asia in 1914   India remained under British rule, while China preserved a precarious political independence. The Dutch Empire in modern-day Indonesia was old, but French control of Indochina was a product of the New Imperialism. Russia continued to expand to the south and to the east as well.

nineteenth century. Russians conquered Muslim areas to the south in the Caucasus and in Central Asia, reaching the border of Afghanistan in 1885. Russia also proceeded to nibble greedily on China's outlying provinces, especially in the 1890s.

The great conquest by the United States was the Philippines, taken from Spain in 1898 through the Spanish-American War. When it quickly became clear that the United States had no intention of granting the independence it had promised, Philippine patriots rose in revolt and were suppressed only after long, bitter fighting. Some Americans protested the taking of the Philippines, but to no avail. Thus another great Western power joined the imperialist ranks in Asia.

Causes of the New Imperialism

Many factors contributed to the late-nineteenth-century rush for empire, which was in turn one aspect of Western society's overall expansion in the age of industry and nationalism. It is little wonder that controversies have raged over interpretation of the New Imperialism, especially since authors of every persuasion have often exaggerated particular aspects in an attempt to prove their own theories. Yet despite complexity and controversy, basic causes are clearly identifiable.

Economic motives played an important role in the extension of political empires, especially in the British Empire. By the late 1870s France, Germany, and the United States were industrializing rapidly behind rising tariff barriers. Great Britain was losing its early economic lead and facing increasingly tough competition in foreign markets. In this changing economic climate, the seizure of Asian and African territory by continental powers in the 1880s raised alarms in Britain. Fearing that France and Germany would seal off their empires with high tariffs, resulting in the permanent loss of future economic opportunities, the British followed suit and began their own push to expand empire.

Actually, the overall economic gains of the New Imperialism proved quite limited before 1914. The new colonies were simply too poor to buy much, and they offered few immediately profitable investments. Nonetheless, even the poorest, most barren desert was jealously prized, and no territory was ever abandoned. This was because colonies became important for political and diplomatic reasons. Each leading country saw colonies as crucial to national security and military power. For instance, safeguarding the Suez Canal played a key role in the British occupation of Egypt, and protecting Egypt in turn led to the bloody conquest of Sudan. Far-flung possessions guaranteed ever-growing navies the safe havens and the dependable coaling stations they needed in time of crisis or war.

Along with economic motives, many people were convinced that colonies were essential to great nations. "There has never been a great power without great colonies," wrote one French publicist. The influential nationalist historian of Germany, Heinrich

Tools for Empire Building   Western technological advances aided Western political ambitions in Africa and Asia. The Maxim machine gun was highly mobile and could lay down a continuous barrage that would decimate charging enemies, as in the slaughter of Muslim soldiers at the Battle of Omdurman in the Sudan. (© Lordprice Collection/Alamy Stock Photo)

von Treitschke, spoke for many when he wrote: "Every virile people has established colonial power. . . . All great nations in the fullness of their strength have desired to set their mark upon barbarian lands and those who fail to participate in this great rivalry will play a pitiable role in time to come."[7]

Treitschke's harsh statement reflects not only the increasing aggressiveness of European nationalism after Bismarck's wars of German unification, but also Social Darwinian theories of brutal competition among races (see Chapter 23). As one prominent English economist argued, the "strongest nation has always been conquering the weaker . . . and the strongest tend to be best." Thus European nations, which saw themselves as racially distinct parts of the dominant white race, had to seize colonies to show they were strong and powerful. Moreover, since victory of the fittest in the struggle for survival was nature's inescapable law, the conquest of "inferior" peoples was just. "The path of progress is strewn with the wreck . . . of inferior races," wrote one professor in 1900. "Yet these dead peoples are, in very truth, the stepping stones on which mankind has risen to the higher intellectual and deeper emotional life of today."[8] Social Darwinism and pseudoscientific racial doctrines fostered imperialist expansion.

So did the industrial world's unprecedented technological and military superiority. Three aspects were particularly important. First, the rapidly firing Maxim machine gun, so lethal at Omdurman, was an ultimate weapon in many another unequal battle. Second, newly discovered quinine proved no less effective in controlling malaria, which had previously decimated whites in the tropics whenever they left breezy coastal enclaves and dared to venture into mosquito-infested interiors. Third, the combination of the steamship and the international telegraph permitted Western powers to quickly concentrate their firepower in a given area when it was needed. Never before—and never again after 1914—would the technological gap between the West and non-Western regions of the world be so great.

Social tensions and domestic political conflicts also contributed mightily to overseas expansion. In Germany and Russia, and in other countries to a lesser extent, conservative political leaders manipulated colonial issues to divert popular attention from the class struggle at home and to create a false sense of national unity. Thus imperial propagandists relentlessly stressed that colonies benefited workers as well as capitalists, providing jobs and cheap raw materials that raised workers' standard of living. Government leaders and their allies in the tabloid press successfully encouraged the masses to savor foreign triumphs and to glory in the supposed increase in national prestige. In short, conservative leaders defined imperialism as a national necessity, which they used to justify the status quo and their hold on power.

Finally, certain special-interest groups in each country were powerful agents of expansion. White settlers in the colonial areas demanded more land and greater state protection. Missionaries and humanitarians wanted to spread religion and stop the slave trade within Africa. Shipping companies wanted lucrative subsidies to protect rapidly growing global trade. Military men and colonial officials foresaw rapid advancement and highly paid positions in growing empires. The actions of such groups pushed the course of empire forward.

A "Civilizing Mission"

Western society did not rest the case for empire solely on naked conquest and a Darwinian racial struggle or on power politics and the need for naval bases on every ocean. Imperialists developed additional arguments for imperialism to satisfy their consciences and answer their critics.

A favorite idea was that Westerners could and should civilize more primitive non-white peoples. According to this view, Westerners shouldered the responsibility for governing and converting the supposed savages under their charge and strove to remake them on superior European models. Africans and Asians would eventually receive the benefits of industrialization and urbanization, Western education, Christianity, advanced medicine, and finally higher standards of living. In time, they might be ready for self-government and Western democracy. Thus the French repeatedly spoke of their imperial endeavors as a sacred "civilizing mission." Other imperialists agreed; as one German missionary put it, a combination of prayer and hard work under German direction would lead "the work-shy native to work of his own free will" and thus lead him to "an existence fit for human beings."⁹ Another argument was that imperial government protected natives from tribal warfare as well as from cruder forms of exploitation by white settlers and business people. In 1899 Rudyard Kipling (1865–1936), who wrote masterfully of Anglo-Indian life and was perhaps the most influential British writer of the 1890s, summarized such ideas in his poem "The White Man's Burden." (See "Evaluating the Evidence 24.2: The White Man's Burden," page 814.)

Many Americans accepted the ideology of the **white man's burden**. It was an important factor in the decision to rule, rather than liberate, the Philippines after the Spanish-American War. Like their European counterparts, these Americans believed that their civilization had reached unprecedented heights and that they had unique benefits to bestow on supposedly less advanced peoples.

Though the colonial administrators and military generals in charge of imperial endeavors were men, European women played a central role in the "civilizing mission." Proponents of imperial expansion actively encouraged women to "serve" in the colonies, and many answered the call. Some women worked as colonial missionaries, teachers, and nurses; others accompanied their husbands overseas. Europeans who embraced the "white man's burden" believed that the presence of white women in the colonies might help stop the spread of what they called "race mixing": the tendency of European men to establish cross-race marriages or relationships

white man's burden The idea that Europeans could and should civilize more primitive nonwhite peoples and that imperialism would eventually provide nonwhites with modern achievements and higher standards of living.

A Missionary School A Swahili schoolboy leads his classmates in a reading lesson in Dar es Salaam in German East Africa in 1903; portraits of Emperor Wilhelm II and his wife look down on the classroom, a reminder of imperial control. Europeans argued that they were spreading the benefits of a superior civilization with schools like this one, which is unusually well built and furnished because of its strategic location in the capital city. Schoolrooms were typically segregated by sex, and lessons for young men and women adhered to Western notions of gender difference. (ullstein bild/Granger, NYC — All rights reserved)

The White Man's Burden

When it was first published in an American illustrated magazine aimed at the middle class in 1899, Rudyard Kipling's well-known poem was read as encouragement for U.S. occupation of the Philippines in the aftermath of the Spanish-American War. It has since been understood as a forceful if somewhat anxious justification for Western imperialism in general.

Take up the White Man's Burden —
    Send forth the best ye breed —
Go, bind your sons to exile
    To serve your captive's need;
To wait, in heavy harness,
    On fluttered folk and wild —
Your new-caught sullen peoples,
    Half devil and half child.

Take up the White Man's burden —
    In patience to abide,
To veil the threat of terror
    And check the show of pride;
By open speech and simple,
    An hundred times made plain,
To seek another's profit
    And work another's gain.

Take up the White Man's burden —
    The savage wars of peace —
Fill full the mouth of Famine,
    And bid the sickness cease;
And when your goal is nearest
    (The end for others sought)
Watch sloth and heathen folly
    Bring all your hope to nought.

Take up the White Man's burden —
    No iron rule of kings,
But toil of serf and sweeper —
    The tale of common things.
The ports ye shall not enter,
    The roads ye shall not tread,

Go, make them with your living
    And mark them with your dead.

Take up the White Man's burden,
    And reap his old reward —
The blame of those ye better
    The hate of those ye guard —
The cry of those ye humor
    (Ah, slowly!) toward the light: —
"Why brought ye us from bondage,
    Our loved Egyptian night?"

Take up the White Man's burden —
    Ye dare not stoop to less —
Nor call too loud on Freedom
    To cloak your weariness.
By all ye will or whisper,
    By all ye leave or do,
The silent sullen peoples
    Shall weigh your God and you.

Take up the White Man's burden!
    Have done with childish days —
The lightly-proffered laurel,
    The easy ungrudged praise:
Comes now, to search your manhood
    Through all the thankless years,
Cold, edged with dear-bought wisdom,
    The judgment of your peers.

EVALUATE THE EVIDENCE

1. What, exactly, is the "white man's burden"? What, according to Kipling, are the costs and rewards of undertaking the "civilizing mission"?
2. Kipling's famous poem is over one hundred years old. Are its assertions for the legitimacy of "westernization" outdated, or do they still have resonance in today's global world?

Source: Reprinted in "The White Man's Versus the Brown Man's Burden," *The Literary Digest*, vol. 18, no. 8 (New York: Funk and Wagnalls, 1899), p. 219.

with indigenous women. If they stayed in the colonies long enough to establish a semipermanent household, European women might oversee native servants. Colonial encounters thus established complicated social hierarchies that entangled race, class, and gender.

Peace and stability under European control also facilitated the spread of Christianity. Catholic and Protestant missionaries—both men and women—competed with Islam south of the Sahara, seeking converts and building schools to spread the Gospel. Many Africans' first real contact with whites was in mission schools. Some peoples, such as the Ibo in Nigeria, became highly Christianized.

Such occasional successes in sub-Saharan Africa contrasted with the general failure of missionary efforts in India, China, and the Islamic world. There Christians often preached in vain to peoples with ancient, complex religious beliefs. Yet the number of Christian believers around the world did increase substantially in the nineteenth century, and missionary groups kept trying.

Orientalism

Even though many Westerners shared a sense of superiority over non-Western peoples, they were often fascinated by foreign cultures and societies. In the late 1970s the influential literary scholar Edward Said (sigh-EED) (1935–2003) coined the term **Orientalism** to describe this fascination and the stereotypical and often racist Western understandings of non-Westerners that dominated nineteenth-century Western thought. Said originally used "Orientalism" to refer to the way Europeans viewed "the Orient," or Arab societies in North Africa and the Middle East. The term caught on, however, and is often used more broadly to refer to Western views of non-Western peoples across the globe.

Said believed that it was almost impossible for people in the West to look at or understand non-Westerners without falling into some sort of Orientalist stereotype. Politicians, scholarly experts, writers and artists, and ordinary people readily adopted "us versus them" views of foreign peoples. The West, they believed, was modern, while the non-West was primitive. The West was white, the non-West colored; the West was rational, the non-West emotional; the West was Christian, the non-West pagan or Islamic. As part of this view of the non-West as radically "other," Westerners imagined the Orient as a place of mystery and romance, populated with exotic, dark-skinned peoples, where Westerners might have remarkable experiences of foreign societies and cultures.

Such views swept through North American and European scholarship, arts, and literature in the late nineteenth century. The emergence of ethnography and anthropology as academic disciplines in the 1880s was part of the process. Inspired by a new culture of collecting, scholars and adventurers went into the field, where they studied supposedly primitive cultures and traded for, bought, or stole artifacts from non-Western peoples. The results of their work were reported in scientific studies, articles, and books, and intriguing objects filled the display cases of new public museums of ethnography and natural history. In a slew of novels published around 1900, authors portrayed romance and high adventure in the colonies and so contributed to the Orientalist worldview. Artists followed suit, and dramatic paintings of ferocious Arab warriors, Eastern slave markets, and the sultan's harem adorned museum walls and wealthy middle-class parlors. Scholars, authors, and artists were not necessarily racists

Orientalism A term coined by literary scholar Edward Said to describe the way Westerners misunderstood and described colonial subjects and cultures.

or imperialists, but they found it difficult to escape Orientalist stereotypes. In the end they helped spread the notions of Western superiority and justified colonial expansion.

Critics of Imperialism

The expansion of empire aroused sharp, even bitter, critics. The forceful attack made by radical English economist J. A. Hobson (1858–1940) in *Imperialism* (1902), a work that influenced Lenin and others, was exemplary. Deeply angered by British tactics during the unpopular South African (Boer) War, Hobson contended that the rush to acquire colonies was due to the economic needs of unregulated capitalism, particularly the need of the rich to find outlets for their surplus capital. Yet, Hobson argued, imperial possessions did not pay off economically for the entire country. Only unscrupulous special-interest groups profited from them, at the expense of both European taxpayers and the natives. Moreover, Hobson argued that the quest for empire diverted popular attention away from domestic reform and the need to reduce the great gap between rich and poor.

Like Hobson, Marxist critics offered a thorough analysis and critique of Western imperialism. Rosa Luxemburg, a radical member of the German Social Democratic Party, argued that capitalism needed to expand into noncapitalist Asia and Africa to maintain high profits. The Russian Marxist and future revolutionary leader Vladimir Lenin concluded that imperialism represented the "highest stage" of advanced monopoly capitalism and predicted that its onset signaled the coming decay and collapse of capitalist society. These and similar arguments were not very persuasive, however. Most people then (and now) were sold on the idea that imperialism was profitable for the homeland and beneficial to the colonized, and the masses developed a broad and genuine enthusiasm for empire.

Hobson and many other critics struck home, however, with their moral condemnation of whites' imperiously ruling nonwhites. They rebelled against crude Social Darwinian thought. "O Evolution, what crimes are committed in thy name!" cried one foe. Another sardonically coined a new beatitude: "Blessed are the strong, for they shall prey on the weak."[10] Kipling and his kind were lampooned as racist bullies whose rule rested on brutality, racial contempt, and the Maxim gun. (See "Evaluating the Evidence 24.3: The Brown Man's Burden," at right.) Similarly, in 1902 in the novel *Heart of Darkness*—a demolishing critique of the Belgian exploitation of the Congo—Polish-born novelist Joseph Conrad (1857–1924) castigated the "pure selfishness" of Europeans in supposedly civilizing Africa. The main character, once a liberal scholar, turns into a savage brute.

Critics charged Europeans with applying a degrading double standard and failing to live up to their own noble ideals. At home, Europeans had won or were winning representative government, individual liberties, and a certain equality of opportunity. In their empires, Europeans imposed military dictatorships. Colonial administrators forced Africans and Asians to work involuntarily, almost like slaves, and subjected them to shameless discrimination. Only by renouncing imperialism, its critics insisted, and giving captive peoples the freedoms Western society had struggled for since the French Revolution would Europeans be worthy of their traditions. These critics provided colonial peoples with a Western ideology of liberation.

The Brown Man's Burden

As soon as it was published, Kipling's "The White Man's Burden" drew mockery from anti-imperialist intellectuals and politicians. In 1899 British publisher and Parliament member Henry Labouchère, known for his inflammatory views on any number of contemporary issues, wrote one of the most famous satires of Kipling's poem.

Pile on the brown man's burden
    To gratify your greed;
Go clear away the "niggers"
    Who progress would impede;
Be very stern, for truly
    'Tis useless to be mild
With new-caught, sullen peoples,
    Half devil and half child.

Pile on the brown man's burden;
    And if ye rouse his hate,
Meet his old-fashioned reasons
    With Maxims up to date.
With shells and dumdum bullets
    A hundred times made plain
The brown man's loss must ever
    Imply the white man's gain.

Pile on the brown man's burden,
    Compel him to be free;
Let all your manifestoes
    Reek with philanthropy.
And if with heathen folly
    He dares your will dispute,
Then in the name of freedom
    Don't hesitate to shoot.

Pile on the brown man's burden,
    And if his cry be sore,
That surely need not irk you—
    Ye've driven slaves before.
Seize on his ports and pastures,
    The fields his people tread;
Go make from them your living,
    And mark them with his dead.

Pile on the brown man's burden,
    Nor do not deem it hard

If you should earn the rancor
    Of these ye yearn to guard,
The screaming of your eagle
    Will drown the victim's sob—
Go on through fire and slaughter,
    There's dollars in the job.

Pile on the brown man's burden,
    And through the world proclaim
That ye are freedom's agent—
    There's no more paying game!
And should your own past history
    Straight in your teeth be thrown,
Retort that independence
    Is good for whites alone.

Pile on the brown man's burden,
    With equity have done;
Weak, antiquated scruples
    Their squeamish course have run,
And though 'tis freedom's banner
    You're waving in the van,
Reserve for home consumption
    The sacred "rights of man"!

And if by chance ye falter,
    Or lag along the course,
If, as the blood flows freely,
    Ye feel some slight remorse,
Hie ye to Rudyard Kipling,
    Imperialism's prop,
And bid him, for your comfort,
    Turn on his jingo stop.

EVALUATE THE EVIDENCE

1. What means does Labouchère use to mock Kipling's poem?
2. What, according to Labouchère, drives the imperial project? Does Kipling or Labouchère make the better case for the causes and effects of Western imperialism? Why?

Source: Reprinted in "The White Man's Versus the Brown Man's Burden," *The Literary Digest*, vol. 18, no. 8 (New York: Funk and Wagnalls, 1899), p. 219.

Responding to Western Imperialism

FOCUS QUESTION

What was the general pattern of non-Western responses to Western expansion?

To Africans and Asians, Western expansion represented a profoundly disruptive assault. Everywhere it threatened existing ruling classes, local economies, and long-standing ways of life. Christian missionaries and European secular ideologies challenged established beliefs and values. Non-Western peoples experienced imperialism as an invasion, one made all the more painful by the power and arrogance of the European intruders.

The Pattern of Response

Generally, the initial response of African and Asian rulers to aggressive Western expansion was to try to drive the unwelcome foreigners away. This was the case in China, Japan, and Sudan, as we have seen. Violent antiforeign reactions exploded elsewhere again and again, as in the lengthy U.S.-Indian wars, but the superior military technology of the industrialized West almost invariably prevailed. Beaten in battle, many Africans and Asians concentrated on preserving their cultural traditions at all costs. Others found themselves forced to reconsider their initial hostility. Some (such as Ismail of Egypt) concluded that the West was indeed superior in some ways and that it was therefore necessary to copy some European achievements, especially if they wished to escape full-blown Western political rule.

Thus it is possible to think of responses to the Western impact as a spectrum, with "traditionalists" at one end, "westernizers" or "modernizers" at the other, and many shades of opinion in between. Both before and after European domination, the struggle among these groups was often intense. With time, however, the modernizers tended to gain the upper hand.

When the power of both the traditionalists and the modernizers was thoroughly shattered by superior force, some Asians and Africans accepted imperial rule. Political participation in non-Western lands was historically limited to small elites, and ordinary people often did what their rulers told them to do. In these circumstances Europeans, clothed in power and convinced of their righteousness, tried to govern smoothly and effectively. At times they received considerable support from both traditionalists (local chiefs, landowners, religious leaders) and modernizers (Western-educated professional classes and civil servants).

Nevertheless, imperial rule was in many ways an imposing edifice built on sand. Support for European rule among subjugated peoples was shallow and weak. Colonized lands were primarily peasant societies, and much of the burden of colonization fell on small farmers who tenaciously fought for some measure of autonomy. When colonists demanded extra taxes or crops, peasants played dumb and hid the extent of their harvest; when colonists asked for increased labor, peasants dragged their feet. These "weapons of the weak" stopped short of open defiance but nonetheless presented a real challenge to Western rule.[11] Moreover, native people followed with greater or lesser enthusiasm the few determined personalities who came to openly oppose the Europeans. Such leaders always arose, both when Europeans ruled directly and when they manipulated native governments, for at least two basic reasons.

First, the nonconformists—the eventual anti-imperialist leaders—developed a burning desire for human dignity, economic emancipation, and political independence, all incompatible with foreign rule. Second, and somewhat ironically, potential leaders found in the Western world the ideologies underlying and justifying their protest. They discovered liberalism, with its credos of civil liberties and political self-determination. They echoed the demands of anti-imperialists in Europe and America that the West live up to its own ideals. Above all, they found themselves attracted to nationalism, which asserted that every people had the right to control its own destiny. After 1917 anti-imperialist revolt would find another European-made weapon in Lenin's version of Marxist socialism. Thus the anti-imperialist search for dignity drew strength from Western thought and culture, as is particularly apparent in the development of three major Asian countries—India, Japan, and China.

Empire in India

India was the jewel of the British Empire, and no colonial area experienced a more profound British impact. Unlike Japan and China, which maintained a real if precarious independence, and unlike African territories, which Europeans annexed only at the end of the nineteenth century, India was ruled more or less absolutely by Britain for a very long time.

Arriving in India on the heels of the Portuguese in the seventeenth century, the British East India Company had conquered the last independent native state by 1848. The last "traditional" response to European rule—an attempt by the existing ruling classes to drive the invaders out by military force—was broken in India in 1857 and 1858. Those were the years of the **Great Rebellion** (which the British called a "mutiny"), an insurrection by Muslim and Hindu mercenaries in the British army that spread throughout northern and central India before it was finally crushed, primarily by loyal indigenous troops from southern India. Britain then established direct control until Indian independence was gained in 1947.

India was ruled by the British Parliament in London and administered by a tiny, all-white civil service in India. In 1900 this elite consisted of fewer than 3,500 top officials, who controlled a population of 300 million. The white elite, backed by white officers and indigenous troops, was competent and generally well disposed toward the welfare of the Indian peasant masses. Yet it practiced strict job discrimination and social segregation, and most of its members quite frankly considered what they saw as the jumble of Indian peoples and castes to be racially inferior. As Lord Kitchener, one of the most distinguished top military commanders in India, stated:

> It is this consciousness of the inherent superiority of the European which has won for us India. However well educated and clever a native may be, and however brave he may prove himself, I believe that no rank we can bestow on him would cause him to be considered an equal of the British officer.[12]

British women played an important part in the imperial enterprise, especially after the opening of the Suez Canal in 1869 made it much easier for civil servants and businessmen to bring their wives and children with them to India. These British families tended to live in their own separate communities, where they occupied large houses with well-shaded porches, handsome lawns, and a multitude of servants. It was the wife's responsibility to manage this complex household. Many officials' wives

The Great Rebellion, 1857–1858

Great Rebellion The 1857 and 1858 insurrection by Muslim and Hindu mercenaries in the British army that spread throughout northern and central India before finally being crushed.

learned to relish their duties, and they directed their households and servants with the same self-confident authoritarianism that characterized their husbands' political rule.

A small minority of British women—many of them feminists, social reformers, or missionaries, both married and single—sought to go further and shoulder what one historian has called the "white women's burden" in India.[13] These women tried especially to improve the lives of Indian women, both Hindu and Muslim, promoting education and legislation to move them closer to the better conditions they believed Western women had attained. Their greatest success was educating some elite Hindu women who took up the cause of reform.

Inspired by the "civilizing mission"—as well as strong feelings of racial and cultural superiority—British imperialists worked energetically to westernize Indian society. Realizing that they needed well-educated Indians to serve as skilled subordinates in both the government and the army, the British established a modern system of secondary education, with all instruction in English. Thus some Indians gained excellent opportunities for economic and social advancement. High-caste Hindus, particularly quick to respond, emerged as skillful intermediaries between the British rulers and the Indian people, and soon they formed a new elite profoundly influenced by Western thought and culture.

This new Indian elite joined British officials and businessmen to promote modern economic development, a second result of British rule. Examples included constructing irrigation projects for agriculture, building the world's third-largest railroad network for good communications, and forming large tea and jute plantations geared to the world economy. Unfortunately, the lot of the Indian masses improved little, for the profits from the increase in production went to indigenous and British elites.

Finally, with a well-educated, English-speaking Indian bureaucracy and steps toward economic development, the British created a unified, powerful state. They placed under the same system of law and administration the different Hindu and Muslim peoples and the vanquished kingdoms of the entire subcontinent—groups that had fought each other for centuries and had been repeatedly conquered by Muslim and Mongol invaders. It was as if Europe, with its many states and varieties of Christianity, had been conquered and united in a single great empire.

Despite these achievements, the decisive reaction to European rule was the rise of nationalism among the Indian elite. No matter how anglicized and necessary a member of the indigenous educated classes became, he or she could never become the white ruler's equal. The top jobs, the best clubs, the modern hotels, and even certain railroad compartments were off limits to darker-skinned Indians. The peasant masses might accept such inequality as the latest version of age-old oppression, but the well-educated, English-speaking elite eventually could not. For them, racial discrimination meant injured pride and bitter injustice. It flagrantly contradicted the cherished Western concepts of human rights and equality that they had learned about in Western schools. Moreover, it was based on dictatorship, no matter how benign.

By 1885, when educated Indians came together to found the predominantly Hindu Indian National Congress, demands were increasing for the equality and self-government that Britain had already granted white-settler colonies, such as Canada and Australia. By 1907, emboldened in part by Japan's success (see the next section), a radical faction in the Indian National Congress called for Indian independence. Although there were sharp divisions between Hindus and Muslims on what shape the Indian future should take, among other issues, Indians were finding an answer to the foreign challenge. The common heritage of British rule and Western ideals, along with the reform and revitalization of the Hindu religion, had created a genuine movement for national independence.

The Example of Japan

When Commodore Matthew Perry arrived in Tokyo in 1853 with his crude but effective gunboat diplomacy, Japan was a complex feudal society. At the top stood a figurehead emperor, but real power was in the hands of a hereditary military governor, the shogun. With the help of a warrior nobility known as samurai, the shogun governed a country of hard-working, productive peasants and city dwellers. The intensely proud samurai were humiliated by the sudden American intrusion and the unequal treaties with Western countries that followed.

When foreign diplomats and merchants began to settle in Yokohama, radical samurai reacted with a wave of antiforeign terrorism and antigovernment assassinations that lasted from 1858 to 1863. In response, an allied fleet of American, British, Dutch, and French warships demolished key forts, further weakening the power and prestige of the shogun's government. Then in 1867 a coalition led by patriotic samurai seized control of the government with hardly any bloodshed and restored the political power of the emperor in the **Meiji Restoration**, a great turning point in Japanese history.

The battle cry of the Meiji (MAY-jee) reformers was "Enrich the state and strengthen the armed forces," and the immediate goal of the new government was to meet the foreign threat. Yet how were these tasks to be accomplished? In a remarkable about-face, the leaders of Meiji Japan dropped their antiforeign attacks. Convinced that Western civilization was indeed superior in its military and industrial aspects, they initiated a series of measures to reform Japan along modern lines. In the broadest sense, the Meiji leaders tried to harness Western industrialization and political reform to protect their country and catch up with Europe.

In 1871 the new leaders abolished the old feudal structure of aristocratic, decentralized government and formed a strong unified state. Following the example of the French Revolution, they dismantled the four-class legal system and declared social equality. They decreed freedom of movement in a country where traveling abroad had been a serious crime. They created a free, competitive, government-stimulated economy. Japan began to build railroads and modern factories. The new generation adopted many principles of a free, liberal society, and, as in Europe, the resulting freedom resulted in a tremendously creative release of human energy.

Yet the overriding concern of Japan's political leadership was always to maintain a powerful state and a strong military. State leaders created a powerful modern navy and completely reorganized the army along European lines, forming a professional officer corps and requiring three years of military service of all males. This army of draftees effectively put down disturbances in the countryside, and in 1877 it crushed a major rebellion by feudal elements protesting the loss of their privileges. In addition, Japan skillfully adapted the West's science and technology, particularly in industry, medicine, and education, and many Japanese studied abroad. The government paid large salaries to attract foreign experts, who were replaced by trained Japanese as soon as possible.

By 1890, when the new state was firmly established, the wholesale borrowing of the early restoration had given way to a more selective emphasis on those things foreign that were in keeping with Japanese tradition. Following the model of the

Meiji Restoration The restoration of the Japanese emperor to power in 1867, leading to the subsequent modernization of Japan.

The Russo-Japanese War, 1904–1905   This 1904 Japanese print portrays the surprise Japanese naval attack on the Russian fleet at Port Arthur as a glorious victory. Though the opening battle was in fact inconclusive, with few losses on either side, the Japanese won the war. Defeat by a supposedly "primitive" Asian nation encouraged reform movements in the Russian Empire and became a factor in the outbreak of the Russian Revolution of 1905 (see Chapter 23). (Universal History Archive/Getty Images)

German Empire, Japan established an authoritarian constitution and rejected democracy. The power of the emperor and his ministers was vast, that of the legislature limited.

Japan also successfully copied the imperialism of Western society. Expansion proved that Japan was strong and cemented the nation together in a great mission. Having "opened" Korea with its own gunboat diplomacy in 1876, Japan decisively defeated China in a war over Korea in 1894 and 1895 and took Formosa (modern-day Taiwan). In the next years, Japan competed aggressively with European powers for influence and territory in China, particularly in Manchuria, where Japanese and Russian imperialism collided. In 1904 Japan launched the Russo-Japanese War (1904–1905) by attacking Russia without a formal declaration of war. After a series of bloody battles, victorious Japan took over Russia's former protectorate in Port Arthur and emerged with a valuable foothold in China (see Map 24.3). By 1910, with the annexation of Korea, Japan had become a major imperialist power.

Japan became the first non-Western country to use an ancient love of country to transform itself and thereby meet the many-sided challenge of Western expansion. Moreover, Japan demonstrated convincingly that a modern Asian nation could defeat and humble a great Western power. Japan's achievement fascinated many Chinese and Vietnamese nationalists and provided patriots throughout Asia and Africa with an inspiring example of national recovery and liberation.

Toward Revolution in China

In 1860 the two-hundred-year-old Qing Dynasty in China appeared on the verge of collapse. Efforts to repel foreigners had failed, and rebellion and chaos wracked the country. Yet the government drew on its traditional strengths and made a surprising comeback that lasted more than thirty years.

Two factors were crucial in this reversal. First, the traditional ruling groups temporarily produced new and effective leadership. Loyal scholar-statesmen and generals quelled disturbances such as the great Tai Ping rebellion. The remarkable empress dowager Tzu Hsi (tsoo shee) governed in the name of her young son, combining shrewd insight with vigorous action to revitalize the bureaucracy.

Second, destructive foreign aggression lessened, for the Europeans had obtained their primary goal of establishing commercial and diplomatic relations. Indeed, some Europeans contributed to the dynasty's recovery. A talented Irishman effectively reorganized China's customs office, increasing government tax receipts, and a sympathetic

American diplomat represented China in foreign lands, helping to strengthen the Chinese government. Such efforts dovetailed with the dynasty's efforts to adopt some aspects of Western government and technology while maintaining traditional Chinese values and beliefs.

The parallel movement toward domestic reform and limited cooperation with the West collapsed under the blows of Japanese imperialism. Defeat in the Sino-Japanese War (1894–1895) and the subsequent harsh peace treaty revealed China's helplessness in the face of aggression, triggering a rush by foreign powers for concessions and protectorates. At the high point of this rush in 1898, it appeared that the European powers might actually divide China among themselves, as they had recently divided Africa. Probably only the jealousy each nation felt toward its imperialist competitors saved China from partition. In any event, the tempo of foreign encroachment greatly accelerated after 1894.

China's precarious position after the war with Japan led to a renewed drive for fundamental reforms. Like the leaders of the Meiji Restoration, some modernizers saw salvation in Western institutions. In 1898 they convinced the young emperor to launch a desperate **hundred days of reform** in an attempt to meet the foreign challenge. More radical reformers, such as the revolutionary Sun Yatsen (1866–1925), who came from the peasantry and was educated in Hawaii by Christian missionaries, sought to overthrow the dynasty altogether and establish a republic.

The efforts at radical reform by the young emperor and his allies threatened the Qing establishment and the empress dowager Tzu Hsi, who had dominated the court for a quarter of a century. In a palace coup, she and her supporters imprisoned the emperor, rejected the reform movement, and put reactionary officials in charge. Hope for reform from above was crushed.

A violent antiforeign reaction swept the country, encouraged by the Qing court and led by a secret society that foreigners called the Boxers. The conservative, patriotic Boxers blamed China's ills on foreigners, charging foreign missionaries with undermining Chinese reverence for their ancestors and thereby threatening the Chinese family and the society as a whole. In the agony of defeat and unwanted reforms, the Boxers and other secret societies struck out at their enemies. In northeastern China, more than two hundred foreign missionaries and several thousand Chinese Christians were killed, prompting threats and demands from Western governments. The empress dowager answered by declaring war on the foreign powers, hoping that the Boxers might relieve the foreign pressure on the government.

The imperialist response was swift and harsh. After the Boxers besieged the embassy quarter in Beijing, foreign governments (including Japan, Britain, France, Germany, and the United States) organized an international force of twenty thousand soldiers to rescue their diplomats and punish China. These troops defeated the Boxers and occupied and plundered Beijing. In 1901 China was forced to accept a long list of penalties, including a heavy financial indemnity payable over forty years.

The years after this heavy defeat were ever more troubled. Anarchy and foreign influence spread as the power and prestige of the Qing Dynasty declined still further. Antiforeign, antigovernment revolutionary groups agitated and plotted. Finally, in 1912 a spontaneous uprising toppled the Qing Dynasty. After thousands of years of emperors, a loose coalition of revolutionaries proclaimed a Western-style republic and called for an elected parliament. The transformation of China under the impact of expanding Western society entered a new phase, and the end was not in sight.

hundred days of reform A series of Western-style reforms launched in 1898 by the Chinese government in an attempt to meet the foreign challenge.

LOOKING BACK LOOKING AHEAD

In the early twentieth century educated Europeans had good reason to believe that they were living in an age of progress. The ongoing triumphs of industry and science and the steady improvements in the standard of living beginning about 1850 were undeniable, and it was generally assumed that these favorable trends would continue. There had also been progress in the political realm. The bitter class conflicts that culminated in the bloody civil strife of 1848 had given way in most European countries to stable nation-states with elected legislative bodies that reflected the general population, responded to real problems, and enjoyed popular support. Moreover, there had been no general European war since Napoleon's defeat in 1815. Only the brief, limited wars connected with German and Italian unification at midcentury had broken the peace in the European heartland.

In the global arena, peace was much more elusive. In the name of imperialism, Europeans (and North Americans) used war and the threat of war to open markets and punish foreign governments around the world. Although criticized by some intellectuals and leftists such as J. A. Hobson, these foreign campaigns resonated with European citizens and stimulated popular nationalism. Like fans in a sports bar, the peoples of Europe followed their colonial teams and cheered them on to victories that were almost certain. Thus imperialism and nationalism reinforced and strengthened each other in Europe, especially after 1875.

This was a dangerous development. Easy imperialist victories over weak states and poorly armed non-Western peoples encouraged excessive pride and led Europeans to underestimate the fragility of their accomplishments as well as the murderous power of their weaponry. Imperialism also made nationalism more aggressive and militaristic. At the same time that European imperialism was dividing the world, the leading European states were also dividing themselves into two opposing military alliances. Thus when the two armed camps stumbled into war in 1914, there would be a superabundance of nationalistic fervor, patriotic sacrifice, and cataclysmic destruction.

Make Connections

Think about the larger developments and continuities within and across chapters.

1. How did the expansion of European empires transform everyday life around the world?

2. Historians often use the term *New Imperialism* to describe the globalization of empire that began in the last decades of the nineteenth century. Was the New Imperialism really that different from earlier waves of European expansion (Chapters 14 and 17)?

3. How did events and trends in European colonies connect to or reflect events and trends in the European homeland?

24 REVIEW & EXPLORE

Review the Main Ideas

Answer the focus questions from each section of the chapter.

◆ What were some of the global consequences of European industrialization between 1815 and 1914? (p. 792)

◆ How was massive migration an integral part of Western expansion? (p. 799)

◆ How did Western imperialism change after 1880? (p. 803)

◆ What was the general pattern of non-Western responses to Western expansion? (p. 818)

Identify Key Terms

Identify and explain the significance of each item below.

neo-Europes (p. 794)

Opium Wars (p. 796)

gunboat diplomacy (p. 797)

global mass migration (p. 799)

nativism (p. 803)

New Imperialism (p. 804)

Afrikaners (p. 805)

Berlin Conference (p. 807)

white man's burden (p. 813)

Orientalism (p. 815)

Great Rebellion (p. 819)

Meiji Restoration (p. 821)

hundred days of reform (p. 823)

NOTES

1. Quoted in J. W. Hall, *Japan: From Prehistory to Modern Times* (New York: Delacorte Press, 1970), p. 250.

2. Quoted in Earl of Cromer, *Modern Egypt* (London, 1911), p. 48.

3. Quoted in T. Blegen, *Norwegian Migration to America*, vol. 2 (Northfield, Minn.: Norwegian-American Historical Association, 1940), p. 468.

4. Quoted in I. Howe, *World of Our Fathers* (New York: Harcourt Brace Jovanovich, 1975), p. 290.

5. Quoted in W. L. Langer, *European Alliances and Alignments, 1871–1890* (New York: Vintage Books, 1931), p. 290.

6. Quoted in J. Ellis, *The Social History of the Machine Gun* (New York: Pantheon Books, 1975), pp. 86, 101. The numbers given for British casualties at the Battle of Omdurman vary; the total casualties quoted here come from an original British army report. See Lieutenant General H. M. L. Rundle, M.G., Chief of Staff, "Herewith Returns of Killed and Wounded of the Expeditionary Force at the Battle of Khartum, on September 2, 1898," Khartum, September 9, 1898, at North East Medals, http://www.britishmedals.us/kevin/other/lgomdurman.html.

7. Quoted in G. H. Nadel and P. Curtis, eds., *Imperialism and Colonialism* (New York: Macmillan, 1964), p. 94.

8. Quoted in W. L. Langer, *The Diplomacy of Imperialism*, 2d ed. (New York: Alfred A. Knopf, 1951), pp. 86, 88.

9. Quoted in S. Conrad, *Globalisation and the Nation in Imperial Germany* (New York: Cambridge University Press, 2010), p. 78.

10. Quoted in Langer, *The Diplomacy of Imperialism*, p. 88.

11. J. C. Scott, *Weapons of the Weak: Everyday Forms of Peasant Resistance* (New Haven: Yale University Press, 1985), p. xvi.

12. Quoted in K. M. Panikkar, *Asia and Western Dominance: A Survey of the Vasco da Gama Epoch of Asian History* (London: George Allen & Unwin, 1959), p. 116.

13. A. Burton, "The White Women's Burden: British Feminists and 'The Indian Women,' 1865–1915," in *Western Women and Imperialism: Complicity and Resistance*, ed. N. Chauduri and M. Strobel (Bloomington: Indiana University Press, 1992), pp. 137–157.

CHAPTER PREVIEW

The Road to War
What caused the outbreak of the First World War?

Waging Total War
How did the First World War differ from previous wars?

The Home Front
In what ways did the war transform life on the home front?

The Russian Revolution
Why did world war lead to revolution in Russia, and what was its outcome?

The Peace Settlement
In what ways was the Allied peace settlement flawed?

Life in World War I
This painting by British artist Paul Nash portrays a supply road on the western front. Nash's somber palette, tiny figures, and Cubist-influenced landscape capture the devastation and anonymous violence of total war.
(*The Menin Road*, 1919/Imperial War Museum, London, UK/Bridgeman Images)

25

War and Revolution

1914–1919

In the summer of 1914 the nations of Europe went willingly to war. They believed they had no other choice. Both peoples and governments confidently expected a short war leading to a decisive victory and thought that European society would be able to go on as before. These expectations were totally mistaken. The First World War was long, indecisive, and tremendously destructive. To the shell-shocked generation of survivors, it was known simply as the Great War because of its unprecedented scope and intensity.

From today's perspective, it is clear that the First World War was closely connected to the ideals and developments of the previous century. Industrialization, which promised a rising standard of living, now produced horrendous weapons that killed and maimed millions. Imperialism, which promised to civilize those the Europeans considered savages, now led to intractable international conflicts. Nationalism, which promised to bring compatriots together in a harmonious nation-state, now encouraged hateful prejudice and chauvinism. The extraordinary violence of world war shook confidence in such nineteenth-century certainties to their core.

The war would have an enormous impact on the century that followed. The need to provide extensive supplies and countless soldiers for the war effort created mass suffering, encouraged the rise of the bureaucratic state, and brought women in increasing numbers into the workplace. Millions were killed or wounded at the front, and millions more grieved these losses. Grand states collapsed: the Russian, Austro-Hungarian, and Ottoman Empires passed into history. The trauma of war contributed to the rise of extremist politics—in the Russian Revolution of 1917 the Bolsheviks established a radical Communist regime, and totalitarian

Fascist movements gained popularity across Europe in the postwar decades. Explaining the war's causes and consequences remains one of the great challenges for historians of modern Europe. ■

The Road to War

FOCUS QUESTION
What caused the outbreak of the First World War?

Historians have long debated why Europeans so readily pursued a war that was long and costly and failed to resolve the problems faced by the combatant nations. There was no single most important cause. Growing competition over colonies and world markets, a belligerent arms race, and a series of diplomatic crises sharpened international tensions. On the home front, new forms of populist nationalism strengthened people's unquestioning belief in "my country right or wrong" while ongoing domestic conflicts encouraged governments to pursue aggressive foreign policies in attempts to bolster national unity. All helped pave the road to war.

Growing International Conflict

The First World War began, in part, because European statesmen failed to resolve the diplomatic problems created by Germany's rise to Great Power status. The Franco-Prussian War and the unification of Germany opened a new era in international relations. By the war's end in 1871, France was defeated, and Bismarck had made Prussia-Germany the most powerful nation in Europe (see Chapter 23). After 1871 Bismarck declared that Germany was a "satisfied" power. Within Europe, he stated, Germany had no territorial ambitions and wanted only peace.

But how was peace to be preserved? Bismarck's first concern was to keep France—bitter over its defeat and the loss of Alsace and Lorraine—diplomatically isolated and without allies. His second concern was the threat to peace posed by the enormous multinational empires of Austria-Hungary and Russia, particularly in southeastern Europe, where the waning strength of the Ottoman Empire had created a threatening power vacuum in the disputed border territories of the Balkans.

Bismarck's accomplishments in foreign policy were effective, but only temporary. From 1871 to the late 1880s, he maintained German leadership in international affairs, and he signed a series of defensive alliances with Austria-Hungary and Russia designed to isolate France. Yet in 1890 the new emperor Wilhelm II incautiously dismissed Bismarck, in part because he disagreed with the chancellor's friendly policy toward Russia. Under Wilhelm II, Bismarck's carefully planned alliance system began to unravel. Germany refused to renew a nonaggression pact with Russia, the centerpiece of Bismarck's system, in spite of Russian willingness to do so. This fateful move prompted long-isolated republican France to court absolutist Russia, offering loans, arms, and diplomatic support. In early 1894 France and Russia became military allies. As a result, continental Europe was divided into two rival blocs. The **Triple Alliance** of Austria, Germany, and Italy faced an increasingly hostile Dual Alliance of Russia and France, and the German general staff began secret preparations for a war on two fronts (Map 25.1).

Triple Alliance The alliance of Austria, Germany, and Italy. Italy left the alliance when war broke out in 1914 on the grounds that Austria had launched a war of aggression.

Chronology

1914–1918	World War I
June 28, 1914	Serbian nationalist assassinates Archduke Franz Ferdinand
August 1914	War begins
September 1914	Battle of the Marne; German victories on the eastern front
October 1914	Ottoman Empire joins the Central Powers
1915	Italy joins the Triple Entente; German submarine sinks the *Lusitania*; Germany halts unrestricted submarine warfare; Battle of Gallipoli
1915–1918	Armenian genocide; German armies occupy large parts of east-central Europe
1916	Battles of Verdun and the Somme
1916–1918	Antiwar movement spreads throughout Europe; Arab rebellion against Ottoman Empire
1917	Germany resumes unrestricted submarine warfare
March 1917	February Revolution in Russia
April 1917	United States enters the war
October–November 1917	Battle of Caporetto
November 1917	Bolshevik Revolution in Russia; Balfour Declaration on Jewish homeland in Palestine
1918	Treaty of Brest-Litovsk; revolution in Germany
1918–1920	Civil war in Russia
1919	Treaty of Versailles; Allies invade Turkey
1923	Treaty of Lausanne recognizes Turkish independence

MAP 25.1

European Alliances at the Outbreak of World War I, 1914

At the start of World War I, Europe was divided into two hostile alliances: the Triple Entente of Britain, France, and Russia, and the Triple Alliance of Germany, Austria-Hungary, and Italy. Italy never fought with the Triple Alliance but instead joined the Entente in 1915.

As rivalries deepened on the continent, Great Britain's foreign policy became increasingly crucial. After 1891 Britain was the only uncommitted Great Power. Many Germans and some Britons felt that the advanced, racially related Germanic and Anglo-Saxon peoples were natural allies. However, the good relations that had prevailed between Prussia and Great Britain since the mid-eighteenth century gave way to a bitter Anglo-German rivalry.

There were several reasons for this ill-fated development. Commercial rivalry in world markets between Germany and Great Britain increased sharply in the 1890s, as Germany became a great industrial power. Germany's ambitious pursuit of colonies further threatened British interests. Above all, Germany's decision in 1900 to expand significantly its battle fleet posed a challenge to Britain's long-standing naval supremacy. In response to German expansion, British leaders prudently shored up their exposed global position with alliances and agreements. Britain improved its often-strained relations with the United States, concluded an alliance with Japan in 1902, and allied with France in the Anglo-French Entente of 1904, which settled all outstanding colonial disputes between Britain and France.

Alarmed by Britain's closer ties to France, Germany's leaders decided to test the strength of their alliance. In 1905 Wilhelm II declared that Morocco—where France had colonial interests—was an independent, sovereign state and demanded that Germany receive the same trading rights as France. Wilhelm II insisted on an international conference in hopes that his saber rattling would settle the Moroccan question to Germany's benefit. But his crude bullying only brought France and Britain closer together, and Germany left the conference empty-handed.

The result of the First Moroccan Crisis in 1905 was something of a diplomatic revolution. Britain, France, Russia, and even the United States began to see Germany as a potential threat. At the same time, German leaders began to see sinister plots to encircle Germany and block its development as a world power. In 1907 Russia, battered by its disastrous war with Japan and the revolution of 1905, agreed to settle its quarrels with Great Britain in Persia and Central Asia and signed the Anglo-Russian Agreement. This agreement laid the foundation of the **Triple Entente** (ahn-TAHNT), an alliance between Britain, Russia, and France.

Germany's decision to expand its navy with a large, enormously expensive fleet of big-gun battleships, known as "dreadnoughts" because of their great size and power, heightened international tensions. German patriots saw a large navy as the legitimate right of a great world power and as a source of national pride. But British leaders saw the German buildup as a military challenge that forced them to spend the "People's Budget" (see Chapter 23) on battleships rather than social welfare. In 1909 the London *Daily Mail* hysterically informed its readers that "Germany is deliberately preparing to destroy the British Empire."[1] By then Britain had sided psychologically, if not officially, with France and Russia.

The leading nations of Europe were divided into two hostile camps, both ill-prepared to deal with the worsening situation in the Balkans. Britain, France, and Russia—the Triple Entente—were in direct opposition to the German-led Triple Alliance (see Map 25.1). This unfortunate treaty system only confirmed the failure of all European leaders to incorporate Bismarck's mighty empire permanently and peacefully into the international system. By 1914 many believed that war was inevitable.

Triple Entente The alliance of Great Britain, France, and Russia prior to and during the First World War.

The Mood of 1914

Diplomatic rivalries and international crises played key roles in the rush to war, but a complete understanding of the war's origins requires an account of the "mood of 1914"—the attitudes and convictions of Europeans around 1914.[2] Widespread militarism (the popular approval of military institutions and their values) and nationalism encouraged leaders and citizens alike to see international relations as an arena for the testing of national power, with war if necessary.

Germany was especially famous for its powerful and aggressive army, but military institutions played a prominent role in affairs of state and in the lives of ordinary people across Europe. In a period marked by diplomatic tensions, politicians relied on generals and military experts to help shape public policy. All the Great Powers built up their armed forces and designed mobilization plans to rush men and weapons to the field of battle. Universal conscription in Germany, France, Italy, Austria-Hungary, and Russia—only Britain still relied on a volunteer army—exposed hundreds of thousands of young men each year to military culture and discipline.

The continent had not experienced a major conflict since the Franco-Prussian War (1870–1871), so Europeans vastly underestimated the destructive potential of modern weapons. Encouraged by the patriotic national press, many believed that war was glorious, manly, and heroic. If they expected another conflict, they thought it would be over quickly. Leading politicians and intellectuals likewise portrayed war as a test of strength that would lead to national unity and renewal. Such ideas permeated European society. As one German volunteer wrote in his diary as he left for the front in 1914, "I believe that this war is a challenge for our time and for each individual, a test by fire, that we may ripen into manhood, become men able to cope with the coming stupendous years and events."[3]

Support for military values was closely linked to a growing sense of popular nationalism, the notion that one's country was superior to all others (see Chapters 21 and 23). Since the 1850s the spread of the idea that members of an ethnic group should live together in a homogeneous, united nation-state had provoked all kinds of international conflicts over borders and citizenship rights. Nationalism drove the spiraling arms race and the struggle over colonies. Broad popular commitment to national interests above all else weakened groups that thought in terms of international communities and consequences. Expressions of antiwar sentiment by socialists, pacifists, and women's groups were seen as a betrayal of country in time of need. Inspired by nationalist beliefs, much of the population was ready for war.

Leading statesmen had practical reasons for promoting militarism and nationalism. Political leaders had long used foreign adventurism and diplomatic posturing to distract the people from domestic conflicts. In Great Britain, leaders faced civil war in Northern Ireland and a vocal and increasingly radical women's movement. In Russia, defeat in the Russo-Japanese War (1904–1905) and the revolution of 1905 had greatly weakened support for the tsarist regime. In Germany, the victory of the Marxist Social Democratic Party in the parliamentary elections of 1912 led government authorities to worry that the country was falling apart. The French likewise faced difficult labor and budget problems.

Determined to hold on to power and frightened by rising popular movements, ruling classes across Europe were willing to gamble on diplomatic brinksmanship and even war to postpone dealing with intractable social and political conflicts.

Victory promised to preserve the privileged positions of elites and rally the masses behind the national cause. The patriotic nationalism bolstered by the outbreak of war did bring unity in the short run, but the wealthy governing classes underestimated the risk of war to themselves. They had forgotten that great wars and great social revolutions very often go hand in hand.

The Outbreak of War

On June 28, 1914, Archduke Franz Ferdinand, heir to the Austro-Hungarian throne, was assassinated by Serbian revolutionaries during a state visit to the Bosnian capital of Sarajevo (sar-uh-YAY-voh). After a series of failed attempts to bomb the archduke's motorcade, Gavrilo Princip, a fanatical member of the radical group the Black Hand, shot the archduke and his wife, Sophie, in their automobile. After his capture, Princip remained defiant, asserting at his trial, "I am a Yugoslav nationalist, aiming for the unification of all Yugoslavs, and I do not care what form of state, but it must be free from Austria."[4]

Princip's deed, in the crisis-ridden borderlands between the weakened Ottoman and Austro-Hungarian Empires, led Europe into world war. In the early years of the twentieth century, war in the Balkans—"the powder keg of Europe"—seemed inevitable. The reason was simple: between 1900 and 1914 the Western powers had successfully forced the Ottoman rulers to give up their European territories. Serbs, Bulgarians, Albanians, and others now sought to establish independent nation-states, and the ethnic nationalism inspired by these changing state boundaries was destroying the Ottoman Empire and threatening Austria-Hungary (Map 25.2). The only questions were what kinds of wars would result and where they would lead.

By the early twentieth century nationalism in southeastern Europe was on the rise. Independent Serbia was eager to build a state that would include all ethnic Serbs and was thus openly hostile to Austria-Hungary and the Ottoman Empire, since both states included substantial Serbian minorities within their borders. To block Serbian expansion, Austria in 1908 annexed the territories of Bosnia and Herzegovina (hehrt-suh-goh-VEE-nuh). The southern part of the Austro-Hungarian Empire now included an even larger Serbian population. Serbians expressed rage but could do nothing without support from Russia, their traditional ally.

The tensions in the Balkans soon erupted into regional warfare. In the First Balkan War (1912), Serbia joined Greece and Bulgaria to attack the Ottoman Empire and then quarreled with Bulgaria over the spoils of victory. In the Second Balkan War (1913), Bulgaria attacked its former allies. Austria intervened and forced Serbia to give up Albania. After centuries, nationalism had finally destroyed the Ottoman Empire in Europe. Encouraged by their success against the Ottomans, Balkan nationalists increased their demands for freedom from Austria-Hungary, dismaying the leaders of that multinational empire.

Within this complex context, the assassination of Archduke Franz Ferdinand instigated a five-week period of intense diplomatic activity that culminated in world war. The leaders of Austria-Hungary concluded that Serbia was implicated in the assassination and deserved severe punishment. On July 23 Austria-Hungary gave Serbia an unconditional ultimatum that would violate Serbian sovereignty. When Serbia replied moderately but evasively, Austria mobilized its armies and declared war on Serbia on July 28. In this way, multinational Austria-Hungary,

MAP 25.2 The Balkans, 1878–1914   After the Congress of Berlin in 1878, the Ottoman Empire suffered large territorial losses but remained a power in the Balkans. By 1914 Ottoman control had given way to ethnic population groups that flowed across political boundaries, and growing Serbian national aspirations threatened Austria-Hungary.

desperate to save its empire, deliberately chose war to stem the rising tide of hostile nationalism within its borders.

From the beginning of the crisis, Germany encouraged Austria-Hungary to confront Serbia and thus bore responsibility for turning a little war into a world war. Emperor Wilhelm II and his chancellor Theobald von Bethmann-Hollweg realized that war between Austria and Russia was likely, for a resurgent Russia would not stand by and watch the Austrians crush the Serbs, who were Russia's traditional allies. Yet Bethmann-Hollweg hoped that, although Russia (and its ally France) would go to war, Great Britain would remain neutral, unwilling to fight in the distant Balkans. With that hope, the German chancellor sent a telegram to Austria-Hungary, which promised that Germany would "faithfully stand by" its ally in case of war. This "blank check" of unconditional support encouraged the prowar faction in Vienna to take a hard line against the Serbs at a time when moderation might still have limited the crisis.

The Schlieffen Plan

Schlieffen Plan Failed German plan calling for a lightning attack through neutral Belgium and a quick defeat of France before turning on Russia.

The diplomatic situation quickly spiraled out of control as military plans and timetables began to dictate policy. Vast Russia required much more time to mobilize its armies than did Germany and Austria-Hungary. And since the complicated mobilization plans of the Russian general staff assumed a two-front war with both Austria and Germany, Russia could not mobilize against one without mobilizing against the other. Therefore, on July 29 Tsar Nicholas II ordered full mobilization, which in effect declared war on both Austria-Hungary and Germany. The German general staff had also long thought in terms of a two-front war. Their misguided **Schlieffen Plan** called for a quick victory over France after a lightning attack through neutral Belgium—the quickest way to reach Paris—before turning on Russia. On August 3 German armies invaded Belgium. Great Britain, infuriated by the German violation of Belgian neutrality, declared war on Germany the following day.

The speed of the so-called July Crisis created shock, panic, and excitement, and a bellicose public helped propel Europe into war. In the final days of July and the first few days of August, massive crowds thronged the streets of Paris, London, St. Petersburg, Berlin, and Vienna. Shouting prowar slogans, the enthusiastic crowds pushed politicians and military leaders toward the increasingly inevitable confrontation. Events proceeded rapidly, and those who opposed the war could do little to prevent its arrival. In a little over a month, a limited Austrian-Serbian war had become a European-wide conflict, and the First World War had begun.

Waging Total War

FOCUS QUESTION

How did the First World War differ from previous wars?

total war A war in which distinctions between the soldiers on the battlefield and civilians at home are blurred, and where the government plans and controls economic and social life in order to supply the armies at the front with supplies and weapons.

When the Germans invaded Belgium in August 1914, they and many others thought that the war would be short and relatively painless. Many sincerely believed that "the boys will be home by Christmas." They were wrong. On the western front in France and the eastern front in Russia, and on the borders of the Ottoman Empire, the belligerent armies bogged down in a new and extremely costly kind of war, later labeled **total war** by German general Erich Ludendorff. Total war meant new roles for soldiers and civilians alike. At the front, total war meant lengthy, deadly battles fought with all the destructive weapons a highly industrialized society could produce. At home, national economies were geared toward the war effort. Governments revoked civil liberties, and many civilians lost lives or livelihoods as occupying armies moved through their towns and cities. The struggle expanded outside Europe, and the Middle East, Africa, East Asia, and the United States were all brought into the maelstrom of total war.

Stalemate and Slaughter on the Western Front

In the face of the German invasion, the Belgian army heroically defended its homeland and fell back in good order to join a rapidly landed British army corps near the Franco-Belgian border. At the same time, Russian armies attacked eastern Germany, forcing the Germans to transfer much-needed troops to the east. Instead of quickly capturing Paris as per the Schlieffen Plan, by the end of August dead-tired German soldiers were advancing slowly along an enormous front in the scorching summer heat. Afraid that armed Belgian partisans (called *francs-tireurs*) were attacking German troops behind the lines, the German occupiers dealt harshly with local resistance. German soldiers executed civilians suspected of joining the partisans and, in an out-of-control tragedy, burned the medieval core of the Belgian city of Louvain. Entente propaganda made the most of the German "Rape of Belgium" and the atrocities committed by German troops.

On September 6 the French attacked a gap in the German line at the Battle of the Marne. For three days, France threw everything into the attack. At one point, the French government desperately requisitioned all the taxis of Paris to rush reserves to the front. Finally, the Germans fell back. France had been miraculously saved (Map 25.3).

With the armies stalled, both sides began to dig trenches to protect themselves from machine-gun fire. By November 1914 an unbroken line of four hundred miles of defensive positions extended from the Belgian coast through northern France and on to the Swiss frontier. Armies on both sides dug in behind rows of trenches, mines, and barbed wire, and slaughter on the western front began in earnest. The cost in lives of **trench warfare** was staggering, the gains in territory minuscule. For ordinary soldiers, conditions in the trenches were atrocious. Recently invented weapons, the products of an industrial age, made battle impersonal, traumatic, and extremely deadly. The machine gun, hand grenades, poison gas, flamethrowers, long-range artillery, the airplane, and the tank were all used to murderous effect. All favored the defense, increased casualty rates, and revolutionized the practice of war.

The leading generals of the combatant nations, who had learned military tactics and strategy in the nineteenth century, struggled to understand trench warfare. For four years they repeated the same mistakes, mounting massive offensives designed to achieve decisive breakthroughs. Brutal frontal assaults against highly fortified trenches might overrun the enemy's frontline, but attacking soldiers rarely captured any substantial territory. The French and British offensives of 1915 never gained more than three miles of territory. In 1916 the unsuccessful German campaign against Verdun left over 700,000 soldiers killed or wounded, and ended with the combatants in their original positions. The results in 1917 were little better. In hard-fought battles on all fronts, millions of young men were wounded or died for no real gain.

Ein Gruss aus dem Schützengraben.

"Greetings from the trenches."   This German postcard shows three soldiers writing letters to their loved ones at home; the card was probably produced on a small, frontline printing press, for quick use by soldiers in the field. The post was typically the only connection between soldiers and their relatives, and over 28 billion pieces of mail passed between home and front on all sides during the war. (© Sammlung Sauer/dpa/Corbis)

trench warfare A type of fighting used in World War I behind rows of trenches, mines, and barbed wire; the cost in lives was staggering and the gains in territory minimal.

MAP 25.3 World War I in Europe and the Middle East, 1914–1918 Trench warfare on the western front was concentrated in Belgium and northern France (inset), while the war in the east and the Ottoman Empire encompassed an enormous territory.

The Battle of the Somme, a great British offensive undertaken in the summer of 1916 in northern France, exemplified the horrors of trench warfare. The battle began with a weeklong heavy artillery bombardment on the German lines, intended to cut the barbed wire fortifications, decimate the enemy trenches, and prevent the Germans from making an effective defense. For seven days and nights, the British artillery fired nonstop on the German lines, delivering about 1.5 million shells. On July 1 the British went "over the top," climbing out of the trenches and moving into no-man's land toward the German lines, dug into a series of ridges about half a mile away.

During the bombardment, the Germans had fled to their dugouts—underground shelters dug deep into the trenches—where they suffered from lack of water, food, and sleep. But they survived. As the British soldiers neared the German lines and the shelling stopped, the Germans emerged from their bunkers, set up their machine guns, and mowed down the approaching troops. In many places, the wire had not been cut by the bombardment, so the attackers, held in place by the wire, made easy targets. About 20,000 British men were killed and 40,000 more were wounded on just the first day, a crushing loss that shook troop morale and public opinion at home. The battle lasted until November, and in the end the British did push the Germans back—a whole seven miles. Some 420,000 British, 200,000 French, and 600,000 Germans were killed or wounded fighting over an insignificant scrap of land.

As the war ground on, exhausted soldiers found it difficult to comprehend or describe the bloody reality of their experiences at the front. As one French soldier wrote:

The Battle of the Somme, 1916

> I went over the top, I ran, I shouted, I hit, I can't remember where or who. I crossed the wire, jumped over holes, crawled through shell craters still stinking of explosives, men were falling, shot in two as they ran; shouts and gasps were half muffled by the sweeping surge of gunfire. But it was like a nightmare mist all around me. . . . Now my part in it is over for a few minutes. . . . Something is red over there; something is burning. Something is red at my feet: blood.[5]

The anonymous, almost unreal qualities of high-tech warfare made their way into the art and literature of the time. In each combatant nation, artists and writers sought to portray the nightmarish quality of total war. Works by artists like Paul Nash, whose painting *The Menin Road* opens this chapter, or the poems of the famous British "trench poets," may do more to capture the experience of the war than contemporary photos or the dry accounts of historians. (See "Evaluating the Evidence 25.1: Poetry in the Trenches," page 838.)

The Widening War

On the eastern front, the slaughter did not immediately degenerate into trench warfare, and the fighting was dominated by Germany. Repulsing the initial Russian attacks, the Germans won major victories at the Battles of Tannenberg and the Masurian Lakes in August and September 1914. Russia put real pressure on the relatively weak Austro-Hungarian army, but by 1915 the eastern front had stabilized in Germany's favor. A staggering 2.5 million Russian soldiers had been killed, wounded,

Poetry in the Trenches

The trauma of the First World War generated an outburst of cultural creation, and each nation had its favored group of artists and writers. Among the most famous were Britain's "trench poets," including John McCrae, Wilfred Owen, and Siegfried Sassoon. All three served in France. McCrae, a medical officer, died of an infection contracted in a field hospital close to the front. Owen was killed in action one week before the end of the war. Sassoon survived, but was always haunted by the death of his close friend Owen and his horrific memories of the fighting.

~

John McCrae, "In Flanders Fields"

In Flanders fields the poppies blow
    Between the crosses, row on row
  That mark our place; and in the sky
  The larks, still bravely singing, fly
Scarce heard amid the guns below.

We are the Dead. Short days ago
We lived, felt dawn, saw sunset glow,
    Loved and were loved, and now we lie
             In Flanders fields.

Take up our quarrel with the foe:
To you from failing hands we throw
    The torch; be yours to hold it high.
    If ye break faith with us who die
We shall not sleep, though poppies grow
           In Flanders fields.

Wilfred Owen, "Dulce et Decorum Est"

Bent double, like old beggars under sacks,
Knock-kneed, coughing like hags, we cursed through
    sludge,
Till on the haunting flares we turned our backs
And towards our distant rest began to trudge.
Men marched asleep. Many had lost their boots,
But limped on, blood-shod. All went lame; all blind;
Drunk with fatigue; deaf even to the hoots
Of gas-shells dropping softly behind.

Gas! GAS! Quick, boys!—An ecstasy
    of fumbling
Fitting the clumsy helmets just in time,
But someone still was yelling out and stumbling
And flound'ring like a man in fire or lime.—

or captured. German armies occupied huge swaths of the Russian Empire in central Europe, including ethnic Polish, Belorussian, and Baltic territories. Yet Russia continued to fight, marking another failure of the Schlieffen Plan.

To govern these occupied territories, the Germans installed a vast military bureaucracy, with some 15,000 army administrators and professional specialists. Anti-Slavic prejudice dominated the mind-set of the occupiers, who viewed the local Slavs as savages and ethnic "mongrels." German military administrators used prisoners of war and refugees as forced labor. They stole animals and crops from local farmers to supply the occupying army or send home to Germany. About one-third of the civilian population died or became refugees under this brutal occupation. In the long run, the German state hoped to turn these territories into German possessions, a chilling forerunner of Nazi policies in World War II.[6]

The changing tides of victory and hopes for territorial gains brought neutral countries into the war (see Map 25.3). Italy, a member of the Triple Alliance since 1882, had declared its neutrality in 1914 on the grounds that Austria had launched a war of aggression. Then in May 1915 Italy switched sides to join the Triple Entente in return for promises of Austrian territory. The war along the Italian-Austrian front was bitter and deadly and cost some 600,000 Italian lives.

Dim through the misty panes and thick green light,
As under a green sea, I saw him drowning.

In all my dreams before my helpless sight
He plunges at me, guttering, choking, drowning.

If in some smothering dreams, you too could pace
Behind the wagon that we flung him in,
And watch the white eyes writhing in his face,
His hanging face, like a devil's sick of sin,
If you could hear, at every jolt, the blood
Come gargling from the froth-corrupted lungs
Bitter as the cud
Of vile, incurable sores on innocent tongues,—
My friend, you would not tell with such high zest
To children ardent for some desperate glory,
The old Lie: *Dulce et decorum est
Pro patria mori.**

Siegfried Sassoon, "Attack"

At dawn the ridge emerges massed and dun
In the wild purple of the glowering sun,
Smouldering through spouts of drifting smoke that
    shroud
The menacing scarred slope; and, one by one,
Tanks creep and topple forward to the wire.

The barrage roars and lifts. Then, clumsily bowed
With bombs and guns and shovels and battle-gear,
Men jostle and climb to meet the bristling fire.
Lines of grey, muttering faces, masked with fear,
They leave their trenches, going over the top,
While time ticks blank and busy on their wrists,
And hope, with furtive eyes and grappling fists,
Flounders in the mud. O Jesu, make it stop!

EVALUATE THE EVIDENCE

1. Each of these poems was written during the war. How does each author bridge the traditional language and rhythm of poetry and the brutality of modern warfare?
2. What messages do the poems have for the reader at home?
3. What do these poems reveal about the effects of World War I on the fine arts and literature?

Sources: John McCrae, *In Flanders Fields and Other Poems* (New York: G. P. Putnam's Sons/Knickerbocker Press, 1919), p. 15; Wilfred Owen, *Poems by Wilfred Owen* (New York: Viking Press, 1921), p. 15; Siegfried Sassoon, *Counter-Attack and Other Poems* (New York: E. P. Dutton, 1918), p. 18.

* It is sweet and fitting/To die for one's country.

In October 1914 the Ottoman Empire joined Austria and Germany, by then known as the Central Powers. The following September Bulgaria followed the Ottoman Empire's lead in order to settle old scores with Serbia. The Balkans, with the exception of Greece, were occupied by the Central Powers.

The entry of the Ottomans carried the war into the Middle East. Heavy fighting between the Ottomans and the Russians in the Caucasus enveloped the Armenians, who lived on both sides of the border and had experienced brutal repression by the Ottomans in 1909. When in 1915 some Armenians welcomed Russian armies as liberators, the Ottoman government, with German support, ordered a mass deportation of its Armenian citizens from their homeland. In this early example of modern ethnic cleansing, often labeled genocide, about 1 million Armenians died from murder, starvation, and disease.

The Armenian Genocide, 1915–1918

British forces landing site, Helles, April 25, 1915

British forces landing site, Suvla Bay, August 6, 1915

Maximum ground gained by Allies

The Battle of Gallipoli

In 1915, at the Battle of Gallipoli, British forces tried and failed to take the Dardanelles and Constantinople from the Ottoman Turks. The invasion force was pinned down on the beaches, and the ten-month-long battle cost the Ottomans 300,000 and the British 265,000 men killed, wounded, or missing.

The British were more successful at inciting the Arabs to revolt against their Ottoman rulers. They bargained with the foremost Arab leader, Hussein ibn-Ali (1856–1931), the chief magistrate (*sharif*) of Mecca, the holiest city in the Muslim world, and ruler for the Ottoman sultan of much of the Ottoman Empire's territory along the Red Sea, an area known as the Hejaz. In a famous exchange of diplomatic notes with Sir Henry McMahon, the British high commissioner in Cairo, Hussein managed in 1915 to win vague British commitments for an independent Arab kingdom. In 1916 Hussein rebelled against the Turks, proclaiming himself king of the Arabs. Hussein was aided by the British liaison officer T. E. Lawrence, who in 1917 helped lead Arab soldiers in a successful guerrilla war against the Turks on the Arabian peninsula.

The British enjoyed similar victories in the Ottoman province of Mesopotamia (today's Iraq). British troops quickly occupied the southern Iraqi city of Basra in 1914, securing their access to the region's oil fields. After a series of setbacks at the hands of Ottoman troops, the British captured Baghdad in 1917. In September 1918 British armies and their Arab allies rolled into Syria, a large and diverse Ottoman territory that included the holy lands of Palestine and the present-day countries of Syria, Lebanon, Jordan, and Israel. This offensive culminated in the triumphal entry of Hussein's son Faisal into Damascus.

Arab patriots in Syria and Iraq now expected a large, unified Arab nation-state to rise from the dust of the Ottoman collapse—though they would later be disappointed by the Western powers (see page 859).

The war spread to East Asia and colonial Africa as well. Japan declared war on Germany in 1914, seized Germany's Pacific and East Asian colonies, and used the opportunity to expand its influence in China. In Africa, instead of rebelling as the Germans hoped, colonial subjects of the British and French generally supported the Allied powers and helped local British and French commanders take over German colonies.

The European world war spilled out of European borders and brought non-European peoples into the conflict. More than a million Africans and Asians served in the various armies of the warring powers; more than double that number served as porters to carry equipment and build defenses. The French, facing a shortage of young men, made especially heavy use of colonial troops from North Africa. Soldiers from India played a key role in Britain's campaigns against the Ottomans, though under the command of native British officers. And large numbers of soldiers came from the British Commonwealth, a voluntary association of former British colonies. Canadians, Australians, and New Zealanders fought with the British; those from Australia and New Zealand (the ANZAC Army Corps) fought with particular distinction in the failed Allied assault on Gallipoli.

After three years of refusing to play a fighting role, the United States was finally drawn into the expanding conflict. American intervention grew out of the war at sea and general sympathy for the Triple Entente. At the beginning of the war, Britain and France established a naval blockade to strangle the Central Powers. No neutral cargo ship was permitted to sail to Germany. In early 1915 Germany retaliated with attacks on supply ships from a murderously effective new weapon, the submarine.

In May 1915 a German submarine sank the British passenger liner *Lusitania*, claiming more than 1,000 lives, among them 139 U.S. citizens. President Woodrow Wilson protested vigorously, using the tragedy to incite American public opinion against the Germans. To avoid almost-certain war with the United States, Germany halted its submarine warfare for almost two years.

Early in 1917 the German military command—hoping that improved submarines could starve Britain into submission before the United States could come to its rescue—resumed unrestricted submarine warfare. This was a reckless gamble, and the United States declared war on Germany in April of that year. Eventually the United States tipped the balance in favor of the British, French, and their allies.

The Home Front

The war's impact on civilians was no less massive than it was on the men crouched in the trenches. Total war encouraged the growth of state bureaucracies, transformed the lives of ordinary women and men, and by the end inspired mass antiwar protest movements.

FOCUS QUESTION
In what ways did the war transform life on the home front?

Mobilizing for Total War

In August 1914 many people greeted the outbreak of hostilities enthusiastically. In every country, ordinary folk believed that their nation was right to defend itself from foreign aggression. With the exception of those on the extreme left, even socialists supported the war. Yet by mid-October generals and politicians had begun to realize that victory would require more than patriotism. Heavy casualties and the stalemate meant each combatant country experienced a desperate need for men and weapons. To keep the war machine moving, national leaders aggressively intervened in society and the economy.

By the late nineteenth century the responsive national state had already shown an eagerness to manage the welfare of its citizens (see Chapter 23). Now, confronted by the crisis of total war, the state intruded even further into people's daily lives. New government ministries mobilized soldiers and armaments, established rationing programs, and provided care for war widows and wounded veterans. Censorship offices controlled news about the course of the war. Government planning boards temporarily abandoned free-market capitalism and set mandatory production goals and limits on wages and prices. Government management of highly productive industrial economies worked: it yielded an effective and immensely destructive war effort on all sides.

Germany went furthest in developing a planned economy to wage total war. As soon as war began, the Jewish industrialist Walter Rathenau convinced the government to set up the War Raw Materials Board to ration and distribute raw materials. Under Rathenau's direction, every useful material from foreign oil to barnyard manure was inventoried and rationed. Moreover, the board launched successful attempts to produce substitutes, such as synthetic rubber and nitrates, for scarce war supplies. Food was rationed in accordance with physical need. Germany failed to tax the war

Women Workers Building a Truck in a London Workshop, 1917   Millions of men on all sides were drafted to fight in the war, creating a serious labor shortage on the home front. When women began to fill jobs formerly reserved for men, they challenged middle-class gender roles. (© Hulton-Deutsch Collection/Corbis)

profits of private firms heavily enough, however. This failure contributed to massive deficit financing, inflation, the growth of a black market, and the eventual re-emergence of class conflict.

Following the terrible Battles of Verdun and the Somme in 1916, German military leaders forced the Reichstag to accept the Auxiliary Service Law, which required all males between seventeen and sixty to work only at jobs considered critical to the war effort. Women also worked in war factories, mines, and steel mills, where they labored, like men, at heavy and dangerous jobs. While war production increased, people lived on little more than one thousand calories a day.

After 1917 Germany's leaders ruled by decree. Generals Paul von Hindenburg and Erich Ludendorff—heroes of the Battle of Tannenberg—drove Chancellor Bethmann-Hollweg from office. With the support of the newly formed ultraconservative Fatherland Party, the generals established a military dictatorship. Hindenburg called for the ultimate mobilization for total war. Germany could win, he said, only "if all the treasures of our soil that agriculture and industry can produce are used exclusively for the conduct of War. . . . All other considerations must come second."[7] Thus in Germany total war led to the establishment of history's first "totalitarian" society, a model for future National Socialists, or Nazis.

Only Germany was directly ruled by a military government, yet leaders in all the belligerent nations took power from parliaments, suspended civil liberties, and ignored democratic procedures. After 1915 the British Ministry of Munitions organized private industry to produce for the war, allocated labor, set wage and price rates, and settled labor disputes. In France, a weakened parliament met without public oversight, and the courts jailed pacifists who dared criticize the state. Once the United States entered the war, new federal agencies such as the War Labor Board and the War Industries Board regulated industry, labor relations, and agricultural production, while the Espionage and Sedition Acts weakened civil liberties. The war may have been deadly for citizen armies, but it was certainly good for the growth of the bureaucratic nation-state.

The Social Impact

The social changes wrought by total war were no less profound than the economic impact, though again there were important national variations. National conscription sent millions of men to the front, exposing many to foreign lands for the first time in their lives. The insatiable needs of the military created a tremendous demand for workers, making jobs readily available. This situation—seldom, if ever, seen before 1914, when unemployment and poverty had been facts of urban life—brought momentous changes.

The need for workers meant greater power and prestige for labor unions. Unions cooperated with war governments on workplace rules, wages, and production schedules in return for real participation in important decisions. The entry of labor leaders and unions into policymaking councils paralleled the entry of socialist leaders into war governments. Both reflected a new government openness to the needs of those at the bottom of society.

The role of women changed dramatically. The production of vast amounts of arms and ammunition required huge numbers of laborers, and women moved into skilled industrial jobs long considered men's work. Women became highly visible in public—as munitions workers, bank tellers, and mail carriers, and even as police officers, firefighters, and farm laborers. Women also served as auxiliaries and nurses at the front. (See "Individuals in Society: Vera Brittain," page 844.)

The war expanded the range of women's activities and helped change attitudes about proper gender roles, but the long-term results were mixed. Women gained experience in jobs previously reserved for men, but at war's end millions of demobilized soldiers demanded their jobs back, and governments forced women out of the workplace. Thus women's employment gains were mostly temporary, except in nursing and social work, already considered "women's work." The great dislocations of war loosened sexual morality, and some women bobbed their hair, shortened their skirts, and smoked in public. Yet supposedly "loose" women were often criticized for betraying their soldier-husbands away at the front. As a result of women's many-sided war effort, the United States, Britain, Germany, Poland, and other countries granted women the right to vote immediately after the war. Yet women's rights movements faded in the 1920s and 1930s, in large part because feminist leaders found it difficult to regain momentum after the crisis of war.

To some extent, the war promoted greater social equality, blurring class distinctions and lessening the gap between rich and poor. This blurring was most apparent in Great Britain, where the bottom third of the population generally lived better than they ever had, for the poorest gained most from the severe shortage of labor. Elsewhere, greater equality was reflected in full employment, distribution of scarce rations according to physical needs, and a sharing of hardships. In general, despite some war profiteering, European society became more uniform and egalitarian.

Death itself had no respect for traditional social distinctions. It savagely decimated the young aristocratic officers who led the charge, and it fell heavily on the mass of drafted peasants and unskilled workers who followed, leading commentators to speak of a "lost generation." Yet death often spared highly skilled workers and foremen. Their lives were too valuable to squander at the front, for they were needed to train the newly recruited women and older unskilled men laboring valiantly in war plants at home.

Growing Political Tensions

During the first two years of war, many soldiers and civilians supported their governments. Patriotic nationalism and belief in a just cause united peoples behind their national leaders. Each government used rigorous censorship and crude propaganda

INDIVIDUALS IN SOCIETY

Vera Brittain

Although the Great War upended millions of lives, it struck Europe's young people with the greatest force. For Vera Brittain (1893–1970), as for so many in her generation, the war became life's defining experience, which she captured forever in her famous autobiography, *Testament of Youth* (1933).

Brittain grew up in a wealthy business family in northern England, bristling at small-town conventions and discrimination against women. Very close to her brother Edward, two years her junior, Brittain read voraciously and dreamed of being a successful writer. Finishing boarding school and overcoming her father's objections, she prepared for Oxford's rigorous entry exams and won a scholarship to its women's college. Brittain fell in love with Roland Leighton, an equally brilliant student from a literary family and her brother's best friend. All three, along with two other close friends, Victor Richardson and Geoffrey Thurlow, confidently prepared to enter Oxford in late 1914.

When war suddenly loomed in July 1914, Brittain shared with millions of Europeans a surge of patriotic support for her government, a prowar enthusiasm she later downplayed in her published writings. She wrote in her diary that her "great fear" was that England would declare its neutrality and commit the "grossest treachery" toward France.* She supported Leighton's decision to enlist, agreeing with his glamorous view of war as "very ennobling and very beautiful." Later, exchanging anxious letters with Leighton in France in 1915, Brittain began to see the conflict in personal, human terms. She wondered if any victory or defeat could be worth her fiancé's life.

Struggling to quell her doubts, Brittain redoubled her commitment to England's cause and volunteered as an army nurse. For the next three years, she served with distinction in military hospitals in London, Malta, and northern France, repeatedly torn between the vision of noble sacrifice and the reality of human tragedy. Having lost sexual inhibitions while caring for mangled male bodies, she longed to consummate her love with Leighton. Awaiting his return on leave on Christmas Day in 1915, she was greeted

Vera Brittain was marked forever by her wartime experiences. (Vera Brittain fonds, William Ready Division of Archives and Research Collections, McMaster University Library)

instead with a telegram: he had been killed two days before.

Leighton's death was the first of several devastating blows that eventually overwhelmed Brittain's idealistic patriotism. In 1917 Thurlow and then Richardson died from gruesome wounds. In early 1918, as the last great German offensive covered the floors of her war-zone hospital with maimed and dying German prisoners, the bone-weary Brittain felt a common humanity and saw only more victims. A few weeks later her brother Edward—her last hope—died in action. When the war ended, she was, she said, a "complete automaton," with her "deepest emotions paralyzed if not dead."

Returning to Oxford and finishing her studies, Brittain gradually recovered. She formed a deep, restorative friendship with another talented woman writer, Winifred Holtby; published novels and articles; and became a leader in the feminist campaign for gender equality. She also married and had children. But her wartime memories were always with her. Finally, Brittain succeeded in coming to grips with them in *Testament of Youth*, her powerful antiwar autobiography. The unflinching narrative spoke to the experiences of an entire generation and became a runaway bestseller. Above all, Brittain captured the contradictory character of the war, in which millions of young people found excitement, courage, and common purpose but succeeded only in destroying their lives with their superhuman efforts and futile sacrifices. Increasingly committed to pacifism, Brittain opposed England's entry into World War II.

QUESTIONS FOR ANALYSIS

1. What were Brittain's initial feelings toward the war? How and why did they change as the conflict continued?
2. Why did Brittain volunteer as a nurse, as many women did? How might wartime nursing have influenced women of her generation?
3. In portraying the contradictory character of World War I for Europe's youth, was Brittain describing the character of all modern warfare?

*Quotes from the excellent study P. Berry and M. Bostridge, *Vera Brittain: A Life* (London: Virago Press, 2001), p. 59; additional quotations are from pp. 80 and 136.

Wartime Propaganda Posters

This famous French propaganda poster from 1918 (left) proclaims "They shall not pass" and expresses the French determination to hold back the German invaders at any cost. The American recruitment poster from 1917 (right) encourages "fighting men" to "join the Navy."

(Private Collection/© Galerie Bilderwelt/Bridgeman Images)

(Private Collection/© Galerie Bilderwelt/Bridgeman Images)

EVALUATE THE EVIDENCE

1. Describe the soldier and sailor pictured on these posters. How do the posters present the war?
2. The French poster was created after France had been at war for four years, while the naval recruitment poster came out before American troops were actively engaged overseas. How might the country of origin and the date of publication have affected the messages conveyed in the posters?

to bolster popular support. (See "Evaluating the Evidence 25.2: Wartime Propaganda Posters," above.) German propaganda pictured black soldiers from France's African empire abusing German women, while the French and British ceaselessly recounted and exaggerated German atrocities in Belgium and elsewhere. Patriotic posters and slogans, slanted news, and biased editorials inflamed national hatreds, helped control public opinion, and encouraged soldiers to keep fighting.

Political and social tensions re-emerged, however, and by the spring of 1916 ordinary people were beginning to crack under the strain of total war. Strikes and protest marches over war-related burdens and shortages flared up on every home front. On

May 1, 1916, several thousand demonstrators in Berlin heard the radical socialist leader Karl Liebknecht (1871–1919) attack the costs of the war effort. Liebknecht was arrested and imprisoned, but his daring action electrified Europe's far left. In France, Georges Clemenceau (zhorzh kleh-muhn-SOH) (1841–1929) established a virtual dictatorship, arrested strikers, and jailed without trial journalists and politicians who dared to suggest a compromise peace with Germany.

In April 1916 Irish republican nationalists took advantage of the tense wartime conditions to step up their rebellion against British rule. During the great Easter Rising, armed republican militias took over parts of Dublin and proclaimed an independent Irish Republic. After a week of bitter fighting, British troops crushed the rebels and executed their leaders. Though the republicans were defeated, the punitive aftermath fueled anti-British sentiment in Ireland. The Rising set the stage for the success of the nationalist Sinn Fein Party and a full-scale civil war for Irish independence in the early 1920s.

On all sides, soldiers' morale began to decline. Numerous French units mutinied and refused to fight after the disastrous French offensive of May 1917. Only tough military justice, including executions for mutiny leaders, and a tacit agreement with the troops that there would be no more grand offensives, enabled the new general-in-chief, Henri-Philippe Pétain (pay-TAN), to restore order. Facing defeat, wretched conditions at the front, and growing hopelessness, Russian soldiers deserted in droves, providing fuel for the Russian Revolution of 1917. After the murderous Battle of Caporetto in northern Italy, which lasted from October to November in 1917, the Italian army collapsed in despair. In the massive battles of 1916 and 1917, the British armies had been "bled dry." Only the promised arrival of fresh troops from the United States stiffened the resolve of the Allies.

The strains were even worse for the Central Powers. In October 1916 a young socialist assassinated the chief minister of Austria-Hungary. The following month, when the aging emperor Franz Joseph died, a symbol of unity disappeared. In spite of absolute censorship, political dissatisfaction and conflicts among nationalities grew. Both Czech and Balkan leaders demanded independent states for their peoples. By April 1917 the Austro-Hungarian people and army were exhausted. Another winter of war would bring revolution and disintegration.

Germans likewise suffered immensely. The British naval blockade greatly limited food imports, and the scarcity of basic necessities had horrific results: some 750,000 German civilians starved to death. For the rest, heavy rationing of everyday goods such as matches, bread, cooking oil, and meat undermined morale. A growing minority of moderate socialists in the Reichstag gave voice to popular discontent when they called for a compromise "peace without annexations or reparations."

Such a peace was unthinkable for the Fatherland Party. Yet Germany's rulers faced growing unrest. When the bread ration was further reduced in April 1917, more than 200,000 workers and women struck and demonstrated for a week in Berlin, returning to work only under the threat of prison and military discipline. That same month, radicals left the Social Democratic Party to form the Independent Social Democratic Party; in 1918 they would found the German Communist Party. Thus Germany, like its ally Austria-Hungary (and its enemy France), was beginning to crack in 1917. Yet it was Russia that collapsed first and saved the Central Powers—for a time.

The Russian Revolution

Growing out of the crisis of the First World War, the Russian Revolution of 1917 was one of modern history's most momentous events. For some, the revolution was Marx's socialist vision come true; for others, it was the triumph of a despised Communist dictatorship. To all, it presented a radically new prototype of state and society.

FOCUS QUESTION
Why did world war lead to revolution in Russia, and what was its outcome?

The Fall of Imperial Russia

Like their allies and enemies, many Russians had embraced war with patriotic enthusiasm in 1914. At the Winter Palace, throngs of people knelt and sang "God Save the Tsar!" while Tsar Nicholas II (r. 1894–1917) repeated the oath Alexander I had sworn in 1812 during Napoleon's invasion of Russia (see Chapter 19), vowing never to make peace as long as the enemy stood on Russian soil. Russia's lower house of parliament, the Duma, voted to support the war. Conservatives anticipated expansion in the Balkans, while liberals and most socialists believed that alliance with Britain and France would bring democratic reforms. For a moment, Russia was united.

Enthusiasm for the war soon waned as better-equipped German armies inflicted terrible losses. By 1915 substantial numbers of Russian soldiers were being sent to the front without rifles; they were told to find their arms among the dead. Russia's battered peasant army nonetheless continued to fight, and Russia moved toward full mobilization on the home front. The government set up special committees to coordinate defense, industry, transportation, and agriculture. These efforts improved the military situation, but overall Russia mobilized less effectively than the other combatants.

One problem was weak leadership. Under the constitution resulting from the revolution of 1905 (see Chapter 23), the tsar had retained complete control over the bureaucracy and the army. A kindly but narrow-minded aristocrat, Nicholas II distrusted the publicly elected Duma and resisted popular involvement in government, relying instead on the old bureaucracy. Excluded from power, the Duma, the educated middle classes, and the masses became increasingly critical of the tsar's leadership. In September 1915 parties ranging from conservative to moderate socialist formed the Progressive bloc, which called for a completely new government responsible to the Duma instead of the tsar. In answer, Nicholas temporarily adjourned the Duma. The tsar then announced that he was traveling to the front in order to lead and rally Russia's armies, leaving the government in the hands of his wife, the strong-willed and autocratic Tsarina Alexandra.

His departure was a fatal turning point. In his absence, Tsarina Alexandra arbitrarily dismissed loyal political advisers. She turned to her court favorite, the disreputable and unpopular Rasputin, an uneducated Siberian preacher whose influence with the tsarina rested on his purported ability to heal Alexis—Alexandra's only son and heir to the throne—from his hemophilia. In a desperate attempt to right the situation, three members of the high aristocracy murdered Rasputin in December 1916. The ensuing scandal further undermined support for the tsarist government.

Imperial Russia had entered a terminal crisis. Tens of thousands of soldiers deserted, swelling the number of the disaffected at home. By early 1917 the cities were wracked by food shortages, heating fuel was in short supply, and the economy was breaking down. In March violent street demonstrations broke out in Petrograd (now named

St. Petersburg), spread to the factories, and then engulfed the city. From the front, the tsar ordered the army to open fire on the protesters, but the soldiers refused to shoot and joined the revolutionary crowd instead. The Duma declared a provisional government on March 12, 1917. Three days later, Nicholas abdicated.

The Provisional Government

February Revolution
Unplanned uprisings accompanied by violent street demonstrations begun in March 1917 (old calendar February) in Petrograd, Russia, that led to the abdication of the tsar and the establishment of a provisional government.

The **February Revolution**, then, was the result of an unplanned uprising of hungry, angry people in the capital, but it was eagerly accepted throughout the country. (The name of the revolution matches the traditional Russian calendar, which used a different dating system.) The patriotic upper and middle classes embraced the prospect of a more determined war effort, while workers anticipated better wages and more food. After generations of autocracy, the provisional government established equality before the law, granting freedoms of religion, speech, and assembly, as well as the right of unions to organize and strike.

Yet the provisional government made a crucial mistake: though the Russian people were sick of fighting, the new leaders failed to take Russia out of the war. A government formed in May 1917 included the fiery agrarian socialist Alexander Kerensky, who became prime minister in July. For the patriotic Kerensky, as for other moderate socialists, the continuation of war was still a national duty. Turning his back on needed reforms, Kerensky refused to confiscate large landholdings and give them to peasants, fearing that such drastic action would complete the disintegration of Russia's peasant army. Human suffering and war-weariness grew, testing the limited strength of the provisional government.

Petrograd Soviet   A huge, fluctuating mass meeting of two to three thousand workers, soldiers, and socialist intellectuals modeled on the revolutionary soviets of 1905.

From its first day, the provisional government had to share power with a formidable rival—the **Petrograd Soviet** (or council) of Workers' and Soldiers' Deputies. Modeled on the revolutionary soviets of 1905, the Petrograd Soviet comprised two to three thousand workers, soldiers, and socialist intellectuals. Seeing itself as a true grassroots product of revolutionary democracy, the Soviet acted as a parallel government. It issued its own radical orders, weakening the authority of the provisional government.

The most famous edict of the Petrograd Soviet was Army Order No. 1, issued in May 1917, which stripped officers of their authority and placed power in the hands of elected committees of common soldiers. Designed to protect the revolution from resistance by the aristocratic officer corps, the order led to a collapse of army discipline.

In July 1917 the provisional government mounted a poorly considered summer offensive against the Germans. The campaign was a miserable failure, and desertions mounted as peasant soldiers returned home to help their families get a share of the land, which peasants were seizing in a grassroots agrarian revolt. By the summer of 1917 Russia was descending into anarchy. It was an unparalleled opportunity for the most radical and talented of Russia's many revolutionary leaders, Vladimir Ilyich Lenin (1870–1924).

Lenin and the Bolshevik Revolution

Born into the middle class, Lenin became an enemy of imperial Russia when his older brother was executed for plotting to kill archconservative Tsar Alexander III in 1887. As a law student, Lenin eagerly studied Marxist socialism, which began to win converts among radical intellectuals during Russia's industrialization in the 1890s. A pragmatic and flexible thinker, Lenin updated Marx's revolutionary philosophy to address existing conditions in Russia.

Three interrelated concepts were central for Lenin. First, he stressed that only violent revolution could destroy capitalism. He tirelessly denounced all "revisionist" theories of a peaceful evolution to socialism (see Chapter 23) as a betrayal of Marx's message of violent class conflict. Second, Lenin argued that under certain conditions a Communist revolution was possible even in a predominantly agrarian country like Russia. Peasants, who were numerous, poor, and exploited, could take the place of Marx's traditional working class in the coming revolutionary conflict.

Third, Lenin believed that the possibility of revolution was determined more by human leadership than by historical laws. He called for a highly disciplined workers' party strictly controlled by a small, dedicated elite of intellectuals and professional revolutionaries. This elite would not stop until revolution brought it to power. Lenin's version of Marxism had a major impact on events in Russia and ultimately changed the way future revolutionaries engaged in radical revolt around the world.

Other Russian Marxists challenged Lenin's ideas. At meetings of the Russian Social Democratic Labor Party in London in 1903, matters came to a head. Lenin demanded a small, disciplined, elitist party dedicated to Communist revolution, while his opponents wanted a more democratic, reformist party with mass membership (like the German SPD). The Russian Marxists split into two rival factions. Lenin called his camp the **Bolsheviks**, or "majority group"; his opponents were Mensheviks, or "minority group." The Bolsheviks had only a tenuous majority of a single vote, but Lenin kept the name for propaganda reasons and they became the revolutionary party he wanted: tough, disciplined, and led from above.

Unlike other socialists, Lenin had not rallied around the national flag in 1914. Observing events from neutral Switzerland, where he lived in exile to avoid persecution by the tsar's police, Lenin viewed the war as a product of imperialist rivalries and an opportunity for socialist revolution. After the February Revolution of 1917, the German government provided Lenin with safe passage across Germany and back into Russia. The Germans hoped Lenin would undermine the sagging war effort of the provisional government. They were not disappointed.

Arriving triumphantly at Petrograd's Finland Station on April 3, Lenin attacked at once. He rejected all cooperation with what he called the "bourgeois" provisional government. His slogans were radical in the extreme: "All power to the soviets"; "All land to the peasants"; "Stop the war now." Lenin was a superb tactician. His promises of "Peace, Land, and Bread" spoke to the expectations of suffering soldiers, peasants, and workers and earned the Bolsheviks substantial popular support. The moment for revolution was at hand.

Yet Lenin and the Bolsheviks almost lost the struggle for Russia. A premature attempt to seize power in July collapsed, and Lenin went into hiding. However, this temporary setback made little difference in the long run. The army's commander in chief, General Lavr Kornilov, led a feeble coup against the provisional Kerensky government in September. In the face of this rightist counter-revolutionary threat,

Bolsheviks Lenin's radical, revolutionary arm of the Russian party of Marxist socialism, which successfully installed a dictatorial socialist regime in Russia.

the Bolsheviks were rearmed. Kornilov's forces disintegrated, but Kerensky lost all credit with the army, the only force that might have saved democratic government in Russia.

Trotsky and the Seizure of Power

Throughout the summer, the Bolsheviks greatly increased their popular support. Party membership soared from 50,000 to 240,000, and in October the Bolsheviks gained a fragile majority in the Petrograd Soviet. Now Lenin's supporter Leon Trotsky (1879–1940), a spellbinding revolutionary orator and radical Marxist, brilliantly executed the Bolshevik seizure of power.

Painting a vivid but untruthful picture of German and counter-revolutionary plots, Trotsky convinced the Petrograd Soviet to form a special military-revolutionary committee in October and make him its leader. Thus military power in the capital passed into Bolshevik hands.

On the night of November 6, militants from Trotsky's committee joined with trusted Bolshevik soldiers to seize government buildings in Petrograd and arrest members of the provisional government. Then they went on to the Congress of Soviets, where a Bolshevik majority—roughly 390 of 650 excited delegates—declared that all power had passed to the soviets and named Lenin head of the new government. John Reed, a sympathetic American journalist, described the enthusiasm that greeted Lenin at the congress:

> Now Lenin, gripping the edge of the reading stand . . . stood there waiting, apparently oblivious to the long-rolling ovation, which lasted several minutes. When it finished, he said simply, "We shall now proceed to construct the Socialist order!" Again that overwhelming human roar.[8]

The Bolsheviks came to power for three key reasons. First, by late 1917 democracy had given way to anarchy: power was there for those who would take it. Second, in Lenin and Trotsky the Bolsheviks had an utterly determined and superior leadership, which both the tsarist and the provisional governments lacked. Third, as Reed's comment suggests, Bolshevik policies appealed to ordinary Russians. Exhausted by war and weary of tsarist autocracy, they were eager for radical changes. (See "Evaluating the Evidence 25.3: Peace, Land, and Bread for the Russian People," at right.) With time, many Russians would become bitterly disappointed with the Bolshevik regime, but for the moment they had good reason to hope for peace, better living conditions, and a more equitable society.

Dictatorship and Civil War

The Bolsheviks' truly monumental accomplishment was not taking power, but keeping it. Over the next four years, they conquered the chaos they had helped create and began to build a Communist society. How was this done?

Lenin had the genius to profit from developments over which the Bolsheviks had little control. Since summer, a peasant revolt had swept across Russia, as impoverished peasants had seized for themselves the estates of the landlords and the church. Thus when Lenin mandated land reform, he merely approved what peasants were

Peace, Land, and Bread for the Russian People

Lenin wrote this dramatic manifesto in the name of the Congress of Soviets in Petrograd, the day after Trotsky seized power in the city. The Bolsheviks boldly promised the Russian people a number of progressive reforms, including an immediate armistice, land reform, democracy in the army, and ample food for all. They also issued a call to arms. The final paragraphs warn of counter-revolutionary resistance and capture the looming descent into all-out civil war.

To Workers, Soldiers, and Peasants!

The . . . All-Russia Congress of Soviets of Workers and Soldiers' Deputies has opened. The vast majority of the Soviets are represented at the Congress. A number of delegates from the Peasants' Soviets are also present. . . . Backed by the will of the vast majority of the workers, soldiers, and peasants, backed by the victorious uprising of the workers and the garrison which has taken place in Petrograd, the Congress takes power into its own hands.

The Provisional Government has been overthrown. The majority of the members of the Provisional Government have already been arrested.

The Soviet government will propose an immediate democratic peace to all the nations and an immediate armistice on all fronts. It will secure the transfer of the land of the landed proprietors, the crown and the monasteries to the peasant committees without compensation; it will protect the rights of the soldiers by introducing complete democracy in the army; it will establish workers' control over production; it will ensure the convocation of the Constituent Assembly at the time appointed; it will see to it that bread is supplied to the cities and prime necessities to the villages; it will guarantee all the nations inhabiting Russia the genuine right to self-determination.

The Congress decrees: all power in the localities shall pass to the Soviets of Workers', Soldiers' and Peasants' Deputies, which must guarantee genuine revolutionary order.

The Congress calls upon the soldiers in the trenches to be vigilant and firm. The Congress of Soviets is convinced that the revolutionary army will be able to defend the revolution against all attacks of imperialism until such time as the new government succeeds in concluding a democratic peace, which it will propose directly to all peoples. The new government will do everything to fully supply the revolutionary army by means of a determined policy of requisitions and taxation of the propertied classes, and also will improve the condition of the soldiers' families.

The Kornilov men—Kerensky, Kaledin and others—are attempting to bring troops against Petrograd. Several detachments, whom Kerensky had moved by deceiving them, have come over to the side of the insurgent people.

Soldiers, actively resist Kerensky the Kornilovite! Be on your guard!

Railwaymen, hold up all troop trains dispatched by Kerensky against Petrograd!

Soldiers, workers in factory and office, the fate of the revolution and the fate of the democratic peace is in your hands!

Long live the revolution!

> November 7, 1917
> The All-Russia Congress of Soviets
> Of Workers' and Soldiers' Deputies
> The Delegates from the Peasants' Soviets

EVALUATE THE EVIDENCE

1. How does Lenin's manifesto embody Bolshevik political goals? Why might it appeal to ordinary Russians in the crisis of war and revolution?
2. What historical conditions made it difficult for the Bolsheviks to fulfill the ambitious promises made at the 1917 congress?

Source: Marxists Internet Archive Library, http://www.marxists.org /archive/lenin/works/1917/oct-26/25b.htm.

already doing. Similarly, urban workers had established their own local soviets or committees and demanded direct control of individual factories. This, too, Lenin ratified with a decree in November 1917.

The Bolsheviks proclaimed their regime a "provisional workers' and peasants' government," promising that a freely elected Constituent Assembly would draw up a new constitution. But free elections in November produced a stunning setback: the

Lenin Rallies the Masses   Bolshevik leader Vladimir Lenin, known for his fiery speeches, addresses a crowd in Moscow's Red Square in October 1917. (Sovfoto/UIG via Getty Images)

Bolsheviks won only 23 percent of the elected delegates. The Socialist Revolutionary Party—the peasants' party—had a clear plurality with about 40 percent of the vote. After the Constituent Assembly met for one day, however, Bolshevik soldiers acting under Lenin's orders disbanded it. By January 1918 Lenin had moved to establish a one-party state.

Lenin acknowledged that Russia had effectively lost the war with Germany and that the only realistic goal was peace at any price. That price was very high. Germany demanded that the Soviet government give up all its western territories, areas inhabited primarily by Poles, Finns, Lithuanians, and other non-Russians—people who had been conquered by the tsars over three centuries and put into the "prisonhouse of nationalities," as Lenin had earlier called the Russian Empire.

At first, Lenin's fellow Bolsheviks refused to accept such great territorial losses. But when German armies resumed their unopposed march into Russia in February 1918, Lenin had his way in a very close vote. A third of old Russia's population was sliced away by the **Treaty of Brest-Litovsk**, signed with Germany in March 1918. With peace, Lenin escaped the disaster of continued war and could pursue his goal of absolute power for the Bolsheviks—now also called Communists—within Russia.

The peace treaty and the abolition of the Constituent Assembly inspired armed opposition to the Bolshevik regime. People who had supported self-rule in November saw that once again they were getting dictatorship. The officers of the old army

Treaty of Brest-Litovsk
Peace treaty signed in March 1918 between the Central Powers and Russia that ended Russian participation in World War I and ceded Russian territories containing a third of the Russian Empire's population to the Central Powers.

organized the so-called White opposition to the Bolsheviks in southern Russia, Ukraine, Siberia, and the area west of Petrograd. The Whites came from many social groups and were united only by their hatred of communism and the Bolsheviks—the Reds.

By the summer of 1918 Russia was in a full-fledged civil war. Eighteen self-proclaimed regional governments—several of which represented minority nationalities—challenged Lenin's government in Moscow. By the end of the year White armies were on the attack. In October 1919 they closed in on central Russia from three sides, and it appeared they might triumph. They did not.

Lenin and the Red Army beat back the counter-revolutionary White armies for several reasons. Most important, the Bolsheviks had quickly developed a better army. Once again, Trotsky's leadership was decisive. At first, the Bolsheviks had preached democracy in the military and had even elected officers in 1917. But beginning in March 1918, Trotsky became war commissar of the newly formed Red Army. He re-established strict discipline and the draft. Soldiers deserting or disobeying an order were summarily shot. Moreover, Trotsky made effective use of former tsarist army officers, who were actively recruited and given unprecedented powers over their troops. Trotsky's disciplined and effective fighting force repeatedly defeated the Whites in the field.

Ironically, foreign military intervention helped the Bolsheviks. For a variety of reasons, but primarily to stop the spread of communism, the Western Allies (including the United States, Britain, France, and Japan) sent troops to support the White armies. Yet their efforts were limited and halfhearted. By 1919, with the Great War over, Westerners were sick of war, and few politicians wanted to get involved in a new military crusade. Allied intervention failed to offer effective aid, though it did permit the Bolsheviks to appeal to the patriotic nationalism of ethnic Russians, in particular former tsarist army officers who objected to foreign involvement in Russian affairs.

Other conditions favored a Bolshevik victory as well. Strategically, the Reds controlled central Russia and the crucial cities of Moscow and Petrograd. The Whites attacked from the fringes and lacked coordination. Moreover, the poorly defined political program of the Whites was a mishmash of liberal republicanism and monarchism incapable of uniting the Bolsheviks' enemies. And while the Bolsheviks promised ethnic minorities in Russian-controlled territories substantial autonomy, the nationalist Whites sought to preserve the tsarist empire.

The Bolsheviks mobilized the home front for the war by establishing a system of centralized controls called **War Communism**. The leadership nationalized banks and industries and outlawed private enterprise. Bolshevik commissars introduced rationing, seized grain from peasants to feed the cities, and maintained strict workplace discipline. Although normal economic activity broke down, these measures maintained labor discipline and kept the Red Army supplied with men and material.

Revolutionary terror also contributed to the Communist victory. Lenin and the Bolsheviks set up a fearsome secret police known as the Cheka, dedicated to suppressing counter-revolutionaries. During the civil war, the Cheka imprisoned and executed without trial tens of thousands of supposed "class enemies." Victims included clergymen, aristocrats, the wealthy Russian bourgeoisie, deserters from the Red Army, and political opponents of all kinds. The tsar and his family were callously

War Communism The application of centralized state control during the Russian civil war, in which the Bolsheviks seized grain from peasants, introduced rationing, nationalized all banks and industry, and required everyone to work.

executed in July 1918. The "Red Terror" of 1918 to 1920 helped establish the secret police as a central tool of the emerging Communist government.

By the spring of 1920 the White armies were almost completely defeated, and the Bolsheviks had retaken much of the territory ceded to Germany under the Treaty of Brest-Litovsk. The Red Army reconquered Belarus and Ukraine, both of which had briefly gained independence. Building on this success, the Bolsheviks moved westward into Polish territory, but they were halted on the outskirts of Warsaw in August 1920 by troops under the leadership of the Polish field marshal and chief of state Jozef Pilsudski. This defeat halted Bolshevik attempts to spread communism farther into Europe, though in 1921 the Red Army overran the independent national governments of the Caucasus. The Russian civil war was over, and the Bolsheviks had won an impressive victory.

The Peace Settlement

FOCUS QUESTION
In what ways was the Allied peace settlement flawed?

Even as civil war raged in Russia and chaos engulfed much of central and eastern Europe, the war in the west came to an end in November 1918. Early in 1919 the victorious Western Allies came together in Paris, where they worked out terms for peace with Germany and created the peacekeeping League of Nations. Expectations were high; optimism was almost unlimited. Nevertheless, the peace settlement of 1919 turned out to be a disappointment for peoples and politicians alike. Rather than lasting peace, the immediate postwar years brought economic crisis and violent political conflict.

The End of the War

In early 1918 the German leadership decided that the time was ripe for a last-ditch, all-out attack on France. The defeat of Russia had released men and materials for the western front. The looming arrival of the first U.S. troops and the growth of dissent at home quickened German leaders' resolve. In the great Spring Offensive of 1918, Ludendorff launched an extensive attack on the French lines. German armies came within thirty-five miles of Paris, but Ludendorff's exhausted, overextended forces never broke through. They were stopped in July at the second Battle of the Marne, where 140,000 American soldiers saw action. The late but massive American intervention tipped the scales in favor of Allied victory.

By September British, French, and American armies were advancing steadily on all fronts. Hindenburg and Ludendorff realized that Germany had lost the war. Not wanting to shoulder the blame, they insisted that moderate politicians should take responsibility for the defeat. On October 4 the German emperor formed a new, more liberal civilian government to sue for peace.

As negotiations over an armistice dragged on, frustrated Germans rose up in revolt. On November 3 sailors in Kiel mutinied, and throughout northern Germany soldiers and workers established revolutionary councils modeled on the Russian soviets. The same day, Austria-Hungary surrendered to the Allies and began breaking apart. Revolution erupted in Germany, and masses of workers demonstrated for peace in Berlin. With army discipline collapsing, Wilhelm II abdicated and fled to

Holland. Socialist leaders in Berlin proclaimed a German republic on November 9 and agreed to tough Allied terms of surrender. The armistice went into effect on November 11, 1918. The war was over.

Revolution in Austria-Hungary and Germany

Military defeat brought turmoil and revolution to Austria-Hungary and Germany, as it had to Russia. Having started the war to preserve an imperial state, the Austro-Hungarian Empire perished in the attempt. The independent states of Austria, Hungary, and Czechoslovakia, and a larger Romania, Italy, and Poland, were carved out of its territories (Map 25.4). For four months in 1919, until conservative nationalists seized power, Hungary became a Marxist republic along Bolshevik lines. A greatly

MAP 25.4 Territorial Changes After World War I World War I brought tremendous changes to eastern Europe. New nations and new boundaries were established, and a dangerous power vacuum was created by the relatively weak states established between Germany and Soviet Russia.

expanded Serbian monarchy gained control of the western Balkans and took the name Yugoslavia.

In late 1918 Germany likewise experienced a dramatic revolution that resembled the Russian Revolution of March 1917. In both cases, a genuine popular uprising welled up from below, toppled an authoritarian monarchy, and created a liberal provisional republic. In both countries, liberals and moderate socialist politicians struggled with more radical workers' and soldiers' councils (or soviets) for political dominance. In Germany, however, moderates from the Social Democratic Party and their liberal allies held on to power and established the Weimar Republic—a democratic government that would lead Germany for the next fifteen years. Their success was a deep disappointment for Russia's Bolsheviks, who had hoped that a more radical revolution in Germany would help spread communism across the European continent.

There were several reasons for the German outcome. The great majority of the Marxist politicians in the Social Democratic Party were moderates, not revolutionaries. They wanted political democracy and civil liberties and favored the gradual elimination of capitalism. They were also German nationalists, appalled by the prospect of civil war and revolutionary terror. Of crucial importance was the fact that the moderate Social Democrats quickly came to terms with the army and big business, which helped prevent total national collapse.

Yet the triumph of the Social Democrats brought violent chaos to Germany in 1918 to 1919. The new republic was attacked from both sides of the political spectrum. Radical Communists led by Karl Liebknecht and Rosa Luxemburg tried to seize control of the government in the Spartacist Uprising in Berlin in January 1919. The Social Democrats called in nationalist Free Corps militias, bands of demobilized soldiers who had kept their weapons, to crush the uprising. Liebknecht and Luxemburg were arrested and then brutally murdered by Free Corps soldiers. In Bavaria, a short-lived Bolshevik-style republic was violently overthrown on government orders by the Free Corps. Nationwide strikes by leftist workers and a short-lived, right-wing military takeover—the Kapp Putsch—were repressed by the central government.

By the summer of 1920 the situation in Germany had calmed down, but the new republican government faced deep discontent. Communists and radical socialists blamed the Social Democrats for the murders of Liebknecht and Luxemburg and the repression in Bavaria. Right-wing nationalists, including the new Nazi Party, despised the government from the start. They spread the myth that the German army had never actually lost the war—instead, the nation was "stabbed in the back" by socialists and pacifists at home. In Germany, the end of the war brought only a fragile sense of political stability.

The Treaty of Versailles

Treaty of Versailles The 1919 peace settlement that ended war between Germany and the Allied powers.

In January 1919 over seventy delegates from twenty-seven nations met in Paris to hammer out a peace accord. The conference produced several treaties, including the **Treaty of Versailles**, which laid out the terms of the postwar settlement with Germany. The peace negotiations inspired great expectations. A young British diplomat later wrote that the victors "were journeying to Paris . . . to found a new order in Europe. We were preparing not Peace only, but Eternal Peace."[9]

This idealism was greatly strengthened by U.S. president Wilson's January 1918 peace proposal, the **Fourteen Points**. The plan called for open diplomacy, a reduction in armaments, freedom of commerce and trade, and the establishment of a **League of Nations**, an international body designed to provide a place for peaceful resolution of international problems. Perhaps most important, Wilson demanded that peace be based on the principle of **national self-determination**, meaning that peoples should be able to choose their own national governments through democratic majority-rule elections and live free from outside interference in territories with clearly defined, permanent borders. Despite the general optimism inspired by these ideas, the conference and the treaty itself quickly generated disagreement.

The "Big Three"—the United States, Great Britain, and France—controlled the conference. Germany, Austria-Hungary, and Russia were excluded, though their lands were placed on the negotiating table. Italy took part, but its role was quite limited. Representatives from the Middle East, Africa, and East Asia attended as well, but their concerns were largely ignored.

Almost immediately, the Big Three began to quarrel. Wilson, who was wildly cheered by European crowds as the champion of democratic international cooperation, was almost obsessed with creating the League of Nations. He insisted that this question come first, for he passionately believed that only a permanent international organization could avert future wars. Wilson had his way—the delegates agreed to create the League, though the details would be worked out later and the final structure was too weak to achieve its grand purpose. Prime Ministers Lloyd George of Great Britain and Georges Clemenceau of France were unenthusiastic about the League. They were primarily concerned with punishing Germany.

The question of what to do with Germany dominated discussions among the Big Three. Clemenceau wanted Germany to pay for its aggression. The war in the west had been fought largely on French soil, and like most French people, Clemenceau wanted revenge, economic retribution, and lasting security for France. This, he believed, required the creation of a buffer state between France and Germany, the permanent demilitarization of Germany, and vast reparation payments. Lloyd George supported Clemenceau, but was less harsh. Wilson disagreed. Clemenceau's demands seemed vindictive, and they violated Wilson's sense of Christian morality and the principle of national self-determination. By April the conference was deadlocked, and Wilson packed his bags to go home.

In the end, Clemenceau, fearful of future German aggression, agreed to a compromise. Clemenceau gave up the French demand for a Rhineland buffer state in return for French military occupation of the region for fifteen years and a formal defensive alliance with the United States and Great Britain. Both Wilson and Lloyd George promised that their countries would come to France's aid in the event of a German attack. The Allies moved quickly to finish the settlement, believing that further adjustments would be possible within the dual framework of a strong Western alliance and the League of Nations.

The various agreements signed at Versailles redrew the map of Europe, and the war's losers paid the price. The new independent nations carved out of the Austro-Hungarian and Russian Empires included Poland, Czechoslovakia, Finland, the Baltic States, and Yugoslavia. The Ottoman Empire was also split apart, or "partitioned," its territories placed under the control of the victors.

Fourteen Points Wilson's 1918 peace proposal calling for open diplomacy, a reduction in armaments, freedom of commerce and trade, the establishment of the League of Nations, and national self-determination.

League of Nations A permanent international organization, established during the 1919 Paris Peace Conference, designed to protect member states from aggression and avert future wars.

national self-determination The notion that peoples should be able to choose their own national governments through democratic majority-rule elections and live free from outside interference in nation-states with clearly defined borders.

The Treaty of Versailles, signed by the Allies and Germany, was key to the settlement. Germany's African and Asian colonies were given to France, Britain, and Japan as League of Nations mandates or administered territories, though Germany's losses within Europe were relatively minor, thanks to Wilson. Alsace-Lorraine was returned to France. Ethnic Polish territories seized by Prussia during the eighteenth-century partition of Poland (see Chapter 16) were returned to a new independent Polish state. Predominantly German Danzig was also placed within the Polish border but as a self-governing city under League of Nations protection. Germany had to limit its army to one hundred thousand men, agree to build no military fortifications in the Rhineland, and accept temporary French occupation of that region.

war guilt clause An article in the Treaty of Versailles that declared that Germany (with Austria) was solely responsible for the war and had to pay reparations equal to all civilian damages caused by the fighting.

More harshly, in Article 231, the famous **war guilt clause**, the Allies declared that Germany (with Austria) was entirely responsible for the war and thus had to pay reparations equal to all civilian damages caused by the fighting. This much-criticized clause expressed French and to some extent British demands for revenge. For the Germans, reparations were a crippling financial burden. Moreover, the clause was a cutting insult to German national pride. Many Germans believed wartime propaganda that had repeatedly claimed that Germany was an innocent victim, forced into war by a circle of barbaric enemies. When presented with these terms, the new German government protested vigorously but to no avail. On June 28, 1919, representatives of the German Social Democrats signed the treaty in Louis XIV's Hall of Mirrors at Versailles, where Bismarck's empire had been joyously proclaimed almost fifty years before (see Chapter 23).

The rapidly concluded Versailles treaties were far from perfect, but within the context of war-shattered Europe they were a beginning. Germany had been punished but not dismembered. A new world organization complemented a traditional defensive alliance of satisfied powers: Britain, France, and the United States. The remaining serious problems, the Allies hoped, could be worked out in the future. Allied leaders had seen speed as essential because they feared that the Bolshevik Revolution might spread. The best answer to Lenin's unending calls for worldwide upheaval, they believed, was peace and tranquillity.

Yet the great hopes of early 1919 had turned to ashes by the end of the year. The Western alliance had collapsed, and a grandiose plan for permanent peace had given way to a fragile truce. There were several reasons for this turn of events. First, the U.S. Senate and, to a lesser extent, the American people rejected Wilson's handiwork. Republican senators led by Henry Cabot Lodge believed that the treaty gave away Congress's constitutional right to declare war and demanded changes in the articles. In failing health, the self-righteous Wilson rejected all compromise. In doing so, he ensured that the Senate would never ratify the treaty and that the United States would never join the League of Nations. Moreover, the Senate refused to ratify treaties forming a defensive alliance with France and Great Britain. America in effect had turned its back on Europe. The new American gospel of isolationism represented a tragic renunciation of international responsibility. Using U.S. actions as an excuse, Great Britain too refused to ratify its defensive alliance with France. Bitterly betrayed by its allies, France stood alone.

A second cause for the failure of the peace was that the principle of national self-determination, which had engendered such enthusiasm, was good in theory but flawed in practice. In Europe, the borders of new states such as Poland, Czechoslovakia, and Yugoslavia cut through a jumble of ethnic and religious groups that often despised each other. The new central European nations would prove to be economically weak and politically unstable, the source of conflict in the years to come. In the colonies, desires for self-determination were simply ignored, leading to problems particularly in the Middle East.

The Peace Settlement in the Middle East

Although Allied leaders at Versailles focused mainly on European issues, they also imposed a political settlement on what had been the Ottoman Empire. Their decisions, made in Paris and at other international conferences, brought radical and controversial changes to the region. The Allies dismantled or partitioned the Ottoman Empire, Britain and France expanded their influence in the region, Jewish peoples were promised a "national homeland" in British-controlled Palestine, and Arab nationalists felt cheated and betrayed.

The British government had encouraged the wartime Arab revolt against the Ottoman Turks and had even made vague promises of an independent Arab kingdom, most clearly in the McMahon-Hussein correspondence (see page 840). However, when the fighting stopped, the British and the French chose instead to honor their own secret wartime agreements to divide and rule the Ottoman lands. Most important was the Sykes-Picot Agreement of 1916, named after the British and French diplomats who negotiated the deal.

In the secret accord, Britain and France agreed that former Ottoman territories would be administered by the European powers under what they called the **mandate system**. Under the terms of the mandates, individually granted to European powers by the League of Nations, former Ottoman territories (and former German colonies) would be placed under the "tutelage" of European authorities until they could "stand alone." France would receive a mandate to govern modern-day Lebanon and Syria and much of southern Turkey, and Britain would control Palestine, Transjordan, and Iraq. Though the official goal of the mandate system was to eventually grant these regions national independence, it quickly became clear that the Allies hardly intended to do so. Critics labeled the system colonialism under another name, and when Britain and France set about implementing their agreements after the armistice, Arab nationalists reacted with understandable surprise and resentment.

British plans for the former Ottoman lands that would become Palestine further angered Arab nationalists. The **Balfour Declaration** of November 1917, written by British foreign secretary Arthur Balfour, had announced that Britain favored a "National Home for the Jewish People" in Palestine, but without discriminating against the civil and religious rights of the non-Jewish communities already living in the region. Some members of the British cabinet believed the declaration would appeal to German, Austrian, and American Jews and thus help the British war effort. Others sincerely supported the Zionist vision of a Jewish homeland (see Chapter 23), which they hoped would also help Britain maintain control of the Suez Canal. Whatever the motives, the declaration enraged Arabs.

In 1914 Jews accounted for about 11 percent of the population in the three Ottoman districts that the British would lump together to form Palestine; the rest of the population was predominantly Arab. Both groups understood that Balfour's "National Home" implied the establishment of some kind of Jewish state that

mandate system The plan to allow Britain and France to administer former Ottoman territories, put into place after the end of the First World War.

Balfour Declaration A 1917 British statement that declared British support of a National Home for the Jewish People in Palestine.

would violate majority rule. Moreover, a state founded on religious and ethnic exclusivity was out of keeping with Islamic and Ottoman tradition, which had historically been more tolerant of religious diversity and minorities than Christian Europe had been.

Though Arab leaders attended the Versailles Peace Conference, their efforts to secure autonomy in the Middle East came to nothing. Only the kingdom of Hejaz—today part of Saudi Arabia—was granted independence. In response, Arab nationalists came together in Damascus as the General Syrian Congress in 1919 and unsuccessfully called again for political independence. The congress proclaimed Syria an independent kingdom; a similar congress declared Iraqi independence.

The Western reaction was swift and decisive. A French army stationed in Lebanon attacked Syria, taking Damascus in July 1920. The Arab government fled, and the French took over. Meanwhile, the British bloodily put down an uprising in Iraq and established control there. Brushing aside Arab opposition, the British mandate in Palestine formally incorporated the Balfour Declaration and its commitment to a Jewish national home. Western imperialism, in the form of the mandate system authorized by the League of Nations, appeared to have replaced Ottoman rule in the Middle East. In the following decades, deadly anti-imperial riots and violent conflicts between Arabs and Jews would repeatedly undermine the region's stability.

The Allies sought to impose even harsher terms on the defeated Turks than on the "liberated" Arabs. A treaty forced on the Ottoman sultan dismembered the Turkish heartland. Great Britain and France occupied parts of modern-day Turkey, and Italy and Greece claimed shares. There was a sizable Greek minority in western Turkey, and Greek nationalists wanted to build a modern Greek empire modeled on long-dead Byzantium. In 1919 Greek armies carried by British ships landed on the Turkish coast at Smyrna (SMUHR-nuh; today's Izmir) and advanced unopposed into the interior, while French troops moved in from the south. Turkey seemed finished.

Turkey survived the postwar invasions. A Turkish National Movement emerged, led by Mustafa Kemal (1881–1938), a prominent general in the successful Turkish defeat of the British at the Battle of Gallipoli. The leaders of the movement overthrew the sultan and refused to acknowledge the Allied dismemberment of their country. Under Kemal's direction, a revived Turkish army gradually mounted a forceful resistance, and despite staggering losses, his troops repulsed the invaders. The Greeks and British sued for peace. In 1923, after long negotiations, the resulting Treaty of Lausanne (loh-ZAN) recognized the territorial integrity of Turkey and solemnly abolished the hated capitulations that the European powers had imposed over the centuries to give their citizens special privileges in the Ottoman Empire.

The peace accords included an agreement for a shattering example of what we would now call "ethnic cleansing," under which Greeks were forced to leave Turkish-majority lands for Greece, while Turks moved from Greece and former Balkan territories to the Turkish mainland. The result, driven by ideals of national self-determination and racial purity, was a humanitarian disaster. Ethnic Greeks constituted about 16 percent of the Turkish population, and now between 1.5 and

2 million people had to pick up and move west. At the same time, 500,000 to 600,000 ethnic Turks moved out of Greece and Bulgaria to the Anatolian peninsula (modern-day Turkey). Very few wanted to leave their homes, and though the authorities set up refugee camps, refugees faced harsh conditions, rampant looting, and physical abuse. In this case, race trumped religion: Muslim Greeks were forced west, and Christian Turks forced east, and the population exchange destroyed a vital, multicultural ethnic patchwork. The agreements at Lausanne became a model for future examples of ethnic cleansing, most notably the exchange of Germans and Slavs in central Europe after the Second World War, and the exchange of Hindus and Muslims that followed Indian independence in 1947.

Kemal, a nationalist without religious faith, believed that Turkey should modernize and secularize along Western lines. He established a republic, was elected president, and created a one-party system—partly inspired by the Bolshevik example—to transform his country. The most radical reforms pertained to religion and culture. For centuries, Islamic religious authorities had regulated most of the intellectual, political, and social activities of Ottoman citizens. Profoundly influenced by the example of western Europe, Kemal set out to limit the place of religion and religious leaders in daily affairs. He decreed a controversial separation of church and state, promulgated law codes inspired by European models, and established a secular public school system. Women received rights that they never had before. By the time of his death in 1938, Kemal had implemented much of his revolutionary program and had moved Turkey much closer to Europe, foretelling current efforts by Turkey to join the European Union as a full-fledged member.

The Human Costs of the War

World War I broke empires, inspired revolutions, and changed national borders on a world scale. It also had immense human costs, and ordinary people in the combatant nations struggled to deal with its legacy in the years that followed. The raw numbers are astonishing: estimates vary, but total deaths on the battlefield numbered about 8 million soldiers. Russia had the highest number of military casualties, followed by Germany. France had the highest proportionate number of losses; about one out of every ten adult males died in the war. The other belligerents paid a high price as well (Figure 25.1). Between 7 and 10 million civilians died because of the war and war-related hardships, and another 20 million people died in the worldwide influenza epidemic that followed the war in 1918.

The number of dead, the violence of their deaths, and the nature of trench warfare made proper burials difficult, if not impossible. Soldiers were typically interred where they fell, and by 1918 thousands of ad hoc military cemeteries were scattered across northern France and Flanders. When remains were gathered, the chaos and danger of the battlefield limited accurate identification. After the war, the bodies were moved to more formal cemeteries, but hundreds of thousands remained unidentified. British and German soldiers ultimately remained in foreign soil, in graveyards managed by national commissions. After some delay, the bodies of most of the French combatants were brought home to local cemeteries.

Millions of ordinary people grieved, turning to family, friends, neighbors, and the church for comfort. Towns and villages across Europe raised public memorials

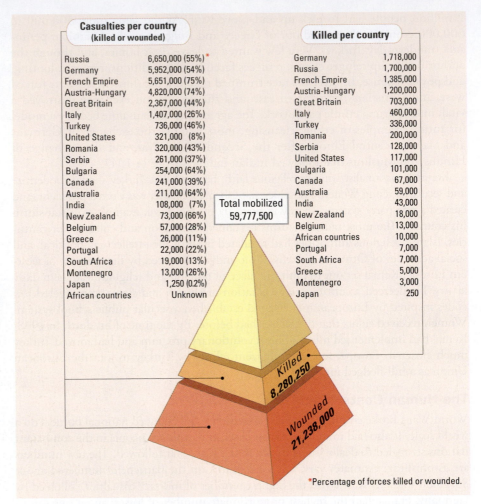

Casualties per country (killed or wounded)		Killed per country	
Russia	6,650,000 (55%)*	Germany	1,718,000
Germany	5,952,000 (54%)	Russia	1,700,000
French Empire	5,651,000 (75%)	French Empire	1,385,000
Austria-Hungary	4,820,000 (74%)	Austria-Hungary	1,200,000
Great Britain	2,367,000 (44%)	Great Britain	703,000
Italy	1,407,000 (26%)	Italy	460,000
Turkey	736,000 (46%)	Turkey	336,000
United States	321,000 (8%)	Romania	200,000
Romania	320,000 (43%)	Serbia	128,000
Serbia	261,000 (37%)	United States	117,000
Bulgaria	254,000 (64%)	Bulgaria	101,000
Canada	241,000 (39%)	Canada	67,000
Australia	211,000 (64%)	Australia	59,000
India	108,000 (7%)	India	43,000
New Zealand	73,000 (66%)	New Zealand	18,000
Belgium	57,000 (28%)	Belgium	13,000
Greece	26,000 (11%)	African countries	10,000
Portugal	22,000 (22%)	Portugal	7,000
South Africa	19,000 (13%)	South Africa	7,000
Montenegro	13,000 (26%)	Greece	5,000
Japan	1,250 (0.2%)	Montenegro	3,000
African countries	Unknown	Japan	250

Total mobilized
59,777,500

Killed
8,280,250

Wounded
21,238,000

*Percentage of forces killed or wounded.

FIGURE 25.1 Casualties of World War I   The losses of World War I were the highest ever for a war in Europe. These numbers are approximate because of problems with record keeping caused by the destructive nature of total war.

to honor the dead and held ceremonies on important anniversaries: on November 11, the day the war ended, and in Britain on July 1, to commemorate the Battle of the Somme. These were poignant and often tearful moments for participants. For the first time, many nations built a Tomb of the Unknown Soldier as a site for national mourning. Memorials were also built on the main battlefields of the war. All expressed the general need to recognize the great sorrow and suffering caused by so much death.

The victims of the First World War included millions of widows and orphans and huge numbers of emotionally scarred and disabled veterans. Countless soldiers suffered from what the British called "shell shock"—now termed post-traumatic stress disorder (PTSD). Contemporary physicians and policymakers poorly understood this

The Human Costs of War   A disabled German veteran works as a carpenter around 1919. The war killed millions of soldiers and left many more permanently disabled, making the sight of men missing limbs or disfigured in other ways a common one in the 1920s. (FPG/Hulton Archive/Getty Images)

complex mental health issue, and though some soldiers suffering from PTSD received medical treatment, others were accused of cowardice and shirking, and were denied veterans' benefits after the war. In addition, some 10 million soldiers came home physically disfigured or mutilated. Governments tried to take care of the disabled and the survivor families, but there was rarely enough money to adequately fund pensions and job-training programs. Artificial limbs were expensive, uncomfortable, and awkward, and some employers refused to hire disabled workers. Crippled veterans were often forced to beg on the streets, a common sight for the next decade.

The German case is illustrative. Nearly 10 percent of German civilians were direct victims of the war in one way or another, and the new German government struggled to take care of them. Veterans' groups organized to lobby for state support, and fully one-third of the federal budget of the Weimar Republic was tied up in war-related pensions and benefits. With the onset of the Great Depression in 1929, benefits were cut, leaving bitter veterans vulnerable to Nazi propagandists who paid homage to the sacrifices of the war while calling for the overthrow of the republican government. The human cost of the war thus had another steep price. Across Europe, newly formed radical right-wing parties, including the German Nazis and the Italian Fascists, successfully manipulated popular feelings of loss and resentment to undermine fragile parliamentary governments.

LOOKING BACK LOOKING AHEAD

When chief of the German general staff Count Helmuth von Moltke imagined the war of the future in a letter to his wife in 1905, his comments were surprisingly accurate. "It will become a war between peoples which will not be concluded with a single battle," the general wrote, "but which will be a long, weary struggle with a country that will not acknowledge defeat until the whole strength of its people is broken."[10] As von Moltke predicted, World War I broke peoples and nations. The trials of total war increased the power of the centralized state and brought down the Austro-Hungarian, Ottoman, and Russian Empires. The brutal violence shocked and horrified observers across the world; ordinary citizens were left to mourn their losses.

Despite high hopes for Wilson's Fourteen Points, the Treaty of Versailles hardly brought lasting peace. The war's disruptions encouraged radical political conflict in the 1920s and 1930s and the rise of totalitarian regimes across Europe, which led to the even more extreme violence of the Second World War. Indeed, some historians believe that the years from 1914 to 1945 might most accurately be labeled a modern Thirty Years' War, since the problems unleashed in August 1914 were only really resolved in the 1950s. This strong assertion contains a great deal of truth. For all of Europe, World War I was a revolutionary conflict of gigantic proportions with lasting traumatic effects.

Make Connections

Think about the larger developments and continuities within and across chapters.

1. While the war was being fought, peoples on all sides of the fighting often referred to the First World War as "the Great War." Why would they find this label appropriate?

2. How did the First World War draw on long-standing political rivalries and tensions among the European powers (Chapters 19, 23, and 24)?

3. To what extent was the First World War actually a "world" war?

25 REVIEW & EXPLORE

Review the Main Ideas

Answer the focus questions from each section of the chapter.

◆ What caused the outbreak of the First World War? (p. 828)

◆ How did the First World War differ from previous wars? (p. 834)

◆ In what ways did the war transform life on the home front? (p. 841)

◆ Why did world war lead to revolution in Russia, and what was its outcome? (p. 847)

◆ In what ways was the Allied peace settlement flawed? (p. 854)

Identify Key Terms

Identify and explain the significance of each item below.

Triple Alliance (p. 828)
Triple Entente (p. 830)
Schlieffen Plan (p. 834)
total war (p. 834)
trench warfare (p. 835)
February Revolution (p. 848)
Petrograd Soviet (p. 848)
Bolsheviks (p. 849)
Treaty of Brest-Litovsk (p. 852)
War Communism (p. 853)
Treaty of Versailles (p. 856)
Fourteen Points (p. 857)
League of Nations (p. 857)
national self-determination (p. 857)
war guilt clause (p. 858)
mandate system (p. 859)
Balfour Declaration (p. 859)

NOTES

1. Quoted in J. Remak, *The Origins of World War I* (New York: Holt, Rinehart & Winston, 1967), p. 84.
2. On the mood of 1914, see J. Joll, *The Origins of the First World War* (New York: Longman, 1992), pp. 199–233.
3. Quoted in G. L. Mosse, *Fallen Soldiers: Reshaping the Memory of the World Wars* (New York: Oxford University Press, 1990), p. 64.
4. Quoted in N. Malcolm, *Bosnia: A Short History* (New York: New York University Press, 1996), p. 153.
5. Quoted in S. Audoin-Rouzeau, *Men at War, 1914–1918: National Sentiment and Trench Journalism in France During the First World War* (Oxford Berg, 1992), p. 69.
6. V. G. Liulevicius, *War Land on the Eastern Front: Culture, National Identity, and German Occupation in World War I* (New York: Cambridge University Press, 2000), pp. 54–89; quotation on p. 71.
7. Quoted in F. P. Chambers, *The War Behind the War, 1914–1918* (London: Faber & Faber, 1939), p. 168.
8. J. Reed, *Ten Days That Shook the World* (New York: International Publishers, 1967), p. 126.
9. Quoted in H. Nicolson, *Peacemaking 1919* (New York: Grosset & Dunlap Universal Library, 1965), pp. 8, 31–32.
10. Quoted in C. Barnett, *The Swordbearers: Supreme Command in the First World War* (New York: Morrow, 1964), p. 40.

CHAPTER PREVIEW

Uncertainty in Modern Thought
How did intellectual developments reflect the general crisis in Western thought?

Modernism in Architecture, Art, Literature, and Music
How did modernism revolutionize Western culture?

An Emerging Consumer Society
How did consumer society change everyday life?

The Search for Peace and Political Stability
What obstacles to lasting peace did European leaders face?

The Great Depression, 1929–1939
What were the causes and consequences of the Great Depression?

Life in the Age of Anxiety
Dadaist George Grosz's disturbing *Inside and Outside* portrays the rampant inequality wrought by the economic crises of the 1920s. Wealthy and bestial elites celebrate a luxurious New Year's Eve "inside," while "outside" a veteran with disabilities begs in vain from uncaring passersby. (Art © Estate of George Grosz/ Licensed by VAGA, New York, NY/ photo: akg-images)

26

The Age of Anxiety

1880–1940

When Allied diplomats met in Paris in early 1919 with their optimistic plans for building a lasting peace, many people looked forward to happier times. After the terrible trauma of total war, they hoped that life would return to normal and would make sense in the familiar prewar terms of peace, progress, and prosperity. Their hopes were in vain. World War I and the Russian Revolution had mangled too many things beyond repair. Great numbers of people felt themselves increasingly adrift in an age of anxiety and continual change.

Late-nineteenth-century thinkers had already called attention to the pessimism, uncertainty, and irrationalism that seemed to accompany modern life. By 1900 radical developments in philosophy and the sciences had substantiated and popularized such ideas. The modernist movement had begun its sweep through literature, music, and the arts, as avant-garde innovators rejected old cultural forms and began to experiment with new ones. Radical innovations in the arts and sciences dominated Western culture in the 1920s and 1930s and remained influential after World War II. A growing consumer society, and the new media of radio and film, transformed the habits of everyday life and leisure.

Even as modern science, art, and culture challenged received wisdom of all kinds, international relations spiraled into crisis. Despite some progress in the mid-1920s, political stability remained short-lived, and the Great Depression that began in 1929 cast millions into poverty and shocked the status quo. Democratic liberalism was besieged by the rise of authoritarian and Fascist governments, and another world conflict seemed imminent. In the early 1920s the French poet and critic Paul Valéry described his widespread "impression of darkness," where "almost all the affairs of men remain in a terrible uncertainty. We think of what has disappeared, and we are almost destroyed by what has been destroyed; we do not know what will be born, and we fear the future, not without reason."[1] Valéry's words captured the gloom and foreboding that dominated the decades between the wars. ■

Uncertainty in Modern Thought

FOCUS QUESTION
How did intellectual developments reflect the general crisis in Western thought?

The decades surrounding the First World War—from the 1880s to the 1930s— brought intense cultural and intellectual experimentation. As people grappled with the costs of the war and the challenges of postwar recovery, philosophers and scientists questioned and even abandoned many of the cherished values and beliefs that had guided Western society since the eighteenth-century Enlightenment and the nineteenth-century triumph of industry and science. Radical intellectuals dismissed the possibility that rational thought could lead to greater human understanding or social progress. Though some thinkers embraced Christianity, others rejected Christian teachings. Modern thought thus dovetailed with the ongoing political and social crises of the 1920s and 1930s.

Historians find it relatively easy to set precise dates for political events, such as the outbreak of wars or the outcome of national elections. Exact dates for the rise and fall of intellectual and cultural developments are more difficult to define. The emergence of modern philosophy, for example, did not follow the clear-cut timelines of political history. Thus to understand the history of modern thought, we must investigate trends dating back to the last decades of the nineteenth century and follow them into the 1950s.

Modern Philosophy

Before 1914 most people still believed in Enlightenment ideals of progress, reason, and individual rights. At the turn of the century supporters of these philosophies had some cause for optimism. Women and workers were gradually gaining support in their struggles for political and social recognition, and the rising standard of living, the taming of the city, and the growth of state-supported social programs suggested that life was indeed improving. Such developments encouraged faith in the ability of a rational human mind to discover the laws of society and then wisely act on them.

Nevertheless, in the late nineteenth century a small group of serious thinkers mounted a determined attack on these optimistic beliefs. These critics rejected the general faith in progress and the rational human mind. The German philosopher Friedrich Nietzsche (NEE-chuh) (1844–1900) was particularly influential, though not until after his death. Never a systematic philosopher, he wrote more as a prophet in a provocative and poetic style. In the first of his *Untimely Meditations* (1873), he argued that ever since classical Athens, the West had

Philosophy with a Hammer German philosopher Friedrich Nietzsche claimed that his "revaluation of all values" was like writing "philosophy with a hammer." His ideas posed a radical challenge to conventional Western thought and had enormous influence on later thinkers. (akg-images)

Chronology

1887	Nietzsche publishes *On the Genealogy of Morals*
1900	Freud publishes *The Interpretation of Dreams*
1913	Stravinsky's *The Rite of Spring* premieres in Paris
1919	Treaty of Versailles; Freudian psychology gains popularity; Keynes publishes *The Economic Consequences of the Peace*; Rutherford splits the atom; Bauhaus school founded
1920s	Existentialism, Dadaism, and Surrealism gain prominence
1922	Eliot publishes *The Waste Land*; Joyce publishes *Ulysses*; Woolf publishes *Jacob's Room*; Wittgenstein writes on logical positivism
1922	First radio broadcast by British Broadcasting Company (BBC)
1923	French and Belgian armies occupy the Ruhr; Corbusier publishes *Towards a New Architecture*
1924	Dawes Plan
1925	Berg's opera *Wozzeck* first performed; Kafka publishes *The Trial*
1926	Germany joins the League of Nations
1927	Heisenberg formulates the "uncertainty principle"
1928	Kellogg-Briand Pact
1929	Faulkner publishes *The Sound and the Fury*
1929–1939	Great Depression
1932	Franklin Roosevelt announces "New Deal for the forgotten man"
1933	The National Socialist Party takes power in Germany
1935	Release of Riefenstahl's documentary film *Triumph of the Will*
1936	Formation of Popular Front in France

overemphasized rationality and stifled the authentic passions and animal instincts that drive human activity and true creativity.

Nietzsche questioned the conventional values of Western society. He believed that reason, progress, and respectability were outworn social and psychological constructs that suffocated self-realization and excellence. Though he was the son of a Lutheran minister, Nietzsche famously rejected religion. In his 1887 book, *On the Genealogy of Morals*, he claimed that Christianity embodied a "slave morality" that glorified weakness, envy, and mediocrity. In one of his most famous lines, an apparent madman proclaims that "God is dead," metaphorically murdered by lackadaisical modern Christians who no longer really believed in him. (See "Evaluating the Evidence 26.1: Friedrich Nietzsche Pronounces the Death of God," page 870.)

Nietzsche painted a dark world, perhaps foreshadowing his own loss of sanity in 1889. He warned that Western society was entering a period of nihilism — the philosophical idea that human life is entirely without meaning, truth, or purpose. Nietzsche asserted that all moral systems were invented lies and that liberalism, democracy, and socialism were corrupt systems designed to promote the weak at the expense of the strong. The West was in decline; false values had triumphed; the death of God left people disoriented and depressed. According to Nietzsche, the only hope for the individual was to accept the meaninglessness of human existence and then make that very meaninglessness a source of self-defined personal integrity and hence liberation. In this way, at least a few superior individuals could free themselves from the humdrum thinking of the masses and become true heroes.

Little read during his active years, Nietzsche's works attracted growing attention in the early twentieth century. Artists and writers experimented with his ideas, which were fundamental to the rise of the philosophy of existentialism in the 1920s.

Friedrich Nietzsche Pronounces the Death of God

In this selection from philosopher Friedrich Nietzsche's
The Gay Science (1882), one of the best-known passages
in his entire body of work, a "madman" pronounces the death
of God and describes the anxiety and despair —
and the opportunities — faced by people in a world
without faith.

The Madman. Haven't you heard of that madman, who on a bright morning day lit a lantern, ran into the marketplace, and screamed incessantly: "I am looking for God! I am looking for God!" Since there were a lot of people standing around who did not believe in God, he only aroused great laughter. Is he lost? asked one person. Did he lose his way like a child? asked another. Or is he in hiding? Is he frightened of us? Has he gone on a journey? Or emigrated? And so they screamed and laughed. The madman leaped into the crowd and stared straight at them. "Where has God gone?" he cried. "I will tell you! *We have killed him.* You and I! All of us are his murderers! But how did we do this? How did we manage to drink up the sea? Who gave us the sponge to wipe away the entire horizon? What were we doing when we unchained this earth from its sun? Where is it going now? Where are we going? Away from all the suns? Aren't we ceaselessly falling? Backward, sideways, forward, in all directions? Is there an up or a down at all? Aren't we just roaming through an infinite nothing? Don't you feel the breath of this empty space? Hasn't it gotten colder? Isn't night and ever more night falling? Don't we have to light our lanterns in the morning? Do we hear anything yet of the noise of the gravediggers who are burying God? Do we smell anything yet of the rot of God's decomposition? Gods decompose too! God is dead! God will stay dead! And we have killed him! How do we console ourselves, the murderers of all murderers? The holiest and mightiest the world has ever known has bled to death against our knives — who will wipe the blood off? Where is the water to cleanse ourselves? What sort of rituals of atonement, what sort of sacred games, will we have to come up with now? Isn't the greatness of this deed too great for us? Don't we have to become gods ourselves simply to appear worthy of it? There has never been a greater deed, and whoever will be born after us will belong to a history greater than any history up to now!"

EVALUATE THE EVIDENCE

1. Does Nietzsche believe that the "death of God" is a positive experience? In what ways can people come to grips with this "great deed"?
2. How does the nihilism expressed in this passage foreshadow many of the main ideas in the philosophy of existentialism?

Source: *Nietzsche and the Death of God: Selected Writings*, trans. and ed. Peter Fritzsche (Boston: Bedford/St. Martin's, 2007), pp. 71–72. Used by permission of Bedford/St. Martin's.

Subsequent generations remade Nietzsche to suit their own needs, and his influence remains enormous to this day.

The growing dissatisfaction with established ideas before 1914 was apparent in other important thinkers as well. In the 1890s French philosophy professor Henri Bergson (1859–1941), for one, argued that immediate experience and intuition were as important as rational and scientific thinking for understanding reality. According to Bergson, a religious experience or mystical poem was often more accessible to human comprehension than a scientific law or a mathematical equation.

The First World War accelerated the revolt against established certainties in philosophy, but that revolt went in two very different directions. In English-speaking countries, the main development was the acceptance of logical positivism in university circles. In the continental countries, the primary development in philosophy was existentialism.

Logical positivism was truly revolutionary. Adherents of this worldview argued that what we know about human life must be based on rational facts and direct observation. They concluded that theology and most traditional philosophy were

logical positivism
A philosophy that sees meaning in only those beliefs that can be empirically proven, and that therefore rejects most of the concerns of traditional philosophy, from the existence of God to the meaning of happiness, as nonsense.

meaningless because even the most cherished ideas about God, eternal truth, and ethics were impossible to prove using logic. This outlook is often associated with the Austrian philosopher Ludwig Wittgenstein (VIHT-guhn-shtine) (1889–1951), who later immigrated to England, where he trained numerous disciples.

In his pugnacious *Tractatus Logico-Philosophicus* (Essay on Logical Philosophy), published in 1922, Wittgenstein argued that philosophy is only the logical clarification of thoughts and that therefore it should concentrate on the study of language, which expresses thoughts. In his view, the great philosophical issues of the ages—God, freedom, morality, and so on—were quite literally senseless, a great waste of time, for neither scientific experiments nor mathematical logic could demonstrate their validity. Statements about such matters reflected only the personal preferences of a given individual. As Wittgenstein put it in the famous last sentence of this work, "Of what one cannot speak, of that one must keep silent." Logical positivism, which has remained dominant in England and the United States to this day, drastically reduced the scope of philosophical inquiry and offered little solace to ordinary people.

On the continent, others looked for answers in **existentialism**. This new philosophy loosely united highly diverse and even contradictory thinkers in a search for usable moral values in a world of anxiety and uncertainty. Modern existentialism had many nineteenth-century forerunners, including Nietzsche, the Danish religious philosopher Søren Kierkegaard (1813–1855), and the Russian novelist Fyodor Dostoyevsky (1821–1881). The philosophy gained recognition in Germany in the 1920s when philosophers Martin Heidegger (1889–1976) and Karl Jaspers (1883–1969) found a sympathetic audience among disillusioned postwar university students. These writers placed great emphasis on the loneliness and meaninglessness of human existence and the need to come to terms with the fear caused by this situation.

Most existential thinkers in the twentieth century were atheists. Often inspired by Nietzsche, they did not believe that a supreme being had established humanity's fundamental nature and given life its meaning. In the words of French existentialist Jean-Paul Sartre (ZHAWN-pawl SAHR-truh) (1905–1980), "existence precedes essence." By that, Sartre meant that there are no God-given, timeless truths outside or independent of individual existence. Only after they are born do people struggle to define their essence, entirely on their own. According to thinkers like Sartre and his lifelong intellectual partner Simone de Beauvoir (1908–1986), existence itself is absurd. Human beings are terribly alone, for there is no God to help them. They are left to confront the inevitable arrival of death and so are hounded by despair. The crisis of the existential thinker epitomized the modern intellectual crisis—the shattering of beliefs in God, reason, and progress.

At the same time, existentialists recognized that human beings must act in the world. Indeed, in the words of Sartre, "man is condemned to be free." Because life is meaningless, existentialists believe that individuals are forced to create their own meaning and define themselves through their actions. Such radical freedom is frightening, and Sartre concluded that most people try to escape it by structuring their lives around conventional social norms. According to Sartre, to escape is to live in "bad faith," to hide from the hard truths of existence. To live authentically, individuals must become "engaged" and choose their own actions in full awareness of their responsibility for their own behavior. Existentialism thus had a powerful ethical component. It placed great stress on individual responsibility and choice, on "being in the world" in the right way.

existentialism A philosophy that stresses the meaninglessness of existence and the importance of the individual in searching for moral values in an uncertain world.

Existentialism had important precedents in the late nineteenth and early twentieth centuries, but the philosophy really came of age in France during and immediately after World War II. The terrible conditions of that war, discussed in the next chapter, reinforced the existential view of and approach to life. After World War II, French existentialists such as Sartre and Albert Camus (1913–1960) became enormously influential. They offered powerful but unsettling answers to the profound moral issues and the crises of the first half of the twentieth century.

The Revival of Christianity

Though philosophers such as Nietzsche, Wittgenstein, and Sartre all argued that religion had little to teach people in the modern age, the decades after the First World War witnessed a tenacious revival of Christian thought. Christianity—and religion in general—had been on the defensive in intellectual circles since the Enlightenment. In the years before 1914 some theologians, especially Protestant ones, had felt the need to interpret Christian doctrine and the Bible so that they did not seem to contradict science, evolution, and common sense. They saw Christ primarily as a great moral teacher and downplayed the mysterious, spiritual aspects of his divinity. Indeed, some modern theologians were embarrassed by the miraculous, unscientific aspects of Christianity and rejected them.

Especially after World War I, a number of thinkers and theologians began to revitalize the fundamental beliefs of Christianity. Sometimes called Christian existentialists because they shared the loneliness and despair of atheistic existentialists, they stressed human beings' sinful nature, their need for faith, and the mystery of God's forgiveness. The revival of Christian belief after World War I was fed by the rediscovery of the work of the nineteenth-century Danish theologian Søren Kierkegaard (KIHR-kuh-gahrd), whose ideas became extremely influential. Kierkegaard believed it was impossible for ordinary individuals to prove the existence of God, but he rejected the notion that Christianity was an empty practice. In his classic *Sickness unto Death* (1849), Kierkegaard mastered his religious doubts by suggesting that people must take a "leap of faith" and accept the existence of an objectively unknowable but nonetheless awesome and majestic God.

In the 1920s the Swiss Protestant theologian Karl Barth (1886–1968) propounded similar ideas. In brilliant and influential writings, Barth argued that human beings were imperfect, sinful creatures whose reason and will are hopelessly flawed. Religious truth is therefore made known to human beings only through God's grace, not through reason. People have to accept God's word and the supernatural revelation of Jesus Christ with awe, trust, and obedience, not reason or logic.

Among Catholics, the leading existential Christian was Gabriel Marcel (1889–1973). Born into a cultivated French family, Marcel found in the Catholic Church an answer to what he called the postwar "broken world." Catholicism and religious belief provided the hope, humanity, honesty, and piety for which he hungered. Marcel and his countryman Jacques Maritain (1882–1973) denounced anti-Semitism and supported closer ties with non-Catholics.

After 1914 religion became much more meaningful to intellectuals than it had been before the war. Between about 1920 and 1950, in addition to Marcel and Maritain, poets T. S. Eliot and W. H. Auden, novelists Evelyn Waugh and Aldous Huxley, historian Arnold Toynbee, writer C. S. Lewis, psychoanalyst Karl Stern, and physicist Max Planck all either converted to a faith or became attracted to religion for the first time. Religion, often of a despairing, existential variety, was one meaningful answer to uncertainty and anxiety and the horrific costs of the First and Second World Wars. In the words of English novelist Graham Greene, a Roman Catholic convert, "One began to believe in heaven because one believed in hell."[2]

The New Physics

Ever since the Scientific Revolution of the seventeenth century, scientific advances and their implications had greatly influenced the beliefs of thinking people. By the late nineteenth century science was one of the main pillars supporting Western society's optimistic and rationalistic worldview. Progressive minds believed that science, unlike religion or philosophical speculation, was based on hard facts and controlled experiments. Unchanging natural laws seemed to determine physical processes and permit useful solutions to more and more problems. All this was comforting, especially to people no longer committed to traditional religious beliefs. And all this was challenged by the new physics.

An important first step came at the end of the nineteenth century with the discovery that atoms were not like hard, permanent little billiard balls. They were actually composed of many far-smaller, fast-moving particles, such as electrons and protons. Polish-born physicist Marie Curie (1867–1934) and her French husband, Pierre, discovered that radium constantly emits subatomic particles and thus does not have a constant atomic weight. Building on this and other work in radiation, German physicist Max Planck (1858–1947) showed in 1900 that subatomic energy is emitted in uneven little spurts, which Planck called "quanta," and not in a steady stream, as previously believed. Planck's discovery called into question the old sharp distinction between matter and energy: the implication was that matter and energy might be different forms of the same thing. The view of atoms as the stable basic building blocks of nature, with a different kind of unbreakable atom for each of the ninety-two chemical elements, was badly shaken.

In 1905 the German-Jewish genius Albert Einstein (1879–1955) went further than the Curies and Planck in undermining Newtonian physics. His **theory of special relativity** postulated that time and space are relative to the viewpoint of the observer and that only the speed of light is constant for all frames of reference in the universe. In order to make his revolutionary and paradoxical idea somewhat comprehensible to the nonmathematical layperson, Einstein used analogies involving moving trains. For example, if a woman in the middle of a moving car got up and walked forward to the door, she had gone, relative to the train, a half car length. But relative to an observer on the embankment, she had gone farther. To Einstein, this meant that time and distance were not natural universals but depended on the position and motion of the observer.

In addition, Einstein's theory stated that matter and energy are interchangeable and that even a particle of matter contains enormous levels of potential energy. These ideas unified an apparently infinite universe with the incredibly small, fast-moving subatomic world. In comparison, the closed framework of the Newtonian physics developed during the Scientific Revolution, exemplified by Newton's supposedly immutable laws of motion and mechanics, was quite limited (see Chapter 16).

theory of special relativity
Albert Einstein's theory that time and space are relative to the observer and that only the speed of light remains constant.

The 1920s opened the "heroic age of physics," in the apt words of Ernest Rutherford (1871–1937), one of its leading pioneers. Breakthrough followed breakthrough. In 1919 Rutherford showed that the atom could be split. By 1944 seven subatomic particles had been identified, the most important of which was the neutron. Physicists realized that the neutron's capacity to shatter the nucleus of another atom could lead to chain reactions of shattered atoms that would release unbelievable force. This discovery was fundamental to the subsequent development of the nuclear bomb.

Although few nonscientists truly understood the revolution in physics, its implications, as presented by newspapers and popular science fiction writers, were disturbing to millions of men and women in the 1920s and 1930s. As unsettling as Einstein's ideas was a notion popularized by German physicist Werner Heisenberg (VER-nuhr HIGH-zuhn-buhrg) (1901–1976). In 1927 Heisenberg formulated the "uncertainty principle," which postulates that nature itself is ultimately unknowable and unpredictable. He suggested that the universe lacked any absolute objective reality. Everything was "relative," that is, dependent on the observer's frame of reference. Such ideas caught on among ordinary people, who found the unstable, relativistic world described by the new physicists strange and troubling. Instead of Newton's dependable, rational laws, there seemed to be only tendencies and probabilities in an extraordinarily complex and uncertain universe. Like modern philosophy, physics no longer provided comforting truths about natural laws or optimistic answers about humanity's place in an understandable world.

Freudian Psychology

With physics presenting an uncertain universe so unrelated to ordinary human experience, questions regarding the power and potential of the rational human mind assumed special significance. The findings and speculations of Sigmund Freud were particularly influential, yet also deeply disturbing.

Before Freud, poets and mystics had probed the unconscious and irrational aspects of human behavior. But most scientists assumed that the conscious mind processed sense experiences in a rational and logical way. Human behavior in turn was the result of rational calculation—of "thinking." Beginning in the late 1880s Freud developed a very different view of the human psyche. Basing his insights on the analysis of dreams and of "hysteria," a sort of nervous breakdown, Freud concluded that human behavior was basically irrational, governed by the unconscious, a mental reservoir that contained vital instinctual drives and powerful memories. Though the unconscious profoundly influenced people's behavior, it was unknowable to the conscious mind, leaving people unaware of the source or meaning of their actions. Freud explained these ideas in his magisterial book *The Interpretation of Dreams*, first published in 1900.

id, ego, and superego
Freudian terms to describe the three parts of the self and the basis of human behavior, which Freud saw as basically irrational.

Freud eventually described three structures of the self—the **id**, the **ego**, and the **superego**—that were basically at war with one another. The primitive, irrational id was entirely unconscious. The source of sexual, aggressive, and pleasure-seeking instincts, the id sought immediate fulfillment of all desires and was totally amoral. Keeping the id in check was the superego, the conscience or internalized voice of parental or social control. For Freud, the superego was also irrational. Overly strict and puritanical, it was constantly in conflict with the pleasure-seeking id. The third component was the ego, the rational self that was mostly conscious and worked to negotiate between the demands of the id and the superego.

For Freud, the healthy individual possessed a strong ego that effectively balanced the id and superego. Neurosis, or mental illness, resulted when the three structures were out of balance. Since the id's instinctual drives were extremely powerful, the danger for individuals and indeed whole societies was that unacknowledged drives might overwhelm the control mechanisms of the ego in a violent, distorted way. Freud's "talking cure"—in which neurotic patients lay back on a couch and shared their innermost thoughts with the psychoanalyst—was an attempt to resolve such unconscious tensions and restore the rational ego to its predominant role.

Yet Freud, like Nietzsche, believed that the mechanisms of rational thinking and traditional moral values could be too strong. In his book *Civilization and Its Discontents* (1930), Freud argued that civilization was possible only when individuals renounced their irrational instincts in order to live peaceably in groups. Such renunciation made communal life possible, but it left basic instincts unfulfilled and so led to widespread unhappiness. Freud gloomily concluded that Western civilization was itself inescapably neurotic.

Freudian psychology and clinical psychiatry had become an international medical movement by 1910, but only after 1919 did they receive more public attention, especially in northern Europe. In the United States, Freud's ideas attained immense popularity after the Second World War. Many opponents and even some enthusiasts interpreted Freud as saying that the first requirement for mental health was an uninhibited sex life—popular understandings of Freud thus reflected and encouraged growing sexual experimentation, particularly among middle-class women. For more serious students, the psychology of Freud and his followers contributed to the weakening of the old easy optimism about the rational and progressive nature of the human mind.

Modernism in Architecture, Art, Literature, and Music

Like the scientists and intellectuals who were part of this increasingly unsettled modern culture, creative artists rejected old forms and old values. **Modernism** in architecture, art, literature, and music meant constant experimentation and a search for new kinds of expression. Even today the modernism of the first half of the twentieth century seems strikingly fresh and original. And though many people still find the varied modern visions of the arts strange and perhaps disturbing, these decades, so dismal in many respects, stand as one of Western society's great artistic eras.

Architecture and Design

Already in the late nineteenth century, architects inspired by modernism had begun to transform the physical framework of urban society. The United States, with its rapid urban growth and lack of rigid building traditions, pioneered the new architecture. In the 1890s the Chicago School of architects, led by Louis H. Sullivan (1856–1924), used inexpensive steel, reinforced concrete, and electric elevators to build skyscrapers and office buildings lacking almost any exterior ornamentation. In the first decade of the twentieth century, Sullivan's student Frank Lloyd Wright (1867–1959) built a series of radically modern houses featuring low lines, open interiors, and mass-produced

FOCUS QUESTION
How did modernism revolutionize Western culture?

modernism A label given to the artistic and cultural movements of the late nineteenth and early twentieth centuries, which were typified by radical experimentation that challenged traditional forms of artistic expression.

building materials. Europeans were inspired by these and other American examples of functional construction, like the massive, unadorned grain elevators of the Midwest.

Promoters of modern architecture argued that buildings and living spaces in general should be ordered according to a new principle: **functionalism**. Buildings, like industrial products, should be "functional"—that is, they should serve, as well as possible, the purpose for which they were made. According to the Franco-Swiss architect Le Corbusier (luh cowr-booz-YAY) (1887–1965), one of the great champions of modernism, "a house is a machine for living in."[3]

functionalism The principle that buildings, like industrial products, should serve as well as possible the purpose for which they were made, without excessive ornamentation.

Le Corbusier's polemical work *Towards a New Architecture*, published in 1923, laid out guidelines meant to revolutionize building design. Le Corbusier argued that architects should affirm and adopt the latest technologies. Rejecting fancy ornamentation, they should find beauty in the clean, straight lines of practical construction and efficient machinery. The resulting buildings, fashioned according to what was soon called the "International Style," were typically symmetrical rectangles made of concrete, glass, and steel.

In Europe, architectural leadership centered in German-speaking countries until Hitler took power in 1933. In 1911 twenty-eight-year-old Walter Gropius (1883–1969) broke sharply with the past in his design of the Fagus shoe factory at Alfeld, Germany—a clean, light, elegant building of glass and iron. In 1919 Gropius merged the schools of fine and applied arts at Weimar into a single interdisciplinary school, the **Bauhaus**. The Bauhaus brought together many leading modern architects, designers, and theatrical innovators. Working as an effective, inspired team, they combined the study of fine art, including painting and sculpture, with the study of applied art in the crafts of printing, weaving, and furniture making. Throughout the 1920s the Bauhaus, with its stress on functionalism and quality design for everyday goods, attracted enthusiastic students from all over the world.

Bauhaus A German interdisciplinary school of fine and applied arts that brought together many leading modern architects, designers, and theatrical innovators.

Another leading modern architect, Ludwig Mies van der Rohe (1886–1969), followed Gropius as director of the Bauhaus in 1930. Like many modernist intellectuals, after 1933 he emigrated to the United States to escape the repressive Nazi regime. His classic steel-frame and glass-wall Lake Shore Apartments in Chicago, built between 1948 and 1951, epitomized the spread and triumph of the modernist International Style in the great building boom that followed the Second World War.

New Artistic Movements

In the decades surrounding the First World War, the visual arts also experienced radical change and experimentation. For the last several centuries, artists had tried to produce accurate representations of reality. Now a new artistic avant-garde emerged to challenge that practice. From Impressionism and Expressionism to Dadaism and Surrealism, a sometimes-bewildering array of artistic movements followed one after another. Modern painting and sculpture became increasingly abstract as artists turned their backs on figurative representation and began to break down form into its constituent parts: lines, shapes, and colors.

Berlin, Munich, Moscow, Vienna, New York, and especially Paris became famous for their radical artistic undergrounds. Commercial art galleries and exhibition halls promoted the new work, and schools and institutions, such as the Bauhaus, emerged to train a generation in modern techniques. Young artists flocked to these cultural centers to participate in the new movements, earn a living making art, and perhaps change the world with their revolutionary ideas.

One of the earliest modernist movements was Impressionism, which blossomed in Paris in the 1870s. French artists such as Claude Monet (1840–1926) and Edgar Degas (1834–1917) and the American Mary Cassatt (1844–1926), who settled in Paris in 1875, tried to portray their sensory "impressions" in their work. Impressionists looked to the world around them for subject matter, turning their backs on traditional themes such as battles, religious scenes, and wealthy elites. Monet's colorful and atmospheric paintings of farmland haystacks and Degas's many pastel drawings of ballerinas exemplify the way Impressionists moved toward abstraction. Capturing a fleeting moment of color and light, in often blurry and quickly painted images, was far more important than making a heavily detailed, precise rendering of an actual object.

In the next decades an astonishing array of new artistic movements emerged one after another. Postimpressionists and Expressionists, such as Vincent van Gogh (1853–1890), built on Impressionist motifs of color and light but added a deep psychological element to their pictures, reflecting the attempt to search within the self and reveal (or "express") deep inner feelings on the canvas.

After 1900 avant-garde artists increasingly challenged the art world status quo. In Paris in 1907 painter Pablo Picasso (1881–1973), along with other artists, established Cubism—a highly analytical approach to art concentrated on a complex geometry of zigzagging lines and sharply angled overlapping planes that exemplified the ongoing trend toward abstract, nonrepresentational art. In 1909 Italian Filippo Tommaso Marinetti (1876–1944) announced the founding of Futurism, a radical art and literary movement determined to transform the mentality of an anachronistic society. According to Marinetti, traditional culture could not deal with the advances of modern technology—automobiles, radios, telephones, phonographs, ocean liners, airplanes, the cinema, the newspaper—and the way these had changed human consciousness. Marinetti embraced the future and cast away the past, calling for radically new art forms that would express the modern condition. (See "Evaluating the Evidence 26.2: The Futurist Manifesto," page 878.)

The shock of World War I encouraged further radicalization. In 1916 a group of international artists and intellectuals in exile in Zurich, Switzerland, championed a new movement they called **Dadaism**, which attacked all the familiar standards of art and delighted in outrageous behavior. The war had shown once and for all that life was meaningless, the Dadaists argued, so art should be meaningless as well. Dadaists tried to shock their audiences with what they called "anti-art," works and public performances that were insulting and entirely nonsensical. A well-known example is a reproduction of Leonardo da Vinci's *Mona Lisa* in which the masterpiece is ridiculed with the addition of a hand-drawn mustache and an obscene inscription. Like Futurists, Dadaists embraced the modern age and grappled with the horrors of modern war. "Art in its execution and direction is dependent on the time in which it lives, and artists are creatures of their epoch," wrote Richard Huelsenbeck (1892–1974), one of the movement's founders. "The highest art will be that which in its conscious content presents the thousand-fold problems of the day, the art which has been visibly shattered by the explosions of last week, which is forever trying to collect its limbs

Dadaism An artistic movement of the 1920s and 1930s that attacked all accepted standards of art and behavior and delighted in outrageous conduct.

The Futurist Manifesto

In the founding manifesto of the Futurist movement, published in 1909, the Italian poet Filippo Tommaso Marinetti called for works of art and literature that embraced the speed and confusion of modernity and the energy and beauty he saw in modern technology.

1. We intend to sing the love of danger, the habit of energy and fearlessness.

2. Courage, audacity, and revolt will be essential elements of our poetry.

3. Up to now literature has exalted a pensive immobility, ecstasy, and sleep. We intend to exalt aggressive action, a feverish insomnia, the racer's stride, the mortal leap, the punch and the slap.

4. We say that the world's magnificence has been enriched by a new beauty: the beauty of speed. A racing car whose hood is adorned with great pipes, like serpents of explosive breath—a roaring car that seems to ride on grapeshot—is more beautiful than the *Victory of Samothrace*.

5. We want to hymn the man at the wheel, who hurls the lance of his spirit across the Earth, along the circle of its orbit.

6. The poet must spend himself with ardor, splendor, and generosity, to swell the enthusiastic fervor of the primordial elements.

7. Except in struggle, there is no more beauty. No work without an aggressive character can be a masterpiece. Poetry must be conceived as a violent attack on unknown forces, to reduce and prostrate them before man.

8. We stand on the last promontory of the centuries! . . . Why should we look back, when what we want is to break down the mysterious doors of the Impossible? Time and Space died yesterday. We already live in the absolute, because we have created eternal, omnipresent speed.

9. We will glorify war—the world's only hygiene— militarism, patriotism, the destructive gesture of freedom-bringers, beautiful ideas worth dying for, and scorn for woman.

10. We will destroy the museums, libraries, academies of every kind, will fight moralism, feminism, every opportunistic or utilitarian cowardice.

11. We will sing of great crowds excited by work, by pleasure, and by riot; we will sing of the multicolored, polyphonic tides of revolution in the modern capitals; we will sing of the vibrant nightly fervor of arsenals and shipyards blazing with violent electric moons; greedy railway stations that devour smoke-plumed serpents; factories hung on clouds by the crooked lines of their smoke; bridges that stride the rivers like giant gymnasts, flashing in the sun with a glitter of knives; adventurous steamers that sniff the horizon; deep-chested locomotives whose wheels paw the tracks like the hooves of enormous steel horses bridled by tubing; and the sleek flight of planes whose propellers chatter in the wind like banners and seem to cheer like an enthusiastic crowd.

EVALUATE THE EVIDENCE

1. Why is Marinetti so fascinated by the products of modern industry, and why does he want to do away with the great institutions of Italian culture?
2. How did Futurism lay the foundation for future radical avant-garde cultural movements?

Source: *Marinetti: Selected Writing* by F. T. Marinetti, edited by R. W. Flint, translated by R. W. Flint and Arthur A. Coppotelli. Translation copyright © 1972 by Farrar, Straus & Giroux, Inc. Reprinted by permission of Farrar, Straus & Giroux, LLC.

after yesterday's crash."[4] After the war, Dadaism became an international movement, spreading to Paris, New York, and particularly Berlin in the early 1920s.

During the mid-1920s some Dadaists were attracted to Surrealism. Surrealists such as Salvador Dalí (1904–1989) were deeply influenced by Freudian psychology and portrayed images of the unconscious in their art. They painted fantastic worlds of wild dreams and uncomfortable symbols, where watches melted and giant metronomes beat time in precisely drawn but impossible alien landscapes.

Many modern artists sincerely believed that art had a radical mission. By calling attention to the bankruptcy of mainstream society, they believed, art had the

Salvador Dalí, *Metamorphosis of Narcissus* Dalí was a leader of the Surrealist art movement, which emerged in the late 1920s. Surrealists were deeply influenced by the theories of Sigmund Freud and used strange and evocative symbols in their work to capture the inner workings of dreams and the unconscious. In this 1937 painting, Dalí plays with the Greek myth of Narcissus, who fell in love with his own reflection and drowned in a pool. What mysterious significance, if any, lies behind this surreal reordering of everyday reality? (© Salvador Dalí, Fundació Gala–Salvador Dalí, Artists Rights Society [ARS], New York 2016/photo: Granger, NYC — All rights reserved)

power to change the world. The sometimes-nonsensical manifestos written by members of the Dadaist, Futurist, and Surrealist movements were meant to spread their ideas, challenge conventional assumptions of all kinds, and foment radical social change.

By the 1920s art and culture had become increasingly politicized. Many avant-garde artists sided with the far left; some became committed Communists. Such artists and art movements had a difficult time surviving the political crises of the 1930s. Between 1933 and 1945, when the National Socialist (Nazi) Party came to power in Germany and brought a second world war to the European continent, hundreds of artists and intellectuals—often Jews and leftists—fled to the United States to escape the war and the repressive Nazi state. After World War II, New York greatly benefited from this transfusion of talent and replaced Paris and Berlin as the world capital of modern art.

Twentieth-Century Literature

In the decades that followed the First World War, Western literature was deeply influenced by the general intellectual climate of pessimism and alienation and the turn toward radical experimentation sweeping through the other arts. The great nineteenth-century novelists had typically written as all-knowing narrators, describing realistic characters and their relationships to an understandable, if sometimes harsh, society (see Chapter 22). Modernist writers now developed new techniques to express new realities. In the twentieth century many authors adopted the limited, often confused viewpoint of a single individual. Like Freud, they focused their attention on the complexity and irrationality of the human mind, where feelings, memories, and desires are forever scrambled. French novelist Marcel Proust (1871–1922), in his semi-autobiographical, multivolume *Remembrance of Things Past* (1913–1927), recalled bittersweet memories of childhood and youthful love and tried to discover their innermost meaning. To do so, Proust lived like a hermit in a soundproof Paris apartment for ten years, withdrawing from the present to dwell on the past.

Some novelists used the **stream-of-consciousness technique**, relying on internal monologues to explore the human psyche. In *Jacob's Room* (1922), the English author

stream-of-consciousness technique A literary technique, found in works by Virginia Woolf, James Joyce, and others, that uses interior monologue—a character's thoughts and feelings as they occur—to explore the human psyche.

Virginia Woolf (1882–1941) created a novel made up of a series of such monologues in which she tried to capture the inner voice in prose. In this and other stories, Woolf portrayed characters whose ideas and emotions from different periods of their lives bubble up as randomly as from a patient on a psychoanalyst's couch. William Faulkner (1897–1962), one of America's greatest novelists, used the same technique in *The Sound and the Fury* (1929), with much of its intense drama confusedly seen through the eyes of a man who is mentally disabled.

The most famous and perhaps most experimental stream-of-consciousness novel is *Ulysses* (1922) by Irish novelist James Joyce (1882–1941). Into an account of a single day in the life of an ordinary man, Joyce weaves an extended ironic parallel between the aimless wanderings of his hero through the streets and pubs of Dublin and the adventures of Homer's hero Ulysses on his way home from Troy. *Ulysses* was surely one of the most disturbing novels of its generation. Abandoning any sense of a conventional plot, breaking rules of grammar, and blending foreign words, puns, bits of knowledge, and scraps of memory together in bewildering confusion, *Ulysses* is intended to mirror modern life: a gigantic riddle impossible to unravel. Since Joyce included frank descriptions of the main character's sexual thoughts and encounters, the novel was considered obscene in Great Britain and the United States and was banned there until the early 1930s.

As creative writers turned their attention from society to the individual and from realism to psychological relativity, they rejected the idea of progress. Some described "anti-utopias," nightmare visions of things to come, as in the T. S. Eliot poem *The Waste Land* (1922), which depicts a world of growing desolation:

> April is the cruelest month, breeding
> Lilacs out of the dead land, mixing
> Memory and desire, stirring
> Dull roots with spring rain.
> . . .
> What are the roots that clutch, what branches grow
> Out of this stony rubbish? Son of man,
> You cannot say, or guess, for you know only
> A heap of broken images, where the sun beats,
> And the dead tree gives no shelter, the cricket no relief,
> And the dry stone no sound of water.[5]

With its biblical references, images of a ruined and wasted natural world, and general human incomprehension, Eliot (1888–1965) expressed the widespread despair that followed the First World War. The Czech writer Franz Kafka (1883–1924) likewise portrayed an incomprehensible, alienating world. Kafka's novels *The Trial* (1925) and *The Castle* (1926) are stories about helpless individuals crushed by inexplicably hostile forces, as is his famous novella *The Metamorphosis* (1915), in which the main character turns into a giant insect. The German-Jewish Kafka died young, at forty-one, and was spared the horror of seeing the world of his nightmares materialize in the Nazi state. In these and many other works, authors between the wars used new literary techniques and dark imagery to capture the anxiety of the age.

Modern Music

Developments in modern music paralleled those in painting and fiction. Composers and performers expressed the emotional intensity and shock of modernism in radically experimental forms. The ballet *The Rite of Spring* by Russian composer Igor Stravinsky (1882–1971), for example, practically caused a riot when it was first performed in Paris in 1913. The combination of pulsating rhythms and dissonant sounds from the orchestra pit with earthy representations of lovemaking by the strangely dressed dancers on the stage shocked audiences accustomed to traditional ballet.

After the First World War, when irrationality and violence had seemed to pervade human experience, modernism flourished in opera and ballet. One of the most powerful examples was the opera *Wozzeck*, by Alban Berg (1885–1935), first performed in Berlin in 1925. Blending a half-sung, half-spoken kind of dialogue with harsh, atonal music, *Wozzeck* is a gruesome tale of a soldier driven by Kafka-like inner terrors and vague suspicions of infidelity to murder his mistress.

Some composers turned their backs on long-established musical conventions. Just as abstract painters arranged lines and color but did not draw identifiable objects, so modern composers arranged sounds without creating recognizable harmonies. Led by Viennese composer Arnold Schönberg (SHURN-buhrg) (1874–1951), they abandoned traditional harmony and tonality. The musical notes in a given piece were no longer united and organized by a key; instead they were independent and unrelated. Schönberg's twelve-tone music of the 1920s arranged all twelve notes of the scale in an abstract mathematical pattern, or "tone row." This pattern sounded like no pattern at all to the ordinary listener and could be detected only by a highly trained eye studying the musical score. Accustomed to the harmonies of classical and romantic music, audiences generally resisted atonal music. Only after the Second World War did it begin to win acceptance.

An Emerging Consumer Society

Fundamental innovations in the basic provision and consumption of goods and services accompanied the radical transformation of artistic and intellectual life. After the First World War, modern business forms of credit, retail, and advertising helped sell increasing numbers of mass-produced goods—the products of a highly industrialized factory system—to ever-larger numbers of people. With the arrival of cinema and radio, commercial entertainment increasingly dominated the leisure time of ordinary people. The consumer revolution had roots in the prosperous decades before World War I and would not be fully consolidated until the 1950s and 1960s. Yet in the interwar years the outlines of a modern consumer society emerged with startling clarity.

FOCUS QUESTION
How did consumer society change everyday life?

Mass Culture

The emerging consumer society of the 1920s is a good example of the way technological developments can lead to widespread social change. The arrival of a highly industrialized manufacturing system dedicated to mass-producing inexpensive goods, the establishment of efficient transportation systems that could bring these goods to national markets, and the rise of professional advertising experts to sell them were all part of a revolution in the way consumer goods were made, marketed, and used by ordinary people.

Contemporaries viewed the new mass culture as a distinctly modern aspect of everyday life. It seemed that consumer goods themselves were modernizing society by changing so many ingrained habits. Some people embraced the new ways; others worried that these changes threatened familiar values and precious traditions.

Critics had good reason to worry. Mass-produced goods had a profound impact on the lives of ordinary people. Housework and private life were increasingly organized around an array of modern appliances, from electric ovens, washing machines, and refrigerators to telephones and radios. The aggressive marketing of fashionable clothing and personal care products, such as shampoo, perfume, and makeup, encouraged a cult of youthful "sex appeal." Advertisements increasingly linked individual attractiveness to the use of brand-name products. The mass production and marketing of automobiles and the rise of tourist agencies opened roads to increased mobility and travel.

Commercialized mass entertainment likewise prospered and began to dominate the way people spent their leisure time. Movies and radio thrilled millions. Professional sporting events drew throngs of fans. Thriving print media brought readers an astounding variety of newspapers, inexpensive books, and glossy illustrated magazines. Flashy restaurants, theatrical revues, and nightclubs competed for evening customers.

Department stores epitomized the emergence of consumer society. Already well established across Europe and the United States by the 1890s, they had become veritable temples of commerce by the 1920s. The typical store sold an enticing variety of goods, including clothing, magazines, housewares, food, and spirits. Larger stores included travel bureaus, movie theaters, and refreshment stands. Aggressive advertising campaigns, youthful and attractive salespeople, and easy credit and return policies helped attract customers in droves.

The emergence of modern consumer culture both undermined and reinforced existing social differences. On one hand, consumerism helped democratize Western society. Since everyone with the means could purchase any good, mass culture helped break down old social barriers based on class, region, and religion. Yet it also reinforced social differences. Manufacturers soon realized they could profit by marketing goods to specific groups. Catholics, for example, could purchase their own popular literature and inexpensive devotional items; young people eagerly bought the latest fashions marketed directly to them. In addition, the expense of many items meant that only the wealthy could purchase them. Automobiles and, in the 1920s, even vacuum cleaners cost so much that ownership became a status symbol.

The changes in women's lives were particularly striking. The new household items transformed how women performed housework. Advice literature of all kinds encouraged housewives to rush out and buy the latest appliances so they could "modernize" the home. Consumer culture brought growing public visibility to women, especially the young. Girls and young women worked behind the counters and shopped in the aisles of department stores, and they went out on the street alone in ways unthinkable in the nineteenth century. Contemporaries spoke repeatedly about the arrival of the **"modern girl,"** a surprisingly independent female who could vote and held a job, spent her salary on the latest fashions, applied makeup and smoked cigarettes, and used her sex appeal to charm any number of young men. The modern

"modern girl" Somewhat stereotypical image of the modern and independent working woman popular in the 1920s.

girl had precedents in the assertive, athletic, and independent "new woman" of the 1890s, but she became a dominant global figure in the 1920s. "The woman of yesterday," wrote one German feminist in 1929, yearned for marriage and children and "honor[ed] the achievements of the 'good old days.'" The "woman of today," she continued, "refuses to be regarded as a physically weak being . . . and seeks to support herself through gainful employment. . . . Her task is to clear the way for equal rights for women in all areas of life."[6]

Despite such enthusiasm, the modern girl was in some ways a stereotype, a product of marketing campaigns dedicated to selling goods to the masses. Few young women could afford to live up to this image, even if they did have jobs. Yet the changes associated with the First World War (see Chapter 25) and the emergence of consumer society did loosen traditional limits on women's behavior.

The emerging consumer culture generated a chorus of complaint from cultural critics of all stripes. On the left, socialist writers worried that its appeal undermined working-class radicalism, because mass culture created passive consumers rather than active, class-conscious revolutionaries. On the right, conservatives complained that money spent on frivolous consumer goods sapped the livelihood of industrious artisans and undermined proud national traditions. Religious leaders protested that modern consumerism encouraged rampant individualism and that greedy materialism was replacing spirituality. Others bemoaned the supposedly loose morals of the modern girl and fretted over the decline of traditional family values.

Despite such criticism—which continued after World War II—consumer society was here to stay. Ordinary people enjoyed the pleasures of mass consumption, and individual identities were tied ever more closely to modern mass-produced goods. Yet the Great Depression of 1929 (see page 891) soon made actual participation in the new world of goods elusive. The promise of prosperity would only truly be realized during the economic boom that followed the Second World War.

The Modern Girl: Image or Reality?   A young woman enjoys a dessert at the Romanesque Café in Berlin in 1924. The independence of this "modern girl," wearing fashionable clothes with a revealing hemline and lacking an escort, transgressed familiar gender roles and shocked and fascinated contemporaries. (bpk, Berlin/Art Resource, NY)

The Appeal of Cinema

Nowhere was the influence of mass culture more evident than in the rapid growth of commercial entertainment, especially cinema and radio. Both became major industries in the interwar years, and an eager public enthusiastically embraced them, spending their hard-earned money and their leisure hours watching movies or listening to radio broadcasts. These mass media overshadowed and began to replace the traditional amusements of people in cities, and then in small towns and villages, changing familiar ways of life.

Cinema first emerged in the United States around 1880, driven in part by the inventions of Thomas Edison. By 1910 American directors and business people had set up "movie factories," at first in the New York area and then in Los Angeles.

Europeans were quick to follow. By 1914 small production companies had formed in Great Britain, France, Germany, and Italy, among others. World War I quickened the pace. National leaders realized that movies offered distraction to troops and citizens and served as an effective means of spreading propaganda. Audiences lined up to see *The Battle of the Somme*, a British film released in August 1916 that was frankly intended to encourage popular support for the war. For the audience, watching this early example of cinematic propaganda could be heart wrenching. "The tears in many people's eyes and the silence that prevailed when I saw the film showed that every heart was full of love and sympathy for our soldiers," wrote one viewer to the *London Times* that September.[7]

Cinema became a true mass medium in the 1920s, the golden age of silent film. The United States was again a world leader, but European nations also established important national studios. Germany's Universal Film Company (or UFA) was particularly renowned. In the massive Babelsberg Studios just outside Berlin, talented UFA directors produced classic Expressionist films such as *Nosferatu* (1922), a creepy vampire story, and *Metropolis* (1927), about a future society in the midst of a working-class revolt. Such films made use of cutting-edge production techniques, thrilling audiences with fast and slow motion, montage sequences, unsettling close-ups, and unusual dissolves.

Film making became big business on an international scale. Studios competed to place their movies on foreign screens, and European theater owners were sometimes forced to book whole blocks of American films to get the few pictures they really wanted. In response, European governments set quotas on the number of U.S. films they imported. By 1926 U.S. money was drawing German directors and stars to Hollywood and consolidating America's international domination. These practices put European producers at a disadvantage until "talkies" permitted a revival of national film industries in the 1930s, particularly in France.

Motion pictures would remain the central entertainment of the masses until after the Second World War and the rise of television. People flocked to the gigantic movie palaces built across Europe in the mid-1920s, splendid theaters that could seat thousands. There they viewed the latest features, which were reviewed by critics in newspapers and flashy illustrated magazines. Cinema audiences grew rapidly in the 1930s. In Great Britain in the late 1930s, one in every four adults went to the movies twice a week, and two in five went at least once a week. Other countries had similar figures.

As these numbers suggest, motion pictures could be powerful tools of indoctrination, especially in countries with dictatorial regimes. Lenin encouraged the development of Soviet film making, believing that the new medium was essential to the social and ideological transformation of the country. Beginning in the mid-1920s, a series of epic films, the most famous of which were directed by Sergei Eisenstein (1898–1948), brilliantly dramatized the Communist view of Russian history. In Nazi Germany, a young and immensely talented woman film maker, Leni Riefenstahl (REE-fuhn-shtahl) (1902–2003), directed a masterpiece of documentary propaganda, *Triumph of the Will*, based on the 1934 Nazi Party rally at Nuremberg. Riefenstahl combined stunning aerial photography with mass processions of young Nazi fanatics and images of joyful crowds welcoming Adolf Hitler. Her film, released in 1935, was a brilliant yet chilling documentary of the rise of Nazism.

The Arrival of Radio

Like film, radio became a full-blown mass medium in the 1920s. Experimental radio sets were first available in the 1880s; the work of Italian inventor Guglielmo Marconi (1874–1937) around 1900 and the development of the vacuum tube in 1904 made possible primitive transmissions of speech and music. But the first major public broadcasts of news and special events occurred only in the early 1920s, in Great Britain and the United States.

Every major country quickly established national broadcasting networks. In the United States such networks were privately owned and were financed by advertising, but in Europe the typical pattern was direct control by the government. In Great Britain, Parliament set up an independent public corporation, the British Broadcasting Corporation (BBC), supported by licensing fees. Whatever the institutional framework, radio enjoyed a meteoric growth in popularity. By the late 1930s more than three out of every four households in both democratic Great Britain and dictatorial Germany had at least one radio.

Like the movies, radio was well suited for political propaganda and manipulation. Dictators such as Hitler and Italy's Benito Mussolini controlled the airwaves and could reach enormous national audiences with their dramatic speeches. In democratic countries, politicians such as American president Franklin Roosevelt and British prime minister Stanley Baldwin effectively used informal "fireside chats" to bolster their popularity.

The Search for Peace and Political Stability

As established patterns of thought and culture were further challenged and mangled by the ferocious impact of World War I, so too was the political fabric stretched and torn. The Versailles settlement had established a shaky truce, not a solid peace. After the war, leaders faced a gigantic task as they sought to create a stable international order within the general context of intellectual crisis, halting economic growth, and political turmoil.

The pursuit of real and lasting peace proved difficult for many reasons. Germany hated the Treaty of Versailles. France was fearful and isolated. Britain was undependable, and the United States turned its back on European problems. Eastern Europe was in ferment, and Communist Russia had an unpredictable future. Moreover, the international economic situation was weak and greatly complicated by war debts and disrupted patterns of trade. Yet from 1925 to late 1929, it appeared that peace and stability were within reach. When the economic collapse of the 1930s mocked these hopes and brought the rise of brutal dictators, the disillusionment of liberals in the democracies intensified.

FOCUS QUESTION
What obstacles to lasting peace did European leaders face?

Germany and the Western Powers

Germany was the key to lasting stability. Yet to Germans of all political parties, the Treaty of Versailles represented a harsh dictated peace, to be revised or repudiated as soon as possible. Germany still had the potential to become the strongest country in Europe but remained a source of uncertainty. Moreover, with ominous implications, France and Great Britain did not see eye to eye on Germany.

Immediately after the war, the French wanted to stress the harsh elements in the Treaty of Versailles. Most of the war in the west had been fought on French soil, and the expected costs of reconstruction, as well as of repaying war debts to the United States, were staggering. Thus French politicians believed that massive reparations from Germany were vital for economic recovery. After having compromised with President Wilson only to be betrayed by America's failure to ratify the treaty, many French leaders saw strict implementation of all provisions of the Treaty of Versailles as France's last best hope. Large reparation payments could hold Germany down indefinitely, ensuring French security.

The British soon felt differently. Before the war Germany had been Great Britain's second-best market in the world; after the war a healthy, prosperous Germany appeared to be essential to the British economy. Many Brits agreed with the analysis of the English economist John Maynard Keynes (1883–1946), who eloquently denounced the Treaty of Versailles in his book *The Economic Consequences of the Peace* (1919). According to Keynes, astronomical reparations and harsh economic measures would impoverish Germany, encourage Bolshevism, and increase economic hardship in all countries. Only a complete revision of the treaty could save Germany—and Europe. Keynes's attack engendered much public discussion and became very influential. It created sympathy for Germany in the English-speaking world, which often paralyzed English and American leaders in their relations with Germany over the next two decades.

In addition, British politicians were suspicious of both France's army—the largest in Europe, and authorized at Versailles to occupy the German Rhineland until 1935—and France's expansive foreign policy. Since 1890 France had looked to Russia as a powerful ally against Germany. But with Russia hostile and Communist, and with Britain and the United States unwilling to make any firm commitments, France turned to the newly formed states of central Europe for diplomatic support. In 1921 France signed a mutual defense pact with Poland and associated itself closely with the so-called Little Entente, an alliance that joined Czechoslovakia, Romania, and Yugoslavia against defeated and bitter Hungary.

While French and British leaders drifted in different directions, the Allied commission created to determine German reparations completed its work. In April 1921 it announced that Germany had to pay the enormous sum of 132 billion gold marks ($33 billion) in annual installments of 2.5 billion gold marks. Facing possible occupation of more of its territory, the young German republic—generally known as the Weimar Republic—made its first payment in 1921. Then in 1922, wracked by rapid inflation and political assassinations and motivated by hostility and arrogance as well, German leaders announced their inability to pay more. They proposed a moratorium on reparations for three years, with the clear implication that thereafter the payments would be either drastically reduced or eliminated entirely.

The British were willing to accept a moratorium, but the French were not. Led by their tough-minded prime minister, Raymond Poincaré (1860–1934), they decided they had to either call Germany's bluff or see the entire peace settlement dissolve to France's great disadvantage. If the Germans refused to pay reparations, France would use occupation to paralyze Germany and force it to accept the Treaty of Versailles. So, despite strong British protests, in early

**French Occupation
of the Ruhr, 1923–1925**

January 1923 French and Belgian armies moved out of the Rhineland and began to occupy the Ruhr district, the heartland of industrial Germany, creating the most serious international crisis of the 1920s.

Strengthened by a wave of German patriotism, the German government ordered the people of the Ruhr to stop working and offer passive resistance to the occupation. The coal mines and steel mills of the Ruhr fell silent, leaving 10 percent of Germany's population out of work. The French responded by sealing off the Ruhr and the Rhineland from the rest of Germany, letting in only enough food to prevent starvation. German opinion was incensed when the French sent over forty thousand colonial troops from North and West Africa to control the territory. German propagandists labeled these troops the "black shame," warning that the African soldiers were savages, eager to brutalize civilians and assault German women. These racist attacks, though entirely unfounded, nonetheless intensified tensions.

By the summer of 1923 France and Germany were engaged in a great test of wills. French armies could not collect reparations from striking workers at gunpoint, but the occupation was paralyzing Germany and its economy. To support the workers and their employers, the German government began to print money to pay its bills, causing runaway inflation. Prices soared as German money rapidly lost all value. People went to the store with bags of banknotes; they returned home with handfuls of groceries. Catastrophic inflation cruelly mocked the old middle-class virtues of thrift, caution, and self-reliance as savings were wiped out. Many Germans felt betrayed. They hated and blamed the Western governments, their own government, big business, the Jews, the workers, and the Communists for their misfortune. Right-wing nationalists—including Adolf Hitler and the newly established National Socialist (Nazi) Party—eagerly capitalized on the widespread discontent.

In August 1923, as the mark lost value and unrest spread throughout Germany, Gustav Stresemann (GOOS-tahf SHTRAY-zuh-mahn) (1878–1929) assumed leadership of the government. Stresemann tried compromise. He called off passive resistance in the Ruhr and in October agreed in principle to pay reparations, but asked for a re-examination of Germany's ability to pay. Poincaré accepted. His hard line had become unpopular in France, and it was hated in Britain and the United States. (See "Individuals in Society: Gustav Stresemann," page 888.) In addition, power in both Germany and France was passing to more moderate leaders who realized that continued confrontation was a destructive, no-win situation. Thus, after five long years of hostility and tension, culminating in a kind of undeclared war in the Ruhr

"Mothers of the World, Did Your Sons Die for This?" In 1923 the French army occupied the industrial district of the Ruhr in Germany in an effort to force reparation payments. The occupying forces included colonial troops from West Africa, and Germans responded with a racist propaganda campaign that cast the West African colonial soldiers as uncivilized savages intent on ravaging German women. (Kharbine-Tarabor/The Art Archive at Art Resource, NY)

German foreign minister Gustav Stresemann is a controversial historical figure. Hailed in the 1920s as a hero of peace, he was denounced as a traitor by radical German nationalists and Hitler's Nazis. After World War II, revisionist historians stressed Stresemann's persistent nationalism and cast doubt on his peaceful intentions. Weimar Germany's most renowned leader is a fascinating example of the restless quest for convincing historical interpretation.

Foreign Minister Gustav Stresemann greets a crowd after accepting the 1926 Nobel Peace Prize in Oslo, Norway. (ullstein bild/ullstein bild via Getty Images)

Stresemann's origins were modest. His parents were Berlin innkeepers and beer retailers, and of their five children only Gustav attended high school. Attracted first to literature and history, Stresemann later turned to economics, earned a doctoral degree, and quickly reached the top as a manager and director of German trade associations. A highly intelligent extrovert with a knack for negotiation, Stresemann became a deputy in the German Reichstag (parliament) in 1907 as a business-oriented liberal and nationalist. When World War I erupted, he believed, like most Germans, that Germany had acted defensively and was not at fault. A strident nationalist, he urged German annexation of conquered foreign territories. Germany's collapse in defeat and revolution devastated Stresemann. He seemed a prime candidate to join the hateful extremism of the far right.

Yet although Stresemann opposed the Treaty of Versailles as unjust and unrealistic, he turned toward the center. He accepted the new Weimar Republic and played a growing role in the Reichstag as the leader of his own small probusiness party. His hour came when French and Belgian troops occupied the Ruhr. Named chancellor in August 1923, he called off passive resistance and began talks with the French. His government also quelled Communist uprisings; put down rebellions in Bavaria, including Hitler's attempted coup; and ended runaway inflation with the introduction of a new currency. Stresemann fought to preserve German unity, and he succeeded.

Voted out as chancellor in November 1923, Stresemann remained as foreign minister in every German government until his death in 1929. Proclaiming a policy of peace and agreeing to pay reparations, he achieved his greatest triumph in the Locarno agreements of 1925. But these agreements did not lead the French to make any further concessions that might have disarmed Germany's extremists. Stresemann made little additional progress in achieving international reconciliation and true sovereignty for Germany. His premature death in office was a serious blow to German pragmatism, encouraging the turn to a more aggressive and nationalist foreign policy.

Stresemann was no fuzzy pacifist. Historians debunking his legend are right in seeing an enduring nationalism in his defense of German interests. But Stresemann, like his French counterpart Aristide Briand, was a statesman of goodwill who wanted peace through mutually advantageous compromise. A realist trained by business and politics in the art of the possible, Stresemann perceived that Germany had to be a satisfied and equal partner for peace to be secure. His unwillingness to guarantee Germany's eastern borders (see Map 25.4, page 855), which is often criticized as contributing to the coming of the Second World War, reflected his conviction that keeping some Germans under Polish and Czechoslovakian rule created a ticking time bomb in Europe. Stresemann was also convinced that war on Poland would almost certainly recreate the Allied coalition that had crushed Germany in 1918.* The mighty coalition that formed after Hitler's 1939 invasion of Poland proved this view prophetic.

QUESTIONS FOR ANALYSIS

1. What did Gustav Stresemann do to promote reconciliation in Europe? How did his policy toward France differ from that toward Poland and Czechoslovakia?
2. What is your interpretation of Stresemann? Does he arouse your sympathy or your suspicion and hostility? Why?

*Robert Grathwol, "Stresemann: Reflections on His Foreign Policy," *Journal of Modern History* 45 (March 1973): 52–70.

in 1923, Germany and France both decided to try compromise. The British, and even the Americans, were willing to help. The first step was to reach an agreement on the reparations question.

Hope in Foreign Affairs

In 1924 an international committee of financial experts headed by American banker Charles G. Dawes met to re-examine reparations from a broad perspective. The resulting **Dawes Plan** (1924) was accepted by France, Germany, and Britain. Germany's yearly reparation payments were reduced and linked to the level of German economic output. Germany would also receive large loans from the United States to promote economic recovery. In short, Germany would get private loans from the United States in order to pay reparations to France and Britain, thus enabling those countries to repay the large war debts they owed the United States.

This circular flow of international payments was complicated and risky, but for a while it worked. With continual inflows of American capital, the German republic experienced a shaky economic recovery. Germany paid about $1.3 billion in reparations in 1927 and 1928, enabling France and Britain to repay the United States. In this way the Americans belatedly played a part in the general economic settlement that, though far from ideal, facilitated a worldwide recovery in the late 1920s.

A political settlement accompanied the economic accords. In 1925 the leaders of Europe signed a number of agreements at Locarno, Switzerland. Germany and France solemnly pledged to accept their common border, and both Britain and Italy agreed to fight either France or Germany if one invaded the other. Stresemann reluctantly agreed to settle boundary disputes with Poland and Czechoslovakia by peaceful means, although he did not agree on permanent borders to Germany's east. In response, France reaffirmed its pledge of military aid to those countries if Germany attacked them. The refusal to settle Germany's eastern borders angered the Poles, and though the "spirit of Locarno" lent some hope to those seeking international stability, political tensions deepened in central Europe.

Other developments suggested possibilities for international peace. In 1926 Germany joined the League of Nations, and in 1928 fifteen countries signed the Kellogg-Briand Pact, initiated by French prime minister Aristide Briand and U.S. secretary of state Frank B. Kellogg. The signing states agreed to "renounce [war] as an instrument of international policy" and to settle international disputes peacefully. The pact made no provisions for action in case war actually occurred and would not prevent the arrival of the Second World War in 1939. In the late 1920s, however, it fostered a cautious optimism and encouraged the hope that the United States would accept its responsibilities as a great world power by contributing to European stability.

Hope in Democratic Government

Domestic politics also offered reason to hope. During the occupation of the Ruhr and the great inflation, republican government in Germany had appeared on the verge of collapse. In 1923 Communists momentarily entered provincial governments, and in November an obscure politician named Adolf Hitler leaped onto a table in a beer hall in Munich and proclaimed a "national socialist revolution." But the young republican government easily crushed Hitler's plot to seize control, and he was

Dawes Plan War reparations agreement that reduced Germany's yearly payments, made payment dependent on economic prosperity, and granted large U.S. loans to promote recovery.

sentenced to prison. In the late 1920s liberal democracy seemed to take root in Weimar Germany. Elections were held regularly, and republican democracy appeared to have growing support among a majority of Germans. A new currency was established, and the economy stabilized. The moderate businessmen who tended to dominate the various German coalition governments were convinced that economic prosperity demanded good relations with the Western powers, and they supported parliamentary government at home.

Sharp political divisions remained, however. Throughout the 1920s Hitler's Nazi Party attracted support from fanatical anti-Semites, ultranationalists, and disgruntled ex-servicemen. Many unrepentant nationalists and monarchists populated the right and the army. On the left, members of Germany's recently formed Communist Party were noisy and active. The Communists, directed from Moscow, reserved their greatest hatred and sharpest barbs for their cousins the Social Democrats, whom they accused of betraying the revolution. Though the working class was divided, a majority supported the nonrevolutionary Social Democrats.

The situation in France was similar to that in Germany. Communists and Socialists battled for workers' support. After 1924 the democratically elected government rested mainly in the hands of coalitions of moderates, with business interests well represented. France's great accomplishment was the rapid rebuilding of its war-torn northeastern region. The expense of this undertaking led, however, to a large deficit and substantial inflation. By early 1926 the franc had fallen to 10 percent of its prewar value, causing a severe crisis. Poincaré was recalled to office, while Briand remained minister for foreign affairs. Poincaré slashed spending and raised taxes, restoring confidence in the economy. The franc was stabilized at about one-fifth of its prewar value, and the economy remained fairly stable until 1930.

Britain, too, faced challenges after 1920. The great problem was unemployment. In June 1921 almost 2.2 million people—or 23 percent of the labor force—were out of work, and throughout the 1920s unemployment hovered around 12 percent, leading to a massive general strike in 1926. Yet the state provided unemployment benefits and supplemented the payments with subsidized housing, medical aid, and increased old-age pensions. These and other measures kept living standards from seriously declining, helped moderate class tensions, and pointed the way toward the welfare state Britain would establish after World War II.

Relative social harmony was accompanied by the rise of the Labour Party as a determined champion of the working class and of greater social equality. Committed to the kind of moderate revisionist socialism that had emerged before World War I (see Chapter 23), the Labour Party replaced the Liberal Party as the main opposition to the Conservatives. This shift reflected the decline of old liberal ideals of competitive capitalism, limited government control, and individual responsibility. In 1924 and from 1929 to 1931, the Labour Party under Ramsay MacDonald (1866–1937) governed the country with the support of the smaller Liberal Party. Yet Labour moved toward socialism gradually and democratically, so as not to antagonize the middle classes.

The British Conservatives showed the same compromising spirit on social issues. In 1922 Britain granted southern, Catholic, Ireland full autonomy after a bitter guerrilla war, thereby removing a key source of prewar friction. Despite conflicts such as the 1926 strike by hard-pressed coal miners, which led to an unsuccessful general strike, social unrest in Britain was limited in the 1920s and 1930s. Developments in both international relations and the domestic politics of the leading democracies across western Europe gave cause for optimism in the late 1920s.

The Great Depression, 1929–1939

This fragile optimism was short-lived. Beginning in 1929, a massive economic downturn struck the entire world with ever-greater intensity. Recovery was slow and uneven, and contemporaries labeled the economic crisis the **Great Depression**, to emphasize its severity and duration. Only with the Second World War did the depression disappear in much of the world.

The social and political consequences of the Great Depression were enormous. Mass unemployment and failing farms made insecurity and unemployment a reality for millions of people (Map 26.1). In Europe and the United States, governments instituted a variety of social welfare programs intended to manage the crisis. Yet the prolonged economic collapse shattered the fragile political stability of the mid-1920s and encouraged the growth of extremists on both ends of the political spectrum. Democratic government faltered, and authoritarian and Fascist parties gained power across Europe.

The Economic Crisis

Though economic activity was already declining moderately in many countries by early 1929, the crash of the stock market in the United States in October of that year initiated a worldwide crisis. The American economy had prospered in the late 1920s, but there were large inequalities in income and a serious imbalance between actual business investment and stock market speculation. Thus net investment—in factories, farms, equipment, and the like—actually fell from $3.5 billion in 1925 to $3.2 billion in 1929. In the same years, as money flooded into stocks, the value of shares traded on the exchanges soared from $27 billion to $87 billion. Such inflated prices should have raised serious concerns about economic solvency, but even experts failed to predict the looming collapse.

This stock market boom—or "bubble" in today's language—was built on borrowed money. Many wealthy investors, speculators, and people of modest means bought stocks by paying only a small fraction of the total purchase price and borrowing the remainder from their stockbrokers. Such buying "on margin" was extremely dangerous. When prices started falling in 1929, the hard-pressed margin buyers had to either put up more money, which was often impossible, or sell their shares to pay off their brokers. Thousands of people started selling all at once. The result was a financial panic. Countless investors and speculators were wiped out in a matter of days or weeks.

The consequences were swift and severe. Stripped of wealth and confidence, battered investors and their fellow citizens started buying fewer goods. Prices fell, production began to slow down, and unemployment began to rise. Soon the entire American economy was caught in a spiraling decline.

FOCUS QUESTION
What were the causes and consequences of the Great Depression?

Great Depression
A worldwide economic depression from 1929 through 1939, unique in its severity and duration and with slow and uneven recovery.

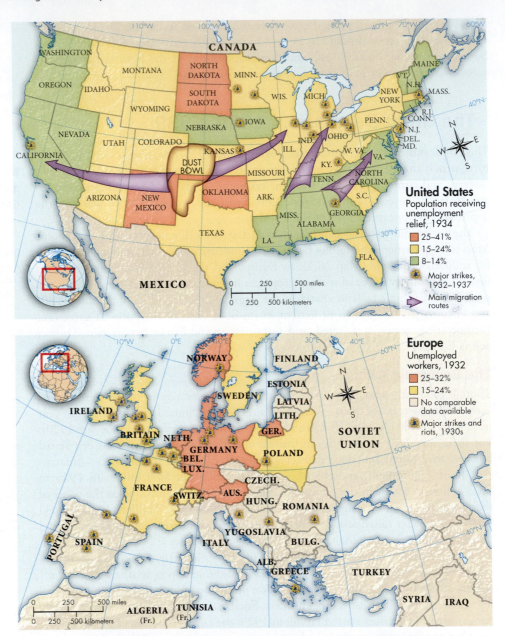

MAP 26.1 The Great Depression in the United States and Europe, 1929–1939 These maps show that unemployment was high almost everywhere, but that national and regional differences were also substantial.

The financial panic triggered an international financial crisis. Throughout the 1920s American bankers and investors had lent large amounts of capital to many countries. Once the panic broke, U.S. bankers began recalling the loans they had made to foreign businesses. Gold reserves began to flow rapidly out of European countries, particularly Germany and Austria, toward the United States. It became very hard for European businesses to borrow money, and panicky Europeans began to withdraw their savings from banks. These banking problems eventually led to the crash of the largest bank in Austria in 1931 and then to general financial chaos. The recall of loans by American bankers also accelerated a collapse in world prices when businesses dumped industrial goods and agricultural commodities in a frantic attempt to get cash to pay their loans.

The financial crisis led to a general crisis of production: between 1929 and 1933 world output of goods fell by an estimated 38 percent. As this happened, each country turned inward and tried to manage the crisis alone. In 1931, for example, Britain went off the gold standard, refusing to convert banknotes into gold, and reduced the value of its money. Britain's goal was to make its goods cheaper and therefore more salable in the world market. But more than twenty other nations, including the United States in 1934, also went off the gold standard, so few countries gained a real advantage from this step — though Britain was an exception. Similarly, country after country followed the example of the United States when in 1930 it raised protective tariffs to their highest levels ever and tried to seal off shrinking national markets for domestic producers. Such actions further limited international trade. Within this context of fragmented and destructive economic nationalism, a recovery did not begin until 1933 and it was a halting one at that.

Although opinions differ, two factors probably best explain the relentless slide to the bottom from 1929 to early 1933. First, the international economy lacked leadership able to maintain stability when the crisis came. Neither Britain nor the United States — the world's economic leaders at the time — successfully stabilized the international economic system in 1929. The American decisions to cut back on international lending and erect high tariffs, as we have seen, had damaging ripple effects.

The second factor was poor national economic policy in almost every country. Governments generally cut their budgets when they should have raised

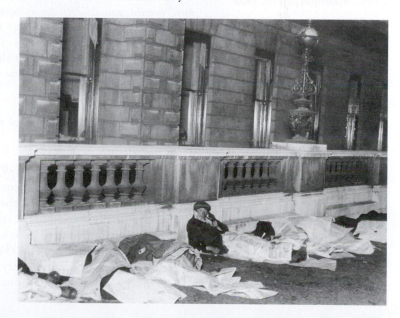

Homelessness in London The Great Depression of the 1930s disrupted the lives of millions across the United States and Europe. The frustration and agony of unemployment are evident in this common scene of homeless Londoners wrapping themselves in newspaper against the cold. (© Mary Evans Picture Library/ The Image Works)

spending and accepted large deficits in order to stimulate their economies. After World War II, this "counter-cyclical policy," advocated by John Maynard Keynes, became a well-established weapon against downturn and depression. But in the 1930s orthodox economists who believed balanced budgets to be the key to economic growth generally regarded Keynes's prescription with horror.

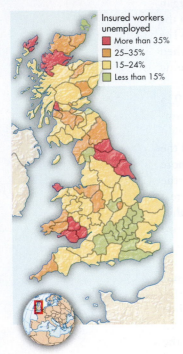

Insured workers unemployed
- More than 35%
- 25–35%
- 15–24%
- Less than 15%

British Unemployment, 1932

Mass Unemployment

The lack of large-scale government spending contributed to the rise of mass unemployment. As the financial crisis led to production cuts, workers lost their jobs and had little money to buy goods. In Britain, where unemployment had averaged 12 percent in the 1920s, it averaged more than 18 percent between 1930 and 1935. Far worse was the case of Germany, where in 1932 one in every three workers was jobless. In the United States, unemployment had averaged only 5 percent in the 1920s. In 1933 it soared to about 30 percent: almost 13 million people were out of work (see Map 26.1).

Mass unemployment created great social problems. Poverty increased dramatically, although in most countries unemployed workers generally received some kind of meager unemployment benefits or public aid that prevented starvation. (See "Evaluating the Evidence 26.3: George Orwell on Life on the Dole," page 896.) Millions of people lost their spirit, condemned to an apparently hopeless search for work. Homes and ways of life were disrupted in millions of personal tragedies. Young people postponed marriages, and birthrates fell sharply. There was an increase in suicide and mental illness. Poverty or the threat of poverty became a grinding reality. In 1932 the workers of Manchester, England, appealed to their city officials—a typical plea echoed throughout the Western world:

> We tell you that thousands of people . . . are in desperate straits. We tell you that men, women, and children are going hungry. . . . We tell you that great numbers are being rendered distraught through the stress and worry of trying to exist without work. . . . If you do not do this—if you do not provide useful work for the unemployed—what, we ask, is your alternative? Do not imagine that this colossal tragedy of unemployment is going on endlessly without some fateful catastrophe. Hungry men are angry men.[8]

Only strong government action could deal with mass unemployment, a social powder keg preparing to explode.

The New Deal in the United States

The Great Depression and the government response to it marked a major turning point in American history. President Herbert Hoover (U.S. pres. 1929–1933) and his administration initially reacted to the stock market crash and economic decline with dogged optimism but limited action. When the full force of the financial crisis struck Europe in the summer of 1931 and boomeranged back to the United States, people's worst fears became reality. Banks failed; unemployment soared. Between 1929 and 1932 industrial production fell by about 50 percent.

In these dire circumstances, Franklin Delano Roosevelt (U.S. pres. 1933–1945) won a landslide presidential victory in 1932 with grand but vague promises of a "New Deal for the forgotten man." Roosevelt's goal was to reform capitalism in order to save it. Though Roosevelt rejected socialism and government ownership of industry, he advocated forceful government intervention in the economy and instituted a broad range of government-supported social programs designed to stimulate the economy and provide jobs.

In the United States, innovative federal programs promoted agricultural recovery, a top priority. Almost half of the American population still lived in rural areas, and the depression hit farmers hard. Roosevelt took the United States off the gold standard and devalued the dollar in an effort to raise American prices and rescue farmers. The Agricultural Adjustment Act of 1933 also aimed at raising prices—and thus farm income—by limiting agricultural production. These measures worked for a while, and in 1936 farmers repaid Roosevelt with overwhelming support in his re-election campaign.

The most ambitious attempt to control and plan the economy was the National Recovery Administration (NRA). Intended to reduce competition among industries by setting minimum prices and wages, the NRA broke with the cherished American tradition of free competition. Though participation was voluntary, the NRA aroused conflicts among business people, consumers, and bureaucrats and never worked well. The program was abandoned when declared unconstitutional by the Supreme Court in 1935.

Roosevelt and his advisers then attacked the key problem of mass unemployment. The federal government accepted the responsibility of employing as many people as financially possible. New agencies like the Works Progress Administration (WPA), set up in 1935, were created to undertake a vast range of projects. One-fifth of the entire U.S. labor force worked for the WPA at some point in the 1930s, constructing public buildings, bridges, and highways. The WPA was enormously popular, and the opportunity of taking a government job helped check the threat of social revolution in the United States.

In 1935 the U.S. government also established a national social security system with old-age pensions and unemployment benefits. The National Labor Relations Act of 1935 gave union organizers the green light by guaranteeing rights of collective bargaining. Union membership more than doubled from 4 million in 1935 to 9 million in 1940. In general, between 1935 and 1938 government rulings and social reforms chipped away at the privileges of the wealthy and tried to help ordinary people.

Programs like the WPA were part of the New Deal's fundamental commitment to use the federal government to provide relief welfare for all Americans. This commitment marked a profound shift from the traditional stress on family support and community responsibility. Embraced by a large majority in the 1930s, this shift in attitudes proved to be one of the New Deal's most enduring legacies.

Despite undeniable accomplishments in social reform, the New Deal was only partly successful in responding to the Great Depression. At the height of the recovery in May 1937, 7 million workers were still unemployed—better than the high of about 13 million in 1933 but way beyond the numbers from the 1920s. The economic situation then worsened seriously in the recession of 1937 and 1938, and unemployment

George Orwell on Life on the Dole

Periodic surges in unemployment were an old story in capitalist economies, but the long-term joblessness of millions in the Great Depression was something new and unexpected. In Britain especially, where the depression followed a weak postwar recovery, large numbers suffered involuntary idleness for years at a time. Whole families lived "on the dole," the weekly welfare benefits paid by the government.

One of the most insightful accounts of unemployed workers was written by the British journalist and novelist George Orwell (1903–1950), who studied the conditions in northern England and wrote The Road to Wigan Pier *(1937), an excerpt of which follows. An independent socialist who distrusted rigid Marxism, Orwell believed that socialism could triumph in Britain if it came to mean commonsense "justice and liberty" for a broad sector of the working classes. Orwell's disillusionment with authoritarian socialism and Soviet-style communism pervades his other famous works,* Animal Farm *(1945) and* 1984 *(1949).*

~

When you see the unemployment figures quoted at two millions, it is fatally easy to take this as meaning that two million people are out of work and the rest of the population is comparatively comfortable. . . . [Adding in the destitute,] you might take the number of underfed people in England (for *everyone* on the dole or thereabouts is underfed) as being, at the very most, five millions.

This is an enormous under-estimate, because, in the first place, the only people shown on unemployment figures are those actually drawing the dole—that is, in general, heads of families. An unemployed man's dependants do not figure on the list unless they too are drawing a separate allowance. . . . In addition there are great numbers of people who are in work but who, from a financial point of view, might equally be unemployed, because they are not drawing anything that can be described as a living wage.

Allow for these and their dependants, throw in as before the old-age pensioners, the destitute and other nondescripts, and you get an *underfed* population of well over ten millions. . . . Take the figures for Wigan, which is typical enough of the industrial and mining districts. . . . The total population of Wigan is a little under 87,000; so that at any moment more than one person in three out of the whole population—not merely the registered workers—is either drawing or living on the dole. . . .

Nevertheless, in spite of the frightful extent of unemployment, it is a fact that poverty—extreme poverty—is less in evidence in the industrial North than it is in London. Everything is poorer and shabbier, there are fewer motor-cars and fewer well-dressed people; but also there are fewer people who are obviously destitute. . . . In the industrial towns the old communal way of life has not yet broken up, tradition is still strong and almost everyone has a family—potentially, therefore, a home. In a town of 50,000 or 100,000 inhabitants there is no casual and as it were unaccounted-for population; nobody sleeping in the streets, for instance. Moreover, there is just this to be said for the unemployment regulations, that they do not discourage people from marrying. A man and wife on twenty-three shillings a week are not far from the starvation line, but they can make a home of sorts; they are vastly better off than a single man on fifteen shillings. . . .

But there is no doubt about the deadening, debilitating effect of unemployment upon everybody, married or single, and upon men more than upon women. . . . Everyone who saw Greenwood's play *Love on the Dole* must remember that dreadful moment when the poor, good, stupid working man beats on the table and cries out, "O God, send me some work!" This was not dramatic exaggeration, it was a touch from life. That cry must have been uttered, in almost those words, in tens of thousands, perhaps hundreds of thousands of English homes, during the past fifteen years.

---

had risen to a staggering 10 million when war broke out in Europe in September 1939. The New Deal never pulled the United States out of the depression; it took the Second World War to do that.

The Scandinavian Response to the Depression

Of all the Western democracies, the Scandinavian countries under Social Democratic leadership responded most successfully to the challenge of the Great Depression. Having grown steadily in the late nineteenth century, the Social Democrats

But, I think not again—or at least, not so often. . . . When people live on the dole for years at a time they grow used to it, and drawing the dole, though it remains unpleasant, ceases to be shameful. Thus the old, independent, workhouse-fearing tradition is undermined. . . .

So you have whole populations settling down, as it were, to a lifetime of the P.A.C. [Public Assistance Committees, which means-tested recipients and set benefit levels]. . . . Take, for instance, the fact that the working class think nothing of getting married on the dole. . . . Life is still fairly normal, more normal than one really has the right to expect. Families are impoverished, but the family-system has not broken up. The people are in effect living a reduced version of their former lives.

Instead of raging against their destiny they have made things tolerable by lowering their standards. But they don't necessarily lower their standards by cutting out luxuries and concentrating on necessities; more often it is the other way about—the more natural way, if you come to think of it. Hence the fact that in a decade of unparalleled depression, the consumption of all cheap luxuries has increased. The two things that have probably made the greatest difference of all are the movies and the mass-production of cheap smart clothes since the war. The youth who leaves school at fourteen and gets a blind-alley job is out of work at twenty, probably for life; but for two pounds ten on the hire-purchase system he can buy himself a suit which, for a little while and at a little distance, looks as though it had been tailored in Savile Row. The girl can look like a fashion plate at an even lower price. . . . You can stand on the street corner, indulging in a private daydream of yourself as Clark Gable or Greta Garbo, which compensates you for a great deal. . . .

Trade since the war has had to adjust itself to meet the demands of underpaid, underfed people, with the result that a luxury is nowadays almost always cheaper than a necessity. One pair of plain solid shoes costs as much as two ultra-smart pairs. . . . And above all there is gambling, the cheapest of all luxuries. Even people on the verge of starvation can buy a few days' hope ("Something to live for," as they call it) by having a penny on a sweepstake. . . . Twenty million people are underfed but literally everyone in England has access to a radio. What we have lost in food we have gained in electricity. Whole sections of the working class who have been plundered of all they really need are being compensated, in part, by cheap luxuries which mitigate the surface of life.

Do you consider all this desirable? No, I don't. But it may be that the psychological adjustment which the working class are visibly making is the best they could make in the circumstances. They have neither turned revolutionary nor lost their self-respect; merely they have kept their tempers and settled down to make the best of things on a fish-and-chip standard. The alternative would be God knows what continued agonies of despair; or it might be attempted insurrections which, in a strongly governed country like England, could only lead to futile massacres and a régime of savage repression.

EVALUATE THE EVIDENCE

1. According to Orwell, "extreme poverty" was less visible in the northern industrial towns than in London. How did family relations contribute to social stability in the face of growing poverty?
2. What were the consequences of long-term unemployment for English workers? How did joblessness change attitudes and behaviors?
3. Judging from Orwell's description, did radical revolution seem likely in England in the Great Depression? Why?

Source: Excerpts from Chapter V in *The Road to Wigan Pier* by George Orwell. Copyright © George Orwell, 1937. Copyright © 1958 and renewed 1986 by the Estate of Sonia B. Orwell. Reprinted by permission of Houghton Mifflin Harcourt Publishing Company, from *The Complete Works of George Orwell*. All rights reserved.

became the largest political party in Sweden and then in Norway after the First World War. In the 1920s they passed important social reform legislation that benefited both peasants and workers and developed a unique kind of socialism. Flexible and nonrevolutionary, Scandinavian socialism grew out of a strong tradition of cooperative community action. Even before 1900 Scandinavian agricultural cooperatives had shown how individual peasant families could join together for everyone's benefit. Labor leaders and capitalists were also inclined to cooperate with one another.

Oslo Breakfast   Scandinavian Social Democrats championed cooperation and practical welfare measures, playing down strident rhetoric and theories of class conflict. The "Oslo Breakfast" portrayed in this pamphlet from the mid-1930s exemplified the Scandinavian approach. It provided every schoolchild in the Norwegian capital with a good breakfast free of charge. (Courtesy, Directorate for Health and Social Affairs, Oslo)

When the economic crisis struck in 1929, socialist governments in Scandinavia built on this pattern of cooperative social action. Sweden in particular pioneered in the use of large-scale deficits to finance public works and thereby maintain production and employment. In ways that paralleled some aspects of Roosevelt's New Deal, Scandinavian governments also increased such social welfare benefits as old-age pensions, unemployment insurance, subsidized housing, and maternity allowances. All this spending required a large bureaucracy and high taxes, first on the rich and then on practically everyone. Yet both private and cooperative enterprise thrived, as did democracy. Some observers saw Scandinavia's welfare socialism as an appealing middle way between sick capitalism and cruel communism or fascism.

Recovery and Reform in Britain and France

In Britain, MacDonald's Labour government and then, after 1931, the Conservative-dominated coalition government followed orthodox economic theory. The budget was balanced, spending was tightly controlled, and unemployed workers received barely enough welfare to live. Nevertheless, the economy recovered considerably after 1932. By 1937 total production was about 20 percent higher than in 1929. In fact, for Britain the years after 1932 were actually somewhat better than the 1920s had been, the opposite of the situation in the United States and France.

This good but by no means brilliant performance reflected the gradual reorientation of the British economy. After going off the gold standard in 1931 and establishing protective tariffs in 1932, Britain concentrated increasingly on the national, rather than the international, market. The old export industries of the Industrial Revolution, such as textiles and coal, continued to decline, but new industries, such as automobiles and electrical appliances, grew in response to British home demand. Moreover, low interest rates encouraged a housing boom. By the end of the decade, there were highly visible differences between the old, depressed industrial areas of the north and the new, growing areas of the south.

Because France was relatively less industrialized and thus more isolated from the world economy, the Great Depression came to it late. But once the depression hit France, it stayed and stayed. Decline was steady until 1935, and a short-lived recovery never brought production or employment back up to predepression levels. Economic stagnation both reflected and heightened an ongoing political crisis. There was no stability in government. As before 1914, the French parliament was made up of many political parties that could never cooperate for long. In 1933, for example, five coalition cabinets formed and fell in rapid succession.

The French, however, had lost the underlying unity that had made government instability bearable before 1914. Fascist organizations agitated against parliamentary democracy and turned to Mussolini's Italy and Hitler's Germany for inspiration. In February 1934 French Fascists rioted and threatened to take over the republic. At the same time, the Communist Party and many workers opposed to the existing system looked to Stalin's Russia for guidance. The vital center of moderate republicanism was weakened by attacks from both sides.

Frightened by the growing strength of the Fascists at home and abroad, the Communists, Socialists, and Radicals formed an alliance — the **Popular Front** — for the national elections of May 1936. Their clear victory reflected the trend toward polarization. The number of Communists in the parliament jumped dramatically from 10 to 72, while the Socialists, led by Léon Blum, became the strongest party in France, with 146 seats. The Radicals — who were actually quite moderate — slipped badly, and the conservatives lost ground to the far right.

In the next few months, Blum's Popular Front government made the first and only real attempt to deal with the social and economic problems of the 1930s in France. Inspired by Roosevelt's New Deal, it encouraged the union movement and launched a far-reaching program of social reform, complete with paid vacations and a forty-hour workweek. Supported by workers and the lower middle class, these measures were quickly sabotaged by rapid inflation and accusations of revolution from Fascists and frightened conservatives. Wealthy people sneaked their money out of the country, labor unrest grew, and France entered a severe financial crisis. Blum was forced to announce a "breathing spell" in social reform.

Political dissension in France was encouraged by the Spanish Civil War (1936–1939), during which authoritarian Fascist rebels overthrew the democratically elected republican government. French Communists demanded that the government support the Spanish republicans, while many French conservatives would gladly have joined Hitler and Mussolini in aiding the Spanish Fascists. Extremism grew, and France itself was within sight of civil war. Blum was forced to resign in June 1937, and the Popular Front quickly collapsed. An anxious and divided France drifted aimlessly once again, preoccupied by Hitler and German rearmament.

Popular Front
A short-lived New Deal–inspired alliance in France led by Léon Blum that encouraged the union movement and launched a far-reaching program of social reform.

LOOKING BACK LOOKING AHEAD

The decades before and especially after World War I brought intense intellectual and cultural innovation. The results were both richly productive and deeply troubling. From T. S. Eliot's poem *The Waste Land* to Einstein's theory of special relativity to the sleek glass and steel buildings of the Bauhaus, the intellectual products of the time stand among the highest achievements of Western arts and sciences. At the same time, mass culture, embodied in cinema, radio, and an emerging consumer society, transformed everyday life. Yet the modern vision was often bleak and cold. Modern art and consumer society alike challenged traditional values, contributing to feelings of disorientation and pessimism that had begun late in the nineteenth century and were exacerbated by the searing events of the war. The situation was worsened by ongoing political and economic turmoil. The Treaty of Versailles had failed to create a lasting peace or resolve the question of Germany's role in Europe. The Great Depression revealed the fragility of the world economic system and cast millions out of work. In the end, perhaps, the era's intellectual achievements and the overall sense of crisis were closely related.

Sigmund Freud captured the general mood of gloom and foreboding in 1930. "Men have gained control over the forces of nature to such an extent that . . . they would have no difficulty in exterminating one another to the last man," he wrote. "They know this, and hence comes a large part of their current unrest, their unhappiness and their mood of anxiety."[9] Freud's dark words reflected the extraordinary human costs of World War I and the horrific power of modern weaponry. They also expressed his despair over the growing popularity of repressive dictatorial regimes. During the interwar years, many European nations — including Italy, Germany, Spain, Poland, Portugal, Austria, and Hungary — would fall one by one to authoritarian or Fascist dictatorships, succumbing to the temptations of totalitarianism. Liberal democracy was severely weakened. European stability was threatened by the radical programs of Soviet Communists on the left and Fascists on the right, and Freud uncannily predicted the great conflict to come.

Make Connections

Think about the larger developments and continuities within and across chapters.

1. How did trends in politics, economics, culture, and the arts and sciences come together to create a general sense of crisis in the 1920s and 1930s?

2. To what extent did the problems of the 1920s and 1930s have roots in the First World War (Chapter 25)?

3. What made modern art and intellectual thought "modern"?

26 REVIEW & EXPLORE

Review the Main Ideas

Answer the focus questions from each section of the chapter.

◆ How did intellectual developments reflect the general crisis in Western thought? (p. 868)

◆ How did modernism revolutionize Western culture? (p. 875)

◆ How did consumer society change everyday life? (p. 881)

◆ What obstacles to lasting peace did European leaders face? (p. 885)

◆ What were the causes and consequences of the Great Depression? (p. 891)

Identify Key Terms

Identify and explain the significance of each item below.

logical positivism (p. 870)
existentialism (p. 871)
theory of special relativity (p. 873)
id, ego, and superego (p. 874)
modernism (p. 875)
functionalism (p. 876)
Bauhaus (p. 876)
Dadaism (p. 877)
stream-of-consciousness technique (p. 879)
"modern girl" (p. 882)
Dawes Plan (p. 889)
Great Depression (p. 891)
Popular Front (p. 899)

NOTES

1. P. Valéry, *Variety*, trans. M. Cowley (New York: Harcourt Brace, 1927), pp. 27–28.
2. G. Greene, *Another Mexico* (New York: Viking Press, 1939), p. 3.
3. C. E. Jeanneret-Gris (Le Corbusier), *Towards a New Architecture* (London: J. Rodker, 1931), p. 15.
4. R. Huelsenbeck, "Collective Dada Manifesto (1920)," in *The Dada Painters and Poets*, ed. Robert Motherwell and Jack D. Flam (Boston: G. K. Hall, 1981), pp. 242–246.
5. From *The Waste Land* by T. S. Eliot. Used by permission of Faber and Faber Ltd.
6. E. Herrmann, *This Is the New Woman* (1929), quoted in *The Weimar Republic Sourcebook*, ed. A. Kaes, M. Jay, and E. Dimendberg (Berkeley: University of California Press, 1994), pp. 206–208.
7. Quoted in R. Smither, ed., *The Battles of the Somme and Ancre* (London: Imperial War Museum, 1993), p. 67.
8. Quoted in S. B. Clough et al., eds., *Economic History of Europe: Twentieth Century* (New York: Harper & Row, 1968), pp. 243–245.
9. S. Freud, *Civilization and Its Discontents* (New York: W. W. Norton, 1961), p. 112.

CHAPTER PREVIEW

Authoritarian States
How were Fascist and Communist totalitarian dictatorships similar and different?

Stalin's Soviet Union
How did Stalin and the Communist Party build a totalitarian state in the Soviet Union?

Mussolini and Fascism in Italy
What kind of government did Mussolini establish in Italy?

Hitler and Nazism in Germany
What policies did Nazi Germany pursue, and how did they lead to World War II?

The Second World War
How did Germany and Japan conquer enormous empires during World War II, and how did the Allies defeat them?

Life at Auschwitz
This rough painting by an anonymous inmate of the Auschwitz-Birkenau Nazi concentration camp is preserved on the ceiling of a camp barracks. Guarded by SS officers, prisoners labor on a drainage canal under the worst conditions, while two carry a dead worker off the field.
(De Agostini/Getty Images)

27

Dictatorships and the Second World War

1919–1945

The intense wave of artistic and cultural innovation in the 1920s and 1930s, which shook the foundations of Western thought, was paralleled by radical developments in the realm of politics. In the age of anxiety, Communist and Fascist states undertook determined assaults on democratic government and individual rights across Europe. On the eve of the Second World War, popularly elected governments survived only in Great Britain, France, Czechoslovakia, the Low Countries, Scandinavia, and Switzerland.

Totalitarian regimes in the Communist Soviet Union, Fascist Italy, and Nazi Germany practiced a ruthless and dynamic tyranny. Their attempts to revolutionize state and society went far beyond traditional forms of conservative authoritarianism. Communist and Fascist states ruled with unprecedented severity. They promised to greatly improve the lives of ordinary citizens and intervened radically in those lives in pursuit of utopian schemes of social engineering. Their drive for territorial expansion threatened neighboring nations. The human costs of these policies were appalling. Millions died as Stalin forced communism on the Soviet Union in the 1930s. Attempts to build a "racially pure" New Order in Europe by Hitler's Nazi Germany led to the deaths of tens of millions more in World War II and the Holocaust, a scale of destruction far beyond that of World War I.

Such brutalities may seem a thing of the distant past that "can't happen again." Yet horrible atrocities in Rwanda, Bosnia, and Sudan show that they continue to plague the world in our time. It remains vital that we understand Europe's era of overwhelming violence in order to guard against the possibility of its recurrence in the future. ■

Authoritarian States

FOCUS QUESTION
How were Fascist and Communist totalitarian dictatorships similar and different?

Both conservative and radical dictatorships took power in Europe in the 1920s and 1930s. Although these two types of dictatorship shared some characteristics, in essence they were quite different. Conservative authoritarian regimes, which had a long history in Europe, were limited in scope. Radical totalitarian dictatorships, based on the ideologies of communism and fascism, were a new and frightening development aimed at the radical reconstruction of society.

Conservative Authoritarianism and Radical Totalitarian Dictatorships

The traditional form of antidemocratic government in European history was conservative authoritarianism. Like Catherine the Great in Russia and Metternich in Austria, the leaders of such governments relied on obedient state bureaucracies in their efforts to control society. Though political opponents were often jailed or exiled, these older authoritarian governments were limited in both power and objectives. They had neither the ability nor the desire to control many aspects of their subjects' lives. As long as the people did not try to change the system, they were typically allowed considerable personal independence.

After the First World War, authoritarianism revived, especially in eastern Europe. What emerged, however, were new kinds of radical dictatorship that went much further than conservative authoritarianism, particularly in the Soviet Union, Germany, and Italy. In addition, both Communist and Fascist political parties became well established in all major European nations and mounted challenges to democratic rule.

totalitarianism A radical dictatorship that exercises "total claims" over the beliefs and behavior of its citizens by taking control of the economic, social, intellectual, and cultural aspects of society.

Some scholars use the term **totalitarianism** to describe these radical dictatorships, which made unprecedented "total claims" on the beliefs and behavior of their citizens. The totalitarian model emphasizes the characteristics that Fascist and Communist dictatorships had in common. One-party totalitarian states used violent political repression and intense propaganda to gain complete power. In addition, the state tried to dominate the economic, social, intellectual, and cultural aspects of people's lives.

Most historians agree that totalitarianism owed much to the experience of total war in 1914 to 1918 (see Chapter 25). World War I required state governments to limit individual liberties and intervene in the economy in order to achieve one supreme objective: victory. Totalitarian leaders were inspired by the example of the modern state at war. They showed a callous disregard for human life and greatly expanded the power of the state in pursuit of social control.

Communist and Fascist dictatorships shared other characteristics. Both rejected parliamentary government and liberal values. Classical liberals (see Chapter 21) sought to limit the power of the state and protect the rights of the individual.

Chronology

1921	New Economic Policy (NEP) in U.S.S.R.
1922	Mussolini gains power in Italy
1924	Mussolini seizes dictatorial powers
1924–1929	Buildup of Nazi Party in Germany
1927	Stalin comes to power in U.S.S.R.
1928	Stalin's first five-year plan
1929	Lateran Agreement; start of collectivization in Soviet Union
1929–1939	Great Depression
1931	Japan invades Manchuria
1932–1933	Famine in Ukraine
1933	Hitler appointed chancellor in Germany; Reichstag passes the Enabling Act, granting Hitler absolute dictatorial power
1935	Nuremberg Laws deprive Jews of citizenship rights
1936	Start of great purges under Stalin; Spanish Civil War begins
1937	Japanese army invades China
1938	Kristallnacht marks beginning of more aggressive anti-Jewish policy in Germany
1939	Germany occupies Czech lands and invades western Poland; Britain and France declare war on Germany, starting World War II; Soviet Union occupies eastern Poland
1940	Germany defeats and occupies France; Battle of Britain begins
1941	Germany invades U.S.S.R.; Japan attacks Pearl Harbor; United States enters war
1941–1945	The Holocaust
1942–1943	Battle of Stalingrad
1944	Allied invasion at Normandy
1945	Soviet and U.S. forces enter Germany; United States drops atomic bombs on Japan; World War II ends

Totalitarians, on the other hand, believed that individualism undermined equality and unity, and rejected democracy in favor of one-party political systems.

A charismatic leader typically dominated the totalitarian state—Stalin in the Soviet Union, Mussolini in Italy, Hitler in Germany. All three created political parties of a new kind, dedicated to promoting idealized visions of collective harmony. They used force and terror to intimidate and destroy political opponents and pursued policies of imperial expansion to exploit other lands. They censored the mass media and instituted propaganda campaigns to advance their goals. Finally, and perhaps most important, totalitarian governments engaged in massive projects of state-controlled social engineering dedicated to replacing individualism with a unified "people" capable of exercising the collective will.

Communism and Fascism

Communism and fascism clearly shared a desire to revolutionize state and society. Yet some scholars—arguing that the differences between the two systems are more important than the similarities—have moved beyond the totalitarian model. What were the main differences between these two systems? To answer this question, it is important to consider the way ideology, or a guiding political philosophy, was linked to the use of state-sponsored repression and violence.

Following Marx, Soviet Communists strove to create an international brotherhood of workers. In the Communist utopia ruled by the revolutionary working class, economic exploitation would supposedly disappear and society would be based on radical social equality (see Chapter 21). Under Stalinism—the name given to the

Communist system during Stalin's rule—the state aggressively intervened in all walks of life to pursue this social leveling. Using brute force to destroy the upper and middle classes, the Stalinist state nationalized private property, pushed rapid industrialization, and collectivized agriculture (see pages 907–916).

The Fascist vision of a new society was quite different. Leaders who embraced **fascism**, such as Mussolini and Hitler, claimed that they were striving to build a new community on a national—not an international—level. Extreme nationalists, and often racists, Fascists glorified war and the military. For them, the nation was the highest embodiment of the people, and the powerful leader was the materialization of the people's collective will.

Like Communists, Fascists promised to improve the lives of ordinary workers. Fascist governments intervened in the economy, but unlike Communist regimes they did not try to level class differences and nationalize private property. Instead, they presented a vision of a community bound together by nationalism. In the ideal Fascist state, all social strata and classes would work together to build a harmonious national community.

Communists and Fascists differed in another crucial respect: the question of race. Where Communists sought to build a new world around the destruction of class differences, Fascists typically sought to build a new national community grounded in racial homogeneity. Fascists embraced the doctrine of **eugenics**, a pseudoscience that maintained that the selective breeding of human beings could improve the general characteristics of a national population. Eugenics was popular throughout the Western world in the 1920s and 1930s and was viewed by many as a legitimate social policy. But Fascists, especially the German National Socialists, or Nazis, pushed these ideas to the extreme.

Adopting a radicalized view of eugenics, the Nazis maintained that the German nation had to be "purified" of groups of people deemed "unfit" by the regime. Following state policies intended to support what they called "racial hygiene," Nazi authorities attempted to control, segregate, or eliminate those of "lesser value," including Jews, Sinti and Roma (often called Gypsies, a term that can have pejorative connotations) and other ethnic minorities, homosexuals, and people suffering from chronic mental or physical disabilities. The pursuit of "racial hygiene" ultimately led to the Holocaust, the attempt to purge Germany and Europe of all Jews and other undesirable groups by mass killing during World War II (see page 931). Though the Soviets readily

fascism A movement characterized by extreme, often expansionist nationalism; anti-socialism; a dynamic and violent leader; and glorification of war and the military.

eugenics A pseudoscientific doctrine saying the selective breeding of human beings can improve the general characteristics of a national population, which helped inspire Nazi ideas about national unity and racial exclusion and ultimately contributed to the Holocaust.

Eugenics in Nazi Germany Nazi "race scientists" believed they could use the eugenic methods of social engineering to build a powerful Aryan race. In this photograph, published in a popular magazine in 1933, a clinician measures a man's nose. Such pseudoscientific methods were used to determine an individual's supposed "racial value." (© Hulton-Deutsch Collection/Corbis)

persecuted specific ethnic groups they believed were disloyal to the Communist state, in general they justified these attacks using ideologies of class rather than race or biology.

Perhaps because both championed the overthrow of existing society, Communists and Fascists were sworn enemies. The result was a clash of ideologies, which was in large part responsible for the horrific destruction and loss of life in the middle of the twentieth century. Explaining the nature of totalitarian dictatorships thus remains a crucial project for historians, even as they look more closely at the ideological differences between communism and fascism.

One important set of questions explores the way dictatorial regimes generated popular consensus. Neither Hitler nor Stalin ever achieved the total control each sought. Nor did they rule alone; modern dictators need the help of large state bureaucracies and the cooperation of large numbers of ordinary people. Which was more important for generating popular support: terror and coercion or material rewards? Under what circumstances did people resist or perpetrate totalitarian tyranny? These questions lead us toward what Holocaust survivor Primo Levi called the "gray zone" of moral compromise, which defined everyday life in totalitarian societies. (See "Individuals in Society: Primo Levi," page 935.)

Stalin's Soviet Union

Lenin's harshest critics claim that he established the basic outlines of a modern totalitarian dictatorship after the Bolshevik Revolution and during the Russian civil war. If so, Joseph Stalin (1879–1953) certainly finished the job. A master of political infighting, Stalin cautiously consolidated his power and eliminated his enemies in the mid-1920s. Then in 1928, as undisputed leader of the ruling Communist Party, Stalin launched the first **five-year plan**—the "revolution from above," as he aptly termed it—the beginning of a radical attempt to transform Soviet society into a Communist state. The ultimate goal of this immensely ambitious effort was to generate new attitudes, new loyalties, and a new socialist humanity. The means were constant propaganda, enormous sacrifice by the people, harsh repression that included purges and executions, and rewards for those who followed the party line. Thus the Soviet Union in the 1930s became a dynamic totalitarian state.

From Lenin to Stalin

By spring 1921 Lenin and the Bolsheviks had won the civil war, but they ruled a shattered and devastated land. Many farms were in ruins, and food supplies were exhausted. In southern Russia, drought combined with the ravages of war to produce the worst famine in generations. Industrial production had broken down completely. In the face of economic disintegration, riots by peasants and workers, and an open rebellion by previously pro-Bolshevik sailors at Kronstadt, Lenin was tough but, as ever, flexible. He repressed the Kronstadt rebels, and in March 1921 he replaced War Communism with the **New Economic Policy (NEP)**, which re-established limited economic freedom in an attempt to rebuild agriculture and industry. During the civil war, the Bolsheviks had simply seized grain without payment. Now peasant producers were permitted to sell their surpluses in free markets, and private traders and small handicraft manufacturers were allowed to reappear. Heavy industry, railroads, and banks, however, remained wholly nationalized.

FOCUS QUESTION
How did Stalin and the Communist Party build a totalitarian state in the Soviet Union?

five-year plan A plan launched by Stalin in 1928, and termed the "revolution from above," aimed at modernizing the Soviet Union and creating a new Communist society with new attitudes, new loyalties, and a new socialist humanity.

New Economic Policy (NEP) Lenin's 1921 policy to re-establish limited economic freedom in an attempt to rebuild agriculture and industry in the face of economic disintegration.

The NEP was a political and economic success. Politically, it was a necessary but temporary compromise with the Soviet Union's overwhelming peasant majority. Realizing that his government was not strong enough to take land from the peasants and turn them into state workers, Lenin made a deal with the only force capable of overturning his government. The NEP brought rapid economic recovery, and by 1926 industrial output surpassed, and agricultural production almost equaled, prewar levels.

In 1924, as the economy recovered and the government partially relaxed its censorship and repression, Lenin died without a chosen successor, creating an intense struggle for power in the inner circles of the Communist Party. The principal contenders were Stalin and Trotsky. Joseph Dzhugashvili (joo-guhsh-VEEL-yih)—later known as Stalin (from the Russian for "steel")—was a good organizer but a poor speaker and writer, and he had no experience outside of Russia. Trotsky, a great and inspiring leader who had planned the 1917 Bolshevik takeover and then created the victorious Red Army, appeared to have all the advantages in the power struggle. Yet Stalin won because he was more effective at gaining the all-important support of the party. Having risen to general secretary of the party's Central Committee in 1922, he used his office to win friends and allies with jobs and promises.

Stalin also won because he was better able to relate Marxist teaching to Soviet realities in the 1920s. Stalin developed a theory of "socialism in one country" that was more appealing to the majority of party members than Trotsky's doctrine of "permanent revolution." Stalin argued that the Russian-dominated Soviet Union had the ability to build socialism on its own. Trotsky maintained that socialism in the Soviet Union could succeed only if a socialist revolution swept throughout Europe. To many Russian Communists, this view sold their country short and promised risky conflicts with capitalist countries. Stalin's willingness to revoke NEP reforms furthermore appealed to young party militants, who detested the NEP's reliance on capitalist free markets.

Stalin's ascendancy had a momentous impact on the policy of the new Soviet state toward non-Russians. The Communists had inherited the vast multiethnic territories of the former Russian Empire. Lenin initially argued that these ethnic groups should have the right to self-determination even if they claimed independence from the Soviet state. In 1922, reflecting such ideas, the Union of Soviet Socialist Republics (or U.S.S.R.) was organized as a federation of four Soviet republics: the Russian

Ethnic Minorities in the U.S.S.R.
The Soviet Union inherited the vast and diverse territories of the former Russian Empire. In this propaganda poster, titled "The Great Stalin Is the Banner of Friendship Between the Peoples of the U.S.S.R.!" the Soviet dictator receives flowers from a diverse group of Soviet citizens, including ethnic Russians and East and Central Asians. This idealized testament to peaceful coexistence within the Soviet empire masked the tensions aroused by Russian domination. How does this poster represent the relationship between Stalin and the Soviet people? (rps — ullstein-bild/Granger, NYC — All rights reserved)

Soviet Federative Socialist Republic, Ukraine, Belorussia, and a Transcaucasian republic. The last was later split into Armenia, Azerbaijan, and Georgia, and five Central Asian republics were established in the 1920s and 1930s (Map 27.1).

In contrast to Lenin, Stalin argued for more centralized Russian control of these ethnic regions. His view would dominate state policy until the breakup of the Soviet Union in the early 1990s. The Soviet republics were granted some cultural independence but no true political autonomy. Party leaders allowed the use of non-Russian languages in regional schools and government institutions, but the right to secede was a fiction, and real authority remained in Moscow, in the hands of the Russian Communist Party. The Stalinists thus established a far-flung Communist empire on the imperial holdings of the former tsars.

MAP 27.1 The Formation of the U.S.S.R.   When the Bolsheviks successfully overthrew the tsarist government and won the civil war that followed, they inherited the vast territories of the former Russian Empire. Following policies instituted by Stalin, they established a Union of Soviet Socialist Republics (U.S.S.R.) that gave limited cultural autonomy but no real political independence to the Soviet republics now under Communist control.

Stalin Justifies the Five-Year Plan

On February 4, 1931, Joseph Stalin delivered the following address, titled "No Slowdown in Tempo!" to the First Conference of Soviet Industrial Managers. Published the following day in Pravda, *the newspaper of the Communist Party, and widely publicized at home and abroad, Stalin's speech reaffirmed the leader's commitment to the breakneck pace of industrialization and collectivization set forth in the first five-year plan. Arguing that more sacrifices were necessary, Stalin sought to rally the people and generate support for the party's program. His address captures the spirit of Soviet ideology in the early 1930s.*

Stalin's concluding idea, that Bolsheviks needed to master technology and industrial management, reflected another major development. The Soviet Union was training a new class of Communist engineers and technicians, who were beginning to replace foreign engineers and "bourgeois specialists," Russian engineers trained in tsarist times who were grudgingly tolerated in the first years after the revolution.

It is sometimes asked whether it is not possible to slow down the tempo somewhat, to put a check on the movement. No, comrades, it is not possible! The tempo must not be reduced! On the contrary, we must increase it as much as is within our powers and possibilities. This is dictated to us by our obligations to the workers and peasants of the U.S.S.R. This is dictated to us by our obligations to the working class of the whole world.

To slacken the tempo would mean falling behind. And those who fall behind get beaten. But we do not want to be beaten. No, we refuse to be beaten! One feature of the history of old Russia was the continual beatings she suffered because of her backwardness. She was beaten by the Mongol khans, . . . the Turkish beys, . . . and the Japanese barons. All beat her—because of her backwardness, cultural backwardness, political backwardness, industrial backwardness, agricultural backwardness. They beat her because to do so was profitable and could be done with impunity. . . . Such is the law of the exploiters—to beat the backward and the weak. It is the jungle law of capitalism. You are backward, you are weak—therefore you are wrong; hence you can be beaten and enslaved. You are mighty—therefore you are right; hence we must be wary of you. That is why we must no longer lag behind.

In the past we had no fatherland, nor could we have had one. But now that we have overthrown capitalism and power is in our hands, in the hands of the people, we have a fatherland, and we will uphold its independence. Do you want our socialist fatherland to be beaten and to lose its independence?

If you do not want this, you must put an end to its backwardness in the shortest possible time and develop a genuine Bolshevik tempo in building up its socialist economy. There is no other way. That is why Lenin said on the eve of the October Revolution: "Either perish, or overtake and outstrip the advanced capitalist countries."

We are fifty or a hundred years behind the advanced countries. We must make good this distance in ten years. Either we do it, or we shall go under. That is what our obligations to the workers and peasants of the U.S.S.R. dictate to us.

But we have yet other, more serious and more important, obligations. They are our obligations to the world proletariat. . . . We achieved victory not solely through the efforts of the working class of the U.S.S.R., but also thanks to the support of the working class of the world.

With cunning skill, Stalin achieved supreme power between 1922 and 1927. First he allied with Trotsky's personal enemies to crush his rival, and then he moved against all who might challenge his ascendancy, including former allies. Stalin's final triumph came at the party congress of December 1927, which condemned all "deviation from the general party line" that he had formulated. The dictator and his followers were ready to launch the revolution from above, radically changing the lives of millions of people.

The Five-Year Plans

The party congress of 1927, which ratified Stalin's consolidation of power, marked the end of the NEP. The following year marked the beginning of the era of socialist five-year plans. The first of these plans had staggering economic objectives. In just five years, total industrial output was to increase by 250 percent, with heavy industry,

Without this support we would have been torn to pieces long ago. . . .

Why does the international proletariat support us? How did we merit this support? By the fact that we were the first to hurl ourselves into the battle against capitalism, we were the first to establish working-class state power, we were the first to begin building socialism. By the fact that we are engaged on a cause which, if successful, will transform the whole world and free the entire working class. But what is needed for success? The elimination of our backwardness, the development of a high Bolshevik tempo of construction. We must march forward in such a way that the working class of the whole world, looking at us, may say:

There you have my advanced detachment, my shock brigade, my working-class state power, my fatherland; they are engaged on their cause, *our* cause, and they are working well; let us support them against the capitalists and promote the cause of the world revolution. Must we not justify the hopes of the world's working class, must we not fulfill our obligations to them? Yes, we must if we do not want to utterly disgrace ourselves.

Such are our obligations, internal and international.

As you see, they dictate to us a Bolshevik tempo of development.

I will not say that we have accomplished nothing in regard to management of production during these years. In fact, we have accomplished a good deal. . . . But we could have accomplished still more if we had tried during this period really to master production, the technique of production, the financial and economic side of it. In ten years at most we must make good the distance that separates us from the advanced capitalist countries. We have all the "objective" possibilities for this. The only thing lacking is the ability to make proper use of these possibilities.

And that depends on us. *Only* on us! . . . If you are a factory manager — interfere in all the affairs of the factory, look into everything, let nothing escape you, learn and learn again. Bolsheviks must master technique. It is time Bolsheviks themselves became experts. . . .

It is said that it is hard to master technique. That is not true! There are no fortresses that Bolsheviks cannot capture. We have solved a number of most difficult problems. We have overthrown capitalism. We have assumed power.

We have built up a huge socialist industry. We have transferred the middle peasants on the path of socialism. We have already accomplished what is most important from the point of view of construction. What remains to be done is not so much: to study technique, to master science. And when we have done that we shall develop a tempo of which we dare not even dream at present. And we shall do it if we really want to.

EVALUATE THE EVIDENCE

1. What reasons does Stalin give to justify an unrelenting "Bolshevik" tempo of industrial and social change? In the light of history, which reason seems most convincing? Why?

2. Imagine that the year is 1931 and you are a Soviet student reading Stalin's speech. Would Stalin's determination inspire you, frighten you, or leave you cold? Why?

3. Some historians argue that Soviet socialism was a kind of utopianism, where the economy, the society, and even human beings could be completely remade and perfected. What utopian elements do you see in Stalin's declaration?

Source: Joseph Stalin, "No Slowdown in Tempo!" *Pravda*, February 5, 1931, excerpted from "Reading No. 14" in *Soviet Economic Development: Operation Outstrip, 1921–1965*, by Anatole G. Mazour.

the preferred sector, growing even faster. Agricultural production was slated to increase by 150 percent, and one-fifth of the peasants in the Soviet Union were to give up their private plots and join collective farms.

Stalin unleashed his "second revolution" for a variety of interrelated reasons. There were, first of all, ideological considerations. Stalin and his militant supporters were deeply committed to socialism as they understood it. They feared a gradual restoration of capitalism and wished to promote the working classes. Moreover, Communist leaders were eager to abolish the NEP's private traders, independent artisans, and property-owning peasants. Economic motivations were also important. A fragile economic recovery stalled in 1927 and 1928, and a new offensive seemed necessary to ensure industrial and agricultural growth. Such economic development would allow the U.S.S.R. to catch up with the West and so overcome traditional Russian "backwardness." (See "Evaluating the Evidence 27.1: Stalin Justifies the Five-Year Plan," above.)

The independent peasantry remained a major problem as well. For centuries the peasants had wanted to own the land, and finally they had it. Sooner or later, Stalinists reasoned, landowning peasants would embrace conservative capitalism and pose a threat to the regime. At the same time, the Communists — mainly urban dwellers — believed that the feared and despised "class enemy" in the villages could be squeezed to provide the enormous sums needed for all-out industrialization.

collectivization of agriculture The forcible consolidation of individual peasant farms into large state-controlled enterprises in the Soviet Union under Stalin.

To resolve these issues, in 1929 Stalin ordered the **collectivization of agriculture** — the forced consolidation of individual peasant farms into large, state-controlled enterprises that served as agricultural factories. Peasants across the Soviet Union were compelled to move off their small plots onto large state-run farms, where their tools, livestock, and produce would be held in common and central planners could control all work.

The increasingly repressive measures instituted by the state first focused on the **kulaks**, the class of well-off peasants who had benefited the most from the NEP. The kulaks were small in number, but propagandists cast them as the great enemy of progress. Stalin called for their "liquidation" and seizure of their property. Stripped of land and livestock, many starved or were deported to forced-labor camps for "re-education."

kulaks The better-off peasants who were stripped of land and livestock under Stalin and were generally not permitted to join collective farms; many of them starved or were deported to forced-labor camps for "re-education."

Forced collectivization led to disaster. Large numbers of peasants opposed to the change slaughtered their animals and burned their crops rather than turn them over to state commissars. Between 1929 and 1933 the number of horses, cattle, sheep, and goats in the Soviet Union fell by at least half. Nor were the state-controlled collective farms more productive. The output of grain barely increased over the first five-year plan, and collectivized agriculture was unable to make any substantial financial contribution to Soviet industrial development in the first five-year plan.

Collectivization in the fertile farmlands of the Ukraine was more rapid and violent than in other Soviet territories. The drive against peasants snowballed into an assault on Ukrainians in general, who had sought independence from Soviet rule after the First World War. Stalin and his associates viewed this peasant resistance as an expression of unacceptable anti-Soviet nationalism. In 1932, as collectivization and deportations continued, party leaders set levels of grain deliveries for the Ukrainian collectives at excessively high levels and refused to relax those quotas or allow food relief when Ukrainian Communist leaders reported that starvation was occurring. The result was a terrible man-made famine in Ukraine in 1932 and 1933, which claimed 3 to 3.5 million lives. (See "Evaluating the Evidence 27.2: Famine and Recovery on a Soviet Collective Farm," at right.)

Collectivization was a cruel but real victory for Stalinist ideologues. Though millions died, by the end of 1938 government representatives had moved 93 percent of peasant households onto collective farms, neutralizing them as a political threat. Nonetheless, peasant resistance had forced the supposedly all-powerful state to make modest concessions. Peasants secured the right to limit a family's labor on the state-run farms and to cultivate tiny family plots, which provided them with much of their food. In 1938 these family plots produced 22 percent of all Soviet agricultural produce on only 4 percent of all cultivated land.

The rapid industrialization mandated by the five-year plans was more successful — indeed, quite spectacular. A huge State Planning Commission, the "Gosplan," was created to set production goals and control deliveries of raw and finished materials.

Famine and Recovery on a Soviet Collective Farm

Fedor Belov describes daily life on a kolkhoz, or collective farm, in the Soviet Ukraine during the famine of the early 1930s and the recovery that followed. Belov, a former collective farm chairman, fled the Soviet Union for the West, where he published this critical account in 1955.

~

In these kolkhozes the great bulk of the land was held and worked communally, but each peasant household owned a house of some sort, a small plot of ground and perhaps some livestock. All the members of the kolkhoz were required to work on the kolkhoz a certain number of days each month; the rest of the time they were allowed to work on their own holdings. They derived their income partly from what they grew on their garden strips and partly from their work in the kolkhoz. . . .

By late 1932 more than 80 per cent of the peasant households in the raion [district] had been collectivized. . . . That year the peasants harvested a good crop and had hopes that the calculations would work out to their advantage and would help strengthen them economically. These hopes were in vain. The kolkhoz workers received only 200 grams of flour per labor day for the first half of the year; the remaining grain, including the seed fund, was taken by the government. The peasants were told that industrialization of the country, then in full swing, demanded grain and sacrifices from them.

That autumn the "red broom" [government agents who requisitioned grain] passed over the kolkhozes and the individual plots, sweeping the . . . "surpluses," [and] everything was collected. . . . As a result, famine, which was to become intense by the spring of 1933, already began to be felt in the fall of 1932.

The famine of 1932–1933 was the most terrible and destructive that the Ukrainian people have ever experienced. The peasants ate dogs, horses, rotten potatoes, the bark of trees, grass—anything they could find. Incidents of cannibalism were not uncommon. The people were like wild beasts, ready to devour one another. And no matter what they did, they went on dying, dying, dying. . . .

There was no one to gather the bumper crop of 1933, since the people who remained alive were too weak and exhausted. More than a hundred persons—office and factory workers from Leningrad—were sent to assist on the kolkhoz; two representatives of the Party arrived to help organize the harvesting. . . .

That summer (1933) the entire administration of the kolkhoz—the bookkeeper, the warehouseman, the manager of the flour mill, and even the chairman himself—were put on trial on charges of plundering the kolkhoz property and produce. All the accused were sentenced to terms of seven to ten years, and a new administration was elected. . . .

After 1934 a gradual improvement began in the economic life of the kolkhoz and its members. . . . In general, from the mid-1930s until 1941, the majority of kolkhoz members in the Ukraine lived relatively well.

EVALUATE THE EVIDENCE

1. How did party leaders respond to widespread starvation? Did government policy contribute to the intensity of the famine in 1932?
2. How did the organization of the collective farm express the basic ideas of communist ideology?

This was a complex and difficult task, and production bottlenecks and slowdowns often resulted. In addition, Stalinist planning favored heavy industry over the production of consumer goods, which led to shortages of basic necessities. Despite such problems, Soviet industry produced about four times as much in 1937 as it had in 1928. No other major country had ever achieved such rapid industrial growth.

Steel was the idol of the Stalinist age. The Soviet state needed heavy machinery for rapid development, and an industrial labor force was created almost overnight as peasant men and women began working in the huge steel mills built across the country. Independent trade unions lost most of their power. The government could assign workers to any job anywhere in the U.S.S.R., and an internal passport system ensured that individuals could move only with permission. When factory managers needed more hands, they called on their counterparts on the collective farms, who sent them millions of "unneeded" peasants over the years. Rapid industrial growth led to urban development: more than 25 million people, mostly peasants, migrated to cities during the 1930s.

The new workers often lived in deplorable conditions in hastily built industrial cities such as Magnitogorsk (Magnetic Mountain City) in the Ural Mountains. Yet they also experienced some benefits of upward mobility. In a letter published in the Magnitogorsk newspaper, an ordinary electrician described the opportunities created by rapid industrialization:

> In old tsarist Russia, we weren't even considered people. We couldn't dream about education, or getting a job in a state enterprise. And now I'm a citizen of the U.S.S.R. Like all citizens I have the right to a job, to education, to leisure. . . . In 1931, I came to Magnitogorsk. From a common laborer I have turned into a skilled worker. . . . I live in a country where one feels like living and learning. And if the enemy should attack this country, I will sacrifice my life in order to destroy the enemy and save my country.[1]

We should read such words with care, since they appeared in a state-censored publication. Yet the enthusiasm was at least partly authentic. The great industrialization drive of 1928 to 1937 was an awe-inspiring achievement, purchased at enormous sacrifice on the part of ordinary Soviet citizens.

Life and Culture in Soviet Society

Daily life was difficult in Stalin's Soviet Union. The lack of housing was a particularly serious problem. Millions were moving into the cities, but the government built few new apartments. A relatively lucky family received one room for all its members and shared both a kitchen and a toilet with others living on the same floor.

There were constant shortages of goods as well. Because consumption was reduced to pay for investment, there was little improvement in the average standard of living in the years before World War II. The average nonfarm wage purchased only about half as many goods in 1932 as it had in 1928. After 1932 real wages rose slowly, but by 1937 workers could still buy only about 60 percent of what they had bought in 1928 and less than they could purchase in 1913. Collectivized peasants experienced greater hardships.

Life was by no means hopeless, however. Idealism and ideology had real appeal for many Communists and ordinary citizens, who saw themselves heroically building the world's first socialist society while capitalism crumbled in a worldwide depression and degenerated into fascism in the West. This optimistic belief in the future of the Soviet Union attracted many disillusioned Westerners to communism in the 1930s. On a more practical level, Soviet workers received important social benefits, such as old-age pensions, free medical services, free education, and day-care centers for children. Unemployment was almost unknown.

Communism also opened possibilities for personal advancement. Rapid industrialization required massive numbers of skilled workers, engineers, and plant managers. In the 1930s the Stalinist state broke with the egalitarian policies of the 1920s and offered tremendous incentives to those who could serve its needs. It paid the mass of unskilled workers and collective farmers very low wages, but provided high salaries and special privileges to its growing technical and managerial elite. This group joined with the political and artistic elites in a new upper class, whose members grew rich and powerful.

The radical transformation of Soviet society had a profound impact on women's lives. Marxists had traditionally believed that both capitalism and middle-class husbands exploited women, and the Russian Revolution of 1917 immediately proclaimed complete equality for women. In the 1920s divorce and abortion were made easily available, and women were urged to work outside the home. After Stalin came to power, he reversed this trend. The government revoked many laws supporting women's emancipation in order to strengthen the traditional family and build up the state's population.

At the same time, women saw lasting changes in education. The Soviets opened higher education to women, who could now enter the ranks of the better-paid specialists in industry and science. Medicine practically became a woman's profession. By 1950, 75 percent of all doctors in the Soviet Union were female.

Alongside such advances, however, Soviet society demanded great sacrifices from women. The vast majority of women had to work outside the home. Wages were so low that it was almost impossible for a family or couple to live only on the husband's earnings. Peasant women continued to work on farms, and millions of women toiled in factories and in heavy construction, building dams, roads, and steel mills in summer heat and winter frost. Men continued to dominate the very best jobs. Finally, rapid change and economic hardship led to many broken families, creating further physical and emotional strains for women. In any event, the massive mobilization of women was a striking characteristic of the Soviet state.

Culture was thoroughly politicized for propaganda and indoctrination purposes. Party activists lectured workers in factories and peasants on collective farms, while newspapers, films, and radio broadcasts endlessly revealed capitalist plots and recounted socialist achievements. Whereas the 1920s had seen considerable modernist experimentation in art and theater, in the 1930s intellectuals were ordered by Stalin to become "engineers of human minds." Following the dictates of "Socialist Realism," they were instructed to exalt the lives of ordinary workers and glorify Russian nationalism. Russian history was rewritten so that early tsars such as Ivan the Terrible and Peter the Great became worthy forerunners of the greatest Russian leader of all — Stalin. Writers and artists who could effectively combine genuine creativity and political propaganda became the darlings of the regime.

Stalin seldom appeared in public, but his presence was everywhere — in portraits, statues, books, and quotations from his writings. Although the government persecuted those who practiced religion and turned churches into "museums of atheism," the state had both an earthly religion and a high priest — Marxism-Leninism and Joseph Stalin.

Stalinist Terror and the Great Purges

In the mid-1930s the great offensive to build socialism and a new society culminated in ruthless police terror and a massive purging of the Communist Party. First used by the Bolsheviks in the civil war to maintain their power, terror as state policy was revived in the collectivization drive against the peasants. Top members of the party and government publicly supported Stalin's initiatives, but there was some grumbling. At a small gathering in November 1932, even Stalin's wife complained bitterly about the misery of the people and the horrible famine in Ukraine. Stalin showered her with insults, and she committed suicide that night. In late 1934 Stalin's number-two man, Sergei Kirov, was mysteriously killed. Stalin—who probably ordered Kirov's murder—blamed the assassination on "Fascist agents" within the party. He used the incident to launch a reign of terror that purged the Communist Party of supposed traitors and solidified his own control.

Murderous repression picked up steam over the next two years. It culminated in the "great purge" of 1936 to 1938, a series of spectacular public show trials in which false evidence, often gathered using torture, was used to incriminate party administrators and Red Army leaders. In August 1936 sixteen "Old Bolsheviks"—prominent leaders who had been in the party since the Russian Revolution—confessed to all manner of contrived plots against Stalin. All were executed. In 1937 the secret police arrested a mass of lesser party officials and newer members, using torture to extract confessions and precipitating more show trials. In addition to the party faithful, union officials, managers, intellectuals, army officers, and countless ordinary citizens were accused of counter-revolutionary activities. At least 6 million people were arrested, and probably 1 to 2 million of these were executed or never returned from prisons and forced-labor camps.

Stalin's mass purges remain baffling, for most historians believe that the victims posed no threat and were innocent of their supposed crimes. Some scholars have argued that the terror was a defining characteristic of the totalitarian state, which must always fight real or imaginary enemies. Certainly the highly publicized purges sent a warning: no one was secure; everyone had to serve the party and its leader with redoubled devotion.

The long-standing interpretation that puts most of the blame for the purges on Stalin has been confirmed by recent research in newly opened Soviet archives. Apparently fearful of active resistance, Stalin and his allies used the harshest measures against their political enemies, real or imagined. Moreover, many in the general population shared such fears. Bombarded with ideology and political slogans, numerous people responded energetically to Stalin's directives. Investigations and trials snowballed into mass hysteria, resulting in a modern witch-hunt that claimed millions of victims. In this view of the 1930s, a deluded Stalin found large numbers of willing collaborators for crime as well as for achievement.[2]

The purges seriously weakened the Soviet Union in economic, intellectual, and military terms. But they left Stalin in command of a vast new state apparatus, staffed by the 1.5 million new party members enlisted to replace the purge victims. Thus more than half of all Communist Party members in 1941 had joined since the purges, and they experienced rapid social advance. Often the children of workers, they had usually studied in the new technical schools, and they soon proved capable of managing the government and large-scale production. Despite their human costs, the great purges thus brought substantial practical rewards to this new generation of committed Communists. They would serve Stalin effectively until his death in 1953, and they would govern the Soviet Union until the early 1980s.

Mussolini and Fascism in Italy

Mussolini's Fascist movement and his seizure of power in 1922 were important steps in the rise of dictatorships in Europe between the two world wars. Mussolini and his supporters were the first to call themselves "Fascists"—revolutionaries determined to create a new totalitarian state based on extreme nationalism and militarism.

FOCUS QUESTION
What kind of government did Mussolini establish in Italy?

The Seizure of Power

In the early twentieth century, Italy was a liberal constitutional monarchy that recognized the civil rights of Italians. On the eve of World War I, the parliament granted universal male suffrage, and Italy appeared to be moving toward democracy. But there were serious problems. Much of the Italian population was still poor, and many peasants were more attached to their villages and local interests than to the national state. Moreover, the papacy, many devout Catholics, conservatives, and landowners remained strongly opposed to liberal institutions, and relations between church and state were often tense. Class differences were also extreme, leading to the development of a powerful revolutionary socialist movement.

World War I worsened the political situation. To win support for the war effort, the Italian government had promised territorial expansion as well as social and land reform, which it could not deliver. Instead, the Versailles treaty denied Italy any territorial gains, and soaring unemployment and inflation after the war created mass hardship. In response, the Italian Socialist Party followed the Bolshevik example, and radical workers and peasants began occupying factories and seizing land in 1920. These actions mobilized the property-owning classes. Moreover, after the war the pope lifted his ban on participation by Catholics in Italian politics, and a strong Catholic party quickly emerged. Thus by 1921 revolutionary socialists, conservatives, Catholics, and property owners were all opposed—though for different reasons—to the liberal government.

Into these crosscurrents of unrest and fear stepped bullying, blustering Benito Mussolini (1883–1945). Mussolini began his political career before World War I as a Socialist Party leader and radical newspaper editor. In 1914 he had urged that Italy join the Allies, a stand for which he was expelled from the Socialist Party. Returning home after being wounded at the front in 1917, Mussolini began organizing bitter war veterans like himself into a band of Fascists—from the Italian word for "a union of forces."

At first Mussolini's program was a radical combination of nationalist and socialist demands. As such, it competed directly with the well-organized Socialist Party and failed to get off the ground. When Mussolini saw that his violent

Mussolini and Hitler   Italian dictator Benito Mussolini and Nazi leader Adolf Hitler, in front of the Shrine of Fallen Nazis, review a military parade passing by in their honor. In September 1937 Mussolini visited Hitler in Germany to cement the Rome-Berlin Axis alliance. (Istituto Nazionale Luce/Alinari via Getty Images)

verbal assaults on rival Socialists won him growing support from conservatives and the frightened middle classes, he shifted gears in 1920 and became a sworn enemy of socialism. Mussolini and his private militia of **Black Shirts** grew increasingly violent. Few people were killed, but Socialist Party newspapers, union halls, and local headquarters were destroyed, and the Black Shirts managed to push Socialists out of city governments in northern Italy.

Fascism soon became a mass movement, one which Mussolini claimed would help the little people against the established interests. In 1922, in the midst of chaos largely created by his Black Shirt militias, Mussolini stepped forward as the savior of order and property. Striking a conservative, anticommunist note in his speeches and gaining the support of army leaders, Mussolini demanded the resignation of the existing government. In October 1922 a band of armed Fascists marched on Rome to threaten the king and force him to appoint Mussolini prime minister of Italy. The threat worked. Victor Emmanuel III (r. 1900–1946) — who himself had no love for the liberal regime — asked Mussolini to take over the government and form a new cabinet. Thus, after widespread violence and a threat of armed uprising, Mussolini seized power using the legal framework of the Italian constitution.

The Regime in Action

Mussolini became prime minister in 1922, but moved cautiously in his first two years in office to establish control of the government. At first, he promised a "return to order" and consolidated his support among Italian elites. Fooled by Mussolini's apparent moderation, the Italian parliament passed a new electoral law that gave two-thirds of the representatives in the parliament to the party that won the most votes. This change allowed the Fascist Party and its allies to win an overwhelming majority in April 1924. Shortly thereafter, a group of Fascist extremists kidnapped and murdered the leading Socialist politician Giacomo Matteotti (JAHK-oh-moh mat-tee-OH-tee). Alarmed, a group of prominent parliamentary leaders demanded that Mussolini's armed squads be dissolved and all violence be banned.

Mussolini may not have ordered Matteotti's murder, but he took advantage of the resulting political crisis. Declaring his desire to "make the nation Fascist," he imposed a series of repressive measures. The government ruled by decree, abolished freedom of the press, and organized fixed elections. Mussolini arrested his political opponents, disbanded all independent labor unions, and put dedicated Fascists in control of Italy's schools. Mussolini trumpeted his goal in a famous slogan: "Everything in the state, nothing outside the state, nothing against the state." By the end of 1926 Italy was a one-party dictatorship under Mussolini's unquestioned leadership.

Mussolini's Fascist Party drew support from broad sectors of the population, in large part because he was willing to compromise with the traditional elites that controlled the army, the economy, and the state. He left big business to regulate itself, and there was no land reform. Mussolini also drew increasing support from the Catholic Church. In the **Lateran Agreement** of 1929, he recognized the Vatican as an independent state, and he agreed to give the church significant financial support in return for the pope's support. Because he was forced to compromise with these conservative elites, Mussolini never established complete totalitarian control.

Mussolini's government nonetheless proceeded with attempts to bring fascism to Italy. The state engineered popular consent by staging massive rallies and sporting events, creating Fascist youth and women's movements, and providing new welfare

Black Shirts Mussolini's private militia that destroyed socialist newspapers, union halls, and Socialist Party headquarters, eventually pushing Socialists out of the city governments of northern Italy.

Lateran Agreement A 1929 agreement that recognized the Vatican as an independent state, with Mussolini agreeing to give the church heavy financial support in return for public support from the pope.

benefits. Newspapers, radio, and film promoted a "cult of the Duce" (leader), portraying Mussolini as a powerful strongman who embodied the best qualities of the Italian people. Like other Fascist regimes, his government was vehemently opposed to liberal feminism and promoted traditional gender roles. Mussolini also gained support by manipulating popular pride in the grand history of the ancient Roman Empire—as one propagandist put it, "Fascism, in its entirety, is the resurrection of Roman-ness."[3]

Mussolini matched his aggressive rhetoric with military action: Italian armies invaded the African nation of Ethiopia in October 1935. After surprising setbacks at the hands of the poorly armed Ethiopian army, the Italians won in 1936, and Mussolini could proudly declare that Italy again had its empire. Though it shocked international opinion, the war resulted in close ties between Italy and Nazi Germany. After a visit to Berlin in the fall of 1937, the Italian dictator pledged support for Hitler and promised that Italy and Germany would "march together right to the end."[4]

Deeply influenced by Hitler's example (see below), Mussolini's government passed a series of anti-Jewish racial laws in 1938. Though the laws were unpopular, Jews were forced out of public schools and dismissed from professional careers. Nevertheless, extreme anti-Semitic persecution did not occur in Italy until late in World War II, when Italy was under Nazi control. Though Mussolini's repressive tactics were never as ruthless as those in Nazi Germany, his government did much to turn Italy into a totalitarian police state.

→ Italian campaigns, 1935–1936

Italy's Ethiopian Campaign, 1935–1936

Hitler and Nazism in Germany

The most frightening dictatorship developed in Nazi Germany. National Socialism (or Nazism) shared some characteristics with Italian fascism, but Nazism was far more interventionist. Under Hitler, the Nazi dictatorship smashed or took over most independent organizations, established firm control over the German state and society, and violently persecuted the Jewish population and non-German peoples. Truly totalitarian in aspiration, Nazi Germany acted with a dynamism, based on racial aggression and territorial expansion, that led to history's most destructive war.

FOCUS QUESTION
What policies did Nazi Germany pursue, and how did they lead to World War II?

The Roots of National Socialism

National Socialism grew out of many complex developments, of which the most influential were nationalism and racism. These two ideas captured the mind of the young Adolf Hitler (1889–1945), and he dominated Nazism until the end of World War II.

The son of an Austrian customs official, Hitler spent his childhood in small towns in Austria. A mediocre student, Hitler dropped out of high school at age fourteen. He then moved to Vienna, where he was exposed to extreme Austro-German nationalists who believed Germans to be a superior people and the natural rulers of central Europe. They advocated the union of Austria with Germany and the violent expulsion of "inferior" peoples as the means of maintaining German domination of the Austro-Hungarian Empire.

In Vienna, Hitler developed an unshakable belief in the crudest distortions of Social Darwinism (see Chapter 24), the superiority of Germanic races, and the inevitability of racial conflict. Exposure to poor eastern European Jews contributed to his

National Socialism A movement and political party driven by extreme nationalism and racism, led by Adolf Hitler; its adherents ruled Germany from 1933 to 1945 and forced Europe into World War II.

anti-Semitic prejudice. Jews, Hitler now claimed, directed an international conspiracy of finance capitalism and Marxist socialism against German culture, German unity, and the German people.

Hitler was not alone. Racist anti-Semitism became wildly popular on the far-right wing of European politics in the decades surrounding the First World War. Such irrational beliefs, rooted in centuries of Christian anti-Semitism, were given pseudo-scientific legitimacy by nineteenth-century developments in biology and eugenics. These ideas came to define Hitler's worldview and would play an immense role in the ideology and actions of National Socialism.

Hitler greeted the outbreak of the First World War as a salvation. The struggle and discipline of war gave life meaning, and Hitler served bravely as a dispatch carrier on the western front. Germany's defeat shattered his world. Convinced that Jews and Marxists had "stabbed Germany in the back," he vowed to fight on.

In late 1919 Hitler joined a tiny extremist group in Munich called the German Workers' Party. In addition to denouncing Jews, Marxists, and democrats, the party promised a uniquely German National Socialism that would abolish the injustices of capitalism and create a mighty "people's community." By 1921 Hitler had gained control of this small but growing party, which had been renamed the National Socialist German Workers' Party, or Nazis for short. Hitler became a master of mass propaganda and political showmanship. In wild, histrionic speeches, he worked his audience into a frenzy with demagogic attacks on the Versailles treaty, Jews, war profiteers, and the Weimar Republic.

In late 1923 that republic seemed on the verge of collapse, and Hitler, inspired by Mussolini's recent victory, organized an armed uprising in Munich—the so-called Beer Hall Putsch. Despite the failure of the poorly planned coup and Hitler's arrest, National Socialism had been born.

Hitler's Road to Power

At his trial, Hitler gained enormous publicity by denouncing the Weimar Republic. He used his brief prison term to dictate his book *Mein Kampf* (My Struggle), where he laid out his basic ideas on "racial purification" and territorial expansion that would define National Socialism.

In *Mein Kampf*, Hitler claimed that Germans were a "master race" that needed to defend its "pure blood" from groups he labeled "racial degenerates," including Jews, Slavs, and others. The German race was destined to triumph and grow, and, according to Hitler, it needed *Lebensraum* (living space). This space could be found to Germany's east, which Hitler claimed was inhabited by the "subhuman" Slavs and Jews. The future dictator outlined a sweeping vision of war and conquest in which the German master race would colonize east and central Europe and ultimately replace the "subhumans" living there. He championed the idea of the leader-dictator, or *Führer* (FYOUR-uhr), whose unlimited power would embody the people's will and lead the German nation to victory. These ideas would ultimately propel the world into the Second World War.

In the years of relative prosperity and stability between 1924 and 1929, Hitler built up the Nazi Party. From the failed beer hall revolt, he had concluded that he had to come to power through electoral competition rather than armed rebellion. To appeal to middle-class voters, Hitler de-emphasized the anticapitalist elements of National Socialism and vowed to fight communism. The Nazis still remained a small splinter group in 1928, when they received only 2.6 percent of the vote in the general elections and only twelve seats in the Reichstag, the German parliament. There the Nazi deputies pursued the legal strategy of using democracy to destroy democracy.

The Great Depression of 1929 brought the ascent of National Socialism. Now Hitler promised German voters economic as well as political salvation. His appeals for "national rebirth" appealed to a broad spectrum of voters, including middle- and lower-class groups — small business owners, officeworkers, artisans, peasants, and skilled workers. Seized by panic as bankruptcies increased, unemployment soared, and the Communists made dramatic election gains, voters deserted conservative and moderate parties for the Nazis. In the election of 1930 the Nazis won 6.5 million votes and 107 seats, and in July 1932 they gained 14.5 million votes — 38 percent of the total. They were now the largest party in the Reichstag.

The breakdown of democratic government helped the Nazis seize power. Chancellor Heinrich Brüning (BROU-nihng) tried to overcome the economic crisis by cutting back government spending and ruthlessly forcing down prices and wages. His conservative policies intensified Germany's economic collapse and convinced many voters that the country's republican leaders were stupid and corrupt, adding to Hitler's appeal.

Division on the left also contributed to Nazi success. Even though the two left-wing parties together outnumbered the Nazis in the Reichstag, the Communists refused to cooperate with the Social Democrats. Failing to resolve their differences, these parties could not mount an effective opposition to the Nazi takeover.

Finally, Hitler excelled in the dirty backroom politics of the decaying Weimar Republic. In 1932 Hitler cleverly gained the support of the conservative politicians in power, who thought they could use Hitler for their own advantage, to resolve the political crisis, but also to clamp down on leftists. They accepted Hitler's demand to be appointed chancellor in a coalition government, reasoning that he could be used and controlled. On January 30, 1933, Adolf Hitler, leader of the most popular political party in Germany, was appointed chancellor by President Hindenburg.

State and Society in Nazi Germany

Hitler moved rapidly and skillfully to establish an unshakable dictatorship that would pursue the Nazi program of racial segregation and spatial expansion. First, Hitler and the Nazi Party worked to consolidate their power. To maintain appearances, Hitler called for new elections. In February 1933, in the midst of an electoral campaign plagued by violence — much of it caused by Nazi toughs — the Reichstag building was partly destroyed by fire. Hitler blamed the Communists and convinced Hindenburg to sign emergency acts that abolished freedom of speech and assembly as well as most personal liberties.

The façade of democratic government was soon torn asunder. When the Nazis won only 44 percent of the vote in the elections, Hitler outlawed the Communist Party and arrested its parliamentary representatives. Then on March 23, 1933, the Nazis pushed through the Reichstag the **Enabling Act**, which gave Hitler dictatorial power for four years. The Nazis' deceitful stress on legality, coupled with divide-and-conquer techniques, disarmed the opposition until it was too late for effective resistance.

Germany became a one-party Nazi state. Elections were farces. The new regime took over the government bureaucracy intact, installing Nazis in top positions. At the same time, it created a series of overlapping Nazi Party organizations responsible solely to Hitler. As recent research has shown, the resulting system of dual government was

Enabling Act An act pushed through the Reichstag by the Nazis that gave Hitler absolute dictatorial power for four years.

riddled with rivalries, contradictions, and inefficiencies. The Nazi state was often disorganized and lacked the all-encompassing unity that its propagandists claimed. Yet this fractured system suited Hitler and his purposes. The lack of unity encouraged competition among state personnel, who worked to outdo each other to fulfill Hitler's vaguely expressed goals. The Führer thus played the established bureaucracy against his personal party government and maintained dictatorial control.

Once the Nazis were firmly in command, Hitler and the party turned their attention to constructing a National Socialist society defined by national unity and racial exclusion. First they eliminated political enemies. Communists, Social Democrats, and trade-union leaders were forced out of their jobs or arrested and taken to hastily built concentration camps. The Nazis outlawed strikes and abolished independent labor unions, which were replaced by the Nazi-controlled German Labor Front.

Hitler then purged the Nazi Party itself of its more extremist elements. The Nazi storm troopers (the SA), the quasi-military band of 3 million toughs in brown shirts who had fought Communists and beaten up Jews before the Nazis took power, now expected top positions in the army. Some SA radicals even talked of a "second revolution" that would create equality among all Germans by sweeping away capitalism. Now that he was in power, however, Hitler was eager to win the support of the traditional military and maintain social order. He decided that the leadership of the SA had to be eliminated. On the night of June 30, 1934, Hitler's elite personal guard—the SS—arrested and executed about one hundred SA leaders and other political enemies. Afterward, the SS grew rapidly. Under its methodical, ruthless leader Heinrich Himmler (1900–1945), the SS took over the political police and the concentration camp system.

The Nazis instituted a policy called "coordination," which forced existing institutions to conform to National Socialist ideology. Professionals—doctors and lawyers, teachers and engineers—saw their previously independent organizations swallowed up by Nazi associations. Charity and civic organizations were also put under Nazi control, and universities, publishers, and writers were quickly brought into line. Democratic, socialist, and Jewish literature was put on ever-growing blacklists. Passionate students and radicalized professors burned forbidden books in public squares. Modern art and architecture—which the Nazis considered "degenerate"—were prohibited. Life became violently anti-intellectual. By 1934 a brutal dictatorship characterized by frightening dynamism and obedience to Hitler was largely in place.

Acting on its vision of racial eugenics, the party began a many-faceted campaign against those deemed incapable of making positive biological contributions to the "master race." The Nazis persecuted a number of groups. Jews headed the list, but Slavic peoples, Sinti and Roma, homosexuals, and Jehovah's Witnesses were also considered social "deviants." Nazi bureaucrats furthermore invented two categories targeted for "racial hygiene": the "hereditarily ill" and "asocials." The "hereditarily ill" included people with chronic mental or physical disabilities, such as schizophrenics, manic depressives, epileptics, and people suffering from what Nazi physicians called "congenital feeblemindedness." The catchall category of "asocials" included common criminals, alcoholics, prostitutes, the "work shy" (or chronically unemployed), beggars and vagrants, and others on the margins of German society.

Nazi leaders used a variety of measures to convince Germans that "racial hygiene" was justified and necessary. In what some historians term the Nazi "racial state," barbarism and race hatred were institutionalized with the force of science and law.[5] New university academies, such as the German Society for Racial Research, wrote studies that measured and defined racial differences; prejudice was thus presented in the guise of enlightened medical science, a means for creating a strong national race. Schoolroom lessons, articles in the popular press, feature films, traveling exhibitions, and even children's board games touted the benefits of racist eugenic practice.

The results were monstrous, a barbaric violation of the ethical norms most of us take for granted. Thousands of innocent people faced social ostracism and then brutal repression, simply because the Nazis deemed them racial outsiders. Convinced by their own racial ideology, Nazi authorities denied outsiders welfare benefits and put them out of work, forced people with disabilities into special hospitals where they could be segregated from "healthy" Germans, and imprisoned homosexuals and "asocials" in concentration camps for "re-education." A series of sterilization laws exemplified the ethical breakdown. Nazi medical workers forcibly sterilized some four hundred thousand German citizens, mainly "asocials" or the "hereditarily ill," so their "degenerate blood" would not pollute the "Aryan race." The eugenics campaign reached a crescendo in 1938, when the authorities initiated a coldhearted euthanasia program — dubbed "mercy killing" by Nazi physicians and administrators — and systematically murdered about seventy thousand Germans with chronic disabilities (see page 931).

From the beginning, German Jews were a special target of Nazi racial persecution. Anti-Jewish propaganda was ever present in Nazi Germany. Ugly posters of stereotypical Jews; feature films and documentaries about the Jewish "menace"; signs in shop windows, banks, and parks forbidding Jewish entry — all and more were used to stigmatize German Jews. Such means were backed up with harsh legal oppression. Shortly after they took power, Nazi authorities issued the Professional Civil Service Restoration Act, which banned Jews from working in government jobs; by 1934 many Jewish lawyers, doctors, professors, civil servants, and musicians had been summarily dismissed from their jobs. In 1935 the infamous Nuremberg Laws classified as Jewish anyone having three or more Jewish grandparents, outlawed marriage and sexual relations between Jews and those defined as German, and deprived Jews of all rights of citizenship. Conversion to Christianity and abandonment of the Jewish faith made no difference. For the vast majority of German citizens not targeted by such laws, the creation of a demonized outsider group may well have contributed to feelings of national unity and support for the Hitler regime.

In late 1938 the assault on the Jews accelerated. During a well-organized wave of violence known as Kristallnacht (or the Night of Broken Glass pogrom), Nazi gangs smashed windows and looted over 7,000 Jewish-owned shops, destroyed many homes, burned down over 200 synagogues, and killed dozens of Jews. German Jews were then rounded up and made to pay for the damage. By 1939 some 300,000 of Germany's 500,000 Jews had emigrated, sacrificing almost all their property in order to escape persecution. Some Germans privately opposed these outrages, but most went along or looked the other way. Historians still debate the degree to which this lack of opposition expressed popular anti-Semitism. In any case, it revealed widespread support for Hitler's government.

Popular Support for National Socialism

Why did millions of ordinary Germans back a brutally repressive, racist regime? A combination of coercion and reward enlisted popular support for the racial state. Using the secret police and the growing concentration camp system in a reign of ruthless terror, the regime persecuted its political and "racial" enemies. Yet for the large majority of ordinary German citizens who were not Jews, Communists, or members of other targeted groups, Hitler's government brought new opportunities. The German "master race" clearly benefited from Nazi policies and programs.

Hitler had promised the masses economic recovery, and he delivered. The Nazi state launched a large public works program to help pull Germany out of the depression. Work began on superhighways, offices, gigantic sports stadiums, and public housing, which created jobs and instilled pride in national recovery. By 1938 unemployment had fallen to 2 percent, and there was a shortage of workers. Between 1932 and 1938 the standard of living for the average worker increased moderately. Business profits rose sharply.

The persecution of Jews brought substantial benefits to ordinary Germans as well. As Jews were forced out of their jobs and compelled to sell their homes and businesses, Germans stepped in to take their place in a process known as Aryanization (named after the "Aryan master race" prized by the Nazis for their supposedly pure German blood). For millions of so-called Aryans, a rising standard of living—at whatever ethical price—was tangible evidence that Nazi promises were more than show and propaganda.

Economic recovery was accompanied by a wave of social and cultural innovation intended to construct what Nazi propagandists called the *Volksgemeinschaft*—a "people's community" for racially pure Germans. The party set up mass organizations to spread Nazi ideology and enlist volunteers for the Nazi cause. Millions of Germans joined the Hitler Youth, the League of German Women, and the German Labor Front. Mass rallies, such as annual May Day celebrations and Nazi Party conventions in Nuremberg, brought together thousands of participants. Glowing reports on such events in the Nazi-controlled press brought the message home to millions more.

As the economy recovered, the government proudly touted a glittering array of inexpensive and enticing people's products. Items such as the Volkswagen (the "People's Car") were intended to link individuals' desire for consumer goods to the collective ideology of the "people's community." Though such programs faltered as the state increasingly focused on rearmament for the approaching war, they suggested to all that the regime was working hard to improve German living standards.

Women played a special role in the Nazi state. Promising to "liberate women from women's liberation," Nazi ideologues championed a return to traditional family values. They outlawed abortion, discouraged women from holding jobs or obtaining higher education, and glorified domesticity and motherhood. Women were cast as protectors of the hearth and home and were instructed to raise young boys and girls in accordance with Nazi ideals. In the later 1930s, facing labor shortages, the Nazis had to reluctantly reverse course and encourage women to enter the labor force. Whatever the employment situation, the millions of women enrolled in Nazi mass organizations, which organized charity drives and other social programs, experienced a sense of freedom and community in these public activities.

Few historians today believe that Hitler and the Nazis brought about a real social revolution, as an earlier generation of scholars thought. Yet Hitler's rule promoted economic growth, and Nazi propagandists continually played up the supposed accomplishments of the regime. The vision of a "people's community," national pride in recovery, and feelings of belonging created by acts of racial exclusion led many Germans to support the regime. Hitler himself remained popular with broad sections of the population well into the war.

Not all Germans supported Hitler, however, and a number of groups actively resisted him after 1933. But opponents of the Nazis were never unified, which helps explain their lack of success. Furthermore, the regime harshly clamped down on dissidents: tens of thousands of political enemies were imprisoned, and thousands were executed. After Communists and socialists were smashed by the SS system, a second group of opponents arose in the Catholic and Protestant churches. Their efforts, however, were directed primarily at preserving religious life, not at overthrowing Hitler. In 1938 and again during the war, a few high-ranking army officers, who feared the consequences of Hitler's reckless aggression, plotted against him, but their plans were unsuccessful.

Aggression and Appeasement

The nazification of German society fulfilled only part of the Nazi agenda. While building the "people's community," the regime aggressively pursued policies meant to achieve territorial expansion for the supposedly superior German race. At first, Hitler carefully camouflaged his expansionist goals. Germany was still militarily weak, and the Nazi leader proclaimed his peaceful intentions. Germany's withdrawal from the League of Nations in October 1933 nonetheless indicated that Gustav Stresemann's policy of peaceful cooperation was dead (see Chapter 26). Then in March 1935 Hitler declared that Germany would no longer abide by the disarmament clauses of the Treaty of Versailles. He established a military draft and began to build up the German army. France and Great Britain protested strongly and warned against future aggressive actions.

Any hope of a united front against Hitler quickly collapsed. Britain adopted a policy of **appeasement**, granting Hitler what he demanded to avoid war. British appeasement, which practically dictated French policy, was motivated in large part by the pacifism of a population still horrified by the memory of the First World War. As in Germany, many powerful conservatives in Britain underestimated Hitler. They believed that Soviet communism was the real danger and that Hitler could be used to stop it. Such strong anticommunist feelings made an alliance between the Western powers and Stalin against Hitler highly unlikely.

When Hitler suddenly marched his armies into the demilitarized Rhineland in March 1936, brazenly violating the treaties of Versailles and Locarno (Map 27.2), Britain refused to act. France could do little without British support. Emboldened, Hitler moved ever more aggressively, enlisting powerful allies in international affairs. Italy and Germany established the so-called Rome-Berlin Axis in 1936. Japan, also under the rule of a Fascist dictatorship, joined the Axis alliance that same year.

At the same time, Germany and Italy intervened in the Spanish Civil War (1936–1939), where their military aid helped General

appeasement The British policy toward Germany prior to World War II that aimed at granting Hitler's territorial demands, including western Czechoslovakia, in order to avoid war.

A Republican Militia in the Spanish Civil War
The enthusiasm of the republican forces of the democratically elected government of Spain could not overcome the rebel Fascist armies of Francisco Franco during the Spanish Civil War (1936–1939). Once in power, Franco ruled over a repressive dictatorial state in Spain until his death in 1975. Women combatants like the *milicianas* pictured here, carrying rifles with their male comrades, made a significant contribution to the republican cause. (Universal History Archive/Getty Images)

MAP 27.2 The Growth of Nazi Germany, 1933–1939   Until March 1939 Hitler's conquests brought ethnic Germans into the Nazi state; then he turned on the Slavic and Jewish peoples he had always hated. He stripped Czechoslovakia of its independence and prepared to attack Poland in September 1939.

Francisco Franco's revolutionary Fascist movement defeat the democratically elected republican government. Republican Spain's only official aid in the fight against Franco came from the Soviet Union, for public opinion in Britain and especially in France was hopelessly divided on whether to intervene.

In late 1937 Hitler moved forward with plans to seize Austria and Czechoslovakia as the first step in his long-contemplated drive for living space in the east. By threatening Austria with invasion, Hitler forced the Austrian chancellor to put local Nazis in control of the government in March 1938. The next day, in the Anschluss (annexation), German armies moved in unopposed, and Austria became part of Greater Germany (see Map 27.2).

Simultaneously, Hitler demanded that territories inhabited mostly by ethnic Germans in western Czechoslovakia — the Sudetenland — be ceded to Nazi Germany. Though democratic Czechoslovakia was allied with France and the Soviet Union and prepared to defend itself, appeasement triumphed again. In negotiations British prime minister Arthur Neville Chamberlain and the French agreed with Hitler that Germany should immediately take over the Sudetenland. Returning to London from the Munich Conference in September 1938, Chamberlain told cheering crowds that he had secured "peace with honor . . . peace for our time." Sold out by the Western powers, Czechoslovakia gave in.

Chamberlain's peace was short-lived. In March 1939 Hitler's armies invaded and occupied the rest of Czechoslovakia. The effect on Western public opinion was electrifying. This time, there was no possible rationale of self-determination for Nazi aggression, since Hitler was seizing ethnic Czechs and Slovaks — not Germans — as captive peoples. When Hitler next used the question of German minorities in Danzig as a pretext to confront Poland, a suddenly militant Chamberlain declared that Britain and France would fight if Hitler attacked his eastern neighbor. Hitler did not take these warnings seriously.

In August 1939, in an about-face that stunned the world, sworn enemies Hitler and Stalin signed a nonaggression pact that paved the road to war. Each dictator promised to remain neutral if the other became involved in open hostilities. An attached secret protocol ruthlessly divided Poland, the Baltic nations, Finland, and a part of Romania into German and Soviet spheres of influence. Stalin agreed to the pact because he remained distrustful of Western intentions and because Hitler offered immediate territorial gain.

For Hitler, everything was now set. On September 1, 1939, German armies and warplanes smashed into Poland from three sides. Two days later, Britain and France, finally true to their word, declared war on Germany. The Second World War had begun.

The Second World War

Nazi Germany's unlimited ambition unleashed an apocalyptic cataclysm. Hitler's armies quickly conquered much of western and eastern Europe, establishing a vast empire of expropriation, destruction, and death. At the same time, Japanese armies overran much of Southeast Asia and created their own racial empire. This reckless aggression brought together a coalition of unlikely but powerful allies determined to halt the advance of fascism: Britain, the United States, and the Soviet Union. After years of slaughter that decimated much of Europe and East Asia, this "Grand Alliance" decisively defeated the Axis powers.

FOCUS QUESTION

How did Germany and Japan conquer enormous empires during World War II, and how did the Allies defeat them?

German Victories in Europe

Using planes, tanks, and trucks in the first example of a blitzkrieg, or "lightning war," Hitler's armies crushed Poland in four weeks. While the Soviet Union quickly took its part of the booty — the eastern half of Poland and the independent Baltic states of Lithuania, Estonia, and Latvia — French and British armies prepared their defenses in the west.

In spring 1940 the Nazi lightning war struck again. After Germany occupied Denmark, Norway, and Holland, motorized columns broke into France through southern Belgium, split the Franco-British forces, and trapped the entire British army on the French beaches of Dunkirk. By heroic efforts, the British withdrew their troops—although equipment could not be saved. Soon after, France was taken by the Nazis. By July 1940 Hitler ruled practically all of continental Europe. Italy was a German ally. Romania, Hungary, and Bulgaria joined the Axis powers, and the Soviet Union, Spain, and Sweden were friendly neutrals. Only the Balkans and Britain, the nation led by the uncompromising Winston Churchill (1874–1965), remained unconquered.

To prepare for an amphibious invasion of Britain, Germany sought to gain control of the air. In the Battle of Britain, which began in July 1940, up to a thousand German planes a day attacked British airfields and key factories, dueling with British defenders high in the skies. Losses were heavy on both sides. In September 1940 Hitler angrily turned from military objectives to indiscriminate bombing of British cities in an attempt to break British morale. British aircraft factories increased production, and the heavily bombed people of London defiantly dug in. By October Britain was beating Germany three to one in the air war, and the Battle of Britain was over. (See "Evaluating the Evidence 27.3: Everyday Life in the London Blitz," at right.) Stymied there, the Nazi war machine invaded and occupied Greece and the Balkans.

Hitler now allowed his lifetime obsession of creating a vast eastern European empire ruled by the master race to dictate policy. In June 1941 he broke his pact with Stalin and launched German armies into the Soviet Union along a vast front (Map 27.3). By October most of Ukraine had been conquered, Leningrad was practically surrounded, and Moscow was besieged. But the Soviets did not collapse, and when a severe winter struck German armies outfitted only in summer uniforms, the invaders retreated. Nevertheless, Hitler and his allies ruled over a vast European empire stretching from eastern Europe to the English Channel. Hitler, the Nazi leadership, and the loyal German army were positioned to greatly accelerate construction of their so-called New Order in Europe.

New Order Hitler's program based on racial imperialism, which gave preferential treatment to the "Nordic" peoples; the French, an "inferior" Latin people, occupied a middle position; and Slavs and Jews were treated harshly as "subhumans."

Europe Under Nazi Occupation

Hitler's New Order was based firmly on the guiding principle of National Socialism: racial imperialism. Occupied peoples were treated according to their place in the Nazi racial hierarchy. All were subject to harsh policies dedicated to ethnic cleansing and the plunder of resources for the Nazi war effort.

Within this **New Order**, the so-called Nordic peoples—the Dutch, Danes, and Norwegians—received preferential treatment, for the Germans believed them related to the Aryan master race. In Holland, Denmark, and Norway, the Nazis established puppet governments of various kinds. Though many people hated the conquerors, the Nazis found willing collaborators who ruled in accord with German needs. France was divided into two parts. The German army occupied the north, including Paris. The southeast remained nominally independent. There the aging First World War general Marshal Henri-Philippe Pétain formed a new French government—the Vichy (VIH-shee) regime—that adopted many aspects of National Socialist ideology and willingly placed French Jews in the hands of the Nazis.

Vichy France, 1940

Everyday Life in the London Blitz

In 1941 Hilde Marchant, a young English journalist, published an account of her experiences in the streets of London during the Battle of Britain the year before. Here she speaks of Mr. Smith, an air raid warden. Mr. Smith, she reported, was neither strong nor brave, but he nonetheless learned to effectively manage the destruction of the blitz.

But perhaps the greatest battle of all in those early days was a personal one. Smith had to adjust his warm, sentimental, domestic nature to the grim agonising sights of the night. He loves humanity, in all its virtue and vice, and it was a shock for him to see the pain and distortion of life around him. Yet he corseted his sentimentality with the months of training he had had and became the handyman of the blitz. . . .

Smith began to tell me about that first night, the night he fell in the road and broke his glasses. A bomb just a few yards from him had hit a block of buildings, and there were eleven people trapped on the ground floor.

"It was a noisy night, but every time we bent low we could hear the groans of the people underneath. I thought I'd be sick. I held a man's hand that was clear. It took us nine hours to get him out. An hour later we got a woman out. They were in a bad way. There was dirt and blood caked on the woman's face. We wiped it off. She must have been about thirty. They both died. We were all a bit quiet. It was the first we'd seen. We couldn't have got them out quicker—we'd torn our hands up dragging the stones away. But it was awful seeing them take the last gasps as they lifted them into the ambulance."

Smith was quiet, even retelling the story, and one of the [other wardens] said:

"It was the first, you see."

Then Smith told me about the next night—the night when he was really "blooded." Incendiaries had started a fire in one of the smaller streets and high explosives began to fall into the fire. Smith approached the houses from the back and got through to the kitchen of one of the houses.

"I fell over something. I picked it up and it was a leg. I stood there with it in my hand wondering what I should do with it. I knew it was a woman's leg. I put it down and went to look for the ambulance. They had got the fire out at the front. The ambulance men brought a stretcher and I showed them the leg. Then we looked farther in and there were pieces all over. All they said was they didn't need a stretcher."

As Smith sat thinking, his whole body seemed to pause. . . .

"You see, how we look at things now is like this. If they're alive you work like the devil to keep 'em alive and get 'em out. . . . If they're dead there's nothing we can do. Getting upset hampers your work."

So Smith learned not to over-indulge his sensitivity on seeing death, or torn limb and flesh. His job was with the spark of life that survived.

EVALUATE THE EVIDENCE

1. Does Marchant's story have a political message for the British people?
2. What does this passage reveal about the resilience of human beings in times of war?

Source: James M. Brophy et al., *Perspectives from the Past: Primary Sources in Western Civilizations*, 4th ed., vol. 2 (New York: W. W. Norton, 2009), pp. 766–767.

In all conquered territories, the Nazis used a variety of techniques to enrich Germany and support the war effort. Occupied nations were forced to pay for the costs of the war and for the occupation itself, and the price was high. Nazi administrators stole goods and money from local Jews, set currency exchanges at favorable rates, and forced occupied peoples to accept worthless wartime scrip. Soldiers were encouraged not only to steal but also to purchase goods at cheap exchange rates and send them home. A flood of plunder thus reached Germany, helping maintain high living standards and preserving home-front morale well into the war. Nazi victory, furthermore, placed national Jewish populations across Europe under German control, allowing the mass murder of Europe's Jews.

MAP 27.3 World War II in Europe and Africa, 1939–1945   This map shows the extent of Hitler's empire before the Battle of Stalingrad in late 1942 and the subsequent advances of the Allies until Germany surrendered on May 8, 1945. Compare this map with Map 27.2 on page 926 to trace the rise and fall of the Nazi empire over time.

In central and eastern Europe, the war and German rule were far more ruthless and deadly than in the west. From the start, the Nazi leadership had cast the war in the east as one of annihilation. The Nazis now set out to build a vast colonial empire where Jews would be exterminated and Poles, Ukrainians, and Russians would be enslaved and forced to die out. According to the plans, ethnic German peasants would resettle the resulting abandoned lands, a "mass settlement space." In pursuit of such goals, large parts of western Poland were incorporated into Germany. Another part of Poland was placed under the rule of a merciless civilian administration.

With the support of military commanders, German policemen, and bureaucrats in the occupied territories, Nazi administrators and Himmler's elite SS corps now implemented a program of destruction and annihilation to create a "mass settlement space" for racially pure Germans. Across the east, the Nazi armies destroyed cities and factories, stole crops and farm animals, and subjected conquered peoples to forced starvation and mass murder. Nazi occupation in the east destroyed the lives of millions.[6]

In response to such atrocities, small but determined underground resistance groups fought back. They were hardly unified. Communists and socialists often disagreed with more centrist or nationalist groups on long-term goals and short-term tactics. In Yugoslavia, for example, Communist and royalist military resistance groups attacked the Germans, but also each other. The resistance nonetheless presented a real challenge to the Nazi New Order. Poland, under German occupation longer than any other nation, had the most determined and well-organized resistance. The Nazis had closed all Polish universities and outlawed national newspapers, but the Poles organized secret classes and maintained a thriving underground press. Underground members of the Polish Home Army, led by the government in exile in London, passed intelligence about German operations to the Allies and committed sabotage. The famous French resistance undertook similar actions, as did groups in Italy, Greece, Russia, and the Netherlands.

The German response was swift and deadly. The Nazi army and the SS tortured captured resistance members and executed hostages in reprisal for attacks. Responding to actions undertaken by resistance groups, the German army murdered the male populations of Lidice (Czechoslovakia) and Oradour (France) and leveled the entire towns, brutal examples of Nazi barbarism in pursuit of a racial New Order. Despite reprisals, Nazi occupiers were never able to eradicate popular resistance to their rule.

Nazi Occupation of Poland and East-Central Europe, 1939–1942

The Holocaust

The ultimate abomination of Nazi racism was the condemnation of all European Jews and other peoples considered racially inferior to extreme racial persecution and then annihilation in the **Holocaust**, a great spasm of racially inspired mass murder.

As already described, the Nazis began to use social, legal, and economic means to persecute Jews and other "undesirable" groups immediately after taking power. Between 1938 and 1940 persecution turned deadly in the Nazi euthanasia (mercy killing) campaign, an important step toward genocide. Just as Germany began the war, some 70,000 people with physical and mental disabilities were forced into special hospitals, barracks, and camps. Deemed by Nazi administrators to be "unworthy lives" who might "pollute" the German race, they were murdered in cold blood. The victims were mostly ethnic Germans, and the euthanasia campaign was stopped after church leaders and ordinary families spoke out. The staff involved took what they learned in implementing this program with them to the extermination camps the Nazis would soon build in the east (Map 27.4).

The German victory over Poland in 1939 brought some 3 million Jews under Nazi control. Jews in German-occupied territories were soon forced to move into urban

Holocaust The systematic effort of the Nazi state to exterminate all European Jews and other groups deemed racially inferior during the Second World War.

A "Transport" Arrives at Auschwitz Upon arrival at Auschwitz in May 1944, Jews from Subcarpathian Rus, a rural district on the border of Czechoslovakia and Ukraine, undergo a "selection" managed by Nazi officers and prisoners in striped uniforms. Camp guards will send the fittest people to the barracks, where they will probably soon die from forced labor under the most atrocious conditions. The aged, ill, very young, or otherwise infirm will be murdered immediately in the Auschwitz gas chambers. The tower over the main gate to the camp, which today opens onto a vast museum complex, is visible in the background. (Galerie Bildwelt/Getty Images)

districts termed "ghettos." In walled-off ghettos in cities large and small—two of the most important were in Warsaw and Lodz—hundreds of thousands of Polish Jews lived in crowded and unsanitary conditions, without real work or adequate sustenance. Over 500,000 people died under these conditions.

The racial violence reached new extremes when Germany invaded the Soviet Union in 1941. Three military death squads known as Special Task Forces (*Einsatzgruppen*) and other military units followed the advancing German armies. They moved systematically from town to town, shooting Jews and other target populations. The victims of these mobile killing units were often forced to dig their own graves in local woods or fields before they were shot. In this way the German armed forces murdered some 2 million civilians.

In late 1941 Hitler and the Nazi leadership, in some still-debated combination, ordered the SS to implement the mass murder of all Jews in Europe. What the Nazi leadership called the "final solution of the Jewish question" had begun. The Germans set up an industrialized killing machine that remains unparalleled, with an extensive network of concentration camps, factory complexes, and railroad transport lines to imprison and murder Jews and other so-called undesirables, and to exploit their labor before they died. In the occupied east, the surviving residents of the ghettos were loaded onto trains and taken to camps such as Auschwitz-Birkenau, the best known of the Nazi killing centers, where over 1 million people—the vast majority of them Jews—were murdered in gas chambers. Some few were put to work as expendable laborers. The Jews of Germany and then of occupied western and central Europe were likewise rounded up, put on trains, and sent to the camps. Even after it was quite clear that Germany would lose the war, the killing continued.

Given the scope and organization of Nazi persecution, there was little opportunity for successful Jewish resistance, yet some Jews did evade or challenge the killing machine. Some brave Jews went underground or masqueraded as Christian to escape Nazi roundups; others fled to rural areas and joined bands of anti-Nazi partisans. Jews also organized secret resistance groups in ghettos and concentration camps. When news

MAP 27.4 The Holocaust, 1941–1945   The leaders of Nazi Germany established an extensive network of ghettos and concentration and extermination camps to persecute their political opponents and those people deemed "racially undesirable" by the regime. The death camps, where the Nazi SS systematically murdered millions of European Jews, Soviet prisoners of war, and others, were located primarily in Nazi-occupied territories in eastern Europe, but the conditions in the concentration camps within Germany's borders were almost as brutal.

of pending deportation to the Treblinka killing center reached the Jews still living in the Warsaw Ghetto in January 1943, poorly armed underground resistance groups opened fire on German troops. The Ghetto Uprising, with sporadic fighting dominated by the vastly superior German forces, lasted until May, when the last Jews were taken to extermination camps and the ghetto was razed to the ground. In Auschwitz itself, in October 1944, a group of Jewish prisoners revolted and burned down one of the camp's crematoriums before all were captured and summarily executed.

The murderous attack on European Jews was the ultimate monstrosity of Nazi "racial hygiene" and racial imperialism. By 1945 the Nazis had killed about 6 million Jews and some 5 million other Europeans, including millions of ethnic Poles and

Russian POWs. (See "Individuals in Society: Primo Levi," at right.) Who was responsible for this terrible crime? Historians continue to debate this critical question. Some lay the guilt on Hitler and the Nazi leadership, arguing that ordinary Germans had little knowledge of the extermination camps or were forced to participate by Nazi terror and totalitarian control. Other scholars conclude that far more Germans knew about and were at best indifferent to the fate of "racial inferiors."

The question remains: what inspired those who actually worked in the killing machine—the "desk murderers" in Berlin who sent trains to the east, the soldiers who shot Jews in the Polish forests, the guards at Auschwitz? Some historians believe that widely shared anti-Semitism led "ordinary Germans" to become Hitler's "willing executioners." Others argue that heightened peer pressure, the desire to advance in the ranks, and the need to prove one's strength under the most brutalizing wartime violence turned average Germans into reluctant killers. The conditioning of racist Nazi propaganda clearly played a role. Whatever the motivation, numerous Germans were somehow prepared to join the SS ideologues and perpetrate ever-greater crimes, from mistreatment to arrest to mass murder.[7]

Japanese Empire and the War in the Pacific

The racist war of annihilation in Europe was matched by racially inspired warfare in East Asia. In response to political divisions and economic crisis, a Fascist government had taken control of Japan in the 1930s. As in Germany and Italy, the Japanese government was highly nationalistic and militaristic, and it was deeply committed to imperial expansion. According to Japanese race theory, the Asian races were far superior to Western ones. In speeches, schools, and newspapers, ultranationalists eagerly voiced the extreme anti-Western views that had risen in the 1920s and 1930s. They glorified the warrior virtues of honor and sacrifice and proclaimed that Japan would liberate East Asia from Western colonialists.

Japan soon acted on its racial-imperial ambitions. In 1931 Japanese armies invaded and occupied Manchuria, a vast territory bordering northeastern China. In 1937 Japan brutally invaded China itself. Seeking to cement ties with the Fascist regimes of Europe, in 1940 the Japanese entered into a formal alliance with Italy and Germany, and in summer 1941 Japanese armies occupied southern portions of the French colony of Indochina (now Vietnam and Cambodia).

The goal was to establish what the Japanese called the Greater East Asia Co-Prosperity Sphere. Under the slogan "Asia for Asians," Japanese propagandists maintained that this expansion would free Asians from hated Western imperialists. By promising to create a mutually advantageous union for long-term development, the Japanese tapped currents of nationalist sentiment, and most local populations were glad to see the Westerners go.

But the Co-Prosperity Sphere was a sham. Real power remained in the hands of the Japanese. They exhibited great cruelty toward civilian populations and prisoners of war, and exploited local peoples for Japan's wartime needs, arousing local populations against them. Nonetheless, the ability of the Japanese to defeat the Western colonial powers set a powerful example for national liberation groups in Asia, which would become important in the decolonization movement that followed World War II.

Japanese expansion from 1937 to 1941 evoked a sharp response from U.S. president Franklin Roosevelt, and Japan's leaders came to believe that war with the United States was inevitable. After much debate, they decided to launch a surprise attack on the U.S. fleet based at Pearl Harbor in the Hawaiian Islands. On December 7, 1941, the

INDIVIDUALS IN SOCIETY

Primo Levi

Most Jews deported to Auschwitz-Birkenau were murdered soon after arriving, but the Nazis used some prisoners as slave laborers, and a few of them survived. Primo Levi (1919–1987), one of these laborers, lived to become one of the most influential witnesses to the Holocaust.

Like much of Italy's small Jewish community, Levi's family belonged to the urban professional classes. Levi graduated from the University of Turin with highest honors in chemistry in 1941. Growing discrimination against Italian Jews led him to join the antifascist resistance two years later. Captured, he was deported to Auschwitz with 650 Italian Jews in February 1944. Stone-faced SS men picked 96 men, Levi among them, and 29 women from this group to work in labor camps; the rest were gassed upon arrival.

Levi and his fellow prisoners were kicked, punched, stripped, branded with tattoos, crammed into huts, and worked unmercifully. Hoping for some prisoner solidarity, Levi found only a desperate struggle of each against all and enormous status differences among prisoners. Many bewildered newcomers, beaten and demoralized by their bosses—the most privileged prisoners—collapsed and died. Others struggled to secure their own privileges, however small, because food rations and working conditions were so abominable that prisoners who were not bosses usually perished in two to three months.

Sensitive and noncombative, Levi found himself sinking into oblivion. But instead of joining the mass of the "drowned," he became one of the "saved"—a complicated surprise with moral implications that he would ponder all his life. As Levi explained in *Survival in Auschwitz* (1947), the usual road to salvation in the camps was some kind of collaboration with German power. Savage German criminals were released from prison to become brutal camp guards; non-Jewish political prisoners competed for jobs entitling them to better conditions; and, especially troubling for Levi, a few Jews plotted and struggled to gain the power of life and death over other Jewish prisoners.

Primo Levi never stopped thinking, writing, and speaking about the Holocaust. (© Gianni Giansanti/Sygma/Corbis)

Though not one of these Jewish bosses, Levi believed that he, like almost all survivors, had entered the "gray zone" of moral compromise. "Nobody can know for how long and under what trials his soul can resist before yielding or breaking," Levi wrote. "The harsher the oppression, the more widespread among the oppressed is the willingness, with all its infinite nuances and motivations, to collaborate."* The camps held no saints, he believed: the Nazi system degraded its victims, forcing them to commit sometimes-bestial acts against their fellow prisoners in order to survive.

For Levi, salvation came from his education. Interviewed by a German technocrat for work in the camp's synthetic rubber program, Levi was chosen for this relatively easy labor because he spoke fluent German, including scientific terminology. Work in the warm camp laboratory offered Levi opportunities to pilfer equipment he could then trade to other prisoners for food and necessities. Levi also gained critical support from three prisoners who refused to do wicked and hateful acts. And he counted luck as essential for his survival: in the camp infirmary with scarlet fever in February 1945 as advancing Russian armies prepared to liberate the camp, Levi was not evacuated by the Nazis and shot to death like most Jewish prisoners.

After the war, Levi was haunted by the nightmare that the Holocaust would be ignored or forgotten. Ashamed that so many people whom he considered better than himself had perished, and wanting the world to understand the genocide in all its complexity so that people would never again tolerate such atrocities, he turned to writing about his experiences. Primo Levi, while revealing Nazi guilt, tirelessly grappled with his vision of individual responsibility and moral ambiguity in a hell designed to make the victims collaborate and persecute each other.

QUESTIONS FOR ANALYSIS

1. Describe Levi's experience at Auschwitz. How did camp prisoners treat each other? Why?
2. What does Levi mean by the "gray zone"?
3. Will a vivid historical memory of the Holocaust help prevent future genocide?

*Primo Levi, *The Drowned and the Saved* (New York: Vintage, 1989), pp. 43, 60. See also Levi, *Survival in Auschwitz: The Nazi Assault on Humanity* (London: Collier Books, 1961). These powerful testimonies are highly recommended.

MAP 27.5 World War II in the Pacific In 1942 Japanese forces overran an enormous amount of territory, which the Allies slowly recaptured in a long, bitter struggle. As this map shows, Japan still held a large Asian empire in August 1945, when the unprecedented devastation of atomic warfare suddenly forced it to surrender.

Japanese sank or crippled every American battleship, but by chance all the American aircraft carriers were at sea and escaped unharmed. Pearl Harbor brought the Americans into the war in a spirit of anger and revenge.

As the Americans mobilized for war, Japanese armies overran more European and American colonies in Southeast Asia. By May 1942 Japan controlled a vast empire (Map 27.5) and was threatening Australia. The Americans pushed back and engaged the Japanese in a series of hard-fought naval battles. In July 1943 the Americans and their

Australian allies opened a successful island-hopping campaign that slowly forced Japan out of its conquered territories. The war in the Pacific was extremely brutal—a "war without mercy," in the words of a leading American scholar—and soldiers on both sides committed atrocities. A product of spiraling violence, mutual hatred, and dehumanizing racial stereotypes, the fighting intensified as the United States moved toward Japan.[8]

The "Hinge of Fate"

While the Nazis and the Japanese built their savage empires, Great Britain, the United States, and the Soviet Union joined together in a military pact Churchill termed the Grand Alliance. This was a matter of circumstance more than of choice. It had taken the Japanese surprise attack to bring the isolationist United States into the war. Moreover, the British and Americans were determined opponents of Soviet communism, and disagreements between the Soviets and the capitalist powers during the course of the war sowed mutual distrust. Stalin repeatedly urged Britain and the United States to open a second front in France to relieve pressure on Soviet forces, but Churchill and Roosevelt refused until the summer of 1944. Despite such tensions, the overriding goal of defeating the Axis powers brought together these reluctant allies.

In one area of agreement, the Grand Alliance concurred on a policy of "Europe first." Only after Hitler was defeated would the Allies mount an all-out attack on Japan, the lesser threat. The Allies also agreed to concentrate on immediate military needs, postponing tough political questions about the eventual peace settlement that might have divided them. To further encourage mutual trust, the Allies adopted the principle of the unconditional surrender of Germany and Japan. This policy cemented the Grand Alliance because it denied Hitler any hope of dividing his foes. It also meant that Soviet and Anglo-American armies would almost certainly be forced to invade and occupy all of Germany, and that Japan would fight to the bitter end.

The military resources of the Grand Alliance were awesome. The United States harnessed its vast industrial base to wage global war and in 1943 outproduced not only Germany, Italy, and Japan, but all of the rest of the world combined. Great Britain became an impregnable floating fortress, a gigantic frontline staging area for a decisive blow to the heart of Germany. After a determined push, the Soviet Union's military strength was so great that it might well have defeated Germany without Western help. Stalin drew heavily on the heroic resolve of the Soviet people, especially those in the central Russian heartland. Broad-based Russian nationalism, as opposed to narrow communist ideology, became a powerful unifying force in what the Soviet people appropriately called the Great Patriotic War of the Fatherland.

The combined might of the Allies forced back the Nazi armies on all fronts (see Map 27.3). Through early 1942 heavy fighting between British and Axis forces had resulted in significant German advances in North Africa. At the Second Battle of El Alamein (el al-uh-MAYN) in October–November 1942, however, British forces decisively defeated combined German and Italian armies and halted Axis penetration of North Africa. Winston Churchill called the battle the "hinge of fate" that opened the door to Allied victory. Shortly thereafter, an Anglo-American force landed in Morocco and Algeria. These French possessions, which were under the control of Pétain's Vichy government, went over to the Allies. Fearful of an Allied invasion across the Mediterranean, German forces occupied Vichy France in November 1942, and the collaborationist French government effectively ceased to exist.

After driving the Axis powers out of North Africa, U.S. and British forces invaded Sicily in the summer of 1943 and mainland Italy that autumn. Mussolini was overthrown by a coup d'état, and the new Italian government publicly accepted unconditional surrender. In response, Nazi armies invaded and seized control of northern and central Italy, and German paratroopers rescued Mussolini in a daring raid and put him at the head of a puppet government. Facing stiff German resistance, the Allies battled their way slowly up the Italian peninsula. The Germans still held northern Italy, but they were clearly on the defensive.

The spring of 1943 brought crucial Allied victories at sea and in the air. In the first years of the war, German submarines had successfully attacked North Atlantic shipping, severely hampering the British war effort. New antisubmarine technologies favored the Allies. Soon massive convoys of hundreds of ships were streaming across the Atlantic, bringing much-needed troops and supplies from the United States to Britain.

The German air force had never really recovered from its defeat in the Battle of Britain. With almost unchallenged air superiority, the United States and Britain now mounted massive bombing raids on German cities to maim industrial production and break civilian morale. By the war's end, hardly a German city of any size remained untouched, and many—including Dresden, Hamburg, and Cologne—lay in ruins.

Great Britain and the United States had made critical advances in the western theater, but the worst German defeats came at the hands of the Red Army on the eastern front. Although the Germans had almost captured the major cities of Moscow and Leningrad in early winter 1941, they were forced back by determined Soviet counterattacks. The Germans mounted a second and initially successful invasion of the Soviet Union in the summer of 1942, but the campaign turned into a disaster. The downfall came at the Battle of Stalingrad, when in November 1942 the Soviets surrounded and systematically destroyed the entire German Sixth Army of 300,000 men. In January 1943 only 123,000 soldiers were left to surrender. Hitler, who had refused to allow a retreat, suffered a catastrophic defeat. For the first time, German public opinion turned decisively against the war. In summer 1943 the larger, better-equipped Soviet armies took the offensive and began to push the Germans back along the entire eastern front (see Map 27.3).

Allied Victory

The balance of power was now clearly in Allied hands, yet bitter fighting continued in Europe for almost two years. Germany, less fully mobilized for war in 1941 than Britain, stepped up its efforts. The German war industry, under the Nazi minister of armaments Albert Speer, put to work millions of prisoners of war and slave laborers from across occupied Europe. Between early 1942 and July 1944, German war production tripled despite heavy Anglo-American bombing.

German resistance against Hitler also failed to halt the fighting. An unsuccessful attempt by conservative army leaders to assassinate Hitler in July 1944 only brought increased repression by the fanatic Nazis who had taken over the government. Closely disciplined by the regime, frightened by the prospect of unconditional surrender, and terrorized by Nazi propaganda that portrayed the advancing Russian armies as rapacious Slavic beasts, the Germans fought on with suicidal resolve.

On June 6, 1944, American and British forces under General Dwight Eisenhower landed on the beaches of Normandy, France, in history's greatest naval invasion. In a hundred dramatic days, more than 2 million men and almost half a million

Nuclear Wasteland at Hiroshima Only a handful of buildings remain standing in the ruins of Hiroshima in September 1945. Fearing the costs of a prolonged ground and naval campaign against the Japanese mainland, the United States dropped atomic bombs on Hiroshima and Nagasaki in August 1945. The bombings ended the war and opened the nuclear age. (AP Photo/AP Images)

vehicles broke through the German lines and pushed inland. Rejecting proposals to strike straight at Berlin in a massive attack, Eisenhower moved forward cautiously on a broad front. Not until March 1945 did American troops cross the Rhine and enter Germany. By spring of 1945 the Allies had finally forced the Germans out of the Italian peninsula. That April, Mussolini was captured in northern Italy by Communist partisans and executed, along with his mistress and other Fascist leaders.

The Soviets, who had been advancing steadily since July 1943, reached the outskirts of Warsaw by August 1944. Anticipating German defeat, the Polish underground Home Army ordered an uprising, so that the Poles might take the city on their own and establish independence from the Soviets. The Warsaw Uprising was a tragic miscalculation. Citing military pressure, the Red Army refused to enter the city. Stalin and Soviet leaders thus allowed the Germans to destroy the Polish insurgents, a cynical move that paved the way for the establishment of a postwar Communist regime. Only after the decimated Home Army surrendered did the Red Army continue its advance. Warsaw lay in ruins, and between 150,000 and 200,000 Poles—mostly civilians—had lost their lives.

Over the next six months, the Soviets moved southward into Romania, Hungary, and Yugoslavia. In January 1945 the Red Army crossed Poland into Germany, and on April 26 met American forces on the Elbe River. The Allies had overrun Europe and closed their vise on Nazi Germany. As Soviet forces fought their way into Berlin, Hitler committed suicide, and on May 8 the remaining German commanders capitulated.

The war in the Pacific also drew to a close. Despite repeated U.S. victories through the summer of 1945, Japanese troops had continued to fight with enormous courage and determination. American commanders believed the invasion and conquest of Japan itself might cost 1 million American casualties and claim 10 to 20 million Japanese lives. In fact, Japan was almost helpless, its industry and dense, fragile wooden cities largely destroyed by intense American bombing. Yet the Japanese seemed determined to fight on, ready to die for a hopeless cause.

After much discussion at the upper levels of the U.S. government, American planes dropped atomic bombs on Hiroshima and Nagasaki in Japan on August 6 and 9, 1945. The mass bombing of cities and civilians, one of the terrible new practices of World War II, now ended in the final nightmare—unprecedented human destruction in a single blinding flash. On August 14, 1945, the Japanese announced their surrender. The Second World War, which had claimed the lives of more than 50 million soldiers and civilians, was over.

LOOKING BACK LOOKING AHEAD

The first half of the twentieth century brought almost unimaginable violence and destruction, leading historian Eric Hobsbawm to label the era the "age of catastrophe."[9] Shaken by the rapid cultural change and economic collapse that followed the tragedy of World War I, many Europeans embraced the radical politics of communism and fascism. Some found appeal in visions of a classless society or a racially pure national community, and totalitarian dictators like Stalin and Hitler capitalized on these desires for social order, building dictatorial regimes that demanded total allegiance to an ideological vision. Even as these regimes rewarded supporters and promised ordinary people a new age, they violently repressed their enemies, real and imagined. The vision proved fatal: the great clash of ideologies that emerged in the 1920s and 1930s led to history's most deadly war, killing millions and devastating large swaths of Europe and East Asia.

Only the reluctant Grand Alliance of the liberal United States and Great Britain with the Communist Soviet Union was able to defeat the Axis powers. After 1945 fascism was finished, discredited by total defeat and the postwar revelation of the Holocaust. To make sure, the Allies would occupy the lands of their former enemies. Rebuilding a devastated Europe proved a challenging but in the end manageable task: once recovery took off, the postwar decades brought an economic boom that led to levels of prosperity unimaginable in the interwar years. Maintaining an alliance between the capitalist West and the Communist East was something else. Trust quickly broke down. Europe would be divided into two hostile camps, and Cold War tensions between East and West would dominate European and world politics for the next fifty years.

Make Connections

Think about the larger developments and continuities within and across chapters.

1. Historians continue to disagree on whether "totalitarianism" is an appropriate way to describe Communist and Fascist dictatorships in Europe. How would you define this term? Is it a useful label to describe state and society under Stalin, Mussolini, and Hitler? Why is the debate over totalitarianism still important today?

2. Why would ordinary people support dictatorships that trampled on familiar political freedoms and civil rights?

3. Summarize the key issues in the origins of World War II and the key turning points in the war itself. Was political ideology the main driving force behind these events or were other factors at play?

27 REVIEW & EXPLORE

Review the Main Ideas

Answer the focus questions from each section of the chapter.

◆ How were Fascist and Communist totalitarian dictatorships similar and different? (p. 904)

◆ How did Stalin and the Communist Party build a totalitarian state in the Soviet Union? (p. 907)

◆ What kind of government did Mussolini establish in Italy? (p. 917)

◆ What policies did Nazi Germany pursue, and how did they lead to World War II? (p. 919)

◆ How did Germany and Japan conquer enormous empires during World War II, and how did the Allies defeat them? (p. 927)

Identify Key Terms

Identify and explain the significance of each item below.

totalitarianism (p. 904)

fascism (p. 906)

eugenics (p. 906)

five-year plan (p. 907)

New Economic Policy (NEP) (p. 907)

collectivization of agriculture (p. 912)

kulaks (p. 912)

Black Shirts (p. 918)

Lateran Agreement (p. 918)

National Socialism (p. 919)

Enabling Act (p. 921)

appeasement (p. 925)

New Order (p. 928)

Holocaust (p. 931)

NOTES

1. Quoted in S. Kotkin, *Magnetic Mountain: Stalinism as a Civilization* (Berkeley: University of California Press, 1997), pp. 221–222.

2. R. Thurston, *Life and Terror in Stalin's Russia, 1934–1941* (New Haven, Conn.: Yale University Press, 1996), esp. pp. 16–106; also M. Malia, *The Soviet Tragedy: A History of Socialism in Russia, 1917–1991* (New York: Free Press, 1995), pp. 227–270.

3. Quoted in C. Duggan, *A Concise History of Italy* (New York: Cambridge University Press, 1994), p. 227.

4. Quoted ibid, p. 234.

5. M. Burleigh and W. Wippermann, *The Racial State: Germany, 1933–1945* (New York: Cambridge University Press, 1991).

6. See, for example, the population statistics on the German occupation of Belarus in C. Gerlach, "German Economic Interests, Occupation Policy, and the Murder of the Jews in Belorussia, 1941–43," in *National Socialist Extermination Policies: Contemporary German Perspectives and Controversies*, U. Herbert, ed. (New York: Berghan Books, 2000), pp. 210–239. See also M. Allen, *The Business of Genocide: The SS, Slave Labor, and the Concentration Camps* (Chapel Hill: University of North Carolina Press, 2002), pp. 270–285.

7. D. Goldhagen, *Hitler's Willing Executioners: Ordinary Germans and the Holocaust* (New York: Vintage Books, 1997); for an alternate explanation, see C. Browning, *Ordinary Men: Reserve Police Battalion 101 and the Final Solution in Poland* (New York: Harper, 1992).

8. J. Dower, *War Without Mercy: Race and Power in the Pacific War* (New York: Pantheon, 1986).

9. E. Hobsbawm, *The Age of Extremes: A History of the World, 1914–1991* (New York: Vintage, 1996), p. 21.

CHAPTER PREVIEW

Postwar Europe and the Origins of the Cold War
Why was World War II followed so quickly by the Cold War?

The Western Renaissance/Recovery in Western Europe
What were the sources of postwar recovery and stability in western Europe?

Developments in the Soviet Union and the East Bloc
What was the pattern of postwar development in the Soviet bloc?

The End of Empires
What led to decolonization after World War II, and how did the Cold War influence the process?

Postwar Social Transformations
How did changes in social relations contribute to European stability on both sides of the iron curtain?

Life in Eastern Europe
This relief sculpture, a revealing example of Socialist Realism from 1952, portrays (from left to right) a mail carrier, a builder, industrial workers, and peasants. It adorns the wall of the central post office in Banská Bystrica, a regional capital in present-day Slovakia (formerly part of Czechoslovakia). Citizens in the Soviet Union and its satellite countries of the East Bloc saw many such works of public art, which idealized the dignity of ordinary laborers and the advantages of communism. (© Georgios Makkas/Alamy Stock Photo)

28

Cold War Conflict and Consensus

1945–1965

The defeat of the Nazis and their allies in 1945 left Europe in ruins. In the immediate postwar years, as Europeans struggled to overcome the effects of rampant death and destruction, the victorious Allies worked to shape an effective peace accord. Disagreements between the Soviet Union and the Western allies emerged during this process and quickly led to an apparently endless Cold War between the two new superpowers—the United States and the Soviet Union. This conflict split much of Europe into a Soviet-aligned Communist bloc and a U.S.-aligned capitalist bloc and spurred military, economic, and technological competition.

Amid these tensions, battered western European countries fashioned a remarkable recovery, building strong democratic institutions and vibrant economies. In the Soviet Union and the "East Bloc" (the label applied to central and eastern European countries governed by Soviet-backed Communist regimes), Communist leaders repressed challenges to one-party rule but also offered limited reforms, leading to stability there as well. Yet the postwar period was by no means peaceful. Anti-Soviet uprisings in East Bloc countries led to military intervention and death and imprisonment for thousands. Colonial independence movements in the developing world sometimes erupted in violence, even after liberation was achieved. Cold War hostilities had an immense impact on the decolonization process, often to the detriment of formerly colonized peoples.

Cold War conflicts notwithstanding, the postwar decades witnessed the construction of a relatively stable social and political consensus in both Communist and capitalist Europe. At the same time, changing class structures, new migration patterns, and new roles for women and youths had a profound impact on European society, laying the groundwork for major transformations in the decades to come. ■

Postwar Europe and the Origins of the Cold War

FOCUS QUESTION
Why was World War II followed so quickly by the Cold War?

In 1945 the Allies faced the momentous challenges of rebuilding a shattered Europe, dealing with Nazi criminals, and creating a lasting peace. Reconstruction began and war crimes were punished, but the Allies found it difficult to cooperate in peacemaking. Motivated by different goals and hounded by misunderstandings, Great Britain and the United States found themselves at loggerheads with the Soviet Union (U.S.S.R.). Though a handful of countries maintained a neutral stance, by 1949 most of Europe was divided into East and West Blocs allied with the U.S.S.R. and the United States, respectively. For the next forty years, the competing superpowers engaged in the **Cold War**, a determined competition for political and military superiority around the world.

Cold War The rivalry between the Soviet Union and the United States that divided much of Europe into a Soviet-aligned Communist bloc and a U.S.-aligned capitalist bloc between 1945 and 1989.

The Legacies of the Second World War

In the summer of 1945 Europe lay in ruins. Across the continent, the fighting had destroyed cities and landscapes and obliterated buildings, factories, farms, rail tracks, roads, and bridges. Many cities—including Leningrad, Warsaw, Vienna, Budapest, Rotterdam, and Coventry—were completely devastated. Postwar observers compared the remaining piles of rubble to moonscapes. Surviving cities such as Prague and Paris were left relatively unscathed, mostly by chance.

The human costs of the Second World War are almost incalculable (Map 28.1). The death toll far exceeded the mortality figures for World War I. At least 20 million Soviets, including soldiers and civilians, died in the war. Between 9 and 11 million noncombatants lost their lives in Nazi concentration camps, including approximately 6 million Jews and over 220,000 Sinti and Roma (sometimes called Gypsies). One out of every five Poles died in the war, including 3 million of Poland's 3.25 million Jews. German deaths numbered 5 million, 2 million of them civilians. France and Britain both lost fewer soldiers than in World War I, but

Displaced Persons in the Ruins of Berlin   The end of the war in 1945 stopped the fighting but not the suffering. For the next two years, millions of displaced persons wandered across Europe searching for sustenance, lost family members, and a place to call home. (Fred Rampage/Getty Images)

Chronology

1945	Yalta Conference; end of World War II in Europe; Potsdam Conference; Nuremberg trials begin	1954–1962	Algerian War of Independence
1945–1960s	Decolonization of Asia and Africa	1955	Warsaw Pact founded
1945–1965	United States takes lead in Big Science	1955–1964	Khrushchev in power; de-Stalinization of Soviet Union
1947	Truman Doctrine; Marshall Plan	1956	Suez crisis
1948	Foundation of Israel	1957	Formation of Common Market; Pasternak publishes *Doctor Zhivago*
1948–1949	Berlin airlift	1961	Building of Berlin Wall
1949	Creation of East and West Germany; formation of NATO; establishment of COMECON	1962	Cuban missile crisis; Solzhenitsyn publishes *One Day in the Life of Ivan Denisovich*
1950–1953	Korean War	1964	Brezhnev replaces Khrushchev as Soviet leader
1953	Death of Stalin		

about 350,000 French civilians were killed in the fighting. Over 400,000 U.S. soldiers died in the European and Pacific campaigns, and other nations across Europe and the globe also lost staggering numbers. In total, about 50 million human beings perished in the conflict.

The destruction of war also left tens of millions homeless—25 million in the U.S.S.R. and 20 million in Germany alone. The wartime policies of Hitler and Stalin had forced some 30 million people from their homes in the hardest-hit war zones of central and eastern Europe. The end of the war and the start of the peace increased their numbers. Some 13 million ethnic Germans fled west before the advancing Soviet troops or were expelled from eastern Europe under the terms of Allied agreements. Forced laborers from Poland, France, the Balkans, and other nations, brought to Germany by the Nazis, now sought to go home. A woman in Berlin described the flow of refugees passing through the city in spring 1945:

> The streets were filled with small, tired caravans of people. . . . All the vehicles looked the same: pitiful handcarts piled high with sacks, crates, and trunks. Often I saw a woman or an older child in front, harnessed to a rope, pulling the cart forward, with the smaller children or a grandpa pushing from behind. There were people perched on top, too, usually very little children or elderly relatives. The old people look terrible amid all the junk, the men as well as the women—pale, dilapidated, apathetic. Half-dead sacks of bones.[1]

These **displaced persons** or DPs—their numbers increased by concentration camp survivors and freed prisoners of war, and hundreds of thousands of orphaned children—searched for food and shelter. From 1945 to 1947 the newly established United Nations Relief and Rehabilitation Administration (UNRRA) opened over 760 DP camps and spent $10 billion to house, feed, clothe, and repatriate the refugees.

For DPs, going home was not always the best option. Soviet citizens who had spent time in the West were seen as politically unreliable by political leaders in the U.S.S.R. Many DPs faced prison terms, exile to labor camps in the Siberian gulag, and even execution upon their return to Soviet territories. Jewish DPs faced

displaced persons Postwar refugees, including 13 million Germans, former Nazi prisoners and forced laborers, and orphaned children.

945

MAP 28.1 The Aftermath of World War II in Europe, ca. 1945–1950 By 1945 millions of people displaced by war and territorial changes were on the move. The Soviet Union and Poland took land from Germany, which the Allies partitioned into occupation zones. Those zones subsequently formed the basis of the East and West German states. Austria was detached from Germany and similarly divided, but the Soviets subsequently permitted Austria to reunify as a neutral state.

unique problems. Their families and communities had been destroyed, and persistent anti-Semitism often made them unwelcome in their former homelands. Many stayed in special Jewish DP camps in Germany for years. After the creation of Israel in 1948 (see page 971), over 330,000 European Jews left for the new Jewish state. By 1952 about 100,000 Jews had also immigrated to the United States; smaller numbers moved to other western European countries, South America, and the British Commonwealth countries. When the last DP camp closed in 1957, the UNRRA had cared for and resettled many millions of refugees, Jews and non-Jews alike.

When the fighting stopped, Germany and Austria had been divided into four occupation zones, each governed by one of the Allies—the United States, the Soviet Union, Great Britain, and France. The Soviets collected substantial reparations from their zone in eastern Germany and from former German allies Hungary and Romania. In Soviet-occupied Germany, administrators seized factories and equipment, even tearing up railroad tracks and sending the rails to the U.S.S.R.

The authorities in each zone tried to punish those guilty of Nazi atrocities. Across Europe, almost 100,000 Germans and Austrians were convicted of war crimes. Many more were investigated or indicted. In Soviet-dominated central and eastern Europe—where the worst crimes had taken place—retribution was particularly intense. There and in other parts of Europe, collaborators, non-Germans who had assisted the German occupiers during the war, were also punished. In the days and months immediately after the war, spontaneous acts of retribution brought some collaborators to account. In both France and Italy, unofficial groups seeking revenge summarily executed some 25,000 persons. French women accused of "horizontal collaboration"—having sexual relations with German soldiers during the occupation—were publicly humiliated by angry mobs. Newly established postwar governments also formed official courts to sanction collaborators or send them to prison. A small number received the death sentence.

In Germany and Austria, occupation authorities set up "denazification" procedures meant to identify and punish former Nazi Party members responsible for the worst crimes and eradicate National Socialist ideology from social and political institutions. At the Nuremberg trials (1945–1946), an international military tribunal organized by the four Allied powers tried the highest-ranking Nazi military and civilian leaders who had survived the war, charging them with war crimes and crimes against humanity. After chilling testimony from victims of the regime, which revealed the full systematic horror of Nazi atrocities, twelve were sentenced to death and ten more to lengthy prison terms.

The Nuremberg trials marked the last time the four Allies worked closely together to punish former Nazis. As the Cold War developed and the Soviets and the Western Allies drew increasingly apart, each carried out separate denazification programs in their own zones of occupation. In the Western zones, military courts at first actively prosecuted leading Nazis. But the huge numbers implicated in Nazi crimes, German opposition to the proceedings, and the need for stability in the looming Cold War made thorough denazification impractical. Except for the worst offenders, the Western authorities had quietly shelved denazification by 1948. The process was similar in the Soviet zone. At first, punishment was swift and harsh. About 45,000 former party officials, upper-class industrialists, and large landowners identified as Nazis were sentenced to prison or death. As in the West, however, former Nazis who cooperated with the Soviet authorities could avoid prosecution. Thus many former Nazis found leading positions in government and industry in both the Soviet and Western zones.

The Peace Settlement and Cold War Origins

In the years immediately after the war, as ordinary people across Europe struggled to come to terms with the war and recover from the ruin, the victorious Allies—the U.S.S.R., the United States, and Great Britain—tried to shape a reasonable and lasting peace. Yet the Allies began to quarrel almost as soon as the unifying threat of Nazi Germany disappeared, and the interests of the Communist Soviet Union and the capitalist Britain and United States increasingly diverged. The hostility between the Eastern and Western superpowers was the sad but logical outgrowth of military developments, wartime agreements, and long-standing political and ideological differences that stretched back to the Russian Revolution.

Once the United States entered the war in late 1941, the Americans and the British had made military victory their highest priority. They did not try to take advantage of the Soviet Union's precarious position in 1942, because they feared that hard bargaining would encourage Stalin to consider making a separate peace with Hitler. Together, the Allies avoided discussion of postwar aims and the shape of the eventual peace settlement and focused instead on pursuing a policy of German unconditional surrender to solidify the alliance. By late 1943 negotiations about the postwar settlement could no longer be postponed. The conference that the "Big Three"—Stalin, Roosevelt, and Churchill—held in the Iranian capital of Teheran in November 1943 proved crucial for determining the shape of the postwar world.

At Teheran, the Big Three jovially reaffirmed their determination to crush Germany, followed by tense discussions of Poland's postwar borders and a strategy to win the war. Stalin, concerned that the U.S.S.R. was bearing the brunt of the fighting, asked his allies to relieve his armies by opening a second front in German-occupied France. Churchill, fearing the military dangers of a direct attack, argued that American and British forces should follow up their Italian campaign with an indirect attack on Germany through the Balkans. Roosevelt, however, agreed with Stalin that an American-British assault through France would be better, though the date for the invasion was set later than the Soviet leader desired. This decision had momentous implications for the Cold War. While the delay in opening a second front fanned Stalin's distrust of the Allies, the agreement on a British-U.S. invasion of France also ensured that the American-British and Soviet armies would come together in defeated Germany along a north-south line, and that Soviet troops would play the predominant role in pushing the Germans out of eastern and central Europe. Thus the basic shape of postwar Europe was cast even as the fighting continued.

When the Big Three met again in February 1945 at Yalta, on the Black Sea in southern Russia, advancing Soviet armies had already occupied Poland, Bulgaria, Romania, Hungary, part of Yugoslavia, and much of Czechoslovakia, and were within a hundred miles of Berlin. The stalled American-British forces had yet to cross the Rhine into Germany. Moreover, the United States was far from defeating Japan. In short, the U.S.S.R.'s position on the ground was far stronger than that of the United States and Britain, which played to Stalin's advantage.

The Allies agreed at Yalta that each of the four victorious powers would occupy a separate zone of Germany and that the Germans would pay heavy reparations to the Soviet Union. At American insistence, Stalin agreed to declare war on Japan after Germany's defeat. As for Poland, the Big Three agreed that the U.S.S.R. would permanently incorporate the eastern Polish territories its army had occupied in 1939 and that Poland would be compensated with German lands to the west. They also agreed in an ambiguous compromise that the new governments in Soviet-occupied Europe would be freely elected but "friendly" to the Soviet Union.

The Big Three In 1945 a triumphant Winston Churchill, an ailing Franklin Roosevelt, and a determined Stalin met at Yalta in southern Russia to plan for peace. Cooperation soon gave way to bitter hostility, and the decisions made by these leaders transformed the map of Europe. (Franklin D. Roosevelt Presidential Library and Museum of the National Archives and Records Administration/U.S. National Archives)

The Yalta compromise over elections in these countries broke down almost immediately. Even before the conference, Communist parties were taking control in Bulgaria and Poland. Elsewhere, the Soviets formed coalition governments that included Social Democrats and other leftist parties but reserved key government posts for Moscow-trained Communists. At the Potsdam Conference of July 1945, the differences over elections in Soviet-occupied Europe surged to the fore. Roosevelt had died and had been succeeded by Harry Truman (U.S. pres. 1945–1953), who demanded immediate free elections throughout central and eastern Europe. Stalin refused point-blank. "A freely elected government in any of these East European countries would be anti-Soviet," he admitted simply, "and that we cannot allow."[2]

Here, then, were the keys to the much-debated origins of the Cold War. While fighting Germany, the Allies could maintain an alliance of necessity. As the war drew to a close, long-standing hostility between East and West re-emerged. Mutual distrust, security concerns, and antagonistic desires for economic, political, and territorial control began to destroy the former partnership.

Stalin, who had lived through two enormously destructive German invasions, was determined to establish a buffer zone of sympathetic states around the U.S.S.R. and at the same time expand the reach of communism and the Soviet state. Stalin believed that only Communists could be dependable allies, and that free elections would result in independent and possibly hostile governments on his western border. With Soviet armies in central and eastern Europe, there was no way short of war for the United States to control the region's political future, and war was out of the question. The United States, for its part, pushed to maintain democratic capitalism and open access to free markets in western Europe. The Americans quickly showed that they, too, were willing to use their vast political, economic, and military power to maintain predominance in their sphere of influence.

West Versus East

The Cold War took shape over the next five years, as both sides hardened their positions. After Japan's surrender in September 1945, Truman cut off aid to the ailing U.S.S.R. In October he declared that the United States would never recognize any government established by force against the will of its people. In March 1946 former British prime minister Churchill ominously informed an American

MAP 28.2 Cold War Europe in the 1950s   The Cold War divided Europe into two hostile military alliances that formed to the east and west of an "iron curtain."

audience that an "iron curtain" had fallen across the continent, dividing Europe into two antagonistic camps (Map 28.2).

The Soviet Union was indeed consolidating its hold on central and eastern Europe. In fact, the Soviets enjoyed some popular support in the region, though this varied from country to country. After all, the Red Army had thrown out the German invaders, and after the abuses of fascism the ideals of Communist equality retained some appeal. Yet the Communist parties in these areas quickly recognized that they lacked enough support to take power in free elections. In Romania, Bulgaria, Poland, and Hungary, Communist politicians, backed by Moscow, repressed their liberal opponents and engineered phony elections that established Communist-led regimes. They purged the last remaining noncommunists from the coalition governments set up after the war and by 1948 had established Soviet-style, one-party Communist dictatorships. The pattern was somewhat different in Czechoslovakia, where Communists enjoyed success in open elections and initially formed a coalition government with other parties. When the noncommunist ministers resigned in February 1948, the Communists took over the government and began Stalinizing the country. This seizure of power in Czechoslovakia greatly contributed to Western fears of limitless Communist expansion.

In western Europe, communism also enjoyed some support. In Italy, which boasted the largest Communist Party outside of the Soviet bloc, Communists won 19 percent of the vote in 1946; French Communists earned 28 percent of the vote the same year. These large, well-organized parties criticized the growing role of the United States in western Europe and challenged their own governments with violent rhetoric and large strikes. At the same time, bitter civil wars in Greece and China pitted Communist revolutionaries against authoritarian leaders backed by the United States.

By early 1947 it appeared to many Americans that the U.S.S.R. was determined to export communism by subversion throughout Europe and around the world. The United States responded with the **Truman Doctrine**, aimed at "containing" communism to areas already under Communist governments, a policy first advocated by U.S. diplomat George Kennan in 1946. The United States, President Truman promised, would use diplomatic, economic, and even military means to resist the expansion of communism anywhere on the globe. In the first examples of containment policies in action, Truman asked Congress to provide military aid to anticommunist forces in the Greek Civil War (1944–1949) and counter the threat of Soviet expansion in Turkey. With American support, both countries remained in the Western bloc. The American determination to enforce containment hardened when the Soviets exploded their own atomic bomb in 1949, raising popular fears of a looming nuclear holocaust. At home and abroad, the United States engaged in an anticommunist crusade. Emotional, moralistic denunciations of Stalin and Communist regimes became part of American public life. By the early 1950s the U.S. government was restructuring its military to meet the Soviet threat, pouring money into defense spending, and testing nuclear weapons that dwarfed the destructive power of atomic bombs.

Military aid and a defense buildup were only one aspect of Truman's policy of containment. In 1947 western Europe was still on the verge of economic collapse. Food was scarce, inflation was high, and black markets flourished. Recognizing that an economically and politically stable western Europe would be an effective block against the popular appeal of communism, U.S. secretary of state George C. Marshall offered Europe economic aid—the **Marshall Plan**—to help it rebuild. As Marshall wrote in a State Department bulletin, "Its purpose should be the revival of a working economy in the world so as to permit the emergence of political and social conditions in which free institutions can exist."[3]

The Marshall Plan was one of the most successful foreign aid programs in history. When it ended in 1951, the United States had given about $13 billion in aid (equivalent to over $200 billion in 2015 dollars) to fifteen western European nations, and Europe's economy was on the way to recovery. Marshall Plan funding was initially offered to East Bloc countries as well, but fearing Western interference in the Soviet sphere, they rejected the offer. In 1949 the Soviets established the **Council for Mutual Economic Assistance (COMECON)**, an economic organization of Communist states intended to rebuild the East Bloc independently of the West. Thus the generous aid of the Marshall Plan was limited to countries in the Western bloc, which further increased Cold War divisions.

Truman Doctrine America's policy geared to containing communism to those countries already under Soviet control.

Marshall Plan American plan for providing economic aid to western Europe to help it rebuild.

Council for Mutual Economic Assistance (COMECON) An economic organization of Communist states meant to help rebuild East Bloc countries under Soviet auspices.

In the late 1940s Berlin, the capital city of Germany, was on the frontline of the Cold War. Like the rest of Germany and Austria, Berlin had been divided into four zones of occupation. In June 1948 the Western allies replaced the currency in the western zones of Germany and Berlin, an early move in plans to establish a separate West German state sympathetic to U.S. interests. The currency reform violated the peace settlement and raised Stalin's fears of the American presence in Europe. In addition, growing ties among Britain, France, Belgium, and the Netherlands convinced Stalin that a Western bloc was forming against the Soviet Union. In response, the Soviet dictator used the one card he had to play—access to Berlin—to force the allies to the bargaining table. Stalin blocked all traffic through the Soviet zone of Germany to Berlin in an attempt to win concessions and perhaps reunify the city under Soviet control. Acting firmly, the Western allies coordinated around-the-clock flights of hundreds of planes over the Soviet roadblocks, supplying provisions to West Berliners and thwarting Soviet efforts to swallow up the western half of the city. After 324 days, the Berlin airlift succeeded, and the Soviets reopened the roads.

Success in breaking the Berlin blockade had several lasting results. First, it paved the way for the creation of two separate German states in 1949: the Federal Republic of Germany (West Germany), aligned with the United States, and the German Democratic Republic (East Germany), aligned with the U.S.S.R. Germany would remain divided for the next forty-one years, a radical solution to the "German problem" that satisfied people fearful of the nation's possible military resurgence.

The Berlin crisis also seemed to show that containment worked, and thus strengthened U.S. resolve to maintain a strong European and U.S. military presence in western Europe. In 1949 the United States formed **NATO** (the North Atlantic Treaty Organization), an anti-Soviet military alliance of Western governments. As one British diplomat put it, NATO was designed "to keep the Russians out, the Americans in, and the Germans down."[4] With U.S. backing, West Germany joined NATO in 1955 and was allowed to rebuild its military to help defend western Europe against possible Soviet attack. That same year, the Soviets countered by organizing the **Warsaw Pact**, a military alliance among the U.S.S.R. and its Communist satellites. In both political and military terms, most of Europe was divided into two hostile blocs.

The superpower confrontation that emerged from the ruins of World War II took shape in Europe, but it quickly spread around the globe. The Cold War turned hot in East Asia. When Soviet-backed Communist North Korea invaded South Korea in 1950, President Truman swiftly sent U.S. troops. In the end, the Korean War was indecisive: the fragile truce agreed to in 1953 left Korea divided between a Communist north and a capitalist south. The war nonetheless showed that though the superpowers might maintain a fragile peace in Europe, they were perfectly willing to engage in open conflict in non-Western territories.

By 1955 the Soviet-American confrontation had become an apparently permanent feature of world affairs. For the next thirty-five years, despite intermittent periods of relaxation, the superpowers would struggle to win political influence and territorial control and to achieve technological superiority. Cold War hostilities helped foster a nuclear arms race, a space race, and the computer revolution, all made possible by stunning advances in science and technology.

NATO The North Atlantic Treaty Organization, an anti-Soviet military alliance of Western governments.

Warsaw Pact Soviet-backed military alliance of East Bloc Communist countries in Europe.

Big Science in the Nuclear Age

During the Second World War, theoretical science lost its innocence when it was joined with practical technology (applied science) on a massive scale. Many leading university scientists went to work on top-secret projects to help their governments fight the war. The development by British scientists of radar to detect enemy aircraft was a particularly important outcome of this new kind of sharply focused research. The air war also greatly stimulated the development of rocketry and jet aircraft. The most spectacular and deadly result of directed scientific research during the war was the atomic bomb, which showed the world both the awesome power and the heavy moral responsibilities of modern science and its high priests.

The impressive results of this directed research inspired a new model for science—Big Science. By combining theoretical work with sophisticated engineering in a large bureaucratic organization, Big Science could tackle extremely difficult problems, from new and improved weapons for the military to better products for consumers. Big Science was extremely expensive, requiring large-scale financing from governments and large corporations.

After the war, scientists continued to contribute to advances in military technologies, and a large portion of all postwar scientific research supported the growing arms race. New weapons such as missiles, nuclear submarines, and spy satellites demanded breakthroughs no less remarkable than those responsible for radar and the first atomic bomb. After 1945 roughly one-quarter of all men and women trained in science and engineering in the West—and perhaps more in the Soviet Union—were employed full-time in the production of weapons to kill other humans. By the 1960s both sides had enough nuclear firepower to destroy each other and the rest of the world many times over.

Sophisticated science, lavish government spending, and military needs came together in the space race of the 1960s. In 1957 the Soviets used long-range rockets developed in their nuclear weapons program to launch Sputnik, the first man-made satellite to orbit the earth. In 1961 they sent the world's first cosmonaut circling the globe. Embarrassed by Soviet triumphs, the United States caught "Sputnikitis" and made an all-out commitment to catch up with the Soviets. The U.S. National Aeronautics and Space Administration (NASA), founded in 1958, won a symbolic victory by landing a manned spacecraft on the moon in 1969. Four more moon landings followed by 1972.

Advanced nuclear weapons and the space race were made possible by the concurrent revolution in computer technology. The search for better weaponry in World War II boosted the development of sophisticated data-processing machines, including the electronic Colossus computer used by the British to break German military codes. The massive mainframe ENIAC (Electronic Numerical Integrator and Computer), built for the U.S. Army at the University of Pennsylvania, went into operation in 1945. The invention of the transistor in 1947 further advanced computer design. From the mid-1950s on, this small, efficient electronic switching device increasingly replaced bulky vacuum tubes as the key computer components. By the 1960s sophisticated computers were indispensable tools for a variety of military, commercial, and scientific uses, foreshadowing the rise of personal computers in the decades to come.

Big Science had tangible benefits for ordinary people. During the postwar green revolution, directed agricultural research greatly increased the world's food supplies. Farming was industrialized and became more and more productive per acre, resulting in far fewer people being needed to grow food. The application of scientific advances to industrial processes made consumer goods less expensive and more available to larger numbers of people. The transistor, for example, was used in computers but also in portable radios, kitchen appliances, and many other consumer products. In sum, in the nuclear age, Big Science created new sources of material well-being and entertainment as well as destruction.

The Western Renaissance/Recovery in Western Europe

FOCUS QUESTION

What were the sources of postwar recovery and stability in western Europe?

In the late 1940s the outlook for Europe appeared bleak. Ruins still covered urban areas, economic conditions were the worst in generations, and Cold War confrontations divided the continent. Yet Europe recovered, with the nations of western Europe in the vanguard. In less than a generation, many western European countries constructed democratic political institutions and entered a period of unprecedented economic growth. As a consumer revolution brought improved living standards and a sense of prosperity to ever-larger numbers of people, politicians entered collective economic agreements and established the European Economic Community, the first steps toward broader European unity.

The Search for Political and Social Consensus

In the first years after the war, economic conditions in western Europe were terrible. Infrastructure of all kinds barely functioned, and runaway inflation and a thriving black market testified to severe shortages and hardships. In 1948, as Marshall Plan dollars poured in, the battered economies of western Europe began to improve. The outbreak of the Korean War in 1950 further stimulated economic activity, and Europe entered a period of rapid economic progress that lasted into the late 1960s. Never before had the European economy grown so fast. By the late 1950s contemporaries were talking about a widespread **economic miracle** that had brought robust growth to most western European countries.

economic miracle Term contemporaries used to describe rapid economic growth, often based on the consumer sector, in post–World War II western Europe.

There were many reasons for this stunning economic performance. American aid got the process off to a fast start. Moreover, economic growth became a basic objective of all western European governments, for leaders and voters alike were determined to avoid a return to the dangerous and demoralizing stagnation of the 1930s.

The postwar governments in western Europe thus embraced new political and economic policies that led to a remarkably lasting social consensus. They turned to liberal democracy and generally adopted Keynesian economics (see Chapter 26) in successful attempts to stimulate their economies. In addition, whether they leaned to the left or to the right, national leaders in the core European states applied an imaginative mixture of government planning and free-market capitalism to promote economic growth. They nationalized (or established government ownership of) significant sectors of the economy, used economic regulation to encourage growth, and established generous welfare provisions, paid for with high taxes, for all citizens. This consensual framework for good government lasted until the middle of the 1970s.

In politics, the Nazi occupation and the war had discredited old ideas and old leaders, and a new team of European politicians emerged to guide the postwar recovery. Across the West, newly formed Christian Democratic parties became important power brokers. Rooted in the Catholic parties of the prewar decades (see Chapters 23 and 27), the **Christian Democrats** offered voters tired of radical politics a center-right vision of reconciliation and recovery. Socialists and Communists, active in the resistance against Hitler, also increased their power and prestige, especially in France and Italy. They, too, provided fresh leadership as they pushed for social change and economic reform.

Across much of continental Europe, the centrist Christian Democrats defeated their left-wing competition. In Italy, the Christian Democrats were the leading party in the first postwar elections in 1946, and in early 1948 they won an absolute majority in the parliament in a landslide victory. In France, the Popular Republican Movement, a Christian Democratic party, provided some of the best postwar leaders after General Charles de Gaulle (duh GOHL) resigned from his position as head of the provisional government in January 1946. West Germans, too, elected a Christian Democratic government from 1949 until 1969.

As they provided effective leadership for their respective countries, Christian Democrats drew inspiration from a common Christian and European heritage. They firmly rejected authoritarianism and narrow nationalism and placed their faith in democracy and liberalism. The anticommunist rhetoric of these steadfast cold warriors was unrelenting. Rejecting the class politics of the left, they championed a return to traditional family values, a vision with great appeal after a war that left many broken families and destitute households; the Christian Democrats often received a majority of women's votes.

Following their U.S. allies, Christian Democrats advocated free-market economics and promised voters prosperity and ample supplies of consumer goods. (See "Evaluating the Evidence 28.1: Western European Recovery and the Promise of Prosperity," page 956.) At the same time, they established education subsidies, family and housing allowances, public transportation, and public health insurance throughout continental Europe. When necessary, Christian Democratic leaders accepted the need for limited government planning. In France, the government established modernization commissions for key industries, and state-controlled banks funneled money into industrial development. In West Germany, the Christian Democrats broke decisively with the straitjacketed Nazi economy and promoted a "social-market economy" based on a combination of free-market liberalism, some state intervention, and an extensive social benefits network.

Though Portugal, Spain, and Greece generally supported NATO and the United States in the Cold War, they proved exceptions to the rule of democratic transformation outside the Soviet bloc. In Portugal and Spain, nationalist authoritarian regimes had taken power in the 1930s. Portugal's authoritarian state was overthrown in a left-wing military coup only in 1974, while Spain's dictator Francisco Franco remained in power until his death in 1975. The authoritarian monarchy established in Greece when the civil war ended in 1949, bolstered by military support and kept in power in a series of army coups, was likewise replaced by a democratic government only in 1975.

By contrast, the Scandinavian countries and Great Britain took decisive turns to the left. Norway, Denmark, and especially Sweden earned a global reputation for long-term

Christian Democrats
Center-right political parties that rose to power in western Europe after the Second World War.

Western European Recovery and the Promise of Prosperity

Christian Democrat Ludwig Erhard, minister for economic affairs (1949–1963) and then chancellor (1963–1966) of West Germany, was an outspoken proponent of liberal capitalism and free markets in the years of the "economic miracle." In this newspaper article from June 16, 1953, Erhard defends the use of consumer credit and the expansion of consumption, starting with the wealthy, as an engine of postwar economic growth.

I have often pointed out that the consumption of quality goods can only be expanded provided we tolerate their use being confined initially to a relatively small number of people in the higher income brackets. If this is not accepted, and if the enjoyment of such goods is regarded as indulgence and made the subject of social obloquy and hostility, then the economy will be forced to abandon production in this sector, and there will be a corresponding loss of potential national income (and jobs) and the growth of the country's productive capacity will be forcibly curtailed. One section of the press actually challenged me to say how an old-age pensioner was to set about getting his refrigerator. To this puerile question I replied that the first motor-cars in America were presumably not run by pensioners but by millionaires, and I do not consider this reply unduly flippant. Does not the history of the world in the last hundred years afford abundant proof of the fact that every single improvement in the standard of living can only be effected step by step, spreading progressively over a gradually mounting proportion of the population? . . .

Ever since 1948 I have been propounding an economic policy which puts the consumer at the very centre of all economic processes, by ensuring freedom of choice to him and restoring him to a position of dignity and power. . . .

Responding to a critique of shoppers purchasing goods on credit, Erhard continues:

At first sight, this argument seems reasonable enough, but in the balance-sheet of the economy as a whole the picture looks different. Consumer credit enables goods to be produced which could otherwise not find a market. . . . Now, consumer credit goes a step further and initiates an expansion of production (e.g. of refrigerators), and this expanded production creates new income which in its turn appears as additional purchasing power on the market. The volume of goods at the disposal of the economy has in other words been built up to a higher level, the national product and the national income have been extended. . . .

In this connection of course the question of magnitude is of vital importance. Consumer credit cannot carry, but can usefully supplement an upswing of the economy as a whole. . . . The use of consumer credit [is] one of the means capable of subserving a general policy aimed at expanded consumption. . . .

Consumer credit can be a means of increasing employment, creating additional returns, and thus enlarging the national product and the national income. The wider the choice of goods available to the consumer, the more active competition becomes, and the more prices will tend to come down, to the benefit of us all.

EVALUATE THE EVIDENCE

1. How, according to Erhard, does expanded consumption and the use of credit lead to economic growth?
2. Why would promises of looming prosperity — such as Erhard's — play an important role in Cold War rhetoric?

Source: Ludwig Erhard, *The Economics of Success*, trans. J. A. Arengo-Jones and D. J. S. Thomson (Princeton: D. Van Nostrand Co., 1963). Used by permission of Ludwig-Erhard-Stiftung e.V.

Social Democratic governance, generous state-sponsored welfare benefits, tolerant lifestyles, and independent attitudes toward Cold War conflicts. In Britain, the social-democratic Labour Party took power after the war and ambitiously established a "cradle-to-grave" welfare state. Although the Labour Party suffered defeats throughout much of the 1950s and early 1960s, its Conservative opponents maintained much of the welfare state when they came to power.

Many British industries were nationalized, including banks, iron and steel industries, and utilities and public transportation networks. The British government gave its citizens free medical services and hospital care, generous retirement pensions, and unemployment benefits, all subsidized by progressive taxation that pegged tax payments to income levels, with the wealthy paying significantly more than those below them. Even though wartime austerity and rationing programs were in place until the mid-1950s, Britain offered the most comprehensive state benefit programs outside Scandinavia. Economic growth and state-sponsored welfare measures meant that, by the early 1960s, western European living standards were higher than ever before.

Toward European Unity

Though there were important regional differences across much of western Europe, politicians and citizens supported policies that brought together limited state planning, strong economic growth, and democratic government, and this political and social consensus accompanied the first tentative steps on the long road toward a more unified Europe. Christian Democrats were committed to cultural and economic cooperation, and other groups shared their dedication. Many European intellectuals believed that only a new "European nation" could effectively rebuild the war-torn continent and reassert the continent's influence in world affairs.

A number of new financial arrangements and institutions encouraged slow but steady moves toward European integration, as did cooperation with the United States. The Bretton Woods agreement of 1944 had already linked Western currencies to the U.S. dollar and established the International Monetary Fund and the World Bank to facilitate free markets and world trade. To receive Marshall Plan aid, the European states were required by the Americans to cooperate with one another, leading to the creation of the Organization for European Economic Cooperation and the Council of Europe in 1948, both of which promoted commerce and cooperation among European countries.

European federalists hoped that the Council of Europe would evolve into a European parliament with sovereign rights, but this did not happen. Britain, with its still-vast empire and its close relationship with the United States, consistently opposed conceding sovereignty to the council. On the continent, many prominent nationalists and Communists agreed with the British view.

Frustrated in political consolidation, European federalists turned to economics as a way of working toward genuine unity. In 1950 two far-seeing French statesmen, the diplomat and political economist Jean Monnet and Foreign Minister Robert Schuman, called for a special international organization to control and integrate all European steel and coal production. Christian Democratic governments in West Germany, Italy, Belgium, the Netherlands, and Luxembourg accepted the French proposal and founded the European Coal and Steel Community in 1951 (the British refused to join). The founding states quickly attained their immediate economic goal—a single, transnational market for steel and coal without national tariffs or quotas. Close economic ties, advocates hoped, would eventually bind the six member nations so closely together that war among them would become unthinkable.

In 1957 the six countries of the Coal and Steel Community signed the Treaty of Rome, which created the European Economic Community, or **Common Market**. The first goal of the treaty was a gradual reduction of all tariffs among the six in order to create a single market almost as large as that of the United States. Other goals included the free movement of capital and labor and common economic policies and institutions. The Common Market encouraged trade among European states, promoted global

Common Market The European Economic Community, created by six western and central European countries in the West Bloc in 1957 as part of a larger search for European unity.

The Place de la Concorde in Paris, 1956
The consumer revolution of the late 1950s brought a rapid increase in the number of privately owned automobiles across western Europe. Major European cities began to experience one of the more unfortunate but increasingly common aspects of postwar life: the traffic jam. (Peter Cornelius/akg-images)

exports, and helped build shared resources for the modernization of national industries. European integration thus increased transnational cooperation even as it bolstered economic growth on the national level.

The development of the Common Market fired imaginations and encouraged the hopes of some for rapid progress toward political as well as economic union. In the 1960s, however, these hopes were frustrated by a resurgence of nationalism. France again took the lead. French president Charles de Gaulle, re-elected to office in 1958, was at heart a romantic nationalist. De Gaulle viewed the United States as the main threat to genuine French (and European) independence. He withdrew all French military forces from what he called an "American-controlled" NATO, developed France's own nuclear weapons, and vetoed the scheduled advent of majority rule within the Common Market. Thus the 1950s and 1960s established a lasting pattern: Europeans would establish ever-closer economic ties, but the Common Market remained a union of independent, sovereign states.

The Consumer Revolution

In the late 1950s western Europe's rapidly expanding economy led to a rising standard of living and remarkable growth in the number and availability of standardized consumer goods. Modern consumer society had precedents in the decades before the Second World War (see Chapter 26), but the years of the "economic miracle" saw the arrival of a veritable consumer revolution: as the percentage of income spent on necessities such as housing and food declined dramatically, near full employment and high wages meant that more Europeans could buy more things than ever before. Shaken by war and eager to rebuild their homes and families, western Europeans embraced the new products of consumer society. Like North Americans, they filled their houses and apartments with modern appliances such as washing machines, and they eagerly purchased the latest entertainment devices of the day: radios, record players, and televisions.

The purchase of consumer goods was greatly facilitated by the increased use of installment purchasing, which allowed people to buy on credit. With the expansion of social security safeguards reducing the need to accumulate savings for hard times and old age, ordinary people were increasingly willing to take on debt, and new banks and credit unions offered loans for consumer purchases on easy terms. The consumer market became an increasingly important engine for general economic growth. For example, the European automobile industry expanded phenomenally after lagging far behind that of the United States since the 1920s. In 1948 there were only 5 million cars in western Europe; by 1965 there were 44 million. Car ownership was democratized and became possible for better-paid workers—the consumer revolution brought a vast array of new items into everyday activities, changing both lifestyles and attitudes.

Visions of consumer abundance became a powerful weapon in an era of Cold War competition. Politicians in both East and West claimed that their respective systems could best provide citizens with ample consumer goods. (See "Evaluating the Evidence 28.2: The Nixon-Khrushchev 'Kitchen Debate,'" page 962.) In the competition over consumption, Western capitalism clearly surpassed Eastern planned economies in the production and distribution of inexpensive products. Western leaders boasted about the abundance of goods on store shelves and promised new forms of social equality in which all citizens would have equal access to consumer items—rather than relying on class leveling mandated by the state, as in the despised East Bloc. The race to provide ordinary people with higher living standards would be a central aspect of the Cold War, as the Communist East Bloc struggled to catch up to Western standards of prosperity.

Developments in the Soviet Union and the East Bloc

While western Europe surged ahead economically and increased its independent political power as American influence gradually waned, East Bloc countries followed a different path. The Soviet Union first tightened its grip on peoples it had "liberated" during the Second World War and then refused to let go. Though limited reforms after Stalin's death in 1953 led to some economic improvement and limited gains in freedoms, postwar recovery in Communist central and eastern Europe proceeded along Soviet lines, and political and social developments there were strongly influenced by developments in the U.S.S.R.

FOCUS QUESTION
What was the pattern of postwar development in the Soviet bloc?

Postwar Life in the East Bloc

The "Great Patriotic War of the Fatherland" had fostered Russian nationalism and a relaxation of dictatorial terror. It also had produced a rare but real unity between Soviet rulers and most citizens. Having made a heroic war effort, the vast majority of the Soviet people hoped in 1945 that a grateful party and government would grant greater freedom and democracy. Such hopes were soon disappointed.

Even before the war ended, Stalin was moving the U.S.S.R. back toward rigid dictatorship. By early 1946 Stalin was arguing that another war was inevitable as long as capitalism existed. Working to extend Communist influence across the globe, the Soviets established the Cominform, or Communist Information Bureau, an international organization dedicated to maintaining Russian control over Communist parties abroad, in western Europe and the East Bloc. Stalin's new superpower foe, the United States, served as an excuse for re-establishing a harsh dictatorship in the U.S.S.R. itself. Stalin reasserted the Communist Party's control of the government and his absolute mastery of the party. Rigid ideological indoctrination, attacks on religion, and the absence of civil liberties were soon facts of life for citizens of the Soviet empire. Millions of supposed political enemies were sent to prison, exile, or forced-labor camps.

As discussed earlier, in the satellite states of central and eastern Europe—including East Germany, Poland, Hungary, Czechoslovakia, Romania, Albania, and Bulgaria— national Communist parties remade state and society on the Soviet model. Though there were significant differences in these East Bloc countries, postwar developments

Rebellion in East Germany   In June 1953 disgruntled construction workers in East Berlin walked off the job to protest low pay and high work quotas, setting off a nationwide rebellion against the Communist regime. The protesters could do little against the Soviet tanks and troops that put down the revolt. (Photo by Wolfgang Albrecht/Deutsches Historisches Museum, Berlin, Germany/© DHM/Bridgeman Images)

followed a similar pattern. Popular Communist leaders who had led the resistance against Germany were ousted and replaced by politicians who supported Stalinist policies. With Soviet backing, national Communist parties absorbed their Social Democratic rivals and established one-party dictatorships subservient to the Communist Party in Moscow. State security services arrested, imprisoned, and sometimes executed dissenters. Show trials of supposedly disloyal Communist Party leaders took place across the East Bloc from the late 1940s into the 1950s, but were particularly prominent in Bulgaria, Czechoslovakia, Hungary, and Romania. They testified to the influence of Soviet advisers and the unrestrained power of the domestic secret police in the satellite states, as well as Stalin's urge to establish complete control—and his increasing paranoia.

Only Josip Broz Tito (TEE-toh) (1892–1980), the resistance leader and Communist chief of Yugoslavia, was able to proclaim political independence and successfully resist Soviet domination. Tito stood up to Stalin in 1948, and because there was no Russian army in Yugoslavia, he got away with it. Though Communist led, Yugoslavia remained outside of the Soviet bloc. The country prospered as a multiethnic state until it began to break apart in 1991.

Within the East Bloc, the newly installed Communist governments moved quickly to restructure national economies along Soviet lines, introducing five-year plans to cope with the enormous task of economic reconstruction. Most industries and businesses were nationalized. These efforts transformed prewar patterns of everyday life, even as they laid the groundwork for industrial development later in the decade.

In their attempts to revive the economy, Communist planners gave top priority to heavy industry and the military. At the same time, East Bloc planners neglected consumer goods and housing, in part because they were generally suspicious of Western-style consumer culture. A glut of consumer goods, they believed, created waste, encouraged rampant individualism, and led to social inequality. Thus, for practical and ideological reasons, the provision of consumer goods lagged in the East Bloc, leading to complaints and widespread disillusionment with the constantly deferred promise of socialist prosperity.

Communist regimes also moved aggressively to collectivize agriculture, as the Soviets had done in the 1930s (see Chapter 27). By the early 1960s independent farmers had virtually disappeared in most of the East Bloc. Poland was the exception: there the Stalinist regime tolerated the existence of private agriculture, hoping to maintain stability in the large and potentially rebellious country.

For many people in the East Bloc, everyday life was hard throughout the 1950s. Socialist planned economies often led to production problems and persistent shortages of basic household items. Party leaders encouraged workers to perform almost super-human labor to "build socialism," often for low pay and under poor conditions. In East Germany, popular discontent with this situation led to open revolt in June 1953. A strike by Berlin construction workers protesting poor wages and increased work quotas led to nationwide demonstrations that were put down with Soviet troops and tanks. At least fifty-five protesters were killed and about five thousand were arrested during the uprising. When the revolt ended, the authorities rescinded the increased work quotas, but despite this apparent concession the protest strengthened the position of hardliner Stalinists within the East German government.

Communist censors purged culture and art of independent voices in aggressive campaigns that imposed rigid anti-Western ideological conformity. In the 1950s and 1960s the Communist states required artists and writers to conform to the dictates of **Socialist Realism**, which idealized the working classes and the Soviet Union. Party propagandists denounced artists who strayed from the party line, and forced many talented writers, composers, and film directors to produce works that conformed to the state's political goals. In short, the postwar East Bloc resembled the U.S.S.R. in the 1930s, although police terror was far less intense (see Chapter 27).

Socialist Realism Artistic movement that followed the dictates of Communist ideals, enforced by state control in the Soviet Union and East Bloc countries in the 1950s and 1960s.

Reform and De-Stalinization

In 1953 the aging Stalin finally died, and the dictatorship that he had built began to change. Even as Stalin's heirs struggled for power, they realized that reforms were necessary because of the widespread fear and hatred created by Stalin's political terrorism. The power of the secret police was curbed, and many forced-labor camps were gradually closed. Change was also necessary to spur economic growth, which had sputtered in the postwar years. Moreover, Stalin's belligerent foreign policy had led directly to a strong Western alliance, which had taken steps to isolate the Soviet Union.

The Soviet leadership was badly split on the question of just how much change could be permitted while still preserving the system. Conservatives wanted to move slowly. Reformers, led by the remarkable Nikita Khrushchev (1894–1971), argued for major innovations. Khrushchev (kroush-CHAWF), who had joined the party as a coal miner in 1918 and risen to a high-level position in Ukraine in the 1930s, emerged as the new Soviet premier in 1955.

To strengthen his position and that of his fellow reformers, Khrushchev launched a surprising attack on Stalin and his crimes at a closed session of the Twentieth Party Congress in 1956. In his famous "secret speech," Khrushchev told Communist delegates startled by his open admission of errors that Stalin had "supported the glorification of his own person with all conceivable methods" to build a propagandistic "cult of personality." The delegates applauded when Khrushchev reported that Stalin had bungled the country's defense in World War II and unjustly imprisoned and tortured thousands of loyal Communists:

[Stalin] discarded the Leninist method of convincing and educating . . . for that of administrative violence, mass repressions, and terror. . . . Mass arrests and deportations of many thousands of people, execution without trial and without normal investigation created conditions of insecurity, fear, and even desperation.[5]

The Nixon-Khrushchev "Kitchen Debate"

During the Cold War, the United States and the Soviet Union waged political battles in Europe, wars of influence in the former colonies, and contests for national prestige in space and the nuclear arms race. But the two superpowers also sparred over which system — communism or capitalism — provided the best lifestyle for its citizens. In an effort to move beyond Cold War tensions, the Americans and Soviets set up public displays in each other's territory. The American National Exhibition in Moscow in 1959 included a model U.S. suburban home, complete with modern kitchen appliances, a television and stereo console, and a Cadillac sedan, all meant to demonstrate the superiority of capitalism.

During a visit to the exhibit, U.S. vice president Richard Nixon and Soviet premier Nikita Khrushchev engaged in an impromptu and sometimes ham-fisted argument over the merits of their respective political systems. As this exchange from the famous "kitchen debate" suggests, dishwashers were also on the frontline of the Cold War.

KHRUSHCHEV: We want to live in peace and friendship with Americans because we are the two most powerful countries and if we live in friendship then other countries will also live in friendship. But if there is a country that is too war-minded we could pull its ears a little and say: Don't you dare; fighting is not allowed now; this is a period of atomic armament; some foolish one could start a war and then even a wise one couldn't finish the war. Therefore, we are governed by this idea in our policy — internal and foreign. How long has America existed? Three hundred years?

NIXON: One hundred and fifty years.

KHRUSHCHEV: One hundred and fifty years? Well then we will say America has been in existence for 150 years and this is the level she has reached. We have existed not quite 42 years and in another seven years we will be on the same level as America. When we catch you up, in passing you by, we will wave to you. Then if you wish we can stop and say: Please follow up. Plainly speaking, if you want capitalism you can live that way. That is your own affair and doesn't concern us. We can still feel sorry for you but since you don't understand us — live as you do understand. . . . [Wrapping his arms about a Soviet workman.] Does this man look like a slave laborer? [Waving at others.] With men with such spirit how can we lose?

NIXON: [Pointing to American workmen.] With men like that we are strong. But these men, Soviet and American, work together well for peace, even as they have worked together in building this exhibition. This is the way it should be. Your remarks are in the tradition of what we have come to expect — sweeping and extemporaneous. Later on we will both have an opportunity to speak and consequently I will not comment on the various points that you raised, except to say this — this color television is one of the most advanced developments in communication that we have. I can only say that if this competition in which you plan to outstrip us is to do the best for both of our peoples and for peoples everywhere, there must be a free exchange of ideas. After all, you don't know everything.

KHRUSHCHEV: If I don't know everything you don't know anything about communism except fear of it.

NIXON: There are some instances where you may be ahead of us, for example in the development of the thrust of your rockets for the investigation of outer space; there may be some instances in which we are ahead of you — in color television, for instance.

KHRUSHCHEV: No, we are up with you on this, too. We have bested you in one technique and also in the other.

NIXON: You see, you never concede anything.

KHRUSHCHEV: I do not give up.

NIXON: Wait till you see the picture [on the TV set]. Let's have far more communication and exchange in this very area that we speak of. We should hear you more on our televisions. You should hear us more on yours.

de-Stalinization The liberalization of the post-Stalin Soviet Union led by reformer Nikita Khrushchev.

The U.S.S.R. now entered a period of genuine liberalization — or **de-Stalinization**, as it was called in the West. Khrushchev's speech was read at Communist Party meetings held throughout the country, and it strengthened the reform movement. The party jealously maintained its monopoly on political power, but Khrushchev brought in new members. Calling for a relaxation of tensions with the West, the new premier announced a policy of "peaceful coexistence." In domestic policies, state planners shifted resources from heavy industry and the military toward consumer goods and

KHRUSHCHEV: That's a good idea. Let's do it like this. You appear before our people. We will appear before your people. People will see and appreciate this. . . .

NIXON: [Halting Khrushchev at the model kitchen in the model house.] You had a very nice house in your exhibition in New York. My wife and I saw and enjoyed it very much. I want to show you this kitchen. It is like those of our houses in California.

KHRUSHCHEV: [After Nixon points to a built-in panel-controlled washing machine.] We have such things.

NIXON: This is the newest model. This is the kind which is built in thousands of units for direct installation in the houses. [He adds that Americans are interested in making life easier for their women.]

Khrushchev remarked that in the Soviet Union, they did not have "the capitalist attitude toward women."

~

NIXON: I think that this attitude toward women is universal. What we want to do is make easier the life of our housewives.

Nixon explained that the house could be built for $14,000 and that most veterans had bought houses for between $10,000 and $15,000.

~

NIXON: Let me give you an example you can appreciate. Our steelworkers, as you know, are on strike. But any steelworker could buy this house. They earn $3 an hour. This house costs about $100 a month to buy on a contract running 25 to 30 years.

KHRUSHCHEV: We have steelworkers and we have peasants who also can afford to spend $14,000 for a house. . . .

KHRUSHCHEV: Don't you have a machine that puts food into the mouth and pushes it down? Many things you've shown us are interesting but they are not needed in life. They have no useful purpose. They are merely gadgets. We have a saying, if you have bedbugs you have to catch one and pour boiling water into the ear.

NIXON: We have another saying. This is that the way to kill a fly is to make it drink whisky. But we have a better use for whisky. [Aside] I like to have this battle of wits with the Chairman. He knows his business. . . .

KHRUSHCHEV: The Americans have created their own image of the Soviet man and think he is as you want him to be. But he is not as you think. You think the Russian people will be dumbfounded to see these things, but the fact is that newly built Russian houses have all this equipment right now. Moreover, all you have to do to get a house is to be born in the Soviet Union. You are entitled to housing. I was born in the Soviet Union. So I have a right to a house. In America, if you don't have a dollar—you have the right to choose between sleeping in a house or on the pavement. Yet you say that we are slaves of communism. . . .

NIXON: We do not claim to astonish the Russian people. We hope to show our diversity and our right to choose. We do not wish to have decisions made at the top by government officials who say that all homes should be built in the same way. Would it not be better to compete in the relative merits of washing machines than in the strength of rockets? Is this the kind of competition you want?

KHRUSHCHEV: Yes that's the kind of competition we want. But your generals say: "Let's compete in rockets. We are strong and we can beat you." But in this respect we can also show you something.

NIXON: To me you are strong and we are strong. In some ways, you are stronger. In others, we are stronger. We are both strong not only from the standpoint of weapons but from the standpoint of will and spirit.

EVALUATE THE EVIDENCE

1. Why did Nixon and Khrushchev focus so heavily on the lives of workers in the United States and the Soviet Union?

2. What does the kitchen debate reveal about the role of consumer goods in the Cold War?

Source: Transcript of the "Kitchen Debate" at the opening of the American National Exhibition at Sokolniki Park in Moscow, July 24, 1959.

agriculture, and relaxed Stalinist workplace controls. Leaders in other Communist countries grudgingly adopted similar reforms, and the East Bloc's generally low standard of living began to improve.

Khrushchev was proud of Soviet achievements and liked to boast that East Bloc living standards and access to consumer goods would soon surpass those of the West. (See "Evaluating the Evidence 28.2: The Nixon-Khrushchev 'Kitchen Debate,'" above.) Soviet and East Bloc reforms did spark a limited consumer revolution. Consumers'

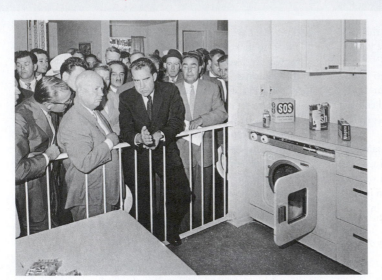

The Kitchen Debate Khrushchev and Nixon discuss the merits of the American way during the famous kitchen debate. Leonid Brezhnev, the future leader of the Soviet Union (from 1964 to 1982), stands on the far right, just behind Nixon. (AP Photo/AP Images)

options were more modest than those in the West, but people in Communist countries also purchased automobiles, televisions, and other consumer goods in increasing numbers in the 1960s.

De-Stalinization created great ferment among writers and intellectuals who sought freedom from the constraints of Socialist Realism, such as Russian author Boris Pasternak (1890–1960), who published his great novel *Doctor Zhivago* in 1957. Appearing in the West but not in the Soviet Union until 1988, *Doctor Zhivago* is both a literary masterpiece and a powerful challenge to communism. It tells the story of a poet who rejects the violence and brutality of the October Revolution of 1917 and the Stalinist years. Mainstream Communist critics denounced Pasternak, whose book was circulated in secret—but in an era of liberalization he was neither arrested nor shot. Other talented writers followed Pasternak's lead, and courageous editors let the sparks fly. Aleksandr Solzhenitsyn (sohl-zhuh-NEET-suhn) (1918–2008) created a sensation when his *One Day in the Life of Ivan Denisovich* was published in 1962. Solzhenitsyn's novel portrays in grim detail life in a Stalinist concentration camp—a life to which Solzhenitsyn himself had been unjustly condemned—and is a damning indictment of the Stalinist past.

Foreign Policy and Domestic Rebellion

Khrushchev also de-Stalinized Soviet foreign policy. "Peaceful coexistence" with capitalism was possible, he argued, and war was not inevitable. Khrushchev negotiated with Western diplomats, agreeing in 1955, for example, to independence for a neutral Austria after ten long years of Allied occupation. As a result, Cold War tensions relaxed considerably between 1955 and 1957. At the same time, Khrushchev began wooing the new nations of Asia and Africa—even those that were not Communist—with promises of support and economic aid.

In the East Bloc states, Communist leaders responded in complex ways to de-Stalinization. In East Germany the regime stubbornly resisted reform, but in Poland and Hungary de-Stalinization stimulated rebelliousness. Poland took the lead in 1956, when extensive popular demonstrations brought a new government to power. The new First Secretary of the Polish Communist Party argued that there were "many roads to socialism." By promising to remain loyal to the Warsaw Pact, the Polish Communists managed to win greater autonomy from Soviet control. The new leadership maintained Communist control even as it tolerated a free peasantry and an independent Catholic Church.

Hungary experienced an ultimately tragic revolution the same year. Led by students and workers—the classic urban revolutionaries—the people of Budapest installed

Imre Nagy (im-rey nadge), a liberal Communist reformer, as the new prime minister in October 1956. Encouraged by extensive popular protests and joined by other Communist reformers, Nagy proposed to democratize Hungary. Though never renouncing communism, he demanded open, multiparty elections, the relaxation of political repression, and other reforms. Bold moves in Hungary raised widespread hopes that Communist states could undergo substantial but peaceful change, driven from within.

At first, it seemed that the Soviets might negotiate, but the breathing space was short-lived. When Nagy announced that Hungary would leave the Warsaw Pact and asked the United Nations to protect the country's neutrality, the Soviets grew alarmed about the possibility that Hungary's independent course would affect other East Bloc countries. On November 4 Soviet troops moved in on the capital city of Budapest and crushed the revolution. Around 2,700 Hungarians died in the crackdown. Fighting was bitter until the end, for the Hungarians hoped that the United Nations would come to their aid. This did not occur—in part because the Western powers were involved in the Suez crisis (see page 972) and were, in general, reluctant to directly confront the Soviets in Europe with military force. When a new, more conservative Communist regime executed Nagy and other protest leaders and sent thousands more to prison, many people in the East Bloc concluded that their best hope was to strive for internal reform without openly challenging Soviet control.

The outcome of the Hungarian uprising weakened support for Soviet-style communism in western Europe—the brutal repression deeply discouraged those who still believed in the possibility of an equitable socialist society, and tens of thousands of Communist Party members in the West resigned in disgust. At the same time, Western politicians saw that the U.S.S.R. would use military force to defend its control of the East Bloc, and that only open war between East and West had the potential to overturn Communist rule there. This price was too high, and it seemed that Communist domination of the satellite states was there to stay.

The Limits of Reform

By late 1962 opposition to Khrushchev's reformist policies had gained momentum in party circles. Khrushchev's Communist colleagues began to see de-Stalinization as a dangerous threat to the authority of the party. Moreover, Khrushchev's policy toward the West was erratic and ultimately unsuccessful. In 1958, in a failed attempt to staunch the flow of hundreds of thousands of disgruntled East German residents who used the open border between East and West Berlin to move permanently to the West, Khrushchev tightened border controls and ordered the Western allies to evacuate the city within six months. In response, the allies reaffirmed their unity in West Berlin, and Khrushchev backed down. Then, with Khrushchev's backing, in 1961 the East German authorities built a wall between East and West Berlin, sealing off West Berlin, in clear violation of existing access agreements between the Great Powers. The recently elected U.S. president, John F. Kennedy (U.S. pres. 1961–1963), insisted publicly that the United States would never abandon Berlin. Privately hoping that the wall would lessen Cold War tensions by easing hostilities in Berlin, Kennedy did little to prevent its construction.

Emboldened by American acceptance of the Berlin Wall and seeing a chance to change the balance of military power decisively, Premier Khrushchev secretly ordered missiles with nuclear warheads installed in Fidel Castro's Communist Cuba in 1962. When U.S. intelligence discovered missile sites under construction, Kennedy countered with a naval blockade of Cuba. After a tense diplomatic crisis, Khrushchev agreed to remove the Soviet missiles in return for American pledges not to disturb Castro's regime. In a secret agreement, Kennedy also promised to remove U.S. nuclear missiles from Turkey.

Khrushchev's influence in the party, already slipping, declined rapidly after the Cuban missile crisis. In 1964 the reformist premier was displaced in a bloodless coup, and he spent the rest of his life under house arrest. Under his successor, Leonid Brezhnev (1906–1982), the U.S.S.R. began a period of limited re-Stalinization and economic stagnation. Almost immediately, Brezhnev (BREHZH-nehf) and his supporters started talking quietly of Stalin's "good points" and downplaying his crimes. This change informed Soviet citizens that further liberalization could not be expected at home. Soviet leaders, determined never to suffer Khrushchev's humiliation in the face of American nuclear superiority, launched a massive arms buildup. Yet Brezhnev and company proceeded cautiously in the mid-1960s and avoided direct confrontation with the United States.

Despite popular protests and changes in leadership, the U.S.S.R. and its satellite countries had achieved some stability by the late 1950s. Communist regimes addressed dissent and uprisings with an effective combination of military force, political repression, and limited economic reform. East and West traded propaganda threats, but both sides basically accepted the division of Europe into spheres of influence. Violent conflicts now took place in the developing world, where decolonization was opening new paths for Cold War confrontation.

The End of Empires

FOCUS QUESTION
What led to decolonization after World War II, and how did the Cold War influence the process?

In the postwar era, in one of world history's great turning points, Europe's long-standing overseas expansion was dramatically reversed. The retreat from imperial control—a process Europeans called **decolonization**—remade the world map. In just two decades, over fifty new nations in Africa, Asia, and the Middle East joined the global community (Map 28.3). In some cases, decolonization proceeded relatively smoothly, with an orderly transition and little violence. In others, the European powers were determined to preserve colonial rule—long a source of profit and national pride—and colonized peoples won independence only after long and bloody struggles.

decolonization The postwar reversal of Europe's overseas expansion caused by the rising demand of the colonized peoples themselves, the declining power of European nations, and the freedoms promised by U.S. and Soviet ideals.

The Cold War had a profound impact on decolonization. Independence movements often had to choose sides in the struggle between the superpowers. After independence was won, both the United States and the Soviet Union struggled to exert influence in the former colonies, and economic growth and political stability remained elusive in much of Europe's former empire. Liberation from colonial domination was a proud achievement that brought fundamental gains in human freedom but left lasting problems for the former colonized and colonizers alike.

Decolonization and the Global Cold War

The most basic cause of imperial collapse was the rising demand of non-Western peoples for national self-determination, racial equality, and personal dignity. This demand spread from intellectuals to ordinary people in nearly every colonial territory after the First World War. By 1939 the colonial powers were already on the defensive; the Second World War prepared the way for the eventual triumph of independence movements.

MAP 28.3 Decolonization in Africa and Asia, 1947 to the Present   Divided primarily along religious lines into two states, British India led the way to political independence in 1947. Most African territories achieved statehood by the mid-1960s as European empires passed away, unlamented.

European empires had been based on an enormous power differential between the rulers and the ruled, a difference that had greatly declined by 1945. Western Europe was economically devastated and militarily weak immediately after the war. Moreover, the Japanese had driven imperial rulers from large parts of East Asia during the war in the Pacific, shattering the myth of European superiority and invincibility. In Southeast Asia, European imperialists confronted strong anticolonial nationalist movements that re-emerged with new enthusiasm after the defeat of the Japanese.

To some degree, the Great Powers regarded their empires very differently after 1945 than before 1914, or even before 1939. Empire had rested on self-confidence and self-righteousness; Europeans had believed their superiority to be not only technical and military but also spiritual, racial, and moral. The horrors of the First and Second World Wars undermined such complacent arrogance and gave opponents of imperialism much greater influence in Europe. Increasing pressure from the United

States, which had long presented itself as an enemy of empire despite its own imperialist actions in the Philippines and the Americas, encouraged Europeans to let go of their former colonies. Indeed, Americans were eager to extend their own influence in Europe's former colonies. Economically weakened, and with their political power and moral authority in tatters, the imperial powers preferred to avoid bloody colonial wars and generally turned to rebuilding at home.

Furthermore, the imperial powers faced dedicated anticolonial resistance. Popular politicians, including China's Mao Zedong, India's Mohandas Gandhi, Egypt's Gamal Abdel Nasser, and many others, provided determined leadership in the struggle against European imperialism. A new generation of intellectuals, such as Jomo Kenyatta of Kenya and Aimé Césaire and Frantz Fanon, both from Martinique, wrote trenchant critiques of imperial power, often rooted in Marxist ideas. (See "Evaluating the Evidence 28.3: Frantz Fanon on Violence, Decolonization, and Human Dignity," at right.) Anticolonial politicians and intellectuals alike helped inspire colonized peoples to resist and overturn imperial rule.

Around the globe, the Cold War had an inescapable impact on decolonization. Liberation from colonial rule had long been a central goal for proponents of Communist world revolution. The Soviets and, after 1949, the Communist Chinese advocated rebellion in the developing world and promised to help end colonial exploitation and bring freedom and equality in a socialist state. They supported Communist independence movements with economic and military aid, and the guerrilla insurgent armed with a Soviet-made AK-47 machine gun became the new symbol of Marxist revolution.

Western Europe and particularly the United States offered a competing vision of independence, based on free-market economics and, ostensibly, liberal democracy—though the United States was often willing to support authoritarian regimes that voiced staunch anticommunism. Like the U.S.S.R., the United States extended economic aid and weaponry to decolonizing nations. The Americans promoted cautious moves toward self-determination in the context of containment, attempting to limit the influence of communism in newly liberated states.

After they had won independence, the leaders of the new nations often found themselves trapped between the superpowers, compelled to voice support for one bloc or the other. Many new leaders followed a third way, adopting a policy of **nonalignment**, remaining neutral in the Cold War and playing both sides for what they could get.

nonalignment Policy of postcolonial governments to remain neutral in the Cold War and play both the United States and the Soviet Union for what they could get.

The Struggle for Power in Asia

The first major fight for independence that followed World War II, between the Netherlands and anticolonial insurgents in the Dutch East Indies (today's Indonesia), in many ways exemplified decolonization in the Cold War world. The Dutch had been involved in Indonesia since the early seventeenth century (see Chapter 14) and had extended their colonial power over the centuries. During World War II, however, the Japanese had overrun the archipelago, encouraging hopes among the locals for independence from Western control. Following the Japanese defeat in 1945, the Dutch returned, hoping to use Indonesia's raw materials, particularly rubber, to support economic recovery at home. But Dutch imperialists faced a determined group of rebels inspired by a powerful combination of nationalism, Marxism, and Islam. Four

Frantz Fanon on Violence, Decolonization, and Human Dignity

Frantz Fanon shocked Western audiences with his assertion that only violence could restore political freedom and human dignity to colonized peoples, an argument forcefully expressed in his famous book The Wretched of the Earth *(1961). Born in the French colony of Martinique in 1925 and educated as a psychiatrist, Fanon held radical views that were profoundly influenced by his work as a doctor in Algeria during the colonial war (1954–1962) that ultimately led to independence from French rule.*

National liberation, national renaissance, the restoration of nationhood to the people, commonwealth: whatever may be the heading used or the new formulas introduced, decolonization is always a violent phenomenon. At whatever level we study it—relationships between individuals, new names for sports clubs, the human admixture at cocktail parties, in the police, on the directing boards of national or private banks—decolonization is quite simply the replacing of a certain "species" of men by another "species" of men. Without any period of transition, there is a total, complete, and absolute substitution. . . .

Decolonization is the meeting of two forces, opposed to each other by their very nature. . . . Their first encounter was marked by violence and their existence together—that is to say the exploitation of the native by the settler—was carried on by dint of a great array of bayonets and cannons. The settler and the native are old acquaintances. . . .

The naked truth of decolonization evokes for us the searing bullets and bloodstained knives which emanate from it. For if the last shall be first, this will only come to pass after a murderous and decisive struggle between the two protagonists. . . . [We] can only triumph if we use all means to turn the scale, including, of course, that of violence. . . .

In the colonial countries the peasants alone are revolutionary, for they have nothing to lose and everything to gain. The starving peasant, outside the class system, is the first among the exploited to discover that only violence pays. For him there is no compromise, no possible coming to terms; colonization and decolonization are only a question of relative strength. . . .

The mobilization of the masses, when it arises out of the war of liberation, introduces into each man's consciousness the ideas of a common cause, of a national destiny, and of a collective history. In the same way the second phase, that of the building-up of the nation, is helped on by the existence of this cement which has been mixed with blood and anger. . . .

At the level of individuals, violence is a cleansing force. It frees the native from his inferiority complex and from his despair and inaction; it makes him fearless and restores his self-respect. . . .

Violence alone, violence committed by the people, violence organized and educated by its leaders, makes it possible for the masses to understand social truths and gives the key to them. Without that struggle, without that knowledge of the practice of action, there's nothing but a fancy dress parade and the blare of the trumpets. There's nothing save a minimum of readaptation, a few reforms at the top, a flag waving: and down there at the bottom an undivided mass, still living in the middle ages, endlessly marking time.

EVALUATE THE EVIDENCE

1. Why, according to Fanon, is violence required for both the political and psychological success of the anti-imperial struggle?
2. How do advocates of nonviolent reform, such as Mohandas Gandhi or Martin Luther King, Jr., challenge Fanon's ideas about the positive potential of violent revolt? Who makes the better case?

Source: Excerpts from *The Wretched of the Earth* by Frantz Fanon, copyright © 1963 by Présence Africaine. Used by permission of Grove/Atlantic, Inc. Any third party use of this material, outside of this publication, is prohibited.

years of deadly guerrilla war followed, and in 1949 the Netherlands reluctantly accepted Indonesian independence. The new Indonesian president became an effective advocate of nonalignment. He had close ties to the Indonesian Communist Party but received foreign aid from the United States as well as the Soviet Union.

A similar combination of communism and anticolonialism inspired the independence movement in parts of French Indochina (now Vietnam, Cambodia, and Laos), though noncommunist nationalists were also involved. France desperately wished to maintain control over these prized colonies and tried its best to re-establish colonial

A Refugee Camp During the Partition of India   A young Muslim man, facing an uncertain future, sits above a refugee camp established on the grounds of a medieval fortress in the northern Indian city of Delhi. In the camp, Muslim refugees wait to cross the border to the newly founded Pakistan. The chaos that accompanied the mass migration of Muslims and Hindus during the partition of India in the late summer and autumn of 1947 cost the lives of up to 1 million migrants and disrupted the livelihoods of millions more. (Margaret-Bourke White/The LIFE Picture Collection/Getty Images)

rule after the Japanese occupation collapsed at the end of World War II. Despite substantial American aid, the French army fighting in Vietnam was defeated in 1954 by forces under the guerrilla leader Ho Chi Minh (hoh chee mihn) (1890–1969), who was supported by the U.S.S.R. and China. Vietnam was divided. As in Korea, a shaky truce established a Communist North and a pro-Western South Vietnam, which led to civil war and subsequent intervention by the United States. Cambodia and Laos also gained independence under noncommunist regimes, though Communist rebels remained active in both countries.

India, Britain's oldest, largest, and most lucrative imperial possession, played a key role in the decolonization process. Nationalist opposition to British rule coalesced after the First World War under the leadership of British-educated lawyer Mohandas (sometimes called "Mahatma," or "Great-Souled") Gandhi (1869–1948), one of the twentieth century's most significant and influential figures. In the 1920s and 1930s Gandhi (GAHN-dee) built a mass movement preaching nonviolent "noncooperation" with the British. In 1935 Gandhi wrested from the frustrated and unnerved British a new, liberal constitution that was practically a blueprint for independence. The Second World War interrupted progress toward Indian self-rule, but when the Labour Party came to power in Great Britain in 1945, it was ready to relinquish sovereignty. British socialists had long been critics of imperialism, and the heavy cost of governing India had become a large financial burden to the war-wracked country.

Britain withdrew peacefully, but conflict between India's Hindu and Muslim populations posed a lasting dilemma for South Asia. As independence neared, the Muslim minority grew increasingly anxious about their status in an India dominated by the Hindu majority. Muslim leaders called for partition—the division of India into separate Hindu and Muslim states—and the British agreed. When independence was made official on August 15, 1947, predominantly Muslim territories on India's eastern and western borders became Pakistan (the eastern section is today's Bangladesh). Seeking relief from ethnic conflict that erupted, some 10 million Muslim and Hindu refugees fled both ways across the new borders, a massive population exchange that left mayhem and death in its wake. In just a few summer weeks, up to 1 million people (estimates vary widely) lost their lives. Then in January 1948 a radical Hindu nationalist who opposed partition assassinated Gandhi, and Jawaharlal Nehru became Indian prime minister.

As the Cold War heated up in the early 1950s, Pakistan, an Islamic republic, developed close ties with the United States. Under the leadership of Nehru, India successfully maintained a policy of nonalignment. India became a liberal, if socialist-friendly, democratic state that dealt with both the United States and the U.S.S.R. Pakistan and India both joined the British Commonwealth, a voluntary and cooperative association of former British colonies that already included Canada, Australia, and New Zealand.

Where Indian nationalism drew on Western parliamentary liberalism, Chinese nationalism developed and triumphed in the framework of Marxist-Leninist ideology. After the withdrawal of the occupying Japanese army in 1945, China erupted again in open civil war. The authoritarian Guomindang (Kuomintang, National People's Party), led by Jiang Jieshi (traditionally called Chiang Kai-shek; 1887–1975), fought to repress the Chinese Communists, led by Mao Zedong (MA-OW zuh-DOUNG) and supported by a popular grassroots uprising. The Soviets gave Mao aid, and the Americans gave Jiang much more. Winning the support of the peasantry by promising to expropriate the holdings of the big landowners, the tougher, better-organized Communists forced the Guomindang to withdraw to the island of Taiwan in 1949. Mao and the Communists united China's 550 million inhabitants in a strong centralized state. Once in power, the "Red Chinese" began building a new society that adapted Marxism to Chinese conditions. The new government promoted land reform, extended education and health-care programs to the peasantry, and introduced Soviet-style five-year plans that boosted industrial production. It also brought Stalinist-style repression—mass arrests, forced-labor camps, and ceaseless propaganda campaigns—to the Chinese people.

Independence and Conflict in the Middle East

In some areas of the Middle East, the movement toward political independence went relatively smoothly. The French League of Nations mandates in Syria and Lebanon had collapsed during the Second World War, and Saudi Arabia and Transjordan had already achieved independence from Britain. But events in the British mandate of Palestine and in Egypt showed that decolonization in the Middle East could follow a dangerous and difficult path.

As part of the peace accords that followed the First World War, the British government had advocated a Jewish homeland alongside the Arab population (see Chapter 25). This tenuous compromise unraveled after World War II. Neither Jews nor Arabs were happy with British rule, and violence and terrorism mounted on both sides. In 1947 the frustrated British decided to leave Palestine, and the United Nations voted in a nonbinding resolution to divide the territory into two states—one Arab and one Jewish. The Jews accepted the plan and founded the state of Israel in 1948.

The Palestinians and the surrounding Arab nations viewed Jewish independence as a betrayal of their own interests, and they attacked the Jewish state as soon as it was proclaimed. The Israelis drove off the invaders and conquered more territory. Roughly nine hundred thousand Arab Palestinians fled or were expelled from their homes, creating a persistent refugee problem. Holocaust survivors from Europe streamed into Israel, as Theodor Herzl's Zionist dream came true (see Chapter 23). The next fifty years saw four more wars between the Israelis and the Arab states and innumerable clashes between Israelis and Palestinians.

Israel, 1948

The Suez Crisis, 1956

The Arab defeat in 1948 triggered a powerful nationalist revolution in Egypt in 1952, led by the young army officer Gamal Abdel Nasser (1918–1970). The revolutionaries drove out the pro-Western king, and in 1954 Nasser became president of an Egyptian republic. A crafty politician, Nasser advocated nonalignment and expertly played the superpowers against each other, securing loans from the United States and purchasing Soviet arms.

In July 1956 Nasser abruptly nationalized the foreign-owned Suez Canal Company, the last symbol and substance of Western power in the Middle East. Infuriated, the British and the French, along with the Israelis, planned a secret military operation. The Israeli army invaded the Sinai Peninsula bordering the canal, and British and French bombers attacked Egyptian airfields. World opinion was outraged, and the United States feared that such a blatant show of imperialism would propel the Arab states into the Soviet bloc. The Americans joined with the Soviets to force the British, French, and Israelis to back down. Egyptian nationalism triumphed: Nasser got his canal, and Israel left the Sinai. The Suez crisis, a watershed in the history of European imperialism, showed that the European powers could no longer maintain their global empires and demonstrated the power and appeal of nonalignment.

Decolonization in Africa

In less than a decade, most of Africa won independence from European imperialism, a remarkable movement of world historical importance. In much of the continent south of the Sahara, decolonization proceeded relatively smoothly. Yet the new African states were quickly caught up in the struggles between the Cold War superpowers, and decolonization all too often left a lasting legacy of violence, economic decline, and political conflict (see Map 28.3).

Starting in 1957 most of Britain's African colonies achieved independence with little or no bloodshed and then entered a very loose association with Britain as members of the British Commonwealth. Ghana, Nigeria, Tanzania, and other countries gained independence in this way, but there were exceptions to this relatively smooth transfer of power. In Kenya, British forces brutally crushed the nationalist Mau Mau rebellion in the early 1950s, but nonetheless recognized Kenyan independence in 1963. In South Africa, the white-dominated government left the Commonwealth in 1961 and declared an independent republic in order to preserve apartheid—an exploitative system of racial segregation enforced by law.

The decolonization of the Belgian Congo was one of the great tragedies of the Cold War. Belgian leaders, profiting from the colony's wealth of natural resources and proud of their small nation's imperial status, maintained a system of apartheid there and dragged their feet in granting independence. These conditions sparked an anticolonial movement that grew increasingly aggressive in the late 1950s under the able leadership of the charismatic Patrice Lumumba. In January 1960 the Belgians gave in and hastily announced that the Congo would be independent six months later, a schedule that was irresponsibly fast. Lumumba was chosen prime minister in democratic elections, but when the Belgians pulled out on schedule, the new government was entirely unprepared. Chaos broke out when the Congolese army attacked Belgian military officers who remained in the country.

Decolonization in the Democratic Republic of the Congo   Flushed with victory, the democratically elected Congolese premier Patrice Lumumba waves as he leaves the National Senate on September 8, 1960. Lumumba had just received a 41–2 vote of confidence that confirmed his leadership position. Four months later he was assassinated in a military coup. (© Bettmann/Corbis)

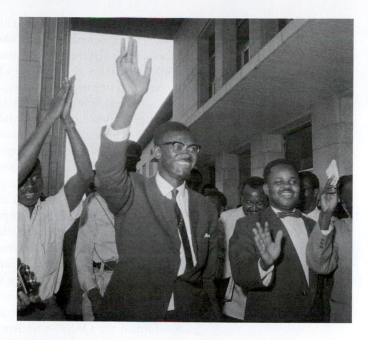

With substantial financial investments in the Congo, the United States and western Europe worried that the new nation might fall into Soviet hands. U.S. leaders cast Lumumba as a Soviet proxy, an oversimplification of his nonalignment policies, and American anxiety increased when Lumumba asked the U.S.S.R. for aid and protection. A cable from the CIA chief in the Congo revealed the way Cold War anxieties framed the situation:

> Embassy and station believe Congo experiencing classic Communist takeover government. . . . Whether or not Lumumba actually Commie or just playing Commie game to assist solidifying his power, anti-West forces rapidly increasing power [in] Congo and there may be little time left in which to take action to avoid another Cuba.[6]

In a troubling example of containment in action, the CIA helped implement a military coup against Lumumba, who was captured and then assassinated. The military set up a U.S.-backed dictatorship under the corrupt general Joseph Mobutu. Mobutu ruled until 1997 and became one of the world's wealthiest men, while the Congo remained one of the poorest, most violent, and most politically torn countries in the world.

French colonies in Africa followed several roads to independence. Like the British, the French offered most of their African colonies the choice of a total break or independence within a kind of French commonwealth. All but one of the new states chose the latter option, largely because they identified with French culture and wanted aid from their former colonizer. The French were eager to help—provided the former colonies accepted close economic ties on French terms. As in the past, the French and their Common Market partners, who helped foot the bill, saw themselves as continuing their civilizing mission in sub-Saharan Africa (see Chapter 24). More important, they saw in Africa raw materials for their factories, markets for their industrial goods, outlets for profitable investment, and good temporary jobs for their engineers and teachers.

Things were far more difficult in the French colony of Algeria, a large Muslim state on the Mediterranean Sea where some 1.2 million white European settlers, including some 800,000 French, had taken up permanent residency by the 1950s. Nicknamed pieds-noirs (literally "black feet"), many of these Europeans had raised families in Algeria for three or four generations, and they enforced a two-tiered system of citizenship, dominating politics and the economy. When Algerian rebels, inspired by Islamic fundamentalism and Communist ideals, established the National Liberation Front

(FLN) and revolted against French colonialism in the early 1950s, the presence of the pieds-noirs complicated matters. Worried about their position in the colony, the pieds-noirs pressured the French government to help them. In response, France sent some 400,000 troops to crush the FLN and put down the revolt.

The resulting Algerian War—long, bloody, and marred by atrocities committed on both sides—lasted from 1954 to 1962. FLN radicals repeatedly attacked pied-noir civilians in savage terrorist attacks, while the French army engaged in systematic torture, mass arrests (often of innocent suspects), and the forced relocation and internment of millions of Muslim civilians suspected of supporting the insurgents. By 1958 French forces had successfully limited FLN military actions, but their disproportionate use of force effectively encouraged many Muslims to support or join the FLN. News reports about torture and abuse of civilians turned significant elements of French public opinion against the war, and international outrage further pressured French leaders to end the conflict. Efforts to open peace talks led to a revolt by the Algerian French and threats of a coup d'état by the French army. In 1958 the immensely popular General Charles de Gaulle was reinstated as French prime minister as part of the movement to keep Algeria French. His appointment at first calmed the army, the pieds-noirs, and the French public.

Yet to the dismay of the pieds-noirs and army hardliners, de Gaulle pragmatically moved toward Algerian self-determination. In 1961 furious pieds-noirs and army leaders formed the OAS (Secret Army Organization) and opened a terrorist revolt against Muslim Algerians and the French government. In April of that year the OAS mounted an all-out but short-lived putsch, taking over Algiers and threatening the government in Paris. Loyal army units defeated the rebellion, the leading generals were purged, and negotiations between the French government and FLN leaders continued. In April 1962, after more than a century of French rule, Algeria became independent under the FLN. Then in a massive postindependence exodus, over 1 million pieds-noirs fled to France and the Americas.

By the mid-1960s most African states had won independence, some through bloody insurrections. There were exceptions: Portugal, for one, waged war against independence movements in Angola and Mozambique until the 1970s. Even in liberated countries, the colonial legacy had long-term negative effects. South African blacks still longed for liberation from apartheid, and white rulers in Rhodesia continued a bloody civil war against African insurgents until 1979. Elsewhere African leaders may have expressed support for socialist or democratic principles in order to win aid from the superpowers. In practice, however, corrupt and authoritarian African leaders like Mobutu in the Congo often established lasting authoritarian dictatorships and enriched themselves at the expense of their populations.

Even after decolonization, western European countries managed to increase their economic and cultural ties with their former African colonies in the 1960s and 1970s. Above all, they used the lure of special trading privileges and provided heavy investment in French- and English-language education to enhance a powerful Western presence in the new African states. This situation led a variety of leaders and scholars to charge that western Europe (and the United States) had imposed a system of **neocolonialism** on the former colonies. According to this view, neocolonialism was a system designed to perpetuate Western economic domination and undermine the promise of political independence, thereby extending to Africa (and much of Asia) the kind of economic subordination that the United States had imposed on Latin America in the nineteenth century.

neocolonialism
A postcolonial system that perpetuates Western economic exploitation in former colonial territories.

Postwar Social Transformations

While Europe staged its astonishing political and economic recovery from the Nazi nightmare and colonized peoples won independence, the basic structures of Western society were also in transition. A changing class structure, new patterns of global migration, and new roles for women and youths had dramatic impacts on everyday life, albeit with different effects in the East Bloc and western Europe. Yet such large-scale changes had transformative effects on both sides of the iron curtain: social and cultural trends joined political and economic recovery to build stability in the postwar decades.

FOCUS QUESTION
How did changes in social relations contribute to European stability on both sides of the iron curtain?

Changing Class Structures

The combination of rapid economic growth, growing prosperity and mass consumption, and the implementation of generous welfare policies went a long way toward creating a new society in Europe after the Second World War. Old class barriers relaxed, and class distinctions became fuzzier.

Changes in the structure of the middle class were particularly influential in this result. In the nineteenth and early twentieth centuries, the model for the middle class had been the independent, self-employed individual who owned a business or practiced a liberal profession such as law or medicine. Ownership of property—frequently inherited property—and strong family ties had often been the keys to wealth and standing within the middle class. After 1945 this pattern changed drastically in western Europe. A new breed of managers and experts—so-called white-collar workers—replaced property owners as the leaders of the middle class. The ability to serve the needs of a big organization largely replaced inherited property and family connections in determining an individual's social position in the middle and upper-middle classes. At the same time, the middle class grew massively and became harder to define.

There were several reasons for these developments. Rapid industrial and technological expansion and the consolidation of businesses created a powerful demand for technologists and managers in large corporations and government agencies. Moreover, the old propertied middle class lost control of many family-owned businesses. Numerous small businesses (including family farms) could no longer turn a profit, so their former owners regretfully joined the ranks of salaried employees.

Similar processes were at work in the Communist states of the East Bloc, where class leveling was an avowed goal of the authoritarian socialist state. The nationalization of industry, expropriation of property, and aggressive attempts to open employment opportunities to workers and equalize wage structures effectively reduced class differences. Communist Party members typically received better jobs and more pay than nonmembers, but by the 1960s the income differential between the top and bottom strata of East Bloc societies was far smaller than in the West.

In both East and West, managers and civil servants represented the model for a new middle class. Well paid and highly trained, often with backgrounds in engineering or accounting, these pragmatic experts were primarily concerned with efficiency and with practical solutions to concrete problems.

The structure of the lower classes also became more flexible and open. Continuing trends that began in the nineteenth century, large numbers of people left the countryside for the city. The population of one of the most traditional and least mobile groups in European society—farmers—drastically declined. Meanwhile, the number of industrial workers in western Europe also began to fall, as new jobs for white-collar and service employees grew rapidly. This change marked a significant transition in the world of labor. The welfare benefits extended by postwar governments also helped promote greater social equality because they raised lower-class living standards and were paid for in part by higher taxes on the wealthy. In general, European workers were better educated and more specialized than before, and the new workforce bore a greater resemblance to the growing middle class of salaried specialists than to traditional industrial workers.

Patterns of Postwar Migration

The 1850s to the 1930s had been an age of global migration, as countless Europeans moved around the continent and the world seeking economic opportunity or freedom from political or religious persecution (see Chapter 24). The 1950s and 1960s witnessed new waves of migration that had a significant impact on European society.

Some postwar migration took place within countries. Declining job prospects in Europe's rural areas encouraged many peasants and small farmers to seek better prospects in cities. In the poorer countries of Spain, Portugal, and Italy, millions moved to more developed regions of their own countries. The process was similar in the East Bloc, where the forced collectivization of agriculture and state subsidies for heavy industry opened opportunities in urban areas. And before the erection of the Berlin Wall in 1961, some 3.5 million East Germans moved to the Federal Republic of Germany, seeking higher pay and a better life.

Many other Europeans moved across national borders seeking work. The general pattern was from south to north. Workers from less developed countries like Italy, Spain, and socialist Yugoslavia moved to the industrialized north, particularly to West Germany, which—having lost 5 million people during the war—was in desperate need of able-bodied workers. In the 1950s and 1960s West Germany and other prosperous countries implemented **guest worker programs** designed to recruit much-needed labor for the booming economy. West Germany signed labor agreements with Italy, Greece, Spain, Portugal, Yugoslavia, Turkey, and the North African countries of Tunisia and Morocco. By the early 1970s there were 2.8 million foreign workers in Germany and another 2.3 million in France, where they made up 11 percent of the workforce.

guest worker programs
Government-run programs in western Europe designed to recruit labor for the booming postwar economy.

Most guest workers were young, unskilled single men who labored for low wages in entry-level jobs and sent much of their pay to their families at home. (See "Individuals in Society: Armando Rodrigues," at right.) According to government plans, these guest workers were supposed to return to their home countries after a specified period. Many built new lives, however, and, to the dismay of the authorities, chose to live permanently in their adoptive countries.

postcolonial migration
The postwar movement of people from former colonies and the developing world into Europe.

Europe was also changed by **postcolonial migration**, the movement of people from the former colonies and the developing world into prosperous Europe. In contrast to guest workers, who joined formal recruitment programs, postcolonial migrants could often claim citizenship rights from their former colonizers and moved spontaneously. Immigrants from the Caribbean, India, Africa, and Asia moved to Britain; people from North Africa, especially Algeria, and from sub-Saharan countries such as Cameroon and the Ivory Coast moved to France; Indonesians migrated to the Netherlands. Postcolonial immigrants also moved to eastern Europe, though in far fewer numbers.

These new migration patterns had dramatic results. Immigrant labor helped fuel economic recovery. Growing ethnic diversity changed the face of Europe and enriched

INDIVIDUALS IN SOCIETY

Armando Rodrigues

Popping flashbulbs greeted Portuguese worker Armando Rodrigues when he stepped off a train in Cologne in September 1964. Celebrated in the national media as West Germany's 1 millionth guest worker, Rodrigues was met by government and business leaders — including the Christian Democratic minister of labor — who presented him with a motorcycle and a bouquet of carnations.

In most respects, Rodrigues was hardly different from the many foreign workers recruited to work in West Germany and other northern European countries. Most foreign laborers were nobodies, written out of mainstream historical texts and treated as statistics. Yet given his moment of fame, Rodrigues is an apt symbol of a troubled labor program that helped turn Germany into a multiethnic society.

By the late 1950s the new Federal Republic desperately needed able-bodied men to fill the low-paying jobs created by rapid economic expansion. The West German government signed labor agreements with several Mediterranean countries to meet this demand. Rodrigues and hundreds of thousands of other young men signed up for the employment program and then submitted to an arduous application process. Rodrigues traveled from his village to the regional Federal Labor Office, where he filled out forms and took written and medical exams. Months later, after he had received an initial one-year contract from a German employer, Rodrigues and twelve hundred other Portuguese and Spanish men boarded a special train reserved for foreign workers and embarked for West Germany.

For labor migrants, life was hard in West Germany. In the first years of the guest worker program, most recruits were men between the ages of twenty and forty who were either single or willing to leave their families at home. They typically filled low-level jobs in construction, mines, and factories, and they lived apart from West Germans in special barracks close to their workplaces, with six to eight workers in a room.

*Quoted in Rita Chin, *The Guest Worker Question in Postwar Germany* (New York: Cambridge University Press, 2007), p. 43.

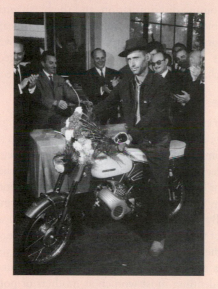

Armando Rodrigues received a standing ovation and a motorcycle when he got off the train in Cologne in 1964. (Horst Ossinger/picture-allliance/dpa/AP Images)

West Germans gave Rodrigues and his fellow migrants a mixed reception. Though they were a welcome source of inexpensive labor, the men who emigrated from what West Germans called "the southern lands" faced discrimination and prejudice. "Order, cleanliness, and punctuality seem like the natural qualities of a respectable person to us," wrote one official in 1966. "In the south, one does not learn or know this, so it is difficult [for a person from the south] to adjust here."*

According to official plans, the so-called guest workers were supposed to return home after a specified period of time. Rodrigues, for one, went back to Portugal in the late 1970s. Others did not. Resisting government pressure, millions of temporary "guests" raised families and became permanent West German residents, building substantial ethnic minorities in the Federal Republic. Because of strict naturalization laws, however, they could not become West German citizens.

Despite the hostility they faced, foreign workers established a lasting and powerful presence in West Germany, and they were a significant factor in the country's swift economic recovery. More than fifty years after Rodrigues arrived in Cologne, his motorcycle is on permanent display in the House of History Museum in Bonn. The exhibit is a remarkable testament to one man's history, to the contribution of migrant labor to West German economic growth, and to the ongoing struggle to come to terms with ethnic difference and integration in a democratic Germany.

QUESTIONS FOR ANALYSIS

1. How did Rodrigues's welcome at his 1964 reception differ from the general attitude toward guest workers in Germany at the time?
2. What were the long-term costs and benefits of West Germany's labor recruitment policies?

the cultural life of the continent. The new residents were not always welcome, however. Adaptation to European lifestyles could be difficult, and immigrants often lived in separate communities where they spoke their own languages. They faced employment and housing discrimination, and the harsh anti-immigrant rhetoric and policies of xenophobic politicians. Even prominent European intellectuals worried aloud that Muslim migrants from North Africa and Turkey would never adopt European values and customs. The tensions that surrounded changed migration patterns would pose significant challenges to social integration in the decades to come.

New Roles for Women

The postwar culmination of a one-hundred-year-long trend toward early marriage, early childbearing, and small family size in wealthy urban societies (see Chapter 22) had revolutionary implications for women. Above all, pregnancy and child care occupied a much smaller portion of a woman's life than in earlier times. The postwar baby boom did make for larger families and fairly rapid population growth of 1 to 1.5 percent per year in many European countries, but the long-term decline in birthrates resumed by the 1960s. By the early 1970s about half of Western women were having their last baby by the age of twenty-six or twenty-seven. When the youngest child trooped off to kindergarten, the average mother had more than forty years of life in front of her.

This was a momentous transition. Throughout history male-dominated society insisted on defining most women as mothers or potential mothers, and motherhood was very demanding. In the postwar years, however, motherhood no longer absorbed the energies of a lifetime, and more and more married women looked for new roles in the world of work outside the family. Three major forces helped women searching for jobs in the changing post–World War II workplace. First, the economic boom created strong demand for labor. Second, the economy continued its gradual shift away from the old male-dominated heavy industries, such as coal, steel, and shipbuilding, and toward the white-collar service industries in which some women already worked, such as government, education, trade, and health care. Third, young women shared fully in the postwar education revolution, positioning them to take advantage of the growing need for officeworkers and well-trained professionals. Thus more and more married women became full-time and part-time wage earners.

In the East Bloc, Communist leaders opened up numerous jobs to women, who accounted for almost half of all employed persons. Many women made their way into previously male professions, including factory work but also medicine and engineering. In western Europe and North America, the percentage of married women in the workforce rose from a range of roughly 20 to 25 percent in 1950 to anywhere from 30 to 60 percent in the 1970s.

All was not easy for women entering paid employment. Married women workers faced widespread and long-established discrimination in pay, advancement, and occupational choice in comparison to men. Moreover, many women could find only part-time work. As the divorce rate rose in the 1960s, part-time work, with its low pay and scanty benefits, often meant poverty for many women with children. Finally, married working women in both the East and West still carried most of the child-rearing and housekeeping responsibilities, leaving them with an exhausting "double burden." Trying to live up to society's seemingly contradictory ideals was one reason that many women accepted part-time employment.

The injustices that married women encountered as wage earners contributed greatly to the movement for women's equality and emancipation that arose in the United States and western Europe in the 1960s. Sexism and discrimination in the workplace—and in the home—grew loathsome and evoked the sense of injustice that drives revolutions and reforms.

Youth Culture and the Generation Gap

The bulging cohort of so-called baby boomers born after World War II created a distinctive and very international youth culture, which brought remarkable changes to postwar youth roles and lifestyles. That subculture, found across western Europe and the United States, was rooted in fashions and musical tastes that set its members off from their elders and fueled anxious comments about a growing "generation gap."

Youth styles in the United States often provided inspiration for movements in Europe. Groups like the British Teddy boys, the West German *Halbstarken* (half-strongs), and the French *blousons noirs* (black jackets) modeled their rebellious clothing and cynical attitudes on the bad-boy characters played by U.S. film stars such as James Dean and Marlon Brando. American jazz and rock 'n' roll spread rapidly in western Europe, aided by the invention of the long-playing record album (or LP) and the 45 rpm "single" in the late 1940s, and the growth of the corporate music industry. American musicians such as Elvis Presley, Bill Haley and His Comets, and Gene Vincent thrilled European youths and worried parents, teachers, and politicians.

Youths played a key role in the consumer revolution. Marketing experts and manufacturers quickly recognized that the young people they now called "teenagers" had money to spend due to postwar prosperity. An array of advertisements and products consciously targeted the youth market. In France, for example, magazine advertising aimed at adolescents grew by 400 percent between 1959 and 1962. As the baby boomers entered their late teens, they eagerly purchased trendy clothing and the latest pop music hits, as well as record players, transistor radios, magazines, hair products, and makeup, all marketed for the "young generation."

The new youth culture became an inescapable part of Western society. One clear sign of this new presence was the rapid growth in the number of universities and college students. Before the 1960s, in North America and Europe, only a small elite received a university education. In 1950 only 3 to 4 percent of western European youths went on to higher education; numbers in the United States were only slightly higher. Then, as government subsidies made education more affordable to ordinary people, enrollments skyrocketed. By 1960 at least three times more European students attended some kind of university than they had before World War II, and the number continued to rise sharply until the 1970s.

The rapid expansion of higher education opened new opportunities for the middle and lower classes, but it also made for overcrowded classrooms. Many students felt that they were not getting the kind of education they needed for jobs in the modern world. At the same time, some reflective students feared that universities were doing nothing but turning out docile technocrats both to stock and to serve "the establishment." Thus it was no coincidence that students became leaders in a counterculture that attacked the ideals of the affluent society of the postwar world and shocked the West in the late 1960s.

LOOKING BACK LOOKING AHEAD

The unprecedented human and physical destruction of World War II left Europeans shaken, searching in the ruins for new livelihoods and a workable political order. A tension-filled peace settlement left the continent divided into two hostile political-military blocs, and the resulting Cold War, complete with the possibility of atomic annihilation, threatened to explode into open confrontation. Albert Einstein voiced a common anxiety when he said, "I do not know with what weapons World War III will be fought, but World War IV will be fought with sticks and stones."

Despite such fears, the division of Europe led to the emergence of a stable world system. In the West Bloc, economic growth, state provision of welfare benefits, and a strong alliance brought social and political consensus. In the East Bloc, a combination of political repression and partial reform likewise limited dissent and encouraged stability. During the height of the Cold War, Europe's former colonies won liberation in a process that was often flawed but that nonetheless resulted in political independence for millions of people. And large-scale transformations, including the rise of Big Science and rapid economic growth, opened new opportunities for women and immigrants and contributed to stability on both sides of the iron curtain.

By the early 1960s Europeans had entered a remarkable age of affluence that almost eliminated real poverty on most of the continent. Superpower confrontations had led not to European war but to peaceful coexistence. The following decades, however, would see substantial challenges to this postwar consensus. Youth revolts and a determined feminist movement, an oil crisis and a deep economic recession, and political dissent and revolution in the East Bloc would shake and remake the foundations of Western society.

Make Connections

Think about the larger developments and continuities within and across chapters.

1. How did the Cold War shape politics and everyday life in the United States and western Europe, the U.S.S.R. and the East Bloc, and the decolonizing world? Why was its influence so pervasive?

2. How were the postwar social transformations in class structures, patterns of migration, and the lives of women and youths related to the broad political and economic changes that followed World War II? How did they differ on either side of the iron curtain?

3. Compare and contrast the treaties and agreements that ended the First and Second World Wars (Chapter 25). Did the participants who shaped the peace accords face similar problems? Which set of agreements did a better job of resolving outstanding issues, and why?

28 REVIEW & EXPLORE

Review the Main Ideas

Answer the focus questions from each section of the chapter.

- Why was World War II followed so quickly by the Cold War? (p. 944)

- What were the sources of postwar recovery and stability in western Europe? (p. 954)

- What was the pattern of postwar development in the Soviet bloc? (p. 959)

- What led to decolonization after World War II, and how did the Cold War influence the process? (p. 966)

- How did changes in social relations contribute to European stability on both sides of the iron curtain? (p. 975)

Identify Key Terms

Identify and explain the significance of each item below.

Cold War (p. 944)

displaced persons (p. 945)

Truman Doctrine (p. 951)

Marshall Plan (p. 951)

Council for Mutual Economic Assistance (COMECON) (p. 951)

NATO (p. 952)

Warsaw Pact (p. 952)

economic miracle (p. 954)

Christian Democrats (p. 955)

Common Market (p. 957)

Socialist Realism (p. 961)

de-Stalinization (p. 962)

decolonization (p. 966)

nonalignment (p. 968)

neocolonialism (p. 974)

guest worker programs (p. 976)

postcolonial migration (p. 976)

NOTES

1. Anonymous, *A Woman in Berlin: Eight Weeks in the Conquered City: A Diary* (New York: Metropolitan Books, 2005), pp. 239–240.

2. Quoted in N. Graebner, *Cold War Diplomacy, 1945–1960* (Princeton, N.J.: Van Nostrand, 1962), p. 17.

3. From a speech delivered by G. Marshall at Harvard University on June 5, 1947, reprinted in *Department of State Bulletin* (June 15, 1947), pp. 1159–1160.

4. Quoted in T. Judt, *Postwar: A History of Europe Since 1945* (New York: Penguin, 2005), p. 150.

5. N. Khrushchev, "On the Cult of Personality and Its Consequences" (1956), quoted in J. M. Brophy et al., *Perspectives from the Past* (New York: W. W. Norton, 2009), pp. 804–805.

6. Quoted in M. Huband, *The Skull Beneath the Skin: Africa After the Cold War* (Boulder: Westview Press, 2001), p. 9.

CHAPTER PREVIEW

Reform and Protest in the 1960s
Why did the postwar consensus of the 1950s break down?

Crisis and Change in Western Europe
What were the consequences of economic decline in the 1970s?

The Decline of "Developed Socialism"
What led to the decline of Soviet power in the East Bloc?

The Revolutions of 1989
Why did revolution sweep through the East Bloc in 1989, and what were the immediate consequences?

Life in a Divided Europe
Watchtowers, armed guards, and minefields controlled the Communist eastern side of the Berlin Wall, a significant symbol of Cold War division in Europe. In the liberal West, to the contrary, ordinary folk turned what was an easily accessible blank wall into an ad hoc art gallery — whimsical graffiti art, like the examples pictured here, covered the western side of the wall.
(Bernd Kammerer/picture-alliance/ dpa/akg-images)

29

Challenging the Postwar Order

1960–1991

As Europe entered the 1960s, the political and social systems forged in the postwar era appeared sound. Centrist politicians in western Europe agreed that managed economic expansion, abundant jobs, and state-sponsored welfare benefits would continue to improve living standards and create social consensus. In the Soviet Union and the East Bloc, although conditions varied by country, modest economic growth and limited reforms amid continued political repression likewise contributed to a sense of stability. Cold War tensions diminished, and it seemed that a remarkable age of affluence would ease political differences and lead to social harmony.

By the late 1960s, however, this hard-won sense of stability had begun to disappear as popular protest movements in East and West arose to challenge dominant certainties. In the early 1970s the astonishing postwar economic advance ground to a halt, with serious consequences. In western Europe, a new generation of conservative political leaders advanced new policies to deal with economic decline and the growth of global competition. New political groups across the political spectrum, from feminists and environmentalists to national separatists and right-wing populists, added to the atmosphere of crisis and conflict.

In the East Bloc, leaders vacillated between central economic control and liberalization and left in place tight controls on social freedom, leading to stagnation and frustration. In the 1980s popular dissident movements emerged in Poland and other satellite states, and efforts to reform the Communist system in the Soviet

Union from the top down snowballed out of control. In 1989, as revolutions swept away Communist rule throughout the entire Soviet bloc, the Cold War reached a dramatic conclusion. ■

Reform and Protest in the 1960s

FOCUS QUESTION
Why did the postwar consensus of the 1950s break down?

In the early 1960s politics and society in prosperous western Europe remained relatively stable. East Bloc governments, bolstered by modest economic growth and state-enforced political conformity, and committed to generous welfare benefits for their citizens, maintained control. As the 1960s progressed, politics in the West shifted noticeably to the left, and Social Democratic governments worked to normalize East-West relations. Amid this more liberalized society, a youthful counterculture emerged among the children of affluence to critique the status quo. In the East Bloc, Khrushchev's limited reforms also inspired rebellions. Thus activists around the world rose in protest against the perceived inequalities of both capitalism and communism, leading to dramatic events in 1968, exemplified in Paris and Prague.

Cold War Tensions Thaw

In western Europe, the first two decades of postwar reconstruction had been overseen for the most part by center-right Christian Democrats, who successfully maintained postwar stability around Cold War politics, free-market economics with limited state intervention, and welfare provisions (see Chapter 28). In the mid- to late 1960s, buoyed by the rapidly expanding economy, much of western Europe moved politically to the left. Socialists entered the Italian government in 1963. In Britain, the Labour Party returned to power in 1964, after thirteen years in opposition. In West Germany, the aging postwar chancellor Konrad Adenauer (1876–1967) retired in 1963, and in 1969 Willy Brandt (1913–1992) became the first Social Democratic West German chancellor; his party would govern Germany until 1982. There were important exceptions to this general trend. Though the tough-minded, independent French president Charles de Gaulle resigned

A West German Leader Apologizes for the Holocaust   In 1970 West German chancellor Willy Brandt knelt before the Jewish Heroes' Monument in Warsaw, Poland, to ask forgiveness for the German mass murder of European Jews and other groups during the Second World War. Brandt's action, captured in photo and film by the onlooking press, symbolized the chancellor's policy of Ostpolitik, the normalization of relations between the East and West Blocs. (bpk, Berlin/photographer: Hanns Hubmann, Inv. HU 17089-071/Art Resource, NY)

Chronology

1961	Building of Berlin Wall suggests permanence of the East Bloc	1973	OPEC oil embargo
1962–1965	Second Vatican Council	1975	Helsinki Accords
1963	Wolf publishes *Divided Heaven;* Friedan publishes *The Feminine Mystique*	1979	Margaret Thatcher becomes British prime minister; founding of West German Green Party; Soviet invasion of Afghanistan
1964	Civil Rights Act in the United States		
1964–1973	Peak of U.S. involvement in Vietnam War	1985	Mikhail Gorbachev named Soviet premier
1966	Formation of National Organization for Women (NOW)	1987	United States and Soviet Union sign arms reduction treaty
1968	Soviet invasion of Czechoslovakia; "May Events" protests in France	1989	Soviet withdrawal from Afghanistan
		1989–1991	Fall of communism in eastern Europe
1971	Founding of Greenpeace	December 1991	Dissolution of the Soviet Union

in 1969, the centrist Gaullists remained in power in France until 1981. And in Spain, Portugal, and Greece, authoritarian regimes remained in power until the mid-1970s.

Despite these exceptions, the general leftward drift eased Cold War tensions. Though the Cold War continued to rage outside Europe and generally defined relations between the Soviet Union and the United States, western European leaders took major steps to normalize relations with the East Bloc. Willy Brandt took the lead. In December 1970 he flew to Poland for the signing of a historic treaty of reconciliation. In a dramatic moment rich in symbolism, Brandt laid a wreath at the tomb of the Polish unknown soldier and another at the monument commemorating the armed uprising of Warsaw's Jewish ghetto against occupying Nazi armies. Standing before the ghetto memorial, a somber Brandt fell to his knees as if in prayer. "I wanted," Brandt said later, "to ask pardon in the name of our people for a million-fold crime which was committed in the misused name of the Germans."[1]

Brandt's gesture at the Warsaw Ghetto memorial and the treaty with Poland were part of his broader, conciliatory foreign policy termed **Ostpolitik** (German for "Eastern policy"). Brandt aimed at nothing less than a comprehensive peace settlement for central Europe and the two postwar German states. Brandt believed that the building of the Berlin Wall in 1961 revealed the limitations of West Germany's official hard line toward the East Bloc. Accordingly, the chancellor negotiated new treaties with the Soviet Union and Czechoslovakia, as well as Poland, that formally accepted existing state boundaries—rejected by West Germany's government since 1945—in return for a mutual renunciation of force or the threat of force. Using the imaginative formula of "two German states within one German nation," he broke decisively with past policy and entered into direct relations with East Germany.

Brandt's Ostpolitik was part of a general relaxation of East-West tensions, termed **détente** (day-TAHNT), which began in the early 1970s. Though Cold War hostilities continued in the developing world, diplomatic relations between the United States and the Soviet Union grew less strained. The superpowers agreed to limit the testing and proliferation of nuclear weapons and in 1975 mounted a joint U.S.-U.S.S.R. space mission.

Ostpolitik German for Chancellor Willy Brandt's new "Eastern policy"; West Germany's attempt in the 1970s to ease diplomatic tensions with East Germany, exemplifying the policies of détente.

détente The progressive relaxation of Cold War tensions that emerged in the early 1970s.

The move toward détente reached a high point when the United States, Canada, the Soviet Union, and all European nations (except isolationist Albania and tiny Andorra) met in Helsinki to sign the Final Act of the Conference on Security and Cooperation in Europe in 1975. Under what came to be called the Helsinki Accords, the thirty-five participating nations agreed that Europe's existing political frontiers could not be changed by force. They also accepted numerous provisions guaranteeing the civil rights and political freedoms of their citizens. The agreement helped diminish Cold War conflict. Although Communist regimes would continue to curtail domestic freedoms and violate human rights guarantees, the accords encouraged East Bloc dissidents, who could now demand that their governments respect international declarations on human rights. (See "Evaluating the Evidence 29.1: Human Rights Under the Helsinki Accords," at right.)

Newly empowered Social Democrats in western Europe also engaged in reform at home. Building on the welfare systems established in the 1950s, politicians increased state spending on public services even further. These Social Democrats did not advocate "socialism" as practiced in the Soviet bloc, where strict economic planning, the nationalization of key economic sectors, and one-party dictatorships ensured rigid state control. To the contrary, they maintained a firm commitment to capitalist free markets and democracy. At the same time, they viewed welfare provisions as a way to ameliorate the inevitable inequalities of a competitive market economy. As a result, western European democracies spent more and more state funds on health care, education, old-age insurance, and public housing, all paid for with very high taxes.

By the early 1970s state spending on such programs hovered around 40 percent of the gross domestic product in France, West Germany, and Great Britain, and even more in Scandinavia and the Netherlands. Center-right Christian Democrats generally supported increased spending on entitlements—as long as the economy prospered. The economic slowdown of the mid-1970s, however, undermined support for the welfare state consensus (see page 995).

The Affluent Society

The political shift to the left in the 1960s was accompanied by rapid social change across western Europe. A decade of economic growth and high wages meant that an expanding middle class could increasingly enjoy the benefits of the consumer revolution that began in the 1950s (see Chapter 28). Yet this so-called age of affluence had clear limits. The living standards of workers and immigrants did not rise as fast as those of the educated middle classes, and the expanding economy did not always reach underdeveloped regions, such as southern Italy. The 1960s nonetheless brought general prosperity to millions, and the construction of a full-blown consumer society had a profound impact on daily life.

Many Europeans now had more money to spend on leisure time and recreational pursuits, and one of the most noticeable leisure-time developments was the blossoming of mass travel and tourism. With month-long paid vacations required by law in most western European countries and with widespread automobile ownership, travel to beaches and ski resorts came within the reach of the middle class and much of the working class. By the late 1960s packaged tours with cheap group airfares and bargain hotel accommodations had made even distant lands easily accessible.

Human Rights Under the Helsinki Accords

At the conclusion of the two-year-long Conference on Security and Cooperation in Europe (1973–1975), the representatives of thirty-five West and East Bloc states solemnly pledged to "respect each other's sovereign equality" and to "refrain from any intervention, direct or indirect . . . in the internal or external affairs . . . of another participating state." East Bloc leaders, pleased that the West had at last officially accepted the frontiers and territorial integrity of the Communist satellite states established after World War II, agreed to recognize a lengthy list of "civil, political, economic, social, cultural and other rights and freedoms."

~

Principle VII on Human Rights and Freedoms, from the Final Act of the Conference on Security and Cooperation in Europe (August 1, 1975).

VII. Respect for human rights and fundamental freedoms, including the freedom of thought, conscience, religion or belief

The participating States will respect human rights and fundamental freedoms, including the freedom of thought, conscience, religion or belief, for all without distinction as to race, sex, language or religion.

They will promote and encourage the effective exercise of civil, political, economic, social, cultural and other rights and freedoms all of which derive from the inherent dignity of the human person and are essential for his free and full development.

Within this framework the participating States will recognize and respect the freedom of the individual to profess and practice, alone or in community with others, religion or belief acting in accordance with the dictates of his own conscience.

The participating States on whose territory national minorities exist will respect the right of persons belonging to such minorities to equality before the law, will afford them the full opportunity for the actual enjoyment of human rights and fundamental freedoms and will, in this manner, protect their legitimate interests in this sphere.

The participating States recognize the universal significance of human rights and fundamental freedoms, respect for which is an essential factor for the peace, justice and well-being necessary to ensure the development of friendly relations and co-operation among themselves as among all States.

They will constantly respect these rights and freedoms in their mutual relations and will endeavor jointly and separately, including in co-operation with the United Nations, to promote universal and effective respect for them.

They confirm the right of the individual to know and act upon his rights and duties in this field.

In the field of human rights and fundamental freedoms, the participating States will act in conformity with the purposes and principles of the Charter of the United Nations and with the Universal Declaration of Human Rights. They will also fulfill their obligations as set forth in the international declarations and agreements in this field, including *inter alia* the International Covenants on Human Rights, by which they may be bound.

EVALUATE THE EVIDENCE

1. How do the Helsinki Accords express the guiding principles of liberal democracy?
2. Why would Communist representatives publicly agree to recognize a list of rights that clearly challenged many of the repressive aspects of one-party rule in the East Bloc?

Source: "The Final Act of the Conference on Security and Cooperation in Europe, Aug. 1, 1975, 14 I.L.M. 1292 (Helsinki Declaration)," University of Minnesota Civil Rights Library, http://www1.umn.edu/humanrts/osce/basics/finact75.htm.

Consumerism also changed life at home. Household appliances that were still luxuries in the 1950s were now commonplace; televisions overtook radio as a popular form of domestic entertainment while vacuum cleaners, refrigerators, and washing machines transformed women's housework. Studies later showed that these new "laborsaving devices" caused women to spend even more time cleaning and cooking to new exacting standards, but at the time electric appliances were considered indispensable to what contemporaries called a "modern lifestyle." The establishment of U.S.-style self-service supermarkets across western Europe changed the way food was produced, purchased, and prepared, and threatened to force independent bakers, butchers, and neighborhood grocers out of business.

Intellectuals and cultural critics greeted the age of affluence with a chorus of criticism. Some worried that rampant consumerism created a bland conformity that wiped out regional and national traditions. The great majority of ordinary people, they argued, now ate the same foods, wore the same clothes, and watched the same programs on television, sapping creativity and individualism. Others complained bitterly that these changes threatened to Americanize Europe. Neither group could do much to stop the spread of consumer culture.

Worries about the Americanization of Europe were overstated. European nations preserved distinctive national cultures even during the consumer revolution, but social change nonetheless occurred. The moral authority of religious doctrine lost ground before the growing materialism of consumer society. In predominantly Protestant lands — Great Britain, Scandinavia, and parts of West Germany — church membership and regular attendance both declined significantly. Even in traditionally Catholic countries, such as Italy, Ireland, and France, outward signs of popular belief seemed to falter. At the **Second Vatican Council**, convened from 1962 to 1965, Catholic leaders agreed on a number of reforms meant to democratize and renew the church and broaden its appeal. They called for new openness in Catholic theology and declared that masses would henceforth be said in local languages rather than in Latin, which few could understand. These resolutions, however, did little to halt the slide toward secularization.

Family ties also weakened in the age of affluence. The number of adults living alone grew remarkably, men and women married later, the nuclear family became smaller and more mobile, and divorce rates rose rapidly. By the 1970s the baby boom of the postwar decades was over, and population growth leveled out across Europe and even began to decline in prosperous northwestern Europe.

Second Vatican Council
A meeting of Catholic leaders convened from 1962 to 1965 that initiated a number of reforms, including the replacement of Latin with local languages in church services, designed to democratize the church and renew its appeal.

The Counterculture Movement

The dramatic emergence of a youthful counterculture, which came of age in the mid-1960s, accompanied growing economic prosperity. The "sixties generation" angrily criticized the comforts of the affluent society and challenged the social and political status quo.

What accounts for the emergence of the counterculture? Simple demographics played an important role. Young soldiers returning home after World War II in 1945 eagerly established families, and the next two decades brought a dramatic increase in the number of births per year in Europe and North America. The children born during the postwar baby boom grew up in an era of political liberalism and unprecedented material abundance. They remembered the horrors of totalitarian government that caused World War II and watched as colonial peoples forged new paths to freedom during the decades of decolonization. The counterculture challenged the growing conformity that seemed to be an inherent part of consumer society and the unequal distribution of wealth that arose from market economics. In short, when the baby boomers came of age in the 1960s, they had the education to see problems like inequality and the lack of social justice, as well as the freedom from want to act on their concerns.

Counterculture movements in both Europe and the United States drew much inspiration from the American civil rights movement. In the late 1950s and early 1960s African Americans effectively challenged institutionalized inequality using the courts, public demonstrations, sit-ins, and boycotts, and thereby threw off a deeply entrenched system of segregation and repression. The landmark Civil Rights Act of 1964, which prohibited discrimination in public services and on the job, and the Voting Rights Act of 1965, which guaranteed all African Americans the right to vote, were the crowning achievements of the long struggle against racism.

If dedicated African Americans and their white supporters could successfully reform entrenched power structures, student leaders reasoned, so could they. In 1964 and 1965, at the University of California–Berkeley, students consciously adapted the tactics of the civil rights movement, including demonstrations and sit-ins, to challenge limits on free speech and academic freedom at the university. Their efforts were contagious. Soon students across the United States and western Europe, where rigid rules controlled student activities at overcrowded universities, were engaged in active protests. The youth movement had come of age, and it mounted a determined challenge to the Western consensus.

Dreaming of economic justice and freer, more tolerant societies, student activists in western Europe and the United States embraced new forms of Marxism, creating a multidimensional and heterogeneous movement that came to be known as the **New Left**. In general, adherents of the various strands of the New Left felt that Marxism in the Soviet Union had been perverted to serve the needs of a repressive totalitarian state but that Western capitalism, with its cold disregard for social equality, was little better. What was needed was a more humanitarian style of socialism that could avoid the worst excesses of both capitalism and Soviet-style communism. New Left critics further attacked what they saw as the conformity of consumer society. The "culture industry," which controlled mass culture, fulfilled only false needs and so contributed to the dehumanization they saw at the core of Western society.

Such rarefied ideas fascinated student intellectuals, but much counterculture activity revolved around a lifestyle rebellion that seemed to have broad appeal. Politics and daily life merged, a process captured in the popular 1960s slogan "the personal is political." Nowhere was this more obvious than in the so-called sexual revolution. The 1960s brought frank discussion about sexuality, a new willingness to engage in premarital sex, and a growing acceptance of homosexuality. Sexual experimentation was facilitated by the development of the birth control pill, which helped eliminate the risk of unwanted pregnancy for millions of women after it went on the market in most western European countries in the 1960s. Much of the new openness about sex crossed generational lines, but for the young the idea of sexual emancipation was closely linked to radical politics. Sexual openness and "free love," the sixties generation claimed, moved people beyond traditional norms and might also shape a more humane society.

The revolutionary aspects of the sexual revolution are easily exaggerated. According to a poll of West German college students taken in 1968, the overwhelming majority wished to establish permanent families on traditional middle-class models. Yet the sexual behavior of young people did change in the 1960s and 1970s. More young people engaged in premarital sex, and they did so at an earlier age than ever before. A 1973 study reported that only 4.5 percent of West German youths born in 1945

New Left A 1960s counter-culture movement that embraced updated forms of Marxism to challenge both Western capitalism and Soviet-style communism.

and 1946 had experienced sexual relations before their seventeenth birthday, but that 32 percent of those born in 1953 and 1954 had done so.[2] Such trends were found in other Western countries and continued in the following decades.

Along with sexual freedom, drug use and rock music inspired lifestyle rebellion. Taking drugs challenged conventional morals; users could "turn on, tune in, and drop out," in the infamous words of the American cult figure Timothy Leary. The popular music of the 1960s championed these alternative lifestyles. Rock bands like the Beatles, the Rolling Stones, and many others sang songs about drugs and casual sex. Counterculture "scenes" developed in cities such as San Francisco, Paris, and West Berlin. Carnaby Street, the center of "swinging London" in the 1960s, was world famous for its clothing boutiques and record stores, revealing the inescapable connections between generational revolt and consumer culture.

The United States and Vietnam

The growth of the counterculture movement was closely linked to the escalation of the Vietnam War. Although many student radicals at the time argued that imperialism was the main cause, American involvement in Vietnam was more clearly a product of the Cold War policy of containment (see Chapter 28). After Vietnam won independence from France in 1954, U.S. president Dwight D. Eisenhower (U.S. pres. 1953–1961) refused to sign the Geneva Accords that temporarily divided the country into a Communist north and an anticommunist south. When the South Vietnamese government declined to hold free elections that would unify the two zones, Eisenhower provided the south with military aid to combat guerrilla insurgents in South Vietnam who were supported by the Communist north. President John F. Kennedy (U.S. pres. 1961–1963) later increased the number of American "military advisers" to 16,000, and in 1964 President Lyndon B. Johnson (U.S. pres. 1963–1969) greatly expanded America's role in the Vietnam conflict, providing South Vietnam with massive military aid and eventually some 500,000 American troops. Though the United States bombed North Vietnam with ever-greater intensity, it did not invade the north or set up a naval blockade.

In the end, the American strategy of limited warfare backfired. The undeclared war in Vietnam, fought nightly on American television, eventually divided the nation. Initial support was strong. The politicians, the media, and the population as a whole saw the war as part of a legitimate defense against the spread of Communist totalitarianism. But an antiwar movement quickly emerged on college campuses, where the prospect of being drafted to fight savage battles in Asian jungles made male stomachs churn. In October 1965 student protesters joined forces with old-line socialists, New Left intellectuals, and pacifists in antiwar demonstrations in fifty American cities. The protests spread to western Europe. By 1967 a growing number of U.S. and European critics denounced the American presence in Vietnam as a criminal intrusion into a complex and distant civil war.

Criticism reached a crescendo after the Vietcong staged the Tet Offensive in January 1968, the Communists' first comprehensive attack on major South Vietnamese cities. The offensive was a military failure. The Vietcong, an army of Communist insurgents and guerrilla fighters located in South Vietnam, suffered heavy losses, but the Tet Offensive signaled that the war was not close to ending, as Washington had claimed. The American people grew increasingly weary of the war and pressured their leaders to stop the fighting. Within months of Tet, President Johnson announced that he would not stand for re-election and called for negotiations with North Vietnam.

President Richard M. Nixon (U.S. pres. 1969–1974) sought to gradually disengage America from Vietnam once he took office. Nixon intensified the bombing campaign against the north, opened peace talks, and pursued a policy of "Vietnamization" designed to give the South Vietnamese responsibility for the war and reduce the U.S. presence. He suspended the draft and cut American forces in Vietnam from 550,000 to 24,000 in four years. In 1973 Nixon finally reached a peace agreement with North Vietnam and the Vietcong that allowed the remaining American forces to complete their withdrawal and gave the United States the right to resume bombing if the accords were broken. Fighting declined markedly in South Vietnam, where the South Vietnamese army appeared to hold its own against the Vietcong.

Although the storm of criticism in the United States passed with the peace settlement, America's disillusionment with the war had far-reaching repercussions. In early 1974, when North Vietnam launched a general invasion against South Vietnamese armies, the U.S. Congress refused to permit any American military response. In 1974 the South Vietnamese were forced to accept a unified country under a Communist dictatorship, ending a conflict that had begun with the anticolonial struggle against the French at the end of World War II.

Student Revolts and 1968

While the Vietnam War had raged, American escalation had engendered worldwide opposition. New Left activists believed that the United States was fighting an immoral and imperialistic war against a small and heroic people, and the counterculture became increasingly radical. In western European and North American cities, students and sympathetic followers organized massive antiwar demonstrations and then extended their protests to support colonial independence movements, demand an end to the nuclear arms race, and call for world peace and liberation from social conventions of all kinds.

Political activism erupted in 1968 in a series of protests and riots that circled the globe. African Americans rioted across the United States after the assassination of civil rights leader Martin Luther King, Jr., and antiwar demonstrators battled police at the Democratic National Convention in Chicago. Young protesters marched for political reform in Mexico City, where police responded by shooting and killing several hundred. Students in Tokyo rioted against the war and for university reforms. Protesters clashed with police in the West and East Blocs as well. Berlin and London witnessed massive, sometimes-violent demonstrations, students in Warsaw protested government censorship, and youths in Prague were in the forefront of the attempt to radically reform communism from within (see page 994).

One of the most famous and perhaps most far-reaching of these revolts occurred in France in May 1968, when massive student protests coincided with a general strike that brought the French economy to a standstill. The "May Events" began when a group of students dismayed by conservative university policies and inspired by New Left ideals occupied buildings at the University of Paris. Violent clashes with police followed. When police tried to clear the area around the university on the night of May 10, a pitched street battle took place. At the end of the night, 460 arrests had been made by police, 367 people were wounded, and about 200 cars

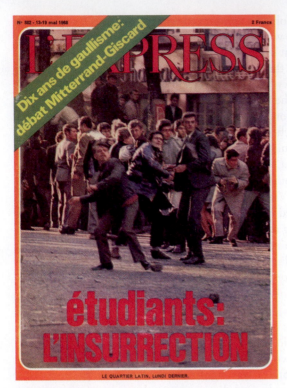

Student Rebellion in Paris   These rock-throwing students in the Latin Quarter of Paris, pictured on the cover of one of France's major newsmagazines, are trying to force education reforms and even topple de Gaulle's government. In May 1968, in a famous example of the protest movements that swept the world in the late 1960s, Parisian rioters clashed repeatedly with France's tough riot police in bloody street fighting. De Gaulle remained in power, but a reform of French education did follow. (Mai 68/Photo © Collection Gregoire/Bridgeman Images)

had been burned by protesters. The slogans that appeared as graffiti scrawled on walls in Paris captured the New Left spirit: "Power to the Imagination"; "Be Realistic, Demand the Impossible"; "Forget Everything You've Been Taught. Start by Dreaming."

The "May Events" might have been a typically short-lived student protest against overcrowded universities, U.S. involvement in Vietnam, and the abuses of capitalism, but the demonstrations triggered a national revolt. By May 18 some 10 million workers were out on strike, and protesters occupied factories across France. For a brief moment, it seemed as if counterculture dreams of a revolution from below would come to pass. The French Fifth Republic was on the verge of collapse, and a shaken President de Gaulle surrounded Paris with troops.

In the end, however, the New Left goals of the radical students contradicted the bread-and-butter demands of the striking workers. When the government promised workplace reforms, including immediate pay raises, the strikers returned to work. President de Gaulle dissolved the French parliament and called for new elections. His conservative party won almost 75 percent of the seats, showing that the majority of the French people supported neither general strikes nor student-led revolutions. The universities shut down for the summer, administrators enacted educational reforms, and the protests had dissipated by the time the fall semester began. The May Events marked the high point of counterculture activism in Europe; in the early 1970s the movement declined.

As the political enthusiasm of the counterculture waned, committed activists disagreed about the best way to continue to fight for social change. Some followed what West German student leader Rudi Dutschke called "the long march through the institutions" and began to work for change from within the system. They ran for office and joined the emerging feminist, antinuclear, and environmental groups that would gain increasing prominence in the following decades (see pages 1000–1004).

Others followed a more radical path. Across Europe, but particularly in Italy and West Germany, fringe New Left groups tried to bring radical change by turning to violence and terrorism. Like the American Weather Underground, the Italian Red Brigades and the West German Red Army Faction robbed banks, bombed public buildings, and kidnapped and killed business leaders and conservative politicians. After spasms of violence in the late 1970s—in Italy, for example, the Red Brigades murdered former prime minister Aldo Moro in 1978—security forces succeeded in incarcerating most of the terrorist leaders, and the movement fizzled out.

Counterculture protests generated a great deal of excitement and trained a generation of activists. In the end, however, the protests of the sixties generation resulted in short-term and mostly limited political change. Lifestyle rebellions involving sex, drugs, and rock music certainly expanded the boundaries of acceptable personal behavior, but they hardly overturned the existing system.

The 1960s in the East Bloc

The building of the Berlin Wall in 1961 suggested that communism was there to stay, and NATO's refusal to intervene showed that the United States and western Europe basically accepted the premise. In the West, the wall became a potent symbol of the repressive nature of communism in the East Bloc, where halting experiments with economic and cultural liberalization brought only limited reform.

East Bloc economies clearly lagged behind those of the West, exposing the weaknesses of central planning. To address these problems, in the 1960s Communist governments implemented cautious forms of decentralization and limited market policies. The results were mixed. Hungary's so-called New Economic Mechanism, which broke up state monopolies, allowed some private retail stores, and encouraged private agriculture, was perhaps most successful. East Germany's New Economic System, inaugurated in 1963, also brought moderate success, though it was reversed when the government returned to centralization in the late 1960s. In other East Bloc countries, however, economic growth flagged.

Recognizing that the overwhelming emphasis on heavy industry was generating popular discontent, Communist planning commissions began to redirect resources to the consumer sector. Again, the results varied. By 1970, for example, ownership of televisions in the more developed nations of East Germany, Czechoslovakia, and Hungary approached that of the affluent nations of western Europe, and other consumer goods were also more available. In Poland, by contrast, the economy stagnated in the 1960s. In the more conservative Albania and Romania, where leaders held fast to Stalinist practices, provision of consumer goods faltered. In general, ordinary people in the East Bloc grew increasingly tired of the shortages of basic consumer goods that seemed an endemic problem in Communist society.

In the 1960s Communist regimes cautiously granted cultural freedoms. In the Soviet Union, the cultural thaw allowed dissidents like Aleksandr Solzhenitsyn to publish critical works of fiction (see Chapter 28), and this relative tolerance spread to other East Bloc countries as well. In East Germany, for example, during the Bitterfeld Movement — named after a conference of writers, officials, and workers held at Bitterfeld, an industrial city south of Berlin — the regime encouraged intellectuals to take a more critical view of life in the East Bloc, as long as they did not directly oppose communism. Author Christa Wolf's novel *Divided Heaven* (1963) is a classic example of the genre. Though the protagonist's boyfriend emigrates to West Germany in search of better work conditions and she sees very real problems in her small-town factory, she remains committed to building socialism.

Cultural openness only went so far, however. The most outspoken dissidents were harassed and often forced to emigrate to the West; other critics contributed to the rise of an underground *samizdat* (SAH-meez-daht) literature that emerged in the Soviet Union and the East Bloc. The label *samizdat*, a Russian term meaning "self-published," referred to books, periodicals, newspapers, and pamphlets published secretly and passed hand to hand by dissident readers because the works directly criticized communism and thus went far beyond the limits of criticism accepted by the state. Samizdat literature emerged

The Invasion of Czechoslovakia Armed with Czechoslovakian flags, courageous Czechs in downtown Prague try to stop a Soviet tank and repel the invasion and occupation of their country by the Soviet Union and its eastern European allies. Realizing that military resistance would be suicidal, the Czechs capitulated to Soviet control. (AP Photo/Libor Hajsky/CTK/AP Images)

in Russia, Poland, and other countries in the mid-1950s and blossomed in the 1960s. These unofficial networks of communication kept critical thought alive and built contacts among dissidents, creating the foundation for the reform movements of the 1970s and 1980s.

The citizens of East Bloc countries sought political liberty as well, and the limits on reform were sharply revealed in Czechoslovakia during the 1968 "Prague Spring" (named for the country's capital city). In January 1968 reform elements in the Czechoslovak Communist Party gained a majority and voted out the long-time Stalinist leader in favor of Alexander Dubček (1921–1992), whose new regime launched dramatic reforms. Educated in Moscow, Dubček (DOOB-chehk) was a dedicated Communist, but he and his allies believed that they could reconcile genuine socialism with personal freedom and party democracy. They called for relaxed state censorship and replaced rigid bureaucratic planning with local decision making by trade unions, workers' councils, and consumers. The reform program—labeled "Socialism with a Human Face"—proved enormously popular.

Remembering that the Hungarian revolution had revealed the difficulty of reforming communism from within (see Chapter 28), Dubček constantly proclaimed his loyalty to the Soviet Union and the Warsaw Pact. But the determination of the Czechoslovak reformers to build a more liberal and democratic socialism nevertheless threatened hardline Communists, particularly in Poland and East Germany, where leaders knew full well that they lacked popular support. Moreover, Soviet leaders feared that a liberalized Czechoslovakia would eventually be drawn to neutrality or even to NATO. Thus the East Bloc leadership launched a concerted campaign of intimidation against the reformers. Finally, in August 1968, five hundred thousand Soviet and East Bloc troops occupied Czechoslovakia. The Czechoslovaks made no attempt to resist militarily, and the arrested leaders surrendered to Soviet demands. The reform program was abandoned, and the Czechoslovak experiment in humanizing communism from within came to an end.

Shortly after the invasion of Czechoslovakia, Soviet premier Leonid Brezhnev (1906–1982) announced that the Soviets would now follow the so-called **Brezhnev Doctrine**, under which the Soviet Union and its allies had the right to intervene militarily in any East Bloc country whenever they thought doing so was necessary to preserve Communist rule. The 1968 invasion of Czechoslovakia was the crucial event of the Brezhnev era: it demonstrated the determination of the Communist elite to maintain the status quo throughout the Soviet bloc, which would last for

Brezhnev Doctrine Doctrine created by Leonid Brezhnev that held that the Soviet Union had the right to intervene in any East Bloc country when necessary to preserve Communist rule.

another twenty years. At the same time, the Soviet crackdown encouraged dissidents to change their focus from "reforming" Communist regimes from within to building a civil society that might bring internal freedoms independent of the regimes (see pages 1007–1010).

Crisis and Change in Western Europe

The great postwar economic boom came to a close in the early 1970s, opening a long period of economic stagnation, widespread unemployment, and social dislocation. As a result, politics in western Europe drifted to the right, and leaders cut taxes and state spending and sold off (or privatized) state-owned companies. A number of new political groups entered national politics, including feminists and environmentalists on the left and neo-nationalists on the right. By the end of the 1980s the postwar consensus based on prosperity, full employment, modest regulation, and generous welfare provisions had been deeply shaken. Led by a new generation of conservative politicians, the West had restructured its economy and entered the information age.

FOCUS QUESTION
What were the consequences of economic decline in the 1970s?

Economic Crisis and Hardship

Starting in the early 1970s the West entered into a long period of economic decline. One of the early causes of the downturn was the collapse of the international monetary system, which since 1945 had been based on the American dollar, valued in gold at $35 an ounce. In the postwar decades the United States spent billions of dollars on foreign aid and foreign wars, weakening the value of American currency. In 1971 President Nixon attempted to reverse this trend by abruptly stopping the exchange of U.S. currency for gold. The value of the dollar fell sharply, and inflation accelerated worldwide. Countries abandoned fixed rates of currency exchange, and great uncertainty replaced postwar predictability in international trade and finance.

Even more damaging to the global economy was the dramatic reversal in the price and availability of energy. The great postwar boom had been fueled in large part by cheap oil from the Middle East. The fate of the developed world was thus increasingly linked to this turbulent region, where strains began to show in the late 1960s. In 1967, in the Six-Day War, Israel quickly defeated Egypt, Jordan, and Syria and occupied more of the former territories of Palestine, angering Arab leaders and exacerbating anti-Western feeling in the Arab states. Economics fed tension between Arab states and the West. Over the years **OPEC**, the Organization of Petroleum Exporting Countries, had watched the price of crude oil decline consistently compared with the rising price of Western manufactured goods. OPEC decided to reverse that trend by presenting a united front against Western oil companies.

OPEC The Organization of Petroleum Exporting Countries.

The stage was thus already set for a revolution in energy prices when Egypt and Syria launched a surprise attack on Israel in October 1973, setting off the fourth Arab-Israeli war. With the help of U.S. weapons, Israel again achieved a quick victory. In response, the Arab members of OPEC declared an embargo on oil shipments to the United States and other industrialized nations that supported Israel in the war, and they simultaneously raised oil prices. Within a year, crude oil prices quadrupled. Western nations realized that the rapid price increase was economically destructive, but together they did nothing. Thus governments, industry, and individuals dealt piecemeal with the so-called oil shock—a "shock" that turned out to be an earthquake.

Coming on the heels of the upheaval in the international monetary system, the revolution in energy prices plunged the world into its worst economic decline since the 1930s. Energy-intensive industries that had driven the economy up in the 1950s and 1960s now dragged it down. Unemployment rose, productivity and living standards declined, and inflation soared. Economists coined a new term—**stagflation**—to describe the combination of low growth and high inflation that drove the worldwide recession. By 1976 a modest recovery was in progress, but in 1979 a fundamentalist Islamic revolution overthrew the shah of Iran. When oil production in that country collapsed, the price of crude oil doubled again, and the world economy succumbed to its second oil shock. Unemployment and inflation rose dramatically before another uneven recovery began in 1982.

Anxious observers, recalling the disastrous consequences of the Great Depression, worried that the European Common Market would disintegrate in the face of severe economic dislocation and that economic nationalism would halt steps toward European unity. Yet the Common Market continued to attract new members. In 1973 Britain finally joined, as did Denmark and Ireland. After replacing authoritarian regimes with democratic governments in the 1970s, Greece joined in 1981, and Portugal and Spain entered in 1986. The nations of the Common Market cooperated more closely in international undertakings, and the movement toward western European unity stayed alive.

The developing world was hit hard by slow growth, and the global economic downturn widened the gap between rich and poor countries. Governments across South America, sub-Saharan Africa, and South Asia borrowed heavily from the United States and western Europe in attempts to restructure their economies, setting the stage for a serious international debt crisis. At the same time, the East Asian countries of Japan and then Singapore, South Korea, and Taiwan started exporting high-tech consumer goods to the West. Competition from these East Asian "tiger economies," whose labor costs were comparatively low, shifted manufacturing jobs away from the highly industrialized countries of northern Europe and North America.

Even though the world economy slowly began to recover in the 1980s, western Europe could no longer create enough jobs to replace those that were lost. By the end of the 1970s, the foundations of economic growth in the industrialized West had begun shifting to high-tech information industries, such as computing and biotechnology, and to services, including medicine, banking, and finance. Scholars spoke of the shift as the arrival of "the information age" or **postindustrial society**. Technological advances streamlined the production of many goods, making many industrial jobs superfluous. In western Europe, heavy industry, such as steel, mining, automobile manufacture, and shipbuilding, lost ground. Factory closings led to the emergence of "rust belts"—formerly prosperous industrialized areas that were now ghost lands, with vacant lots, idle machinery, and empty inner cities. The highly industrialized Ruhr district in northwest West Germany and the once-extensive factory regions around Birmingham (Great Britain) and Detroit, Michigan, were classic examples. By 1985 the unemployment rate in western Europe had risen to its highest level since the Great Depression. Nineteen million people were jobless.

stagflation Term coined in the early 1980s to describe the combination of low growth and high inflation that led to a worldwide recession.

postindustrial society A society that relies on high-tech and service-oriented jobs for economic growth rather than heavy industry and manufacturing jobs.

The crisis struck countless ordinary people, and there were heartbreaking human tragedies—bankruptcies, homelessness, and mental breakdowns. The punk rock songs of the late 1970s captured the mood of hostility and cynicism among young people. Yet on the whole, the welfare system fashioned in the postwar era prevented mass suffering and degradation. The responsive, socially concerned national state undoubtedly contributed to the preservation of political stability and democracy in the face of economic difficulties that might have brought revolution and dictatorship in earlier times.

With the commitment of governments to supporting social needs, government spending in most European countries continued to rise sharply during the 1970s and early 1980s. In 1982 western European governments spent an average of more than 50 percent of all national income on social programs, as compared to only 37 percent fifteen years earlier. Across western Europe, people were willing to see their governments increase spending, but they resisted higher taxes. This imbalance contributed to the rapid growth of budget deficits, national debts, and inflation. While this increased spending was generally popular, a powerful reaction against government's ever-increasing role had set in by the late 1970s that would transform governance in the 1980s.

The New Conservatism

The transition to a postindustrial society was led to a great extent by a new generation of conservative political leaders, who believed they had viable solutions for restructuring the relations between the state and the economy. During the thirty years following World War II, both Social Democrats and the more conservative Christian Democrats had usually agreed that economic growth and social stability were best achieved through full employment and high wages, some government regulation, and generous welfare provisions. In the late 1970s, however, with a weakened economy and increased global competition, this consensus began to unravel. Whether politics turned to the right, as in Great Britain, the United States, and West Germany, or to the left, as in France and Spain, leaders moved to cut government spending and regulation in attempts to improve economic performance.

The new conservatives of the 1980s followed a philosophy that came to be known as **neoliberalism** because of its roots in the free market, laissez-faire policies favored by eighteenth-century liberal economists such as Adam Smith (see Chapter 21). Neoliberal theorists like U.S. economist Milton Friedman argued that governments should cut support for social services, including housing, education, and health insurance; limit business subsidies; and retreat from regulation of all kinds. (Neoliberalism should be distinguished from modern American liberalism, which supports welfare programs and some state regulation of the economy.) Neoliberals also called for **privatization**—the sale of state-managed industries to private owners. Placing government-owned industries such as transportation and communication networks and heavy industry in private hands, they argued, would both reduce government spending and lead to greater workplace efficiency. The main goal was to increase private profits, which neoliberals believed were the real engine of economic growth.

The effects of neoliberal policies are best illustrated by events in Great Britain. The broad shift toward greater conservatism, coupled with growing voter dissatisfaction with high taxes and runaway state budgets, helped elect Margaret Thatcher (1925–2013) prime minister in 1979. A member of the Conservative Party and a

neoliberalism Philosophy of 1980s conservatives who argued for privatization of state-run industries and decreased government spending on social services.

privatization The sale of state-managed industries such as transportation and communication networks to private owners; a key aspect of broader neoliberal economic reforms meant to control government spending, increase private profits, and foster economic growth, which were implemented in western Europe in response to the economic crisis of the 1970s.

convinced neoliberal, Thatcher was determined to scale back the role of government, and in the 1980s—the "Thatcher years"—she pushed through a series of controversial free-market policies that transformed Britain. Thatcher's government cut spending on health care, education, and public housing; reduced taxes; and privatized or sold off government-run enterprises. In one of her most popular actions, Thatcher encouraged low- and moderate-income renters in state-owned housing projects to buy their apartments at rock-bottom prices. This initiative, part of Thatcher's broader privatization campaign, created a whole new class of property owners, thereby eroding the electoral base of Britain's socialist Labour Party. (See "Individuals in Society: Margaret Thatcher," at right.)

Though Thatcher never eliminated all social programs, her policies helped replace the interventionist ethos of the welfare state with a greater reliance on private enterprise and the free market. This transition involved significant human costs. In the first three years of her government, heavy industries such as steel, coal mining, and textiles shut down, and unemployment rates in Britain doubled to over 12 percent. The gap between rich and poor widened, and increasing poverty led to discontent and crime. Strikes and working-class protests sometimes led to violent riots. Street violence often had racial overtones: immigrants from former British colonies in Africa, India, and the Caribbean, dismayed with poor jobs and racial discrimination, clashed repeatedly with police. Thatcher successfully rallied support by leading a British victory over Argentina in the brief Falklands War (1982), but over time her position weakened. By 1990 Thatcher's popularity had fallen to record lows, and she was replaced by Conservative Party leader John Major.

In the United States, two-term president Ronald Reagan (U.S. pres. 1981–1989) followed a similar path, though his success in cutting government was more limited. Reagan's campaign slogan—"government is not the solution to our problem, government is the problem"—summed up a movement in line with Thatcher's ideas, which was labeled the conservative movement in the United States. With widespread popular support and the agreement of most congressional Democrats as well as Republicans, Reagan pushed through major across-the-board cuts in income taxes in 1981. But Reagan and Congress failed to limit government spending, which increased as a percentage of national income in the course of his presidency. A massive military buildup was partly responsible, but spending on social programs—despite Reagan's pledges to rein them in—also grew rapidly. The harsh recession of the early 1980s required the government to spend more on unemployment benefits, welfare benefits, and medical treatment for the poor. Moreover, Reagan's antiwelfare rhetoric mobilized the liberal opposition and eventually turned many moderates against him. The budget deficit soared, and U.S. government debt tripled in a decade.

West Germany also turned to the right. After more than a decade in power, the Social Democrats foundered, and in 1982 Christian Democrat Helmut Kohl (b. 1930) became the new chancellor. Like Thatcher, Kohl cut taxes and government spending. His policies led to increasing unemployment in heavy industry but also to solid economic growth. By the mid-1980s West Germany was one of the most prosperous countries in the world. In foreign policy, Kohl drew close to President Reagan. The chancellor agreed to deploy U.S. cruise missiles and nuclear-armed Pershing missiles on West German territory, a decision that contributed to renewed superpower tensions. In power for sixteen years, Kohl and the Christian Democrats

Margaret Thatcher, the first woman elected to lead a major European state, was one of the late twentieth century's most significant political leaders. The controversial "Iron Lady" attacked socialism, promoted capitalism, and changed the face of modern Britain.

Raised in a lower-middle-class family in a small city in southeastern England, Thatcher entered Oxford in 1943 to study chemistry. She soon discovered a passion for politics and was elected president of student conservatives. Four years after her graduation, she ran for Parliament in 1950 in a solidly Labour district to gain experience. Articulate and attractive, she won the attention of Denis Thatcher, a wealthy businessman who drove her to campaign appearances in his Jaguar. Married a year later, the new Mrs. Thatcher abandoned chemistry, went to law school, gave birth to twins, and became a tax attorney. In 1959 she returned to politics and won a seat in that year's Conservative triumph.

For the next fifteen years Thatcher served in Parliament and held various ministerial posts when the Conservatives governed. In 1974, as the economy soured and the Conservatives lost two close elections, a rebellious Thatcher adroitly ran for the leadership of her party and won. Five years later, as the Labour government faced rampant inflation and crippling strikes, Thatcher promised to reduce union power, lower taxes, and promote free markets. Attracting swing votes from skilled workers, the Conservatives gained a majority, and she became prime minister.

A self-described "conviction politician," Thatcher rejected postwar Keynesian efforts to manage the economy, arguing that governments created inflation by printing too much money. Thus her government reduced the supply of money and credit and refused to retreat when interest rates and unemployment soared. Her popularity plummeted. But Thatcher remained in office, in part through an aggressive foreign policy. In 1982 the generals ruling Argentina suddenly seized the nearby Falkland Islands, home to 1,800 British citizens. A staunch nationalist, Thatcher detached a naval armada that recaptured the islands without a hitch. Britain admired Thatcher's determination and patriotism, and she was re-elected in 1983.

Margaret Thatcher as prime minister.
(Dave Caulkin/AP Photo/AP Images)

Thatcher's second term was the high point of her influence. Her commitment to privatization transformed British industry. More than fifty state-owned companies, ranging from the state telephone monopoly to the nationalized steel trust, were sold to private investors. Small investors were offered shares at bargain prices to promote "people's capitalism." Thatcher curbed the power of British labor unions, most spectacularly in 1984, when the once-mighty coal miners rejected more mine closings and doggedly struck for a year; the "Iron Lady" stood firm and beat them. This outcome had a profound psychological impact on the public, who blamed her for growing unemployment. Thatcher was also accused of mishandling a series of protest hunger strikes undertaken by the Irish Republican Army—in 1981 ten IRA members starved themselves to death in British prisons—but she refused to compromise with those she labeled criminals. As a result, the revolt in Northern Ireland entered one of its bloodiest phases.

Despite these problems, Thatcher was elected to a third term in 1987. Afterward, she became increasingly stubborn, overconfident, and uncaring. Working with her ideological soul mate, U.S. president Ronald Reagan, she opposed greater political and economic unity within the European Community. This, coupled with rising inflation, stubborn unemployment, and an unpopular effort to assert financial control over city governments, proved her undoing. In 1990, as in 1974, party stalwarts suddenly revolted and elected a new Conservative leader. The transformational changes of the Thatcher years nonetheless endured, consolidated by her Conservative successor, John Major, and largely accepted by the new Labour prime minister, the moderate Tony Blair, who served in office from 1997 to 2007.

QUESTIONS FOR ANALYSIS

1. "Thatcherism" has become a shorthand label for the neoliberal ideologies that gained popularity in the 1970s and 1980s. How did the policies promoted by Thatcher's government embody neoliberal ideas?
2. Would you say that Thatcher was a successful British leader? Why or why not?

governed during the opening of the Berlin Wall in 1989, the reunification of East and West Germany in 1990, and the end of the Cold War.

The most striking temporary exception to the general drift to the right in European politics was François Mitterrand (1916–1996) of France. After his election as president in 1981, Mitterrand and his Socialist Party led France on a lurch to the left. This marked a significant change in French politics, which had been dominated by center-right parties for some twenty-five years. Working at first in a coalition that included the French Communist Party, Mitterrand launched a vast program of nationalization and public investment designed to spend the country out of economic stagnation. By 1983 this attempt had clearly failed, and Mitterrand's Socialist government made a dramatic about-face. The Socialists were compelled to reprivatize industries they had just nationalized. They imposed a wide variety of austerity measures and maintained those policies for the rest of the decade.

Despite persistent economic crises and high social costs, by 1990 the developed nations of western Europe and North America were far more productive than they had been in the early 1970s. Western Europe was at the center of the emerging global economy, and its citizens were far richer than those in Soviet bloc countries (see page 1005). Even so, the collapse of the postwar consensus and the remaking of Europe in the transitional decades of the 1970s and 1980s helped generate new forms of protest and dissent across the political spectrum.

Challenges and Victories for Women

The 1970s marked the arrival of a diverse and widespread feminist movement devoted to securing genuine gender equality and promoting the general interests of women. Three basic reasons accounted for this dramatic development. First, ongoing changes in underlying patterns of motherhood and paid work created novel conditions and new demands (see Chapter 28). Second, a vanguard of feminist intellectuals articulated a powerful critique of gender relations, which stimulated many women to rethink their assumptions and challenge the status quo. Third, taking a lesson from the civil rights movement in the United States and protests against the Vietnam War, dissatisfied women recognized that they had to band together if they were to influence politics and secure fundamental reforms.

Feminists could draw on a long heritage of protest, stretching back to the French Revolution and the women's movements of the late nineteenth century (see Chapters 19 and 22). They were also inspired by recent writings,

Feminist Protest in London, 1982   In a protest organized by the grassroots Women's Fightback Network, women march for equal pay and employment opportunity. (Roberto Koch/Contrasto/Redux)

such as the foundational book *The Second Sex* (1949) by the French writer and philosopher Simone de Beauvoir (1908–1986). Beauvoir, who worked closely with the existentialist philosopher Jean-Paul Sartre, analyzed the position of women within the framework of existential thought. Drawing on history, philosophy, psychology, biology, and literature, Beauvoir argued that women had almost always been trapped by particularly inflexible and limiting conditions. Only through courageous action and self-assertive creativity could a woman become a completely free person and escape the role of the inferior "other" that men had constructed for her gender. (See "Evaluating the Evidence 29.2: Simone de Beauvoir's Feminist Critique of Marriage," page 1002.)

The Second Sex inspired a generation of women intellectuals, and by the late 1960s and the 1970s "second-wave feminism" had spread through North America and Europe. In the United States, writer and organizer Betty Friedan's (1921–2006) pathbreaking study *The Feminine Mystique* (1963) pointed the way. Friedan called attention to the stifling aspects of women's domestic life, devoted to the service of husbands and children. Housewives lived in a "gilded cage," she concluded, because they were usually not allowed to hold professional jobs or become mature adults and genuine human beings. In 1966 Friedan helped found the National Organization for Women (NOW) to press for women's rights. NOW flourished, growing from seven hundred members in 1967 to forty thousand in 1974.

Many other women's organizations rose in Europe and North America. The diverse groups drew inspiration from Marx, Freud, or political liberalism, but in general feminists attacked patriarchy (the domination of society by men) and sexism (the inequalities faced by women simply because they were female). Throughout the 1970s a proliferation of publications, conferences, and institutions devoted to women's issues reinforced the emerging international movement. Advocates of women's rights pushed for new statutes governing the workplace: laws against discrimination, acts requiring equal pay for equal work, and measures such as maternal leave and affordable day care designed to help women combine careers and family responsibilities.

The movement also addressed gender and family questions, including the right to divorce (in some Catholic countries), legalized abortion, the needs of single mothers, and protection from rape and physical violence. In almost every country, the effort to decriminalize abortion served as a catalyst in mobilizing an effective, self-conscious women's movement—and, as in the United States, in creating opposition to it.

In countries that had long placed women in a subordinate position, the legal changes were little less than revolutionary. In Italy, for example, new laws abolished restrictions on divorce and abortion that had been strengthened by Mussolini and defended energetically by the Catholic Church in the postwar era. By 1988 divorce and abortion were common in Italy, which had the lowest birthrate in Europe. While the women's movement of the 1970s won new rights for women, subsequently it became more diffuse, a victim of both its successes and the resurgence of an antifeminist opposition.

The Rise of the Environmental Movement

Like feminism, environmentalism had roots in the 1960s counterculture. Early environmentalists drew inspiration from writers like U.S. biologist Rachel Carson, whose book *Silent Spring*, published in 1962, was quickly translated into twelve European

Simone de Beauvoir's Feminist Critique of Marriage

Having grown up in Paris in a middle-class family and become a teacher, novelist, and intellectual, Simone de Beauvoir turned increasingly to feminist concerns after World War II. Her most influential work was The Second Sex *(1949), a massive declaration of independence for contemporary women.*

As an existentialist, Beauvoir believed that all individuals must accept responsibility for their lives and strive to overcome the tragic dilemmas they face (see Chapter 26). Studying the experience of women since antiquity, Beauvoir argued that men had generally used education and social conditioning to create a dependent "other," a negative nonman who was not permitted to grow and strive for freedom. Marriage — on men's terms — was part of this unjust and undesirable process. Beauvoir's conclusion that some couples could establish free and equal unions was based in part on her own experience with philosopher Jean-Paul Sartre, her encouraging companion and longtime lover.

All human existence is transcendence and immanence at the same time; to go beyond itself, it must maintain itself; to thrust itself toward the future, it must integrate the past into itself; and while relating to others, it must confirm itself in itself. These two moments are implied in every living movement: for *man*, marriage provides the perfect synthesis of them; in his work and political life, he finds change and progress, he experiences his dispersion through time and the universe; and when he tires of this wandering, he establishes a home, he settles down, he anchors himself in the world; in the evening he restores himself in the house, where his wife cares for the furniture and children and safeguards the past

she keeps in store. But the wife has no other task save the one of maintaining and caring for life in its pure and identical generality; she perpetuates the immutable species, she ensures the even rhythm of the days and the permanence of the home she guards with locked doors; she is given no direct grasp on the future, nor on the universe; she goes beyond herself toward the group only through her husband as mouthpiece.

Marriage today still retains this traditional form. . . . The male's vocation is action; he needs to produce, fight, create, progress, go beyond himself toward the totality of the universe and the infinity of the future; but traditional marriage does not invite woman to transcend herself with him; it confines her in immanence. She has no choice but to build a stable life where the present, prolonging the past, escapes the threats of tomorrow, that is, precisely to create a happiness. . . .

It is through housework that the wife comes to make her "nest" her own; this is why, even if she has "help," she insists on doing things herself; at least by watching over, controlling, and criticizing, she endeavors to make her servants' results her own. By administrating her home, she achieves her social justification; her job is also to oversee the food, clothing, and care of the familial society in general. Thus she too realizes herself as an activity. But, as we will see, it is an activity that brings her no escape from her immanence and allows her no individual affirmation of herself. . . .

Few tasks are more similar to the torment of Sisyphus than those of the housewife; day after day, one must wash dishes, dust furniture, mend clothes that will be dirty, dusty, and torn again. The housewife wears herself out running on the spot; she does nothing; she only perpetuates the present;

languages. Carson's chilling title referred to a future spring, when people in developed society would wake up and hear no birds singing, because they had all been killed by the rampant use of pesticides. The book had a striking impact on the growth of environmental movements in Europe and North America.

By the 1970s the destructive environmental costs of industrial development in western Europe and the East Bloc were everywhere apparent. The mighty Rhine River, which flows from Switzerland, past France, and through Germany and the Netherlands, was an industrial sewer. The forests of southwestern Germany were dying from acid rain, a result of smokestack emissions. The pristine coast of Brittany, in northwest France, was fouled by oil spills from massive tanker ships. Rapid industrialization in the East Bloc, undertaken with little regard for environmental impact, severely polluted waterways, contaminated farmlands and forests, and degraded air she never gains the sense that she is conquering a positive Good, but struggles indefinitely against Evil. . . .

Washing, ironing, sweeping, routing out tufts of dust in the dark places behind the wardrobe, this is holding away death but also refusing life: for in one movement time is created and destroyed; the housewife only grasps the negative aspect of it. . . .

So the wife's work within the home does not grant her autonomy; it is not directly useful to the group, it does not open onto the future, it does not produce anything. It becomes meaningful and dignified only if it is integrated into existences that go beyond themselves, toward the society in production or action: far from enfranchising the matron, it makes her dependent on her husband and children; she justifies her existence through them: she is no more than an inessential mediation in their lives. . . .

The drama of marriage is not that it does not guarantee the wife the promised happiness — there is no guarantee of happiness — it is that it mutilates her; it dooms her to repetition and routine. The first twenty years of a woman's life are extraordinarily rich; she experiences menstruation, sexuality, marriage, and motherhood; she discovers the world and her destiny. She is mistress of a home at twenty, linked from then on to one man, a child in her arms, now her life is finished forever. Real activity, real work, are the privilege of man: her only occupations are sometimes exhausting but never fulfill her. . . .

Marriage must combine two autonomous existences, not be a withdrawal, an annexation, an escape, a remedy. . . . The couple should not consider itself a community, a closed cell: instead, the individual as individual has to be integrated into a society in which he can thrive without assistance; he will then be able to create links in pure generosity with another individual equally adapted to the group, links founded on the recognition of two freedoms.

This balanced couple is not a utopia; such couples exist sometimes even within marriage, more often outside of it; some are united by a great sexual love that leaves them free in their friendships and occupations; others are linked by a friendship that does not hamper their sexual freedom; more rarely there are still others who are both lovers and friends but without seeking in each other their exclusive reason for living. Many nuances are possible in the relations of a man and a woman: in companionship, pleasure, confidence, tenderness, complicity, and love, they can be for each other the most fruitful source of joy, richness, and strength offered to a human being.

EVALUATE THE EVIDENCE

1. How did Beauvoir's analysis of marriage and marriage partners express the main ideas of existential philosophy?
2. To what extent does a married woman benefit from a "traditional" marriage, according to Beauvoir? Why?
3. What was Beauvoir's solution to the situation she described? Was her solution desirable? Realistic?
4. What have you learned about the history of women that supports or challenges Beauvoir's analysis? Include developments since World War II and your own reflections.

Source: Excerpt from THE SECOND SEX by Simone de Beauvoir and translated by Constance Borde and Sheila Malovany-Chevallier, translation copyright © 2009 by Constance Borde and Sheila Malovany-Chevallier. Used by permission of Alfred A. Knopf, an imprint of the Knopf Doubleday Publishing Group, a division of Penguin Random House LLC. All rights reserved. Any third-party use of this material, outside of this publication, is prohibited. Interested parties must apply directly to Penguin Random House LLC for permission.

quality. Nuclear power plants across Europe were generating toxic waste that would last for centuries; serious accidents at nuclear plants — at Three Mile Island in Pennsylvania (1979) and at Chernobyl in Soviet Ukraine (1986) — revealed nuclear power's potential to create human and environmental disaster (Map 29.1). These were just some examples of the environmental threats that inspired a growing environmental movement to challenge government and industry to clean up their acts.

Environmentalists had two main agendas. First, they worked to lessen the ill effects of unbridled industrial development on the natural environment. Second, they argued that local environmental problems often increased human poverty, inequality, and violence around the globe, and they sought ways to ameliorate the impact of environmental decline on human well-being. Environmental groups pursued their goals in various ways. Some used the mass media to reach potential

Nuclear power plants
- Over 50
- 10–50
- Under 10

Acid rain levels
- High
- Medium
- Low

— Severely polluted river
— Oil tanker disaster, 1970s–1990s

Chernobyl nuclear accident April 26, 1986

MAP 29.1 Pollution in Europe, ca. 1990 Despite attempts to remedy the negative consequences of the human impact on the environment, pollution remains a significant challenge for Europeans in the twenty-first century.

supporters; some worked closely with politicians and public officials to change government policies. Others took a more activist stance. In Denmark in March 1969, in a dramatic example, student protesters at the University of Copenhagen took over a scientific conference on natural history. They locked the conference hall doors, sprayed the professors in attendance with polluted lake water, and held up an oil-doused duck, shouting, "Come and save it . . . you talk about pollution, why don't you do anything about it!"[3]

Environmental protesters also built new institutions, particularly in North America and western Europe. In 1971 Canadian activists established Greenpeace, a nongovernmental organization dedicated to environmental conservation and protection. Greenpeace quickly grew into an international organization, with strong support in Europe and the United States. In West Germany in 1979 environmentalists founded the Green Party, a political party to fight for environmental causes. The West German Greens met with astounding success when they elected members to parliament in 1983, the first time in sixty years that a new political party had been seated in Germany. Their success was a model for like-minded activists in Europe and North America, and Green Party members were later elected to parliaments in Belgium, Italy, and Sweden. In the East Bloc, government planners increasingly recognized and tried to ameliorate environmental problems in the 1980s, but official censorship meant that groups like the Greens would not emerge there until after the end of Communist rule.

Separatism and Right-Wing Extremism

The 1970s also saw the rise of determined separatist movements across Europe. In Ireland, Spain, Belgium, and Switzerland—and in Yugoslavia and Czechoslovakia in the East Bloc—regional ethnic groups struggled for special rights, political autonomy, and even national independence. This separatism was most violent in Spain and Northern Ireland, where well-established insurgent groups used terrorist attacks to win government concessions. In the ethnic Basque region of northern Spain, the ETA (short, in the Basque language, for Basque Homeland and Freedom) tried to use bombings and assassinations to force the government to grant independence. After the death in 1975 of Fascist dictator Francisco Franco, who had ruled Spain for almost forty years, a new constitution granted the Basque region special autonomy, but it was not enough. The ETA stepped up its terrorist campaigns, killing over four hundred people in the 1980s.

The Provisional Irish Republican Army (IRA), a paramilitary organization in Northern Ireland, used similar tactics. Though Ireland had won autonomy in 1922, Great Britain retained control of six primarily Protestant counties in the north of the island (see Chapter 26). In the late 1960s violence re-emerged as the IRA, hoping to unite these counties with Ireland, attacked British security forces, which it saw as an occupying army. On Bloody Sunday in January 1972, British soldiers shot and killed thirteen demonstrators, who had been protesting anti-Catholic discrimination in the town of Derry, and the violence escalated. For the next thirty years the IRA attacked soldiers and civilians in Northern Ireland and in Britain itself. Over two thousand British soldiers, civilians, and IRA members were killed during "the Troubles" before negotiations between the IRA and the British government opened in the late 1990s; a settlement was finally reached in 1998.

Mainstream European politicians also faced challenges from newly assertive political forces on the far right. Right-wing political parties such as the National Front in France, the Northern League in Italy, the Austrian Freedom Party, and the National Democratic Party in West Germany were founded or gained popularity in the 1970s and 1980s. Populist leaders like Jean-Marie Le Pen, the founder of the French National Front, opposed European integration and called for a return to traditional national customs, often at the expense of the non-European immigrants who were a growing proportion of western Europe's working-class population (see Chapter 28). New right-wing politicians promoted themselves as the champions of ordinary (white) workers, complaining that immigrants swelled welfare rolls and stole jobs from native-born Europeans. Though their programs at times veered close to open racism, in the 1980s they began to win seats in national parliaments.

The Decline of "Developed Socialism"

In the postwar decades the Communist states of the East Bloc had achieved a shaky social consensus based on a rising standard of living, an extensive welfare system, and political repression. When the Marxist utopia still had not arrived in the 1970s, Communist leaders told citizens that an egalitarian society would be realized sometime in the future; until then, they would have to accept the system as it was. In the long run, leaders promised, "developed socialism" would prove better than capitalism. Such claims were an attempt to paper over serious tensions in socialist society. Everyday life could be difficult. Limits on personal and political freedoms encouraged the growth of determined reform movements, and a revival of Cold War tensions accompanied the turn to the right in the United States and western Europe in the 1980s.

When Mikhail Gorbachev burst on the scene in 1985, the new Soviet leader opened an era of reform that was as sweeping as it was unexpected. Although many believed that Gorbachev would soon fall from power, his reforms rapidly transformed Soviet culture and politics and drastically reduced Cold War tensions. But communism, which Gorbachev wanted so desperately to revitalize, continued to stagnate and decline.

State and Society in the East Bloc

By the 1970s many of the professed goals of communism had been achieved. Communist leaders in central and eastern Europe and the Soviet Union adopted the term **developed socialism** (sometimes called "real existing socialism") to describe the accomplishments of their societies. Agriculture had been thoroughly collectivized, and though Poland was an exception, 80 to 90 percent of Soviet and East Bloc farmers worked on huge collective farms. Industry and business had been nationalized,

FOCUS QUESTION
What led to the decline of Soviet power in the East Bloc?

developed socialism A term used by Communist leaders to describe the socialist accomplishments of their societies, such as nationalized industry, collective agriculture, and extensive social welfare programs.

and only a small portion of the economy remained in private hands in most East Bloc countries. The state had also done much to level class differences. Though some people—particularly party members—clearly had greater access to opportunities and resources, the gap between rich and poor was far smaller than in the West. An extensive system of government-supported welfare benefits included free medical care, guaranteed employment, inexpensive public transportation, and large subsidies for rent and food.

Everyday life under developed socialism was defined by an uneasy mixture of outward conformity and private disengagement—or apathy. The Communist Party dominated public life. Party-led mass organizations for youth, women, workers, and sports groups staged huge rallies, colorful festivals, and new holidays that exposed citizens to the values of the socialist state. East Bloc citizens might grudgingly participate in party-sponsored public events, but at home, and in private, they often grumbled about and sidestepped the Communist authorities.

East Bloc living standards were well above those in the developing world, but below those in the West. Centralized economic planning continued to lead to shortages, and people complained about the poor quality and lack of choice of the most basic goods. Under these conditions, informal networks of family and friends helped people find hard-to-get goods and offered support beyond party organizations. Though the secret police persecuted those who openly challenged the system and generated mountains of files on ordinary people, they generally left alone those who demonstrated the required conformity.

Women in particular experienced the contradictions of the socialist system. Official state policy guaranteed equal rights for women and encouraged them to join the workforce in positions formerly reserved for men, and an extensive system of state-supported child care freed women to accept these employment opportunities and eased the work of parenting. Yet women rarely made it into the upper ranks of business or politics, and they faced the same double burden as those in the West (see Chapter 28). In addition, government control of the public sphere meant that the independent groups dedicated to feminist reform that emerged in the West in the 1970s developed more slowly in the East Bloc and the Soviet Union. Women could complain to the Communist authorities about unequal or sexist conditions at work or at home, but until the 1980s they could not build private, nongovernmental organizations to lobby for change.

Though everyday life was fairly comfortable in the East Bloc, a number of deeply rooted structural problems undermined popular support for Soviet-style communism. These fundamental problems would contribute to the re-emergence of civic dissent and ultimately to the revolutions of 1989. East Bloc countries—like those in the West—were hard hit by the energy crisis and stagflation of the 1970s. For a time, access to inexpensive oil from the Soviet Union, which had huge resources, helped prop up faltering economies, but this cushion began to fall apart in the 1980s. For a number of reasons, East Bloc leaders refused to make the economic reforms that might have made developed socialism more effective.

First, a move toward Western-style postindustrial society would have required fundamental changes to the Communist system. As in the West, it would have hurt the already-tenuous living standard of industrial workers. But Communist East Bloc states were publicly committed to supporting the working classes, including coal miners, shipbuilders, and factory and construction workers. To pursue the neoliberal reforms undertaken in the West would have undermined popular support for the government among these basic constituencies, which was already tenuous at best.

Second, East Bloc regimes refused to cut spending on the welfare state because that was, after all, one of the proudest achievements of socialism. Third, the state continued to provide subsidies to heavy industries such as steel and mining. High-tech industries failed to take off in Communist Europe, in part because the West maintained embargoes on technology exports. The industrial goods produced in the East Bloc became increasingly uncompetitive in the new global system. To stave off total collapse, governments borrowed massive amounts of hard currency from Western banks and governments, helping to convince ordinary people that communism was bankrupt, and setting up a cycle of indebtedness that helped bring down the entire system in 1989.

Economic decline was not the only reason people increasingly questioned one-party Communist rule. The best career and educational opportunities were reserved for party members or handed out as political favors, leaving many talented people underemployed and resentful. Tight controls on travel continually called attention to the burdens of daily life in a repressive society. The one-party state had repeatedly quashed popular reform movements, retreated from economic liberalization, and jailed or exiled dissidents, even those who wished to reform communism from within. Though many East Bloc citizens still found the promise of Marxist egalitarian socialism appealing, they increasingly doubted the legitimacy of Soviet-style communism: the dream of distributing goods "from each according to his means, to each according to his needs" (as Marx had once put it) hardly made up for the great structural weaknesses of developed socialism.

Dissent in Czechoslovakia and Poland

Stagnation in the East Bloc encouraged small numbers of dedicated people to try to change society from below. Developments in Czechoslovakia and Poland were the most striking and significant, and determined protest movements re-emerged in both countries in the mid-1970s. Remembering a history of violent repression and Soviet invasion, dissenters carefully avoided direct challenges to government leaders. Nor did they try to reform the Communist Party from within, as Dubček and his followers had attempted in Prague in 1968. Instead, they worked to build a civil society from below — to create a realm of freedom beyond formal politics, where civil liberties and human rights could be exercised independent of the Communist system.

In Czechoslovakia in 1977 a small group of citizens, including future Czechoslovak president Václav Havel (VAH-slahf HAH-vuhl) (1936–2011), signed a manifesto that came to be known as Charter 77. The group criticized the government for ignoring the human rights provision of the Helsinki Accords and called on Communist leaders to respect civil and political liberties. They also criticized censorship and argued for improved environmental policies. (See "Evaluating the Evidence 29.3: Dissent in the Czechoslovak Socialist Republic," page 1008.) Despite immediate state repression, the group challenged passive acceptance of Communist authority and voiced public dissatisfaction with developed socialism.

In Poland, an unruly satellite from the beginning, the Communists had failed to dominate society to the extent seen elsewhere in the East Bloc. Most agricultural land remained in private hands, and the Catholic Church thrived. The Communists also failed to manage the economy effectively. The 1960s brought stagnation, and in 1970 Poland's working class rose again in angry protest. A new Communist leader

Dissent in the Czechoslovak Socialist Republic

First published in West Germany in January 1977, the Manifesto of the Czechoslovak dissident group Charter 77 called on the Communist regime to recognize the human rights codified in the country's 1960 constitution, the 1975 Helsinki Accords (see "Evaluating the Evidence 29.1: Human Rights Under the Helsinki Accords," page 987), and other international agreements on civil and political rights. The 243 courageous individuals who signed the Charter faced harsh state retaliation and their opposition had little immediate impact, but their ideas expressed a deep desire for civil rights and helped lay the intellectual foundations for the revolutions of 1989.

The human rights and freedoms underwritten by these covenants [on international civil and political rights, including the Helsinki Accords, signed by the Czechoslovak government] constitute features of civilized life for which many progressive movements have striven throughout history and whose codification could greatly assist humane developments in our society.

We accordingly welcome the Czechoslovak Socialist Republic's accession to those agreements.

Their publication, however, serves as a powerful reminder of the extent to which basic human rights in our country exist, regrettably, on paper alone.

The right to freedom of expression, for example, guaranteed by Article 19 of the first-mentioned covenant, is in our case purely illusory. Tens of thousands of our citizens are prevented from working in their own fields for the sole reason that they hold views differing from official ones, and are discriminated against and harassed in all kinds of ways by the authorities and public organizations. Deprived as they are of any means to defend themselves, they become victims of a virtual apartheid. . . .

Freedom of religious confession, emphatically guaranteed by Article 18 of the first covenant, is continually curtailed by arbitrary official action. . . .

This state of affairs likewise prevents workers and others from exercising the unrestricted right to establish trade unions and other organizations to protect their economic and social interests. . . .

Further civic rights, including the explicit prohibition of "arbitrary interference with privacy, family, home or correspondence" (Article 17 of the first covenant), are seriously vitiated by the various forms of interference in the private life of citizens exercised by the Ministry of the Interior, for example by bugging telephones and houses, opening mail, following personal movements, searching homes, setting up networks of neighborhood informers (often recruited by illicit threats or promises) and in other ways. . . .

Clause 2, Article 12 of the first covenant, guaranteeing every citizen the right to leave the country, is consistently violated, or under the pretense of "defense of national security" is subjected to various unjustifiable conditions (Clause 3). . . .

Responsibility for the maintenance of rights in our country naturally devolves in the first place on the political and state authorities. Yet not only on them: everyone bears his share of responsibility for the conditions that prevail and accordingly also for the observance of legally enshrined agreements, binding upon all individuals as well as upon governments.

It is this sense of co-responsibility, our belief in the importance of its conscious public acceptance and the general need to give it new and more effective expression that led us to the idea of creating Charter 77, whose inception we today publicly announce. . . .

We believe that Charter 77 will help to enable all citizens of Czechoslovakia to work and live as free human beings.

EVALUATE THE EVIDENCE

1. Why does the Charter call on ordinary citizens to take responsibility for observing the "legally enshrined agreements" on human rights?
2. How did the 1975 Helsinki Accords provide a legal basis for dissidents to challenge the Czechoslovak one-party state?

Source: "Appendix D: Manifesto of Charter 77 — Czechoslovakia," in *Czechoslovakia (Former): A Country Study*, Library of Congress, https://archive.org/details/czechoslovakiaco00gawd.

came to power, and he wagered that massive inflows of Western capital and technology, especially from rich and now-friendly West Germany, could produce a Polish economic miracle. Instead, bureaucratic incompetence and the first oil shock in 1973 sent the economy into a nosedive. Workers, intellectuals, and the church became increasingly restive. Then the real Polish miracle occurred: Cardinal Karol Wojtyla (KAH-rohl voy-TIH-wah), archbishop of Kraków, was elected pope in 1978 as John Paul II. In June 1979 he returned to Poland from Rome, preaching love of Christ and country and the "inalienable rights of man." The pope drew enormous crowds and electrified the Polish nation.

In August 1980 strikes broke out across Poland; at the gigantic Lenin Shipyards in Gdansk (formerly known as Danzig) sixteen thousand workers laid down their tools and occupied the plant. As other workers joined "in solidarity," the strikers advanced the ideals of civil society, including the right to form trade unions free from state control, freedom of speech, release of political prisoners, and economic reforms. After the strikers occupied the shipyard for eighteen days, the government gave in and accepted the workers' demands in the Gdansk Agreement. In a state in which the Communist Party claimed to rule on behalf of the proletariat, a working-class revolt had won an unprecedented, even revolutionary, victory.

Led by feisty Lenin Shipyards electrician and devout Catholic Lech Wałęsa (lehk vah-WEHN-suh) (b. 1943), the workers proceeded to organize a free and democratic trade union called **Solidarity**. As had been the case in Czechoslovakia, Solidarity worked cautiously to shape an active civil society. Joined by intellectuals and supported by the Catholic Church, it became a national union with a full-time staff of 40,000 and 9.5 million members. Cultural and intellectual freedom blossomed in Poland, and Solidarity enjoyed tremendous public support. But Solidarity's leaders pursued a self-limiting revolution, meant only to defend the concessions won in the Gdansk Agreement. Solidarity thus practiced moderation, refusing to challenge directly the Communist monopoly on political power. At the same time, the ever-present threat of calling a nationwide strike gave them real leverage in ongoing negotiations with the Communist bosses.

Solidarity's combination of strength and moderation postponed a showdown, as the Soviet Union played a waiting game of threats and pressure. After a confrontation in March 1981, Wałęsa settled for minor government concessions, and Solidarity dropped plans for a massive general strike. Criticism of Wałęsa's moderate leadership gradually grew, and Solidarity lost its cohesiveness. The worsening economic crisis also encouraged radical actions among disgruntled Solidarity members, and the Polish Communist leadership shrewdly denounced the union for promoting economic collapse and provoking a possible Soviet invasion. In December 1981 Wojciech Jaruzelski (VOY-chehk yahr-oo-ZEHL-skee), the general who headed Poland's Communist government, suddenly proclaimed martial law and arrested Solidarity's leaders.

Outlawed and driven underground, Solidarity survived in part because of the government's unwillingness (and probably its inability) to impose full-scale terror. Moreover, millions of Poles decided to continue acting as if they were free—the hallmark of civil society—even though they were not. Cultural and intellectual life remained extremely vigorous as the Polish economy continued to deteriorate. Thus popular support for outlawed Solidarity remained strong under martial law in the 1980s, preparing the way for the union's political rebirth toward the end of the decade.

Solidarity Independent Polish trade union that worked for workers' rights and political reform throughout the 1980s.

The rise and survival of Solidarity showed that ordinary Poles would stubbornly struggle for greater political and religious liberty, cultural freedom, trade-union rights, patriotic nationalism, and a more humane socialism. Not least, Solidarity's challenge encouraged fresh thinking in the Soviet Union, ever the key to lasting change in the East Bloc.

From Détente Back to Cold War

The Soviets and the leaders of the Soviet satellite states faced challenges from abroad as optimistic hopes for détente in international relations gradually faded in the late 1970s. Brezhnev's Soviet Union ignored the human rights provisions of the Helsinki agreement, and East-West political competition remained very much alive outside Europe. Many Americans became convinced that the Soviet Union was taking advantage of détente, steadily building up its military might and pushing for political gains and revolutions in Africa, Asia, and Latin America. The Soviet invasion of Afghanistan in December 1979, designed to save an increasingly unpopular Marxist regime, alarmed the West. Many Americans feared that the oil-rich states of the Persian Gulf would be next, and once again they looked to the NATO alliance and military might to thwart Communist expansion.

President Jimmy Carter (U.S. pres. 1977–1981) tried to lead NATO beyond verbal condemnation of the Soviet Union and urged economic sanctions against it, but only Great Britain among the European allies supported the American initiative. The alliance showed the same lack of concerted action when the Solidarity movement rose in Poland. Some observers concluded that NATO had lost the will to act decisively in dealing with the Soviet bloc.

The Atlantic alliance endured, however, and the U.S. military buildup launched by Carter in his last years in office was greatly accelerated by President Reagan, who was swept into office in 1980 by a wave of patriotism and economic discontent. The new American leadership acted as if the military balance had tipped in favor of the Soviet Union, which Reagan anathematized as the "evil empire." Increasing defense spending enormously, the Reagan administration deployed short-range nuclear missiles in western Europe and built up the navy to preserve American power in the post-Vietnam age. The broad shift toward greater conservatism in the 1980s gave Reagan invaluable allies in western Europe. Margaret Thatcher worked well with Reagan and was a forceful advocate for a revitalized Atlantic alliance, and under Helmut Kohl West Germany likewise worked with the United States to coordinate military and political policy toward the Soviet bloc.

Gorbachev's Reforms in the Soviet Union

Cold War tensions aside, the Soviet Union's Communist elite seemed safe from any challenge from below in the early 1980s. A well-established system of administrative controls stretched downward from the central ministries and state committees to provincial cities and from there to factories, neighborhoods, and villages. At each level of this massive state bureaucracy, the overlapping hierarchy of the 17.5-million-member Communist Party maintained tight state control. Organized opposition was impossible, and average people left politics to the bosses.

Although the massive state and party bureaucracy safeguarded the elite, it promoted widespread apathy and stagnation. When the ailing Brezhnev finally died in 1982, his

The Soviet War in Afghanistan, 1979–1989

Afghanistan
Soviet Union
Soviet invasion
Controlled by Soviet forces

UZBEKISTAN   KIRGHIZIA
TAJIKISTAN
Dushanbe
TURKMENISTAN
Mary
Mazar-e Sharif
Kabul
Peshawar
Herat
Kandahar
IRAN   PAKISTAN
INDIA

successor, the long-time chief of the secret police, Yuri Andropov (1914–1984), tried to invigorate the system. Relatively little came of his efforts, but they combined with a sharply worsening economic situation to set the stage for the emergence in 1985 of Mikhail Gorbachev (b. 1931), the most vigorous Soviet leader in a generation.

A lawyer and experienced Communist Party official, Gorbachev was smart, charming, and tough. He believed in communism, but realized that the Soviet Union was failing to keep up with the West and was losing its superpower status. Thus Gorbachev tried to revitalize the Soviet system with fundamental reforms. An idealist who wanted to improve conditions for ordinary citizens, Gorbachev understood that the enormous expense of the Cold War arms race had had a disastrous impact on living conditions in the Soviet Union; improvement at home, he realized, required better relations with the West.

In his first year in office, Gorbachev attacked corruption and incompetence in the bureaucracy and consolidated his power. He condemned alcoholism and drunkenness, which were deadly scourges of Soviet society, and worked out an ambitious reform program designed to transform and restructure the economy in order to provide for the real needs of the Soviet population. To accomplish this economic restructuring, or **perestroika** (pehr-uh-STROY-kuh), Gorbachev and his supporters permitted an easing of government price controls on some goods, more independence for state enterprises, and the creation of profit-seeking private cooperatives to provide personal services. These timid reforms initially produced a few improvements, but shortages grew as the economy stalled at an intermediate point between central planning and free-market mechanisms. By late 1988 widespread consumer dissatisfaction posed a serious threat to Gorbachev's leadership and the entire reform program.

Gorbachev's bold and far-reaching campaign for greater freedom of expression was much more successful. Very popular in a country where censorship, dull uniformity, and outright lies had long characterized public discourse, the newfound openness, or **glasnost** (GLAZ-nohst), of the government and the media marked an astonishing break with the past. Long-banned émigré writers sold millions of copies of their works in new editions, while denunciations of Stalin and his terror became standard fare in plays and movies. In another example of glasnost in action, after several days of hesitation the usually secretive Soviet government issued daily reports on the 1986 nuclear plant accident at Chernobyl, one of the worst environmental disasters in history. Indeed the initial openness in government pronouncements quickly went much further than Gorbachev intended and led to something approaching free speech, a veritable cultural revolution.

Mikhail Gorbachev　Soviet president Mikhail Gorbachev (center, with red tie) walks with a crowd of delegates to the twenty-eighth and last congress of the Soviet Communist Party in July 1990. Gorbachev took office in 1985 with the goal of reforming communism from within. His plans spiraled out of control. By 1991 the Soviet Union and the East Bloc had disintegrated into independent, noncommunist states. (© Pascal Le Segretain/Sygma/Corbis)

perestroika Economic restructuring and reform implemented by Premier Mikhail Gorbachev in the Soviet Union in 1985.

glasnost Soviet premier Mikhail Gorbachev's popular campaign for openness in government and the media.

Democratization was another element of reform. Beginning as an attack on corruption in the Communist Party, it led to the first free elections in the Soviet Union since 1917. Gorbachev and the party remained in control, but a minority of critical independents was elected in April 1989 to a revitalized Congress of People's Deputies. Millions of Soviets then watched the new congress for hours on television as Gorbachev and his ministers saw their proposals debated and even rejected. Thus millions of Soviet citizens took practical lessons in open discussion, critical thinking, and representative government. An active civil society was emerging—a new political culture at odds with the Communist Party's monopoly of power and control.

Democratization also ignited demands for greater political and cultural autonomy and even national independence among non-Russian minorities living in the fifteen Soviet republics. The Soviet population numbered about 145 million ethnic Russians and 140.6 million non-Russians, including 55 million Muslims in the Central Asian republics and over 44 million Ukrainians. Once Gorbachev opened the doors to greater public expression, tensions flared between central Soviet control and national separatist movements. Independence groups were particularly active in the Baltic Soviet socialist republics of Lithuania, Latvia, and Estonia; in western Ukraine; and in the Transcaucasian republics of Armenia, Azerbaijan, and Georgia.

Finally, Gorbachev brought reforms to the field of foreign affairs. He withdrew Soviet troops from Afghanistan in February 1989 and sought to reduce East-West tensions. Of enormous importance, the Soviet leader sought to halt the arms race with the United States and convinced President Reagan of his sincerity. In a Washington summit in December 1987, the two leaders agreed to eliminate all land-based intermediate-range missiles in Europe, setting the stage for more arms reductions. Gorbachev pledged to respect the political choices of the peoples of East Bloc countries, repudiating the Brezhnev Doctrine and giving encouragement to reform movements in Poland, Czechoslovakia, and Hungary. By early 1989 it seemed that if Gorbachev held to his word, the tragic Soviet occupation of eastern Europe might wither away, taking the long Cold War with it once and for all.

The Revolutions of 1989

FOCUS QUESTION
Why did revolution sweep through the East Bloc in 1989, and what were the immediate consequences?

In 1989 Gorbachev's plan to reform communism from within snowballed out of control. A series of largely peaceful revolutions swept across eastern Europe, overturning existing Communist regimes (Map 29.2). The revolutions of 1989 had momentous consequences. First, the peoples of the East Bloc gained political freedom after about forty years of dictatorial Communist rule. Second, West Germany absorbed its East German rival, and a reunified Germany emerged as the most influential country in Europe. Third, as Gorbachev's reforms boomeranged, a complicated anticommunist revolution swept through the Soviet Union, and the multinational empire broke into a large Russia and fourteen other independent states. The Cold War came to an end, and the United States suddenly stood as the world's only superpower.

The Collapse of Communism in the East Bloc

The collapse of Communist rule in the Soviet satellite states surprised many Western commentators, who had expected Cold War divisions to persist for many years. Yet while the revolutions of 1989 appeared to erupt quite suddenly, long-standing, structural

MAP 29.2 Democratic Movements in Eastern Europe, 1989 Countries that had been satellites in the orbit of the Soviet Union began to set themselves free in 1989.

weaknesses in the Communist system had in some ways made revolt inevitable. East Bloc economies never really recovered from the economic catastrophe of the 1970s. State spending on outdated industries and extensive welfare systems led to massive indebtedness to Western banks and undermined economic growth, while limits on personal and political freedoms fueled a growing sense of injustice (see page 1006).

In this general climate of economic stagnation and popular anger, Solidarity and the Polish people led the way to revolution. In 1988 widespread strikes, raging inflation, and the outlawed Solidarity's refusal to cooperate with the military government had brought Poland to the brink of economic collapse. Poland's frustrated Communist leaders offered to negotiate with Solidarity if the outlawed union's leaders could get the strikers back to work and resolve the political stalemate and the economic crisis. The subsequent agreement in April 1989 legalized Solidarity and declared that a large minority of representatives to the Polish parliament would be chosen by free elections that June. Still guaranteed a parliamentary majority and expecting to win many of the contested seats, the Communists believed that their rule was guaranteed for four years and that Solidarity would keep the workers in line.

Lacking access to the state-run media, Solidarity succeeded nonetheless in mobilizing the country and winning all but one of the contested seats in an overwhelming victory. Moreover, many angry voters crossed off the names of unopposed party candidates, so that the Communist Party failed to win the majority its leaders had anticipated. Solidarity members jubilantly entered the Polish parliament, and a dangerous stalemate quickly developed. But Lech Wałęsa, a gifted politician who always repudiated violence, adroitly obtained a majority by securing the allegiance of two minor procommunist parties that had been part of the coalition government after World War II. In August 1989 Tadeusz Mazowiecki (Ta-DAY-ush MAH-zoe-vee-ETS-key) (1927–2013), the editor of one of Solidarity's weekly newspapers, was sworn in as Poland's new noncommunist prime minister.

In its first year and a half, the new Solidarity government cautiously introduced revolutionary political changes. It eliminated the hated secret police, the Communist ministers in the government, and finally Communist Party leader Jaruzelski himself, but it did so step-by-step in order to avoid confrontation with the army or the Soviet Union. In economics, however, the Solidarity government was radical from the beginning. It applied economic shock therapy, an intense dose of neoliberal policy designed to make a clean break with state planning and move quickly to market mechanisms and private property (see Chapter 30). Thus the government abolished controls on many prices on January 1, 1990, and reformed the monetary system with a big bang.

Hungary followed Poland. Hungary's moderate Communist Party leader János Kádár (KAH-dahr) had permitted liberalization of the rigid planned economy after the 1956 uprising in exchange for political loyalty and continued Communist control. In May 1988, in an effort to retain power by granting modest political concessions, the party replaced the ill and aging Kádár with a reform-minded Communist. But liberal opposition groups rejected piecemeal progress, and in the summer of 1989 the Hungarian Communist Party agreed to hold free elections the following March. Welcoming Western investment and moving rapidly toward multiparty democracy, Hungary's Communists now enjoyed considerable popular support, and they believed, quite mistakenly, that they could defeat the opposition in the upcoming elections.

In an effort to strengthen their support at home, the Hungarians opened their border to East Germans and tore down the barbed wire curtain separating Hungary from Austria. Tens of thousands of dissatisfied East German "vacationers" then poured into Hungary, crossed into Austria as refugees, and continued on to immediate resettlement in thriving West Germany.

The flight of East Germans fed the rapid growth of a homegrown, spontaneous protest movement in East Germany. Workers joined intellectuals, environmentalists, and Protestant ministers in huge candlelight demonstrations, arguing that a democratic but still socialist East Germany was both possible and desirable. These "stayers" failed to convince the "leavers," however, who continued to depart en masse. In a desperate attempt to stabilize the situation, the East German government opened the Berlin Wall in November 1989, and people danced for joy atop that grim symbol of the prison state. A new, reformist government took power and scheduled free elections.

In Czechoslovakia, Communist rule began to dissolve peacefully in November to December 1989. This so-called **Velvet Revolution** grew out of popular demonstrations led by students and joined by intellectuals and a dissident playwright-turned-moral-revolutionary named Václav Havel (1936–2011). When the protesters took control of the streets, the Communist government resigned, leading to a power-sharing arrangement termed the "Government of National Understanding." As 1989 ended, the Czechoslovakian assembly elected Havel president.

In Romania, popular revolution turned violent and bloody. There the dictator Nicolae Ceaușescu (chow-SHESS-koo) (1918–1989) had long combined tight party control with stubborn independence from Moscow. Faced with mass protests in December 1989, Ceaușescu ordered his ruthless security forces to quell unrest, sparking an armed uprising. Perhaps 750 people were killed in the fighting; the numbers were often exaggerated. After the dictator and his wife were captured and executed by a military court, Ceaușescu's forces were defeated. A coalition government emerged, although the legacy of Ceaușescu's long and oppressive rule left a troubled country.

Velvet Revolution
The term given to the relatively peaceful overthrow of communism in Czechoslovakia; the label came to signify the collapse of the East Bloc in general in 1989 to 1990.

German Unification and the End of the Cold War

The dissolution of communism in East Germany that began in 1989 reopened the "German question" and raised the threat of renewed Cold War conflict over Germany. Taking power in October 1989, East German reform Communists, enthusiastically supported by leading intellectuals and former dissidents, wanted to preserve socialism by making it genuinely democratic and responsive to the needs of the people. They argued for a "third way" that would go beyond the failed Stalinism they had experienced and the ruthless capitalism they saw in the West. These reformers supported closer ties with West Germany but feared unification, hoping to preserve a distinct East German identity with a socialist system.

Over the next year, however, East Germany was absorbed into an enlarged West Germany, much as a faltering company is swallowed by a stronger rival and ceases to exist. Three factors were particularly important in this outcome. First, in the first week after the Berlin Wall was opened, almost 9 million East Germans—roughly half of

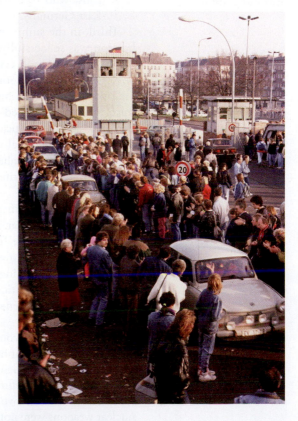

The Opening of the Berlin Wall   The sudden and unanticipated opening of the Berlin Wall on November 10, 1989, dramatized the spectacular fall of communism throughout east-central Europe. West Berliners welcomed the East Germans who piled into their "Trabi" automobiles to cross the border. Millions of East German citizens traveled into West Berlin and the Federal Republic of Germany in the first few days after the surprise relaxation of inter-German travel controls. (© DPA/Courtesy Everett Collection)

The Reunification of Germany, 1990

Former boundary between East and West Germany

the total population—poured across the border into West Germany. Almost all returned to their homes in the east, but the joy of warm welcomes from long-lost friends and relatives and the exhilaration of crossing a long-closed border aroused long-dormant hopes of unity among ordinary citizens.

Second, West German chancellor Helmut Kohl and his closest advisers skillfully exploited the historic opportunity handed them. Sure of support from the United States, whose leadership he had steadfastly followed, in November 1989 Kohl presented a ten-point plan for step-by-step unification in cooperation with both East Germany and the international community. Kohl then promised the struggling citizens of East Germany an immediate economic bonanza—a generous though limited exchange of East German marks in savings accounts and pensions into much more valuable West German marks. This offer helped popularize the conservative-liberal Alliance for Germany, a well-financed political party established in East Germany with the support of Kohl's West German Christian Democrats. In March 1990 the Alliance won almost 50 percent of the votes in an East German parliamentary election, outdistancing the Party of Democratic Socialism (the renamed East German Communist Party) (16 percent) and the revived Social Democratic Party (22 percent). The Alliance for Germany quickly negotiated an economic and political union on favorable terms with Kohl. The rapid pace of reunification quickly overwhelmed those who argued for the preservation of an independent socialist society in East Germany.

Third, in the summer of 1990 the crucial international aspect of German unification was successfully resolved. Unification would once again make Germany the strongest state in central Europe and would directly affect the security of the Soviet Union. But Gorbachev swallowed hard—Western cartoonists showed Stalin turning over in his grave—and negotiated the best deal he could. In a historic agreement signed by Gorbachev and Kohl in July 1990, Kohl solemnly affirmed Germany's peaceful intentions and pledged never to develop nuclear, biological, or chemical weapons. The Germans sweetened the deal by promising enormous loans to the hard-pressed Soviet Union. In October 1990 East Germany merged into West Germany, forming a single nation under the West German laws and constitution.

The peaceful reunification of Germany accelerated the pace of agreements to liquidate the Cold War. In November 1990 delegates from twenty-two European countries joined those from the United States and the Soviet Union in Paris and agreed to a scaling down of all their armed forces. The delegates also solemnly affirmed that all existing borders in Europe, including those of unified Germany and the emerging Baltic States, were legal and valid. The Paris Accord was for all practical purposes a general peace treaty bringing an end to both World War II and the Cold War.

Peace in Europe encouraged the United States and the Soviet Union to scrap a significant portion of their nuclear weapons in a series of agreements. In September 1991 a confident President George H. W. Bush canceled the around-the-clock alert status for American bombers outfitted with atomic bombs, and a floundering Gorbachev quickly followed suit with his own forces. For the first time in four decades, Soviet and American nuclear weapons were not standing ready for mutual destruction.

The Disintegration of the Soviet Union

As 1990 began, the tough work of dismantling some forty-five years of Communist rule had begun in all but two East Bloc states—tiny Albania and the vast Soviet Union. The great question now became whether the Soviet Union would follow its former satellites.

In February 1990, as competing Russian politicians noisily presented their programs and nationalists in the non-Russian republics demanded autonomy or independence from the Soviet Union, the Communist Party suffered a stunning defeat in local elections throughout the country. As in East Bloc countries, democrats and anticommunists won clear majorities in the leading cities of the Russian Soviet Federative Socialist Republic (S.F.S.R.), by far the largest republic in the Soviet Union. Moreover, in Lithuania the people elected an uncompromising nationalist as president, and the newly chosen parliament declared Lithuania an independent state.

Gorbachev responded by placing an economic embargo on Lithuania, but he refused to use the army to crush the separatist government. The result was a tense political stalemate that undermined popular support for Gorbachev. Separating himself further from Communist hardliners, Gorbachev asked Soviet citizens to ratify a new constitution that formally abolished the Communist Party's monopoly of political power and expanded the power of the Congress of People's Deputies. While retaining his post as party secretary, Gorbachev then convinced a majority of deputies to elect him president of the Soviet Union.

Despite his victory, Gorbachev's power continued to erode, and his unwillingness to risk a universal suffrage election for the presidency strengthened his great rival, Boris Yeltsin (1931–2007). A radical reform Communist, Yeltsin embraced the democratic movement, and in May 1990 he was elected parliamentary leader of the Russian Soviet Republic. He boldly announced that Russia would put its interests first and declare its independence from the Soviet Union, broadening the base of the anticommunist movement by joining the patriotism of ordinary Russians with the democratic aspirations of big-city intellectuals. Gorbachev tried to save the Soviet Union with a new treaty that would link the member republics in a looser, freely accepted confederation, but six of the fifteen Soviet republics rejected his plan.

Opposed by democrats and nationalists, Gorbachev was also challenged by the Communist old guard. In August 1991 a gang of hardliners kidnapped him and his family in the Caucasus and tried to seize the Soviet government. The attempted coup collapsed in the face of massive popular resistance that rallied around Yeltsin. As the spellbound world watched on television, Yeltsin defiantly denounced the rebels from atop a stalled tank in central Moscow and declared the "rebirth of Russia." The army supported Yeltsin, and Gorbachev was rescued and returned to power as head of the Soviet Union.

The leaders of the coup had wanted to preserve Communist power, state ownership, and the multinational Soviet Union; they succeeded in destroying all three. An anticommunist revolution swept Russia as Yeltsin and his supporters outlawed the Communist Party and confiscated its property. Locked in a personal and political duel with Gorbachev, Yeltsin and his democratic allies declared Russia independent, withdrew from the Soviet Union, and changed the country's name from the Russian Soviet Republic to the Russian Federation. All the other Soviet republics also withdrew. Gorbachev resigned on December 25, 1991, and the next day the Supreme Soviet dissolved itself, marking the end of the Soviet Union. The independent republics of the old Soviet Union then established a loose confederation, the Commonwealth of Independent States, which played only a minor role in the 1990s.

LOOKING BACK LOOKING AHEAD

The unexpected collapse of Communist Europe capped three decades of turbulent change. In the 1960s the counterculture challenged the status quo and steered western Europe to the left as reformists attempted (but failed) to liberalize East Bloc communism. In the 1970s a global recession had devastating effects in the West and East Blocs alike. In the 1980s conservative Western leaders pushed neoliberal plans to revive growth and meet growing global competition. In the East Bloc, structural problems and spontaneous revolt brought down communism, dissolved the Soviet Union, and ended the Cold War.

With the world economy on the road to recovery and new free-market systems in place across the former East Bloc, all of Europe would now have the opportunity to enter the information age. After forty years of Cold War division, the continent regained an underlying unity as faith in democratic government and market economics became the common European creed. In 1991 hopes for peaceful democratic progress were almost universal. According to philosopher Francis Fukuyama, the world had reached "the end of history"—the end of the Cold War, he argued, would lead to peaceful development based on growing tolerance, free-market economics, and liberal democracy.

The post–Cold War years saw the realization of some of these hopes, but the new era brought its own problems and tragedies. New ethnic and nationalist tensions flared, leading to a disastrous civil war in the former Yugoslavia. The struggle to rebuild the shattered societies of the former East Bloc countries was far more difficult than the people living in them had hoped. Poor economic growth continued to complicate attempts to deal with the wide-open global economy. New conflicts with Islamic nations in the Middle East involved some European nations in war. The European Union expanded, but political disagreements, environmental issues, increased anxiety about non-Western immigrants, and a host of other problems undermined moves toward true European unity. History was far from over—the realities of a post–Cold War world continued to produce difficult challenges as Europe entered the twenty-first century.

Make Connections

Think about the larger developments and continuities within and across chapters.

1. How did the revolts that shook western European countries and the East Bloc develop out of issues left unresolved in the 1950s era of postwar reconstruction (Chapter 28)?

2. Both East and West Blocs faced similar economic problems in the 1970s, yet communism collapsed in the East and capitalism recovered. How do you account for the difference? Were economic problems the main basis for popular opposition to communism?

3. What were some of the basic ideas behind the neoliberal economic policies that emerged in the West in the 1970s and 1980s? Why are they still popular today?

29 REVIEW & EXPLORE

Review the Main Ideas

Answer the focus questions from each section of the chapter.

◆ Why did the postwar consensus of the 1950s break down? (p. 984)

◆ What were the consequences of economic decline in the 1970s? (p. 995)

◆ What led to the decline of Soviet power in the East Bloc? (p. 1005)

◆ Why did revolution sweep through the East Bloc in 1989, and what were the immediate consequences? (p. 1012)

Identify Key Terms

Identify and explain the significance of each item below.

Ostpolitik (p. 985)

détente (p. 985)

Second Vatican Council (p. 988)

New Left (p. 989)

Brezhnev Doctrine (p. 994)

OPEC (p. 995)

stagflation (p. 996)

postindustrial society (p. 996)

neoliberalism (p. 997)

privatization (p. 997)

developed socialism (p. 1005)

Solidarity (p. 1009)

perestroika (p. 1011)

glasnost (p. 1011)

Velvet Revolution (p. 1015)

NOTES

1. Quoted in Kessing's Research Report, *Germany and East Europe Since 1945: From the Potsdam Agreement to Chancellor Brandt's "Ostpolitik"* (New York: Charles Scribner's Sons, 1973), pp. 284–285.

2. M. Mitterauer, *The History of Youth* (Oxford: Basil Blackwell, 1992), p. 40.

3. See R. Guha, *Environmentalism: A Global History* (New York: Longman, 2000), p. 79.

CHAPTER PREVIEW

Reshaping the Soviet Union and the Former East Bloc

How did life change in Russia and the former East Bloc countries after 1989?

The New Global System

How did globalization affect European life and society?

Ethnic Diversity in Contemporary Europe

What are the main causes and effects of growing ethnic diversity in contemporary Europe?

Confronting Long-Term Challenges

What challenges will Europeans face in the coming decades?

Life in a Globalizing World

This French-American collaboration, titled *The Standing March*, was exhibited on the façade of the National Assembly building in Paris during the United Nations–sponsored climate conference in December 2015, when world leaders gathered to negotiate an international deal to control climate change. Using cutting-edge technology, the creators projected a video of faces from around the world to remind the negotiators about the impact of global warming on ordinary people.

(*The Standing March* is the collaborative work by the French artist known as JR and the U.S. filmmaker Darren Aronofsky/photo: Eric Feferberg/AFP/Getty Images)

30

Life in an Age of Globalization

1990 TO THE PRESENT

On November 9, 2009, the twentieth anniversary of the opening of the Berlin Wall, jubilant crowds filled the streets around the Brandenburg Gate at the former border between East and West Berlin. World leaders and tens of thousands of onlookers applauded as former Polish president Lech Wałęsa pushed over a line of one thousand eight-foot-tall foam dominos, symbolizing the collapse of communism.

The crowd had reason to celebrate. The revolutions of 1989 had opened a new chapter in European and world history. Capitalism spread across the former East Bloc and Soviet Union (now the Russian Federation and fourteen other republics), along with the potential for political reform. Some of these hopes were realized, but the new era also brought problems and tragedies. The process of remaking formerly Communist societies was more difficult than expected. At the same time, across the West and around the world, globalization, the digital revolution, and the ongoing flow of immigrants into western Europe had impacts both positive and negative.

As Europeans faced serious tensions and complex changes in the twenty-first century, they also came together to form a strong new European Union that would prove a formidable economic competitor to the United States. Ties between western Europe and the United States began to loosen, but Europe and North America—as well as the rest of the world—confronted common challenges. Finding solutions to problems in the Middle East and addressing challenges regarding economic growth, energy needs, the environment, and human rights would require not only innovation but also creative cooperation.   ■

Reshaping the Soviet Union and the Former East Bloc

FOCUS QUESTION

How did life change in Russia and the former East Bloc countries after 1989?

Establishing stable democratic governments in the former East Bloc countries and the diverse territories of the Soviet Union, now divided into fifteen republics with Russia at its core, was not easy. While Russia initially moved toward economic reform and political openness, by 2010 it had returned to its authoritarian traditions. Stability proved elusive in many of the former Soviet Socialist Republics, and conflict undermined Russia's relations with some of these new nation-states.

The transformation of the Communist East Bloc was also difficult. After a period of tense reform, some countries, such as Poland, the Czech Republic, and Hungary, established relatively prosperous democracies and joined NATO and then the European Union. Others, such as Romania and Bulgaria, lagged behind. In multiethnic Yugoslavia, the collapse of communism and the onset of a disastrous civil war broke the country apart. All these changes produced mixed results for ordinary folk.

Economic Shock Therapy in Russia

Politics and economics were closely intertwined in Russia after the dissolution of the Soviet Union (see Chapter 29). President Boris Yeltsin (pres. 1991–1999), his democratic supporters, and his economic ministers wanted to create conditions that would prevent a return to communism and right the faltering economy. Following the example of Poland (see Chapter 29), and agreeing with neoliberal Western advisers who argued that a quick turn to free markets would speed economic growth, Russian reformers opted in January 1992 for liberalization at breakneck speed.

To implement the plan, the Russians abolished price controls on most consumer goods, with the exception of bread, vodka, oil, and public transportation. The government launched a rapid privatization program, selling formerly state-owned industries and agricultural concerns to private investors. As a result, thousands of factories and mines were turned over to new private companies. In an attempt to share the wealth privatization was expected to generate, each citizen received a voucher worth 10,000 rubles (about $22) to buy stock in these private companies. Ownership of these formerly public assets, however, usually remained in the hands of the old bosses—the managers and government officials from the Communist era—undermining the reformers' goal of worker participation.

President Yeltsin and his economic advisers believed that shock therapy would revive production and bring widespread prosperity. The results were quite different. Prices increased 250 percent on the very first day and kept on soaring, increasing by a factor of twenty-six in the course of 1992. At the same time, production fell a staggering 20 percent. Nor did the situation stabilize quickly. After 1995 inflation still raged, though at slower rates, and output continued to fall. According to most estimates,

Chronology

1980s–1990s	Emergence of globalization	**2004**	Train bombings in Madrid by Islamic extremists
1990s–2010s	New waves of legal and illegal immigration to Europe	**2005**	Young Muslims riot in France; subway bombing in London by Islamic extremists
1991	Maastricht Treaty	**2008**	Worldwide financial crisis begins
1991–2001	Civil war in Yugoslavia	**2009**	Ratification of Treaty of Lisbon; young Muslims riot in France
1992–1997	Decline of Russian economy		
1993	Creation of the European Union	**2011**	Start of Arab Spring
1999	Protests against WTO in Seattle	**2012–2013**	Mass protests against government austerity plans in Greece and Spain
2000–2008	Resurgence of Russian economy under Putin	**2013**	France legalizes same-sex marriage
2001	September 11 terrorist attack on the United States; war in Afghanistan begins	**2014**	Russian Federation annexes Crimea; pro-Russian insurrection in eastern Ukraine
2002	Euro replaces national currencies in Eurozone	**2014–2015**	Rise of the Islamic State
2003–2011	Iraq War	**2015–2016**	Greek debt crisis; EU immigration emergency

Russia produced from one-third to one-half less in 1996 than it had in 1991. The Russian economy crashed again in 1998 in the wake of Asia's financial crisis.

Rapid economic liberalization worked poorly in Russia for several reasons. Soviet industry had been highly monopolized and strongly tilted toward military goods. Production of many items had been concentrated in one or two gigantic factories or in interconnected combines. With privatization, these powerful state monopolies became powerful private monopolies that cut production and raised prices in order to maximize profits. Moreover, Yeltsin's government handed out enormous subsidies to corporate managers and bureaucrats, ostensibly to reinforce faltering firms and avoid bankruptcies, but also to buy political allegiance. New corporate leaders included criminals who intimidated would-be rivals in attempts to prevent the formation of competing businesses.

Runaway inflation and poorly executed privatization brought a profound social revolution to Russia. The new capitalist elite—the so-called Oligarchs—acquired great wealth and power, while large numbers of people fell into abject poverty and the majority struggled to make ends meet. Managers, former Communist officials, and financiers who came out of the privatization process with large shares of the old state monopolies stood at the top. The Oligarchs, Yeltsin's main supporters, maintained control with corrupt business practices and rampant cronyism. The new elite held more wealth than ever before.

At the other extreme, the vast majority of people saw their savings become practically worthless. Pensions lost much of their value, living standards drastically declined, and many people sold their personal goods to survive. Under these conditions, effective representative government failed to develop, and many Russians came to equate democracy with the corruption, poverty, and national decline they experienced throughout the 1990s. Yeltsin became increasingly unpopular; only the backing of the Oligarchs kept him in power.

Russian Revival Under Vladimir Putin

This widespread disillusionment set the stage for the rise of Vladimir Putin (POO-tihn) (b. 1952), who was elected president as Yeltsin's chosen successor in 2000 and re-elected in a landslide in March 2004. A colonel in the secret police during the Communist era, Putin maintained relatively liberal economic policies but re-established semi-authoritarian political rule. Critics labeled Putin's system an "imitation democracy," and indeed a façade of democratic institutions masked authoritarian rule from above in postcommunist Russia.[1] Putin's government maintained control with rigged elections, weak parliamentary rule, the intimidation of political opponents, and the distribution of state-owned public assets to win support of the new elite. Yet Putin's argument that the transition to free markets required strong political rule to control corruption and prevent a collapse into complete chaos resonated with ordinary Russians worried about the disintegration of the Communist state. The president enjoyed strong popular support, at least in the first years of his rule.

Putin's government combined authoritarian politics with economic reform. The regime clamped down on the excesses of the Oligarchs, lowered corporate and business taxes, and re-established some government control over key industries. Such reforms—aided greatly by high world prices for oil and natural gas, Russia's most important exports—led to a decade of economic expansion, encouraging the growth of a new middle class. In 2008, however, the global financial crisis and a rapid drop in the price of oil caused a downturn, and the Russian stock market collapsed. The government initiated a $200 billion rescue plan, and the economy stabilized and returned to modest growth in 2010.

During his first two terms as president, Putin's domestic and foreign policies proved immensely popular with a majority of Russians. His housing, education, and health-care reforms significantly improved living standards. Putin repeatedly evoked the glories of Russian history, expressed pride in the accomplishments of the Soviet Union, and downplayed the abuses of the Stalinist system; he thus capitalized on popular feelings of Russian patriotism. In addition, the Russian president centralized power in the Kremlin, increased military spending, and expanded the secret police. Putin's carefully crafted manly image and his forceful international diplomacy soothed the country's injured pride and symbolized its national revival.

In foreign relations, the president generally championed assertive anti-Western policies in an attempt to bolster Russia's status as a great Eurasian power and world player. (See "Evaluating the Evidence 30.1: President Putin on Global Security," at right.) Putin forcefully opposed the expansion of NATO into the former East Bloc and regularly challenged U.S. and NATO foreign policy goals. In the Syrian civil war that broke out in 2011, for example, Russian backing of Syrian president Bashar al-Assad flew in the face of U.S. attempts to depose him. Putin's support in summer 2015 for a deal to limit Iran's nuclear capabilities marked a rare moment of Russian cooperation with the United States, the EU, and the United Nations.

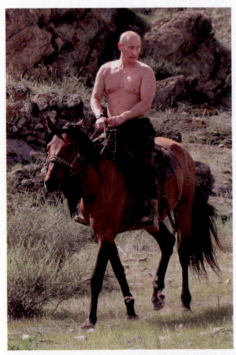

Vladimir Putin on Vacation in 2009   After two terms as Russian president (2000–2008), Putin served as prime minister for four years before returning to the presidency in 2012. Putin's high approval ratings were due in part to his carefully crafted image of strength and manliness. (Alexsey Druginyn/AFP/Getty Images)

President Putin on Global Security

In this wide-ranging speech, delivered to representatives of over forty nations at the Munich Conference on Security Policy in 2007, Russian president Vladimir Putin explained his views on achieving global security. He attacked the militarization of outer space, the expansion of NATO into former East Bloc countries, and unlimited nuclear proliferation — all key elements of Russian foreign policy after communism — but reserved his sternest comments for U.S. actions in what he called a "unipolar world."

What is a unipolar world? However one might embellish this term, at the end of the day it . . . is [a] world in which there is one master, one sovereign. And at the end of the day this is pernicious not only for all those within this system, but also for the sovereign itself because it destroys itself from within. . . .

I consider that the unipolar model is not only unacceptable but also impossible in today's world. . . . The model itself is flawed because at its basis there is and can be no moral foundations for modern civilization. . . .

Today we are witnessing an almost uncontained hyper use of force — military force — in international relations, force that is plunging the world into an abyss of permanent conflicts. As a result we do not have sufficient strength to find a comprehensive solution to any one of these conflicts. Finding a political settlement also becomes impossible.

We are seeing a greater and greater disdain for the basic principles of international law. And independent legal norms are, as a matter of fact, coming increasingly closer to one state's legal system. One state and, of course, first and foremost the United States, has overstepped its national borders in every way. This is visible in the economic, political, cultural and educational policies it imposes on other nations. Well, who likes this? Who is happy about this? . . .

But do we have the means to counter these threats [of authoritarian regimes and the proliferation of weapons of mass destruction]? Certainly we do. It is sufficient to look at recent history. Did not our country have a peaceful transition to democracy? Indeed, we witnessed a peaceful transformation of the Soviet regime — a peaceful

transformation! And what a regime! With what a number of weapons, including nuclear weapons! Why should we start bombing and shooting now at every available opportunity? Is it the case when without the threat of mutual destruction we do not have enough political culture, respect for democratic values and for the law? . . .

The use of force can only be considered legitimate if the decision is sanctioned by the UN. And we do not need to substitute NATO or the EU for the UN. When the UN will truly unite the forces of the international community and can really react to events in various countries, when we will leave behind this disdain for international law, then the situation will be able to change. Otherwise the situation will simply result in a dead end, and the number of serious mistakes will be multiplied. . . .

The stones and concrete blocks of the Berlin Wall have long been distributed as souvenirs. But we should not forget that the fall of the Berlin Wall was possible thanks to a historic choice — one that was also made by our people, the people of Russia — a choice in favour of democracy, freedom, openness and a sincere partnership with all the members of the big European family.

And now they are trying to impose new dividing lines and walls on us — these walls may be virtual but they are nevertheless dividing, ones that cut through our continent. And is it possible that we will once again require many years and decades, as well as several generations of politicians, to dissemble and dismantle these new walls?

EVALUATE THE EVIDENCE

1. Putin's speech often seems overly general or vague. Exactly which U.S. actions draw his concern, and why would he worry about them?
2. How do Putin's words reflect the diminished stature of Russia in global affairs after the end of the Cold War? Why does he claim that "new walls" are being built between Russia and the West?

Source: Global Research, http://www.globalresearch.ca/the-universal-indivisible-character-of-global-security/4741.

Putin's Russia has taken an aggressive and at times interventionist stance toward the Commonwealth of Independent States, a loose confederation of most of the former Soviet republics (Map 30.1). The annexation of the Crimea in 2014 and support for insurrectionist pro-Russian rebels in eastern Ukraine are only the latest examples.

Putin's government moved decisively to limit political opposition at home. The 2003 arrest and imprisonment for tax evasion and fraud of the corrupt oil billionaire Mikhail Khodorkovsky, an Oligarch who had openly supported opposition parties, showed early on that Putin and his United Russia Party would use state powers to stifle dissent. Though the Russian constitution guarantees freedom of the press, the government cracked down on the independent media. Using a variety of tactics, officials and pro-government businessmen influenced news reports and intimidated critical journalists. The suspicious murder in 2006 of journalist Anna Politkovskaya, a prominent critic of the government's human rights abuses and its war in Chechnya, reinforced Western worries that the country was returning to Soviet-style press censorship.

Putin stepped down when his term limits expired in 2008. His handpicked successor, Dmitry Medvedev (mehd-VEHD-yehf) (b. 1965), easily won election that year and then appointed Putin prime minister, leading observers to believe that the former president was still the dominant figure. This suspicion was confirmed when Putin won the presidential election of March 2012 with over 60 percent of the vote. International observers agreed that the election itself was democratic, but reported irregularities during the vote-counting process. Some fifteen thousand protesters marched through downtown Moscow to protest election fraud and the authoritarian aspects of Putin's rule, and demonstrations accompanied the president's inauguration that May.

Tensions between political centralization and openness continue to define Russia's difficult road away from communism. On one hand, Putin's return to the presidency seemed to reinforce Russia's system of authoritarian central control. On the other, the fact that mass assemblies and marches against the president took place with relatively little repression attests to some degree of political openness and new limits on Russian state power in the twenty-first century.

Coping with Change in the Former East Bloc

Developments in the former East Bloc paralleled those in Russia in important ways. The former satellites worked to replace state planning and socialism with market mechanisms and private property. Western-style electoral politics also took hold.

New leaders across the former East Bloc faced similar economic problems: how to restructure Communist economic systems and move state-owned businesses and property into private hands. Under Soviet-style communism, central planners determined production and distribution goals and often set wage and price controls; now former East Bloc countries would adopt market-based economic systems. In addition, industries, businesses, and farms, considered the "people's property" and managed by the state in the name of the entire population, would now be privatized.

The methods of restructuring and privatization varied from country to country. Poland's new leaders turned to "shock therapy," the most rapid and comprehensive form of economic transformation, advocated by neoliberal Western institutions, including the International Monetary Fund and the World Bank. Starting in 1990, the Poles liberalized prices and trade policies, raised taxes, cut spending to reduce

MAP 30.1 Russia and the Successor States, 1991–2015 After the failure of an attempt in August 1991 to depose Gorbachev, an anticommunist revolution swept the Soviet Union. The republics that formed the Soviet Union each declared their sovereignty and independence, with Russia, under President Boris Yeltsin, being the largest. Eleven of the fourteen republics then joined with Russia to form a loose confederation called the Commonwealth of Independent States, but the integrated economy of the Soviet Union dissolved into separate national economies, each with its own goals and policies. Conflict continued to simmer over these goals and policies, as evidenced by the ongoing civil war in Chechnya, the struggle between Russia and Georgia over South Ossetia, the Russian annexation of the Crimea, and the Ukrainian separatist movement.

budget deficits, and quickly sold state-owned industries to private investors. As they would in Russia a few years later, these radical moves at first brought high inflation and a rapid decline in living standards, which generated public protests and strikes. But because the plan had the West's approval, Poland received Western financial support that eased the pain of transition. By the end of the decade, the country had one of the strongest economies in the former East Bloc.

Other countries followed alternate paths. Czechoslovakia took a more gradual approach. As in Russia, the Czechoslovak state issued vouchers to its citizens, which they could use to bid for shares in privatized companies. In Slovenia, one of the countries carved out of the former Yugoslavia, privatization included the transfer of up to 60 percent of company ownership to employees. In Estonia, reformers experimented with employee ownership, vouchers, and worker cooperatives. Compared to Poland's approach, privatization in all three countries was slower, continued more practices from the Communist past, and caused less social disruption.

Economic growth in the former Communist countries was varied, but most observers agreed that Poland, the Czech Republic, and Hungary were the most successful. Each met the critical challenge of economic reconstruction more successfully than did Russia, and each could claim to be the economic leader in the former East Bloc, depending on the criteria selected. The reasons for these successes included considerable experience with limited market reforms before 1989, flexibility and lack of dogmatism in government policy, and an enthusiastic embrace of capitalism by a new entrepreneurial class. In its first five years of reform, Poland created twice as many new businesses as did Russia in a comparable period, despite having only a quarter of Russia's population.

Poland, the Czech Republic, and Hungary also did far better than Russia in creating new civic institutions, legal systems, and independent media outlets that reinforced political freedom and national revival. Lech Wałęsa in Poland and Václav Havel in Czechoslovakia were elected presidents of their countries and proved as remarkable in power as in opposition (see Chapter 29). After Czechoslovakia's Velvet Revolution in 1989, the Czechoslovak parliament accepted a "velvet divorce" in 1993, when Slovakian nationalists wanted to break off and form their own state, creating the separate Czech and Slovak Republics. Above all, and in sharp contrast to Russia, the popular goal of adopting the liberal democratic values of western Europe reinforced political moderation and compromise. In 1999 Poland, Hungary, and the Czech Republic were accepted into NATO, and in 2004 they and Slovakia gained admission to the European Union (EU) (see page 1034).

Romania and Bulgaria lagged behind in the postcommunist transition. Western traditions were weaker there, and both countries were poorer than their more successful neighbors. Romania and Bulgaria did make progress after 2000, however, and joined NATO in 2004 and the EU in 2007.

The social consequences of rebuilding the former East Bloc were similar to those in Russia, though people were generally spared the widespread shortages and misery that characterized Russia in the 1990s. Ordinary citizens and the elderly were once again the big losers, while the young and former Communist Party members were the big winners. Inequalities between richer and poorer regions also increased. Capital cities such as Warsaw, Prague, and Budapest concentrated wealth, power, and opportunity as never before, while provincial centers stagnated and old industrial areas declined. Crime, corruption, and gangsterism increased in both the streets and the executive suites.

Though few former East Bloc residents wanted to return to communism, some expressed longings for the stability of the old system. They missed the guaranteed jobs and generous social benefits provided by the Communist state, and they found the individualism and competitiveness of capitalism cold and difficult. One Russian woman living on a pension of $448 a month in 2003 summed up the dilemma: "What we want is for our life to be as easy as it was in the Soviet Union, with the guarantee of a good, stable future and low prices—and at the same time this freedom that did not exist before."[2]

The question of whether or how to punish former Communist leaders who had committed political crimes or abused human rights emerged as a pressing issue in the former East Bloc. Germany tried major offenders and opened the records of the East German secret police (the Stasi) to the public, and by 1996 more than a million former residents had asked to see their files.[3] Other countries designed various means to deal with former Communist elites who might have committed crimes, with right-wing leaders generally taking a more punitive stand. The search for fair solutions proceeded slowly and with much controversy, a reminder of the troubling legacies of communism and the Cold War.

Tragedy in Yugoslavia

The great postcommunist tragedy occurred in Yugoslavia, which under Josip Broz Tito had been a federation of republics under centralized Communist rule (see Chapter 28). After Tito's death in 1980, power passed increasingly to the sister republics, which encouraged a revival of centuries-old regional and ethnic conflicts that were exacerbated by charges of ethnically inspired massacres during World War II and a dramatic economic decline in the mid-1980s.

The revolutions of 1989 accelerated the breakup of Yugoslavia. Serbian president Slobodan Milošević (1941–2006), a former Communist bureaucrat, wished to strengthen the federation's centralized government under Serbian control. In 1989 Milošević (mee-LOH-sheh-veech) severely limited self-rule in the Serbian province of Kosovo, where ethnic Albanians constituted the overwhelming majority, but which held a medieval battleground that he claimed was sacred to Serbian identity. In 1990 Milošević supported calls to grab land from other republics and unite all Serbs, regardless of where they lived, in a "greater Serbia" (which included Kosovo). Milošević's moves strengthened the cause of national separatism in the federation, and in June 1991 relatively wealthy Slovenia and Croatia declared their independence. Milošević ordered the Yugoslavian federal army to invade both areas to assert Serbian control. The Serbs were quickly repulsed in Slovenia, but managed to take about 30 percent of Croatia.

In 1992 the civil war spread to Bosnia-Herzegovina, which had also declared its independence. Serbs—about 30 percent of that region's population—refused to live under the more numerous Bosnian Muslims, or Bosniaks (Map 30.2). Yugoslavia had once been a tolerant and largely successful multiethnic state with different groups living side by side and often intermarrying. The new goal of the armed factions in the Bosnian civil war was **ethnic cleansing**: the attempt to establish ethnically homogeneous territories by intimidation, forced deportation, and killing. The Yugoslavian army and irregular militias attempted to "cleanse" the territory of its non-Serb residents,

ethnic cleansing The attempt to establish ethnically homogeneous territories by intimidation, forced deportation, and killing.

MAP 30.2 **The Breakup of Yugoslavia, 1991–2006**   Yugoslavia had the most ethnically diverse population in eastern Europe. The republic of Croatia had substantial Serbian and Muslim minorities. Bosnia-Herzegovina had large Muslim, Serbian, and Croatian populations, none of which had a majority. In June 1991 Serbia's brutal effort to seize territory and unite all Serbs in a single state brought a tragic civil war.

unleashing ruthless brutality, with murder, rape, destruction, and the herding of refugees into concentration camps. Before the fighting in Bosnia ended, some three hundred thousand people were dead, and millions had been forced to flee their homes.

While appalling scenes of horror not seen in Europe since the Holocaust shocked the world, the Western nations had difficulty formulating an effective, unified response. The turning point came in July 1995 when Bosnian Serbs overran Srebrenica—a Muslim city previously declared a United Nations safe area. Serb forces killed about eight thousand of the city's Bosniak civilians, primarily men and boys. Public outrage prompted NATO to bomb Bosnian Serb military targets intensively, and the Croatian army drove all the Serbs from Croatia. In November 1995 President Bill Clinton helped the warring sides hammer out a complicated accord that gave Bosnian Serbs about 49 percent of Bosnia and gave Bosniaks and the Roman Catholic Bosnian Croats the rest. Troops from NATO countries patrolled Bosnia to keep the peace; by 2013 only one thousand remained, suggesting that the situation had significantly improved.

Srebrenica Refugees More than 2,300 Bosnian Muslims packed into NATO trucks to flee the Serbian encirclement of Srebrenica in the spring of 1995. That July, the Serbian army massacred approximately 8,000 civilians in the city, and outraged public opinion in western Europe and North America finally led to decisive intervention against Serbia. In early 2016 twelve of the Serbian military leaders believed responsible were still on trial for crimes against humanity at the United Nations International Criminal Tribunal; eighty had been sentenced by the international court. (Michel Euler/AP Photo/AP Images)

The Kosovo Albanians, who hoped to establish self-rule, gained nothing from the Bosnian agreement. Frustrated Kosovar militants formed the Kosovo Liberation Army (KLA) and began to fight for independence. Serbian repression of the Kosovars increased, and in 1998 Serbian forces attacked both KLA guerrillas and unarmed villagers, displacing 250,000 people.

When Milošević refused to withdraw Serbian militias from Kosovo and accept self-government (but not independence) for Kosovo, NATO began bombing Serbia in March 1999. Serbian paramilitary forces responded by driving about 865,000 Albanian Kosovars into exile. NATO redoubled its destructive bombing campaign, which eventually forced Milošević to withdraw and allowed the Kosovars to regain their homeland. A United Nations and NATO peacekeeping force occupied Kosovo, ending ten years of Yugoslavian civil wars. Although U.S.-led NATO intervention finally brought an end to the conflict, the failure to take a stronger stand in the early years led to widespread and unnecessary suffering in the former Yugoslavia.

The war-weary and impoverished Serbs eventually voted the still-defiant Milošević out of office, and in July 2001 a new pro-Western Serbian government turned him over to a war crimes tribunal in the Netherlands to stand trial for crimes against humanity. After blustering his way through the initial stages of his trial, Milošević died in 2006 before the proceedings were complete. In 2008, after eight years of administration by the United Nations and NATO peacekeeping forces, the Republic of Kosovo declared its independence from Serbia. The United States and most states of the European Union recognized the declaration. Serbia and Russia did not, and the long-term status of this troubled emerging state remained uncertain.

Instability in the Former Soviet Republics

The collapse of the Soviet Union led to the establishment of the Russian Federation and fourteen other newly independent republics and brought major changes to east-central Europe and south-central Asia (see Map 30.1). In many ways, the transformation of this vast and diverse region paralleled the experience of the former East Bloc countries and Russia itself. Though most of the fourteen new republics, which included almost one-half of the former Soviet Union's total population, adopted some sort of liberal market capitalism, political reforms varied broadly. In the Baltic republics, where Gorbachev's perestroika had quickly encouraged powerful separatist movements, reformers established working democratic government. While Ukrainians struggled to construct a working democratic system, elsewhere—in Belarus, Kazakhstan and the other Central Asian republics, and the new republics in the Caucasus—systems of "imitation democracy" and outright authoritarian rule took hold.

Though Putin encouraged the former Soviet republics to join the Commonwealth of Independent States, a loose confederation dominated by Russia that supposedly represented regional common interests, stability and agreement proved elusive. Popular protests and revolts challenged local politicians and Russian interests alike. In Georgia, the so-called Rose Revolution (November 2003) brought a pro-Western, pro-NATO leader to power. In Ukraine, the Orange Revolution (November 2004–January 2005) challenged the results of a national election and expressed popular nationalist desires for more distance from Russia. Similar **Color Revolutions** in Belarus, Kyrgyzstan, and Moldova exemplified the unpredictable path toward democratization in the new republics that bordered the powerful Russian Federation.

Putin took an aggressive and at times interventionist stance toward anti-Russian revolt in the Commonwealth of Independent States and the Russian borderlands. Conflict has been particularly intense in the oil-rich Caucasus, where an unstable combination of nationalist separatism and ethnic and religious tensions challenges Russian dominance. Since the breakup of the Soviet Union, Russian troops have repeatedly invaded Chechnya (CHEHCH-nyuh), a tiny Muslim republic with 1 million inhabitants on Russia's southern border that declared its independence in 1991. Despite ultimate Russian victory in the Chechen wars, the cost of the conflict was high. Thousands lost their lives, and both sides committed serious human rights abuses. Moscow declared an end to military operations in April 2009, but Chechen insurgents, inspired by nationalism and Islamic radicalism, continued to fight. Russia also intervened in the independent state of Georgia, which won independence when the Soviet Union collapsed in 1991. Russian troops also invaded Georgia in 2008 to support a separatist movement in South Ossetia (ah-SEE-shuh), which eventually established a breakaway independent republic recognized only by Russia and a handful of small states.

Revolution broke out again in Ukraine in February 2014, and when popular protests brought down the pro-Russian government, Putin's response was rapid and radically interventionist. In late February Russian troops marched into Crimea, a strategically valuable peninsula in the Black Sea where pro-Russian sentiment ran high. The territory, with a major naval base in the city of Sevastopol and large reserves of oil and natural gas, was incorporated into the Russian Federation. Then, in response to the anti-Russian policies of the new Ukrainian government, in April 2014 a group of armed rebels took over the regional capital Donetsk and other cities in eastern Ukraine and declared the establishment of the separatist, pro-Russian Donetsk and Luhansk "People's Republics" (see Map 30.1).

A full-scale military assault by Ukrainian government troops failed to push back or defeat the separatist forces. According to Ukrainian and U.S. sources, only direct Russian intervention, including substantial supplies of weaponry and troops, prevented the defeat of the insurrection. In response, the United States and the European

Color Revolutions A series of popular revolts and insurrections that challenged regional politicians and Russian interests in the former Soviet republics during the first decade of the twenty-first century.

Union placed economic sanctions on Russia, and since February 2015 a shaky cease-fire has dampened hostilities in eastern Ukraine. Yet the outcome of the conflict remains uncertain, a telling example of the way great power interests continue to create instability in the former Soviet republics.

The New Global System

Contemporary observers often assert that the world has entered a new era of **globalization**. Such assertions do not mean that there were never international connections before. Europe has long had close—sometimes productive, sometimes destructive—ties to other parts of the world. Yet new global relationships and increasing interdependence did emerge in the last decades of the twentieth century.

First, the growth of multinational corporations restructured national economies on a global scale. Second, an array of international governing bodies, such as the European Union, the United Nations, the World Trade Organization, and a number of nongovernmental organizations (or NGOs), increasingly set policies that challenged the autonomy of traditional nation-states. Finally, the expansion and ready availability of highly efficient computer and media technologies led to ever-faster exchanges of information and entertainment around the world. Taken together, these global transformations had a remarkable impact, both positive and negative, on many aspects of Western society.

FOCUS QUESTION
How did globalization affect European life and society?

globalization The emergence of a freer, more technologically connected global economy, accompanied by a worldwide exchange of cultural, political, and religious ideas.

The Global Economy

Though large business interests had long profited from international trade and investment, multinational corporations grew and flourished in a world economy increasingly organized around policies of free-market neoliberalism, which relaxed barriers to international trade (see Chapter 29). Multinational corporations built global systems of production and distribution that generated unprecedented wealth and generally escaped the control of regulators and politicians acting on the national level.

Conglomerates such as Siemens and Vivendi exemplified this business model. Siemens, with international headquarters in Berlin and Munich and offices around the globe, is one of the world's largest engineering companies, with vast holdings in energy, construction, health care, financial services, and industrial production. Vivendi, an extensive media and telecommunications company headquartered in Paris, controls a vast international network of producers and products, including music and film, publishing, television broadcasting, pay-TV, Internet services, and video games.

The development of sophisticated personal computer technologies and the Internet at the end of the twentieth century, coupled with the deregulation of national and international financial systems, further encouraged the growth of international trade. The ability to rapidly exchange information and capital meant that economic activity was no longer centered on national banks or stock exchanges, but rather flowed quickly across international borders. Large cities like London, Moscow, New York, and Hong Kong became global centers of banking, trade, and financial services. The influence of financial and insurance companies, communications conglomerates, and energy and legal firms headquartered in these global cities extended far beyond the borders of the traditional nation-state.

At the same time, the close connections between national economies also made the entire world vulnerable to economic panics and downturns. In 1997 a banking crisis in Thailand spread to Indonesia, South Korea, and Japan and then echoed around the world. The resulting slump in oil and gas prices hit Russia especially hard, leading to high inflation, bank failures, and the collapse of the Russian stock market. The crisis then spread to Latin America, plunging most countries there into a severe economic downturn. A decade later, a global recession triggered by a crisis in the U.S. housing market and financial system created the worst worldwide economic crisis since the Great Depression of the 1930s (see page 1056).

The New European Union

European Union (EU) The economic, cultural, and political alliance of twenty-eight European nations.

Global economic pressures encouraged the expansion and consolidation of the European Common Market, which in 1993 proudly rechristened itself the **European Union (EU)** (Map 30.3). The EU added the free movement of capital and services and eventually individuals across national borders to the existing free trade in goods. In addition, member states sought to create a monetary union in which all EU countries would share a single currency. Membership in the monetary union required states to meet strict financial criteria defined in the 1991 **Maastricht Treaty**, which also set legal standards and anticipated the development of common policies on defense and foreign affairs.

Maastricht Treaty The basis for the formation of the European Union, which set financial and cultural standards for potential member states and defined criteria for membership in the monetary union.

Western European elites and opinion makers generally supported the economic integration embodied in the Maastricht Treaty. They felt that membership requirements, which imposed financial discipline on national governments, would combat Europe's ongoing economic problems and viewed the establishment of a single European currency as an irreversible historic step toward basic political unity. This unity would allow Europe as a whole to regain its place in world politics and to deal with the United States as an equal.

Support for the Maastricht Treaty was hardly universal. Ordinary people, leftist political parties, and right-wing nationalists expressed considerable opposition to the new rules. Many people resented the EU's ever-growing bureaucracy in Brussels, which imposed common standards on everything from cheese production to day care, supposedly undermining national customs and local traditions. Moreover, increased unity meant yielding still more power to distant "Eurocrats" and political insiders, which limited national sovereignty and democratic control.

Above all, many citizens feared that the European Union would operate at their expense. Joining the monetary union required national governments to meet stringent fiscal standards, impose budget cuts, and contribute to the EU operating budget. The resulting reductions in health care and social benefits hit ordinary citizens and did little to reduce high unemployment. When put to the public for a vote, ratification of the Maastricht Treaty was usually very close. In France, for example, the treaty passed with just 50.1 percent of the vote. Even after the treaty was ratified, battles over budgets, benefits, and high unemployment continued throughout the EU in the 1990s.

Then in 2002, brand-new euros finally replaced the national currencies of all Eurozone countries. The establishment of the European monetary union built confidence in member nations and increased their willingness to accept new members. On May 1, 2004, the European Union began admitting its former East Bloc

MAP 30.3 The European Union, 2016   No longer divided by ideological competition and the Cold War, much of today's Europe has banded together in a European Union that facilitates the open movement of people, jobs, and currency across national borders.

neighbors. By 2016, with the recent admission of Croatia, the EU was home to about 500 million citizens in twenty-eight countries. It included most of the former East Bloc and, with the Baltic nations, three republics of the former Soviet Union.

This rapid expansion underscored the need to reform the EU's unwieldy governing structure. In June 2004 a special commission presented a new EU constitution that created a president, a foreign minister, and a voting system weighted to reflect the populations of the different states. The proposed constitution moved toward a more centralized federal system, though each state retained veto power over taxation, social policy, foreign affairs, and other sensitive areas. After many contentious referendum campaigns across the continent, the constitution failed to win the unanimous support required to take effect. Ultimately, nationalist fears about losing sovereignty and cultural identity outweighed the perceived benefits of a more unified Europe. Fears that an unwieldy European Union would grow to include Ukraine, Georgia, and Muslim Turkey—countries with cultures and histories that were very different from those of western Europe—were particularly telling.

Though the constitution did not go into effect, the long postwar march toward greater European unity did not stop. In 2007 the rejected constitution was replaced with the Treaty of Lisbon. The new treaty kept many sections of the constitution, but further streamlined the EU bureaucracy and reformed its political structure. When the Treaty of Lisbon went into effect on December 1, 2009, after ratification by all EU states, it capped a remarkable fifty-year effort to unify what had been a deeply divided and war-torn continent.

Yet profound questions about the meaning of European unity and identity remained. Would the European Union expand as promised to include the postcommunist nations of the former Soviet Union, and if so, how could Muslim Turkey's long-standing application be ignored? Could a union of twenty-eight diverse countries have any real cohesion and common identity? Would the EU remain closely linked with the United States in NATO, or would it develop an independent defense policy? Could member states agree on an economic policy to master the stubborn recession that emerged in 2008 and the Greek debt crisis of 2015 and keep the nineteen-state Eurozone intact (see page 1057)? Would they be able to manage the refugee crisis that emerged in 2015? The EU struggled to shape institutions and policies to address these complicated issues.

Supranational Organizations

Beyond the European Union, the trend toward globalization empowered a variety of other supranational organizations that had tremendous reach. National governments still played the leading role in defining and implementing policy, but they increasingly had to take the policies of institutions such as the United Nations and the World Trade Organization into consideration.

The United Nations (UN), established in 1945 after World War II, remains an important player on the world stage. Representatives from all independent countries meet in the UN General Assembly in New York City to try to forge international agreements. UN agencies deal with issues such as world hunger and poverty, and the International Court of Justice in The Hague, Netherlands, hears cases that violate international law. The UN also sends troops in attempts to preserve peace between warring parties—as in Yugoslavia in the 1990s. While the smaller UN Security Council has broad powers, including the ability to impose sanctions to punish uncooperative states and even to endorse military action, its five permanent members—the United States, Russia, France, Great Britain, and China—can each veto resolutions introduced in that body. The predominance of the United States and western European powers on the Security Council has led some critics to accuse the UN of implementing Western neocolonial policies (see Chapter 28). Others argue that UN policies should never take precedence over national needs, and UN resolutions are at times ignored or downplayed.

A trio of nonprofit international financial institutions have also gained power in a globalizing world. Like the United Nations, the World Bank and the International Monetary Fund (IMF) were established in the years following World War II. Initially founded to help rebuild war-torn Europe, these organizations now provide loans to the developing world. Their funding comes primarily from donations from the United States and western Europe, and they typically extend loans on the condition that recipient countries adopt neoliberal economic reforms, including budget reduction, deregulation, and privatization. In the 1990s the World Bank and the IMF played especially active roles in shaping economic and social policy in the former East Bloc.

The third economic supranational, the **World Trade Organization (WTO)**, is one of the most powerful supranational financial institutions. It sets trade and tariff agreements for over 150 member countries, thus helping manage a large percentage of the world's import-export policies. Like the IMF and the World Bank, the WTO generally promotes neoliberal policies.

The rise of these institutions, which typically represent the shared interests of national governments, was paralleled by the emergence of a variety of **nongovernmental organizations (NGOs)**. Some NGOs act as lobbyists on specific issues; others conduct international programs and activities. Exemplary NGOs include Doctors Without Borders, a charitable organization of physicians headquartered in France; Greenpeace, an international environmental group; and Oxfam, a British-based group dedicated to alleviating famine, disease, and poverty in the developing world. Though financed by donations from governments and private citizens, NGOs' annual budgets can total hundreds of millions of dollars and their work can be quite extensive.

The Human Side of Globalization

Globalization transformed the lives of millions of people, as the technological changes associated with postindustrial society (see Chapter 29) remade workplaces and lifestyles around the world. Low labor costs in the industrializing world—including the former East Bloc, Latin America, and East Asia—encouraged corporations to outsource labor-intensive manufacturing jobs to these regions. Widespread adoption of neoliberal free-trade policies and low labor costs in developing countries made it less expensive to manufacture steel, automotive parts, computer components, and all manner of consumer goods in developing countries and then import them for sale in the West. In the 1990s China, with its low wages and rapidly growing industrial infrastructure, emerged as an economic powerhouse that supplied goods across the world—even as the West's industrial heartlands continued to decline. Under these conditions, a car made by Volkswagen could still be sold as a product of high-quality German engineering despite being assembled in Chattanooga, Tennessee, using steel imported from South Korea and computer chips made in Taiwan.

The outsourcing of manufacturing jobs dramatically changed the nature of work in western Europe and North America. In France in 1973, for example, some 40 percent of the employed population worked in industry—in mining, construction, manufacturing, and utilities. About 49 percent worked in services, including retail, hotels and restaurants, transportation, communications, financial and business services, and social and personal services. In 2004 only 24 percent of the French worked in industry, and a whopping 72 percent worked in services. The numbers varied

World Trade Organization (WTO) A powerful supranational financial institution that sets trade and tariff agreements for over 150 member countries and so helps manage a large percentage of the world's import-export policies. Like the IMF and the World Bank, the WTO promotes neoliberal policies around the world.

nongovernmental organizations (NGOs) Independent organizations with specific agendas, such as humanitarian aid or environmental protection, that conduct international programs and activities.

Antiglobalization Activism French protesters carry the figure of Ronald McDonald through the streets to protest the trial of José Bové, a prominent leader in campaigns against the human and environmental costs associated with globalization. Bové was accused of demolishing a McDonald's franchise in a small town in southern France. With its worldwide fast-food restaurants that pay little attention to local traditions, McDonald's has often been the target of antiglobalization protests. (Witt/Haley/Sipa)

country by country, yet across Europe the trend was clear: by 2005 only about one in three workers was still employed in the once-booming manufacturing sector.[4]

The deindustrialization of Europe established a multitiered society with winners and losers. At the top was a small, affluent group of experts, executives, and professionals—about one-quarter of the population—who managed the new global enterprises. In the second, larger tier, the middle class struggled with stagnating incomes and a declining standard of living as once-well-paid industrial workers faced stubborn unemployment and cuts in both welfare and workplace benefits. Many were forced to take low-paying jobs in the retail service sector.

In the bottom tier—in some areas as much as a quarter of the population—a poorly paid underclass performed the unskilled jobs of a postindustrial economy or were chronically unemployed. In western Europe and North America, inclusion in this lowest segment of society was often linked to race, ethnicity, and a lack of educational opportunity. Recently arrived immigrants had trouble finding jobs and often lived in unpleasant, hastily built housing, teetering on the edge of poverty. In London, unemployment rates among youths and particularly young black men soared above those of their white compatriots. Frustration over these conditions, coupled with anger at a police shooting, boiled over in immigrant neighborhoods across the city in August 2011, when angry youths rioted in the streets, burning buildings and looting stores.

Geographic contrasts further revealed the unequal aspects of globalization. Regions in Europe that had successfully shifted to a postindustrial economy, such as northern Italy and southern Germany and Austria, enjoyed prosperity. Lagging behind were regions historically dependent on heavy industry, such as the former East Bloc countries and the factory districts north of London, or underdeveloped areas, such as rural sections of southern Italy, Spain, and Greece. In addition, a global north-south divide increasingly separated Europe and North America—both still affluent despite their economic problems—from the industrializing nations of Africa and Latin America. Though India, China, and other East Asian nations experienced solid growth, other industrializing nations struggled to overcome decades of underdevelopment.

The human costs of globalization resulted in new forms of global protest. Critics accused global corporations and financial groups of doing little to address problems caused by their activities, such as social inequality, pollution, and unfair labor practices. The Slow Food movement that began in Italy, for example, criticized American-style fast-food chains that proliferated in Europe and the world in the 1990s. Cooking with local products and traditional methods, followers argued, was healthier and kept jobs and profits in local neighborhoods. The fast-food giant McDonald's was often targeted as an example of the ills of corporate globalization. José Bové, a French farmer and antiglobalization activist, made world headlines by driving his truck through the windows of a McDonald's in a small French village to protest the use of hormone-fed beef and genetically modified foods as well as the reach of corporate capital.

The general tone of the antiglobalization movement was captured at the 1999 meeting of the WTO in Seattle, Washington. Tens of thousands of protesters from around the world, including environmentalists, consumer and antipoverty activists, and labor rights groups, marched in the streets and disrupted the meeting. Comparable demonstrations took place at later meetings of the WTO, the World Bank, and other supranational groups.

Similar feelings inspired the Occupy movement, which began in the United States in 2011 and quickly spread to over eighty countries. Under the slogan "We are the 99 percent," thousands of people camped out in (or "occupied") public places to protest the rapidly growing social inequality that divided a tiny wealthy elite (the "1 percent") from the vast majority of ordinary people. Though the diverse groups in the Occupy movement failed to mount a sustained and successful challenge to the public officials and business leaders who profited from globalization, their calls for greater social equality and democracy showed that the struggle for reform continued.

Life in the Digital Age

The growing sophistication of information technologies—a hallmark of the globalizing age—has had a profound and rapidly evolving effect on patterns of communications, commerce, and politics. As tiny digital microchips replaced bulky transistors and the Internet grew in scope and popularity, more and more people organized their everyday lives around the use of ever-smaller and more powerful high-tech devices.

Leisure-time pursuits were a case in point. The arrival of cable television, followed swiftly by DVDs and then online video streaming, enabled individuals to watch full-length movies or popular television shows on their personal computers or smartphones at any time and greatly diversified the options for home entertainment. Europe's once-powerful public broadcasting systems, such as the BBC, were forced to compete with a variety of private enterprises, including Netflix, a U.S. online video provider that entered the European media market in 2014. Music downloads and streaming audio files replaced compact discs, which themselves had replaced vinyl records and cassettes; digital cameras eliminated the need for expensive film; e-book readers, including Kindles and iPads, offered a handheld portable library; smartphone apps provided an apparently endless variety of conveniences and distractions.

Digitalization transformed familiar forms of communication in a few short decades. Many of these changes centered on the Internet, which began its rapid expansion around the globe in the late 1980s. In the first decade of the twenty-first century, the evolution of the cell phone into the smartphone, with its multimedia telecommunications features and more functions and power than the desktop computers of the previous decade, hastened the change. The growing popularity of Internet-based communication tools such as e-mail, text messaging, Facebook, Twitter, and other social media changed the way friends, families, and businesses kept in touch. Letter writing with pen and paper became a quaint relic of the past. Skype, first introduced in 2003, offered personal computer and smartphone users video telecommunications around the world. The old-fashioned "landline," connected

Edward Snowden — traitor or hero? When the former CIA operative leaked a trove of classified documents about American surveillance programs to the world press, he was praised by some, vilified by others, and ultimately indicted on espionage charges by the U.S. government.

Snowden perhaps seems an unlikely candidate for masterminding the biggest intelligence leak in history. Born in 1983, the gun-owning, political conservative never finished high school and took computer classes at a community college. In 2006 he got a job in information technology with the CIA. From 2009 to 2013 he worked as a contractor for the National Security Agency.

As a systems analyst with a high-level security clearance, Snowden had access to highly classified NSA materials. Over the years, he grew increasingly outraged by the extent of secret government surveillance. In contravention of NSA regulations, he began to copy files on a personal thumb drive and ultimately collected tens of thousands of top-secret documents from NSA archives.

In January 2013 a journalist working for the liberal British newspaper the *Guardian* and an American documentary film maker received e-mails from an anonymous source asking for an exchange of encrypted (highly encoded) information. "I am a senior member of the intelligence community," read the anonymous e-mail. "This won't be a waste of your time."* Enticed, they agreed to meet the source in a Hong Kong hotel. There Snowden disclosed his identity and handed over a

selection of documents. Recognizing a scoop, the *Guardian* revealed the secret surveillance programs. Other media outlets pounced on the story, and Snowden's revelations became a global sensation.

The explosive news reports described extensive U.S. spy programs that shocked people around the world. The leaks revealed that the NSA had collected phone records from virtually every person in the United States and had misled the U.S. Congress about the extent of the surveillance. The agency had accessed the Internet servers of major telecommunications providers and could thus collect information about e-mail messages, Internet searches, and individual friends and contacts from Facebook and Google. The documents described programs that monitored the telephone calls of notable politicians in friendly nations. Chancellor Angela Merkel of Germany, a close ally of the United States, was infuriated to find out that the NSA had tapped her cell phone; so were the presidents of Mexico and Brazil, among others.

The response took many forms. Foreign leaders were dismayed by the extensive leaks from a major allied security service and by the pervasiveness of U.S. surveillance programs. Conservative pundits and U.S. officials condemned Snowden, arguing that the leaked materials revealed secret antiterrorism operations and could even endanger the lives of agents in the field. As President Barack Obama put it, "If any individual who objects to government policy can take it in their own

to a stationary telephone, seemed ready to join the vinyl LP and the handwritten letter in the junk bin of history.

Entire industries were dramatically changed by the emergence of the Internet. With faster speeds and better online security came online shopping. People increasingly relied on the Internet to purchase goods from clothes to computers to groceries. Online file sharing of books and popular music transformed the publishing and music industries, while massive online retailers such as Amazon and eBay, which sell millions of goods across the globe without physical storefronts, transformed familiar retail systems.

The rapid growth of the Internet and social media raised complex questions related to personal privacy and politics. Governments and businesses used online tracking systems to amass an extraordinary amount of information on individuals and then monitor their political activities or target them with advertising. Privacy hands to publicly disclose classified information, then we will not be able to keep our people safe, or conduct foreign policy."†

Proponents of civil liberties, defenders of the right to online privacy, and critics of U.S. foreign policy nonetheless welcomed Snowden's revelations. "It is time for President Obama to offer clemency to Edward Snowden, the courageous U.S. citizen who revealed the Orwellian reach of the National Security Agency's sweeping surveillance of Americans," wrote a liberal commentator in the *Washington Post*. "His actions may have broken the law, but his act . . . did the nation a great service."‡

Fearing for his freedom, Snowden went underground in Hong Kong. Several weeks later, he surfaced in Russia, where he received an offer of temporary asylum. Snowden now lives somewhere around Moscow, where he continues to comment on electronic surveillance and privacy rights.

Former NSA contractor and antisurveillance whistleblower Edward Snowden receives the 2015 Bjornson Prize from the Norwegian Academy of Literature and Freedom of Expression. (© SVEIN OVE EKORNESVAAG/epa/Corbis)

QUESTIONS FOR ANALYSIS

1. Why did the arrival of the digital age lead to heated debates about the individual's right to privacy?
2. Where would you draw the line between the need for online privacy and the government's need to collect personal information in order to protect society from terrorist attacks? Where does Snowden fit in?

*Luke Harding, "How Edward Snowden Went from Loyal NSA Contractor to Whistleblower," *Guardian*, February 1, 2014, http://www.theguardian.com/world/2014/feb/01/edward-snowden-intelligence-leak-nsa-contractor-extract.

†Josh Gerstein, "Obama Hits Snowden over NSA Leaks," *Politico*, January 17, 2014, http://www.politico.com/story/2014/0ç1/barack-obama-edward-snowden-nsa-leaks-102316.

‡Katrina vanden Heuval, "Justice for Edward Snowden," *Washington Post*, October 28, 2014.

advocates worked with government regulators to shape laws that might preserve key elements of online privacy, and in general, rules were more stringent in Europe than in the United States.

The vast amount of information circulating on the Internet could also lead to the exposure of government and business secrets. The numerous materials posted online by the nonprofit organization WikiLeaks, dedicated to the publication of secret information and news leaks, documented numerous examples of government and corporate misconduct. The classified U.S. National Security Agency information leaked in 2013 by former CIA contractor Edward Snowden embarrassed U.S. diplomats and fueled further debates about Internet surveillance, national security, and privacy protection. (See "Individuals in Society: Edward Snowden," above.) In addition, individuals could use smartphones and social media sites to organize protest campaigns. Facebook and Twitter, for example, helped mobilize demonstrators in Egypt during the Arab Spring (see page 1055) and allowed members of the Occupy movement to share news and shape strategy. A number of authoritarian states from North Korea to Iran to Cuba, recognizing the disruptive powers of the Internet, strictly limited online access.

Ethnic Diversity in Contemporary Europe

FOCUS QUESTION
What are the main causes and effects of growing ethnic diversity in contemporary Europe?

As the twenty-first century opened and ongoing globalization transformed European society and politics, Europeans witnessed the remaking of their ethnic communities. First, Europe experienced a remarkable decline in birthrates that seemed to predict a shrinking and aging population in the future. Second, the peaceful, wealthy European Union attracted rapidly growing numbers of refugees and immigrants from the former Soviet Union and East Bloc, North Africa, and the Middle East. The unexpected arrival of so many newcomers raised perplexing questions about ethnic diversity and the costs and benefits of multiculturalism.

The Prospect of Population Decline

In 2016 population rates were still growing rapidly in many poor countries but not in the world's industrialized nations. In 2000 families in developed countries had only 1.6 children on average; only in the United States did families have, almost exactly, the 2.1 children necessary to maintain a stable population. In Europe, where birthrates had been falling since the 1950s, national fertility rates ranged from 1.2 to 1.8 children per woman of childbearing age. By 2013 Italy and Ireland, once known for large Catholic families, had each achieved one of Europe's lowest birthrates—a mere 1.3 babies per woman. None of the twenty-eight countries in the EU had birthrates above 2.0; the average fertility rate was about 1.55 children per woman.[5]

If the current baby bust continues, the long-term consequences could be dramatic, though hardly predictable. At the least, Europe's population would decline and age. Projections for Germany are illustrative. Total German population, barring much greater immigration, would gradually decline from about 81 million in 2015 to just under 72 million around 2050. The number of people of working age would fall, and due to longer life spans, nearly a third of the population would be over sixty. Social security taxes paid by the shrinking labor force would need to soar to meet the skyrocketing costs of pensions and health care for seniors—a recipe for generational conflict. As the premier of Bavaria, Germany's biggest state, has warned, the prospect of demographic decline is a "ticking time bomb under our social welfare system and entire economy."[6]

Why, in times of peace, did Europeans fail to reproduce? Studies showed that European women and men in their twenties, thirties, and early forties still wanted two or even three children—like their parents. But unlike their parents, young couples did not realize their ideal family size. Many women postponed the birth of their first child into their thirties in order to finish their education and establish careers. Then, finding that balancing a child and a career was more difficult than anticipated, new mothers tended to postpone and eventually forgo having a second child. The better educated and the more economically successful a woman was, the more likely she was to have just one child or no children at all. In addition, the uneven, uninspiring European economic conditions since the mid-1970s played a role. High unemployment fell heavily on young people, especially after the recession of 2008, convincing youths to delay settling down and having children.

In 2013 some population experts concluded that European birthrates had stabilized, though women continued to postpone having children. Moreover, the frightening implications of dramatic population decline emerged as a major public issue. Opinion leaders, politicians, and the media started to advocate for larger families and propose policies to provide more support for families with children. Europeans may yet respond with enough vigor to reverse their population decline and avoid societal crisis.

Changing Immigration Flows

As European demographic vitality waned in the 1990s, a surge of migrants from the former Soviet Bloc, Africa, and most recently the Middle East headed for western Europe. Some migrants entered the European Union legally, with proper documentation, but increasing numbers were smuggled in past beefed-up border patrols. Large-scale immigration, both documented and undocumented, emerged as a critical and controversial issue.

Historically a source rather than a destination of immigrants, western Europe saw rising numbers of immigrants in postcolonial population movements beginning in the 1950s, augmented by the influx of manual laborers in its boom years from about 1960 until about 1973 (see Chapter 28). A new and different surge of migration into western Europe began in the 1990s. The collapse of communism in the East Bloc and savage civil wars in Yugoslavia drove hundreds of thousands of refugees westward. Equally brutal conflicts in Somalia and Rwanda, the U.S.-led invasions of Afghanistan and Iraq, and then the turmoil in North Africa and the Middle East unleashed by the "Arab Spring," brought hundreds of thousands more. In 2013 immigration to the EU from nonmember countries topped 1.7 million people.

Undocumented or irregular immigration into the European Union also exploded. The number of irregular migrants is difficult to quantify, but in 2014 approximately 260,000 non-European nationals were turned back at Europe's borders, while almost 550,000 irregular migrants already lived in the EU. That same year, about 275,000 migrants entered Europe irregularly, an increase of almost 140 percent from 2013.[7]

Why was Europe such an attractive destination for non-European migrants, regular and irregular? First, even with all the economic problems of western Europe, economic opportunity undoubtedly was a major attraction for immigrants. Germans, for example, earned on average three and a half times more than neighboring Poles, who in turn earned much more than people farther east and in North Africa. In 1998 most European Union states abolished all border controls; entrance into one country allowed for unimpeded travel almost anywhere (though Ireland and the United Kingdom opted out of this agreement). This meant that irregular migrants could enter across the relatively lax borders of Greece and south-central Europe, and then move north across the continent in search of refuge and jobs.

Second, EU immigration policy offered migrants the possibility of acquiring asylum status, if they could demonstrate that they faced severe persecution, based on race, nationality, religion, political belief, or membership in a specific social group in their home countries. Many migrants turned to Europe as they fled civil wars in Syria and Iraq, violence in Libya, and poverty and harsh social and political repression in parts of Africa. The rules for attaining asylum status varied by nation, though Germany and

Europe's Refugee Crisis   A volunteer helps Middle Eastern refugees ashore at the Greek island of Lesbos on November 29, 2015. Exhausted and emotional, they traveled by boat from Turkey. Under Europe's system of open internal borders, the island's thinly patrolled, easily accessible coastline, within sight of the Turkish coast, offered a tempting entry into the European Union for migrants ultimately seeking residence in Germany or Sweden. In fall and early winter of 2015–2016, about five thousand refugees reached Europe each day along the so-called Balkan migrant route. Their unprecedented numbers stoked anti-immigrant tensions across Europe and called into question the internal open-border system. (Oage Elif Kizil/Anadolu Agency/Getty Images)

Sweden offered relatively liberal policies, housing for applicants, and high benefit payments (still only about $425 per month, per adult). The regulations were nonetheless restrictive: though numerous migrants applied for asylum, after an average fifteen-month wait many were rejected, classified as illegal job seekers, and expelled.

Irregular immigration was aided by powerful criminal gangs that smuggled people for profit. In the 1990s these gangs contributed to the large number of young female illegal immigrants from eastern Europe, especially Russia and Ukraine. Often lured by criminals promising jobs as maids or waitresses, these women were often trafficked into the most prosperous parts of Europe and forced into prostitution.

More recently, immigration flows have shifted to reflect the dislocation that emerged in North Africa and the Middle East in the wake of the failed "Arab Spring" and the war against the Islamic State (see page 1055). Smugglers with a callous disregard for the well-being of their charges can demand thousands of euros to bring undocumented migrants from North Africa and the Middle East across the Mediterranean into Spain and Italy; the safer and less expensive route across Turkey and Greece and the north into more prosperous European countries is particularly well traveled (Map 30.4).

In the summer of 2015 the migration issue reached crisis proportions. Tens of thousands of migrants, most displaced by war in Syria and Iraq, entered Hungary through Serbia and struggled to travel into more hospitable Austria, Germany, and northern Europe. Others continued to enter the EU through the relatively accessible Greek islands. As Germany promised homes for eight hundred thousand migrants and encouraged other EU nations to take their share, thousands of migrants choked train and bus stations on the Hungarian-Austrian border. Others languished in quickly established refugee camps built in northern Greece and the Hungarian countryside, and Hungary's anti-immigrant government quickly built a 108-mile razor-wire fence along the border with Serbia to squelch further movement.

The discovery of seventy-one dead migrants locked in an abandoned truck on an Austrian highway—and the deaths of thousands more who in the last several years attempted to cross the Mediterranen in rudimentary rubber rafts and leaky

MAP 30.4 Major Migration Routes into Contemporary Europe In the wake of wars and the collapse of the Arab Spring, in-migration from northern Africa and the Middle East into Europe reached crisis proportions. Aided by smugglers, thousands of migrants traveled two main routes: through Libya and across the Mediterranean Sea into southern Italy, and across Turkey to close-by Greek islands and then north through the Balkans. Countries with relatively lenient refugee regulations, such as Sweden and Germany, were favorite destinations. Under the so-called Schengen Agreement, the EU's open-border policy made travel through Europe fairly easy. As the number of migrants increased in fall 2015 and spring 2016, however, European politicians began to close national borders, and many migrants were stranded in quickly built refugee camps.

boats—underscored the venality of the smugglers and the human costs of uncontrolled immigration. As this text was being written, European leaders were still struggling to contain the humanitarian crisis caused by the largest movement of peoples across Europe since the end of World War II, with little end in sight.

Toward a Multicultural Continent

By 2015 immigration to Europe had profoundly changed the ethnic makeup of the continent, though the effects were unevenly distributed. One way to measure the effect of these new immigrants is to consider the rapid rise of their numbers. Since the 1960s the foreign population of western European nations has grown by two to ten times. In the Netherlands in 1960, only 1 percent of the population was foreign-born. In 2006 the foreign born made up 10 percent. Over the same years the proportion of immigrants grew from 1.2 percent to 12.3 percent in Germany and from 4.7 percent to almost 11 percent in France.[8] In 2005 immigrants constituted about 10 percent of most western European nations (though a far smaller share of the former East Bloc nations). For centuries the number of foreigners living in Europe had been relatively small. Now, permanently displaced ethnic groups, or **diasporas**, brought ethnic diversity to the continent.

diasporas Enclaves of ethnic groups settled outside of their homelands.

The new immigrants were divided into two main groups. A small percentage were highly trained specialists who could find work in the upper ranks of education, business, and high-tech industries. Engineers from English-speaking India, for example, could find positions in international computer companies. Most immigrants, however, did not have access to high-quality education or language training, which limited their employment opportunities and made integration more difficult. They often lived in separate city districts marked by poor housing and crowded conditions, which set them apart from more established residents. Districts of London were home to tens of thousands of immigrants from the former colonies, and in Paris North Africans dominated some working-class *banlieues* (suburbs).

A variety of new cultural forms, ranging from sports and cuisine to music, the fine arts, and film, brought together native and foreign traditions and transformed European lifestyles. Food was a case in point. Recipes and cooks from former colonies in North Africa enlivened French cooking, while the döner kebab—the Turkish version of a gyro sandwich—became Germany's "native" fast food. Indian restaurants proliferated across Britain, and controversy raged when the British foreign minister announced in 2001 that chicken tikka masala—a spicy Indian stew—was Great Britain's new national dish.[9]

multiculturalism The mixing of ethnic styles in daily life and in cultural works such as film, music, art, and literature.

The **multiculturalism** and ethnic diversity associated with globalization have inspired numerous works in literature, film, and the fine arts. From rap to reggae to rai, multiculturalism has also had a profound effect on popular music, a medium with a huge audience. Rai, which originated in the Bedouin culture of North Africa, exemplified the new pop music forms that emerged from cultural mixing. In the 1920s rai traveled with Algerian immigrants to France. In its current form, it blends Arab and North African folk music, U.S. rap, and French and Spanish pop styles. Lyrics range from sentimental love stories to blunt and sometimes critical descriptions of daily life in immigrant communities.

The growth of immigration and ethnic diversity created rich social and cultural interactions but also generated controversy and conflict in western Europe. In most EU nations, immigrants can become full citizens if they meet certain legal qualifications;

adopting the culture of the host country is not a requirement. This legal process has raised questions about who, exactly, could or should be European, and about the way these new citizens might change European society. The idea that cultural and ethnic diversity could be a force for vitality and creativity has run counter to deep-seated beliefs about national homogeneity. Some commentators have accused the newcomers of taking jobs from unemployed native Europeans and undermining national unity. Government welfare programs intended to support struggling immigrants have been criticized by some as a misuse of money, especially in times of economic downturn.

Europe and Its Muslim Population

General concerns with migration often fused with fears of Muslim migrants and Muslim residents who have grown up in Europe. Islam is now the largest minority religion in Europe. The EU's 15 to 20 million Muslims outnumber Catholics in Europe's mainly Protestant north, and they outnumber Protestants in Europe's Catholic south. Major cities have substantial Muslim minorities. Muslim residents make up about 25 percent of the population in Marseilles and Rotterdam, 15 percent in Brussels, and about 10 percent in Paris, Copenhagen, and London.[10]

Worries increased after the September 11, 2001, al-Qaeda attack on New York's World Trade Center (see page 1052) and the subsequent war in Iraq. Terrorist attacks in Europe organized by Islamist extremists heightened anxieties. On a morning in March 2004, radical Moroccan Muslims living in Spain exploded bombs planted on trains bound for Madrid, killing 191 commuters and wounding 1,800 more. A year later, an attack on the London transit system carried out by British citizens of Pakistani descent killed over 50 people. Since then, a number of attacks have kept Islamist terrorism in the public eye — including the murderous January 2015 assault on the staff of the satiric French magazine *Charlie Hebdo*, which had published cartoons critical of the Prophet Muhammad, and the even more deadly attacks in Paris in November 2015, when extremists motivated by the ideologies of the Islamic State killed 130 people.

The vast majority of Europe's Muslims clearly supported democracy and rejected violent extremism, but these spectacular attacks and other assaults by Islamist militants nonetheless sharpened the debate on immigration. Security was not the only focus of concern. Critics across the political spectrum warned that Europe's rapidly growing Muslim population posed a dire threat to the West's liberal tradition, which embraced

Terrorist Attacks in Paris, November 2015
At a makeshift memorial made of flowers, candles, and messages left by mourners and passersby, onlookers observe a moment of silence for the victims of the November 13, 2015, terrorist attacks in central Paris. Islamic State jihadists claimed responsibility for the series of coordinated assaults, which killed 130 people and wounded hundreds more at a concert hall (Le Bataclan), restaurants, and the national stadium. (Jacques Demarthon/AFP/Getty Images)

freedom of thought, representative government, toleration, separation of church and state, and, more recently, equal rights for women and gays. Islamist extremists and radical clerics living in Europe, critics proclaimed, rejected these fundamental Western values and preached the supremacy of Islamic laws for Europe's Muslims.

Secular Europeans at times had a hard time understanding the depths of Muslim spirituality. French attempts to enforce a ban on wearing the hijab (the headscarf worn by many faithful Muslim women) in public schools expressed the tension between Western secularism and Islamic religiosity on a most personal level and evoked outrage and protests in the Muslim community. As busy mosques came to outnumber dying churches in European cities, nationalist politicians exploited widespread doubts that immigrant populations from Muslim countries would ever assimilate into Western culture. A Danish-Muslim imam (spiritual leader) captured the dilemma: "The Danish shelves for faith and spirituality are empty," he reported. "They fill them instead with fear of the 'strong foreigner.'"[11] Time was on the side of Euro-Islam, critics warned. Europe's Muslim population, estimated at 20 million in 2010, appeared likely to grow to 30 million by 2025 and to increase rapidly thereafter—even though that total would only be 4 percent of Europe's then-projected 750 million people.

By the 1990s in France, some 70 percent of the population believed that there were "too many Arabs," and 30 percent supported right-wing politician Jean-Marie Le Pen's calls to rid France of its immigrants altogether.[12] In the last decade, Le Pen's National Front and other anti-immigration, far-right political parties, such as the Danish People's Party and Austria's Freedom Party, have made impressive gains in national elections. Their success has been aided by bigotry and popular misconceptions. According to one 2013 poll, about 50 percent of respondents in Spain, Germany, France, Switzerland, Britain, and Sweden believe that "Islam is not compatible with the West." Other polls show that Europeans routinely overestimate the number of Muslims in Europe. In France, for example, the public believes that 31 percent of the population is Muslim, when the actual number is about 8 percent; the British believe that 21 percent of the population is Muslim, when the actual number is only 5 percent.[13]

In Germany, tens of thousands of people have joined the anti-immigrant movement called Pegida (Patriotic Europeans Against the Islamization of the West), and in the first six months of 2015 the German authorities recorded over two hundred attacks against migrant housing or against the migrants themselves. Immigration and the supposed "Islamization" of Europe, along with fundamentalist terrorism, have become highly charged political issues, and conservative and far-right pundits and politicians across Europe offer a variety of diagnoses and solutions to these perceived problems.

Admitting that Islamist extremism could pose a serious challenge, some observers focused instead on the issue of integration. Whereas the first generation of Muslim migrants—predominantly Turks in Germany, Algerians in France, Pakistanis in Britain, and Moroccans in the Netherlands—had found jobs as unskilled workers in Europe's great postwar boom, they and their children had been hard hit after 1973 by the general economic downturn and the decline of manufacturing. Immigrants also suffered from a lack of educational opportunities. Provided with modest welfare benefits and housed minimally in dilapidated housing projects, many second- and third-generation Muslim immigrants were outcasts in their adopted countries. To these observers, economics, inadequate job training, and discrimination had more influence on immigrant attitudes about their host communities than did religion and extremist teachings.

This argument was strengthened by widespread rioting by Muslim youths in France in 2005 and again in 2007 and 2009. Almost always French by birth, language, and education, marauding groups labeled "Arabs" in press reports torched hundreds of automobiles night after night in Paris suburbs and other large cities. (See "Evaluating the Evidence 30.2: William Pfaff, Will the French Riots Change Anything?" page 1050.) The rioters complained bitterly of high unemployment, systematic discrimination, and exclusion, and studies sparked by the rioting showed that religious ideology had almost no influence on their thinking.

A minority used such arguments to challenge anti-immigrant, anti-Muslim discrimination and its racist overtones. They argued that Europe badly needed newcomers—preferably talented newcomers—to limit the impending population decline and provide valuable technical skills. Some asserted that Europe should recognize that Islam has for centuries been a European religion and a vital part of European life. This recognition might open the way to political and cultural acceptance of European Muslims and head off the resentment that can drive a tiny minority to separatism and acts of terror.

Confronting Long-Term Challenges

Russian irredentism, uncontrolled immigration, and radical Islamic terrorism posed major problems for Europeans in the second decade of the twenty-first century. Yet with goodwill, one could believe that these might be temporary crises, resolvable with determined government action. At the same time, European societies faced a number of interconnected challenges that seemed to pose longer-term challenges. The growing distance in international affairs between the United States and Europe revealed differences in social values and political goals, though both struggled to deal with turmoil in the Muslim world. A persistent economic recession had a devastating impact on the lives of millions and called into question the unity of the Eurozone. Climate change and environmental degradation exposed the dangers of industrial development and the heavy dependence on fossil fuels for energy. At the same time, the relative wealth of European societies in the global context provoked serious thinking about European identity and Europe's humanitarian mission in the community of nations.

FOCUS QUESTION
What challenges will Europeans face in the coming decades?

Growing Strains in U.S.-European Relations

In the fifty years after World War II, the United States and western Europe generally maintained close diplomatic relations. Though they were never in total agreement, they usually worked together to promote international consensus under U.S. guidance, as represented by the NATO alliance. For example, a U.S.-led coalition that included thousands of troops from France and the United Kingdom and smaller contributions from other NATO allies attacked Iraqi forces in Kuwait in the 1990–1991 Persian Gulf War, freeing the small nation from attempted annexation

William Pfaff, Will the French Riots Change Anything?

In late November 2005 young Muslim males rioted for several nights in the suburbs of Paris and other French cities. Receiving saturation coverage from the media, their explosion of car burning and arson ignited controversy and debate throughout France and across Europe. Similar outbreaks occurred in 2007 and 2009. What caused the riots, and why did they persist? Anti-immigrant conservatives interpret the outbursts as an example of the inevitable conflict between Christians and Muslims. More liberal observers have blamed dismal living conditions and failures of assimilation.

One penetrating commentary, written after the unrest in 2005 and aimed at an American audience, came from William Pfaff, a noted author and political columnist with many years of European experience. As you read Pfaff's analysis, note in particular the portrait he draws of daily life in France's immigrant ghettos and the role of religion in French Muslim society.

~

The rioting in France's ghetto suburbs is a phenomenon of futility—but a revelation nonetheless. It has no ideology and no purpose other than to make a statement of distress and anger. It is beyond politics. It broke out spontaneously and spread in the same way, communicated by televised example, ratified by the huge attention it won from the press and television and the politicians, none of whom had any idea what to do.

It has been an immensely pathetic spectacle, whose primary meaning has been that it happened. It has been the most important popular social phenomenon in France since the student uprisings of 1968. But those uprisings . . . had consequences for power. The new riots have nothing to do with power.

They started with the accidental electrocutions of two boys hiding from the police, who they thought were after them. The police say there was no pursuit and they had no interest in the boys. However, under the policies of the minister of interior—the presidential candidate Nicolas Sarkozy—there had been a general police crackdown in these ugly suburban clusters of deteriorating high-rise apartments built years ago to house immigrant workers. They were meant to be machines for living. The police attention meant random identity checks, police suspicion, and harassment of young men hanging about—maybe dealing in drugs, maybe simply doing nothing because there is nothing for them to do. (In the past, they at least had to do national military service, which was a strong integrative force, but now France has a professional army.)

Their grandfathers came to France, mostly from North Africa, to do the hard labor in France's industrial reconstruction after the Second World War. Their fathers saw the work gradually dry up as Europe's economies slowed, following the first oil shock in the early 1970s. After that came unemployment. The unemployment rate in the zones where there has been the most violence is nearly 40 percent and among young people it is higher. Many of the young men in these places have never been offered a job. When they applied, their names often excluded them.

Their grandfathers were hard-working men. Their fathers saw their manhood undermined by unemployment. These young men are doomed to be boys. They often take their frustration out on their sisters and girlfriends, who are more likely to have done well in school and found jobs—and frequently a new life—outside the ghetto. . . .

The Muslim mothers and wives of the French ghetto are often confined in the home. Drugs are big business in the American ghetto; they are not that big in France. The crimes of the French ghetto are robbery and shoplifting, stealing mobile phones, stealing cars for joyrides, burning them afterward to eliminate fingerprints, or burning cars just for the hell of it, as well as robbing middle-class students in the

by Iraqi dictator Saddam Hussein. Over time, however, the growing power of the European Union and the new unilateral thrust of Washington's foreign policy created strains in traditional transatlantic relations.

The growing gap between the United States and Europe had several causes. For one, the European Union was now the world's largest trading block, challenging the predominance of the United States. Prosperous European businesses invested heavily in the United States, reversing a decades-long economic relationship in which investment dollars had flowed the other way. For another, under Presidents George W. Bush city and making trouble on suburban trains, looking for excitement.

Religion is important . . . in the French ghetto, it provides the carapace that protects against the France that excludes Muslims. To the European Muslim, it seems that all of the powerful in the world are in collusion to exclude Muslims—or are at war with them. The war in Iraq, on television, is the constant backdrop to Muslim life in Europe. There are itinerant imams who can put the young ghetto Muslim on the road to danger and adventure in Afghanistan, Pakistan, Iraq—or elsewhere. There are plenty more who preach a still deeper ghettoization: a retreat inside Islamic fundamentalism, totally shutting out a diabolized secular world.

One would think there would be a revolutionary potential in these ghettos, vulnerability to a mobilizing ideology. This seems not to be so. We may be living in a religious age, but it is not one of political ideology. In any case, it is difficult to imagine how the marginalized, thirteen- to twenty-three-year-old children of the Muslim immigration could change France other than by what they are doing, which is to demonstrate that the French model of assimilating immigrants as citizens, and not as members of religious or ethnic groups, has failed for them. It has failed because it has not seriously been tried.

The ghettoization of immigrant youth in France is the consequence of negligence. It has been as bad as the ghettoization through political correctness of Muslims in Britain and the Netherlands, where many people who thought of themselves as enlightened said that assimilation efforts were acts of cultural aggression. The immigrant in France is told that he or she is a citizen just like everyone else, with all the rights and privileges of citizenship—including the right to be unemployed.

Nicolas Sarkozy's zero tolerance of crime and of the petty mafias in the ghetto contributed to touching off these riots, but until recently he was the only French politician to say there has to be affirmative action to get an immigrant elite out of the ghettos and into important roles in French life, where they can pull their communities after them. Some affirmative action has been attempted in recruiting candidates for the elite *grandes écoles* [state schools] that train the French administrative and political class, where the cultural hurdles are immense for candidates. Virtually no children of the Muslim immigration are prominent in mainstream electoral politics; the political parties have yet to make a serious effort to include them. The present government has one junior minister of Algerian origin. I am not aware of any Muslims of immigrant origin in French diplomacy or the top ranks of police and military.*

President Jacques Chirac has announced a civilian national service agency to give training and employment to 50,000 young people from the troubled zones by 2007. The age of apprenticeship has been lowered to fourteen, with a corresponding drop in the age of compulsory academic schooling and new measures to support apprenticeships. There will be more money for schools, local associations, and housing construction and renovation. This is change. Whether it is enough, and in time, is another matter.

EVALUATE THE EVIDENCE

1. Describe the situation of young Muslims in France. What elements of their situation strike you most forcefully? How might these contribute to ongoing outbreaks of civic unrest?

2. France has maintained that, since all citizens are equal, they should all be treated the same way. Why has this policy failed for French Muslims? What alternatives would you suggest? Why?

Source: William Pfaff, "The French Riots: Will They Change Anything?" *The New York Review of Books*, vol. 52, no. 20, December 15, 2005, pp. 88–89. Copyright © 2005 by William Pfaff.

* In 2013 William Pfaff added the following comment: "This no longer is true. All recent French government cabinets have included appointments of immigrant origin or descent."

(U.S. pres. 2001–2009) and Barack Obama (U.S. pres. 2009–), the United States often ignored international opinion in pursuit of its own interests. Citing the economic impact, Washington refused to ratify the Kyoto Protocol of 1997, which was intended to limit global warming and which had been agreed to by nearly two hundred countries. Nor did the United States join the International Criminal Court, a global tribunal meant to prosecute individuals accused of crimes against humanity, which nearly 140 states agreed to join. These positions troubled EU leaders, as did unflagging U.S. support for Israel in the ongoing Palestinian-Israeli crisis.

A values gap between the United States and Europe contributed to cooler relations. Ever more secular Europeans had a hard time understanding the religiosity of many Americans. Relatively lax gun control laws and use of capital punishment in the United States were viewed with dismay in Europe, where most countries had outlawed private handgun ownership and abolished the death penalty. Despite President Obama's health-care reforms—which evoked controversy among Americans—U.S. reluctance to establish a single-payer, state-funded program surprised Europeans, who saw their own such programs as highly advantageous.

Hardball geopolitical issues relating to NATO further widened the gap. The dissolution of the Communist Warsaw Pact left NATO without its Cold War adversaries. Yet NATO continued to expand, primarily in the territories in the former East Bloc—the defensive belt the Soviet Union had established after World War II. NATO's expansion angered Russia's leaders, particularly when President Bush moved to deploy missile defense systems in Poland and the Czech Republic in 2008. Even within the alliance there were tensions. By 2009, with twenty-eight member states, it was difficult to shape unanimous support for NATO actions. France, for example, did not support NATO's engagement in Bosnia in 1995 because the alliance failed to get UN approval for the action, and in 2011 Germany and Poland refused to back NATO air strikes against the Libyan regime. As the EU expanded, some argued that Europe should determine its own military and defense policy without U.S. or NATO guidance.

American-led wars in Afghanistan and Iraq, undertaken in response to the September 11 terrorist attacks against the United States, further strained U.S.-European relations. On the morning of September 11, 2001, passenger planes hijacked by terrorists destroyed the World Trade Center towers in New York City and crashed into the Pentagon. Perpetrated by the radical Islamist group al-Qaeda, the attacks took the lives of more than three thousand people from many countries and put the personal safety of ordinary citizens at the top of the West's agenda.

Immediately after the September 11 attacks, the peoples and governments of Europe and the world joined Americans in heartfelt solidarity. Over time, however, tensions between Europe and the United States re-emerged and deepened markedly, particularly after President Bush declared a unilateral U.S. **war on terror**—a determined effort to fight terrorism in all its forms, around the world. The main acts in Bush's war on terror were a U.S.-led war in Afghanistan, which started in 2001, and another in Iraq, which lasted from 2003 to 2011. Both succeeded in quickly bringing down dictatorial regimes. At the same time, they fomented anti-Western sentiment in the Muslim world and failed to stop regional violence driven by ethnic and religious differences.

The U.S. invasion of Iraq and subsequent events caused some European leaders, notably in France and Germany, to question the rationale for and indeed the very effectiveness of a "war" on terror. Military victory, even over rogue states, would hardly end terrorism, since terrorist groups easily moved across national borders. Terrorism, they concluded, was better fought through police and intelligence measures. Europeans certainly shared U.S. worries about stability in the Middle East, and they faced their own problems with Islamist terrorism, especially after the Madrid and London train bombings of 2004 and 2005, and the attacks in Paris in 2015. But European leaders worried that the tactics used in the Iraq War, exemplified by Washington's readiness to use its military without international agreements or UN backing, violated international law.

war on terror American policy under President George W. Bush to fight global terrorism in all its forms.

American conduct of the war on terror also raised serious human rights concerns. The revelation of the harsh interrogation techniques used on prisoners held by American forces and abuse of prisoners in Iraq shocked many Europeans. U.S. willingness to engage in "extraordinary rendition"—secretly moving terrorism suspects to countries that allow coercive interrogation techniques—caused further concern.

The election of Barack Obama, America's first African American president, in 2008, and his re-election in 2012, brought improvement to U.S.-European foreign relations. Upon election, Obama announced that he would halt deployment of missiles in central Europe and reduce nuclear arms, easing tensions with Russia. He took U.S. troops out of Iraq in 2011 and Afghanistan in 2014, and quietly shelved the language of the "war on terror." Despite these changes, many Europeans continued to find U.S. willingness to undertake unilateral military action disturbing—American drone attacks on suspected terrorists along the Afghanistan-Pakistan border were particularly unpopular.[14] In the long run, though ties with the United States remained firm, European states increasingly responded independently to global affairs.

Turmoil in the Muslim World

Over the past decade, civil wars, terrorist sectarian attacks, civilian dislocation and misery, and a loss of social, political, and economic stability have shaken much of the Muslim world in North Africa and the Middle East. In many ways, these problems were the results of recent historical events. Yet the turmoil in North Africa and the Middle East, along with Islamic challenges to Western interests and policies, had a much deeper history, which included the legacies of European colonialism and the mandate system established after World War I, Cold War power plays, and the Palestinian-Israeli conflict.

Radical political Islam, a mixture of traditional religious beliefs and innovative social and political reform ideas, was at first a reaction against the foreign control and secularization represented by the mandate system established in the Middle East after World War I (see Chapter 25). Groups like the **Muslim Brotherhood**, founded in Egypt in 1928, called for national liberation from European control and a return to shari'a law (based on Muslim legal codes), and demanded land reform, extensive social welfare programs, and economic independence. The appeal of such ideas crossed class lines and national borders. By the 1960s the Brotherhood had established chapters across the Middle East and North Africa, and a variety of other groups and leaders advocated similar ideas about the need for Islamic revival and national autonomy. The broad spectrum of Islamist ideas is difficult to summarize, but adherents tended to fall into two main groups: a moderate or centrist group that worked peacefully to reform society within existing institutions, and a much smaller, more militant minority willing to use violence to achieve its goals.

Decolonization and the Cold War sharpened anti-Western and particularly anti-U.S. sentiments among radical Islamists. As the western European powers loosened their ties to the Middle East, the Americans stepped in. Applying containment policy to limit the spread of communism, and eager to preserve steady supplies of oil, the United States supported secular, authoritarian regimes friendly to U.S. interests in Egypt, Saudi Arabia, Iran, and elsewhere. Such regimes often played on U.S. concerns about communism or the threat of radical Islam to bolster American support.

Muslim Brotherhood
Islamic social and political reform group founded in Egypt in 1928 that called for national liberation from European control and a return to shari'a law (based on Muslim legal codes), and demanded land reform, extensive social welfare programs, and economic independence.

U.S. policies in the Middle East at times produced "blowback," or unforeseen and unintended consequences. One example was the Iranian revolution of 1979, when Islamist radicals antagonized by Western intervention, state corruption, and secularization overthrew the U.S.-supported shah and established an Islamic republic. The successful revolution encouraged militant Islamists elsewhere. So did the example of the mujahideen, the Muslim guerrilla fighters in Afghanistan who successfully fought off the Soviet army from 1979 to 1989 (see Chapter 29). U.S. military aid and arms, funneled to the mujahideen during the war, also generated blowback. Many of the U.S.-armed mujahideen would go on to support the Taliban, a militant Islamist faction that came to rule Afghanistan in 1996. The Taliban established a strict Islamist state based on shari'a law that denied women's right to education and banned Western movies and music. The Taliban also provided a safe haven for the Saudi-born millionaire Osama bin Laden and the al-Qaeda terrorist network.

As a result of these policies, the United States, along with western Europe, became the main target for Islamist militants. During the 1990s bin Laden and al-Qaeda mounted several terrorist attacks on U.S. installations, leading up to the horrific September 11 assault. After that attack, President Bush declared with some justification that the terrorists "hate our freedoms: our freedom of religion, our freedom of speech, our freedom to vote."[15] In public calls for jihad (or struggle) against the United States and the West, however, bin Laden gave a more pragmatic list of grievances, including U.S. support for Israel in the Israeli-Palestinian crisis, the sanctions on Iraq that followed the Persian Gulf War, and the presence of U.S. military bases in Saudi Arabia—seen as an insult to the Muslim holy sites in Mecca and Medina.[16]

The Bush administration hoped that the invasions of Afghanistan—a direct response to the September 11 attacks—and Iraq would end the terrorist attacks and bring peace and democracy to the Middle East, but both brought chaos instead. The military campaign in Afghanistan quickly achieved one of its goals, bringing down the Taliban, and the United States installed a friendly government. But U.S. troops failed to find bin Laden or disable al-Qaeda, and Taliban insurgents mounted a determined and lasting guerrilla war.

With heavy fighting still under way in Afghanistan in late 2001, the Bush administration turned its attention to Saddam Hussein's Iraq, arguing that it was necessary to expand the war on terror to other hostile regimes in the Middle East. U.S. leaders effectively played on American fears of renewed terrorism and charged that Saddam Hussein was still developing weapons of mass destruction in flagrant disregard of his 1991 promise to end all such programs. Some Americans shared the widespread doubts held by Europeans about the legality—and wisdom—of an American attack on Iraq, especially after UN inspectors found no weapons of mass destruction in the country. Though they failed to win UN approval, in March 2003 the United States and Britain, with token support from a handful of other European states, invaded Iraq.

The U.S.-led invasion quickly overwhelmed the Iraqi army, and Saddam's dictatorship collapsed in April, but America's subsequent efforts to establish a stable pro-American Iraq proved difficult. Poor postwar planning and management by administration officials was one factor, but there were others. Iraq, a creation of Western imperialism after the First World War (see Chapter 25), was a fragile state with three distinct groups: non-Arab Kurds, Arab Sunni Muslims,

Iraq, ca. 2010

and Arab Shi'ite Muslims. By 2006 deadly sectarian conflicts among these groups and against the United States and its Iraqi supporters had taken hold. Casualties in Iraq began to decline after President Bush sent additional troops to the country in 2007, and when President Obama took office in 2009 his administration moved forward with agreements to withdraw all U.S. forces in 2011. The shaky Iraqi government continued to struggle with ethnic divisions and terrorist violence, however.

Although U.S. commandos finally killed Osama bin Laden in Pakistan in May 2011, the apparently unwinnable guerrilla war in Afghanistan became increasingly unpopular in the United States and among NATO allies in Europe. Though the conflict continued, President Obama withdrew U.S. combat troops from the country in 2014.

In early 2011 an unexpected chain of events that came to be called the **Arab Spring** further destabilized the Middle East and North Africa. In a provincial town in Tunisia, a poor fruit vendor set himself on fire to protest official harassment. His death eighteen days later unleashed a series of spontaneous mass protests that brought violence, chaos, and regime change; six weeks later, Tunisia's authoritarian president fled the country, opening the way for reform. Massive popular demonstrations calling for more open democratic government and social tolerance broke out across the Middle East. In Egypt, demonstrators forced the resignation of President Hosni Mubarak, a U.S.-friendly leader who had ruled for thirty years. An armed uprising in Libya, supported by NATO air strikes, brought down the dictatorial government of Muammar Gaddafi that October. A civil war broke out in Syria in July 2011, but dragged on into 2016 as Bashar al-Assad, with Russian support, hurled his army at the rebels and Western powers disagreed about what to do. Protests arose in other countries in the region as well, evoking a mixed response of repression and piecemeal reform.

As the popular movements inspired by the Arab Spring faltered, the emergence of the **Islamic State** (sometimes called ISIS or ISIL) suggested that events in the Middle East had spiraled out of control. The Islamic State, an extremist Islamist militia dedicated to the establishment of a new caliphate to unify Muslims around the world, grew out of al-Qaeda and the various other insurgent groups fighting in Iraq and the Syrian civil war. By summer 2015 Islamic State soldiers had taken control of substantial parts of central Syria and Iraq—including Mosul, Ramadi, and Fallujah, cities central to U.S. combat missions in the Iraq war. Over 4 million Syrians and Iraqis lost their homes during the fighting, and hundreds of thousands streamed north in attempts to find asylum in Europe (see page 1044).

In the territories under their control, Islamic State militants set up a terroristic government based on an extremist reading of shari'a law. Islamic State terror tactics included the violent persecution of sectarian religious groups; use of sexual assault and rape as tools of conquest; mass executions and beheadings of military, political, or sectarian enemies; and the "cultural cleansing" (destruction and looting) of ancient cultural monuments and shrines that failed to meet its stringent religious ideals, most recently in the classical city of Palmyra in Syria. All these actions were well documented in widespread Internet propaganda campaigns; videos recorded by militants, intended to demonstrate their power and entice recruits, were regularly posted on the Internet.

In summer 2016, as this was being written, the outcome of the turmoil in the Middle East was difficult to predict. The Arab Spring seemed, for the most part, a

Arab Spring A series of popular revolts in several countries in the Middle East and North Africa that sought an end to authoritarian, often Western-supported regimes.

Islamic State A radical Islamist militia in control of substantial parts of central Syria and Iraq, where it applies an extremist version of shari'a law.

dismal failure. The young activists who sought greater political and social liberties from authoritarian regimes quickly lost control of the changes they unleashed. Multiple players now vied for power: military leaders and old elites, local chieftains representing ethnic or sectarian interests, and moderate and radical Islamists. In Egypt, the first open elections in decades brought to power representatives of the moderate wing of the Muslim Brotherhood; a year later, military leaders overthrew this elected government. In Libya, Yemen, and especially Syria, persistent civil wars undermined the search for stability. The hold of the Islamic State was likewise difficult to shake. In Iraq, air strikes by a U.S.-NATO coalition and assaults by Iraqi ground troops only slowly repulsed the extremists.

In the period leading up to 2016, Western policymakers grappled in vain for clear and effective ways to help defeat the Islamic State and bring order to the region. Their efforts were especially freighted, since the turmoil in the Muslim world was at the center of many of Europe's problems. These included the immigration emergency of 2015–2016, the persistent extremist Islamist terrorist attacks, the destabilization of Europe's energy supplies, and the disastrous human rights crisis faced by millions of Middle East residents.

The Global Recession and the Viability of the Eurozone

While chaos and change roiled the Muslim world, economic crisis sapped growth and political unity in Europe and North America. In 2008 the United States entered a deep recession, caused by the burst of the housing boom, bank failures, and an overheated financial securities market. The U.S. government spent massive sums to recharge the economy. Banks, insurance agencies, auto companies, and financial services conglomerates received billions of dollars in federal aid. By 2016 the economy had improved and much of the housing market had recovered, though some critics claimed that income inequality was higher than ever.

The 2008 recession swept across Europe, where a housing bubble, high national deficits, and a weak bond market made the crisis particularly acute. One of the first countries affected, and one of the hardest hit, was Iceland, where the currency and banking system collapsed outright. Other countries followed—Ireland and Latvia made deep and painful cuts in government spending to balance national budgets. By 2010 Britain was deeply in debt, and Spain, Portugal, and especially Greece were close to bankruptcy.

Anti-Austerity Protests in Greece   With protest marches and a rally in front of the Greek parliament, thousands of anti-austerity voters celebrated the results of the July 2015 Greek referendum in the streets of Athens. The popular vote soundly rejected a bailout deal proposed by the IMF, the European Common Bank, and the European Union, which would have required the Greek government to implement harsh austerity measures. Just days after the vote, Greek leaders backed down and accepted the plan anyway. (© Bjorn Kietzmann/Demotix/Corbis)

This sudden "euro crisis" put the very existence of the Eurozone in question. The common currency grouped together countries with vastly divergent economies. Germany and France, the zone's two strongest economies, felt pressure to provide financial support to ensure the stability of far weaker countries, including Greece and Portugal. They did so with strings attached: recipients of EU support were required to reduce deficits through austerity measures. Even so, the transfer of monies within the Eurozone angered the citizens of wealthier countries, who felt they were being asked to subsidize countries in financial difficulties of their own making. Such feelings were particularly powerful in Germany, forcing Chancellor Angela Merkel (r. 2005–), the nation's first woman chancellor, to move cautiously in providing financial stimulus to troubled Eurozone economies.

The difficulty dealing with the stubborn Greek debt crisis prompted debates about the viability of a single currency for nations with vastly different economies as well as widespread speculation that the Eurozone might fall apart. In 2010 and 2012 Greece received substantial bailouts from the IMF, the European Common Bank, and the European Union (the so-called Troika). In return for loans and some debt relief, Greek leaders were required to implement a painful austerity plan—which meant raising taxes, privatizing state-owned businesses, reforming labor markets, and drastically reducing government spending on employee wages, pensions, and other popular social benefits. Greek unemployment hit a record 25 percent in 2012, and more than half of young adults lacked jobs. Rampant joblessness meant declining tax revenues, and the Greek economy continued to weaken. As the government cut popular social programs, demonstrators took to the streets to protest declining living standards and the lack of work; in Athens, protests large and small were almost a daily occurrence.

The 2015 Greek elections brought the left-wing Syriza Party and the charismatic prime minister Alexis Tsipras to power. In the Thessaloniki Programme, Tsipras and his party promised voters a tough stand against the Troika's fiscal demands and an end to austerity. (See "Evaluating the Evidence 30.3: The Thessaloniki Programme," page 1058.) Yet Troika negotiators, led by Germany, maintained an uncompromising line: if Tsipras and Syriza failed to meet Greek debt payments, they would be forced into a "Grexit" (a Greek exit from the Eurozone). After a dramatic series of events, which included a resounding "no" vote in a Greek referendum on the deal proposed by the Troika, Tsipras backtracked and accepted further austerity measures in return for yet another bailout loan. Among other conditions, Greek leaders promised to sell off about 50 billion euros' worth of government-owned property, including airports, power plants and energy assets, roads and railroads, and the national post office.

Even as the Greek crisis shook European unity, in June 2016 Great Britain voted to leave the EU altogether. The campaign for the "Brexit" (British exit from the EU) was intense. The narrow victory of those wanting "out" showed that many Brits did not want "Eurocrats" in Brussels intruding on national policy and did not appreciate the EU's relatively open immigration policies. Prime Minister David Cameron (r. 2010–2016) resigned immediately. Though Britain had two years to negotiate the terms of the exit, global financial markets fell, far-right populist parties on the continent rejoiced, and EU supporters expressed deep concern about the future of the union.

The Thessaloniki Programme

Under the leadership of soon-to-be Greek prime minister Alexis Tsipras, the left-wing Syriza Party unanimously adopted the Thessaloniki Programme in September 2014. The reformist manifesto called for a "European Debt Conference" to write down Greece's public debt and end the austerity policies enforced by bailout deals with the EU, and announced a series of measures to grow the Greek economy. In elections in January 2015, Syriza took power from the center-right government led by Prime Minister Antonis Samaras. Though Tsipras boldly announced that the terms of the Programme were "non-negotiable," in July 2015 his government accepted a new EU bailout and a new round of strict austerity requirements.

～

We demand immediate parliamentary elections and a strong negotiation mandate with the goal to:

Write-off the greater part of public debt's nominal value so that it becomes sustainable in the context of a "European Debt Conference." It happened for Germany in 1953. It can also happen for the South of Europe and Greece.

Include a "growth clause" in the repayment of the remaining part so that it is growth-financed and not budget-financed.

Include a significant grace period ("moratorium") in debt servicing to save funds for growth.

Exclude public investment from the restrictions of the Stability and Growth Pact.

A "European New Deal" of public investment financed by the European Investment Bank.

Quantitative easing by the European Central Bank with direct purchases of sovereign bonds.

Finally, we declare once again that the issue of the Nazi Occupation forced loan from the Bank of Greece is open for us. Our partners know it. It will become the country's official position from our first days in power.

On the basis of this plan, we will fight and secure a socially viable solution to Greece's debt problem so that our country is able to pay off the remaining debt from the creation of new wealth and not from primary surpluses, which deprive society of income.

With that plan, we will lead with security the country to recovery and productive reconstruction by:

Immediately increasing public investment by at least €4 billion.

Gradually reversing all the Memorandum injustices.

Gradually restoring salaries and pensions so as to increase consumption and demand.

Providing small and medium-sized enterprises with incentives for employment, and subsidizing the energy cost of industry in exchange for an employment and environmental clause.

Investing in knowledge, research, and new technology in order to have young scientists, who have been massively emigrating over the last years, back home.

Rebuilding the welfare state, restoring the rule of law and creating a meritocratic state.

We are ready to negotiate and we are working towards building the broadest possible alliances in Europe.

The present Samaras government is once again ready to accept the decisions of the creditors. The only alliance which it cares to build is with the German government.

This is our difference and this is, at the end, the dilemma:

European negotiation by a SYRIZA government, or acceptance of the creditors' terms on Greece by the Samaras government.

EVALUATE THE EVIDENCE

1. How did the Thessaloniki Programme challenge the economic policies promoted by international organizations like the European Union and the International Monetary Fund?
2. Why did Tsipras and the Syriza Party drop these demands? How do you think the Greek public responded to that action?

Source: "Syriza: The Thessaloniki Programme," Syriza, http://www.syriza.gr/article/SYRIZA---THE-THESSALONIKI-PROGRAMME.html#.VfXCt87WFJk.

Dependence on Fossil Fuels

One of the most significant long-term challenges facing Europe and the world in the early twenty-first century was the need for adequate energy resources. Maintaining standards of living in industrialized countries and modernizing the developing world required extremely high levels of energy use, and supplies were heavily dependent on fossil fuels: oil, coal, and natural gas. In 2011 Europe and Russia combined had about 12 percent of the world's population but annually consumed about 34 percent of the world's natural gas production, 22 percent of oil production, and 13 percent of coal output. Scientists warned that such high levels of usage were unsustainable over the long run and predicted that fossil fuel supplies will eventually run out, especially as the countries of the developing world—including giants such as India and China—increased their own rates of consumption.[17]

Struggles to control and profit from these shrinking resources often resulted in tense geopolitical conflicts. The need to preserve access to oil, for example, has led to a transformation in military power in the post–Cold War world. Between 1945 and 1990 the largest areas of military buildup were along the iron curtain in Europe and in East Asia, as U.S. forces formed a bulwark against the spread of communism. Today military power is increasingly concentrated in oil-producing areas such as the Middle East, which holds about 65 percent of the world's oil reserves. One scholar labeled conflicts in the Persian Gulf and Central Asia "resource wars" because they are fought, in large part, to preserve the West's access to the region's energy supplies.[18]

The global struggle for ample energy has placed Russia, which in 2011 became the world's number-one oil producer (surpassing Saudi Arabia) and the number-two natural gas producer, in a powerful but strained position. The Russian invasions of Chechnya and Georgia, and intervention in Ukraine, were attempts to maintain political influence in these territories, but also to preserve Russian control of the region's rich energy resources.

Beyond military action, Russian leaders readily use their control over energy to assert political influence. The Russian corporation Gazprom, one of the world's largest producers of natural gas, sells Europe about 30 percent of its natural gas, and the EU treads softly with Russia to maintain this supply. Russia is willing to play hardball: it has engaged in over fifty politically motivated disruptions of natural gas supply in the former Soviet republics, including one in January 2009 when Russia shut off supplies to Ukraine for three weeks, resulting in closed factories and no heat for hundreds of thousands of people. "Yesterday tanks, today oil," a Polish politician remarked about Russia's willingness to use energy to exert influence in central Europe.[19]

Oil pipeline
Gas pipeline
Supplied by Russia

Primary Oil and Gas Pipelines to Europe, ca. 2005

Climate Change and Environmental Degradation

Even setting aside the question of the supply of fossil fuels, their use has led to serious environmental problems. Burning oil and coal releases massive amounts of carbon dioxide (CO_2) into the atmosphere, the leading cause of **climate change**, or global warming. While the future effects of climate change are difficult to predict, the vast majority of climatologists agree that global warming is proceeding far more quickly than previously predicted and that some climatic disruption is now unavoidable.

climate change Changes in long-standing weather patterns caused primarily by carbon dioxide emissions from the burning of fossil fuels.

Rising average temperatures already play havoc with familiar weather patterns, melting glaciers and polar ice packs, and drying up freshwater resources. Moreover, in the next fifty years rising sea levels may well flood low-lying coastal areas around the world.

Since the 1990s the EU has spearheaded efforts to control energy consumption and contain climate change. EU leaders have imposed tight restrictions on CO_2 emissions, and Germany, the Netherlands, and Denmark have become world leaders in harnessing alternative energy sources such as solar and wind power. Some countries, hoping to combat the future effects of global warming, have also taken pre-emptive measures. The Dutch government, for example, has spent billions of dollars constructing new dikes, levees, and floodgates. These efforts provided models for U.S. urban planners after floodwaters churned up by Hurricane Sandy swamped low-lying swaths of New York City in October 2012.

Environmental degradation encompasses a number of problems beyond climate change. Overfishing and toxic waste threaten the world's oceans and freshwater lakes, which once seemed to be inexhaustible sources of food and drinking water. The disaster that resulted when an offshore oil rig exploded in the Gulf of Mexico in April 2010, spewing millions of gallons of oil into the gulf waters, underscored the close connections between energy consumption and water pollution. Deforestation, land degradation, soil erosion, and overfertilization; species extinction related to habitat loss; the accumulation of toxins in the air, land, and water; the disposal of poisonous nuclear waste—all will continue to pose serious problems in the twenty-first century.

Though North American and European governments, NGOs, and citizens have taken a number of steps to limit environmental degradation and regulate energy use, the overall effort to control energy consumption has been an especially difficult endeavor, underscoring the interconnectedness of the contemporary world. Rapidly industrializing countries such as India and China—the latter surpassed the United States in 2008 as the largest emitter of CO_2—have had a difficult time balancing environmental concerns and the energy use necessary for economic growth. Because of growing demand for electricity, for example, China currently accounts for about 47 percent of the world's coal consumption, causing hazardous air pollution in Chinese cities and contributing to climate change.[20]

Can international agreements and good intentions make a difference? In December 2015 representatives of almost two hundred nations met at the annual United Nations Climate Change Conference in Paris, France. They extended the Kyoto Protocol on climate change, set ambitious goals for the reduction of CO_2 emissions by 2020, and promised to help developing countries manage the effects of climate change. Such changes would require substantial modifications in the planet's consumption of energy derived from fossil fuels, however, and the ultimate success of ambitious plans to limit the human impact on the environment remains uncertain.

Promoting Human Rights

Though regional differences persisted in the twenty-eight EU member states, Europeans entering the twenty-first century enjoyed some of the highest living standards in the world, the sweet fruit of more than fifty years of peace, security, and overall economic growth. The recent agonies of barbarism and war in the former Yugoslavia as well as the memories of the horrors of World War II and the Holocaust cast in bold relief the ever-present reality of collective violence. For some Europeans, the realization that they had so much and so many others had so little kindled a desire to help. As a result, European intellectuals and opinion makers began to envision a new historic mission for Europe: the promotion of domestic peace and human rights in lands plagued by instability, violence, and oppression.

European leaders and humanitarians believed that more global agreements and new international institutions were needed to set moral standards and to regulate countries, leaders, armies, corporations, and individuals. In practice, this meant more curbs on the sovereign rights of the world's states, just as the states of the European Union had imposed increasingly strict standards of behavior on themselves in order to secure the rights and welfare of EU citizens. As one EU official concluded, the European Union has a "historical responsibility" to make morality "a basis of policy" because "human rights are more important than states' rights."[21]

In practical terms, this mission raised questions. Europe's evolving human rights policies would require military intervention to stop civil wars and to prevent tyrannical governments from slaughtering their own people. Thus the EU joined the United States to intervene militarily to stop the killing and protect minority rights in Bosnia, Croatia, and Kosovo. The EU states vigorously supported UN initiatives to verify compliance with anti–germ warfare conventions, outlaw the use of land mines, and establish a new international court to prosecute war criminals.

Europeans also broadened definitions of individual rights. Having abolished the death penalty in the EU, they condemned its continued use in China, the United States, and other countries. At home, Europe expanded personal rights. The pacesetting Netherlands gave pensions and workers' rights to prostitutes and provided assisted suicide (euthanasia) for the terminally ill. The Dutch recognized same-sex marriage in 2001. By the time France followed suit in 2013, nine western European countries had legalized same-sex marriage and twelve others recognized alternative forms of civic union. (The United States Supreme Court guaranteed the right to same-sex marriage in June 2015.) The countries of the former East Bloc, where people were generally less supportive of gay rights, lagged behind in this regard.

Europeans extended their broad-based concept of human rights to the world's poorer countries. Such efforts often included sharp criticism of globalization and unrestrained neoliberal capitalism. For example, Europe's moderate Social Democrats joined human rights campaigners in 2001 to secure drastic price cuts from international pharmaceutical corporations selling drugs to combat Africa's AIDS crisis. Advocating greater social equality and state-funded health care, European socialists embraced morality as a basis for the global expansion of human rights.

The record was not always perfect. Critics accused the European Union (and the United States) of selectively promoting human rights in their differential responses to the Arab Spring—the West was willing to act in some cases, as in Libya, but dragged its feet in others, as in Egypt and Syria. The conflicted response to the immigration emergency of 2015 underscored the difficulties of shaping unified human rights policies that would satisfy competing political and national interests. Attempts to extend rights to women, indigenous peoples, and immigrants remained controversial. Even so, the general trend suggested that Europe's leaders and peoples alike took very seriously the ideals articulated in the 1948 UN Universal Declaration of Human Rights.

LOOKING BACK LOOKING AHEAD

The twenty-first century opened with changes and new challenges for the Western world. The collapse of the East Bloc brought more-representative government to central and eastern Europe, but left millions struggling to adapt to a different way of life in market economies. High-tech information systems that quickened the pace of communications and the global reach of new supranational institutions made the world a smaller place, yet globalization left some struggling to maintain their livelihoods. New contacts between peoples, made possible by increased migration, revitalized European society, but the massive influx of refugees in 2015–2016 raised concerns about cultural tolerance and the EU's open internal borders policy.

One thing is sure: despite the success of European democracy and liberalism, and despite the high living standards enjoyed by most Europeans, the challenges won't go away. The search for solutions to environmental degradation and conflicts between ethnic and religious groups, and the promotion of human rights across the globe, will clearly occupy European and world leaders for some time to come.

However these issues play out, the study of the past puts the present and the future in perspective. Others before us have trodden the paths of uncertainty and crisis, and the historian's ability to analyze and explain the choices they made helps us understand our current situation and helps save us from exaggerated self-pity in the face of our own predicaments. Perhaps our Western heritage may rightly inspire us with measured pride and self-confidence. We stand, momentarily, at the head of the long procession of Western civilization. Sometimes the procession has wandered, or backtracked, or done terrible things. But it has also carried the efforts and sacrifices of generations of toiling, struggling ancestors. Through no effort of our own, we are the beneficiaries of those sacrifices and achievements. Now that it is our turn to carry the torch onward, we may remember these ties with our forebears.

To change the metaphor, we in the West are like card players who have been dealt many good cards. Some of them are obvious, such as our technical and scientific heritage, our environmental resources, and our commitment to human rights and individual freedoms. Others are not so obvious, sometimes half-forgotten or even hidden up the sleeve. Think, for example, of the almost-miraculous victory of peaceful revolution in the East Bloc in 1989 — an expression of what Czech playwright-turned-president Václav Havel called "the power of the powerless." Here we again see the regenerative strength of the Western ideals of individual rights and democratic government. We hold a good hand.

Our study of history, of mighty struggles and fearsome challenges, of shining achievements and tragic failures, gives a sense of the essence of life itself: the process of change over time. Again and again we have seen how peoples and societies evolve, influenced by ideas, human passions, and material conditions. This process of change will continue as the future becomes the present and then the past. Students of history are better prepared to make sense of this unfolding process because they have closely observed it. They understand that change is rooted in existing historical forces, and they have tools to explore the intricate web of activity that propels life forward. Students of history are prepared for the new and unexpected in human development, for they have already seen great breakthroughs and revolutions. They have an understanding of how things really happen.

Make Connections

Think about the larger developments and continuities within and across chapters.

1. Did people's lives really change dramatically during the wave of globalization that emerged in the late twentieth century? How have they stayed the same?

2. The globalization of today's world seems inseparable from advances in digital technology. How are the two connected? Were there other times in the history of Western society during which technological developments drove social, political, or cultural change?

3. How are the challenges that confront Europeans in the twenty-first century rooted in events and trends that came before?

30 REVIEW & EXPLORE

Review the Main Ideas

Answer the focus questions from each section of the chapter.

◆ How did life change in Russia and the former East Bloc countries after 1989? (p. 1022)

◆ How did globalization affect European life and society? (p. 1033)

◆ What are the main causes and effects of growing ethnic diversity in contemporary Europe? (p. 1042)

◆ What challenges will Europeans face in the coming decades? (p. 1049)

Identify Key Terms

Identify and explain the significance of each item below.

ethnic cleansing (p. 1029)
Color Revolutions (p. 1032)
globalization (p. 1033)
European Union (EU) (p. 1034)
Maastricht Treaty (p. 1034)
World Trade Organization (WTO) (p. 1037)
nongovernmental organizations (NGOs) (p. 1037)
diasporas (p. 1046)
multiculturalism (p. 1046)
war on terror (p. 1052)
Muslim Brotherhood (p. 1053)
Arab Spring (p. 1055)
Islamic State (p. 1055)
climate change (p. 1059)

NOTES

1. P. Anderson, "Managed Democracy," *London Review of Books*, August 27, 2015, pp. 19–27.

2. Quoted in T. Judt, *Postwar: A History of Europe Since 1945* (New York: Penguin, 2005), p. 691.

3. Ibid., pp. 698–699.

4. *Quarterly Labor Force Statistics*, vol. 2004/4 (Paris: OECD Publications, 2004), p. 64.

5. "Fertility Statistics," Eurostat: Statistics Explained, accessed August 7, 2015, http://ec.europa.eu/eurostat/statistics-explained/index.php/Fertility_statistics.

6. Quoted in *The Economist*, January 6, 2001, p. 6.

7. European Commission, *European Migration Network Annual Report on Immigration and Asylum 2014*, p. 9; European Commission, Migration and Home Affairs, "Irregular Migration and Return," accessed August 7, 2015, http://ec.europa.eu/dgs/home-affairs/what-we-do/policies/irregular-migration-return-policy/index_en.htm.

8. Mark Mazower, *Dark Continent: Europe's Twentieth Century* (New York: Vintage, 2000), p. 415; *United Nations International Migration Report 2006* (UN Department of Economic and Social Affairs), http://www.un.org/esa/populationpublications/2006_MigrationRep/report.htm.

9. L. Collingham, *Curry: A Tale of Cooks and Conquerors* (London: Oxford University Press, 2006), pp. 2, 9.

10. J. Klausen, *The Islamic Challenge: Politics and Religion in Western Europe* (New York: Oxford University Press, 2006), p. 16; Malise Ruthven, "The Big Muslim Problem!" *New York Review*, December 17, 2009, p. 62.

11. Quoted in Klausen, *The Islamic Challenge*, p. 16.

12. J. Gross, D. McMurray, and T. Swedenborg, "Rai, Rap, and Ramadan Nights: Franco-Maghribi Cultural Identities," in *Political Islam: Essays from Middle East Report*, ed. Joel Beinin and Joe Stork (London: I. B. Tauris, 1997), p. 258.

13. "Islam in Europe," *Wall Street Journal*, January 7, 2015, http://www.economist.com/blogs/graphicdetail/2015/01/daily-chart-2.

14. "Global Opinion of Obama Slips, International Policies Faulted," *Pew Research Global Attitudes Research Project*, June 13, 2012, http://www.pewglobal.org/2012/06/13/global-opinion-of-obama-slips-international-policies-faulted/.

15. Quoted in "Text: President Bush Addresses the Nation," *Washington Post Online*, September 20, 2001, http://www.washingtonpost.com/wp-srv/nation/specials/attacked/transcripts/bushaddress_092001.html.

16. See M. H. Hunt, ed., *The World Transformed, 1945 to the Present: A Documentary Reader* (Boston: Bedford/St. Martin's), pp. 410–411.

17. Statistics in *BP Statistical Review of World Energy June 2012*, http://www.bp.com/en_no/norway/media/press-releases-and-news/2012/bp-statistical-review-of-world-energy-2012.html.

18. M. T. Klare, *Resource Wars: The New Landscape of Global Conflict* (New York: Henry Holt, 2001), pp. 25–40.

19. A. E. Kramer, "Eastern Europe Fears New Era of Russian Sway," *New York Times*, October 13, 2009, p. A1.

20. Edward Wong, "Beijing Takes Steps to Fight Pollution as Problem Worsens," *New York Times*, January 31, 2013, p. A4.

21. Quoted in *International Herald Tribune*, June 15, 2001, p. 6.

Glossary

Afrikaners Descendants of the Dutch settlers in the Cape Colony in southern Africa. (p. 805)

al-Andalus The part of the Iberian Peninsula under Muslim control in the eighth century, encompassing most of modern-day Spain. (p. 224)

anticlericalism Opposition to the clergy. (p. 392)

apostolic succession The doctrine that all bishops can trace their spiritual ancestry back to Jesus's apostles. (p. 191)

appeasement The British policy toward Germany prior to World War II that aimed at granting Hitler's territorial demands, including western Czechoslovakia, in order to avoid war. (p. 925)

aqueducts Canals, channels, and pipes that brought freshwater into cities. (p. 169)

Arab Spring A series of popular revolts in several countries in the Middle East and North Africa that sought an end to authoritarian, often Western-supported regimes. (p. 1055)

Arianism A theological belief that originated when Arius, a priest of Alexandria, denied that Christ was co-eternal with God the Father. (p. 189)

Atlantic slave trade The forced migration of Africans across the Atlantic for slave labor on plantations and in other industries; the trade reached its peak in the eighteenth century and ultimately involved more than 12 million Africans. (p. 564)

Aztec Empire A large and complex Native American civilization in modern Mexico and Central America that possessed advanced mathematical, astronomical, and engineering technology. (p. 442)

Babylonian Captivity The period from 1309 to 1376 when the popes resided in Avignon rather than in Rome. The phrase refers to the seventy years when the Hebrews were held captive in Babylon. (p. 339)

Balfour Declaration A 1917 British statement that declared British support of a National Home for the Jewish People in Palestine. (p. 859)

barracks emperors The emperors of the middle of the third century, so called because they were military commanders. (p. 181)

Battle of Peterloo The army's violent suppression of a protest that took place at Saint Peter's Fields in Manchester in reaction to the revision of the Corn Laws. (p. 704)

Bauhaus A German interdisciplinary school of fine and applied arts that brought together many leading modern architects, designers, and theatrical innovators. (p. 876)

Berlin Conference A meeting of European leaders held in 1884 and 1885 in order to lay down some basic rules for imperialist competition in sub-Saharan Africa. (p. 807)

bishops Christian Church officials with jurisdiction over certain areas and the power to determine the correct interpretation of Christian teachings. (p. 180)

Black Death Plague that first struck Europe in 1347 and killed perhaps one-third of the population. (p. 326)

"Black Legend" The notion that the Spanish were particularly ruthless and cruel in their conquest and domination of the Americas, an idea often propagated by Spain's rivals. (p. 459)

Black Shirts Mussolini's private militia that destroyed socialist newspapers, union halls, and Socialist Party headquarters, eventually pushing Socialists out of the city governments of northern Italy. (p. 918)

blood sports Events such as bullbaiting and cockfighting that involved inflicting violence and bloodshed on animals and that were popular with the eighteenth-century European masses. (p. 589)

Bloody Sunday A massacre of peaceful protesters at the Winter Palace in St. Petersburg in 1905, triggering a revolution that overturned absolute tsarist rule and made Russia into a conservative constitutional monarchy. (p. 769)

Bolsheviks Lenin's radical, revolutionary arm of the Russian party of Marxist socialism, which successfully installed a dictatorial socialist regime in Russia. (p. 849)

Book of the Dead Egyptian funerary manuscripts, written to help guide the dead through the difficulties they would encounter on the way to the afterlife. (p. 25)

bourgeoisie The middle-class minority who owned the means of production and, according to Marx, exploited the working-class proletariat. (p. 695)

boyars The highest-ranking members of the Russian nobility. (pp. 244, 485)

Brezhnev Doctrine Doctrine created by Leonid Brezhnev that held that the Soviet Union had the right to intervene in any East Bloc country when necessary to preserve Communist rule. (p. 994)

Bronze Age The period in which the production and use of bronze implements became basic to society. (p. 12)

caliph A successor, as chosen by a group of Muhammad's closest followers. (p. 224)

cameralism View that monarchy was the best form of government, that all elements of society should serve the monarch, and that, in turn, the state should use its resources and authority to increase the public good. (p. 534)

canon law Church law, which had its own courts and procedures. (p. 268)

caravel A small, maneuverable, three-mast sailing ship developed by the Portuguese in the fifteenth century that gave the Portuguese a distinct advantage in exploration and trade. (p. 434)

carnival The few days of revelry in Catholic countries that preceded Lent and that included drinking, masquerading, dancing, and rowdy spectacles that upset the established order. (p. 589)

Cartesian dualism Descartes's view that all of reality could ultimately be reduced to mind and matter. (p. 517)

cathedral The church of a bishop and the administrative headquarters of a diocese. (p. 318)

charivari Degrading public rituals used by village communities to police personal behavior and maintain moral standards. (p. 578)

chivalry Code of conduct in which fighting to defend the Christian faith and protecting one's countrymen were declared to have a sacred purpose. (p. 262)

Christendom The term used by early medieval writers to refer to the realm of Christianity. (p. 281)

Christian Democrats Center-right political parties that rose to power in western Europe after the Second World War. (p. 955)

Christian humanists Northern humanists who interpreted Italian ideas about and attitudes toward classical antiquity and humanism in terms of their own religious traditions. (p. 368)

civilization A large-scale system of human political, economic, and social organizations; civilizations have cities, laws, states, and often writing. (p. 5)

civitas The city and surrounding territory that served as a basis of the administrative system in the Frankish kingdoms, based on Roman models. (p. 228)

class-consciousness Awareness of belonging to a distinct social and economic class whose interests might conflict with those of other classes. (p. 674)

climate change Changes in long-standing weather patterns caused primarily by carbon dioxide emissions from the burning of fossil fuels. (p. 1059)

Cold War The rivalry between the Soviet Union and the United States that divided much of Europe into a Soviet-aligned Communist bloc and a U.S.-aligned capitalist bloc between 1945 and 1989. (p. 944)

collectivization of agriculture The forcible consolidation of individual peasant farms into large state-controlled enterprises in the Soviet Union under Stalin. (p. 912)

college of cardinals A special group of high clergy with the authority and power to elect the pope and the responsibility to govern the church when the office of the pope is vacant. (p. 265)

Color Revolutions A series of popular revolts and insurrections that challenged regional politicians and Russian interests in the former Soviet republics during the first decade of the twenty-first century. (p. 1032)

Columbian exchange The exchange of animals, plants, and diseases between the Old and the New Worlds. (p. 451)

Combination Acts British laws passed in 1799 that outlawed unions and strikes, favoring capitalist business people over skilled artisans. Bitterly resented and widely disregarded by many craft guilds, the acts were repealed by Parliament in 1824. (p. 676)

comitatus A war band of young men in a barbarian tribe who were closely associated with the chief, swore loyalty to him, and fought with him in battle. (p. 198)

comites A senior official or royal companion, later called a count, who presided over the civitas. (p. 228)

commercial revolution The transformation of the European economy as a result of changes in business procedures and growth in trade. (p. 304)

common law A body of English law established by King Henry II's court that in the next two or three centuries became common to the entire country. (p. 260)

Common Market The European Economic Community, created by six western and central European countries in the West Bloc in 1957 as part of a larger search for European unity. (p. 957)

communes Sworn associations of free men in Italian cities led by merchant guilds that sought political and economic independence from local nobles. (p. 359)

community controls A pattern of cooperation and common action in a traditional village that sought to uphold the economic, social, and moral stability of the closely knit community. (p. 578)

companionate marriage Marriage based on romantic love and middle-class family values that became increasingly dominant in the second half of the nineteenth century. (p. 733)

conciliarists People who believed that the authority in the Roman Church should rest in a general council composed of clergy, theologians, and laypeople, rather than in the pope alone. (p. 340)

confraternities Voluntary lay groups organized by occupation, devotional preference, neighborhood, or charitable activity. (p. 342)

Congress of Vienna A meeting of the Quadruple Alliance (Russia, Prussia, Austria, and Great Britain), restoration France, and smaller European states to fashion a general peace settlement that began after the defeat of Napoleon's France in 1814. (p. 683)

conquistador Spanish for "conqueror"; Spanish soldier-explorers, such as Hernán Cortés and Francisco Pizarro, who sought to conquer the New World for the Spanish crown. (p. 433)

constitutionalism A form of government in which power is limited by law and balanced between the authority and power of the government, on the one hand, and the rights and liberties of the subjects or citizens on the other hand; could include constitutional monarchies or republics. (p. 492)

consuls Primary executives in the Roman Republic, elected for one-year terms, who commanded the army in battle, administered state business, and supervised financial affairs. (p. 126)

consumer revolution The wide-ranging growth in consumption and new attitudes toward consumer goods that emerged in the cities of northwestern Europe in the second half of the eighteenth century. (p. 592)

Continental System A blockade imposed by Napoleon to halt all trade between continental Europe and Britain, thereby weakening the British economy and military. (p. 635)

Copernican hypothesis The idea that the sun, not the earth, was the center of the universe. (p. 510)

Corn Laws British laws governing the import and export of grain, which were revised in 1815 to prohibit the importation of foreign grain unless the price at home rose to improbable levels, thus benefiting the aristocracy but making food prices high for working people. (p. 703)

Cossacks Free groups and outlaw armies originally comprising runaway peasants living on the borders of Russian territory from the fourteenth century onward. By the end of the sixteenth century they had formed an alliance with the Russian state. (p. 486)

cottage industry A stage of industrial development in which rural workers used hand tools in their homes to manufacture goods on a large scale for sale in a market. (p. 552)

Council for Mutual Economic Assistance (COMECON) An economic organization of Communist states meant to help rebuild East Bloc countries under Soviet auspices. (p. 951)

courts Magnificent households and palaces where signori and other rulers lived, conducted business, and supported the arts. (p. 360)

Covenant An agreement that the Hebrews believed to exist between themselves and Yahweh, in which he would consider them his chosen people if they worshipped him as their only god. (p. 43)

craft guild A band of producers in a town that regulated most aspects of production of a good in that town. (p. 299)

Crimean War A conflict fought between 1853 and 1856 over Russian desires to expand into Ottoman territory; Russia was defeated by France, Britain, and the Ottomans, underscoring the need for reform in the Russian Empire. (p. 766)

Crusades Wars sponsored by the papacy for the recovery of Jerusalem and surrounding territories from the Muslims in the late eleventh to the late thirteenth centuries. (p. 276)

Crystal Palace The location of the Great Exhibition in 1851 in London; an architectural masterpiece made entirely of glass and iron. (p. 657)

cuneiform Sumerian form of writing; the term describes the wedge-shaped marks made by a stylus. (p. 15)

Dadaism An artistic movement of the 1920s and 1930s that attacked all accepted standards of art and behavior and delighted in outrageous conduct. (p. 877)

Dawes Plan War reparations agreement that reduced Germany's yearly payments, made payment dependent on economic prosperity, and granted large U.S. loans to promote recovery. (p. 889)

debate about women Debate among writers and thinkers in the Renaissance about women's qualities and proper role in society. (p. 380)

debt peonage A form of serfdom that allowed a planter or rancher to keep his workers or slaves in perpetual debt bondage by periodically advancing food, shelter, and a little money. (p. 563)

decolonization The postwar reversal of Europe's overseas expansion caused by the rising demand of the colonized peoples themselves, the declining power of European nations, and the freedoms promised by U.S. and Soviet ideals. (p. 966)

deism Belief in a distant, noninterventionist deity; common among Enlightenment thinkers. (p. 523)

Delian League A military alliance led by Athens aimed at protecting the Aegean Islands, liberating Ionia from Persian rule, and keeping the Persians out of Greece. (p. 76)

democracy A type of Greek government in which all citizens administered the workings of government. (p. 69)

de-Stalinization The liberalization of the post-Stalin Soviet Union led by reformer Nikita Khrushchev. (p. 962)

détente The progressive relaxation of Cold War tensions that emerged in the early 1970s. (p. 985)

developed socialism A term used by Communist leaders to describe the socialist accomplishments of their societies, such as nationalized industry, collective agriculture, and extensive social welfare programs. (p. 1005)

diasporas Enclaves of ethnic groups settled outside their homelands. (p. 1046)

diocese An administrative unit in the later Roman Empire; adopted by the Christian Church as the territory under the authority of a bishop. (p. 186)

displaced persons Postwar refugees, including 13 million Germans, former Nazi prisoners and forced laborers, and orphaned children. (p. 945)

Domesday Book A general inquiry about the wealth of his lands ordered by William of Normandy. (p. 253)

Dreyfus affair A divisive case in which Alfred Dreyfus, a Jewish captain in the French army, was falsely accused and convicted of treason. The Catholic Church sided with the anti-Semites against Dreyfus; after Dreyfus was declared innocent, the French government severed all ties between the state and the church. (p. 776)

Duma The Russian parliament that opened in 1906, elected indirectly by universal male suffrage but controlled after 1907 by the tsar and the conservative classes. (p. 769)

economic liberalism A belief in free trade and competition based on Adam Smith's argument that the invisible hand of free competition would benefit all individuals, rich and poor. (p. 558)

economic miracle Term contemporaries used to describe rapid economic growth, often based on the consumer sector, in post–World War II western Europe. (p. 954)

Edict of Nantes A document issued by Henry IV of France in 1598, granting liberty of conscience and of public worship to Calvinists, which helped restore peace in France. (p. 419)

empiricism A theory of inductive reasoning that calls for acquiring evidence through observation and experimentation rather than deductive reason and speculation. (p. 516)

Enabling Act An act pushed through the Reichstag by the Nazis that gave Hitler absolute dictatorial power for four years. (p. 921)

enclosure The movement to fence in fields in order to farm more effectively, at the expense of poor peasants who relied on common fields for farming and pasture. (p. 546)

encomienda system A system whereby the Spanish crown granted the conquerors the right to forcibly employ groups of Indians in exchange for providing food, shelter, and Christian teaching. (p. 447)

English Peasants' Revolt Revolt by English peasants in 1381 in response to changing economic conditions. (p. 346)

enlightened absolutism Term coined by historians to describe the rule of eighteenth-century monarchs who, without renouncing their own absolute authority, adopted Enlightenment ideals of rationalism, progress, and tolerance. (p. 533)

Enlightenment The influential intellectual and cultural movement of the late seventeenth and eighteenth centuries that introduced a new worldview based on the use of reason, the scientific method, and progress. (p. 520)

Epicureanism A system of philosophy based on the teachings of Epicurus, who viewed a life of contentment, free from fear and suffering, as the greatest good. (p. 111)

estates The three legal categories, or orders, of France's inhabitants: the clergy, the nobility, and everyone else. (p. 621)

Estates General A legislative body in prerevolutionary France made up of representatives of each of the three classes, or estates. It was called into session in 1789 for the first time since 1614. (p. 621)

ethnic cleansing The attempt to establish ethnically homogeneous territories by intimidation, forced deportation, and killing. (p. 1029)

eugenics A pseudoscientific doctrine that maintains that the selective breeding of human beings can improve the general characteristics of a national population, which helped inspire Nazi ideas about "race and space" and ultimately contributed to the Holocaust. (p. 906)

European Union (EU) The economic, cultural, and political alliance of twenty-eight European nations. (p. 1034)

evolution The idea, applied by thinkers in many fields, that stresses gradual change and continuous adjustment. (p. 745)

excommunication A penalty used by the Christian Church that meant being cut off from the sacraments and all Christian worship. (p. 266)

existentialism A philosophy that stresses the meaninglessness of existence and the importance of the individual in searching for moral values in an uncertain world. (p. 871)

Factory Acts English laws passed from 1802 to 1833 that limited the workday of child laborers and set minimum hygiene and safety requirements. (p. 666)

fascism A movement characterized by extreme, often expansionist nationalism; anti-socialism; a dynamic and violent leader; and glorification of war and the military. (p. 906)

February Revolution Unplanned uprisings accompanied by violent street demonstrations begun in March 1917 (old calendar February) in Petrograd, Russia, that led to the abdication of the tsar and the establishment of a provisional government. (p. 848)

Fertile Crescent An area of mild climate and abundant wild grain where agriculture first developed, in present-day Lebanon, Israel, Jordan, Turkey, and Iraq. (p. 9)

feudalism A term devised by later scholars to describe the political system in which a vassal was generally given a piece of land in return for his loyalty. (p. 246)

fief A piece of land granted by a feudal lord to a vassal in return for service and loyalty. (p. 246)

First Triumvirate The name later given to an informal political alliance among Caesar, Crassus, and Pompey in which they agreed to advance one another's interests. (p. 147)

"five good emperors" The five Roman emperors (Nerva, Trajan, Hadrian, Antoninus Pius, and Marcus Aurelius) of the second century C.E. whose reigns were relatively prosperous and stable. (p. 165)

Five Pillars of Islam The five practices Muslims must fulfill according to the shari'a, or sacred law, including the profession of faith, prayer, fasting, giving alms to the poor, and pilgrimage to Mecca. (p. 223)

five-year plan A plan launched by Stalin in 1928 and termed the "revolution from above," aimed at modernizing the Soviet Union and creating a new Communist society with new attitudes, new loyalties, and a new socialist humanity. (p. 907)

flagellants People who believed that the plague was God's punishment for sin and sought to do penance by flagellating (whipping) themselves. (p. 330)

Fourteen Points Wilson's 1918 peace proposal calling for open diplomacy, a reduction in armaments, freedom of commerce and trade, the establishment of the League of Nations, and national self-determination. (p. 857)

friars Men belonging to certain religious orders who did not live in monasteries but out in the world. (p. 274)

Fronde A series of violent uprisings during the early reign of Louis XIV triggered by growing royal control and increased taxation. (p. 473)

functionalism The principle that buildings, like industrial products, should serve as well as possible the purpose for which they were made, without excessive ornamentation. (p. 876)

German Social Democratic Party (SPD) A German working-class political party founded in the 1870s, the SPD championed Marxism but in practice turned away from Marxist revolution and worked instead in the German parliament for social and workplace reform. (p. 773)

germ theory The idea that disease was caused by the spread of living organisms that could be controlled. (p. 722)

Girondists A moderate group that fought for control of the French National Convention in 1793. (p. 628)

glasnost Soviet premier Mikhail Gorbachev's popular campaign for openness in government and the media. (p. 1011)

globalization The emergence of a freer, more technologically connected global economy, accompanied by a worldwide exchange of cultural, political, and religious ideas. (p. 1033)

global mass migration The mass movement of people from Europe in the nineteenth century; one reason that the West's impact on the world was so powerful and many-sided. (p. 799)

Gothic An architectural style typified by pointed arches and large stained-glass windows. (p. 318)

Grand Empire The empire over which Napoleon and his allies ruled, encompassing virtually all of Europe except Great Britain and Russia. (p. 635)

Great Depression A worldwide economic depression from 1929 through 1939, unique in its severity and duration and with slow and uneven recovery. (p. 891)

Greater Germany A liberal plan for German national unification that included the German-speaking parts of the Austrian Empire, put forth at the national parliament in 1848 but rejected by Austrian rulers. (p. 713)

Great Famine (Europe) A terrible famine in 1315–1322 that hit much of Europe after a period of climate change. (p. 324)

Great Famine (Ireland) The result of four years of potato crop failure in the late 1840s in Ireland, a country that had grown dependent on potatoes as a dietary staple. (p. 706)

Great Fear The fear of noble reprisals against peasant uprisings that seized the French countryside and led to further revolt. (p. 624)

Great Rebellion The 1857 and 1858 insurrection by Muslim and Hindu mercenaries in the British army that spread throughout northern and central India before finally being crushed. (p. 819)

Great Schism The division, or split, in church leadership from 1378 to 1417 when there were two, then three, popes. (p. 340)

guest worker programs Government-run programs in western Europe designed to recruit labor for the booming postwar economy. (p. 976)

guild system The organization of artisanal production into trade-based associations, or guilds, each of which received a monopoly over its trade and the right to train apprentices and hire workers. (p. 556)

gunboat diplomacy The use or threat of military force to coerce a government into economic or political agreements. (p. 797)

gynaeceum Women's quarters at the back of an Athenian house where the women of the family and the female slaves worked, ate, and slept. (p. 83)

Hammurabi's law code A proclamation issued by Babylonian king Hammurabi to establish laws regulating many aspects of life. (p. 21)

Hanseatic League A mercantile association of towns begun in northern Europe that allowed for mutual protection and trading rights. (p. 303)

Haskalah The Jewish Enlightenment of the second half of the eighteenth century, led by the Prussian philosopher Moses Mendelssohn. (p. 539)

Hellenistic A term that literally means "like the Greek," used to describe the period after the death of Alexander the Great, when Greek culture spread. (p. 98)

Hellenization The spread of Greek ideas, culture, and traditions to non-Greek groups across a wide area. (p. 99)

helots Unfree residents of Sparta forced to work state lands. (p. 71)

heresy A religious practice or belief judged unacceptable by church officials. (p. 180)

Holocaust The systematic effort of the Nazi state to exterminate all European Jews and other groups deemed racially inferior during the Second World War. (p. 931)

Holy Alliance An alliance formed by the conservative rulers of Austria, Prussia, and Russia in September 1815 that became a symbol of the repression of liberal and revolutionary movements all over Europe. (p. 687)

Holy Office The official Roman Catholic agency founded in 1542 to combat international doctrinal heresy. (p. 414)

Holy Roman Empire The loose confederation of principalities, duchies, cities, bishoprics, and other types of regional governments stretching from Denmark to Rome and from Burgundy to Poland. (p. 256)

Homestead Act An American law enacted during the Civil War that gave western land to settlers, reinforcing the concept of free labor in a market economy. (p. 766)

hoplites Heavily armed citizens who served as infantrymen and fought to defend the polis. (p. 69)

Huguenots French Calvinists. (p. 418)

humanism A program of study designed by Italians that emphasized the critical study of Latin and Greek literature with the goal of understanding human nature. (p. 364)

hundred days of reform A series of Western-style reforms launched in 1898 by the Chinese government in an attempt to meet the foreign challenge. (p. 823)

Hundred Years' War A war between England and France from 1337 to 1453, with political and economic causes and consequences. (p. 332)

id, ego, and superego Freudian terms to describe the three parts of the self and the basis of human behavior, which Freud saw as basically irrational. (p. 874)

illegitimacy explosion The sharp increase in out-of-wedlock births that occurred in Europe between 1750 and 1850, caused by low wages and the breakdown of community controls. (p. 579)

imperator Title given to a Roman general after a major victory that came to mean "emperor." (p. 154)

Inca Empire The vast and sophisticated Peruvian empire centered at the capital city of Cuzco that was at its peak from 1438 until 1532. (p. 443)

indulgence A document issued by the Catholic Church lessening penance or time in purgatory, widely believed to bring forgiveness of all sins. (pp. 277, 394)

Industrial Revolution A term first coined in 1799 to describe the burst of major inventions and economic expansion that began in Britain in the late eighteenth century. (p. 650)

industrious revolution The shift that occurred as families in northwestern Europe focused on earning wages instead of producing goods for household consumption; this reduced their economic self-sufficiency but increased their ability to purchase consumer goods. (p. 555)

infidel A disparaging term used for a person who does not believe in a particular religion. (p. 227)

Institutes of the Christian Religion, The Calvin's formulation of Christian doctrine, which became a systematic theology for Protestantism. (p. 411)

Iron Age Period beginning about 1100 B.C.E., when iron became the most important material for tools and weapons. (p. 36)

iron law of wages Theory proposed by English economist David Ricardo suggesting that the pressure of population growth prevents wages from rising above the subsistence level. (p. 657)

Islamic State A radical Islamist militia in control of substantial parts of central Syria and Iraq, where it applies an extremist version of shari'a law. (p. 1055)

Jacobin Club A political club in revolutionary France whose members were well-educated radical republicans. (p. 627)

Jacquerie A massive uprising by French peasants in 1358 protesting heavy taxation. (p. 344)

janissary corps The core of the sultan's army, composed of slave conscripts from non-Muslim parts of the empire; after 1683 it became a volunteer force. (p. 491)

Jansenism A sect of Catholicism originating with Cornelius Jansen that emphasized the heavy weight of original sin and accepted the doctrine of predestination; it was outlawed as heresy by the pope. (p. 601)

Jesuits Members of the Society of Jesus, founded by Ignatius Loyola, whose goal was the spread of the Roman Catholic faith. (p. 417)

Junkers The nobility of Brandenburg and Prussia, they were reluctant allies of Frederick William in his consolidation of the Prussian state. (p. 482)

just price The idea that prices should be fair, protecting both consumers and producers, and that they should be imposed by government decree if necessary. (p. 590)

Karlsbad Decrees Issued in 1819, these repressive regulations were designed to uphold Metternich's conservatism, requiring the German states to root out subversive ideas and squelch any liberal organizations. (p. 688)

Kievan Rus A confederation of Slavic territories, with its capital at Kiev, ruled by descendants of the Vikings. (p. 244)

kulaks The better-off peasants who were stripped of land and livestock under Stalin and were generally not permitted to join collective farms; many of them starved or were deported to forced-labor camps for "re-education." (p. 912)

Kulturkampf Bismarck's attack on the Catholic Church within Germany from 1870 to 1878, resulting from Pius IX's declaration of papal infallibility. (p. 773)

Kush Kingdom in Nubia that adopted hieroglyphics and pyramids, and later conquered Egypt. (p. 38)

labor aristocracy The highly skilled workers, such as factory foremen and construction bosses, who made up about 15 percent of the working classes from about 1850 to 1914. (p. 729)

laissez faire A doctrine of economic liberalism that calls for unrestricted private enterprise and no government interference in the economy. (p. 690)

Lateran Agreement A 1929 agreement that recognized the Vatican as an independent state, with Mussolini agreeing to give the church heavy financial support in return for public support from the pope. (p. 918)

latifundia Huge agricultural estates owned by wealthy absentee landowners and worked by slaves. (p. 142)

law of inertia A law formulated by Galileo that states that motion, not rest, is the natural state of an object, and that an object continues in motion forever unless stopped by some external force. (p. 511)

law of universal gravitation Newton's law that all objects are attracted to one another and that the force of attraction is proportional to the objects' quantity of matter and inversely proportional to the square of the distance between them. (p. 513)

League of Nations A permanent international organization, established during the 1919 Paris Peace Conference, designed to protect member states from aggression and avert future wars. (p. 857)

liberalism The principal ideas of this movement were equality and liberty; liberals demanded representative government and equality before the law as well as individual freedoms such as freedom of the press, freedom of speech, freedom of assembly, freedom of worship, and freedom from arbitrary arrest. (p. 690)

logical positivism A philosophy that sees meaning in only those beliefs that can be empirically proven, and that therefore rejects most of the concerns of traditional philosophy, from the existence of God to the meaning of happiness, as nonsense. (p. 870)

Luddites Group of handicraft workers who attacked factories in northern England in 1811 and later, smashing the new machines that they believed were putting them out of work. (p. 673)

Maastricht Treaty The basis for the formation of the European Union, which set financial and cultural standards for potential member states and defined criteria for membership in the monetary union. (p. 1034)

ma'at The Egyptian belief in a cosmic harmony that embraced truth, justice, and moral integrity; it gave the kings the right and duty to govern. (p. 24)

Magna Carta A peace treaty intended to redress the grievances that particular groups had against King John; it was later viewed as the source of English rights and liberty more generally. (p. 261)

mandate system The plan to allow Britain and France to administer former Ottoman territories, put into place after the end of the First World War. (p. 859)

manorialism A system in which peasant residents of manors, or farming villages, provided work and goods for their lord in exchange for protection. (p. 247)

manumission The freeing of individual slaves by their masters. (p. 138)

Marshall Plan American plan for providing economic aid to western Europe to help it rebuild. (p. 951)

Marxism An influential political program based on the socialist ideas of German radical Karl Marx, which called for a working-class revolution to overthrow capitalist society and establish a Communist state. (p. 694)

Meiji Restoration The restoration of the Japanese emperor to power in 1867, leading to the subsequent modernization of Japan. (p. 821)

mercantilism A system of economic regulations aimed at increasing the power of the state based on the belief that a nation's international power was based on its wealth, specifically its supply of gold and silver. (p. 477)

merchant guild A band of merchants in a town that prohibited nonmembers from trading in that town. (p. 299)

Messiah In Jewish belief, a savior who would bring a period of peace and happiness for Jews. (p. 176)

Methodists Members of a Protestant revival movement started by John Wesley, so called because they were so methodical in their devotion. (p. 599)

millet system A system used by the Ottomans whereby subjects were divided into religious communities, with each millet (nation) enjoying autonomous self-government under its religious leaders. (p. 491)

Mines Act of 1842 English law prohibiting underground work for all women and girls as well as for boys under ten. (p. 668)

Minoan A wealthy and vibrant culture on Crete from around 1900 B.C.E. to 1450 B.C.E., ruled by a king with a large palace at Knossos. (p. 64)

"modern girl" Somewhat stereotypical image of the modern and independent working woman popular in the 1920s. (p. 882)

modernism A label given to the artistic and cultural movements of the late nineteenth and early twentieth centuries, which were typified by radical experimentation that challenged traditional forms of artistic expression. (p. 875)

Mountain, the Led by Robespierre, the French National Convention's radical faction, which seized legislative power in 1793. (p. 628)

multiculturalism The mixing of ethnic styles in daily life and in cultural works such as film, music, art, and literature. (p. 1046)

Muslim Brotherhood Islamic social and political reform group founded in Egypt in 1928 that called for national liberation from European control and a return to shari'a law (based on Muslim legal codes), and demanded land reform, extensive social welfare programs, and economic independence. (p. 1053)

Mycenaean A Bronze Age culture that flourished in Greece from about 1650 B.C.E. to 1100 B.C.E., building fortified palaces and cities. (p. 65)

mystery religions Belief systems that were characterized by secret doctrines, rituals of initiation, and sometimes the promise of rebirth or an afterlife. (p. 87)

Napoleonic Code French civil code promulgated in 1804 that reasserted the 1789 principles of the equality of all male citizens before the law and the absolute security of wealth and private property, as well as restricting rights accorded to women by previous revolutionary laws. (p. 633)

National Assembly The first French revolutionary legislature, made up primarily of representatives of the third estate and a few from the nobility and clergy, in session from 1789 to 1791. (p. 624)

nationalism The idea that each people had its own genius and specific identity that manifested itself especially in a common language and history, and often led to the desire for an independent political state. (p. 691)

national self-determination The notion that peoples should be able to choose their own national governments through democratic majority-rule elections and live free from outside interference in nation-states with clearly defined borders. (p. 857)

National Socialism A movement and political party driven by extreme nationalism and racism, led by Adolf Hitler; its adherents ruled Germany from 1933 to 1945 and forced Europe into World War II. (p. 919)

nativism Policies and beliefs, often influenced by nationalism, scientific racism, and mass migration, that give preferential treatment to established inhabitants over immigrants. (p. 803)

NATO The North Atlantic Treaty Organization, an anti-Soviet military alliance of Western governments. (p. 952)

natural law A Stoic concept that a single law that was part of the natural order of life governed all people. (p. 112)

natural philosophy An early modern term for the study of the nature of the universe, its purpose, and how it functioned; it encompassed what we would call "science" today. (p. 508)

Navigation Acts A series of English laws that controlled the import of goods to Britain and British colonies. (p. 560)

neocolonialism A postcolonial system that perpetuates Western economic exploitation in former colonial territories. (p. 974)

neo-Europes Settler colonies with established populations of Europeans, such as North America, Australia, New Zealand, and Latin America, where Europe found outlets for population growth and its most profitable investment opportunities in the nineteenth century. (p. 794)

neoliberalism Philosophy of 1980s conservatives who argued for privatization of state-run industries and decreased government spending on social services. (p. 997)

Neolithic era The period after 9000 B.C.E., when people developed agriculture, domesticated animals, and used tools made of stone and wood. (p. 6)

New Christians A term for Jews and Muslims in the Iberian Peninsula who accepted Christianity; in many cases they included Christians whose families had converted centuries earlier. (p. 385)

New Economic Policy (NEP) Lenin's 1921 policy to re-establish limited economic freedom in an attempt to rebuild agriculture and industry in the face of economic disintegration. (p. 907)

New Imperialism The late-nineteenth-century drive by European countries to create vast political empires abroad. (p. 804)

New Left A 1960s counterculture movement that embraced updated forms of Marxism to challenge both Western capitalism and Soviet-style communism. (p. 989)

New Order Hitler's program based on racial imperialism, which gave preferential treatment to the "Nordic" peoples; the French, an "inferior" Latin people, occupied a middle position; and Slavs and Jews were treated harshly as "subhumans." (p. 928)

nonalignment Policy of postcolonial governments to remain neutral in the Cold War and play both the United States and the Soviet Union for what they could get. (p. 968)

nongovernmental organizations (NGOs) Independent organizations with specific agendas, such as humanitarian aid or environmental protection, that conduct international programs and activities. (p. 1037)

oligarchy A type of Greek government in which citizens who owned a certain amount of property ruled. (p. 70)

OPEC The Organization of Petroleum Exporting Countries. (p. 995)

open-field system System in which the arable land of a manor was divided into two or three fields without hedges or fences to mark individual holdings. (p. 288)

Opium Wars Two mid-nineteenth-century conflicts between China and Great Britain over the British trade in opium, which were designed to "open" China to European free trade. In defeat, China gave European traders and missionaries increased protection and concessions. (p. 796)

Orientalism A term coined by literary scholar Edward Said to describe the way Westerners misunderstood and described colonial subjects and cultures. (p. 815)

Orthodox Church Eastern Christian Church in the Byzantine Empire. (p. 214)

Ostpolitik German for Chancellor Willy Brandt's new "Eastern policy"; West Germany's attempt in the 1970s to ease diplomatic tensions with East Germany, exemplifying the policies of détente. (p. 985)

pagan Originally referring to those who lived in the countryside, it came to mean those who practiced religions other than Judaism or Christianity. (p. 176)

Paleolithic era The period of human history up to about 9000 B.C.E., when tools were made from stone and bone and people gained their food through foraging. (p. 6)

pastoralism An economic system based on herding flocks of goats, sheep, cattle, or other animals beneficial to humans. (p. 10)

paterfamilias The oldest dominant male of the family, who held great power over the lives of family members. (p. 135)

patriarchy A society in which most power is held by older adult men, especially those from the elite groups. (p. 11)

patricians The Roman hereditary aristocracy, who held most of the political power in the republic. (p. 129)

patronage Financial support of writers and artists by cities, groups, and individuals, often to produce specific works or works in specific styles. (p. 358)

patron-client system An informal system of patronage in which free men promised their votes to a more powerful man in exchange for his help in legal or other matters. (p. 132)

pax Romana The "Roman peace," a period during the first and second centuries C.E. of political stability and relative peace. (p. 157)

Peace of Utrecht A series of treaties, from 1713 to 1715, that ended the War of the Spanish Succession, ended French expansion in Europe, and marked the rise of the British Empire. (p. 478)

Peace of Westphalia The name of a series of treaties that concluded the Thirty Years' War in 1648 and marked the end of large-scale religious violence in Europe. (p. 469)

People's Budget A bill proposed after the Liberal Party came to power in Britain in 1906, it was designed to increase spending on social welfare services but was initially vetoed in the House of Lords. (p. 776)

perestroika Economic restructuring and reform implemented by Premier Mikhail Gorbachev in the Soviet Union in 1985. (p. 1011)

Petrine Doctrine A doctrine stating that the popes (the bishops of Rome) were the successors of Saint Peter and therefore heirs to his highest level of authority as chief of the apostles. (p. 191)

Petrograd Soviet A huge, fluctuating mass meeting of two to three thousand workers, soldiers, and socialist intellectuals modeled on the revolutionary soviets of 1905. (p. 848)

pharaoh The title given to the king of Egypt in the New Kingdom, from a word that meant "great house." (p. 24)

philosophes A group of French intellectuals who proclaimed that they were bringing the light of knowledge to their fellow humans in the Age of Enlightenment. (p. 522)

Phoenicians Seafaring people from Canaan who traded and founded colonies throughout the Mediterranean and spread the phonetic alphabet. (p. 38)

Pietism A Protestant revival movement in early-eighteenth-century Germany and Scandinavia that emphasized a warm and emotional religion, the priesthood of all believers, and the power of Christian rebirth in everyday affairs. (p. 598)

Platonic ideals In Plato's thought, the eternal unchanging ideal forms that are the essence of true reality. (p. 89)

plebeians The common people of Rome, who were free but had few of the patricians' advantages. (p. 129)

polis Generally translated as "city-state," it was the basic political and institutional unit of Greece in the Hellenic period. (p. 67)

politiques Catholic and Protestant moderates who held that only a strong monarchy could save France from total collapse. (p. 419)

polytheism The worship of many gods and goddesses. (p. 12)

popolo Disenfranchised common people in Italian cities who resented their exclusion from power. (p. 359)

Popular Front A short-lived New Deal–inspired alliance in France led by Léon Blum that encouraged the union movement and launched a far-reaching program of social reform. (p. 899)

postcolonial migration The postwar movement of people from former colonies and the developing world into Europe. (p. 976)

postindustrial society A society that relies on high-tech and service-oriented jobs for economic growth rather than heavy industry and manufacturing jobs. (p. 996)

Praetorians Imperial bodyguard created by Augustus. (p. 164)

predestination The teaching that God has determined the salvation or damnation of individuals based on his will and purpose, not on their merit or works. (p. 412)

primogeniture An inheritance system in which the oldest son inherits all land and noble titles. (p. 254)

principate Official title of Augustus's form of government, taken from *princeps*, meaning "first citizen." (p. 154)

privatization The sale of state-managed industries such as transportation and communication networks to private owners; a key aspect of broader neoliberal economic reforms meant to control government spending, increase private profits, and foster economic growth, which were implemented in western Europe in response to the economic crisis of the 1970s. (p. 997)

proletarianization The transformation of large numbers of small peasant farmers into landless rural wage earners. (p. 549)

proletariat The industrial working class who, according to Marx, were unfairly exploited by the profit-seeking bourgeoisie. (p. 695)

Protectorate The English military dictatorship (1653–1658) established by Oliver Cromwell following the execution of Charles I. (p. 495)

Protestant The name originally given to followers of Luther, which came to mean all non-Catholic Western Christian groups. (p. 396)

Ptolemy's *Geography* A second-century-C.E. work that synthesized the classical knowledge of geography and introduced the concepts of longitude and latitude. Reintroduced to Europeans about 1410 by Arab scholars, its ideas allowed cartographers to create more accurate maps. (p. 434)

public sphere An idealized intellectual space that emerged in Europe during the Enlightenment, where the public came together to discuss important issues relating to society, economics, and politics. (p. 532)

Punic Wars A series of three wars between Rome and Carthage in which Rome emerged the victor. (p. 132)

Puritans Members of a sixteenth- and seventeenth-century reform movement within the Church of England that advocated purifying it of Roman Catholic elements, like bishops, elaborate ceremonials, and wedding rings. (p. 494)

putting-out system The eighteenth-century system of rural industry in which a merchant loaned raw materials to cottage workers, who processed them and returned the finished products to the merchant. (p. 552)

Qur'an The sacred book of Islam. (p. 220)

rationalism A secular, critical way of thinking in which nothing was to be accepted on faith, and everything was to be submitted to reason. (p. 520)

Realism A literary movement that, in contrast to Romanticism, stressed the depiction of life as it actually was. (p. 747)

reconquista The Christian term for the conquest of Muslim territories in the Iberian Peninsula by Christian forces. (p. 258)

Red Shirts The guerrilla army of Giuseppe Garibaldi, who invaded Sicily in 1860 in an attempt to liberate it, winning the hearts of the Sicilian peasantry. (p. 760)

Reform Bill of 1832 A major British political reform that increased the number of male voters by about 50 percent and gave political representation to new industrial areas. (p. 704)

regular clergy Men and women who lived in monastic houses and followed sets of rules, first those of Benedict and later those written by other individuals. (p. 193)

Reichstag The popularly elected lower house of government of the new German Empire after 1871. (p. 773)

Reign of Terror The period from 1793 to 1794 during which Robespierre's Committee of Public Safety tried and executed thousands suspected of treason and a new revolutionary culture was imposed. (p. 630)

relics Bones, articles of clothing, or other objects associated with the life of a saint. (p. 210)

religious orders Groups of monastic houses following a particular rule. (p. 270)

Renaissance A French word meaning "rebirth," used to describe the rebirth of the culture of classical antiquity in Italy during the fourteenth to sixteenth centuries. (p. 358)

representative assemblies Deliberative meetings of lords and wealthy urban residents that flourished in many European countries between 1250 and 1450. (p. 338)

republicanism A form of government in which there is no monarch and power rests in the hands of the people as exercised through elected representatives. (p. 493)

revisionism An effort by moderate socialists to update Marxist doctrines to reflect the realities of the late nineteenth century. (p. 787)

Rocket The name given to George Stephenson's effective locomotive that was first tested in 1829 on the Liverpool and Manchester Railway at 35 miles per hour. (p. 656)

rococo A popular style in Europe in the eighteenth century, known for its soft pastels, ornate interiors, sentimental portraits, and starry-eyed lovers protected by hovering cupids. (p. 531)

Roma et Augustus Patriotic cult encouraged by Augustus and later emperors in which the good of Rome and the good of the emperor were linked. (p. 157)

Romanesque An architectural style with rounded arches and small windows. (p. 318)

Romanticism An artistic movement at its height from about 1790 to the 1840s that was in part a revolt against classicism and the Enlightenment, characterized by a belief in emotional exuberance, unrestrained imagination, and spontaneity in both art and personal life. (p. 695)

runic alphabet Writing system developed in some barbarian groups that helps give a more accurate picture of barbarian society. (p. 196)

sacraments Certain rituals defined by the church in which God bestows benefits on the believer through grace. (p. 195)

salon Regular social gathering held by talented and rich Parisians in their homes, where philosophes and their followers met to discuss literature, science, and philosophy. (p. 530)

sans-culottes The laboring poor of Paris, so called because the men wore trousers instead of the knee breeches of the aristocracy and middle class; the word came to refer to the militant radicals of the city. (p. 629)

satraps Administrators in the Persian Empire who controlled local government, collected taxes, heard legal cases, and maintained order. (p. 55)

Schlieffen Plan Failed German plan calling for a lightning attack through neutral Belgium and a quick defeat of France before turning on Russia. (p. 834)

Scholastics University professors in the Middle Ages who developed a method of thinking, reasoning, and writing in which questions were raised and authorities cited on both sides of a question. (p. 312)

Second Industrial Revolution The burst of industrial creativity and technological innovation that promoted strong economic growth in the last third of the nineteenth century. (p. 744)

second revolution From 1792 to 1795, the second phase of the French Revolution, during which the fall of the French monarchy introduced a rapid radicalization of politics. (p. 628)

Second Triumvirate A formal agreement in 43 B.C.E. among Octavian, Mark Antony, and Lepidus to defeat Caesar's murderers. (p. 150)

Second Vatican Council A meeting of Catholic leaders convened from 1962 to 1965 that initiated a number of reforms, including the replacement of Latin with local languages in church services, designed to democratize the church and renew its appeal. (p. 988)

secular clergy Priests and bishops who staffed churches where people worshipped and who were not cut off from the world. (p. 193)

Senate The assembly that was the main institution of power in the Roman Republic, originally composed only of aristocrats. (p. 126)

sensationalism The idea that all human ideas and thoughts are produced as a result of sensory impressions. (p. 521)

separate spheres A gender division of labor with the wife at home as mother and homemaker and the husband as wage earner. (pp. 666, 737)

serfs Peasants bound to the land by a relationship with a manorial lord. (p. 247)

signori Government by one-man rule in Italian cities such as Milan; also refers to these rulers. (p. 360)

simony The buying and selling of church offices, a policy that was officially prohibited but often practiced. (p. 265)

Social Darwinism A body of thought drawn from the ideas of Charles Darwin that applied the theory of biological evolution to human affairs and saw the human race as driven by an unending economic struggle that would determine the survival of the fittest. (p. 746)

socialism A backlash against the emergence of individualism and the fragmentation of industrial society, and a move toward cooperation and a sense of community; the key ideas were economic planning, greater social equality, and state regulation of property. (p. 693)

Socialist Realism Artistic movement that followed the dictates of Communist ideals, enforced by state control in the Soviet Union and East Bloc countries in the 1950s and 1960s. (p. 961)

Socratic method A method of inquiry used by Socrates based on asking questions, through which participants developed their critical thinking skills and explored ethical issues. (p. 89)

Solidarity Independent Polish trade union that worked for workers' rights and political reform throughout the 1980s. (p. 1009)

Sophists A group of thinkers in fifth-century-B.C.E. Athens who applied philosophical speculation to politics and language and were accused of deceit. (p. 89)

Spanish Armada The fleet sent by Philip II of Spain in 1588 against England as a religious crusade against Protestantism. Weather and the English fleet defeated it. (p. 411)

spinning jenny A simple, inexpensive, hand-powered spinning machine created by James Hargreaves in 1765. (p. 651)

stadholder The executive officer in each of the United Provinces of the Netherlands, a position often held by the princes of Orange. (p. 500)

stagflation Term coined in the early 1980s to describe the combination of low growth and high inflation that led to a worldwide recession. (p. 996)

Statute of Kilkenny Law issued in 1366 that discriminated against the Irish, forbidding marriage between the English and the Irish, requiring the use of the English language, and denying the Irish access to ecclesiastical offices. (p. 352)

steam engines A breakthrough invention by Thomas Savery in 1698 and Thomas Newcomen in 1705 that burned coal to produce steam, which was then used to operate a pump; the early models were superseded by James Watt's more efficient steam engine, patented in 1769. (p. 654)

Stoicism A philosophy, based on the ideas of Zeno, that people could be happy only when living in accordance with nature and accepting whatever happened. (p. 112)

stream-of-consciousness technique A literary technique, found in works by Virginia Woolf, James Joyce, and others, that uses interior monologue—a character's thoughts and feelings as they occur—to explore the human psyche. (p. 879)

Struggle of the Orders A conflict in which the plebeians sought political representation and safeguards against patrician domination. (p. 130)

suffrage movement A militant movement for women's right to vote led by middle-class British women around 1900. (p. 741)

sultan The ruler of the Ottoman Empire; he owned all the agricultural land of the empire and was served by an army and bureaucracy composed of highly trained slaves. (p. 490)

sumptuary laws Laws that regulated the value and style of clothing and jewelry that various social groups could wear as well as the amount they could spend on celebrations. (p. 307)

sweated industries Poorly paid handicraft production, often carried out by married women paid by the piece and working at home. (p. 730)

Tanzimat A set of reforms designed to remake the Ottoman Empire on a western European model. (p. 771)

tariff protection A government's way of supporting and aiding its own economy by laying high taxes on imported goods from other countries, as when the French responded to cheaper British goods flooding their country by imposing high tariffs on some imported products. (p. 661)

Test Act Legislation, passed by the English Parliament in 1673, to secure the position of the Anglican Church by stripping Puritans, Catholics, and other dissenters of the right to vote, preach, assemble, hold public office, and teach at or attend the universities. (p. 497)

tetrarchy Diocletian's four-part division of the Roman Empire. (p. 186)

theory of special relativity Albert Einstein's theory that time and space are relative to the observer and that only the speed of light remains constant. (p. 873)

Thermidorian reaction A reaction to the violence of the Reign of Terror in 1794, resulting in the execution of Robespierre and the loosening of economic controls. (p. 632)

thermodynamics A branch of physics built on Newton's laws of mechanics that investigated the relationship between heat and mechanical energy. (p. 744)

Torah The first five books of the Hebrew Bible, containing the most important legal and ethical Hebrew texts; later became part of the Christian Old Testament. (p. 42)

totalitarianism A radical dictatorship that exercises "total claims" over the beliefs and behavior of its citizens by taking control of the economic, social, intellectual, and cultural aspects of society. (p. 904)

total war A war in which distinctions between the soldiers on the battlefield and civilians at home are blurred, and where the government plans and controls economic and social life in order to supply the armies at the front with supplies and weapons. (p. 834)

Treaty of Brest-Litovsk Peace treaty signed in March 1918 between the Central Powers and Russia that ended Russian participation in World War I and ceded Russian territories containing a third of the Russian empire's population to the Central Powers. (p. 852)

Treaty of Paris The treaty that ended the Seven Years' War in Europe and the colonies in 1763, and ratified British victory on all colonial fronts. (p. 562)

Treaty of Tordesillas The 1494 agreement giving Spain everything to the west of an imaginary line drawn down the Atlantic and giving Portugal everything to the east. (p. 439)

Treaty of Verdun Treaty signed in 843 by Charlemagne's grandsons dividing the Carolingian Empire into three parts and setting the pattern for political boundaries in Europe still in use today. (p. 240)

Treaty of Versailles The 1919 peace settlement that ended war between Germany and the Allied powers. (p. 856)

trench warfare A type of fighting used in World War I behind rows of trenches, mines, and barbed wire; the cost in lives was staggering and the gains in territory minimal. (p. 835)

tribunes Plebeian-elected officials; tribunes brought plebeian grievances to the Senate for resolution and protected plebeians from the arbitrary conduct of patrician magistrates. (p. 131)

Triple Alliance The alliance of Austria, Germany, and Italy. Italy left the alliance when war broke out in 1914 on the grounds that Austria had launched a war of aggression. (p. 828)

Triple Entente The alliance of Great Britain, France, and Russia prior to and during the First World War. (p. 830)

troubadours Poets who wrote and sang lyric verses celebrating love, desire, beauty, and gallantry. (p. 315)

Truman Doctrine America's policy geared to containing communism to those countries already under Soviet control. (p. 951)

tyranny Rule by one man who took over an existing government, generally by using his wealth to gain a political following. (p. 69)

Union of Utrecht The alliance of seven northern provinces (led by Holland) that declared its independence from Spain and formed the United Provinces of the Netherlands. (p. 420)

utilitarianism The idea of Jeremy Bentham that social policies should promote the "greatest good for the greatest number." (p. 721)

vassal A warrior who swore loyalty and service to a noble in exchange for land, protection, and support. (p. 246)

Velvet Revolution The term given to the relatively peaceful overthrow of communism in Czechoslovakia; the label came to signify the collapse of the East Bloc in general in 1989 to 1990. (p. 1015)

vernacular literature Writings in the author's local dialect, that is, in the everyday language of the region. (p. 315)

viceroyalties The name for the four administrative units of Spanish possessions in the Americas: New Spain, Peru, New Granada, and La Plata. (p. 446)

virtù The quality of being able to shape the world according to one's own will. (p. 365)

War Communism The application of centralized state control during the Russian civil war, in which the Bolsheviks seized grain from peasants, introduced rationing, nationalized all banks and industry, and required everyone to work. (p. 853)

war guilt clause An article in the Treaty of Versailles that declared that Germany (with Austria) was solely responsible for the war and had to pay reparations equal to all civilian damages caused by the fighting. (p. 858)

war on terror American policy under President George W. Bush to fight global terrorism in all its forms. (p. 1052)

Warsaw Pact Soviet-backed military alliance of East Bloc Communist countries in Europe. (p. 952)

water frame A spinning machine created by Richard Arkwright that had a capacity of several hundred spindles and used waterpower; it therefore required a larger and more specialized mill — a factory. (p. 651)

wergeld Compensatory payment for death or injury set in many barbarian law codes. (p. 199)

wet-nursing A widespread and flourishing business in the eighteenth century in which women were paid to breast-feed other women's babies. (p. 582)

white man's burden The idea that Europeans could and should civilize more primitive nonwhite peoples and that imperialism would eventually provide nonwhites with modern achievements and higher standards of living. (p. 813)

World Trade Organization (WTO) A powerful supranational financial institution that sets trade and tariff agreements for over 150 member countries and so helps manage a large percentage of the world's import-export policies. Like the IMF and the World Bank, the WTO promotes neoliberal policies around the world. (p. 1037)

Yahweh The sole god in Hebrew monotheism; later anglicized as Jehovah. (p. 40)

Young Turks Fervent patriots who seized power in a 1908 coup in the Ottoman Empire, forcing the conservative sultan to implement reforms. (p. 772)

Zionism A movement dedicated to building a Jewish national homeland in Palestine, started by Theodor Herzl. (p. 783)

Zoroastrianism Religion based on the ideas of Zoroaster that stressed devotion to the god Ahuramazda alone and that emphasized the individual's responsibility to choose between good and evil. (p. 56)

Index

A Note about the Index: Names of individuals appear in boldface. Letters in parentheses following pages refer to the following:

(d) documents
(b) boxed features
(i) illustrations, including photographs and artifacts
(m) maps
(f) figures, including charts and graphs

Aachen, 235, 237, 256, 257
Abandoned children, 291–292, 582
Abbasid Empire, 235
Abbess, 236, 271. *See also* Nuns
Abbey. *See* Monasticism; Monks and monasteries
Abbot, 270, 271, 273
'Abd al-'Aziz, 225*(d)*
Abdülhamid II (Ottomans), 772
Abelard, Peter, 313
Abolition: of British slave trade, 677; of serfdom (Russia), 767; of slavery, 565, 766. *See also* Emancipation
Aborigines, Australian, 794
Abortion and abortion rights, 583, 1001
Abraham (Hebrew leader), 43, 222, 226
Abrahamic religions, 43
Absenteeism, clerical, 392
Absolute monarchy and absolutism, 543; armies and, 471; in Austria, 465; in Byzantine Empire, 187; in China, 527; enlightened, 532–539, 569; in France, 469, 472–473, 473–474, 477–478, 477*(m)*; in Prussia, 465; in Rome, 187; in Russia, 486–487, 534; state-building and, 469–471
Abstract art, 877
Abu Bakr, 224
Ab Urbe Condita (Livy), 161
Abu Simbel: temples at, 32
Academies: artistic, 376; Platonic, 89; scientific, 514*(d),* 518, 519, 523
Achaean League, 135
Achaeans (Mycenaeans), 66
Achilles, 66–67
Acid rain, 1002
Acre, Crusaders in, 279
Acropolis: of Athens, 80*(d),* 80*(i)*; defined, 69

Actium, Battle of, 150
Activism. *See* specific issues
Act of Union (1707), 525
Adad-nirari II (Assyria), 47
Adams, Abigail, "Remember the Ladies," 619, 619*(d)*
Adams, John, 615, 619
Adenauer, Konrad, 984
Administration. *See* Government
Adoption: Hammurabi on, 21; of Roman heirs, 164
Adrianople, Battle of, 203
Adriatic Sea, trade and, 245, 302*(m)*
Adultery: French punishment of, 261*(i)*; Hammurabi on, 21; Ovid on, 163; in Rome, 163
Advertising, 881, 882
Aegean region, 62, 63*(m)*; Persia and, 55. *See also* Greece
Aeneas (Troy), 124, 161
Aeneid (Virgil), 153, 160–161
Aequi people, 126
Aeschylus, 81
Aetolian League, 98, 134
Affluence: in 1960s, 986–988; after Second World War, 979. *See also* Wealth
Afghanistan: Bactria in, 95; Hellenistic, 99–100; Rome and, 175; Taliban and, 1054; U.S. and, 1052; warfare in, 1055
Africa: cities in, 430; colonies in, 805, 806*(m)*; decolonization in, 966, 967*(m),* 972–974; diamonds in, 808*(b)*; domesticated animals in, 10; England (Britain) and, 805, 806*(m),* 807–809; Europeans and, 805–809, 806*(m)*; First World War and, 840; France and, 805, 807, 809; Germany and, 805, 807, 858; gold in, 790*(i),* 807; humans in, 6; immigrants from, 976; imperialism in, 805–809, 806*(m)*; inequality in, 1038; Italy and, 805; migration from, 1043; mission schools in, 813*(i),* 815; neocolonialism in, 974; railroads in, 793, 809; religious beliefs in Americas and, 567; Scramble for, 805–809; Second World War in, 930*(m)*; slavery and, 430–431, 542*(i),* 564, 566; smelting in, 36; Soviets and, 964; trade and, 428; trading states of,

430–431. *See also* North Africa; specific locations
African Americans: in 1960s, 989; civil rights movement and, 989, 991. *See also* Slaves and slavery
Africans: European ideas about, 459–460; as French soldiers, 887; marriage in colonies and, 567. *See also* Africa; Slaves and slavery
Afrikaners, 805, 807–809, 808*(b)*
Afroeurasia: humans in, 6; trade in, 427, 428–429, 428*(m)*
Afterlife: Christianity and, 177; Egyptian concept of, 25; in Greek mystery religions, 87; Zoroastrians and, 56
Against the Murderous, Thieving Hordes of the Peasants (Luther), 401
Agamemnon, 66–67
Age of Anxiety, 866*(i),* 867–868
Age of Discovery, 427, 805. *See also* Exploration
Age of exploration. *See* Age of Discovery; Exploration
Agincourt, battle at, 335
Agora, 69, 126
Agricultural Adjustment Act (U.S., 1933), 895
Agriculture: in 17th and 18th centuries, 551–552; ancient, 8–9; collectivization of, 767, 912, 960; commercial, 481; developed socialism and, 1005; development of, 9–11; in Egypt, 23, 24, 26, 798; in England, 547–549; in Great Depression, 895; in Greece, 61; in Hammurabi's code, 21; Hellenistic, 104; Industrial Revolution and, 648–649; in Italy, 142; in Low Countries, 546–547; in Mesopotamia, 12–13; in Middle Ages (High), 289, 289*(i)*; Muslims and, 226; Neolithic era and, 6; open-field system in, 288; in Rome, 188; in Russia, 767, 769; in Scandinavia, 897; slavery for, 765. *See also* Farms and farming; Manors and manorialism; Peasants; Serfs and serfdom
Ahuramazda (god), 55, 56, 57*(i)*
AIDS: drug costs for, 1061
Air force, in Second World War, 938
Airlift: in Berlin, 952

Air pollution, 1002; industrialization and, 721. *See also* Pollution

Air pump, 504*(i)*, 508

Akan peoples, gold from, 430

Akhenaton (Egypt), 30, 31*(b)*

Akkad and Akkadians, 17, 19–20, 22, 46

Alans, 203

Alaric I (Visigoth), 203

Albania: economy in, 993; ethnic Albanians and, 1029, 1031, 1031*(i)*; Rome and, 173; Second Balkan War and, 832. *See also* East Bloc

Alberti, Leon Battista, 365–366

Albert of Mainz, 394

Albert of Wallenstein, 469

Albert the Bear (Germany), 281

Albigensian heresy, 267–268

Alchemy, 515

Alcibiades (Athens), 77

Alcmene (goddess), 87

Alcohol and alcoholism: drinking as recreation and, 589; of working class, 731

Alcuin, 231, 236–237

Ale, 290

Alexander I (Russia), 634, 635, 636, 637, 683, 685, 847; Holy Alliance and, 687

Alexander II (Russia), 767

Alexander III (Russia), 768, 848

Alexander VI (Pope), 362, 386, 439

Alexander the Great, 79, 93; Arrian on, 97*(d)*; conquests by, 94–96, 95*(m)*; Italy, Sicily, and, 122; political legacy of, 96–98. *See also* Hellenistic world

Alexandra (Russia), 847

Alexandria: culture of, 103; Europeans in, 798; founding of, 94; library in, 103; riots in, 798–799; trade in, 430

Alexis (Russia), 847

Alfonso VI (Castile and León), 368

Alfonso VIII (Castile), 258

Alfonso X (Castile), 311

Alfred (Wessex), 202, 252

Algebra, 227, 506

Algebra (al-Khwarizmi), 227

Algeria: France and, 708, 770, 805; independence for, 973–974; in Second World War, 937

Algerian War (1954–1962), 974

Ali (fourth caliph), 224

Ali, Ibrahim (Egypt), 771

Ali, Ismail (Egypt), 798

Ali, Muhammad (Egypt), 770, 771, 797–798

Allah (God), 222

Allegory of the Tudor Dynasty, 408*(i)*

Alliance(s): Delian League as, 76; before First World War, 828–830, 829*(m)*; after First World War, 857; Holy Alliance, 687–688; Little Entente and, 886; Roman, 126; Second Coalition as, 633; after Second World War, 952; Sumerian, 17; Theban, 79. *See also* specific alliances

Alliance for Germany, 1016

Allies (First World War), 840, 846; German reparations and, 886; Russian civil war and, 853; after war, 857, 858, 859, 860

Allies (Second World War). *See* Grand Alliance (Second World War)

Allies, Roman, 133

Almanacs, 588

Almohad dynasty, 258

Almoravid dynasty, 258

Alphabet: Greek, 40, 125; Phoenician, 40; Roman, 40, 125. *See also* Writing

Alps: Hannibal and, 133

al-Qaeda, 1047, 1054

Alsace, 478, 763–764, 775, 828. *See also* Alsace-Lorraine

Alsace-Lorraine, 858

Alva, duke of, 420

Amalgamated Society of Engineers, 677

Amarna, Egypt, 30, 31*(b)*

Ambrose (Bishop of Milan), 190–191, 191*(i)*, 194–195

Amendments: to U.S Constitution, 618

Amenhotep III (Egypt), 29, 30

America(s): Columbian exchange and, 451; conversion in, 567; Creoles in, 565; naming of, 439; silver from, 478. *See also* New World; North America; specific locations

American Indians. *See* Native Americans

Americanization: fears of, 988

American National Exhibition (Moscow, 1959), 962*(d)*

American Revolution: background to, 613–614; Cincinnatus and, 127; Constitution (U.S.) and, 617–618; France and, 617; independence from Britain and, 609, 616–617; liberty, equality, and, 618–619; origins of, 614–616

Amiens: revolt in, 472; Treaty of, 634

Ammianus Marcellinus (Rome), 203

Amnesty: by Napoleon, 634

Amon (god), 25, 30

Amon-Ra (god), 25, 30, 36*(i)*

Amorites, 20

Amphoras, 96*(i)*; Greek shipments in, 106

Amsterdam, 456, 521, 547

Anabaptists, 400*(b)*

Anagni, papacy and, 270, 340

Anarchism: in Russia, 767, 850; in Spain and Italy, 787

Anatolia (Turkey), 62, 687; Assyria and, 37; cultural contacts of, 23; Cyrus in, 54; after First World War, 861; Greeks in, 66; iron smelting in, 35, 36; Persia and, 54. *See also* Turkey

Anatomy, 517–518, 518*(i)*

Anaximander (Greece), 745

Ancient world. *See* specific issues and locations

al-Andalus, 224, 226

Andalusia, 224

Andropov, Yuri, 1011

Anesthesia, 603

Angevin dynasty, 253–254, 255*(m)*

Angles (England), 202

Anglican Church. *See* Church of England

Anglo-French Entente (1904), 830

Anglo-Russian Agreement (1907), 830

Anglo-Saxons: *Beowulf* and, 239*(d)*; helmet of, 202*(i)*; Viking defeat of, 242

Angola, 805, 974

Angra Mainyu (god), 56

Animals: in Columbian exchange, 451; domestication of, 10; as food, 7

Anjou, 253–254, 383

Anne (Saint), 295

Anne of Austria, 473

Anne of Denmark, 580

Annulment: for Henry VIII (England), 268*(i)*

Anointment, of kings, 231, 472

Anomie, 747

Anschluss, in Austria, 926

Anthony (saint), 192

Anthropology, 815

Antibiotics, 722

Anticlericalism, 392, 686

Anticolonialism, 968; and communism, 968–971

Anticommunism: after Second World War, 951

Anti-Corn Law League, 704*(i)*, 705

Antifederalists (U.S.), 618

Antiglobalization: activism toward, 1038–1039

Antigone (Sophocles), 82*(d)*

Antigonid dynasty (Macedonia), 98, 133

Antigonus I, 98

Anti-imperialism, 791, 816, 817*(d)*, 818–819

Antioch: as Crusader kingdom, 277

Antiochus III (Seleucids), 110
Antiochus IV Epiphanes (Seleucids), 110
Anti-Semitism: Catholic existentialist denunciation of, 872; Dreyfus affair and, 776; in Italy, 919; modern, 781–783, 782(b); nationalism and, 778, 781–783; in Nazi Germany, 919–920; in Spain, 387; Zionism and, 783. See also Holocaust; Jews and Judaism
Antiseptic principle, 722
Anti-Socialist Laws (Germany), 774, 783, 786
Antiwar movement: before First World War, 831; in Vietnam War, 990, 991
Antonine plague, 170, 180
Antonines (Rome), 165–167
Antoninus Pius (Rome), 165, 167
Antony, Mark (Rome), 146(b), 150
Anubis (god), 26
ANZAC Army Corps, in First World War, 840
Apartheid policy, in South Africa, 808(b), 972, 974
Apennine Mountains, 122, 267
Apocalyptic belief, Jews, Christianity, and, 176
Apostolic succession, 191
Apothecaries, 290, 602, 603
Appalachian Mountains region: settlement in, 615
Appeasement, of Hitler, 925–927
Appliances: in 1960s, 987
Apprentices, 300, 347, 371, 433, 577, 652–653
Aqueducts, 139, 169–170, 170(i)
Aquinas, Thomas, 313, 508
Aquitaine, 253–254, 332, 335
Arabi, Ahmed, 798, 799
Arabia, 455
Arabian Sea, Alexander at, 96
Arabic language: in Egypt, 798; Phoenician alphabet and, 40; scholarship in, 506
Arabic numerals, 227
Arab-Israeli wars, 971, 995
Arabs and Arab world: Africa and, 805; culture and, 227; expansion of, 220, 222–223, 222(m); First World War and, 840; after First World War, 859–860; Israel and, 971; Jerusalem and, 277; medicine in, 227; Muslim world and, 1053–1056; Six-Day War and, 995; in Spain, 386; Suez crisis and, 972, 972(m); trade and, 430. See also Crusades; Islam; Middle East; Muslims; specific locations

Arab Spring (2011), 1055–1056; destabilization after, 1055; refugees from, 1043, 1044; social media and, 1041–1042
Aragon, 227, 362, 384, 386(d); Great Schism and, 340
Ara Pacis (Roman altar), 163(d), 163(i)
Arawak language, 438
Archaic Age (Greece), 67
Archaic Period (Egypt), 24
Archbishop of Canterbury, 346, 494
Archilochus (soldier-poet), 86
Archimedes (scientist), 113, 114(b), 114(i)
Architecture: Assyrian, 50; of cathedrals, 317–319, 318(i); Chicago School of, 875–876; Greek, 81; Hellenistic, 101; "International Style" of, 876; modernism in, 875–876; Persian, 57; Renaissance, 377; Roman, 174; women and, 377
Archon (chief magistrate): in Athens, 74
Arête (excellence), 67, 90
Argentina, 800; Italian agricultural workers in, 802; migrants in, 801
Arguin (settlement), 436
Arianism, 189–190, 205, 206, 212
Aristarchus (Samos), 113
Aristocracy: in 19th century, 726; Carolingian, 230, 237, 245–246; in England, 499, 776; European, 286; in France, 707; of labor, 729; Merovingian, 230; in Paris, 662(i); Roman, 131, 190, 201; wealth of, 726. See also Nobility
Aristophanes, 82–83, 84(b), 84(i), 89
Aristotle, 90; Alexander the Great and, 94; medieval medical study and, 311; sciences and, 508–509; on slavery, 460; translation into Latin, 205, 227, 507
Arkwright, Richard, 651, 652(b)
Armada (Spain), 411, 411(i)
Armagnacs (France), 383
Armed forces: in 17th century, 471; Akkadian, 19–20; Assyrian, 35, 47–49; after Cold War, 1016; colonial, in First World War, 840; Egyptian, 26, 798; before First World War, 831; French, 465, 477, 631, 632, 755; Greek, 69; Hellenistic, 101; Mycenaean, 65; nobility in, 488; professionalization of, 471, 477; Prussian, 484, 484(i), 761; Russian, 488–489, 847, 848, 853. See also Military; Soldiers; specific battles and wars
Armenia and Armenians, 909; in Austrian Empire, 686; genocide against, 839,

839(m); independence groups and, 1012
Armistice, in First World War, 854–855
Arms race: before First World War, 831. See also Nuclear arms race
Army Order No. 1 (Russia, 1917), 848
Arnold of Brescia, 267
Arouet, François Marie. See Voltaire
Arrian (historian), on Alexander, 97(d)
Arsinoe II (Egypt), 98(i)
Art(s): Assyrian, 50; Baroque, 500–501; Catholicism and, 601; decorative (minor) vs. major, 376–377; on First World War, 826(i), 837; in France, 476; Greek, 79–83; Greek influence on Roman, 139; Hellenistic, 101, 112–113, 112(i); in late Middle Ages, 331; Mannerist, 375; Mesopotamian, 17(i); Minoan, 64; modernism in, 875–881; Mycenaean, 65, 65(i); Nazis on, 922; Orientalism in, 815–816; Paleolithic, 7; Persian, 56–57, 57(i); politicization of, 879; Realism in, 747–748, 748(i); in Renaissance, 373–378, 374(i), 378(i); Romanticism in, 698–700; Socialist Realism in, 961; Soviet, 915, 942(i); visual, 876–879; women in, 376–377. See also Architecture; Literature; Painting; specific works and artists
Artemisium, battle at, 75
Arthur (legendary king), 202, 315
Arthur (Prince of Wales, England), 384, 407
Artillery: Archimedes and, 114(b). See also Weapons
Artisans: capitalists and, 676; Carolingian, 234; in Egypt, 26; in France, 661; guilds and, 299–301, 347, 556; in industry, 676; in lower classes, 729; in social hierarchy, 466; wives and widows of, 301, 347, 348(d). See also Labor; Workers
Art of Love, The (Ovid), 161–163, 162(d)
Aryan race, 780, 923
Asceticism, 193, 416; during Black Death, 330
Asclepius (god), 108, 117
Ashurbanipal (Assyria), 50
Asia: in 1914, 810(m); banking crisis in (1997), 1034; decolonization in, 934, 966, 967(m); domesticated animals in, 10; Dutch and, 570, 810; emigration from, 802–803; England and, 571, 810, 810(m); financial crisis in, 1023; First World War in, 840; German

Asia (continued)
  colonies in, 858; humans in, 6; immigrants from, 802, 803, 976; imperialism in, 810–811, 810(m), 818–822; industrialization in, 663, 664; inequality in, 1038; Japan and, 822, 934; power struggle in, 968–971; railroads in, 793; sea routes to, 427, 439, 440; Soviets and, 964; trade and empire in, 570–571; use of term, 4. See also Asia Minor; specific locations
Asia Minor: Greek culture in, 103. See also Anatolia; Near East; specific locations
Asiento, 479(m), 562
Aspendos, Turkey, 174
al-Assad, Bashar, 1024, 1055
Assassinations. See specific individuals
Assemblies: colonial American, 615; of French clergy, 621; in Rome, 129, 130. See also Estates (assemblies); National assembly (France); specific assemblies
Assignats (French paper currency), 626
Assimilation: barbarian, 200–206; into Christianity, 207–208; of Franks and Romans, 205; nationalism and, 781
Assyria and Assyrian Empire, 35–36, 46–50, 48(m); Alexander the Great in, 94; archaeological discovery of, 50; arts and architecture of, 50; destruction of, 50; government and culture of, 49–50; Hebrews and, 42, 46, 48–49, 49(i), 51(d); Medes and, 52; military of, 47–49; military technology of, 48; Neo-Assyrian Empire and, 47
Astell, Mary, 519
Astrakhan, 486
Astrolabe (baby), 313
Astrolabe (instrument), 227(i), 313, 435, 435(i)
Astrology, 515
Astronomy: ancient, 12; cartography and, 509; Hellenistic, 113; Muslim, 227(i), 506; professorships in, 507–508; Ptolemaic, 509; Scientific Revolution and, 509–510, 510–512. See also Scientific Revolution; Universe
Astyages (Medes), 53(b)
Asylum status, 803, 1043–1044
Atahualpa (Inca), 444
Atheism: of existential thinkers, 871
Athena (goddess): Parthenon and, 80(d), 80(i)
Athens, 62, 65, 67; Acropolis of, 80(i); democracy in, 73–74; empire of, 76; gender roles in, 85; growth of, 73–74;

Peloponnesian War and, 76–78; after Peloponnesian War, 78–79; Persian Wars and, 75; philosophers in, 89–90; sex and sexuality in, 85–86; slaves in, 83; Sparta and, 76; Syracuse and, 77–78
Athletics. See Sports
Atlantic Ocean region: economy in, 562–563; Enlightenment in, 568–570; identities and communities of, 567; Industrial Revolution and, 648; Magyars in, 244; revolutionary ideas in, 613; in Second World War, 938; slavery in, 677; slave trade in, 432, 564–565, 565(i); trade in, 559–570
Atlantis, 64
Atom, 873; Greek concept of, 516; subatomic particles and, 874
Atomic power: in Second World War, 939, 939(i). See also Nuclear weapons
Atomic theory, 111
Aton (Aten) (god), 30, 31(b)
Atonal music, 881
"Attack" (Sassoon), 839(d)
Attica, 62; Spartan invasion of, 77
Attila (Huns), 203
Auden, W. H., 872
Auerstädt, battle at, 635
Augsburg, Peace of, 406, 407, 469
Augsburg Confession, 406
Augustine of Canterbury, 207–208, 393–394
Augustine of Hippo (Saint), 194–195, 196, 216, 236, 261, 412; on sacraments, 293
Augustus (Octavian, Rome), 150, 154–164, 210; Ara Pacis (altar) for, 163(d), 163(i), 167; as Caesar's heir, 146(b); Cleopatra and, 146(b); as emperor, 155; family of, 163–164; as imperator, 154, 154(i); Res Gestae and, 157, 158–159(d); successors to, 164–168; Virgil and, 161
Augustus, use of title, 186, 234
Auschwitz-Birkenau, 902(i), 932, 932(i), 933
Austen, Jane, 525
Austerlitz, Battle of, 635
Australia: Aborigines in, 794; Asian immigrants in, 802, 803; British settlement of, 571; European immigrants to, 800; First World War and, 840; Second World War and, 936
Austria, 533; 1846 rebellion in, 708; absolutism in, 465, 533; Catholic

Church in, 537, 598; denazification in, 947; Denmark and, 761; Enlightenment in, 537; in First Coalition, 628; First World War and, 855, 855(m); France and, 478, 629, 759; Freedom Party in, 1048; French Revolution and, 627, 628; Garibaldi and, 760; Germany and, 828; growth to 1748, 483(m); Habsburgs and, 404, 469, 481–482, 483(m); Hungary and, 778; independence of (1955), 964; Italy and, 757, 758–759; Metternich and, 683–684, 685–686; Napoleon and, 634, 635; Nazi Germany and, 926; occupation zones in, 947; Ottomans and, 772; partition of Poland and, 536(m), 537; Prussia and, 537, 713, 760–761, 762, 763; Rome and, 157; in Seven Years' War, 613; state-building in, 481–482, 483(m), 537; in Third Coalition, 634; Thirty Years' War and, 469; war guilt clause and, 858; War of the Austrian Succession and, 537, 562. See also Austria-Hungary; specific rulers
Austria-Hungary: dual monarchy of, 778; First World War and, 827, 832–833, 846, 854, 857; industrialization in, 659, 659(f); nationalism in, 778, 832; revolution in, 855–856; socialists in, 784, 787; streetcars in, 725. See also First World War
Austrian Empire, 686; 1848 revolutions in, 710–712, 711(m); German language in, 713; peoples of (1815), 686; reaction in, 711–712. See also Austria
Austrian Freedom Party, 1005
Austrian Netherlands, 628, 629, 634. See also Belgium
Austro-Hungarian Empire. See Austria-Hungary
Austro-Prussian War, 762, 762(m)
Authoritarianism, 753, 903; in Africa, 974; in Greece, 955; Internet disruptions and, 1042; in Japan, 822; nationalism and, 753, 754, 756; New Imperialism and, 791; in Portugal, 955; in Russia, 1026; before Second World War, 904–907; in Spain, 955. See also specific locations
Authority. See Power (authority)
Autocracy: before 1848, 702; Metternich and, 688
Automobiles: after Second World War, 958–959, 958(i)
Auxiliaries: Roman, 126, 155

Auxiliary Service Law (Germany), 843
Avant-garde artists, 877, 879
Avars, 203, 210–211, 232
Avesta (Zoroastrian texts), 56
Avicenna, 227
Avignon, papacy in, 339, 340, 341, 342
Axis powers (Second World War), 925, 927, 937–938. See also Italy; Japan; Nazi Germany; Second World War
Ay Khanoum (city), 101(i)
Azerbaijan, 909, 1012
Azores, 436
Aztec Empire, 375, 442–443, 442(m), 443(i)

Baal (god), 41, 41(i)
Babies. See Children
Baby boom, 978, 988; youth culture, generation gap, and, 979
Babylon and Babylonians, 19; Amorites and, 20; Assyrians and, 35, 46, 50; creation myth of, 16; Hammurabi and, 20–22; Neo-Babylonians and, 51–52; Persian capture of, 53(b). See also Neo-Babylonians
Babylonian Captivity: of Catholic Church, 339–340, 392; of Hebrews, 42, 53(b)
Bach, Johann Sebastian, 501
Bacon, Francis, 516, 517
Bacterial revolution, 722–723. See also Disease
Bactria, 95, 98, 227; Greek culture in, 99–100, 101(i), 104; Persia and, 54
Baghdad, 234, 235, 313, 506, 840
Bahamas, 438
Bailiffs, 287
Balance of power: after Congress of Vienna, 682, 683–685, 766; expansion and, 478, 537; in Italian Renaissance, 360–362, 361(i); Napoleon and, 635; after Napoleonic Wars, 682. See also specific locations
Baldwin, Stanley, radio and, 885
Balfour, Arthur, 859
Balfour Declaration (1917), 782(b), 859–860
Balkan migrant route, 1044(i)
Balkan region: 1878–1914, 833(m); copper in, 12; First and Second Balkan wars in, 832; First World War and, 839, 855(m), 856; nationalism and, 772, 832; Ottomans and, 489–490, 772, 833(m); repatriation to, 801; Rome and, 157; in Second World War, 928;

slaves from, 432. See also specific locations
Baltic region: Christianity in, 280; democratic governments in, 1032; in EU, 1035; after First World War, 857; independence groups in, 1012; Nazi Germany and, 927; plague in, 327; Russia and, 487, 767; in Thirty Years' War, 469. See also specific locations
Balzac, Honoré de, 748
Bandits, fur-collar crime and, 351
Bangladesh, 970
Banking: in Belgium, 662; crisis in (1997), 1034; in Florence, 358, 360(i), 374; in France, 620, 756; in Great Depression, 893, 894; industrial, 662; in Ottoman Empire, 771; in Rome, 172. See also Economy
Banlieues (suburbs): in Paris, 1046
Baptism, 296; of Huguenots, 474; of indigenous people, 457
Baptistery (Florence), doors of, 373
Baptists, 399
Bar (French county), 383
Barbados, 445, 446; Jews in, 567
Barbarians: assimilation and, 200–206; Christianity and, 206, 207–210; customary and written law of, 197, 205; ethnicity of, 196–197; in Italy, 211; migrations by, 200–206, 201(m), 219; religion of, 200; Rome and, 185; slavery and, 197; society of, 197–199; Tacitus on, 197, 198(d)
Barbarossa, Frederick. See Frederick I Barbarossa
Barometer, 508
Baroque period, arts of, 500–501, 601
Barracks emperors (Rome), 181, 186
Barter, 70. See also Trade
Barth, Karl, 872
Basil (Saint), 192
Basilicas, 191, 284(i), 318, 375
Basques and Basque region: Charlemagne and, 232; separatists in Spain and, 1004
Basra, Iraq, 840
Bastille (Paris), storming of, 608(i), 614, 780
Batavia (Jakarta), Java, 570
Batavian Republic, 634
Bath, England, 139(i), 596
Bathhouses, 596
Baths and bathing: in 18th century, 596; medieval public, 349(i); in Rome, 139–140, 139(i)
Battering rams, 115

Battle(s): Etruscan, 124; Roman naval, 132. See also specific battles and wars
Battle of Britain, 928, 929(d)
Battle of the Somme, The (movie), 884
Bauhaus, 876
Bavaria: Charlemagne and, 232; demographic decline in, 1042; after First World War, 856; Magyars in, 244; Rome and, 157
Bayeux tapestry, 250(i)
Bayle, Pierre, 521
BBC, 885
Beatles, 990
Beattie, James, 529
Beauvais, cathedral in, 319
Beauvoir, Simone de, 871; Second Sex, The, and, 1001, 1002–1003(d)
Beccaria, Cesare, 526
Bechuanaland (Botswana), 807
Becket, Thomas, 260, 353
Bede (historian), 202, 238(b), 238(i)
Bedouins, 220
Beer Hall Putsch, 889, 920
Beethoven, Ludwig van, 701–702
Beguines, 276
Beijing (Peking), China: Boxer Rebellion and, 823
Belarus (Belorussia), 485, 539, 854, 909, 1032
Belgian Congo. See Congo
Belgian partisans (francs-tireurs), 835
Belgium: Africa and, 805, 816; Congo and, 972; in First World War, 834; in Grand Empire, 635; independence of, 680(i), 688, 708; industrialization in, 659, 659(f); in Kingdom of the Netherlands, 685; Nazis and, 928; railroads in, 662; Rhineland and, 887; Ruhr region and, 887; separatism in, 1004; socialists in, 784. See also Flanders; Low Countries; Netherlands
Belorussia (Belarus), 485, 539, 854, 909, 1032
Belov, Fedor, on Soviet collective farm, 913(d)
Benedict of Nursia (Saint) and Benedictines: Rule of, 192–193, 214, 273; schools of, 193, 270
Benefices (clerical offices), 392–393
Benet Biscop (Saint), 237, 238(b)
Bengal, 571
Bentham, Jeremy, 721
Beowulf, 239–240, 239(d)
Berbers, as Moors, 224
Berg, Alban, 881
Bergson, Henri, 870

Berlin, 712; airlift to, 952; riots in (1848), 712, 781; scientific academy in, 519; in Second World War, 939; student protests in, 991; war protest in, 845–846; zones in, 952

Berlin Conference (1884, 1885), 807

Berlin Wall, 965, 982(i); Brandt and, 985; migration before, 976; opening of (1989), 1014–1016, 1015(i); as symbol, 993

Bermuda, 446

Bernal, Martin, 86–87

Bernstein, Eduard, 787

Bertin, Rose, 595(b), 595(i)

Bethmann-Hollweg, Theobald von, 833, 842

Beutelsbach, peasants in, 602

Bible: cosmology and, 510; in Czech language, 341; in England, 408; Erasmus and, 370; Gospels and, 176; in Greek language, 110; of Gutenberg, 371; Hebrew, 40, 41, 42, 49; in Latin, 193; literacy and, 588; reading of, 323; Vulgate, 193. *See also* New Testament; Old Testament

Big Science: consumer benefits of, 954; in nuclear age, 953–954

Big Three: in First World War, 857; in Second World War, 948

Bill of Rights: in England, 497–498; in United States, 618

Bills of exchange, 304

Bin Laden, Osama, 1054, 1055

Birth control: in 19th century, 740; breast-feeding and, 582; pill for, 989; premarital sex and, 578

Births and birthrate, 581; in 17th century, 550; decline in, 739–740, 740(f), 799, 978, 1042–1043; in Italy, 1001; after Second World War, 988. *See also* Childbirth

Bishops (Christian), 180, 191, 416, 494; Carolingian, 231, 232; Merovingian, 229–230, 231; of Rome, 191. *See also* Pope(s); specific bishops

Bismarck, Otto von, 761–764, 773; alliance system of, 828; Berlin Conference and, 807

Bjørnson, Martinius, 802

Black Athena: The Afroasiatic Roots of Classical Civilization (Bernal), 86–87

Black Death: course of, 328(m); effects of, 330–332, 428, 432; in Florence, 327, 358; fresco from, 331(i); labor after, 330, 480–481; pathology of, 326–327; population and, 327–328, 549;

scapegoats for, 330–331; spread of, 327–329, 328(m); treatment of, 329. *See also* Plague

Black Hand (Serbian radicals), 832

"Black Legend," 459

Black market, in First World War Germany, 842

Black people. *See* Africa; African Americans; Africans; Slaves and slavery

Black Prince. *See* Edward (Black Prince, England)

Black Sea region: Genoese trade and, 432; Greeks and, 71(m); Huns in, 203

Black Shirts (Italy), 918

Blair, Tony, 999(b)

Blake, William, 673, 696

Blanc, Louis, 694, 709

"Blank check" before First World War, 833

Blitz, in London, 928, 929(d)

Blitzkrieg (lightning war), 927

Blockade(s): of Berlin, 952; in First World War, 840–841, 846; by Napoleon, 635

Blocs (political): before First World War, 828. *See also* East Bloc; West Bloc

Bloodletting: illness and, 603

"Blood purity," 352

Blood sports, 589

Bloody Sunday (Ireland), 1005

Bloody Sunday massacre (Russia), 769, 770(d)

"Blowback": to U.S. policy in Middle East, 1054

Blum, Léon, 899

Boats. *See* Ships and shipping

Boccaccio, Giovanni, 329, 330

Boeotia, 62

Boers and Boer (South African) War, 807–809, 808(b), 816

Boethius, 205

Bohemia: in Austrian Empire, 712; battle of Sadowa in, 762; Black Death in, 328; Christianity in, 281; Estates in, 481; Habsburgs in, 481–482, 686; independent church in, 413; nationalism in, 712; Reformation in, 392; Wyclif's ideas in, 341

Bohemian phase, of Thirty Years' War, 469

Boleyn, Anne, 407, 408

Bolívar, Simón, 690

Bologna: university in, 310, 311, 331, 509

Bolshevik Revolution, 848–850, 858

Bolsheviks, 827, 849, 850, 851–852, 853, 854, 907. *See also* Communist Party and communism; Russia; Soviet Union

Bombs and bombings: atomic, 874; by Fenians, 777(i); in Second World War,

939, 939(i); in Vietnam War, 990. *See also* Terrorism

Bonaparte family: Joseph, 635. *See also* Napoleon I (Napoleon Bonaparte); Napoleon III (Louis Napoleon)

Boniface (missionary), 230

Boniface VIII (Pope), 266, 269–270, 269(d), 339

Book of Common Prayer, 409, 494

Book of hours, in France, 289(i)

Book of the Dead (Egypt), 25–26

Book of Three Virtues (Christine de Pizan), 348(d)

Books: in Enlightenment, 532; printing and, 370–373; prohibited, 372, 415, 518. *See also* Literature; specific authors and works

Bora, Katharina von, 401, 403(i)

Bordeaux, revolt in, 472

Borders: in Europe, 334(m), 471; after First World War, 858–859, 889; against migrants, 803; migration into EU and, 1043; Roman, 143, 144, 167, 181; of Russia, 767. *See also* Boundaries; Frontiers

Borgia family: Cesare, 362, 368; Lucrezia, 368; Rodrigo (Pope Alexander VI), 368, 386, 439

Borodino, Battle of, 637

Borrowing: in Great Depression, 891, 893

Bosnia and Bosnians, 243, 832; atrocities and, 903–904; human rights and, 1061

Bosnia-Herzegovina: Muslims, Serbs, and Croatians in, 1029, 1030(m)

Bosnian Muslims (Bosniaks), 1029, 1030

Bosnian Serbs, 1030

Boston Tea Party, 616

Botany, 507, 513, 514–515, 527

Botswana, 807

Botticelli, Sandro, 375, 378(i)

Boucher, François, 595(i)

Boule (Athenian council), 74

Boulton, Matthew, 654

Boundaries: of Europe, 334(m), 471. *See also* Borders; Frontiers

Bourbon dynasty (France), 775; enlightened absolutism of, 569; restoration of, 637, 684, 707

Bourgeoisie: in France, 709; Marx on, 695; nobility and, 610

Boutham, Yorkshire, England, 307

Bové, José, 1038–1039, 1038(i)

Boxers (Chinese secret society), 823

Boyars, 244, 485, 488, 489(i)

Boycotts: by African Americans, 989; by women in American colonies, 619

Boyle, Robert, and Boyle's law, 518
Boyne, Battle of the, 497
Boys: Spartan, 72. *See also* Children; Families; Men
Brahe, Tycho, 510, 512
Branches of government: in United States, 618
Brandenburg, 482. *See also* specific rulers
Brandenburg-Prussia, growth to 1748, 483*(m)*
Brando, Marlon, 979
Brandt, Willy, 984, 984*(i)*, 985
Brazil: Christianity in, 417; European immigrants to, 800; Portugal and, 439, 444; racial/ethnic characteristics of, 450, 450*(i)*; slavery in, 444, 454, 564; sugar in, 444, 455
Brazza, Pierre de, 807
Bread: in diet, 290, 451, 467–468; riots over, 171, 472, 590
Breast-feeding: in 18th century, 582–583; in 19th century, 739; in Rome, 137–138
Bremen, 301
Brennus (Gauls), 127
Brest-Litovsk, Treaty of, 852, 854
Brethren and Sisters of the Common Life, 342
Breton language, 196–197
Bretton Woods agreement (1944), 957
Brexit (British exit from EU), 1057
Brezhnev, Leonid, 966, 1010
Brezhnev Doctrine, 994–995, 1012
Briand, Aristide, 888*(b)*, 889, 890
Bridget of Kildare, 207
Bridget of Sweden, 344
Briefe and True Report of the New Found Land of Virginia, A (Hariot), 449*(d)*
"Bright Star" (Keats), 697*(d)*
Bristol, 542*(i)*
Britain: Battle of, 928; Roman, 167*(m)*, 172. *See also* England (Britain)
British Commonwealth: African former colonies in, 972; First World War soldiers from, 840; Jewish migration and, 946; Pakistan and India in, 971. *See also* specific countries
British East India Company, 562*(i)*, 570, 571, 616, 819
British Empire: India and, 570*(i)*, 819; after Seven Years' War, 613–617. *See also* Colonies and colonization; England (Britain); specific locations
British Ministry of Munitions, 842
British North America: Enlightenment and, 568–569. *See also* Colonies and colonization; North America

Brittain, Edward, 844*(b)*
Brittain, Vera, 844*(b)*, 844*(i)*
Brittany, 383
Broadcasting, 885
Bronze, 12
Bronze Age, 6, 12; Greek Helladic period as, 61, 62–67; Hyksos and, 28
Bronze Age Collapse, 33, 35–36, 62, 65
Brothels, 309, 347, 349, 349*(i)*, 403, 736. *See also* Prostitution
Brothers of the Christian Schools, 587
"Brown Man's Burden, The" (Labouchère), 817*(d)*
Bruges, 299, 301, 303
Brunelleschi, Filippo, 373, 374
Brunhilda (Merovingian), 229
Bruni, Leonardo, 364, 365, 367
Brüning, Heinrich, 921
Brunswick (duke of), 628
Brussels, 299, 680*(i)*
Brutus (Rome), 149
Bubbles: economic, 891
Bubonic plague, 326, 327, 468, 604; disappearance of, 551; Justinian plague and, 213. *See also* Black Death
Buda, 414
Budapest: Hungarian revolution (1956) and, 965
Budgets: deficits in United States, 998; in Great Depression, 893–894
Buffer state, after First World War, 857
Building. *See* Architecture; Housing
Bulgaria: Balkan Wars and, 832; First World War and, 839; Rome and, 157; after Second World War, 950; Turks in, 861. *See also* East Bloc
Bulgars, 203, 210
Bullbaiting, 590
Bullfighting, 309
Bulls: on Crete, 64, 64*(i)*
Bureaucracy: 17th-century state-building and, 471, 484; in Austria, 537, 778; Crusades and, 279; in England, 253, 408; in European countries, 382, 772; in Germany, 921–922; Hellenistic, 101, 103; in Inca Empire, 443; in India, 820; military in First World War, 838; Ottoman, 490–491; in Prussia, 484, 534, 761, 763; in Russia, 488, 847; in Soviet Union, 1010; training for, 258
Burgher (bourgeois), 298, 333
Burgundians (France), 196, 204, 205, 336, 383, 387
Burgundy, 333; Holy Roman Empire and, 387, 404; Magyars in, 244; Netherlands and, 387, 404

Burials: Christian, 178; First World War and, 861. *See also* Funerals; Tombs
Burke, Edmund, 627, 686
Bush, George H. W., 1016
Bush, George W., 1050–1051; Afghanistan and Iraq invasions and, 1054; war on terror and, 1052
Business: in Middle Ages (High), 303–304; social classes and, 975; women in, 673. *See also* Commerce; Commercial revolution; Merchant(s); Trade
Butler, Josephine, 737
Byblos: trade of, 39*(d)*
Byron, George Gordon, Lord, 697, 699*(b)*, 703
Byzantine Empire, 186*(m)*, 211*(m)*; attacks on, 210–211; Black Death in, 328; Charlemagne and, 232; Crusades and, 279; Huns and, 203; intellectual thought in, 213; Irene as empress of, 235; Islam and, 506; popes and, 235, 276; strength of, 210–212; Vikings in, 244. *See also* Constantinople; Eastern Roman Empire
Byzantine-Greek-Christian empire, 220
Byzantium. *See* Byzantine Empire; Constantinople

Cabot, John, 439–441
Cabral, Pedro Álvares, 439, 444
Caesar, as title, 186
Caesar, Julius (Rome), 145–150, 145*(i)*; assassination of, 149; Cleopatra and, 146*(b)*; in Gaul, 160, 201; humanists on, 364; plot against, 148–149*(d)*
Caesarion (Rome), 146*(b)*
Cairo, 430, 506, 798
Calais, 336
Calcagus (Scottish chieftain), 157
Calculus, 521
Calendars: Christian, 292; in Egypt, 23; Russian, 848
Calicut, India, 429, 433, 437
Caligula (Rome), 164
Caliph, 224
Caliphate, of Córdoba, 258
Calvin, John, and Calvinism, 407, 411–413; in France, 418–419; in Netherlands, 420; Peace of Augsburg and, 469; predestination and, 412; in Scotland, 494; spread of, 412–413, 415*(m)*; teachings of, 419; Wesley on, 600
Cambodia, 934; independence of, 969, 970

Cambyses (Persia), 54, 55
Camels, caravan trade and, 106
Cameralism, in Prussia, 534
Cameron, David, 1057
Cameroon(s), 807
Campania, 122
Camus, Albert, 872
Canaan, 28, 41, 41*(i)*, 66
Canada: European immigrants to, 800; First World War and, 840; France and, 440–441, 445–446, 477; fur trade in, 441, 445; Loyalists in, 617; Seven Years' War and, 613. *See also* New France
Canals: in England, 649; in Panama, 794; Persian, 55; Suez, 794, 798, 798*(m)*, 811, 819, 859, 972, 972*(m)*
Canary Islands: Greece and, 70
Candide or Optimism (Voltaire), 521
Cannae, Battle of, 133
Cannon, in Hundred Years' War, 335, 338
Canonical Gospels, 176
Canon law, 190, 268, 311
Canon of Medicine (Avicenna), 227
Canterbury, Becket in, 260
Canterbury Tales (Chaucer), 352
Canton. *See* Guangzhou (Canton), China
Canute (Viking), 252
Cape Colony, 805, 807, 809
Cape of Good Hope, 437; passage to East Indies and, 559
Capetian dynasty (France), 254–255, 332. *See also* specific rulers
Cape Town, 456, 805
Capital (financial): exports of, 794; labor and, 672–677
Capital (Marx), 694, 694*(i)*
Capital cities. *See* specific cities
Capitalism: commercial revolution and, 304, 306; in England, 676; in First World War, 841; Hitler and, 920; imperialism and, 816; Marx on, 695; Smith, Adam, and, 558–559; socialism and, 693; in Soviet Union, 912; Weber and, 746–747; West and, 5
Capitoline Hill (Rome), 126
Capitularies, 229, 233*(d)*
Capitulary de Villis, The, 233*(d)*
Caporetto, Battle of, 846
Caracalla (Rome), 181
Caravan trade, 106, 220, 430; Black Death spread by, 327
Caravel, 434
Carbon dioxide, 1059

Cardinals, 340, 375
Caribbean region: European exploration of, 437–439; European settlement in, 442; France and, 641; immigrants from, 976; mixed-race children in, 566; after Seven Years' War, 613; slaves in, 454, 564. *See also* West Indies; specific locations
Carlos III (Spain), 569
Carlos IV (Spain), 569
Carmelite order, 416
Carnaby Street (London), 990
Carnival, 589–590
Carolingian Empire, 245–248; capitularies in, 233*(d)*; end of, 240–241, 240*(m)*, 254, 270; rise of, 230–231; society in, 236–237
Carolingian minuscule, 236, 236*(i)*
Carolingian Renaissance, 236–237, 248
Carson, Rachel, 1001–1002
Carter, Jimmy, 1010
Cartesian dualism, 517
Carthage: Cato the Elder on, 141; Greece and, 70; Phoenician founding of, 40; Punic Wars and, 132–134; Rome and, 127
Cartier, Jacques, 440–441
Cartography, 434, 509, 513
Cassatt, Mary, 877
Cassius (Rome), 149
Caste, in India, 819
Castiglione, Baldassare, 366–367
Castile, 227, 258, 384, 386*(d)*, 479; Great Schism and, 340. *See also* Ferdinand and Isabella (Spain); Spain
Castle, The (Kafka), 880
Castlereagh, Robert, 684
Casualties. *See* specific battles and wars
Catacombs, Christian, 178
Çatal Hüyük, 11–12
Catalonia, 227, 472, 480
Catapults, 115–116
Cateau-Cambrésis, Treaty of, 418
Cathars. *See* Albigensian heresy
Cathedrals, 191; medieval, 317–319, 318*(i)*, 320; stained glass in, 264*(i)*; wedding door in, 305*(b)*
Catherine de' Medici, 418, 419
Catherine of Aragon, 384, 407, 409
Catherine the Great (Russia), 534–537, 535*(i)*, 539, 617
Catholic Church: in 16th century, 392–393; in American colonies, 567; anti-Nazi opponents in, 925; Babylonian Captivity of, 339–340, 390; baroque arts and, 500–501; in

Britain, 207, 495; Charles V and, 406; Christendom and, 382; Christian existentialists and, 872; Constantine and, 189; Copernican hypothesis and, 510, 518–519; divorce, abortion, and, 1001; education and, 775; in England, 340, 393, 408–409, 495; Enlightenment and: 569; in France, 416, 597, 626, 631, 634, 755, 775, 776; in Germany, 413, 416, 773; Great Schism in, 340, 392; Gregorian reforms in, 265; heresy and, 267–268; hierarchy of, 191, 597–598; Holy Roman Empire and, 406, 597; immigration and, 445, 804*(d)*; in Ireland, 495–496, 705, 777; in Italy, 518–519, 757, 918; mass in local languages and, 988; in Middle Ages (later period), 331; missionaries of, 815; Napoleon III and, 755; Orthodox Christianity and, 213–215; piety in, 601; in Poland, 1007; in Portugal, 597; reforms of, 391, 413, 414–417; schisms in, 188–189, 331; Second Vatican Council and, 988; in Spain, 393, 416, 597; Thirty Years' War and, 469. *See also* Christianity; Councils (Christian); Counter-Reformation; Protestantism; Reformation
Catholic Counter-Reformation. *See* Counter-Reformation
Catholic Enlightenment, 525
Catholic League, 469
Catholic Reformation (Counter-Reformation). *See* Counter-Reformation (Catholic Reformation)
Cato the Elder (Marcus Cato), 133, 140–141
Caucasus region: First World War in, 839; Russia and, 536, 767, 772, 810*(m)*, 811, 854
Caudillos, in South America, 690
Cavaignac, Louis, 710
Cavendish, Margaret, 519
Cavour, Camillo Benso di, 758, 759, 760
Cayenne, 446
Ceaușescu, Nicolae, 1015
Celestial spheres, 508–509, 509*(i)*, 510
Celibacy, 576; clerical, 194, 265, 266; Luther and Zwingli on, 401
Celtic peoples, 196–197; Christianity of, 207; in Gaul and Britain, 201–202. *See also* Gaul and Gauls
Cenobitic monastery, at Tabennisi, 192

Censors (Rome), 130, 141

Censorship: in First World War, 841, 843, 846; in Russia, 767; in totalitarian countries, 905

Center Party (Germany), 773

Central Africa: Belgium and, 807; France and, 807

Central America: conversion in, 567. *See also* Latin America; South America; specific countries

Central Asia: former Soviet republics in, 1032; nomads from, 200, 203; Russia and, 767, 810(*m*), 811; Soviet republics in, 909; trade and, 301. *See also* specific locations

Central Europe: 1848 revolutions in, 711(*m*); absolutism in, 469, 471; Jews and, 781, 783; nationalism in, 692; in Second World War, 930–931; states in, 256–257, 256(*m*). *See also* specific locations

Centralization: in East Germany, 993; state-building and, 251, 470, 471

Central Powers (First World War), 839, 840, 846

Centuriate Assembly (Rome), 129

Centuries (Rome), 129

Césaire, Aimé, 968

Ceuta, Morocco, 436

Ceylon, 456

Chadwick, Edwin, 675, 721, 722

Chaldeans, 51–52

Châlons, battle at, 203

Chamberlain, Houston Stewart, 780

Chamberlain, Neville, 927

Chamber of Accounts (France), 255

Chamber of Deputies (France), 707

Champagne, France, fairs in, 302

Champlain, Samuel de, 445

Chansons de geste, 315

Charcoal, 654

Chariots, 28, 47, 172

Charity: foundling homes as, 583; schools as, 587

Charivari, 578–579

Charlemagne: Abbasid Empire and, 235; Carolingian Renaissance and, 236–237; conquests by (768–814), 228, 232(*m*); coronation of, 234–235; marriages of, 232–233; successors to, 254; as warrior-ruler, 231–232

Charles I (England), 469, 494, 497

Charles I (Spain), 448, 459

Charles II (England), 497, 560

Charles II (France), 478

Charles IV (France), 332

Charles V (Holy Roman Empire, Spain): abdication by, 407; empire of, 387, 405(*m*); exploration and, 424, 439; Henry VIII and, 407–408; Luther and, 395, 404; Netherlands under, 404, 419; papacy and, 340; religion and, 406; slavery in Americas and, 454

Charles VI (France), 338

Charles VII (France), 336, 383

Charles VIII (France), 362, 363(*d*)

Charles X (France), 707, 707(*i*), 708

Charles XII (Sweden), 488

Charles Martel, 230, 231

Charles the Bald, 240, 242

Charles the Bold (Burgundy), 383

Charles the Great. *See* Charlemagne

Charles the Simple, 242

Charlie Hebdo (magazine): terrorist attack on, 1047

Charters: Charter 77, 1007, 1008(*d*); in France, 707; of Medina, 221. *See also* Magna Carta

Chartist movement (England), 677, 705

Châtelet, Madame du, 523

Chaucer, Geoffrey, 352

Chaumont, Treaty of, 637

Chechnya, 1027(*m*), 1032, 1059

Checks and balances, 617–618

Cheka, 853, 854. *See also* Secret police

Chemistry, 744

Chernobyl nuclear accident, 1003, 1011

Chicago: Mies van der Rohe buildings in, 876; student protests in, 991

Chicago School of architects, 875–876

Chieftains, of barbarian tribes, 197–199

Childbearing: decline in, 739–740, 740(*f*)

Childbirth: in Greece, 85; medicine and, 117; in Middle Ages, 291; midwifery and, 604. *See also* Births and birthrate; Midwives

Childcare: in 18th century, 581–583; working women and, 666–667

Child labor: debate over laws for, 667(*d*); in factories, 646(*i*), 665–666; in mines, 669(*i*); workdays of, 666

Children: in 18th century, 584–585; in 19th century, 739–741; abandonment of, 291–292; disciplining of, 584–585; education and, 581–587; as factory workers, 652–653; Germanic, 198(*d*); in Hebrew society, 44; infanticide and, 104, 583–584; in Middle Ages, 254(*d*), 263–264, 271; middle-class, 740; in nobility, 263–264; in patriarchal society, 466–467; as peasants, 287–288; in Rome, 137–138; Spartan,

73; wardship in Norman England, 254(*d*); women workers and, 978; in workforce, 610; working-class, 741. *See also* Child labor; Families; Illegitimacy

Children's Stories and Household Tales (Brothers Grimm), 698, 700–701(*d*)

Chilperic (Merovingian), 208(*d*), 231

China: Boxer Rebellion in, 823; communism in, 951, 968; Enlightenment attitudes toward, 526–527; Hellenism and, 100; imperialism in, 795–797, 810(*m*), 823; industrialization in, 658, 659, 659(*f*), 664; Japan and, 822, 823, 840, 934; nationalism in, 971; navigation technology from, 434, 435, 507; opening to West, 429, 795–797; opium trade and, 795–797; papermaking in, 507; plague in 1890s, 326; pollution and, 1060; population of, 429; reform and, 823; revolution in (1912), 823; Roman trade and, 175; Russia and, 768, 811; scientific activity in, 507; silver and, 455; trade and, 303, 428, 429, 455; traditionalism in, 508

Chinggis Khan, Crusades and, 279

Chirac, Jacques, 1051(*d*)

Chivalry, 202, 262–263, 263(*i*)

Chocolate: drinking of, 590(*i*)

Choir monks, 273

Cholera, 723

Cholula, Mexico, 442

Chopin, Frédéric, 701

Chrétien de Troyes, 315

Christ: use of term, 177. *See also* Jesus of Nazareth

Christendom, 281. *See also* Christianity

Christian III (Denmark), 407

Christian IV (Denmark), 469

Christian Church. *See* Catholic Church; Christianity; Protestant Reformation; Reformation; specific churches

Christian Democrats, 955, 966; in Europe, 984; European unification and, 957; in Germany, 955, 998, 1016; after Second World War, 955

Christian existentialism, 872

Christian humanists, 368–370, 391

Christianity: in 16th century, 392–393; Arian, 189–190, 205, 206, 212; in barbarian states, 206, 207–210; Carolingians and, 236–237; Charlemagne and, 236; church hierarchy in, 180; Columbus and, 437–438; conversion to, 178, 189(*m*),

Christianity (*continued*)
190, 206, 207–210, 457; expansion of, 190–195, 216, 280–281; gender and sexuality in, 193–194; Great Schism and, 340; in Iberian Peninsula, 280; imperialism and, 815; in Ireland, 280; Justinian and, 215(*d*); Metternich on, 686; middle-class values and, 728; Muslims and, 225, 226–227; mystery religions and, 118; Nestorian, 190, 212; Nicene, 189–190, 206; Nietzsche on, 869; revival after First World War, 872–873; rise of, 176; in Roman Empire, 175–180, 185, 188–189; saints and sacraments in, 195, 266, 293, 416; in Spain, 280, 393, 416; spread of, 177–179, 189(*m*); in West, 5; women in, 178. *See also* Cathedrals; Church(es); Jesus of Nazareth; Missions and missionaries; Orthodox Church; Reformation; Saint(s); specific groups
Christian Socialist Party (Vienna), 783
Christine de Pizan, 347, 348(*d*), 381
Church(es): in 1960s, 988; Christian in Roman Empire, 180; hierarchy in 18th century, 597–598; in medieval villages, 318; in Middle Ages (High), 317–319; in United States, 732; working-class, 732. *See also* Religion(s); specific groups
Church and state, 776, 861
Church councils. *See* Councils; specific councils
Churchill, Winston: "iron curtain" speech of, 950, 950(*m*); Second World War and, 928, 937; at wartime conferences, 948, 949(*i*)
Church of England (Anglican Church), 408, 409–410, 497; abolition of privileges of, 777; Ireland and, 705; Puritans and, 494; schools and, 587; Wesley and, 599
Church of Ireland, 409
Church of Scotland. *See* Presbyterianism
Cicero, Marcus Tullius: Caesar and, 148–149(*d*); humanists on, 364; rebellion ended by, 145
Cimbri people, 144
Cincinnati, Ohio, 127
Cincinnatus (Rome), 126
Cinema. *See* Movies
Circumcision, in Judaism, 296
Circumnavigation of earth, 439
Cistercians, 271
Cîteaux, 271

Cities and towns: in 17th century, 481; in 19th century, 716, 717, 718–725; care of sick in, 329–330; in Dutch Republic, 547; in England, 718–721; Etruscan, 124; European, of 100,000 or more, 719(*m*); as global centers, 1033; Greek, 69; guilds in, 556–557, 556(*i*); Hellenistic, 93, 99–100, 106, 110; industrial life in, 671–672; infant-mortality in, 582–583; Iran and, 52; in Italy, 257, 267, 358–359; leisure and recreation in, 589; market days in, 574(*i*); Mesopotamian trade and, 22; in Middle Ages, 234, 235, 285, 298–299, 306–309; military camps as, 172; Muslim populations in, 1047; public health in, 721; public transportation in, 725; Roman, 138–139, 142, 157, 173; rural migration to, 800; after Second World War, 944; sex in medieval, 347, 349–350; trade and, 430; urban planning and, 723–724, 723(*m*); Uruk as, 13, 14. *See also* City-states; Polis (Greece); Urban areas; Urban planning; Villages; Walled cities; specific locations
Citizens and citizenship: in Athens, 74, 85; in Greece, 69–70, 85; Hellenistic, 101, 102, 110; for immigrants in Europe, 1046–1047; immigration and, 803, 804(*d*); national, 779–780; in nation-state, 753–754; in Rome, 128, 136, 141, 148, 155, 168, 181; in Russia, 767; in Saint-Domingue, 640; sovereignty of, 74; in Sparta, 72
City of God (Augustine), 195, 196, 216
City-states: Greek, 67, 98, 135; in Italy, 360–362, 361(*m*), 499, 757; Mesopotamian, 20; polis as, 67; Sumerian, 14–15, 17, 68. *See also* Greece; specific locations
Civic morality, 525
Civil Code: in France, 1804, 633; in Germany, 1906, 742
Civil Constitution of the Clergy (France), 626
Civilization(s): characteristics of, 5–6; European, 248; Western, 4. *See also* Classical culture; Culture(s); Society; specific civilizations
Civilization and Its Discontents (Freud), 875
Civil law: in Rome, 130
Civil liberties: in First World War, 842; in Italy, 757
Civil Rights Act (U.S., 1964), 989

Civil rights movement (U.S.), 989, 991
Civil servants: in middle class, 975
Civil service: in India, 819; in Rome, 167. *See also* Bureaucracy
Civil war(s): in England, 495, 495(*m*); in France, 383, 419; in Greece, 955; for Irish independence, 846; in Netherlands, 420; in Rome, 145–147, 145–150, 153, 180–181; in Russia, 852–854, 907; in Spain, 899; in United States, 765; in Yugoslavia, 1029–1030. *See also* specific locations
Civitas, 228
Clans, Arab, 220, 221, 224
Clare of Assisi, 275
Class conflict: in Germany, 842
Class-consciousness, 674, 676
Classes: in 19th century, 725–726; clothing as sign of, 268, 307–308; consumerism and, 882; in East Bloc, 1006; in England, 703, 705; in Europe after deindustrialization, 1038; factory owners as, 672, 673; French estates as, 621–624; income inequality and, 726, 792–793; in Italy, 917; liberalism and, 691; Marx on, 694–695; in Renaissance, 380–381; after Second World War, 975–976; sumptuary laws and, 307–308. *See also* Estates (social orders); Hierarchy; Nobility; Orders; specific groups
Classical culture: as art topic, 476; in barbarian states, 205; Renaissance and, 364–366, 368–370; Scholastics and, 312–313
Classical Greece: life and culture in, 79–90; warfare in, 75–79
Classical liberalism, 691
Classicism, 696
Claudians (Rome), 164
Claudius (Rome), 164
Cleisthenes (Athens), 74
Clemenceau, Georges, 846, 857
Clement V (Pope), 339
Clement VII (Pope), 340, 407
Cleon (Athens), 77, 84
Cleopatra VII (Egypt), 47, 93, 98, 146(*b*), 146(*i*), 147, 150; Horace on, 161
Clergy: in 14th century, 329, 339, 342; in 18th century, 597; anticlericalism and, 392; Catholic Reformation and, 392, 414, 416; celibacy of, 265, 266, 291; criticism of, 392; education and training of, 414, 416; in France, 621; in Middle Ages, 246, 265–266; during plague, 329; sexual morality of, 265,

266; in social hierarchy, 466; taxation of, 269(d); university students as, 314; on veneration of relics and saints, 208–209(d). *See also* Friars; Monasticism; Monks and monasteries; Pope(s); Priests and priestesses; Religious orders

Clermont (steam ship), 656

Client kingdoms: Rome and, 143

Climate: in 17th century, 466; Bronze Age Collapse and, 32–33; of Italy, 122; in Middle Ages (later period), 323, 324; warming of, 8

Climate change, 466, 1059–1060

Climate Change Conference (Paris), 1060

Clinton, Bill: Bosnia and, 1030

Clive, Robert, 571

Clocks, 508

Clotaire (Merovingians), 229(i)

Cloth and cloth industry. *See* Clothing; Textiles and textile industry

Clothing: class and, 307; consumerism and, 594; for Jews and Muslims, 268, 308; legal distinctions of, 307–308; middle-class, 728. *See also* Fashion; Textiles and textile industry

Clouds, The (Aristophanes), 89

Clover, 545

Clovis (Franks), 205, 228

Cluny, monastic reform and, 270–271

Coal and coal industry: child labor in, 669(i); in England, 649; as fuel, 654, 655; men and women workers in, 668; in Ukraine, 768

Cockerill, William and **John,** 661, 673

Code Napoleon. *See* Civil Code, in France

Code Noir (Black Code), in Saint-Domingue, 638–639

Code of Hammurabi. *See* Hammurabi (Babylon)

Codes of law. *See* Law codes; specific codes

Codex (Justinian), 212

Coercive Acts (1774), 616

Coffee, 591

Coffeehouses, 532

Coins: in Aspendos, 174; Augustus on, 157; of Cleopatra, 146(i); Greek, 70; in Hellenistic world, 105–106; in Lydia, 54; Merovingian, 228; Roman, 143(i), 182, 186, 188(i); silver, 186, 303–304; Venetian, 432

Coke, 655

Colbert, Jean-Baptiste, 446, 477, 478, 556–557

Cold War, 944–954; in 1960s, 985; Berlin Wall and, 965, 982(i); consumerism

during, 959; decolonization and, 966–968; détente and, 985–986, 1010; in East Asia, 952; end of, 1016; Helsinki Accords and, 986; thaw in, 984–986. *See also* Soviet Union

Coleridge, Samuel Taylor, 696, 697; *Lyrical Ballads,* 697

Collaborators, Second World War and, 947

Collective bargaining: in Germany, 787; in United States, 895

Collectivization: of agriculture, 767; in East Bloc, 960; Soviet, 912, 913(d)

College of cardinals, 265, 268, 282

Colleges. *See* Universities

Colloquy of Marburg, 398

Cologne, Germany: bombing of, 938; Rome and, 175; urban planning in, 724

Colonies and colonization, 790(i), 792–793; in 19th century, 791; administration of, 446–447; in Africa, 805–809, 806(m); African slaves in, 565–567; American Revolution and, 613–619; in Australia, 571; British Commonwealth and, 971; British trade and, 560; Caesar and, 148; chartered companies in, 445; Columbian exchange and, 451; decolonization and, 792; disease in, 448, 449(d), 451, 478; Dutch, 560; economic motives for, 793–794, 811; elites in, 565; English, 444–445, 567; exports from, 562–563; fabric costs and, 594; First World War and, 840; after First World War, 858, 859; French, 445–446, 563, 638, 709, 775, 973–974; global inequality and, 792–793; Greek, 70, 71(m), 122; Hellenistic, 101–102; lifestyle in Americas, 449–450; mandate system and, 858, 859; mixed-race people in, 567; nationalism and, 831; neocolonialism and, 974; Phoenician, 40, 40(m); population loss in, 448; racism in, 610–611; Spanish, 446, 447–448, 569–570; trade in, 793–794; Western culture in, 4; women in, 446, 450. *See also* Decolonization; Imperialism; New imperialism; specific colonies

Colonna. *See* Martin V (Pope)

Color Revolutions, 1032

Colossus computer, 953

Columbian exchange, 451, 545

Columbus, Christopher: background of, 437; crusade against Islam and, 280; exploration by, 433, 437–438, 438(m),

440–441(d); motivations of, 437–438, 457

Combination Acts (England, 1799), 676

COMECON (Council for Mutual Economic Assistance), 951

Comedy (drama), 84, 112–113; Latin, 139

Cominform (Communist Information Bureau), 959

Comitatus, Germanic, 198–199

Comites, 228–229

Commandments. *See* Ten Commandments

Commentaries on the Gallic Wars (Caesar), 145–146

Commerce: economic development and, 793; Hellenistic, 105–106; after Hundred Years' War, 337–338; in Jewish society, 45; Roman, 174–175. *See also* Economy; Trade

Commercial agriculture, in Egypt, 798

Commercial revolution, 304, 306

Committee of Public Safety (France), 629, 630, 631

Committee of Union and Progress (CUP), 772

Commodus (Rome), 181

Common law, in England, 260, 282

Common Market, 957–958, 996. *See also* European Economic Community

Common people: diets of, 591; in Enlightenment, 532; in Europe, 575; in France, 621, 625–626; literature of, 588; in Rome, 129. *See also* Lifestyle; Peasants; specific groups

Commons (England), 338

Common Sense (Paine), 588–589, 616

Commonwealth of Independent States, 1017, 1027(m); Putin and, 1032

Communes: northern Italian cities as, 358–359. *See also* Paris Commune (1871)

Communication(s): in global markets, 793; industrialization and, 672; nationalism and, 779; in Persia, 55. *See also* Writing

Communion. *See* Eucharist

Communist Manifesto, The (Marx and Engels), 695

Communist Party and communism: anticolonialism and, 968–971; in China, 971; Cominform and, 959; containment policy toward, 951, 952, 990, 1053; decolonization and, 968; in East Bloc, 943, 951, 952, 959–961, 1005–1007, 1012–1015; end of Soviet Union and, 1017; fascism and, 905–907; after First World War, 856; in France, 899; in Germany, 846, 856;

Communist Party and communism (*continued*)
in Hungary, 855; Marx and, 695; Nazi Germany and, 921, 925; punishment for former leaders and, 1029; in Russia, 827, 852, 853; after Second World War, 955; Soviet Union and, 903, 907–916, 959, 1005; totalitarianism and, 903, 904; in Vietnam, 991. *See also* Bolsheviks; China; Soviet Union; specific locations

Community: of Atlantic world, 565–567; controls over marriage, 578; Greek notion of, 69

Companionate marriage, 733

Company, use of term, 303

Compass, 434–435

Compostela. *See* Santiago de Compostela

Computers, 953

Concentration camps: in Boer War, 809; casualties of Nazi camps, 944; Nazi, 902*(i)*, 922, 932–933, 932*(i)*

Conciliarists, 340–341

Concilium plebis (Rome), 129, 154

Concord: fighting in (1775), 616

Concordat of 1801, 634

Concordat of Bologna, 383, 418

Concordia (Harmony), 402*(i)*

Concubines: clerical, 416; in Egypt, 28

Condition of the Working Class in England, The (Engels), 674

Condorcet, marquis de, 530

Condottieri, 360

Confederate States of America, 765

Confederation: Holy Roman Empire as, 256

Confederation Diet, 688

Confession, of sin, 209, 268, 292, 423

Confessions, The (Augustine), 195

Confirmation, 293

Conflicts. *See* Violence; War(s) and warfare; specific battles and wars

Confraternities, 342

Confucianism, 526–527

Congo, 417, 807, 816, 972–973, 973*(i)*

Congo Free State, 807

Congo River region, 807

Congregationalists, 399

Congress (U.S.), 150–151

Congress of Berlin (1878), 833*(m)*

Congress of People's Deputies (Soviet Union), 1012

Congress of Soviets, 850, 851*(d)*

Congress of Vienna (1814), 682, 682*(m)*, 683–684, 685; balance of power after, 682, 683–685; Crimean War and, 766; Italy after, 757

Congress System, 685

Connecticut, 445

Conquistadors, 433, 444, 566

Conrad, Joseph, 816

Conscious: Freud on, 874

Conscription. *See* Draft (military)

Conservatism: in 1970s and 1980s, 995–1000; in Germany, 842; Holy Alliance and, 687–688; Karlsbad Decrees and, 688; Metternich and, 685–687; nationalism and, 754; Reagan and, 998; in South America, 688–690; Thatcher and, 997–998, 999*(b)*; in West Germany, 998–1000. *See also* Authoritarianism; Right wing

Conservative authoritarianism, 904–905

Conservative Party (England), 776, 890–891, 898, 956, 997–998

Consistory (Geneva), 412

Consolation of Philosophy, The (Boethius), 205

Constable, John, 700

Constantine (Rome), 186–190, 210, 211

Constantine (the African), medical training and, 311

Constantinople (Istanbul): attacks on, 211–212, 213; bishop of Rome and, 187; in First World War, 840; Mongols at, 210–211; Ottoman Turks in, 211–212, 431, 433, 451, 485, 489, 491; sack by Crusaders, 279; trade and, 303; universities in, 506; Vikings in, 243. *See also* Byzantine Empire; Crusades; Eastern Roman Empire

Constituent Assembly: in France, 710; in Prussia, 713; in Russia, 851, 852

Constitution: in Austrian Empire, 710–711; in EU, 1035–1036; in European countries, 772; in France, 626, 630–631, 709, 755, 756; in German Confederation, 710–711, 713; of German Empire, 781; in Germany, 713; in Haiti, 643; in Hungary, 778; in Italy, 757; in Japan, 822; in Prussia, 712, 713, 763; in Rome, 154; in Russia, 769, 847; in Soviet Union, 1017; in United States, 150–151, 399–401, 492, 523, 617–618, 619

Constitutional Charter (France), 707, 708

Constitutional Convention (U.S.), 617

Constitutionalism, 466, 492, 499

Constitutional liberalism: in Prussia, 713

Constitutional monarchy: in England, 497–499, 703; in France, 626; in Kingdom of the Two Sicilies, 688;

National Assembly (France) and, 626; in Prussia, 712; in Russia, 769; in Spain, 688. *See also* Parliamentary monarchy

Consuls (Rome), 126, 129; Caesar as, 147

Consumer goods: in East Bloc, 960, 993; long-distance trade in, 428–429, 431–432; after Second World War, 954; in Soviet Union, 962–963, 1011. *See also* Goods and services

Consumer revolution: in 18th century, 587, 592–596; in 1950s, 958–959, 979

Consumers and consumerism: in 1960s, 987–988; in East Bloc, 993; after First World War, 881–885; self-identity of, 592–593

Consumption: in Soviet Union, 914

Contagious disease. *See* Disease

Contagious Diseases Acts (England, 1864 to 1886), 737

Containment policy, 951, 952, 990, 1053

Continental Army (U.S.), 619

Continental Congress: First (1774), 616; Second (1776), 616

Continental Europe: industrialization in, 659–661, 660*(m)*; Nazis in, 928; rural industry in, 553; after Verdun Treaty, 240, 240*(m)*. *See also* Europe; specific locations

Continental System: of Napoleon, 635, 636

Contraception. *See* Birth control

Contubernium (marriage-like relationship), 136

Convents: lifestyle in, 271, 273–274; Merovingian, 229*(i)*. *See also* Monasticism; Monks and monasteries; Nuns; specific orders

Conversion (Christian), 178, 567; of barbarians, 189*(m)*, 190, 206, 207–210; of Clovis, 205; of Constantine, 188; of Huguenots to Catholicism, 520–521; of indigenous people, 457; of Irish, 206–207; of Jews, 387, 538*(b)*, 538*(i)*; process of, 207–210; of Slavs, 243; of women, 193–194. *See also* Christianity

Conversion (Islam), 222–223

Conversos, 387

Conway, Anne, 519

Cook, James, 527, 571

Cooperatives: Owen and, 677

Coordination policy: in Nazi Germany, 922

Copenhagen: environmental protests in, 1004

Copernicus, Nicolaus, and Copernican hypothesis, 113, 506, 509–510

Copper: for coins, 303–304; trade in, 12, 24, 455

Corcyra, Athens and, 76

Córdoba: caliphate in, 258; as cultural center, 225–226, 234, 313, 506; growth of, 299

Corinne (Staël), 699(b)

Corinth, 62; Athens and, 76; Rome and, 135

Corn Laws (England, 1815), 703, 704(i), 793

Coronation, of Charlemagne, 234–235

Corporate banks, 662

Corporations: industrialization and, 727; limited liability of, 662. *See also* Business; Economy; Guilds and guild system

Corps of engineers: Assyrian, 48

Corpus Juris Civilis, 212–213

Corsica: Rome and, 132

Cort, Henry, 655

Cortes (Spanish parliament), 338, 385

Cortés, Hernán, 442–443

Cosmology, of Aristotle, 508–509, 509(i)

Cosmonauts, 953

Cossacks (Russia), 486, 487, 489, 770(d)

Cottage industry, 552, 669–670; in England, 648(m); industrious revolution and, 555; putting-out system in, 552–553; water frame and, 651; workers in, 555, 665

Cotton and cotton industry: Britain and, 793; consumption of cotton goods and, 672; in England, 651; in India, 793; slavery and, 564, 677, 765, 765(m); in United States, 765, 765(m); workers for, 664–665. *See also* Textiles and textile industry

Cotton Mills and Factories Act (Britain, 1819), 667

Council for Mutual Economic Assistance (COMECON), 951

Council of Elders (France), 632

Council of Europe, 957

Council of 500 (France), 632

Councils: Athenian, 74; Spartan, 72

Councils (Christian): of bishops, 180; of Constance (1414–1418), 341, 342; at Pisa (1409), 341; of Trent, 414–416

Counterculture, 984, 988–990, 992–993

Counter-Reformation (Catholic Reformation), 413, 414–417, 601

Countryside. *See* Rural areas

Counts: Carolingian, 232, 246; Merovingian, 228–229. *See also* Nobility; specific individuals

Coup d'état: by Napoleon I, 632; by Napoleon III, 755; in Soviet Union, 1017; by Young Turks, 772

Courbet, Gustav, 748

Court (legal): in medieval towns, 475–476; papal curia and, 268. *See also* Judiary and judicial system

Court (royal): Merovingian, 230

Courtier, The (Castiglione), 366–367

Courtiers. *See* Nobility

Courtly love, 316–317(d)

Court of Star Chamber (England), 384

Courtship: middle-class, 733

Covenant: between Yahweh and Jews, 43

Cowpox, 605

Cowrie shells: trade in, 571

"Cradles of civilization," 5–6

Cradock, Fanny, 594

Craft guilds, 299–301

Crafts. *See* Art(s); specific types

Cranmer, Thomas, 408, 409

Crassus (Rome), 145, 147

Creation myths: Mesopotamian, 16

Crécy, battle at, 335

Credit: consumer goods and, 279; after Second World War, 958

Cremation, Christianity and, 178

Creoles, 565, 567; Enlightenment and, 570; in Saint-Domingue, 638, 639; in South America, 688, 689–690

Crescent of Islam, 222

Crete, 62, 63(m); Minoans in, 63–64, 64(i); Mycenaean attack on, 65

Crimea: Russia and, 766, 1026, 1027(m), 1032

Crime and criminals: in former East Bloc, 1029; fur-collar, 351; gangs of smugglers and, 1044; Hammurabi on, 21–22; in Middle Ages (High), 261, 261(i), 309; in Russia, 1023; war crimes and, 947. *See also* Law(s); Law codes

Crimean Tartars, in Russia, 536

Crimean War, 766, 766(m)

Crisis of the third century (Rome), 181

Croatia: "Dance of Death" in, 331(i); in EU, 1035; human rights and, 1061; Rome and, 173; Serbs in, 1029, 1030

Croatians (Croats), 243, 686, 712, 778

Croesus (Lydia), 54

Crompton, Samuel, 651, 652–653(b), 653(i)

Cromwell, Oliver, 495–496, 560, 650

Cromwell, Thomas, 408

Crop rotation, 193, 287, 288, 544, 545, 546; in England, 547

Crops: in 17th century, 545; ancient, 8–9; in Columbian exchange, 451; in Muslim world, 226, 245. *See also* Agriculture; Farms and farming; specific crops

Crosby, Alfred, 794

Cross-cultural connections. *See* Intellectual thought; Trade; specific cultures

Crowd, The (Le Bon), 747

Crucifixion of Jesus, 177

Cruel sports, 731

Crusades, 278(m), 296; Albigensian, 281; background and motives of, 276–277; consequences of, 279–280; course of, 277–279; Frederick II and, 258; holy war and, 258, 276, 277, 280; Jews attacked during, 280; Muslims and, 277, 278–279, 280; Richard I in, 260–261; women in, 278

Crystal Palace, 657, 716(i), 717

Cuba, 438, 440(d), 442; Chinese immigrants in, 802

Cuban missile crisis, 965–966

Cubism, 826(i)

Cugoana, Ottobah, 529

Cult(s): of Duce, 919; of Isis, 109–110; of Roma et Augustus, 157; of Roman emperor, 179; ruler, 98; of saints, 292–293

Cultural cleansing, 1055

Cultural exchange: in Rome, 172; along Silk Road, 106. *See also* Columbian exchange

Cultural relativism, 460

Culture(s): in ancient Near East, 13(m); Assyrian, 49–50; in classical Greece, 79–83, 88–90; of Crete, 64; of early Middle Ages, 235–240; in East Bloc, 993; in Fertile Crescent, 22–23; in French Revolution, 631; Greek, 66, 102–103; Greek influence on, 138–140; Greek in Hellenistic cities, 102; Hellenistic, 93, 108; after Hundred Years' War, 351; immigrants and, 1046; leisure, recreation, and, 589–590; mass, 881–883; middle-class, 727–728; Minoan, 64; Mycenaean, 64–65; nation building and, 779; Nubian, 38; Orientalism in, 815–816; Paleolithic, 7; Persian, 56–57; Phoenician, 40; politicization of, 879; popular, 587–590; Roman, 138–140, 159–160, 172; Soviet, 914–915. *See also* Art(s); Classical culture; Intellectual thought; Literature; specific locations

Cuneiform writing, 40; Akkadian, 20, 22; Assyrian, 50; Mesopotamian commerce, culture, and, 23; Sumerian, 15, 15(f)

Cure for Love, The (Ovid), 163

Curia, papal, 268

Curie, Marie and **Pierre,** 873

Currency: Bretton Woods agreement and, 957; common, 779; cowrie shells as, 571; euro as, 1034; in France, 626; in Germany, 890. *See also* Coins; Euro; Money

Curriculum: in elementary schools, 586

Cuzco, 444

Cybele (goddess), 101(i)

Cyril (missionary), 215

Cyrillic alphabet, 215

Cyrus the Great (Persia), 42, 52–55, 53(b), 53(i)

Czechoslovakia: Brandt and, 985; dissent in, 1007; economy in, 993; after First World War, 855, 855(m), 857, 858–859, 886; Germany and, 888(b), 985; invasion of, 994, 994(i); in Little Entente, 886; Nazis and, 926, 927; Prague Spring in, 994, 1007; after Second World War, 886; separatism in, 1004; Sudetenland and, 927; Velvet Revolution in, 1015. *See also* Czech Republic; East Bloc

Czech people, 243; in Austrian Empire, 686, 712, 778; Nazi Germany and, 927

Czech Republic, 1028; Hus and, 341; after Soviet Union, 1028. *See also* Bohemia

Dadaism, 877–878

Da Gama, Vasco, 430(i), 432, 435

Daily life. *See* Lifestyle

D'Alembert, Jean le Rond, 523–524, 530, 532

Dalí, Salvador, 878, 879(i)

Dalmatia, 173, 232

Damascus: Paul and, 177–178; Umayyad capital at, 224

Dance of Death, 331, 331(i)

Dancing, 309

Danegeld (tax), 242

Danelaw, 242–243

Danish People's Party, 1048

Danish phase, of Thirty Years' War, 469

Dante Alighieri, 352, 353

Danton, Georges Jacques, 628, 631

Danube River region, 210–211, 770; Rome and, 157, 167, 172, 181

Danzig, 858; as Gdansk, 1009

Dardanelles, in First World War, 840

Dar es Salaam, missionary school in, 813(i)

Darius I (Persia), 55, 56, 57(i)

Darius III (Persia), Alexander the Great and, 94, 96(i)

Dark Age (Greece), 62

Dark Ages: Merovingian period as, 228; Petrarch on, 364

Darwin, Charles, 745–746

Dating method, Christian, 238(b)

Datini, Francesco, 305(b), 305(i)

Daumier, Honoré, 748, 748(i)

Dauphin (France), 336

David (Michelangelo), 374(i)

David of Bethlehem (Israel), 42, 176

Dawes, Charles G., 889

Dawes Plan, 889

Day of Judgment: Muslim, 223, 226

D-Day landing. *See* Normandy

Dean, James, 979

Deane, John, 488(d)

Death: in Christianity, 296–298; from famine, 324, 324(i); First World War and, 843. *See also* Black Death; Mortality

Death camps. *See* Concentration camps; Holocaust

Death rate. *See* Mortality

"Debate about women," 379

De Beers Mining Company, 808(b)

Debt: Egyptian, 798; in France, 620; in Rome, 131; from Seven Years' War, 614

Debt crisis: in Greece (2015), 1036, 1057

Debt peonage, 563

Decameron, The (Boccaccio), 329

Decentralization: of Europe, 251; feudalism and, 246–247; of former Carolingian Empire, 246–247, 251

De-Christianization, in France, 631

Decius (Rome), 179

Declaration of Independence (U.S.), 612, 616

Declaration of Pillnitz, 627

Declaration of the Rights of Man and of the Citizen (France), 611, 625

Declaration of the Rights of Woman (de Gouges), 626

Decolonization, 792, 966–974; in Africa, 966, 967(m), 972–974; anti-Western sentiments and, 1053; in Asia, 934, 967(m), 968–971; Cold War and, 966; of Congo, 972, 973(i); Fanon on, 968, 969(d); in India, 970–971; after Second World War, 934. *See also* Anticolonialism; Colonies and colonization; Imperialism; specific locations

Decretum (Gratian), 311

Deductive reasoning, 516–517, 521

Deeds of Otto, The (Hroswitha of Gandersheim), 256

Deffand, Madame du, 530

Deficit financing: in Germany, 842

Degas, Edgar, 877

De Gaulle, Charles, 955, 958, 974, 984–985, 992

Degenerate art, Nazis on, 922

De Gouges, Olympe, 626, 631

Dei, Benedetto, 359

Deindustrialization, of Europe, 664, 1038

Deism, 523, 568–569, 599–600

Deities. *See* Gods and goddesses; specific deities

Delacroix, Eugène, 698; *Massacre at Chios,* 702(i)

Delian League, 76, 79

Delos, 76

Delphi: Pythian games at, 88

Delphic oracle, 54, 100

Deme (land unit), 74

Demesne, 287

Demeter (goddess), 87

Democracy: in Athens, 73–74; in England, 776; after First World War, 856, 889–891; Greek, 69–70

Democracy in America (Tocqueville), 710

Democratic movements: in eastern Europe (1989), 1013(m); in Soviet Union, 1017

Democratic National Convention (Chicago, 1968), 991

Democratization: in Soviet Union, 1012

Democritus (Greece), 88, 111

Demography: in 18th century, 550–551; crisis of, 550; population decline and, 1042. *See also* Population

Demonstrations. *See* Protest(s)

Demos, in Athens, 74

Denazification: after Second World War, 947

Denmark: Christianity in, 280; in Common Market, 996; environmental protests in, 1004; Nazis and, 928; Protestantism in, 407; Russia and, 487; Saxons from, 202; Schleswig-Holstein and, 761; Social Democrats in, 955; Thirty Years' War and, 469; Vikings from, 240, 241; West Africa and, 446. *See also* Scandinavia

Denmark-Norway, Protestantism in, 407

Dentistry, 727

Depressions. *See* Economy; Great Depression

Deregulation: of guilds, 558–559

Descartes, René, 516–517, 521

Desertion, in First World War, 846, 847, 848

Dessalines, Jean Jacques, 643

De-Stalinization: in East Bloc states, 962–964, 964–965

Détente, 985–986, 1010

Determinism, of Spinoza, 521

Developed socialism, decline of, 1005–1007

Developing world: economic slowdown in, 996

Devolution: human, 6–7

Dhimmis (protected people), 226

Dialects, 691

Dialogue on the Two Chief Systems of the World (Galileo), 518

Diamonds, in Africa, 808(b)

Diasporas, of displaced ethnic groups, 1046

Diaz, Bartholomew, 433, 437

Dictators and dictatorships: Caesar and, 147; Clemenceau and, 846; Communist, 950–951; in Congo, 973; military, in First World War, 842; Napoleon I as, 632; radical totalitarian, 904–905; radio and, 885; in Rome, 126; Second World War and, 903–939; in Soviet Union, 959; Sulla and, 145. *See also* specific locations and individuals

Diderot, Denis: Catherine the Great and, 534–535; on China, 527; *Encyclopedia* by, 523–524; portrait of, 535(i); "Supplement to Bougainville's Voyage," 528–529(d)

Dido (Carthage), 161

Diet (food): bread in, 290, 451, 467–468; Carolingian, 234; of common people, 590–591; Greek, 83; Hellenistic, 106–107; imports in, 591; Jewish laws for, 45–46; Muslim laws for, 223; of peasants, 289, 467–468; in Rome, 169; Sumerian, 14. *See also* Food(s)

Diet (political): in Germany, 338; in Hungary, 413–414; Imperial (1530), 406; of Speyer (1529), 397; of Worms (1521), 395, 424

Digest (Justinian), 212

Digital age, 1039–1042

Digitalization, 1039–1040

Dijon, revolt in, 472

Dioceses: Christian, 191; Roman, 186

Diocletian (Rome), 179, 186–190, 191

Diodoros Siculus (historian), 104, 105, 115

Diogenes Laertes, 111

Dionysus (god), 81, 88

Diphtheria, 723

Diplomacy: before First World War, 828–830, 831, 833–834; gunboat, 797, 821, 822; in Italian Renaissance, 362; Roman, 126. *See also* Alliance(s); Balance of power

Directory (France), 633

Disabled people: after First World War, 862–863, 863(i); Nazis and, 906, 923

Disarmament: Nazi Germany and, 925

Discourses on Livy (Machiavelli), 368

Discovery. *See* Age of Discovery; Expansion; Voyages

Discrimination: in India, 820. *See also* specific groups

Discus Thrower (statue), 81(i)

Disease: in American colonies, 448, 449(d), 451, 478; bacterial revolution and, 722–723; Black Death as, 326–327; in Columbian exchange, 451; in Egypt, 23; epidemic, 550; famine and, 468; germ theory of, 722; Hellenistic medicine and, 117, 311–312; infectious, 451; medieval treatment of, 237, 290; miasmatic theory of, 722; plague and, 326–332, 468; public health and, 721; in Rome, 170; in wars, 116–117. *See also* specific conditions

Displaced persons (DPs): after Second World War, 944(i), 945–946. *See also* Refugees

Disraeli, Benjamin, 776

Dissection, 117, 170

Dissent: in Czechoslovakia, 1007, 1008(d); in Nazi Germany, 924–925; in Poland, 1007–1010

Dissidents, in Russia, 769

Distribution of income, 725–726; in 19th century, 725–726

Diversity. *See* specific groups

Divided Heaven (Wolf), 993

Divine Comedy (Dante), 352

Divine Office, 273, 306

Divine right of kings, 474, 494, 497. *See also* Absolute monarchy and absolutism

Division of labor, 10–11; sexual, 666–669; Smith, Adam, on, 557, 558(d)

Divorce: in Egypt, 27–28; in France, 626; in Middle Ages, 266, 295; in Protestantism, 402–403; right to, 1001; women and, 978

Doctors. *See* Medicine; Physicians

Doctors Without Borders, 1037

Doctor Zhivago (Pasternak), 964

Dogmatic school of medicine, 117

Dole, Orwell on, 896–897(d)

Dollar (U.S.), 995

Doll's House, A (Ibsen), 734

Dome of the Rock, 221(i)

Domesday Book (England), 253, 255

Domestication: of animals, 10; of plants, 8–9

Domestic service and servants. *See* Servants

Domestic sphere: family in, 556

Dominicans (religious order), 274, 457, 567

Domitian (Rome), 165

Donatello, 374

Donetsk People's Republic, 1032

Dorians, 66

Dostoyevsky, Fyodor, 871

Double monasteries, 236, 239

Dowry: in Babylon, 21; in Middle Ages, 264; in Rome, 136; in Sumer, 18–19

DPs. *See* Displaced persons

Draco (Athens), 73

Draconian (term), 73

Draft (military): in Egypt, 798; before First World War, 831; in First World War, 842; in France, 631; in new nation-states, 779; in Prussia, 484; in Rome, 126, 142; in Vietnam War, 991

Drama: Greek, 81–83; Hellenistic, 112–113; music halls, vaudeville, and, 731–732; vernacular, 316

Dresden, 938

Dreyfus, Alfred, and Dreyfus affair, 776, 780, 782(b)

Drinking. *See* Alcohol and alcoholism; Water

Drone attacks, by U.S., 1053

Droz, Gustav, 739, 740

Drugs, counterculture and, 990

Druids, 200

Dual Alliance, 828

Dual government: in Nazi Germany, 921–922

Dualism: Cartesian, 517; for ethnic groups, 351; in Manichaeism, 194; in Zoroastrianism, 56

Dual monarchy. *See* Austria-Hungary

Dubček, Alexander, 994, 1007

Duce, cult of, 919(i)

Duchy, 332. *See also* specific duchies

Du Coudray (Madame), 604

Due process of law, in Magna Carta, 261, 494

Dukes, Merovingian, 229

"Dulce et Decorum Est" (Owen), 838–839(d)

Duma (Russia), 769, 847, 848

Dunkirk, 928

Dürer, Albrecht, 374–375

Durkheim, Émile, 747

Dutch: Asia and, 456; in Cape Town, 456, 805; colonization by, 805, 810; decolonization and, 968–969; Navigation Acts and, 560; Spain and, 456, 480, 499; trade by, 456, 491. *See also* Dutch Republic; Holland; Netherlands

Dutch East India Company, 454, 456, 570

Dutch East Indies: independence for, 968–969. *See also* East Indies; Indonesia

Dutch Republic: in 17th century, 499–500; agriculture in, 545, 546–547; constitutionalism in, 466, 469, 499; England and, 560; family life in, 499(i), 500; France and, 478, 634; French Huguenots in, 500; government of, 499–500; religious toleration in, 500, 520–521; rural industry in, 553; shipbuilding in, 500. *See also* Dutch; Netherlands; United Provinces

Dutch West India Company, 454, 456

Duties. *See* Tariffs

Duties of Man, The (Mazzini), 759(d)

Dutschke, Rudi, 992

Dyes: synthetic, 744

Dynasties: in Egypt, 24, 28, 97–98; patriarchal hereditary, 17. *See also* Hundred Years' War; specific dynasties

Dzhugashvili, Joseph. *See* Stalin, Joseph

Early Middle Ages, 218(i). *See also* Middle Ages

Earth: Aristotle on, 508–509; circumference of, 115; circumnavigation of, 439. *See also* Astronomy; Universe

Earth-centered universe, 113

Earthquakes: Mycenaean, 66

East: concepts of, 4; Hellenistic, 139; Roman cities in, 174. *See also* Asia; Middle East; Near East; specific locations

East Africa: Germany and, 807, 809, 813(i); *Homo sapiens* in, 7; slave trade and, 431

East Asia: economies in, 996; First World War and, 840; imperialism and, 967

East Berlin: Berlin Wall and, 965; strike in, 961

East Bloc: in 1960s, 993; Brezhnev Doctrine in, 994–995; classes in, 975; collapse of communism in, 1012–1015; de-Stalinization in, 964–965; economies in, 993; end of Soviet Union and, 1017; EU and, 1034–1035; lifestyle in, 959–961, 963–964; pollution in, 1002–1003; Prague Spring in, 994; reforms and rebellions in, 984; refugees from, 1043; after Second World War, 4–5, 943, 944, 949–952, 959–961; show trials in, 960; after Soviet Union, 1026–1029; state and society in, 1005–1007; western Europe and, 985; worker migration in, 976; World Bank, IMF, and, 1037. *See also* Berlin Wall; Eastern Europe; Soviet Union; specific locations

East-central Europe, Nazis and, 930–931, 931(m)

Eastern Christian Church. *See* Orthodox Church

Eastern Europe: absolutism in, 471, 480–484; Black Death in, 328; Christianity in, 280; democratic movements in (1989), 1013(m); German settlers in, 281; Jews and, 781, 781(i), 783; lifestyle in, 942(i); marriage in, 576; nationalism in, 692; Nazis and, 928; peasants in, 467, 480–481, 545; Reformation in, 407, 413–414; refugees from, 1043; in Second World War, 930–931; serfdom in, 467, 480–481; Slavs and Vikings in, 219, 243–244; society in former East Bloc, 1028–1029. *See also* East Bloc; Europe; Orthodox Church; specific locations

Eastern front: in First World War, 837–841; in Second World War, 938

Eastern Roman Empire, 205–206, 210, 211; plague in, 326. *See also* Byzantine Empire

Eastern world, 4

Easter Rising, 846

East German Communist Party, 1016

East Germany, 952; Brandt and, 985; economy in, 993; Hungarian border with, 1014; New Economic System in, 993; rebellion in (1953), 960(i); after Second World War, 959; Soviets and, 965; West German reunification with, 1000, 1015–1016. *See also* East Bloc; Germany

East India Company: British, 562(i), 570, 571, 616, 651, 819; Dutch, 570

East Indies: Dutch and, 456, 810, 968–969; passage to, 559. *See also* Indonesia

East Prussia, 781

East Slavs, 243

Eating: utensils for, 303. *See also* Diet (food); Food

Ebbo (Reims archbishop), 237(i)

Eburacum (York), 172

Ecbatana (Hamadan, Iran), 52

Ecclesia (Athenian assembly of citizens), 74

Ecclesiastical History (Orderic Vitalis), 291

Ecclesiastical History of the English People (Bede), 238(b)

Eck, Johann, 395

Eckhart (Meister), 343(b), 343(i)

Economic Consequences of the Peace, The (Keynes), 886

Economic liberalism, 557–559, 691

Economic miracle, 954

Economic planning. *See* Planned economies

Economics: European unity and, 957. *See also* Keynes, John Maynard; Smith, Adam

Economy: in 17th century, 468, 477; in 1960s, 986; Asian financial crisis and, 1023; in Atlantic region, 560, 562–563; Black Death and, 330; of China, 429; in East Bloc, 993, 1006–1007; Egypt-Byblos, 39(d); energy prices and, 996; in England, 886; equality in, 612; European expansion and, 432–433; European recovery in Great Depression, 898–899; in First World War, 841–842; in former Communist countries, 1028; in France, 624, 625, 709–710, 756, 890; in French Revolution, 629–630, 632; in Germany, 886, 887, 890, 924; global, 793–794, 1033–1034; Great Depression and, 891–899; Greek, 70, 75; of Hellenistic world, 104–107; immigration and, 804(d); in India, 820; mercantilism and, 477; moral, 590; Mycenaean, 65; New Imperialism and, 811; Ottoman, 771–773; plantation, in U.S., 764–765; in Poland, 1014; in Roman Empire, 181–182; in Russia, 767, 768, 847, 1023–1024; Soviet, 907–908, 1011; Thirty Years' War and, 469; in western Europe, 986, 995–997; women workers and, 978. *See also* Capitalism; Commerce; Economics; Globalization; Great Depression; Socialism; Trade; specific issues and locations

Edessa, 277

Edict of Milan, 188

Edict of Nantes, 419, 473, 500

Edict of Restitution, 469

Edison, Thomas, movies and, 883–884

Edo (Tokyo, Japan). *See* Tokyo

Education: in Byzantine Empire, 214; children and, 581–587; church clergy and, 597; of craftsmen, 300; elementary schools and, 586–587; in France, 755, 775; free, 772, 775, 779; in Hebrew society, 44; of immigrants, 1046; middle class and, 727; in monasteries and convents, 214; nationalism and, 775; of nobility, 263–264; for physicians, 603; in Renaissance, 366–367; in Rome, 138, 169; after Second World War, 979; in Turkey, 861; underclass and, 1038; universities and, 746; for women, 530, 915. *See also* Literacy; Schools; Universities

Education of a Christian Prince, The (Erasmus), 370

Edward (Black Prince, England), 335

Edward (Canute's heir, England), 252

Edward I (England), 269, 280

Edward II (England), 325, 333(i)

Edward III (England), 332–333, 333(i), 335, 338, 353, 358

Edward IV (England), 384

Edward VI (England), 408(i), 409

"Effective occupation" of African territory, 807

Eggley, Ann, 670–671(d)

Ego, 874

Egypt, 23–32; agriculture in, 23, 24, 26, 798; Alexander the Great in, 94; anticolonialism in, 968; Arab Spring in, 1042; *Book of the Dead* in, 25–26; Cleopatra VII in, 146(b); decline of, 37–38; dynasties in, 24; empire in, 28; England and, 798–799, 805, 809; families in, 27–28; First Intermediate Period in, 24, 25; France and, 633,

798; gods and goddesses in, 24, 25–26, 30; Greeks in, 102; Hatshepsut in, 29, 31(b), 31(i); Hebrew Exodus from, 41; Hittites and, 30–32, 37; Hyksos in, 28–29; industrialization in, 663; iron in, 37; Islam and, 222; kingdoms in, 24–25; Kush and, 38; labor in, 26; lifestyle in, 27(d); marriage in, 27–28, 30; Middle Kingdom in, 25; modernization of, 771, 798; Napoleon in, 797; Nasser in, 968, 972; nationalist revolution in, 798–799; Nefertiti in, 30, 31(b), 31(i); New Kingdom in, 2(i), 25, 28–30, 38, 65; Nile River region and, 23–24, 25, 26; Nubia and, 25, 28; Old Kingdom in, 25; Ottoman Empire and, 770, 771, 797–798; Ptolemies in, 103; revolution in (2011), 1055; Roman conquest of, 93; as Roman province, 146(b); Saladin in, 279; Sea Peoples and, 37; Second Intermediate Period in, 28; Six-Day War and, 995; society in, 26; Third Intermediate Period in, 25, 37–38; trade in, 24, 39(d), 430–431; unification of, 24; wars in, 30; writing in, 26. *See also* Ptolemies (Egypt); specific dynasties

Egyptian Nationalist Party, 798

Einhard, on Charlemagne, 231, 234, 235

Einsatzgruppen, 932

Einstein, Albert, 505, 873

Eisenhower, Dwight, 938–939, 990

Eisenstein, Sergei, 884

El Alamein, Second Battle of, 937

Elba: Napoleon at, 637–638, 684, 685

Elbe River, 939

Eleanor of Aquitaine, 254, 260–261, 332

"Elect," Calvinists and, 412

Elections: in England, 704; in France (1797), 632; in Germany, 921; in Hungary, 1014; in Russia, 851–852; after Second World War, 949; in Soviet Union, 1012

Electors: in Holy Roman Empire, 404; of Saxony, 399

Electricity, 744; streetcars and, 725

Elementary Forms of Religious Life, The (Durkheim), 747

Elementary schools, 586–587, 775

Elements of Geometry, The (Euclid), 113, 227

Eleonore of Portugal, 404

Elephantine papyri, 45(d)

Eleusinian mysteries, 87

Eliot, George (Mary Ann Evans), 748–749

Eliot, T. S., 872, 880

Elisabeth-Charlotte (Germany), "Letter from Versailles," 475(d)

Elites: colonial, 565; consumer economy and, 427; fashion and, 594; in France, 634; governing, 773; in Hellenistic cities, 99, 103; in India, 820; labor, 729; mixed-race populations in, 566; in multinational empires, 687; non-Western, 791; in Persian government, 55; recreation and, 590; wealth gap and, 726. *See also* Aristocracy; Nobility

Elizabeth (Bohemia), 519

Elizabeth I (England): on "blackamoores," 379; female rulers and, 382, 493; literature under, 403; religion and, 409–410, 410(d); Spanish Armada and, 411, 411(i); Tudor dynasty and, 408(i), 409

Ellis, Sarah Stickney, *Women of England, The: Their Social Duties and Domestic Habits,* 675(d)

Elmo (Saint), 293

Emancipation: of Jews, 781; of slaves in French territories, 641. *See also* Abolition

Emigration: from Asia, 802–803; from Europe, 799–800, 800(f), 801–802; of Jews, 781(i), 783; origins and destinations of (1851–1960), 801(f); use of term, 799. *See also* Immigrants and immigration; Migrants and migration

Emile, or On Education (Rousseau), 585

Emperors: barracks, 181; Charlemagne as, 234–235; cult of Roman, 179; Friedrich Wilhelm and, 713; origin of term, 147; in Rome, 155. *See also* Empire(s); Holy Roman Empire; specific emperors and empires

Empire(s): in Asia and Pacific region, 571; Assyrian, 35–36, 46–50; Athenian, 76; Austrian, 686; of Charlemagne, 232, 232(m); Communist, 909, 909(m); decolonization and, 966–974; in eastern Mediterranean, 29(m); Egyptian, 28; French-English competition over, 560–562; in Mesopotamia, 19–23; Muslim, 508; Neo-Babylonian, 51–52; New Imperialism and, 803–805; Ottoman, 508; Spartan, 78. *See also* Colonies and colonization; Decolonization; Emperors; Imperialism; New imperialism; specific locations and rulers

Empiricism, 516

Employment: in putting-out system, 553; in rural textile industry, 554; after Second World War, 958, 975–976; of women, 555, 741, 842, 843. *See also* Labor; Unemployment; Workers

Enabling Act (Germany, 1933), 921

Enclosure, 546, 547, 548*(d)*, 649

Encomienda system, 447–448, 449

Encyclopedia (Diderot and d'Alembert), 523–524, 529, 530, 534–535

Energy: for industry, 718; new physics and, 873; nuclear power plants and, 1003; prices of, 996; Russian controls over, 1059. *See also* Steam power; specific sources

Energy crisis: in East Bloc, 1006

Engels, Friedrich, 674, 694

Engine. *See* Steam power

Engineering, 727; Roman, 128

England (Britain): Africa and, 805, 806*(m)*, 807–809, 808*(b)*, 972; agriculture in, 545, 547; Asia and, 571, 810, 810*(m)*; Australia and, 571; Black Death and, 345; Bristol in, 542*(i)*; capitalism in, 676; Catholic Church in, 340, 393, 408–409; China trade and, 795–797; cities in, 718–721; civil war in, 493–495, 495*(m)*; class differences in, 779; clocks in, 306; colonies of, 444–445, 567, 805; common law in, 260, 282; constitutional monarchy in, 466, 469; Contagious Diseases Acts in, 737; cottage industry in, 648*(m)*; Crimean War and, 766; deaths in Second World War, 944–945; debt in, 1056; dole in, 896–897*(d)*; economic recovery in, 898–899; Egypt and, 798, 799, 805; emigrants from, 800, 800*(f)*; enclosure in, 546, 547; Exchequer and, 253; exploration by, 439–440; exports by, 562, 793; famine in, 325; before First World War, 830, 831; First World War and, 834, 837, 837*(m)*, 840, 843, 846; after First World War, 885, 886, 890; foreign investment by, 794, 795*(m)*; France and, 253–254, 332–339, 334*(m)*, 383, 478, 560–562, 634, 830; in Great Depression, 893, 896–897*(d)*; Great Schism and, 340; guilds in, 557; hospitals in, 291; Hundred Years' War and, 332–339, 334*(m)*, 337–339, 345; illegitimacy in, 578; immigrants in, 801, 998; imperialism by, 805; income in, 725, 792*(f)*; India and, 571,

819–821, 970; industrialization in, 648–658, 659*(f)*; IRA and, 1004–1005; Ireland and, 497, 777, 831, 846; Irish famine and, 706; iron industry in, 655–656; Jews in, 294, 386–387, 781*(i)*, 801; labor in, 345, 675–677, 786; Labour Party in, 984; laissez-faire in, 691; laws in, 311; liberalism in, 703–705; literacy in, 353; mandates of, 858, 859–860; maritime trade of, 560; medicinal plants in, 603; mercantilism of, 496, 560; mortality decline in, 722*(f)*; movies in, 884; Muslims in, 1048; Napoleon and, 634, 635; Navigation Acts of, 560; navy of, 471; Nazi Germany and, 925; neoliberalism in, 997–999; nonagricultural workers in, 670; Normandy and, 250*(i)*, 252–254, 335; Ottoman Empire and, 771, 859–860; peasants in, 325; plague in, 327; politics after Second World War, 956–957; Poor Law (1834) in, 721; population growth in, 549*(f)*, 657; Protestantism in, 407; public health movement in, 721; Puritans in, 494; railroads in, 656, 660, 660*(m)*; Realism in, 748–749; religious divides in, 493–495; reparations after First World War and, 857; Restoration in, 497, 498, 498*(d)*; rights in, 261; rivalry with Germany, 830; Romantics in, 696–698, 700; Scientific Revolution and, 516, 517, 518; Second World War and, 927, 928, 937, 938–939; servants in, 730; Seven Years' War and, 613; silver in, 303; slave trade and, 478, 479*(m)*, 677; socialists in, 787; social welfare in, 776; Spain and, 478; spinners in, 555; streetcars in, 725; taxation in, 253, 336, 346; taxation of American colonies by, 615–616; in Third Coalition, 634; Thirty Years' War and, 469, 494; trade and, 432; transportation in, 648*(m)*; in Triple Entente, 829*(m)*, 830; Turkey and, 860; urban areas in, 718–721; U.S. independence from, 616–617; Vikings in, 242–243, 245, 252; voting rights in, 776–777; welfare state in, 998; William of Normandy in, 252–253; workers in, 665. *See also* Britain; British East India Company; Decolonization; First World War; London; Parliament (England); Second World War; specific dynasties

English East India Company. *See* British East India Company

English language, 30

English Peasants' Revolt (1381), 346

Enheduana (Ur), 20

ENIAC (Electronic Numerical Integrator and Computer), 953

Enkidu (Sumer), 18–19*(d)*

Enlightened absolutism, 532–539, 569

Enlightenment: Atlantic, 568–570; Catholic clergy and, 598; childhood and, 585; coffeehouses in, 532; culture in, 532; defined, 520; early, 520–522; Industrial Revolution and, 648; Jews in, 538*(b)*, 538*(i)*, 539, 539*(m)*; literature and, 588–589; Methodism and, 599–600; philosophes in, 522–524, 522*(i)*; political ideas and, 610; race and, 527–529, 780; religious tolerance and, 521–522; rise and spread of, 520–526; science in, 505–506, 519; Scottish, 557, 568; women in, 519, 523, 530–531

Enlil (god), 14, 16, 17

Ennius, 139

Enslaved peoples. *See* Slaves and slavery

Entertainment: leisure, recreation, and, 589–590; mass, 882; medieval, 308*(i)*, 309; in Rome, 171–172. *See also* specific types

Entrepreneurs: world markets and, 794

Environment and environmentalism, 1001–1004; agriculture and, 10; crops and, 8; degradation of, 1059–1060; global warming and, 1020; industrialization and, 720, 1003–1004; Mesopotamia and, 13–15; urbanization, industrialization, and, 720. *See also* Pollution

Epaminondas (Thebes), 78–79

Ephors (overseers), 72

Epic literature: *Epic of Gilgamesh,* 17, 18–19*(d),* 50; of Hesiod, 62, 67; of Homer, 62, 66–67; of Virgil, 160–161. *See also* Philosophy; specific works

Epicurus and Epicureanism, 111

Epidemics, 550; Columbian exchange and, 451; influenza (1918), 861. *See also* Disease; specific conditions

Epirus, 127

Epitaphs, in Rome, 137, 172

Equality: 18th-century demands for, 611–612; in First World War, 843; in Ottoman Empire, 771, 772; for women, 699*(b)*. *See also* Rights; Women

Equiano, Olaudah, 529, 565, 566(d)
Erasistratus, 117
Erasmus, Desiderius, 370, 391, 395, 396
Eratosthenes, 113–115
Erechtheum, 81
Eremetical monasticism, 192
Espionage and Sedition Acts (U.S.), 842
Essay Concerning Human Understanding
   (Locke), 521–522
Essay on the Principle of Population
   (Malthus), 657
Essays (Montaigne), 460
Estates (assemblies): Bohemian, 481; Dutch,
   499, 500; Prussian, 482, 483, 484
Estates (land): in Rome, 142
Estates (social orders), in France, 621–624
Estates General (France), 474, 621, 622
Estates of Normandy (assembly), 468
Estonia: reforms in, 1028; Russia and, 489;
   Soviet Union and, 927, 1012
ETA (Basque Homeland and Freedom),
   1004
Ethelbert (Kent), 207
Ethics: Jewish, 43. *See also* Morality
Ethiopia: Italy and, 805, 919, 919(m)
Ethnic cleansing: Armenian genocide as,
   839; in Bosnian civil war, 1029–1030;
   exchange of Hindus and Muslims after
   Indian independence, 861; of Germans
   and Slavs after Second World War,
   861; of Greeks in Turkey, 860–861; of
   Turks in Greece and Bulgaria, 861
Ethnic groups: Albanians in Kosovo and,
   1031(i); in Austrian Empire, 686,
   687(m), 778; in Austro-Hungarian
   Empire, 778; churches and, 732;
   diversity in contemporary Europe,
   1042–1049; German, 927, 945; in
   Middle Ages, 351–352; migration
   patterns and, 976–978; nationalism
   and, 691–692, 754, 780–781; Nazis
   and, 906–907; in Russia, 853;
   separatism and, 1004; in Soviet Union,
   908–909, 908(i); underclass and, 1038.
   See also Minorities; specific groups
Ethnography, 815
Etruria, 127
Etruscans, 120(i), 122, 124, 124(i),
   124(m), 125
EU. *See* European Union
Euboea, 62
Eucharist (Lord's Supper), 292, 398
Euclid, 113, 227, 507
Eugenics, 906, 906(i), 922, 923
Euphrates River region, 12, 13, 19
Euripides, 81–82, 139

Euro, 1034, 1057
Europe: Americanization of, 988; Asia and,
   810–811; assumption of superiority by,
   611–612; Atlantic colonies of,
   565–567; cities of 100,000 or more
   and, 719 (m); counterculture in, 989;
   deindustrialization of, 688, 1038;
   domesticated animals in, 10; economic
   recovery in, 898–899; Egypt and, 798;
   emigration from, 799–800, 800(f),
   801–802, 801(f); ethnic diversity in,
   1042–1049; First World War in,
   836(m); former African colonies of,
   974; global inequality and, 1038;
   global trade and, 559; human rights
   policies in, 1061; industry and
   population in 18th century, 554(m);
   long-term challenges in, 1049–1061;
   market days and, 574(i); migration
   into, 1043–1046, 1045(m); mortality
   decline in, 722–723; multiculturalism
   in, 1046–1047; Muslims in,
   1047–1049; after Napoleonic Wars,
   682–690; nationalism in, 753–754;
   Obama and, 1053; outsourcing and,
   1037; after Peace of Utrecht, 479(m);
   pollution in (ca. 1990), 1004(m);
   population decline in, 1042;
   population in, 799–800; price
   revolution in, 549–550; religious
   divisions in (ca. 1555), 415(m);
   Scientific Revolution in, 506–508;
   Second World War in, 930(m); after
   Second World War, 943–954;
   separatism in, 1004–1005; Seven Years'
   War and, 612–613, 614(m); slaves and,
   430–431; after Thirty Years' War,
   470(m); trade in, 302(m), 428, 431;
   unity of, 1036; urban reforms in,
   723–724; U.S. relations with,
   1049–1053; use of term, 4; voyages of
   discovery by, 432–441, 436(m);
   witches and witchcraft in, 421–423,
   422(i), 602
European Coal and Steel Community, 957
European Common Bank, 1056(i), 1057
European Economic Community, 957. *See
   also* Common Market
European Enlightenment, 520–522
European monetary union, 1034
European Union (EU), 1021, 1034; in
   2016, 1035(m); economic sanctions on
   Russia by, 1032–1033; euro and, 1034,
   1057; exits from, 1057; globalization
   and, 1033; human rights and, 1061;
   immigration into, 1043; Poland,

Hungary, Czech Republic, and
   Slovakia in, 1028; Turkey and, 861
Europe first policy: in Second World War,
   937
Eurozone: global recession and,
   1056–1057; unity of, 1049
Eurymedon (Kopru) River, 174
Eusebius (bishop), 188
Euthanasia, in Nazi Germany, 923
Evans, Mary Ann. *See* Eliot, George
Evolution: Darwin's theory of, 745–746;
   Greek proposal of, 745
Evolutionary Socialism (Bernstein), 787
Exchange. *See* Culture(s); Trade
Exchange rates, 995
Exchequer (England), 253
Exclusionary policies: in neo-Europes, 803
Excommunication: Gregory VII on, 266,
   267; of Luther, 395
Executive: in Rome, 126; in United States,
   618
Existentialism, 871–872; Beauvoir and,
   1002(d); Christian, 872; Nietzsche
   and, 869
Exodus (Hebrew), 41, 42(m)
Exorcism, 602
Expansion: Carolingian, 234, 246; English,
   808(b); European, 432–441, 436(m),
   471; French, 383(m), 477(m), 478,
   634–635, 708; Greek, 70–71, 71(m);
   Hittite, 32; Italian, 917; by Japan, 822,
   934–937; by Nazi Germany, 919, 920,
   921, 925–927; population growth and,
   799–800; Prussian, 533, 763; of
   Rome, 132–135, 134(m), 156–160,
   156(m), 167; of Russia, 766, 767, 768,
   768(m); in United States, 765;
   Western, 791. *See also* Exploration;
   Imperialism; New Imperialism
Expeditions, scientific, 513–515
Experimental method, 509, 516, 517, 519,
   525
Experimentation: in Scientific Revolution,
   504(i), 505, 516
Exploration: by China, 429; European,
   432–441, 436(m); Genoese, 432;
   overseas, 436(m); by Portugal,
   435–436; reasons for, 432–434; by
   Spain, 437–438; technology and,
   434–435, 435(i); by Vespucci, 439. *See
   also* Space exploration; Voyages; specific
   explorers
Exports: colonial, 562; English, 793; of
   English technology, 661; foreign
   investments as, 794; Greek, 106. *See
   also* Trade; specific goods

Expressionism, 877; in films, 884

Extended families, 576

Extermination camps. *See* Concentration camps

Extinction: of species, 1060

Extreme unction, 296

Facebook, 1041–1042

Factories: apprenticeships in, 652–653; in cities, 718; closings of, 996; in continental Europe, 661; families and children in, 665–666; labor aristocracy in, 729; labor in, 649, 729; labor movement and, 675–677; machine-powered, 650, 653; owners of, 672, 673; in Russia, 768; sexual division of labor and, 666–669; technology and, 650–653; wages in, 669; workers in, 664–665, 730

Factories (trading): French, 445; Hansa merchants and, 303; Portuguese, 436–437

Factory Acts (England, 1802 to 1833), 666

Fairs: after Hundred Years' War, 337–338; urban, 302

Fairy tales, 698, 700–701*(d)*

Faisal (Syria), 840

Faith: salvation by, 394. *See also* Religion(s)

Faith healing, 602–603

Families: in 17th century, 499*(i)*; in 19th century, 732–743; in 1960s, 988; in ancient societies, 11; barbarian, 197; British, in India, 819–820; Carolingian, 230, 232–233; Dutch, 499*(i)*; in Egypt, 27; emigration process and, 802; in English colonies, 567; in Greece, 86; as handloom weavers, 553–554; Hebrew, 44; Jewish contract for, 45*(d)*; medieval, 289; medieval weddings and, 294; Merovingian, 229; middle-class, 738*(i)*; nuclear, 576–577; patriarchal, 466–467; Roman, 135–138, 163–164; in Soviet Union, 915; Spartan, 72; survivor families after First World War, 862, 863; women and girls in labor market and, 555; in workplace, 665–666. *See also* Marriage

Famine, 550; in 17th century, 468; in Ireland, 705–707, 777; in Middle Ages (later period), 323, 324–325, 324*(i)*; in Rome, 180; in Ukraine, 912

Fanon, Frantz, 968, 969*(d)*

Far East. *See* Asia; specific locations

Farms and farming: ancient, 10; collective, 912, 913*(d)*; communal, 544; in East Bloc, 1005; in Egypt, 26; in Hammurabi's code, 21; Hellenistic, 104; Mesopotamian, 13; open-field system in, 288; Roman, 142, 181, 188; Soviet collectivization and, 912, 913*(d)*; workers in, 675. *See also* Agriculture; Manors and manorialism; Peasants; Serfs

Farnese, Alexander (Cardinal). *See* Paul III (Pope)

Fasces, 125

Fascism: communism and, 905–907; in England, 899; after First World War, 828; in France, 899; in Germany, 899; in Italy, 863, 899, 917–918; totalitarianism and, 904. *See also* Italy; Nazi Germany

Fascist Party (Italy), 126

Fashion: in 18th century, 594; for women, 593*(b)*, 593*(i)*. *See also* Clothing

Fashoda, 809

Fast-food chains: criticisms of, 1038

Father Goriot (Balzac), 748

Fatherland Party (Germany), 842, 846

Fathers: in 19th century, 739–740; in patriarchal society, 466–467; in Roman families, 135–136. *See also* Families

Faulkner, William, 880

Feast days, 208–209, 276, 290

February Revolution (Russia), 848, 849

Federalists: in Europe, 957; in United States, 618

Federal Republic of Germany. *See* West Germany

Federal system: in EU, 1036; in German Empire, 773

Feminine Mystique, The (Friedan), 1001

Feminism, 1000–1001, 1000*(i)*; feminist movement and, 741–743; after First World War, 882–883. *See also* Women

Fenians (Ireland), 777, 777*(i)*

Ferdinand I (Holy Roman Empire), 711, 712

Ferdinand I (Two Sicilies), 688

Ferdinand II (Holy Roman Empire), 392, 481

Ferdinand III (Holy Roman Empire), 482

Ferdinand VII (Spain), 635

Ferdinand and Isabella (Spain), 384, 385–386, 386*(d)*, 387; Columbus and, 433, 438, 440–441*(d)*; Holy Roman Empire and, 407

Ferrara: as city-state, 360; university at, 509

Ferry, Jules, 807, 810

Fertile Crescent, 9; cultural exchange in, 22–23, 28. *See also* Mesopotamia; Middle East; Near East; Sumer and Sumerians; specific peoples

Fertility: declining, 1042; medieval diet and, 289

Festivals: Pan-Hellenic, 88

Feudalism, 199, 246–247, 382. *See also* Middle Ages

Ficino, Marsilio, 364

Fief, 246

Fifth Republic (France), 992

Films. *See* Movies

Final Act of the Conference on Security and Cooperation (1975), 986

"Final solution," 932

Finance(s): in France, 899; in Great Depression, 894–895; in western Europe, 957. *See also* Panics; Taxation

Financial crash: of 1873, 662, 781; of 1929, 891, 894; in Russia (1998), 1023

Financial crisis: Asian banking crisis (1997) and, 1034

Finland: Christianity in, 280; after First World War, 857; Nazi Germany and, 927

Finland Station, Lenin at, 849

Fireside chats (F. D. Roosevelt), 885

First Balkan War, 832

First Coalition: against France, 628

First Continental Congress (1774), 616

First Crusade, 277, 280

First estate (France), clergy as, 621

First Intermediate Period (Egypt), 24, 25

First International, 784, 785

First Messenian War, 71

First Moroccan Crisis (1905), 830

First Punic War, 132

First Triumvirate (Rome), 147

First World War, 826*(i)*, 827–828; alliances in, 828–830, 829*(m)*; armistice in, 854–855; art on, 826*(i)*, 837; capitalism in, 841; casualties in, 835, 837, 838, 839, 840, 861, 862*(f)*; consumer society after, 881–885; democracy after, 889–891; eastern front in, 837–841; England after, 886; in Europe, 834–837, 836*(m)*; events leading to, 828–834; Hitler and, 920; homefront in, 841–846; human costs of, 861–863; Italy and, 838, 917; Jewish homeland and, 859–860; Lenin and, 852; Middle East and, 836*(m)*, 859–861; mobilization for, 834, 841–842, 847; mutinies in, 846;

outbreak of, 832–834; peace settlement after, 856–860; poetry from, 837, 838–839(d); propaganda posters from, 845(b); reparations after, 857, 858, 886, 888(b), 889; Russia in, 834, 837–838, 847, 852; social impact of, 842–843; territorial changes after, 855(m); as total war, 834, 841; United States and, 840–841, 854; Versailles Treaty after, 856–859; western front in, 834–837; women in, 842, 842(i), 843, 844(b)

First Zionist Congress (Basel), 782(b), 783

Fish and fishing industry: in Canada, 441; Hellenistic, 106–107; in Middle Ages (early period), 218(i); overfishing and, 1060; Sumerian, 14

"Five good emperors" (Rome), 164, 165–168

Five Pillars of Islam, 223

Five-year plans: in Soviet Union, 907, 910–911(d), 910–914

Flagellants, 330

Flanders: agriculture in, 545, 547; France and, 478; merchant influence in, 306; military cemeteries in, 861; peasants in, 325, 344, 346; Renaissance painters in, 374; rural industry in, 553; towns in, 301–302; trade and, 301–302, 303, 333, 432. See also Holland; Low Countries

Flaubert, Gustave, 748

Flavian dynasty (Rome), 164, 165

Flemish language and people. See Flanders

FLN. See National Liberation Front (FLN, Algeria)

Floods: in Mesopotamia, 13–14; by Nile, 23; Noah in Bible and, 14

Florence: arts in, 373, 374(i); banks in, 358, 360(i); as city-state, 360; growth of, 299, 358–359; Medici family in, 361, 362, 366; plague in, 327–328; same-sex relations in, 350; Savonarola in, 362, 365

Florida, 613

Flying shuttle, 553

Foederati, 200

Food(s): in 18th century, 590–591; ancient, 8–11; of Columbian exchange, 451; ethnic, 1046; in First World War, 841, 847; in Germanic society, 198(d); for industrial workers, 672; in Middle Ages (later period), 290; open-field system and, 544; Paleolithic, 7; of peasants, 290; population increase and, 551; in Rome, 170–171. See also

Agriculture; Diet (food); Grain; Spice trade

Foragers, 3, 7, 9; crops and, 8

Forced labor: in American colonies, 448–449; in First World War, 838; Nazi, 932(i), 945; in Soviet Union, 912, 959, 961. See also Slaves and slavery

Foreign aid: to Greece, 951

Foreign competition, tariffs and, 773

Foreign investment, 794; European, to 1914, 795(m)

Foreign policy: Bismarck and, 828; domestic issues and, 773; in England, 384; before First World War, 828–830; in Germany, 774; of Putin, 1024; Soviet, 964–965; of Spain, 385. See also specific locations

Foreign relations: U.S.-European, 1052–1053

Foreign workers, in Russia, 768

Forests: wood fuel and, 654

Formosa (Taiwan), 822

Fortuna (fate), 368

Forum (Rome), 126

Fossil fuels: dependence on, 1059, 1060; Russian controls over, 1059

Foundation myths: Roman, 124–125

Foundlings: in 18th century, 582, 583–584; in 19th century, 739; infanticide and, 582, 583–584

Fourier, Charles, 693

Fourteen Points, 857, 864

Fourth Crusade, 279

Fourth Lateran Council (1215), 268, 281; on clothing for Jews and Muslims, 308; on sacraments, 293

France: 1830 revolution in, 707–708, 707(i); 1848 revolution in, 708, 709–710, 711(m); absolutism in, 469, 472–473, 473–474, 477–478, 477(m); Africa and, 805, 807, 809; Algeria and, 708, 770, 805, 973–974; Alsace and, 763–764, 775; American Revolution and, 617; Angevin dynasty in, 253–254; anti-Semitism in, 776; artisan production in, 661; Asia and, 810, 810(m); Austria and, 533; banking in, 662; Black Death in, 327; Bourbon restoration in, 637, 684, 707; bourgeoisie in, 709; Burgundy and, 383; Calvinism and, 418–419; Capetian dynasty in, 254–255; Catholic Church in, 418–419, 597, 626, 631, 634, 755, 775, 776; Charlemagne and, 231; Civil

Constitution of the Clergy in, 626; civil war in, 333, 383, 419; clocks in, 306; colonial independence from, 973–974; colonies of, 445–446, 563; Common Market and, 958; communism in, 951; Constituent Assembly in, 710; constitutional monarchy in, 626; constitution in, 626, 755; deaths in Second World War, 944–945; de-Christianization in, 631; de Gaulle in, 955, 958, 974, 984–985; Dreyfus affair in, 776; economy in, 624, 625, 898–899; education in, 755 775; Egypt and, 633, 798; emancipation of slaves in territories of, 641; England and, 253–254, 332–339, 334(m), 383, 560–562, 830; estates (social orders) in, 621–624; expansion of, 383(m), 477(m), 478, 634–635; exploration by, 440–441; before First World War, 830, 831; First World War and, 835, 837, 840, 842, 846, 854; after First World War, 857, 885; First World War casualties in, 861; foreign investments by, 794, 795(m); Germany and, 828; government of, 255, 473, 626, 755, 756; Great Fear in (1789), 624, 624(m); Great Schism and, 340; Greece and, 70; guest worker in, 976; guilds in, 556, 557, 559; Habsburgs, Burgundy, and, 404; Habsburg-Valois wars and, 362, 406, 418; hospitals in, 291; Hundred Years' War and, 332–339, 334(m), 345, 383; after Hundred Years' War, 337–339; illegitimacy in, 578; immigrants to, 801; India and, 571; industrialists in, 673; industrialization in, 659, 659(f); inflation in, 890; Italy and, 634, 757–758; Jesuits in, 417; Jews in, 294, 386–387, 781(i); judicial system in, 259–260; kingdom of, 255, 255(m); labor unions in, 786; liberalism in, 710; literacy in (ca. 1789), 588(m); in Little Entente, 886; mandates of, 858, 859, 860; medieval, 287; Merovingians in, 228; mixed-race people in colonies, 567; as modern state, 775–776; mortality decline in, 722(f); Muslims in, 1047, 1048, 1049; Napoleon I in, 633–638; after Napoleon I, 684–685; Napoleon III and, 754–757, 763; National Front in, 1005; nationalism in, 691, 756; nativism in, 803; nobility in, 255, 621–622, 623, 626; Normandy and, 383; North Africa

France *(continued)*
and, 937; Ottoman Empire and, 859; philosophes in, 522–524, 522*(i)*; Popular Front in, 899; Protestantism in, 406, 407, 418–419; Prussia and, 762*(m)*, 763–764; public health movement in, 721; Realism in, 748, 748*(i)*; regional allegiances in, 779; religion and, 390*(i)*, 416, 418–419; reparations after First World War and, 857, 858; representative government in, 338; republicans in, 710; republic in, 628–629, 709–710, 755, 775–776; revolutionary era in, 609; Rhineland and, 886, 887; Romanticism in, 696, 698; Ruhr occupation by, 886*(m)*, 887–889, 887*(i)*; Ruhr region and, 887; Russia and, 766, 828; Saint-Domingue and, 573, 638–643; Scientific Revolution and, 517; Second Republic in, 755; Second World War and, 927, 928; Second World War collaborators in, 947; Seven Years' War and, 613; socialism in, 709, 710, 784, 787; Socialist Party in, 1000; society in, 624–625; Spain and, 418, 478, 480; streetcars in, 725; student protests in, 991–992; third estate in, 621–622, 621*(i)*, 623–624; Third Republic in, 775–776; Thirty Years' War and, 469, 494; uprisings in, 472, 473; Versailles Treaty and, 857, 858; Vichy government in, 928, 928*(m)*, 937; Vietnam and, 970; voting in, 755; war on terror and, 1052; wars under Louis XIV, 477–478; women in, 634; workers in, 1037–1038. *See also* First World War; French Revolution; Napoleon I (Napoleon Bonaparte); Paris; Second World War; specific leaders and wars
Francesco di Bernardone. *See* Francis (Saint)
Franche-Comté, 478
Francis (Saint), 274, 275, 275*(d)*
Francis I (France), 273*(i)*, 383, 418
Franciscans, 457, 567
Franco, Francisco, 925*(i)*, 926, 955, 1004
Franco-Prussian War, 762*(m)*, 763–764, 775, 828, 831
Frankfurt: parliament in, 713
Frankfurt Assembly, Jewish rights and, 781
Frankish kingdom, 205, 228. *See also* Carolingian Empire; Charlemagne; Franks; Merovingian dynasty
Franklin, Benjamin, 530, 568, 617

Franks, 196, 199, 205, 245. *See also* Frankish kingdom
Franz II (Austria), 628, 635, 683
Franz Ferdinand (Austria-Hungary), 832
Franz Joseph (Austria-Hungary), 712, 778, 846
Frederick I (Barbarossa, Holy Roman Empire), 256–257, 256*(m)*, 267, 279
Frederick I (Prussia), 484
Frederick II (Holy Roman Empire), 257*(i)*
Frederick II (the Great, Prussia): Jews and, 539; on partition of Poland, 537; War of the Austrian Succession and, 533
Frederick III ("the Ostentatious") (Elector of Brandenburg). *See* Frederick I (Prussia)
Frederick III (Holy Roman Empire), 404
Frederick William (Great Elector, Brandenburg), 482–484
Frederick William I (the "Soldiers' King") (Prussia), 484, 484*(i)*, 533
Free Corps (Germany), 856
Freedom Party (Austria), 1048
"Free love," counterculture and, 989
Free-market capitalism: after Second World War, 954, 955
Free-market neoliberalism, 1033
Free people of color: in Americas, 566; in Saint-Domingue, 638, 640
Free trade, 690; Britain and, 793; in EU, 1034; Germany and, 773; neoliberal policies of, 1037; in Ottoman Empire, 771; Smith and, 560
French and Indian War, 613. *See also* Seven Years' War
French Indochina. *See* Indochina
French language, 172, 351, 460, 476, 522
French phase, of Thirty Years' War, 469
French Revolution (1789), 609, 620–626; background to, 620–624; culture in, 631; de-Christianization in, 631; Declaration of the Rights of Man and of the Citizen and, 611, 625; economy in, 629–630, 632; Industrial Revolution and, 678; insurrection in (1793), 629*(m)*; international reactions to, 627–628; Jacobins in, 627–628; Jews and, 626; National Convention and, 628; peasants in, 624–625, 629; Reign of Terror in, 630–631; religions during, 626; sans-culottes in, 629, 630*(d)*; second revolution in, 628–629; Thermidorian Reaction in, 631–632; women during, 625, 631. *See also* Guillotine (France)

Frescoes: Croatian, during Black Death, 331*(i)*; Renaissance, 356*(i)*, 375; women and, 378
Freud, Sigmund, 874–875, 879
Freundlich, Matthaus, 568–569*(b)*
Friars, 274–276, 393–394, 457
Friedan, Betty, 1001
Friedman, Milton, 997
Friedrich, Casper David, 698–700
Friedrich Wilhelm III (Prussia), 683
Friedrich Wilhelm IV (Prussia), 712, 713, 760
Frobisher, Martin, 440
Fronde (France), 473
Frontiers: of Carolingian Empire, 240, 240*(m)*; Roman, 155, 156, 157, 165, 167. *See also* Borders; Boundaries
Fronts (military). *See* Eastern front; Western front
Fruit, 590–591
Fuel: wood as, 654. *See also* Energy; specific types
Führer, Hitler as, 920, 921. *See also* Hitler, Adolf
Fulbert, 313
Functionalism, 876
Fundamentalism, Islamic, 996
Fundamentalist terrorism, 1047, 1047*(i)*, 1048
Fundamental Laws (Russia), 769
Funerals: in Egypt, 24, 25*(i)*; medieval, 296; Roman inscription and, 137*(d)*
Fur-collar crime, 350–351
Fur trade, in Canada, 441, 445

Gaddafi, Muammar, 1055
Gaelic languages, 196–197
Gaius Appuleius Diocles (Roman charioteer), 172
Gaius Duilius (Roman admiral), triumphal column of, 133*(i)*
Gaius Gracchus (Rome), 143
Gaius Marius. *See* Marius (Gaius Marius)
Galen (physician), 170, 507, 517
Galilei, Galileo: Inquisition and, 518–519; on moon, 512*(d)*; *Sidereal Messenger, The,* and, 511–512, 512*(d)*; telescope of, 511–512, 511*(i)*, 512*(d)*
Gallican Church: in France, 597
Gallipoli, Battle of, 840, 840*(m)*, 860
Gambetta, Léon, 775
Gambling, 309
Gandhi, Mohandas ("Mahatma"), 968, 970

Gan Ying (China), 175

Gapon, Father, 770(d)

Garden of Love (Rubens), 501(i)

Garibaldi, Giuseppe, 760

Garrisons: Roman army as, 168; towns and, 172

Gas, natural, 1059, 1059(m)

Gas chambers: Nazi, 932(i)

Gas lighting, 672

Gattinara (chancellor), 404

Gaugamela, battle at, 94

Gaul and Gauls: Franks and, 205, 228; Merovingian, 205; Rome and, 156, 160, 164, 172–173. *See also* Celtic peoples; Germanic peoples

Gays. *See* Homosexuality

Gaza, Alexander the Great in, 94

Gazprom, 1059

Gdansk, strikes in, 1009

Gdansk Agreement, 1009

Gedrosian Desert, Alexander in, 96

Gender and gender issues: Christianity and, 193–194; clothing distinctions and, 594; consumer culture and, 882–883; division of labor and, 287; equality and, 611; feminist movement and, 1001; in First World War, 843; in Greece, 85; hierarchy of, 11; marriage equality and, 577; medical treatments and, 312; in medieval universities, 314; in Renaissance, 376–377, 381–382; same-sex relations and, 350; sexual division of labor as, 666–669; witchcraft trials and, 421. *See also* Homosexuality; Men; Sex and sexuality; Voting and voting rights; Women

General Assembly (UN), 1036

General History of the Things of New Spain (Florentine Codex), 458(d)

General Syrian Congress (1919), 860

Generation gap: youth culture and, 979

Geneva: Calvin and, 412

Geneva Accords (1954), 990

Genius: Renaissance concept of, 375–376, 376(d)

Genoa: plague carried from, 327; trade and, 302, 379, 432

Genocide: against Armenians, 839, 839(m). *See also* Ethnic cleansing; Holocaust

Gentiles, Paul on, 178

Geoffrey of Anjou, 253

Geography: Eratosthenes and, 115; globalization inequality and, 1038; of Greece, 62; of Iran, 52; of Italy, 122, 123(m); in Mesopotamia, 13; *Periplus*

of the Erythraean Sea and, 116(d). *See also* specific locations

Geography (Ptolemy), 434, 438, 439, 507, 509

Geometry: Descartes and, 516; Euclid and, 113, 227

Geopolitics: U.S.-European relations and, 1052

George III (England), 616

Georgia (country), 909, 1027(m); EU and, 1036; independence groups in, 1012; Rose Revolution in, 1032; Russian intervention in, 1032, 1059

Georgics (Virgil), 160

German Confederation, 760, 761, 762; Karlsbad Decrees and, 688, 689(d); liberals in, 710–711; after Napoleonic Wars, 685, 688; nationalists in, 692; Prussia and, 712–713; reestablishment of, 713

German Confederation of the Rhine (1806), 635, 635(m)

German Customs Union (Zollverein), 760

German Democratic Republic. *See* East Germany

German East Africa, 807, 809, 813(i)

German Empire, 763, 773–774. *See also* Germany; Holy Roman Empire

Germanic languages, 196–197

Germanic peoples: Huns and, 203; migrations by, 202; religion of, 200. *See also* Barbarians; specific groups

Germanization, 781

German language, 343(b), 351, 482; in Austrian Empire, 713

German Peasants' War (1525), 399, 401

German people: in Austria, 712, 778; as barbarians, 196–197; after Second World War, 945

German Social Democratic Party (SPD), 773. *See also* Social Democrats, in Germany (SPD)

German Trade Union Congress, 787

German Workers' Party, 920

Germany: Africa and, 805, 807, 809; anti-immigrant movement in, 1048; Asia and, 810, 810(m); Austria and, 828; banking in, 662; Black Death in, 327; Catholic Church in, 267, 393, 413, 773; Charlemagne and, 231; Civil Code in (1906), 742; clocks in, 306; colonies of, 807, 840, 858; Crusaders and Jews in, 280; denazification in, 947; elementary schools in, 587; emigrants from, 800, 800(f); ethnic Germans and, 945; before First World

War, 830, 831; First World War and, 833, 834–835, 837–838, 854–855, 861; after First World War, 854–855, 856, 863, 885–889; foreign investments by, 794, 795(m); Greater and Lesser, 713; as Great Power, 828; Great Schism and, 340; guest workers in, 976; guilds in, 557; Habsburg-Valois wars in, 406; homefront in (First World War), 841–842, 846; immigrants to, 801; industrialists in, 673; industrialization in, 659, 659(f), 800; inflation in, 887; Jews in, 781(i); Karlsbad Decrees and, 688; labor in, 786–787; lay investiture and, 256; Lenin and, 849; Luther and Lutheranism in, 404–405, 413; Magyars in, 244–245; medical research in, 722; medieval, 287; Merovingians in, 228; migrants to, 1043–1044, 1044(i); militarism in, 831; military government in, 842; mortality decline in, 722(f); movies in, 884; Napoleon and, 634, 635; after Napoleonic Wars, 685; nationalism in, 764, 773, 888(b); nativism in, 803; occupation zones in, 947; planned economy in, 841–842; Poland and, 888(b), 985; population in, 550, 1042; Prussia and, 712–713; public health movement in, 721; radical Reformation in, 399, 401; religious wars in, 404–405; Renaissance art in, 374–375; reparations and, 857, 858, 886, 889; reunification of, 1000, 1015–1016, 1016(m); revolution in, 854–855, 856; Rhineland and, 886; rivalry with Britain, 830; Rome and, 156–157, 165; Ruhr region and, 886(m), 887–889; Russia and, 852; serfdom and, 481; in Seven Years' War, 613; Social Democratic Party in, 773–774, 784, 785(d), 787; socialists in, 787; social welfare in, 774; split into East and West, 952; "Storm and Stress" movement in, 696; streetcars in, 725; Stresemann in, 887, 888(b), 888(i); Thirty Years' War and, 465, 469; unification of, 713, 760–764, 762(m), 764(i), 779; Versailles Treaty and, 885; veterans after First World War, 863, 863(i); voting rights in, 763; war guilt clause and, 858; war on terror and, 1052; Weimar Republic in, 856; witch-hunts in, 421; women in, 742. *See also* First World War; German Empire; Holy Roman Empire; Nazi Germany; Second World War

Germ theory, of disease, 722
Gerousia (Spartan council), 72
Gesù, Church of, 500
Géza (Magyar), 245
Ghana, 430, 972
Ghent, 299, 301
Ghettos, for Jews, 539, 781, 932
Ghiberti, Lorenzo, 373
Gibbon, Edward, 157, 158, 205, 584
Gibraltar: in al-Andalus, 224; England and, 478
Gilgamesh, 17, 18–19(d)
Gillray, James, 605(i)
Gioberti, Vincenzo, 757
Giotto, 374
Girls: slave trade and, 432; in workforce, 577. See also Children; Families; Women
Girondists, 628, 629
Gladiators (Rome), 171–172, 171(i)
Gladstone, William, 777
Glasgow: Irish workers in, 665; lifestyle in, 671
Glasnost, 1011
Glass-making, 175
Global economy, 1033–1034; birth of, 427, 455–456; after Columbus, 447–456; currency exchange and, 995; industrialization and, 792–799; recession in, 1056–1057; seaborne trading empires in, 453(m); silver trade and, 455. See also Economy
Globalization, 1020(i), 1021–1022, 1033–1042; economic, 1033–1034; human side of, 1037–1039; supranational organizations and, 1036–1037
Global mass migration, 799
Global security, Putin on, 1025(d)
Global trade, 559–571; foods and, 591
Global warming, 1020, 1059; Kyoto Protocol and, 1051
Glorious Revolution (England, 1688–1689), 497, 498, 498(d), 612
GNP. See Gross national product
Goa, 437, 455
Göbekli Tepe, 9, 9(i)
Gobineau, Arthur de, 780
Gods and goddesses: ancient polytheism and, 12; Babylonian, 20; barbarian, 200; Egyptian, 24, 25–26, 30; Greek, 67, 86–88, 128; in Hellenistic world, 107–110; Mesopotamian, 16; Persian, 55–56; Roman, 108, 126, 127–128, 138, 172, 176, 179, 200; Sumerian, 14. See also Religion(s); Yahweh; specific gods and goddesses

Gold: in Africa, 430, 436, 790(i), 807; alchemy and, 515; for coins, 303–304; as coins in Lydia, 54; in Great Depression, 893; in Hellenistic world, 105; in New World, 438, 444
Golden age: of Latin literature, 160; in Netherlands, 468, 499
Golden Jubilee, of Victoria (England), 780
Gold standard: in Great Depression, 893, 895, 898; Nixon and, 995
Goods and services: Hellenistic, 105; purchase of, 672; trade in industrial and luxury, 106. See also Consumer goods; Consumption
Gorbachev, Mikhail, 1005; end of Cold War and, 1016; German reunification and, 1016; reforms by, 1010–1012
Gospels, 176, 177; at Lindisfarne, 237, 239; of Matthew, 237(i)
Gosplan, 912–913
Gothic architecture, of cathedrals, 248, 318–319, 318(i)
Gothic language, Bible in, 206
Goths. See Ostrogoths; Visigoths
Government: 17th-century state-building and, 471, 484, 492–493; in 1848 revolutions, 708; of American colonies, 446–447; Assyrian, 49–50; Carolingian, 232–233, 233(d); clergy and, 393; constitutional, 492, 686; of England, 493–499, 703–704, 998; of EU, 1035–1036; in First World War, 841–842, 843; of France, 255, 626, 630–631, 755, 756, 776, 899; by Franks, 228–229; of German Empire, 773; in Great Depression, 898; Greek, 62, 69–70; Hellenistic, 98, 101; industrialization and, 650, 660, 661; of Italian Renaissance cities, 358–359; of Italy, 760, 918; Machiavelli on, 367–368; Minoan, 64; Montesquieu on, 523; Mycenaean, 65; of Napoleonic France, 633–634; of nation-states, 753–754; of Persian Empire, 55; polis as, 67; postwar European, 954–957; in Prussia, 534, 761, 763; public health and, 721; by Puritans in England, 495–496; representative, 612; of Roman Empire, 154–155, 167; of Roman Republic, 129–130; of Rome, 126; of Russia, 767, 848, 1024; before Second World War, 903; after Second World War, 949; sovereignty of people and, 611; of Sparta, 72; Sumerian, 14; types of, 523; of United States, 617–618,

895–896; workers' living standards and, 559. See also Absolute monarchy and absolutism; Constitutional monarchy; Law(s); Representative government; specific locations
Government planning: by Christian Democrats, 955; after Second World War, 954
Goya, Francisco, 637
Gracchi brothers. See Gaius Gracchus (Rome); Tiberius Gracchus (Rome)
Grain: English Corn Laws and, 703; regulation of, 559; in Rome, 171; in Russia, 767; trade in, 106
Granada: population of, 299; reconquista and, 258, 259(m), 386; Spain and, 384
Gran Colombia, 690
Grand Alliance: against Louis XIV, 478
Grand Alliance (Second World War), 927, 937–938; postwar occupation by, 947; victory by, 938–939; after war, 943–944. See also Alliance(s); England (Britain); France; Soviet Union; specific alliances
Grand Duchy of Moscow, 485
Grand Duchy of Tuscany, 361–362
Grand Empire (Napoleon), 635–638
Grand jury, 260
Grand National Consolidated Trades Union, 677
Granicus River, battle at, 94
Grapes: Phoenician, 39
Gratian, 311
Gravitation, 513
Great Britain (England). See England (Britain)
Great Depression (1929–1939), 863, 891–899; economic crisis in, 891–894; in Europe, 892(m); homelessness in, 893(i); Nazi Germany and, 921; in Scandinavia, 896–898; unemployment in, 894, 894(m); in United States, 891–893, 892(m)
Great Elector. See Frederick William (Great Elector, Brandenburg)
Greater East Asia Co-Prosperity Sphere, 934
Greater Germany, 713; Austria in, 926
Greater Serbia, 1029
Great Exhibition in London (1851), 657
Great Famine: in Ireland, 705–707; in northern Europe, 324–325
Great Fear (France, 1789), 624, 624(m)
Great Northern War, 488
Great Panathenaea, 80

Great Powers, 685; competition among, 766, 828–830; at Congress of Vienna, 682(m), 684(i), 757; empires of, 967–968; before First World War, 829(m), 831; Greece and, 702–703; in Italy, 757, 760; Prussia as, 533, 764; Russia as, 487, 489

"Great purges," in Soviet Union, 916

Great Rebellion (India), 819, 819(m)

"Great Reforms," in Russia, 766–768

Great Schism, in Catholic Church, 340, 340(m), 392

Great Silk Road, 106

Great Trek, 805

Great War. See First World War

Greco-Roman culture: barbarians and, 200, 205; Christianity and, 195, 207–208; West in, 4

Greece: agriculture in, 61; anti-austerity protests in, 1056(i); authoritarianism in, 955; in Bronze (Helladic) Age, 62–67; colonies of, 70; in Common Market, 996; communism in, 951; Dark Age in, 62; debt crisis in (2015), 1036; economy in, 75; Etruscans and, 120(i); expansion by, 70–71, 71(m); exports from, 106; First Balkan War and, 832; First World War and, 839; foreign aid to, 951; geography and settlement of, 62; gods and goddesses of, 67, 86–88, 128; government in, 69–70; Hellenistic, 98; households and work in, 83; independence of, 702–703, 703(m), 770; Macedonia and, 75, 79; migration through, 1044; national liberation in, 702–703; Persian Wars and, 75–76; philosophy in, 88–90; Phoenicians and, 40; polis in, 67–74; politics in, 62; recession in, 1056–1057; refugees in, 1044, 1044(i); Rome and, 134; in Second World War, 931; slaves in, 83; society and culture of, 61–90; Turkey and, 860–861; war and turmoil in, 75–79; on West-East distinction, 4. See also Alexander the Great; Athens; Hellenistic world; Minoan civilization; Mycenae and Mycenaeans; Sparta

Greek culture and people: Cato on, 140; in Hellenistic world, 100–102, 124(i); Rome and, 138–140; in Turkey, 860–861

Greek fire, 213

Greek language: alphabet of, 40; Byzantine literature in, 507; of Dorians, 66; in Hellenistic world, 102; Jews and, 110;

Renaissance and, 363, 370; in Rome, 139. See also Classical culture

Greek Orthodox Church. See Orthodox Church

Greene, Graham, 873

Greenland: in "little ice age," 324; Vikings in, 242, 324

Green Party, 1004

Greenpeace, 1004, 1037

Gregorian reforms, 265–266

Gregory I ("the Great," Pope), 191–192, 207

Gregory VII (Pope), 265–266, 267

Gregory of Tours, on relics, 208–209(d)

Grenadiers, in Prussia, 484, 484(i)

Grexit (Greek exist from the Eurozone), 1057

Grimm, Jacob and **Wilhelm,** 698; *Children's Stories and Household Tales,* 700–701(d)

Gropius, Walter, 876

Gross national product (GNP): in England, 657

Grosz, George, 966(i)

Grumbach, Argula von, 403

Guadeloupe, 446, 563, 641

Guanajuato, 454

Guangzhou (Canton), China, foreign merchants in, 795, 796, 796(i)

Guerrilla warfare: in South Africa, 809; against Turks on Arabian peninsula, 840

Guest worker programs, 976, 977(b), 977(i)

Guilds and guild system, 556–559, 556(i); capitalist attacks on, 676; craft, 477; exclusions from, 556, 557; French, 559; investors in, 346; women and, 347, 557. See also specific locations

Guillotine (France), 628, 631, 632, 632(i)

Guinea worm disease, 23

Guinefort (saint), 295

Gulf of Mexico, oil rig disaster in, 1060

Gulf War. See Persian Gulf War

Gunboat diplomacy, 797, 821, 822

Gunpowder, 435

Guns. See Weapons

Guomindang (Kuomintang), 971

Gustavus Adolphus (Sweden), 469

Gustavus Vasa (Sweden), 407

Gutenberg, Johann, 370–371, 371(i)

Guzmán, Gaspar de. See Olivares, count-duke of (Gaspar de Guzmán)

Gynaeceum (women's quarters), 83, 85

Gypsies: Nazis and, 906, 922, 944

Haarlem, Spanish troops in, 420(i)

Habsburg dynasty, 613; in Austria, 481–482, 483(m), 533; Austrian Empire and, 686, 711; Catholicism of, 597; Charles V and, 404; education and, 587; France and, 628; in Hungary, 414, 482, 712; Ottomans and, 491; peoples of (1815), 67(m); in Thirty Years' War, 469

Habsburg-Valois wars, 362, 406, 418

Haciendas, 448, 449

Hades (god), 87, 108

Hadith, 221, 224

Hadrian (Rome), 165, 167

Hadrian's Wall, 167

Hagab (Hebrews), 46(i)

Hagiographies, 293

Hague, The, 1036

Haiti, 563; independence of, 641(m); revolution in (1791–1804), 609, 638–643. See also L'Ouverture, Toussaint; Saint-Domingue

Halicarnassus, 75

Hall of Mirrors (Versailles): First World War treaty signed in, 858; German unification and, 763, 764(i)

Hamadan (Ecbatana, Iran), 52

Hamburg, 301, 303, 938

Hamilcar Barca (Carthage), 132–133

Hammurabi (Babylon): law code of, 19, 20–22, 21(i)

Han China. See China

Hancock, John, 617

Handicapped people. See Disabled people

Handloom weaving, 553–554, 652

Hanging gardens (Babylon), 51–52

Hannibal (Carthage), 132–133, 134

Hanseatic League (Hansa), 303, 303(m), 304(i)

Hanukkah, 110

Hapiru people. See Hebrews

Harald III (Norway), 252

Hardy, Thomas, 749

Harem, 492(b), 530

Hargreaves, James, 651

Hariot, Thomas, on Roanoke colony, 449(d)

Harkort, Fritz, 661, 673

Harold Godwinson, 252

Harun-al-Rashid (Abbasid caliph), 235

Harvests: of hay, 289(i); in "little ice age," 324, 468

Harvey, William, 517–518

Hasdrubal (Carthage), 133

Haskalah (Jewish movement), 539

Hastings, Battle of, 252

Hatshepsut (Egypt), 29, 31*(b)*, 31*(i)*

Hattusa (Hittite city), 37

Hattusili I (Hittites), 32

Hattusili III (Hittites), 32

Haussmann, Georges, 723–724, 723*(m)*, 724

Havel, Václav, 1007, 1015, 1028, 1062

Hawaii: Asian immigrants to, 802, 803*(i)*; Pearl Harbor attack in, 934–936

Health: bacterial revolution and, 722; improvements in, 551; medieval, 312*(d)*; public health movement and, 721, 722; in Rome, 170; state-funded health care and, 1061. *See also* Disease; Medicine

Heart of Darkness (Conrad), 816

Hebrew language: Phoenician alphabet and, 40

Hebrews, 40–46; Assyria and, 42, 46, 48–49, 49*(i)*, 51*(d)*; Bible of, 40, 42–43, 49; Exodus of, 41, 42*(m)*; family and society of, 44–46; religion of, 35, 42–44; seal of, 46*(i)*; state of, 41–42, 42*(m)*; Yahweh's Covenant with, 43. *See also* Israel; Jews and Judaism

Hegel, Georg, 694

Heidegger, Martin, 871

Heisenberg, Werner, 874

Hejaz, 840. *See also* Saudi Arabia

Helena (mother of Constantine), 188, 208*(d)*

Helene (Roman slave), 168–169

Heliocentric theory, 113, 509–510, 510–512, 518

Helladic period (Bronze Age, Greece), 61, 62–67

Hellenic Greece, 60*(i)*, 61, 122. *See also* Greece

Hellenistic world, 62, 93–117; ca. 263 B.C.E., 100; agriculture in, 104; arts in, 103*(i)*; bureaucrats in, 101; economy of, 104–107; Etruscans and, 124*(i)*; Greek colonies in, 122; Greek people and culture in, 100–102; Greeks and non-Greeks in, 102–104; Jews in, 110; kings in, 98; lifestyle in, 99–100; marriage in, 92*(i)*; medicine in, 117; philosophy in, 110–113; religions in, 107–110; Rome and, 121, 135, 141; science in, 113–117; trade in, 105–106. *See also* Alexander the Great; Greece; Mystery religions

Hellenization, 99

Heloise, Abelard and, 313

Helots (unfree residents), 71, 72

Helsinki Accords (1975), 986, 1007, 1008*(d)*; human rights in, 986, 987*(d)*, 1010

Henry ("the Navigator," Portugal), 435–436

Henry I (England), 253, 260

Henry II (England), 253–254, 260, 332

Henry II (France), 418

Henry III (England), 332

Henry III (France), 419

Henry IV (England), 383–384

Henry IV (France), 419, 472, 473, 477

Henry IV (Germany, Holy Roman Empire), 266, 267

Henry V (England), 335

Henry VI (England), 384

Henry VII (England), 384

Henry VIII (England), 384, 408*(i)*; Protestant Reformation and, 400*(b)*, 407–409

Henry of Navarre (France). *See* Henry IV (France)

Hera (goddess), 87

Heraclitus (Greece), 88

Heraclius I (Byzantine Empire), 211

Herakles (Hercules), 87, 128

Hercules Victor, temple of, 128

Heredity: male, 17

Herero people, 809

Heresy, 180; Albigensian, 267–268; Arianism as, 189–190; Beguines and, 276; Consistory and, 412; Eckhart and, 343*(b)*; German, 413–414; Hus and, 341, 342, 342*(i)*; in Middle Ages, 267

Hermits, 192

Hernández, Francisco, 513

Herodotus (historian): on Cyrus the Great, 53*(b)*, 54; on Persian Empire, 75, 76

Heroes: Sumerian, 16–17

Herophilus, 117

Herzegovina, 832. *See also* Bosnia-Herzegovina

Herzl, Theodor, 782*(b)*, 782*(i)*, 783, 971

Hesiod, 62, 67; *Works and Days*, 66, 68*(d)*

Hetaerae (Greek courtesans), 85, 85*(i)*

Hezekiah (Judah): Assyrians and, 48–49, 49*(i)*

Hierarchy: in 17th-century society, 466–468; in barbarian society, 197–199; in Christian churches, 180, 268, 597–598; colonial social, 815; of gender, 11; racial, 567; in Renaissance society, 379–382; social, 10–11, 26, 379–382; in Sumerian society, 17–18; of wealth, 380–381. *See also* Classes; specific groups

Hieratic writing, in Egypt, 26

Hieroglyphic writing, 26, 40

Higher education: after Second World War, 979. *See also* Education; Schools; Universities

High Middle Ages: agriculture in, 289, 289*(i)*; children in, 287; churches in, 317–319; cities and towns in, 298–299, 306–309; Crusades in, 276–280; economy in, 298–306; home life in, 289–291; law and justice in, 259–260, 261–262; lifestyle in, 250*(i)*, 284*(i)*, 292; literature and architecture and, 315–320; manors in, 287; Muslims and Jews in, 294; nation-states in, 252, 384; nobility in, 303; papacy in, 282, 339; popular religion in, 292–298; universities in, 309–314; urban life in, 298–299, 306–309; use of term, 248; village life in, 286–292. *See also* Crusades; Middle Ages

High-tech industries: in East Bloc, 1007

Highways. *See* Roads and highways

Hijab, in France, 1048

Hijra, 221

Hilda of Whitby (Saint), 207, 239

Hildegard of Bingen, 272*(b)*, 272*(i)*

Hilim (Pasha), 771*(i)*

Himmler, Heinrich, 922, 931

Hindenburg, Paul von, 842, 854, 921

Hindus, in India, 819, 820, 970

Hippocrates, 88, 117, 227, 311

Hiroshima, atomic bombing of, 939, 939*(i)*

Hispania (Spain). *See* Iberian peninsula; Spain

Hispaniola, 438, 439, 440*(d)*, 442, 446, 447, 448, 638, 640

Historical and Critical Dictionary (Bayle), 521

History, 3; Romanticism and, 696; Russian, 915; time periods in, 6. *See also* specific individuals

History of the Decline and Fall of the Roman Empire, The (Gibbon), 205

History of the Two Indies (Raynal), 529

Hitler, Adolf, 783, 889–890; anti-Semitism and, 922, 923; appeasement of, 925; fascism and, 906; film and, 884; after First World War, 887; Mussolini and, 917*(i)*; Nazism and, 919–927, 926*(m)*; radio and, 885; Rhineland and, 925; rise to power, 920–921; as totalitarian leader, 905. *See also* Holocaust; Nazi Germany; Second World War

Hittites: Assyrians and, 46; Egypt and, 30–32, 37; end of empire, 30–32, 35, 65; language of, 32

Hobbes, Thomas, 496

Hobsbawm, Eric, 940

Hobson, J. A., 816

Ho Chi Minh, 970

Hogarth, William, 600(i)

Hohenstaufen dynasty, 256–257

Hohenzollern dynasty, 482

Holidays: Christian, 208–209; national, 780; nationalism and, 780

Holland: Brethren and Sisters of the Common Life in, 342; in Kingdom of the Netherlands, 685; Nazis and, 928, 931. See also Dutch entries; Low Countries; Netherlands

Holocaust, 931–934, 932(i), 933(m); German apology for, 984(i); Levi, Primo, on, 935(b)

Holtby, Winifred, 844(b)

Holy Alliance, 687–688

Holy Land. See Crusades; Israel; Jerusalem; Palestine

Holy Office, 414–415, 518. See also Inquisition

Holy Roman Empire: Black Death in, 328; Catholic Church in, 597; under Charles V, 405, 406–407, 418; as confederation, 256; Habsburgs and, 405; Jews in, 294; laws and justice in, 260; Otto I and, 256; papacy and, 266–267; Protestantism in, 406, 418; Prussian electors and, 483; Sicily and, 256(m); Thirty Years' War and, 468–469. See also Germany; Habsburg dynasty; specific locations and rulers

Homage. See Feudalism

Home, Sweet Home, 738(i)

Home Army (Poland), 931

Home front, in First World War, 841–846

Homelessness: in London, 893(i); after Second World War, 944

Homer, 62, 66–67

Home rule, for Ireland, 777, 777(i)

Homestead Act (U.S., 1862), 766

Hominids, 6–7

Homo sapiens, 7

Homosexuality: in 18th century, 581; gay rights and, 1061; Nazis and, 906, 923; subcultures and, 581. See also Same-sex relationships

Hong Kong, 796

Honorius of Autun, 264, 286

Hoover, Herbert, 894

Hoplites (infantry), 69, 73(i)

Horace, 139, 161

Hormuz, 437

Horse collar, 289

Horses: in Americas, 451; for plowing, 289; Portuguese trade in, 455

Horus (god), 25, 26, 110(i)

Hospitals: for foundlings, 583; germ theory and, 722; medieval, 291

Hot-air balloons, 594(i)

Households: Greek, 83; medieval, 234; Merovingian royal, 229; in Middle Ages (High), 264–265, 289, 290; separate spheres and, 666–667, 737–739; workers in, 346

House of Commons (England), 704, 776, 777

House of Lords (England), 704, 776, 777

House of Orange. See specific rulers

House of Trade (Spain), 445

Housing: in 19th-century cities, 718–719; ancient, 9; consumerism and, 594–596; crisis in (2008), 1034; in Egypt, 27; in England, 718–719, 899; of foragers, 7; in Germanic society, 198(d); in industrial cities, 721; in London, 724; mass transit and, 725; in Middle Ages (later period), 289–290; middle-class, 728; in Paris, 724; of rural textile workers, 55; transportation and, 725

Hroswitha of Gandersheim, 226, 256

Hudson Bay region, 478; cession to Britain, 562

Huelsenbeck, Richard, 877

Hugh Capet, 254

Hugo, Victor, 98

Huguenots (France), 418, 473, 474, 520–521. See also Protestantism

Human(s): evolution of society and, 6–12; in Greece, 61; migration of, 7

Human body: ideal proportions in, 311–312, 377(i); study of, 517–518, 518(i). See also Medicine

Human Comedy, The (Balzac), 748

Humanism: Christian, 368–370, 391; Christian Church reforms and, 415; Jesuits and, 417; in Renaissance, 364–366, 507; schools and, 366–367

Human rights: in 18th century, 611; emigration for, 802; in Helsinki Accords, 986, 987(d); promotion of, 1060–1061; war on terror and, 1053

Human trafficking, 1044

Hume, David, 525, 527–529

Hunchback of Notre Dame, The (Hugo), 698

Hundred Days, of Napoleon, 638, 707

Hundred days of reform (China), 823

Hundred Years' War, 255, 332–339, 334(i), 344, 382

Hungarian people: in Austrian Empire, 414, 482; origins of term, 244

Hungary: 1848 revolution in, 711, 712; anti-immigrant government in, 1044; Austrian Empire and, 482, 483(m), 711, 778; Black Death in, 328; borders opened by, 1014; Celtic-speaking peoples in, 201; Christianity in, 281; economy in, 993; elections in, 1014; after First World War, 855, 855(m), 886; Habsburgs in, 414, 482, 686; independence and, 778; kingdom of, 686, 712; Magyars in, 245; nobility in, 482; Ottomans and, 406, 414, 482, 491; Reformation in, 413–414; revolution in (1956), 964–965; Rome and, 157; Russia and, 712; after Second World War, 950; after Soviet Union, 1028. See also Austria-Hungary; East Bloc; Magyars

Huns, 200; invasions by, 203, 210

Hunter-gatherers: in Greece, 61

Hunting: Paleolithic, 7

Hürrem (Ottomans), 491, 492–493(b), 493(i)

Hurricane Sandy, 1060

Hus, Jan, 341, 341(i), 342, 414

Husbands. See Families; Marriage; Men

Hussein, Saddam, 1054

Hussein ibn-Ali, 840, 859

Hussites, 341(m), 413

Huxley, Aldous, 872

Hydraulic projects, Sumerian, 13–14

Hydrostatics, 115(b)

Hygiene: in 19th century, 721; Black Death and, 327, 329; improvements in, 596

Hyksos people, in Egypt, 28–29

Hymns: by Enheduana, 20

"Hymn to Aton," 31(b)

Hyphasis River, Alexander the Great at, 96

Iaroslav the Wise (Kiev), 244

Iberian Peninsula: blacks in, 379; Catholic control of books in, 258; Celtic-speaking peoples in, 201; Enlightenment and, 569; Muslims in, 224–226, 245; reconquista in, 258, 259(m), 277, 279, 294; Rome and, 134; unification of, 385(m), 387; Visigoths in, 204. See also Portugal; Reconquista; Spain

Ibn-Sina. *See* Avicenna
Ibo people, 815
Ibsen, Henrik, 734
Ice age, little ice age and, 324, 468
Iceland: Christianity in, 280; Viking settlement in, 245
Iconoclasm, 419
Icons and iconography, 188*(i),* 213
Id, 874
Ideas. *See* Intellectual thought
Identity: in Atlantic world, 567; consumerism and, 592–593, 596; in French Revolution, 631; of homosexual men, 581; national, 692, 779, 780; of workers, 677
Ideograms, 15*(f),* 40
Ideologies: Communist vs. Fascist, 907; nationalism as, 691–692, 753. *See also* specific ideologies
Ides of March, 149
Ignatius. *See* Loyola, Ignatius
Île-de-France, 318
Iliad (Homer), 66
Illegitimacy: in 18th century, 583–584; in 19th century, 739; explosion of, 579–580; foundlings and, 583–584; premarital sex and, 578
Illness. *See* Disease; Health; Medicine
Illumination (illustrations), 273
Illyria, 173
Imams, 224; Danish-Muslim, 1048
IMF. *See* International Monetary Fund
Imitation of Christ, The (Thomas à Kempis), 342
Immigrants and immigration: to Akkad, 20; changes in, 1043–1046; in England, 998; ethnic groups and, 1046; from Europe, 801–802; Irish, 706; Muslims as, 978; nativism and, 803; of postwar Jews, 946–947; rights of, 1061; right-wing extremists and, 1005; after Second World War, 976–978; types of, 1046; U.S. restrictions on, 803, 804*(d);* use of term, 799. *See also* Emigration; Migrants and migration
Immortality, in Christianity, 392
Imperator, 154; Augustus as, 154, 154*(i);* Caesar as, 147
Imperialism: Africa and, 805–810, 806*(m);* Asia and, 810–812m 810*(m);* Athenian, 76; critics of, 816, 817*(d);* decolonization and, 966–968, 967*(m);* European, 934; First World War and, 827; French, 708; by Japan, 810*(m),* 822; mandate system and, 860;

nationalism and, 824; responses to, 818–823; Russian, 768; scientific racism, nationalism, and, 780; Western, 771–772. *See also* Empire(s); New Imperialism; specific empires
Imperialism (Hobson), 816
Imperial Rescript (1856), 771
Imports: to England, 562, 793; foods as, 591; tariffs on, 661, 771
Impressionism, 877
Inanna (goddess), 16, 20
Inca Empire, 443–444, 450*(i)*
Income: disparities in, 803; distribution of, 725–726; of immigrants, 802; in industrialized countries, nonindustrialized countries, and Great Britain (1750–1970), 792*(f);* inequality of, 726, 792–793; Merovingian, 228. *See also* Wages
Indentured laborers, Asian emigrants as, 802
Indentured servants, 445
Independence: of African territories, 805; of American colonies, 616–617; of Belgium, 680*(i),* 688; Communists and, 968; Greek, 702–703, 703*(m),* 770; of Haiti, 609, 641*(m),* 643; of India, 819; liberalism and, 686; of Lithuania, 1017; in Middle East, 971–972; of Portugal, 480; of Russia from Soviet Union, 1017; in South America, 690. *See also* American Revolution; Decolonization; specific locations
Independent Social Democratic Party (Germany), 846
Index of Prohibited Books, 415
India: in 1805, 571*(m);* Alexander the Great and, 96; anticolonialism in, 968; Britain and, 570*(i),* 571, 793, 819–820; British East India Company in, 819; British women in, 819–820; Christianity in, 417; cotton cloth from, 651; cotton in, 793; decolonization of, 970–971; First World War soldiers from, 840; France and, 613; Greek culture in, 104; Hellenism and, 100; Hindus in, 819, 820; immigrants from, 976; imperialism in, 810*(m);* independence for, 819; industrialization in, 658, 659, 659*(f),* 663; Islam and, 224; Muslims in, 819, 820; nationalism in, 820–821; partition of, 970–971, 970*(i);* plague in (1890s), 326; pollution and, 1060; Seven Years' War and, 614*(m);*

smelting in, 36; specialists from, 1046; textile workers and industrialization in, 663; trade and, 301, 428, 429, 430*(i),* 446, 793; water route to, 115; "white women's burden" in, 820
Indian National Congress, 820–821
Indian Ocean region: Atlantic economy and, 563; trade and, 427, 428–429, 428*(m),* 430, 435, 447, 570–571
Indians: origin of term, 438. *See also* Native Americans
Indictments, in English criminal justice system, 260
Indigenous peoples: in American colonies, 566, 569; conversion to Christianity, 567; imperialism and, 813–815, 818; neo-European impact on, 794; rights of, 1061; in South America, 688. *See also* specific groups
Individualism: Romantics and, 696
Indochina, 810, 810*(m);* independence movement in, 969–970; Japan and, 934. *See also* specific locations
Indo-European languages: migration of speakers, 30–32; of nomads, 52
Indo-Greek states, 104
Indonesia, 968–969; banking crisis in, 1034. *See also* East Indies
Inductive reasoning, 516–517
Indulgences, 277, 296, 341, 394–395, 394*(i),* 416
Indus River region: Alexander at, 96
Industrial banks, 662
Industrialists, class of, 673, 674
Industrialization: agents of, 661–663; child mortality and, 672; comparative country data about, 658–659; in continental Europe, 658–663; in England, 704; First World War and, 827; in Germany, 800; global, 663–664; global inequality and, 792–793; government and, 660, 661; middle classes and, 727; New Imperialism and, 811; population growth and, 657; responses to, 673–675; of Russia, 766, 767, 768; slavery and, 677; society and, 672; Soviet, 912–913, 914–915; Western civilization and, 747; world economy and, 792–799. *See also* specific locations
Industrializing nations: inequality in, 1038; labor costs in, 1037
Industrial Revolution, 647–648, 650, 756, 792; in England, 563, 648–658, 656*(m);* factories of, 664–665; French

Revolution and, 678; lifestyle in, 646(*i*); living standards and, 669–672, 718; Second, 659, 744–745; urban conditions and, 718–721

Industrious revolution, 555–556

Industry: in 18th-century Europe, 554(*m*); developed socialism and, 1005; in East Bloc, 993, 1007; in England, 899; English nationalization of, 956; environmental damage from, 1002–1003; in First World War, 842, 842(*i*); labor aristocracy in, 729; machines in factories and, 650; population and, 657–658; in Roman provinces, 174–175; rural, 552–556; in Russia, 907; science in, 744–745; Soviet, 910–911, 912–913; sweated, 730–731; workers in, 654–655, 669–670, 729, 730, 975–976. *See also* Cottage industry; Industrialization; specific industries

Infanticide, 104; foundlings and, 583–584

Infant mortality, 581; in 18th century, 581–582; breast-feeding and, 582–583; in foundling homes, 584; wet-nursing and, 582. *See also* Childbirth; Midwives

Infantry. *See* Armed forces; Hoplites; Military

Infection: bacteria and, 722

Infectious disease. *See* Disease

Infidels: holy war against, 277

"In Flanders Fields" (McCrae), 838(*d*)

Inflation: Black Death and, 330; in France, 890; in Germany, 842, 886, 887; Great Depression and, 891; price revolution as, 549–550; in Rome, 182; in Russia, 1022; in Spain, 455, 479; in western Europe, 997

Influenza epidemic (1918), 861

Information age, 995, 996

Information technologies, 1039–1042

Ingeborg (Denmark), 268

Inheritance: Hammurabi on, 21; by primogeniture, 254–255; Qur'an on, 223; in Rome, 136

Innocent III (Pope), 268, 279

Inoculation: against smallpox, 551, 604–605, 605(*i*), 672

Inquiry into the Nature and Causes of the Wealth of Nations, An (Smith), 525, 557

Inquisition: friars and, 274–275; Roman, 414–415, 422; Spain and, 287, 416, 420, 422; witchcraft trials and, 422

Inside and Outside (Grosz), 866(*i*)

Installment purchasing, 958

Institutes of the Christian Religion, The (Calvin), 411

Insurance: public health, 776. *See also* Welfare

Intellectual thought: in 1960s, 988; in Alexandria, 103; anti-intellectualism in Nazi Germany and, 922; in Carolingian Renaissance, 237; in Enlightenment, 520–526; exchange of ideas and, 12; feminist, 1000; on global inequality, 792–793; idea movement and, 506; medieval European centers of, 506; medieval theology, philosophy, and, 227; modern philosophy and, 868–872; movement of ideas, 506; nationalism and, 779–780; in Northumbria, 237, 239–240; orthodoxy in, 508; printing and, 363; in Protestant Reformation, 398–399; on race, 780; religion and, 872–873; in Renaissance, 363–373, 507; on revisionism, 787; science and, 744–746; Scientific Revolution and, 516–519; in Soviet Union, 915, 964; uncertainty in, 868–875. *See also* Art(s); Culture(s); Enlightenment; Ideologies; Industrial Revolution; Literature; Philosophy; Religion(s); Renaissance; Scientific Revolution; specific individuals

Intendants (in France), 473

Intermarriage: Ireland and, 352; Roman Empire and, 173

International agreements. *See* Alliance(s); specific treaties

International conference, on Morocco, 830

International Court of Justice, 1036

International Criminal Court: U.S. and, 1051

International Monetary Fund (IMF), 957, 1026, 1037, 1056(*i*), 1057

International organizations. *See* League of Nations; United Nations (UN); specific organizations

"International Style": of architecture, 876

International trade. *See* Trade

International Working Men's Association (First International), 784, 785. *See also* Workers International

Internet, 1033, 1039

Interpretation of Dreams, The (Freud), 874

Interracial relationships. *See* Mixed races

Inuit people, 324

Invasions: in 9th and 10th centuries, 240, 241(*m*); of Czechoslovakia, 994, 994(*i*); of England by Anglo-Saxons, 202; of Iraq, 1054; of Normandy, 938–939; Viking, 202, 240–241, 252. *See also* Migrants and migration; specific locations and invaders

Inventions. *See* Industrial Revolution; Technology; specific inventions and inventors

Investment: European in U.S., 1050–1051; foreign, 794, 795(*m*)

Ionia, 62; Greek exploration from, 70; Persia and, 76, 78; Pre-Socratics in, 88; Trojan War in, 65

IRA. *See* Provisional Irish Republican Army

Iran: fundamental Islamic revolution in, 996; nomads in, 52; Putin and, 1024; revolution in (1979), 1054; Rome and, 175. *See also* Medes and Media; Persia; Persian Empire

Iraq: Britain and, 859, 860; in First World War, 840; Hussein in, 1054; Islamic State and, 1055; migrants from, 1043, 1044; Persian Gulf War and, 1049–1050. *See also* Mesopotamia; Nineveh

Iraq war, 1047, 1052; collapse after, 1054–1055

Ireland: Catholicism vs. Protestantism in, 495–496, 777; Christianity in, 280; Church of, 409; in Common Market, 996; conversion to Christianity, 206–207; economy in, 1056; emigration from, 800, 800(*f*), 801; England and, 494, 495–496, 497, 777, 890–891; exports to, 562; famine in, 777; First World War and, 846; furs and, 303; Great Famine in, 705–707; home rule for, 777, 777(*i*); nationalism in, 707; population of, 706; potato failure in, 705; repatriation to, 801; revolts in, 494; separatism in, 1004; workers from, 665

Irene (Byzantine Empire), 235

Irish Republic, 846

Irish Republican Army (IRA), 1004–1005

Irish Republican Brotherhood (Fenians), 777, 777(*i*)

Irnerius, 311

Iron Age, 6, 36

Iron and iron industry, 12; of barbarian groups, 197; in Egypt, 37; in England, 655; in Meroë, 38; in Middle Ages (High), 288–289; Mycenaean, 65; smelting and, 35, 36; technology of, 36–37, 655–656

Iron curtain, 950, 950(*m*)

Iron law of wages, 657
Irrationalism: after First World War, 868
Irregular immigration: into EU, 1043
Irrigation: Mesopotamian, 13
Isabella (Castile), 385–386, 386(d), 387. *See also* Ferdinand and Isabella (Spain)
Isabella (France), 332, 333(i)
Isabella d'Este, 380
Isaiah (prophet), 43
Isis (goddess), 25, 26, 87, 110(i); cult of, 109–110
Islam: Black Death and, 327; Christian missionaries and, 815; Enlightenment attitudes toward, 527; in Europe, 224–226; in Pakistan, 971; radical political, 1053; in Spain, 224–226; spread of, 220–228, 222(m); teachings of, 222–223; in Turkey, 861; in West, 5. *See also* Arabs and Arab world; Crusades; Muslims
Islamic law, 224
Islamic State (ISIS, ISIL), 1055; immigration and, 1044; terrorism by, 1047(i)
Islamic world, conflicts in, 1053–1056
Islamists: Taliban and, 1054
Islamization, fears of, 1048
Island-hopping campaign, in Second World War, 937
Islands. *See* specific locations
Isolationism: after First World War, 858; of Japan, 797; in United States, 937
Israel: in 1948, 971(m), 972; ancient, 40, 42; Arab-Israeli wars and, 971, 995; Assyria and, 47; establishment of, 782(b); First World War and, 840; Jewish migration to, 946; Sinai Peninsula and, 972; Six-Day War and, 995. *See also* Hebrews; Jews and Judaism; Palestine
Israelites, 41
Issus, Battle of, 94, 96(i)
Istanbul. *See* Constantinople
Istria, 232
Italian language, 172
Italian people, in Austrian Empire, 686
Italy: Africa and, 805; anti-Semitism in, 919; Austria and, 762; as barbarian state, 199, 203; Black Death in, 327; city-states in, 301, 360–362, 362(i), 499, 757; clocks in, 306; Congress of Vienna and, 757; divorce and abortion in, 1001; emigration from, 800, 800(f), 801, 802; Ethiopia and, 919, 919(m); Etruscan culture in, 124; fascism in, 863, 917–918; First World

War and, 838, 846; after First World War, 855, 855(m); France and, 634; geography of, 122, 123(m); Greater Germany and, 713; Great Schism and, 340; Greece and, 70; Habsburg-Valois wars and, 362, 406; Holy Roman Empire in, 257; hospitals in, 291; industrialization in, 659, 659(f); Jews in, 294; Justinian and, 211; Lombardy-Venetia and, 711; Magyars in, 244; Mazzini on, 759(d); merchants in, 201, 205, 206, 299, 358–359; after Napoleonic Wars, 685; Napoleon III and, 758–759, 760; nationalists and nationalism in, 692, 757–760, 762(i); Nazi Germany and, 919, 925; New Left in, 992; northern cities in, 257, 267, 358–359; Northern League in, 1005; Red Brigades in, 992; Renaissance in, 358–362, 361(m), 373, 374–375; Rome and, 121, 123(m), 126–127, 165; science in, 518–519; in Second World War, 938; Second World War collaborators in, 947; slave trade and, 380, 431–432; socialism in, 787, 917, 984; Triple Alliance and, 828, 829(m); Turkey and, 860; unification of, 757–760, 758(m), 779; voting rights in, 757, 760. *See also* Lombardy-Venetia; Roman Empire; Roman Republic; Rome
Ius gentium (law of the peoples), 130
Ius naturale (natural law), 130
Ivanhoe (Scott), 696
Ivan III the Great (Russia), 485
Ivan IV the Terrible (Russia), 485, 486

Jacobin Club (France), 627–628, 631
Jacobites (England), 497
Jacob's Room (Woolf), 879–880
Jacquerie uprising, 344–345
James I (England), 494, 516, 580, 596
James II (England), 497
James V (Scotland), 413
Jameson Raid, 808(b)
Jamestown colony, 445
Janissary corps, Ottoman, 490–491
Jansen, Cornelius, 601
Jansenism, 601
Jansz, Anna (Rotterdam), 400(b), 400(i)
Japan: in Axis powers, 925; banking crisis in, 1034; British alliance with, 830; China and, 822, 840; Christianity in, 417; European imperialism and, 797,

821; expansion by, 822; before First World War, 830; in First World War, 840; German colonies and, 858; imperialism by, 810(m), 822, 823; industrialization in, 663, 664; Pearl Harbor attack by, 934–936; Portugal and, 455; Russia and, 768, 822, 822(i); Second World War and, 927, 934–937, 948; Sino-Japanese War and, 823; surrender in Second World War by, 939, 949; United States and, 797, 821. *See also* Second World War
Jaruzelski, Wojciech, 1009, 1014
Jaspers, Karl, 871
Jaurès, Jean, 787
Java, 570, 810
Jefferson, Thomas, 529, 612, 616
Jehovah. *See* Yahweh
Jehovah's Witnesses: Nazis and, 922
Jena, battle at, 635
Jenner, Edward, 605, 605(i)
Jerome (Saint), 191(i), 193, 194, 207–208
Jerusalem: Antiochus and, 110; Assyrian siege of, 48–49, 49(i); Babylonians and, 51; Crusades and, 258, 276, 277; as Hebrew capital, 41; Rome and, 165; Saladin in, 279
Jesuits: Catholicism extended by, 413, 417, 597–598; as missionaries, 417, 457, 526, 567; schools run by, 417
Jesus of Nazareth, 175, 176–177, 222; Muslims and, 226. *See also* Arianism; Christianity
Jet aircraft, 953
Jewelry: Persian, 56
Jewish State, The:... (Herzl), 782(b)
Jews and Judaism: Aryanization of Nazi Germany and, 924; in Atlantic world, 567; in Austria, 598, 686; Balfour Declaration and, 782(b), 859–860; Black Death and, 330–331; clothing of, 268, 308; Crusader attacks on, 280; Cyrus the Great and, 53(b), 55; death and, 298; deaths in Second World War, 944; as DPs after Second World War, 945–947; emancipation of, 781; in England, 280, 294, 386–387, 801; Enlightenment and, 538(b), 539, 539(i); family life of, 44–45; in France, 294, 386–387, 626, 776, 928; Hebrews and, 40–46; Hellenistic, 99, 110; Hitler and, 919–920; Holocaust and, 931–934, 932(i), 933(m), 935(b); in Holy Roman Empire, 294; in Iberian Peninsula, 225–226, 384(m), 386–387; immigration and, 801, 802;

Jesus and, 175, 176–177; Judaea and, 165; legal commentaries by, 311; legal restrictions on, 308; in Middle Ages, 294, 325; money-lending and, 280, 325; Muslims and, 225–226, 226–227; nationalism and, 778, 781; Nazis and, 906, 919–920, 922, 923, 928, 929, 930; in Pale of Settlement, 539, 539(m); reconquista and, 567; religion of, 42–44; religious toleration and, 490; repatriation and, 801; Rome and, 167; in Russia, 767, 781(i); in Spain, 225–226, 384(m), 386–387; sumptuary laws for, 308; weddings and, 294; in West, 5. *See also* Anti-Semitism; Hebrews; Israel; Zionism

Jiang Jieshi (Chiang Kai-shek), 971

Jihad, 222–223, 1047(i)

Joanna of Castile, 387

Joan of Arc (France), 335–337, 337(d), 383(m); trial of, 337(d)

John (England), 255, 261, 268

John II (Portugal), 435

John VI Kantakouzenos (Byzantine Empire), 328, 330

John Chrysostom (Saint), 214

John of Spoleto, 340

John Paul II (Pope), 1009

Johnson, Lyndon B.: Vietnam and, 990, 991

Joliet, Louis, 477

Jonson, Ben, on death of son, 584

Jordan: First World War and, 840; Six-Day War and, 995. *See also* Transjordan

Joseph II (Austria): Enlightenment and, 537; Jews and, 539, 598; religion and, 539, 598, 602

Journeymen's guilds, 300, 347, 557

Joyce, James, 880

Judaea: Christianity and, 175, 176; Jewish revolt in, 110, 165

Judah: Assyria and, 47; Babylonians and, 51; as Jewish state, 40, 42; name of Judaism taken from, 40

Judaism. *See* Hebrews; Jews and Judaism

Judeo-Christian Scriptures, Muslims on, 226

Judiciary and judicial system: in Middle Ages (High), 259–260, 262; in United States, 618. *See also* Court (legal); Law(s)

Jugurtha (Numidia), 143–144

Julia (Augustus' daughter), 164

Julia (Caesar's daughter), 147

Julio-Claudians (Rome), 164

Julius II (Pope), 373, 375

July Crisis, First World War and, 834

"June Days" (Paris), 710

Junkers, 482–483, 484

Jupiter (Jupiter Optimus Maximus), 128; temple of, 126

Jury trial, in England, 260

Justinian (Byzantine Empire): *Code* of, 212–213, 311; conquests by, 205–206, 211, 213; Theodora and, 214–215(b)

Just price, 590

Ka'ba, 220, 221

Kádár, János, 1014

Kaddish, 298

Kadesh, Battle of, 32

Kaffa, Black Death and, 327

Kafka, Franz, 880

Kalmar, Union of, 280

Kampuchea. *See* Cambodia

Kant, Immanuel, 526

Kapp Putsch, 856

Karlsbad Decrees (1819), 688, 689(d), 713

Kashrut (Jewish dietary laws), 45–46

Kay, John, 553

Kazakhstan, 1032

Kazan, 486

Keats, John, 697; "Bright Star," 697(d)

Kellogg, Frank B., 889

Kellogg-Briand Pact (1928), 889

Kemal, Mustafa, 860, 861

Kennedy, John F.: Berlin Wall and, 965; Vietnam and, 990

Kenya, 972; anticolonialism in, 968

Kenyatta, Jomo, 968

Kepler, Johannes, 510–511, 512, 515, 518

Kerensky, Alexander, 848, 850

Kershaw, Patience, 671(d)

Keynes, John Maynard, 886, 894

Khan. *See* China; Mongols

Khartoum, massacre at, 809

Khazars, 203

Khedive (Egypt), 798, 799

Khodorkovsky, Mikhail, 1026

Kholops (Russian slaves), 244

Khrushchev, Nikita: Cuban missile crisis and, 966; de-Stalinization and reform by, 961; "kitchen debate" and, 959, 962–963(d), 964(i)

al-Khwarizmi, 227

Kiel, mutiny at, 854

Kierkegaard, Søren, 871, 872

Kiev: Jews in, 802; Mongols in, 485; Rus territories and, 243–244

Kievan Rus, 244, 244(m), 245

Kilwa, 430

King, Martin Luther, Jr., 991

Kingdom of Sardinia-Piedmont, 759

Kingdom of the Two Sicilies, 688, 758(m), 760

Kin groups, 11

Kings and kingdoms, 38; Anglo-Saxon, 202; Assyrian, 47, 49–50; Carolingian, 231–232; Christianity and, 277, 280; Crusader, 277, 279–280, 281; in Egypt, 24–25, 29, 97–98; in England, 332, 384; in France, 255, 255(m), 332; Frankish, 230–231; Hebrew, 42; Hellenistic, 97–98, 102–103, 108; in Hungary, 686, 712; of Lombardy-Venetia, 686; Merovingian, 205, 228–230, 229(i); Mesopotamian, 16; Minoan, 64; Mycenaean, 65; Naples as, 257; in Near East, 35; Ptolemaic, 97–98; Seleucid, 98; of Sicily, 256(m), 257–258; in Spain, 480; in Sumer, 16–17. *See also* Empire(s); Monarchs and monarchies; specific locations and rulers

King's Peace (Greece-Persia), 78

Kinship: among workers, 665. *See also* Families

Kipling, Rudyard, 813; criticisms of, 816; "White Man's Burden, The," 813, 814(d)

Kirov, Sergei, 916

"Kitchen debate," 959, 962–963(d), 964(i)

Kitchener, Horatio H., 809, 819

Knights: as fur-collar criminals, 351; in Hundred Years' War, 333, 338; origin and status of, 246; Teutonic, 281. *See also* Nobility

Knights, The (Aristophanes), 84(b)

Knights Templars, 277–278

Knossos, Crete: palace at, 64, 64(i)

Knowledge. *See* Intellectual thought

Knox, John, 413

Koch, Robert, 722

Kohl, Helmut, 998–1000, 1010, 1016

Koine (Greek dialect), 102

Kongo, 453

Korea: Japanese annexation of, 822; Russia and, 768

Korean War, 952; economy and, 954

Kornilov, Lavr, 849

Kosovo, 1029; ethnic Albanians in, 1029, 1031; human rights and, 1061; independence from Serbia, 1031

Kraków, 281

Kristallnacht, 923

Kulaks, in Soviet Union, 912

Kulturkampf, 773, 780

Kurds, 1054–1055

Kush, 36, 36(i), 38, 38(m)

Kuwait, 1049–1050

Kyoto Protocol (1997), 1060; U.S. and, 1051

Kyrgyzstan, 1032

Labor: in 17th century, 480–481; agricultural, 10; Black Death and, 330; capital and, 672–677; in Egypt, 26; for factories, 649; in First World War, 838, 842; Greek, 83; guest worker programs and, 976; guilds and, 346–347; Hellenistic, 104, 105; immigration of, 802, 1043–1046, 1045 (m); in industrializing world, 1037; of peasants, 480–481; in putting-out system, 552–553; of serfs, 480–481; slaves as, 677; Smith, Adam, on, 557, 558(d); specialization of, 10; of working classes, 665, 728. See also Child labor; Forced labor; Gender and gender issues; Peasants; Serfs and serfdom; Slaves and slavery; Strikes; Workers; Working classes

Labor aristocracy, 729

Labor laws, 666

Labor strikes. See Strikes

Labor unions: in England, 675–677, 776; in First World War, 843; in France, 756; liberalism and, 691; Marxism and, 787; in Nazi Germany, 922; outlawing of, 676; socialism and, 786–787; in United States, 895. See also Guilds and guild system; Trade unions; Workers

Labouchère, Henry, "Brown Man's Burden, The," 817(d)

Labour Party (England), 787, 890, 956, 984, 998

Lachish (Jewish town), Assyrian attack on, 51(d), 51(i)

Ladies National Association, 737

Lafayette, marquis de, 617, 625

Laissez faire, 690

Lamarck, Jean-Baptiste, 745

Lamartine, Alphonse de, 698

Lancaster, house of, 384

Land: in 17th century, 544–546; Carolingian, 233(d), 234; drainage of,

547; enclosure of, 546; in England and Scotland, 548–549; Hammurabi on, 21; Merovingian, 228; in Poland, 1007; population increase and, 800; for Roman veterans, 155; in Rome, 130, 142–143, 155, 188; in Russia, 767, 850; serfdom and, 188, 481; in Sumer, 17. See also Agriculture

Landed aristocracy, 726

Landlords: in Egypt, 798; in Ireland, 705

Landowners: in England and Scotland, 548

Langport, battle at, 495

Language(s): in Austria, 686, 778; of Celts and Germans, 196–197; English, 30; Etruscan, 124; in Greece, 102; Hittite, 32; Indo-European, 30–32; Latin, 160–163; Magyar, in Hungary, 778; Nahuatl, 457; national, 692; nation building and, 779; Phoenician alphabet and, 40; Romance, 172; Semitic, 20; vernacular, 207; Wittgenstein on, 871. See also specific languages

Languedoc, prostitution in, 347, 349

Laos: independence of, 969, 970

Lares (household deities), 138

La Salle, Jean-Baptiste de, 587

La Salle, Robert de, 446

Las Casas, Bartolomé de, 458, 459(i)

Last Judgment, in Zoroastrianism, 56

Last Supper, The (Leonardo da Vinci), 376(d), 377(d), 377(i)

Late antiquity, 185–217

Lateen sail, 435

Late-marriage pattern: in Europe, 576–577

Lateran Agreement (1929), 918

Lateran Councils: of 1059, 265; Fourth (1215), 268

Lateran Palace, 188

Later Middle Ages: Black Death and society during, 326–332, 354; Catholic Church in, 331, 339–344; climate change and famine in, 323, 324–325, 324(i); ethnic groups in, 351–352; Hundred Years' War during, 332–339, 334(m); life and death in, 322(i); popular revolts in, 344–346, 345(m); same-sex relations in, 350; society in, 325, 351–352; urban conditions in, 346–347, 349; witches and, 421; women in, 347, 349, 350. See also Middle Ages

Latifundia (Roman estates), 142

Latin alphabet, runes and, 196(i)

Latin America: England and, 562; financial crisis in, 1034; industrialization in,

663–664; inequality in, 1038; railroads in, 793. See also South America; specific locations

Latin Christianity. See Catholic Church; Christianity

Latin language, 160; in barbarian states, 205; Bible in, 193; in Byzantine Empire, 185, 213; in Carolingian Renaissance, 237; Catholic mass and, 988; Celtic adoption of, 201; in church services, 292; decline of, 364; Greek and Persian learning and, 205, 227, 507; in Hungary, 245; literature in, 315, 363, 370; Renaissance and, 363, 370; in Rome, 139; for scholarship, 476

Latin people: Rome and, 127

Latin West, 186(m). See also Western Roman Empire

Latium, 122; Rome and, 126

Latvia, 539; economy in, 1056; Russia and, 489, 769; Soviet Union and, 927, 1012

Laud, William, 494

Lausanne, Treaty of, 860–861

Lavater, Johann Caspar, 538(b), 538(i)

Law(s): canon, 190, 268, 311; Carolingian, 232; child labor, 667(d); church, 268–270; Danelaw, 242–243; in England, 260, 282, 311; in France, 259–260; in Holy Roman Empire, 260; Islamic, 1053; Jewish, 43; labor, 666; against labor unions, 786; marriage age and, 576; Merovingian, 228–229; in Prussia, 534; Roman, 130, 159; in Russia, 535; serfs and, 481; witch trials and, 421–422. See also Canon law; Law codes; Mosaic law; Natural law; specific laws

Law (scientific): of motion and mechanics, 513; of universal gravitation, 513

Law codes: barbarian, 197, 199; of Draco (Athens), 73; English common law and, 260, 282; of Hammurabi, 19, 20–22, 21(i); of Jews, 43, 46; of Justinian, 212–213, 311; Napoleonic, 633; in Rome, 131; Salic, 199, 332; Ten Commandments as, 41(i), 43

Lawrence, T. E., 840

Laws of the Twelve Tables (Rome), 131, 136

Layard, A. H., on Nineveh, 50

Lay investiture, 256, 266

Laypeople: in government administration, 353; in Middle Ages (later period), 353

Lay piety, 342

Lay preachers: Methodist, 601

Leaders: totalitarian, 905

League of Armed Neutrality, 617

League of Nations, 857; Germany and, 889, 925; mandates of, 858, 859, 971; United States and, 858

Learning: ancient Greek, 506, 507; in monasteries and convents, 229(i), 236, 273; Muslim, 225–226, 227, 227(i); in Northumbria, 237, 239–240. *See also* Education; Intellectual thought; Renaissance; Schools; Universities

Leary, Timothy, 990

Lebanon: First World War and, 840; as French mandate, 859, 860, 971

Lebensraum (living space), 920, 926

Le Bon, Gustav, 747

Lechfeld, Battle of, 244–245, 256

Le Corbusier, 876

Left (political): in 1960s, 984, 985; in Germany, 921. *See also* New Left; Socialism

Legal system. *See* Law(s)

Legions and legionaries (Roman), 126, 127, 142, 144, 155

Legislation. *See* Law(s); specific acts

Legislative Assembly (France), 627, 628

Legislature: in United States, 618. *See also* Assemblies; specific bodies

Legnano, battle at, 257

Lehmus, Emilie, 742(b), 743(b)

Leibniz, Gottfried Wilhelm von, 521, 526

Leighton, Roland, 844(b)

Leisure: in 18th century, 589–590; in digital age, 1039–1040; mass travel, tourism, and, 986; of middle class, 727; of working class, 731–732

Lenin, Vladimir Ilyich, 852(i); Bolshevik Revolution and, 848–850; dictatorship and, 850–852; film and, 884; on imperialism, 816; Marxism of, 849; New Economic Policy of, 907–908; "Peace, Land, and Bread for the Russian People," 851(d); peasants and, 908; Soviet Union after, 907

Leningrad (St. Petersburg). *See* St. Petersburg

Lent, carnival and, 589

Leo I (Pope), 191, 203, 234, 235

Leo IX (Pope), 265

Leo X (Pope), 383, 394

Leo XIII (Pope), 776

León, Spain, 227, 258

Leonardo da Vinci, 375, 376–377(b), 377(i)

Leopold II (Belgium), 805

Leopold II (Holy Roman Empire), 537

Le Pen, Jean-Marie, 1005, 1048

Lepidus (Rome), 150

Leprosariums, 291

Lesbians: 18th-century subculture of, 581. *See also* Homosexuality

Lesbos, 86

Lesser Germany, 713

Le Tellier, François. *See* Louvois, marquis de

Levi, Primo, 907, 935(b)

Leviathan (Hobbes), 496

Lewis, C. S., 872

Lex Canuleia (Rome), 131

Lexington: fighting in (1775), 616

Liberal arts, 364

Liberal capitalism: in Ottoman Empire, 771

Liberal democracy, after Second World War, 954

Liberalism: in 18th century, 611, 612; anti-imperialism and, 819; in Austrian Empire, 710–711; defined, 690; economic, 557–559, 691; in England, 703–705; in France, 710, 756; in German Federation, 710–711; in Germany, 713; Karlsbad Decrees and, 688; laissez faire and, 690; Metternich on, 686; middle class and, 754, 756; nationalism and, 692; reforms of, 688; vs. totalitarianism, 904–905. *See also* Neoliberalism

Liberal Party (England), 776, 777, 890

Liberia, 805

Liberty(ies): 18th-century demands for, 611–612; Christian, 396–397(d); medieval use of term, 299

Libraries: in Alexandria, 103; Assyrian, 50; in Córdoba, 226; in Enlightenment, 532

Libya: migration from, 1043; uprising in, 1055

Licinian-Sextian laws (Rome), 131

Licinius (Rome), 131

Lidice, Czechoslovakia, Nazis in, 931

Liebknecht, Karl, 846, 856

Life of St. Cuthbert (Bede), 238(i)

Life span: in Middle Ages, 289. *See also* Mortality

Lifestyle: in 17th century, 500; in 19th century, 716(i); in 1960s, 986; agriculture and, 10; Black Death and, 325; Carolingian, 232–234; in China, 971; in cities, 306–307, 716(i), 718–721, 718–725; in classical Greece,

79–88; in Cold War, 959; consumerism and, 594–596; in digital age, 1039–1042; domestic, 499(i), 500; Dutch, 499(i), 500; in East Bloc, 959–961, 1006; in Eastern Europe, 942(i); in Egypt, 27–28, 27(d); in England, 890; in Europe, 1060–1061; family, 732–743; in First World War, 826(i); in French royal court, 474–476, 475(i); Hellenistic, 99–100; of immigrants, 1046; Industrial Revolution and, 646(i); in Mesopotamia, 21, 22–23; in Middle Ages, 234; middle-class, 673, 737–738; in monasteries, 192–193, 271, 273–274; of Muslim immigrants, 1048–1049; in Paris, 592–593(d); population growth and, 799; in Roman Empire, 152(i), 168–175; in Roman Republic, 138–140; Romanticism and, 696; of rural textile workers, 553–555; in Russia, 1023; socialist, 784–785(b); in Soviet Union, 914–915; in trench warfare, 835, 835(i); urban, 306–309, 718–721; in western Europe, 957; of workers, 786; working-class, 669–672, 738–739. *See also* Children; Families; Health; Marriage; Middle classes; specific locations

Lighting: gas, 672

Lightning war, 927

Limerick, Treaty of, 497

Limited liability: corporate, 662

Limited warfare: in Vietnam, 990

Lincoln, Abraham, 765, 766

Lindisfarne, 237, 239

Linear A script, 64, 66

Linear B script, 65, 66

Linnaeus, Carl, 514–515

Linné, Carl von, 527

Lin Zexu, 796, 796(i)

Lisbon, 379, 437, 453

Lisbon, Treaty of, 1036

Lister, Joseph, 722

Liszt, Franz, 701

Literacy: Bible reading and, 323; in Carolingian Renaissance, 237; in England, 353, 649; in France, 476, 588(m); growth of, 588, 779; Hellenistic, 101; in Middle Ages (later period), 352–353; nationalism and, 779; popular literature and, 587–589; of priests, 392; printing and, 371, 372–373. *See also* Literature

Literature: in 20th century, 879–881; Dance of Death and, 331, 331(i); in East Bloc 1960s, 994; Enlightenment, 532; essays and, 460; in France, 460; Greek, 363; Greek influence on Roman, 139; in Latin language, 160–163, 363; multiculturalism and, 1046; Orientalism and, 815; popular, 587–589; Realist, 748–749; Romantic, 696–698; Soviet, 964; travel, 515, 526–527, 528–529(d); women and, 530. See also Drama; Epic literature; Poets and poetry; specific writers and works

Lithuania, 413, 539; independence of, 1017; Soviet Union and, 927, 1012

Little Entente, 886

"Little ice age," 468

Liturgy: in England, 409; in monastic houses, 273

Liverpool: Irish workers in, 665

Liverpool and Manchester Railway, 656

Livery, of nobility, 307

Lives of the Most Excellent Painters, Sculptors, and Architects, The (Vasari), 365

Livestock, 10; in England, 547

Livia (Rome), 163

Living standards. See Lifestyle

Livy (historian), 125, 161

Lloyd George, David, 776, 857

Loans: to Germany, 889

Locarno agreements, 888(b), 889, 925

Locke, John: constitutional theories of, 568; Essay Concerning Human Understanding, 521–522; on role of government, 612; Two Treatises of Government, 498, 498(d)

Lodge, Henry Cabot, 804(d), 858

Lodz, Jewish ghetto in, 932

Logical positivism, 870–871

Lollards, 341

Lombards, 206; as Arian Christians, 206; papacy and, 230

Lombardy, 232, 685; Sardinia-Piedmont and, 759

Lombardy-Venetia, Kingdom of, 686, 711

Londinium (London), 172

London: in 19th century, 717, 720(d); in 1960s, 990; blitz in, 928, 929(d); Crystal Palace exhibition in, 657, 716(i), 717; first impressions of, 720(d); founding of, 172; growth of, 563; homelessness in, 893(i); immigrants in, 1046; poverty in, 724(i); scientific academy in, 519;

student protests in, 991; terrorist attack in, 1047; working-class leisure in, 731–732

Long-distance trade, in Middle Ages, 301–303

Long Parliament (England), 494

Looms, 553

Lords: of manors, 292; medieval, 247. See also Aristocracy; Nobility

Lord's Supper, 179

Lorenzo de' Medici, 361, 365, 373

Lorraine, 478, 763–764, 775, 828. See also Alsace-Lorraine

Lost generation, in First World War, 843

Lothair, 240

Louis II (Hungary), 413, 414

Louis IX (France), 259, 279, 332

Louis XI "Spider King" (France), 383

Louis XII (France), 383

Louis XIII (France), 472, 473, 596

Louis XIV (France): absolutism of, 472–473, 473–474, 522–523; acquisitions of, 477(m); arts and, 476; Charles II (England) and, 478, 497; death of, 478; guilds and, 556–557; portrait of, 474(i); religion and, 473, 474, 497, 500, 520–521; revolts against, 472, 473; in royal court, 464(i); Versailles and, 474–476; wars of, 465, 471, 477–478, 560–562

Louis XV (France), 531, 531(i), 559, 620–621

Louis XVI (France): constitutional monarchy and, 627; finances and, 620; guillotining of, 628; personality of, 621

Louis XVIII (France), 637–638, 685, 690, 707

Louisiana, 446, 477, 613

Louis Napoleon. See Napoleon III (Louis Napoleon)

Louis Philippe (France), 708, 709, 748

Louis the German, 240

Louvain, burning of, 835

L'Ouverture, Toussaint, 640–643, 642(b), 642(i)

Louvois, marquis de (François le Tellier), 477

Love: courtly, 316–317(d); marriage and, 733–734; Platonic idea of, 365. See also Marriage; Sex and sexuality

Low Countries: agriculture in, 546–547; enclosure in, 546; famine in, 325; Hundred Years' War and, 333; Protestantism in, 419, 420; textile industry in, 299; towns in, 299. See also Belgium; Holland; Netherlands

Lower classes: morality of, 736. See also Classes

Lower Egypt, 24

Lower middle class, 727

Loyalists: in American Revolution, 616–617

Loyola, Ignatius, 417

Lübeck, 301, 303, 304(i)

Lucretia (Rome), 125, 136–137

Luddites, 673–674, 674(i)

Ludendorff, Erich, 834, 842, 854

Lueger, Karl, 783

Lug (Gallic god), 160

Lugalzagesi (Umma king), 17

Lugdunum (Lyons), 160

Luhansk People's Republic, 1032

Lumumba, Patrice, 972–973, 973(i)

Lunéville, Treaty of, 634

Lusitania (ship), 841

Lutetia Parisiorum (Paris), 172

Luther, Martin, 392, 393–395, 398–399; Erasmus and, 370; on Eucharist, 398; excommunication of, 395; German New Testament of, 398; on indulgences, 395; marriage of, 401, 403(i); "Ninety-five Theses" of, 395, 404, 462; On Christian Liberty, 396–397(d); peasants' rebellion and, 401. See also Lutheranism; Protestantism

Lutheranism: Augsburg Confession and, 406; in Germany, 404–405, 407; in Holy Roman Empire, 406; in Hungary, 414; in Poland-Lithuania, 413; Protestant revival and, 598

Luxembourg, Holy Roman Empire and, 404

Luxemburg, Rosa, 816, 856

Luxury goods: Roman women and, 456(i); trade and, 106, 175, 279, 303, 427, 431, 455, 570

Lycurgus and Lycurgan regimen, 72

Lydia, Turkey, 54; coins in, 70

Lyons, France, 175, 242, 418, 472

Lyrical Ballads (Wordsworth and Coleridge), 697

Maastricht Treaty (1991), 1034

Ma'at (cosmic harmony), 24

Macao settlement, 455

Maccabees, Revolt of the, 110

MacDonald, Ramsay, 890, 898

Macedonia: Greece and, 79, 100; Persia and, 55; Rome and, 134–135. See also

Alexander the Great; Philip II (Macedonia)

Macedonians, 243

Machiavelli, Niccolò, 367–368, 370

Machine guns, 809

Machines. *See* Industry

Madame Bovary (Flaubert), 748

Madeira Islands, 436

Magdeburg, 242, 263(i)

Magellan, Ferdinand, 424, 439, 462

Magenta, Battle of, 758

Magi (priestly class), 55

Magic: Hellenistic religion and, 107–108, 108(i), 109(d)

Magna Carta (England), 260–261

Magna Graecia, 122

Magnitogorsk (city), 914

Magyars, 778; in Austrian Empire, 686, 778; invasions and migrations by, 244–245; Lutheranism and, 414. *See also* Hungary

Mahmud II (Ottomans), 771

Maine, France, 253–254, 383

Main River region, 762

Maintenon, Madame de, 476

Mainz, Jews of, 280

Major, John, 999(b)

Malacca, 429, 437, 455

Malaria, 812

Malay Archipelago, 439, 810

Malay Peninsula, Portuguese and, 455

Maldive Islands, 571

Malindi (city), 430

Malthus, Thomas, 657, 673, 745–746

Mamluks (Egypt), 279, 430

Manchester, England: in Great Depression, 894; lifestyle in, 671; Peterloo Battle in, 704; strike in, 676

Manchu dynasty (China). *See* Qing (Manchu) dynasty (China)

Manchuria: Japan and, 822, 934; Russia and, 768

Mandate system, 858, 859, 971; Islam and, 1053

Mani (Persia), 194

Manichaeism, 193

Manifest destiny, in U.S., 766

Manila, trade in, 455, 456

Mannerism, as art style, 375

Manors and manorialism: Carolingian, 247; courts and, 247; in Middle Ages (High), 287, 292. *See also* Feudalism; Serfs and serfdom

Mantegna, Andrea, 374

Mantinea, Battle of, 79

Mantua, 480; as city-state, 360

Manual on the Art of Childbirth (Coudray), 604

Manufacturing: Industrial Revolution and, 648; Muslim workers and, 1048–1049; outsourcing of jobs in, 1037; rural, 553; trade and, 107, 793, 794. *See also* Industrialization; Industry; specific industries

Manumission: in Rome, 138, 168–169. *See also* Abolition

Manuscripts: in monasteries, 236, 237, 273

Mao Zedong, 968, 971

Maps: by Eratosthenes, 115

Marathon, Battle of, 75

Marcel, Gabriel, 872

Marchant, Hilde, on London blitz, 929(d)

Marconi, Guglielmo, 885

Marcus Aurelius (Rome), 157, 165, 180–181, 181(i)

Marcus Aurelius Ammonio, slave of, 168–169

Marduk (god), 16, 20, 54

"Mare nostrum" (our sea), Mediterranean as, 135

Margaret of Valois, 419

Margrete I (Union of Kalmar), 280–281

Marguerite (France), 278

Maria Theresa (Austria): Catholic Church and, 598; education and, 587; Frederick the Great and, 533, 562; reforms of, 537; Seven Years' War and, 613

Marie Antoinette (France), 595, 628; fashion and, 595

Marie de' Medici, 501

Marie of Champagne, 315

Marinetti, Filippo Tommaso, 877

Maritain, Jacques, 872

Maritime trade: in Rome, 175. *See also* Seaborne trade

Marius (Gaius Marius, Rome), 144–145

Market(s): commercial rivalry in, 830; Dutch, 547; European, 574(i); foods in, 591; in medieval towns, 306–307; national, 779; Phoenician, 39–40; worldwide, 793–794. *See also* Trade

Marketing, 882

Marne: Battle of the (first), 835; Battle of the (second), 854

Marquette, Jacques, 477

Marriage: age at, 263, 264; Astell on, 530; Beauvoir on, 1002–1003(d); Catholic, 268, 268(i); Christianity and, 179, 193–194, 278, 294–296; of clergy, 265, 266; companionate, 733; in Crusades, 278; in Egypt, 27–28, 30; in

English colonies, 567; Hammurabi on, 21; Hellenistic, 92(i); illegitimacy explosion and, 579–580; in Islam, 294; in Jewish society, 44, 294–296; late marriage, nuclear families, and, 576–577; in Middle Ages (High), 264, 294–296, 295(i); in Middle Ages (later period), 325, 347; middle-class, 733; of Muslims, 278, 294; nobility-bourgeoisie, 610; noble, 381; in Norman England, 254(d); in Ottoman Empire, 491; as political alliance, 229, 230, 233; premarital sex and, 578–579; Protestantism and, 401–403, 402(i); in Renaissance, 382; in Rome, 136, 163–164; as sacrament, 266, 268, 268(i), 293; same-sex, 1061; unmarried men and, 382; women and, 382, 401–403; women workers and, 978–979. *See also* Separate spheres

Marseilles: origins of, 70; plague in, 552(i)

Marshall, Alfred, 744

Marshall, George C., 951

Marshall Plan, 951, 957

Marsiglio of Padua, 340

Martel, Charles. *See* Charles Martel

Martial law: in England, 495; in Poland, 1009–1010

Martin V (Pope), 342

Martinique, 446, 563, 641; Fanon and, 968, 969(d)

Martin of Tours (Saint), 206

Martyrs (Christian), 178, 179

Marx, Karl, and Marxism, 674, 694–695, 694(i); on fears of socialism, 754; Germany and, 773–774; labor unions and, 786–787; Lenin and, 849; Marxist critique of imperialism, 816; New Left and, 989; Paris Commune and, 784–785; in Russia, 766, 767, 787; social classes and, 726; socialism and, 694–695, 784–785; social sciences and, 746; Soviet Union and, 905; Workers International party of, 784. *See also* Marxism-Leninism

Marxian socialism, 694–695, 784–785, 819, 848–849

Marxism-Leninism: in China, 971; in Soviet Union, 915

Mary (mother of Jesus), 226, 293, 295, 318(i), 344, 457

Mary I Tudor (England), 407, 408(i)

Mary II (England), 497, 498(d), 500

Mary, Queen of Scots, 411, 413

Maryland, 445

Mary of Burgundy, 404

Masonic lodges, 532

Mass (Catholic), 292

Massachusetts Bay Colony, 445

Massacre at Chios (Delacroix), 702*(i)*

Mass culture, 881–883; in 1960s, 989. *See also* Culture(s)

Mass education: teacher status and, 727

Mass entertainment, 882

Mass media. *See* Media (communications); specific media

Mass migration, global, 799, 803

Mass mobility, in late 19th century, 803

Mass politics, after 1870, 772

Mass production, 882

Mass transit, 725

Mass unemployment, 894, 895. *See also* Unemployment

Masurian Lakes, Battle of, 837

Materialism, 267

Mathematical Principles of Natural Philosophy (Newton). *See Principia Mathematica* (Newton)

Mathematics: Arabic learning and, 506; Descartes and, 516–517; education in, 649; of Eratosthenes, 113–115; geometry and, 113; Hellenistic, 113–115; Mesopotamian, 16, 22; natural philosophy and, 511; of Newton, 513; professorships in, 507–508

Matilda (England), 253

Matilda (Tuscany), 267

Matteotti, Giacomo, 918

Matter, new physics on, 873

Matthew (Saint), Gospel of, 237*(i)*

Mau Mau rebellion, 972

Mauryan Empire: Greek culture in, 104

Maximilian (archduke, Austria), 771*(i)*

Maxim machine gun, 809, 811*(i)*, 812

May Day, 785, 786*(i)*

"May Events" (France), 991

Mayor of the palace, 230, 231

Mazarin, Jules, 473

Mazowiecki, Tadeusz, 1014

Mazzini, Giuseppe, 757, 759*(d)*, 780

McCrae, John, "In Flanders Fields," 838*(d)*

McDonald's, 1038–1039, 1038*(i)*

McMahon, Henry, 840, 859

Mecca: Arabs in, 220; as holy site, 221; Hussein ibn-Ali in, 840; Ka'ba in, 220, 221; pilgrimage to, 430

Mechanics: Hellenistic, 117

Mechanistic universe, 516, 517, 523

Mechanization: Industrial Revolution and, 650

Medes and Media, 34*(i)*, 35; Babylon and, 50, 51; in Iran, 52; Magi and, 55; Persian Empire and, 52, 53*(b)*

Media (communications): in digital age, 1039–1042. *See also* specific media

Medici family, 362, 367–368, 376; Catherine de', 418, 419; Cosimo de', 361; Lorenzo de', 361, 365, 373; Marie de', 501; Piero, 361; Savonarola and, 362, 365

Medicinal plants, 603

Medicine, 602–605; in 18th century, 551; advances in, 672; apothecaries and, 602, 603; in Arab world, 312*(i)*; Byzantine, 213; faith healing and, 602–603; Hellenistic, 117; Hippocrates and, 88; Islamic, 227, 312*(i)*; medieval, 227, 237, 290; in Rome, 170; schools of, 237, 311–312; Soviet women in, 915; spices as, 603; women in, 742–743*(b)*. *See also* Health

Medieval period. *See* Middle Ages

Medina: Arabs in, 220; as holy site, 221

Meditations (Marcus Aurelius), 180–181

Mediterranean region: Alexander the Great in, 94; Egypt and, 24; empires and migrations in, 29*(m)*; Genoese trade and, 432; Greek expansion in, 70, 71*(m)*; Muslims in, 431; Persia and, 52, 54; Phoenician settlements in, 40*(m)*; Punic Wars in, 132–134; Rome and, 135; Sea Peoples in, 37; trade and, 303, 431–432, 451. *See also* Rome; specific locations

Medvedev, Dmitry, 1026

Megara, Athens and, 76

Meiji Restoration (Japan), 821

Mein Kampf (Hitler), 920

Mejid, Abdul (Sultan, Ottomans), 771

Melesippus (Sparta), 76–77, 78

Memoirs (Catherine the Great), 534

Memorials: to First World War, 861–862; Greek, 79–80

Men: childbirth and, 604; gender hierarchy and, 11; gender roles and, 350; in Greece, 85; marriage age for, 263; in medieval universities, 314; in Roman families, 135–136; same-sex relations among, 350, 580–581; Spartan, 72; in Sumer, 18–19. *See also* Families; Fathers; Gender and gender issues; Marriage

Menander, 112–113

Mendeleev, Dmitri, 744

Mendelssohn, Moses, 538*(b)*, 538*(i)*, 539

Menes (Narmer, Egypt), 24

Ménétra, Jacques-Louis, autobiography of, 586*(d)*

Menin Road, The (Nash), 826*(i)*, 837

Mensheviks, 849

Mercantilism, 560; British, 496, 563; colonial competition and, 445; defined, 304; French, 477, 563; Industrial Revolution and, 648; Spanish, 563

Mercenaries: of Alexander the Great, 95; Carthaginian, 132

Merchant(s): African, 564; Carolingian, 234, 248; demand and, 594; English, 560; European, in China, 795–796; French, 563; Hellenistic trade and, 106; hierarchy of wealth and, 380–381; in Italy, 201, 205, 206, 299, 358–359; in medieval towns, 248; in Middle Ages (High), 303, 320; money-lending and, 304; Roman, 129, 172; rural textile workers and, 555; slaves imported by, 431–432; in social hierarchy, 466; woolen decline and, 325. *See also* Merchant guilds; Trade

Merchant guilds, 299–301

Mercier, Louis-Sébastien, 592–593*(d)*

Merian, Maria Sibylla, 519

Merici, Angela, 416–417

Merk, J. C., 484*(i)*

Merkel, Angela, 1057

Meroë, 38

Merovech, 205

Merovingian dynasty, 205, 228–230, 229*(i)*

Merry Family, The (Steen), 499*(i)*

Mesoamerica: botanical knowledge of, 513–514, 514*(d)*

Mesopotamia: agriculture in, 12–13; Assyria and, 46–50; civilization in, 12–19; culture of, 17*(i)*; empires in, 19–23; environment of, 13–15; in First World War, 840; lifestyle in, 21; myths from, 16–17, 20; Neo-Babylonians in, 51–52; religion in, 16–17; trade in, 22–23, 429; writing in, 15–16, 15*(f)*, 22. *See also* Babylon and Babylonians; City-states; Neo-Babylonians; Sumer and Sumerians

Messenia, 71–72

Messiah, 176, 177

Mestizos, 450, 567, 688

Metallurgy, 513

Metals. *See* specific metals

Metamorphosis (Kafka), 880

Metamorphosis of Narcissus (Dali), 879

Metaurus, Battle of, 133

Methodists and Methodism, 567, 599–601; Hogarth on, 600(i); Wesley on, 599(d)

Methodius (missionary), 215

Metics (resident foreigners): in Greece, 70

Métis, 567

Metropolis, 70–71

Metropolis (film), 884

Metternich, Klemens von, 686(i); 1848 revolutions and, 710, 711; on balance of power, 683–684; conservatism and, 685–687; Greece and, 702; Holy Alliance and, 687–688; Italy and, 757; Napoleon and, 637

Mexican-American War, 765

Mexico: Aztec Empire in, 442–443; Cortés in, 442–443; silver in, 448, 454; Spanish conquest of, 442–443

Mexico City, 442, 457; mining school in, 570; student protests in, 991

Miasmatic theory of disease, 722

Michael III (Byzantine Empire), 215

Michelangelo, 373, 374(i), 375, 501

Michelet, Jules, 696

Microchips, 1039

Microscope, 508

Middle Ages: cities and towns in, 234, 235; creativity in, 375; long-distance trade in, 301–303; society and economy in, 373; use of term, 219. *See also* Carolingian Empire; Early Middle Ages; High Middle Ages; specific periods

Middle classes, 717; in 19th century, 726; advice for women in, 675(d); culture and values of, 727–728; education of, 727; in England, 705, 776; family lifestyles of, 402(i); in France, 756; French reforms and, 709; industrialization and, 673; Jews in, 781; lifestyle of, 727–728; marriage and families in, 733–734; mass transit and, 725; morality of, 734–735; people and occupations of, 726–727; prostitution and, 736; in Prussia, 761, 763; in Russia, 766, 769, 848; after Second World War, 975; sentimental pleasures of, 738(i); separate spheres in, 737–739; urban transportation and, 725; women in, 673

Middle East: Arab Spring and, 1055; Crimean War in, 766; decolonization in, 966; empires in, 220; First World War and, 836(m), 839; independence in, 971–972; industrialization in, 663;

oil in, 995–996, 1059; refugees from, 1043, 1044(i), 1055; trade and, 428, 430–431; turmoil in, 1053; U.S. regime support in, 1053–1054. *See also* Arabs and Arab world; Crusades; Islam; Muslims; Near East; specific locations

Middle Kingdom (Egypt), 25

Middlemarch: A Study of Provincial Life (Eliot), 748–749

Midwives, 117, 291, 296, 602, 604

Mies van der Rohe, Ludwig, 876

Migrant labor, 790(i)

Migrants and migration: in 9th and 10th centuries, 240, 241(m); barbarian, 200–206, 201(m), 219; changes in, 1043–1046; in eastern Mediterranean, 29(m); European, 801; German attacks against, 1048; by Germanic peoples, 201(m), 203; global mass, 799; Greece and, 61, 66, 102; human, 7; of Hyksos, 28; Indian partition and, 970, 970(i); from Ireland, 706; in Middle Ages (later period), 351; by Muslims, 978; population pressure and, 799–800; postcolonial, 976; routes into Europe, 1045(m); after Second World War, 976–978; smuggling gangs and, 1044; use of term, 799. *See also* Emigration; Immigrants and immigration; specific groups and locations

Migration chain, 802

Milan, 759; as city-state, 360; growth of, 299, 358; Sforza family in, 361

Militants: Islamic State, 1055

Militarism: before First World War, 831

Military: under Alexander the Great, 94–96, 95(m); Assyrian, 35, 46, 47–49; in Crimean War, 766; in First World War, 840, 846; French, 634–635; French withdrawal from NATO and, 958; German, 858; imperialism and, 791, 792, 812, 823; Italian, 919, 919(m); in Japan, 821; in Nazi Germany, 922; in Prussia, 484, 484(i); Roman, 126, 129, 130–131, 134–135, 144, 155, 168; Roman roads and, 157; Russian, 488–489, 768, 847, 848; in Second World War, 937; space race and, 953; in Sumer, 17. *See also* Armed forces; Soldiers; specific battles and wars

Military dictatorship: in Germany (First World War), 842

Military draft. *See* Draft (military)

Military technology, 35; Assyrian, 48; in Hundred Years' War, 335, 335(i), 338; imperialism and, 811(i), 812. *See also* Weapons; specific weapons

Millet, Jean-François, 748

Millet (nation) system, in Ottoman Empire, 491

Mills: water and wind-driven, 288; workers in, 665. *See also* Factories; Textiles and textile industry

Milošević, Slobodan, 1029, 1031

Mines Act (England, 1842), 668

Mines and mining: Asian immigrants and, 802, 803; child labor in, 669(i); coal and, 654; pumping water from, 654; workers in, 665, 670–671(d). *See also* Gold; Silver; Trade

Ming dynasty (China), 429, 484

Minoan civilization, 62, 63–64, 64(i)

Minorca, 478

Minorities: in Austrian Empire, 712; ethnic, 692; rights of, 1061; in Russia, 769; in Soviet Union, 1012. *See also* specific groups

Minor orders: marriage and, 347; university students as, 314

Minting: in medieval towns, 298, 303–304

Minuscule, Carolingian, 236, 236(i)

Misogyny: in Christianity, 194; in Renaissance, 381

Missal, 237

Missi dominici (Carolingian officials), 232

Missiles: Bush, George W., and, 1052; Cuban missile crisis and, 965–966

Missions and missionaries: activities of, 206–207, 280; in American colonies, 448, 457, 458(d), 567; to barbarians, 206; to British Isles, 192; Carolingian, 230; in China, 797, 823; Columbus and, 437–438; conversion process by, 207–210; Eastern Orthodox, 244; imperialism and, 812, 813, 813(i), 815; Jesuit, 417, 457, 526; Moravians and, 215; Nestorian, 190; in New World, 448, 457, 458(d); Protten, Rebecca, as, 568–569(b). *See also* Monks and monasteries; specific orders

Mississippi River region, 617; France and, 446

Mithra (god), 55

Mithridates, 144; Pompey and, 145

Mitterrand, François, 1000

Mixed races, 448, 450, 567

Mobility. *See* Mass mobility; Social mobility

Mobilization: for First World War, 831, 832–833, 847; for total war, 841–842

Mobutu, Joseph, 973

Moctezuma II (Mexica Empire), 442–443

Modena, as city-state, 360

"Modern girl," 882–883, 883*(i)*

Modernism, in arts, 875–881

Modernization: of Egypt, 771, 798; in Japan, 821; of Ottoman Empire, 769–772; as response to imperialism, 818, 821; of Russia, 488, 488*(d),* 489, 766–769; of Turkey, 861

Mogadishu, 430

Mohács, Battle of, 414

Mohammed. *See* Muhammad

Mohammed II (Ottoman Empire), 431

Moldova, 1032

Molesmes, abbey of, 271

Molière (Jean-Baptiste Poquelin), 476

Molson, John, 656

Moluccas, 439

Mombasa, 430

Mona Lisa (Leonardo da Vinci), 376*(d);* Dadaist version of, 877

Monarchical period (Rome), 121

Monarchs and monarchies: in 17th century, 466; absolutism and, 502, 533; Assyrian, 46–49; cameralism and, 534; in England, 252–254, 493, 497–499; enlightened absolutism in, 532–539; in France, 332–333, 634, 709; in Germany, 713; in Greece, 69; Hellenistic, 101, 121; in Italy, 760; parliamentary, 753, 760; in social hierarchy, 466; women rulers and, 382, 493. *See also* Absolute monarchy and absolutism; Constitutional monarchy; Kings and kingdoms; specific rulers

Monasticism (Christian): eremetic and cenobitic, 192; *Rule of Saint Benedict* and, 192–193. *See also* Monks and monasteries

Monet, Claude, 877

Monetary system: in Poland, 1014; in United States, 995

Money: in France, 620, 626; for trade, 105–106. *See also* Coins; Currency; Economy

Moneylending: by Jews, 280, 304, 325; by Knights Templars, 278

Mongols, 484–485; Avars as, 203, 210–211; Louis IX (France) and, 279; in Russia, 484–485; trade and, 429

Monism, 521

Monks and monasteries: Benedictine, 192–193; Carolingian, 270;

Charlemagne and, 236; children sent to, 271, 291–292; double, 236, 239; in England, 408; in France, 626; lifestyle of, 192–193, 271, 273–274; monastic revival and, 270–271; in Orthodox Christianity, 214, 215; schools and, 193, 214, 274, 310, 310*(m);* in Spain, 479. *See also* Convents; Friars; Missions and missionaries; Monasticism; specific orders

Monnet, Jean, 957

Monopolies: guilds as, 557

Monotheism, 5; of Hebrews, 40, 43; of Zoroastrians, 56

Montagu, Mary Wortley, 527, 604–605

Montaigne, Michel de, 457, 460–461, 584

Montenegro: independence of, 772; Rome and, 173

Montesquieu, baron de (Charles-Louis de Secondat), 522–523, 527, 530, 612; constitutional theories of, 568

Montpellier: revolt in, 472

Montreal, 441, 445

Monuments: in Egypt, 24, 28

Monument to the Battle of the Nations (Leipzig), 780

Moon: U.S. landings on, 953

Moors, 224–225, 461

Morale, in First World War, 846

Morality: civic, 525; fascism and, 907; middle-class, 728; middle-class and working-class sexuality and, 734–736; Nietzsche on, 869; in Rome, 163–164; working-class, 729–730. *See also* Ethics

Moratorium, on German reparations, 886

Moravia, 215, 243

Moravians, 567; in St. Thomas, 568–569*(b);* Wesley and, 600

More, Thomas, 366, 368–369, 369*(d),* 370, 400*(b),* 408

Moriscos (former Muslims), Spanish expulsion of, 479

Moro, Aldo, 992

Morocco, 436, 830; in Second World War, 937

Mortagne, siege at castle of, 335*(i)*

Mortality: in 17th century, 550; from Black Death, 326, 327–328, 329; child, 672; in cities, 721; decline in, 550–551, 722–723, 722*(f),* 799; of medieval clergy, 329; of Native Americans, 448; from plague, 326, 327–328, 329; in slave trade, 454. *See also* Death; Infant mortality

Mortimer, Roger, 333*(i)*

Mosaic law, 223

Mosaics, of gladiators, 171*(i)*

Moscow: autonomy of, 485; in Second World War, 928; suburbs of, 767; as Third Rome, 215

Moses, 41, 41*(i),* 43, 226

Moses (Michelangelo), 375

Mosques: in Europe, 1048

Mothers and motherhood: in 19th century, 739–740. *See also* Breast-feeding; Childbirth; Children; Marriage; Wet-nursing; Women

Motion: Newton and, 513

Motion pictures. *See* Movies

Moulin Rouge, 731*(i)*

Mountain, the (France), 628, 629

Mountains. *See* specific mountains and ranges

Movable type, 371, 371*(i)*

Movement of peoples: in Hellenistic world, 101–102. *See also* Immigrants and immigration; Migrants and migration

Movies, 882, 883–884

Mozambique, 805, 974

Mubarak, Hosni, 1055

Mughal Empire, 508

Mughals (India), 571

Muhammad, 220–222, 527

Mujahideen, 1054

Mulatto, 450, 688; Protten, Rebecca, as, 568–569*(b)*

Mule: spinning, 651

Multiculturalism: European, 1046–1047

Multiethnic state: Austrian Empire as, 686; nationalism in, 692; Yugoslavia as, 960, 1029

Mummification: in Egypt, 26, 30, 102

Mundus Novus, 439

Munich, Beer Hall Putsch in, 889, 920

Munich Conference (1938), 927

Munitions. *See* Armed forces; Weapons

Münster, Germany, 399

Murder, in Middle Ages, 262

Mursili I (Hittites), 32

Musa (Mansa), 430

Musa ibn Nusair, 225*(d)*

Music: baroque, 501; by Hildegard of Bingen, 272*(b);* in medieval celebrations, 309; Mesopotamian, 17*(i);* middle class and, 728; modern, 881; multiculturalism and, 1046; punk rock, 997; rock, 990; in Roman Empire, 160*(i);* Romantic, 700–702; youth culture and, 979

Music halls: working class and, 731–732

Muslim Brotherhood, 1053, 1056

Muslims: in Algeria, 708; Black Death and, 327–328; in Bosnia, 1029; Byzantine Empire and, 211; Christians and, 225, 226–227; clothing of, 268, 308; Crusades and, 277, 278–279, 280; death and, 297; Enlightenment and, 527; in EU, 1036; in Europe, 1047–1049; French riots by, 1050–1051(d); in India, 819, 970, 970(i); Jews and, 225–226, 226–227; in Middle Ages, 258, 294; migration to Europe by, 978; as Moors, 224–225, 461; in Ottoman Empire, 485, 772; papermaking by, 226, 315; population in Europe, 1048; reconquista and, 567; scholarship of, 506; Shi'ite (Shi'a), 223–224; in Sicily, 257; slave sales to, 242; in Spain, 224–226, 258, 387, 454–455, 479; in Sudan, 809; sumptuary laws for, 308; Sunni, 223–224; turmoil in Muslim world and, 1053–1056; weddings of, 294; women and, 492–493(b). *See also* Arabs and Arab world; Islam

Mussolini, Benito: Fascist Italy under, 126, 906, 917–919; Hitler and, 917(i); overthrow of, 939; radio and, 885; in Second World War, 938; as totalitarian leader, 905

Mustafa Kemal. *See* Kemal, Mustafa (Atatürk)

Mutinies: in First World War, 846, 854

Mycenae and Mycenaeans, 62, 64–66

Myron of Athens (sculptor), 81(i)

Mystery plays, 316

Mystery religions: Christianity as, 118, 178; Greek, 87; Hellenistic, 108–110

Mysticism, Christian, 272(b), 339, 342, 344

Myths: Celtic, 202; Mesopotamian, 16–17, 20; Roman foundation, 124–125. *See also* Philosophy; Religion

Nabta Playa, 12

Nagasaki: atomic bombing of, 939; Portuguese trade with, 455

Nagy, Imre, 965

Nahuatl language, 457

Nahum (prophet), 50

Nama people, 809

Namban-jin (southern barbarians), 426(i)

Nanjing (Nanking), 429; Treaty of (1842), 796

Napata, Kush, 38

Naples: 1848 revolt in, 708; Enlightenment in, 526; kingdom of, 360; University of, 258

Napoleon I (Napoleon Bonaparte), 632, 633–638; Austria and, 634; Egypt and, 797; at Elba, 637–638, 684, 685; empire of, 635–638; expansion in Europe, 634–638, 636(m); Grand Empire of, 635–638; Hundred Days of, 638; Russian invasion by, 637; at Waterloo, 685

Napoleon III (Louis Napoleon), 710, 763, 775; election of, 754, 755, 756; Italian unification and, 758–759, 760; Paris modernization and, 723; Second Empire of, 756; Second Republic of, 755; urban planning and, 723

Napoleonic Code (France), 633, 634

Napoleonic Wars, 633, 634–637, 638, 770, 780; Europe after, 682–690; tariffs after, 661

Naram-Sin (Akkad), 20(i)

Narmer (Menes, Egypt), 24

Narva, battle at, 488

Naseby, battle at, 495

Nash, Paul, 826(i), 837

Nasmyth, James, 655(i)

Nasser, Gamal Abdul, 968, 972

Natal, 809

Nation (state). *See* Nationalism; State (nation); specific nations

National Aeronautics and Space Administration (NASA), 953

National Assembly (France), 624–625, 627; constitutional monarchy and, 626; guilds and, 559; Napoleon III and, 755, 756; Paris Commune and, 775; reforms by, 775; Saint-Domingue and, 639–640; social changes made by, 624–625

National Convention (France), 628, 629, 631, 632, 641

National debt. *See* Debt

National Democratic Party (West Germany), 1005

National Front (France), 1005, 1048

National Guard (France), 625, 709, 710

National independence: liberalism and, 686

Nationalism, 691–692, 753; after 1870, 778; anti-imperialism and, 819; anti-Semitism and, 781–783; Arab, 859, 860; in Austrian Empire, 711–712; Austro-German, 919; in Austro-Hungarian Empire, 778; authoritarianism and, 754, 756; in China, 971; Czech, 712; in Egypt, 798–799; ethnic minorities and, 780–781, 832; First World War and, 827, 831, 832–833; in France, 333, 338–339, 707–708, 756; in French Revolution, 631; in Germany, 764, 773, 779, 887, 888(b), 890; in Greece, 702–703; growth of, 779–780; after Hundred Years' War, 338–339; in Hungary, 711; immigrants and, 803, 1048; imperialism and, 824; in India, 820–821, 970–971; in Ireland, 707, 777; in Italy, 752(i), 757–760, 779; Magyar, 778; Metternich and, 686–687; in Middle Ages (later period), 333; nation-states and, 753–754, 778–780; New Imperialism and, 811–812; in Ottoman Empire, 772, 832; in Prussia, 763; racism and, 780–781; Romanticism and, 698; in Russia, 767, 853; after Second World War, 955; socialism and, 783; in Soviet Union, 937; totalitarian governments and, 906; in United States, 766. *See also* Patriotism

Nationality: in Austrian Empire, 686, 687(m); repatriation and, 801. *See also* Ethnic groups; Minorities

Nationalization: in East Bloc, 1005–1006; economic, 954; in England, 956–957; in France, 1000; by Soviets, 907; of Suez Canal, 972; under War Communism, 853

National Labor Relations Act (U.S., 1935), 895

National Liberals (Germany), 773

National Liberation Front (FLN, Algeria), 973–974

National Organization for Women (NOW), 1001

National People's Party. *See* Guomindang (Kuomintang)

National Recovery Administration (NRA), 895

National security, New Imperialism and, 811

National Security Agency (NSA, U.S.): Internet information leaks and, 1041; Snowden and, 1040–1041(b)

National self-determination, 857, 858–859; U.S. and, 968

National Socialism, 879, 887, 919, 920; support for, 923–925. *See also* Nazi Germany

National Socialist German Workers' (Nazi) Party. *See* Nazi Germany; Nazi Party

National state. *See* State (nation)

Nation building. *See* Nationalism; State-building

Native Americans: after American Revolution, 618; baptism and conversion of, 457; Columbus and, 438, 440–441*(d)*; debates on treatment of, 457–459; diseases of, 448, 449*(d)*, 451, 478; European settlement and, 615; as forced labor, 448–449; marriage in colonies, 567; neo-European impact on, 794; population loss by, 448, 457; in Seven Years' War, 562, 613; U.S. wars with, 818; Wesley, John, and, 600

Native peoples. *See* Indigenous peoples; specific groups

Nativism, 803; in United States, 803, 804*(d)*

NATO (North Atlantic Treaty Organization), 952; bombing of Serbia by, 1030; disagreements in, 1052; EU and, 1036; France and, 958; Kosovo occupied by, 1031; Poland, Hungary, and Czech Republic in, 1028; Putin's opposition to, 1024, 1025*(d)*; U.S.-European relations and, 1010, 1049–1050

Natural gas, 1059, 1059*(m)*

Natural History (Pliny the Elder), 166*(b)*

Naturalism, Realism as, 747

Natural law: in Rome, 130; Rousseau on, 531; Stoics on, 112

Natural philosophy, 505, 507, 508, 511, 521

Natural resources. *See* specific resources

Natural rights, 498–499

Natural selection, 745–746

Nature: Romanticism and, 696, 700

Navarre, 227, 297*(d)*, 384

Navigation: mathematics for, 508; technology and, 226, 434–435. *See also* Maritime trade; Ships and shipping

Navigation Acts (England), 562, 650; of 1651, 496, 560; of 1660, 560; of 1663, 560

Navy: Athenian, 78; British, 471, 560; Carthaginian, 132; in Crimean War, 766; before First World War, 830; in First World War, 840–841, 846; German, 830; Greek, 75; Hellenistic, 101; Japanese, 821, 822*(i)*; Persian, 75–76; Roman, 132; in Second World War, 936, 938–939. *See also* Ships and shipping; specific battles and wars

Nazareth. *See* Jesus of Nazareth

Nazi Germany, 919–927; aggression by, 925–927; anti-Semitism in, 919–920; Aryanization of, 924; central and eastern Europe under, 930–931, 931*(m)*; deaths in Second World War, 944; economy in, 924; ethnic Germans and, 927; eugenics in, 906, 906*(i)*, 922, 923; former Nazis in postwar positions, 947; Great Depression and, 921; growth of, 887, 890, 926*(m)*; Holocaust and, 931–934, 932*(i)*, 933*(m)*; Italy and, 919; New Order in, 903, 928, 931; punishment of war crimes and, 947; Second World War and, 927–934; Sixth Army of, 938; Soviets and, 927, 928; Spanish Civil War and, 925–926; state and society in, 921–923; Sudetenland and, 927; totalitarianism in, 919, 934; women in, 924. *See also* Germany; Hitler, Adolf; Second World War

Nazi Party (Germany), 856, 921; film about, 884; support for, 863. *See also* Hitler, Adolf; Nazi Germany

Near East: cultures in, 13*(m)*; kingdoms and empires in, 35–57; steel in, 37. *See also* East; Middle East; specific locations

Nebuchadnezzar II (Neo-Babylonian empire), 51

Necropolis of Monterozzi, 120*(i)*

Nefertiti (Egypt), 30, 31*(b)*, 31*(i)*

Nehru, Jawaharlal, 970, 971

Nelson, Horatio, at Trafalgar, 634

Neo-Assyrian Empire, 47

Neo-Babylonians, empire of, 51–52

Neocolonialism, 974; UN and, 1036

Neo-Europes, 794; Asian immigration to, 803; European emigrants to, 799

Neoliberal free-trade policies, 1037

Neoliberalism, 997; East Bloc and, 1006–1007; free-market, 1033

Neolithic (New Stone) era, 6; food in, 10; trade in, 12

NEP. *See* New Economic Policy

Nero (Rome), 164, 166*(b)*

Nerva (Rome), 165

Nestorian Christians, 190, 212

Netflix, 1039

Netherlands: 1830 revolt in, 708; Belgian independence from, 680*(i)*, 688, 708; Burgundian, 404; under Charles V, 404, 419; Dutch East Indies and, 968–969; Dutch Republic and, 499; France and, 478; global warming in, 1060; golden age in, 468, 499; in

Grand Empire, 635; Holy Roman Empire and, 404; independence from Spain, 499; Jansz, Anna, in, 400*(b)*; Kingdom of the, 684; medieval, 287; radical Reformation in, 399; revolts in, 472; Spanish, 420, 456, 478, 479*(m)*. *See also* Austrian Netherlands; Dutch entries; Holland; Low Countries

Neurosis: Freud on, 875

Neutrality: First World War and, 838

New Amsterdam: British seizure of, 560

New Christians, 387

Newcomen, Thomas, 654

New conservatism: in 1980s, 997–1000

New Deal (United States), 894–896

New Economic Mechanism (Hungary), 993

New Economic Policy (NEP), 907–908

New Economic System (East Germany), 993

New England: exploration of, 440; religious factors in settlement of, 445

Newfoundland: cession to Britain, 562; England and, 439–440, 478; Vikings in, 242

New France, 446, 450, 613

New Harmony, Indiana, 677

New Haven, 445

New Imperialism: in Africa, 805–810, 806*(m)*; in Asia, 810–811, 810*(m)*, 818–822; causes of, 811–812; as "civilizing mission," 813–815, 820; critics of, 811, 816, 817*(d)*; by Europeans, 791, 803–805; as national necessity, 812; responses to, 818–823; Rhodes and, 807, 808*(b)*, 808*(i)*. *See also* Colonies and colonization; Imperialism; specific locations

New Jerusalem, radical Reformation and, 399

New Kingdom (Egypt), 2*(i)*, 25, 28–30, 38, 65

New Laws, 448

New Left, 989, 990, 991

New Model Army, 494–495

New Order (Nazi Germany), 903, 928, 931

New physics, 873–874

News. *See* Media (communications)

New South Wales, 571

New Spain, 457, 513

New Stone period. *See* Neolithic (New Stone) era

New Testament, 176, 177; Erasmus on, 370, 396; in German, 398; Vulgate Bible and, 193

Newton, Isaac, 506, 512–513, 515, 517, 520, 521, 523, 744

New World, 442–444, 459(i); crops from, 545; diseases in, 448, 449(d), 451; English settlement in, 444–445; European "discovery" of, 437–439; French settlement in, 445–446. *See also* America(s); Colonies and colonization; specific locations and regions

New York (colony): settlement of, 445

New York City: al-Qaeda attack in, 1047, 1052; arts in, 879; British seizure of, 560

New Zealand, 800, 840

NGOs. *See* Nongovernmental organizations

Nicaea, council at (325 C.E.), 189

Nice, 760; France and, 628

Nicene Christianity, 189–190, 206

Nicene Creed, 189–190

Nicholas I (Russia), 688, 712

Nicholas II (Russia), 768, 769, 834, 847, 853–854

Nicias, Peace of, 77

Nietzsche, Friedrich, 868–869, 868(i), 871

Nigeria, 972

Nihilism, 869

Nile River region: Egypt and, 23–24, 25, 26; England and, 809

"Ninety-five Theses on the Power of Indulgences" (Luther), 395, 404, 462

Nineveh, 50; battles at, 47, 211; palace carving from, 51(d), 51(i)

Nitrogen: in soil, 544, 545

Nixon, Richard M.: "kitchen debate" and, 959, 962–963(d), 964(i); monetary system and, 995; Vietnam War and, 991

Noah (Bible), 14, 460

Nobility: in 17th century, 471, 479–480; in barbarian society, 199; bourgeoisie and, 610; Carolingian, 234, 262; Crusades and, 279; French, 418, 621–622, 623, 626; Hungarian, 482; in Italian Renaissance, 358; liberal ideas and, 612; Magyar, 778; in Middle Ages (High), 262–265; origins and status of, 262–263; power and responsibility of, 264–265; in Renaissance, 381; Russian, 488, 536; same-sex relations of, 580; in social hierarchy, 466. *See also* Aristocracy; Counts

Nomads: Bedouins as, 220; Hebrews as, 41; Indo-European, 52; in Iran, 52

Nonaggression pact: German-Russian, 828; Hitler-Stalin, 927

Nonalignment policy, 968, 971

Nongovernmental organizations (NGOs), 1033, 1037

Nonindustrial countries. *See* Colonies and colonization; Industrialization

Nonwhites. *See* Race and racism; White people; specific groups

Nordic peoples: Hitler and, 928

Norman Conquest (1066), 252–253

Normandy: England and, 250(i), 252–254, 335; France and, 335, 336; in Hundred Years' War, 335, 336; Second World War landing in, 938–939; Vikings in, 242, 245

Normans: in Sicily, 225, 277. *See also* Normandy; Vikings

North (United States, Union), 764, 765, 766

North Africa: Arab Spring and, 1055; colonial independence and, 973–974; Europeans in, 436; First World War troops from, 840; immigrants from, 976; Islam and, 222, 224; Justinian and, 211; Muslim turmoil in, 258; in Second World War, 937; trade in, 301; turmoil in, 1053; Vandals in, 204. *See also* specific locations

North America: Christianity in, 417; conversion in, 567; English exports to, 562; environmental protests in, 1004; outsourcing and, 1037; revolutionary era in, 609; Seven Years' War in, 613, 614(m); underclass in, 1038; Vikings and, 245; War of the Spanish Succession and, 479(m). *See also* America(s); New World; specific locations

North Atlantic Treaty Organization. *See* NATO

Northern Europe: Christianity in, 280; exploration by, 439–441; Great Famine in, 324–325. *See also* Christian humanists; specific locations

Northern Ireland: IRA and, 1004–1005. *See also* Ulster

Northern League (Italy), 1005

North German Confederation, 763

North Korea, 952. *See also* Korea; Korean War

Northmen. *See* Normandy; Vikings

Northumbria, learning in, 237, 239–240

North Vietnam, 970, 990, 991. *See also* Vietnam; Vietnam War

Norway: emigration from, 802; Germanic tribes from, 202; Great Depression in, 898(i); Nazis and, 928; Protestant Reformation in, 407; Social Democrats in, 897, 955; Vikings from, 240, 242. *See also* Scandinavia

Nosferatu (film), 884

Notre Dame Cathedral (Paris), 318(i), 319; school of, 312

Nova Scotia, 478; cession to Britain, 562

Novels. *See* Literature

Novgorod, 485

NOW. *See* National Organization for Women

Nubia, 38, 103(i); Abu Simbel in, 32; cylinder sheath from, 36(i); Egypt and, 25, 28; Persia and, 55

Nuclear arms race, 966, 991; Gorbachev and, 1012, 1016

Nuclear families, 576–577; in age of affluence, 988

Nuclear power plants, 1003

Nuclear weapons: Big Science and, 953–954; bomb and, 874; development of, 953; end of Cold War and, 1016; French, 958; Soviet, 1016. *See also* Atomic power

Numeracy: in England, 649

Numerals: Arabic, 227; in Mesopotamia, 22

Numidia, Rome and, 143–144

Nuns: Carolingian, 236; Gregorian reforms and, 266; lifestyle of, 271, 273–274; Protestant Reformation and, 403; Scholastica and, 193. *See also* Convents; specific orders

Nuremberg Laws (1935), 923

Nuremberg trials, 947

Nurses and nursing, 727; in middle class, 727; women in, 604, 741, 843

Nutrition. *See* Diet (food); Food; Health

OAS (Secret Army Organization), in Algeria, 974

Obama, Barack: on classified information, 1040–1041(b); European interests and, 1053; Iraq and, 1055

Obsidian, 11–12

Occam. *See* William of Occam

Occident, 4

Occupation (military): after First World War, 857; by France, 628–629; in Second World War, 929, 931, 948

Occupation (work): for Jews, 44–45, 781; of middle classes, 726–727; of Puritans, 496(i); of working classes, 728–731. *See also* Employment; Labor

Occupy movement, 1039, 1042
Oceans and ocean regions: global warming and, 1060. *See also* specific ocean regions
Octavian. *See* Augustus
October Manifesto (Russia), 769
Odoacer (Ostrogoths), 204
Odyssey (Homer), 66, 67
Oedipus at Colonus (Sophocles), 81
Oedipus the King (Sophocles), 81
"Of Cannibals" (Montaigne), 460, 461
Of Natural Characters (Hume), 527
Ogé, Vincent, 640
Ohio River region: settlement in, 615; in Seven Years' War, 613
Oikist (Greek leader), 71
Oil and oil industry: Gulf of Mexico disaster and, 1060; in Iran, 996; OPEC and, 995–996; pipelines to Europe (ca. 2005), 1059*(m)*; U.S. regime support in Middle East and, 1053–1054
Oil shocks, 996, 1009
Olaf II (Norway), 280
Old Babylonian period, 20
Old Bolsheviks, 916
Old Kingdom (Egypt), 25
Old Stone period. *See* Paleolithic (Old Stone) era
Old Testament, 40; Copernican system and, 518; Torah and, 42; Vulgate Bible and, 193. *See also* Bible
Oleg (Varangian), 243–244
Oligarchs, in Russia, 1023, 1026
Oligarchy: in Greece, 70; in Italian government, 360
Olivares, Count-Duke of (Gaspar de Guzmán), 480
Olives: Greek, 106; in Rome, 174
Olympia, festivals in, 88
Olympic games, 75, 88
Olympus, Mount, 87
Omdurman, battle at, 809, 812
On Christian Liberty (Luther), 396–397*(d)*
On Crimes and Punishments (Beccaria), 526
One Day in the Life of Ivan Denisovich (Solzhenitsyn), 964
On Floating Bodies (Archimedes), 115*(b)*
On Germany (Staël), 698
Online. *See* Internet
"On My First Son" (Jonson), 584
On Plane Equilibriums (Archimedes), 114*(b)*
On the Different Races of Man (Kant), 528
On the Genealogy of Morals (Nietzsche), 869
On the Immortality of the Soul (Mendelssohn), 538*(b)*

On the Inequality of the Human Races (Gobineau), 780
On the Origin of Species by the Means of Natural Selection (Darwin), 745–746
On the Revolutions of the Heavenly Spheres (Copernicus), 509, 517
On the Structure of the Human Body (Vesalius), 517
OPEC (Organization of Petroleum Exporting Countries), 995–996
Open-field system, 288; legacy of, 544–545, 546
Open-field village: community controls of illegitimacy in, 578
Opium, trade in, 795–797
Opium Wars: first (1839–1842), 796; second (1856–1860), 796–797
Oppenheim, Moritz, 538*(i)*
Oppian Law, 140
Optimates (Rome), 144, 145
Oracles: at Delphi, 54, 100
Oradour, France, Nazis in, 931
Orange Free State, 807
Orange Revolution (Ukraine), 1032
Orchestra, 700–701
Orderic Vitalis (monk), 291
Orders: social classes as, 621. *See also* Clergy; Estates (social orders); Nobility; Peasants; Religious orders
Oresteia, The (Aeschylus), 81
Organization for European Economic Cooperation, 957
Organization of Petroleum Exporting Countries. *See* OPEC
Organization of Work (Blanc), 694, 709
Organized religion: skepticism toward, 599–600. *See also* Religion(s)
Orient, 4, 429. *See also* Asia; specific locations
Orientalism, 815–816
Original sin, 195, 585, 601
Orléans, battle at, 336
Orléans, duchess of, 475*(d)*
Orlov, Gregory, 534
Orthodox Church: Byzantine church as, 185; Catholic Church and, 213–215; in Ottoman Empire, 702, 772; vs. Roman Christianity, 276; in Russia, 486, 487, 687; Slavs in, 243. *See also* Christianity
Orwell, George, on life on the dole, 896–897*(d)*
Oseberg ship, 242, 242*(i)*
Osiris (god), 25, 26, 56, 108
"Oslo Breakfast," as welfare, 898*(i)*
Ostia, 122

Ostpolitik policy, 984*(i)*, 985
Ostrogoths, 199, 204, 205–206
Oswiu (Northumbria), 207
Othello (Shakespeare), 461
Otto I (Germany), 256, 265, 280, 281
Ottoman Empire, 489–491, 682*(m)*; in 1566, 490*(m)*; Armenian deportation from, 839, 839*(m)*; Austria and, 491, 686–687; Balkan wars and, 832; Egypt and, 770, 771; expansion of, 431; before First World War, 832, 833*(m)*; First World War and, 827, 839, 840; after First World War, 857, 859–861; government of, 490–491, 771; Greece and, 702, 703; Hungary and, 406, 414, 482; Jews in, 490, 859; military in, 491; modernization of, 769–772; nationalism in, 772, 832; reform in, 771–772; religion in, 772; religious toleration in, 485, 490, 491, 771; Russia and, 487, 537, 766, 766*(m)*, 767, 770, 772; trade and, 431, 433, 451, 491, 771; Transylvania and, 414, 482, 483*(m)*; women in, 527. *See also* Ottoman Turks; Turkey
Ottoman Turks, 687; Constantinople and, 211–212, 431, 433, 451, 485, 489, 491; Greece and, 702; Hungary and, 406, 491; Vienna and, 406. *See also* Ottoman Empire; Turks
Outsourcing: of manufacturing jobs, 1037–1038
Overland trade, 106
Overseas expansion. *See* Expansion; Exploration; specific locations
Ovid, 161–162; *Art of Love, The,* 161–163, 162*(d)*; on Roman household gods, 138
Owen, Robert, 666, 676–677, 693, 786
Owen, Wilfred, "Dulce et Decorum Est," 838–839*(d)*
Oxfam, 1037
Oxus River, 34*(i)*
"Ozymandias" (Shelley), 697*(d)*

Pachomius, 192
Pacific Ocean region: Atlantic economy and, 563; Cook in, 571; First World War and, 840; Magellan in, 424, 439; Second World War in, 934–937, 936*(m)*; trade and empire in, 570–571; United States and, 797
Pacifism: in First World War, 842; in Vietnam War, 990

Padua, university at, 509

Pagans and paganism, Christianity and, 176, 205, 230

Paine, Thomas, 588–589, 616

Painting: baroque, 501, 501*(i)*; of First World War, 826*(i)*, 837; Realism in, 374; in Renaissance, 374, 375–378, 376–377*(b)*; by women, 377–378. *See also* Art(s); specific works and artists

Pakistan: Alexander in, 96; Indian partition and, 970–971, 970*(i)*

Palaces: in Italian Renaissance, 360; Minoan, 64, 64*(i)*; Mycenaean, 65. *See also* specific palaces

Pale of Settlement, 539, 539*(m)*, 801

Paleolithic (Old Stone) era, 6, 7–8, 8*(d)*, 8*(i)*

Palermo, 472, 760

Palestine, 771; Arab refugees from, 971; Balfour Declaration and, 859–860; British and, 859, 971; First World War and, 840; Israel and, 971; Jews in, 782*(b)*, 783, 859–860; Seljuk Turks in, 277; Six-Day War and, 995; trade and, 431. *See also* Israel

Palimpsest (manuscript), 114*(i)*

Panama Canal, 794

Pan-Hellenic festivals, 88

Panics: financial, 893; witch, 423

Pantheon (Rome), 167

Papa, Mama, and Baby (Droz), 739

Papacy: Anagni and, 270, 340; in Avignon, 339, 340, 341, 342; Babylonian Captivity of, 339–340; banking and, 358; Carolingians and, 231; criticisms of, 340–342; Crusades and, 276–277, 279, 281; Great Schism and, 340, 340*(m)*, 342, 392; Habsburgs and, 537; Habsburg-Valois wars and, 418; Holy Roman Empire and, 266–267, 281; Iberian Peninsula and, 258–259, 259*(m)*, 447; Italy and, 757; Luther and, 395; in Middle Ages (High), 265–270, 269*(d)*; wealth of, 362. *See also* Catholic Church; Pope(s); Protestant Reformation; specific popes

Papal bull, 269, 269*(d)*

Papal curia, 268

Papal infallibility, 773

Papal States, 360, 760

Paper: in China, 371; Muslims and, 226, 315, 371; printing and, 371

Papyrus, 26, 103, 108*(i)*

Paracelsus, 517

Pareja, Juan de, 452*(b)*, 452*(i)*

Paris: 1830 revolution in, 707*(i)*, 708; 1848 revolutions and, 709–710; aristocracy in, 662*(i)*; Bastille in, 608*(i)*; fashion in, 594; founding of, 172; foundling homes and, 583; Franco-Prussian War in, 763, 775; growth of, 299; Huguenots in, 418, 419; immigrant suburbs in, 1046; "June Days" in, 710; lifestyle in, 592–593*(d)*; modernization of, 723–724, 723*(m)*; population of, 724; protests in, 991–992, 992*(i)*; revolutionary attitude in, 614; Saint Bartholomew's Day massacre in, 419; scientific academy in, 519; in Second Empire, 754*(i)*; after Second World War, 944; socialism in, 694; terrorism in, 1047*(i)*; University of, 313, 331. *See also* France; French Revolution; Paris, Treaty of; Parlement of Paris

Paris, Treaty of: of 1259, 332; of 1763, 562, 571, 613; of 1783, 617; in 1815, 685; during Napoleonic Wars, 684

Paris Accord (1990), 1016

Paris Commune (1871), 775, 784–785

Parish churches, 597

Paris peace conference (1919). *See* Versailles, Treaty of

Parlement of Paris, 259, 473

Parliament: in German Confederation, 713; in Germany, 713; in Prussia, 763. *See also* Parliament (England)

Parliament (England): American colonies and, 615; Charles I and, 494; Cromwell and, 495; India and, 819; voting rights and, 776. *See also* House of Commons (England); House of Lords (England)

Parliamentary monarchy, 753; in Italy, 760. *See also* Constitutional monarchy

Parsis: Zoroastrians as, 56

Parthenon (Athens), 80*(d)*, 80*(i)*

Parthia and Parthians, 98; Greek culture and, 99–100, 104; Persia and, 54; Rome and, 175

Partisans: anti-Nazi, in Second World War, 932–933; Belgian, in First World War, 835

Partitions: of Africa, 806*(m)*; of India, 970–971, 970*(i)*. *See also* East Germany; West Germany; specific locations

Party of Democratic Socialism, 1016

Pasargadae (city), 53*(i)*

Passover, 41, 177

Pasternak, Boris, 964

Pasteur, Louis, and pasteurization, 722

Pastoralism, 10; of Hebrews, 41

Pastures, 544

Paterfamilias (Rome), 135–136

Patriarchy: ancient, 11; Sumerian, 17

Patricians (Rome), 129, 131, 136

Patrick (Saint), 206–207, 280

Patriotism: in American Revolution, 127; in First World War, 841, 843–844; in French Revolution, 631; in Germany, 764; of Paris Commune, 784–785. *See also* Nationalism

Patriots: in American Revolution, 616

Patronage: of arts and letters, 531, 531*(i)*; in French court, 475; in Renaissance, 358, 375, 377*(d)*; of scientists, 510

Patron-client system (Rome), 132

Patron saints, 210

Paul III (Pope), 414–416

Paul of Tarsus (Saint), 177–178, 412

Pax deorum, 127

Pax Romana, 157–159, 175. *See also* Roman Empire

Payne (coal master), 670*(d)*

Peace: Bismarck on, 828; after First World War, 885–891; after Second World War, 947–949. *See also* Pax Romana; specific wars and treaties

"Peace, Land, and Bread for the Russian People" (Lenin), 851*(d)*

Peaceful coexistence policy, 962–963, 964

Peacekeeping: by UN, 1036

Peace of Augsburg, 406, 407, 469

Peace of God, 276

Peace of Utrecht (1713), 478, 479*(m)*, 562

Peace treaties. *See* specific treaties

Pearl Harbor, Japanese attack on, 934–936

Peasants: in 17th century, 467*(i)*; in Austria, 711; at carnival, 589; Christianity and, 601–602; cottage industry and, 552; in Egypt, 798; in England, 346; in France, 344–345, 710; in French Revolution, 624–625, 629; in Germany, 401; in Ireland, 777; in Italy, 917; labor of, 467, 467*(i)*; marriage age of, 576; in Middle Ages, 244, 286; open-field system and, 288, 544; response to imperialism, 818; revolts by, 344–346, 345*(m)*; in Russia, 486, 486*(i)*, 767, 849, 850–851, 908; as serfs, 286; social order and, 286, 466; Soviet, 912, 916; Soviet women as, 915; taxation of, 544–545; in working classes, 728. *See also* Agriculture; Land; Manors and manorialism; Serfs and serfdom

Peel, Robert (English prime minister), 705

Peel, Robert (factory owner), 667(d)

Pegida (Patriotic Europeans Against the Islamization of the West), 1048

Peloponnesian War, 75, 76–78, 77(m)

Peloponnesus, 62; Messenia in, 71

Penance, 208–209, 276, 293, 395

Penates (household deities), 138

Pendulum clock, 508

Peninsulares, 688

Penitentials, 209–210

Penn, William, 497

Pennsylvania, 445

Pensions: in England, 776; after First World War, 863; in Germany, 774

Pentagon: terrorist attack on, 1052

Peonage, debt, 563

People, the: government and, 692

People of color: in Americas, 566, 689–690. See also specific groups

People's Budget (England), 776, 830

People's Charter (England, 1838), 705

People's Party: in Denmark, 1048

People's Republic of China. See China

"People's Will" (Russia), 767

Perestroika, 1011

Pergamum: in Hellenistic period, 98, 99; Rome and, 135

Pericles (Athens): arts under, 79–83; leadership by, 76

Periculoso (papal decree), of Boniface VIII, 266

Periodic law and table, 744

Periokoi (free Spartans), 71

Periplus of the Erythraean Sea, 116(d)

Permanent revolution, Trotsky on, 908

Perry, Matthew, 797, 821

Persecution: of Christians, 179

Persephone (goddess), 87

Persepolis, 55, 57, 94

Persia: Ionia and, 78; Medes and, 50; Medese in, 53(b); Safavid, 431; Sassanid, 220. See also Iran; Persian Empire

Persian Empire, 34(i), 35–36, 48(m), 52–57; Alexander the Great and, 93, 94, 95(m); communication and trade in, 55; conquests by, 54; consolidation of, 52–55; gods and goddesses in, 55–56; Greece and, 75; Judah in, 42; Medes and, 34(i), 35; Phoenician alphabet and, 40; religion in, 55–56; trade and, 431

Persian Gulf region: Lugalzagesi and, 17; Soviet Union and, 1010

Persian Gulf War (1990–1991), 1049–1050

Persian Letters, The (Montesquieu), 522–523, 527, 530

Persian Wars, 75–76, 75(m)

Personal computers, 953; technologies for, 1033

Peru: Chinese immigrants in, 802; Inca Empire in, 443–444; Spain and, 444, 448

Pétain, Henri-Philippe, 846, 928, 938

Peter (Saint), 191, 266

Peter III (Russia), 533, 534

Peterloo, Battle of, 704

Peter the Great (Russia), 485, 487–489, 488(d), 489(i)

Petrarch, Francesco, 364

Petrine Doctrine, 191

Petrograd. See St. Petersburg

Petrograd Soviet, 848, 850

Petroleum. See Oil and oil industry

Pfaff, William, "Will the French Riots Change Anything?," 1050–1051(d)

Phalanx (military), 69; Macedonian, 134

Phalanxes (self-sufficient communities), 693

Pharaoh (Egypt), 24, 28, 29; Ptolemy as, 97–98; woman as, 29, 31. See also Egypt

Pharmaceuticals: costs of, 1061

Pharsalus, Battle of, 147

Philip (Burgundy, Holy Roman Empire), 387, 407

Philip I (France), 255, 266

Philip II Augustus (France): England and, 261; French unification under, 255; Roman Catholic Church and, 268; Third Crusade and, 279

Philip II (Macedonia), 75, 79, 115

Philip II (Spain), 387, 424; Armada and, 411, 411(i); Mary Tudor and, 408(i), 409, 410–411; Netherlands and, 419–420; scientific knowledge and, 513; state debt, silver trade, and, 455

Philip III (Spain), 480

Philip IV the Fair (France): expelling Jews, 280; pope and, 269; Roman Catholic Church and, 339; sons of, 325, 332; Templars and, 278

Philip IV (Spain), 472, 480

Philip V (Macedonia), 133, 134–135

Philip V (Spain), 478

Philip VI (France), 332–333

Philip of Anjou. See Philip V (Spain)

Philippines: Portugal and, 455, 456; U.S. conquest of, 810(m), 811, 813

Philistines, 41–42; Mycenaean Greeks as, 66

Philosophes, 522–524, 522(i), 535

Philosophy: Greek, 61, 88–90; Hellenistic, 110–113; medieval, 313; modern, 868–872. See also Enlightenment; Intellectual thought; Science; specific philosophers

Phoenicia and Phoenicians, 36, 38–40; Alexander the Great and, 94; alphabet of, 40; Assyria and, 47; Mediterranean settlements of, 39–40, 40(m); trade by, 38–39, 39(d), 40; in Tunisia, 39–40

Phonetic alphabet, 15(f), 40

Physicians: in 18th century, 602, 603; Arab, 227; Hellenistic, 311–312; in Middle Ages, 237. See also Medicine

Physics: Aristotle and, 90; new physics, 873–874; Newton and, 506, 513

Picasso, Pablo, 877

Pico della Mirandola, Giovanni, 365

Pictographic writing, 15(f)

Picts (Scotland), 202

Piedmont, 757, 758

Pieds-noirs (Algeria), 973, 974

Piero della Francesca, 374

Pietà (Michelangelo), 375

Pietism, 598–599; Wesley and, 600

Piety: Catholic, 601

Pig iron, 654

Pilate, Pontius, 175, 177

Pilgrimage of Grace (England), 408–409

Pilgrims: guide to Santiago de Compostela, 297(d); to Jerusalem, 277; medieval, 296–297

Pill, the: for birth control, 989

Pilsudski, Jozef, 854

Pippin I (Carolingian), 230

Pippin III (Carolingian), 230–231

Piracy: in Hellenistic world, 106

Pisistratus (Athens), 74

Pius VII (Pope), 634

Pius IX (Pope), 757, 773

Pizarro, Francisco, 444

Place de la Concord (Paris), 958(i)

Place value: in Mesopotamian mathematics, 22

Plague: in 17th century, 468; in 1890s, 326; Antonine (smallpox), 170, 180; in Athens, 77; bubonic, 326, 468, 551; clerical medical care during, 329; in Marseilles, 552(i); treatment of, 329–330. See also Black Death

Planck, Max, 873

Planetary motion: Aristotle and, 508–509; Kepler's laws of, 510–511

Planned economies: in First World War, 841–842; in French Revolution,

629–630; in Poland, 1014; socialism and, 693

Plantations: agricultural slavery and, 444, 764–765; of Creoles, 565; immigrant labor for, 802, 803; sugar, 444; zones of (ca. 1700), 564(m)

Plants: in Columbian exchange, 451; medicinal, 603. *See also* Agriculture; Crops; specific crops

Plassey, Battle of, 571

Plato, 89–90; Academy of, 89; on love, 85–86; Renaissance thinkers and, 364–365, 366

Platonic ideals, 89

Platonic love, 86, 365

Plautus, 139

Plays. *See* Drama

Plebeians (Rome), 129, 130–131, 136

Plessis, Armand Jean du. *See* Richelieu, Cardinal

Pliny the Elder (Rome), 166(b)

Plow, 10; medieval, 285, 288; plow agriculture, 11

Pluralism: in church, 416; in European societies, 225; in Middle Ages (later period), 351–352

Plutarch (historian): on Roman slavery, 168

Plymouth colony, 445

Pneumonic transmission (plague), 326. *See also* Black Death; Plague

Poets and poetry: *Beowulf* and, 239–240, 239(d); of courtly love, 316–317(d); epic poems and, 17; from First World War, 837, 838–839(d); Latin, 139, 160; Romantic, 673, 696–698. *See also* Epic literature; Literature; specific poets and works

Pogroms, 387, 781, 783, 801

Poincaré, Raymond, 886, 890

Poitiers: battle at (732), 230; battle at (1356), 335

Poland: 1830 rebellion in, 708; agriculture in, 960; Black Death in, 327, 328; Catholic Church in, 243; Christianity in, 281; deaths in Second World War, 944; dissent in, 1007–1010; economy in, 993, 1026–1028; after First World War, 855, 855(m), 857, 858–859, 886, 888(b), 889; French pact with, 886; Germany and, 888(b), 985; Jews in, 539, 931–932; Nazis and, 927, 931–932, 931(m); partitions of, 536–537, 536(m), 858; revolt in (1956), 964; Russia and, 487, 685, 767, 854; Second World War and,

927, 930, 931, 939; after Second World War, 948, 950; serfdom and, 481; Solidarity movement in, 1009–1010, 1013–1014; after Soviet Union, 1028; Teutonic Knights and, 281. *See also* East Bloc

Poland-Lithuania, 413

Polis (Greece), 67, 68–74; colonies of, 70–71

Polish Home Army, 931

Polish people, 767, 769, 778, 781; in Austrian Empire, 686; emigration by, 801; Nazi murders of, 933–934

Politeuma (political corporation), 110

Political parties: anti-Semitic, nationalist, 783; in Germany, 773; after Second World War, 955. *See also* specific parties and locations

Political thought: in Renaissance, 367–368. *See also* Politics; specific individuals and ideologies

Politics: 1775–1815, 609; in 1960s, 984; after Alexander the Great, 96–98; in England, 776; Enlightenment ideas and, 610; in France, 1000; Greek, 61, 62; after Hundred Years' War, 338; Minoan, 64; in Poland, 1014; in Rome, 130–132; Sumerian, 17; in western Europe, 382–387. *See also* Government; specific locations

Politiques (France), 419

Politkovskaya, Anna, 1026

Pollution: in cities, 721; environmental costs of, 1002–1003; industrialization and, 721. *See also* Environment

Polo, Marco, 429

Poltava, battle at, 489

Polybius (historian), 133–134, 141

Polygamy: in barbarian society, 197; Hebrew, 44

Polygyny, in Islam, 223

Polytheism, 12; in Greece, 86. *See also* Gods and goddesses; Religion

Pomerania, 469

Pompadour, Madame de, 531, 531(i)

Pompeii: destruction of, 165, 166(b), 166(i)

Pompey (Rome), 145, 147

Pondicherry, 571

Pontus, king of, 147

Poor Clares, 275

Poorhouses: factories as, 665

Poor Laws (England): of 1834, 721

Poor people: foods of, 590–591. *See also* Peasants; Poverty

Pope(s), 191; Holy Roman Emperor and, 407–408; in Italy, 257; Lateran Palace

and, 188; in Middle Ages (High), 251; in Renaissance, 375. *See also* Crusades; Great Schism; Papacy; specific popes

Popolo, in Italy, 358–359

Popp, Adelheid, 784–785(b)

Popular culture: literature and, 587–589

Populares (Rome), 144, 145

Popular Front (France), 899

Popular Republican Movement (France), 955

Population: in 17th century, 469, 484; in 18th century, 550–551, 554(m); Black Death and, 327–328; of China, 429; of cities, 718; decline in, 325; diet and growth of, 289; of Dutch Republic, 546–547; in England, 549(f); in Europe, 300(m); explosion of, 549–552, 799–800; growth of, 290, 551(f), 610; of indigenous people, 448, 457; industry and, 657–658; of Ireland, 706; in medieval cities, 299; of neo-Europes, 794; Paleolithic, 8; of Paris, 724; of Poland-Lithuania, 413; of Spain, 387, 454; after Thirty Years' War, 484

Poquelin, Jean-Baptiste. *See* Molière

Port Arthur, 768, 822

Portico of the Caryatids, 81

Portraits: in Renaissance, 375

Portugal: Africa and, 805; Catholic Church in, 597; colonies of, 974; in Common Market, 996; emigration from, 801; empire of, 435–437; exploration by, 435–437, 451; Great Schism and, 340; independence of, 480; India and, 819; Indian Ocean trade and, 456, 570; Japan and, 455; Phoenicians and, 40; recession in, 1056, 1057; revolts in, 472, 480; after Second World War, 955; slave trade and, 379, 380, 451, 453, 453(m), 454, 455; Spain and, 227, 384, 387, 439, 480; trade by, 436–437, 455, 491; Treaty of Tordesillas and, 439, 444

Portuguese language, 172

Postcolonial migration, 976, 1043

Postimpressionists, 877

Postindustrial society, 996, 1006; globalization and, 1037–1039

Post office, 779

Post-traumatic stress disorder (PTSD), 862–863

Postwar period. *See* Second World War; specific issues

Potatoes, 545, 591, 706

Potato famine (Ireland, 1845–1851), 705

Potosí, 454

Potsdam Conference (1945), 949

Pottery: in Egypt, 24; in Greece, 66; Mesopotamian, 14; Roman, 175; trade in, 106

Poverty: in 19th century, 725; consumer revolution and, 610; in England, 720–721; in France, 624; of Franciscans, 275; in Great Depression, 894; in Greek Dark Age, 66; in Ireland, 705– 706; of Jews, 783; marriage age and, 576; public health and, 721; of rural textile workers, 555; socialism and, 693; urban, 724(i). *See also* Poor people; Wealth; Wealth gap

Power (authority): hierarchies of, 11; New Imperialism and, 811; in Rome, 131, 145(i); separation of, 523; in Sumer, 17. *See also* Absolute monarchy and absolutism; Constitutional monarchy

Power (energy). *See* Energy

Powhatan Confederacy, 445

Praetor (Rome), 129–130

Praetorian Guard, 164–165

Prague, 341; 1848 revolt in, 712; nationalists in, 712; after Second World War, 944; student protests in, 991

Prague Spring (1968), 994, 1007

Praise of Folly, The (Erasmus), 370

Pravda, 910(d)

Prayer meetings: Jansenism and, 601

Preaching Friars, Dominicans as, 274

Predestination: Calvin on, 412; Wesley on, 600

Preferred status, 803

Pregnancy: birthrates and, 582–583; infanticide and, 583; marriage and, 580; of servant girls, 577–578. *See also* Childbirth; Illegitimacy

Prehistory, 3

Premarital sex, 578–579, 735–736, 989–990

Presbyterianism: education and, 587

Pre-Socratic philosophers, 88, 111

Prester John, 431

Price(s): Black Death and, 330; energy, 996; in First World War, 841; in Great Depression, 891, 895; just, 590. *See also* Inflation; Silver, from Americas

Price revolution: European, 549–550

Priests and priestesses: Catholic, 776; married, 265; medieval, 292; in Sumer, 16, 17. *See also* Clergy; Religious orders

Prignano, Bartolomeo. *See* Urban VI (Pope)

Primavera (Botticelli), 378(i)

Primogeniture, 254–255, 263; children given to monasteries and, 291–292

Prince(s): origin of term, 154

Prince, The (Machiavelli), 367, 370

Princeps civitatis (Rome), 154

Princip, Gavrilo, 832

Principate (Rome), 154–155

Principia Mathematica (Newton), 513, 520, 523

Printing: in Enlightenment, 508, 532; growth in Europe, 372(m); Protestantism and, 392, 398; in Renaissance, 363, 370–373, 371(i); Scientific Revolution and, 508. *See also* Books

Printing press, 363, 370–373, 371(i); Protestant Reformation and, 392, 398

Prior and prioress, 271

Priskos (Byzantine Empire), 211

Prisoners of war (POWs): Nazi murders of, 933–934; as slaves, 18

Private enterprise, 690, 691

Private property. *See* Property

Privatization, 997, 998; in former East Bloc, 1028; in France, 1000; in Russia, 1022, 1023

Proclamation Line, 615

Procopius (historian), 213

Procurator (governor), 166(b)

Production: Black Death and, 330; in First World War, 841; in Great Depression, 893, 894; Hellenistic, 105; mass, 882; in putting-out system, 553; in Roman Empire, 173(m). *See also* specific products and industries

Productivity: labor and, 559

Products: Greek, 106

Professional Civil Service Restoration Act (Nazi Germany), 923

Professionalization, of armies, 471, 477

Professions: in 19th century, 727; in Byzantine Empire, 187; middle-class, 727; women in, 742–743(b), 915, 978. *See also* Occupations

Profit(s): in 1980s, 997

Progressive bloc, in Russia, 847

Proletarianization, 549

Proletariat, 695; Marx on, 695; in Russia, 767

Propaganda: in First World War, 843–845, 845(d); German, 858; imperialist, 812; movies and, 884; Nazi, 934, 938; radio and, 885; in Soviet Union, 915

Property: inheritance of, 136; in Kievan Rus, 244; ownership of, 498–499, 975; rights to, 612; women's rights to, 223. *See also* Inheritance; Land

Prophets: Hebrew, 43. *See also* Muhammad

Propylaea, 80

Prosperity: in Roman provinces, 172–174

Prostitution: in 18th century, 580; in 19th century, 736–737; clothing of, 308; female immigrants and, 1044; in Middle Ages, 347, 349; in Roman baths, 140; for servant girls, 577–578; sex and, 580–581; stigmatization of, 737

Protective tariffs, 61, 773

Protectorate(s): in Africa, 807; in China, 823; in England, 495–496; by Germany, 807

Protest(s): in 1968, 991–993; counterculture and, 984, 988–990, 992–993; in East Germany, 960(i), 961; environmental, 1004; feminist, 1000(i); in First World War, 845–846; in France, 991–992, 992(i); in late 1960s, 983; in Poland, 1007–1010; in Russia, 688, 766, 847–848; student, 991–993; against Vietnam War, 990, 991. *See also* Antiwar movement; Revolts and rebellions; specific locations

Protestant Ethic and the Spirit of Capitalism, The (Weber), 746

Protestantism: American missionaries and, 567; anti-Nazi opponents and, 925; baroque arts and, 501; Calvin and, 407, 411–413, 419; church hierarchy and, 597; in France, 418–419, 474, 626; in Germany, 404–407; in Ireland, 777; Luther and, 398–399, 404–405; marriage in, 401–403, 402(i); missionaries and, 815; as New World settlers, 445; printing press and, 392, 398; religious violence and, 418–419, 474; revival of, 598–601; schools and, 587; spread of, 407–414; in Switzerland, 406; Thirty Years' War and, 469; use of term, 396–397; Zwingli and, 395–397, 406. *See also* Christianity; Edict of Nantes; Huguenots; Lutheranism; specific individuals

Protestant Reformation: early period in, 392–403; Erasmus and, 370. *See also* Reformation

Protestant Union, 469

"Protocols of the Elders of Zion, The," 783

Protten, Jacob, 569(b)

Protten, Rebecca, 568–569(b)

Proudhon, Pierre-Joseph, 693

Proust, Marcel, 879

Provence, 383

Providence, 445

Provinces: Roman, 155, 172–174. *See also* Colonies and colonization

Provincial Assembly of Saint-Domingue, 640

Provisional government, in Russia, 848, 849, 850

Provisional Irish Republican Army (IRA), 1004–1005

Prussia, 712–713; in 17th century, 482–484, 483*(m)*; 1848 revolutions and, 712–713; absolutism in, 484, 533; Austria and, 760–761, 762, 762*(m)*; cameralism in, 534; Constituent Assembly in, 713; Enlightenment in, 526, 533–534; in First Coalition, 628; France and, 478, 533, 629; Franco-Prussian War and, 763–764; French Revolution and, 627, 628; German Confederation and, 712; Junkers in, 482–483, 484; Kulturkampf in, 773; military in, 484, 484*(i)*; Napoleon and, 635; after Napoleonic Wars, 684, 685; Napoleon III and, 763; nobility in, 534; peasants in, 480–481, 534; in Seven Years' War, 533, 613; Silesia, 562; state-building in, 482–484, 483*(m)*; Teutonic Knights and, 281; unification and, 713. *See also* Brandenburg-Prussia; Germany; specific rulers

Psalms: book of, 43; children and, 44

Psalter, 227

Psychology and psychiatry, Freud and, 874–875

Ptolemies (Egypt) and Ptolemaic dynasty, 97–98; Cleopatra VII, 47, 93, 98, 146*(b)*, 146*(i)*, 147, 150; Hellenistic kingdom of, 97–98, 103; Ptolemy I Soter and, 98, 108; Ptolemy II, Arsinoe II, and, 98*(i)*; Ptolemy III, 113–115; Ptolemy XIII and, 146*(b)*, 147; Rome and, 135. *See also* Egypt

Ptolemy, Claudius (scientist), 113; *Geography* by, 434, 438, 439, 507, 509

Public art: in Soviet Union, 942*(i)*

Public broadcasting, 1039

Public education. *See* Education

Public health, 551, 772, 799; in cities, 721; movement for, 721; prostitutes and, 737

Public opinion, Napoleon III on, 756

Public speaking: in Rome, 169

Public sphere, in Enlightenment, 532

Public transportation, 725

Public works, in France, 756

Puddling furnace, 655

Pugachev, Emelian, 535–536

Pullein, Samuel, 514*(d)*

Punic Wars, 132–134; Rome and, 123*(m)*

Punishment: in Hammurabi's code, 21–22; by Hebrew god, 43; in Middle Ages (High), 261, 261*(i)*; for premarital sex, 578–579; by Sumerian gods, 16

Punk rock, 997

Purgatory, 276, 296, 342, 353, 394

Purges, in Soviet Union, 916

Purification: of spirituality, 602

Puritans: Anglican Church and, 494; in England, 409; occupations of, 496*(i)*; Protectorate of, 495–496

"Purity of blood" laws, 352, 387

Putin, Vladimir, 1024*(i)*; Commonwealth of Independent States and, 1032; on global security, 1025*(d)*; Russia under, 1024–1026

Putting-out system, 552–553, 650–651

Pydna, Battle of, 134–135

Pyramids: in Egypt, 24

Pyrenees, Treaty of the, 480

Pyrrhus (Epirus), 127

Pythian games, 88

Qing (Manchu) dynasty (China), 508, 795, 796, 822, 823

Quadruple Alliance, 637, 682, 683, 684–685

Quaestors (Rome), 129

Quakers, 399, 445, 497, 567

Quanta, 873

Quebec, 445, 477; in Seven Years' War, 613

Queens. *See* Monarchs and monarchies; specific individuals

Querelle des dames (debate about women), 530–531

Quilon, India, 429

Quinine, 812

Quintilian (Rome), 169

Quintus Lucretius Vespillo (Rome), 137*(d)*

Qur'an, 220–221, 223, 224, 294; death and, 297

Ra (god), 25*(i)*, 30

Race and racism: toward African soldiers, 887, 887*(i)*; in American colonies, 566; biblical justification for, 460;

"blood," racial inheritance, and, 352; Enlightenment and, 527–529, 780; eugenics and, 906, 906*(i)*, 922, 923; in European colonies, 610–611; Holocaust and, 931–934, 932*(i)*, 933*(m)*; ideas about, 459–460; in Japan, 934; mixed races and, 448, 450; nationalism and, 780–781; Nazis and, 906, 922–923; Orientalism and, 815; "purity of blood" laws and, 352, 387; in Renaissance society, 379–380; scientific justifications of, 527–529, 778, 780; Shakespeare and, 461; underclass and, 1038. *See also* Ethnic groups; Holocaust; Slaves and slavery; specific groups

Race laws, 566

Race mixing: white women in colonies and, 813–815

Racial hygiene: in Nazi Germany, 922–923

Racine, Jean, 476

Racing, chariot, 172

Radar, 953

Radegund (Saint), 208*(d)*, 229*(i)*

Radiation, 873

Radical Reformation, 399, 401

Radical republicanism: nationalism and, 692

Radicals and radicalism: in arts, 878–879; Paris Commune and, 775

Radical socialism: in France, 710

Radio, 882, 885

al-Rahman, Abd III (Umayyad caliph), 227

Ra-Horus (god), 25

Railroads, 672, 779; in continental Europe, 662; in England, 656, 660, 660*(m)*; in France, 756; Prussia and, 762; in Russia, 767, 768; steam power and, 656; trade and, 793–794

Raimon de Cornet, on Avignon papacy, 339

Rai music, 1046

Rákóczy, Francis, 482

Ramadan, 223

Ramesses II (Egypt), 32

Ramesses III (Egypt), 37

Rape, 349–350

"Rape of Belgium" (First World War), 835

Raphael Sanzio, 375

Rasputin, Grigori, 847

Rathenau, Walter, 841

Rationalism, 757; defined, 520; irrationalism after First World War and, 868

Rationing: in First World War, 841, 846; under War Communism, 853

"Ratting," 729(i)

Ravenna, Ostrogoths in, 204

Raw materials: in Egypt, 24; in England, 649; in First World War, 841; Industrial Revolution and, 648; trade and, 794

Raynal, abbé, 529

Razin, Stenka, 487, 535

Reaction: to 1848 revolutions, 711; in German states, 713

Reactionaries: in Russia, 767, 768

Reading: in Enlightenment, 532. *See also* Education; Literacy

Reagan, Ronald, 998–1000; Gorbachev and, 1012; military and, 1010; Thatcher and, 998, 999

"Real existing socialism," 1005

Realism: in arts, 374, 747–748, 748(i); in literature, 748–749, 749(d)

Reason: Romanticism and, 695; witches and, 423. *See also* Enlightenment; Rationalism

Reasoning: deductive, 516–517, 521; inductive, 516–517

Rebellions. *See* Revolts and rebellions

Recession: of 1937 and 1938, 895–896; of 1980s, 998; Eurozone unity and, 1049; global (2008), 1034, 1056–1059

Reconquista (reconquest), 258, 259(m), 277, 279, 294, 386, 567; exploration and, 433, 447–448

Record-keeping: Sumerian, 17. *See also* Writing

Recovery: in Great Depression, 895, 898–899; after Second World War, 954–959

Recreation: in 18th century, 589–590. *See also* Leisure

Red Army (Soviet Union), 854; great purge and, 916; Lenin, Trotsky, and, 853; in Second World War, 938, 939

Red Army Faction (West Germany), 992

Red Brigades (Italy), 991

Red China, 971. *See also* China

Reds, in Russian civil war, 853

Red Sea region, 220, 840

Red Shirts, of Garibaldi, 760

"Red Terror" (1918–1920), 853–854

Reed, John, 850

Re-exports: English, 563

Reflections on the Revolution in France (Burke), 627

Reform(s): before 1848, 702–708; in 1960s, 984–995; in Austria, 537; of Catholic Church, 265–266, 267, 340, 414–416, 988; in Czechoslovakia, 994;

de-Stalinization and, 961–964; in Egypt, 771; in factories, 665; in former Soviet republics, 1032; in France, 620, 709, 775, 899; liberal, 688; in Ottoman Empire, 771–772; by Putin, 1024; religious, 597–598; in Rome, 142–143, 147–148; in Russia, 766–768, 769, 850–851, 851(d); in Soviet Union, 959, 961–964, 965–966, 1010–1012; urban, 723–724. *See also* Protestant Reformation; Reformation; specific reforms

Reformation, 388, 424; early period in, 392–403; in eastern Europe, 407, 413–414; European witch-hunt and, 421–423, 422(i). *See also* Protestant Reformation

Reform Bill (England): of 1832, 704; of 1867, 776; of 1884, 776

Refugees: from civil wars, 1043; to Europe, 1042, 1043–1045, 1044(i); First World War and, 838, 861; in Greece, 1044; in India, 970(i); from Middle East, 1055; Palestinian, 971; after Second World War, 945–947

Regular clergy, 193

Regulation: economic, 560; laissez faire and, 690; after Second World War, 954; Smith, Adam, and, 557

Reichstag (Germany), 773, 774, 784, 842, 846, 921

Reign of Terror, in French Revolution, 630–631

Relativity theory, 873

Relics of saints, 208–209(d), 210, 602

Religion(s): in 16th-century Europe, 415(m); in 18th century, 596–602; Abrahamic, 43; in Americas, 567; barbarians and, 200; Black Death and, 329–330; in Catholic countries, 601; Chaldean, 51; education and, 587; in Egypt, 25–26; Elizabeth I on, 410(d); Enlightenment principles and, 520–521; in Europe (ca. 1555), 415(m); after First World War, 872–873; in French Muslim society, 1051; Greek public and personal, 86–88; Hebrew, 35; in Hellenic Greece, 60(i); in Hellenistic world, 107–110; industrialists and, 673; of Jews, 42–44; magic and, 107–108; marginal beliefs and practices in, 601–602; in Mesopotamia, 16–17; Metternich on, 686; in Middle Ages (later period), 285, 292–298; Minoan, 64; Muslim in

France, 1051(d); mystery, 108–110; in Ottoman Empire, 485, 771, 772; Paleolithic spirituality and, 7; Persian, 55–56; rituals and, 11; Roman, 127–128; science and, 518–519; in West, 5; of working class, 732. *See also* Crusades; Cult(s); Gods and goddesses; specific groups

Religious orders: in Catholic Reformation, 393, 416–417; of friars, 270–271; New World missionaries and, 567; teaching orders, 587. *See also* Monks and monasteries; specific orders

Religious toleration: in Austria, 598; Dutch, 500, 520–521; Enlightenment and, 535, 539; in France, 626; Islamic, 860; for Jews, 539; in late antiquity, 188; in Ottoman Empire, 485, 490, 491, 771, 860

Religious wars: in France, 390(i)

"Remember the Ladies" (Abigail Adams), 619, 619(d)

Remembrance of Things Past (Proust), 879

Renaissance, 424; art and artists in, 373–378, 374(i), 378(i); Carolingian, 236–237, 248; education in, 366; humanism in, 364–366, 368–370, 507; intellectual thought in, 363–373; in Italy, 358–362, 361(m); political thought in, 367–368; politics and state in, 382–387; race and slavery in, 379–380; society in, 379–382; use of term, 357; women in arts of, 378

"Renaissance man," 366, 376(d)

Renan, Ernest, 780

Reparations: after First World War, 857, 858, 886, 888(b), 889; after Second World War, 947

Repartimiento labor system, 448

Repatriation, of immigrants, 801

Representative assemblies, 338, 382, 470

Representative government, 612; liberals and, 691; in Russia, 1023

Reproduction, in Europe, 1042–1043

Republic(s): in France, 628–629, 709–710, 755, 775–776; in Germany, 855, 856; in Italy, 361, 499; in Rome, 126, 129–132; in Soviet Union, 908–909; in Soviet Union (former), 1031–1033; after Soviet Union, 1022; in Turkey, 861. *See also* Dutch Republic; England (Britain); Roman Republic; specific locations

Republicanism, 753; Dutch, 493, 499; English, 493; in Italian cities, 360, 361, 499; nationalism and, 692

Republicans: in France, 710, 775; liberal ideology of, 691; in Paris (1848), 709–710; in Spanish Civil War, 925(i)

Republic of Letters, in Enlightenment, 522, 524

Res Gestae Divi Augusti (Augustus), 157, 158–159(d)

Resistance: in First World War, 835; to Nazis, 924–925, 931, 932, 938

Resources: population and, 657; of Russian fossil fuels, 1059. *See also* Raw materials; specific resources and locations

Re-Stalinization, 966

Restoration: of Bourbon dynasty, 637, 684, 707; in England, 497, 498, 498(d)

Return of the Native, The (Hardy), 749

Reunification: of Germany, 1000, 1015–1016, 1016(m)

Revisionism: labor unions and, 787

Revisionist socialism, 787

Revolts and rebellions: in 14th century, 345(m); in 17th century, 472; in 1848, 708–713; in Algeria, 708; in Austrian Empire, 711; in France, 991–992, 992(i); in India, 571, 819, 819(m); in Ireland, 846; by Italian Red Shirts, 760; in Italy, 759; by Jacquerie, 344–345; by Jews, 110, 165, 167; by Mycenaean slaves, 65; against Napoleon, 635–636; by peasants, 344–346, 345(m), 399, 401; in Poland, 708, 964; in Rome, 138, 145; in Russia, 535–536, 850; in Saint-Domingue, 639(i), 640–643; in South America, 688–690; student (1968), 991–993. *See also* War(s) and warfare; specific revolts

Revolution(s): 1775–1815, 609; 1815–1850, 681; of 1830, 680(i), 707–708, 707(i); before 1848, 702–708; of 1848, 681, 708–713, 711(m), 753, 757, 781; of 1989, 984, 1012–1017, 1029; in Austrian Empire, 710–712; in China (1912), 823; consumer, 592–596; demands in, 612; in Germany, 854–855; in Haiti, 638–643; in Hungary (1956), 964–965; in Iran, 996, 1054; Lenin on, 849; social change and, 610–611; in South America, 688–690; in Ukraine (2014), 1032. *See also* American Revolution; French Revolution; Russian Revolution entries; specific revolutions and types

"Revolutionary Etude" (Chopin), 701

Revolutionary War in America. *See* American Revolution

Rhineland: after First World War, 857, 858, 886, 887; France and, 628, 629, 857; Hitler march into, 925; Magyars in, 244

Rhine River region: France and, 634; pollution in, 1002; Prussia and, 482; as Roman frontier, 157, 181; in Second World War, 939

Rhode Island, 445

Rhodes, Cecil, 807, 808(b), 808(i)

Rhodesia, 807, 974

Rhodes scholarships, 808(b)

Ricardo, David, 657, 673

Rice and rice industry, 445

Richard I the Lion-Hearted (England), 260–261, 279

Richard II (England), Peasants' Revolt and, 346, 353

Richard III (England), 384

Richardson, Victor, 844(b)

Richelieu, Cardinal (Armand Jean du Plessis), 469, 473, 474

Riefenstahl, Leni, 884

Riga, 281

Rigaud, André, 643

Rights: 18th-century demands for, 61; American Revolution and, 613–614; of Egyptian women, 28; in Hellenistic cities, 99; human, 1060–1061; individual, 1061; natural, 498–499; for women, 861

Right to work, 691

Right wing: anti-Semitism of, 920; extremism of, 1005; in Germany after First World War, 856; immigration issue and, 1048; nationalism and, 778. *See also* Conservatism

Riots: in 17th century, 472; bread, 171, 590; in Egypt, 798–799; Luddite, 674(i); by Muslims in France, 1049, 1050–1051(d)

Rite of Spring, The (Stravinsky), 881

Rituals, 11; Christian, 295; in French court, 475; Greek, 60(i), 87; Hellenistic religious, 107–108; nationalism and, 780; penance, 276, 277; Roman, 179. *See also* Sacraments

Rivers: in England, 649. *See also* specific rivers and river regions

Roads and highways: in Paris, 724; Persian, 55; Roman, 128, 157, 167, 168, 205

Road to Wigan Pier, The (Orwell), 896–897(d)

Roanoke, English colony in, 445, 449(d)

Robert (France), 254

Robert of Geneva. *See* Clement VII

Robespierre, Maximilien, 627, 628, 629, 631, 632, 632(i)

Robin Hood, 351

Rocket (locomotive), 656

Rockets, 953

Rock music, counterculture and, 990

Rococo style, 531, 531(i)

Rocroi, battle at, 480

Rodrigues, Armando, as guest worker, 977(b), 977(i)

Roger II (Sicily), 257–258

Roger de Hauteville, 257

Rolling mills, 454

Rolling Stones, 990

Roma (Gypsies), 906, 922, 944

Roma et Augustus, cult of, 157

Roman alphabet, in Hungary, 245

Roman Catholic Church. *See* Catholic Church

Romance languages, 172

Roman Empire, 121, 153–182; army in, 168; under Augustus, 154–164; after Augustus, 164–168; barbarians and, 200; barracks emperors in, 186; boundaries of, 167; Britain in, 167(m), 201–202; Carolingians and, 235; China and, 175; Christianity in, 175–180, 179; citizenship in, 128, 136, 141, 148, 155, 168; civil wars in, 153, 180–181; crisis of the third century in, 181; culture of, 159–160; disarray in, 180–182; division into western and eastern, 186(m); economy in, 181–182, 186, 187–188; entertainment in, 171–172; expansion of, 156–160, 156(m), 167; under "five good emperors," 165–168; under Flavians, 164; Gaul and, 172–173; government of, 154–155, 167; health and medicine in, 170–171; industry in provinces and, 174–175; Jews in, 167; lifestyle in, 152(i), 168–169, 168–175; music in, 160(i); Pax Romana and, 157–159, 175; political issues in, 186–187; prosperity in, 172–174; provinces of, 155, 172–174; religion in, 186; Sallust on, 135; same-sex relationships in, 164; slavery in, 168–169; succession in, 164–168, 182; trade and commerce in, 173(m), 174–175; urban areas in, 169–171. *See also* Byzantine Empire; Classical culture; Eastern Roman Empire; Holy Roman Empire; Roman Republic; Rome; Western Roman Empire

Romanesque architecture, 318
Romania: economy in, 993; after First World War, 855, 855(m); independence of, 772; in Little Entente, 886; Nazi Germany and, 927; revolution in, 1015; Rome and, 157; after Second World War, 950. *See also* East Bloc
Romanian language, 172
Romanian people: in Austrian and Austro-Hungarian Empires, 686, 712, 778
Romanization, 173–174
Roman language: Phoenician alphabet and, 40. *See also* Latin language
Romanov family (Russia): Catherine the Great and, 534; Michael, 486–487. *See also* specific rulers
Roman Republic, 126, 129–132; American Constitution and, 150–151; borders of, 143, 144; civil wars in, 145–147, 150; expansion of, 132–135, 134(m); families in, 135–138; government of, 129–130; Greece and, 134, 138–140; late period in, 141–150; "Liberators" in, 150; lifestyle in, 138; Macedonia and, 134–135; military in, 144; Numidia and, 143–144; political violence in, 143–145; Punic Wars and, 123(m), 132–134; society in, 135–141. *See also* Roman Empire; Rome; specific rulers
Romanticism, 695–702; in arts, 698–700, 747; Greeks and, 703; in literature, 673, 696–698, 699(b); in music, 700–702; nationalism and, 698; poets of, 696–698
Rome: Carthage and, 127; civil law in, 130; East-West distinction in, 4; Egypt and, 93; founding of, 124–126; gods in, 108; Hellenistic world and, 121; Italy and, 121, 123(m), 126–127; military in, 126, 129, 130–131; monarchical period in, 121; religion in, 127–128; republic(s) in, 126; rise of, 122; roads and highways in, 168; Seleucid and Ptolemaic kingdoms and, 98; society in, 130–132; Syracuse and, 114(b); trade in, 126, 128; voters in, 143(i); wars in, 126; women in, 136, 140. *See also* Roman Empire; Roman Republic; Sacks of Rome
Rome (city), 123(m), 138–139; chariot racing in, 172; entertainment in, 171–172; Fascists in, 918; food in, 170–171; in Kingdom of Italy, 760;

lifestyle in, 168–169; Renaissance art in, 375
Rome, Treaty of (1957), 957
Rome-Berlin Axis alliance, 925
Romulus and **Remus,** 124–125
Romulus Augustus (Rome), 204
Roosevelt, Franklin Delano: Great Depression and, 895; Japan and, 934–936; radio and, 885; at wartime conferences, 948, 949(i)
Rose Revolution (Georgia), 1032
Rotation of crops. *See* Crop rotation
Rotten boroughs: in England, 704
Rousseau, Jean-Jacques, 592(d); constitutional theories of, 568; *Emile, or On Education,* 585; on foundling homes, 583; on natural man, 524; political theory of, 524; Romantic movement and, 524, 697; on women, 531
Roxana (wife of Alexander the Great), 96
Royal Annals (Franks), 235
Royal courts. *See* Court (royal)
Royal Navy (England), 560
Royal Society (England), 514(d), 518
Royalty: same-sex relations of, 580. *See also* Kings and kingdoms; Monarchs and monarchies; specific rulers
Rubber: synthetic, 841
Rubens, Peter Paul, 501, 501(i)
Rubicon River, Caesar at, 147
Rudolph II (Holy Roman Empire), 510
Rudolphine Tables, 510
Ruhr region, 886(m), 887–889, 887(i); industrial decline in, 996
Rule of Saint Benedict, The, 192–193, 214
Rule of the Little Brothers of Saint Francis, 274
Ruler cults, 98
Rump Parliament, 495
Runes: on whalebone chest, 196(i)
Runic alphabet, 196
Rural areas: in Greece, 69; housing in, 721; industrial growth in, 552–556; manufacturing in, 553; movement to cities from, 800; in Roman Republic, 138; workers in textile industry in, 553–555. *See also* Agriculture; Farms and farming; Peasants; Serfs and serfdom
Russia: absolutism in, 469, 533, 534; army in, 488–489; Byzantines and, 215; Catherine the Great in, 534–537, 535(i); civil war in, 852–854, 907; Cossacks in, 486, 487, 489; Crimea and, 766, 1026, 1027(m), 1032; East

Slavs in, 243; economic shock therapy in, 1022–1023; economy in, 767, 768; education in, 488; emigration from, 801, 802; European immigrants to, 800; expansion of, 484–485, 486(m), 536–537, 536(m), 766, 767, 768(m); before First World War, 830, 831; in First World War, 834, 837–838, 839, 846, 847, 848, 861; foreign experts in, 487, 488, 488(d); fossil fuel resources of, 1059; France and, 766, 828; Germany and, 828; government in, 488; Hungary and, 712, 778; imperialism of, 768, 810–811, 810(m); industrialization in, 659, 659(f), 663, 766, 767, 768; Japan and, 822; Jews in, 767, 781(i), 783; Kosovo and, 1031; League of Armed Neutrality and, 617; Lenin and, 848–850, 850–853; minorities in, 769; modernization of, 488–489, 534–535, 766–769; Napoleon and, 635, 636, 637; after Napoleonic Wars, 685; nationalism in, 767; nobility in, 488, 536; Oligarchs in, 1023; Ottoman Empire and, 487, 537, 772; peasants in, 486, 486(i), 489; Poland and, 487, 536–537, 536(m), 685, 708; protest in (1825), 688; provisional government in, 848, 849; Prussia and, 760; railroads in, 767, 768; reforms in, 487–489, 535, 766–768; revolutionary movement in, 767, 769; in Second World War, 937; Serbia and, 832; serfs in, 487, 535–536, 544, 767; socialists in, 767, 787; after Soviet Union, 1022–1023; state-building in, 487; and successor states (1991–2015), 1027(m); in Third Coalition, 634; trade and, 303, 487; Ukraine and, 486, 487; U.S. and EU sanctions on, 1032–1033; War Communism in, 853. *See also* First World War; Russian Revolution (1905); Russian Revolution (1917); Second World War; Soviet Union; specific rulers and wars
Russian Empire, 465, 767, 781, 852, 857; Austrian Empire and, 686–687; in First World War, 827. *See also* Russia; Soviet Union
Russian Federation, 1017; republics bordering, 1032
Russian Revolution (1905), 768–769, 770(d), 831
Russian Revolution (1917), 827, 846, 847–850; Bolshevik Revolution,

848–850, 858; February Revolution, 848, 849
Russian Soviet Federative Republic (S.F.S.R.), 908–909, 1017. *See also* Soviet Union
Russification, 781
Russo-Japanese War (1904–1905), 768, 822, 822*(i)*, 831
Russo-Turkish War (1877–1878), 772
Rust belts, 996
Rutherford, Ernest, 874
Rwanda: atrocities in, 903–904; refugees from, 1043

SA. *See* Storm troopers (SA)
Sabine peoples, 125
Sacks: of Athens, 75; of Constantinople, 279; of Rome, 127, 245, 362
Sacraments, 195, 266, 292, 293, 416
Sacrifice: Greek, 60*(i)*; Hellenistic, 108–109
Sadowa, Battle of, 762
Safavid Empire, 431, 508
Saguntum, battle at, 133
Sahagún, Bernardino de, 458*(d)*
Sahara, trade in, 430
Said, Edward, 815
Sailors, 433–434. *See also* Ships and shipping
Saint(s): in medieval religion, 292–293; relics of, 208–209*(d)*, 210, 602; veneration of, 292–293. *See also* specific saints
Saint Bartholomew's Day massacre, 419
St. Christophe, West Indies, 446
Saint-Domingue: France and, 446, 573, 613, 614*(m)*, 638–643; independence of, 643; race laws in, 566–567; revolt in, 640–643; slave revolt in, 609
St. Helena, Napoleon at, 638
St. Lawrence River region, 440–441, 446
Saint Peter's Basilica, 375
St. Petersburg, 767; in 1825, 688; construction of, 489; Russian Revolutions and, 769, 847–848, 850
Saint Peter's Fields (Manchester), 704
Saint-Simon, duke of, 476
Saint-Simon, Henri de, 693
Saladin (Salah al-Din), 279
Salamis, battle at, 75–76
Salerno, medical school in, 237, 310, 311–312
Salian Franks, law code of, 199, 332
Salimbene of Parma, 275*(d)*

Sallust (historian), on Rome, 135
Salons: women in, 476, 519, 530, 699*(b)*
Salt: trade in, 107
Salvation: in Christianity, 179; Wesley on, 600
Samaras, Antonis, 1058*(d)*
Samaria: as Israel capital, 42
Same-sex relationships: in Greece, 85, 86; male, 580; marriage and, 1061; in Middle Ages, 350; in Rome, 164; in Sparta, 73. *See also* Homosexuality
Samizdat literature, 993–994
Samnites, 127
Samurai, 821
Sand, George (Armandine-Aurore-Lucile Dudevant), 698
Sanitation: Black Death and, 326; in cities, 719–720, 721, 724*(i)*; in medieval cities, 307; in Roman cities, 169–170; surgery and, 603
San Martín, José de, 690
San Salvador (Bahamas), 438
Sans-culottes (France), 629, 630*(d)*, 632
Santiago de Compostela, pilgrim's guide to, 297*(d)*
Santo Domingo, 640
Sappho, 86
Saracens. *See* Muslims
Sarajevo, Franz Ferdinand assassination in, 832
Sardinia: Greece and, 70; Rome and, 132; Russian expansion and, 766
Sardinia-Piedmont, Italian unification and, 757, 758*(m)*, 759, 760
Sargon (Akkad), 19–20, 46
Sargon II (Assyria), 47
Sarkozy, Nicolas, 1051*(d)*
Sartre, Jean-Paul, 871–872, 1001
Sassanid Persians, 211
Sassanid-Persian-Zoroastrian empire, 220
Sassoon, Siegfried, "Attack," 839*(d)*
Satellites (space), 953
Satellite states: in central and eastern Europe, 959–962; Soviet, 964–965. *See also* East Bloc
Satraps: in Persia, 55
Saudi Arabia: oil in, 1059
Saul (Israel), 42
Savonarola, Girolamo, 362, 363*(d)*, 365
Savoy: French acquisition of, 628, 760
Saxons, 202; Charlemagne and, 231. *See also* Anglo-Saxons
Saxony: education in, 587; Magyars in, 244; Otto I in, 256; Prussia and, 685
Scandinavia: Black Death in, 327; Christianity in, 280; Great Depression

in, 896–898; medieval, 287; Social Democrats in, 955. *See also* specific locations
Schisms: in Catholic Church, 188–189, 331. *See also* Reformation
Schleswig-Holstein, 761
Schlieffen Plan, 834, 834*(m)*, 838
Schliemann, Heinrich, 67
Scholarship. *See* Intellectual thought
Scholastica (Saint), 193
Scholastics, 312–313
Schönberg, Arnold, 881
Schönbrunn palace, 482
Schools: Catholic, 776; elementary, 586–587, 775; in England, 353, 497; humanist, 366–367; Jesuit, 417; mission, 813*(i)*, 815; monastic and cathedral, 193, 236, 274, 310, 310*(m)*; at Notre Dame Cathedral, 312; primary, 371; religious, 497; for scribes, 15–16. *See also* Education; Universities; specific schools
Schubert, Franz, 696
Schuman, Robert, 957
Science: in 19th century, 743–746; Big Science and, 953; Enlightenment and, 502; Greek, 61, 88–90; Hellenistic, 113–117; in industry, 744–745; methods of, 516–517; popularization of, 504*(i)*; race defined by, 780; religion and, 518–519; society and, 519; use of term, 508; witches and, 423; women in, 519, 523. *See also* Mathematics; Medicine; Philosophy; Scientific Revolution; specific fields
Scientific expeditions, 513–515
Scientific laws. *See* Law (scientific); specific scientists and laws
Scientific method, 516–517
Scientific racism, 778, 780, 803
Scientific Revolution: Copernican hypothesis and, 506, 509–510; Enlightenment and, 502; farming and, 545; Industrial Revolution and, 648; magic and alchemy in, 515; Newton and, 506, 512–513
Scipio Aemilianus (Rome), 133–134, 140–141
Scipio Africanus (Rome), 133, 141
Scivias (Hildegard of Bingen), 272*(i)*
"Scorched earth" policies, of British, 809
Scotland: Calvinism and, 412–413; elementary schools in, 587; England and, 494, 525; famine in, 325; Great Schism and, 340
Scots, 202

Scott, Walter, 696, 705

Scottish Enlightenment, 525, 557, 568

Scramble for Africa, 805–809, 806*(m)*

Scribes: Carolingian, 236, 237; in Egypt, 26; in Sumer, 15–16

Scriptures: Catholic Reformation and, 415–416; Christian, 176, 180, 226; education and, 587; Hebrew, 22, 41, 110; Luther on, 394, 396–397*(d)*, 398, 401; Zwingli and, 396, 398, 401

Sculpture: Greek, 79–80, 81*(i)*; Hellenistic, 103*(i)*; in Renaissance, 374; Roman, 139; Venus figures and, 8*(i)*. *See also* specific works and artists

Scythia, 55

Seaborne trade: Hellenistic, 106. *See also* Maritime trade; Trade

Sea Peoples, 37, 42, 66

Secession, in U.S., 765, 765*(m)*

Secondary education, 775

Second Athenian Confederacy, 78

Second Balkan War, 832

Second Battle of El Alamein, 937

Second Coalition (1798), 633, 634

Second Continental Congress (1776), 616

Second Empire (France), 754*(i)*, 756, 763

Second estate (France), nobility as, 621, 621*(i)*

Second front: in Second World War, 948

Second Industrial Revolution, 659, 744–745

Second Intermediate Period (Egypt), 28

Second International, 785, 787

Second Messenian War, 72

Second Punic War, 133, 134; Archimedes and, 114*(b)*

Second Reform Bill (England, 1867), 776

Second Republic (France), 709

Second revolution: in French Revolution, 628–629; in Soviet Union, 911

Second Sex, The (Beauvoir), 1001, 1002–1003*(d)*

Second Triumvirate, 150

Second Vatican Council, 988

Second World War, 927–939; in Africa, 930*(m)*; aftermath of (ca. 1945–1950), 946*(m)*; Atlantic region in, 938; atomic power in, 939, 939*(i)*; authoritarianism before, 904–907; casualties in, 939, 944; dictatorships and, 903–939; East-West division after, 4–5; economy and, 896; end of, 939; in Europe, 930*(m)*; Europe after, 943, 944–954; Japan in, 934–937; Nazi Germany and, 927–934; in Pacific Ocean region, 934–937, 936*(m)*;

refugees after, 945–947; second front in, 948; society after, 975–979; totalitarian states before, 864; western Europe after, 954–959. *See also* specific locations and battles

Secret History (Procopius), 213, 214*(b)*

Secret police: in Poland, 1014; in Russia, 783, 853, 854

Secular clergy, 193

Secularism: in Turkey, 861

Secularization: in 1960s, 988

Security Council (UN), 1036

Sedan, battle at, 763, 780

Seed drills, 546*(i)*

Seleucids, 98; Greek culture and, 103; Jews and, 110; overthrow of, 100; Rome and, 133, 134

Seleucus Nicator, 98

Self-determination. *See* National self-determination

Self-government: of medieval villages and towns, 287

Seljuk Turks, 277

Semiramis (Shammuramat, Assyria), 47

Semiskilled workers, 730

Semites. *See* Arabs and Arab world; Jews and Judaism

Semitic languages, 20

Senate (Rome), 121, 125, 126, 127, 129, 130, 144, 154–155

Senate (U.S.): Versailles Treaty and, 858

Senegal, 807

Seniors: pension and health care for, 1042

Sennacherib (Assyria), 48–49, 49*(i)*, 51*(d)*, 51*(i)*

Sensationalism, Locke on, 521

Sense and Sensibility (Austen), 525

Senses: Hume and, 525; Locke and, 521

Separate spheres, 666, 669, 675*(d)*, 737–739

Separation of church and state: in France, 391

Separation of powers, 523

Separatism: in Ireland, 1004; in Lithuania, 1017; right-wing extremism and, 1004–1005; in South Ossetia, 1032; in Spain, 1004; in Yugoslavia, 1029

September 11, 2001, terrorist attacks, 1052

Septimius Severus (Rome), 179, 181

Sepúlveda, Juan Ginés de, 459

Serapis (god), 108, 109

Serbia, 1030*(m)*; autonomy of, 770; First World War and, 832, 856; independence of, 772; Kosovo independence from, 1031; Milošević

in, 1029; Rome and, 157; Srebrenica and, 1030, 1031*(i)*

Serbs, 243; in Austria-Hungary, 833; in Austrian Empire, 686, 712; Kosovo and, 1029

Serfs and serfdom: in 17th century, 480–481, 534; in Austria, 480–481, 537, 711; debt peonage and, 563; in eastern Europe, 544; in England, 346; medieval transition to, 247; in Middle Ages (High), 286; peasants and, 247; in Prussia, 534; in Russia, 487, 767; in western Europe, 544. *See also* Peasants

Serious Proposal to the Ladies, A (Astell), 530

Servants: in 19th century, 730, 740; black, 379–380, 380*(i)*; domestic, 73, 308–309, 347, 349, 452*(b)*, 475, 557, 583, 665, 666, 675–676, 728, 730, 740; in England, 675–676; girls as, 577; in Middle Ages (High), 308–309; of middle class, 728; native, in colonies, 815

Servetus, Michael, 412

Service industries: employees in, 976; women in, 978

Settlement(s): in Americas, 438, 442; European neo-Europes and, 794; of Greece, 62; of Italy, 122, 124; in North America, 615; Paleolithic, 7; permanent, 3; Phoenician, 39–40, 40*(m)*. *See also* Colonies and colonization; Provinces; specific locations

Seventh Crusade, 278, 279

Seven Years' War, 562, 612–613, 614*(m)*; England and, 533, 613; France and, 533, 613, 620; Prussia and, 533, 534, 613; Russia and, 533, 534

Seville, 258, 379, 446

Sewage and sewage systems, 169–170; in England, 551, 721; in Paris, 724; public health movement and, 721

Sex and sexuality: in Carolingian Empire, 232; of children, 740; Christian notions of, 193–194; in cities, 347, 349–350; coal workers' conditions and, 668; First World War and, 843; Freud and, 875; in Greece, 85–86; in Hebrew society, 44; illegitimacy and, 579–580; in Islam, 223; in medieval urban areas, 347, 349–350; in middle and working classes, 734–736; premarital sex and, 578–579; prostitution and, 580–581, 736–737; Protestantism and, 401–403;

servant girls and, 577; Zweig on, 734–735(d). *See also* Gender and gender issues; Homosexuality; Prostitution; Same-sex relationships

Sexism: feminist movement and, 1001

Sextius (Rome), 131

Sexual division of labor, 666–669. *See also* Gender and gender issues

Sexual revolution, in 1960s, 989

Seymour, Jane, 408

Sforza family, 361; Francesco, 377(d)

Shah of Iran, overthrow of, 1054

Shakespeare, William, 457

Shalmaneser III (Assyria), 47

Shamash (god), 20, 21(i)

Shammuramat (Semiramis, Assyria), 48

Shari'a (sacred law), 224, 1053

Sharif, 840

Shelley, Percy Bysshe, 697; *Ozymandias,* 697(d)

Shell shock, after First World War, 862–863

Sheriff (England), 252

Shi'ite (Shi'a) Muslims, 223–224, 431, 1055

Ships and shipping: Black Death spread on, 326–327; British Navigation Acts and, 496; caravel and, 434; dreadnoughts, 830; Dutch, 500; Hellenistic trade and, 106; in Italian Renaissance, 358; Navigation Acts and, 560; steam power for, 794; steamships and, 656; Venetian, 301–302; Viking, 240, 242, 242(i). *See also* Maritime trade; Navy; Seaborne trade

Shiraz, Iran, 55

Shock therapy: in Polish economy, 1026–1027; in Russian economy, 1022–1023

Shogun (Japan), 821

Short Account of the Destruction of the Indies (Las Casas), 459(i)

Show trials: in East Bloc, 960; Soviet, 916

Siberia, 486, 487, 688, 767

Sicily, 122; Athens and, 78; Garibaldi in, 760; Greece and, 70; Kingdom of, 256(m), 257–258; Kingdom of the Two Sicilies and, 257, 688; medical knowledge in, 311, 312(i); Muslims and, 245, 294; Normans in, 225, 277; Phoenician colonies in, 40; Rome and, 132; in Second World War, 938; Spain and, 472; Vikings and, 242, 245. *See also* Kingdom of the Two Sicilies

Sickness unto Death (Kierkegaard), 872

Sieges: by Assyrians, 51(d), 51(i); weapons for, 115. *See also* Sacks, of Rome; specific wars

Siena: as city-state, 360

Siete Partidas (Alfonso X), 311

Sieyès, Emmanuel Joseph: *What Is the Third Estate?,* 622–623(d), 623

Sigismund (Germany), 342

Sigismund I (Poland), 413

Signori (rulers), 360

Silent film, 884

Silent Spring (Carson), 1001–1002

Silesia, 469, 533, 537, 562; in Seven Years' War, 613

Silk Road, 106

Silk trade, 106, 175, 303, 431, 455, 456

Silkworms, 514(d)

Silver: from Americas, 448, 454–455, 478; China as buyer of, 455; for coins, 303–304; European sources of, 303; Spain and, 454–455, 478

Simony, 414, 416

Sin: Christianity and, 178; confessing of, 209, 268, 292; Jesus on, 178; original, in children, 585

Sinai Peninsula: Israel invasion of, 972; phonetic signs in, 40

Sinn Fein Party (Ireland), 846

Sino-Japanese War, 823

Sinti (Gypsies), 922, 944

Sistine Chapel, 373, 375

Sit-ins, 989

Siwah, Alexander the Great at, 94

Six Acts (England), 704

Six-Day War (1967), 995

Sixtus IV (Pope), 287

Skepticism, 460, 521, 525

Skilled workers, 728–730, 843; in Soviet Union, 914–915

Skype, 1039–1040

Skyscrapers, 875

Slaves and slavery: abolition and, 565; in Africa, 430–431; African, 542(i), 807; in American colonies, 454; after American Revolution, 618; in Athens, 73; in barbarian society, 197; in Egypt, 28; Equiano on ending, 566(d); in French colonies, 709; Greek, 70, 83; Haiti and, 638, 643; as industrial labor, 677; in Middle Ages (High), 308; Mycenaean, 65; plantation agriculture and, 444, 446; in Renaissance society, 379–380; in Rome, 136, 138, 168; in Saint-Domingue, 638–639, 639(i); sugar and, 444, 446, 451, 453–454; in

Sumer, 17–18; in United States, 643, 764–765, 765(m), 766; Visigoths and, 202–203; as wet nurses, 138; women as, 450. *See also* Africa; Africans; Race and racism; Serfs and serfdom; Slave trade; specific groups

Slave trade, 802; African, 564, 805, 807; Atlantic, 564–565, 565(i); Carolingian, 248; England and, 478, 562; Industrial Revolution and, 648; Italy and, 380, 431–432; Portugal and, 451, 453, 453(m), 454, 455, 564; ships in, 454; shore method of, 564; Spain and, 562; transatlantic, 454, 456; Viking, 242; wealth from, 610. *See also* Slaves and slavery

Slavic alphabet, 215

Slavs: in Austrian Empire, 686, 778; in eastern Europe, 218, 243–244, 281; in First World War, 838; Ibrahim Ibn Jakob on, 243; immigration and, 243; Mongols and, 485; Nazis and, 920, 922; Vikings and, 244. *See also* Russia

Slovakia: public art in, 942(i)

Slovak Republic, 1028

Slovaks, 243, 927

Slovenes, 243, 686

Slovenia, 1028, 1029

Slow Food movement, 1038

Smallpox: conquest of, 604–605; inoculation against, 551, 672; in New World, 451; in Rome, 170, 180

Smelting, 12; of coke, 656; of iron, 35, 36, 38

Smith, Adam, 525; classical liberalism, and, 691; on economic freedom, 676; economic liberalism and, 557–559, 691; on guilds, 556; on trade, 559

Smugglers: of people for profit, 1044

Smyrna (Izmir), 860

Snowden, Edward, 1040–1041(b), 1041(i)

Social classes. *See* Classes

Social Contract, The (Rousseau), 524

Social Darwinism, 746, 780, 808(b), 812, 816; Hitler and, 919–920

Social Democratic Labor Party, in Russia, 849

Social Democrats: East-West relations and, 984; in Germany (SPD), 773–774, 784, 785(d), 787, 816, 831, 846, 856, 858, 984; Nazis and, 921; reforms by, 986; Russian, 784; in Scandinavia, 896–898, 955–956; after Second World War, 949

Social engineering, 905

Social hierarchy. *See* Hierarchy

Socialism: decline of "developed," 1005–1007; defined, 693; in East Bloc, 1005–1007; in England, 787; First World War and, 841, 843; in France, 709, 710, 787; in Germany, 743, 774, 787, 846; Hitler and, 920, 925; with a Human Face (Czechoslovakia), 994; in Italy, 917, 984; labor unions and, 786–787; Marxism and, 694–695, 766, 784–785; nationalism and, 783; New Left and, 989; organized religion and, 732; Popp, Adelheid, and, 784–785(b); revisionism and, 787; in Russia, 848; in Scandinavia, 897–898; scientific, 694; after Second World War, 955; in Soviet Union, 908; state, 774; women and, 784–785(b), 1006; Zola and, 748. *See also* Communist Party and communism

Socialism in one country: Stalin and, 908

Socialist parties: in France, 1000; growth of, 783–785

Socialist Realism, 915, 942(i), 961

Socialist Revolutionary Party (Russia), 852

Social media, 1039–1040

Social mobility: in Middle Ages (High), 286; of peasants, 286; in Rome, 187

Social programs: in western Europe, 997. *See also* Welfare

Social sciences, 746–747

Social security, in Germany, 774, 783

Social War (Rome), 144

Social welfare. *See* Welfare

Social work, women in, 843

Society: before 18th-century revolutions, 610–611; in 19th century, 717; anomie in, 747; capital-labor conflicts in, 672; Carolingian, 232–234; consumer culture and, 882; Darwin's theory and, 746; drinking and, 731; in Egypt, 26; enclosure and, 548; evolution of, 6–12; in First World War, 842–843; in France, 624–625; Great Depression and, 891–899; guilds in, 557; Hebrew, 44–46; hierarchies in, 10–11; after Hundred Years' War, 338; income inequality, status, and, 726; nationalism and, 692; in Nazi Germany, 921–923; Persian, 57; Roman, 130–132, 135–141; after Second World War, 975–979; Soviet, 914–915; Spartan, 72–73; Sumerian, 18–19; Weber on, 746–747; in western Europe, 545; youth culture in, 979. *See also* Culture(s); Estates (social orders);

Families; Orders; Rural areas; Social mobility; Urban areas

Society of Friends. *See* Quakers

Society of Jesus. *See* Jesuits

Society of the Cincinnati, 127

Sociology, 746–747

Socrates, 77, 89

Socratic method, 89

Sodomy, 580

Soil: open-field system and, 544

Solar system. *See* Astronomy; Heliocentric theory; Universe

Soldiers: African in French military, 887; age of, 72; colonial in First World War, 840; in First World War, 835, 835(i), 837, 846, 861; Hellenistic, 101; Mycenaean, 65; Roman, 127, 155, 168; Russian, 847, 853; after Second World War, 988. *See also* Armed forces; Military

Solferino, Battle of, 759

Solidarity movement, 1009–1010, 1013–1014

Solomon (Israel), 42

Solon (Athens), 73–74

Solzhenitsyn, Aleksandr, 964, 993

Somalia: refugees from, 1043

Somme, Battle of the, 837, 837(m), 842, 862

Sophia (Austria), 712

Sophie (Austria-Hungary), 832

Sophists, 89

Sophocles, 81; *Antigone* by, 82(d)

Sound and the Fury, The (Faulkner), 880

South (U.S.), 764–765, 765(m)

South Africa: apartheid in, 808(b), 972; colonialism in, 790(i), 805; independence of, 972, 974; Union of, 808(b), 809

South African (Boer) War, 807–809, 808(b), 816

South America: conservatism in, 688–689; conversion in, 567; economies in, 996; Jewish migration to, 946; silver from, 448, 478. *See also* Latin America; specific locations

South Asia, 429; economies in, 996

South China Sea, trade in, 428–429

Southeast Asia: Japanese invasions in, 927; in Second World War, 936. *See also* specific locations

Southern Europe: conservatism in, 688

South Korea, 952; banking crisis in, 1034. *See also* Korea; Korean War

South Ossetia, 1027(m), 1032

South Vietnam, 970, 990, 991. *See also* Vietnam

Southwest Africa, Germans in, 807, 809

Sovereignty: of citizens, 74; of the people, 611

Soviet bloc. *See* East bloc

Soviets (councils), 848, 851, 856

Soviet Union (former), 1022–1023; instability of former republics, 1031–1033; republics in EU, 1035

Soviet Union (U.S.S.R.): Afghanistan and, 1010, 1010(m); Brandt and, 985; central and eastern postwar Europe and, 950–952; collectivization in, 912; COMECON and, 951; deaths in Second World War, 944; democratization in, 1012; de-Stalinization and reforms in, 961–964; détente and, 985–986, 1010; disintegration of, 1017; East Bloc revolts against, 964–965; end of, 1017; five-year plans in, 907, 910–911(d), 910–914; foreign aid to, 949; foreign policy in, 964–965; formation of, 908–909, 909(m); industry in, 912–913; intellectual thought in, 964; limits of reform in, 965–966; movies in, 884; Nazi Germany and, 928, 938; public art in, 942(i); reforms in, 1010–1012; Second World War and, 927, 938, 939; after Second World War, 944–945, 948–949, 959–966; Socialist Realism in, 915, 942(i), 961; society and culture in, 914–915; under Stalin, 907–916; steel in, 913–914; Suez crisis and, 972; terror and purges in, 915–916; women in, 915. *See also* Arms race; Cold War; East Bloc; Lenin, Vladimir Ilyich; Russia; Russian Revolution (1917); Second World War

Space exploration: joint U.S.-U.S.S.R. mission, 985; space race and, 953

Spain: absolutism in, 469, 478–480; American Revolution and, 617; in Americas, 442–444, 448; aristocrats in, 479–480; Black Death in, 327; black people in, 379; Bourbon dynasty in, 569; Calvinism and, 420; Catholic Church in, 393, 416, 597; cession of West African slave trade by, 562; chocolate mills in, 590(i); Christianity in, 393; cities and towns in, 299; colonies of, 446, 447–448, 459, 459(i); in Common Market, 996; conquistadors from, 566; constitutional monarchy in, 688; *cortes* in, 338, 385; Dutch and, 456, 480,

499; emigration from, 801; exploration by, 433, 437–438, 439, 442–444; France and, 418, 478, 480; Greece and, 70; Habsburg-Valois wars and, 418; inflation in, 455, 479; Inquisition in, 287, 416; Jesuits in, 417; Jews and, 225–226, 385(m), 386–387, 454–455; Louis XIV and, 560–562; Magyars in, 244; mixed-race people in colonies, 567; monasteries in, 479; Muslims and, 224–226, 258, 387, 454–455, 479; Napoleon and, 635–636; Netherlands and, 420, 420(i), 420(m), 456; papermaking in, 315; Phoenician colonies in, 40; Portugal and, 439; recession in, 1056; reconquista in, 258, 259(m), 277, 279, 294; Rome and, 133, 134, 156; Santo Domingo and, 640; after Second World War, 955; separatism in, 1004; after Seven Years' War, 613; silver in, 454–455, 478; slave trade and, 478, 479(m); Thirty Years' War and, 469, 480, 494; trade and, 455, 563; Treaty of Tordesillas and, 439; unification of, 384–387, 385(m); Vandals in, 204, 224; Visigoths in, 204, 224; War of the Spanish Succession and, 478, 479(m), 482. *See also* Exploration; Silver; Spanish Civil War

Spanish America: Columbian exchange and, 451; Enlightenment and, 569; mixed races in, 448, 450. *See also* Latin America

Spanish-American War, 811, 813

Spanish Armada, 411, 411(m)

Spanish Civil War, 899, 925–926; republicans in, 925(i)

Spanish Empire, trade and, 456

Spanish language, 172

Spanish Netherlands, 420, 479(m)

Sparta, 67, 71–73; Athens and, 76; empire of, 78; hoplite in, 73(i); Peloponnesian War and, 76–79; Persian Wars and, 75; polis of, 69

Spartacist Uprising (Berlin, 1919), 856

Spartacus (Roman slave), 145

Special-interest groups: imperialism and, 812, 816

Specialization: of labor, 10, 11–12

Special Task Forces *(Einsatzgruppen)*, 932

Species extinction, 1060

Spectator sports, 731

Speculation: medieval, 325

Speer, Albert, 938

Spencer, Herbert, 746

Spending: conservatism of 1980s and, 997; on space race, 953; on welfare, 986. *See also* Finance(s)

Spheres of influence: of Russia, 768; after Second World War, 949

Spice Islands. *See* Moluccas

Spices and spice trade, 303, 429, 430(i), 431, 433, 455, 456(i), 570; apothecaries and, 603

Spinning, 651; by women, 288, 650(i)

Spinning jenny, 650(i), 651, 652(b)

Spinning mule, 651, 652(b)

Spinoza, Baruch, 521, 527

Spinsters: use of term, 554

Spirit of Laws, The (Montesquieu), 523

Spiritual Exercises (Loyola), 417

Spirituality: Muslim, 1048; Paleolithic, 7

Sports: blood sports, 589; medieval, 308(i), 309; ratting as, 729(i); working-class, 731

SPQR (Senate and the Roman People), 129, 154

Spring Offensive (1918), 854

Sputnik, 953

Srebrenica: massacre at, 1030; refugees from, 1031(i)

Sri Lanka. *See* Ceylon

SS squads (Nazi Germany), 922, 931, 932, 933(m)

Stadholder (Dutch), 500

Staël, Germaine de, 698, 699(b), 699(i)

Stagflation, 996; in East Bloc, 1006

Stained glass, 264(i), 319

Stålhammar, Ulrika Elenora, 581

Stalin, Joseph, and Stalinism, 905–906; death of, 959; five-year plans of, 910–911(d), 910–914; NEP and, 908; purges by, 916; Second World War and, 937; Soviet Union under, 903, 907–916; as totalitarian leader, 905; at wartime conferences, 948, 949(i)

Stalingrad, Battle of, 938

Stamp Act (1765), 615

Standard of living. *See* Lifestyle

Standing March, The, 1020(i)

Stanley, Henry M., 807

Starvation: in First World War Germany, 846. *See also* Famine

Stasi (East German secret police), 1029

State (nation), 692; citizens of, 779–780; in England, 776–777; First World War and, 841–842; in France, 775–776; in Germany, 773–774, 921–922; Hebrew, 41–42, 42(m); in Italy, 752(i); origins of modern, 251; rise of, 753–754; Roman, 129–130. *See also* Government; Nationalism; specific states

State-building: in 17th century, 469–471, 482; in Austria, 481–482, 483(m), 537; in Prussia, 482–484, 483(m); in Russia, 487

State Planning Commission: in Soviet Union, 912–913

Status. *See* Classes; Hierarchy

Statute of Kilkenny (Ireland, 1368), 352

Statute of Laborers (England, 1351), 345

Steam hammers, 655(i)

Steam power: in iron industry, 655; profits from, 675(d); steam engine and, 654–655, 718; steamships and, 656, 812; transportation and, 656, 794; water travel and, 656

Steel: in Near East, 37; in Soviet Union, 913–914; in Ukraine, 768

Steen, Jan, 499(i)

Stele: in Akkad, 20(i); in Egypt, 25(i)

Stephen I (Hungary), 245

Stephen II (Pope), 231

Stereotypes: in Nazi Germany, 923; Orientalism as, 815, 816

Sterilization, 722; in Nazi Germany, 923

Stern, Karl, 872

Sternpost rudder, 435

Stoa (school), 112

Stock market crash: of 1873, 781; of 1929, 894

Stoicism, 112, 180

Stolypin, Pyotr, 769

Stone Age, 6. *See also* Neolithic (New Stone) era; Paleolithic (Old Stone) era

Stonehenge, 12

"Storm and Stress" movement (Germany), 696

Storm troopers (SA), 922

Straits of Magellan, 432, 439

Strasbourg: France and, 478; wedding door of cathedral, 305(b)

Strategos (military leader), in Athens, 74

Stravinsky, Igor, 881

Stream-of-consciousness technique, in literature, 879–880

Streetcars, 725

Stresemann, Gustav, 887, 888(b), 888(i), 889, 925

Strikes (labor): in Berlin, 960; in England, 676, 998; in First World War, 845, 846; in France, 756; in Germany, 856; in Manchester, 676; in Nazi Germany, 922; outlawing of, 676; in Poland, 1009

Strozzi family, 374

Struggle of the Orders (Rome), 130–131
Students: in medieval universities, 314; protests by, 991–993
Subatomic particles, 873, 874
Subculture: homosexual, 581; youth, 979
Submarines: in First World War, 841; nuclear, 953; in Second World War, 938
Sub-Saharan Africa: decolonization and, 973; immigrants from, 976; missionaries in, 815. *See also* Africa; Slaves and slavery; Slave trade; specific locations
Subsidies: for education, 979
Suburbs, 725; of immigrants in Paris, 1046; in Russia, 767
Subversion: Soviet, 951
Succession: primogeniture as, 254–255; in Rome, 164–168, 182. *See also* War of the Austrian Succession; War of the Spanish Succession
Successor states: to Soviet Union, 1027*(m)*
Sudan, 430, 770, 809; atrocities in, 903–904; Kush in, 38
Sudetenland, 927
Suez Canal, 794, 798, 798*(m)*; British control of, 811, 859; British India and, 819
Suez crisis (1956), 972, 972*(m)*
Suffrage movement, 741–742, 741*(i)*, 776–777. *See also* Universal suffrage; Voting and voting rights
Sugar and sugar industry: in Americas, 444, 446; in Brazil, 444, 446; as crop, 453–454; Genoa and, 432; slavery and, 444, 446, 451, 453–454, 564; trade in, 303; in West Indies, 446
Suicide (Durkheim), 747
Suleiman the Magnificent (Ottoman), 414, 491
Sulla (Rome), 144, 145
Sullivan, Louis H., 875
Sultans, Ottoman, 490, 491
Sumer and Sumerians: agriculture and, 13; city-states of, 14–15, 17, 68; government of, 14, 17; myths from, 16–17; politics and society in, 17–19; pottery of, 14; scribes and schools in, 15–16; writing in, 15–16, 15*(f)*. *See also* Mesopotamia
Summa (reference books), 313
Summa Theologica (Thomas Aquinas), 313
Sumptuary laws, 307–308
Sun-centered (heliocentric) solar system, 113, 509
Sunna, 224
Sunni Muslims, 223–224, 431, 1054–1055

Sun Yatsen, 823
Superego, 874
Supermarkets: in 1960s, 987–988
Supernatural: in ancient societies, 8. *See also* Religion(s)
Superpowers, 952; détente and, 985
Supranational organizations, 1036–1037
Supreme Sacred Congregation of the Roman and Universal Inquisition. *See* Holy Office; Inquisition
Sura, 221
Surgeons and surgery: in 18th century, 602, 603. *See also* Medicine
Surplus, agricultural, 24
Surrealism, 877
Survival in Auschwitz (Levi), 935*(b)*
Survival of the fittest, 780
Swahili people, 813*(i)*
"Swallows": Italian emigrants as, 802
Sweated industries, 730–731
Sweden: Christianity in, 280; emigration from, 802; Germanic tribes from, 202; in Great Depression, 898; migrants to, 1044, 1044*(i)*; mortality decline in, 722*(f)*; Protestant Reformation in, 407; Russia and, 487–488; Social Democrats in, 897, 955; in Third Coalition, 634; Vikings from, 240. *See also* Scandinavia
Swedish Church, 407
Swedish phase, of Thirty Years' War, 469
Switzerland: 1830 revolt in, 708; 1847 civil war in, 708; Protestantism in, 399, 406; radical Reformation in, 399; religious wars in, 404–406; separatism in, 1004; witch-hunts in, 421
Sykes-Picot Agreement (1916), 859
Syllabus of Errors (Pius IX), 757
Symbols, nationalism and, 780
Symposia, 85*(i)*
Synthetic dyes, 644
Syphilis, 736
Syracuse, 77; Rome and, 114*(b)*, 133
Syria: Akkad and, 20; Alexander the Great in, 94; Babylonians and, 51; caravans to, 220; civil war in, 1055; Egypt and, 32, 771; First World War and, 840; as French mandate, 859, 860, 971; Greek culture in, 103; Islam and, 222; Islamic State and, 1055; Maccabees and, 110; Mesopotamian culture and, 22; migrants from, 1043, 1044; Russia and, 1024; Saladin in, 279; Six-Day War and, 995; trade and, 431
Syriza Party (Greece), 1057, 1058*(d)*
System of Nature, The (Linné), 527

Tacitus (historian): on Germanic society, 197, 198*(d)*; on Roman peace, 157–158
Tai Ping rebellion, 822
Taiwan, 822, 971
Tajikistan, Persian Empire in, 34*(i)*
Taliban, 1054
Talleyrand, Charles, 684
Talmud, 46; academies for study of, 311
Tannenberg, Battle of, 837, 842
Tanzania, 972
Tanzimat ("Reorganization"), 771
Tarentum, 127
Tariffs: in Common Market, 957; in England, 703, 899; in France, 477; in Germany, 773; Great Depression and, 893; industrialization and, 663; protective, 661; in Russia, 768. *See also* Taxation
Tarquin (Etruscans), 125
Tarquinia, 120*(i)*
Tartars: in Russia, 536. *See also* Mongols
Taxation: in 17th century, 471, 472; American Revolution and, 613; Carolingian, 232, 246; of clergy, 269*(d)*; Danegeld as, 242; in England, 253, 338, 776, 957; English, of American colonies, 615–616; in First World War Germany, 841–842; in France, 255, 344, 620; Hellenistic, 104; after Hundred Years' War, 338; income, 726; Merovingian, 228; by Napoleon, 635; papal, 392; of peasants, 544–545; population decline and, 1042; in Rome, 181; after Second World War, 976. *See also* Tariffs
Tea, consumption of, 591
Tea Act (1773), 616
Teachers and teaching, 727, 741; in Enlightenment, 585; status of, 727. *See also* Education; Schools
Technology: bronze and, 12; in East Bloc, 1007; English, 661; factories and, 650–653; Hundred Years' War and, 335, 335*(i)*, 338; imperialism and, 811*(i)*, 812; Industrial Revolution and, 649; in industry, 647; iron, 35, 36–37; in Japan, 821; Muslim, 226; papermaking and, 226, 315, 507; Persian water handling and, 57; personal computer, 1033; in Russia, 487. *See also* Industrial Revolution; Information age; Military technology; Science; Tools; Weapons
Teenagers. *See* Students; Young people; Youth culture

Teheran Conference (1943), 948

Telegraph: transoceanic, 794; world communications and, 812

Telephones, in digital age, 1039–1040

Telescope, 508, 511–512, 511(i), 512(d)

Television, 1039

Tell el Amarna, Egypt, 27

Tempest, The (Shakespeare), 461

Templars. *See* Knights Templars

Temples: Egyptian, 30; Greek, 79–81; Hellenistic, 107; in Jerusalem, 42, 165; Persian carvings on, 57; in Rome, 126; Sumerian, 14, 16; in Uruk, 13. *See also* specific sites

Tenant farmers: in Ireland, 705

Ten Commandments, 41(i), 43

Ten Hours Act (England, 1847), 705

Ten-hour workday, 677

Tennis Court Oath (France, June 20, 1789), 624

Tenochtitlan, 442–443, 442(m), 443(i), 458(d)

Terence, 139

Terra sigillata (pottery), 175, 416

Territorial churches, Protestant, 597

Territorial expansion. *See* Expansion

Terror, the, in French Revolution, 630–631

Terrorism: al-Qaeda and, 1047; in Europe, 1047, 1047(i); fighting of, 1052; in France, 1047, 1047(i), 1050; Islamic State, 1055; in Paris, 1047(i); "Red Terror" (1918–1920), 853–854; by samurai, 821; Soviet terror and, 915–916; in United States, 1047, 1052

Tess of the D'Urbervilles (Hardy), 749

Test Act (England, 1673), 497

Testament of Youth (Brittain), 844(b)

Tet Offensive, 990–991

Tetrarchy (Rome), 186–187

Teutoburg Forest, Battle of, 157

Teutone people, 144

Teutonic Knights, 281

Tewfiq (Egypt), 798

Textiles and textile industry, 765; in England, 650–651, 653; in France, 477; long-distance trade and, 427, 431; in rural areas, 553–555. *See also* Cotton and cotton industry; Woolen industry

Thailand: banking crisis in, 1034

Thales (Greece), 88

Thatcher, Margaret, 997–998, 999(b), 1010; Reagan and, 998, 999(b)

Theater. *See* Drama

Thebes, 65; after Peloponnesian War, 78–79

Themistocles (Athens), 75

Theoderic (Ostrogoths), 205

Theodicy (Leibniz), 521

Theodora (Byzantine Empire), 214–215(b), 215(i)

Theodore, penitential of, 209–210

Theodosian Code, 212

Theodosius I (Rome), 190–191

Theodosius II (Byzantine Empire), 211

Theogony (Hesiod), 67

Theology: Christian, 314; medieval, 314

Theophrastus, 507

Theory of special relativity, 873

Thera, island of, 64

Thermidorian reaction, 631–632

Thermodynamics, 744

Thermometer, 508

Thermopylae, battle at, 75

Thessaloniki Programme, 1057, 1058(d)

Thiers, Adolphe, 775

Third Balkan War. *See* First World War

Third-Class Carriage, The (Daumier), 748, 748(i)

Third Coalition: against France, 634–635

Third Crusade, 279

Third estate (France), 621–622, 621(i), 623–624

Third Intermediate Period (Egypt), 25(i), 37–38

Third of May, The (Goya), 637

Third Punic War, 133–134, 141

Third Reform Bill (England, 1884), 776

Third Republic (France), 775–776

Third Symphony (Beethoven), 701

Thirteenth Amendment (U.S.), 766

Thirty Years' War: causes of, 413; England and, 469, 494; Europe after, 470(m); France and, 465, 469, 494; Habsburgs and, 469; phases of, 469; popular revolts during, 472; population change and, 469, 550; Spain and, 469, 480, 494, 499; state-building after, 469–471

Thomas à Kempis, 342

Thomas Aquinas. *See* Aquinas, Thomas

Thomism, 314

Thought. *See* Intellectual thought

Thrace, 55, 202

Thralls (slaves), 242

Three Mile Island nuclear accident, 1003

Thucydides: on Athens, 78

Thurlow, Geoffrey, 844(b)

Thutmose II (Egypt), 31

Thutmose III (Egypt), 31

Tiamat (goddess), 16

Tiberius (Rome), 164, 175

Tiberius Gracchus (Rome), 142–143

Tiber River region, 122

Tiburtius, Franziska, 742–743(b), 743(i)

Tiger economies, 996

Tiglath-pileser III (Assyria), 49

Tigris River region, 12, 13, 19, 47

Tilsit, Treaty of, 635

Time, clocks and, 306

"Time of Troubles" (Russia), 486

Time periods: historical, 6

Times (London): eyewitness account of Bloody Sunday (1905) in, 770(d)

Titian, 375, 379(i)

Tito, Josip Broz, 960, 1029

Titus (Rome), 165

Tiye (Egypt), 29

Tlaxcala people, 442

Tocqueville, Alexis de, 710

Tod, James, 562(i)

Tofts, Mary, 600(i)

Togo, 807

Tokyo: Commodore Perry in, 797, 821; student protests in, 991

Toledo, 227, 258, 313

Toleration. *See* Religious toleration

Tolstoy, Leo, 749

Tombs: in Egypt, 24, 25, 28, 30; Etruscan, 120(i); Roman, 137; of Unknown Soldier (First World War), 862

Tönnies, Ferdinand, 747

Tools, 6; ancient, 11–12; early, 7; Egyptian, 26, 28; iron, 36–37. *See also* specific tools

Topkapi palace, 491

Torah, 42–43, 45

Tordesillas, Treaty of, 439, 444

Torture: Soviet, 916

Tory government (England), 703–704

Totalitarianism, 827–828, 903, 904; in Fascist Italy, 919; First World War and, 864; in First World War Germany, 842; in Nazi Germany, 919, 934; radical, 904–905. *See also* Communist Party and communism; Nazi Germany; Soviet Union

Total war: in First World War, 834, 841, 864; in French Revolution, 629–631

Touraine, 253–254

Tourism: in 1960s, 986

Tournai, 299

Tournament, 263

Toussaint L'Ouverture. *See* L'Ouverture, Toussaint

Towards a New Architecture (Le Corbusier), 876

Towns. *See* Cities and towns

Toxic waste, 1060

Toynbee, Arnold, 872

Tractatus Logico-Philosophicus (Wittgenstein), 871

Trade: in 13th-century Europe, 301–303; Afroeurasian, 427, 428–429, 428(m); Akkadian, 20; in Asia and Pacific, 570–571; in Atlantic world, 559–570; barriers to, 1033; Champagne fairs and, 302; with China, 795–797; colonial, 478, 793–794; Common Market and, 957–958; copper in, 12; in cowrie shells, 571; cross-cultural connections and, 11–12; Crusades and, 279; in Egypt, 24; English, 562–563, 648; Etruscan, 124; exchange of ideas in, 12; expansion of, 301–303; after First World War, 885; free, 771, 773; global economy and, 1033; in Great Depression, 893; Greek, 70; Hellenistic, 105–106; after Hundred Years' War, 337–338; of iron weapons, 36–37; with Japan, 797; long-distance, 301–303; Mesopotamian, 22–23; in Middle Ages (High), 285, 301–303; Minoan, 63–64; Minoan-Mycenaean, 65; Neolithic, 12; in opium, 795–797; Ottoman Empire and, 771; overland, 106; in Persia, 55; Phoenician, 38–39, 40; Roman, 126, 128, 173(m), 174–175; seaborne, 453(m); shore method of, 564; silk, 106; Spanish, 478; standardization of customs and languages, 106; Sumerian, 14; in Venice, 302–303, 361. *See also* Business; Commerce; Free trade; Maritime trade; Slave trade; Spice trade; specific locations

Trade unions: in Britain, 675–677; in France, 775; German, 787. *See also* Labor unions; Solidarity movement

Trading companies: in Italy, 305(b)

Trading posts: European, 805; Portuguese, 436–437

Traditionalists' response, to imperialism, 818

Trafalgar, Battle of, 634

Tragedy (drama), 112

Training. *See* Education

Trajan (Rome), 156(m), 165, 167, 179

Transcaucasian republics, 909, 1012

Transistors, 953, 1039

Transjordan: Britain and, 859. *See also* Jordan

Translation: of Greek works into Latin, 139

Transportation: in cities, 718, 720; in continental Europe, 662; in England,

648(m); in industrial cities, 720–721; industrialization and, 672; nationalism and, 779; in Paris, 723(m); public, 725; in Russia, 767; steam-powered, 656; trade and, 793–794. *See also* Automobiles; Railroads; Roads and highways; Ships and shipping; specific types

Trans-Siberian Railway, 767, 768(m)

Transubstantiation, 416

Transvaal, 807, 808(b)

Transylvania, 414, 482, 483(m)

Travel: in 1960s, 986. *See also* Expansion; Exploration

Travels of Sir John Mandeville, The, 434

Treasure of the City of Ladies, The (Christine de Pizan), 348(d)

Treaties: with African chiefs, 807; Chinese-European, 797; Egyptian-Hittite, 32; of Lisbon, 1036; Rome-Carthage, 132; Sparta-Athens, 76; U.S.-Japanese, 797, 821. *See also* Alliance(s); specific treaties

Treatment: for Black Death, 329

Treblinka, 933

Treitschke, Heinrich von, 779, 811–812

Trench warfare: in First World War, 835–837, 835(i), 861; poetry from, 837, 838–839(d)

Trent, Council of, 414–416

Trial, The (Kafka), 880

Trials: Nuremberg, 947; by ordeal, 261; Soviet show trials and, 916

Tribes: barbarian, 197–199; Greek demes as, 74; Hebrew, 41

Tribunes (Rome), 131

Triennial Act (England, 1641), 494

Trinity (Christian), 180

Triple Alliance, 828, 829(m), 830, 838

Triple Entente, 829(m), 830, 838, 840

Tripoli, as Crusader kingdom, 277

Triremes, 75

Triumph of the Will, The (Riefenstahl), 884

Troika (IMF, European Common Bank, and European Union), Greece and, 1057

Trojan War, 65, 66–67

Troppau, Austria, conference at, 688

Trotsky, Leon, 850, 853, 908

Troubadours, 315, 339

"Troubles, the," in Ireland, 1005

Troy, 67, 124

Truman, Harry, 949

Truman Doctrine, 951

Tsars (Russia), 485. *See also* specific tsars

Tsipras, Alexis, 1057, 1058(d)

Tudor dynasty (England), 384, 407–408, 408(i). *See also* specific rulers

Tull, Jethro, 547

Tunisia: Phoenicians in, 39–40; protests in, 1055

Turgot, Anne-Robert-Jacques, 559

Turia inscription (Rome), 137(d)

Turkey: ancient, 9, 9(i); in classical Greece, 63(m); England and, 860; EU and, 1036; after First World War, 860–861; France and, 859, 860; Greeks in, 860–861; immigrant movement across, 1044; modernization and secularization of, 861; refugee crisis and, 1044(i); Rome and, 174; Young Turks and, 772. *See also* Anatolia; Lydia, Turkey; Ottoman Empire

Turkish National Movement, 860

Turkmenistan, Hellenistic, 100

Turks: after First World War, 861; Hungary and, 414. *See also* Ottoman Empire; Ottoman Turks; Seljuk Turks; Turkey

Turner, Joseph M. W., 700

Tuscany, 759; trade and, 303

Tutankhamon (Egypt), 30

Twentieth Party Congress, 961

Twitter, 1041–1042

Two Sicilies, Kingdom of. *See* Kingdom of the Two Sicilies

Two Treatises of Government (Locke), 498, 498(d)

Tyche (goddess), 107–108, 111

Typhoid, 468, 723

Typhus, 723

Tyrants and tyranny: in Greece, 69, 74, 126; Locke on, 612

Tyre, Alexander the Great in, 94

Tyrtaeus (Sparta), 72

Tzu Hsi (China), 822, 823

Ukraine, 909; collectivization in, 912; Crimea and, 1032; East Slavs in, 243; EU and, 1036; industry in, 768; Jews in, 539; Nazis and, 928; Orange Revolution in (2004–2005), 1032; revolution in (2014), 1032; Russia and, 487, 489, 767, 769, 854, 1026; Russian natural gas to, 1059; separatism in, 1027(m); serfdom in, 536; Slavs in, 485; after Soviet Union, 1032; Soviet Union and, 1012

Ulfilas (Bishop), 206

Ulrich of Richental, 341(i)

Ulster: Catholics in, 705; opposition to home rule in, 777. *See also* Northern Ireland

Ultraconservatives, in Germany, 842

Ultranationalism: in Germany, 890; in Japan, 934

Ulysses (Joyce), 880

al-Umari, 430

Umayyad Dynasty, 224, 227

Umma (city), 17

Umma (faith community), 221

UN. *See* United Nations

Unam Sanctam, 269, 269(d)

Uncertainty: in modern thought, 868–875; principle of, 874

Unconscious: Freud on, 874, 875

Underclass, 1038

Underground (resistance), in Second World War, 931

Undocumented immigration: into EU, 1043, 1044

Unemployment: in England, 776, 890; in France, 709, 756; in Germany, 924; in Great Depression, 894, 894(m), 895–896; Orwell on dole and, 896–897(d); population decline and, 1043; in western Europe, 996

Unification: of Egypt, 24; of Germany, 713, 760–764, 762(m), 764(i), 779, 828; of Italy, 757–760, 758(m), 779; of Spain, 384–387, 385(m); of western Europe, 957–958. *See also* Reunification

Unigeniture, in Russia, 489

Union of Kalmar, 280

Union of South Africa, 808(b), 809

Union of Soviet Socialist Republics (U.S.S.R.). *See* Soviet Union

Union of Utrecht, 420(m)

Unions. *See* Labor unions

United Kingdom. *See* England (Britain)

United Nations (UN): Climate Change Conference (Paris), 1060; globalization and, 1033; Hungary and, 964; Palestine division and, 971; *Standing March, The,* and, 1020(i); as supranational organization, 1036; Universal Declaration of Human Rights, 1061

United Nations Relief and Rehabilitation Administration (UNRRA), 945

United Provinces, 420, 454, 499. *See also* Dutch Republic

United States: Congo and, 973; Constitution of, 617–618; counterculture in, 989; deaths in

Second World War, 945; economic sanctions on Russia by, 1033; England and, 830; European immigrants to, 800; European relations with, 1049–1053; in First World War, 840–841, 846, 854; First World War home front in, 842; after First World War, 858, 885; flight from Germany to, 879; gold standard and, 893; Great Depression in, 891–893, 892(m); human rights and, 1061; immigration to, 802, 803; imperialism by, 810–811, 810(m), 813; industrialization in, 659, 659(f), 663; Islamist terrorism in, 1047; isolationism in, 858; Japan and, 797; Jewish migration to, 946; migrants in, 801; movies in, 883; nation building in, 764–766; nativism in, 803, 804(d); NATO alliance and, 1049–1050; New Deal in, 894–896; oil shipments to, 995–996; pollution and, 1060; public health movement in, 721; Putin and, 1024; religion and social conservatism in, 732; reparations after First World War and, 857; slavery in, 764–765, 765(m), 766; student protests in, 991; Suez crisis and, 972; Versailles Treaty and, 858; Vietnam War and, 990–991; Weather Underground in, 992; women in, 843. *See also* Arms race; Cold War; First World War; Second World War

Unity movement, in western Europe, 957–958

Universal Declaration of Human Rights, 1061

Universal gravitation, law of, 513

Universalism: of Christianity, 178

Universal suffrage, male, 754, 755, 756, 763, 779

Universe: Aristotle on, 508–509; Copernicus on, 506, 509–510; earth-centered, 113; Newton on, 506; Pre-Socratics on, 88; sun-centered, 113

Universities, 257, 285, 309–314; during Black Death years, 331; in Enlightenment, 519, 540; in Europe, 309–314, 310(m), 506; French protests in, 992; friars and, 274–275; in Middle Ages, 274–275, 309–314, 331, 506, 540; of Naples, 257; origins of, 310; Scientific Revolution and, 519; students in, 314; women in, 314, 519, 523, 742. *See also* specific schools

Unskilled workers, 730

Untimely Meditations (Nietzsche), 868–869

Upper classes, 695; in Russia, 848. *See also* Aristocracy; Classes; Nobility

Upper Egypt, 24

Uprisings. *See* Revolts and rebellions; Riots

Upward mobility. *See* Social mobility

Ur, 20

Ural Mountains, 486

Urban II (Pope), 277

Urban VI (Pope), 339–340

Urban VIII (Pope), 518

Urban areas: in 17th century, 481, 486; in 19th century, 717, 718–725; clergy in, 393; conflicts in, 346–347; guilds in, 556–557; Hellenistic, 99–100; immigrants in, 802; improvements in, 723–724; Jewish society in, 44–45; lifestyle in, 306–309; London in 19th century, 720(d); poverty in, 724(i); public transportation in, 725; reform of, 723–724; in Rome, 138–139, 157, 169–171; workers in, 665; working classes in, 728, 738–739. *See also* Cities and towns

Urban planning, 723–724

Ure, Andrew, 675

Ursuline order, 416–417

Uruk, 13, 16, 17, 18–19(d)

U.S.S.R. *See* Soviet Union

Usury: Christians and, 304; Jews and, 304; Muslims and, 223

Utilitarianism, 721

Utopia (More), 366, 369(d), 370, 408

Utopian socialism, 693

Utrecht: Peace of, 478, 479(m), 562; Union of, 420

Vaccines, 722. *See also* Inoculation

Vacuum, 504(i), 516, 517, 518

Valens (Rome), 202

Valmy, Battle of, 628

Valois dynasty (France): Habsburg-Valois wars and, 362, 406; Hundred Years' War and, 332

Values: middle-class, 727–728; Nietzsche and, 869; U.S.-European gap in, 1052

Vandals, 204, 224; as Arian Christians, 206

Van der Weyden, Rogier, 374

Van Eyck, Jan, 374

Van Gogh, Vincent, 877

Varangians, 243

Varus (Rome), 157

Vasa family. *See* Gustavus Vasa (Sweden)

Vasari, Giorgio, 357, 364, 365, 375, 376, 376(d), 388

Vassals, 246, 248

Vatican: Lateran Agreement (1929) and, 918; Second Vatican Council and, 988. *See also* Catholic Church; Papacy

Vegetables, 590, 591

Vehicles. *See* Transportation

Velázquez, Diego, 452*(b)*, 452*(i)*

Velvet Revolution, 1015, 1028

Venerable Bede. *See* Bede

Venereal disease, 736

Venetia, 232, 685, 762

Venice: as city-state, 360, 361; growth of, 299; in Kingdom of Italy, 760; Renaissance arts in, 375; trade by, 301–302, 431–432

Venus figures, Paleolithic, 8*(d)*, 8*(i)*

Verdun: Battle of, 835, 842; Treaty of, 240, 240*(m)*

Vergil, Polydore, 384

Vermuyden, Cornelius, 547

Vernacular languages: Anglo-Saxon as, 239–240; Bible in, 193; *Canterbury Tales* in, 352, 353; *Divine Comedy* in, 352, 353

Vernacular literature, 315–317, 352–353

Verrocchio, Andrea del, 376*(d)*

Versailles, Treaty of, 856–859, 885, 888*(b)*, 917, 925

Versailles palace: construction and renovations in, 474–475; court at, 620; Estates General in, 474; "Letter from Versailles" and, 475*(d)*; life at, 474–476, 475*(i)*; Louis XIV and, 472–473, 474; women's march to, 625, 625*(i)*. *See also* Hall of Mirrors (Versailles)

Vesalius, Andreas, 517

Vespasian (Rome), 164, 165, 166*(b)*

Vestal virgins, 127–128

Vesuvius, Mount, 165, 166*(b)*

Veterans: after First World War, 862–863, 863*(i)*; in Rome, 142, 155

Viceroyalties, in Spanish New World, 446

Vichy France, 928, 928*(m)*, 937

Victor Emmanuel II (Italy), 757, 758, 760; national monument to (Rome), 780

Victor Emmanuel III (Italy), 918

Victoria (England): Chinese letter to, 796; Golden Jubilee of, 780; lifestyle and, 738*(i)*

Vienna, 783; Black Death in, 328; Congress of, 682, 683–684; Ottoman siege of, 406; palaces in, 482; revolt in, 712; revolution of 1848 in, 711, 781; Treaty of, 684*(i)*; urban planning in, 724

Vietcong, 990–991

Vietnam: independence movement in, 969–970; Japan and, 934; after Vietnam War, 991

Vietnam War: antiwar movement in, 990; United States and, 990–991

Vikings: in eastern Europe, 243–244; in England, 252; in Greenland, 245, 324; invasions and migrations by, 202, 240–241, 252; ships of, 240, 242, 242*(i)*; slave trade of, 242; Slavs and, 244; use of term, 240; in western Europe, 242. *See also* Normans

Villages, 3; agriculture and, 9–10; communal farming in, 544; medieval, 287, 288, 290; weddings in, 579–580. *See also* Cities and towns; Manors and manorialism

Ville-Marie. *See* Montreal

Vindication of the Rights of Man, A (Wollstonecraft), 627

Vindication of the Rights of Woman, A (Wollstonecraft), 627

Violence: Arab-Jewish, 860; human rights and, 1060–1061; in Ireland, 777, 777*(i)*; against Jews, 294; in Middle Ages (later period), 294, 351; as response to imperialism, 818; in Rome, 143–145. *See also* War(s) and warfare

Virgil, 153, 160–161, 353

Virginia: colony of, 445

Virgin Mary. *See* Mary (mother of Jesus)

Virtù, in arts and political thought, 365, 367–368

Viscounts, Carolingian, 232

Visigoths, 196, 202–203, 205; as Arian Christians, 206; in Rome, 195; in Spain, 204, 224, 225*(d)*

Visual arts: after First World War, 876–879

Vitruvian Man (Leonardo), 377*(i)*

Vodou (voodoo), 640

Volcanoes: in Crete, 64

Volga River region, 486

Volksgemeinschaft, 924

Voltaire, 521, 522*(d)*, 523, 524–526, 527, 533, 534, 535*(i)*

Von Moltke, Helmuth, 864

Vortigern (Briton), 202

Voting and voting rights: in American colonies, 615; Chartist movement and, 677; in England, 499, 704, 776; in France, 622, 754, 755, 756; in Germany, 763; in Hungary, 778; in Italy, 757, 760; in Rome, 143*(i)*;

Russia, 769; in United States, 618, 989; for women, 499, 618–619, 742, 843. *See also* Universal suffrage

Voyages: European voyages of discovery, 432–441, 436*(m)*, 462; Genoese, 432

Vulgate Bible, 193

Wages: in 19th century, 725–726; from 1840s on, 672; Black Death and, 330; in England, 345; in factories, 669; in First World War, 841; in France, 756; gender differences in, 648; iron law of, 657; for rural textile workers, 555; of urban workers, 308–309. *See also* Income

Waksman, Selman, 329

Waldo, Peter, and Waldensians, 267–268

Wales: mortality decline in, 722*(f)*

Wałesa, Lech, 1009, 1014, 1021, 1028

Walking city, 718

Walled cities, medieval, 306

Walls: Roman, 167

War and Peace (Tolstoy), 749

War(s) and warfare: army size and, 471; demography and, 550; Egyptian, 30; in France, 477–478; Hellenistic, 116–117; Hyksos and, 28; Mycenaean, 65; Napoleonic, 633, 634–637, 638; Rome and, 126, 143–145; in Saint-Domingue, 640; over slave trade, 564; Spartan, 71–72; submarine (First World War), 841; Sumerian, 14–15; total, 834, 841. *See also* Civil war(s); Military; Navy; Trench warfare; Weapons; specific battles and wars

War Communism, in Russia, 853, 907

War crimes: Milošević and, 1031; punishment after Second World War, 947

War guilt clause, 858

War Industries Board (U.S.), 842

War Labor Board (U.S.), 842

War of Independence. *See* American Revolution

War of the Austrian Succession, 533, 533*(m)*, 537, 562, 571, 620

War of the Spanish Succession, 478, 479*(m)*, 482, 560–562

War on terror, 1052–1053

War Raw Materials Board, 841

Warriors: Christian, 231; Egypt, 25

Warrior-saints, 277

Warsaw: Jewish ghetto in, 932, 985

Warsaw Pact, 952, 964, 965

Warsaw Uprising, 939

Warships. *See* Ships and shipping

Wars of the Roses (England), 384

Washington, George, 617

Waste Land, The (Eliot), 880

Wastes. *See* Sanitation; Sewage systems

Water and water resources: aqueducts and, 139, 169–170, 170*(i)*; for drinking, 722; in England, 551, 651; in mines, 654; public health and, 721; travel by, 656

Water frame, 651

Waterloo: Napoleon at, 638, 685

Water mills, 285, 288

Water pollution. *See* Pollution

Water supply: Persian, 57

Waterways. *See* Canals; Rivers; specific river regions

Watt, James, 654–655, 673

Waugh, Evelyn, 872

Wealth: in 19th century, 725–726; of Croesus, 54; diet and, 591; distribution of income and, 725–726; in foraging societies, 7; hierarchies of, 11; industrial, 647; of industrialists, 673; inequalities of, 610; mercantilism and, 477; of middle classes, 726–727; Renaissance and, 373; socialism and, 693

Wealth gap, 998; in 19th century, 726; in East Bloc, 1006; global inequality and, 792–793

Wealth of Nations (Smith). *See Inquiry into the Nature and Causes of the Wealth of Nations* (Smith)

Weapons: Archimedes and, 114*(b)*; Assyrian, 47–48; in Crimean War, 766; in Egypt, 28; in First World War, 835; in Hundred Years' War, 335, 335*(i)*, 338; imperialism and, 809, 811*(i)*; iron, 38; Mycenaean, 65, 65*(i)*; trade and, 431. *See also* Nuclear weapons; specific weapons

Weather. *See* Climate

Weather Underground (U.S.), 992

Weavers and weaving, 226, 288, 325; handloom, 652. *See also* Textiles and textile industry

Weber, Max, 746–747

Weddings: medieval religion and, 294; in Rome, 136; Strasbourg Cathedral door for, 305*(b)*; in villages, 579*(i)*. *See also* Marriage

Weights and measures: national identity and, 779; standard, 779

Weimar Republic (Germany), 856, 863, 886, 888*(b)*, 890, 921

Welfare, 772; Christian, 179; in East Bloc, 1006, 1007; in England, 776, 957, 998; in Germany, 774; for immigrants, 1047; "Oslo Breakfast" as, 898*(i)*; in Scandinavia, 956; after Second World War, 976; Social Democrats and, 986

Welfare socialism, in Scandinavia, 898

Welfare state, in Britain, 998

Wenamun (Egypt), "Report of Wenamun, The," 39*(d)*

Wends people, 243

Wergeld (monetary value), 199

Werner, Anton von, 764*(i)*

Wesley, John, 584, 598–601; "Advice to Methodists," 599*(d)*; Pietism and, 598–599

Wesley, Susannah, 584

Wessex, 202, 252

West, the, 4–5. *See also* Western world

West Africa, 805; cotton cloth from, 651; England and, 446, 562, 809; France and, 446, 807; Portugal and, 436–437; slave trade and, 431; trade in, 446

West Berlin, 952; Berlin Wall and, 965. *See also* Berlin

West Bloc: after Second World War, 944, 949–953

Western Asia. *See* Asia Minor; specific locations

Western Christian church. *See* Catholic Church

Western civilization, 4–5, 6

Western Europe: Charlemagne in, 231–232, 232*(m)*; classes after Second World War, 975–976; communism in, 951; crisis and change in, 995–1005; East Bloc and, 985; economies in, 995–997; environmental protests in, 1004; guest workers in, 976; industrialization in, 659; Jews in, 781; marriage in, 576; migration into, 1043; peasants in, 286, 467–468; pollution in, 1002–1003; recovery in, 956*(d)*; after Second World War, 954–959; serfdom decline in, 286; social conditions in, 544; underclass in, 1038; Vikings in, 242, 243; welfare provisions in, 986. *See also* Europe; Western world; specific locations

Western front, in First World War, 834–837

Western Hemisphere. *See* America(s); New World; specific locations

Westernization: of Indian society, 820; as response to imperialism, 489, 818, 821; in Russia, 534

Western Roman Empire: barbarians and, 200, 201–202, 204; end of, 205, 210, 216; Huns in, 210. *See also* Byzantine Empire; Roman Empire

Western world: capitalism in, 5; "civilizing" of nonwhites by, 813–815, 820; concepts of, 4; expansion by, 791; industrialization in, 659; opening of China to, 795–797; Orientalism and, 815–816. *See also* specific locations

West Germany, 952; Christian Democrats in, 955, 998; conservatism in, 998–1000; East German movement into, 1014; East German reunification with, 1000, 1015–1016; Green Party in, 1004; guest workers in, 976, 977*(b)*, 977*(i)*; Holocaust apology in, 984*(i)*; National Democratic Party in, 1005; New Left in, 992; premarital sex in, 989–990; Red Army Faction in, 992; relations with East Germany, 985; Social Democrats in, 984. *See also* Germany

West Indies: colonial sugar trade and, 446; England and, 446, 562

Westphalia, Peace of, 469

Wet nurses, 138, 293, 582

What Is Enlightenment? (Kant), 526

What Is Property? (Proudhon), 693

What Is the Third Estate? (Sieyès), 622–623*(d)*, 623

Wheat, 106, 451

Wheel, Sumerian, 14

Whig Party (England), 704

"Whig view," of Britain, 776

White-collar workers, 727, 975, 976; women as, 978

White man's burden, 813

"White Man's Burden, The" (Kipling), 813, 814*(d)*

White Mountain, Battle of the, 469

White people: in Americas, 566; New Imperialism and, 812, 813–814, 816; in Saint-Domingue, 638–639; Social Darwinism and, 812; South Africa and, 972; supposed superiority of, 780; in United States, 765

Whites, in Russian civil war, 853, 854

White women's burden, 820

Widows: of artisans, 301, 347; in medieval villages, 254; of sailors, 434. *See also* Women

WikiLeaks, 1041

Wilhelm I (Germany), 761, 763, 764*(i)*
Wilhelm II (Germany), 774, 833; abdication by, 854–855; Bismarck dismissal by, 828; Morocco and, 830
Wilhelm III (Prussia), 685
Wilkinson, John, 655
William III of Orange (king of England), 497, 498*(d)*, 500, 580
William and **Mary** (England). *See* William III of Orange (king of England)
William of Normandy (the Conqueror), 250*(i)*, 252, 266
William of Occam, 340
William the Pious of Aquitaine, 270
Wilson, Isabel, 671*(d)*
Wilson, Woodrow, 841, 857, 858; Versailles Treaty and, 886
Wine: Greek, 106
Winter Palace (St. Petersburg), 769, 847
Witches and witchcraft: European persecution of, 421–423, 422*(i)*, 602; pamphlets about, 422*(i)*, 423
Witte, Sergei, 768
Wittenberg, Luther at, 395
Wittgenstein, Ludwig, 871
Wives. *See* Families; Marriage; Women
Wojtyla, Karol. *See* John Paul II (Pope)
Wolf, Christa, 993
Wollstonecraft, Mary, 531, 627
Women: in 1970s, 1000–1001; age at marriage, 264; in American colonies, 447, 450; as apprentices, 301; in arts, 377–378; in barbarian society, 197, 199; British, in India, 819–820; business opportunities for, 673; in Byzantine Empire, 215*(d)*; Carolingian, 236, 246; cathedral windows of, 264*(i)*; Christianity and, 178, 193–194; "civilizing mission" of imperialism and, 813–815; confraternities of, 342; consumer culture and, 882–883; conversion of, 193–194; at courts, 475*(d)*, 476; in Crusades, 278; debate about, 381; diet improvements and, 289; division of labor and, 287; as domestic servants, 308–309, 730; education for, 264, 366; in Egypt, 27–28; employment of, 555; in Enlightenment, 519, 523, 530–531; equality for, 699*(b)*; fashion for, 539*(i)*, 593*(b)*, 593*(i)*, 594; in First World War, 842, 842*(i)*, 843, 844*(b)*; in France, 332, 475, 476, 625, 626, 634; in French Revolution, 631; gender hierarchy and, 11; gender roles and, 287; in Greece, 69–70, 85; in

guilds, 347, 557; in Hebrew society, 44; Hellenistic, 98, 101, 102; inheritance by, 136; in Hebrew society, 44; in Islam, 223; in Italy, 918–919; literacy of, 588; march to Versailles by, 625, 625*(i)*; marriage and, 264; medieval, 246, 287; Merovingian, 229; in middle class, 675*(d)*, 727–728, 737–739; as midwives, 604; Muslim, 492–493*(b)*; in Nazi Germany, 924; in nobility, 264–265; in nursing, 604; in Ottoman Empire, 527; in patriarchal society, 466–467; as pharaoh, 29; prostitution and, 580, 736–737; in Protestantism, 402–403; protests by, 1000*(i)*; in Renaissance, 378, 381–382; rights of, 1061; in Rome, 136, 140; Rousseau on, 531; as rulers, 332, 381; in rural textile industry, 553–555; in salons, 476, 519, 530; same-sex relationships of, 164, 350, 581; in sciences, 519; as seamstresses, 557; after Second World War, 978–979; separate spheres and, 666, 669, 675*(d)*, 737–739; as servants, 676; sexual division of labor and, 287, 666; socialism and, 693, 784–785*(b)*, 1006; in Soviet Union, 915; Spartan, 72–73; spinning by, 650*(i)*; suffrage movement and, 741–742, 741*(i)*; in Sumer, 18–19; trafficking in, 1044; in Turkey, 861; universities and, 314, 519, 523; as unmarried workers, 668; voting rights for, 618–619, 776–777, 843; witch-hunts and, 421; as workers, 287, 555, 577, 610, 666, 668, 978; working-class, 729, 730–731, 739. *See also* Families; Feminism; Gender and gender issues; Marriage; Midwives; Nuns; Service and servants; specific individuals
Women of England, The: Their Social Duties and Domestic Habits (Ellis), 675*(d)*
Women's Fightback Network, 1000*(i)*
Women's movement, 1000–1001
Women's rights, 1001; in Turkey, 861
Women's rights movements, 843
"Women's work," 668
Woodblock printing, 370
Woolen industry: 17th-century decline in, 468; England and, 174, 302, 336, 384; trade and, 303, 333, 384, 431. *See also* Textiles and textile industry
Woolf, Virginia, 880

Wordsworth, William, 673, 696, 697–698; *Lyrical Ballads,* 697
Work: gender division of, 287; Greek, 83; marriage, families, and, 577–578. *See also* Labor; Peasants; Workers
Workday: limits on, 666, 677
Workers: in Austrian Empire, 711; in cities, 718; communism and, 905–906; conditions for, 675; debt peonage and, 563; in factories, 664–665; families and children as, 287; in First World War, 838, 842, 843; in France, 754, 756; in Germany, 774; government and, 559; in Great Depression, 896–897*(d)*; guest worker, 976; industrial, 654–655, 669–670; industrious revolution and, 555–556; in Italy, 917; in labor unions, 786–787; Marxism and, 695; in middle class, 975–976; in mines, 670–671*(d)*; nonagricultural, 670; in Russia, 767, 768, 848, 851; socialism and, 784, 786; Soviet, 913–914; in textile industry, 553–555; unmarried women as, 668; white-collar, 975; women as, 555, 666, 668, 842, 842*(i)*, 843, 978. *See also* Employment; Industrialization; Industry; Labor; Labor unions; Peasants; Serfs and serfdom; Unemployment; Working classes
Workers International: French Section of, 784
Working classes, 717, 726; in England, 705; leisure and religion of, 731–732; leisure of, 731–732; living standards for, 669–672; Marx on, 694; people and occupations of, 728–731; in Poland, 1007–1010; prostitution and, 736; religion and, 732; socialism and, 695, 784, 786; solidarity of, 676; upper, 729–730; wage laborers as, 665; women's lives in, 738. *See also* Workers
Workplace: conditions in, 664–665; women in, 843, 978
Works and Days (Hesiod), 66, 68*(d)*
Workshops: in Paris, 709–710
Works Progress Administration (WPA, U.S.), 895
World Bank, 957, 1026, 1037
World economy. *See* Global economy
World of Yesterday, The (Zweig), 734–735*(d)*
World Trade Center: al-Qaeda attack on, 1047, 1052

World Trade Organization (WTO), 1037; globalization and, 1033; protests against (1999), 1039; as supranational organization, 1036

Worldview: in Enlightenment, 520; in Scientific Revolution, 506

World War I. *See* First World War

World War II. *See* Second World War

Worms: conference at (1122), 267; Diet of (1521), 395, 424; Jews of, 280

Wozzeck (Berg), 881

Wretched of the Earth, The (Fanon), 969(d)

Wright, Frank Lloyd, 875–876

Wright, Joseph, 504(i)

Writers. *See* Literature

Writing: Akkadian, 20; Assyrian, 50; civilization and, 5–6; in Egypt, 26; Etruscan, 124; Linear A, 64, 66; Linear B, 65, 66; in Mesopotamia, 15–16, 15(f), 22; Phoenician alphabet and, 40; Sumerian, 15–16, 15(f), 17; in Uruk, 13. *See also* Alphabet; Hieroglyphic writing; Literature

Württemberg: education in, 587

Wyclif, John, 340–341

Xenophon (historian): on Nineveh, 50; on Sparta, 73

Xerxes I (Persia), 55, 75, 94

Xhosa people, 805

Yahweh, 40, 42, 177; Covenant with Jews, 43; Hezekiah and, 49

Yalta Conference (1945), 948, 949(i)

Yellow fever, 723

Yeltsin, Boris, 1017, 1022–1023, 1027(m)

Yemen, 220

Yokohama, Westerners in, 821

York, house of, 384

York, England, founding of, 172

Young, Arthur, on benefits of enclosure, 547, 548(d)

Young Italy, 759(d)

Young people: as immigrants, 801, 802; in Italy, 918–919. *See also* Students

Young Turks, 772

Youth culture: after Second World War, 979. *See also* Counterculture; Students

Ypres, 301

Ypsilanti, Alexander, 702

Yucatán peninsula, 442

Yugoslavia: breakup of, 1029–1031, 1030(m); civil war in former, 1029–1030; after First World War, 856, 857, 859; in Little Entente, 886; refugees from, 1043; Second World War and, 931; separatism in, 1004; Tito in, 960

Zacatecas, 454

Zacharias (pope), 231

Zama, battle at, 133

Zambia, 807

Zanzibar, 809

Zapolya, Janos, 414

Zarathustra. *See* Zoroaster and Zoroastrianism

al-Zarqali, Abu Isaq Ibrahim (astronomer), 227(i)

Zealots, 176

Zemstvo, 767

Zeno (Cyprus), 112

Zeno (Rome), 204

Zeus (god), 87, 88, 108, 128

Zeus-Amon, oracle of, 94

Zheng He, voyages of, 428(m), 429

Ziggurat, 14

Zimbabwe, 807

Zinzendorf, Count, 569

Zionism, 782(b), 783, 859, 971

Zola, Émile, 748, 749(d), 776

Zollverein, 661, 760

Zones of occupation: in Berlin, 952; after Second World War, 947

Zoning: in cities, 724

Zoology, 513

Zoroaster and Zoroastrianism, 56

Zulu people, 790(i), 805

Zurich, 398, 399

Zweig, Stephan, on middle-class youth and sexuality, 734–735(d)

Zwingli, Ulrich, 395–397, 398–399, 401; death of, 406; on Eucharist, 398; marriage of, 401

THE CONTEMPORARY WORLD

ARCTIC OCEAN

RUSSIAN FEDERATION

NORWAY
FINLAND
SWEDEN
ESTONIA
LATVIA
LITHUANIA
DEN.
NETH.
GERMANY
BEL.
LUX.
CZ.
SWITZ.
SLK.
AUS. HUNG.
SLN.
CR. B.H. SE.
ITALY
MO.
KO.
ALB.
POLAND
BELARUS
UKRAINE
MOLDOVA
ROMANIA
BULGARIA
MAC.
GREECE
MALTA
TUNISIA
CYPRUS
LEBANON
ISRAEL
West Bank
Gaza Strip
GEORGIA
ARMENIA
AZERBAIJAN
TURKEY
SYRIA
IRAQ
IRAN
ALGERIA
LIBYA
EGYPT
JORDAN
KUWAIT
BAHRAIN
QATAR
SAUDI
ARABIA
UNITED ARAB
EMIRATES
OMAN
YEMEN

KAZAKHSTAN
UZBEKISTAN
TURKMENISTAN
KYRGYZSTAN
TAJIKISTAN
AFGHANISTAN
PAKISTAN

MONGOLIA

CHINA

N. KOREA
S. KOREA
JAPAN

NEPAL
BHUTAN
INDIA
BANGLADESH
MYANMAR
(BURMA)
LAOS
THAILAND
VIETNAM
CAMBODIA
Taiwan

PACIFIC
OCEAN

PHILIPPINES

Mariana Is.
(U.S.)

Guam
(U.S.)

MARSHALL
IS.

NIGER
CHAD
SUDAN
NIGERIA
BENIN
TOGO
CAMEROON
CENTRAL
AFRICAN
REP.
SOUTH
SUDAN
ETHIOPIA
EQ. GUINEA
GABON
CONGO
DEM. REP.
OF
THE CONGO
RWANDA
BURUNDI
UGANDA
KENYA
TANZANIA
ERITREA
DJIBOUTI
SOMALIA

MALDIVES

SRI
LANKA

BRUNEI
MALAYSIA
SINGAPORE

PALAU

INDONESIA

FEDERATED STATES
OF MICRONESIA

NAURU

KIRIBATI

TUVALU

SÃO
TOMÉ
& PRÍNCIPE
ANGOLA
ZAMBIA
NAMIBIA
BOTSWANA
ZIMBABWE
MALAWI
MOZAMBIQUE
COMOROS
SEYCHELLES
MADAGASCAR
MAURITIUS

INDIAN
OCEAN

PAPUA
NEW
GUINEA
TIMOR
LESTE

SOLOMON
IS.

VANUATU

FIJI

SOUTH
AFRICA
SWAZILAND
LESOTHO

AUSTRALIA

New
Caledonia
(Fr.)

NEW
ZEALAND

Tasmania
(Aust.)

ANTARCTICA

20°E   40°E   60°E   80°E

ABBREVIATIONS	
ALB.	ALBANIA
AUS.	AUSTRIA
BEL.	BELGIUM
B.H.	BOSNIA AND HERZEGOVINA
CR.	CROATIA
CZ.	CZECH REPUBLIC
DEN.	DENMARK
HUNG.	HUNGARY
KO.	KOSOVO
LUX.	LUXEMBOURG
MAC.	MACEDONIA
MO.	MONTENEGRO
NETH.	NETHERLANDS
SE.	SERBIA
SLK.	SLOVAKIA
SLN.	SLOVENIA
SWITZ.	SWITZERLAND

About the Authors

John P. McKay (Ph.D., University of California, Berkeley) is professor emeritus at the University of Illinois. He has written or edited numerous works, including the Herbert Baxter Adams Prize–winning book *Pioneers for Profit: Foreign Entrepreneurship and Russian Industrialization, 1885–1913*.

Bennett D. Hill (Ph.D., Princeton), late of Georgetown University, published *Church and State in the Middle Ages* and numerous articles and reviews, and was one of the contributing editors to *The Encyclopedia of World History*. He taught for many years at the University of Illinois and was a Benedictine monk of St. Anselm's Abbey in Washington, D.C.

John Buckler (Ph.D., Harvard University), late of the University of Illinois, published numerous works, including *Theban Hegemony, 371–362 B.C.*; *Philip II and the Sacred War*; and *Aegean Greece in the Fourth Century B.C.* With Hans Beck, he published *Central Greece and the Politics of Power in the Fourth Century*.

Clare Haru Crowston (Ph.D., Cornell University) teaches at the University of Illinois, where she is currently professor of history and department chair. She is the author of *Credit, Fashion, Sex: Economies of Regard in Old Regime France* and *Fabricating Women: The Seamstresses of Old Regime France, 1675–1791*, which won the Berkshire and Hagley Prizes. She edited two special issues of the *Journal of Women's History*, has published numerous journal articles and reviews, and is one of the editors of the *Journal of Social History* and past president of the Society for French Historical Studies.

Merry E. Wiesner-Hanks (Ph.D., University of Wisconsin–Madison) taught first at Augustana College in Illinois, and since 1985 at the University of Wisconsin–Milwaukee, where she is currently UWM Distinguished Professor in the department of history. She is the Senior Editor of the *Sixteenth Century Journal*, one of the editors of the *Journal of Global History*, and the author or editor of more than twenty books, including *A Concise History of the World* (2015). She is the former Chief Reader for Advanced Placement World History.

Joe Perry (Ph.D., University of Illinois at Urbana-Champaign) is associate professor of modern German and European history at Georgia State University. He has published numerous articles and is author of *Christmas in Germany: A Cultural History*. His current research interests focus on issues of consumption, gender, and popular culture in West Germany and Western Europe after World War II.